S0-EIE-950

Justin
Bunz
No

OHIO

HOLT

Elements of LITERATURE

Second Course

correlated to

Ohio

Academic Content Standards for Language Arts

CONTENTS

HOLT, RINEHART AND WINSTON

Ohio
The Buckeye State

State Capitol, Columbus

COVER PHOTO CREDITS: (c), Chad Ehlers/Stone/Getty Images; (br), © Image source/Corbis; (bkgd), Travelpix Ltd/Getty Images; (inset), Chris Clinton/ Stone+/Getty Images.

Acknowledgments and other credits appear on pages 1075–1083, which are an extension of the copyright page.

Printed in the United States of America

ISBN-13: 978-0-55-400669-7
ISBN-10: 0-55-400669-3

1 2 3 4 5 048 10 09 08

State flower, scarlet carnation

State bird, red male cardinal

Ohio Academic Content Standards for Language Arts

READING

Acquisition of Vocabulary

CONTEXTUAL UNDERSTANDING

>1 Define unknown words through context clues and the author's use of comparison, contrast and cause and effect.

What does it mean? Clues from surrounding words and sentences can help you define new words.

EXAMPLE: Using Context Clues For practice using context clues, see pages 297, 304, 478, and 662.

CONCEPTUAL UNDERSTANDING

>2 Apply knowledge of connotation and denotation to determine the meaning of words.

What does it mean? **Denotations** are dictionary meanings of words; **connotations** are feelings and ideas that have become attached to the words.

EXAMPLE: Understanding Connotation and Denotation See pages 683 and 701 for information on connotations and denotations.

>3 Identify the relationships of pairs of words in analogical statements (e.g., synonyms and antonyms) and infer word meanings from these relationships.

What does it mean? Word relationships—such as opposites, or antonyms—can help you learn new words.

EXAMPLE: Understanding Words and Analogies See pages 402 and 532 for helpful lessons on word analogies.

>4 Infer the literal and figurative meaning of words and phrases and discuss the function of figurative language, including metaphors, similes and idioms.

Goldenrod, rural Ohio

What does it mean? Interpreting figurative language in a work can add to your understanding and enjoyment of it.

EXAMPLE: Understanding Idioms For practice with idioms, see pages 278 and 424. See pages 294 and 402 for practice with metaphors and similes.

>5 Examine and discuss the ways that different events (e.g., cultural, political, social, technological, and scientific events) impact and change the English language.

What does it mean? Migrating groups, invaders, traders, and new inventions have all affected the development of the English language.

EXAMPLE: Understanding the History of English See pages 86 and 830 to learn more about the development of the English language.

STRUCTURAL UNDERSTANDING

>6 Use knowledge of Greek, Latin and Anglo-Saxon roots, prefixes and suffixes to understand complex words and new subject-area vocabulary (e.g., unknown words in science, mathematics and social studies).

What does it mean? You will break words into parts—roots and affixes—and use the meanings of those parts to understand new terms.

EXAMPLE: Analyzing Word Structure For roots, prefixes, and suffixes, see pages 510, 542, 545, 611, 625, 833, and 914.

TOOLS AND RESOURCES

>7 Determine the meanings and pronunciations of unknown words by using dictionaries, thesauruses, glossaries, technology and textual features, such as definitional footnotes or sidebars.

What does it mean? Use reference sources and text features to aid your comprehension and pronunciation of new words.

EXAMPLE: Using Tools and Resources You will find on-page footnotes giving vocabulary classifications, pronunciations, and definitions for unfamiliar words in reading selections. On pages 1067–1076, you will find English and Spanish glossaries.

Reading Process: Concepts of Print, Comprehension Strategies and Self-Monitoring Strategies

COMPREHENSION STRATEGIES

>1 Apply reading comprehension strategies, including making predictions, comparing and contrasting, recalling and summarizing and making inferences and drawing conclusions.

What does it mean? Effective readers use a variety of reading comprehension strategies to fully grasp texts.

EXAMPLE: Making Inferences See information on making inferences (pages 154, 157, and 163), making predictions (page 259), drawing conclusions (pages 371 and 417), and retelling (pages 23 and 24).

>2 Answer literal, inferential, evaluative and synthesizing questions to demonstrate comprehension of grade-appropriate print texts and electronic and visual media.

What does it mean? For maximum comprehension, you will not only recall facts, but also draw conclusions, predict outcomes, and evaluate and synthesize what you read.

EXAMPLE: Answering Questions See the Reading Check and Literary Focus questions at the end of the selections. For example, see the wide range of questions on page 85 for "Flowers for Algernon."

SELF-MONITORING STRATEGIES

>3 Monitor own comprehension by adjusting speed to fit the purpose, or

Columbus skyline

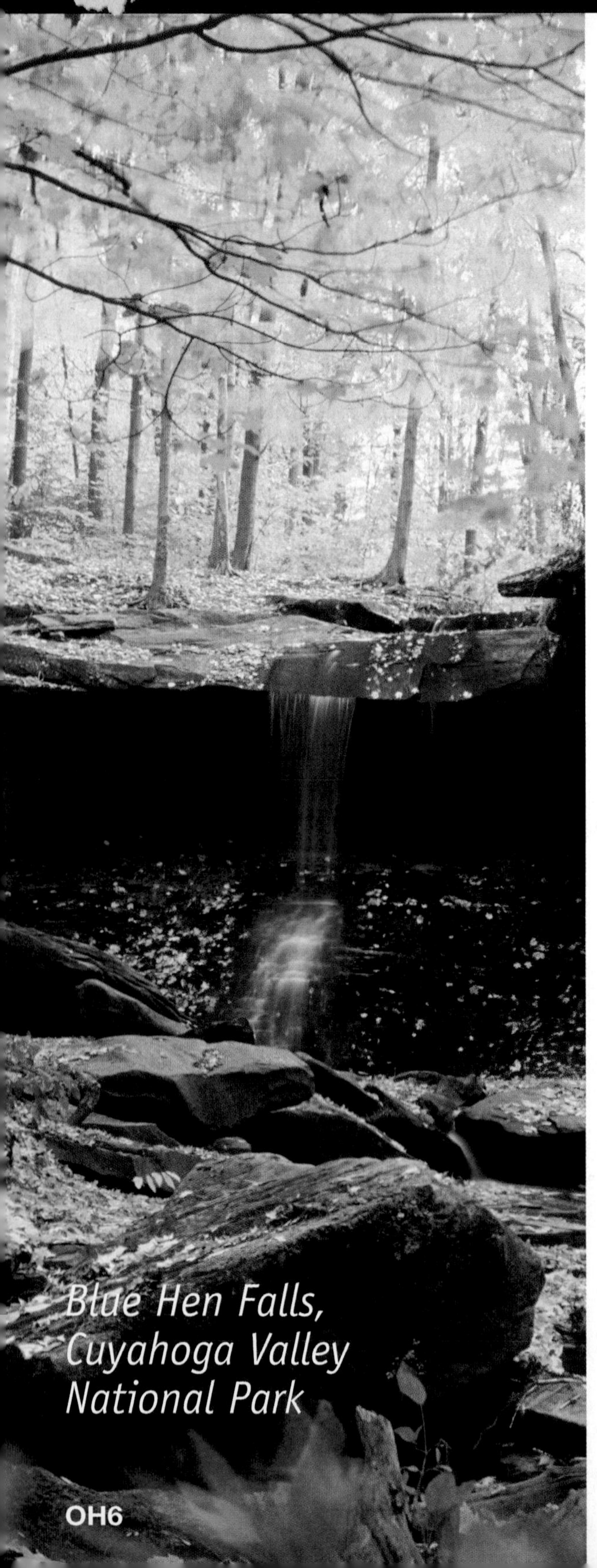
Blue Hen Falls, Cuyahoga Valley National Park

by skimming, scanning, reading on, looking back, note taking or summarizing what has been read so far in text.

What does it mean? If you find yourself getting confused as you read, slow down and use strategies to get back on track.

EXAMPLE: Self-Monitoring Comprehension Learn about taking notes and outlining (page 491) and understanding informative texts (pages 598–599). See also the many self-monitoring reading questions in selections such as "The Inn of Lost Time" on pages 33–48.

INDEPENDENT READING

>4 Use criteria to choose independent reading materials (e.g., personal interest, knowledge of authors and genres or recommendations from others).

What does it mean? To find good reading material, you might try choosing works according to personal interest, knowledge of authors and genres, or recommendations from others.

EXAMPLE: Reading Independently Read On, at the end of each collection, suggests books for independent reading (see, for example, pages 480–481).

>5 Independently read books for various purposes (e.g., for enjoyment, for literary experience, to gain information or to perform a task).

What does it mean? You may choose books for enjoyment, for literary experience, to gain information, or to perform a task.

EXAMPLE: Reading Independently Read On, at the end of each collection, suggests books for independent reading (see, for example, pages 480–481).

Reading Applications: Informational, Technical and Persuasive Text

>1 Compare and contrast text features, including format and headers of various informational texts in terms of their structure and purpose.

What does it mean? You will learn to analyze text features to find information quickly.

EXAMPLE: Using Text Features See page 221 for information about text features.

>2 Identify and use the organizational structure of a text, such as chronological, compare-contrast, cause-effect, problem-solution, and evaluate its effectiveness.

What does it mean? Recognizing the organizational pattern an author uses can enhance your understanding of a text.

EXAMPLE: Understanding Text Structures For help in identifying and understanding comparison and contrast, see pages 337 and 492; cause and effect, pages 331, 333, and 335; and chronological order, page 486.

>3 Compare and contrast the treatment, scope and organization of ideas from different sources on the same topic.

What does it mean? You will learn to use different sources to analyze a topic from different perspectives.

EXAMPLE: Comparing Texts See page 221 for information about comparing texts. See also the different selections on the Battle of Shiloh (pages 545–561).

>4 Analyze information found in maps, charts, tables, graphs, diagrams, cutaways and overlays.

What does it mean? You will learn to read graphic elements and understand the information they convey.

EXAMPLE: Analyzing Graphic Features For practice reading maps, see page 603 and the maps that appear throughout the text (see, for example, page 547). For practice reading diagrams, see pages 5, 50, 112, and 417.

>5 Assess the adequacy, accuracy and appropriateness of an author's details, identifying persuasive techniques (e.g., bandwagon, testimonial and emotional word repetition) and examples of bias and stereotyping.

What does it mean? You will analyze how an author appeals to an audience and examine the techniques, details, and evidence that develop a viewpoint.

EXAMPLE: Identifying Persuasive Techniques See the Writing Skills Review, "Persuasive Essay," on page 593. See also "Presenting a Persuasive Speech" (pages 584–585).

>6 Identify the author's purpose and intended audience for the text.

What does it mean? You will learn how authors use different types of writing to present their ideas.

EXAMPLE: Identifying Author's Purpose For information about the purpose of a text, see pages 112 and 126–127.

>7 Analyze an author's argument, perspective or viewpoint and explain the development of key points.

What does it mean? You will learn how to identify the author's main idea and evaluate supporting details.

EXAMPLE: Analyzing an Author's Argument Learn about the main idea and supporting details on page 486, and coherence and internal consistency on page 487.

>8 Recognize how writers cite facts, draw inferences and present opinions in informational text.

What does it mean? As you read a text, ask yourself whether the author's statements can be proved or not—whether they are facts or opinions.

EXAMPLE: Analyzing Inferences See the information on supported and unsupported inferences (pages 154, 157, 163, and 805).

>9 Distinguish the characteristics of consumer materials (e.g., warranties, product information, instructional materials), functional or workplace documents (e.g., job-related materials, memoranda, instructions) and public documents (e.g., speeches or newspaper editorials).

What does it mean? Use the features and organization of real-world documents to aid your understanding.

EXAMPLE: Analyzing Consumer and Workplace Documents See all of Collection 6 (pages 596–665) on analyzing consumer and public documents.

Reading Applications: Literary Text

>1 Identify and explain various types of characters (e.g., flat, round, dynamic, static) and how their interactions and conflicts affect the plot.

What does it mean? You will examine characters in literary texts and analyze the techniques authors use to bring their characters to life.

EXAMPLE: Analyzing Character and Conflict See pages 150–151, 163, and 208 for information on character and pages 5, and 15 for information on conflict.

>2 Analyze the influence of setting in relation to other literary elements.

What does it mean? Time, place, and atmosphere are elements of setting.

EXAMPLE: Analyzing Setting For information about setting, see pages 5–9.

>3 Explain how authors pace action and use subplots, parallel episodes and climax.

What does it mean? Understanding plot structure—the rising action, climax, and resolution—can help you follow the action in a story.

EXAMPLE: Analyzing Plot See the essay on plot (pages 4–5).

>4 Compare and contrast different points of view (e.g., first person and third person limited, omniscient, objective and subjective), and explain how voice affects literary text.

What does it mean? Point of view affects what readers learn about events and people in the text.

EXAMPLE: Analyzing Point of View See page 303 for information about the narrator and pages 221 and 948 for instruction on objective and subjective writing.

>5 Identify and explain universal themes across different works by the same author and by different authors.

What does it mean? As you read works from different time periods and countries,

you will learn to look for universal themes and symbols.

EXAMPLE: Identifying Universal Themes In Collection 8, you will compare and contrast universal themes in several groups of works (see pages 917–921 on Anne Frank and pages 923–925 on the civil war in the former Yugoslavia).

>6 Explain how an author's choice of genre affects the expression of theme or topic.

What does it mean? You will analyze how genre—or particular type of writing—affects the way an author communicates a message.

EXAMPLE: Understanding Genres See "Comparing Themes Across Genres," pages 306–307.

>7 Identify examples of foreshadowing and flashback in a literary text.

What does it mean? Authors use foreshadowing and flashback to play with time and add to the impact of story events.

EXAMPLE: Identifying Foreshadowing and Flashback You will encounter many examples of foreshadowing and flashback as you read the fiction and drama selections in this textbook.

>8 Explain ways in which the author conveys mood and tone through word choice, figurative language, and syntax.

What does it mean? The word choices and sentence structures contribute to a story's atmosphere or feeling (mood) and to the writer's attitude (tone).

EXAMPLE: Analyzing Mood See page 5 and 366 for information about mood and tone.

>9 Examine symbols used in literary texts.

What does it mean? You will learn how authors make symbols work and how readers make sense of them.

EXAMPLE: Understanding Symbols For information about symbols, see pages 366 and 372.

Cleveland

WRITING

Writing Processes

PREWRITING

>1 Generate writing ideas through discussions with others and from printed material, and keep a list of writing ideas.

What does it mean? Writing ideas may come from a vivid memory or a chat with a friend. Keep a list of such ideas to avoid writer's block.

EXAMPLE: Generating Writing Ideas In each of the Writing Workshops, you will find specific suggestions for generating ideas. See, for example, "Idea Starters" on page 231.

>2 Conduct background reading, interviews or surveys when appropriate.

What does it mean? When you write expository or persuasive papers, you will often have to do research by reading or conducting interviews.

EXAMPLE: Preparing for Writing On pages 658–659 you will learn how to conduct an interview. On page 955 you will find advice on background reading and gathering information for a research report.

>3 Establish a thesis statement for informational writing or a plan for narrative writing.

What does it mean? You will learn to build any type of writing around a central idea.

EXAMPLE: Focusing Your Writing The persuasive Writing Workshop gives advice on writing a thesis statement (see page 575). See also page 128 for planning a personal narrative.

>4 Determine a purpose and audience and plan strategies (e.g., adapting focus, content structure and point of view) to address purpose and audience.

What does it mean? Before you write, you will want to decide why you are writing and who your audience is.

EXAMPLE: Determining Purpose and Audience It's essential to identify your purpose and audience before you begin writing. For instruction on audience and purpose, see "Think About Audience and Purpose" (page 128).

>5 Use organizational strategies (e.g., notes and outlines) to plan writing.

What does it mean? You will learn how to organize your ideas by jotting them down in outlines, diagrams, and webs.

EXAMPLE: Using Organizational Strategies See information on outlines (page 232), charts (pages 5 and 1008), and Venn diagrams (page 996).

DRAFTING, REVISING AND EDITING

>6 Organize writing with an effective and engaging introduction, body and a conclusion that summarizes, extends or elaborates on points or ideas in the writing.

What does it mean? This indicator asks you to follow the standard organizational pattern when writing essays and narratives.

EXAMPLE: Organizing Writing In each Writing Workshop a writer's framework gives tips about an essay's introduction, body, and conclusion (see pages 126 and 230).

>7 Vary simple, compound and complex sentence structures.

What does it mean? You will learn to vary sentence structures so that your sentences flow smoothly instead of having a choppy, singsong quality.

EXAMPLE: Varying Sentences For information about sentences, see pages 1050–1051 in the Language Handbook.

>8 Group related ideas into paragraphs, including topic sentences following paragraph form, and maintain a consistent focus reinforced by parallel structures across paragraphs.

What does it mean? You will learn to organize your paragraphs so that they have a main idea and supporting evidence.

EXAMPLE: Writing Effective Paragraphs See pages 349–351 for tips about writing effective paragraphs.

>9 Use precise language, action verbs, sensory details, colorful modifiers and style as appropriate to audience and purpose.

What does it mean? Vivid, precise words and a distinctive voice will help interest readers in your ideas.

EXAMPLE: Using Effective Language See pages 87 and 543 on using action verbs and appropriate modifiers.

>10 Use available technology to compose text.

What does it mean? Word processors, Internet resources, and audio recorders can help you create written work.

EXAMPLE: Using Technology to Create Graphics For help with the visual design of your texts, see "Creating Graphics for Technical Documents" (pages 1021–1022).

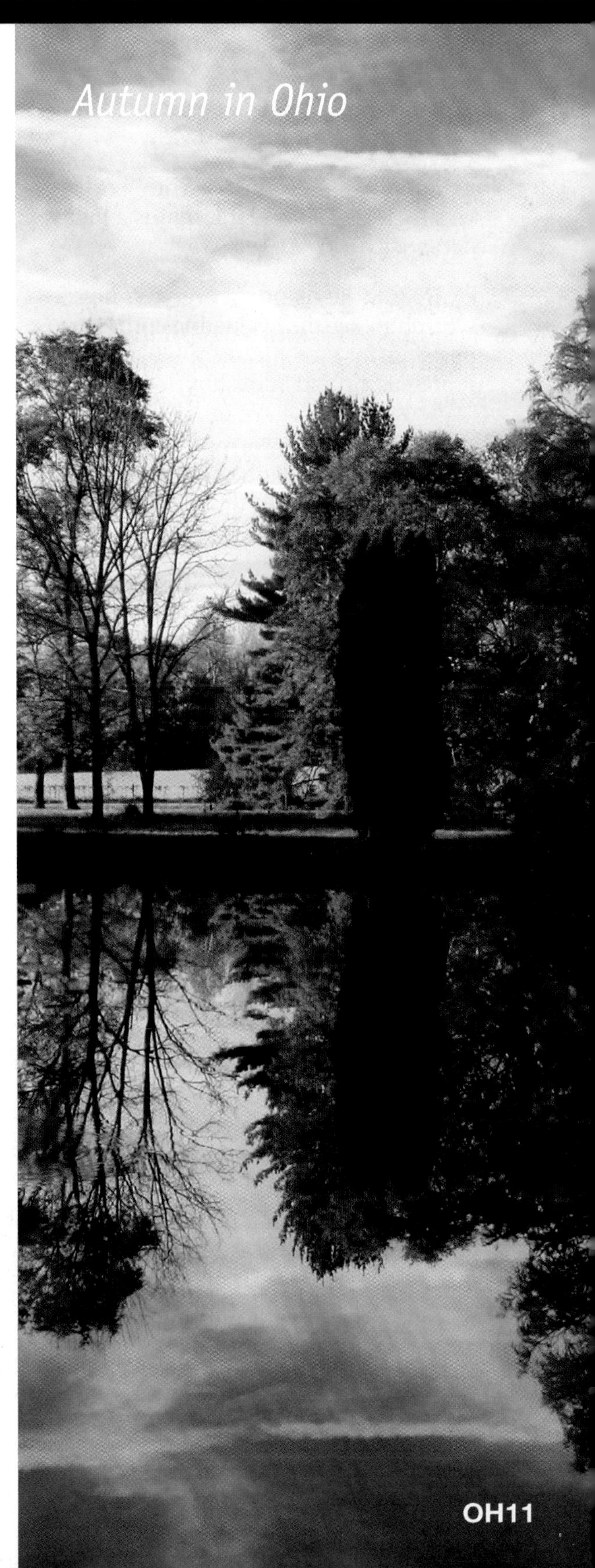
Autumn in Ohio

>11 Reread and analyze clarity of writing and consistency of point of view.

What does it mean? Revise your work to be sure it is clear and maintains a focused perspective.

EXAMPLE: Revising In every Writing Workshop, see the Evaluating and Revising (for example, page 466) and the Proofreading and Publishing (see page 469).

>12 Add and delete information and details to better elaborate on a stated central idea, and to more effectively accomplish purpose.

What does it mean? Sometimes you will need to add or delete information to support your point more effectively.

EXAMPLE: Elaborating Ideas Several of the Writing Workshops include information about elaborating within the Evaluating and Revising feature (see, for example, page 234).

>13 Rearrange words, sentences and paragraphs, and add transitional words and phrases to clarify meaning.

What does it mean? Varying sentence structure and using transitional words can improve the flow of your work and clarify your meaning.

EXAMPLE: Revising for Clarity See the revising techniques in every Writing Workshop (for example, page 234). You can focus on one writer's revisions of several paragraphs on pages 131–132. You can also learn about transitions by reading the Mini-Lesson on page 132.

>14 Use resources and reference materials (e.g., dictionaries and thesauruses) to select more effective vocabulary.

What does it mean? Reference works are great tools for improving word choice.

EXAMPLE: Using Resources You will use a dictionary to find etymologies (page 176). You can also use the glossaries at the back of this book (see pages 1067–1076).

>15 Proofread writing, edit to improve conventions (e.g., grammar, spelling, punctuation and capitalization), and identify and correct fragments and run-ons.

Toledo, Ohio

What does it mean? You will check written work for correct grammar, spelling, punctuation, and capitalization.

EXAMPLE: Proofreading Every Writing Workshop has proofreading tips (see page 351 for an example). You will find proofreaders' marks on page 1017.

>16 Apply tools (e.g., rubric, checklist and feedback) to judge the quality of writing.

What does it mean? To assess whether your writing meets high standards, you can use rubrics and peer feedback.

EXAMPLE: Using Tools to Evaluate Writing Workshops list evaluation criteria and provide guidelines for revision (for example, page 234).

PUBLISHING

>17 Prepare for publication (e.g., for display or for sharing with others) writing that follows a format appropriate to the purpose, using such techniques as electronic resources, principles of design (e.g., margins, tabs, spacing and columns) and graphics (e.g., drawings, charts and graphs) to enhance the final product.

What does it mean? After you've worked hard to create a written work, you will want to publish it for others to appreciate.

EXAMPLE: Publishing You may decide to post your writing online or create a classroom anthology. At the end of each Writing Workshop, you will find publishing suggestions (for example, see page 237). For help creating graphics, see pages 1021–1022.

Writing Applications

>1 Write narratives that: (a) sustain reader interest by pacing action and developing engaging plot (e.g., tension and suspense); use literary devices to enhance style and (b) tone; and (c) create complex characters in a definite, believable setting.

What does it mean? This indicator asks you to write focused, interesting narratives.

EXAMPLE: Writing Narratives You will find step-by-step guidance in two narrative Writing Workshops: "Personal Narrative" (page 126) and "Short Story" (page 230).

>2 Write responses to literature that organize an insightful interpretation around several clear ideas, premises or images and support judgments with specific references to the original text, to other texts, authors and to prior knowledge.

What does it mean? You will learn to write thoughtful interpretations of literary works.

EXAMPLE: Responding to Literature You will have many opportunities to write brief responses to literature. You will also write an essay in the Writing Workshop, "Response to Literature," (page 344).

>3 Write business letters, letters to the editor and job applications that: (a) address audience needs, stated purpose and context in a clear and efficient manner; (b) follow the conventional style appropriate to the text using proper technical terms; (c) include appropriate facts and details; (d) exclude extraneous details and inconsistencies; and (e) provide a sense of closure to the writing.

What does it mean? Learning to write business letters is something that will help you long after you graduate from school.

EXAMPLE: Writing a Business Letter See the Writing Workshop, "Business Letters and Memos," page 648.

>4 Write informational essays or reports, including research, that: (a) pose relevant and tightly drawn questions that engage the reader; (b) provide a clear and accurate perspective on the subject; (c) create an organizing structure appropriate to the purpose, audience and context; (d) support the main ideas with facts, details, examples and explanations from sources; and (e) document sources and include bibliographies.

What does it mean? You will learn to write effective, informative research papers.

EXAMPLE: Writing Informational Essays and Reports The Writing Workshop "Technical Documents" (page 462) guides you through every step in the process of planning, drafting, and revising.

>5 Write persuasive compositions that: (a) establish and develop a controlling idea; (b) support arguments with detailed evidence; (c) exclude irrelevant information; and (d) cite sources of information.

What does it mean? This indicator asks you to write persuasive essays that are clear and organized.

EXAMPLE: Writing Persuasive Essays See the Writing Workshop "Persuasive Writing" (page 574).

>6 Produce informal writings (e.g., journals, notes and poems) for various purposes.

What does it mean? You will learn to write effectively in informal contexts.

EXAMPLE: Writing Informally Writing Focus features offer many opportunities to write informally. For example, you will write a character sketch (page 218), an outline (page 229), and a paragraph (page 452).

Writing Conventions

SPELLING

>1 Use correct spelling conventions.

What does it mean? Don't rely on a computer spellchecker. Learn or look up the words you use in your writing.

EXAMPLE: Using Correct Spelling See pages 1062–1064 in the Language Handbook for spelling rules.

PUNCTUATION AND CAPITALIZATION

>2 Use correct punctuation and capitalization.

What does it mean? Correct punctuation and capitalization help make your writing clear and authoritative.

EXAMPLE: Using Correct Punctuation See instruction on capitalization (pages 1052–1054) and punctuation (pages 1054–1062) in the Language Handbook.

GRAMMAR AND USAGE

>3 Use all eight parts of speech (e.g., noun, pronoun, verb, adverb, adjective, conjunction, preposition, interjection).

What does it mean? Understanding the functions of the eight parts of speech can help you use them more effectively in your writing.

EXAMPLE: Using Parts of Speech
For information about the parts of speech, see the Grammar Links on pages 29, 51, and 87. In the Language Handbook, see parts of speech (pages 1023–1029), subject-verb agreement (pages 1030–1032), pronoun usage (pages 1037–1038), and modifiers (pages 1039–1040).

>4 Use clauses (e.g., main, subordinate) and phrases (e.g., gerund, infinitive, participial).

What does it mean? A clause is a group of words with a subject and verb, and it is used as part of a sentence. A phrase is a group of related words that is used as a single part of speech.

EXAMPLE: Using Clauses and Phrases
See clauses (pages 1044–1045) and phrases (pages 1041–1043) in the Language Handbook.

>5 Use parallel structure to present items in a series and items juxtaposed for emphasis.

What does it mean? Parallel structure means using the same grammatical form to express like concepts. For example, the sentence "We used to swim, ski, and hike" has three parallel verb forms.

EXAMPLE: Using Parallel Structure For examples of parallel structure, see page 1055 on punctuating items in a series.

>6 Use proper placement of modifiers.

What does it mean? A misplaced modifier may be confusing or unintentionally funny, as in this example: "Barking and jumping into the pool, I saw a big dog."

EXAMPLE: Using Modifiers See the Grammar Link on page 581 and "Placement of Modifiers" on page 1040 in the Language Handbook.

>7 Maintain the use of appropriate verb tenses.

What does it mean? Avoid shifting verb tenses unless the shift is to achieve a particular effect—for example, in a flashback.

EXAMPLE: Using Verb Tenses For practice choosing the correct verb tense, see the Grammar Link on page 523. See also page 1034 in the Language Handbook.

Rhododendron and azalea gardens

>8 Conjugate regular and irregular verbs in all tenses correctly.

What does it mean? This indicator asks you to use the different tenses of verbs correctly.

EXAMPLE: Using Verbs Correctly See the Grammar Link on page 523 and "Using Verbs" on pages 1033–1036 in the Language Handbook.

RESEARCH

>1 Compose open-ended questions for research, assigned or personal interest, and modify questions as necessary during inquiry and investigation.

What does it mean? You will learn to choose research topics and to adapt and refine them.

EXAMPLE: Choosing a Topic For help with selecting and developing a topic for a research report, see pages 954–961.

>2 Identify appropriate sources and gather relevant information from multiple sources (e.g., school library catalogs, online databases, electronic resources, and Internet-based resources).

What does it mean? You will learn how to find and choose appropriate resources.

EXAMPLE: Finding and Using Sources On page 955, you will find information about primary and secondary sources.

>3 Explain the usefulness and accuracy of sources by determining their validity (e.g., authority, accuracy, objectivity, publication date and coverage) and define primary and secondary sources.

What does it mean? You will learn how to evaluate research sources.

EXAMPLE: Evaluating Sources See "Evaluating Web Sources" on pages 1014–1015).

>4 Select an appropriate structure for organizing information in a systematic way (e.g., notes, outlines, charts, tables and graphic organizers).

What does it mean? You will learn to use outlines, charts, and graphic organizers to keep track of your information.

EXAMPLE: Taking Notes For information on preparing source cards and taking notes, see pages 956 and 1004.

>5 Compile and organize the important information and select appropriate sources to support central ideas, concepts and themes.

What does it mean? Solid research requires you to find information and support in the sources you choose and to organize that information.

EXAMPLE: Organizing Information For information on how to sort your notes for an outline, see page 956.

>6 Integrate quotations and citations into written text to maintain a flow of ideas.

What does it mean? In your writing, you will use quotations and citations effectively and fluently.

EXAMPLE: Using Quotations For information about using direct quotations, see pages 1059–1060. For an example of a citation in a text, see the Student Model on page 960.

>7 Use style guides to produce oral and written reports that give proper credit for sources and include an acceptable format for source acknowledgement.

What does it mean? Style guides such as the MLA Handbook for Writers of Research Papers show how to cite and credit your research sources.

EXAMPLE: Documenting Sources Follow the format for documenting sources that your teacher requires. See page 1016 for the MLA (Modern Language Association) style for documenting sources.

>8 Use a variety of communication techniques, including oral, visual, written or multimedia reports, to present information that supports a clear position about the topic research question and to maintain an appropriate balance between researched information and original ideas.

What does it mean? Use written and oral reports, visuals, and multimedia to present research and ideas.

EXAMPLE: Creating Multimedia Presentations See "Giving and Listening to an Informative Speech" (page 964).

COMMUNICATION: ORAL AND VISUAL

LISTENING AND VIEWING

>1 Apply active listening strategies (e.g., monitoring message for clarity, selecting and organizing essential information, noting cues such as changes in pace).

What does it mean? To be sure you understand what a speaker says, you need to ask questions, take note of gestures, and make eye contact.

EXAMPLE: Listening Actively You will listen actively as you listen to a speech and analyze and evaluate others' speeches (page 964–965).

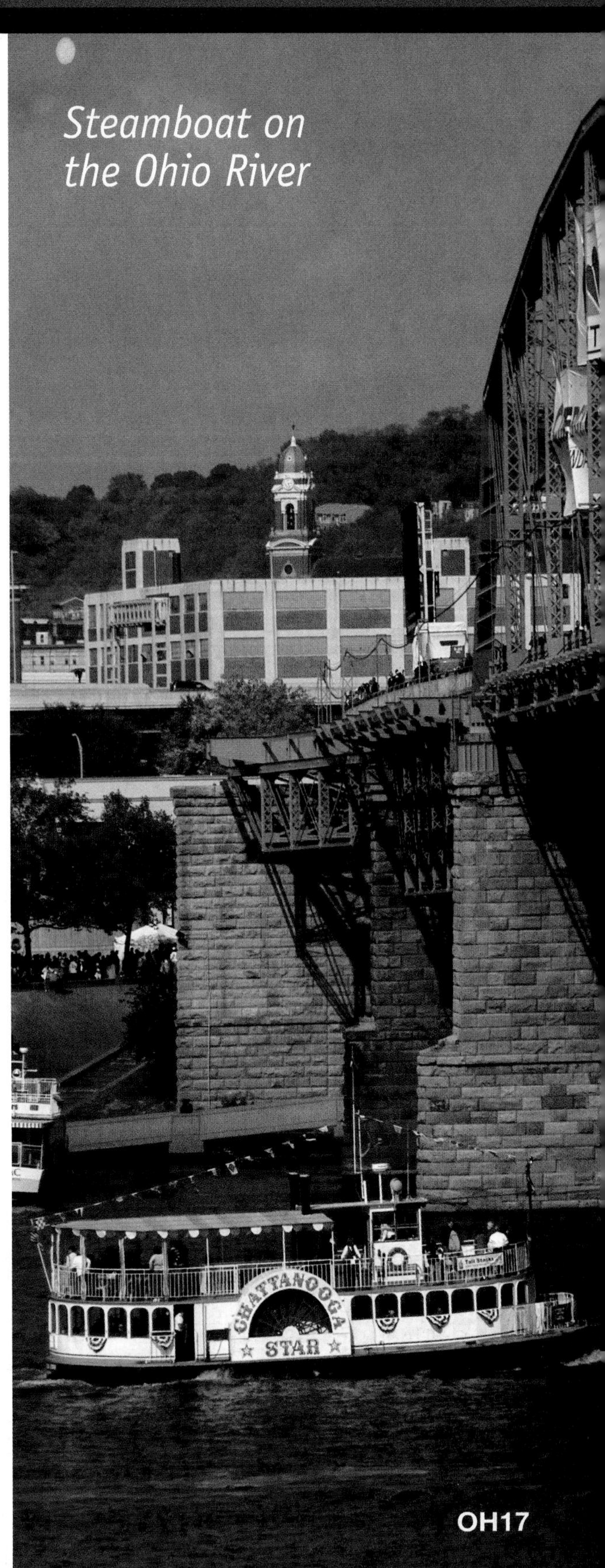

Steamboat on the Ohio River

>2 Identify and analyze the persuasive techniques (e.g., bandwagon, testimonial, glittering generalities, emotional word repetition and bait and switch) used in presentations and media messages.

What does it mean? You will learn to recognize and explain the persuasive techniques speakers use.

EXAMPLE: Identifying Persuasive Techniques See page 585, "Guidelines for Evaluating a Persuasive Speech," and pages 1018–1020, "Evaluating Persuasive Images in the Media."

>3 Determine the credibility of the speaker (e.g., hidden agendas, slanted or biased material) and recognize fallacies of reasoning used in presentations and media messages.

What does it mean? Become a savvy listener by learning to analyze and evaluate speakers' messages and agendas.

EXAMPLE: Analyzing a Speaker's Argument When you listen to a speaker, listen carefully for fallacious reasoning (pages 998–999). For help in analyzing a speaker's believability, see page 585 on "Guidelines for Evaluating a Persuasive Speech."

>4 Identify the speaker's choice of language and delivery styles (e.g., repetition, appeal to emotion, eye contact) and how they contribute to meaning.

What does it mean? You will learn to recognize speaking strategies and their effect on an audience.

EXAMPLE: Evaluating Diction and Delivery Style See the strategies for making a narrative speech (page 136) and the questions for evaluating persuasive speeches (page 585).

SPEAKING SKILLS AND STRATEGIES

>5 Demonstrate an understanding of the rules of the English language and select language appropriate to purpose and audience.

What does it mean? Effective communicators know how to use standard English, both formal and informal, to reach audiences.

EXAMPLE: Using Standard English The conventions of standard English apply to speaking as well as writing. In the Language Handbook, review the sections on grammar (pages 1023–1064) and usage (pages 1065–1066).

>6 Adjust volume, phrasing, enunciation, voice modulation and inflection to stress important ideas and impact audience response.

What does it mean? This indicator asks you to use effective delivery techniques when giving a speech.

EXAMPLE: Using Verbal Techniques You will find suggestions on verbal techniques in every Listening and Speaking Workshop. See, for example, pages 137 and 472.

>7 Vary language choices as appropriate to the context of the speech.

What does it mean? You will learn to choose your words to fit the audience and the occasion.

EXAMPLE: Using Appropriate Language For information about how to adapt your language to fit your purpose and audience, see pages 126 and 230.

SPEAKING APPLICATIONS

>8 Deliver informational presentations (e.g., expository, research) that: (a) demonstrate understanding of the topic and present events ideas in a logical sequence; (b) support the controlling idea or thesis with well-chosen and relevant facts, details, examples, quotations, statistics, stories and anecdotes; (c) include an effective introduction and conclusion and use a consistent organizational structure (e.g., cause-effect, compare-contrast, problem-solution); (d) use appropriate visual materials (e.g., diagrams, charts, illustrations) and available technology; and (e) draw from multiple sources, including both primary and secondary sources, and identify sources used.

What does it mean? This indicator asks you to give informational speeches that are organized and thorough.

EXAMPLE: Delivering Informational Presentations For step-by-step help in preparing an informational presentation, see "Giving and Listening to an Informative Speech" (page 964).

>9 Deliver formal and informal descriptive presentations that convey relevant information and descriptive details.

What does it mean? You will learn to give engaging and informative descriptive presentations.

EXAMPLE: Delivering Descriptive Presentations You will use description in delivering your oral narrative (page 136).

>10 Deliver persuasive presentations that: (a) establish and develop a logical and controlled argument; (b) include relevant evidence, differentiating between evidence and opinion to support a position and to address counter-arguments or listener bias; and (c) consistently use common organizational structures as appropriate (e.g., cause-effect, compare-contrast, problem-solution).

What does it mean? You will learn to convince your listeners of your point of view and persuade them to take action..

EXAMPLE: Delivering Persuasive Presentations See page 584 for help with planning and delivering a persuasive speech.

Farmland, Cambridge

Taking Ohio's Reading and Writing Tests

You have probably already taken national or statewide standardized tests. These tests become more important as you approach high school. Ohio's middle school achievement tests in reading and writing measure your mastery of the skills and knowledge described in Ohio's **Academic Content Standards.** The **reading test** contains reading passages and three types of questions (multiple-choice questions, short-answer questions, and extended-response questions) based on several reading passages. In the **writing test,** you may answer multiple-choice questions and short-answer questions and write essays in response to prompts.

The tips and practice in this section will help you prepare for the standardized tests in reading and in writing that you will take throughout your school career.

Marblehead Lighthouse, Lake Erie

Taking Reading Tests

Use the following tips and practice test to prepare for Ohio's reading test.

TIP 1 LOOK AHEAD. Skim the test. You will find several passages—literary and informational texts of various lengths. Notice which passages have questions that require a written response.

TIP 2 PLAN YOUR TIME. Estimate how long you can spend on each passage and set of questions. Plan to spend up to five minutes answering a short-answer question and up to fifteen minutes for an extended-response question. Check often to see if you need to work faster.

TIP 3 READ EVERYTHING CAREFULLY. Do not skip anything. Pay careful attention to the directions, the reading passages, and each entire question.

TIP 4 FOR DIFFICULT MULTIPLE-CHOICE QUESTIONS, MAKE EDUCATED GUESSES. Choose your answer only after reading all four choices carefully. You can usually eliminate one or two answers you know are wrong. Then, make an educated guess about the remaining choices. If you cannot answer a question, skip it and come back to it later.

TIP 5 ANSWER ALL PARTS OF SHORT-ANSWER AND EXTENDED-RESPONSE QUESTIONS. A written-response question is worth more points than a multiple-choice question. The test may not label short-answer and extended-response items, but your answer will be the right length if you answer *all* parts of the question. Be sure your explanation is logical and clearly related to the question and passage. Use examples from the passage as support. Also, use complete sentences.

TIP 6 MARK YOUR ANSWER CAREFULLY. Do not lose your place on the answer document. For multiple-choice questions, match your answer carefully to each question's number. Make any changes neatly. Review your answer document to make sure you filled in the correct space for every question.

Practice Reading Test

This practice test includes two reading passages, each followed by sample questions like those you might see on Ohio's reading achievement test.

Directions: After reading each passage, choose the best answer to each question. You may refer to the passages as often as necessary.

A Strange, Funny-Looking Vegetable

by Milton Meltzer

1 One day in the 1530s a scouting party of Spaniards entered an Inca village, high in the Andes in what we now call Peru. Reports of cruel and greedy white invaders had already spread throughout the mountains, and the villagers had fled at word of their coming. The Spaniards went from empty house to empty house, hunting for loot. They found only maize (corn), beans, and a strange vegetable that was like nothing they had ever seen.

2 The vegetable came in many sizes, tiny as a nut to big as an apple. Its shape ranged from an irregular ball to a twisted oblong. Its skin was white, yellow, blue, purple, red, brown. Inside, its color could be white, yellow, purple, pink. The Spaniards were not impressed. They had come to the Andes searching for gold, silver, and precious stones. What good was this funny-looking vegetable?

3 Gradually they found out. First of all, it was the staple food of these mountain people. Secondly, the vegetable was believed to have healing powers. Raw slices were fixed to broken bones, pressed against the head to cure aching, eaten with other food to end a bellyache. The Incas also rubbed it on their bodies to cure skin diseases and carried slices to prevent rheumatism.

4 The Inca name for the vegetable was *papa.* It means a tuber, a short, fleshy underground stem or root. . . . When the Spaniards tasted the potato, they found it delicious—"a dainty dish even for Spaniards,"one conquistador admitted.

5 The diet of the common people of Peru was mainly vegetarian. . . . The main diet was maize and other vegetables in the lowlands. In the highlands, where maize would not grow, it was the potato above all that people depended on. We now know that the native peoples living along the western coast of South America were growing and eating potatoes two thousand years before Columbus set sail. . . .

6 When the Spaniards discovered the rich silver mines of Potosí (now in Bolivia) in 1545, they were quick to see the use of the potato, fresh or freeze dried, as food for the Inca they forced to work for them. It didn't take long for speculators in Spain to see a new way to get rich. They sailed across the Atlantic, bought up potatoes cheaply from the Inca farmers, and sold them at high prices to the native workers in the mines.

7 Here is a strange twist of history: The annual $100-billion value of the potato crop is three times greater than the value of all the gold and silver the Spanish lugged away from the Americas. The potatoes they took so lightly turned out to be worth far more than the gold and silver they killed for.

RP.8.2

>1 What did the Spaniards hope to find in the Andes?

A. a lost civilization
B. cheap labor for European factories
C. gold, silver, and precious stones
D. food for their starving soldiers

EXPLANATION: Skim the passage to look for key words. The correct answer, C, is stated in paragraph 2.

RA.I.8.7

>2 The writer's viewpoint toward the Spanish conquistadors is

A. sympathetic.
B. critical.
C. approving.
D. admiring.

EXPLANATION: Notice the words the writer uses to describe the Spanish conquistadors (cruel, greedy). The correct answer is B.

Terminal Tower, Cleveland

VO.8.1

>3 In paragraph 7, **lugged** means

A. dragged.
B. discovered.
C. imported.
D. destroyed.

EXPLANATION: The most useful context clue is the word away. You can eliminate B, C, and D, since none of these meanings go with away. The correct answer is A.

RP.8.1

>4 According to the passage, which of the following is probably true about Inca society?

A. The Incas developed great wealth from mining.
B. The Incas were a trusting people who welcomed outsiders.
C. The Incas had extensive agricultural knowledge.
D. The Incas had a highly developed religion and built great temples.

EXPLANATION: A is wrong because the text mentions only forced labor in mines owned by the Spanish. B is wrong because the text says the Incas fled from the Spanish. D may be true, but the article gives no information on the Inca religion. C is correct.

Corn fields, rural Ohio

WA.8.2

>5 Write a summary of the article, using your own words but keeping the organizational structure the writer used. Write your response on a separate sheet of paper. Then, read the sample response below.

Sample Response

In the 1530s, Spaniards searched an Inca village for gold and silver. They were disappointed to find only corn, beans, and lots of an unusual vegetable called a "papa," the Inca name for "potato." Later, they learned that the potato was both useful and tasty. The Incas thought it had healing powers, and it had been a major part of their diet for two thousand years. Spanish speculators bought potatoes cheaply from the Inca farmers and sold them at a profit to the Inca workers in the silver mines. Today, the annual potato crop is worth three times as much as all the gold and silver the Spanish found.

The following is an excerpt from the beginning of a short story.

from The Open Window

by Saki

1 "My aunt [Mrs. Sappleton] will be down presently, Mr. Nuttel," said a very self-possessed young lady of fifteen; "in the meantime you must try and put up with me."

2 Framton Nuttel endeavored to say the correct something which should duly flatter the niece of the moment without unduly discounting the aunt that was to come. Privately he doubted more than ever whether these formal visits on a succession of total strangers would do much toward helping the nerve cure which he was supposed to be undergoing.

3 "I know how it will be," his sister had said when he was preparing to migrate to this rural retreat; "you will bury yourself down there and not speak to a living soul, and your nerves will be worse than ever from moping.

I shall just give you letters of introduction to all the people I know there. Some of them, as far as I can remember, were quite nice." . . .

4 "Do you know many of the people round here?" asked the niece, when she judged that they had had sufficient silent communion.

5 "Hardly a soul," said Framton. "My sister was staying here, at the rectory, you know, some four years ago, and she gave me letters of introduction to some of the people here." . . .

6 "Then you know practically nothing about my aunt?" pursued the self-possessed young lady.

7 "Only her name and address," admitted the caller. . . .

8 "Her great tragedy happened just three years ago," said the child; "that would be since your sister's time."

9 "Her tragedy?" asked Framton. . . .

10 "You may wonder why we keep that window wide open on an October afternoon," said the niece, indicating a large French window that opened onto a lawn.

11 "It is quite warm for the time of the year," said Framton, "but has that window got anything to do with the tragedy?"

12 "Out through that window, three years ago to a day, her husband and her two young brothers went off for their day's shooting. They never came back. In crossing the moor to their favorite snipe-shooting ground, they were all three engulfed in a treacherous piece of bog. It had been that dreadful wet summer, you know, and places that were safe in other years gave way suddenly without warning. Their bodies were never recovered. That was the dreadful part of it." Here the child's voice lost its self-possessed note and became falteringly human. "Poor aunt always thinks that they will come back someday, they and the little brown spaniel that was lost with them, and walk in at that window just as they used to do. That is why the window is kept open every evening till it is quite dusk. Poor dear aunt, she has often told me how they went out, her husband with his white waterproof coat over his arm, and Ronnie, her youngest brother, singing, 'Bertie, why do you bound?' as he always did to tease her, because she said it got on her nerves. Do you know, sometimes on still, quiet evenings like this, I almost get a creepy feeling that they will all walk in through that window—"

RP.8.2

>6 Which of the following adjectives does not describe Framton Nuttel?

A. nervous
B. confident
C. tense
D. worried

EXPLANATION: Notice the word not in the question. The only adjective that does not describe the character is B, confident. B is the correct answer.

VO.8.6

>7 The author uses the word discounting in paragraph 2. The prefix *dis–* comes from Latin, and it means "to do the opposite of." Framton Nuttel does not want to discount the aunt; he wants to treat her with

A. respect.
B. rudeness.
C. pity.
D. amusement.

EXPLANATION: In this context, the word *discounting* means "not counting" or "making unimportant." Nuttel wants to say something flattering to the niece that does not make the aunt seem unimportant. In other words, he wants to treat the aunt with respect. A is the correct answer.

RA.8.7

>8 The purpose of the flashback in paragraph 3 is to

A. introduce an important character.
B. introduce the theme of loneliness.
C. explain an important mystery.
D. explain the basic story situation.

EXPLANATION: You can eliminate A and C; the sister does not seem important, and there is no mention of a mystery. B seems possible, but in the context of the passage as a whole, D is the better choice. D explains why Framton Nuttel is there waiting for Mrs. Sappleton.

RA.8.4

>9 The third-person limited point of view allows the reader to learn the thoughts and feelings of

A. the fifteen-year-old niece.
B. Framton Nuttel.
C. Mrs. Sappleton.
D. all of the characters.

EXPLANATION: The passage reveals the thoughts and feelings of Framton Nuttel, not of the niece or her aunt and, therefore, not all of the characters. B is the correct answer.

RA.8.8

>10 What mood does the writer create in this story excerpt? Give examples from the passage of details and word choices the author uses to create this mood. Write your response on a separate sheet of paper. Then, read the sample response below.

Sample Response

At first, Saki creates a very quiet mood. The dialogue between Framton Nuttel and the niece is boringly polite. As the story continues, Saki gradually creates a mood of sadness and fear with the niece's description of "the tragedy." The niece's voice changes from "self-possessed" to "falteringly human." The girl also describes having a "creepy feeling." These details and word choices bring a sense of approaching doom to the story.

Taking Writing Tests

On a writing test, you might answer multiple-choice and short-answer questions about writing processes and respond to prompts that assess writing applications and conventions. The sample questions that follow will prepare you for the kinds of questions you may see on the Ohio graduation test in writing. You will take this test in Grade 10.

Here is the first part of Caroline's rough draft of an essay about soccer. Use this rough draft to answer the questions that follow.

(1) Anyone can tell you that baseball, football, and basketball are popular sports in the United States. (2) My favorite sport is tennis. (3) However, soccer is the world's most popular sport. (4) It is played in almost every country. (5) What makes it so appealing? (6) The game moves quickly and demands that players be in top physical condition and that they work together as a team.

(7) Historians say that games like soccer have been played for over two thousand years. (8) A professional soccer team has eleven players. (9) Only goalkeepers can use their arms or hands; the rest of the players hit the ball with their feet, head, or other body parts. (10) Soccer has been an Olympic event since 1900, but the game goes back a very long way. (11) As in hockey, a point is scored when the ball enters the goal of the opposing team.

WP.8.13

>1 Which transition fits best at the beginning of sentence 8?

A. However,
B. Therefore,
C. As a result,
D. Today,

EXPLANATION: Try out each transition. Only one makes sense in the context, tying together the ideas in sentences 7 and 8. The correct answer is D.

WP.8.13

>2 Sentence 10 is out of place. Where should it go?

A. before sentence 1
B. before sentence 5
C. before sentence 7
D. after sentence 11

EXPLANATION: Try out sentence 10 in each of the suggested places. Because of the clause "but the game goes back a very long way," sentence 10 fits in only one place. The correct answer is C.

WP.8.12

>3 Which sentence should Caroline delete because it destroys the paragraph's unity?

A. 2
B. 3
C. 5
D. 7

EXPLANATION: Although sentence 2 is about sports, it does not fit in with the other sentences in the paragraph. The correct answer is A.

WA.8.5

>4 Caroline's purpose for writing is informative. Using ideas from the passage as well as your own ideas, write a persuasive paragraph to convince fellow students to play soccer. Write your response on a separate sheet of paper. Then, read the sample response below.

Sample Response

Would you like to get fit and have fun doing it? If so, you should play soccer. Soccer players run almost constantly. Instead of running on a boring track, soccer players run on a grass field and play a game. The game is very fast, so there is no time to think about anything except the game. You might build great friendships with people on your team or even with people on the opposing team. When the game is finished, you will have had an energetic physical workout, a mental break, and a great time. What could be better?

Responding to Writing Prompts

This section of a writing test may ask you to write narrative, persuasive, or expository responses to prompts. Use the steps of the writing process to develop each response.

Sample Writing Prompt and Response

WA.8.4

Older generations have much to teach. They have experienced many of the situations that await you as you grow older. Write a paper about the life experiences of an older person you know or about what younger people can learn from older generations.

Here is one writer's response to the sample writing prompt. It would likely receive a high score.

The writer introduces the focus of her essay.

The writer discusses a significant event in her grandmother's life.

The writer discusses a second significant event.

The writer discusses more significant events and continues to emphasize her grandmother's character.

The writer concludes by restating the focus of the essay.

My Grandmother

Last year, I created a family tree for a history assignment. The tree showed four generations of relatives. For help in gathering information, I went to my grandmother. She had all the information I needed—and more. I learned a lot about my family that day. Most of all, though, I learned what amazing experiences my grandmother has had.

My grandmother went through some tough times when she was a young girl. She was born into a Jewish family in Hungary and, because of the Nazis, had to go into hiding during World War II. She and her family stayed with a farmer who hid them. They lived in constant fear that they would be caught, but they made it through.

After the war, my grandmother and her family moved to Budapest. For a while, they were safe and happy, but everything changed when the Russians invaded the country. People were not allowed to leave freely, so they had to escape. On the night they left for Vienna, all they took was a change of clothes. The escape was very dangerous. As they walked across the border, there was gunfire all around them. Again, they made it through.

When my grandmother was fourteen, she moved here. Moving here was hard for her because she had to leave her home and all of her friends again. She had gotten through difficult times before, though. In America, she worked hard in school and eventually went to college, where she met my grandfather. After they got married, she had a family of her own—two girls and two boys. Even with so much to do in helping to raise a family, she still somehow made the time to go to law school and then later to run her own law firm.

Today, my grandmother is still going strong. She is a great example. When she tells me stories about her life, I feel inspired. She went through such tough times to get to where she is now.

Evaluating Your Writing

Each essay will receive a score based on a rubric. Here are some criteria for a high score:

- The paper **focuses** clearly on the subject of the prompt.
- The topic is fully **developed** through strong examples and details. Ideas flow naturally.
- The organizational structure is logical throughout the paper.
- **Vocabulary** is chosen carefully to achieve the **purpose. Sentence structure** is generally varied. Vocabulary and sentence structure contribute to an identifiable personal **style** and **voice.**
- The paper demonstrates concern for the target **audience.**
- Errors in **mechanics** do not interfere with understanding.

HOLT

Elements of LITERATURE

Second Course

How To Use Your READER/WRITER Notebook

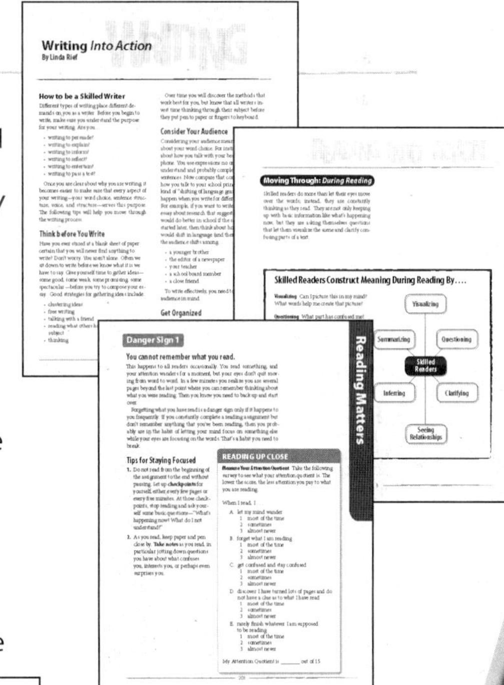

You've been in school long enough to know that you can't write in your textbooks. But, many times, you need a place to capture your thoughts about what you are reading or write your ideas down on paper. Your *Reader/Writer Notebook* is a place where you can do just that.

Want to improve your skills?

By now, you can read and write, but are you as strong as you want to be? In your *Reader/Writer Notebook*, you'll find helpful tips from real experts on how to become a better reader and writer. You can also take a survey to help you see how you think as a reader and as a writer.

Thinking like a Reader

In your notebook, you can track how much you read, what you read, and how you react to each piece. This habit helps you understand what you like or don't like to read, but more importantly, you can chart how reading changes you. Just as musicians can quickly tell you music that they enjoy playing and athletes can reaccount their victories, you can know what makes you a reader.

Your teachers probably tell you to take notes about what you are reading, but that task is easier said than done! A blank piece of paper doesn't tell you how to take notes, but your *Reader/Writer Notebook* outlines space for you to take notes on up to 30 different reading selections.

Thinking like a Writer

When you read, you are also learning how to be a writer, so your *Reader/Writer Notebook* makes space to take your writing notes within your reading notes. There is lots of space for sketching out your ideas and trying out drafts, too. You can work on the Writing Workshops and Your Turn activities from your textbook in your RWN notebook.

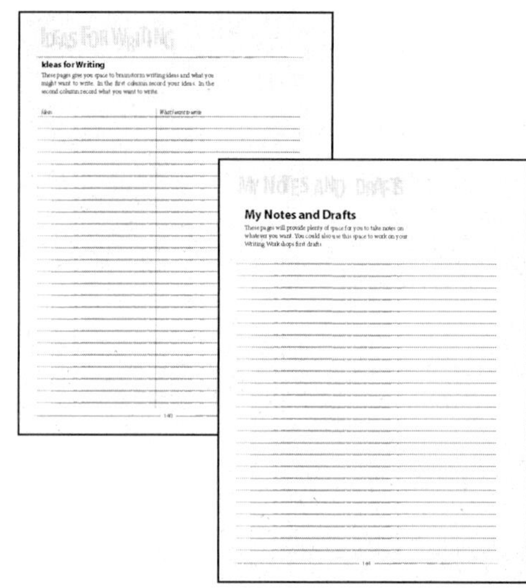

Finding the Right Words

You can't read or write without words. As you read, you run across new words or words that you know that are used in a new way. As you write, you try to find the best way to express what you want to say. For both of these reasons, vocabulary is an important part of being a reader/writer. Your notebook helps you increase your personal vocabulary by helping you take better notes as you read and write. It also has a handy reference list of all the word parts and academic vocabulary found in your textbook and graphic organizers to help you tackle new words.

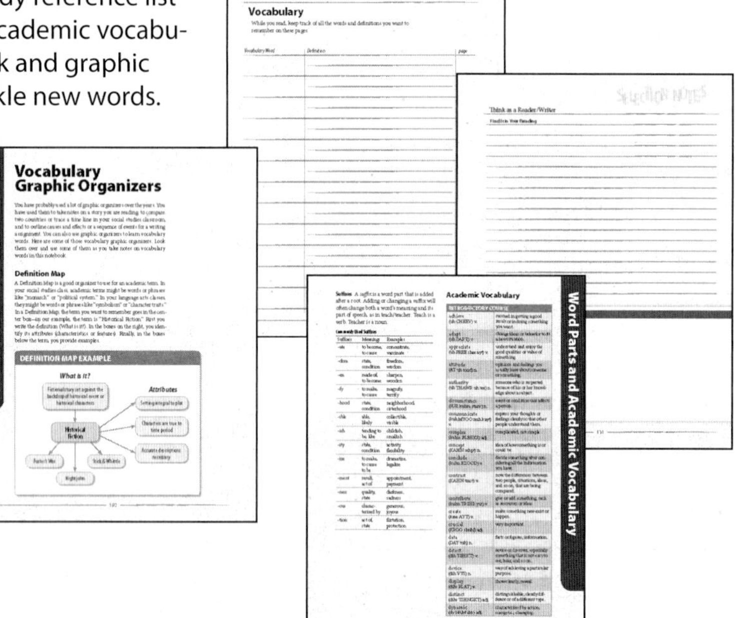

Program Authors

Kylene Beers is the senior program author for *Elements of Literature*. A former middle school teacher, she is now Senior Reading Advisor to Secondary Schools for Teachers College Reading and Writing Project at Columbia University. She is the author of *When Kids Can't Read: What Teachers Can Do* and co-editor (with Linda Rief and Robert E. Probst) of *Adolescent Literacy: Turning Promise into Practice*. The former editor of the National Council of Teachers of English (NCTE) literacy journal *Voices from the Middle*, Dr. Beers assumed the NCTE presidency in 2008. With articles in *English Journal, Journal of Adolescent and Adult Literacy, School Library Journal, Middle Matters,* and *Voices from the Middle,* she speaks both nationally and internationally as a recognized authority on struggling readers. Dr. Beers has served on the review boards of *English Journal, The ALAN Review,* the Special Interest Group on Adolescent Literature of the International Reading Association, and the Assembly on Literature for Adolescents of the NCTE. She is the 2001 recipient of the Richard W. Halley Award given by NCTE for outstanding contributions to middle school literacy.

Carol Jago is a teacher with thirty-two years of experience at Santa Monica High School in California. The author of nine books on education, she continues to share her experiences as a writer and as a speaker at conferences and seminars across the country. Her wide and varied experience in standards assessment and secondary education in general has made her a sought-after speaker. As an author, Ms. Jago also works closely with Heinemann Publishers and with the National Council of Teachers of English. Her longtime association with NCTE led to her June 2007 election to a four-year term on the council's board. During that term she will serve for one year as president of the council. She is also active with the California Association of Teachers of English (CATE) and has edited CATE's scholarly journal *California English* since 1996. Ms. Jago served on the planning committees for the 2009 NAEP Reading Framework and the 2011 NAEP Writing Framework.

Deborah Appleman is professor and chair of educational studies and director of the Summer Writing Program at Carleton College in Northfield, Minnesota. Dr. Appleman's primary research interests include adolescent response to literature, multicultural literature, and the teaching of literary theory in high school. With a team of classroom teachers, she co-edited *Braided Lives,* a multicultural literature anthology. In addition to many articles and book chapters, she is the author of

Linda Rief, Alfred Tatum, Kylene Beers, Patrick Schwarz, and Carol Jago

PROGRAM AUTHORS continued

Critical Encounters in High School English: Teaching Literary Theory to Adolescents and co-author of *Teaching Literature to Adolescents*. Her most recent book, *Reading for Themselves,* explores the use of extracurricular book clubs to encourage adolescents to read for pleasure. Dr. Appleman was a high school English teacher, working in both urban and suburban schools. She is a frequent national speaker and consultant and continues to work weekly in high schools with students and teachers.

Leila Christenbury is a former high school English teacher and currently professor of English education at Virginia Commonwealth University, Richmond. The former editor of *English Journal,* she is the author of ten books, including *Writing on Demand, Making the Journey,* and *Retracing the Journey: Teaching and Learning in an American High School.* Past president of the National Council of Teachers of English, Dr. Christenbury is also a former member of the steering committee of the National Assessment of Educational Progress (NAEP). A recipient of the Rewey Belle Inglis Award for Outstanding Woman in English Teaching, Dr. Christenbury is a frequent speaker on issues of English teaching and learning and has been interviewed and quoted on CNN and in the *New York Times, USA Today, Washington Post, Chicago Tribune,* and *US News & World Report*.

Leila Christenbury, Héctor Rivera, Sara Kajder, Eric Cooper, and Deborah Appleman

Sara Kajder, author of *Bringing the Outside In: Visual Ways to Engage Reluctant Readers* and *The Tech-Savvy English Classroom,* is an assistant professor at Virginia Polytechnic Institute and State University (Virginia Tech). She has served as co-chair of NCTE's Conference on English Education (CEE) Technology Commission and of the Society for Information Technology and Teacher Education (SITE) English Education Committee. Dr. Kajder is the recipient of the first SITE National Technology Leadership Fellowship in English Education; she is a former English and language arts teacher for high school and middle school.

Linda Rief has been a classroom teacher for twenty-five years. She is author of *The Writer's-Reader's Notebook, Inside the Writer's-Reader's Notebook, Seeking Diversity, 100 Quickwrites,* and *Vision and Voice* as well as the co-author (with Kylene Beers and Robert E. Probst) of *Adolescent Literacy: Turning Promise into Practice*. Ms. Rief has written numerous chapters and journal articles, and she co-edited the first five years of *Voices from the Middle*. During the summer she teaches graduate courses at the University of New Hampshire and Northeastern University. She is a national and international consultant on adolescent literacy issues.

Program Consultants

Mabel Rivera, Harvey Daniels, Margaret McKeown, and Isabel Beck

Isabel L. Beck is professor of education and senior scientist at the University of Pittsburgh. Dr. Beck has conducted extensive research on vocabulary and comprehension and has published well over one hundred articles and several books, including *Improving Comprehension with Questioning the Author* (with Margaret McKeown) and *Bringing Words to Life: Robust Vocabulary Instruction* (with Margaret McKeown and Linda Kucan). Dr. Beck's numerous national awards include the Oscar S. Causey Award for outstanding research from the National Reading Conference and the William S. Gray Award from the International Reading Association for lifetime contributions to the field of reading research and practice.

Margaret G. McKeown is a senior scientist at the University of Pittsburgh's Learning Research and Development Center. Her research in reading comprehension and vocabulary has been published extensively in outlets for both research and practitioner audiences. Recognition of her work includes the International Reading Association's (IRA) Dissertation of the Year Award and a National Academy of Education Spencer Fellowship. Before her career in research, Dr. McKeown taught elementary school.

Amy Benjamin is a veteran teacher, literacy coach, consultant, and researcher in secondary-level literacy instruction. She has been recognized for excellence in teaching from the New York State English Council, Union College, and Tufts University. Ms. Benjamin is the author of several books about reading comprehension, writing instruction, grammar, and differentiation. Her most recent book (with Tom Oliva) is *Engaging Grammar: Practical Advice for Real Classrooms,* published by the National Council of Teachers of English. Ms. Benjamin has had a long association and leadership role with the NCTE's Assembly for the Teaching of English Grammar (ATEG).

Eric Cooper is the president of the National Urban Alliance for Effective Education (NUA) and co-founder of the Urban Partnership for Literacy with the IRA. He currently works with the NCTE to support improvements in urban education and collaborates with the Council of the Great City Schools. In line with his educational mission to support the improvement of education for urban and minority students, Dr. Cooper writes, lectures, and produces educational documentaries and talk shows to provide advocacy for children who live in disadvantaged circumstances.

Harvey Daniels is a former college professor and classroom teacher, working in urban and suburban Chicago schools. Known for his pioneering work on student book clubs, Dr. Daniels is author and co-author of many books, including *Literature Circles: Voice and Choice in Book Clubs and Reading Groups* and *Best Practice: Today's Standards for Teaching and Learning in America's Schools.*

Ben Garcia is associate director of education at the Skirball Cultural Center in Los Angeles, California, where he oversees school programs and teacher professional development. He is a board member of the Museum Educators of Southern California and presents regularly at conferences in the area of visual arts integration across curricula. Prior to the Skirball, he worked with classroom teachers for six years in the *Art and Language Arts* program at the J. Paul Getty Museum. Recent publications include *Art and Science: A Curriculum for K–12 Teachers* and *Neoclassicism and the Enlightenment: A Curriculum for Middle and High School Teachers.*

PROGRAM CONSULTANTS continued

Judith L. Irvin taught middle school for several years before entering her career as a university professor. She now teaches courses in curriculum and instructional leadership and literacy at Florida State University. Dr. Irvin's many publications include *Reading and the High School Student: Strategies to Enhance Literacy* and *Integrating Literacy and Learning in the Content Area Classroom*. Her latest book, *Taking Action: A Leadership Model for Improving Adolescent Literacy,* is the result of a Carnegie-funded project and is published by the Association for Supervision and Curriculum Development.

Victoria Ramirez is the interim education director at the Museum of Fine Arts, Houston, Texas, where she plans and implements programs, resources, and publications for teachers and serves as liaison to local school districts and teacher organizations. She also chairs the Texas Art Education Association's museum division. Dr. Ramirez earned a doctoral degree in curriculum and instruction from the College of Education at the University of Houston and an M.A.T. in museum education from George Washington University. A former art history instructor at Houston Community College, Dr. Ramirez currently teaches education courses at the University of Houston.

Héctor H. Rivera is an assistant professor at Southern Methodist University, School of Education and Human Development. Dr. Rivera is also the director of the SMU Professional Development/ESL Supplemental Certification Program for Math and Science Teachers of At-Risk Middle and High School LEP Newcomer Adolescents. This federally funded program develops, delivers, and evaluates professional development for educators who work with at-risk newcomer adolescent students. Dr. Rivera is also collaborating on school reform projects in Guatemala and with the Institute of Arctic Education in Greenland.

Mabel Rivera is a research assistant professor at the Texas Institute for Measurement, Evaluation, and Statistics at the University of Houston. Her current research interests include the education of and prevention of reading difficulties in English-language learners. In addition, Dr. Rivera is involved in local and national service activities for preparing school personnel to teach students with special needs.

Robin Scarcella is a professor at the University of California at Irvine, where she also directs the Program in Academic English/English as a Second Language. She has a Ph.D. in linguistics from

Amy Benjamin, Ben Garcia, Robin Scarcella, and Judith Irvin

the University of Southern California and an M.A. degree in education-second language acquisition from Stanford University. She has taught all grade levels. She has been active in shaping policies affecting language assessment, instruction, and teacher professional development. In the last four years, she has spoken to over ten thousand teachers and administrators. She has written over thirty scholarly articles that appear in such journals as the *TESOL Quarterly* and *Brain and Language*. Her most recent publication is *Accelerating Academic English: A Focus on the English Learner*.

Patrick Schwarz is professor of special education and chair of the Diversity in Learning and Development department for National-Louis University, Chicago, Illinois. He is author of *From Disability to Possibility* and *You're Welcome* (co-written with Paula Kluth), texts that have inspired teachers worldwide to reconceptualize inclusion to help all children. Other books co-written with Paula

Kluth include *Just Give Him the Whale* and *Inclusion Bootcamp*. Dr. Schwarz also presents and consults worldwide through Creative Culture Consulting.

Alfred W. Tatum is an associate professor in the Department of Curriculum and Instruction at the University of Illinois at Chicago (UIC), where he earned his Ph.D. He also serves as the director of the UIC Reading Clinic. He began his career as an eighth-grade teacher, later becoming a reading specialist. Dr. Tatum has written more than twenty-five articles, chapters, and monographs and is the author of *Teaching Reading to Black Adolescent Males: Closing the Achievement Gap*. His work focuses on the literacy development of African American adolescent males, particularly the impact of texts on their lives.

UNIT INTRODUCTION WRITERS ON WRITING

UNIT 1 SHORT STORIES

Ursula K. Le Guin

"A short story can be an adventure, or a warning, or a portrait, or a picture of a whole way of life. . . ."

UNIT 2 NONFICTION

Joseph Bruchac

"Nonfiction shows us that we live in a world of wonders and infinite possibilities."

UNIT 3 POETRY

Aimee Nezhukumatathil

"And ultimately for me, connection, communicating—that's what writing poetry is all about."

UNIT 4 DRAMA

Cassandra Medley

"All of us have the potential to create and retell stories—we all gossip, tell lies, retell favorite stories, and recreate versions of our own and other people's lives."

Critical Reviewers

Dee Ambrose-Stahl
Ligonier Valley High School
Ligonier, Pennsylvania

Melinda Bogart
Switzerland Point Middle School
St. Augustine, Florida

Abigayl Brown
Valley Stream Memorial
Junior High School
Valley Stream, New York

Kim Brown
Buckeye Valley Middle School
Delaware, Ohio

Kathryn Abbey Chwalisz
Glenridge Middle School
Orlando, Florida

Parniece Crawford
Lockhart Middle School
Orlando, Florida

Chrissy Cuenca
Winston Park K-8 Center
Miami, Florida

Heather Dick
Amherst Junior High School
Amherst, Ohio

Sabrina R. Dorsey
General Ray Davis Middle School
Stockbridge, Georgia

Gloria Feather
Independence Middle School
Pittsburgh, Pennsylvania

Lisa Anne Flowers
Olympia High School
Orlando, Florida

Sandi Green
Swanson Middle School
Arlington, Virginia

Bobbi Ann Hammill
Elderton High School
Elderton, Pennsylvania

Pat Harris
Bryant Middle School
Bryant, Arkansas

Clifford Hartline
Harrison Middle School
Grand Rapids, Michigan

Carolyn Matthews
Memphis City Schools
Memphis, Tennessee

Patricia Mentgen
John P. Freeman Optional School
Memphis, Tennessee

Jennifer Nzeza
Booker Middle School
Sarasota, Florida

Marcia Rosen
Independence Middle School
Pittsburgh, Pennsylvania

Shahara M. Ruth
Tucker Middle School
Tucker, Georgia

Donna Scheidt
Highland Middle School
Highland, Indiana

Patricia Sherman
Baldwin Middle School
Baldwin, New York

Laura Jeannine Simon
Princeton Community
Middle School
Cincinnati, Ohio

Jennifer Warford
Boone County Schools
Florence, Kentucky

FIELD-TEST PARTICIPANTS

Brandi Anzaldua
North Richland Middle School
North Richland Hills, Texas

Lisa Archibald
Pasco Middle School
Dade City, Florida

Julie Bruce-Magee
Kathleen & Tim Harney
Middle School
Las Vegas, Nevada

Cheryl Carter
Murchison Middle School
Austin, Texas

Marcie Chesin
Lake Bluff Middle School
Lake Bluff, Illinois

Wendy Clancy
Dodson Middle School
Rancho Palos Verdes, California

Cynthia Colson
Forest Middle School
Forest, Virginia

Donna Dekersky
Jeaga Middle School
West Palm Beach, Florida

Michelle Dobelbower
North Richland Middle School
North Richland Hills, Texas

Kathy Dubose
Murchison Middle School
Austin, Texas

Janice Heller
Eisenhower Middle School
Oregon, Ohio

Barbara Henry
Smith Middle School
Beaumont, Texas

Ashley Highsmith
Austin Middle School
Beaumont, Texas

Karen Houser
Marsteller Middle School
Bristow, Virginia

Janice Ingersoll
Portsmouth Middle School
Portland, Oregon

Monica Jordan
Murchison Middle School
Austin, Texas

Mary Klein
Liberty Middle School
Powell, Ohio

Carol Kubaska
Lehi Elementary School
Mesa, Arizona

Patty Martinez
Murchison Middle School
Austin, Texas

Craig May
Walker Middle School
Salem, Oregon

Ikema Morris
Rays of Hope School
Sanford, Florida

Beth Morse
Fairbanks Middle School
Milford Center, Ohio

Michael Mullan
Alice B. Landrum Middle School
Ponte Vedra Beach, Florida

Marjean Nielsen
Hornell Junior High School
Hornell, New York

Katy Roskowski
Becker Middle School
Las Vegas, Nevada

Alma Alvarez Salazar
Webster Middle School
Los Angeles, California

Michael Sedlak
Justice Myron E. Leavitt
Middle School
Las Vegas, Nevada

Diana Snyder
Charles A. Mooney Middle School
Cleveland, Ohio

Sandra Thomason
Liberty Middle School
Powell, Ohio

Dr. Jane N. White
Alice B. Landrum Middle School
Ponte Vedra Beach, Florida

Contents in Brief

Ohio Academic Content Standards for Language Arts for each collection can be found in the full Table of Contents on pages A4, A6, A8, A10, A12, A14, A16, and A18.

UNIT 1 Short Stories

COLLECTION 1 • Plot and Setting

COLLECTION 2 • Characters

COLLECTION 3 • Theme

COLLECTION 4 • Style

Short Stories

COLLECTION 1 Plot and Setting

"Be careful what you set your heart upon—for it will surely be yours."
—James Baldwin

What Do You Think? What kinds of wishes might cause more heartache than joy?

Ohio Academic Content Standards for Language Arts

Acquisition of Vocabulary VO.8.1; VO.8.4; VO.8.5
Reading Process RP.8.1; RP.8.3; RP.8.4; RP.8.5
Reading Applications RA.I.8.9; RA.L.8.1; RA.L.8.2; RA.L.8.3; RA.L.8.4; RA.L.8.7
Writing Processes WP.8.3; WP.8.5; WP.8.8; WP.8.11; WP.8.13; WP.8.14; WP.8.15
Writing Applications WA.8.1.a; WA.8.1.c; WA.8.3.c; WA.8.4.a; WA.8.4.b; WA.8.4.c; WA.8.4.d; WA.8.5.a; WA.8.5.b; WA.8.5.c; WA.8.6
Writing Conventions WC.8.1; WC.8.3; WC.8.8
Research R.8.2; R.8.5; R.8.8
Communication: Oral and Visual C.8.6; C.8.7; C.8.8.a; C.8.9

Literary Selections

Comparing Texts

Informational Text Focus

UNIT 1

Short Stories

COLLECTION 2 Characters

"No matter what accomplishments you make, somebody helps you."
—Althea Gibson

What Do You Think? To whom do we turn for help in times of need?

Ohio Academic Content Standards for Language Arts

Acquisition of Vocabulary VO.8.1; VO.8.4; VO.8.6; VO.8.7
Reading Process RP.8.1; RP.8.2; RP.8.4; RP.8.5
Reading Applications RA.I.8.2; RA.L.8.1; RA.L.8.2; RA.L.8.3; RA.L.8.5; RA.L.8.8
Writing Processes WP.8.5; WP.8.9; WP.8.10; WP.8.11; WP.8.13; WP.8.14
Writing Applications WA.8.1.a; WA.8.1.c; WA.8.3.d; WA.8.3.e; WA.8.4.a; WA.8.4.c; WA.8.4.d; WA.8.4.e; WA.8.5.a; WA.8.5.b; WA.8.5.c; WA.8.6
Writing Conventions WC.8.1; WC.8.3
Research R.8.5
Communication: Oral and Visual C.8.4; 9C.8.6; 9C.8.9

Informational Text Focus

UNIT 1

Short Stories

COLLECTION 3 Theme

"You never really understand a person until you consider things from his point of view."
—**Harper Lee**

What Do You Think? Is it harder to understand others or ourselves?

Ohio Academic Content Standards for Language Arts

Acquisition of Vocabulary VO.8.1; VO.8.4; VO.8.7
Reading Process RP.8.1; RP.8.4; RP.8.5
Reading Applications RA.I.8.2; RA.L.8.1; RA.L.8.4; RA.L.8.5; RA.L.8.8
Writing Processes WP.8.3; WP.8.5; WP.8.6; WP.8.7; WP.8.10; WP.8.11; WP.8.12; WP.8.14; WP.8.16
Writing Applications WA.8.2; WA.8.4.a; WA.8.4.b; WA.8.4.c; WA.8.4.d; WA.8.5.a; WA.8.5.b; WA.8.5.c; WA.8.5.d; WA.8.6
Writing Conventions WC.8.1; WC.8.3; WC.8.4
Research R.8.2; R.8.5; R.8.8
Communication: Oral and Visual C.8.5; C.8.6; C.8.7; C.8.8.a; C.8.8.c; C.8.9

Informational Text Focus

UNIT 1

Short Stories

COLLECTION 4 Style

"Could it think, the heart would stop beating."
—Fernando Pessoa

What Do You Think? Is it better to act from the mind or from the heart?

Ohio Academic Content Standards for Language Arts

Acquisition of Vocabulary VO.8.1; VO.8.4; VO.8.7
Reading Process RP.8.1; RP.8.2; RP.8.4; RP.8.5
Reading Applications RA.I.8.3; RA.I.8.6; RA.I.8.7; RA.L.8.2; RA.L.8.3; RA.L.8.5; RA.L.8.8; RA.L.8.9
Writing Processes WP.8.5; WP.8.6; WP.8.7; WP.8.9; WP.8.10; WP.8.11; WP.8.14; WP.8.15
Writing Applications WA.8.2; WA.8.3.a; WA.8.3.b; WA.8.3.c; WA.8.4.b; WA.8.4.c; WA.8.4.d; WA.8.5.a; WA.8.6
Writing Conventions WC.8.1; WC.8.3
Research R.8.5; R.8.8
Communication: Oral and Visual C.8.1; 9C.8.4; C.8.8.a; C.8.8.b; C.8.8.d; C.8.9

Comparing Texts

Informational Text Focus

UNIT 2

Nonfiction

COLLECTION 5 Elements of Nonfiction

"Fall down seven times; stand up eight times."
—Japanese proverb

What Do You Think? What qualities help people overcome hard times?

Ohio Academic Content Standards for Language Arts

Acquisition of Vocabulary VO.8.1; VO.8.3; VO.8.4; VO.8.6; VO.8.7
Reading Process RP.8.1; RP.8.3; RP.8.4; RP.8.5
Reading Applications RA.I.8.1; RA.I.8.2; RA.I.8.5; RA.I.8.6; RA.I.8.7; RA.I.8.8; RA.L.8.3; RA.L.8.6
Writing Processes WP.8.3; WP.8.5; WP.8.6; WP.8.11; WP.8.16
Writing Applications WA.8.1.a; WA.8.3.d; WA.8.3.e; WA.8.4.b; WA.8.4.c; WA.8.4.d; WA.8.5.a; WA.8.5.b; WA.8.5.c; WA.8.5.d; WA.8.6
Writing Conventions WC.8.1; WC.8.3; WC.8.6; WC.8.7
Communication: Oral and Visua C.8.2; C.8.3; C.8.5; C.8.9; C.8.10.a; C.8.10.b; C.8.10.c

Literary Selections

Comparing Texts

Informational Text Focus

UNIT 2

Nonfiction

COLLECTION 6 Reading for Life

"Problems can become opportunities when the right people come together." —**Robert Redford**

What Do You Think? How can we solve the problems we face in daily life?

Ohio Academic Content Standards for Language Arts

Acquisition of Vocabulary VO.8.1; VO.8.4; VO.8.7
Reading Process RP.8.1; RP.8.3; RP.8.4; RP.8.5
Reading Applications RA.I.8.1; RA.I.8.4; RA.I.8.9
Writing Processes WP.8.5; WP.8.10; WP.8.11; WP.8.15
Writing Applications WA.8.3.a; WA.8.3.b; WA.8.3.c; WA.8.3.d; WA.8.3.e; WA.8.4.b; WA.8.5.b; WA.8.5.d; WA.8.6
Writing Conventions WC.8.1; Research R.8.3
Communication: Oral and Visual C.8.4

Using Information to Solve a Problem

UNIT 3

Poetry

COLLECTION 7 Poetry

"The poetry and the songs that you are supposed to write, I believe are in your heart. You just have to open up your heart and not be afraid to get them out." **—Judy Collins**

What Do You Think? How important is it that we express our feelings?

Ohio Academic Content Standards for Language Arts

Acquisition of Vocabulary VO.8.1; VO.8.2; VO.8.4; VO.8.7
Reading Process RP.8.1; RP.8.2; RP.8.3; RP.8.4; RP.8.5
Reading Applications RA.L.8.5; RA.L.8.6; RA.L.8.8; RA.L.8.9
Writing Processes WP.8.1; WP.8.2; WP.8.3; WP.8.4; WP.8.5; WP.8.6; WP.8.9; WP.8.10; WP.8.11; WP.8.14; WP.8.17
Writing Applications WA.8.1.a; WA.8.1.b; WA.8.2; WA.8.4.b; WA.8.4.c; WA.8.4.d; WA.8.5.a; WA.8.5.c; WA.8.6
Writing Conventions WC.8.1; 8R.8.5
Research R.8.8
Communication: Oral and Visual C.8.8.d; C.8.8.e; C.8.9

Literary Selections

Drama

COLLECTION 8 Elements of Drama

"There is a thin line that separates laughter and pain, comedy and tragedy, humor and hurt. And how do you know laughter if there is no pain to compare it with?" **—Erma Bombeck**

What Do You Think? How can we do the best with what we've been given?

Ohio Academic Content Standards for Language Arts

Acquisition of Vocabulary VO.8.1; VO.8.4; VO.8.5; VO.8.6; VO.8.7
Reading Process RP.8.1; RP.8.3; RP.8.4; RP.8.5;
Reading Applications RA.I.8.1; RA.I.8.2; RA.L.8.1; RA.L.8.5; RA.L.8.6; RA.L.8.7; RA.L.8.8
Writing Processes WP.8.3; WP.8.4; WP.8.5; WP.8.10; WP.8.11
Writing Applications WA.8.1.a; WA.8.1.b; WA.8.4.a; WA.8.4.b; WA.8.4.c; WA.8.4.d; WA.8.4.e; WA.8.6
Writing Conventions WC.8.2; WC.8.3
Research R.8.1; R.8.3; R.8.4; R.8.5; R.8.6; R.8.7; R.8.8
Communication: Oral and Visual C.8.1; C.8.2; C.8.3; C.8.4; C.8.5; C.8.8.a; C.8.8.e; C.8.9

Literary Selections

Comparing Texts

Informational Text Focus

RESOURCE CENTER

Selections by Alternative Themes

Selections are listed here in alternative theme groupings.

CULTURAL DIVERSITY

FAMILY ALBUM

HUMOR AND SATIRE

LEARNING FROM HISTORY

PERSONAL CHALLENGES

THE POWER OF LOVE

THE STRANGE AND MYSTERIOUS

SURPRISES

SELECTIONS BY ALTERNATIVE THEMES continued

VOICES OF COURAGE

SCIENCE AND CURRENT AFFAIRS

Skills, Workshops, and Features

SKILLS

LITERARY FOCUS ESSAYS BY SARA KAJDER

INFORMATIONAL TEXT FOCUS ESSAY

BY CAROL JAGO

READING FOCUS ESSAYS BY KYLENE BEERS

LITERARY SKILLS

IINFORMATIONAL TEXT SKILLS

READING SKILLS FOR LITERARY TEXTS

READING SKILLS FOR INFORMATIONAL TEXTS

VOCABULARY SKILLS

ACADEMIC VOCABULARY

LANGUAGE COACH

VOCABULARY DEVELOPMENT

WORKSHOPS

WRITING WORKSHOPS

MEDIA WORKSHOP

PREPARING FOR TIMED WRITING

LISTENING AND SPEAKING WORKSHOPS

FEATURES

ANALYZING VISUALS

LITERARY PERSPECTIVES

CROSS-CURRICULAR LINKS

GRAMMAR LINKS

SKILLS REVIEWS

LANGUAGE HANDBOOK

SPELLING HANDBOOK

COMMUNICATIONS HANDBOOK

MEDIA HANDBOOK

Why Be a Reader/Writer?

by **Kylene Beers**

ONCE UPON A TIME

B.B. Wolf stood by the judge's desk, asking for mercy. He'd been accused of terrorizing a young girl named Red and a trio of pigs.

"Sure, I may have scared Red," he explained, "but that was just a prank! You found her grandmother at Jack B. Nimble's Athletic Club, so you know I didn't eat her."

"What about the two houses you've destroyed?" the judge asked.

"Cheap construction," B.B. argued, "made of hay and sticks! If I could blow them over, how could they have survived the first big storm to blow through?"

The judge was not entirely convinced. He thought of all the peace and quiet that could be had by simply sending this one unruly character away. But then he thought that everyone deserved a second chance. The Wolf's lawyer—a sly fox—negotiated probation, with conditions. B.B. Wolf could stay in the forest if he would become a vegetarian and perform community service with Habitat for Humanity®.

Surprisingly, B.B. discovered that he loved vegetables. And he was much better at building houses than blowing them over. And they all lived happily ever after . . . until a fe-fi-fo-fumming giant moved into the neighborhood.

WHAT YOU KNOW + WHAT YOU READ

You probably understood this silly tale because you have prior knowledge of some other stories—"Little Red Riding Hood" and "The Three Little Pigs." It also makes more sense if you know something about courtroom dramas, Habitat for Humanity®, the "Jack Be Nimble" nursery rhyme, and "Jack and the Beanstalk." Without that information, this silly story might just be confusing.

Reading becomes more meaningful when you use what you know to shape your understanding. When you combine the old with the new, you unlock new and exciting doors.

CONFIDENTIAL

Beyond Grading

Understanding what you read is important for more reasons than just making good grades. Reading is also a way to learn, to grow, to ponder over the ideas provided by what you read. Sometimes you read just for fun—to relax, to be entertained, to escape from the ordinary world. But even fun reading can inform you and give you new perspectives of yourself and the world. (Maybe B.B.'s story says something about second chances.)

Sometimes YOU will be the writer, helping your readers to learn and grow. But when you write, you can also learn and grow. Because of this you'll find opportunities in this book to use writing to explore your thoughts, feelings, and opinions—ways to sharpen your understanding on any topic and to grow as a person.

COMMUNITY SERVICE CASE #AA-85945
DEFENDANT: B. B. WOLF

Kylene Beers

Creating Change

I once saw a bumper sticker that said:

When you change the way you look at things, **the things you look at change.**

Reading and writing are powerful ways to help change the way you look at things. Eighth grade should be a year of many changes. If you think of reading and writing as merely chores to be completed, consider changing the way you look at them. Try to see them as opportunities that connect what is on the page and what is already in your head. If you do that, then you'll have found the best reason for being a reader and a writer—to create new understandings about yourself and the world around you.

Kylene Beers

Senior Author, *Elements of Literature*

How to Use Your Textbook

Getting to know a new textbook is like getting to know a new video game. In each case, you have to figure out how the game or book is structured, as well as its rules. Knowing how your book is structured, you can be successful from the start.

UNIT 1

Short Stories

Writers on Writing

Ursula K. Le Guin on Short Stories Ursula K. Le Guin has written hundreds of short stories and many books for adults, young adults, and children, including the Catwing series and the Books of Earthsea. She is best known for her fantasy and science fiction writing, which explores ideas about culture, gender, race, and class.

"There have been short stories as long as there have been people. In the ages before we had writing, we told our stories aloud—animal fables, legends of gods and heroes, folk tales, joke tales, ghost stories. We still tell tall tales around a campfire and read bedtime stories aloud to little kids. The modern short story grew out of all those forms. Writers and readers love the short story because it can tell so much in so few words.

There are almost as many ways to write short stories as there are short stories. Some stories are very neat, with a tight, jack-in-the-box plot that pops a surprise out at the end. O. Henry was such a master of this kind of story that his name is still used to describe it. Many stories have no trick ending, but their plots are full of action and suspense. Other stories go along without very much happening and end quietly. A story that seems to have little action can still deeply involve your mind and emotions and imagination. What makes it a story is that *something happens.* It may happen through conflict or violence, or it may be a quiet discovery, something learned, or lost. But at the end of the story, *something has changed.*

If you want to write fiction, the short story is the best place to start. But 'short' isn't 'easy'! A story can start out almost anywhere, but it can't just stop anywhere. During a story, *something changes.* The writer needs to know beforehand: What's going to change as this story happens? Where is it all going to end up? And how is it going to get there? You don't have to know every detail beforehand, but you need to have the idea of it in your head. Then, knowing where you're going, you don't have to go in a big rush. You can take it easy, so long as you keep following your story to where it's headed. And always remember to bring the reader along with you!

A short story can be an adventure, or a warning, or a portrait, or a picture of a whole way of life, or a meditation about right and wrong, or a dream, or a nightmare. Many stories are written purely for entertainment and nothing more. Many are written to show people something fascinating or wonderful or terrible about our life on earth, to let us share the writer's deepest thoughts and feelings.

All storytellers use fiction to tell what they think is true. They have always done this, and always will, because often the only way to tell the truth, and to get people to listen to the truth, is to make it into a story."

Think as a Writer Le Guin writes that "often the only way to tell the truth, and to get people to listen to the truth, is to make it into a story." What truths can you teach through a story? What truths have you learned through a story?

Writers on Writing 1

Writers on Writing

If you think about the authors of the selections in your book, you may think they are a rare breed like astronauts or underwater explorers. **Writers on Writing** introduces you to authors whose stories, poems, plays, or articles began with experiences that were transformed by the author's words.

Collection Opener

What is the focus of each collection, or section of the book? What does the image suggest about what the collection will cover? On the right, you'll see a bold heading that says "Plot and Setting" or "Character." These are the **literary skills** you will study in the collection. Also in bold type is the **Informational Text Focus** for the collection. These are the skills you use to read a newspaper or Web site. Keep the **What Do You Think?** question in mind as you go through the collection. Your answers may even surprise you.

COLLECTION 4

Style

INFORMATIONAL TEXT FOCUS

Evaluating a Summary

"Could it think, the heart would stop beating."

—Fernando Pessoa

What Do You Think Is it better to act from the mind or from the heart?

Heart flowers (20th century) by St. Pierre. Haitian art.

Learn It Online

For more about style, watch the video "A Matter of Style" on:

go.hrw.com L8-365 Go

364 Unit 1 • Collection 4

Style 365

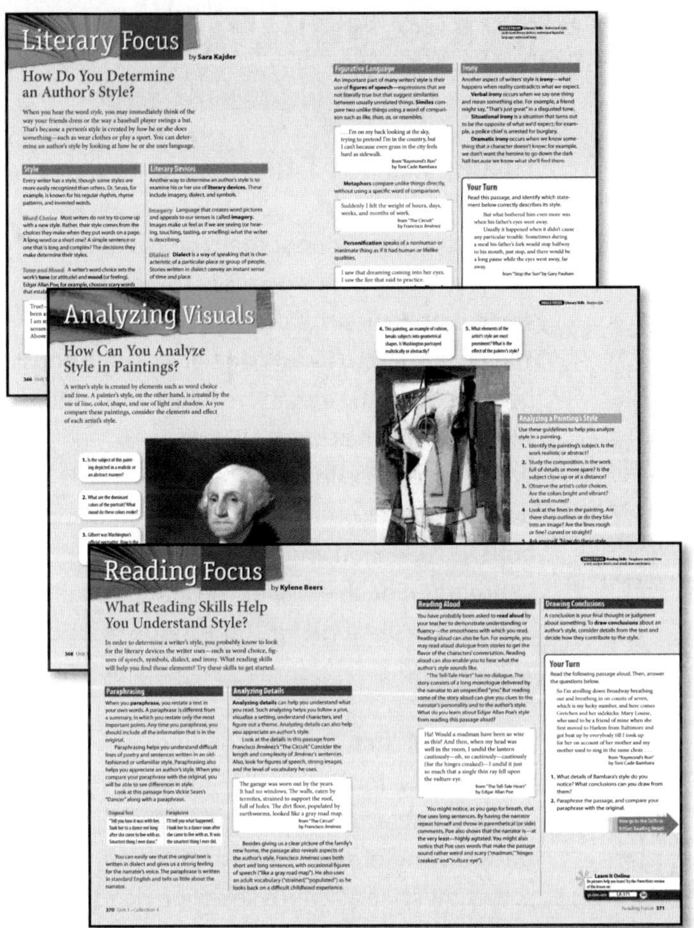

Literary Focus

Like a set of rules or a map, the **Literary Focus** shows you how literary elements work in stories and poems, helping you navigate through selections more easily. The Literary Focus will help you get to your destination—understanding and enjoying the selection.

Analyzing Visuals

Visuals are all around you: murals on buildings, magazine ads, or video-game graphics. Because you see images daily, you probably know quite a bit about analyzing them. **Analyzing Visuals** helps you apply these skills to understand the literary elements that drive the selections.

Reading Focus

Your mind is working all the time as you read, even if you're not aware of it. Still, all readers, even very good ones, sometimes don't understand what they've read. **Reading Focus** gives you the skills to help you improve your reading.

Reading Model

You tend to do things more quickly and easily if you have a model to follow. The **Reading Model** shows you the literary and reading skills that you will practice in the collection so that you can learn them more quickly and easily.

Wrap Up

Think of **Wrap Up** as a bridge that gives you a chance to practice the skills on which the collection will focus. It also introduces you to the **Academic Vocabulary** you will study in the collection: the language of school, business, and standardized tests. To be successful in school, you'll need to understand and use its language.

How to Use Your Textbook

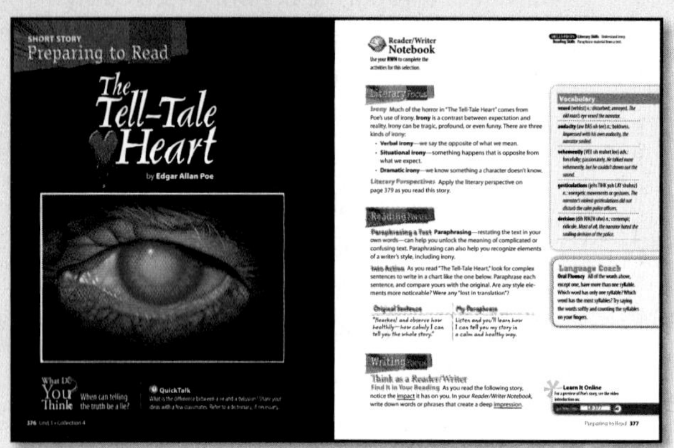

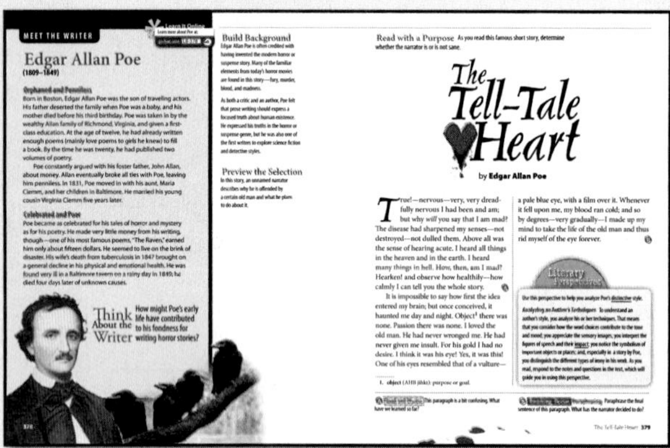

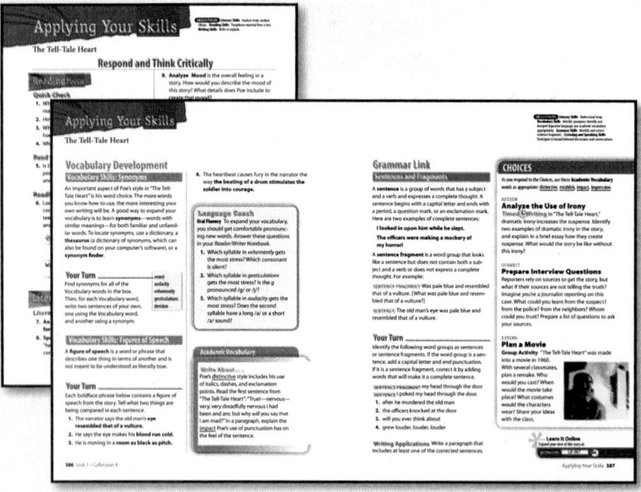

Literary Selection Pages

Preparing to Read

If you have ever done something complicated, you know that things go more smoothly with some preparation. It's the same with reading. The **Preparing to Read** page gives you a boost by presenting the literary, reading, and writing skills you'll learn about and use as you read the selection. The list of **Vocabulary** words gives the words you need to know for reading both the selection and beyond the selection. **Language Coach** explains the inner workings of English—like looking at the inside of a clock.

Selection

Meet the Writer gives you all kinds of interesting tidbits about the authors who wrote the selections in this book. **Build Background** provides information you sometimes need when a selection deals with unfamiliar times, places, and situations. **Preview the Selection** presents the selection's main character, like a movie trailer that hints at what is to come. **Read with a Purpose** helps you set a goal for your reading. It helps you answer the question, "What's the point of this selection?"

Applying Your Skills

If you have a special talent or hobby, you know that you have to practice to master it. In **Applying Your Skills,** you will apply the reading, literary, vocabulary, and language skills from the Preparing to Read page that you practiced as you read the selection. This gives you a chance to check on how you are mastering these skills.

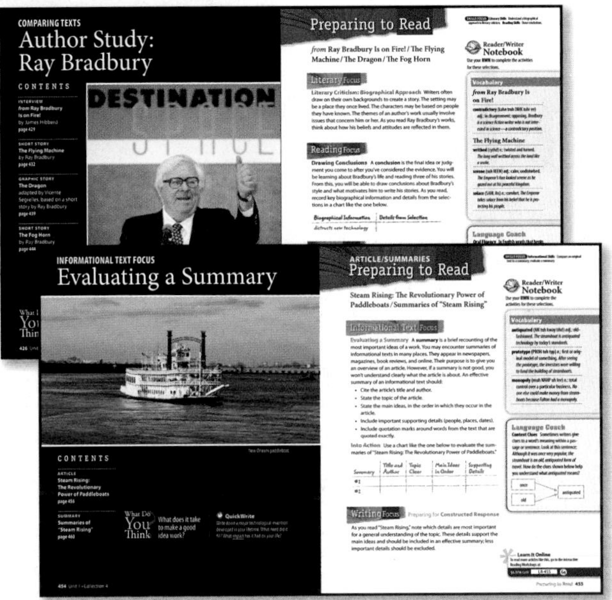

COMPARING TEXTS

Author Study: Ray Bradbury

Preparing to Read

INFORMATIONAL TEXT FOCUS

Evaluating a Summary

ARTICLE/SUMMARIES

Preparing to Read

Comparing Texts
You probably compare people, places, and things all the time, such as a favorite singer's new songs with her previous album. In **Comparing Texts,** you will compare different works—sometimes by the same author, sometimes by different authors—that have something in common.

Informational Text Focus
If you've ever read a web site or followed a technical manual, you've been reading informational text. The skills you use in this type of reading are different from the ones you use for literary text. **Informational Text Focus** helps you gain the skills that will enable you to be a more successful reader in daily life and on standardized tests.

Preparing for Standardized Tests
Do you dread test-taking time? Do you struggle over reading the passage and then choosing the correct answer? **Preparing for Standardized Tests** can reduce your "guesses" and give you the practice you need to feel more confident during testing.

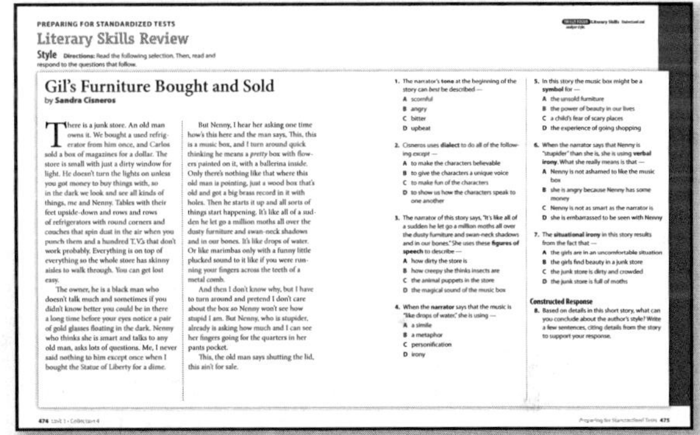

PREPARING FOR STANDARDIZED TESTS

Literary Skills Review

Gil's Furniture Bought and Sold

by Sandra Cisneros

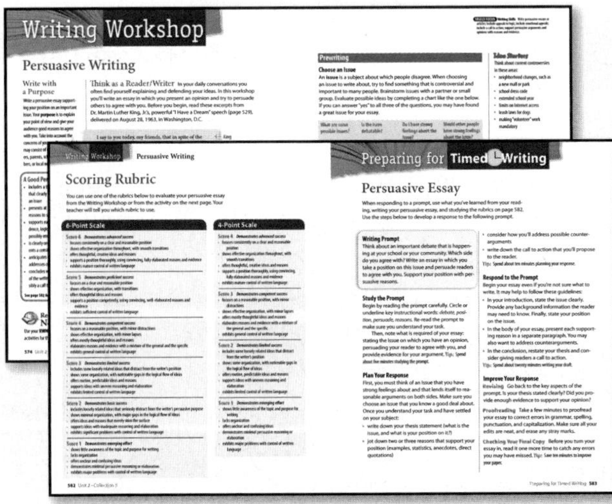

Writing Workshop

Persuasive Writing

Scoring Rubric

Preparing for Timed Writing

Persuasive Essay

Writing Workshop
Does a blank piece of paper send shivers up your spine? The **Writing Workshop** will help you tackle the page. It takes you step-by-step through developing an effective piece of writing. Models, annotations, graphic organizers, and charts take the "What now?" out of writing for different purposes and audiences.

Preparing for Timed Writing
What's your idea of a nightmare? Maybe it's trying to respond to a writing prompt. **Preparing for Timed Writing** helps you practice for on-demand, or timed, writing so that you can realize your dreams of success.

UNIT 1

Short Stories
Writers on Writing

Ursula K. Le Guin on Short Stories

Ursula K. Le Guin has written hundreds of short stories and many books for adults, young adults, and children, including the Catwing series and the Books of Earthsea. She is best known for her fantasy and science fiction writing, which explores ideas about culture, gender, race, and class.

"There have been short stories as long as there have been people. In the ages before we had writing, we told our stories aloud—animal fables, legends of gods and heroes, folk tales, joke tales, ghost stories. We still tell tall tales around a campfire and read bedtime stories aloud to little kids. The modern short story grew out of all those forms. Writers and readers love the short story because it can tell so much in so few words.

There are almost as many ways to write short stories as there are short stories. Some stories are very neat, with a tight, jack-in-the-box plot that pops a surprise out at the end. O. Henry was such a master of this kind of story that his name is still used to describe it. Many stories have no trick ending, but their plots are full of action and suspense. Other stories go along without very much happening and end quietly. A story that seems to have little action can still deeply involve your mind and emotions and imagination. What makes it a story is that *something happens.* It may happen through conflict or violence, or it may be a quiet discovery, something learned, or lost. But at the end of the story, *something has changed.*

If you want to write fiction, the short story is the best place to start. But 'short' isn't 'easy'! A story can start out almost anywhere, but it can't just stop anywhere. During a story, *something changes.* The writer needs to know beforehand: What's going to change as this story happens? Where is it all going to end up? And how is it going to get there? You don't have to know every detail beforehand, but you need to have the idea of it in your head. Then, knowing where you're going, you don't have to go in a big rush. You can take it easy, so long as you keep following your story to where it's headed. And always remember to bring the reader along with you!

A short story can be an adventure, or a warning, or a portrait, or a picture of a whole way of life, or a meditation about right and wrong, or a dream, or a nightmare. Many stories are written purely for entertainment and nothing more. Many are written to show people something fascinating or wonderful or terrible about our life on earth, to let us share the writer's deepest thoughts and feelings.

All storytellers use fiction to tell what they think is true. They have always done this, and always will, because often the only way to tell the truth, and to get people to listen to the truth, is to make it into a story."

Think as a Writer

Le Guin writes that "often the only way to tell the truth, and to get people to listen to the truth, is to make it into a story." What truths can you teach through a story? What truths have you learned through a story?

Les Maries de la Tour Eiffel (1928) by Marc Chagall. Oil on canvas, .89 x 1.16 m.

COLLECTION 1

Plot and Setting

INFORMATIONAL TEXT FOCUS

Text Structures

"Be careful what you set your heart upon—for it will surely be yours."

—James Baldwin

What Do You Think?

What kinds of wishes might cause more heartache than joy?

Learn It Online

Learn how to analyze plot and setting in novels at the *NovelWise* site online:

go.hrw.com L8-3 

Literary Focus

by **Sara Kajder**

What Are Plot and Setting?

When you describe your favorite TV show to friends, you probably tell them what happens (plot) as well as where and when it happens (setting). These are essential elements of all stories. Understanding the elements of a story can make you a better audience—and storyteller!

Plot

Plot **Plot** is a chain of related events that tells what happens in a story. One event causes another to occur, which causes another to occur, and so on.

Most plots are built from these basic elements:

- **Exposition** is the part of the story in which we are introduced to the characters, setting, and the basic story conflict. In some stories, the exposition occurs over several pages or even chapters; in some, the exposition is very short—perhaps confined to a paragraph or two; and in some stories, the exposition is skipped as characters plunge into action.
- **Rising action** is the part of the story in which the main character faces a series of conflicts on his or her journey toward reaching a goal.
- **Climax** is the point at which we learn the outcome of the story's main conflict. Very often, the climax is also the emotional high point of the story.
- **Resolution** is the closing part of the story in which we learn how the characters have dealt with the outcome of the conflict.

Here is how a plot is traditionally diagrammed. Note that the climax is the high point of the story.

Subplots Long stories usually have **subplots**—minor plots that are part of the larger story. In "Flowers for Algernon," Charlie's relationship with Miss Kinnian and his problems at work are subplots to the story's main plot.

Parallel Episodes When elements of the plot are repeated, we refer to those events as parallel episodes. Parallel episodes are very common in fairy tales. Each of the wishes in "Those Three Wishes" is a parallel episode.

RA.L.8.3 Explain how authors pace action and use subplots, parallel episodes and climax. RA.L.8.2 Analyze the influence of setting in relation to other literary elements.

Setting

Setting as Background The time and place in which a story takes place is called its **setting.** Depending on the story and the writer, setting can be a background story element or a key part of the story.

In this example, the story's setting is mentioned in the very first sentence of the work; we are immediately taken to the time and place of the story's action

> The dark sky, filled with angry, swirling clouds, reflected Greg Ridley's mood as he sat on the stoop of his building.
>
> from "The Treasure of Lemon Brown" by Walter Dean Myers

Setting as Conflict Sometimes the setting is central to a story's main conflict. Fierce winter, broiling sun, or a raging hurricane, for example, may be the main problem that faces a story's character.

Mood The overall atmosphere or emotional effect of a work of literature is referred to as the work's mood. Mood is created by the writer's word choice and is described with adjectives, such as *scary, uplifting, tense,* and *nostalgic.* A story's setting often plays a role in creating mood.

> As we walked from the bamboo grove, I saw the familiar clump of bamboo shoots, and we found ourselves standing in the same clearing again. Before our eyes was the thatched house.
>
> from "The Inn of Lost Time" by Lensey Namioka

Your Turn Analyze Plot and Setting

Map out the plot structure of a story you know well. The story could be from a book, a TV show, or a movie. Use a story map like this:

Characters:

Conflict (what keeps the characters from getting what they want):

Major Story Events:
1.
2.
3.
(and so on)

Climax (how the conflicts are resolved):

Resolution:

Make note of any **parallel episodes** and of any instances where the story's **setting** affects the **plot.** If you can find **subplots** in your story, fill out another chart just like this one.

Learn It Online

To understand the role of literary elements in novels, visit *NovelWise* at:

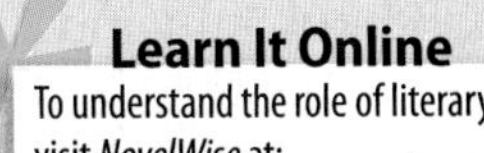

Analyzing Visuals

How Can You Analyze Setting and Mood in a Painting?

When you visit a new place for the first time, often what strikes you first is the **setting**. For example, you may visit a neighborhood that is beautiful, calm, and quiet or one that is chaotic and full of people. In literature, writers create setting and **mood** through their use of words; artists, however, create setting and mood through their choice of color, shapes, shadows, and brushstrokes, among other things.

Analyzing a Painting

Use these guidelines to help you analyze a painting.

1. Identify the painting's subject. An artist creates a painting around a focal point, or the point of main interest.
2. Find details that help set the scene—the particular place and time period of the painting.
3. What is the mood of the painting? How do colors and shapes in the painting help to create that mood?
4. Imagine yourself in the painting. What connection, if any, can you make between the subject of the work and your own experience?

Your Turn Write About Setting

Flip through this book, and find a painting that has an interesting setting. Write a description of the setting, and point out ways the artist used shapes, colors, shadows, and so on, to create that setting.

1. This is Mont Blanc. At 15,774 ft, it's the tallest peak in Western Europe. How does the artist convey the mountain's height?

2. In winter, temperatures on Mont Blanc average 18°F. How do the colors and shapes help convey the coldness of the **setting?**

3. How would you describe this painting's **mood**? What has the artist done to create that mood?

Ascending a Cliff (c. 1827), Artist unknown. Color lithograph.

Reading Focus

by **Kylene Beers**

What Reading Skills Help You Understand Plot and Setting?

Do you ever find yourself confused by a story you are reading? For example, you may suddenly wonder what is happening, or maybe you have forgotten who one of the characters is or why a character is in an unexpected place. Using these reading skills can help you keep the story straight.

Summarizing

To keep track of the plot, stop from time to time and **summarize,** or retell in your own words the most important events of the story.

Here is an example of a summary of the traditional story "The Three Little Pigs."

> "The Three Little Pigs" is a folk tale in which three pigs build houses—one straw, one wood, and one brick. A hungry wolf blows down the houses of straw and wood, but the pigs run to safety in the brick house, which the wolf cannot blow down. When the wolf tries to climb down the chimney he lands in a pot of soup.

Summarizing Tips A good summary should

1. state the title and author
2. identify the main character
3. describe the setting
4. relate the main events
5. use time-order words like *first, then,* and *when*
6. keep events in the right order
7. explain how the story ends

Analyzing Details

When you read a short story, analyzing details helps you understand the plot, get to know the characters, and **visualize,** or picture, the setting.

Look especially for these details as you read the stories in this collection.

characters' actions
conflicts and problems
order of events
→ **plot**

location of the events
time period of the story
customs of the time
→ **setting**

In this example, the story details tell us about a conflict the story's main character is facing.

> Im skared. Lots of people who work here and the nurses and the people who gave me the tests came to bring me candy and wish me luck. I hope I have luck.
>
> from "Flowers for Algernon"
> by Daniel Keyes

RP.8.1 Apply reading comprehension strategies, including making predictions, comparing and contrasting, recalling and summarizing and making inferences and drawing conclusions. **RA.L.8.3** Explain how authors pace action and use subplots, parallel episodes and climax.

Tracking Story Events

Many stories are told in **chronological** order, or the time order in which they happen. Keep track of a story's events by making a chart like this:

The chart above will work for the main events of a story, but you'll find that most stories are a bit more complicated.

"The Inn of Lost Time" is actually three stories in one. Two guests trade stories with a farmer and his wife. To keep track of story events, you'll probably want to make three separate events charts.

Main Story:

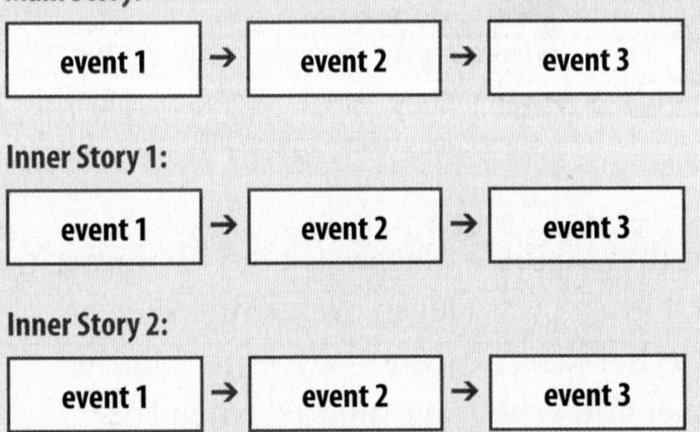

As you read "Flowers for Algernon," first track the story events as a whole. Then identify the events that form subplots and parallel episodes.

Main Story:

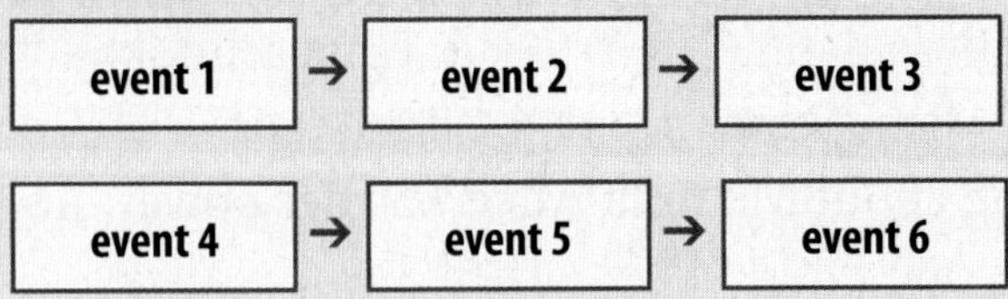

Your Turn Apply Reading Skills

As you read the following passage, keep track of the story events and look for details about the plot and setting. Afterward, summarize the most important events.

The second day of our journey was a particularly grueling one, with several steep hills to climb. As the day was drawing to its close, we began to consider where we should spend the night. I knew that within an hour's walking was a hot-spring resort known to have several attractive inns.

But Tokubei, my employer, said he was already very tired and wanted to stop. He had heard of the resort and knew the inns there were expensive. Wealthy as he was, he did not want to spend more money than he had to.

While we stood talking, a smell reached our noses, a wonderful smell of freshly cooked rice. Suddenly I felt ravenous. From the way Tokubei swallowed, I knew he was feeling just as hungry.

from "The Inn of Lost Time"
by Lensey Namioka

Now go to the Skills in Action: Reading Model

Learn It Online

To become an expert at summarizing, visit the interactive Reading Workshops on:

go.hrw.com L8-9

SHORT STORY

Girl, 1963, by Roy Lichtenstein. © Estate of Roy Lichtenstein.

Analyzing Visuals **Viewing and Interpreting** Does the woman in this painting remind you of Melinda Alice? Why or why not?

Read with a Purpose

Read this story to find out what Melinda Alice does with the wishes she is granted.

Those Three Wishes

by **Judith Gorog**

No one ever said that Melinda Alice was nice. That wasn't the word used. No, she was clever, even witty. She was called—never to her face, however—Melinda Malice.[1] Melinda Alice was clever and cruel. Her mother, when she thought about it at all, hoped Melinda would grow out of it. To her father, Melinda's very good grades mattered.

It was Melinda Alice, back in the eighth grade, who had labeled the shy, myopic[2] new girl "Contamination" and was the first to pretend that anything or anyone touched by the new girl had to be cleaned, inoculated,[3] or avoided. High school had merely given Melinda Alice greater scope for her talents.

Reading Focus

Analyzing Details Details that reveal the time and place of the story are "back in the eighth grade" and "High school."

The surprising thing about Melinda Alice was her power; no one trusted her, but no one avoided her either. She was always

1. **malice** (MAL ihs): a wish to hurt others; ill will.
2. **myopic** (my AHP ihk): nearsighted.
3. **inoculated** (ih NAHK yuh layt ihd): vaccinated.

included, always in the middle. If you had seen her, pretty and witty, in the center of a group of students walking past your house, you'd have thought, "There goes a natural leader."

Melinda Alice had left for school early. She wanted to study alone in a quiet spot she had because there was going to be a big math test, and Melinda Alice was not prepared. That A mattered; so Melinda Alice walked to school alone, planning her studies. She didn't usually notice nature much, so she nearly stepped on a beautiful snail that was making its way across the sidewalk.

"Ugh. Yucky thing," thought Melinda Alice, then stopped. Not wanting to step on the snail accidentally was one thing, but now she lifted her shoe to crush it.

"Please don't," said the snail.

"Why not?" retorted Melinda Alice.

"I'll give you three wishes," replied the snail evenly.

"Agreed," said Melinda Alice. "My first wish is that my next," she paused a split second, "my next thousand wishes come true." She smiled triumphantly and opened her bag to take out a small notebook and pencil to keep track.

Melinda Alice was sure she heard the snail say, "What a clever girl," as it made it to the safety of an ivy bed beside the sidewalk.

During the rest of the walk to school, Melinda was occupied with wonderful ideas. She would have beautiful clothes. "Wish number two, that I will always be perfectly dressed," and she was just that. True, her new outfit was not a lot different from the one she had worn leaving the house, but that only meant that Melinda Alice liked her own taste.

After thinking awhile, she wrote, "Wish number three. I wish for pierced ears and small gold earrings." Her father had not allowed Melinda to have pierced ears, but now she had them anyway. She felt her new earrings and shook her beautiful hair in delight. "I can have anything: stereo, tapes, TV videodisc, moped, car, anything! All my life!" She hugged her books to herself in delight.

By the time she reached school, Melinda was almost an altruist;[4] she could wish for peace. Then she wondered, "Is the snail that

---

4. **altruist** (AL troo ihst): person who helps others without expecting anything in return.

Literary Focus

Plot and Setting Here the writer explains Melinda Alice's **conflict**—she is not prepared for her math test—and describes the **setting**—a sidewalk on the way to school.

Reading Focus

Summarizing Here's one way to summarize what has happened: "Melinda Alice almost steps on a snail, who offers her three wishes. Her first wish is to be granted her next thousand wishes."

Reading Focus

Tracking Story Events Melinda Alice has now made three wishes: to have a thousand wishes, to be perfectly dressed, and to have pierced ears and earrings.

powerful?" She felt her ears, looked at her perfect blouse, skirt, jacket, shoes. "I could make ugly people beautiful, cure cripples . . ." She stopped. The wave of altruism had washed past. "I could pay people back who deserve it!" Melinda Alice looked at the school, at all the kids. She had an enormous sense of power. "They all have to do what I want now." She walked down the crowded halls to her locker. Melinda Alice could be sweet; she could be witty. She could—The bell rang for homeroom. Melinda Alice stashed her books, slammed the locker shut, and just made it to her seat.

"Hey, Melinda Alice," whispered Fred. "You know that big math test next period?"

"Oh, no," grimaced Melinda Alice. Her thoughts raced; "That stupid snail made me late, and I forgot to study."

"I'll blow it," she groaned aloud. "I wish I were dead."

Literary Focus

Plot Melinda Alice makes her final wish here at the **climax** of the story—the point when we know what will happen. But the **resolution**, or final part of the story, is left to your imagination.

Read with a Purpose What do you think about the way Melinda Alice handles her wishes?

MEET THE WRITER

Judith Gorog
(1938–)

World Traveler

Judith Gorog has been traveling all her life. Born in Wisconsin, she has lived in many parts of the United States and also in Germany and Italy. She has traveled far and wide—to Peru, Japan, Europe, and Indonesia.

All along the way, Judith wrote stories. She says, "I have always written, and began to write stories for children when I was a child, making up stories and plays and rewriting the Greek myths with myself taming Pegasus."

Think About the Writer Based on the information above, how would you describe the author?

SKILLS IN ACTION

Wrap Up

RP.8.1 Apply reading comprehension strategies, including making predictions, comparing and contrasting, recalling and summarizing and making inferences and drawing conclusions. RA.L.8.2 Analyze the influence of setting in relation to other literary elements.

Into Action: Story Map

"Those Three Wishes" is a very short story with a dramatic climax. Fill in a story map like the one below to summarize the story.

Characters:
Melinda Alice
& snail

Conflict:

Major story events:
1.
2.
3.

Climax:

Resolution:

Talk About . . .

1. With a partner, discuss the plot and setting of "Those Three Wishes." Try to use each Academic Vocabulary word listed at the right at least once in your discussion.

Write About . . .

Answer the following questions about "Those Three Wishes."

2. Using the structure in your story map above, write a summary of the story's plot.
3. Would the story's outcome have been more effective if it had included a resolution? Why or why not?
4. What theme, or insight about life, does the story reveal?

Writing Focus

Think as a Reader/Writer

The short stories in Collection 1 have interesting plots and settings. The Writing Focus activities on the Preparing to Read pages will guide you in understanding how writers construct their plots and settings. On the Applying Your Skills pages, you'll have a chance to practice using those writers' techniques.

Academic Vocabulary for Collection 1

Talking and Writing About Stories

Academic Vocabulary is the language you use to write and talk about literature. Use these words to discuss the stories you read in this collection. The words are underlined throughout the collection.

effective (uh FEHK tihv) *adj.:* bringing about a desired result. *I found the ending of the story to be surprising but effective.*

outcome (OWT kuhm) *n.:* result; ending. *The outcome of this story is left to the reader's imagination.*

reveal (rih VEEL) *v.:* make known. *Melinda Alice's cruel actions reveal her personality.*

structure (STRUHK chuhr) *n.:* arrangement of parts. *A plot diagram shows the structure of the story.*

Your Turn

Copy these Academic Vocabulary words into your *Reader/Writer Notebook*, and try to use them as you answer questions about the stories in the collection.

SHORT STORY

Preparing to Read

THE TREASURE OF LEMON BROWN

by **Walter Dean Myers**

Music Lesson #2 (2000) by Colin Bootman. Oil on board.

What Do You Think?

What things in life are really important?

QuickWrite

Think about something important you would like to teach or tell someon
younger than you. What would it be? How would you do it?

Reader/Writer Notebook

Use your **RWN** to complete the activities for this selection.

RA.L.8.1 Identify and explain various types of characters and how their interactions and conflicts affect the plot. **RP.8.1** Apply reading comprehension strategies, including making predictions, comparing and contrasting, recalling and summarizing and making inferences and drawing conclusions.

Literary Focus

Conflict The plot of a story almost always involves **conflict**. Usually a conflict arises when a character wants something very badly but is prevented from getting it. A story can have **external conflicts**—struggles with outside forces, such as a blizzard—or **internal conflicts**—struggles within a character's heart or mind, such as fighting shyness. In "The Treasure of Lemon Brown," the main character has many conflicts, both external and internal.

TechFocus As you read the story, pay attention to how one character describes music called the "blues." Make a list of details to research for a short presentation.

Reading Focus

Summarizing A **summary** is a brief restatement of important plot events. Unlike a retelling, which is a paraphrase of an entire story, a summary touches on only the key plot events.

Into Action Use a Somebody Wanted But So chart to record the major conflicts in the story. Once you have filled in the chart, review the conflicts you've listed to help you summarize the story.

Somebody (character)	Wanted (goal or desire)	But (conflict)	So (resolution)
Greg	wants to play basketball	but his dad wants him to study	

Writing Focus

Think as a Reader/Writer

Find It in Your Reading Walter Dean Myers uses precise details to portray New York City's Harlem. As you read, jot down in your *Reader/Writer Notebook* some of the details that help you imagine this urban neighborhood.

Vocabulary

impromptu (ihm PRAHMP too) *adj.:* unplanned. *Greg's friends had an impromptu checkers tournament.*

tentatively (TEHN tuh tihv lee) *adv.:* in an uncertain or hesitant way. *Greg pushed tentatively on the apartment door.*

intently (ihn TEHNT lee) *adv.:* with close attention. *Greg listened intently to the sounds in the room.*

probing (PROHB ihng) *v.* used as *adj.:* searching or investigating. *Greg, probing his leg, did not find any injuries.*

ominous (AHM uh nuhs) *adj.:* threatening. *After the crash, Greg heard only an ominous silence.*

Language Coach

Related Words An *omen* is an event that hints at a future event. Although an omen could indicate a happy event to come, omens are usually associated with upcoming danger. Which of the words on the list above is formed from the word *omen*?

Learn It Online

Listen to a professional actor read this story at:

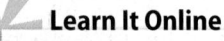

go.hrw.com  L8-15 

MEET THE WRITER

Walter Dean Myers

(1937–)

Michael L. Printz AWARD

Fostering a Talent

Walter Dean Myers was born in Martinsburg, West Virginia; he was one of eight children. Myers's mother died when he was two, and when he was three, his father sent him and two of his sisters to New York City to be raised by foster parents. The Deans guided him through the rough times of his youth and taught him to appreciate both storytelling and education. When he became a published writer, Myers added their name to his to show how important they were to him.

"My foster father was a wonderful man. He gave me the most precious gift any father could give to a son: He loved me. . . . My foster mother understood the value of education. . . . She also understood the value of a story, how it could serve as a refuge for people like us."

Think About the Writer What do you think inspired Myers to become a writer?

Build Background

This story is set in Harlem, a neighborhood in New York City. After World War I, Harlem was the center of an African American literary explosion called the Harlem Renaissance. Important writers, such as Langston Hughes and Zora Neale Hurston, lived in Harlem during this time. Though Harlem has always been a vibrant place, full of life, many of the buildings were not maintained for many years and were abandoned. Recently, however, Harlem has enjoyed a new wave of development and restoration.

Preview the Selection

In this story, you'll meet a boy named **Greg,** who learns some life lessons from an unlikely person he meets in an unlikely place.

Read with a Purpose Read this story to find out what Lemon Brown treasures most of all.

THE TREASURE OF LEMON BROWN

by **Walter Dean Myers**

The dark sky, filled with angry, swirling clouds, reflected Greg Ridley's mood as he sat on the stoop of his building. His father's voice came to him again, first reading the letter the principal had sent to the house, then lecturing endlessly about his poor efforts in math.

"I had to leave school when I was thirteen," his father had said; "that's a year younger than you are now. If I'd had half the chances that you have, I'd . . ."

Greg had sat in the small, pale-green kitchen listening, knowing the lecture would end with his father saying he couldn't play ball with the Scorpions. He had asked his father the week before, and his father had said it depended on his next report card. It wasn't often the Scorpions took on new players, especially fourteen-year-olds, and this was a chance of a lifetime for Greg. He hadn't been allowed to play high school ball, which he had really wanted to do, but playing for the Community Center team was the next best thing. Report cards were due in a week, and Greg had been hoping for the best. But the principal had ended the suspense early when she sent that letter saying Greg would probably fail math if he didn't spend more time studying.

"And you want to play *basketball*?" His father's brows knitted over deep-brown eyes. "That must be some kind of a joke. Now you just get into your room and hit those books." **A**

That had been two nights before. His father's words, like the distant thunder that now echoed through the streets of Harlem, still rumbled softly in his ears.

A **Reading Focus** **Summarizing** What does Greg want? What keeps him from getting it?

It was beginning to cool. Gusts of wind made bits of paper dance between the parked cars. There was a flash of nearby lightning, and soon large drops of rain splashed onto his jeans. He stood to go upstairs, thought of the lecture that probably awaited him if he did anything except shut himself in his room with his math book, and started walking down the street instead. Down the block there was an old tenement that had been abandoned for some months. Some of the guys had held an impromptu checkers tournament there the week before, and Greg had noticed that the door, once boarded over, had been slightly ajar. **B**

Pulling his collar up as high as he could, he checked for traffic and made a dash across the street. He reached the house just as another flash of lightning changed the night to day for an instant, then returned the graffiti-scarred building to the grim shadows. He vaulted over the outer stairs and pushed tentatively on the door. It was open, and he let himself in. **C**

The inside of the building was dark except for the dim light that filtered through the dirty windows from the street lamps. There was a room a few feet from the door, and from where he stood at the entrance, Greg could see a squarish patch of light on the floor. He entered the room, frowning at the musty smell. It was a large room that might have been someone's parlor at one time. Squinting, Greg could see an old table on its side against one wall, what looked like a pile of rags or a torn mattress in the corner, and a couch, with one side broken, in front of the window.

He went to the couch. The side that wasn't broken was comfortable enough, though a little creaky. From this spot he could see the blinking neon sign over the bodega[1] on the corner. He sat awhile, watching the sign blink first green, then red, allowing his mind to drift to the Scorpions, then to his father. His father had been a postal worker for all Greg's life and was proud of it, often telling Greg how hard he had worked to pass the test. Greg had heard the story too many times to be interested now.

For a moment Greg thought he heard something that sounded like a scraping against the wall. He listened carefully, but it was gone.

Outside, the wind had picked up, sending the rain against the window with a force that shook the glass in its frame. A car passed, its tires hissing over the wet street and its red taillights glowing in the darkness.

Greg thought he heard the noise again. His stomach tightened as he held himself still and listened intently. There weren't any more scraping noises, but he was sure

1. **bodega** (boh DAY guh): small grocery store.

B **Literary Focus** **Conflict** What internal conflict does Greg have when it starts to rain?

C **Read and Discuss** What is Greg doing?

Vocabulary **impromptu** (ihm PRAHMP too) *adj.:* unplanned.
tentatively (TEHN tuh tihv lee) *adv.:* in an uncertain or hesitant way.
intently (ihn TEHNT lee) *adv.:* with close attention.

Analyzing Visuals **Viewing and Interpreting** Does the boy in this portrait remind you of Greg? Why or why not?

Jim (1930) by William H. Johnson. Oil on canvas, (21 5/8" x 21 1/4").

he had heard something in the darkness—something breathing!

He tried to figure out just where the breathing was coming from; he knew it was in the room with him. Slowly he stood, tensing. As he turned, a flash of lightning lit up the room, frightening him with its sudden brilliance. He saw nothing, just the overturned table, the pile of rags, and an old newspaper on the floor. Could he have been imagining the sounds? He continued listening, but heard nothing and thought that it might have just been rats. Still, he thought, as soon as the rain let up he would leave. He went to the window and was about to look out when he heard a voice behind him.

"Don't try nothin', 'cause I got a razor here sharp enough to cut a week into nine days!"

Greg, except for an involuntary tremor in his knees, stood stock-still. The voice was high and brittle, like dry twigs being broken, surely not one he had ever heard before. There was a shuffling sound as the person who had been speaking moved a step closer. Greg turned, holding his breath, his eyes straining to see in the dark room. **D**

The upper part of the figure before him was still in darkness. The lower half was in the dim rectangle of light that fell unevenly from the window. There were two feet, in cracked, dirty shoes from which rose legs that were wrapped in rags.

"Who are you?" Greg hardly recognized his own voice.

"I'm Lemon Brown," came the answer. "Who're you?"

"Greg Ridley."

"What you doing here?" The figure shuffled forward again, and Greg took a small step backward.

"It's raining," Greg said.

"I can see that," the figure said.

The person who called himself Lemon Brown peered forward, and Greg could see him clearly. He was an old man. His black, heavily wrinkled face was surrounded by a halo of crinkly white hair and whiskers that seemed to separate his head from the layers of dirty coats piled on his smallish frame. His pants were bagged to the knee, where they were met with rags that went down to the old shoes. The rags were held on with strings, and there was a rope around his middle. Greg relaxed. He had seen the man before, picking through the trash on the corner and pulling clothes out of a Salvation Army box. There was no sign of the razor that could "cut a week into nine days." **E**

"What are you doing here?" Greg asked.

"This is where I'm staying," Lemon Brown said. "What you here for?"

"Told you it was raining out," Greg said, leaning against the back of the couch until he felt it give slightly.

"Ain't you got no home?"

"I got a home," Greg answered.

"You ain't one of them bad boys looking for my treasure, is you?" Lemon Brown cocked his head to one side and squinted one eye. "Because I told you I got me a razor."

"I'm not looking for your treasure," Greg answered, smiling. "*If* you have one."

"What you mean, *if* I have one," Lemon Brown said. "Every man got a treasure. You

---

D **Literary Focus** **Conflict** What new conflict is Greg facing?

E **Read and Discuss** What does this information suggest about Lemon Brown?

don't know that, you must be a fool!"

"Sure," Greg said as he sat on the sofa and put one leg over the back. "What do you have, gold coins?"

"Don't worry none about what I got," Lemon Brown said. "You know who I am?"

"You told me your name was orange or lemon or something like that."

"Lemon Brown," the old man said, pulling back his shoulders as he did so, "they used to call me Sweet Lemon Brown."

"Sweet Lemon?" Greg asked.

"Yessir. Sweet Lemon Brown. They used to say I sung the blues so sweet that if I sang at a funeral, the dead would commence to rocking with the beat. Used to travel all over Mississippi and as far as Monroe, Louisiana, and east on over to Macon, Georgia. You mean you ain't never heard of Sweet Lemon Brown?"

"Afraid not," Greg said. "What . . . what happened to you?"

"Hard times, boy. Hard times always after a poor man. One day I got tired, sat down to rest a spell and felt a tap on my shoulder. Hard times caught up with me." **F**

"Sorry about that."

"What you doing here? How come you didn't go on home when the rain come? Rain don't bother you young folks none."

"Just didn't." Greg looked away.

"I used to have a knotty-headed boy just like you." Lemon Brown had half walked, half shuffled back to the corner and sat down against the wall. "Had them big eyes like you got. I used to call them moon eyes. Look into them moon eyes and see anything you want."

GREG TURNED, HOLDING HIS BREATH, HIS EYES STRAINING TO SEE IN THE DARK ROOM.

"How come you gave up singing the blues?" Greg asked.

"Didn't give it up," Lemon Brown said. "You don't give up the blues; they give you up. After a while you do good for yourself, and it ain't nothing but foolishness singing about how hard you got it. Ain't that right?"

"I guess so." **G**

"What's that noise?" Lemon Brown asked, suddenly sitting upright.

Greg listened, and he heard a noise outside. He looked at Lemon Brown and saw the old man was pointing toward the window.

Greg went to the window and saw three men, neighborhood thugs, on the stoop. One was carrying a length of pipe. Greg looked back toward Lemon Brown, who moved quietly across the room to the window. The old man looked out, then beckoned frantically for Greg to follow

---

F **Literary Focus** **Conflict** What do you think Lemon Brown means by "hard times"? What kinds of conflict might he have faced? Explain your answer.

G **Reading Focus** **Summarizing** What kept Lemon Brown from continuing his career as a blues singer?

Analyzing Visuals **Viewing and Interpreting** How is the view of Harlem seen in this photograph similar to Walter Dean Myers's description? How is it different?

him. For a moment Greg couldn't move. Then he found himself following Lemon Brown into the hallway and up darkened stairs. Greg followed as closely as he could. They reached the top of the stairs, and Greg felt Lemon Brown's hand first lying on his shoulder, then probing down his arm until he finally took Greg's hand into his own as they crouched in the darkness.

"They's bad men," Lemon Brown whispered. His breath was warm against Greg's skin.

"Hey! Ragman!" a voice called. "We know you in here. What you got up under them rags? You got any money?"

Silence.

"We don't want to have to come in and hurt you, old man, but we don't mind if we have to."

Lemon Brown squeezed Greg's hand in his own hard, gnarled fist.

There was a banging downstairs and a light as the men entered. They banged around noisily, calling for the ragman.

"We heard you talking about your treasure." The voice was slurred. "We just want to see it, that's all."

"You sure he's here?" One voice seemed to come from the room with the sofa.

"Yeah, he stays here every night."

"There's another room over there; I'm going to take a look. You got that flashlight?"

"Yeah, here, take the pipe too."

Greg opened his mouth to quiet the sound of his breath as he sucked it in uneasily. A beam of light hit the wall a few feet opposite him, then went out.

"Ain't nobody in that room," a voice said. "You think he gone or something?"

"I don't know," came the answer. "All I know is that I heard him talking about some kind of treasure. You know they found that shopping-bag lady with that money in her bags."

"Yeah. You think he's upstairs?"

"HEY, OLD MAN, ARE YOU UP THERE?"

Silence.

"Watch my back, I'm going up." **H**

There was a footstep on the stairs, and the beam from the flashlight danced crazily along the peeling wallpaper. Greg held his breath. There was another step and a loud crashing noise as the man banged the pipe against the wooden banister. Greg could feel his temples throb as the man slowly neared them. Greg thought about the pipe, wondering what he would do when the man reached them—what he *could* do.

Then Lemon Brown released his hand and moved toward the top of the stairs. Greg looked around and saw stairs going up to the next floor. He tried waving to Lemon Brown, hoping the old man would see him in the dim light and follow him to the next floor. Maybe, Greg thought, the man wouldn't follow them up there. Suddenly, though, Lemon Brown stood at the top of the stairs, both arms raised high above his head.

"There he is!" a voice cried from below.

"Throw down your money, old man, so I won't have to bash your head in!"

Vocabulary **probing** (PROHB ihng) *v.* used as *adj.*: searching or investigating.

H **Reading Focus** **Summarizing** What has happened to put Greg and Lemon Brown in danger?

Lemon Brown didn't move. Greg felt himself near panic. The steps came closer, and still Lemon Brown didn't move. He was an eerie sight, a bundle of rags standing at the top of the stairs, his shadow on the wall looming over him. Maybe, the thought came to Greg, the scene could be even eerier.

Greg wet his lips, put his hands to his mouth, and tried to make a sound. Nothing came out. He swallowed hard, wet his lips once more, and howled as evenly as he could.

"What's that?"

As Greg howled, the light moved away from Lemon Brown, but not before Greg saw him hurl his body down the stairs at the men who had come to take his treasure. There was a crashing noise, and then footsteps. A rush of warm air came in as the downstairs door opened; then there was only an ominous silence.

Greg stood on the landing. He listened, and after a while there was another sound on the staircase.

"Mr. Brown?" he called.

"Yeah, it's me," came the answer. "I got their flashlight." **I**

Greg exhaled in relief as Lemon Brown made his way slowly back up the stairs.

"You OK?"

"Few bumps and bruises," Lemon Brown said.

"I think I'd better be going," Greg said, his breath returning to normal. "You'd better leave, too, before they come back."

"They may hang around outside for a while," Lemon Brown said, "but they ain't getting their nerve up to come in here again. Not with crazy old ragmen and howling spooks. Best you stay awhile till the coast is clear. I'm heading out west tomorrow, out to East St. Louis."

"They were talking about treasures," Greg said. "You *really* have a treasure?"

"What I tell you? Didn't I tell you every man got a treasure?" Lemon Brown said. "You want to see mine?"

"If you want to show it to me," Greg shrugged.

"Let's look out the window first, see what them scoundrels be doing," Lemon Brown said.

They followed the oval beam of the flashlight into one of the rooms and looked out the window. They saw the men who had tried to take the treasure sitting on the curb near the corner. One of them had his pants leg up, looking at his knee.

"You sure you're not hurt?" Greg asked Lemon Brown.

"Nothing that ain't been hurt before," Lemon Brown said. "When you get as old as me, all you say when something hurts is, 'Howdy, Mr. Pain, sees you back again.' Then when Mr. Pain see he can't worry you none, he go on mess with somebody else."

Greg smiled.

"Here, you hold this." Lemon Brown gave Greg the flashlight.

He sat on the floor near Greg and carefully untied the strings that held the rags on his right leg. When he took the rags away, Greg saw a piece of plastic. The old man

---

Vocabulary **ominous** (AHM uh nuhs) *adj.:* threatening.

I **Reading Focus** **Summarizing** How do Lemon Brown and Greg scare off the thugs?

carefully took off the plastic and unfolded it. He revealed some yellowed newspaper clippings and a battered harmonica.

"There it be," he said, nodding his head. "There it be."

Greg looked at the old man, saw the distant look in his eye, then turned to the clippings. They told of Sweet Lemon Brown, a blues singer and harmonica player who was appearing at different theaters in the South. One of the clippings said he had been the hit of the show, although not the headliner. All of the clippings were reviews of shows Lemon Brown had been in more than fifty years ago. Greg looked at the harmonica. It was dented badly on one side, with the reed holes on one end nearly closed.

"WHAT I TELL YOU? DIDN'T I TELL YOU EVERY MAN GOT A TREASURE?" LEMON BROWN SAID.

"I used to travel around and make money for to feed my wife and Jesse—that's my boy's name. Used to feed them good, too. Then his mama died, and he stayed with his mama's sister. He growed up to be a man, and when the war come, he saw fit to go off and fight in it. I didn't have nothing to give him except these things that told him who I was, and what he come from. If you know your pappy did something, you know you can do something too.

"Anyway, he went off to war, and I went off still playing and singing. 'Course by then I wasn't as much as I used to be, not without somebody to make it worth the while. You know what I mean?"

"Yeah," Greg nodded, not quite really knowing.

"I traveled around, and one time I come home, and there was this letter saying Jesse got killed in the war. Broke my heart, it truly did. **J**

"They sent back what he had with him over there, and what it was is this old mouth fiddle and these clippings. Him carrying it around with him like that told me it meant something to him. That was my treasure, and when I give it to him, he treated it just like that, a treasure. Ain't that something?" **K**

"Yeah, I guess so," Greg said.

"You *guess* so?" Lemon Brown's voice rose an octave[2] as he started to put his treasure back into the plastic. "Well, you got to guess, 'cause you sure don't know nothing. Don't know enough to get home when it's raining."

"I guess . . . I mean, you're right."

"You OK for a youngster," the old man said as he tied the strings around his leg, "better than those scalawags what come here looking for my treasure. That's for sure."

"You really think that treasure of yours was worth fighting for?" Greg asked.

2. **octave** (AHK tihv): musical term for the span of eight whole notes.

J **Literary Focus** **Conflict** What type of conflict does Lemon Brown face?

K **Read and Discuss** What do we learn about Lemon Brown's treasure?

Harmonica.

"Against a pipe?"

"What else a man got 'cepting what he can pass on to his son, or his daughter, if she be his oldest?" Lemon Brown said. "For a big-headed boy, you sure do ask the foolishest questions."

Lemon Brown got up after patting his rags in place and looked out the window again.

"Looks like they're gone. You get on out of here and get yourself home. I'll be watching from the window, so you'll be all right."

Lemon Brown went down the stairs behind Greg. When they reached the front door, the old man looked out first, saw the street was clear, and told Greg to scoot on home.

"You sure you'll be OK?" Greg asked.

"Now, didn't I tell you I was going to East St. Louis in the morning?" Lemon Brown asked. "Don't that sound OK to you?"

"Sure it does," Greg said. "Sure it does. And you take care of that treasure of yours."

"That I'll do," Lemon said, the wrinkles about his eyes suggesting a smile. "That I'll do." **L**

The night had warmed and the rain had stopped, leaving puddles at the curbs. Greg didn't even want to think how late it was. He thought ahead of what his father would say and wondered if he should tell him about Lemon Brown. He thought about it until he reached his stoop, and decided against it. Lemon Brown would be OK, Greg thought, with his memories and his treasure.

Greg pushed the button over the bell marked "Ridley," thought of the lecture he knew his father would give him, and smiled. **M**

L **Read and Discuss** What has happened between the boy and the old man?

M **Literary Focus** **Conflict** Is Greg's conflict with his father over playing basketball resolved? Explain.

Applying Your Skills

RA.L.8.1 Identify and explain various types of characters and how their interactions and conflicts affect the plot. RA.L.8.3 Explain how authors pace action and use subplots, parallel episodes and climax. *Also covered* RP.8.1; WA.8.6

The Treasure of Lemon Brown

Respond and Think Critically

Reading Focus

Quick Check

1. Why does Greg go to the abandoned building?
2. What does Lemon Brown reveal to Greg about his past?

Read with a Purpose

3. What is Lemon Brown's treasure? Why does it mean so much to him?

Reading Skills: Summarizing

4. Review the chart that you made as you read the story. Then, add a row to your chart and write a brief summary of the story.

Somebody	Wanted	But	So
Greg	wants to play basketball	but his dad wants him to study	Greg avoids going home.

My summary:

Literary Focus

Literary Analysis

5. **Interpret** What does Lemon Brown mean when he says that everyone's got a treasure?
6. **Infer** What does Greg's encounter with Lemon Brown reveal to him about his own treasures?
7. **Infer** Why do you think Greg decides not to tell his father about Lemon Brown?
8. **Evaluate** Myers has said that in his writing he has to "counter" values conveyed by TV. Is that a worthwhile goal? If Myers asked you whether his story is effective at challenging the values on TV, what would you say?

Literary Skills: Conflict

9. **Analyze** Think about the various conflicts that Greg faces during the story. How does his handling of them change during the course of the story? Use story details to support your ideas.
10. **Interpret** What internal conflict has Greg resolved at the end of the story?

Literary Skills Review: Resolution

11. **Analyze** In the **resolution** of a story, conflicts are resolved. Identify three important external conflicts in the story. How is each one resolved?

Writing Focus

Think as a Reader/Writer

Use It in Your Writing Myers based his description of Harlem on his memories of growing up there. Look back at the details of the setting you jotted down in your *Reader/Writer Notebook*. Then, write a description of your own neighborhood. Like Myers, use precise details to make your description true to life.

What does Greg learn is important in life? Is what he learns also important to you? Why or why not?

Applying Your Skills

The Treasure of Lemon Brown

Vocabulary Development

History of the English Language

Now you know what Lemon Brown's treasure is. But where does the word *treasure* come from? About 60 percent of English words, including *treasure,* come from the Latin language.

Latin was spoken by the Romans. The Roman Empire reached its height in the A.D. 100s and 200s. At that time, the Roman army conquered much of the Western world, including most of Europe and the Middle East as well as northern Africa. The Roman soldiers spoke Latin and spread their language around the world. In fact, Latin is the basis for all the Romance languages (French, Portuguese, Spanish, Italian, and Romanian).

Eventually, in A.D. 1066, William the Conqueror, a Norman (from Normandy, in France) invaded England and became king. He spoke French—a Latin-based language—which influenced the English language. When the English pilgrims came to America in 1620, they brought the English language with them.

Your Turn

impromptu
tentatively
intently
probing
ominous

Study the following Latin words and meanings. Then, write each matching Vocabulary word in the third column.

Latin Word	Meaning	Vocabulary Word
probare	test or examine	
tentare	feel; try	
ominosous	full of foreboding	
promere	bring out	
intendere	strain	

Language Coach

Related Words Related words share the same base word but have different beginnings or endings. Challenge yourself to list two related words for each of the following words: *tentatively, intently, probing,* and *ominous.*

Academic Vocabulary

Talk About . . .

What are some effective ways to gain trust? In a group, discuss the reasons that Greg and Lemon Brown come to trust one another. What does this trust reveal about them? How does this new friendship affect the story's outcome? Try to use some examples from the text as well as the underlined Academic Vocabulary words in your discussion.

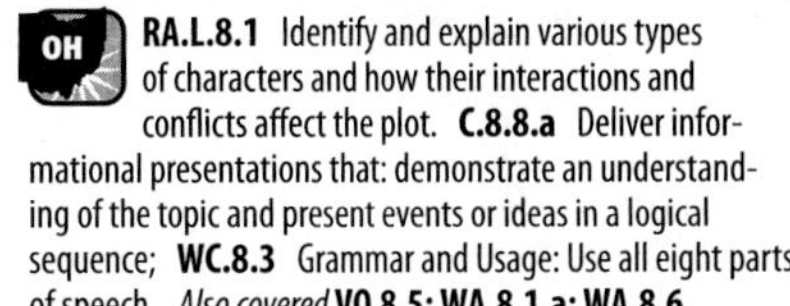
RA.L.8.1 Identify and explain various types of characters and how their interactions and conflicts affect the plot. **C.8.8.a** Deliver informational presentations that: demonstrate an understanding of the topic and present events or ideas in a logical sequence; **WC.8.3** Grammar and Usage: Use all eight parts of speech. *Also covered* **VO.8.5; WA.8.1.a; WA.8.6**

Grammar Link

Nouns and Pronouns

Nouns are one of the basic buildings blocks of the English language. A noun is a word that is used to name a person, a place, a thing, or an idea.

Persons	Greg, Lemon Brown, street thugs
Places	Greg's front stoop, abandoned building
Things	couch, pipe, harmonica, flashlight
Ideas	fear, danger, love, sadness

Sometimes you can use a short word—a **pronoun**—in place of one or more nouns to avoid repetition.

Here is a sentence without pronouns:

When Lemon Brown crashed into the thugs, Lemon Brown scared the thugs away.

Here is the same sentence with pronouns:

When Lemon Brown crashed into the thugs, **he** scared **them** away.

The word that a pronoun stands for is called its antecedent. In the above sentences, *Lemon Brown* and *thugs* are the antecedents for the pronouns.

Your Turn

Rewrite the following sentences by replacing the repeated nouns with pronouns.

1. Greg wanted to play basketball because basketball was Greg's favorite sport.
2. Because Greg's father valued education, Greg's father wanted Greg to study harder.
3. The thugs attacked Lemon Brown to get Lemon Brown's treasure.

CHOICES

As you respond to the Choices, use these **Academic Vocabulary** words as appropriate: effective, outcome, reveal, structure.

REVIEW

Write a Scene

With a classmate, write a scene with dialogue between Greg and his father that reveals their main conflict. Consider the following:

- What does Greg's father say in his lecture?
- How does Greg respond?
- Is there an effective outcome to the disagreement that will satisfy them both?

Perform the dialogue for your class.

CONNECT

Research the Blues

TechFocus In the course of the story, we learn that Lemon Brown was a blues musician. Learn more about blues music by using the Internet to perform research. You might, for example, find out about the life of a musician such as B. B. King or trace the evolution of the guitar in blues music. Use presentation software to share your findings with the class.

EXTEND

Describe a Keepsake

Timed Writing Lemon Brown's treasure is a keepsake, an object that has value as a remembrance. Write an essay describing a keepsake of your own. Imagine what it would reveal to someone who found it. Structure your essay with a short introduction, body, and conclusion. Use precise details to help readers visualize the object.

SHORT STORY

Preparing to Read

The Inn of Lost Time

by **Lensey Namioka**

What Do You Think?

What is the most precious thing a person can have?

QuickWrite

Make a list of things in life that most people think are important. Then, number the list in order of importance to you.

Takachiho Mountain and Yufu Mountain (Yufu Mountain side) (Edo Period, c. 1808) by Tanomura Chikuden. Pair of hanging scrolls, color on silk. 95.8 x 35.8 cm

The Museum of the Imperial Collections, Sannomaru Schozokan.

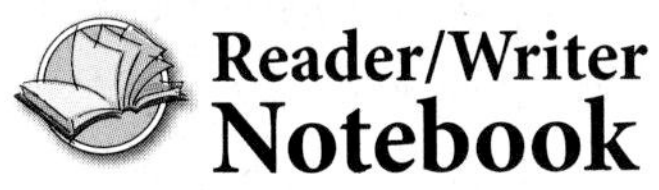

Reader/Writer
Notebook

Use your **RWN** to complete the activities for this selection.

RA.L.8.2 Analyze the influence of setting in relation to other literary elements. **RA.L.8.3** Explain how authors pace action and use subplots, parallel episodes and climax.

Literary Focus

Setting and Mood Have you ever shivered through a movie that takes place in Antarctica or dripped with sweat while watching a desert scene? If so, you have experienced the power of the setting of a story. The **setting** is the time and place of a story. It also includes the customs and behaviors of that time and place.

Setting can create the **mood,** or atmosphere, of a story. If the story's setting is a rain-drenched, dismal day, for example, the mood will probably be gloomy. On the other hand, the writer may create a festive mood with a sunny day and the sound of laughter. Good writers are effective at creating specific settings and moods that help us enter the physical worlds of the characters.

TechFocus As you read this story, which is based on a folk tale, think about some folk tales that you have heard before.

Reading Focus

Analyzing Details Writers use well-chosen details to advance their plots and create memorable settings. For instance, in "The Inn of Lost Time," Lensey Namioka uses details of place and time to set the story in the historical time period of sixteenth-century Japan.

Into Action Use a chart like the one below to record details from the "The Inn of Lost Time" that help create setting.

Detail: Place	Detail: Time	Detail: Custom
a Japanese farmhouse	nighttime; sixteenth century	people drink tea by a fire and tell stories

Writing Focus

Think as a Reader/Writer

Find It in Your Reading The mythic and historical meet in "The Inn of Lost Time." As you read, record in your *Reader/Writer Notebook* some of the descriptive words Lensey Namioka uses to create the haunting setting in "The Inn of Lost Time."

Vocabulary

desolate (DEHS uh liht) *adj.:* lonely; miserable. *Zenta was desolate when he woke up alone and freezing cold.*

poignant (POYN yuhnt) *adj.:* causing sadness or pain; touching. *Matsuzo felt tears welling up as the poignant story ended.*

ruefully (ROO fuhl lee) *adv.:* with regret and embarrassment. *Zenta thought ruefully of all the trouble he had caused.*

grueling (GROO uhl ihng) *adj.:* very tiring; demanding. *After a grueling journey, they arrived exhausted.*

traumatic (traw MAT ihk) *adj.:* emotionally painful; causing shock. *The shock of the loss was especially traumatic to Tokubei.*

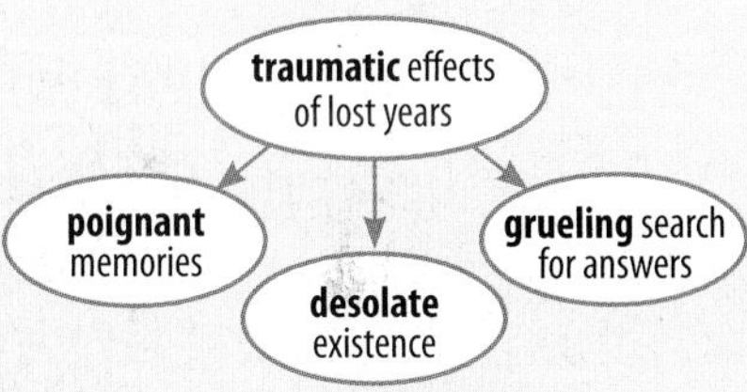

Language Coach

Oral Fluency Sometimes you can't tell how to pronounce English words from their spelling. The last syllable of *chocolate,* for instance, does not sound like the word *late.* Instead, it's pronounced "iht." What word in the list above has an *-ate* ending? How is it pronounced?

Learn It Online

For a preview of this story, see the *PowerNotes* video introduction on:

go.hrw.com L8-31 

MEET THE WRITER

Lensey Namioka

(1929–)

From Mathematician to Storyteller

Lensey Namioka was born in Beijing, China, and moved to the United States when she was a child. Before she became a writer, Namioka studied and taught math. However, she always loved telling stories, and eventually she began writing novels for young adults. Her award-winning novels have a wide range of settings, including China, Japan, and modern-day America. Her books explore a range of subjects—from growing up as an immigrant in America to medieval Japanese samurai culture.

A Rich Heritage

Namioka says, "For my writings, I draw heavily on my Chinese cultural heritage and on my husband's Japanese cultural heritage." A trip to her husband's hometown in Japan (where she visited a medieval castle on a hill with the name "Namioka") sparked her interest in Japanese feudal history.

"I decided I liked being a writer better than being a mathematician."

Think About the Writer What historical period captures Lensey Namioka's imagination?

Build Background

"The Inn of Lost Time" was written in modern times, but it is set in sixteenth-century Japan, when samurai, members of the warrior class, roamed the land. To structure her tale, Lensey Namioka uses an age-old technique that is still popular today—the frame story, or story within a story. In fact, this story has *two* stories within it. One is an ancient Japanese folk tale that may remind you of "Rip Van Winkle," a popular American story, in which a man sleeps for fifty years. The other is a tale about something that happened to one of the samurai.

Preview the Selection

Some of Namioka's most popular stories, including "The Inn of Lost Time," recount the adventures of **Zenta** and **Matsuzo**, a pair of wandering samurai searching for work in long-ago Japan. In this story, they stop for the night at a farmhouse, where Zenta tells a tale about a time he unraveled an intriguing mystery.

Read with a Purpose Read this story to solve a mystery set in ancient Japan.

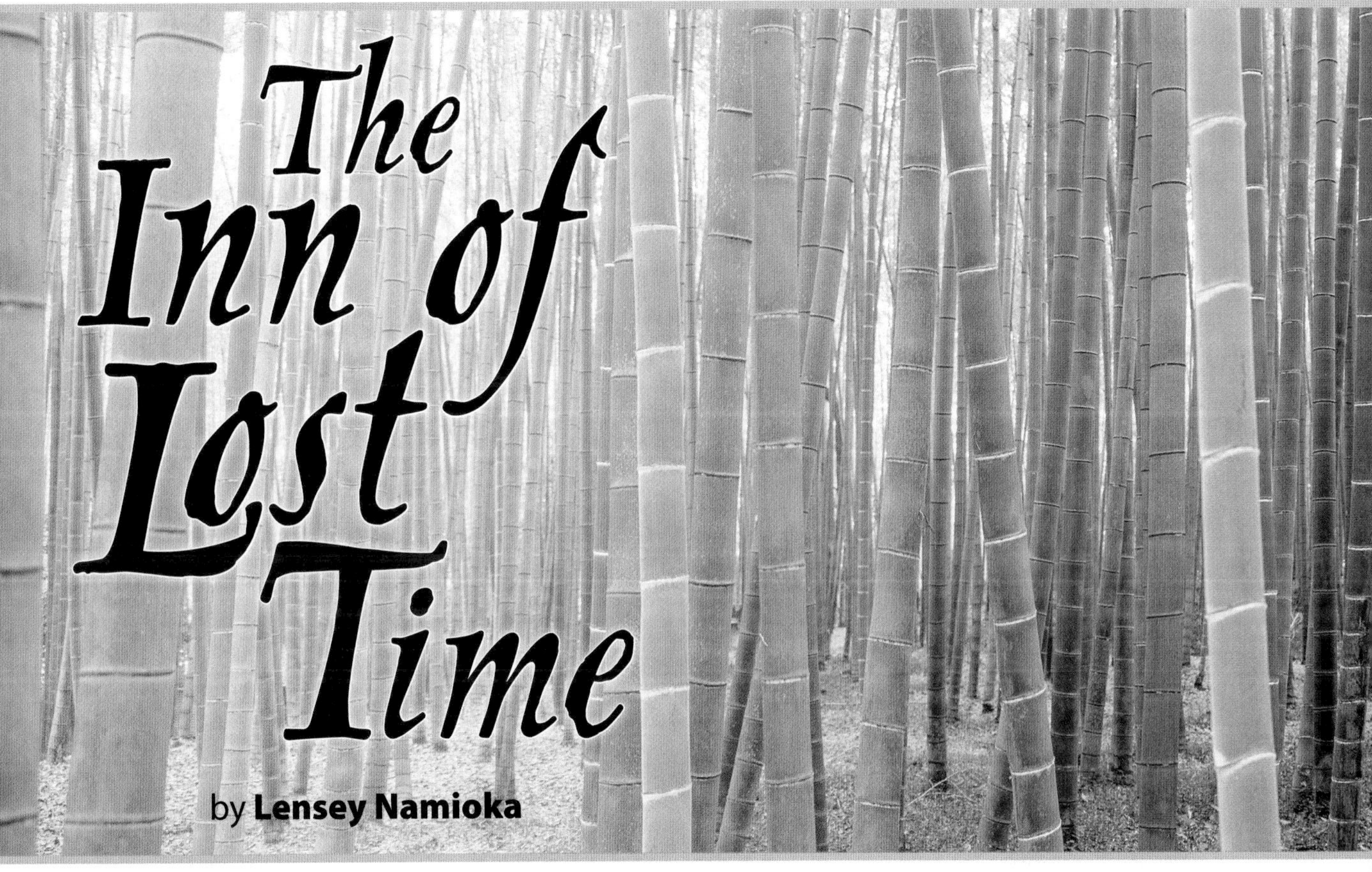

The Inn of Lost Time

by **Lensey Namioka**

"Will you promise to sleep if I tell you a story?" said the father. He pretended to put on a stern expression.

"Yes! Yes!" the three little boys chanted in unison. It sounded like a nightly routine.

The two guests smiled as they listened to the exchange. They were wandering ronin, or unemployed samurai, and they enjoyed watching this cozy family scene.

The father gave the guests a helpless look. "What can I do? I have to tell them a story, or these little rascals will give us no peace." Clearing his throat, he turned to the boys. "All right. The story tonight is about Urashima Taro."

Instantly the three boys became still. Sitting with their legs tucked under them, the three little boys, aged five, four, and three, looked like a descending row of stone statuettes. Matsuzo, the younger of the two ronin, was reminded of the wayside half-body statues of Jizo, the God of Travelers and Protector of Children.

Behind the boys the farmer's wife took up a pair of iron chopsticks and stirred the ashes of the fire in the charcoal brazier.[1] A momentary glow brightened the room. The lean faces of the two ronin, lit by the fire, suddenly looked fierce and hungry. **A**

The farmer knew that the two ronin were supposed to use their arms in defense of the weak. But in these troubled times, with the country torn apart by civil wars, the samurai didn't always live up to their honorable code.

Then the fire died down again and the subdued red light softened the features of the two ronin. The farmer relaxed and began his story. **B**

At the end of the story the boys were close to tears. Even Matsuzo found himself deeply touched.

The tale of Urashima Taro is familiar to every Japanese. No doubt the three little boys had heard their father tell it before—and more than once. But they listened with rapt attention.

> Urashima Taro, a fisherman, rescued a turtle from some boys who were battering it with stones. The grateful turtle rewarded Taro by carrying him on his back to the bottom of the sea, where he lived happily with the Princess of the Undersea. But Taro soon became homesick for his native village and asked to go back on land. The princess gave him a box to take with him but warned him not to peek inside.
>
> When Taro went back to his village, he found the place quite changed. In his home he found his parents gone, and living there was another old couple. He was stunned to learn that the aged husband was his own son, whom he had last seen as a baby! Taro thought he had spent only a pleasant week or two undersea with the princess. On land, seventy-two years had passed! His parents and most of his old friends had long since died.
>
> Desolate, Taro decided to open the box given him by the princess. As soon as he looked inside, he changed in an instant from a young man to a decrepit old man of more than ninety.

At the end of the story the boys were close to tears. Even Matsuzo found himself deeply touched. He wondered why the farmer had told his sons such a poignant bedtime story. Wouldn't they worry all evening instead of going to sleep? **C**

But the boys recovered quickly. They were soon laughing and jostling each other,

---

1. **brazier** (BRAY zhuhr): metal container that holds burning coals or charcoal, used to warm a room or cook food.

A **Reading Focus** **Analyzing Details** What details help create the mood, or atmosphere, in this farmhouse?

B **Read and Discuss** What has the author told us so far?

C **Literary Focus** **Mood** How does the mood of the story affect its listeners?

Vocabulary **desolate** (DEHS uh liht) *adj.:* lonely; miserable.

poignant (POYN yuhnt) *adj.:* causing sadness or pain; touching.

and they made no objections when their mother shooed them toward bed. Standing in order of age, they bowed politely to the guests and then lay down on the mattresses spread out for them on the floor. Within minutes the sound of their regular breathing told the guests that they were asleep.

Zenta, the older of the two ronin, sighed as he glanced at the peaceful young faces. "I wish I could fall asleep so quickly. The story of Urashima Taro is one of the saddest that I know among our folk tales."

The farmer looked proudly at his sleeping sons. "They're stout lads. Nothing bothers them much."

The farmer's wife poured tea for the guests and apologized. "I'm sorry this is only poor tea made from coarse leaves."

Zenta hastened to reassure her. "It's warm and heartening on a chilly autumn evening."

"You know what I think is the saddest part of the Urashima Taro story?" said Matsuzo, picking up his cup and sipping the tea. "It's that Taro lost not only his family and friends but a big piece of his life as well. He had lost the most precious thing of all: time."

The farmer nodded agreement. "I wouldn't sell even one year of my life for money. As for losing seventy-two years, no amount of gold will make up for that!" **D**

Zenta put his cup down on the floor and looked curiously at the farmer. "It's interesting that you should say that. I had an opportunity once to observe exactly how much gold a person was willing to pay for some lost years of his life." He smiled grimly. "In this case the man went as far as one gold piece for each year he lost."

"That's bizarre!" said Matsuzo. "You never told me about it."

"It happened long before I met you," said Zenta. He drank some tea and smiled ruefully. "Besides, I'm not particularly proud of the part I played in that strange affair." **E**

"Let's hear the story!" urged Matsuzo. "You've made us all curious."

The farmer waited expectantly. His wife sat down quietly behind her husband and folded her hands. Her eyes looked intently at Zenta.

"Very well, then," said Zenta. "Actually, my story bears some resemblance to that of Urashima Taro. . . ."

It happened about seven years ago, when I was a green, inexperienced youngster not quite eighteen years old. But I had had a good training in arms, and I was able to get a job as a bodyguard for a wealthy merchant from Sakai.

As you know, wealthy merchants are relatively new in our country. Traditionally the rich have been noblemen, landowners, and warlords with thousands of followers. Merchants, regarded as parasites in our society, are a despised class. But our civil wars have made people unusually mobile and stim-

D **Literary Focus** **Setting** How has the mood changed since the farmer told his story?

E **Read and Discuss** What does this conversation reveal?

Vocabulary **ruefully** (ROO fuhl lee) *adv.:* with regret and embarrassment.

ulated trade between various parts of the country. The merchants have taken advantage of this to conduct business on a scale our fathers could not imagine. Some of them have become more wealthy than a warlord with thousands of samurai under his command.

The man I was escorting, Tokubei, was one of this new breed of wealthy merchants. He was trading not only with outlying provinces but even with the Portuguese[2] from across the sea. On this particular journey he was not carrying much gold with him. If he had, I'm sure he would have hired an older and more experienced bodyguard. But if the need should arise, he could always write a message to his clerks at home and have money forwarded to him. It's important to remember this. **F**

The second day of our journey was a particularly grueling one, with several steep hills to climb. As the day was drawing to its close, we began to consider where we should spend the night. I knew that within an hour's walking was a hot-spring resort known to have several attractive inns.

But Tokubei, my employer, said he was already very tired and wanted to stop. He had heard of the resort and knew the inns there were expensive. Wealthy as he was, he did not want to spend more money than he had to.

While we stood talking, a smell reached our noses, a wonderful smell of freshly cooked rice. Suddenly I felt ravenous. From the way Tokubei swallowed, I knew he was feeling just as hungry.

We looked around eagerly, but the area was forested and we could not see very far in any direction. The tantalizing smell seemed to grow and I could feel the saliva filling my mouth.

"There's an inn around here somewhere," muttered Tokubei. "I'm sure of it."

We followed our noses. We had to leave the well-traveled highway and take a narrow, winding footpath. But the mouthwatering smell of the rice and the vision of fluffy, freshly aired cotton quilts drew us on.

The sun was just beginning to set. We passed a bamboo grove, and in the low evening light the thin leaves turned into little golden knives. I saw a gilded[3] clump of bamboo shoots. The sight made me think of the delicious dish they would make when boiled in soy sauce.

We hurried forward. To our delight we soon came to a clearing with a thatched house standing in the middle. The fragrant smell of rice was now so strong that we were certain a meal was being prepared inside. **G**

2. **Portuguese**: The Portuguese were the first Europeans to reach Japan, arriving in 1543. Until they were expelled, in the 1630s, they traded extensively with the Japanese.

3. **gilded:** here, appearing to be coated with gold.

F Reading Focus Analyzing Details What do the details Zenta gives about his employer suggest about the setting of his story?

G Literary Focus Mood What mood is created through the description of the house and its surroundings?

Vocabulary **grueling** (GROO uhl ihng) *adj.:* very tiring; demanding.

Analyzing Visuals

Viewing and Interpreting How do these color choices help the artist convey the warrior aspect of the samurai? In what way do the samurai in this story differ from this one?

The Actor Ichikawa Danjuro VII as a Samurai Warrior by Utagawa Kunisada. Surimono-woodblock print.

Standing in front of the house was a pretty girl beaming at us with a welcoming smile. "Please honor us with your presence," she said, beckoning.

There was something a little unusual about one of her hands, but, being hungry and eager to enter the house, I did not stop to observe closely.

You will say, of course, that it was my duty as a bodyguard to be suspicious and to look out for danger. Youth and inexperience should not have prevented me from wondering why an inn should be found hidden away from the highway. As it was, my stomach growled, and I didn't even hesitate but followed Tokubei to the house.

Before stepping up to enter, we were given basins of water to wash our feet. As the girl handed us towels for drying, I saw what was unusual about her left hand: She had six fingers.

Tokubei had noticed it as well. When the girl turned away to empty the basins, he nudged me. "Did you see her left hand? She had—" He broke off in confusion as the girl turned around, but she didn't seem to have heard.

The inn was peaceful and quiet, and we soon discovered the reason why. We were the only guests. Again, I should have been suspicious. I told you that I'm not proud of the part I played.

Tokubei turned to me and grinned. "It seems that there are no other guests. We should be able to get extra service for the same amount of money." **H**

The girl led us to a spacious room which was like the principal chamber of a private residence. Cushions were set out for us on the floor and we began to shed our traveling gear to make ourselves comfortable.

The door opened and a grizzled-haired man entered. Despite his vigorous-looking face his back was a little bent, and I guessed his age to be about fifty. After bowing and greeting us, he apologized in advance for the service. "We have not always been innkeepers here," he said, "and you may find the accommodations lacking. Our good intentions must make up for our inexperience. However, to compensate for our inadequacies, we will charge a lower fee than that of an inn with an established reputation."

Tokubei nodded graciously, highly pleased by the words of our host, and the evening began well. It continued well when the girl came back with some flasks of wine, cups, and dishes of salty snacks.

While the girl served the wine, the host looked with interest at my swords. From the few remarks he made, I gathered that he was a former samurai, forced by circumstances to turn his house into an inn.

Having become a bodyguard to a tight-fisted merchant, I was in no position to feel superior to a ronin-turned-innkeeper. Socially, therefore, we were more or less equal.

We exchanged polite remarks with our host while we drank and tasted the salty snacks. I looked around at the pleasant room. It showed excellent taste, and I especially admired a vase standing in the alcove. **I**

My host caught my eyes on it. "We still have a few good things that we didn't have to sell," he said. His voice held a trace of bitterness. "Please look at the panels of these doors. They were painted by a fine artist."

Tokubei and I looked at the pair of sliding doors. Each panel contained a landscape painting, the right panel depicting a winter scene and the left one the same scene in late summer. Our host's words were no idle boast. The pictures were indeed beautiful.

Tokubei rose and approached the screens for a closer look. When he sat down again, his eyes were calculating. No doubt he was trying to estimate what price the paintings would fetch. **J**

After my third drink I began to feel very tired. Perhaps it was the result of drinking on an empty stomach. I was

---

H **Reading Focus** **Analyzing Details** Which details of this inn's setting seem comforting? Which details seem threatening?

I **Literary Focus** **Mood** What adjective would you use to describe the mood of this evening?

J **Read and Discuss** What is Zenta suggesting about Tokubei?

SOCIAL STUDIES LINK

Kojima Takanori Writing a Poem on a Cherry Tree, from the series *'Pictures of Flowers of Japan'* (1895) by Ogata Gekko. Woodblock print.

The Samurai

This story's main character, Zenta, is a samurai (SAM u ry), a member of the warrior class in feudal Japan. The samurai were proud, disciplined warriors who led a life based on duty and sacrifice. They followed a code called Bushido, which required them to show absolute obedience and loyalty to their lords and to place their honor above anything else, including their own lives. The samurai class lost its privileges and began to die out when feudalism was abolished in Japan in 1871. You may be surprised to hear that these disciplined warriors produced many of Japan's famous arts, including the tea ceremony and flower arrangement.

One of the great movies of the twentieth century is *The Seven Samurai* (1954), directed by Akira Kurosawa. In the movie, set in the sixteenth century, a group of samurai who are looking for work hire themselves out to protect a village threatened by bandits. The movie has been called an "eastern western" because the seven samurai remind people of the heroic cowboys of American western movies.

Ask Yourself

Do Zenta and Matsuzo seem to follow the ways and codes of the samurai? Explain.

glad when the girl brought in two dinner trays and a lacquered container of rice. Uncovering the rice container, she began filling our bowls.

Again I noticed her strange left hand with its six fingers. Any other girl would have tried to keep that hand hidden, but this girl made no effort to do so. If anything, she seemed to use that hand more than her other one when she served us. The extra little finger always stuck out from the hand, as if inviting comment.

The hand fascinated me so much that I kept my eyes on it and soon forgot to eat. After a while the hand looked blurry. And then everything else began to look blurry. The last thing I remembered was the sight of Tokubei shaking his head, as if trying to clear it.

When I opened my eyes again, I knew that time had passed, but not how much time. My next thought was that it was cold. It was not only extremely cold but damp.

I rolled over and sat up. I reached immediately for my swords and found them safe on the ground beside me. *On the ground?* What was I doing on the ground? My last memory was of staying at an inn with a merchant called Tokubei.

The thought of Tokubei put me into a panic. I was his bodyguard, and instead of watching over him, I had fallen asleep and had awakened in a strange place.

I looked around frantically and saw that he was lying on the ground not far from where I was. Had he been killed?

I got up shakily, and when I stood up, my head was swimming. But my sense of urgency gave some strength to my legs. I stumbled over to my employer and to my great relief found him breathing—breathing heavily, in fact.

When I shook his shoulder, he grunted and finally opened his eyes. "Where am I?" he asked thickly.

It was a reasonable question. I looked around and saw that we had been lying in a bamboo grove. By the light I guessed that it was early morning, and the reason I felt cold and damp was that my clothes were wet with dew. K

"It's cold!" said Tokubei, shivering and climbing unsteadily to his feet. He looked around slowly, and his eyes became wide with disbelief. "What happened? I thought we were staying at an inn!"

His words came as a relief. One of the possibilities I had considered was that I had gone mad and that the whole episode with the inn was something I had imagined. Now I knew that Tokubei had the same memory of the inn. I had not imagined it.

But why were we out here on the cold ground, instead of on comfortable mattresses in the inn?

"They must have drugged us and robbed us," said Tokubei. He turned and looked at me furiously. "A fine bodyguard you are!"

There was nothing I could say to that. But at least we were both alive and unharmed. "Did they take all your money?" I asked.

Tokubei had already taken his wallet out of his sash and was peering inside. "That's funny! My money is still here!"

This was certainly unexpected. What did the innkeeper and his strange daughter intend to do by drugging us and moving us outside?

At least things were not as bad as we had feared. We had not lost anything except a comfortable night's sleep, although from the heaviness in my head I had certainly slept deeply enough—and long enough too. Exactly how much time had elapsed since we drank wine with our host?

All we had to do now was find the highway again and continue our journey. Tokubei suddenly chuckled. "I didn't even have to pay for our night's lodging!"

As we walked from the bamboo grove, I saw the familiar clump of bamboo shoots, and we found ourselves standing in the same clearing again. Before our eyes was the thatched house. Only it was somehow different. Perhaps things looked different in the daylight than at dusk.

But the difference was more than a change of light. As we approached the house slowly, like sleepwalkers, we saw that the thatching was much darker.

K **Literary Focus** **Setting** Where are Zenta and Tokubei now? What details reveal this information?

On the previous evening the thatching had looked fresh and new. Now it was dark with age. Daylight should make things appear brighter, not darker. The plastering of the walls also looked more dingy. **L**

Tokubei and I stopped to look at each other before we went closer. He was pale, and I knew that I looked no less frightened. Something was terribly wrong. I loosened my sword in its scabbard.[4]

We finally gathered the courage to go up to the house. Since Tokubei seemed unable to find his voice, I spoke out. "Is anyone there?"

After a moment we heard shuffling footsteps and the front door slid open. The face of an old woman appeared. "Yes?" she inquired. Her voice was creaky with age.

What set my heart pounding with panic, however, was not her voice. It was the sight of her left hand holding on to the frame of the door. The hand was wrinkled and crooked with the arthritis of old age—and it had six fingers.

I heard a gasp beside me and knew that Tokubei had noticed the hand as well.

The door opened wider and a man appeared beside the old woman. At first I thought it was our host of the previous night. But this man was much younger, although the resemblance was strong. He carried himself straighter and his hair was black, while the innkeeper had been grizzled and slightly bent with age. **M**

When I opened my eyes again, I knew that time had passed, but not how much time.

"Please excuse my mother," said the man. "Her hearing is not good. Can we help you in some way?"

Tokubei finally found his voice. "Isn't this the inn where we stayed last night?"

The man stared. "Inn? We are not innkeepers here!"

"Yes, you are!" insisted Tokubei. "Your daughter invited us in and served us with wine. You must have put something in the wine!"

The man frowned. "You are serious? Are you sure you didn't drink too much at your inn and wander off?"

"No, I didn't drink too much!" said Tokubei, almost shouting. "I hardly drank at all! Your daughter, the one with six fingers on her hand, started to pour me a second cup of wine . . ." His voice trailed off, and he stared again at the left hand of the old woman.

"I don't have a daughter," said the man slowly. "My mother here is the one who has six fingers on her left hand, although I hardly think it polite of you to mention it."

4. **scabbard:** case for the blade of a sword.

L Literary Focus Setting How does this setting differ from the setting of the inn on the previous night?

M Reading Focus Analyzing Details Consider the careful descriptions of the old woman and the man. What do these details suggest?

"I'm getting dizzy," muttered Tokubei, and began to totter.

"I think you'd better come in and rest a bit," the man said to him gruffly. He glanced at me. "Perhaps you wish to join your friend. You don't share his delusion about the inn, I hope?"

"I wouldn't presume to contradict my elders," I said carefully. Since both Tokubei and the owner of the house were my elders, I wasn't committing myself. In truth, I didn't know what to believe, but I did want a look at the inside of the house.

The inside was almost the same as it was before but the differences were there when I looked closely. We entered the same room with the alcove and the pair of painted doors. The vase I had admired was no longer there, but the doors showed the same landscapes painted by a master. I peered closely at the pictures and saw that the colors looked faded. What was more, the left panel, the one depicting a winter scene, had a long tear in one corner. It had been painstakingly mended, but the damage was impossible to hide completely. **N**

Snow-laden grasses [and] Snow-laden pine branches (Edo Period) by Ogata Kenzan. Fan; ink and color on paper. A. 7 5/8 x 19 1/2 in. B. 7 5/8 x 19 7/16 in.

Tokubei saw what I was staring at and he became even paler. At this stage we had both considered the possibility that a hoax of some sort had been played on us. The torn screen convinced Tokubei that our host had not played a joke: The owner of a valuable painting would never vandalize it for a trivial reason.

As for me, I was far more disturbed by the sight of the sixth finger on the old woman's hand. Could the young girl have disguised herself as an old crone? She could put rice powder in her hair to whiten it, but she could not transform her pretty straight fingers into old fingers twisted with arthritis. The woman here with us now was genuinely old, at least fifty years older than the girl. **O**

It was this same old woman who finally gave us our greatest shock. "It's interesting that you should mention

---

N **Read and Discuss** What has happened?

O **Reading Focus** **Analyzing Details** Zenta observes details of his surroundings very carefully. What conclusions might he be drawing?

an inn, gentlemen," she croaked. "My father used to operate an inn. After he died, my husband and I turned this back into a private residence. We didn't need the income, you see."

"Your . . . your . . . f-father?" stammered Tokubei.

"Yes," replied the old woman. "He was a ronin, forced to go into inn keeping when he lost his position. But he never liked the work. Besides, our inn had begun to acquire an unfortunate reputation. Some of our guests disappeared, you see."

Even before she finished speaking, a horrible suspicion had begun to dawn on me. Her *father* had been an innkeeper, she said, her father who used to be a ronin. The man who had been our host was a ronin-turned-innkeeper. Could this mean that this old woman was actually the same person as the young girl we had seen?

I sat stunned while I tried to absorb the implications. What had happened to us? Was it possible that Tokubei and I had slept while this young girl grew into a mature woman, got married, and bore a son, a son who was now an adult? If that was the case, then we had slept for fifty years!

The old woman's next words confirmed my fears. "I recognize you now! You are two of the lost guests from our inn! The other lost ones I don't remember so well, but I remember *you* because your disappearance made me so sad. Such a handsome youth, I thought; what a pity that he should have gone the way of the others!"

A high wail came from Tokubei, who began to keen[5] and rock himself back and forth. "I've lost fifty years! Fifty years of my life went by while I slept at this accursed inn!"

Snow-laden grasses [and] Snow-laden pine branches (Edo Period) by Ogata Kenzan. Fan; ink and color on paper. A. 7 5/8 x 19 1/2 in. B. 7 5/8 x 19 7/16 in.

The inn was indeed accursed. Was the fate of the other guests similar to ours? "Did anyone else return as we did, fifty years later?" I asked.

The old woman looked uncertain and turned to her son. He frowned thoughtfully. "From time to time wild-looking people have come to us with stories similar to yours. Some of them went mad with the shock."

---

5. **keen:** wail.

Tokubei wailed again. "I've lost my business! I've lost my wife, my young and beautiful wife! We had been married only a couple of months!"

A gruesome chuckle came from the old woman. "You may not have lost your wife. It's just that she's become an old hag like me!"

That did not console Tokubei, whose keening became louder. Although my relationship with my employer had not been characterized by much respect on either side, I did begin to feel very sorry for him. He was right: He had lost his world.

As for me, the loss was less traumatic. I had left home under extremely painful circumstances and had spent the next three years wandering. I had no friends and no one I could call a relation. The only thing I had was my duty to my employer. Somehow, someway, I had to help him.

"Did no one find an explanation for these disappearances?" I asked. "Perhaps if we knew the reason why, we might find some way to reverse the process."

The old woman began to nod eagerly. "The priestess! Tell them about the shrine priestess!"

"Well," said the man, "I'm not sure if it would work in your case. . . ."

"What? What would work?" demanded Tokubei. His eyes were feverish.

"There was a case of one returning guest who consulted the priestess at our local shrine," said the man. "She went into a trance and revealed that there was an evil spirit dwelling in the bamboo grove here. This spirit would put unwary travelers into a long, unnatural sleep. They would wake up twenty, thirty, or even fifty years later."

"Yes, but you said something worked in his case," said Tokubei.

The man seemed reluctant to go on. "I don't like to see you cheated, so I'm not sure I should be telling you this."

"Tell me! Tell me!" demanded Tokubei. The host's reluctance only made him more impatient.

"The priestess promised to make a spell that would undo the work of the evil spirit," said the man. "But she demanded a large sum of money, for she said that she had to burn some very rare and costly incense before she could begin the spell."

At the mention of money Tokubei sat back. The hectic[6] flush died down on his face and his eyes narrowed. "How much money?" he asked.

The host shook his head. "In my opinion the priestess is a fraud and makes outrageous claims about her powers. We try to have as little to do with her as possible."

6. **hectic:** feverish.

Vocabulary **traumatic** (traw MAT ihk) *adj.:* emotionally painful; causing shock.

"Yes, but did her spell work?" asked Tokubei. "If it worked, she's no fraud!"

"At least the stranger disappeared again," cackled the old woman. "Maybe he went back to his own time. Maybe he walked into a river."

Tokubei's eyes narrowed further. "How much money did the priestess demand?" he asked again.

"I think it was one gold piece for every year lost," said the host. He hurriedly added, "Mind you, I still wouldn't trust the priestess."

"Then it would cost me fifty gold pieces to get back to my own time," muttered Tokubei. He looked up. "I don't carry that much money with me."

"No, you don't," agreed the host.

Something alerted me about the way he said that. It was as if the host knew already that Tokubei did not carry much money on him.

Meanwhile Tokubei sighed. He had come to a decision. "I do have the means to obtain more money, however. I can send a message to my chief clerk and he will remit the money when he sees my seal."

"Your chief clerk may be dead by now," I reminded him.

"You're right!" moaned Tokubei. "My business will be under a new management and nobody will even remember my name!"

"And your wife will have remarried," said the old woman, with one of her chuckles. I found it hard to believe that the gentle young girl who had served us wine could turn into this dreadful harridan.[7]

"Sending the message may be a waste of time," agreed the host.

"My business will be under a new management and nobody will even remember my name!"

"What waste of time!" cried Tokubei. "Why shouldn't I waste time? I've wasted fifty years already! Anyway, I've made up my mind. I'm sending that message."

"I still think you shouldn't trust the priestess," said the host.

That only made Tokubei all the more determined to send for the money. However, he was not quite resigned to the amount. "Fifty gold pieces is a large sum. Surely the priestess can buy incense for less than that amount?"

"Why don't you try giving her thirty gold pieces?" cackled the old woman. "Then the priestess will send you back thirty years, and your wife will only be middle-aged." **P**

While Tokubei was still arguing with himself about the exact sum to send for, I decided to have a look at the

7. **harridan:** spiteful old woman.

P **Read and Discuss** What is this passage telling us?

bamboo grove. "I'm going for a walk," I announced, rising and picking up my sword from the floor beside me.

The host turned sharply to look at me. For an instant a faint, rueful smile appeared on his lips. Then he looked away.

Outside, I went straight to the clump of shoots in the bamboo grove. On the previous night—or what I perceived as the previous night—I had noticed that clump of bamboo shoots particularly, because I had been so hungry that I pictured them being cut up and boiled.

The clump of bamboo shoots was still in the same place. That in itself proved nothing, since bamboo could spring up anywhere, including the place where a clump had existed fifty years earlier. But what settled the matter in my mind was that the clump looked almost exactly the way it did when I had seen it before, except that every shoot was about an inch taller. That was a reasonable amount for bamboo shoots to grow overnight.

Overnight. Tokubei and I had slept on the ground here overnight. We had not slept here for a period of fifty years.

Analyzing Visuals **Viewing and Interpreting**

How would you describe the expression on this woman's face? Might the farmer's wife have reacted similarly when the samurai came to visit? Explain.

Young Servant Girl, series of Kabuki theatre, ukiyo-e print, 19th century.

Once I knew that, I was able to see another inconsistency: the door panels with the painted landscapes. The painting with the winter scene had been on the *right* last night and it was on the *left* this morning. It wasn't simply a case of the panels changing places, because the depressions in the panel for the handholds had been reversed. In other words, what I saw just now was not a pair of paintings faded and torn by age. They were an entirely different pair of paintings. Q

But how did the pretty young girl change into an old woman? The answer was that if the screens could be different ones, so could the women. I had seen one woman, a young girl, last night. This morning I saw a different woman, an old hag.

The darkening of the thatched roof? Simply blow ashes over the roof. The grizzled-haired host of last night could be the same man who claimed to be his grandson today. It would be a simple matter for a young man to put gray in his hair and assume a stoop.

And the purpose of the hoax? To make Tokubei send for fifty pieces of gold, of course. It was clever of the man to accuse the shrine priestess of fraud and pretend reluctance to let Tokubei send his message.

I couldn't even feel angry toward the man and his daughter—or mother, sister, wife, whatever. He could have killed me and taken my swords, which he clearly admired. Perhaps he was really a ronin and felt sympathetic toward another one.

When I returned to the house, Tokubei was looking resigned. "I've decided to send for the whole fifty gold pieces." He sighed.

"Don't bother," I said. "In fact, we should be leaving as soon as possible. We shouldn't even stop here for a drink, especially not of wine."

Tokubei stared. "What do you mean? If I go back home, I'll find everything changed!"

"Nothing will be changed," I told him. "Your wife will be as young and beautiful as ever."

"I don't understand," he said. "Fifty years . . ."

"It's a joke," I said. "The people here have a peculiar sense of humor, and they've played a joke on us."

Tokubei's mouth hung open. Finally he closed it with a snap. He stared at the host, and his face became first red and then purple. "You—you were trying to swindle me!" He turned furiously to me. "And you let them do this!"

"I'm not letting them," I pointed out. "That's why we're leaving right now."

"Are you going to let them get away with this?" demanded Tokubei. "They might try to swindle someone else!"

"They only went to this much trouble when they heard of the arrival of a fine

Q **Literary Focus** **Setting** What details of the setting provide clues to the mystery of the inn?

fat fish like you," I said. I looked deliberately at the host. "I'm sure they won't be tempted to try the same trick again."

"And that's the end of your story?" asked Matsuzo. "You and Tokubei just went away? How did you know the so-called innkeeper wouldn't try the trick on some other luckless traveler?"

"And that's the end of your story?" asked Matsuzo.

Zenta shook his head. "I didn't know. I merely guessed that once the trick was exposed, they wouldn't take the chance of trying it again. Of course I thought about revisiting the place to check if the people there were leading an honest life."

"Why didn't you?" asked Matsuzo. "Maybe we could go together. You've made me curious about that family now."

"Then you can satisfy your curiosity," said Zenta, smiling. He held his cup out for more tea, and the farmer's wife came forward to pour.

Only now she used both hands to hold the pot, and for the first time Matsuzo saw her left hand. He gasped. The hand had six fingers.

"Who was the old woman?" Zenta asked the farmer's wife.

"She was my grandmother," she replied. "Having six fingers is something that runs in my family."

At last Matsuzo found his voice. "You mean this is the very house you visited? This is the inn where time was lost?"

"Where we *thought* we lost fifty years," said Zenta. "Perhaps I should have warned you first. But I was almost certain that we'd be safe this time. And I see that I was right."

He turned to the woman again. "You and your husband are farmers now, aren't you? What happened to the man who was the host?"

"He's dead," she said quietly. "He was my brother, and he was telling you the truth when he said that he was a ronin. Two years ago he found work with another warlord, but he was killed in battle only a month later."

Matsuzo was peering at the pair of sliding doors, which he hadn't noticed before. "I see that you've put up the faded set of paintings. The winter scene is on the left side."

The woman nodded. "We sold the newer pair of doors. My husband said that we're farmers now and that people in our position don't need valuable paintings. We used the money to buy some new farm implements."

She took up the teapot again. "Would you like another cup of tea?" she asked Matsuzo.

Staring at her left hand, Matsuzo had a sudden qualm. "I—I don't think I want any more."

Everybody laughed. 

R **Read and Discuss** Why do you think the author ends the story this way?

Applying Your Skills

RA.L.8.2 Analyze the influence of setting in relation to other literary elements. RA.L.8.3 Explain how authors pace action and use subplots, parallel episodes and climax. WA.8.1.c Write narratives that: create complex characters in a definite, believable setting.

The Inn of Lost Time

Respond and Think Critically

Reading Focus

Quick Check

1. Where does the frame story begin and end?
2. What happens in the old Japanese folk tale told by the farmer?
3. In Zenta's story, what do Zenta and his employer think happened to them the night they stayed at the "inn of lost time"?
4. What is revealed to them later? What actually occurred?

Read with a Purpose

5. Did you solve the mystery before or along with Zenta? What clues gave the deceivers away?

Reading Skills: Analyzing Details

6. Review the details of setting that you listed on your chart. Circle details that helped create specific moods. Then, use this chart to answer questions 9 and 10.

Detail: Place	Detail: Time	Detail: Custom
a Japanese farmhouse	nighttime; sixteenth century	people drink tea by a fire and tell stories

Literary Focus

Literary Analysis

7. **Interpret** What connection did you discover between the inn in Zenta's story and the inn in the frame story? Do you think this was an effective way to structure the story? Explain.
8. **Infer** Why do you think the farmer's wife and her family changed their ways?

Literary Skills: Setting and Mood

9. **Analyze** How does the setting of the story affect the story's action? Could this story have taken place in any time and place? Explain.
10. **Draw Conclusions** Look back at your chart of story details that describe setting. What overall mood do these details create?

Literary Skills Review: Suspense

11. **Analyze** The uncertainty or anxiety that a reader feels about what will happen next is called **suspense.** Describe ways in which Lensey Namioka builds suspense in this tale.

Writing Focus

Think as a Reader/Writer

Use It in Your Writing The details Lensey Namioka uses in "The Inn of Lost Time" help create a believable and haunting picture of the past. Write a scene that takes place in another time and place of your choosing. Choose precise descriptive words to establish the setting of this time and place.

Matsuzo calls time "the most precious thing of all." After reading this story, do you agree or disagree with Matsuzo? Explain.

Applying Your Skills

The Inn of Lost Time

Vocabulary Development

Verify Word Meanings

There are many ways to test and verify a word's meaning. You might come up with examples or comparisons or try restating the meaning of the word in slightly different terms. All these strategies lead to a better understanding of a word's meaning.

A word map is an effective tool to help you clarify how a word can be used. See the word map below for the Vocabulary word *desolate*.

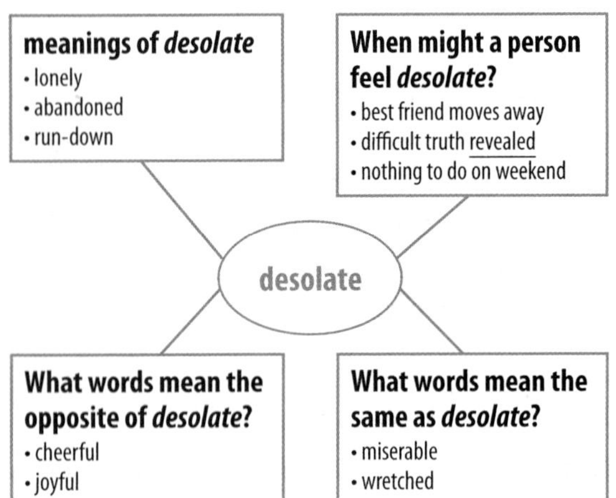

meanings of desolate

Your Turn

• best friend moves away
• difficult truth revealed
• nothing to do on weekend
desolate
What words mean the same as desolate?
poignant
ruefully
grueling
traumatic

Make a word map for each of the Vocabulary words from the list. Use your word maps as you answer the following questions.

1. What is the opposite of a **desolate** mood?
2. The movie was **poignant**—it left me feeling incredibly __________.
3. What experience might lead someone to smile **ruefully**?
4. Our trip was very difficult. It became especially **grueling** when __________.
5. Name three historical events that would have been **traumatic** to experience.

Language Coach

Oral Fluency The *gn* letter combination can be pronounced in a number of ways. Look up the following words in a dictionary, and write down how each *gn* letter combination is pronounced: *lasagna, campaign, signal.*

Academic Vocabulary

Talk About . . .

The farmer in "The Inn of Lost Time" says he would not sell even one year of his life for money. What do you think? What might be the outcome of selling a year of your life? What might a willingness to sell a year of one's life reveal about someone's personality?

Learn It Online
For more great vocabulary information, use Word Watch at:
go.hrw.com
L8-50
Go

WA.8.5.a Write persuasive compositions that: establish and develop a controlling idea; C.8.9 Deliver formal and informal descriptive presentations that convey relevant information and descriptive details. WC.8.3 Grammar and Usage: Use all eight parts of speech. Also covered VO.8.4; RA.L.8.2

Grammar Link

Adjectives

What do the phrases *lively boy* and *feisty lion* have in common? Both include a noun modified by an adjective. An adjective is a word that describes a noun (such as *boy* or *lion*) or a pronoun (such as *he, she,* or *them*). Adjectives typically answer one of the following questions: *What kind? Which one? How much* or *how many?* Examples of adjectives are underlined in the chart below.

What kind?	salty snacks fine artist landscape painting
Which one (or ones)?	that inn this young girl any bamboo shoots
How much or many?	fifty years many hills six fingers

Your Turn

Identify the adjective(s) in each sentence or phrase below from "The Inn of Lost Time."

1. "He pretended to put on a stern expression."
2. "The lean faces of the two ronin . . ."
3. "The grateful turtle rewarded Taro . . ."
4. ". . . the mouthwatering smell of the rice . . ."
5. ". . . with several steep hills to climb."

Writing Applications Write three sentences of your own using three different types of adjectives: those answering *What kind?;* those answering *Which one (or ones)?;* and those answering *How much or many?*

CHOICES

As you respond to the Choices, use these **Academic Vocabulary** words as appropriate: effective, outcome, reveal, structure.

REVIEW

Write to Persuade

Timed Writing Is it better to travel alone or with a friend, such as the samurai from the story? Write a short essay to convince others of your opinion. Structure your essay with an introduction stating your opinion, specific examples for support, and a conclusion.

CONNECT

Present a Story

TechFocus A custom in medieval Japan was to gather and tell stories. Select a folk tale to make into a digital story or short video to share with your classmates. Bring the story to life with music, maps, photographs, and pictures.

EXTEND

Discuss a Movie

Group Activity With classmates, watch Akira Kurosawa's classic film *The Seven Samurai.* What do you learn about this time period in Japanese history—what did the film reveal about the class system, the civil wars, and the samurai code?

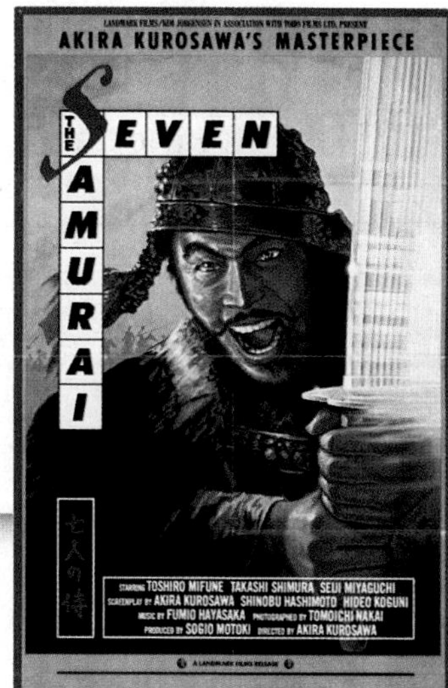

SHORT STORY

Preparing to Read

Flowers for Algernon

by **Daniel Keyes**

What Do You Think?

When is knowledge power? When is ignorance bliss?

QuickWrite

Why might a person hesitate to tell a friend something upsetting? Write down your thoughts.

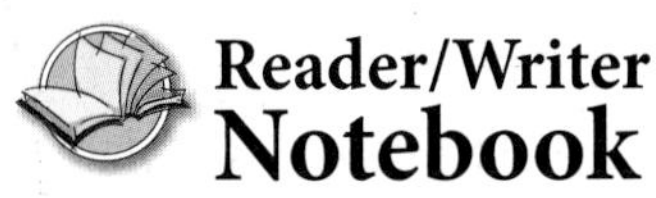

Reader/Writer Notebook

Use your **RWN** to complete the activities for this selection.

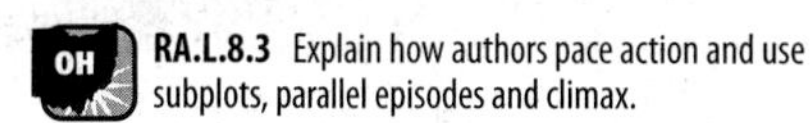

RA.L.8.3 Explain how authors pace action and use subplots, parallel episodes and climax.

Literary Focus

Subplots and Parallel Episodes A long short story, like the one that follows, sometimes has a complex plot, a plot that consists of intertwined stories. A complex plot may include

- **subplots**—less important plots that are part of the larger story
- **parallel episodes**—deliberately repeated plot events

As you read "Flowers for Algernon," watch for new settings, characters, or conflicts that are introduced into the story. These may signal that a subplot is beginning. To identify parallel episodes, take note of similar situations or events that occur in the story.

Literary Perspectives Apply the literary perspective described on page 55 as you read this story.

Reading Focus

Tracking Story Events To follow a story's plot and identify subplots and parallel episodes, pause every now and then to think about what has happened so far.

Into Action Use a chart like the one below to **track story events.** Underline events that introduce new settings, characters, or conflicts. Circle any event that is similar to an event that happened earlier.

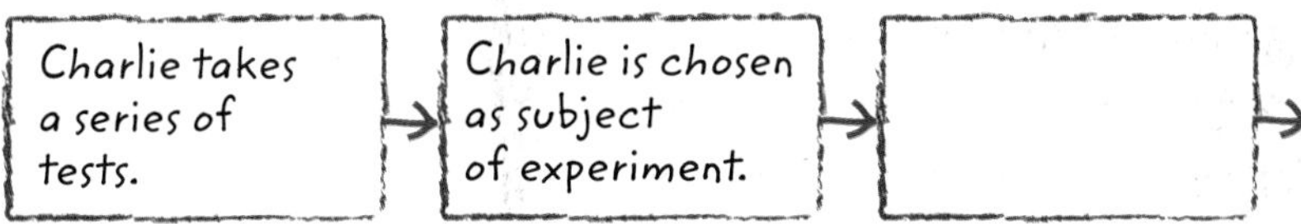

Charlie takes a series of tests.
Charlie is chosen as subject of experiment.

Writing Focus

Think as a Reader/Writer

Find It in Your Reading In this story, events unfold through a character's journal entries. In your *Reader/Writer Notebook* note how Keyes develops Charlie's character through that character's use of language (his word choice, spelling, and grammar).

Vocabulary

misled (mihs LEHD) *v.:* fooled; led to believe something wrong. *Joe and Frank misled Charlie into believing they were his friends.*

regression (rih GREHSH uhn) *n.:* return to an earlier or less advanced condition. *After its regression, the mouse could no longer find its way through a maze.*

obscure (uhb SKYOOR) *v.:* hide. *He wanted to obscure the fact that he was losing his intelligence.*

deterioration (dih tihr ee uh RAY shuhn) *n.* used as an *adj:* worsening; declining. *Charlie could predict mental deterioration syndromes by using his formula.*

introspective (ihn truh SPEHK tihv) *adj.:* looking inward. *Charlie was introspective about all the changes he went through.*

Language Coach

Word Origins Which Vocabulary word above looks as if it is derived from the Latin verb *specere*, meaning "to see"? What other words do you know that contain the word part *-spec-*?

Learn It Online
Expand your story experience by visiting Literature Links at:

go.hrw.com L8-53 Go

MEET THE WRITER

Daniel Keyes

(1927–)

"Fascinated by the . . . Human Mind"

Born in Brooklyn, New York, Daniel Keyes says that he is "fascinated by the complexities of the human mind." In fact, he studied psychology so that he could create more believable characters in his stories.

Unhelpful "Advice"

When Keyes was looking for a publisher for "Flowers for Algernon," he was advised to change the ending of his story to a happy, "Hollywood" ending. Keyes refused. His decision proved to be a good one. His story became famous around the world and was made into a novel, a play, a movie, and even a musical.

> "When I went to Tokyo, they . . . brought me gifts, flowers, candy, letters, and I sat there thinking, 'I feel like a rock star.'"

Think About the Writer What might Keyes's refusal to change his story say about him?

Build Background

You will find terms dealing with psychology and science in "Flowers for Algernon." Here are some terms to know:

- **Rorschach** (RAWR shahk) **test:** psychological test in which people describe the images suggested to them by a series of inkblots. See page 59 for an example.
- **IQ:** short for *intelligence quotient;* a number that is meant to show how intelligent someone is. An IQ score is determined from an intelligence test.
- **hypothesis:** a theory to be proved. In the story, the doctors' hypothesis is that they can improve intelligence through surgery.

Preview the Selection

In this story you'll meet **Charlie Gordon,** who undergoes experimental surgery to increase his intelligence. Charlie keeps a journal to record his progress and to share how the experiment affects his life.

Read with a Purpose Read this story to find out what Charlie gains and loses as he participates in a medical experiment.

Flowers for Algernon

by **Daniel Keyes**

Part 1

progris riport 1—martch 5 1965

Dr. Strauss says I shud rite[1] down what I think and evrey thing that happins to me from now on. I dont know why but he says its importint so they will see if they will use me. I hope they use me. Miss Kinnian says maybe they can make me smart. I want to be smart. My name is Charlie Gordon. I am 37 years old and 2 weeks ago was my brithday. I have nuthing more to rite now so I will close for today.

progris riport 2—martch 6

I had a test today. I think I faled it. and I think that maybe now they wont use me. What happind is a nice young man was in the room and he had some white cards with ink spillled all over them. He sed Charlie what do you see on this card. I was very

1. **shud rite:** should write. To understand Charlie's misspelled words, try sounding them out and reading the surrounding words for clues to the meaning.

Literary Perspectives

Use this literary perspective to help you analyze the story's main character.

Analyzing Credibility in Literature Literature often requires that we believe in things that are not true, such as talking animals. Even so, we expect the characters and plots to be believable, or credible.

Analyzing the credibility of the narrator is especially important in "Flowers for Algernon." Consider these questions as you read: How might the narrator's perceptions of the world differ from yours? How is he unlike any narrator you have met before? As you read, be sure to notice the notes and questions in the text, which will guide you in using this perspective.

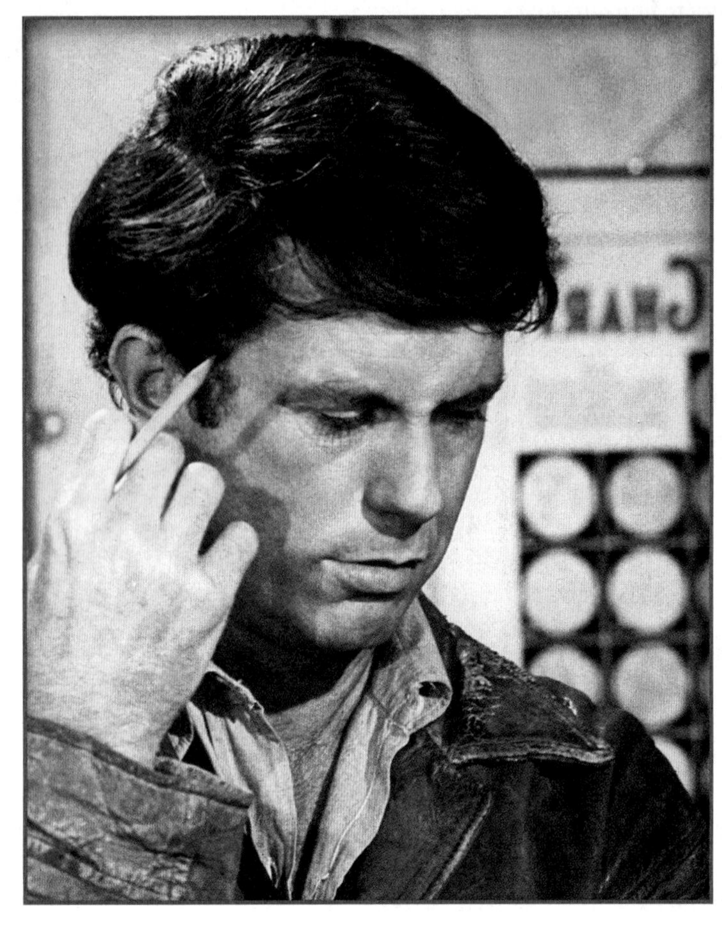

skared even tho I had my rabits foot[2] in my pockit because when I was a kid I always faled tests in school and I spillled ink to.

I told him I saw a inkblot. He said yes and it made me feel good. I thot that was all but when I got up to go he stopped me. He said now sit down Charlie we are not thru yet. Then I dont remember so good but he wantid me to say what was in the ink. I dint see nuthing in the ink but he said there was picturs there other pepul saw some picturs. I coudnt see any picturs. I reely tryed to see. I held the card close up and then far away. Then I said if I had my glases I coud see better I usally only ware my glases in the movies or TV but I said they are in the closit in the hall. I got them. Then I said let me see that card agen I bet Ill find it now.

I tryed hard but I still coudnt find the picturs I only saw the ink. I told him maybe I need new glases. He rote somthing down on a paper and I got skared of faling the test. I told him it was a very nice inkblot with littel points all around the eges. He looked very sad so that wasnt it. I said please let me try agen. Ill get it in a few minits becaus Im not so fast somtimes. Im a slow reeder too in Miss Kinnians class for slow adults but I'm trying very hard.

He gave me a chance with another card that had 2 kinds of ink spillled on it red and blue.

He was very nice and talked slow like Miss Kinnian does and he explaned it to me that it was a *raw shok.*[3] He said pepul see things in the ink. I said show me where. He said think. I told him I think a inkblot but that wasnt rite eather. He said what does it remind you—pretend something. I closd my eyes for a long time to pretend. I told him I pretned a fowntan pen with ink

2. **rabits foot:** The hind foot of a rabbit is sometimes used as a good-luck charm.

3. **raw shok:** Charlie is trying to spell *Rorschach.*

leeking all over a table cloth. Then he got up and went out.

I dont think I passd the *raw shok* test. **A**

progris report 3—martch 7

Dr Strauss and Dr Nemur say it dont matter about the inkblots. I told them I dint spill the ink on the cards and I coudn't see anything in the ink. They said that maybe they will still use me. I said Miss Kinnian never gave me tests like that one only spelling and reading. They said Miss Kinnian told that I was her bestist pupil in the adult nite scool becaus I tryed the hardist and I reely wantid to lern. They said how come you went to the adult nite scool all by yourself Charlie. How did you find it. I said I askd pepul and sumbody told me where I shud go to lern to read and spell good. They said why did you want to. I told them becaus all my life I wantid to be smart and not dumb. But its very hard to be smart. They said you know it will probly be tempirery. I said yes. Miss Kinnian told me. I dont care if it herts.

Later I had more crazy tests today. The nice lady who gave it me told me the name and I asked her how do you spellit so I can rite it in my progris riport. THEMATIC APPERCEPTION TEST. I dont know the frist 2 words but I know what *test* means. You got to pass it or you get bad marks. This test lookd easy becaus I coud see the picturs. Only this time she dint want me to tell her the picturs. That mixd me up. I said the man yesterday said I shoud tell him what I saw in the ink she said that dont make no difrence. She said make up storys about the pepul in the picturs.

I told her how can you tell storys about pepul you never met. I said why shud I make up lies. I never tell lies any more becaus I always get caut.

She told me this test and the other one the raw-shok was for getting personalty. I laffed so hard. I said how can you get that thing from inkblots and fotos. She got sore and put her picturs away. I dont care. It was sily. I gess I faled that test too. **B**

Later some men in white coats took me to a difernt part of the hospitil and gave me a game to play. It was like a race with a white mouse. They called the mouse Algernon. Algernon was in a box with a lot of twists and turns like all kinds of walls and they gave me a pencil and a paper with lines and lots of boxes. On one side it said START and on the other end it said FINISH. They said it was *amazed* and that Algernon and me had the same *amazed* to do. I dint see how we could have the same *amazed* if Algernon had a box and I had a paper but I dint say nothing. Anyway there wasnt time because the race started.

One of the men had a watch he was trying to hide so I wouldnt see it so I tryed not to look and that made me nervus.

Anyway that test made me feel worser than all the others because they did it over 10 times with difernt *amazeds* and Algernon won every time. I dint know that mice were so smart. Maybe thats because

---

A **Read and Discuss** What situation has the author set up?

B **Read and Discuss** How does Charlie handle his latest test?

Algernon is a white mouse. Maybe white mice are smarter then other mice. **C**

progis riport 4—Mar 8

Their going to use me! Im so exited I can hardly write. Dr Nemur and Dr Strauss had a argament about it first. Dr Nemur was in the office when Dr Strauss brot me in. Dr Nemur was worryed about using me but Dr Strauss told him Miss Kinnian rekemmended me the best from all the people who she was teaching. I like Miss Kinnian becaus shes a very smart teacher. And she said Charlie your going to have a second chance. If you volenteer for this experament you mite get smart. They dont know if it will be perminint but theirs a chance. Thats why I said ok even when I was scared because she said it was an operashun. She said dont be scared Charlie you done so much with so little I think you deserv it most of all.

So I got scaird when Dr Nemur and Dr Strauss argud about it. Dr Strauss said I had something that was very good. He said I had a good *motor-vation.*[4] I never even knew I had that. I felt proud when he said that not every body with an eye-q of 68 had that thing. I dont know what it is or where I got it but he said Algernon had it too. Algernons *motor-vation* is the cheese they put in his box. But it cant be that because I didnt eat any cheese this week. **D**

Then he told Dr Nemur something I dint understand so while they were talking I wrote down some of the words.

He said Dr Nemur I know Charlie is not what you had in mind as the first of your new brede of intelek** (coudnt get the word) superman. But most people of his low ment** are host** and uncoop** they are usualy dull apath** and hard to reach. He has a good natcher hes intristed and eager to please.

Dr Nemur said remember he will be the first human beeng ever to have his intelijence trippled by surgicle meens.

Dr Strauss said exakly. Look at how well hes lerned to read and write for his low mentel age its as grate an acheve** as you and I lerning einstines therey of **vity[5] without help. That shows the intenss motor-vation. Its comparat** a tremen** achev** I say we use Charlie.

I dint get all the words and they were talking to fast but it sounded like Dr Strauss was on my side and like the other one wasnt.

Then Dr Nemur nodded he said all right maybe your right. We will use Charlie. When he said that I got so exited I jumped up and shook his hand for being so good to me. I told him thank you doc you wont be sorry for giving me a second chance. And I mean it like I told him. After the operashun Im gonna try to be smart. Im gonna try awful hard. **E**

---

4. **motor-vation:** motivation, the force or inner drive that makes someone want to do or accomplish something; here, Charlie's desire to learn.

5. **einstines therey of **vity:** theory of relativity, developed by Albert Einstein (1879–1955) and deals with matter, time, space, and energy.

C **Read and Discuss** What has the author hinted at now?

D **Reading Focus** **Tracking Story Events** What is the conflict between Dr. Strauss and Dr. Nemur?

E **Literary Perspectives** **Analyzing Credibility** Now that you have read this progress report, do you think Charlie will be a credible narrator? Why or why not?

progris ript 5—Mar 10

Im skared. Lots of people who work here and the nurses and the people who gave me the tests came to bring me candy and wish me luck. I hope I have luck. I got my rabits foot and my lucky penny and my horse shoe. Only a black cat crossed me when I was comming to the hospitil. Dr Strauss says dont be supersitis Charlie this is sience. Anyway Im keeping my rabits foot with me.

I asked Dr Strauss if Ill beat Algernon in the race after the operashun and he said maybe. If the operashun works Ill show that mouse I can be as smart as he is. Maybe smarter. Then Ill be abel to read better and spell the words good and know lots of things and be like other people. I want to be smart like other people. If it works permin-int they will make everybody smart all over the wurld.

They dint give me anything to eat this morning. I dont know what that eating has to do with getting smart. Im very hungry and Dr Nemur took away my box of candy. That Dr Nemur is a grouch. Dr Strauss says I can have it back after the operashun. You cant eat befor a operashun . . .

Progress Report 6—Mar 15

The operashun dint hurt. He did it while I was sleeping. They took off the bandijis from my eyes and my head today so I can make a PROGRESS REPORT. Dr Nemur who looked at some of my other ones says I spell PROGRESS wrong and he told me how to spell it and REPORT too. I got to try and remember that.

I have a very bad memary for spelling. Dr Strauss says its ok to tell about all the things that happin to me but he says I shoud tell more about what I feel and what I think. When I told him I dont know how to think he said try. All the time when the bandijis were on my eyes I tryed to think. Nothing happened. I dont know what to think about. Maybe if I ask him he will tell me how I can think now that Im suppose to get smart. What do smart people think about. Fancy things I suppose. I wish I knew some fancy things alredy.

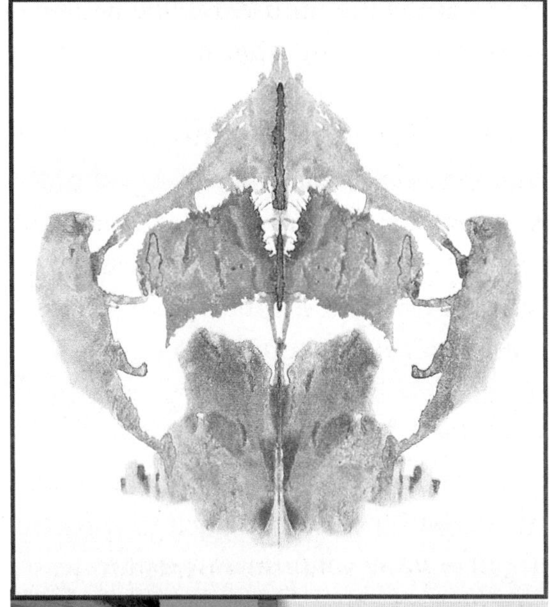

Analyzing Visuals Viewing and Interpreting
The image above is a Rorschach test. What do you see? Why do you think Charlie has difficulty with the test?

Progress Report 7—mar 19

Nothing is happining. I had lots of tests and different kinds of races with Algernon. I hate that mouse. He always beats me. Dr Strauss said I got to play those games. And he said some time I got to take those tests over again. Thse inkblots are stupid. And those pictures are stupid too. I like to draw a picture of a man and a woman but I wont make up lies about people. **F**

I got a headache from trying to think so much. I thot Dr Strauss was my frend but he dont help me. He dont tell me what to think or when Ill get smart. Miss Kinnian dint come to see me. I think writing these progress reports are stupid too.

Progress Report 8—Mar 23

Im going back to work at the factery. They said it was better I shud go back to work but I cant tell anyone what the operashun was for and I have to come to the hospitil for an hour evry night after work. They are gonna pay me mony every month for lerning to be smart.

Im glad Im going back to work because I miss my job and all my frends and all the fun we have there.

Dr Strauss says I shud keep writing things down but I dont have to do it every day just when I think of something or something speshul happins. He says dont get discoridged because it takes time and it happins slow. He says it took a long time with Algernon before he got 3 times smarter then he was before. Thats why Algernon beats me all the time because he had that operashun too. That makes me feel better. I coud probly do that *amazed* faster than a reglar mouse. Maybe some day Ill beat Algernon. Boy that would be something. So far Algernon looks like he mite be smart perminent.

Mar 25 (I dont have to write PROGRESS REPORT on top any more just when I hand it in once a week for Dr Nemur to read. I just have to put the date on. That saves time)

We had a lot of fun at the factery today. Joe Carp said hey look where Charlie had his operashun what did they do Charlie put some brains in. I was going to tell him but I remembered Dr Strauss said no. Then Frank Reilly said what did you do Charlie forget your key and open your door the hard way. That made me laff. Their really my friends and they like me.

Sometimes somebody will say hey look at Joe or Frank or George he really pulled a Charlie Gordon. I don't know why they say that but they always laff. This morning Amos Borg who is the 4 man at Donnegans used my name when he shouted at Ernie the office boy. Ernie lost a packige. He said Ernie for godsake what are you trying to be a Charlie Gordon. I dont understand why he said that. I never lost any packiges. **G**

Mar 28 Dr Strauss came to my room tonight to see why I dint come in like I was suppose to. I told him I dont like to race with Algernon any more. He said I dont have to for a while but I shud come in. He had a present for me only it wasnt a present but just for lend. I thot it was a little television but it wasnt. He said I got to turn it on when I go to sleep. I said your kidding why shud I turn it on when Im going to sleep. Who ever herd of a thing like that. But he said if I want to get smart I got to

---

F **Reading Focus** **Tracking Story Events** How is Charlie's spelling now? What does his spelling indicate?

G **Literary Focus** **Subplot** The author has introduced a new setting: Charlie's workplace. What is it like? How do his co-workers behave?

do what he says. I told him I dint think I was going to get smart and he put his hand on my sholder and said Charlie you dont know it yet but your getting smarter all the time. You wont notice for a while. I think he was just being nice to make me feel good because I dont look any smarter.

Oh yes I almost forgot. I asked him when I can go back to the class at Miss Kinnians school. He said I wont go their. He said that soon Miss Kinnian will come to the hospitil to start and teach me speshul. I was mad at her for not comming to see me when I got the operashun but I like her so maybe we will be frends again. **H**

Mar 29 That crazy TV kept me up all night. How can I sleep with something yelling crazy things all night in my ears. And the nutty pictures. Wow. I dont know what it says when Im up so how am I going to know when Im sleeping.

Dr Strauss says its ok. He says my brains are lerning when I sleep and that will help me when Miss Kinnian starts my lessons in the hospitl (only I found out it isnt a

---

H **Read and Discuss** What does this conversation between Dr. Strauss and Charlie let us know?

hospitil its a labatory). I think its all crazy. If you can get smart when your sleeping why do people go to school. That thing I dont think will work. I use to watch the late show and the late late show on TV all the time and it never made me smart. Maybe you have to sleep while you watch it. **I**

PROGRESS REPORT 9—April 3

Dr Strauss showed me how to keep the TV turned low so now I can sleep. I dont hear a thing. And I still dont understand what it says. A few times I play it over in the morning to find out what I lerned when I was sleeping and I dont think so. Miss Kinnian says Maybe its another langwidge or something. But most times it sounds american. It talks so fast faster then even Miss Gold who was my teacher in 6 grade and I remember she talked so fast I coudnt understand her.

I told Dr Strauss what good is it to get smart in my sleep. I want to be smart when Im awake. He says its the same thing and I have two minds. Theres the *subconscious*[6] and the *conscious* (thats how you spell it). And one dont tell the other one what its doing. They don't even talk to each other. Thats why I dream. And boy have I been having crazy dreams. Wow. Ever since that night TV. The late late late late late show.

I forgot to ask him if it was only me or if everybody had those two minds.

(I just looked up the word in the dictionary Dr Strauss gave me. The word is *subconscious. adj. Of the nature of mental operations yet not present in consciousness; as, subconscious conflict of desires.*) Theres more but I still dont know what it means. This isnt a very good dictionary for dumb people like me.

Anyway the headache is from the party. My frends from the factery Joe Carp and Frank Reilly invited me to go with them to Muggsys Saloon for some drinks. I dont like to drink but they said we will have lots of fun. I had a good time.

Joe Carp said I shoud show the girls how I mop out the toilet in the factory and he got me a mop. I showed them and everyone laffed when I told that Mr Donnegan said I was the best janiter he ever had because I like my job and do it good and never come late or miss a day except for my operashun.

I said Miss Kinnian always said Charlie be proud of your job because you do it good.

6. **subconscious** (suhb KAHN shuhs): mental activity that takes place below the level of consciousness (KAHN shuhs nihs), or full awareness.

I **Reading Focus** **Tracking Story Events** Why does Dr. Strauss give Charlie the "crazy TV"? What is its purpose?

Everybody laffed and we had a good time and they gave me lots of drinks and Joe said Charlie is a card when hes potted. I dont know what that means but everybody likes me and we have fun. I cant wait to be smart like my best frends Joe Carp and Frank Reilly.

I dont remember how the party was over but I think I went out to buy a newspaper and coffe for Joe and Frank and when I came back there was no one their. I looked for them all over till late. Then I dont remember so good but I think I got sleepy or sick. A nice cop brot me back home. Thats what my landlady Mrs Flynn says.

But I got a headache and a big lump on my head and black and blue all over. I think maybe I fell but Joe Carp says it was the cop they beat up drunks some times. I don't think so. Miss Kinnian says cops are to help people. Anyway I got a bad headache and Im sick and hurt all over. I dont think Ill drink anymore. J

April 6 I beat Algernon! I dint even know I beat him until Burt the tester told me. Then the second time I lost because I got so exited I fell off the chair before I finished. But after that I beat him 8 more times. I must be getting smart to beat a smart mouse like Algernon. But I dont *feel* smarter. K

I wanted to race Algernon some more but Burt said thats enough for one day. They let me hold him for a minit. Hes not so bad. Hes soft like a ball of cotton. He blinks and when he opens his eyes their black and pink on the eges.

I said can I feed him because I felt bad to beat him and I wanted to be nice and make frends. Burt said no Algernon is a very specshul mouse with an operashun like mine, and he was the first of all the animals to stay smart so long. He told me Algernon is so smart that every day he has to solve a test to get his food. Its a thing like a lock on a door that changes every time Algernon goes in to eat so he has to lern something new to get his food. That made me sad because if he couldnt lern he would be hungry.

I dont think its right to make you pass a test to eat. How woud Dr Nemur like it to have to pass a test every time he wants to eat. I think Ill be frends with Algernon.

April 9 Tonight after work Miss Kinnian was at the laboratory. She looked like she was glad to see me but scared. I told her dont worry Miss Kinnian Im not smart yet and she laffed. She said I have confidence in you Charlie the way you struggled so hard to read and right better than all the others. At werst you will have it for a littel wile and your doing somthing for sience.

We are reading a very hard book. I never read such a hard book before. Its called *Robinson Crusoe* about a man who gets merooned on a dessert Iland. Hes smart and figers out all kinds of things so he can have a house and food and hes a good swimmer. Only I feel sorry because hes all alone and has no frends. But I think their must be somebody else on the iland

---

J Reading Focus Tracking Story Events What do you think happened to Charlie?

K Literary Focus Parallel Episodes Charlie races Algernon again. How have their situations changed?

because theres a picture with his funny umbrella looking at footprints. I hope he gets a frend and not be lonely.

April 10 Miss Kinnian teaches me to spell better. She says look at a word and close your eyes and say it over and over until you remember. I have lots of truble with *through* that you say *threw* and *enough* and *tough* that you dont say *enew* and *tew*. You got to say *enuff* and *tuff*. Thats how I use to write it before I started to get smart. Im confused but Miss Kinnian says theres no reason in spelling.

Apr 14 Finished *Robinson Crusoe*. I want to find out more about what happens to him but Miss Kinnian says thats all there is. *Why*

Apr 15 Miss Kinnian says Im lerning fast. She read some of the Progress Reports and she looked at me kind of funny. She says Im a fine person and Ill show them all. I asked her why. She said never mind but I shoudnt feel bad if I find out that everybody isnt nice like I think. She said for a person who god gave so little to you done more then a lot of people with brains they never even used. I said all my frends are smart people but there good. They like me and they never did anything that wasnt nice. Then she got something in her eye and she had to run out to the ladys room.

Apr 16 Today, I lerned, the *comma*, this is a comma (,) a period, with a tail, Miss Kinnian, says its importent, because, it makes writing better, she said, sombeody, coud lose, a lot of money, if a comma, isnt, in the, right place, I dont have, any money, and I dont see, how a comma, keeps you from losing it,

But she says, everybody, uses commas, so Ill use, them too,

Apr 17 I used the comma wrong. Its punctuation. Miss Kinnian told me to look up long words in the dictionary to lern to spell them. I said whats the difference if you can read it anyway. She said its part of your education so now on Ill look up all the words Im not sure how to spell. It takes a long time to write that way but I think Im remembering. I only have to look up once and after that I get it right. Anyway thats how come I got the word *punctuation* right. (Its that way in the dictionary). Miss Kinnian says a period is punctuation too, and there are lots of other marks to lern. I told her I thot all the periods had to have tails but she said no.

You got to mix them up, she showed? me" how. to mix! them(up,. and now; I can! mix up all kinds" of punctuation, in! my writing? There, are lots! of rules? to lern; but Im gettin'g them in my head.

One thing I? like about, Dear Miss Kinnian: (thats the way it goes in a business letter if I ever go into business) is she, always gives me' a reason" when—I ask. She's a gen'ius! I wish! I cou'd be smart" like, her;

(Punctuation, is; fun!)

April 18 What a dope I am! I didn't even understand what she was talking about. I read the grammar book last night and it explanes the whole thing. Then I saw it was the same way as Miss Kinnian was trying to tell me, but I didn't get it. I got up in the middle of the night, and the whole thing straightened out in my mind. **L**

Miss Kinnian said that the TV working in my sleep helped out. She said I reached a plateau. Thats like the flat top of a hill.

After I figgered out how punctuation worked, I read over all my old Progress Reports from the beginning. Boy, did I have crazy spelling and punctuation! I told Miss Kinnian I ought to go over the pages and fix all the mistakes but she said, "No, Charlie, Dr. Nemur wants them just as they are. That's why he let you keep them after they were photostated, to see your own progress. You're coming along fast, Charlie."

That made me feel good. After the lesson I went down and played with Algernon. We don't race anymore.

April 20 I feel sick inside. Not sick like for a doctor, but inside my chest it feels empty like getting punched and a heartburn at the same time.

I wasn't going to write about it, but I guess I got to, because it's important. Today was the first time I ever stayed home from work.

Last night Joe Carp and Frank Reilly invited me to a party. There were lots of girls and some men from the factory. I remembered how sick I got last time I drank too much, so I told Joe I didn't want anything to drink. He gave me a plain Coke

---

L **Read and Discuss** What does Charlie's ability to read and understand a grammar book indicate?

instead. It tasted funny, but I thought it was just a bad taste in my mouth.

We had a lot of fun for a while. Joe said I should dance with Ellen and she would teach me the steps. I fell a few times and I couldn't understand why because no one else was dancing besides Ellen and me. And all the time I was tripping because somebody's foot was always sticking out.

Then when I got up I saw the look on Joe's face and it gave me a funny feeling in my stomack. "He's a scream," one of the girls said. Everybody was laughing.

Frank said, "I ain't laughed so much since we sent him off for the newspaper that night at Muggsy's and ditched him."

"Look at him. His face is red."

"He's blushing. Charlie is blushing."

"Hey, Ellen, what'd you do to Charlie? I never saw him act like that before."

I didn't know what to do or where to turn. Everyone was looking at me and laughing and I felt naked. I wanted to hide myself. I ran out into the street and I threw up. Then I walked home. It's a funny thing I never knew that Joe and Frank and the others liked to have me around all the time to make fun of me.

Now I know what it means when they say "to pull a Charlie Gordon."

I'm ashamed. (M)

PROGRESS REPORT 10

April 21 Still didn't go into the factory. I told Mrs. Flynn my landlady to call and tell Mr. Donnegan I was sick. Mrs. Flynn looks at me very funny lately like she's scared of me.

I think it's a good thing about finding out how everybody laughs at me. I thought about it a lot. It's because I'm so dumb and I don't even know when I'm doing something dumb. People think it's funny when a dumb person can't do things the same way they can.

Anyway, now I know I'm getting smarter every day. I know punctuation and I can spell good. I like to look up all the hard words in the dictionary and I remember them. I'm reading a lot now, and Miss Kinnian says I read very fast. Sometimes I even understand what I'm reading about, and it stays in my mind. There are times when I can close my eyes and think of a page and it all comes back like a picture.

Besides history, geography, and arithmetic, Miss Kinnian said I should start to learn a few foreign languages. Dr. Strauss gave me some more tapes to play while I sleep. I still don't understand how that conscious and unconscious mind works, but Dr. Strauss says not to worry yet. He asked me to promise that when I start learning college subjects next week I wouldn't read any books on psychology—that is, until he gives me permission.

I feel a lot better today, but I guess I'm still a little angry that all the time people were laughing and making fun of me because I wasn't so smart. When I become intelligent like Dr. Strauss says, with three times my I.Q. of 68, then maybe I'll be like

---

(M) **Reading Focus** **Tracking Story Events** What happens when Charlie goes out with Joe and Frank?

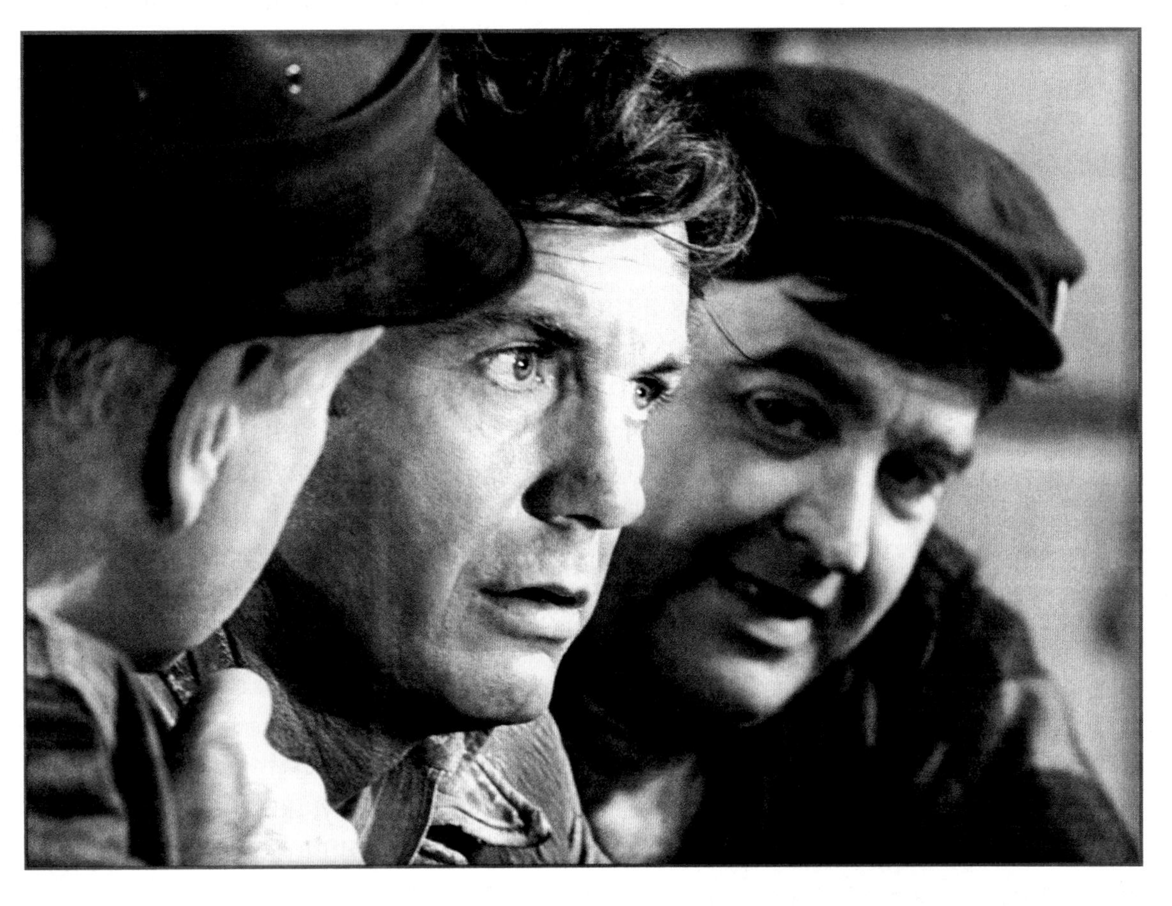

everyone else and people will like me and be friendly. **N**

I'm not sure what an I.Q. is. Dr. Nemur said it was something that measured how intelligent you were—like a scale in the drugstore weighs pounds. But Dr. Strauss had a big argument with him and said an I.Q. didn't weigh intelligence at all. He said an I.Q. showed how much intelligence you could get, like the numbers on the outside of a measuring cup. You still had to fill the cup up with stuff.

Then when I asked Burt, who gives me my intelligence tests and works with Algernon, he said that both of them were wrong (only I had to promise not to tell them he said so). Burt says that the I.Q. measures a lot of different things including some of the things you learned already, and it really isn't any good at all.

So I still don't know what I.Q. is except that mine is going to be over 200 soon. I didn't want to say anything, but I don't see how if they don't know *what* it is, or *where*

N **Read and Discuss** Now that Charlie is becoming aware of his past limitations, how does he connect intelligence to the way people treat each other?

it is—I don't see how they know *how much* of it you've got.

Dr. Nemur says I have to take a *Rorschach Test* tomorrow. I wonder what *that* is.

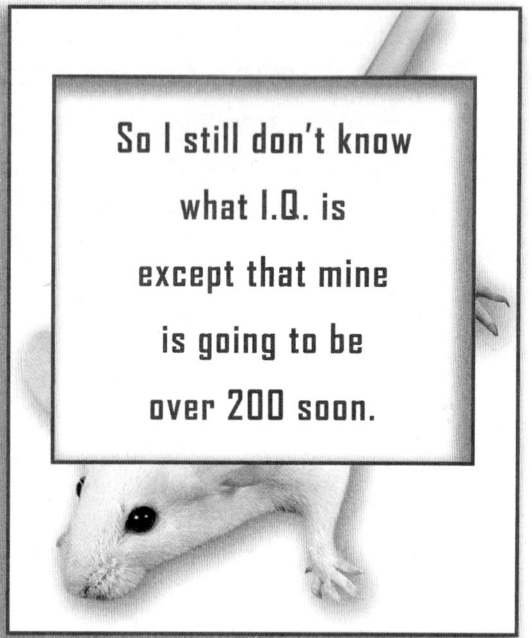
So I still don't know what I.Q. is except that mine is going to be over 200 soon.

April 22 I found out what a *Rorschach* is. It's the test I took before the operation—the one with the inkblots on the pieces of cardboard. The man who gave me the test was the same one.

I was scared to death of those inkblots. I knew he was going to ask me to find the pictures and I knew I wouldn't be able to. I was thinking to myself, if only there was some way of knowing what kind of pictures were hidden there. Maybe there weren't any pictures at all. Maybe it was just a trick to see if I was dumb enough to look for something that wasn't there. Just thinking about that made me sore at him.

"All right, Charlie," he said, "you've seen these cards before, remember?"

"Of course I remember."

The way I said it, he knew I was angry, and he looked surprised. "Yes, of course. Now I want you to look at this one. What might this be? What do you see on this card? People see all sorts of things in these inkblots. Tell me what it might be for you—what it makes you think of."

I was shocked. That wasn't what I had expected him to say at all. "You mean there are no pictures hidden in those inkblots?"

He frowned and took off his glasses. "What?"

"Pictures. Hidden in the inkblots. Last time you told me that everyone could see them and you wanted me to find them too."

He explained to me that the last time he had used almost the exact same words he was using now. I didn't believe it, and I still have the suspicion that he misled me at the time just for the fun of it. Unless—I don't know any more—could I have been *that* feebleminded?

We went through the cards slowly. One of them looked like a pair of bats tugging at something. Another one looked like two men fencing with swords. I imagined all sorts of things. I guess I got carried away. But I didn't trust him any more, and I kept turning them around and even looking on the back to see if there was anything there I was supposed to catch. While he was making his notes, I peeked out of the corner of my eye to read it. But it was all in code that looked like this:

WF + A DdF-Ad orig. WF-A SF + obj

Vocabulary **misled** (mihs LEHD) *v.:* fooled; led to believe something wrong.

The test still doesn't make sense to me. It seems to me that anyone could make up lies about things that they didn't really see. How could he know I wasn't making a fool of him by mentioning things that I didn't really imagine? Maybe I'll understand it when Dr. Strauss lets me read up on psychology. **O**

April 25 I figured out a new way to line up the machines in the factory, and Mr. Donnegan says it will save him ten thousand dollars a year in labor and increased production. He gave me a twenty-five-dollar bonus.

I wanted to take Joe Carp and Frank Reilly out to lunch to celebrate, but Joe said he had to buy some things for his wife, and Frank said he was meeting his cousin for lunch. I guess it'll take a little time for them to get used to the changes in me. Everybody seems to be frightened of me. When I went over to Amos Borg and tapped him on the shoulder, he jumped up in the air.

People don't talk to me much anymore or kid around the way they used to. It makes the job kind of lonely. **P**

April 27 I got up the nerve today to ask Miss Kinnian to have dinner with me tomorrow night to celebrate my bonus.

At first she wasn't sure it was right, but I asked Dr. Strauss and he said it was okay. Dr. Strauss and Dr. Nemur don't seem to be getting along so well. They're arguing all the time. This evening when I came in to ask Dr. Strauss about having dinner with Miss Kinnian, I heard them shouting. Dr. Nemur was saying that it was *his* experiment and *his* research, and Dr. Strauss was shouting back that he contributed just as much, because he found me through Miss Kinnian and he performed the operation. Dr. Strauss said that someday thousands of neurosurgeons might be using his technique all over the world.

Dr. Nemur wanted to publish the results of the experiment at the end of this month. Dr. Strauss wanted to wait a while longer to be sure. Dr. Strauss said that Dr. Nemur was more interested in the Chair of Psychology at Princeton than he was in the experiment. Dr. Nemur said that Dr. Strauss was nothing but an opportunist who was trying to ride to glory on *his* coattails.

When I left afterwards, I found myself trembling. I don't know why for sure, but it was as if I'd seen both men clearly for the first time. I remember hearing Burt say that Dr. Nemur had a shrew of a wife who was pushing him all the time to get things published so that he could become famous. Burt said that the dream of her life was to have a big shot husband.

Was Dr. Strauss really trying to ride on his coattails?

April 28 I don't understand why I never noticed how beautiful Miss Kinnian really is. She has brown eyes and feathery brown hair that comes to the top of her neck. She's

---

O **Literary Perspectives** **Analyzing Credibility** How are Charlie's relationships changing? If you only know about these characters through Charlie's eyes, are you getting the whole story?

P **Literary Focus** **Subplot** What events are taking place where Charlie works?

only thirty-four! I think from the beginning I had the feeling that she was an unreachable genius—and very, very old. Now, every time I see her she grows younger and more lovely.

We had dinner and a long talk. When she said that I was coming along so fast that soon I'd be leaving her behind, I laughed.

"It's true, Charlie. You're already a better reader than I am. You can read a whole page at a glance while I can take in only a few lines at a time. And you remember every single thing you read. I'm lucky if I can recall the main thoughts and the general meaning."

"I don't feel intelligent. There are so many things I don't understand."

She took out a cigarette and I lit it for her. "You've got to be a *little* patient. You're accomplishing in days and weeks what it takes normal people to do in half a lifetime. That's what makes it so amazing. You're like a giant sponge now, soaking things in. Facts, figures, general knowledge. And soon you'll begin to connect them, too. You'll see how the different branches of learning are related. There are many levels, Charlie, like steps on a giant ladder that take you up higher and higher to see more and more of the world around you.

"I can see only a little bit of that, Charlie, and I won't go much higher than I am now, but you'll keep climbing up and up, and see more and more, and each step will open new worlds that you never even knew existed." She frowned. "I hope . . . I just hope to God—"

"What?"

"Never mind, Charles. I just hope I wasn't wrong to advise you to go into this in the first place."

I laughed. "How could that be? It worked, didn't it? Even Algernon is still smart."

We sat there silently for a while and I knew what she was thinking about as she watched me toying with the chain of my rabbit's foot and my keys. I didn't want to think of that possibility any more than elderly people want to think of death. I knew that this was only the beginning. I knew what she meant about levels because I'd seen some of them already. The thought of leaving her behind made me sad.

I'm in love with Miss Kinnian. **Q**

PROGRESS REPORT 11

April 30 I've quit my job with Donnegan's Plastic Box Company. Mr. Donnegan insisted that it would be better for all concerned if I left. What did I do to make them hate me so?

The first I knew of it was when Mr. Donnegan showed me the petition. Eight hundred and forty names, everyone connected with the factory, except Fanny Girden. Scanning the list quickly, I saw at once that hers was the only missing name. All the rest demanded that I be fired.

Joe Carp and Frank Reilly wouldn't talk to me about it. No one else would either,

---

Q Literary Focus Subplot What complication has arisen in the relationship between Miss Kinnian and Charlie?

except Fanny. She was one of the few people I'd known who set her mind to something and believed it no matter what the rest of the world proved, said, or did—and Fanny did not believe that I should have been fired. She had been against the petition on principle and despite the pressure and threats she'd held out.

"Which don't mean to say," she remarked, "that I don't think there's something mighty strange about you, Charlie. Them changes. I don't know. You used to be a good, dependable, ordinary man—not too bright maybe, but honest. Who knows what you done to yourself to get so smart all of a sudden. Like everybody around here's been saying, Charlie, it's not right."

"But how can you say that, Fanny? What's wrong with a man becoming intelligent and wanting to acquire knowledge and understanding of the world around him?"

She stared down at her work and I turned to leave. Without looking at me, she said: "It was evil when Eve listened to the snake and ate from the tree of knowledge. It was evil when she saw that she was naked. If not for that none of us would ever have to grow old and sick, and die."

Once again now I have the feeling of shame burning inside me. This intelligence has driven a wedge between me and all the people I once knew and loved. Before, they laughed at me and despised me for my ignorance and dullness; now, they hate me for my knowledge and understanding. What in God's name do they want of me?

They've driven me out of the factory. Now I'm more alone than ever before . . . Ⓡ

Ⓡ **Literary Perspectives** **Analyzing Credibility** How are Charlie's tone and personality changing? Does he seem more or less credible?

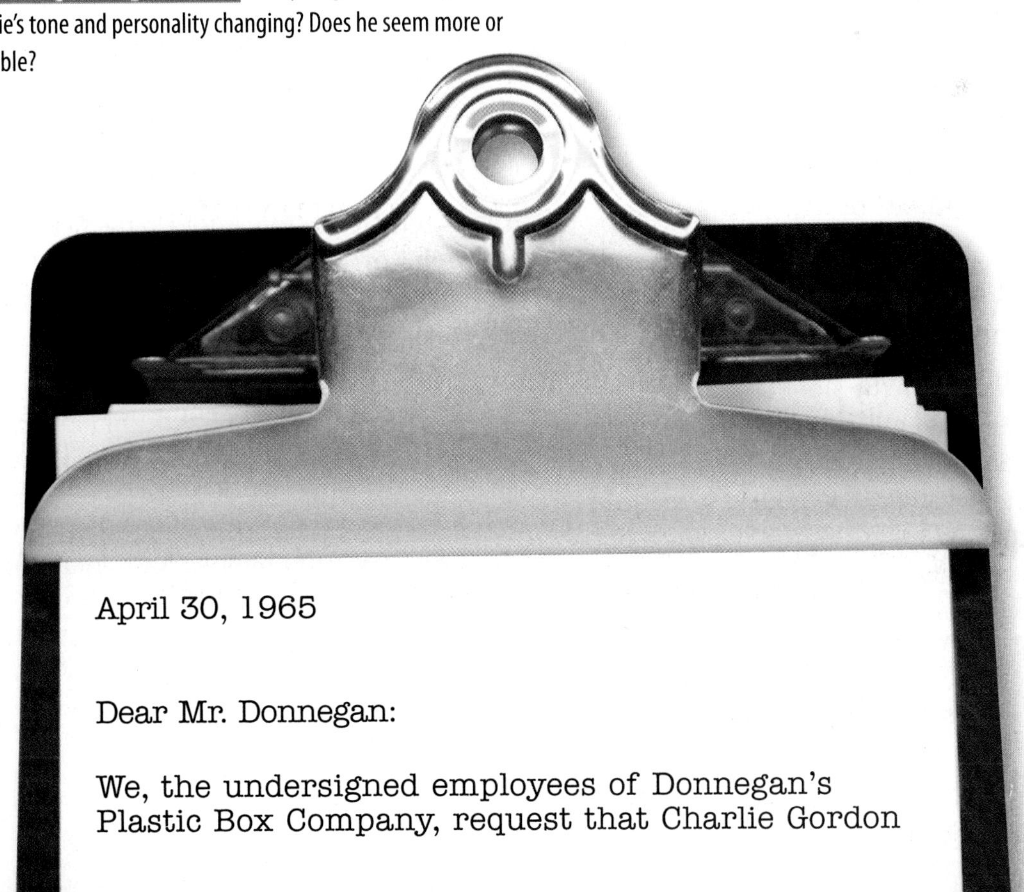
April 30, 1965

Dear Mr. Donnegan:

We, the undersigned employees of Donnegan's Plastic Box Company, request that Charlie Gordon

Applying Your Skills

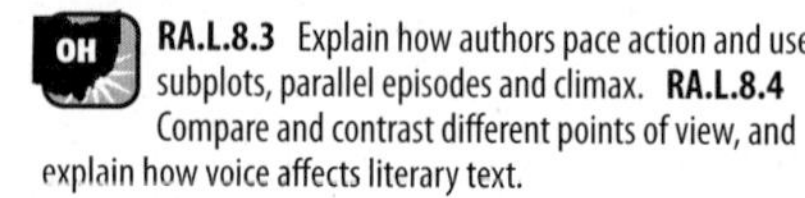

RA.L.8.3 Explain how authors pace action and use subplots, parallel episodes and climax. **RA.L.8.4** Compare and contrast different points of view, and explain how voice affects literary text.

Flowers for Algernon, Part 1

Respond and Think Critically

Reading Focus

Quick Check

1. Why does Charlie want to be in the experiment?
2. Why does Dr. Strauss think Charlie would be a good subject for the experiment?
3. Who is Algernon? What does he have in common with Charlie?
4. What are some signs that Charlie's operation has been effective? How is he changing?

Reading Skills: Tracking Story Events

5. Look over your tracking chart, and re-read the story events that you have underlined. This review will help you piece together the subplots. Next, briefly describe the subplots you have found, noting conflicts and complications that are developing.

Literary Focus

Literary Analysis

6. **Interpret** What does it mean "to pull a Charlie Gordon"?
7. **Evaluate** Early in the story, Dr. Strauss tells Dr. Nemur that Charlie's learning to read and write is as impressive as their learning a difficult scientific theory without help (page 58). What does Dr. Strauss mean? Challenge or defend his statement.
8. **Compare and Contrast** Re-read Fanny's comments about the changes in Charlie (page 71). How are Charlie's experiences similar to those of Adam and Eve in the Bible? (Look especially at the entry for April 30. You may want to compare Charlie's description with the Biblical account in Genesis 2:25–3:24.)
9. **Connect** Re-read the last few lines in Part 1. What do you think about people who dislike others who are different from them?

Literary Skills: Subplots and Parallel Episodes

10. **Analyze** Charlie takes a Rorschach test twice. How do these parallel episodes reveal what is happening to Charlie?
11. **Infer** An important subplot in this story involves Charlie's relationship with Miss Kinnian. What have you learned about Charlie through this subplot?

Literary Skills Review: First-Person Point of View

12. **Extend** This story is told in the **first-person point of view,** in which one of the characters tells the story as "I" and readers know only what the character tells them. In "Flowers for Algernon," we experience everything through Charlie's eyes and see how he thinks and how he often misunderstands a situation. Choose one of Charlie's journal entries, and retell it from the point of view of one of the other characters, for example, Joe Carp for April 3 or Miss Kinnian for April 15.

Flowers for Algernon

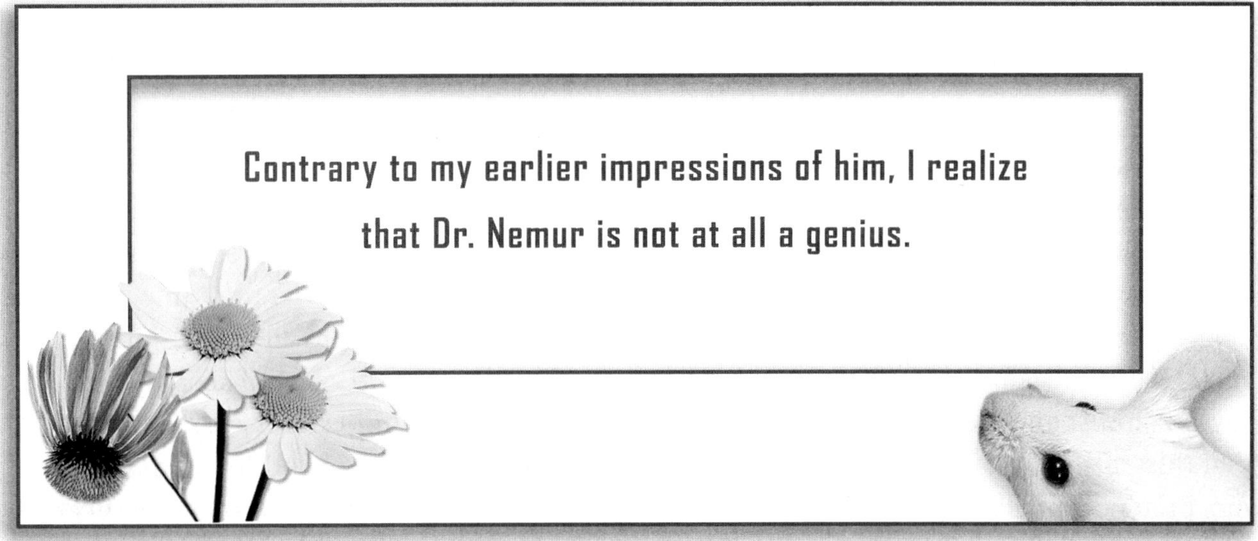
Contrary to my earlier impressions of him, I realize that Dr. Nemur is not at all a genius.

Part 2

May 15 Dr. Strauss is very angry at me for not having written any progress reports in two weeks. He's justified because the lab is now paying me a regular salary. I told him I was too busy thinking and reading. When I pointed out that writing was such a slow process that it made me impatient with my poor handwriting, he suggested that I learn to type. It's much easier to write now because I can type nearly seventy-five words a minute. Dr. Strauss continually reminds me of the need to speak and write simply so that people will be able to understand me. **A**

I'll try to review all the things that happened to me during the last two weeks. Algernon and I were presented to the American Psychological Association sitting in convention with the World Psychological Association last Tuesday. We created quite a sensation. Dr. Nemur and Dr. Strauss were proud of us.

I suspect that Dr. Nemur, who is sixty—ten years older than Dr. Strauss—finds it necessary to see tangible results of his work. Undoubtedly the results of pressure by Mrs. Nemur.

Contrary to my earlier impressions of him, I realize that Dr. Nemur is not at all a genius. He has a very good mind, but it struggles under the specter of self-doubt. He wants people to take him for a genius. Therefore, it is important for him to feel that his work is accepted by the world. I believe that Dr. Nemur was afraid of further delay because he worried that someone else might make a discovery along these lines and take the credit from him.

Dr. Strauss on the other hand might be called a genius, although I feel that his

---

A Reading Focus **Tracking Story Events** What does Dr. Strauss's request about writing and speaking simply tell you about Charlie's progress?

areas of knowledge are too limited. He was educated in the tradition of narrow specialization; the broader aspects of background were neglected far more than necessary—even for a neurosurgeon.

I was shocked to learn that the only ancient languages he could read were Latin, Greek, and Hebrew, and that he knows almost nothing of mathematics beyond the elementary levels of the calculus of variations. When he admitted this to me, I found myself almost annoyed. It was as if he'd hidden this part of himself in order to deceive me, pretending—as do many people, I've discovered—to be what he is not. No one I've ever known is what he appears to be on the surface.

Dr. Nemur appears to be uncomfortable around me. Sometimes when I try to talk to him, he just looks at me strangely and turns away. I was angry at first when Dr. Strauss told me I was giving Dr. Nemur an inferiority complex. I thought he was mocking me and I'm oversensitive at being made fun of.

How was I to know that a highly respected psychoexperimentalist like Nemur was unacquainted with Hindustani and Chinese? It's absurd when you consider the work that is being done in India and China today in the very field of his study.

I asked Dr. Strauss how Nemur could refute Rahajamati's attack on his method and results if Nemur couldn't even read them in the first place. That strange look on Dr. Strauss's face can mean only one of two things. Either he doesn't want to tell Nemur what they're saying in India, or else—and this worries me—Dr. Strauss doesn't know either. I must be careful to speak and write clearly and simply so that people won't laugh.

May 18 I am very disturbed. I saw Miss Kinnian last night for the first time in over a week. I tried to avoid all discussions of intellectual concepts and to keep the conversation on a simple, everyday level, but she just stared at me blankly and asked me what I meant about the mathematical variance equivalent in Dorbermann's Fifth Concerto.

When I tried to explain she stopped me and laughed. I guess I got angry, but I suspect I'm approaching her on the wrong level. No matter what I try to discuss with her, I am unable to communicate. I must review Vrostadt's equations on *Levels of Semantic Progression*. I find that I don't communicate with people much anymore. Thank God for books and music and things I can think about. I am alone in my apartment at Mrs. Flynn's boardinghouse most of the time and seldom speak to anyone. **B**

May 20 I would not have noticed the new dishwasher, a boy of about sixteen, at the corner diner where I take my evening meals if not for the incident of the broken dishes.

They crashed to the floor, shattering and sending bits of white china under the

---

B **Read and Discuss** Charlie found it hard to communicate with others before his operation. What new problem is hampering his efforts to connect with others?

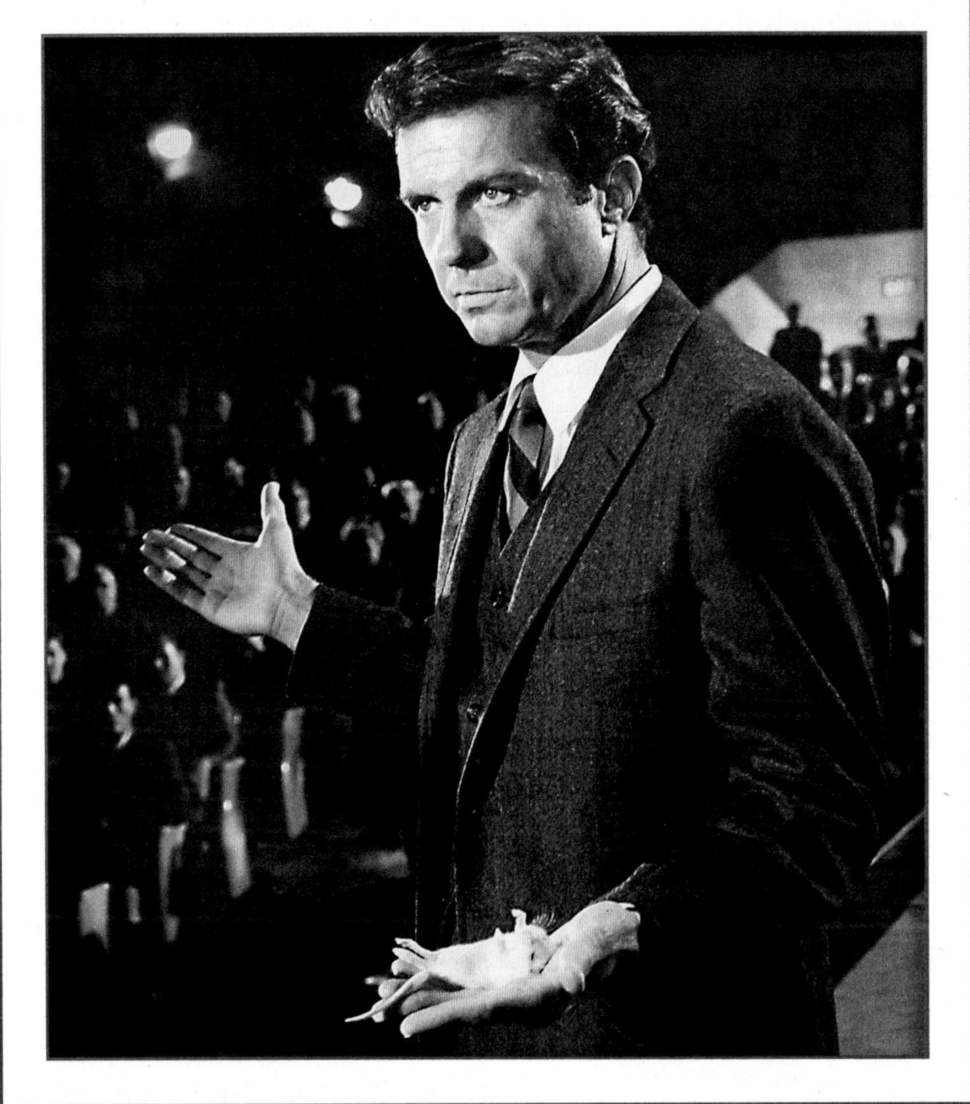

tables. The boy stood there, dazed and frightened, holding the empty tray in his hand. The whistles and catcalls[1] from the customers (the cries of "Hey, there go the profits!" . . . "Mazel tov!"[2] . . . and "Well, *he* didn't work here very long . . ." which invariably seem to follow the breaking of glass or dishware in a public restaurant) all seemed to confuse him. **C**

When the owner came to see what the excitement was about, the boy cowered as if he expected to be struck and threw up his arms as if to ward off the blow.

"All right! All right, you dope," shouted the owner, "don't just stand there! Get the

1. **catcalls:** shouts and whistles made to express disapproval or ridicule, so called because people used to make noises like a cat's cry to show disapproval.
2. **mazel tov** (MAH zuhl tohv): Yiddish expression conveying "congratulations."

C **Literary Focus** **Parallel Episodes** How does the dishwasher's experience resemble episodes from Charlie's own life?

broom and sweep that mess up. A broom . . . a broom, you idiot! It's in the kitchen. Sweep up all the pieces."

The boy saw that he was not going to be punished. His frightened expression disappeared and he smiled and hummed as he came back with the broom to sweep the floor. A few of the rowdier customers kept up the remarks, amusing themselves at his expense.

Only a short time ago,
I learned that people
laughed at me. Now I
can see that unknow-
ingly I joined with them
in laughing at myself.

"Here, sonny, over here there's a nice piece behind you . . ."

"C'mon, do it again . . ."

"He's not so dumb. It's easier to break 'em than to wash 'em . . ."

As his vacant eyes moved across the crowd of amused onlookers, he slowly mirrored their smiles and finally broke into an uncertain grin at the joke which he obviously did not understand.

I felt sick inside as I looked at his dull, vacuous smile, the wide, bright eyes of a child, uncertain but eager to please. They were laughing at him because he was mentally retarded.

And I had been laughing at him too.

Suddenly, I was furious at myself and all those who were smirking at him. I jumped up and shouted, "Shut up! Leave him alone! It's not his fault he can't understand! He can't help what he is! But for God's sake . . . he's still a human being!"

The room grew silent. I cursed myself for losing control and creating a scene. I tried not to look at the boy as I paid my check and walked out without touching my food. I felt ashamed for both of us.

How strange it is that people of honest feelings and sensibility, who would not take advantage of a man born without arms or legs or eyes—how such people think nothing of abusing a man born with low intelligence. It infuriated me to think that not too long ago I, like this boy, had foolishly played the clown.

And I had almost forgotten.

I'd hidden the picture of the old Charlie Gordon from myself because now that I was intelligent it was something that had to be pushed out of my mind. But today in looking at that boy, for the first time I saw what I had been. *I was just like him!*

Only a short time ago, I learned that people laughed at me. Now I can see that unknowingly I joined with them in laughing at myself. That hurts most of all. **D**

D **Read and Discuss** What has Charlie learned about himself in the diner?

I have often re-read my progress reports and seen the illiteracy, the childish naiveté,[3] the mind of low intelligence peering from a dark room, through the keyhole, at the dazzling light outside. I see that even in my dullness I knew that I was inferior, and that other people had something I lacked—something denied me. In my mental blindness, I thought that it was somehow connected with the ability to read and write, and I was sure that if I could get those skills I would automatically have intelligence too.

Even a feeble-minded man wants to be like other men.

A child may not know how to feed itself, or what to eat, yet it knows of hunger.

This then is what I was like. I never knew. Even with my gift of intellectual awareness, I never really knew.

This day was good for me. Seeing the past more clearly, I have decided to use my knowledge and skills to work in the field of increasing human intelligence levels. Who is better equipped for this work? Who else has lived in both worlds? These are my people. Let me use my gift to do something for them.

Tomorrow, I will discuss with Dr. Strauss the manner in which I can work in this area. I may be able to help him work out the problems of widespread use of the technique which was used on me. I have several good ideas of my own.

There is so much that might be done with this technique. If I could be made into a genius, what about thousands of others like myself? What fantastic levels might be achieved by using this technique on normal people? On *geniuses*?

There are so many doors to open. I am impatient to begin. **E**

Progress Report 12

May 23 It happened today. Algernon bit me. I visited the lab to see him as I do occasionally, and when I took him out of his cage, he snapped at my hand. I put him back and watched him for a while. He was unusually disturbed and vicious.

May 24 Burt, who is in charge of the experimental animals, tells me that Algernon is changing. He is less cooperative, he refuses to run the maze any more; general motivation has decreased. And he hasn't been eating. Everyone is upset about what this may mean. **F**

May 25 They've been feeding Algernon, who now refuses to work the shifting-lock problem. Everyone identifies me with Algernon. In a way we're both the first of our kind. They're all pretending that Algernon's behavior is not necessarily significant for me. But it's hard to hide the fact that some of the other animals who were used in this experiment are showing strange behavior.

Dr. Strauss and Dr. Nemur have asked me not to come to the lab anymore. I know what they're thinking but I can't accept it. I am going ahead with my plans to carry their research forward. With all due respect to

3. **naiveté** (nah eev TAY): simplicity; foolish innocence.

E **Literary Perspectives** **Analyzing Credibility** Do you find Charlie's transformation credible? Why or why not?

F **Read and Discuss** What is going on with Algernon?

both of these fine scientists, I am well aware of their limitations. If there is an answer, I'll have to find it out for myself. Suddenly, time has become very important to me.

May 29 I have been given a lab of my own and permission to go ahead with the research. I'm on to something. Working day and night. I've had a cot moved into the lab. Most of my writing time is spent on the notes which I keep in a separate folder, but from time to time I feel it necessary to put down my moods and my thoughts out of sheer habit.

I find the *calculus of intelligence* to be a fascinating study. Here is the place for the application of all the knowledge I have acquired. In a sense it's the problem I've been concerned with all my life.

May 31 Dr. Strauss thinks I'm working too hard. Dr. Nemur says I'm trying to cram a lifetime of research and thought into a few weeks. I know I should rest, but I'm driven on by something inside that won't let me stop. I've got to find the reason for the sharp regression in Algernon. I've got to know *if* and *when* it will happen to me.

Vocabulary **regression** (rih GREHSH uhn) *n.:* return to an earlier or less advanced condition.

June 4

LETTER TO DR. STRAUSS (*copy*)

Dear Dr. Strauss:

Under separate cover I am sending you a copy of my report entitled, "The Algernon-Gordon Effect: A Study of Structure and Function of Increased Intelligence," which I would like to have you read and have published.

As you see, my experiments are completed. I have included in my report all of my formulae, as well as mathematical analysis in the appendix. Of course, these should be verified.

Because of its importance to both you and Dr. Nemur (and need I say to myself, too?) I have checked and rechecked my results a dozen times in the hope of finding an error. I am sorry to say the results must stand. Yet for the sake of science, I am grateful for the little bit that I here add to the knowledge of the function of the human mind and of the laws governing the artificial increase of human intelligence.

I recall your once saying to me that an experimental *failure* or the *disproving* of a theory was as important to the advancement of learning as a success would be. I know now that this is true. I am sorry, however, that my own contribution to the field must rest upon the ashes of the work of two men I regard so highly.

Yours truly,

Charles Gordon

encl.: rept

June 5 I must not become emotional. The facts and the results of my experiments are clear, and the more sensational aspects of my own rapid climb cannot obscure the fact that the tripling of intelligence by the surgical technique developed by Drs. Strauss and Nemur must be viewed as having little or no practical applicability (at the present time) to the increase of human intelligence.

As I review the records and data on Algernon, I see that although he is still in his physical infancy, he has regressed mentally. Motor activity is impaired; there is a general reduction of glandular activity; there is an accelerated loss of coordination.

There are also strong indications of progressive amnesia. **G**

As will be seen by my report, these and other physical and mental deterioration syndromes can be predicted with statistically significant results by the application of my formula.

The surgical stimulus to which we were both subjected has resulted in an intensification and acceleration of all mental processes. The unforeseen development, which I have taken the liberty of calling the *Algernon-Gordon Effect,* is the logical extension of the entire intelligence speed-up. The hypothesis here proven may be described simply in the following terms: Artificially increased intelligence deteriorates at a rate of time directly proportional to the quantity of the increase.

I feel that this, in itself, is an important discovery.

G Reading Focus Tracking Story Events What changes is Algernon experiencing?

Vocabulary **obscure** (uhb SKYUR) v.: hide.
deterioration (dih tihr ee uh RAY shuhn) *n.* used as *adj.:* worsening; declining.

As long as I am able to write, I will continue to record my thoughts in these progress reports. It is one of my few pleasures. However, by all indications, my own mental deterioration will be very rapid.

I have already begun to notice signs of emotional instability and forgetfulness, the first symptoms of the burnout. **H**

June 10 Deterioration progressing. I have become absent-minded. Algernon died two days ago. Dissection shows my predictions were right. His brain had decreased in weight and there was a general smoothing out of cerebral convolutions as well as a deepening and broadening of brain fissures.[4]

I guess the same thing is or will soon be happening to me. Now that it's definite, I don't want it to happen.

I put Algernon's body in a cheese box and buried him in the backyard. I cried.

June 15 Dr. Strauss came to see me again. I wouldn't open the door and I told him to go away. I want to be left to myself. I have become touchy and irritable. I feel the darkness closing in. It's hard to throw off thoughts of suicide. I keep telling myself how important this introspective journal will be.

It's a strange sensation to pick up a book that you've read and enjoyed just a few months ago and discover that you don't remember it. I remembered how great I thought John Milton was, but when I picked up *Paradise Lost* I couldn't understand it at all. I got so angry I threw the book across the room.

I've got to try to hold on to some of it. Some of the things I've learned. Oh, God, please don't take it all away.

June 19 Sometimes, at night, I go out for a walk. Last night I couldn't remember where I lived. A policeman took me home. I have the strange feeling that this has all happened to me before—a long time ago. I keep telling myself I'm the only person in the world who can describe what's happening to me.

June 21 Why can't I remember? I've got to fight. I lie in bed for days and I don't know who or where I am. Then it all comes back to me in a flash. Fugues of amnesia.[5] Symptoms of senility—second childhood. I can watch them coming on. It's so cruelly logical. I learned so much and so fast. Now my mind is deteriorating rapidly. I won't let it happen. I'll fight it. I can't help thinking of the boy in the restaurant, the blank expression, the silly smile, the people laughing at him. No—please—not that again . . .

June 22 I'm forgetting things that I learned recently. It seems to be following the classic pattern—the last things learned

4. **brain fissures** (FIHSH uhrz): grooves in the surface of the brain.

5. **fugues** (fyoogz) **of amnesia** (am NEE zhuh): temporary states of forgetfulness.

H **Read and Discuss** What has Charlie learned about his condition?

Vocabulary **introspective** (ihn truh SPEHK tihv) *adj.:* looking inward.

are the first things forgotten. Or is that the pattern? I'd better look it up again. . . .

I re-read my paper on the *Algernon-Gordon Effect* and I get the strange feeling that it was written by someone else. There are parts I don't even understand.

Motor activity impaired. I keep tripping over things, and it becomes increasingly difficult to type.

June 23 I've given up using the typewriter completely. My coordination is bad. I feel that I'm moving slower and slower. Had a terrible shock today. I picked up a copy of an article I used in my research, Krueger's *Uber psychische Ganzheit*, to see if it would help me understand what I had done. First I thought there was something wrong with my eyes. Then I realized I could no longer read German. I tested myself in other languages. All gone. **1**

June 30 A week since I dared to write again. It's slipping away like sand through my fingers. Most of the books I have are too hard for me now. I get angry with them because I know that I read and understood them just a few weeks ago.

I keep telling myself I must keep writing these reports so that somebody will know what is happening to me. But it gets harder to form the words and remember spellings. I have to look up even simple words in the dictionary now and it makes me impatient with myself.

Dr. Strauss comes around almost every day, but I told him I wouldn't see or speak to anybody. He feels guilty. They all do. But I don't blame anyone. I knew what might happen. But how it hurts.

July 7 I don't know where the week went. Todays Sunday I know becuase I can see through my window people going to church. I think I stayed in bed all week but I remember Mrs. Flynn bringing food to me a few times. I keep saying over and over Ive got to do something but then I forget or maybe its just easier not to do what I say Im going to do.

I think of my mother and father a lot these days. I found a picture of them with me taken at a beach. My father has a big ball under his arm and my mother is holding me by the hand. I dont remember them the way they are in the picture. All I remember is my father drunk most of the time and arguing with mom about money.

He never shaved much and he used to scratch my face when he hugged me. My mother said he died but Cousin Miltie said he heard his mom and dad say that my father ran away with another woman. When I asked my mother she slapped my face and said my father was dead. I dont think I ever

---

1 Reading Focus **Tracking Story Events** What is happening to Charlie?

found out which was true but I don't care much. (He said he was going to take me to see cows on a farm once but he never did. He never kept his promises . . .) **J**

July 10 My landlady Mrs Flynn is very worried about me. She says the way I lay around all day and dont do anything I remind her of her son before she threw him out of the house. She said she doesn't like loafers. If Im sick its one thing, but if Im a loafer thats another thing and she wont have it. I told her I think Im sick.

I try to read a little bit every day, mostly stories, but sometimes I have to read the same thing over and over again because I dont know what it means. And its hard to write. I know I should look up all the words in the dictionary but its so hard and Im so tired all the time.

Then I got the idea that I would only use the easy words instead of the long hard ones. That saves time. I put flowers on Algernons grave about once a week. Mrs Flynn thinks Im crazy to put flowers on a mouses grave but I told her that Algernon was special.

July 14 Its sunday again. I dont have anything to do to keep me busy now because my television set is broke and I dont have any money to get it fixed. (I think I lost this months check from the lab. I dont remember)

I get awful headaches and asperin doesnt help me much. Mrs Flynn knows Im really sick and she feels very sorry for me. Shes a wonderful woman whenever someone is sick.

July 22 Mrs Flynn called a strange doctor to see me. She was afraid I was going to die. I told the doctor I wasnt too sick and that I only forget sometimes. He asked me did I have any friends or relatives and I said no I dont have any. I told him I had a friend called Algernon once but he was a mouse and we used to run races together. He looked at me kind of funny like he thought I was crazy.

He smiled when I told him I used to be a genius. He talked to me like I was a baby and he winked at Mrs Flynn. I got mad and chased him out because he was making fun of me the way they all used to.

July 24 I have no more money and Mrs Flynn says I got to go to work somewhere and pay the rent because I havent paid for over two months. I dont know any work but the job I used to have at Donnegans Plastic Box Company. I dont want to go back there because they all knew me when I was smart and maybe theyll laugh at me. But I don't know what else to do to get money.

July 25 I was looking at some of my old progress reports and its very funny but I cant read what I wrote. I can make out some of the words but they dont make sense.

Miss Kinnian came to the door but I said go away I dont want to see you. She cried and I cried too but I wouldnt let her in because I didn't want her to laugh at me. I told her I didn't like her any more. I told her I didnt want to be smart any more. Thats not true. I still love her and I still want to

J **Read and Discuss** What clues in the journal entry of July 7 suggest that Charlie is undergoing more change?

be smart but I had to say that so shed go away. She gave Mrs Flynn money to pay the rent. I dont want that. I got to get a job. **K**

Please . . . please let me not forget how to read and write . . . **L**

July 27 Mr Donnegan was very nice when I came back and asked him for my old job of janitor. First he was very suspicious but I told him what happened to me then he looked very sad and put his hand on my shoulder and said Charlie Gordon you got guts.

Everybody looked at me when I came downstairs and started working in the toilet sweeping it out like I used to. I told myself Charlie if they make fun of you dont get sore because you remember their not so smart as you once thot they were. And besides they were once your friends and if they laughed at you that doesnt mean anything because they liked you too.

One of the new men who came to work there after I went away made a nasty crack he said hey Charlie I hear your a very smart fella a real quiz kid. Say something intelligent. I felt bad but Joe Carp came over and grabbed him by the shirt and said leave him alone you lousy cracker or Ill break your neck. I didn't expect Joe to take my part so I guess hes really my friend.

Later Frank Reilly came over and said Charlie if anybody bothers you or trys to take advantage you call me or Joe and we will set em straight. I said thanks Frank and I got choked up so I had to turn around and go into the supply room so he wouldnt see me cry. Its good to have friends. **M**

K **Literary Focus** **Subplot** Why does Charlie send Miss Kinnian away?

L **Read and Discuss** What do Charlie's words "Please . . . please let me not forget how to read and write . . ." show us about his state of mind and what he's feeling?

M **Literary Focus** **Subplot** What is the resolution of the subplot of Charlie and his co-workers?

July 28 I did a dumb thing today I forgot I wasnt in Miss Kinnians class at the adult center any more like I use to be. I went in and sat down in my old seat in the back of the room and she looked at me funny and she said Charles. I dint remember she ever called me that before only Charlie so I said hello Miss Kinnian Im redy for my lesin today only I lost my reader that we was using. She startid to cry and run out of the room and everybody looked at me and I saw they wasnt the same pepul who used to be in my class.

Then all of a suddin I rememberd some things about the operashun and me getting smart and I said holy smoke I reely pulled a Charlie Gordon that time. I went away before she come back to the room.

Thats why Im going away from New York for good. I dont want to do nothing like that agen. I dont want Miss Kinnian to feel sorry for me. Evry body feels sorry at the factery and I dont want that eather so Im going someplace where nobody knows that Charlie Gordon was once a genus and now he cant even reed a book or rite good.

Im taking a cuple of books along and even if I cant reed them Ill practise hard and maybe I wont forget every thing I lerned. If I try reel hard maybe Ill be a littel bit smarter then I was before the operashun. I got my rabits foot and my luky penny and maybe they will help me.

If you ever reed this Miss Kinnian dont be sorry for me Im glad I got a second chanse to be smart becaus I lerned a lot of things that I never even new were in this world and Im grateful that I saw it all for a littel bit. I dont know why Im dumb agen or what I did wrong maybe its becaus I dint try hard enuff. But if I try and practis very hard maybe Ill get a littl smarter and know what all the words are. I remember a littel bit how nice I had a feeling with the blue book that has the torn cover when I red it. Thats why Im gonna keep trying to get smart so I can have that feeling agen. Its a good feeling to know things and be smart. I wish I had it rite now if I did I would sit down and reed all the time. Anyway I bet Im the first dumb person in the world who ever found out somthing importent for sience. I remember I did somthing but I dont remember what. So I gess its like I did it for all the dumb pepul like me.

Good-by Miss Kinnian and Dr Strauss and evreybody. And P.S. please tell Dr Nemur not to be such a grouch when pepul laff at him and he woud have more frends. Its easy to make frends if you let pepul laff at you. Im going to have lots of frends where I go.

P.P.S. Please if you get a chanse put some flowrs on Algernons grave in the bakyard . . . Ⓝ

Ⓝ **Read and Discuss** How does Charlie's plan to leave New York shed light on what he's thinking and feeling about his experience?

Applying Your Skills

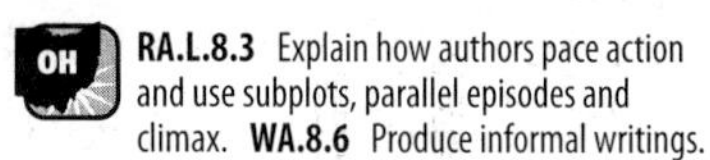
OH

RA.L.8.3 Explain how authors pace action and use subplots, parallel episodes and climax. **WA.8.6** Produce informal writings.

Flowers for Algernon, Part 2

Respond and Think Critically

Reading Focus

Quick Check

1. At the beginning of Part 2, what conflicts is Charlie having with the doctors? with himself?
2. How does Charlie react when the boy in the diner drops the dishes?
3. What does Charlie's research reveal about the outcome of the experiment?
4. What are some of the signals that tell you that Charlie's mental state is getting worse?
5. At the end of the story, why does Charlie decide to leave New York?

Read with a Purpose

6. What has Charlie gained and lost by the end of the story? How does his loss affect him?

Reading Skills: Tracking Story Events

7. Update your chart now that you have finished the story. Below your chart, write a summary of the story.

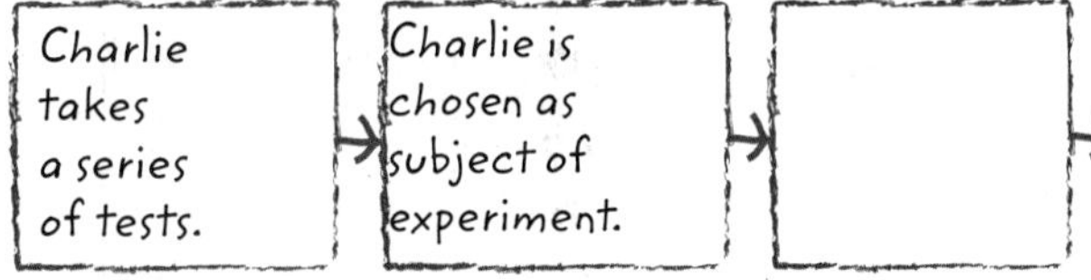

Charlie takes a series of tests.
Charlie is chosen as subject of experiment.

Literary Focus

Literary Analysis

8. **Analyze** How did the author's use of Charlie's journal to tell his story impact the way we as readers understand Charlie's experience?
9. **Extend** What do you think becomes of Charlie after the story ends? Why?
10. **Literary Perspectives** At the beginning of the story, Charlie's credibility as a narrator is affected by his intelligence. Was that also true as he became smarter? Which Charlie did you find more trustworthy—the original Charlie or the altered Charlie?

Literary Skills: Subplots and Parallel Episodes

11. **Analyze** What is the outcome of the subplot about Charlie and Miss Kinnian's relationship?
12. **Analyze** In addition to the Rorschach tests, what parallel episodes are in the story? What purpose do the parallel episodes serve?

Writing Focus

Think as a Reader/Writer

Use It in Your Writing Review your notes on the details Keyes uses to convey story events and the changes Charlie undergoes. Now, write a journal entry about an interesting event in your life. Include details that will make the events, and your experience of them, clear to your readers.

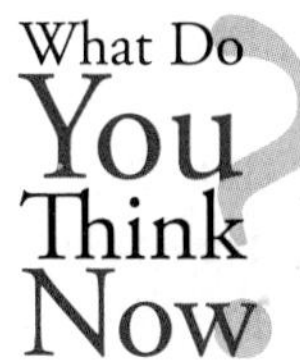

What Do You Think Now? In Charlie's case, was ignorance bliss? Would he have been better off if he had not had the operation? Explain.

Applying Your Skills

Flowers for Algernon

Vocabulary Development

History of the English Language

Digging into the Past
Where did English come from? England, of course! Not entirely. Today's English developed over a long period of time and from many sources. The history of English can be divided into three periods: Old English (A.D. 450–1066), Middle English (1066–1485), and Modern English (1485 to the present).

Old English In the fifth century, the Anglo-Saxons migrated from northern Europe to Britain. The Anglo-Saxons developed a new language, combining their old Germanic language and the Celtic language of the people native to Britain. Soon Vikings, from Scandinavia, invaded. Their language, Norse, was added to the language of Britain. We call this new language Old English. Here are three Old English words that survive today: *horse, night, wife.*

Middle English In the year 1066, William the Conqueror, from Normandy in France, conquered England. Soon French and Latin words were added to the mix. These borrowings from Anglo-Saxon, Norse, Latin, and French gave English the large, rich vocabulary it has today. Here are three words derived from French: *government, justice, literature.*

Modern English In 1485, Henry VII, the first Tudor king, came to the throne of England. The House of Tudor helped promote all things English—including the language. Printed books helped make it possible for all English people to speak, read, and write the same language.

Your Turn

Use a dictionary to find the origin of each Vocabulary word at the right. Then, make a word map like the one below. The word *obscure* is done for you.

misled
regression
obscure
deterioration
introspective

obscure	
Derivation	OFr *obscur* < L *obscurus*, "covered over"
Meaning	verb, "to hide or conceal"; adjective, "not clear," "not easily understood"
Sample sentences	"The moon is **obscured** by a cloud." "Their reasons for leaving are **obscure**."

Language Coach

Word Origins Which two Vocabulary words share word origins with these words from Spanish? How can you tell?

introspectivo deteriorar

Academic Vocabulary

Write About . . .
Do you think it is ethical, or morally acceptable, to use human subjects for medical experiments? How should experiments be conducted to ensure they are effective and have a safe outcome?

Learn It Online
To expand your vocabulary knowledge, visit Word Watch at:

go.hrw.com L8-86 Go

R.8.2 Identify appropriate sources and gather relevant information from multiple sources. **WA.8.1.a** Write narratives that: sustain reader interest by pacing action and developing an engaging plot; **WA.8.4.b** Write informational essays or reports, including research, that: provide a clear and accurate perspective on the subject *Also covered* **WC.8.8; VO.8.5**

Grammar Link

Verbs

A **verb** is a word used to express action or a state of being. The verb's role in a sentence is to tell you something about the subject. Three types of verbs are **helping verbs, action verbs,** and **linking verbs**.

- A **helping verb** helps the main verb express action or a state of being. It does not stand alone. Some common helping verbs are *is, being, do, have, could.*

  EXAMPLE Charlie **has decided** to move to New York. [The main verb is *decided*.]

- An **action verb** expresses physical action or mental action, such as *fly, jog, celebrate, regret.*

  EXAMPLE Algernon **finishes** the maze quickly.

- A **linking verb** connects the subject to a word or words that identify or describe the subject. Some common linking verbs are *am, seem, was, remain, feel.*

  EXAMPLE Charlie **becomes** smarter than most people.

Your Turn

Fill in each blank below with a verb that fits the meaning of the sentence. Look in the brackets to see which type of verb to use.

1. Charlie _____ decided to have experimental surgery. [helping]
2. At first, Charlie _____ the same. [linking]
3. Later, he _____ at an astonishing rate. [action]
4. Charlie _____ understand several languages. [helping]
5. At the story's end, Charlie _____ to his former state. [action]

CHOICES

As you respond to the Choices, use these **Academic Vocabulary** words as appropriate: effective, outcome, reveal, structure.

REVIEW

Write a Story

Choose a familiar story, perhaps from a fairy tale, TV show, or movie. Then, select a minor character from that story to further develop. Then, develop a short narrative that provides more information about that character. Include elements of plot such as exposition, climax, and resolution.

CONNECT

Analyze the Story

Timed Writing Although the outcome of the experiment was not good for Charlie, he experienced many new things. Which lesson or experience do you think was the most important for him? In a short essay, explain your answer and support it with evidence from the story.

EXTEND

Research Psychological Tests

What sorts of psychological tests measure personality, intellect, and aptitudes? Are they effective? Perform research to find out. Record your findings in a chart that lists each test name, when it was developed and by whom, and what information the test reveals.

Learn It Online
Find more great works of science fiction by visiting *NovelWise* at:
go.hrw.com
L8-87
Go

Comparing and Contrasting Stories

CONTENTS

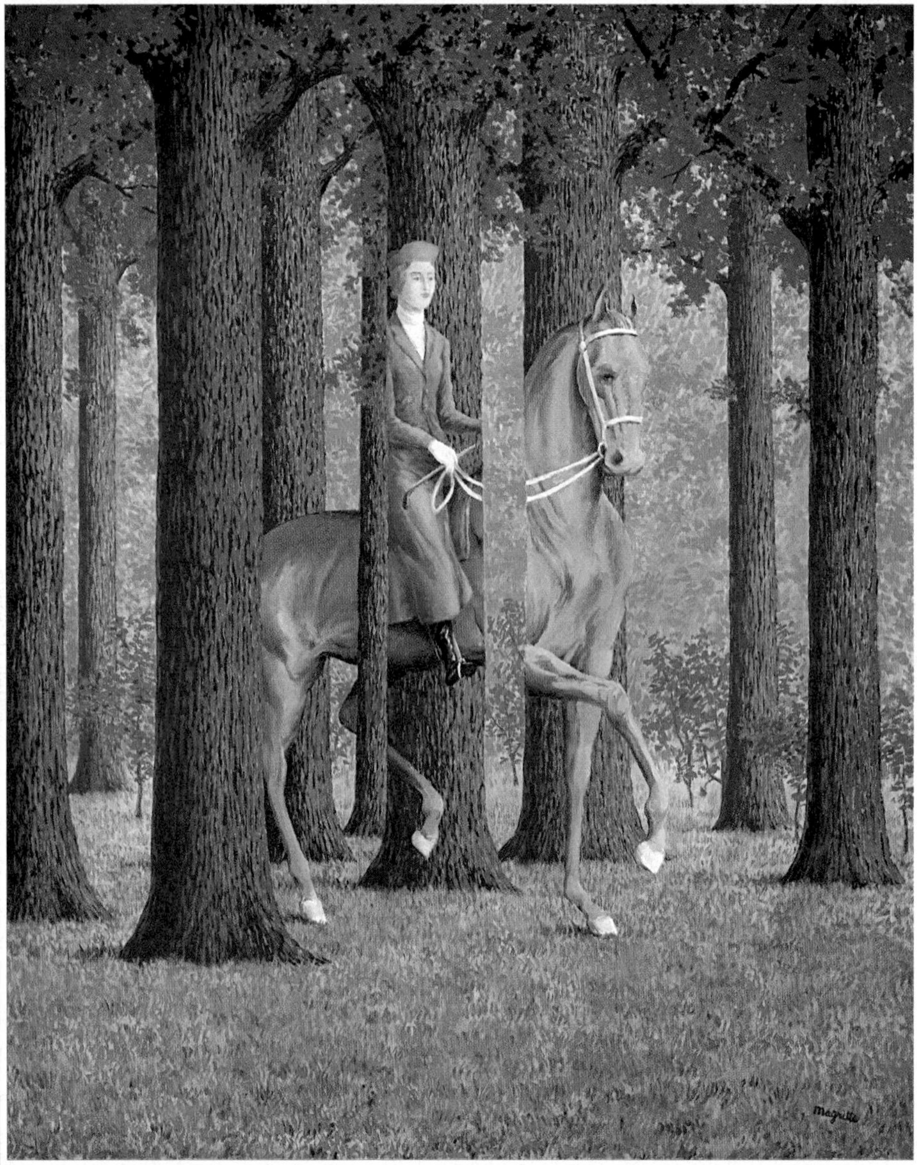

Le Blanc-Seing, the Blank Signature (1965) by René Magritte. Oil on canvas (81.3 x 65.1 cm).

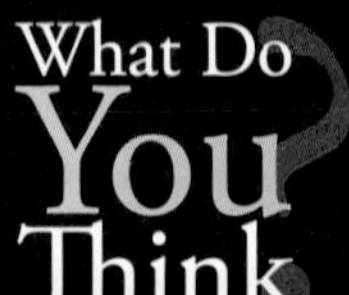

Is what we want the same as what is good for us?

QuickWrite

If you were given the chance to have any wish fulfilled, would you wish for something for yourself or for another person or group? Jot down your thoughts.

Preparing to Read

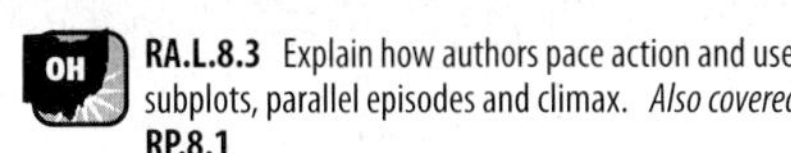
RA.L.8.3 Explain how authors pace action and use subplots, parallel episodes and climax. *Also covered* RP.8.1

The Monkey's Paw / Aunty Misery

Use your **RWN** to complete the activities for these selections.

Vocabulary

The Monkey's Paw

amiably (AY mee uh blee) *adv.:* good-naturedly. *Before the visitor arrives, father and son are amiably playing a competitive game of chess.*

presumptuous (prih ZUHMP choo uhs) *adj.:* overly bold or confident; expecting too much. *Is it presumptuous to think one can overcome fate?*

credulity (kruh DOO luh tee) *n.:* quality of believing too readily. *The father is ashamed of his own credulity as he tries out the monkey's paw.*

Aunty Misery

hospitality (hahs puh TAL uh tee) *n.:* friendly or generous treatment of guests. *In return for her hospitality, Aunty Misery is granted a wish.*

gnarled (nahrld) *adj.:* covered with knots; twisted. *The ancient tree was twisted and gnarled.*

Language Coach

Related Words The Latin word *credere* means "trust" or "believe in." Which word on the list above is related to that Latin word? Challenge yourself to list two other words that are derived from *credere.*

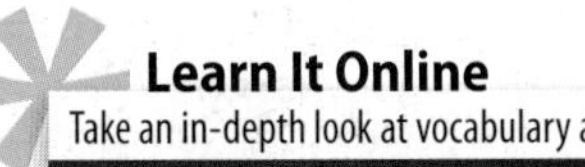
Learn It Online
Take an in-depth look at vocabulary at:
go.hrw.com L8-89 

Literary Focus

Literary Patterns Stories, whether in books or in movies, often contain patterns. One familiar pattern involves the number three. (Think of Charles Dickens's *A Christmas Carol,* in which Scrooge is visited by three ghosts.) Such patterns are repeated in tales from various cultures and periods of history. Some patterns are formed within a single story, as certain plot events are repeated. We call these repetitive structures within a story **parallel episodes.**

Reading Focus

Comparing and Contrasting When you compare and contrast stories, you look for ways that they are similar to and different from each other. Doing so helps you appreciate how storytellers from different cultures and times capture common human experiences.

Into Action As you read the following stories, create a chart like the one below to help you keep track of patterns you find both within and across the stories.

	"The Monkey's Paw"	"Aunty Misery"
Parallel episodes within a story		
Literary patterns across stories	mysterious guest arrives	

Writing Focus

Think as a Reader/Writer

Find It in Your Reading Notice how the two author's sentences differ—one uses short and simple sentences; the other, long and complex sentences. How do these different styles create distinct moods? Write examples in your *Reader/Writer Notebook.*

MEET THE WRITERS

W. W. Jacobs
(1863–1943)

Watching the Ships Go By

The oldest child in a large family, William Wymark Jacobs grew up in London, near the River Thames, where his father worked on the docks. As a teenager, Jacobs spent many hours on the docks, watching ships come and go and listening to the stories of the sailors. These experiences are reflected in his short stories and novels, many of which include seafaring characters.

While Jacobs is best known today for his horror stories, he was actually one of the most popular humorists of his time. "The Monkey's Paw" is his most famous story.

(top) William Wymark Jacobs (1910) by Carton Moore-Park. Oil on canvas.

Judith Ortiz Cofer
(1952–)

Bridge Between Two Cultures

Judith Ortiz Cofer was born in Puerto Rico but moved with her family to Paterson, New Jersey, when she was two years old. Her father had joined the U.S. Navy and was stationed at the Brooklyn Naval Yard. Whenever her father was sent to sea, Cofer returned to Puerto Rico with the rest of the family. As a result, Cofer found herself divided between two worlds. Fortunately she was able to find refuge in books.

> "I absorbed literature . . . as a creature who breathed ink. Each writer . . . taught me that language could be tamed. I realized that I could make it perform. I had to believe the work was important to my being: to use my art as a bridge between my cultures."

Think About the Writers

How did their fathers' jobs affect both Jacobs and Cofer?

Preview the Selections

In "The Monkey's Paw" an English family, **the Whites,** receive a visit from an old friend, **Sergeant Major Morris,** who has returned after years in India. The visitor brings with him an odd souvenir.

In "Aunty Misery" you'll meet an old woman, **Aunty Misery,** who uses the one wish she is granted in a surprising way.

SHORT STORY

THE MONKEY'S PAW

by **W. W. Jacobs**

Read with a Purpose
Read to discover what happens when a family is given the opportunity to make a wish.

– 1 –

Without, the night was cold and wet, but in the small parlor of Laburnam Villa the blinds were drawn and the fire burned brightly. Father and son were at chess, the former, who possessed ideas about the game involving radical changes, putting his king into such sharp and unnecessary perils that it even provoked comment from the white-haired old lady knitting placidly by the fire.

"Hark at the wind," said Mr. White, who, having seen a fatal mistake after it was too late, was amiably desirous of preventing his son from seeing it.

"I'm listening," said the latter, grimly surveying the board as he stretched out his hand.

"Check."[1]

"I should hardly think that he'd come tonight," said his father, with his hand poised over the board.

"Mate," replied the son.

"That's the worst of living so far out," bawled Mr. White, with sudden and unlooked-for violence; "of all the beastly, slushy, out-of-the-way places to live in, this is the worst. Pathway's a bog,[2] and the road's a torrent. I don't know what people

1. **check:** in the game of chess, the situation of a king in danger of being captured when the opposing player makes his or her next move. Checkmate is a move that leaves the opponent's king unable to move safely and means winning the game.
2. **bog:** swamp; very wet ground.

Vocabulary **amiably** (AY mee uh blee) *adv.:* good-naturedly.

Analyzing Visuals **Viewing and Interpreting** The story's mood so far has been light. What is the mood of the image above?

are thinking about. I suppose because only two houses on the road are let,[3] they think it doesn't matter."

"Never mind, dear," said his wife soothingly; "perhaps you'll win the next one."

Mr. White looked up sharply, just in time to intercept a knowing glance between mother and son. The words died away on his lips, and he hid a guilty grin in his thin gray beard.

"There he is," said Herbert White, as the gate banged to loudly and heavy footsteps came toward the door. **A**

3. **let:** rented.

The old man rose with hospitable haste, and, opening the door, was heard condoling[4] with the new arrival. The new arrival also condoled with himself, so that Mrs. White said, "Tut, tut!" and coughed gently as her husband entered the room, followed by a tall burly man, beady of eye and rubicund of visage.[5]

"Sergeant Major Morris," he said, introducing him.

4. **condoling:** expressing sympathy (here, about the bad weather).

5. **rubicund** (ROO buh kuhnd) **of visage** (VIHZ ihj): red-faced.

A **Read and Discuss** What has the author told us about this family so far?

The sergeant major shook hands, and, taking the proffered seat by the fire, watched contentedly while his host got out whiskey and tumblers and stood a small copper kettle on the fire.

At the third glass his eyes got brighter, and he began to talk, the little family circle regarding with eager interest this visitor from distant parts, as he squared his broad shoulders in the chair and spoke of wild scenes and doughty[6] deeds, of wars and plagues and strange peoples.

"Twenty-one years of it," said Mr. White, nodding at his wife and son. "When he went away he was a slip of a youth in the warehouse. Now look at him."

"He don't look to have taken much harm," said Mrs. White politely.

"I'd like to go to India myself," said the old man, "just to look around a bit, you know." **B**

"Better where you are," said the sergeant major, shaking his head. He put down the empty glass and, sighing softly, shook it again.

"I should like to see those old temples and fakirs[7] and jugglers," said the old man. "What was that you started telling me the other day about a monkey's paw or something, Morris?"

"Nothing," said the soldier hastily. "Leastways, nothing worth hearing."

"Monkey's paw?" said Mrs. White curiously.

6. **doughty** (DOW tee): brave.

7. **fakirs** (fuh KIHRZ): in India, holy men thought to have miraculous powers.

"Well, it's just a bit of what you might call magic, perhaps," said the sergeant major offhandedly.

His three listeners leaned forward eagerly. The visitor absent-mindedly put his empty glass to his lips and then set it down again. His host filled it for him.

"To look at," said the sergeant major, fumbling in his pocket, "it's just an ordinary little paw, dried to a mummy."

He took something out of his pocket and proffered it. Mrs. White drew back with a grimace, but her son, taking it, examined it curiously.

"And what is there special about it?" inquired Mr. White as he took it from his son and, having examined it, placed it upon the table.

"It had a spell put on it by an old fakir," said the sergeant major, "a very holy man. He wanted to show that fate ruled people's lives, and that those who interfered with it did so to their sorrow. He put a spell on it so that three separate men could each have three wishes from it."

His manner was so impressive that his hearers were conscious that their light laughter jarred somewhat.

"Well, why don't you have three, sir?" said Herbert White cleverly.

The soldier regarded him in the way that middle age is wont to regard presumptuous youth. "I have," he said quietly, and his blotchy face whitened.

"And did you really have the three wishes granted?" asked Mrs. White.

B **Read and Discuss** What have we learned about Sergeant Major Morris?

Vocabulary **presumptuous** (prih ZUHMP choo uhs) *adj.:* overly bold or confident; expecting too much.

"I did," said the sergeant major, and his glass tapped against his strong teeth.

"And has anybody else wished?" inquired the old lady.

"The first man had his three wishes, yes," was the reply. "I don't know what the first two were, but the third was for death. That's how I got the paw." **C**

His tones were so grave that a hush fell upon the group.

"If you've had your three wishes, it's no good to you now, then, Morris," said the old man at last. "What do you keep it for?"

The soldier shook his head. "Fancy,[8] I suppose," he said slowly. "I did have some idea of selling it, but I don't think I will. It has caused enough mischief already. Besides, people won't buy. They think it's a fairy tale, some of them, and those who do think anything of it want to try it first and pay me afterward."

"If you could have another three wishes," said the old man, eyeing him keenly, "would you have them?"

"I don't know," said the other. "I don't know."

He took the paw, and dangling it between his forefinger and thumb, suddenly threw it upon the fire. White, with a slight cry, stooped down and snatched it off.

"Better let it burn," said the soldier solemnly.

"If you don't want it, Morris," said the old man, "give it to me."

"I won't," said his friend doggedly. "I threw it on the fire. If you keep it, don't blame me for what happens. Pitch it on the fire again, like a sensible man." **D**

The other shook his head and examined his new possession closely. "How do you do it?" he inquired.

"Hold it up in your right hand and wish aloud," said the sergeant major, "but I warn you of the consequences."

"Sounds like *The Arabian Nights,*" said Mrs. White, as she rose and began to set the supper. "Don't you think you might wish for four pairs of hands for me?"

Her husband drew the talisman[9] from his pocket and then all three burst into laughter as the sergeant major, with a look of alarm on his face, caught him by the arm.

"If you must wish," he said, gruffly, "wish for something sensible."

Mr. White dropped it back into his pocket, and placing chairs, motioned his friend to the table. In the business of supper, the talisman was partly forgotten, and afterward the three sat listening in an enthralled fashion to a second installment of the soldier's adventures in India.

"If the tale about the monkey's paw is not more truthful than those he has been telling us," said Herbert, as the door closed behind their guest, just in time for him to

8. **fancy:** here, feeling that has no apparent cause. *Fancy* can also mean "imagination," as it does later in the story.

9. **talisman** (TAL ihs muhn): something thought to have magic power.

C **Read and Discuss** What has the sergeant major told us about the monkey's paw?

D **Reading Focus** **Contrasting** Contrast the Whites' attitude about the paw with the sergeant major's. What might the sergeant major's reaction reveal about future events?

catch the last train, "we shan't make much out of it."

"Did you give him anything for it, Father?" inquired Mrs. White, regarding her husband closely.

"A trifle," said he, coloring slightly. "He didn't want it, but I made him take it. And he pressed me again to throw it away."

"Likely," said Herbert, with pretended horror. "Why, we're going to be rich, and famous, and happy. Wish to be an emperor, Father, to begin with: then you can't be bossed around."

He darted round the table, pursued by the maligned Mrs. White armed with an antimacassar.[10]

Mr. White took the paw from his pocket and eyed it dubiously. "I don't know what to wish for, and that's a fact," he said slowly. "It seems to me I've got all I want."

"If you only cleared the house, you'd be quite happy, wouldn't you?" said Herbert, with his hand on his shoulder. "Well, wish for two hundred pounds,[11] then; that'll just do it."

His father, smiling shamefacedly at his own credulity, held up the talisman, as his son, with a solemn face somewhat marred by a wink at his mother, sat down at the piano and struck a few impressive chords.

"I wish for two hundred pounds," said the old man distinctly. **E**

A fine crash from the piano greeted the words, interrupted by a shuddering cry from the old man. His wife and son ran toward him.

"It moved," he cried, with a glance of disgust at the object as it lay on the floor. "As I wished, it twisted in my hand like a snake."

"Well, I don't see the money," said his son, as he picked it up and placed it on the table, "and I bet I never shall."

"It must have been your fancy, Father," said his wife, regarding him anxiously.

He shook his head. "Never mind, though; there's no harm done, but it gave me a shock all the same."

They sat down by the fire again while the two men finished their pipes. Outside, the wind was higher than ever, and the old man started nervously at the sound of a door banging upstairs. A silence unusual and depressing settled upon all three, which lasted until the old couple rose to retire for the night. **F**

"WHY, WE'RE GOING TO BE RICH, AND FAMOUS, AND HAPPY."

10. **antimacassar** (an tee muh KAS uhr): small cover placed on the back or arms of a chair to keep it clean.
11. **two hundred pounds:** British money equivalent to about one thousand dollars at the time of this story.

E **Literary Focus** **Patterns** In stories involving wishes, the first wish often determines how the rest of the characters' wishes will play out. Do you think Mr. White made a good first wish? Explain.

Vocabulary **credulity** (kruh DOO luh tee) *n.:* quality of believing too readily.

F **Read and Discuss** What effect is created when the narrator says, "A silence unusual and depressing settled upon all three . . ."?

"I expect you'll find the cash tied up in a big bag in the middle of your bed," said Herbert, as he bade them good night, "and something horrible squatting up on top of the wardrobe[12] watching you as you pocket your ill-gotten gains."

– 2 –

In the brightness of the wintry sun next morning as it streamed over the breakfast table Herbert laughed at his fears. There was an air of prosaic wholesomeness about the room which it had lacked on the previous night, and the dirty, shriveled little paw was pitched on the sideboard with a carelessness which betokened no great belief in its virtues.[13]

"I suppose all old soldiers are the same," said Mrs. White. "The idea of our listening to such nonsense! How could wishes be granted in these days? And if they could, how could two hundred pounds hurt you, Father?"

"Might drop on his head from the sky," said the frivolous Herbert.

"Morris said the things happened so naturally," said his father, "that you might if you so wished attribute it to coincidence."

"Well, don't break into the money before I come back," said Herbert, as he rose from the table. "I'm afraid it'll turn you into a mean, avaricious man, and we shall have to disown you." **G**

His mother laughed, and followed him to the door, watched him down the road, and returning to the breakfast table, was very happy at the expense of her husband's credulity. All of which did not prevent her from scurrying to the door at the postman's knock, nor prevent her from referring somewhat shortly to retired sergeant majors of bibulous habits[14] when she found that the post brought a tailor's bill.

"Herbert will have some more of his funny remarks, I expect, when he comes home," she said, as they sat at dinner.

"I dare say," said Mr. White, pouring himself out some beer; "but for all that, the thing moved in my hand; that I'll swear to."

"You thought it did," said the old lady soothingly.

"I say it did," replied the other. "There was no thought about it. I had just—What's the matter?"

His wife made no reply. She was watching the mysterious movements of a man outside, who, peering in an undecided fashion at the house, appeared to be trying to make up his mind to enter. In mental connection with the two hundred pounds, she noticed that the stranger was well dressed and wore a silk hat of glossy newness. Three times he paused at the gate, and then walked on again. The fourth time he stood with his hand upon it, and then with sudden resolution flung it open and walked up the path. Mrs. White at the same moment placed her hands behind her, and hurriedly unfastening the strings of her apron, put that useful article of apparel beneath the cushion of her chair. **H**

12. **wardrobe:** movable closet.

13. **virtues:** here, powers.

14. **bibulous** (BIHB yuh luhs) **habits:** tendency to drink heavily.

G **Read and Discuss** What does the breakfast conversation tell us about the family's view of the paw?

H **Literary Focus** **Patterns** How is this stranger's arrival part of a pattern? What other visitor have the Whites entertained?

She brought the stranger, who seemed ill at ease, into the room. He gazed furtively at Mrs. White, and listened in a preoccupied fashion as the old lady apologized for the appearance of the room, and her husband's coat, a garment which he usually reserved for the garden. She then waited patiently for him to broach his business, but he was at first strangely silent.

"I—was asked to call," he said at last, and stooped and picked a piece of cotton from his trousers. "I come from Maw and Meggins."

The old lady started. "Is anything the matter?" she asked breathlessly. "Has anything happened to Herbert? What is it? What is it?"

Her husband interposed. "There, there, Mother," he said hastily. "Sit down and don't jump to conclusions. You've not brought bad news, I'm sure, sir," and he eyed the other wistfully.

"I'm sorry—" began the visitor.

"Is he hurt?" demanded the mother wildly.

The visitor bowed in assent. “Badly hurt,” he said quietly, “but he is not in any pain.”

“Oh, thank God!” said the old woman, clasping her hands. “Thank God for that! Thank—”

She broke off suddenly as the sinister meaning of the assurance dawned upon her and she saw the awful confirmation of her fears in the other’s averted face. She caught her breath, and turning to her husband, laid her trembling old hand upon his. There was a long silence.

“He was caught in the machinery,” said the visitor at length, in a low voice.

“Caught in the machinery,” repeated Mr. White, in a dazed fashion, “yes.”

He sat staring blankly out at the window, and taking his wife’s hand between his own, pressed it as he had been wont to do in their old courting days nearly forty years before.

“He was the only one left to us,” he said, turning gently to the visitor. “It is hard.”

The other coughed, and, rising, walked slowly to the window. “The firm wished me to convey their sincere sympathy with you in your great loss,” he said, without looking around. “I beg that you will understand I am only their servant and merely obeying orders.”

There was no reply; the old woman’s face was white, her eyes staring, and her breath inaudible; on the husband’s face was a look such as his friend the sergeant might have carried into his first action.

“I was to say that Maw and Meggins disclaim all responsibility,” continued the other. “They admit no liability at all, but in consideration of your son’s services they wish to present you with a certain sum as compensation.”

THERE WAS NO REPLY; THE OLD WOMAN’S FACE WAS WHITE.

Mr. White dropped his wife’s hand, and rising to his feet, gazed with a look of horror at his visitor. His dry lips shaped the words, “How much?”

“Two hundred pounds,” was the answer.

Unconscious of his wife’s shriek, the old man smiled faintly, put out his hands like a sightless man, and dropped, a senseless heap, to the floor. **I**

– 3 –

In the huge new cemetery, some two miles distant, the old people buried their dead, and came back to a house steeped in shadow and silence. It was all over so quickly that at first they could hardly realize it, and remained in a state of expectation as though of something else to happen—something else which was to lighten this load, too heavy for old hearts to bear. But the days passed, and expectations gave place to resignation—the hopeless resignation of the old, sometimes miscalled apathy. Sometimes they hardly exchanged a word, for now they had nothing to talk about, and their days were long to weariness.

I **Read and Discuss** What do the Whites think of the magic of the paw now?

It was about a week after that that the old man, waking suddenly in the night, stretched out his hand and found himself alone. The room was in darkness, and the sound of subdued weeping came from the window. He raised himself in bed and listened.

"Come back," he said tenderly. "You will be cold."

"It is colder for my son," said the old woman, and wept afresh.

The sound of her sobs died away on his ears. The bed was warm, and his eyes heavy with sleep. He dozed fitfully, and then slept until a sudden wild cry from his wife awoke him with a start.

"*The paw!*" she cried wildly. "The monkey's paw!"

He started up in alarm. "Where? Where is it? What's the matter?"

She came stumbling across the room toward him. "I want it," she said quietly. "You've not destroyed it?"

"It's in the parlor, on the bracket,"[15] he replied, marveling. "Why?"

She cried and laughed together, and bending over, kissed his cheek.

"I only just thought of it," she said hysterically. "Why didn't I think of it before? Why didn't *you* think of it?"

"Think of what?" he questioned.

"The other two wishes," she replied rapidly. "We've only had one."

"Was not that enough?" he demanded fiercely.

"No," she cried triumphantly; "we'll have one more. Go down and get it quickly, and wish our boy alive again." **J**

The man sat up in bed and flung the bedclothes from his quaking limbs. "You are mad!" he cried, aghast.

"Get it," she panted; "get it quickly, and wish—Oh, my boy, my boy!"

Her husband struck a match and lit the candle. "Get back to bed," he said unsteadily. "You don't know what you are saying."

"We had the first wish granted," said the old woman feverishly; "why not the second?"

"A coincidence," stammered the old man.

"Go and get it and wish," cried his wife, quivering with excitement.

The old man turned and regarded her, and his voice shook. "He has been dead ten days, and besides he—I would not tell you else, but—I could only recognize him by his clothing. If he was too terrible for you to see then, how now?"

"Bring him back," cried the old woman, and dragged him toward the door. "Do you think I fear the child I have nursed?" **K**

He went down in the darkness, and felt his way to the parlor, and then to the mantelpiece. The talisman was in its place, and a horrible fear that the unspoken wish might bring his mutilated son before him ere he could escape from the room seized upon him, and he caught his breath as he found that he had lost the direction of the door.

15. **bracket:** wall shelf held up by supports.

J **Literary Focus** **Patterns** The wishes in this story form parallel episodes. How is the second wish similar to the first? How is it different?

K **Read and Discuss** What does Mr. White think of his wife's idea?

His brow cold with sweat, he felt his way round the table, and groped along the wall until he found himself in the small passage with the unwholesome thing in his hand.

Even his wife's face seemed changed as he entered the room. It was white and expectant, and to his fears seemed to have an unnatural look upon it. He was afraid of her.

"*Wish!*" she cried, in a strong voice.

"It is foolish and wicked," he faltered.

"*Wish!*" repeated his wife.

He raised his hand. "I wish my son alive again." **L**

The talisman fell to the floor, and he regarded it fearfully. Then he sank trembling into a chair as the old woman, with burning eyes, walked to the window and raised the blind.

He sat until he was chilled with the cold, glancing occasionally at the figure of the old woman peering through the window. The candle end, which had burned below the rim of the china candlestick, was throwing pulsating shadows on the ceiling and walls, until, with a flicker larger than the rest, it expired. The old man, with an unspeakable sense of relief at the failure of the talisman, crept back to his bed, and a minute or two afterward the old woman came silently and apathetically beside him.

Neither spoke, but both lay silently listening to the ticking of the clock. A stair creaked, and a squeaky mouse scurried noisily through the wall. The darkness was oppressive, and after lying for some time screwing up his courage, the husband took the box of matches, and striking one, went downstairs for a candle.

At the foot of the stairs the match went out, and he paused to strike another, and at the same moment a knock, so quiet and stealthy as to be scarcely audible, sounded on the front door.

The matches fell from his hand. He stood motionless, his breath suspended until the knock was repeated. Then he turned and fled swiftly back to his room, and closed the door behind him. A third knock sounded through the house.

"*What's that?*" cried the old woman, starting up.

"A rat," said the old man, in shaking tones—"a rat. It passed me on the stairs."

His wife sat up in bed listening. A loud knock resounded through the house. **M**

"It's Herbert!" she screamed. "It's Herbert!"

She ran to the door, but her husband was before her, and catching her by the arm, held her tightly.

"What are you going to do?" he whispered hoarsely.

"It's my boy; it's Herbert!" she cried, struggling mechanically. "I forgot it was two miles away. What are you holding me for? Let go. I must open the door."

"For God's sake don't let it in," cried the old man, trembling.

"You're afraid of your own son," she cried, struggling. "Let me go. I'm coming, Herbert; I'm coming."

There was another knock, and another. The old woman with a sudden wrench

---

L **Read and Discuss** Why does Mr. White go along with the idea?

M **Literary Focus** **Patterns** What pattern does this event—the knocking at the door—continue?

broke free and ran from the room. Her husband followed to the landing, and called after her appealingly as she hurried downstairs. He heard the chain rattle back and the bottom bolt drawn slowly and stiffly from the socket. Then the old woman's voice, strained and panting.

"The bolt," she cried loudly. "Come down. I can't reach it."

But her husband was on his hands and knees groping wildly on the floor in search of the paw. If he could only find it before the thing outside got in. A perfect fusillade[16] of knocks reverberated through the house, and he heard the scraping of a chair as his wife put it down in the passage against the door. He heard the creaking of the bolt as it came slowly back, and at the same moment he found the monkey's paw, and frantically breathed his third and last wish.

The knocking ceased suddenly, although the echoes of it were still in the house. He heard the chair drawn back and the door opened. A cold wind rushed up the staircase, and a long loud wail of disappointment and misery from his wife gave him courage to run down to her side, and then to the gate beyond. The street lamp flickering opposite shone on a quiet and deserted road. **N**

16. **fusillade** (FYOO suh lahd): here, something resembling a rapid, continuous series of gunshots.

N **Read and Discuss** What exactly happened?

Applying Your Skills

RA.L.8.3 Explain how authors pace action and use subplots, parallel episodes and climax. RA.L.8.7 Identify examples of foreshadowing and flashback in a literary text. *Also covered* RP.8.1; VO.8.4; WA.8.1.c

The Monkey's Paw

Respond and Think Critically

Reading Focus

Quick Check

1. How do the Whites come to own the monkey's paw?
2. Why is Mr. White's first wish for only two hundred pounds?
3. What final wish does Mr. White make? Why does he make that wish?

Read with a Purpose

4. How does the monkey's paw change the Whites' lives?

Reading Skills: Comparing and Contrasting

5. Continue filling in your chart, and use it to help you answer questions 13 and 14.

	"The Monkey's Paw"
Parallel episodes within a story	
Literary patterns across stories	mysterious guest arrives magical object

Vocabulary Check

Match the Vocabulary words with their definitions.

6. **amiably**
7. **presumptuous**
8. **credulity**

a. quality of believing too readily
b. overly confident
c. pleasantly

Literary Focus

Literary Analysis

9. **Identify** What does the sergeant major say that **foreshadows,** or hints at, the Whites' fate?
10. **Analyze** The fakir who put the spell on the paw wanted to show that one shouldn't try to change fate. In your opinion, was he effective in making his point? Why or why not?
11. **Evaluate** Do you think that, knowing what he does, the sergeant major should have allowed his friend to have the monkey's paw and wish on it? Explain.
12. **Evaluate** Discuss the idea of "maternal instincts" and how that notion played a role in the Whites' differing views on allowing their son to enter the house.

Literary Skills: Literary Patterns

13. **Identify** What parallel episodes did you find within "The Monkey's Paw"?
14. **Extend** What literary patterns in this story have you encountered in other works of literature or in movies? Explain.

Writing Focus

Think as a Reader/Writer

Use It in Your Writing Choose a setting from real life or from your imagination. Using an energetic, long-sentenced style like Jacobs's, write a paragraph describing this setting. What effect does this prose style create?

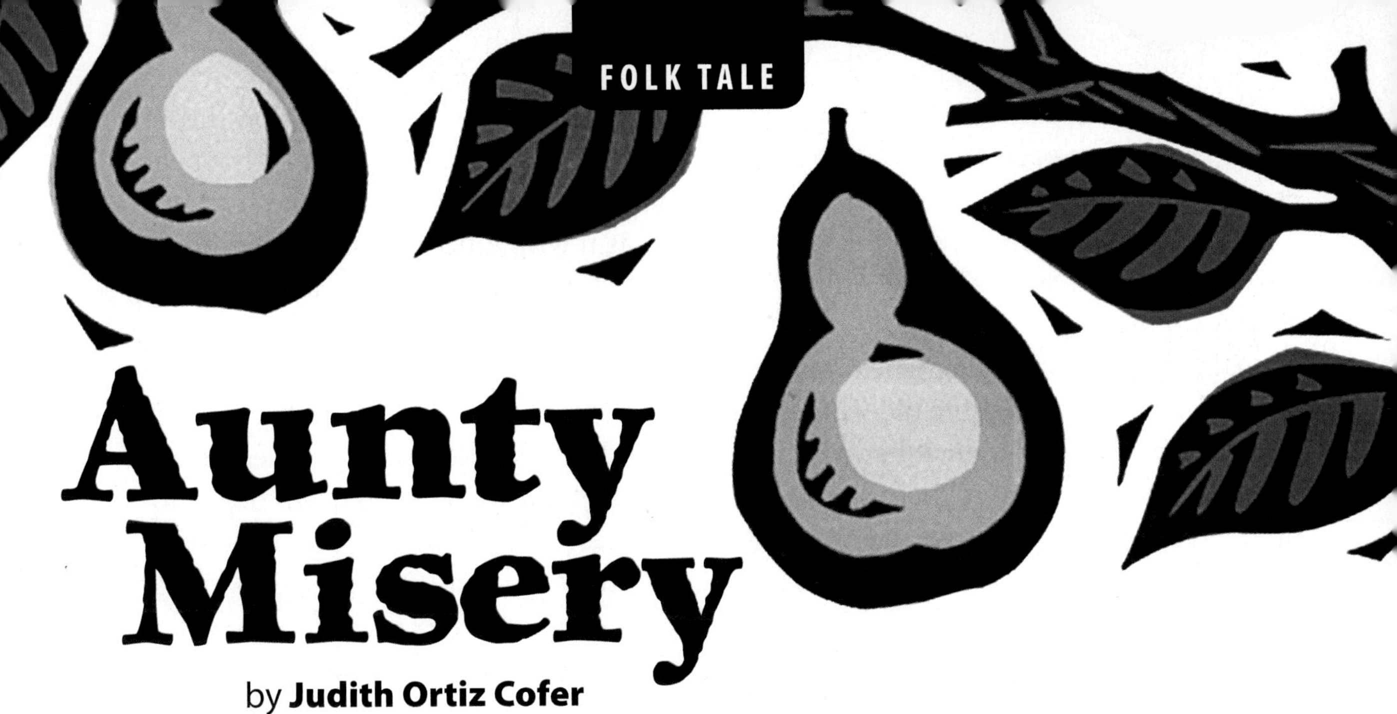

Aunty Misery

by **Judith Ortiz Cofer**

Read with a Purpose

Read "Aunty Misery" to learn the consequences of a simple wish.

Preparing to Read for this selection is on page 89.

Build Background

"Aunty Misery" is a folk tale, a story that has been passed on by word of mouth from one generation to another. Often, folk tales contain fantastic elements and try to explain why things are the way they are.

This is a story about an old, a very old woman who lived alone in her little hut with no other company than a beautiful pear tree that grew at her door. She spent all her time taking care of this tree. The neighborhood children drove the old woman crazy by stealing her fruit. They would climb her tree, shake its delicate limbs, and run away with armloads of golden pears, yelling insults at *la Tia Miseria,*[1] Aunty Misery, as they called her. **A**

1. **la Tia Miseria** (lah TEE ah mee say REE ah).

One day, a traveler stopped at the old woman's hut and asked her for permission to spend the night under her roof. Aunty Misery saw that he had an honest face and bid the pilgrim come in. She fed him and made a bed for him in front of her hearth. In the morning the stranger told her that he would show his gratitude for her hospitality by granting her one wish. **B**

"There is only one thing that I desire," said Aunty Misery.

"Ask, and it shall be yours," replied the stranger, who was a sorcerer in disguise.

A **Read and Discuss** What has the author told us so far?

B **Reading Focus** **Comparing** What similarities do you notice between this story and "The Monkey's Paw"?

Vocabulary **hospitality** (hahs puh TAL uh tee) *n.:* friendly or generous treatment of guests.

"I wish that anyone who climbs up my pear tree should not be able to come back down until I permit it."

"Your wish is granted," said the stranger, touching the pear tree as he left Aunty Misery's house.

And so it happened that when the children came back to taunt the old woman and to steal her fruit, she stood at her window watching them. Several of them shimmied up the trunk of the pear tree and immediately got stuck to it as if with glue. She let them cry and beg her for a long time before she gave the tree permission to let them go on the condition that they never again steal her fruit, or bother her.

Time passed and both Aunty Misery and her tree grew bent and gnarled with age. One day another traveler stopped at her door. This one looked untrustworthy to her, so before letting him into her home the old woman asked him what he was doing in her village. He answered her in a voice that was dry and hoarse, as if he had swallowed a desert: "I am Death, and I have come to take you with me." **C**

Thinking fast, Aunty Misery said, "All right, but before I go I would like to pluck some pears from my beloved tree to remember how much pleasure it brought me in this life. But I am a very old woman and cannot climb to the tallest branches where the best fruit is. Will you be so kind as to do it for me?"

With a heavy sigh like wind through a tomb, Señor Death climbed the pear tree. Immediately he became stuck to it as if with glue. And no matter how much he cursed and threatened, Aunty Misery would not allow the tree to release Death.

Many years passed and there were no deaths in the world. The people who make their living from death began to protest loudly. The doctors claimed no one bothered to come in for examinations or treatments anymore, because they did not fear dying; the pharmacists' business suffered too because medicines are, like magic potions, bought to prevent or postpone the inevitable; priests and undertakers were unhappy with the situation also, for obvious reasons. There were also many old folks tired of life who wanted to pass on to the next world to rest from miseries of this one. **D**

La Tia Miseria was blamed by these people for their troubles, of course. Not wishing to be unfair, the old woman made a deal with her prisoner, Death: if he promised not ever to come for her again, she would give him his freedom. He agreed. And that is why there are two things you can always count on running into in this world: Misery and Death: *La miseria y la muerte.*[2]

2. **y la muerte** (ee lah MWEHR tay).

C **Literary Focus** **Patterns** What parallel episodes can you find in both "Aunty Misery" and "The Monkey's Paw"?

Vocabulary **gnarled** (nahrld) *adj.:* covered with knots; twisted.

D **Read and Discuss** What is the connection between Death being stuck in Aunty Misery's tree and what is going on in the rest of the world?

Applying Your Skills

Aunty Misery

RA.L.8.3 Explain how authors pace action and use subplots, parallel episodes and climax. **RP.8.1** Apply reading comprehension strategies, including making predictions, comparing and contrasting, recalling and summarizing and making inferences and drawing conclusions. *Also covered* **VO.8.4; WA.8.1.c**

Respond and Think Critically

Reading Focus

Quick Check

1. Who is Aunty Misery's first visitor? What wish of hers does he grant?
2. What bargain does Aunty Misery make with her second visitor?

Read with a Purpose

3. What happens as a result of Aunty Misery's wish?

Reading Skills: Comparing and Contrasting

4. Now, fill in the second column of your chart. Use your chart to answer questions 10 and 11.

	"The Monkey's Paw"	"Aunty Misery"
Parallel episodes within a story	three wishes	
Literary patterns across stories	mysterious guest arrives magical object	

Vocabulary Check

Match the Vocabulary words with their definitions.

5. **gnarled**   **a.** twisted
6. **hospitality**   **b.** generosity

Literary Focus

Literary Analysis

7. **Identify** What story clues reveal that Aunty Misery is clever?
8. **Interpret** The folk tale states that there are two things you can always count on in this world: misery and death. What does that saying mean?
9. **Extend** According to the folk tale, what happens in the world when there is no death? What other effects can you imagine if there were no death?

Literary Skills: Literary Patterns

10. **Identify** What parallel episodes can you find in "Aunty Misery"?
11. **Interpret** Compare the outcomes of Aunty Misery's wish with those of Mr. White's wishes. What can you conclude about the consequences of human desire?

Writing Focus

Think as a Reader/Writer

Use It in Your Writing Cofer uses short, simple sentences in the telling of this folk tale. Choose a setting that intrigues you—it can be imaginary or real. Using Cofer's simple style, try writing a paragraph that describes the setting. Observe the effect of this style. Now, rewrite your paragraph using longer, more complex sentences. How does the overall effect of the description change?

COMPARING TEXTS

Wrap Up

RP.8.1 Apply reading comprehension strategies, including making predictions, comparing and contrasting, recalling and summarizing and making inferences and drawing conclusions. **WA.8.4.d** Write informational essays or reports, including research, that: support the main ideas with facts, details, examples and explanations from sources *Also covered* **RA.L.8.3**

The Monkey's Paw / Aunty Misery

Writing Focus

Writing a Comparison-Contrast Essay

Use It in Your Writing Write an essay comparing the patterns you find within and across "The Monkey's Paw" and "Aunty Misery." To help plan your essay, review the chart you completed after you read each story. The chart will help you focus on story elements that are similar and different. Also, ask yourself these questions:

- How does the pattern of wishes set in motion each story's events?
- What are the outcomes of Mr. White's and Aunty Misery's wishes? How are these outcomes similar and different?
- What does the ending of each story suggest about the consequences of people's desires being fulfilled?

You do not have to write about all of these elements in your essay. Explore the elements that most interest you.

There are two basic ways you can organize the body of your essay:

1. **The Block Method** If you choose this organizational structure, you will discuss one story at a time. Your first few paragraphs might look like this:

   Paragraph 1: "The Monkey's Paw" (parallel episodes; other literary patterns; lesson about life)

   Paragraph 2: "Aunty Misery" (parallel episodes; other literary patterns; lesson about life)

2. **The Point-by-Point Method** If you use this organizational structure, you will discuss each literary element in turn, explaining how it is used in each story. Your first three paragraphs might look like this:

   Paragraph 1: Parallel episodes in "The Monkey's Paw" and in "Aunty Misery"

   Paragraph 2: Common literary patterns in "The Monkey's Paw" and in "Aunty Misery"

   Paragraph 3: Lessons about life in "The Monkey's Paw" and in "Aunty Misery"

At the end of your essay, tell which story you prefer and why. Which story challenged you more as a reader? Explain your opinions.

Evaluation Criteria for a Comparison-Contrast Essay

An effective comparison-contrast essay

- uses the opening paragraph to clearly state what is being compared and contrasted
- conveys a main idea in a thesis statement
- is organized logically and effectively
- cites appropriate details or passages from the text to support ideas
- has been carefully proofread for spelling, punctuation, and grammar errors

What Do You Think Now?

After reading these stories, what new idea about wishes and desires do you have? Explain.

Text Structures

CONTENTS

What Do You Think? How can science help us fulfill our wishes?

QuickWrite

List some of the ways that science has changed our lives, for better or for worse.

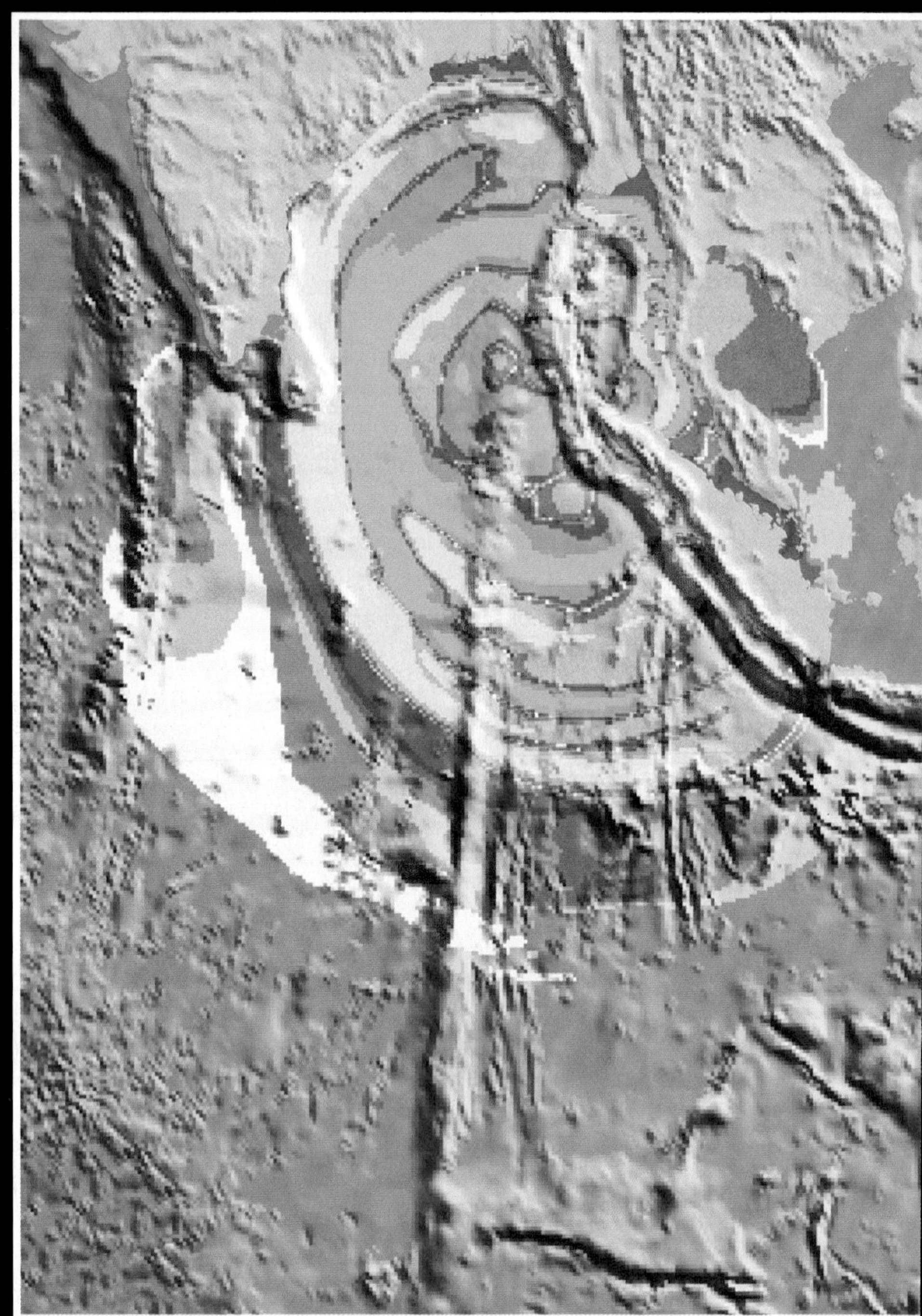

Tsunami two hours after earthquake.

TEXTBOOK CHAPTER
Preparing to Read

RA.I.8.9 Distinguish the characteristics of consumer materials, functional or workplace documents and public documents. *Also covered* **RP.8.3**

Physical Science

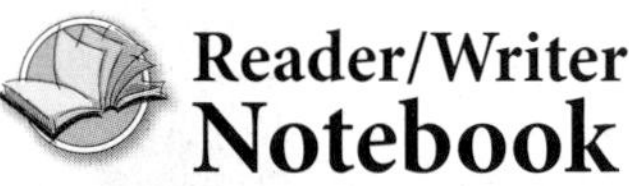

Use your **RWN** to complete the activities for this selection.

Informational Text Focus

Structure and Purpose of a Textbook The pages of a textbook are filled with useful information, but you have to know how to find it. Here are some of the features that will help you find your way through a textbook:

- **Table of Contents** This list appears at the front of the book and shows the book's structure and the major topics covered.
- **Headings** These words in large bold type signal key topics of a section; subheadings divide text into more specific topics.
- **Diagrams** Diagrams such as graphs, charts, and outlines visually present an idea or concept.
- **Captions** Text that is placed beneath an illustration, photo, or diagram helps to explain the image's significance.
- **Text Styles** Boldface text and italicized text draw your attention to key ideas and terms.

Into Action The headings in a textbook can help when you take notes. As you read the chapter in *Physical Science,* write each main heading on a separate notecard. Take notes about the most important ideas under each heading.

I. What Are Scientific Methods?	II. Asking a Question	III. Forming a Hypothesis
• ways scientists solve problems • use steps	• observations lead to questions • example—Czarnowski and Triantafyllou	

Vocabulary

observation (ahb zuhr VAY shuhn) *n.:* act of noticing. *Scientists can learn about glaciers from careful observation of their movements.*

hypothesis (hy PAHTH uh sihs) *n.:* possible explanation or answer. *Once a scientist has developed a hypothesis to answer a scientific question, he or she has to test the hypothesis.*

necessarily (nehs uh SAIR uh lee) *adv.:* unavoidably; in every case. *Conclusions based on only one experiment are not necessarily reliable or true.*

Language Coach

Prefixes A thesis is an idea or theory. Which word on the list above contains the word *thesis*? What prefix is added to *thesis*? How does that prefix alter the meaning of the word?

Writing Focus

Preparing for **Constructed Response**

Textbooks often use examples to help clarify information. As you read the textbook chapter that follows, record the examples you find in your *Reader/Writer Notebook*.

Learn It Online

Do pictures help you learn? Try the *PowerNotes* version of this lesson on:

go.hrw.com L8-109 

Read with a Purpose

Read to learn about scientific methods and how and why scientists use them.

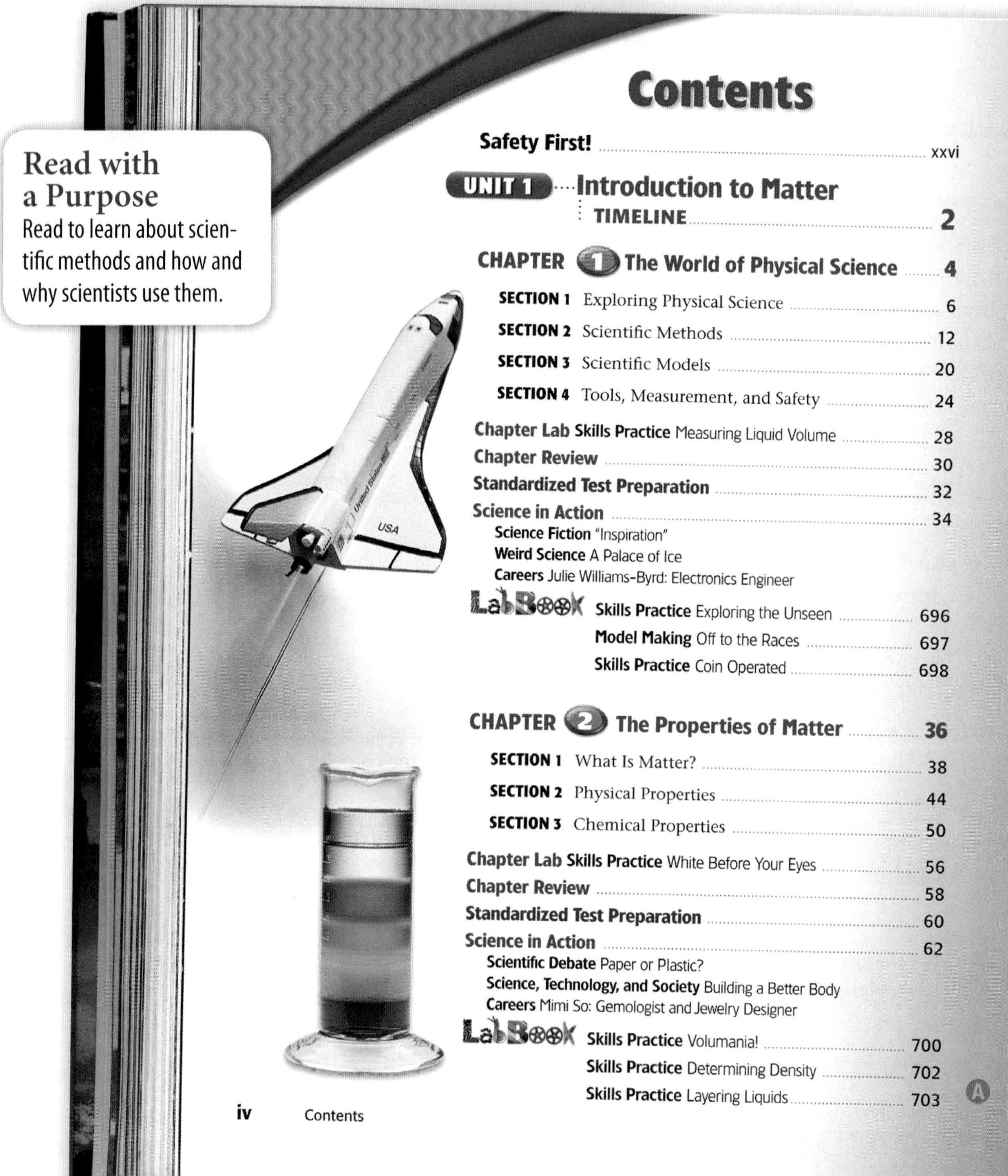

Contents

A

A **Informational Focus** **Structure and Purpose** Where is the topic of Scientific Methods covered?

B
Contents
v

B Informational Focus Structure and Purpose What does this table of contents tell you about the structure of this textbook?

SECTION 2

Scientific Methods

Imagine that you are trying to improve ships. Would you study the history of shipbuilding? Would you investigate different types of fuel? Would you observe animals that move easily through water, such as dolphins and penguins?

Two scientists from the Massachusetts Institute of Technology (MIT) thought that studying penguins was a great way to improve ships! James Czarnowski (zahr NOW SKEE) and Michael Triantafyllou (tree AHN ti FEE loo) used scientific methods to develop *Proteus* (PROH tee uhs), the penguin boat. In the next few pages, you will learn how these scientists used scientific methods to answer their questions.

What You Will Learn

- Explain what scientific methods are.
- Explain how scientific methods are used to answer questions.
- Describe how a hypothesis is formed and tested.
- Identify methods that are used to analyze data.
- Explain how a conclusion can support or disprove a hypothesis.
- List methods of communicating data.

Vocabulary

scientific methods
observation
hypothesis
data

READING STRATEGY

Reading Organizer As you read this section, make a flowchart of the steps used in scientific methods.

What Are Scientific Methods?

Scientific methods are the ways in which scientists answer questions and solve problems. As scientists look for answers, they often use the same steps. But there is more than one way to use the steps. Look at **Figure 1.** This figure is an outline of the six steps on which scientific methods are based. Scientists may use all of the steps or just some of the steps during an investigation. They may even repeat some of the steps or do the steps in a different order. How they choose to use the steps depends on what works best to answer their question.

scientific methods a series of steps followed to solve problems

Figure 1 Steps of Scientific Methods

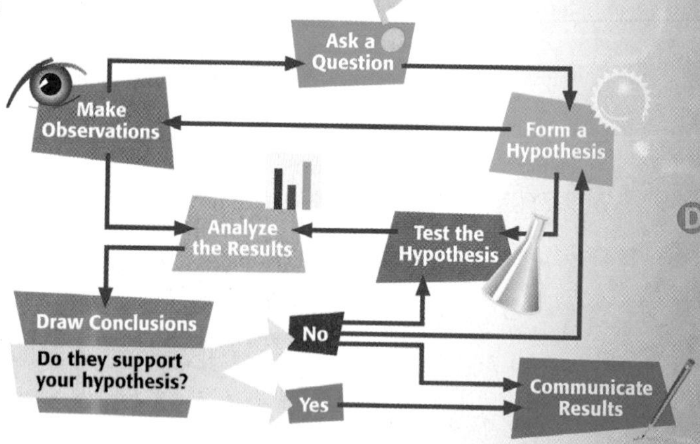

D

12 Chapter 1 The World of Physical Science

C **Read and Discuss** What have we learned about scientific methods?

D **Informational Focus** **Structure and Purpose** What is the purpose of this diagram?

Asking a Question

Asking a question helps focus the purpose of an investigation. Scientists often ask a question after making many observations. **Observation** is any use of the senses to gather information. Noting that the sky is blue or that a cotton ball feels soft is an observation. Measurements are observations that are made with tools, such as the ones shown in **Figure 2.** Keep in mind that observations can be made (and should be accurately recorded) at any point during an investigation. E

Reading Check What is the purpose of asking questions? *(See the Appendix for answers to Reading Checks.)*

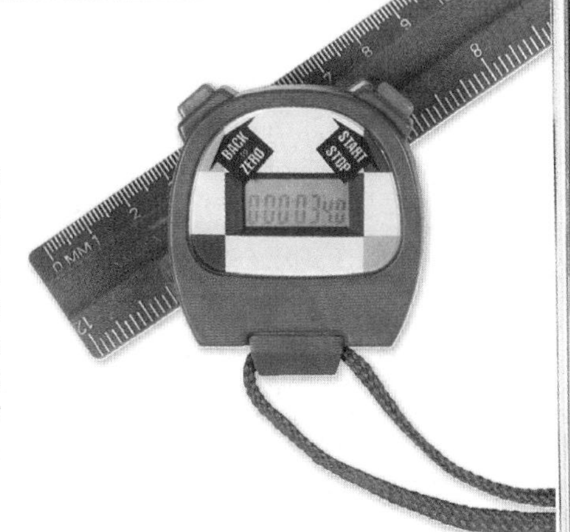

Figure 2 *Stopwatches and rulers are among the many tools used to make observations.*

observation the process of obtaining information by using the senses

A Real-World Question

Czarnowski and Triantafyllou, shown in **Figure 3,** are engineers, scientists who put scientific knowledge to practical use. Czarnowski was a graduate student at the Massachusetts Institute of Technology. He and Triantafyllou, his professor, worked together to observe boat propulsion (proh PUHL shuhn) systems. Then, they investigated how to make these systems work better. A propulsion system is what makes a boat move. Most boats have propellers to move them through the water.

Czarnowski and Triantafyllou studied the efficiency (e FISH uhn see) of boat propulsion systems. *Efficiency* compares energy output (the energy used to move the boat forward) with energy input (the energy supplied by the boat's engine). From their observations, Czarnowski and Triantafyllou learned that boat propellers are not very efficient.

Figure 3 *James Czarnowski* (left) *and Michael Triantafyllou* (right) *made observations about how boats work in order to develop* Proteus.

E **Read and Discuss** What do "asking a question" and "observation" have to do with scientific methods?

Vocabulary **observation** (ahb zuhr VAY shuhn) *n.:* act of noticing.

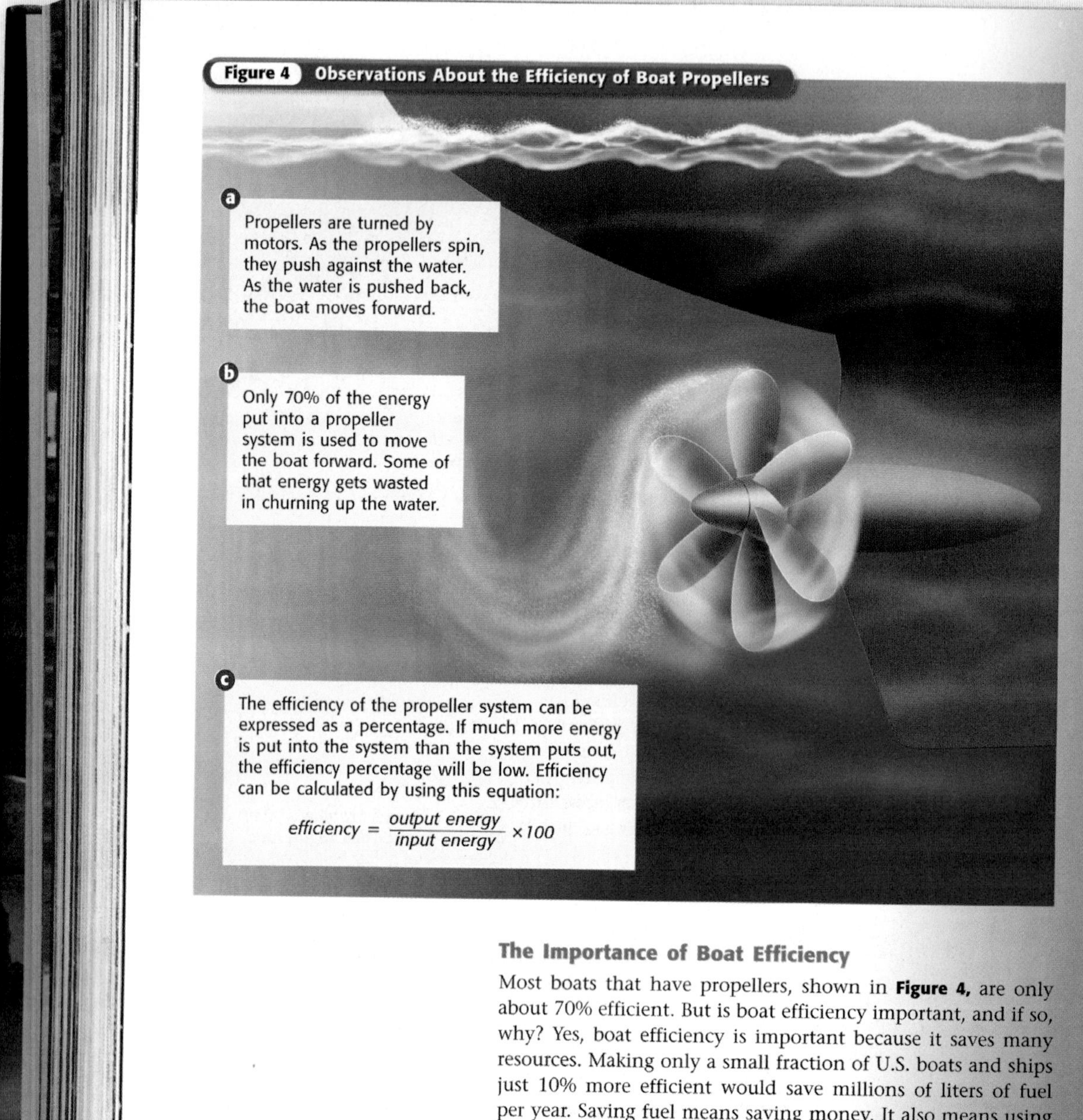

Figure 4 Observations About the Efficiency of Boat Propellers
a
Propellers are turned by motors. As the propellers spin, they push against the water. As the water is pushed back, the boat moves forward.
b
Only 70% of the energy put into a propeller system is used to move the boat forward. Some of that energy gets wasted in churning up the water.
c
The efficiency of the propeller system can be expressed as a percentage. If much more energy is put into the system than the system puts out, the efficiency percentage will be low. Efficiency can be calculated by using this equation:
$$efficiency = \frac{output\ energy}{input\ energy} \times 100$$

The Importance of Boat Efficiency

Most boats that have propellers, shown in **Figure 4,** are only about 70% efficient. But is boat efficiency important, and if so, why? Yes, boat efficiency is important because it saves many resources. Making only a small fraction of U.S. boats and ships just 10% more efficient would save millions of liters of fuel per year. Saving fuel means saving money. It also means using less of Earth's supply of fossil fuels. Based on their observations and all of this information, Czarnowski and Triantafyllou were ready to ask a question: How can boat propulsion systems be made more efficient? F

Reading Check **Why is boat efficiency important?**

14 Chapter 1 The World of Physical Science

F **Informational Focus** **Structure and Purpose** What purpose do the labels next to Figure 4 serve?

Figure 5 *Penguins use their flippers to "fly" underwater. As they pull their flippers toward their body, they push against the water, which propels them forward.*

Read with a Purpose
Why are understanding and applying scientific methods important?

Forming a Hypothesis

Once you've asked your question and made observations, you are ready to form a hypothesis (hie PAHTH uh sis). A **hypothesis** is a possible explanation or answer to a question. You can use what you already know and what you have observed to form a hypothesis.

A good hypothesis is testable. In other words, information can be gathered or an experiment can be designed to test the hypothesis. A hypothesis that is not testable isn't necessarily wrong. But there is no way to show whether the hypothesis is right or wrong.

hypothesis an explanation that is based on prior scientific research or observations and that can be tested

A Possible Answer from Nature

Czarnowski and Triantafyllou wanted to base their hypothesis on an example from nature. Czarnowski had made observations of penguins swimming at the New England Aquarium. He observed how quickly and easily the penguins moved through the water. **Figure 5** shows how penguins propel themselves. Czarnowski also observed that penguins, like boats, have a rigid body. These observations led to a hypothesis: A propulsion system that imitates the way that a penguin swims will be more efficient than a propulsion system that uses propellers.

Making Predictions

Before scientists test a hypothesis, they often predict what they think will happen when they test the hypothesis. Scientists usually state predictions in an if-then statement. The engineers at MIT might have made the following prediction: *If* two flippers are attached to a boat, *then* the boat will be more efficient than a boat powered by propellers. G

CONNECTION TO Biology

Adaptations Penguins, though flightless, are better adapted to water and extreme cold than any other birds are. Research these amazing birds to learn how they are adapted to their environment. Also, investigate the speed at which penguins can swim. Present this information in a poster.

G **Informational Focus** **Structure and Purpose** What are the headings and subheadings on this page? What information do those heads reveal?

Vocabulary **hypothesis** (hy PAHTH uh sihs) *n.:* possible explanation or answer.
necessarily (nehs uh SAIR uh lee) *adv.:* unavoidably; in every case.

Applying Your Skills

RA.I.8.9 Distinguish the characteristics of consumer materials, functional or workplace documents and public documents. **WA.8.4.b** Write informational essays or reports, including research, that: provide a clear and accurate perspective on the subject *Also covered* **VO.8.4**

Physical Science

Practicing the Standards

Informational Text and Vocabulary

1. Which question can you answer by reading the **table of contents** for *Physical Science*?
   A Where will I find information about organizing scientific data?
   B What is the scientific definition of *efficiency*?
   C How is the design of the *Proteus* different from the design of other boats?
   D What is the difference between controlled and variable parameters?

2. Which of the following text features helps explain the parts and significance of a **diagram**?
   A Headings
   B Italics
   C Captions
   D Table of contents

3. What kinds of details appear in **boldface** type in *Physical Science*?
   A Main ideas and chapter summaries
   B Names of scientists and inventors
   C Vocabulary words and references to figures
   D Diagram labels and key questions

4. *Necessarily* means —
   A Uncertainly
   B Unfriendly
   C Unavoidably
   D Unimportant

5. If you make a *hypothesis*, you —
   A avoid a dangerous situation
   B analyze the results of an experiment
   C solve one problem but create another
   D come up with a possible explanation

6. What do you need to make an *observation*?
   A Your senses
   B Your imagination
   C Your encyclopedia
   D Your beliefs

Writing Focus Constructed Response

What features of the textbook excerpt did you find most useful in helping you understand the concepts being explained? Give reasons for your response.

What Do You Think Now?

How do scientific methods help us use science to fulfill our wishes?

NEWSPAPER ARTICLE

Preparing to Read

RA.I.8.9 Distinguish the characteristics of consumer materials, functional or workplace documents and public documents.

Hawaiian Teen Named Top Young Scientist

Reader/Writer Notebook

Use your **RWN** to complete the activities for this selection.

Informational Text Focus

Structure and Purpose of a Newspaper Article You can find factual information about current events in newspaper articles. Newspaper articles use the following features to answer the questions *who? what? when? where? why?* and *how?*

- **Headline** A headline usually appears in bold type and identifies the topic.
- **Dateline** The location from which the article was reported and the date appear in the dateline.
- **Byline** A byline gives the name of the reporter or news agency that created the article.
- **Lead** The lead appears at the beginning of the article and states the key event. Most leads grab readers' interest with a catchy or bold statement.
- **Tone** Tone is the writer's attitude toward the subject. The tone of many newspaper articles is serious and straightforward. The tone of magazine articles can be light, lively, or humorous.

Newspaper articles often follow an **inverted pyramid** structure: The most important information is presented first, followed by key details. Less-important details are placed last.

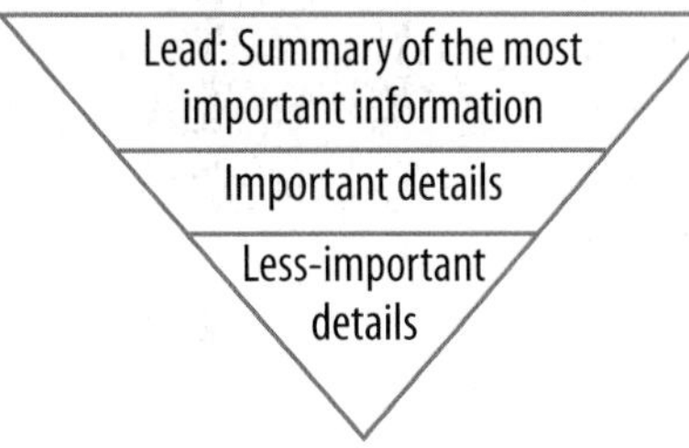

Vocabulary

scholarship (SKAHL uhr shihp) *n.:* money given to help a student continue to study. *The winner of the science challenge receives a generous scholarship for college.*

competition (kahm puh TIHSH uhn) *n.:* contest. *In this competition the winner will be the student who creates the best science project.*

Language Coach

Suffixes When the suffix *–ship* is added to a noun, it creates another noun that means "the quality or state of" that noun. One definition of the Vocabulary word *scholarship* is "state of being a scholar." See if you can list at least three other words that contain the suffix *–ship.*

Writing Focus Preparing for **Constructed Response**

When writing for an assessment, you will often be asked to share your opinion about a topic. As you read, think about how this article relates to your own ideas about science fairs and school contests. Jot down your thoughts in your *Reader/Writer Notebook.*

Learn It Online

Learn more about the structure of newspaper articles with the interactive Reading Workshops on:

go.hrw.com L8-117 

NEWSPAPER ARTICLE

Hawaiian Teen Named Top Young Scientist

from **Honolulu Advertiser**, October 27, 2006

Read with a Purpose

Read the following article to find out what it takes to become an award-winning young scientist.

Build Background

The Discovery Channel Young Scientist Challenge began in 1998. Each year, tens of thousands of middle school students enter science fairs around the country. After a semifinalist round, the best entries are selected to compete for the title of Top Young Scientist of the Year.

HONOLULU (AP) — A Hawaiian teen has won a $20,000 scholarship and the title America's Top Young Scientist of the Year.

"Right now, I'm more or less in shock," said Nolan Kamitaki, 14. "I was just happy to be in the national competition. I didn't expect this at all." **A**

The Discovery Channel Young Scientist Challenge is for student grades 5 through 8. The winners were announced Wednesday.

Kamitaki is now a freshman at Waiakea High School. To get to the national competition in Washington, D.C., he first had to win his school science fair, district science fair and then state science fair.

He entered with a project analyzing the effect arsenic[1] in local soils has had on Big Island school children. He also competed against 40 finalists in a series of challenges at the National Institutes of Health.

Nolan Kamataki (center), with the second and third place winners

"I tested for arsenic levels first in the soils of the Keaau and Hilo area, and I tested hair samples of students who attend nearby schools," Kamitaki said. "After reading newspaper

1. **arsenic:** a poisonous element.

A Informational Focus **Structure and Purpose** Do these first two paragraphs follow the inverted pyramid organization? Explain.

Vocabulary **scholarship** (SKAHL uhr shihp) *n.:* money given to help a student continue to study.
competition (kahm puh TIHSH uhn) *n.:* contest.

An aerial view near Hilo, one of the areas where Kamitaki tested the soil for arsenic.

Analyzing Visuals

Viewing and Representing What information does this image add to the newspaper article?

articles, I realized there is a big problem with arsenic in the Keaau area where a hotel is about to be built. I decided if it is a problem for tourists, it is definitely a problem for kids who go to the schools there."

Wayne Kamitaki is still having a hard time believing his son won. "He felt he had a chance, but we didn't want him to get too excited. The odds were difficult," he said. "We're so proud of him." The younger Kamitaki said he hasn't yet decided what he'd like to study in college, but he's leaning toward medicine or physics.

His father said he hopes his son's win will encourage other students in the islands. "He's from the public school system from Hawaii. Hawaii is such a small state and sometimes it is overlooked," he said. "Hopefully this shows people that Hawaii's kids can compete." **B**

Maryland Teen Takes Second Place **C**

A freshman at Montgomery Blair High School took second place in the Discovery Channel's Young Scientist Challenge for the science project he and a friend did at Robert Frost Middle School last year.

Jacob Hurwitz will get a $10,000 scholarship as a result. He and his partner Scott Yu presented their project called "Discombobulated,"[2] which took people with various education levels, family histories, and other factors and looked at their understanding of word permutations.[3]

The results, not surprisingly, indicated that those who attended preschool or whose parents went to college did better, while those who often missed class did the worst.

2. **discombobulated** (dihs kuhm BAHB yuh lay tihd): slang term that means "very confused."
3. **permutations:** here, the different forms of related words, such as *perspective, respected, spectacles.*

Read with a Purpose What qualities do you think helped the competition winners succeed?

B **Read and Discuss** What have we learned about Nolan Kamitaki?

C **Informational Focus** **Structure and Purpose** What new topic does this subheading introduce?

NEWSPAPER ARTICLE
Applying Your Skills

RA.I.8.9 Distinguish the characteristics of consumer materials, functional or workplace documents and public documents. **WA.8.5.b** Write persuasive compositions that: support arguments with detailed evidence; *Also covered* **VO.8.4**

Hawaiian Teen Named Top Young Scientist

Practicing the Standards

Informational Text and Vocabulary

1. What information do you learn in the **lead** of this newspaper article?
   - **A** The winner's science fair project was about arsenic.
   - **B** There are high levels of arsenic in some of Hawaii's soil.
   - **C** Students from the fifth through eighth grades compete in this national science contest.
   - **D** A teenager from Hawaii was named America's Top Young Scientist.

2. In what feature of a newspaper article would you find the place where the story was reported?
   - **A** Headline
   - **B** Lead
   - **C** Dateline
   - **D** Byline

3. Which of the following statements from the article answers both *where?* and *who?* questions?
   - **A** "The Discovery Channel Young Scientist Challenge is for student grades 5 through 8."
   - **B** "Wayne Kamitaki is still having a hard time believing his son won."
   - **C** "Kamitaki is now a freshman at Waiakea High School."
   - **D** "The winners were announced Wednesday."

4. A *competition* is one kind of —
   - **A** strategy
   - **B** understanding
   - **C** reward
   - **D** contest

5. The purpose of a *scholarship* is to help a student —
   - **A** remember facts
   - **B** avoid tests
   - **C** skip a grade
   - **D** afford to keep studying

Writing Focus Constructed Response

Winning a contest feels great, but losing is not so fun. Do you think that contests such as science fairs are good for students? Share your opinion, and give examples to support it.

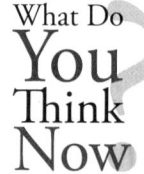

What Do You Think Now?

Nolan Kamitaki's scientific study won him a prize. What other benefits might his study have had?

INSTRUCTIONS

Preparing to Read

The Scientific Method

RA.I.8.9 Distinguish the characteristics of consumer materials, functional or workplace documents and public documents.

Informational Text Focus

Structure and Purpose of Instructions Effective instructions can tell you how to do anything from making a pizza to building a robot. It's important to read instructions carefully before you begin any project. The quality of your results—and sometimes your safety—depends on how well you read and follow instructions. Pay attention to these elements when you read instructions:

- **Headings** Large or boldface words that summarize each step.
- **Signal Words** Numbers and words like *first, next, then,* and *last* tell you the correct order to follow.
- **Tone** Most instructions are written in a direct style with few unnecessary words.
- **Technical Vocabulary** Many instructions include words that are related to the task. Recipes, for example, include cooking terms; instructions for experiments use scientific language.

Into Action A sequence chart can help you summarize the most important steps in any instructions. Create a sequence chart like the one below to show the steps of the experiment you will read about. You may need to add more boxes.

First
Hold a ruler between someone's fingers at the one-inch mark.

↓

Then

↓

Last

Writing Focus

Preparing for **Constructed Response**

In your *Reader/Writer Notebook,* note how the writer of these instructions uses numbers, letters, and text features such as boldface to make the steps of the experiment clear and easy to follow.

Use your **RWN** to complete the activities for this selection.

Vocabulary

formulated (FAWR myuh lay tihd) *v.:* formed in one's mind; developed. *Once she formulated her hypothesis, she could begin the experiment.*

correlate (KAWR uh layt) *v.:* show the connection between things. *It is important to correlate the results of your experiment to make sure that your cause and effect are really related.*

verify (VEHR uh fy) *v.:* show to be true; confirm. *To verify the results of an experiment, you must repeat it and get the same results.*

Language Coach

Word Forms The Vocabulary words above are all verbs. *Formulation, correlation,* and *verification* are noun forms of the Vocabulary words. In your *Reader/Writer Notebook,* jot down the definitions of these noun forms in your own words. Consult a dictionary if you need help.

Learn It Online
There's more to words than just definitions. Get the whole story on:

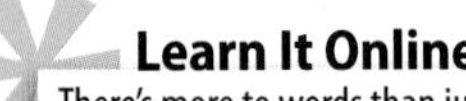

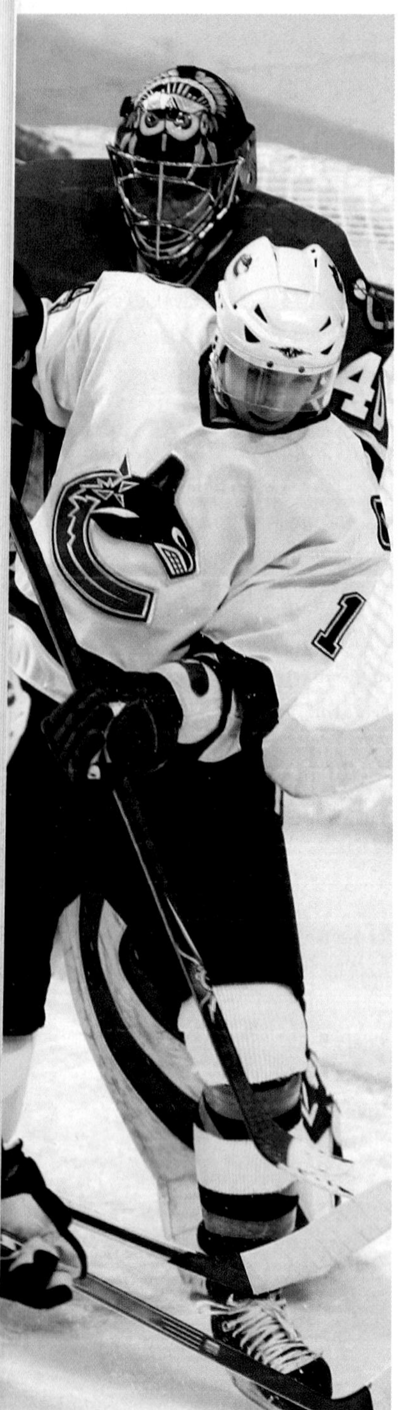

The Scientific Method

from **Current Science**

Read with a Purpose

Read the following selection to learn how to conduct your own experiment.

One of the ways that science differs from other branches of knowledge is that scientists follow their own special path of inquiry. That path is called the *scientific method.* The basic steps in the scientific method are as follows:

1. State the problem. A

Often the first step in the scientific method involves simply noticing something—making an observation. For example, you have a friend who is very good at sports. Your friend also seems to have very fast reflexes—he or she responds very quickly when a ball or a puck is coming his or her way.

Could it be that having fast reflexes is what has made your friend a star athlete? In asking yourself that question, you have come up with a *research question.*

2. Gather information.

To answer your question, you might begin by gathering information on the subject from science books and journals. You might try to find out whether other scientists have explored the same question. You might also try to find out as much as you can about human reflexes and how best to test them.

A **Informational Focus** **Structure and Purpose** Why are the headings numbered?

3. Form a hypothesis.

Using all of the information you've gathered, you are then ready to suggest a possible solution to your problem in the form of a *hypothesis,* or an educated guess. In this case, you hypothesize that having fast reflexes determines a person's success at sports.

Once you've formulated your hypothesis, you must test it. You must find evidence that either supports or disproves your hypothesis. **B**

4. Perform experiments.

In other words, you must perform an experiment. Experiments are performed according to specific directions. By following those directions, scientists can be confident that the information they uncover will clearly support or disprove the hypothesis.

For a study of human reflexes, you might perform a reaction-time test following these directions.

A. Hold one end of a ruler so that the other end is dangling between a subject's open thumb and middle finger. The 1-inch mark on the ruler should hang right between the subject's two open fingers.

B. Without warning, drop the ruler. The subject must catch the ruler between his or her two fingers.

C. Note the spot where the subject caught the ruler. The lower the inch number at the point where the subject caught the ruler, the faster the subject's reaction time. Record the result. **C**

Perform the reaction-time test on many subjects who are the same age but who have achieved different levels of athletic success. Some subjects will be top athletes; others will be average athletes; still others will be people who don't play sports well at all.

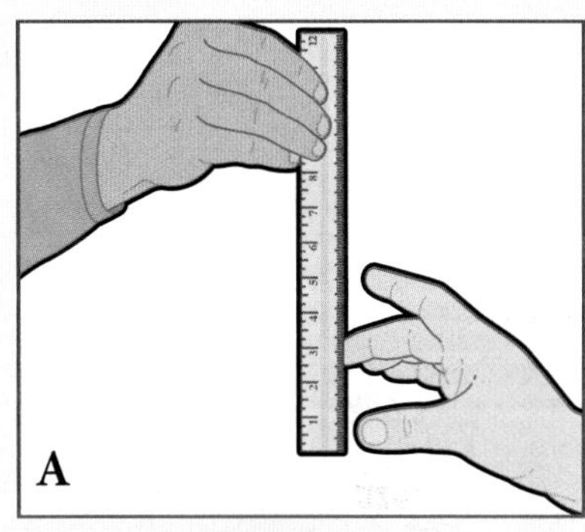

A

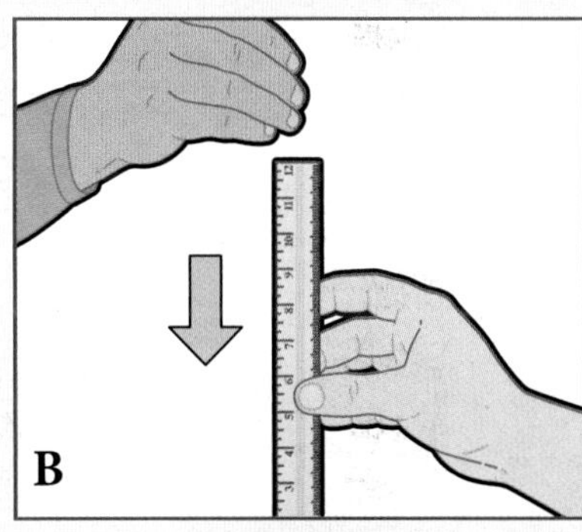

B

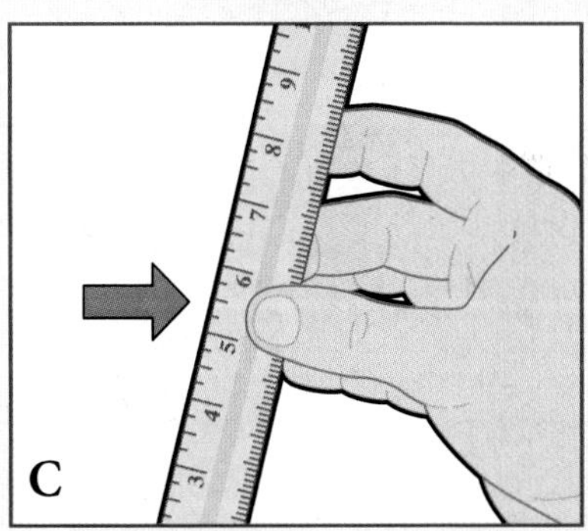

C

B **Read and Discuss** What has the author told us about the scientific method?

C **Informational Focus** **Structure and Purpose** What structural element makes the instructions for this reaction-time experiment clear?

Vocabulary **formulated** (FAWR myuh lay tihd) *v.:* formed in one's mind; developed.

5. Record and analyze data.

Once all your subjects have been tested and you have recorded all your data, you must *analyze* the data. In this study, you will need to correlate your results. In other words, you will need to see whether there exists a match between the subjects' athletic ability and their individual scores on the ruler test. If the correlation is strong, you will find that top athletes did indeed have fast reaction times on the ruler test and poor athletes had slow reaction times on the ruler test.

6. Reach a conclusion.

With your evidence in hand, you can arrive at a *conclusion,* one that either supports or does not support the hypothesis. In this case, you might find, as many other scientists have found, that reaction time doesn't determine athletic achievement. **D**

7. Repeat the process.

In order to be satisfied that the data and your conclusion were accurate, you must verify the results—that is, repeat the experiment. Before other scientists accept your conclusion, they may repeat the experiment, too.

Even if scientists accept your conclusion, one answer inevitably leads to at least another question. In this case, you might want to find out whether fast reflexes are something a person is born with or whether they can be learned. The pursuit of scientific knowledge never ends.

Read with a Purpose What experiments might you undertake?

D Informational Focus **Structure and Purpose** Why are the terms *analyze* and *conclusion* italicized?

Vocabulary **correlate** (KAWR uh layt) *v.:* show the connection between things.
verify (VEHR uh fy) *v.:* show to be true; confirm.

INSTRUCTIONS

Applying Your Skills

RA.I.8.9 Distinguish the characteristics of consumer materials, functional or workplace documents and public documents. **WA.8.3.c** Write business letters, letters to the editor and job applications that: include appropriate facts and details; *Also covered* **VO.8.4**

The Scientific Method

Practicing the Standards

Informational Text and Vocabulary

1. Which of these actions form the first step of the scientific method?

A Form an explanation for something confusing.

B Conduct an experiment to test your ideas.

C Notice something that you cannot explain.

D Make sure that the results of an experiment are accurate.

2. Which **text structure** tells you when to do the steps in these instructions?

A boldface heads

B instructional tone

C numbered list

D technical vocabulary

3. What is the **tone** of these instructions?

A Clear and direct

B Light and amusing

C Overstated and exaggerated

D Strong and emotional

4. When you *correlate* data, you show how the results are —

A important

B related

C perfect

D random

5. How can you *verify* the results of an experiment?

A Show that the results are always true.

B Share the results with others.

C Change the results to match your hypothesis.

D Throw out results that do not make sense.

6. A scientist who has *formulated* a hypothesis has —

A received results in a test

B developed an explanation

C tested his or her theory

D incorrectly tested it

Writing Focus Constructed Response

Create guidelines for students to follow during a fire drill. Use features such as numbering, lettering, and headings to structure the steps and ensure a safe outcome.

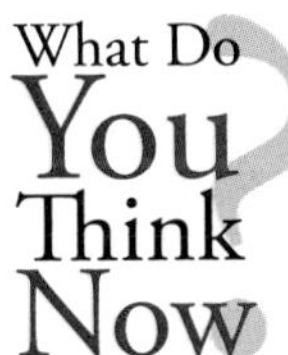

What Do You Think Now?

How can pursuing a career in science fulfill both one's personal wishes and those of nonscientists?

Writing Workshop

Personal Narrative

Write with a Purpose

Write a personal narrative about a significant experience in your life. Include important and vivid details as you tell what happened, and explain why this experience continues to be meaningful to you. Your **purpose** for writing is to entertain your **audience** by sharing a meaningful event.

A Good Personal Narrative

- focuses on a single incident
- is told from your point of view, using the pronoun "I"
- relates events in a clear order, usually chronological
- includes transitions that help readers follow the events
- includes sensory details and vivid verbs that bring the people, places, and events to life
- makes clear what the experience means to the writer

See page 134 for complete rubric.

Reader/Writer Notebook

Use your **RWN** to complete the activities for this workshop.

Think as a Reader/Writer

In this collection, you've seen the techniques writers use, and you've also practiced some of those techniques. Now it's time to tell about your own experiences by using vivid details that will engage your reader. A good personal narrative not only tells what happened but reveals why the experience is important to the writer—and perhaps to the reader, too. To get started, take a few minutes to read this excerpt from *Woodsong* by Gary Paulsen.

> There was a point where an old logging trail went through a small, sharp-sided gully—a drop of fifty or so feet—then scooted across a frozen stream and up the other side. It might have been a game trail that was slightly widened or an old foot trail that had not caved in. Whatever it was, I came onto it in the middle of January. The dogs were very excited. New trails always get them tuned up and they were fairly smoking as we came to the edge of the gully.
>
> I did not know it was there and had been letting them run, not riding the sled brake to slow them, and we virtually shot off the edge.
>
> The dogs stayed on the trail, but I immediately lost all control and went flying out into space with the sled. As I did, I kicked sideways, caught my knee on a sharp snag, and felt the wood enter under the kneecap and tear it loose.
>
> I may have screamed then.

← Details such as these make the **setting** clear.

← Paulsen tells his story by using the **first-person point of view.**

← Use of **transitions** helps to make the order of events clear.

← The author shares his **personal experiences** through details like these.

Think About the Professional Model

With a partner, discuss the following questions about the model.

1. What specific sensory details does the writer include?
2. Why do you think the experience was significant to the writer?

OH **WA.8.1.a** Write narratives that: sustain reader interest by pacing action and developing an engaging plot; **WP.8.8** Drafting, Revising and Editing: Group related ideas into paragraphs, including topic sentences following paragraph form, and maintain a consistent focus reinforced by parallel structures across paragraphs. **WP.8.15** Drafting, Revising and Editing: Proofread writing, edit to improve conventions and identify and correct fragments and run-ons. **WP.8.13** Drafting, Revising and Editing: Rearrange words, sentences and paragraphs, and add transitional words and phrases to clarify meaning.

Prewriting

Choose a Topic

Use the Idea Starters in the margin to help you recall some memorable experiences that you enjoy telling people about. Ask yourself the following questions about each experience on your list:

- What specific details, such as sights, sounds, smells, and sensations, do I remember about the experience?
- What does the incident reveal about me or about someone else?
- Why does this experience continue to be important to me?
- Why might reading about it be important or interesting for someone else?
- Am I comfortable sharing my thoughts about the incident with my readers?

Gather Details

As you decide what experience you would like to write about, gather the details that you want to include. Ask yourself these *5 W-How?* questions:

- *Who* was involved in the experience, and what did he or she say?
- *What* happened, and in what order did events occur?
- *When* did I have this experience?
- *Where* did the events happen?
- *Why* did the events happen? What set them in motion?
- *How* did I feel about the events at the time, and how do I feel now? *How* do I want my readers to feel about my experience?

To be sure that you recall the details clearly and coherently, create a chart of events like the one below:

Time	Experience	Details
when I was 13	I was the only middle school student to become a varsity cross-country runner.	I dedicated myself to running; I easily passed the older racers.

Idea Starters

- a childhood adventure
- going to a family reunion
- my first day of middle school
- winning or losing a big game
- attending a birthday party

Your Turn

Get Started Making notes in your **RWN,** decide on a specific experience to write about. Then, use a chart like the one on the left to gather details about the experience. Your notes and chart will help you plan your personal narrative.

Learn It Online
An interactive graphic organizer can help you generate and organize ideas. Try one at:

Think About Audience and Purpose

Before you begin your draft, think about your **audience** and about your **purpose** for writing. This will help you decide what details to include and what ideas to emphasize. Jot down answers to the following questions:

- Who will my narrative be read by? Will it be read by my classmates? my teacher? my family? What information will they need to understand my story?
- Why am I writing about this experience? Do I want to make my audience laugh—or cry? Do I want them to understand something about me or about the world we live in?

Plan Your Narrative

What will you include in your personal narrative? Use an outline like the one below to help you plan your personal narrative.

Plan for a Personal Narrative

Write what the experience means to you: ____________

Introduction (in the words you'll actually use): ____________

Body (Order of events):

1. ____________
2. ____________
3. ____________
4. ____________

Conclusion (in the words you'll actually use): ____________

Here is one writer's outline for a personal narrative. Use this model to help you create your own plan.

Personal Narrative

This experience was significant to me because I learned that the most important thing is to do your best.

Introduction: "This is going to be the year for me," I thought.

Body:

1. *I prepared to win the first race by training hard, so that I would make the varsity team.*
2. *In the race, I ran as fast as I could, and only one runner kept up.*
3. *The other runner at first fell behind but caught up with me at the end.*
4. *I won a varsity letter and met my goal.*

Conclusion: Proud of myself, I thought, "I did my best this year, and next year I'll do even better."

Peer Review

Share your completed plan with a peer. Ask your peer to offer concrete suggestions for improving your plans for your personal narrative.

Your Turn

Plan Your Narrative To help you decide what to include in your personal narrative, make a **personal narrative plan.** Then review your plan, asking yourself which details you should emphasize and which you could add to make your narrative more effective. Remember to keep in mind your **purpose** and **audience.**

Drafting

Keep Point of View Consistent

In a personal narrative you'll use the **first-person point of view** pronouns (*I, me, my*) to refer to yourself. Be sure to use your natural voice—the words and phrases you would use when telling the story to your friends. Your **tone** reveals your attitude about your topic.

Framework for a Personal Narrative

Introduction
- Begin with an engaging first sentence.
- Include details about when and where the experience took place.

Body
- Relay the order of events using sensory details and vivid verbs.
- Include your thoughts and feelings as the events unfold.

Conclusion
- Reveal why the experience is meaningful.

Use Sensory Details and Vivid Verbs

Because Gary Paulsen wants us to appreciate the action and the danger of his adventure, he uses **sensory details** such as "fairly smoking" and "flying out into space." You want your readers to appreciate how exciting or fun or challenging your experience was to you.

One way to grab and hold readers' attention is to use **vivid verbs**—verbs that place the reader right in the middle of the action. Verbs help set the tone and the pace of an essay. For example, instead of *I took,* you might write *I grabbed, grasped,* or *snatched*. Instead of *We walked*, you might write *We hiked, strolled*, or *staggered*, depending on what you are trying to communicate.

Grammar Link **Punctuating a Series of Verbs**

When you write a personal narrative, you may have more than one action verb in a sentence. Study the following sentence from *Woodsong.* Be sure to follow the rules for punctuating a series of verbs when you write your personal narrative.

> As I did, I kicked sideways, caught my knee on a sharp snag, and felt the wood enter under the kneecap . . .

- If there are more than two verbs in a series, you should usually separate the verbs or verb phrases with a comma, as in the example above.
- If all of the verbs or verb phrases are joined by *and, or,* or *nor,* do not follow the above rule. You do not need commas to separate the verbs or verb phrases. Here are two examples:

  I played and I sang and I danced.

  Sara will dance or sing or play an instrument in the talent show.

Writing Tip

When the last two verbs in a series are joined by *and*, the comma before the *and* is sometimes omitted. To review the rules for using commas in a series, see the Language Handbook.

Your Turn

Write Your Draft After creating your framework, use it to help you write a draft of your personal narrative. Think about the following questions as you write your draft:
- What **tone** should I use in my narrative?
- How can the use of sensory details and vivid verbs bring the experience to life?
- Have I used commas correctly with series of action verbs?

Peer Review

Work with a partner and review each other's drafts. Answer each question on the chart to the right to see how you could improve your drafts. Be sure to take notes about what your partner suggests.

Evaluating and Revising

Read the questions in the left column of the chart, and use the tips in the middle column to make revisions to your personal narrative. The right column suggests techniques that you can use to revise your draft.

Personal Narrative: Guidelines for Content and Organization

Evaluation Questions	Tips	Revision Techniques
1. Does your introduction grab your reader's attention and set the scene?	**Put stars** next to interesting statements. **Circle** details that show when and where the experience happened.	**Add** an attention-getting quotation or statement. **Add** details about where and when the event took place.
2. Are events in chronological order?	**Number the events.** Check that the sequence shows the actual order of events.	**Rearrange** events in the order in which they occurred. **Add** transitions to link events.
3. Are the details describing people, places, and events vivid and precise?	**Highlight** sensory details. In the margin, note which senses the sensory details appeal to.	**Elaborate** with sensory details, if necessary. **Delete** irrelevant details.
4. Have you used vivid action verbs?	**Circle** vivid verbs.	**Replace** vague, passive verbs with vivid verbs.
5. Is your choice of words and details appropriate for your audience and purpose?	**Put a box around** difficult or technical words. **Put brackets around** passages that do not support your purpose.	**Replace** difficult words with easier ones, or add explanations. **Rephrase** passages to help you achieve your purpose.
6. Have you included your thoughts and feelings?	**Put a check mark** next to statements of your feelings and thoughts.	**Add** specific details about feelings and thoughts, if necessary.
7. Does your conclusion reveal why the experience is meaningful?	**Underline** your statement about why the experience is meaningful.	**Add** a statement that explains why the experience is important to you.

Read this student's draft, the comments on its structure, and some suggestions for how the narrative could be made even stronger.

Student Draft

Today Is the Day

by Alex Bloom, Gray Middle School

"This is going to be the year for me," I thought. To achieve the standards I set for myself, I worked out every spare minute. As the season progressed, I focused even more on my running, securing a position on the school's track team. But I wanted more. Determined to be the only varsity cross-country runner from middle school, I pushed myself the extra mile. I made running part of my daily routine. I drank, ate, and slept running. I was determined to be prepared to win the first race of the year.

← The student's first-person **point of view** is established right away and maintained throughout the narrative.

Bang! The race began. "I can do this," I thought. I quickly passed most of the racers from the other teams, putting myself in the front of the pack. My hair blew from side to side in the wind, and my uniform was no longer neat. I sped past the rest of the racers, leaving them behind. Only one runner stayed with me throughout the race. We flew around every turn with speed and precision, competing, challenging each other. He fell back as I powered up the hill, I moved ahead, gaining distance. I turned into the final corner.

← The experience of the race highlights the personal narrative. **Vivid verbs** help create a sense of action and forward movement.

MINI-LESSON How to Add Descriptive Details

Notice that Alex's description of the race doesn't really help readers picture it. Alex might add details to the second paragraph to make the descriptions even more vivid to the reader.

Alex's Revision of Paragraph Two

Bang! The race began. "I can do this," I thought. I quickly passed most of the racers from the other teams, putting myself in the front of the pack. My ^long^ hair blew from side to side in the wind, and my ^bright red^ uniform was ~~no longer neat~~ ^drenched in sweat^. I sped past the rest of the racers, leaving them behind. Only one runner ^, a gangly freshman,^ stayed with me throughout the race.

Your Turn

Add Details Read your draft and then ask yourself: What sensory details and descriptive information would help my readers picture events better?

After writing the **climax** of the narrative, Alex reflects on what it means.

The final sentence of the narrative helps reveal the significance of Alex's experience.

Student Draft *continues*

I stepped carefully on the uneven surface, hoping not to twist my ankle. "I want to win this race," I thought. I used every bit of energy left in my exhausted body, but the other runner suddenly appeared right behind me. I guess you could call it a photo finish because we crossed the finish line neck and neck, but he won by inches. Then it hit me. It didn't matter if I won or not because I tried my hardest.

The season ended. An awards ceremony was held in the school cafeteria. The coach called everybody's name, and then he finally called mine. "This is the moment," I thought. "This is the moment of truth." I received a varsity letter, reaching the goal I had set. I was also named the Outstanding Middle School Runner of the Year. Proud of myself, I thought, "I did my best this year, and next year I'll do even better."

MINI-LESSON How to Add Transitions

In the final paragraph of his draft, Alex jumps from the end of the season to an awards ceremony. Then, he describes the coach calling "everybody's name." Alex does not use transitions to connect these ideas, and the sentences seem choppy. How can Alex describe what happened and make the passage of time clear? Transitions will help.

Alex revised the paragraph, adding transitions to show the passage of time and to connect the ideas. Transitions are written in blue.

Alex's Draft of Paragraph Four

The season ended. An awards ceremony was held in the school cafeteria. The coach called everybody's name, and then he finally called mine.

Alex's Revision of Paragraph Four

After many more races, the season ended. *I was excited when I went to the* ~~An~~ awards ceremony in the school cafeteria *later that month. Soon* the coach called everybody's name, and then he finally called mine. . . .

Your Turn

Add Transitions Read your draft and then ask yourself:

- Does each sentence flow logically from one idea to another?
- What transitional words, phrases, or sentences should I add to make my ideas flow more logically?

Proofreading and Publishing

Proofreading

Re-read your personal narrative, and look for errors in grammar, usage, spelling, and punctuation. Make sure that you have used commas correctly in any series of verbs or verb phrases.

Proofreading Partners Trade papers with a partner to proofread each other's work and discuss any possible changes. Then, prepare your final copy to share with your audience.

Grammar Link **Fixing Run-on Sentences**

As you read over your narrative, be sure that you have a period at the end of every complete thought. In the second paragraph of his draft, Alex's writing was not clear because he had a run-on sentence. To fix the run-on sentence, Alex needed to fix the punctuation.

He fell back as I powered up the hill, I moved ahead, gaining distance.

Notice how Alex separated the run-on sentence into two complete sentences simply by changing the comma to a period.

Publishing

Share your personal narrative with your audience. Here are some ways to share your essay:

- Give a copy of your narrative to friends, family members, and classmates. If you wish, add photographs or illustrations to your narrative.
- Read your narrative aloud to a group.

Reflect on the Process Thinking about how you wrote your personal narrative will help you in other writing that you'll do. In your **RWN,** make notes about what you learned and answer the following questions:

1. How did writing a personal narrative help you to better understand how you feel about your experience or what the importance of the experience might be?
2. What techniques did you use to convey the importance of that experience to your readers?

Proofreading Tip

Reading your narrative aloud may help you catch errors that you do not see when scanning the page. As you read aloud, pay attention to places where you stumble over phrases. There might be punctuation errors that you need to correct. Also pay attention to places where one thought runs into another without punctuation. These might be run-on sentences that need to end with a period.

Your Turn

Proofread and Publish Take time to proofread your work. Check to be sure you have fixed any run-on sentences. Also, correct any errors in punctuating a series of verbs. Some places where you could submit your work are:

- an online literary magazine
- your personal Web page
- a class anthology

Scoring Rubric

You can use one of the rubrics below to evaluate your personal narrative from the Writing Workshop or your response to the on-demand prompt on the next page.

6-Point Scale

Score 6 *Demonstrates advanced success*
- focuses consistently on a clear controlling idea
- shows effective organization throughout, with smooth transitions
- offers a thoughtful, creative approach to the narrative
- develops the narrative thoroughly, using incidents, details, and explanation
- exhibits mature control of written language

Score 5 *Demonstrates proficient success*
- focuses on a clear controlling idea
- shows effective organization, with transitions
- offers a thoughtful approach to the narrative
- develops the narrative competently, using incidents, details, and explanation
- exhibits sufficient control of written language

Score 4 *Demonstrates competent success*
- focuses on a clear controlling idea, with minor distractions
- shows effective organization, with minor lapses
- offers a mostly thoughtful approach to the narrative
- develops the narrative adequately, using some incidents, details, and explanation
- exhibits general control of written language

Score 3 *Demonstrates limited success*
- includes some loosely related ideas that distract from the controlling idea
- shows some organization, with noticeable gaps in the logical flow of ideas
- offers a routine, predictable approach to the narrative
- develops the narrative with uneven use of incidents, details, and explanation
- exhibits limited control of written language

Score 2 *Demonstrates basic success*
- includes loosely related ideas that seriously distract from the writer's controlling idea
- shows minimal organization, with major gaps in the logical flow of ideas
- offers a narrative that merely skims the surface
- develops the narrative with inadequate use of incidents, details, and explanation
- exhibits significant problems with control of written language

Score 1 *Demonstrates emerging effort*
- shows little awareness of the topic and purpose for writing
- lacks organization
- offers an unclear and confusing narrative
- develops the narrative in only a minimal way, if at all
- exhibits major problems with control of written language

4-Point Scale

Score 4 *Demonstrates advanced success*
- focuses consistently on a clear controlling idea
- shows effective organization throughout, with smooth transitions
- offers a thoughtful, creative approach to the narrative
- develops the narrative thoroughly, using incidents, details, and explanation
- exhibits mature control of written language

Score 3 *Demonstrates competent success*
- focuses on a clear controlling idea, with minor distractions
- shows effective organization, with minor lapses
- offers a mostly thoughtful approach to the narrative
- develops the narrative adequately, using some incidents, details, and explanation
- exhibits general control of written language

Score 2 *Demonstrates limited success*
- includes some loosely related ideas that distract from the controlling idea
- shows some organization, with noticeable gaps in the logical flow of ideas
- offers a routine, predictable approach to the narrative
- develops the narrative with uneven use of incidents, details, and explanation
- exhibits limited control of written language

Score 1 *Demonstrates emerging effort*
- shows little awareness of the topic and purpose for writing
- lacks organization
- offers an unclear and confusing narrative
- develops the narrative in only a minimal way, if at all
- exhibits major problems with control of written language

Preparing for **Timed Writing**

Personal Narrative

When responding to a prompt asking you to write a personal narrative, use what you have learned from this collection's Writing Workshop, the rubric on page 134, and the steps below.

Writing Prompt

Write a narrative in which you relate a significant personal experience. Use sensory details and vivid verbs to describe the experience, and tell readers why the experience is still meaningful to you.

Study the Prompt

Be sure to read the prompt carefully, and identify all parts of your task. Circle or underline key instructional words: *personal, narrative, details, significant,* and *experience*. Reread the prompt to make sure you understand your task.

Note that your narrative should not only describe the events of this experience but also the meaning the experience had for you.

Tip: Spend about five minutes studying the prompt.

Plan Your Response

First, think of some personal experiences that you feel comfortable writing about. Choose the most meaningful of those experiences as the subject of your narrative. Once you have settled on your subject, take notes on the following:

- specific details that you remember about the experience
- what the experience reveals about you or someone else
- why the experience is still important to you

Tip: Spend about fifteen minutes planning your response.

Respond to the Prompt

Using the notes you've just made, draft your narrative. Follow these guidelines:

- In the introduction, grab the reader's attention with an interesting opener, and set the scene with sensory details.
- In the body of your narrative, relate the events of your experience in a clear order, usually chronological.
- In the conclusion, state why the experience is meaningful to you.
- Remember to use a consistent first-person point of view.

Tip: Spend about twenty minutes writing your draft.

Improve Your Response

Revising Go back to the key aspects of the prompt. Have you used sensory details and vivid verbs? Have you used transitions to guide the reader?

Proofreading Take a few minutes to proofread your personal narrative to correct errors in grammar, spelling, punctuation, and capitalization. Make sure that all of your edits are neat, and erase any stray marks.

Checking Your Final Copy Before you turn in your personal narrative, read it one more time to catch any errors that you may have missed. You'll be glad that you took the extra time for one final review.

Tip: Save ten minutes to improve your paper.

Presenting an Oral Narrative

Speak with a Purpose

Adapt your written narrative into an oral narrative. After you have practiced delivering your narrative, present it to your class.

Think as a Reader/Writer Good stories aren't always fiction. They can be true stories about experiences that people have lived through. In fact, you probably tell such stories all the time—when you tell your friends about skiing over the weekend or about the time you had to rescue your cat from a tree. In this workshop you will turn a true story, or a personal narrative, into an oral presentation.

Adapt Your Personal Narrative

Make It Interesting

Think about how to tell your story so that you will capture your audience's attention. Remember, since your audience is listening to your narrative, not reading it, they have only one chance to understand what you are saying. Use these tips to help you develop an oral presentation your listeners will enjoy.

- **Background Information** Include extra information your listeners might need to understand your narrative.
- **Realistic Dialogue** Try to re-create the actual words of the people involved in the events.
- **Specific Action** Describe events directly and clearly.
- **Word Choice** Use vivid verbs and precise nouns to describe people, settings, and things. Use verbs that express either physical or mental activity (as opposed to *be* verbs such as *is, were, am,* and *been*).
- **Sensory Details** Select words that appeal to one or more of the five senses—sight, hearing, touch, taste, and smell.
- **Organization** Tell your story in chronological order. Use transitions to help listeners follow your story.
- **Conclusion** Sum up your story by sharing with listeners why your experience was memorable, fun, scary, or eye-opening.

Streamline

After you consider what to include, look back at your written narrative and consider what you can exclude. Remember that some words that are necessary for your readers may not be needed for your listeners—who will be receiving additional information through your delivery.

Use your **RWN** to complete the activities for this workshop.

OH **C.8.9** Deliver formal and informal descriptive presentations that convey relevant information and descriptive details. **C.8.7** Vary language choices as appropriate to the context of the speech. **C.8.6** Adjust volume, phrasing, enunciation, voice modulation and inflection to stress important ideas and impact audience response.

Deliver Your Personal Narrative

Engage Your Audience

Acting out information, rather than depending solely on your words, is an effective—and often more interesting—way to communicate an idea. **Verbal techniques,** the manner in which you use your voice, and **nonverbal techniques,** the manner in which you use your body, can help you communicate your message. For example, instead of telling your audience that a character is angry, you can show them by using facial expressions (such as scowling or glaring), raising the pitch of your voice to a shrill level, or changing the tone of your voice to sound irritated.

Verbal Techniques	Nonverbal Techniques
Volume No matter how loudly or softly you speak, be sure your audience can understand you.	**Facial Expressions** Smiling or frowning, looking puzzled or surprised can help you convey your meaning.
Rate Speak fast enough not to bore your listeners and slowly enough that they can follow your presentation.	**Gestures** Pointing, reaching, or banging can add emphasis to what you say, but be careful not to gesture needlessly.
Pitch Qualities of pitch, or modulation—such as high, low, shrill, musical, or rumbling—can help clarify your meaning.	**Posture** Whether you stand straight or slouch can influence the way your audience reacts to what you say.
Tone Your attitude toward what you are saying, such as amused, angry, or serious, should be clear from the tone of your voice.	**Appearance** You may want to dress more formally for a serious presentation but wear casual clothes for a humorous one.

Practice! Practice!

Practice your presentation in front of a mirror. Then, try a rehearsal in front of friends. Listen to their feedback, and consider their ideas as you practice and improve your presentation.

Note It

To avoid finding yourself tongue-tied when you present your personal narrative, jot down some notes. Your notes should be brief and easy to read so that you can glance at them without losing eye contact with your audience.

A Good Oral Presentation

- focuses on a single, important event
- contains details that allow listeners to visualize the people, settings, and events in the narrative
- is clearly organized so that listeners can easily follow the story
- holds listeners' attention through effective verbal and nonverbal techniques

Speaking Tip

Don't forget to breathe, and avoid rushing through your story. One way to stay in control is to pay attention to the punctuation in the written version of your narrative. Pause briefly for commas. Pause longer at periods. Allow your voice to convey the emotions indicated by question marks and exclamation points.

Learn It Online
Bring your presentation to a wider audience. Use the *Digital Storytelling* mini-site at:

go.hrw.com L8-137 

Literary Skills Review

Plot and Setting **Directions:** Read the passage. Then, answer each question that follows.

from The Cay by **Theodore Taylor**

In the novel The Cay, *Phillip, an eleven-year-old boy who is blind, is shipwrecked on a very small island, or cay, with a West Indian seaman named Timothy and a cat. Timothy dies while protecting Phillip during a hurricane. In this part of the story, Phillip is trying to make it on his own.*

The sun came out strong in the morning. I could feel it on my face. It began to dry the island, and toward noon, I heard the first cry of a bird. They were returning.

By now, I had taught myself to tell time, very roughly, simply by turning my head toward the direct warmth of the sun. If the angle was almost overhead, I knew it was around noon. If it was low, then of course, it was early morning or late evening.

There was so much to do that I hardly knew where to start. Get a campfire going, pile new wood for a signal fire, make another rain catchment for the water keg, weave a mat of palm fibers to sleep on. Then make a shelter of some kind, fish the hole on the reef, inspect the palm trees to see if any coconuts were left—I didn't think any could be up there—and search the whole island to discover what the storm had deposited. It was enough work for weeks, and I said to Stew Cat, "I don't know how we'll get it all done." But something told me I must stay very busy and not think about myself.

I accomplished a lot in three days, even putting a new edge on Timothy's knife by honing it on coral. I jabbed it into the palm nearest my new shelter, so that I would always know where it was if I needed it. Without Timothy's eyes, I was finding that in my world, everything had to be very precise; an exact place for everything.

On the fifth day after the storm, I began to scour the island to find out what had been cast up. It was exciting, and I knew it would take days or weeks to accomplish. I had made another cane and beginning with east beach, I felt my way back and forth, reaching down to touch everything that my cane struck; sometimes having to spend a long time trying to decide what it was that I held in my hands.

I found several large cans and used one of them to start the "time" can again, dropping five pebbles into it so that the reckoning would begin again from the night of

RA.L.8.3 Explain how authors pace action and use subplots, parallel episodes and climax. **RA.L.8.1** Identify and explain various types of characters and how their interactions and conflicts affect the plot. *Also covered* **RA.L.8.2**

the storm. I discovered an old broom, and a small wooden crate that would make a nice stool. I found a piece of canvas, and tried to think of ways to make pants from it, but I had no needle or thread.

Other than that, I found many shells, some bodies of dead birds, pieces of cork, and chunks of sponge, but nothing I could really put to good use.

It was on the sixth day after the storm, when I was exploring on south beach, that I heard the birds. Stew Cat was with me, as usual, and he growled when they first screeched. Their cries were angry, and I guessed that seven or eight might be in the air.

I stood listening to them; wondering what they were. Then I felt a beat of wing past my face, and an angry cry as the bird dived at me. I lashed out at it with my cane, wondering why they were attacking me.

Another dived down, screaming at me, and his bill nipped the side of my head. For a moment, I was confused, not knowing whether to run for cover under sea grape, or what was left of it, or try to fight them off with my cane. There seemed to be a lot of birds.

Then one pecked my forehead sharply, near my eyes, and I felt blood run down my face. I started to walk back toward camp, but had taken no more than three or four steps when I tripped over a log. I fell into the sand, and at the same time, felt a sharp pain in the back of my head. I heard a raging screech as the bird soared up again. Then another bird dived at me.

I heard Stew Cat snarling and felt him leap up on my back, his claws digging into my flesh. There was another wild screech, and Stew Cat left my back, leaping into the air.

His snarls and the wounded screams of the bird filled the stillness over the cay. I could hear them battling in the sand. Then I heard the death caw of the bird.

I lay still a moment. Finally, I crawled to where Stew Cat had his victim. I touched him; his body was rigid and his hair was still on edge. He was growling, low and muted.

Then I touched the bird. It had sounded large, but it was actually rather small. I felt the beak; it was very sharp.

Slowly, Stew Cat began to relax.

Wondering what had caused the birds to attack me, I felt around in the sand. Soon, my hand touched a warm shell. I couldn't blame the birds very much. I'd accidentally walked into their new nesting ground.

They were fighting for survival, after the storm, just as I was. I left Stew Cat to his unexpected meal and made my way slowly back to camp.

RA.L.8.3 Explain how authors pace action and use subplots, parallel episodes and climax. **RA.L.8.2** Analyze the influence of setting in relation to other literary elements. *Also covered* **WA.8.2**

1. What details tell you that the setting of this story is a tropical island?
   A. palm trees and coconuts
   B. warm sun
   C. a wooden crate
   D. returning birds

2. What aspect of the setting creates conflict for Phillip?
   A. destruction from the hurricane
   B. using the sun to tell time
   C. no coconuts left to eat
   D. items left by the storm

3. What detail of the setting adds horror to the story's mood?
   A. Timothy's knife
   B. Stew Cat
   C. a signal fire
   D. attacking birds

4. The climax of the story occurs when
   A. Phillip is alone with Stew Cat.
   B. Phillip hones his knife.
   C. Phillip trips over a log.
   D. Stew Cat kills the bird .

5. Phillip has an internal conflict over whether to
   A. build a campfire or hut.
   B. walk all around the island.
   C. run for cover or fight the birds.
   D. praise or scold Stew Cat.

Phillip hears birds screeching.		Stew Cat kills a bird.

6. If you were tracking the events of this passage in chronological order, which of the following events would you place in the empty box that appears above?
   A. Birds lay eggs in the sand.
   B. Birds attack Phillip.
   C. Stew Cat eats the bird.
   D. Phillip runs back to camp.

Short Answer

7. Identify the resolution, or how the problem of the story is solved. Use information from the passage to support your answer.

Extended Response

8. Describe one external conflict and one internal conflict that Phillip has. Is either of them resolved by the end of the story? Which one do you think makes surviving more difficult for Phillip? Explain.

Informational Skills Review

Text Structures **Directions:** Read the following documents. Then, read and respond to the questions that follow.

TEXTBOOK

CHAPTER 10

The Roman World 509 B.C.–A.D. 476

As the Roman Republic expanded to include new territories, it was transformed into an empire. Power rested in the hands of emperors, who gained increasing control over society. Under the rules of the early emperors, a long period of relative peace descended over the empire. This period of peace allowed trade and culture to flourish. . . .

NEWSPAPER ARTICLE

Violinist Stephanie Chang wows audience with virtuoso performance

Los Angeles, CA, November 10 — In one of the best concerts of the year, 28-year-old Stephanie Chang gave an electrifying performance of Beethoven's Violin Concerto. Ms. Chang, a native Californian, captivated the audience with a powerful blend of technique and emotion. . . .

INSTRUCTIONAL MANUAL

How to Use Your Wireless Headset Unit

Turning the unit on:

Press and hold main button for one second. Unit is on when blue light is flashing.

Linking the unit with your cell phone:

1. Press and hold main button and volume button simultaneously for five seconds. Blue light will remain lit.
2. Activate remote search for external devices from your cell phone.
3. Once your cell phone finds the unit, you will be asked to verify. Choose "Yes."
4. Your unit is now ready to be used with your phone.

RA.I.8.9 Distinguish the characteristics of consumer materials, functional or workplace documents and public documents.

1. What kind of text feature is "The Roman World 509 B.C.–A.D. 476"?
   A. byline
   B. dateline
   C. heading
   D. caption

2. What organizational pattern do the excerpts from the textbook and newspaper article follow?
   A. The main idea is introduced first and is followed by supporting details.
   B. Supporting details build up to the main idea.
   C. Details are presented in cause-and-effect order.
   D. The texts are organized chronologically.

3. Which of the following best describes the purpose of the newspaper article?
   A. to teach people how to perform activities
   B. to tell of current events
   C. to help readers categorize information
   D. to provide an overview of a historical event

4. The newspaper dateline tells of
   A. a recent violin concert.
   B. wireless headsets for cell phones.
   C. the exact time the events happened.
   D. the place and date the article was written.

5. Which of the following does the instructional manual not do?
   A. tell the user how to turn on the wireless headset
   B. provide customer service information
   C. describe how to link the headset to a cell phone
   D. give step-by-step directions

Short Answer

6. Identify and explain the tone of the instruction manual. Use information from the passage to support your answer.

Extended Response

7. If you were to write an instructional manual, what text features would you use? List at least three types of text features, and explain why those features would help you present your information clearly.

Vocabulary Skills Review

OH **VO.8.1** Define unknown words through context clues and the author's use of comparison, contrast and cause and effect.

Multiple-Meaning Words

Directions: Choose the answer in which the boldfaced word is used in the same way it is used in the passage.

1. "You used to be a good, dependable, ordinary man—not too bright maybe, but honest. Who knows what you done to yourself to get so **smart** all of a sudden."
   A. Your new outfit looks smart.
   B. The scientist was a smart person.
   C. Don't be smart with me, young man!
   D. Does the cut on your finger still smart?

2. "He hasn't been eating. Everyone is upset about what this may **mean**."
   A. Charlie's friends were mean to him.
   B. The mean rainfall in that part of the world is one inch per year.
   C. David Wells throws a mean fastball.
   D. High intelligence doesn't necessarily mean high achievement.

3. "I am grateful for the little bit that I here add to the knowledge of the function of the human **mind**."
   A. Did Charlie mind being teased?
   B. Who will mind the lab tonight?
   C. A mind is a terrible thing to waste.
   D. That nasty dog should mind its owner.

4. "Then Frank Reilly said what did you do Charlie forget your **key** and open your door the hard way."
   A. Play that song in the key of G major.
   B. The awards ceremony was a key event.
   C. Ken locked the car with the key inside.
   D. The answer key to the test is incorrect.

5. "I tried not to look at the boy as I paid my **check** and walked out without touching my food."
   A. This test will check your word power.
   B. Waiter, bring the check, please.
   C. The doctors tried to check Algernon's decline.
   D. Have you cashed that check yet?

6. "Seeing the past more clearly, I have decided to use my knowledge and skills to work in the **field** of increasing human intelligence levels."
   A. I hope to get a job in the field of economics.
   B. The children ran toward the building, through the field.
   C. Can you field any telephone calls while I'm away?
   D. Our school hopes to have a new baseball field soon.

Academic Vocabulary

Directions: Choose the correct definition for the boldfaced Academic Vocabulary word.

7. The manual we read was **effective**.
   A. logical or rational
   B. difficult and challenging
   C. clear and simple
   D. useful or helpful

WA.8.1.a Write narratives that: sustain reader interest by pacing action and developing an engaging plot; *Also covered* **WP.8.12**

Writing Skills Review

Personal Narrative **Directions:** Read the following paragraph from a personal narrative. Then, answer each question that follows.

(1) It was a cool October evening as I stood backstage all dressed up in my black leotard and tights with a gold-sequined belt. (2) My hair was pulled back in a bun, and a strong flowery smell of hair spray wafted around me. (3) My brother had teased me and called my outfit "silly," but I felt beautiful. (4) I was seven years old, and I knew that my first dance performance would be perfect. (5) I had eaten spaghetti, my favorite meal, for dinner. (6) As I pranced proudly onto the stage and into the hot, bright stage lights, I swelled with confidence. (7) Just as I neared my position on stage, my enthusiasm interfered with my footing, and I tripped. (8) On my knees on the stage floor, I could hear my brother's distinctive laugh and feel the heat rushing to my face. (9) I remembered my dance teacher's advice: "If you make a mistake, keep smiling and move on." (10) I held my tears and jumped up from the floor like a graceful ballerina. (11) I wouldn't let a little fall stop me from enjoying my night in the spotlight.

---

1. Which of the following additions would *best* help the writer develop the ideas introduced in this paragraph?
   A. Description of the main character's mother
   B. Description of the main character's expressions
   C. Description of the actions of the other dancers
   D. Description of the car ride to the performance

2. Which of the following sentences is *least* necessary for the paragraph's coherence?
   A. Sentence 2
   B. Sentence 3
   C. Sentence 5
   D. Sentence 7

3. What should the writer add to this paragraph or to a later passage to make the personal narrative complete?
   A. A reflection on the importance of this event
   B. An explanation of the history of dance recitals
   C. A description of the dance's choreography
   D. A summary of the events leading up to the fall

4. The **tone** of this story would best be described as a mixture of —
   A. anger and confidence
   B. confidence and sadness
   C. confusion and sadness
   D. embarrassment and confidence

Read On

Fiction

Kit's Wilderness

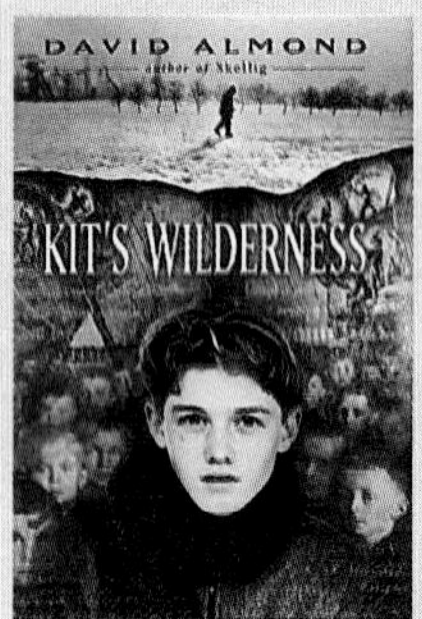

When a well-behaved thirteen-year-old named Kit Watson moves to Stoneygate, he encounters John Askew, a boy with a knack for getting into trouble. As they get to know each other, Kit finds they have something in common: Both can see ghosts of children who have died in Stoneygate's mines. In David Almond's *Kit's Wilderness,* Kit hopes this bond will help reveal John's goodness.

Ella Enchanted

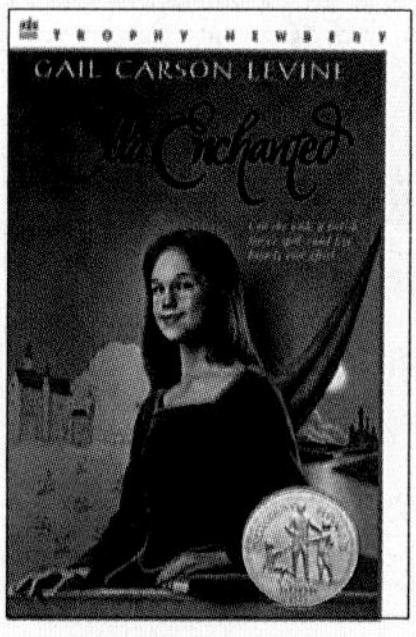

On the day she was born, Ella received a gift from a fairy. However, Ella has never appreciated the gift because it is the gift of obedience. She has to do whatever anyone tells her to do. Gail Carson Levine's *Ella Enchanted,* a Newbery Medal winner, is a retelling of the Cinderella story. In this version, however, the heroine goes on a mission to change the way things are. Ella won't allow ogres, elves, or fairy godmothers to get in her way.

Hatchet

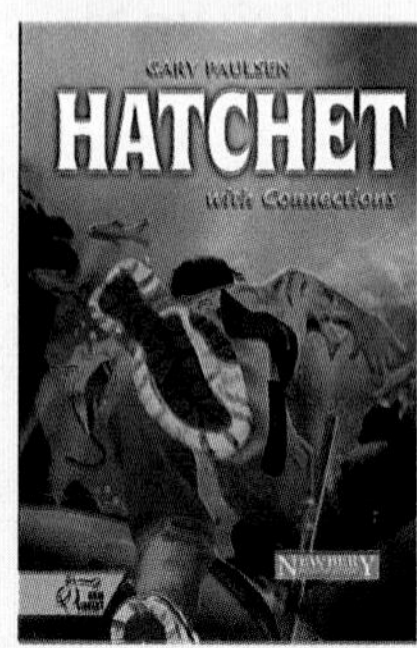

Young Brian finds himself stranded alone in the Canadian wilderness after a plane crash. With only his wits and a hatchet to rely on for survival, Brian learns some memorable lessons about nature, growing up, and himself. Lovers of survival and adventure stories will find themselves engrossed in Gary Paulsen's Newbery Honor book *Hatchet.*

Ice Drift

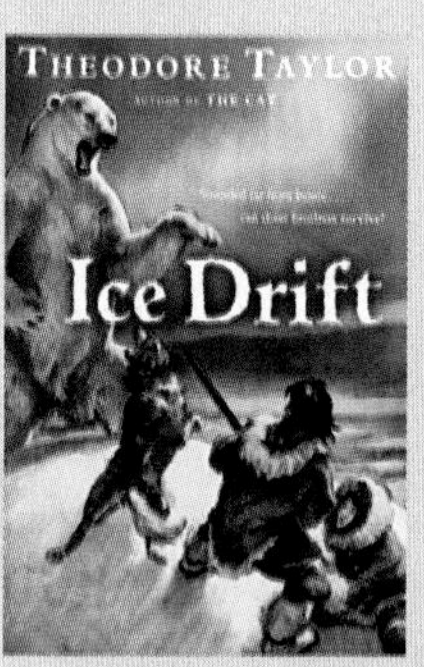

When Alika and Sulu, two Inuit brothers, find themselves trapped on a floating island of ice in the Arctic, they must use all their knowledge and survival skills to stay alive. Alika, his little brother Sulu, and their dog Jamka must hunt for food, fend off polar bears, and endure the bitter subzero cold. *Ice Drift* by Theodore Taylor is a survival story that expertly weaves a gripping plot with a stark and deadly setting into a heart-pounding adventure.

Nonfiction

Samurai

Most people know that samurai were great warriors. Did you also know that in ancient Japan, samurai were the only people permitted to carry swords? In *Samurai,* Caroline Leavitt tells this warrior class's exciting story, spanning hundreds of years. Even though the age of the samurai came to an end when Japan opened its doors to the Western world, the spirit of these warriors has lasted until the present day. Beautiful illustrations complement this exciting work.

Guinea Pig Scientists: Bold Self-Experimenters in Science and Medicine

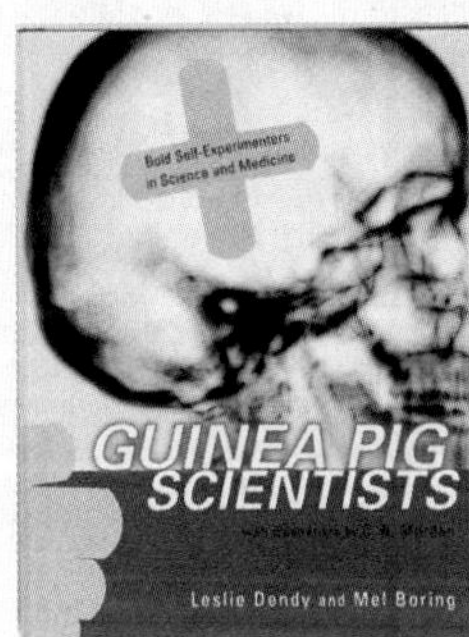

The "guinea pig" in the title is a person who offers himself or herself as a subject in a scientific experiment—as Charlie does in "Flowers for Algernon." In *Guinea Pig Scientists,* Mel Boring and Leslie Dendy tell the stories of ten scientists who experimented on themselves. Be sure not to try any of these experiments yourself, but enjoy reading the fascinating—if sometimes gruesome—tales.

Black Pioneers of Science and Invention

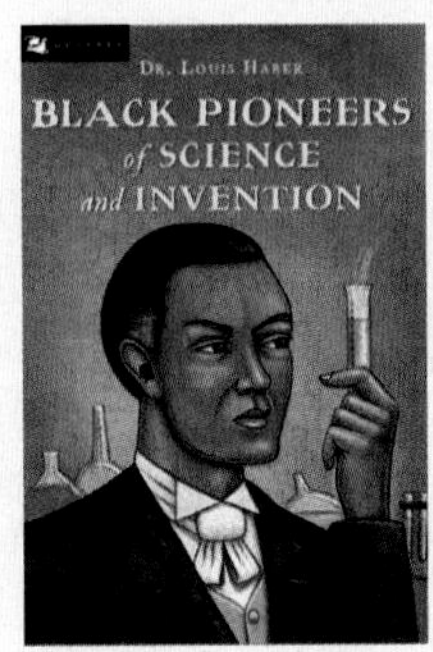

Many African Americans have made important contributions that have improved the lives of all Americans. Louis Haber tells the stories of fourteen such people in *Black Pioneers of Science and Invention.* Included are Benjamin Banneker, astrologist and surveyor; Granville T. Woods, inventor of many railroad improvements; George Washington Carver, chemist who discovered hundreds of uses for peanuts and other agricultural products; and more.

Forensics

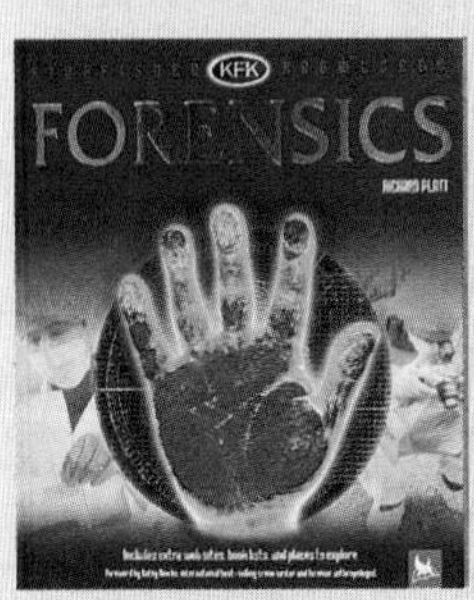

Forensics, or the science of crime investigation, is a popular topic in TV shows and movies. Read Richard Platt's overview of the subject to learn how forensics is really done. Topics such as ballistics, counterfeit money, DNA evidence, and identification of tsunami victims are explored and are illustrated with detailed color photos.

Learn It Online

Explore other novels and find tips for enjoying them at:

go.hrw.com L8-147 

W. H. Johnson

COLLECTION 2

Characters

INFORMATIONAL TEXT FOCUS

Comparing Treatment, Scope, and Organization of Ideas

"No matter what accomplishments you make, somebody helps you."

—Althea Gibson

What Do You Think? To whom do we turn for help in times of need?

Off to War (c. 1942–1944) by William H. Johnson. Oil on plywood (25 1/8" x 32 5/8").

Learn It Online
Take a different look at this collection with *PowerNotes* online:

go.hrw.com L8-149 Go

Literary Focus

by **Sara Kajder**

How Do Writers Introduce You to Their Characters?

Have you ever gotten to know a character so well that you were a little sad when the story was over? How is it that a writer can create a character in his or her mind, transfer that character to the page, and make you feel as though you have met a real person?

Characterization

The way a writer reveals character is called **characterization.** Poor characterization can make even a real person seem uninteresting. Good characterization can make readers feel that even fantasy characters live and breathe.

Creating Characters A writer may simply tell you directly that a character is mean-tempered or thrifty or honest. This kind of characterization is called **direct characterization.** You don't have to do any detective work to figure the character out.

However, writers generally prefer to *show* their characters in action, giving readers the chance to decide for themselves what the character is like. This method is called **indirect characterization.**

Direct Characterization In the example that follows, Yoshiko Uchida states directly what the character is like: You know immediately three things about him: he's arrogant, he's cruel, and he's young.

> Many long years ago, there lived an arrogant and cruel young lord who ruled over a small village in the western hills of Japan.
>
> from "The Wise Old Woman"
> by Yoshiko Uchida

Indirect Characterization Now, contrast the previous example of direct characterization with the following examples of ways that writers show indirect characterization.

Below, Naomi Shihab Nye describes the **appearance** of her character. You can infer that Mr. Hamadi takes pride in his appearance and dresses conservatively. What might this say about his personality?

> Usually Hamadi was wearing a white shirt, shiny black tie, and a jacket that reminded Susan of the earth's surface just above the treeline on a mountain—thin, somehow purified.
>
> from "Hamadi"
> by Naomi Shihab Nye

O. Henry shows readers through Jimmy's **actions** that all the beauty of nature is having no effect on Jimmy. His attention is set on one thing: food.

> Disregarding the song of the birds, the waving green trees, and the smell of the flowers, Jimmy headed straight for a restaurant.
>
> from "A Retrieved Reformation"
> by O. Henry

OH **RA.L.8.8** Explain ways in which the author conveys mood and tone through word choice, figurative language, and syntax. **RA.L.8.1** Identify and explain various types of characters and how their interactions and conflicts affect the plot.

Notice how Ken Mochizuki uses his character's **words** to give readers an insight into Mr. Sugihara's personality. What Mr. Sugihara says to his son reflects his calmness, sensitivity, and selflessness.

> "I cannot help these people yet," he calmly told me. "But when the time comes, I will help them all that I can."
>
> from "Passage to Freedom: The Sugihara Story" by Ken Mochizuki

In the following example, Maya Angelou shows readers what her character is like by revealing the character's **thoughts and feelings** of admiration for Mrs. Flowers.

> Although she warned that she hadn't tried her hand at baking sweets for some time, I was certain that like everything else about her the cookies would be perfect.
>
> from "Mrs. Flowers" by Maya Angelou

O. Henry gives the reader a view of the character from another angle: through other characters' reactions. Through the **character relationship** between Jimmy Valentine and the warden, the reader learns two things: (1) Jimmy has done wrong, and (2) another person believes that Jimmy is still a good person and has the potential to change.

> "Now, Valentine," said the warden, "you'll go out in the morning. Brace up, and make a man of yourself. You're not a bad fellow at heart. Stop cracking safes, and live straight."
>
> from "A Retrieved Reformation" by O. Henry

Motivation

Why did your best friend suddenly develop an interest in sports? What could possibly have possessed your brother to think he could dance?

We always wonder about people's **motivation**—why people behave the way they do. In real life we may never learn the answer, but in literature you will find plenty of clues to characters' motives. One of the pleasures of reading stories is using these clues to find out what makes characters tick. You discover their motivations from paying attention to what they say and do and thinking about what happens to them.

Your Turn Analyze a Character

Choose a character from a story you have read recently, and fill in a chart like the one below:

Character profile of ____________

Method of Characterization	Details in Story
Indirect Characterization	
Appearance	
Actions	
Words	
Thoughts	
Relationships with Others	
Direct Characterization	
What the Writer Says	

Learn It Online
Build your understanding using *PowerNotes* at:
go.hrw.com L8-151 Go

Analyzing Visuals

How Can You Learn About Characters in a Painting?

In short stories, you get to know **characters** through description, appearance, dialogue, and actions. In visual art, you can learn about characters by observing their appearance, facial expressions, body language, and how they relate to the setting they are in and to those around them. The use of color, light, and shadow in a painting can also create a mood that helps convey the characters' situations.

Analyzing a Painting

Use these guidelines to help you analyze a painting.

1. Look carefully at the facial expression and body language of the subjects. Are they cheerful? worried? shocked? amused?
2. Analyze the characters' appearance—clothing, hair, jewelry, and so on. What does their appearance tell you about them?
3. What do the characters' actions suggest about their personalities? Do the characters seem comfortable in that setting?
4. Examine the lighting in the painting. Is it dark and shadowy? bright? dramatic? How does it affect the image mood?

Look at the detail of the painting to help you answer the questions on page 153.

Detail of *Crispin et Scapin (The Two Clowns)*.

RA.L.8.8 Explain ways in which the author conveys mood and tone through word choice, figurative language, and syntax.

Crispin et Scapin (*The Two Clowns*) (c.1864) by Honoré Daumier.
Oil on canvas, 60.5 x 82 cm. R.F. 2057.

1. What does the body language of the two **characters** reveal about their relationship to each other?

2. What does the facial expression of the clown on the left suggest about what he is thinking?

3. What **mood** do the lighting, shadows, and colors create in this painting?

Your Turn Write About a Character

Look through the textbook to find a painting or photograph of a character that interests you. List three inferences you can make about that character based on his or her appearance, action, and facial expression.

Reading Focus

by **Kylene Beers**

What Reading Skills Help You Understand Characters?

Getting to know people is sometimes hard. You may sometimes wonder why in the world they are acting the way they do. It can take time and careful observation to figure them out. It is the same with characters in a story. When you are confused by a story's characters, try these strategies to make sense of what they do.

Making Inferences

When you see a group of classmates giggling in the hallway, what do you think is happening? If the students have been mean to you before, you may decide they are laughing at you. If they are your friends, you may think someone is telling a funny story about something that happened in class. You make **inferences,** or guesses, based on your observations and your prior experiences.

Hints for Making Inferences To make an inference about a character in a story, combine the information the writer gives you with what you already know. As you read, keep these questions in mind.

- What does the writer tell you about how the character looks and acts? What do you know about people who look and act that way?
- What does the writer tell you about problems the character faces? What do you know about similar situations?
- What does the writer tell you about the way people respond to the character? What do such responses usually tell you about a person?

Making Connections

You may not realize it, but you have a wealth of knowledge to draw from—simply from reading stories, meeting people, and experiencing or hearing about world events. **Making connections** to what you already know will help you understand the stories you read. When you are getting to know a character in a book, think about how he or she *is* or *isn't* like other people you know or have heard about.

Connection Chart As you read about the characters in this collection, use a chart like this one based on *Passage to Freedom: The Sugihara Story* to connect to what you already know about people:

Character:	Mr. Sugihara
Situation:	He wants to save refugees, but doing so is risky.
Personal Connection:	I once stood up for someone who was being bullied, and I was scared I would be a target.
World Connection:	I read about a man in Rwanda who saved many lives in spite of danger to his own.
Literary Connection:	

RP.8.1 Apply reading comprehension strategies, including making predictions, comparing and contrasting, recalling and summarizing and making inferences and drawing conclusions. **RA.L.8.1** Identify and explain various types of characters and how their interactions and conflicts affect the plot.

Making Judgments

As you get to know a character in a story, you'll start **making judgments** about him or her. Just like a judge in a courtroom, you will need to base your judgments on **evidence.** In the case of a story, the evidence will come from the text. Use this information to make judgments about characters. Here is a judgment a reader made about the title character in "Hamadi":

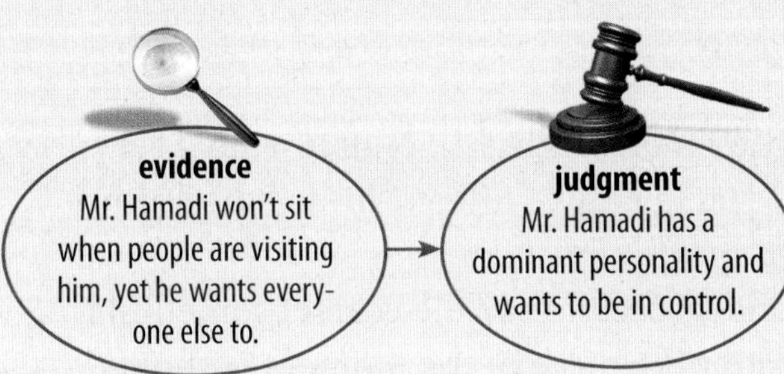

evidence
Mr. Hamadi won't sit when people are visiting him, yet he wants everyone else to.
judgment
Mr. Hamadi has a dominant personality and wants to be in control.

Adjusting Your Judgments Keep in mind that for your judgments to be valid, they must be based on evidence in the text. However, don't be surprised if your judgments change as you learn more about a character. In your reading—and in life—you must modify your judgments as you gain new information. New evidence in "Hamadi" leads the reader to adjust her original judgment:

new evidence
Mr. Hamadi lives humbly and speaks patiently. He doesn't seem controlling.
updated judgment
I think Mr. Hamadi just wants his visitors to be comfortable.

Your Turn Apply Reading Skills

Read the following passage from "A Retrieved Reformation" and then answer the questions below.

> Pulling out from a wall a folding bed, Jimmy slid back a panel in the wall and dragged out a dust-covered suitcase. He opened this and gazed fondly at the finest set of burglar's tools in the East. . . .
>
> In half an hour Jimmy went downstairs and through the café. He was now dressed in tasteful and well-fitting clothes and carried his dusted and cleaned suitcase in his hand.

1. What can you infer about how long it has been since Jimmy has used his tools?
2. What connection can you make, knowing that Jimmy carries his suitcase with him?
3. Based on this evidence, what is your opinion of Jimmy? Is he a good or bad man, or a bit of both?

Now go to the Skills in Action: Reading Model.

Learn It Online

For tips on applying reading strategies to longer works, visit:

go.hrw.com L8-155 

SHORT STORY

Read with a Purpose Read "The Open Window" to discover how a family story affects a nervous visitor.

The Open Window

by **Saki**

Literary Focus

Characterization The author, Saki, directly characterizes the young lady when he writes that she is "a very self-possessed young lady of fifteen." *Self-possessed* means "composed" or "in control of one's feelings or actions." Once you know this information, you can look for ways that her actions support this characterization.

Literary Focus

Characterization Through his sister's words, we learn that Framton has a nervous personality and tends to isolate himself and mope around.

"My aunt will be down presently, Mr. Nuttel," said a very self-possessed young lady of fifteen; "in the meantime you must try and put up with me."

Framton Nuttel endeavored to say the correct something which should duly flatter the niece of the moment without unduly discounting the aunt that was to come. Privately he doubted more than ever whether these formal visits on a succession of total strangers would do much toward helping the nerve cure which he was supposed to be undergoing.

"I know how it will be," his sister had said when he was preparing to migrate to this rural retreat; "you will bury yourself down there and not speak to a living soul, and your nerves will be worse than ever from moping. I shall just give you letters of introduction to all the people I know there. Some of them, as far as I can remember, were quite nice."

Framton wondered whether Mrs. Sappleton, the lady to whom he was presenting one of the letters of introduction, came into the nice division.

"Do you know many of the people round here?" asked the niece, when she judged that they had had sufficient silent communion.

"Hardly a soul," said Framton. "My sister was staying here, at the rectory,[1] you know, some four years ago, and she gave me letters of introduction to some of the people here."

1. **rectory:** house in which the minister of a parish lives.

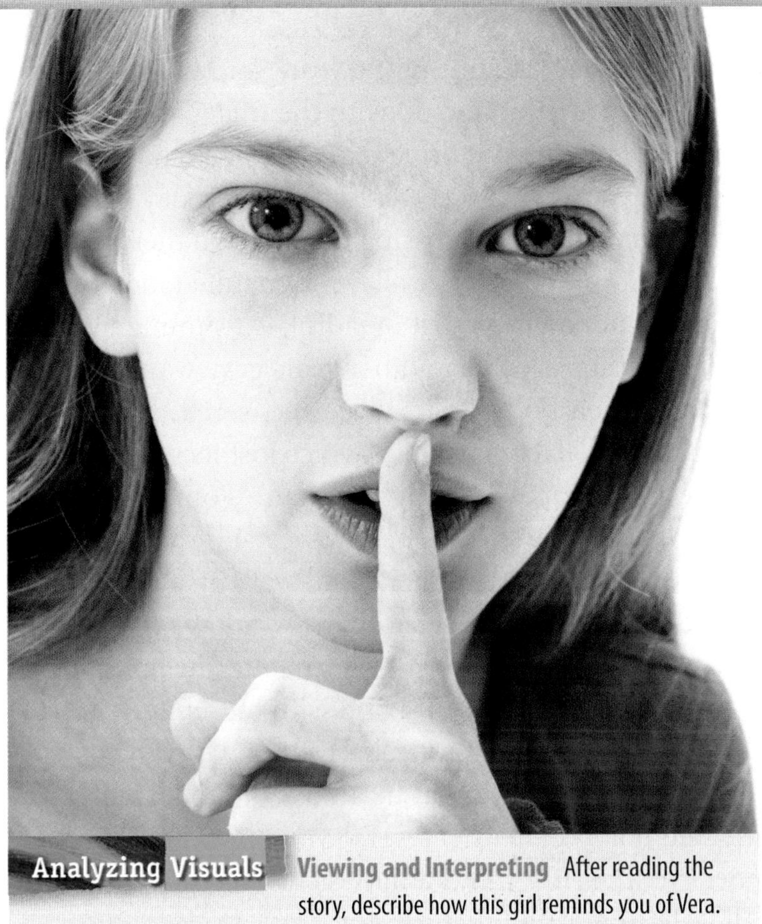

Analyzing Visuals **Viewing and Interpreting** After reading the story, describe how this girl reminds you of Vera.

He made the last statement in a tone of distinct regret.

"Then you know practically nothing about my aunt?" pursued the self-possessed young lady.

"Only her name and address," admitted the caller. He was wondering whether Mrs. Sappleton was in the married or widowed state. An undefinable something about the room seemed to suggest masculine habitation.

"Her great tragedy happened just three years ago," said the child; "that would be since your sister's time."

"Her tragedy?" asked Framton; somehow, in this restful country spot, tragedies seemed out of place.

"You may wonder why we keep that window wide open on an October afternoon," said the niece, indicating a large French window[2] that opened onto a lawn.

Reading Focus

Making Inferences You can infer from his "tone of distinct regret" that Framton isn't thrilled about having to meet new people.

2. **French window:** pair of doors that have glass panes from top to bottom and open in the middle.

"It is quite warm for the time of the year," said Framton, "but has that window got anything to do with the tragedy?"

"Out through that window, three years ago to a day, her husband and her two young brothers went off for their day's shooting. They never came back. In crossing the moor to their favorite snipe-shooting[3] ground, they were all three engulfed in a treacherous piece of bog. It had been that dreadful wet summer, you know, and places that were safe in other years gave way suddenly without warning. Their bodies were never recovered. That was the dreadful part of it." Here the child's voice lost its self-possessed note and became falteringly human. "Poor aunt always thinks that they will come back someday, they and the little brown spaniel that was lost with them, and walk in at that window just as they used to do. That is why the window is kept open every evening till it is quite dusk. Poor dear aunt, she has often told me how they went out, her husband with his white waterproof coat over his arm, and Ronnie, her youngest brother, singing, 'Bertie, why do you bound?' as he always did to tease her, because she said it got on her nerves. Do you know, sometimes on still, quiet evenings like this, I almost get a creepy feeling that they will all walk in through that window——"

She broke off with a little shudder. It was a relief to Framton when the aunt bustled into the room with a whirl of apologies for being late in making her appearance.

"I hope Vera has been amusing you?" she said.

"She has been very interesting," said Framton.

"I hope you don't mind the open window," said Mrs. Sappleton briskly; "my husband and brothers will be home directly from shooting, and they always come in this way. They've been out for snipe in the marshes today, so they'll make a fine mess over my poor carpets. So like you menfolk, isn't it?"

She rattled on cheerfully about the shooting and the scarcity of birds and the prospects for duck in the winter. To Framton, it was all purely horrible. He made a desperate but only partially successful effort to turn the talk onto a less ghastly topic; he was conscious that his hostess was giving him only a fragment of her attention, and her eyes were constantly straying past him to the

Reading Focus

Making Connections The character of the aunt may remind you of other characters from television, movies, or books. Many stories have a character who wants something so badly that he or she has lost touch with reality.

Literary Focus

Characterization Notice Vera's and Framton's reactions to the creepy story of the missing family members. Vera shudders, and Framton is uncomfortable.

---

3. **snipe-shooting:** A snipe is a kind of bird that lives in swampy areas.

open window and the lawn beyond. It was certainly an unfortunate coincidence that he should have paid his visit on this tragic anniversary.

"The doctors agree in ordering me complete rest, an absence of mental excitement, and avoidance of anything in the nature of violent physical exercise," announced Framton, who labored under the tolerably widespread delusion that total strangers and chance acquaintances are hungry for the least detail of one's ailments and infirmities, their cause and cure. "On the matter of diet they are not so much in agreement," he continued.

"No?" said Mrs. Sappleton, in a voice which only replaced a yawn at the last moment. Then she suddenly brightened into alert attention—but not to what Framton was saying.

"Here they are at last!" she cried. "Just in time for tea, and don't they look as if they were muddy up to the eyes!"

Framton shivered slightly and turned toward the niece with a look intended to convey sympathetic comprehension. The child was staring out through the open window with dazed horror in her eyes. In a chill shock of nameless fear Framton swung round in his seat and looked in the same direction.

In the deepening twilight three figures were walking across the lawn toward the window; they all carried guns under their arms, and one of them was additionally burdened with a white coat hung over his shoulders. A tired brown spaniel kept close at their heels. Noiselessly they neared the house, and then a hoarse young voice chanted out of the dusk: "I said, Bertie, why do you bound?"

Framton grabbed wildly at his stick and hat; the hall door, the gravel drive, and the front gate were dimly noted stages in his headlong retreat. A cyclist coming along the road had to run into the hedge to avoid imminent collision.

"Here we are, my dear," said the bearer of the white mackintosh, coming in through the window, "fairly muddy, but most of it's dry. Who was that who bolted out as we came up?"

"A most extraordinary man, a Mr. Nuttel," said Mrs. Sappleton; "could only talk about his illnesses and dashed off without a word of goodbye or apology when you arrived. One would think he had seen a ghost."

Reading Focus

Making Judgments Using the information Saki gives us, we can make the judgment that Framton is a bit of a bore, going on and on about his health.

Reading Focus

Making Judgments Now that we know more about the situation, it is time to adjust our judgment about Mrs. Sappleton.

"I expect it was the spaniel," said the niece calmly; "he told me he had a horror of dogs. He was once hunted into a cemetery somewhere on the banks of the Ganges[4] by a pack of pariah dogs[5] and had to spend the night in a newly dug grave with the creatures snarling and grinning and foaming just above him. Enough to make anyone lose their nerve."

Romance at short notice was her specialty.

Literary Focus

Motivation The author tells us in the last sentence why Vera has been making up stories. *Romance,* here, doesn't refer to a love affair. Instead, it refers to a story that has adventurous, mysterious, or heroic characters and plot.

4. **Ganges** (GAN jeez): river in northern India and Bangladesh.
5. **pariah** (puh RY uh) **dogs:** wild dogs.

Read with a Purpose How does Framton Nuttel react to what happens after Vera tells her story? Do you feel sorry for him? Why or why not?

MEET THE WRITER

Saki
(1870–1916)

Hector Hugh Munro "Saki", 1912 (1912) by E. O. Hoppé.

Mischief and Mayhem

Saki is the pen name of Hector Hugh Munro. He was born in Burma (now called Myanmar) in Southeast Asia, where his father, a Scottish military officer, was posted. Later, in England, Saki's mother died, and he and his siblings were raised by their grandmother and two aunts.

Although living with his strict and often-bickering aunts was an unpleasant experience, it helped Saki develop the mischievous sense of humor that later made his writing famous.

Saki is well-known for his funny yet often creepy stories. It has been said that when we read his stories, "our laughter is only a note or two short of a scream of fear."

Think About the Writer What elements of Saki's humor do you see in "The Open Window"?

SKILLS IN ACTION

Wrap Up

RA.L.8.1 Identify and explain various types of characters and how their interactions and conflicts affect the plot. *Also covered* **RP.8.1; VO.8.7**

Into Action: Character Flowchart

Practice analyzing a character by completing a flowchart like the one below for either Framton Nuttel or for Vera. Then, write a character description that is two or three sentences long.

Character Details from Text:

My Inference:

My Connection:

My Judgment:

Talk About . . .

1. Discuss Vera's character with a partner. Is she cruel, or basically harmless? Support your opinion with details from the text. Try to use each Academic Vocabulary word listed at the right at least once in your discussion.

Write About . . .

2. What can you tell about Vera and Framton from the way they interact?
3. In what way is Vera's story a critical factor of Saki's tale?
4. Think about Framton's response when the hunters return home. How might his response to this incident have kept Vera from getting into trouble?

Writing Focus

Think as a Reader/Writer

In Collection 2, you will read several stories with interesting characters. The Writing Focus activities on the Preparing to Read pages will help you focus on the ways an author can reveal a character's personality. On the Applying Your Skills pages, you will have an opportunity to try an author's techniques out for yourself.

Academic Vocabulary for Collection 2

Talking and Writing About Stories

Academic Vocabulary is the language you use to write and talk about literature. Use the following words to discuss the characters in this collection. These words are underlined throughout the collection.

incident (IHN suh duhnt) *n.:* event or occurrence. *What did the character's behavior during the scary incident reveal about her?*

factor (FAK tuhr) *n.:* something that has an influence on something else. *Factors to consider when analyzing a character are his or her appearance, actions, and relationships.*

interact (ihn tuhr AKT) *v.:* behave toward one another. *Characters reveal their personalities when they interact.*

response (rih SPAHNS) *n.:* reply or reaction. *To learn more about a character, observe his or her response to a stressful event.*

Your Turn

Copy these Academic Vocabulary words into your *Reader/Writer Notebook,* and try to use them as you answer questions about the stories in the collection.

SHORT STORY

Preparing to Read

HAMADI

by **Naomi Shihab Nye**

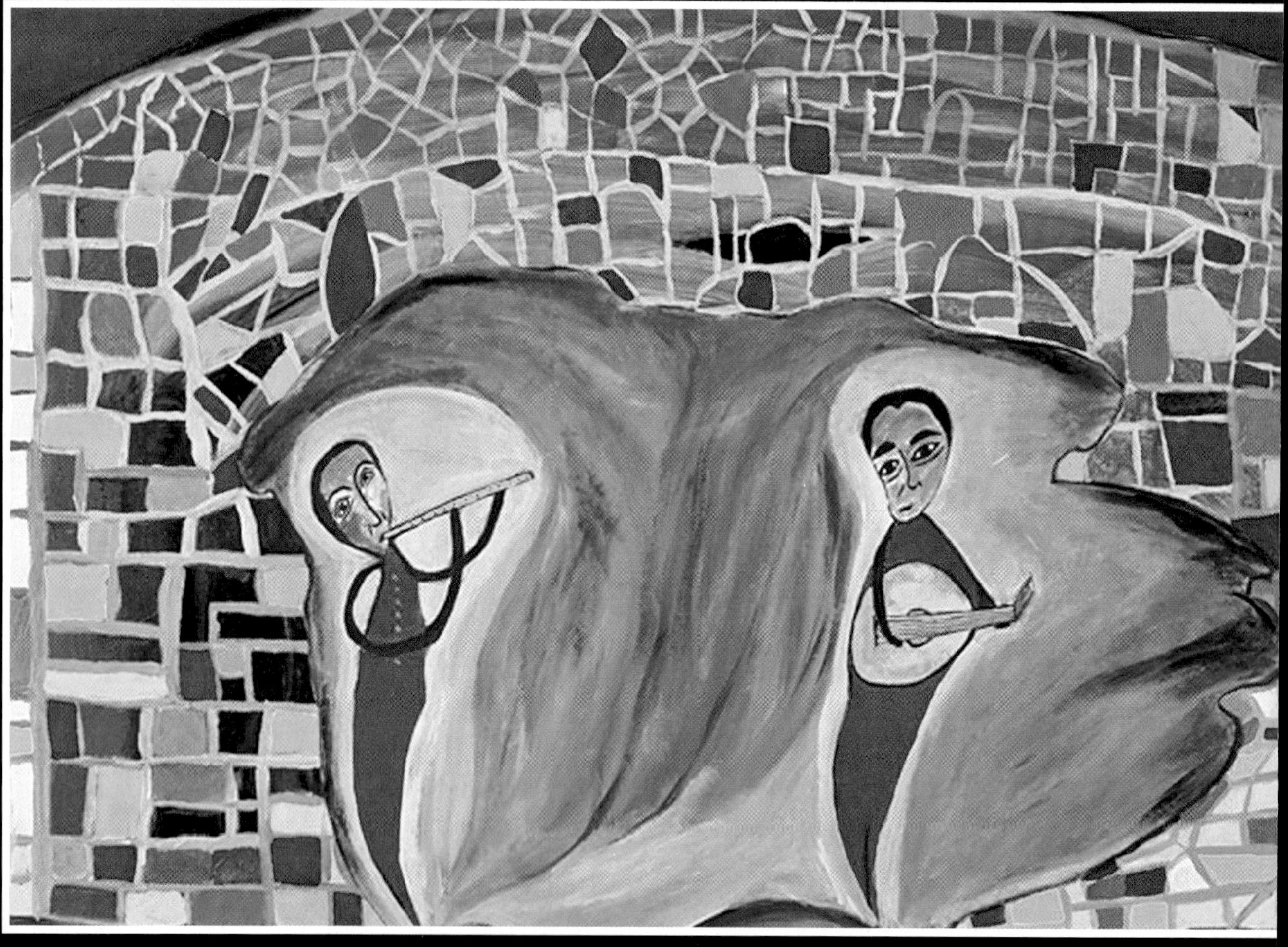

The Musicians (1995) by Zahi Khamis. Acrylic on paper. www.PalestinianArt.com; www.ZahiArt.com

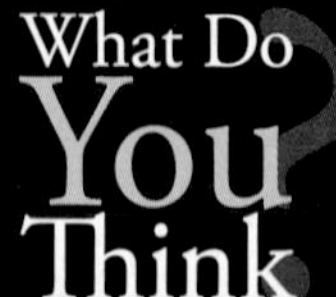

What can people who are different from us teach us about ourselves?

QuickWrite

Think of a friend who is very different from you. Write for a few minutes about what he or she has taught you.

Reader/Writer Notebook

Use your **RWN** to complete the activities for this selection.

OH **RA.L.8.8** Explain ways in which the author conveys mood and tone through word choice, figurative language, and syntax. **RP.8.1** Apply reading comprehension strategies, including making predictions, comparing and contrasting, recalling and summarizing and making inferences and drawing conclusions.

Literary Focus

Characterization To analyze **characters** in a story, gather information about their appearance, actions, and other characters' reactions to them. Pay attention to *what* they say and *how* they say it. In some stories, the author may even tell you what a character is thinking.

Literary Perspectives Apply the literary perspective described on page 165 as you read this story.

Reading Focus

Making Inferences To make an inference, examine a set of facts and ask yourself what you can guess, or **infer,** based on what you know from your own experience. To analyze a character, make inferences based on your own experience and evidence from the text.

Into Action Use the organizer below to analyze the character of Mr. Hamadi. As you read, write down details about him and details from your own experience, expanding the organizer as needed. Then, make inferences about Mr. Hamadi's character.

Details About Mr. Hamadi	My Experience
dresses nicely; wears a tie	seems overdressed for a casual visit
My Inference:	

Writing Focus

Think as a Reader/Writer

Find It in Your Reading As you read this story, notice the adverbs Naomi Shihab Nye uses to describe Mr. Hamadi's actions, for example, "He turned *dramatically.*" Write some of those adverbs in your *Reader/Writer Notebook*. For help identifying adverbs, turn to page 177.

Vocabulary

tedious (TEE dee uhs) *adj.:* repetitive; boring. *Susan prepares family recipes, even though the work is tedious.*

archaic (ar KAY ihk) *adj.:* out of date; old-fashioned. *Mr. Hamadi's stately manners seem archaic.*

vaguely (VAYG lee) *adv.:* unclearly. *Because of her shyness, Tracy only vaguely mumbles a hello.*

inquiring (ihn KWYR ihng) *v.:* looking for answers; asking. *By inquiring about the people around him, Mr. Hamadi shows that he cares.*

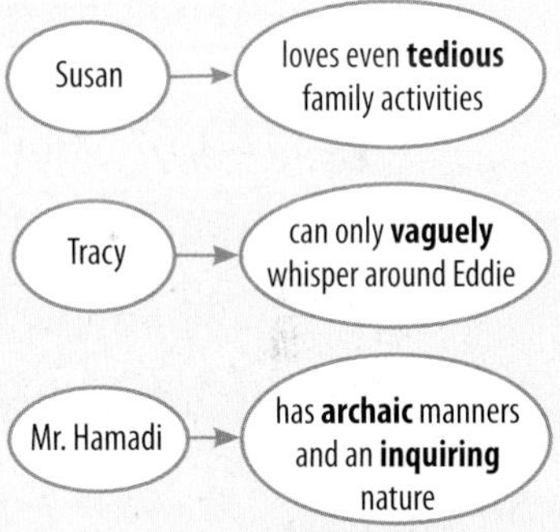

Language Coach

Word Origins *Taedet* is a Latin word that means "it disgusts or offends." Which Vocabulary word on the list above comes to us from this Latin word? How can you tell?

Learn It Online

Improve your comprehension and understanding of words at:

go.hrw.com L8-163 

MEET THE WRITER

Naomi Shihab Nye

(1952–)

The Makings of a Writer

Naomi Shihab Nye was born in St. Louis, Missouri. Her American mother read her poetry aloud, and her Palestinian father told her stories of his homeland. As a child, Nye read constantly. Her love of reading led naturally to writing, and she published her first poems when she was seven. She is best known as a poet, but she also writes fiction for children and young adults.

A Sampling of Cultures

When Nye was a teenager, her family returned to Jerusalem, where she completed a year of high school and immersed herself in the culture of her father's homeland. From there her family moved to San Antonio, Texas, a city with a rich Latino culture. Nye absorbed this culture from her neighbors and still lives in an inner-city San Antonio neighborhood.

"I hope that my characters are brave and strong. I want them to use their voices. I want young people to be reminded, always, that voices are the best tools we have."

Think About the Writer What details in the biography suggest that Nye values cultural connections?

Preview the Selection

Like Naomi Shihab Nye, **Susan,** the main character in this story, is a Palestinian-American who has spent time in Jerusalem. When she decides to invite a family friend to a school function, she finds that people of different cultures can connect in surprising ways.

Old Jerusalem, Israel.

Read with a Purpose Read to find out how Mr. Hamadi makes a difference to the people around him.

HAMADI

by **Naomi Shihab Nye**

> "It takes two of us to discover truth:
> one to utter it and one to understand it."
> KAHLIL GIBRAN, *Sand and Foam*

Susan didn't really feel interested in Saleh Hamadi until she was a freshman in high school carrying a thousand questions around. Why this way? Why not another way? Who said so and why can't I say something else? Those brittle women at school in the counselor's office treated the world as if it were a yardstick and they had tight hold of both ends.

Sometimes Susan felt polite with them, sorting attendance cards during her free period, listening to them gab about fingernail polish and television. And other times she felt she could run out of the building yelling. That's when she daydreamed about Saleh Hamadi, who had nothing to do with any of it. Maybe she thought of him as escape, the way she used to think about the Sphinx at Giza[1] when she was younger. She would picture the golden Sphinx sitting quietly in the desert with sand blowing around its face, never changing its expression. She would think of its wry, slightly crooked mouth and how her grandmother looked a little like that as she waited for her bread to bake in the old village north of Jerusalem.[2]

1. **Sphinx at Giza:** Giza is a city in Egypt, where there is a giant statue of a sphinx, a mythological creature with the body of a lion and a human head.

2. **Jerusalem:** major city of the Middle East.

Literary Perspectives

Use this perspective to help you find connections between the author and this story.

Analyzing Biographical Context Because authors typically write about things they care deeply about and know well, the events and circumstances of their lives are often reflected in their fictional works. To examine ways in which Naomi Shihab Nye's life may have influenced the characters, settings, and themes of "Hamadi," read the Meet the Writer section. Then you can make generalizations about how Nye's life and interests have informed the creation of "Hamadi." Also use the questions in the text to guide you in using this perspective.

Susan's family had lived in Jerusalem for three years before she was ten and drove out to see her grandmother every weekend. They would find her patting fresh dough between her hands, or pressing cakes of dough onto the black rocks in the *taboon,* the rounded old oven outdoors. Sometimes she moved her lips as she worked. Was she praying? Singing a secret song? Susan had never seen her grandmother rushing.

Now that she was fourteen, she took long walks in America with her father down by the drainage ditch at the end of their street. Pecan trees shaded the path. She tried to get him to tell stories about his childhood in Palestine. She didn't want him to forget anything. She helped her American mother complete tedious kitchen tasks without complaining—rolling grape leaves around their lemony rice stuffing, scrubbing carrots for the roaring juicer. Some evenings when the soft Texas twilight pulled them all outside, she thought of her far-away grandmother and said, "Let's go see Saleh Hamadi. Wouldn't he like some of that cheese pie Mom made?" And they would wrap a slice of pie and drive downtown. Somehow he felt like a good substitute for a grandmother, even though he was a man. **A**

Usually Hamadi was wearing a white shirt, shiny black tie, and a jacket that reminded Susan of the earth's surface just above the treeline on a mountain—thin, somehow purified. He would raise his hands high before giving advice.

"It is good to drink a tall glass of water every morning upon arising!" If anyone doubted this, he would shake his head. "Oh Susan, Susan, Susan," he would say.

He did not like to sit down, but he wanted everyone else to sit down. He made Susan sit on the wobbly chair beside the desk and he made her father or mother sit in the saggy center of the bed. He told them people should eat six small meals a day. **B**

They visited him on the sixth floor of the Traveler's Hotel, where he had lived so long nobody could remember him ever traveling. Susan's father used to remind him of the apartments available over the Victory Cleaners, next to the park with the fizzy pink fountain, but Hamadi would shake his head, pinching kisses at his spartan[3] room. "A white handkerchief spread across a tabletop, my two extra shoes lined by the wall, this spells 'home' to me, this says 'mi casa.' What more do I need?"

Hamadi liked to use Spanish words. They made him feel expansive, worldly. He'd learned them when he worked at the fruits and vegetables warehouse on Zarzamora Street, marking off crates of apples and avocados on a long white pad. Occasionally

3. **spartan:** simple; not luxurious.

A **Literary Perspectives** **Analyzing Biographical Context** How does Susan feel about her heritage? How might those feelings relate to Nye's recollections of her childhood?

B **Literary Focus** **Characterization** What do Mr. Hamadi's interactions with others suggest about him?

Vocabulary **tedious** (TEE dee uhs) *adj.:* repetitive; boring.

Analyzing Visuals

Viewing and Interpreting How does the man in the photograph compare to your impressions of Hamadi?

he would speak Arabic, his own first language, with Susan's father and uncles, but he said it made him feel too sad, as if his mother might step into the room at any minute, her arms laden with fresh mint leaves. He had come to the United States on a boat when he was eighteen years old and he had never been married. "I married books," he said. "I married the wide horizon." **C**

"What is he to us?" Susan used to ask her father. "He's not a relative, right? How did we meet him to begin with?"

Susan's father couldn't remember. "I think we just drifted together. Maybe we met at your uncle Hani's house. Maybe that old Maronite[4] priest who used to cry after every service introduced us. The priest once shared an apartment with Kahlil Gibran[5] in New York—so he said. And Saleh always says he stayed with Gibran when he first got

4. **Maronite:** The Maronite Church is in Lebanon and is part of the Eastern Catholic Church.
5. **Kahlil Gibran** (kah LEEL jih BRAHN) (1883–1931): Lebanese writer who wrote about religious and philosophical topics. One of his most famous books written in English is *The Prophet.*

C Reading Focus **Making Inferences** What can you infer about Mr. Hamadi's mother?

off the boat. I'll bet that popular guy Gibran has had a lot of roommates he doesn't even know about."

Susan said, "Dad, he's dead."

"I know, I know," her father said.

Later Susan said, "Mr. Hamadi, did you really meet Kahlil Gibran? He's one of my favorite writers." Hamadi walked slowly to the window of his room and stared out. There wasn't much to look at down on the street—a bedraggled flower shop, a boarded-up tavern with a hand-lettered sign tacked to the front, GONE TO FIND JESUS. Susan's father said the owners had really gone to Alabama.

Hamadi spoke patiently. "Yes, I met brother Gibran. And I meet him in my heart every day. When I was a young man—shocked by all the visions of the new world—the tall buildings—the wild traffic—the young people without shame—the proud mailboxes in their blue uniforms—I met him. And he has stayed with me every day of my life."

"But did you really meet him, like in person, or just in a book?"

He turned dramatically. "Make no such distinctions, my friend. Or your life will be a pod with only dried-up beans inside. Believe anything can happen." **D**

Susan's father looked irritated, but Susan smiled. "I do," she said. "I believe that. I want fat beans. If I imagine something, it's true, too. Just a different kind of true." **E**

Susan's father was twiddling with the knobs on the old-fashioned sink. "Don't they even give you hot water here? You don't mean to tell me you've been living without hot water?"

On Hamadi's rickety desk lay a row of different "Love" stamps issued by the post office.

"You must write a lot of letters," Susan said.

"No, no, I'm just focusing on that word," Hamadi said. "I particularly like the globe in the shape of a heart," he added.

"Why don't you take a trip back to your village in Lebanon?" Susan's father asked. "Maybe you still have relatives living there."

Hamadi looked pained. "'Remembrance is a form of meeting,' my brother Gibran says, and I do believe I meet with my cousins every day."

D **Literary Focus** **Characterization** What does this statement tell you about Mr. Hamadi's approach to life?

E **Read and Discuss** What is on Susan's mind?

"But aren't you curious? You've been gone so long! Wouldn't you like to find out what has happened to everybody and everything you knew as a boy?" Susan's father traveled back to Jerusalem once each year to see his family.

"I would not. In fact, I already know. It is there and it is not there. Would you like to share an orange with me?" **F**

His long fingers, tenderly peeling. Once when Susan was younger, he'd given her a lavish ribbon off a holiday fruit basket and expected her to wear it on her head. In the car, Susan's father said, "Riddles. He talks in riddles. I don't know why I have patience with him." Susan stared at the people talking and laughing in the next car. She did not even exist in their world. **G**

Susan carried *The Prophet* around on top of her English textbook and her Texas history. She and her friend Tracy read it out loud to one another at lunch. Tracy was a junior—they'd met at the literary magazine meeting where Susan, the only freshman on the staff, got assigned to do proofreading. They never ate in the cafeteria; they sat outside at picnic tables with sack lunches, whole wheat crackers and fresh peaches. Both of them had given up meat.

Tracy's eyes looked steamy. "You know that place where Gibran says, 'Hate is a dead thing. Who of you would be a tomb?'"

Susan nodded. Tracy continued. "Well, I hate someone. I'm trying not to, but I can't help it. I hate Debbie for liking Eddie and it's driving me nuts."

"Why shouldn't Debbie like Eddie?" Susan said. "*You* do."

Tracy put her head down on her arms. A gang of cheerleaders walked by giggling. One of them flicked her finger in greeting.

"In fact, we *all* like Eddie," Susan said. "Remember, here in this book—wait and I'll find it—where Gibran says that loving teaches us the secrets of our hearts and that's the way we connect to all of Life's heart? You're not talking about liking or loving, you're talking about owning."

Tracy looked glum. "Sometimes you remind me of a minister."

Susan said, "Well, just talk to me someday when *I'm* depressed." **H**

Susan didn't want a boyfriend. Everyone who had boyfriends or girlfriends seemed to have troubles. Susan told people she had a boyfriend far away, on a farm in Missouri, but the truth was, boys still seemed like cousins to her. Or brothers. Or even girls.

A squirrel sat in the crook of a tree, eyeing their sandwiches. When the end-of-lunch bell blared, Susan and Tracy jumped—it always seemed too soon. Squirrels were lucky; they didn't have to go to school.

F **Reading Focus** **Making Inferences** What might Mr. Hamadi expect to find if he traveled back to his home?

G **Literary Perspectives** **Analyzing Biographical Context** What might Nye say about the different ways Susan and her father see Hamadi?

H **Read and Discuss** What does this conversation teach us?

Susan's father said her idea was ridiculous: to invite Saleh Hamadi to go Christmas caroling with the English Club. "His English is archaic, for one thing, and he won't know *any* of the songs."

"How could you live in America for years and not know 'Joy to the World' or 'Away in a Manger'?"

"Listen, I grew up right down the road from 'Oh Little Town of Bethlehem' and I still don't know a single verse."

"I want him. We need him. It's boring being with the same bunch of people all the time."

Susan's father said her idea was ridiculous: to invite Saleh Hamadi to go Christmas caroling with the English Club.

So they called Saleh and he said he would come—"thrilled" was the word he used. He wanted to ride the bus to their house, he didn't want anyone to pick him up. Her father muttered, "He'll probably forget to get off." Saleh thought "caroling" meant they were going out with a woman named Carol. He said, "Holiday spirit—I was just reading about it in the newspaper."

Susan said, "Dress warm."

Saleh replied, "Friend, my heart is warmed simply to hear your voice."

All that evening Susan felt light and bouncy. She decorated the coffee can they would use to collect donations to be sent to the children's hospital in Bethlehem. She had started doing this last year in middle school, when a singing group collected $100 and the hospital responded on exotic onion-skin stationery that they were "eternally grateful." I

Her father shook his head. "You get something into your mind and it really takes over," he said. "Why do you like Hamadi so much all of a sudden? You could show half as much interest in your own uncles."

Susan laughed. Her uncles were dull. Her uncles shopped at the mall and watched TV. "Anyone who watches TV more than twelve minutes a week is uninteresting," she said.

Her father lifted an eyebrow.

"He's my surrogate[6] grandmother," she said. "He says interesting things. He makes me think. Remember when I was little and he called me The Thinker? We have a con-

6. **surrogate:** used as a substitute for something else.

I **Literary Focus** **Characterization** What do you think is Susan's motivation for raising money for the hospital?

Vocabulary **archaic** (ar KAY ihk) *adj.:* out of date; old-fashioned.

nection." She added, "Listen, do you want to go too? It's not a big deal. And Mom has a *great* voice. Why don't you both come?" **J**

A minute later her mother was digging in the closet for neck scarves, and her father was digging in the drawer for flashlight batteries.

Saleh Hamadi arrived precisely on time, with flushed red cheeks and a sack of dates stuffed in his pocket. "We may need sustenance on our journey." Susan thought the older people seemed quite giddy as they drove down to the high school to meet the rest of the carolers. Strands of winking lights wrapped around their neighbors' drainpipes and trees. A giant Santa tipped his hat on Dr. Garcia's roof.

Her friends stood gathered in front of the school. Some were smoothing out song sheets that had been crammed in a drawer or cabinet for a whole year. Susan thought holidays were strange; they came, and you were supposed to feel ready for them. What if you could make up your own holidays as you went along? She had read about a woman who used to have parties to celebrate the arrival of fresh asparagus in the local market. Susan's friends might make holidays called Eddie Looked at Me Today and Smiled.

Two people were alleluia-ing in harmony. Saleh Hamadi went around the group formally introducing himself to each person and shaking hands. A few people laughed silently when his back was turned. He had stepped out of a painting, or a newscast, with his outdated long overcoat, his clunky old man's shoes and elegant manners.

Susan spoke more loudly than usual. "I'm honored to introduce you to one of my best friends, Mr. Hamadi." **K**

"Good evening to you," he pronounced musically, bowing a bit from the waist.

What could you say back but "Good evening, sir." His old-fashioned manners were contagious.

They sang at three houses that never opened their doors.

They sang "We Wish You a Merry Christmas" each time they moved on. Lisa had a fine, clear soprano. Tracy could find the alto harmony to any line. Cameron and Elliot had more enthusiasm than accuracy. Lily, Rita, and Jeannette laughed every time they said a wrong word and fumbled to find their places again. Susan loved to see how her mother knew every word of every verse without looking at the paper, and how her father kept his hands in his pockets and seemed more interested in examining people's mailboxes or yard displays than in trying to sing. And Saleh Hamadi—what language was he singing in? He didn't even seem to be pronouncing words, but humming deeply from his throat. Was he saying, "Om"? Speaking Arabic? Once he caught

---

J **Read and Discuss** What strikes you about father and daughter in this conversation?

K **Literary Focus** **Characterization** Based on what you know about Susan, why do you think she spoke more loudly than usual?

her looking and whispered, "That was an Aramaic word that just drifted into my mouth—the true language of the Bible, you know, the language Jesus Christ himself spoke." **L**

By the fourth block their voices felt tuned up and friendly people came outside to listen. Trays of cookies were passed around and dollar bills stuffed into the little can. Thank you, thank you. Out of the dark from down the block, Susan noticed Eddie sprinting toward them with his coat flapping, unbuttoned. She shot a glance at Tracy, who pretended not to notice. "Hey, guys!" shouted Eddie. "The first time in my life I'm late and everyone else is on time! You could at least have left a note about which way you were going." Someone slapped him on the back. Saleh Hamadi, whom he had never seen before, was the only one who managed a reply. "Welcome, welcome to our cheery group!"

Eddie looked mystified. "Who is this guy?"

Susan whispered, "My friend."

Eddie approached Tracy, who read her song sheet intently just then, and stuck his face over her shoulder to whisper, "Hi." Tracy stared straight ahead into the air and whispered "Hi" vaguely, glumly. Susan shook her head. Couldn't Tracy act more cheerful at least?

L **Read and Discuss** How is the caroling going?

Vocabulary **vaguely** (VAYG lee) *adv.:* unclearly.

They were walking again. They passed a string of blinking reindeer and a wooden snowman holding a painted candle.

Eddie fell into step beside Tracy, murmuring so Susan couldn't hear him anymore. Saleh Hamadi was flinging his arms up high as he strode. Was he power walking? Did he even know what power walking was? Between houses, Susan's mother hummed obscure songs people hardly remembered: "What Child Is This?" and "The Friendly Beasts."

Lisa moved over to Eddie's other side. "I'm *so excited* about you and Debbie!" she said loudly. "Why didn't she come tonight?"

Eddie said, "She has a sore throat."

Tracy shrank up inside her coat. **M**

Lisa chattered on. "James said we should make our reservations *now* for dinner at the Tower after the Sweetheart Dance, can you believe it? In December, making a reservation for February? But otherwise it might get booked up!"

Saleh Hamadi tuned into this conversation with interest; the Tower was downtown, in his neighborhood. He said, "This sounds like significant preliminary planning! Maybe you can be an international advisor someday." Susan's mother bellowed, "Joy to the World!" and voices followed her, stretching for notes. Susan's father was gazing off into the sky. Maybe he thought about all the

M **Reading Focus** **Making Inferences** What inference can you make about Tracy's response to this situation?

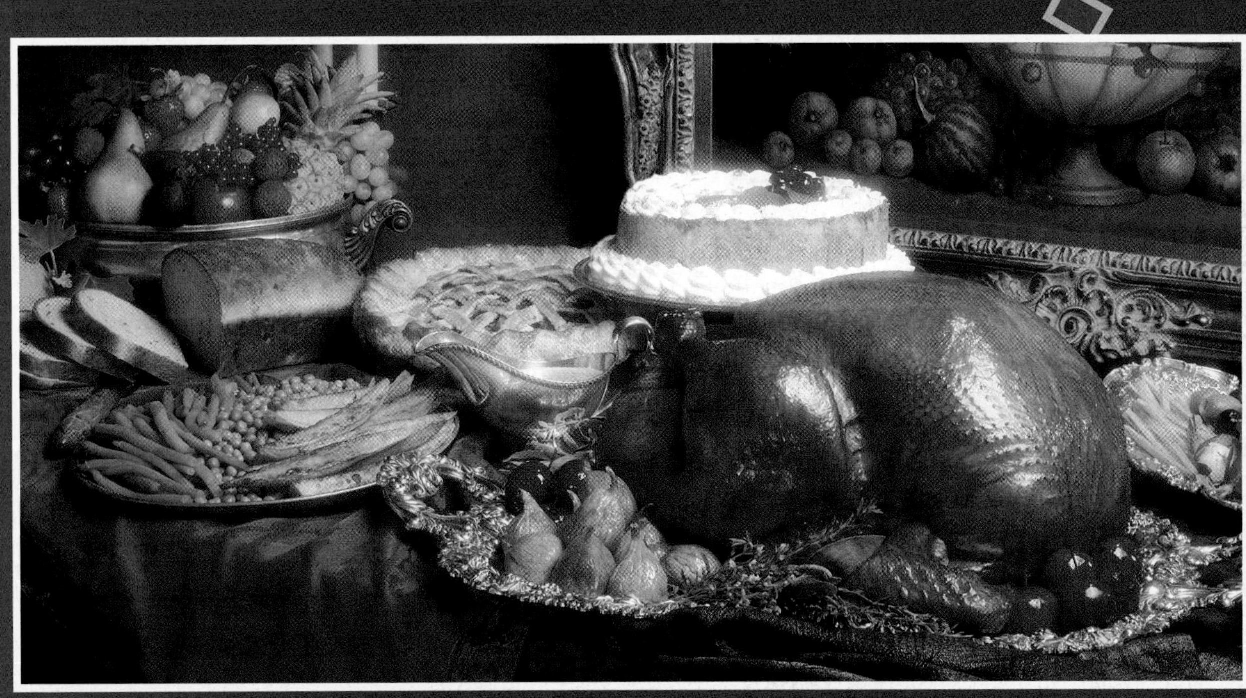

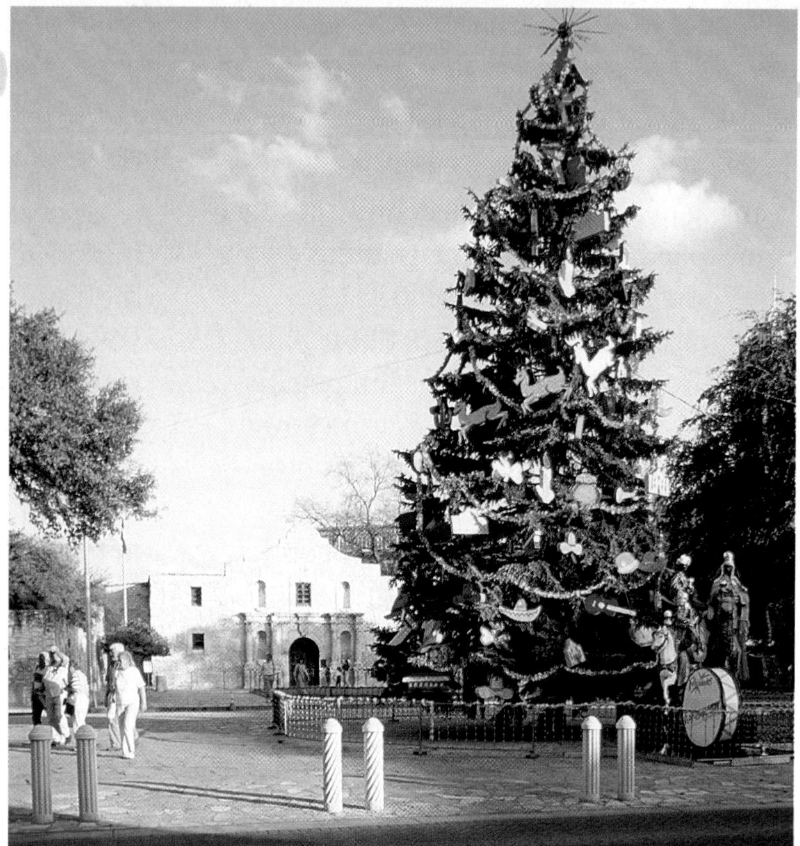

refugees in camps in Palestine far from doorbells and shutters. Maybe he thought about the horizon beyond Jerusalem when he was a boy, how it seemed to be inviting him, "Come over, come over." Well, he'd come all the way to the other side of the world, and now he was doomed to live in two places at once. To Susan, immigrants seemed bigger than other people, and always slightly melancholy. They also seemed doubly interesting. Maybe someday Susan would meet one her own age.

Two thin streams of tears rolled down Tracy's face. Eddie had drifted to the other side of the group and was clowning with Cameron, doing a tap dance shuffle. "While fields and floods, rocks, hills and plains, repeat the sounding joy, repeat the sounding joy . . ." Susan and Saleh Hamadi noticed her. Hamadi peered into Tracy's face, inquiring, "Why? Is it pain? Is it gratitude? We are such mysterious creatures, human beings!"

Tracy turned to him, pressing her face against the old wool of his coat, and wailed. The song ended. All eyes were on Tracy and this tall, courteous stranger who would never in a thousand years have felt comfortable stroking her hair. But he let her stand there, crying, as Susan stepped up firmly on the other side of Tracy, putting her arms around her friend. And Hamadi said something Susan would remember years later, whenever she was sad herself, even after college, a creaky anthem sneaking back into her ear, "We go on. On and on. We don't stop where it hurts. We turn a corner. It is the reason why we are living. To turn a corner. Come, let's move." **N**

Above them, in the heavens, stars lived out their lonely lives. People whispered, "What happened? What's wrong?" Half of them were already walking down the street.

Vocabulary **inquiring** (ihn KWYR ihng) *v.:* looking for answers; asking.

N **Literary Perspectives** **Analyzing Biographical Context** What do you think Susan and Nye feel about Hamadi?

Applying Your Skills

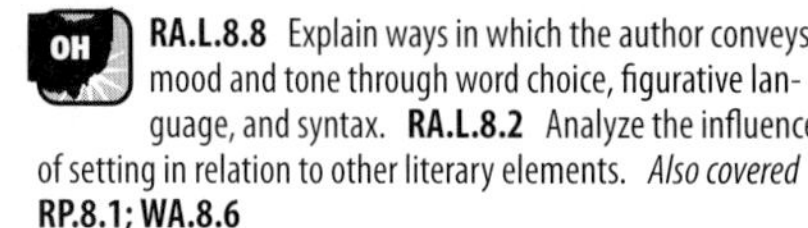

RA.L.8.8 Explain ways in which the author conveys mood and tone through word choice, figurative language, and syntax. **RA.L.8.2** Analyze the influence of setting in relation to other literary elements. *Also covered* **RP.8.1; WA.8.6**

Hamadi

Respond and Think Critically

Reading Focus

Quick Check

1. What does Susan find puzzling about Mr. Hamadi?
2. What does Mr. Hamadi teach Susan?

Read With a Purpose

3. How does Mr. Hamadi affect the people around him? Support your answer with examples from the story.

Reading Skills: Making Inferences

4. What inferences did you make about Mr. Hamadi? Use the information from your inference chart to write a short description of the character of Mr. Hamadi.

My Inferences:
Description:

Literary Focus

Literary Analysis

5. **Interpret** How does the quotation "It takes two of us to discover truth: one to utter it and one to understand it" relate to the story?
6. **Analyze** What do you think Mr. Hamadi represents to Susan?
7. **Interpret** What **theme,** or insight about life, is conveyed in this story?
8. **Literary Perspectives** Review the information from Meet the Writer. Do you think Nye's real life may have inspired the characters of Susan and Mr. Hamadi? Explain.

Literary Skills: Characterization

9. **Identify** Find three story details that help you to understand the essence of Susan's character.
10. **Analyze** Is Mr. Hamadi a contented man or a sad one? What story details support your ideas?

Literary Skills Review: Setting

11. **Analyze** A story's **setting** is its place and time. An important factor in a story, setting provides atmosphere and also meaning. How does having Christmas as a part of the setting of "Hamadi" add meaning to the story?

Writing Focus

Think as a Reader/Writer

Use It in Your Writing One way Nye develops her characters is by describing what they do. Write a short action-based character sketch about someone you admire. Instead of relying only on adjectives to describe your subject, focus on the subject's actions, and use adverbs to show how he or she does them. Turn to page 177 to learn more about adverbs.

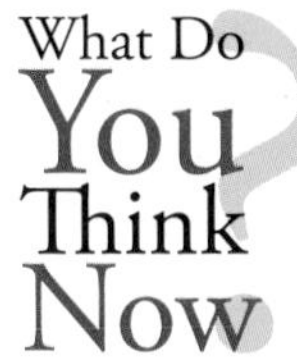

What Do You Think Now

What do you think of Mr. Hamadi's advice to Tracy? What can we learn from people who are outwardly different from us?

Applying Your Skills

Hamadi

Vocabulary Development

Etymology

Languages aren't invented. They develop over time. **Etymology** is the study of how languages develop. Each word has a history of its own. Just look in your dictionary to discover a word's past. For each entry, you'll find an abbreviated word history. Look at the bracketed portion of the entry below. (The symbol < means "derived from" or "came from.")

gratitude (GRAT uh tood) *n.* [Fr < ML *gratitudo* < L *gratus,* pleasing] thankfulness.

The abbreviation *Fr* stands for *French, ML* for *Middle Latin,* and *L* for *Latin.* The words in italics, *gratitudo* and *gratus,* are the ancestor words, in Middle Latin and Latin, that *gratitude* came from. Note the meaning of *gratus:* "pleasing." How are *pleasing* and *thankfulness* related? (You are thankful for the pleasing things in life, right?)

The next time you learn a new word, look up its etymology to find out how it came to be part of your language.

Your Turn

tedious
archaic
vaguely
inquiring

Look up each Vocabulary word in a dictionary. In your *Reader/Writer Notebook,* write the ancestor word each Vocabulary word has come from. Next, write down the meaning of the ancestor word.

EXAMPLE: *popular;* Ancestor word: Latin *populus,* meaning "people."

Language Coach

Word Origins Just as people may have lots of relatives—siblings, aunts, uncles, and cousins—words have relatives too. It's not unusual for ten or more words to spring from a common origin.

See if you can place three of the Vocabulary words into their word families, as shown below.

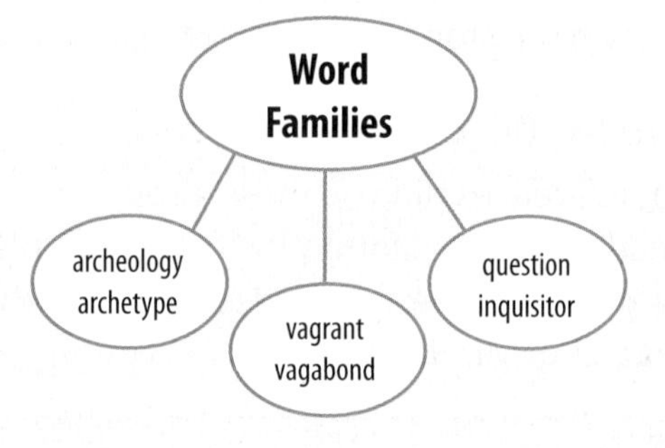

Academic Vocabulary

Write About . . .

What can you learn about Susan and her father by the way they interact? Think about the factors in the story that support your response.

RA.L.8.8 Explain ways in which the author conveys mood and tone through word choice, figurative language, and syntax. WA.8.6 Produce informal writings. WA.8.5.a Write persuasive compositions that: establish and develop a controlling idea; *Also covered* VO.8.6; VO.8.7; WC.8.3; C.8.4

Grammar Link

Adverbs

Did you know that *not* and *here* are adverbs? Identifying and using adverbs correctly can be tricky because they do so many different jobs. Adverbs can tell *where, how, when,* and *to what extent.* They can modify verbs, other adverbs, and adjectives. Look at the examples below.

MODIFYING A VERB: Susan thought deeply about Mr. Hamadi's words.

MODIFYING AN ADVERB: Susan's mother sang incredibly enthusiastically.

MODIFYING AN ADJECTIVE: The children's hospital was "eternally grateful" for Susan's donation.

Once you start looking, you'll find adverbs hiding everywhere! Look at this adverb-packed sentence.

Mr. Hamadi arrived there (where) early (when), to find the carolers utterly (to what extent) eager to celebrate merrily (how).

Your Turn

Complete each sentence with an adverb that answers the question in parentheses.

1. The carolers walked ____________ the street. (Where?)
2. Lisa chattered ____________ (How?)
3. Mr. Hamadi was ____________ sympathetic. (To what extent?)
4. Tracy heard the news and began crying ____________. (When?)
5. Susan ____________ hugged her friend as she wept. (How?)

CHOICES

As you respond to the Choices, use these **Academic Vocabulary** words as appropriate: incident, factor, interact, response.

REVIEW

Create a Character

Imagine that you are creating a television show about an outlandish **character.** Design a storyboard for the opening sequence of your show (five to six boxes), using a separate piece of paper for each box. Use captions for lines of dialogue and character descriptions.

CONNECT

Write a Letter

Timed Writing Mr. Hamadi is a "fish out of water" when he goes caroling with the English Club. Imagine that you want to invite someone who wouldn't usually be part of the group to come with you to a favorite activity. Write a one-page letter to that person in which you persuade him or her to join you. Give reasons and examples to support your argument.

EXTEND

Conduct an Interview

Listening and Speaking Interview someone who seems different from you, either in culture or interests. Ask the following questions:

- Where were your parents born?
- What are your favorite foods?
- What do you most enjoy doing?
- What is most important to you in life?

Read your notes back to make sure you recorded your subject's answers correctly. Have you discovered any common ground with the person?

SHORT STORY

Preparing to Read

A Retrieved Reformation

by **O. Henry**

What Do You Think

Everyone makes mistakes. When is it a good idea to give someone a second chance?

QuickWrite

Think of a situation in which a person should be given a second chance. What might the person learn from a chance to try again?

Reader/Writer Notebook

Use your **RWN** to complete the activities for this selection.

RA.L.8.1 Identify and explain various types of characters and how their interactions and conflicts affect the plot. **RP.8.1** Apply reading comprehension strategies, including making predictions, comparing and contrasting, recalling and summarizing and making inferences and drawing conclusions.

Literary Focus

Motivation What makes people do the things they do? In literature as in life, a person's **motivation,** or reason for acting a certain way, is not always clear. To analyze motivation as you read, ask yourself, "What clues tell me why the character did that?"

TechFocus As you read, compose an e-mail listing some questions you would like to ask Jimmy Valentine. Phrase your questions in such a way that his responses can't be yes or no.

Reading Focus

Making Connections To make connections to a story, consider what you already know and how it relates to what you're reading. Use the connections you make to help you understand the characters' behavior.

Into Action To make connections as you read, fill in a chart like the one below:

The Character	Did This	It reminded me of . . .	And helped me understand . . .
Warden	lectured Jimmy	a movie I saw where the warden spoke to a prisoner	the warden wants to help Jimmy lead an honest life
Jimmy			

Writing Focus

Think as a Reader/Writer

Find It in Your Reading As you read this story, use your *Reader/Writer Notebook* to record some vivid adjectives O. Henry uses to describe his characters, particularly the main character. Remember that adjectives are words that describe nouns and pronouns.

Vocabulary

rehabilitate (ree huh BIHL uh tayt) *v.:* restore to good standing. *The prison warden hopes Jimmy will rehabilitate himself.*

clemency (KLEHM uhn see) *n.:* mercy; tolerance. *Well-behaved prisoners may get clemency in the form of shorter sentences.*

elusive (ih LOO sihv) *adj.:* hard to catch. *The safecracker was elusive; the detectives found it difficult to catch him.*

anguish (ANG gwihsh) *n.:* emotional pain. *The thought of losing his beloved causes Jimmy great anguish.*

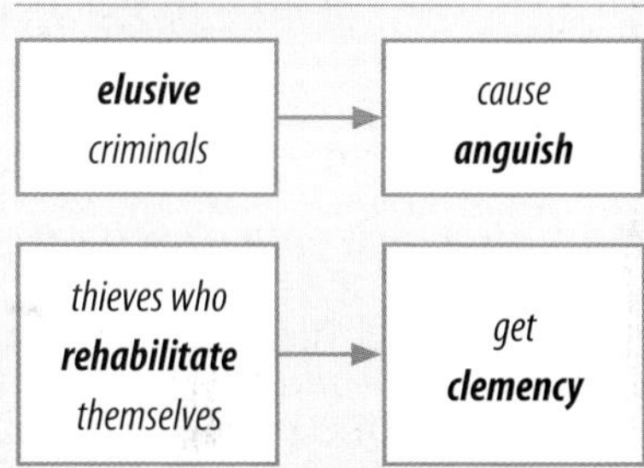

Language Coach

Oral Fluency With a partner, take turns reading aloud the example sentences for each Vocabulary word. If you have difficulty pronouncing any of the Vocabulary words, refer to the pronunciation guides provided.

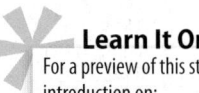

Learn It Online

For a preview of this story, see the video introduction on:

go.hrw.com L8-179

MEET THE WRITER

Learn It Online
Get more on the author's life at:
go.hrw.com L8-180 Go

O. Henry
(1862–1910)

A Career Begun in Prison

O. Henry (the pen name of William Sydney Porter) is famous for beginning his career as a short-story writer in prison, where he was sentenced to serve three years for embezzlement. This fame would not have pleased O. Henry, who was mortified by his imprisonment and told fellow inmates, "I will forget that I ever breathed behind these walls." Some people believe that he took his pen name from the name of a prison guard, Orrin Henry.

A Colorful Life

After serving his prison term, O. Henry moved to New York City. He took to life in the city, frequenting its many cafes and stores. He often recorded snatches of conversation he thought were interesting, later using them in his writing. After being inspired by the energy of the city, he would often lock himself in a room for three or four days to write. About this habit O. Henry said:

> "I have to get a story off my chest as soon as possible. . . . I have to top it off while my interest is still hot. Once I begin to yarn, I must finish without stopping or it kinda goes dead on me."

Think About the Writer How might O. Henry's time in prison have affected his life and his stories?

Build Background

O. Henry based the character of Jimmy Valentine—the criminal with a heart—on a safecracker he met in prison. The story was later made into a Broadway play called *Alias Jimmy Valentine.*

Preview the Selection

Jimmy Valentine is a career criminal and an expert safecracker. As the story opens, Valentine is about to be released from prison. A guard warns him to change his ways, but it seems unlikely Valentine will listen.

Read with a Purpose Read this short story to find out what critical decision Jimmy Valentine is forced to make.

A Retrieved Reformation

by **O. Henry**

A guard came to the prison shoeshop, where Jimmy Valentine was assiduously[1] stitching uppers, and escorted him to the front office. There the warden handed Jimmy his pardon, which had been signed that morning by the Governor. Jimmy took it in a tired kind of way. He had served nearly ten months of a four-year sentence. He had expected to stay only about three months, at the longest. When a man with as many friends on the outside as Jimmy Valentine had is received in the "stir," it is hardly worthwhile to cut his hair. **A**

"Now, Valentine," said the warden, "you'll go out in the morning. Brace up, and make a man of yourself. You're not a bad fellow at heart. Stop cracking safes, and live straight."

"Me?" said Jimmy, in surprise. "Why, I never cracked a safe in my life."

"Oh, no," laughed the warden. "Of course not. Let's see, now. How was it you happened to get sent up on that Springfield job? Was it because you wouldn't prove an alibi for fear of compromising somebody in extremely high-toned society? Or was it simply a case of a mean old jury that had it in for you? It's always one or the other with you innocent victims."

"Me?" said Jimmy, still blankly virtuous. "Why, warden, I never was in Springfield in my life!"

"Take him back, Cronin!" smiled the warden, "and fix him with outgoing clothes. Unlock him at seven in the morning, and let him come to the bullpen.[2] Better think over my advice, Valentine." **B**

At a quarter past seven on the next morning Jimmy stood in the warden's outer office. He had on a suit of the villainously fitting, ready-made clothes and a pair of the stiff, squeaky shoes that the state furnishes to its discharged compulsory[3] guests.

1. **assiduously** [uh SIHJ yoo uhs lee]: steadily and busily.

2. **bullpen:** a barred room where prisoners are held temporarily.

3. **compulsory:** forced.

A **Reading Focus** **Making Connections** What kind of person generally has a lot of friends?

B **Read and Discuss** What does the conversation between Jimmy and the warden tell us about Jimmy?

THE SATURDAY EVENING POST
By The House of KUPPENHEIMER
The Beaufort
YOU will recognize the Beaufort as one of the pronounced style hits of the season. It stands for a group of advanced Kuppenheimer Models that offer the young man a wide range of choice and an opportunity to express his individuality. Prices $20 to $45. Write for our Book "Styles for Men."
HOUSE OF KUPPENHEIMER
Chicago

Analyzing Visuals Viewing and Interpreting

How does the man in this advertisement compare with your mental image of Jimmy Valentine?

The clerk handed him a railroad ticket and the five-dollar bill with which the law expected him to rehabilitate himself into good citizenship and prosperity. The warden gave him a cigar, and shook hands. Valentine, 9762, was chronicled on the books, "Pardoned by Governor," and Mr. James Valentine walked out into the sunshine.

Disregarding the song of the birds, the waving green trees, and the smell of the flowers, Jimmy headed straight for a restaurant. There he tasted the first sweet joys of liberty in the shape of a broiled chicken and a bottle of white wine—followed by a cigar a grade better than the one the warden had given him. From there he proceeded leisurely to the depot. He tossed a quarter into the hat of a blind man sitting by the door and boarded his train. Three hours set him down in a little town near the state line. He went to the café of one Mike Dolan and shook hands with Mike, who was alone behind the bar.

"Sorry we couldn't make it sooner, Jimmy, me boy," said Mike. "But we had that protest from Springfield to buck against, and the governor nearly balked. Feeling all right?"

"Fine," said Jimmy. "Got my key?"

He got his key and went upstairs, unlocking the door of a room at the rear. Everything was just as he had left it. There on the floor was still Ben Price's collar button that had been torn from that eminent detective's shirt band when they had overpowered Jimmy to arrest him.

Vocabulary **rehabilitate** (ree huh BIHL uh tayt) *v.:* restore to good standing.

Pulling out from a wall a folding bed, Jimmy slid back a panel in the wall and dragged out a dust-covered suitcase. He opened this and gazed fondly at the finest set of burglar's tools in the East. It was a complete set, made of specially tempered steel, the latest designs in drills, punches, braces and bits, jimmies, clamps, and augers,[4] with two or three novelties invented by Jimmy himself, in which he took pride. Over nine hundred dollars they had cost him to have made at ——, a place where they make such things for the profession. **C**

In half an hour Jimmy went downstairs and through the café. He was now dressed in tasteful and well-fitting clothes and carried his dusted and cleaned suitcase in his hand.

"Got anything on?" asked Mike Dolan genially.

"Me?" said Jimmy, in a puzzled tone. "I don't understand. I'm representing the New York Amalgamated Short Snap Biscuit Cracker and Frazzled Wheat Company."

This statement delighted Mike to such an extent that Jimmy had to take a seltzer and milk on the spot. He never touched "hard" drinks.

A week after the release of Valentine, 9762, there was a neat job of safe burglary done in Richmond, Indiana, with no clue to the author. A scant eight hundred dollars was all that was secured. Two weeks after that a patented, improved, burglarproof safe in Logansport was opened like a cheese to the tune of fifteen hundred dollars, currency; securities and silver untouched. That began to interest the rogue-catchers. Then an old-fashioned bank safe in Jefferson City became active and threw out of its crater an eruption of bank notes amounting to five thousand dollars. The losses were now high enough to bring the matter up into Ben Price's class of work. By comparing notes, a remarkable similarity in the methods of the burglaries was noticed. Ben Price investigated the scenes of the robberies, and was heard to remark:

"That's Dandy Jim Valentine's autograph. He's resumed business. Look at that combination knob—jerked out as easy as pulling up a radish in wet weather. He's got the only clamps that can do it. And look how clean those tumblers were punched out! Jimmy never has to drill but one hole. Yes, I guess I want Mr. Valentine. He'll do his bit next time without any short-time or clemency foolishness." **D**

Ben Price knew Jimmy's habits. He had learned them while working on the Springfield case. Long jumps, quick getaways, no confederates,[5] and a taste for good society—these ways had helped Mr. Valentine to become noted as a successful dodger of retribution.[6] It was given out that

4. **drills . . . augers** (AW guhrz): tools for working with metal.

5. **confederates:** accomplices, or fellow criminals.

6. **retribution** (reht ruh BYOO shuhn): punishment.

C **Literary Focus** **Motivation** What reasons might Jimmy have for retrieving his suitcase?

D **Read and Discuss** What is Jimmy doing now?

Vocabulary **clemency** (KLEHM uhn see) *n.:* mercy; tolerance.

Ben Price had taken up the trail of the elusive cracksman, and other people with burglarproof safes felt more at ease. **E**

One afternoon Jimmy Valentine and his suitcase climbed out of the mail hack[7] in Elmore, a little town five miles off the railroad down in the blackjack country of Arkansas. Jimmy, looking like an athletic young senior just home from college, went down the board sidewalk toward the hotel.

A young lady crossed the street, passed him at the corner, and entered a door over which was the sign "The Elmore Bank." Jimmy Valentine looked into her eyes, forgot what he was, and became another man. She lowered her eyes and colored slightly. Young men of Jimmy's style and looks were scarce in Elmore.

Jimmy collared a boy that was loafing on the steps of the bank as if he were one of the stockholders, and began to ask him questions about the town, feeding him dimes at intervals. By and by the young lady came out, looking royally unconscious of the young man with the suitcase, and went her way.

"Isn't that young lady Miss Polly Simpson?" asked Jimmy, with specious guile.[8]

"Naw," said the boy. "She's Annabel Adams. Her pa owns this bank. What'd you come to Elmore for? Is that a gold watch chain? I'm going to get a bulldog. Got any more dimes?" **F**

Jimmy went to the Planters' Hotel, registered as Ralph D. Spencer, and engaged a room. He leaned on the desk and declared his platform[9] to the clerk. He said he had come to Elmore to look for a location to go into business. How was the shoe business, now, in the town? He had thought of the shoe business. Was there an opening?

The clerk was impressed by the clothes and manner of Jimmy. He, himself, was something of a pattern of fashion to the thinly gilded[10] youth of Elmore, but now he perceived his shortcomings. While trying to figure out Jimmy's manner of tying his four-in-hand,[11] he cordially gave information.

Yes, there ought to be a good opening in the shoe line. There wasn't an exclusive shoe store in the place. The dry goods and general stores handled them. Business in all lines was fairly good. Hoped Mr. Spencer would decide to locate in Elmore. He would find it a pleasant town to live in, and the people very sociable.

Mr. Spencer thought he would stop over in the town a few days and look over the situation. No, the clerk needn't call the boy. He would carry up his suitcase, himself; it was rather heavy. **G**

---

7. **mail hack:** horse-drawn carriage used to carry mail from one town to another.
8. **with specious** (SPEE shuhs) **guile** (gyl): in a tricky way that appears to be innocent.
9. **platform:** here, intentions, or plans.
10. **thinly gilded:** only seeming to be well-dressed. To be gilded is to be covered with a layer of gold.
11. **four-in-hand:** a necktie.

E Reading Focus Making Connections Think of other detectives you've seen or read about. How is Ben Price like them?

F Read and Discuss What is happening now? What do Jimmy's encounters with the people on the street tell us about him?

G Literary Focus Motivation Why do you think Jimmy wants to set up a shoe business in town?

Vocabulary **elusive** (ih LOO sihv) *adj.:* hard to catch.

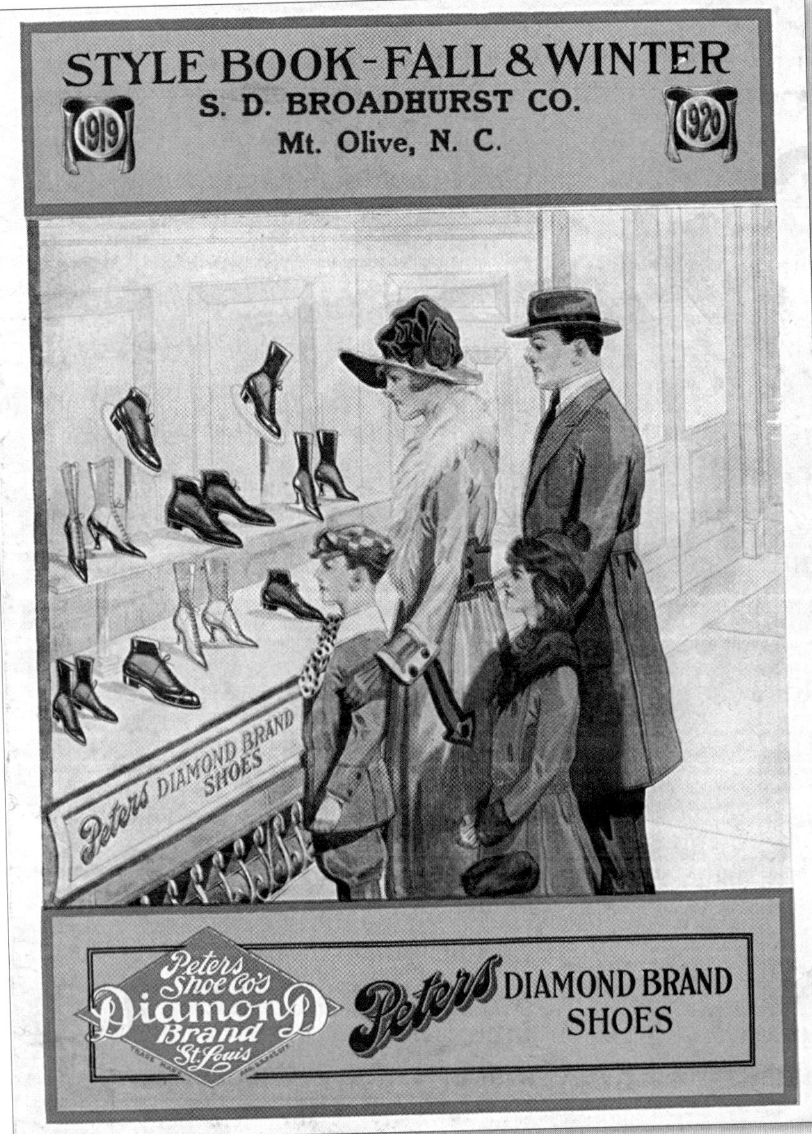

STYLE BOOK-FALL & WINTER
S. D. BROADHURST CO.
Mt. Olive, N. C.
1919
1920
Peters DIAMOND BRAND SHOES
Peters Shoe Co's Diamond Brand St. Louis
Peters DIAMOND BRAND SHOES

Socially he was also a success and made many friends. And he accomplished the wish of his heart. He met Miss Annabel Adams and became more and more captivated by her charms.

At the end of a year the situation of Mr. Ralph Spencer was this: he had won the respect of the community, his shoe store was flourishing, and he and Annabel were engaged to be married in two weeks. Mr. Adams, the typical, plodding country banker, approved of Spencer. Annabel's pride in him almost equaled her affection. He was as much at home in the family of Mr. Adams and that of Annabel's married sister as if he were already a member. **H**

One day Jimmy sat down in his room and wrote this letter, which he mailed to the safe address of one of his old friends in St. Louis:

Mr. Ralph Spencer, the phoenix[12] that arose from Jimmy Valentine's ashes—ashes left by the flame of a sudden and alterative attack of love—remained in Elmore and prospered. He opened a shoe store and secured a good run of trade.

12. **phoenix** (FEE nihks): bird in ancient Egyptian mythology. It was believed that the phoenix burned itself up and that from its ashes a new bird arose.

Dear Old Pal:

I want you to be at Sullivan's place, in Little Rock, next Wednesday night, at nine o'clock. I want you to wind up some little matters for me. And, also, I want to make you a present of my little kit of tools. I know you'll be glad to get them—you couldn't duplicate the lot for a thousand dollars. Say, Billy, I've quit

H **Read and Discuss** How are things looking for Jimmy?

the old business—a year ago. I've got a nice store. I'm making an honest living, and I'm going to marry the finest girl on earth two weeks from now. It's the only life, Billy—the straight one. I wouldn't touch a dollar of another man's money now for a million. After I get married I'm going to sell out and go West, where there won't be so much danger of having old scores brought up against me. I tell you, Billy, she's an angel. She believes in me; and I wouldn't do another crooked thing for the whole world. Be sure to be at Sully's, for I must see you. I'll bring along the tools with me.

Your old friend,
Jimmy **I**

On the Monday night after Jimmy wrote this letter, Ben Price jogged unobtrusively into Elmore in a livery buggy.[13] He lounged about town in his quiet way until he found out what he wanted to know. From the drugstore across the street from Spencer's shoe store, he got a good look at Ralph D. Spencer.

"Going to marry the banker's daughter, are you, Jimmy?" said Ben to himself, softly. "Well, I don't know!" **J**

The next morning Jimmy took breakfast at the Adamses'. He was going to Little Rock that day to order his wedding suit and buy something nice for Annabel. That would be the first time he had left town since he came to Elmore. It had been more than a year now since those last professional "jobs," and he thought he could safely venture out.

After breakfast quite a family party went downtown together—Mr. Adams, Annabel, Jimmy, and Annabel's married sister with her two little girls, aged five and nine. They came by the hotel where Jimmy still boarded, and he ran up to his room and brought along his suitcase. Then they went on to the bank. There stood Jimmy's horse and buggy and Dolph Gibson, who was going to drive him over to the railroad station.

All went inside the high, carved oak railings into the banking room—Jimmy included, for Mr. Adams' future son-in-law was welcome anywhere. The clerks were pleased to be greeted by the good-looking, agreeable young man who was going to marry Miss Annabel. Jimmy set his suitcase down. Annabel, whose heart was bubbling with happiness and lively youth, put on Jimmy's hat and picked up the suitcase. "Wouldn't I make a nice drummer?"[14] asked Annabel. "My! Ralph, how heavy it is! Feels like it was full of gold bricks."

"Lot of nickel-plated shoehorns in there," said Jimmy, coolly, "that I'm going to return. Thought I'd save express charges by taking them up. I'm getting awfully economical." **K**

The Elmore Bank had just put in a new safe and vault. Mr. Adams was very

13. **livery buggy:** hired horse and carriage.

14. **drummer:** here, a traveling salesperson.

I **Literary Focus** **Motivation** Why does Jimmy write the letter?

J **Literary Focus** **Motivation** What has motivated Ben Price to visit Elmore?

K **Read and Discuss** Now what has happened? Why is Jimmy's suitcase so heavy?

proud of it and insisted on an inspection by everyone. The vault was a small one, but it had a new patented door. It fastened with three solid steel bolts thrown simultaneously with a single handle, and had a time lock. Mr. Adams beamingly explained its workings to Mr. Spencer, who showed a courteous but not too intelligent interest. The two children, May and Agatha, were delighted by the shining metal and funny clock and knobs. **L**

While they were thus engaged, Ben Price sauntered in and leaned on his elbow, looking casually inside between the railings. He told the teller that he didn't want anything; he was just waiting for a man he knew.

Jealousy (detail) (1892) by Tihamer Margitay.

Suddenly there was a scream or two from the women and a commotion. Unperceived by the elders, May, the nine-year-old girl, in a spirit of play had shut Agatha in the vault. She had then shot the bolts and turned the knob of the combination as she had seen Mr. Adams do.

The old banker sprang to the handle and tugged at it for a moment. "The door can't be opened," he groaned. "The clock hasn't been wound nor the combination set."

Agatha's mother screamed again, hysterically.

"Hush!" said Mr. Adams, raising his trembling hand. "All be quite for a moment. Agatha!" he called as loudly as he could. "Listen to me." During the following silence they could just hear the faint sound of the child wildly shrieking in the dark vault in a panic of terror.

L **Reading Focus** **Making Connections** Judging by what you've learned about criminals, will Jimmy be tempted to steal from the safe? Why or why not?

"My precious darling!" wailed the mother. "She will die of fright! Open the door! Oh, break it open! Can't you men do something?"

"There isn't a man nearer than Little Rock who can open that door," said Mr. Adams, in a shaky voice. "Spencer, what shall we do? That child—she can't stand it long in there. There isn't enough air, and, besides, she'll go into convulsions[15] from fright." **M**

Agatha's mother, frantic now, beat the door of the vault with her hands. Somebody wildly suggested dynamite. Annabel turned to Jimmy, her large eyes full of anguish, but not yet despairing. To a woman nothing seems quite impossible to the powers of the man she worships.

"Can't you do something, Ralph—*try,* won't you?"

He looked at her with a queer, soft smile on his lips and in his keen eyes.

"Annabel," he said, "give me that rose you are wearing, will you?"

Hardly believing that she heard him aright, she unpinned the bud from the bosom of her dress, and placed it in his hand. Jimmy stuffed it into his vest pocket, threw off his coat, and pulled up his shirt sleeves. With that act Ralph D. Spencer passed away, and Jimmy Valentine took his place.

"Get away from the door, all of you," he commanded, shortly.

15. **convulsions:** shaking fits.

He set his suitcase on the table, and opened it out flat. From that time on he seemed to be unconscious of the presence of anyone else. He laid out the shining, queer implements swiftly and orderly, whistling softly to himself as he always did when at work. In a deep silence and immovable, the others watched him as if under a spell.

In a minute Jimmy's pet drill was biting smoothly into the steel door. In ten minutes—breaking his own burglarious record—he threw back the bolts and opened the door. **N**

Agatha, almost collapsed, but safe, was gathered into her mother's arms.

Jimmy Valentine put on his coat, and walked outside the railings toward the front door. As he went he thought he heard a far-away voice that he once knew call "Ralph!" But he never hesitated.

At the door a big man stood somewhat in his way.

"Hello, Ben!" said Jimmy, still with his strange smile. "Got around at last, have you? Well, let's go. I don't know that it makes much difference, now."

And then Ben Price acted rather strangely.

"Guess you're mistaken, Mr. Spencer," he said. "Don't believe I recognize you. Your buggy's waiting for you, ain't it?"

And Ben Price turned and strolled down the street. **O**

M **Read and Discuss** What is happening? What mood has the author created?

N **Literary Focus** **Motivation** Valentine knows he may get caught if he opens the safe. Why do you think he opens it anyway?

O **Literary Focus** **Motivation** Why doesn't Price arrest Valentine?

Vocabulary **anguish** (ANG gwihsh) *n.:* emotional pain.

Applying Your Skills

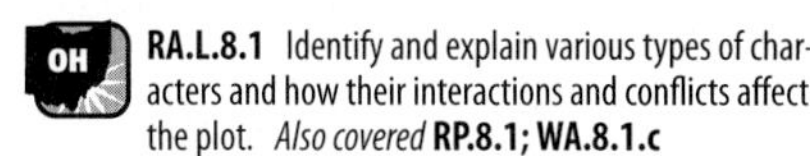

RA.L.8.1 Identify and explain various types of characters and how their interactions and conflicts affect the plot. *Also covered* **RP.8.1; WA.8.1.c**

A Retrieved Reformation

Respond and Think Critically

Reading Focus

Quick Check

1. Who is Ben Price, and what is his opinion of Jimmy?
2. What decision does Ben Price make at the story's end?

Read with a Purpose

3. What critical decision does Jimmy Valentine make when the girl gets locked in the safe? What risk is he taking?

Reading Skills: Making Connections

4. Complete the chart you made as you read "A Retrieved Reformation." What stories or life experiences did this story bring to mind? How did making connections help you understand the story?

The Character	Did This	It reminded me of . . .	And helped me understand . . .

Literary Focus

Literary Analysis

5. **Interpret** What is the significance of Jimmy's name change to Ralph D. Spencer?
6. **Infer** What can you infer about the type of person Ben Price is when he lets Jimmy go?
7. **Make Judgments** Do you believe Ben Price makes the right decision at the end of the story? Why or why not?
8. **Extend** Do you think that Jimmy has really given up stealing for good? Explain.

Literary Skills: Motivation

9. **Evaluate** What factors cause Jimmy to change his criminal ways? Do you think his reformation is believable? Why or why not?
10. **Analyze** What might be Ben Price's motivation for letting Jimmy go free at the story's end? Why did Price have a change of heart?

Literary Skills Review: Conflict

11. **Interpret** Conflict is a struggle between two or more forces. **External conflict** is between a character and another character or force. **Internal conflict** occurs inside a character's mind. What is the external conflict in this story? (Hint: It's between two characters.) What is Valentine's inner conflict? When does it occur?

Writing Focus

Think as a Reader/Writer

Use It in Your Writing The descriptive words O. Henry uses help you get to know the characters. Write a short description of someone you know. Use vivid adjectives to bring the person to life for your reader.

What Do You Think Now?

Has reading "A Retrieved Reformation" changed your ideas about giving people second chances? Why or why not?

Applying Your Skills

A Retrieved Reformation

Vocabulary Development

Influences in English

The histories of English words can give us a glimpse of the history of the English-speaking peoples themselves. Thousands of words that we use every day have come into English from other languages. Some countries have tried to prevent foreign words from entering their languages. English, however, has always been like a giant sponge, absorbing words from every group with which it comes in contact. The Vocabulary words in "A Retrieved Reformation" all come from Latin.

- **rehabilitate** L *re–*, "again," + L *habilitare*, "make suitable"
- **clemency** L *clemens*, "merciful"
- **elusive** L *elusus*, "trick, fool"
- **anguish** L *angustia*, "tightness, distress"

Your Turn

Match each Vocabulary word with a related word that springs from the same Latin word.

1. rehabilitate	**a.** clement
2. anguish	**b.** elude
3. elusive	**c.** anger
4. clemency	**d.** habit

Language Coach

Oral Fluency People in many professions, such as newscasters and actors, need to be able to speak fluently and clearly. To do that, they practice speaking aloud.

With a partner, take turns reading the following "news item" aloud as if you were a television anchor reporting the event. Remember to refer to the pronunciations of the words on page 179 if you need help. Practice makes perfect!

News Item:
Following a period of good behavior, Jasper "Fingers" Johnson was shown **clemency** and released from prison one year into his sentence. Sadly, the master criminal was unable to **rehabilitate** himself, and he returned to his old ways, stealing pianos. Despite law enforcement's best efforts, "Fingers" remains **elusive.** His relatives wait with **anguish,** unsure of the fate that lies in store for Johnson once he is finally recaptured.

Academic Vocabulary

Talk About . . .
With a partner, act out an incident that might take place a year after the story ends, when Valentine meets Price unexpectedly. What would be their initial response to each other? What would they discuss, and how would the two interact?

RA.L.8.1 Identify and explain various types of characters and how their interactions and conflicts affect the plot. **WC.8.3** Grammar and Usage: Use all eight parts of speech. *Also covered* **VO.8.7; VO.8.6; WA.8.5.b**

Grammar Link

Prepositions

Prepositions tell you how a noun or pronoun relates to another word. Notice how a change of preposition changes the meaning of the following sentences. The prepositions are boldface.

The officer chased the criminal **with** the police car.

The officer chased the criminal **into** the police car.

The officer chased the criminal **under** the police car.

The officer chased the criminal **around** the police car.

The officer chased the criminal **out of** the police car.

Your Turn

Complete the following sentences by choosing the appropriate preposition from the list.

into after with beween to

1. Valentine left prison __________ serving his sentence.
2. Soon after, Valentine fell in love __________ Annabel Adams.
3. After deciding to give up his old ways, Valentine sent a letter __________ his old friend.
4. The situation was dire; Valentine used his tools to break __________ the safe.
5. The interaction __________ Valentine and Price at the end of the story was rather unusual.

CHOICES

As you respond to the Choices, use these **Academic Vocabulary** words as appropriate: incident, factor, interact, response.

REVIEW

Conduct an Interview

TechFocus How and why do you think Jimmy Valentine began safecracking? Imagine interviewing him. Write a blog entry about your experience in the interview. What did you think of him? What did you discover about his **motivations**?

CONNECT

Analyze a Character

Timed Writing Jimmy Valentine turns out to be different from how Ben Price thought he was. Write a paragraph explaining your first impression of Jimmy Valentine. Then, write another paragraph describing whether your opinion of him changed at all by the end of the story. Use details to explain your ideas.

EXTEND

Pitch a TV Series

Group Project How does Jimmy explain his knowledge of safes to Annabel and her family? Does he still get married, or is he booted out of town? Imagine "A Retrieved Reformation" is the first episode of a new TV series. Develop a plan for future episodes. "Pitch" your ideas to the class, explaining why viewers will watch.

SHORT STORY

Preparing to Read

PASSAGE TO FREEDOM: THE SUGIHARA STORY

by **Ken Mochizuki**

The Hall of Names in the Yad Vashem Holocaust Memorial in Jerusalem.

When is it more important to help others than to protect yourself?

QuickWrite

What advice would you give someone who had to choose between what he or she was told to do and what he or she thought was right?

Reader/Writer Notebook

Use your **RWN** to complete the activities for this selection.

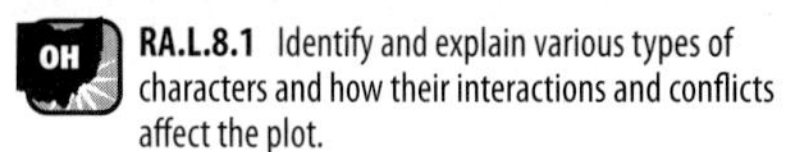

RA.L.8.1 Identify and explain various types of characters and how their interactions and conflicts affect the plot.

Literary Focus

Character Relationships In "Passage to Freedom" the author reveals the character of Mr. Sugihara not by telling the reader about him but by showing the reader his relationships with others and how he treats them. As you read, take note of the ways Mr. Sugihara interacts with his family, with the refugees, and with the Japanese government. What do these interactions reveal about his character?

Reading Focus

Making Judgments You make a judgment when you decide whether something is good or bad, interesting or boring. Every day, you make judgments, including judgments about what you read.

Into Action Using a chart like the one below, answer the following questions to help you make judgments about Mr. Sugihara.

How does Mr. Sugihara treat . . .	My Judgment:
his family? He considers their needs and asks them to help him decide what to do.	
the wartime refugees?	
others in his government?	

Writing Focus

Think as a Reader/Writer

Find It in Your Reading The writer begins the story with the saying "The eyes tell everything about a person" and then uses images of people's eyes throughout the story. As you come across these descriptions, list them in your *Reader/Writer Notebook.*

TechFocus As you read, make a list of keywords for an Internet search to find out more about refugees in the world today.

Vocabulary

diplomat (DIHP luh mat) *n.:* person who handles issues with other countries. *A Japanese diplomat, Mr. Sugihara represents his country in Lithuania.*

refugees (rehf yuh JEEZ) *n.:* people who seek refuge, or safety, especially in another country. *The refugees desperately need to go to Japan.*

superiors (suh PIHR ee uhrz) *n.:* people of higher rank. *The diplomat had to ask permission from his superiors.*

fate (fayt) *n.:* what becomes of someone or something. *The fate of the refugees is unknown: Will they survive?*

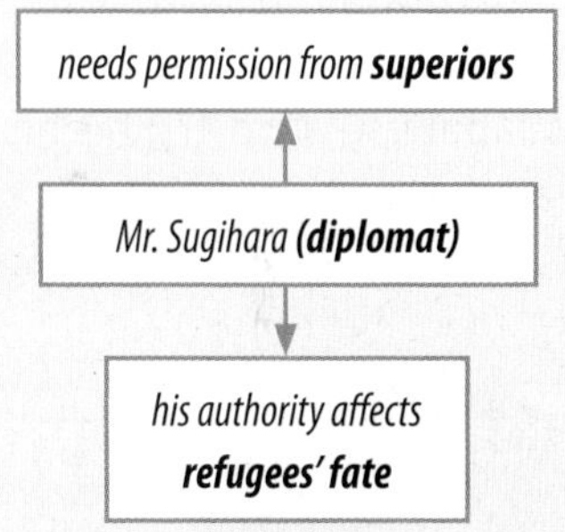

Language Coach

Suffixes When added to the word *super,* meaning "above," the suffix *–ior* makes a word that means "someone who is above." Copy these words into your *Reader/Writer Notebook* and try to figure out their meanings: *anterior, ulterior,* and *inferior.*

Learn It Online

Take a closer look at words. Increase your comprehension with Word Watch at:

go.hrw.com L8-193 

MEET THE WRITER

Ken Mochizuki

(1954–)

One Person Can Make a Difference

Ken Mochizuki says that he wrote "Passage to Freedom" because he wanted to show that one person can make a difference in the world: Chiune Sugihara, the real-life subject of this story, issued about 6,000 visas to refugees. The descendants of those refugees now number more than 40,000.

Telling the Story

"Passage to Freedom" was Mochizuki's first try at writing historical fiction for young people. First, he gathered all the facts. Then he had to figure out how he could tell the story from the point of view of a five-year-old boy. He decided to tell the story in the first person, as if he were that boy himself.

Eliminating Stereotypes

Mochizuki, who was born in Seattle, Washington, speaks at schools about his work writing books for young people. He tries to challenge stereotypes by pointing out that although he has Japanese ancestry, his first language is English, he doesn't wear glasses or practice any martial arts, and as a student he wasn't particularly good at math.

Think About the Writer How has Mochizuki shown that one person can make a difference?

Build Background

"Passage to Freedom" is a work of historical fiction. The story is fictional because the writer has created the character who is telling the story. The writer also made up some details and dialogue. The story is historical because it is based on real events and people. In fact, the real Hiroki Sugihara—who was the basis for the made-up narrator in the story—has written an Afterword, which you will read after the selection.

Preview the Selection

In this story the narrator's father, **Mr. Sugihara,** must choose between what his government tells him to do and what his conscience tells him to do.

Read with a Purpose Read to discover the risks a Japanese diplomat takes in a time of war.

PASSAGE TO FREEDOM: THE SUGIHARA STORY

by **Ken Mochizuki**

There is a saying that the eyes tell everything about a person.

At a store, my father saw a young Jewish boy who didn't have enough money to buy what he wanted. So my father gave the boy some of his. That boy looked into my father's eyes and, to thank him, invited my father to his home.

That is when my family and I went to a Hanukkah[1] celebration for the first time. I was five years old. **A**

In 1940, my father was a diplomat representing the country of Japan. Our family lived in a small town in the small country called Lithuania. There was my father and mother, my Auntie Setsuko, my younger brother Chiaki, and my three-month-old baby brother, Haruki. My father worked in his office downstairs.

1. **Hanukkah** (HAH noo kah): Jewish festival celebrated in December.

In the mornings, birds sang in the trees. We played with girls and boys from the neighborhood at a huge park near our home. Houses and churches around us were hundreds of years old. In our room, Chiaki and I played with toy German soldiers, tanks, and planes. Little did we know that the real soldiers were coming our way.

Then one early morning in late July, my life changed forever. **B**

My mother and Auntie Setsuko woke Chiaki and me up, telling us to get dressed quickly. My father ran upstairs from his office.

"There are a lot of people outside," my mother said. "We don't know what is going to happen."

In the living room, my parents told my brother and me not to let anybody see us looking through the window. So, I parted

A **Literary Focus** **Character Relationships** What does this incident suggest about Mr. Sugihara and how he treats people?

Vocabulary **diplomat** (DIHP luh mat) *n.:* person who handles issues with other countries.

B **Read and Discuss** What has the author told us about the narrator and his family? What is the author doing when he writes, "Then one early morning in late July, my life changed forever"?

the curtains a tiny bit. Outside, I saw hundreds of people crowded around the gate in front of our house.

The grown-ups shouted in Polish, a language I did not understand. Then I saw the children. They stared at our house through the iron bars of the gate. Some of them were my age. Like the grown-ups, their eyes were red from not having slept for days. They wore heavy winter coats—some wore more than one coat, even though it was warm outside. These children looked as though they had dressed in a hurry. But if they came from somewhere else, where were their suitcases?

"What do they want?" I asked my mother.

"They have come to ask for your father's help," she replied. "Unless we help, they may be killed or taken away by some bad men."

Some of the children held on tightly to the hands of their fathers, some clung to their mothers. One little girl sat on the ground, crying.

I felt like crying, too. "Father," I said, "please help them." **C**

My father stood quietly next to me, but I knew he saw the children. Then some of the men in the crowd began climbing over the fence. Borislav and Gudje, two young men who worked for my father, tried to keep the crowd calm. **D**

My father walked outside. Peering through the curtains, I saw him standing on the steps. Borislav translated what my father said: He asked the crowd to choose five people to come inside and talk.

My father met downstairs with the five men. My father could speak Japanese, Chinese, Russian, German, French, and English. At this meeting, everyone spoke Russian.

I couldn't help but stare out the window and watch the crowd, while downstairs, for two hours, my father listened to frightening stories. These people were refugees—people who ran away from their homes because, if they stayed, they would be killed. They were Jews from Poland, escaping from the Nazi soldiers who had taken over their country.

The five men had heard my father could give them visas—official written permission to travel through another country. The hundreds of Jewish refugees outside hoped to travel east through the Soviet Union and end up in Japan. Once in Japan, they could go to another country. Was it true? the men asked. Could my father issue these visas? If he did not, the Nazis would soon catch up with them.

My father answered that he could issue a few, but not hundreds. To do that, he would have to ask for permission from his government in Japan.

That night, the crowd stayed outside our house. Exhausted from the day's excitement, I slept soundly. But it was one of the worst nights of my father's life. He had to make a decision. If he helped these people, would he put our family in danger? If the Nazis found out, what would they do? **E**

But if he did not help these people, they could all die.

C **Literary Focus** **Character Relationships** Why do you think the boy asks his father to help the people?

D **Read and Discuss** What is going on now?

E **Reading Focus** **Making Judgments** What decision does Mr. Sugihara face? What do you think his response should be? Why?

Vocabulary **refugees** (rehf yuh JEEZ) *n.:* people who seek refuge, or safety, especially in another country.

SOCIAL STUDIES **LINK**

Passage to Freedom: The Sugihara Story

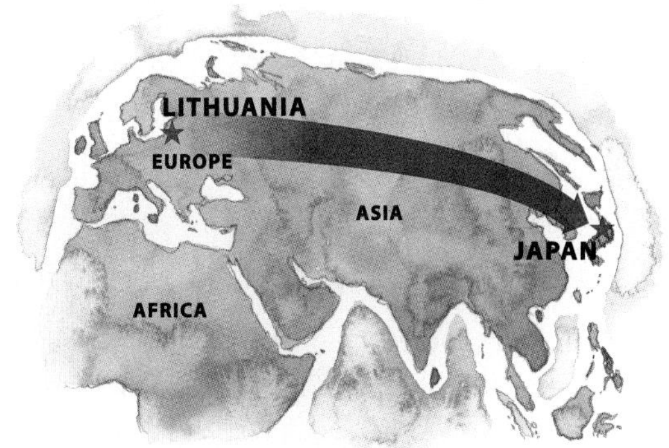

"Passage to Freedom: The Sugihara Story" takes place in 1940, during the chaos of World War II. During this time, Nazi Germany was invading much of Western Europe and beginning its plan to rid Europe of Jewish people. Soviet Russia, at the time an ally of Germany, had invaded the small Baltic countries of Estonia, Latvia, and Lithuania, where this story takes place. It was not until more than a year later, on December 7, 1941, that Japan bombed Pearl Harbor and the United States entered the war.

The Jewish refugees from Poland in "Passage to Freedom" hope to travel east through the Soviet Union to Japan. Once in Japan, they will try to go to other countries where they can be safe.

Ask Yourself

With a partner, use the map above to trace the path the refugees will take. What qualities would a person need to survive such a journey?

My mother listened to the bed squeak as my father tossed and turned all night.

The next day, my father said he was going to ask his government about the visas. My mother agreed it was the right thing to do. My father sent his message by cable. Gudje took my father's written message down to the telegraph office.

I watched the crowd as they waited for the Japanese government's reply. The five representatives came into our house several times that day to ask if an answer had been received. Any time the gate opened, the crowd tried to charge inside.

Finally, the answer came from the Japanese government. It was "no." My father could not issue that many visas to Japan. For the next two days, he thought about what to do.

Hundreds more Jewish refugees joined the crowd. My father sent a second message to his government, and again the answer was "no." We still couldn't go outside. My little brother Haruki cried often because we were running out of milk.

I grew tired of staying indoors. I asked my father constantly, "Why are these people here? What do they want? Why do they have to be here? Who are they?"

My father always took the time to explain everything to me. He said the refugees needed his help, that they needed permission from him to go to another part of the world where they would be safe.

"I cannot help these people yet," he calmly told me. "But when the time comes, I will help them all that I can."

My father cabled his superiors yet a third time, and I knew the answer by the look in his eyes. That night, he said to my mother, "I have to do something. I may have to disobey my government, but if I don't, I will be disobeying God."

The next morning, he brought the family together and asked what he should do. This was the first time he ever asked all of us to help him with anything.

My mother and Auntie Setsuko had already made up their minds. They said we had to think about the people outside before we thought about ourselves. And that is what my parents had always told me—that I must think as if I were in someone else's place. If I were one of those children out there, what would I want someone to do for me?

I said to my father, "If we don't help them, won't they die?"

With the entire family in agreement, I could tell a huge weight was lifted off my father's shoulders. His voice was firm as he told us, "I will start helping these people."

Outside, the crowd went quiet as my father spoke, with Borislav translating.

"I will issue visas to each and every one of you to the last. So, please wait patiently." **F**

The crowd stood frozen for a second. Then the refugees burst into cheers. Grown-ups embraced each other, and some reached to the sky. Fathers and mothers hugged their children. I was especially glad for the children.

My father opened the garage door and the crowd tried to rush in. To keep order, Borislav handed out cards with numbers. My

Vocabulary **superiors** (suh PIHR ee uhrz) *n.:* people of higher rank.

F **Read and Discuss** Why would the father have a "huge weight" lifted from his shoulders when he is planning to disobey his government?

(left) Chiune Sugihara, c. 1937. (middle) Polish-Jewish refugees lined up outside Japanese consulate in Kaunas, Lithuania, waiting for visas from Sugihara. (right) Reunion of Chiune Sugihara, left, and Zorach Warhaftig, Israeli Religious Minister and Sugihara survivor in Jerusalem, 1968.

Analyzing Visuals **Viewing and Interpreting** How do these accompanying photos effect the impact that Mochizuki's writing has on you, the reader? Explain.

father wrote out each visa by hand. After he finished each one, he looked into the eyes of the person receiving the visa and said, "Good luck." G

Refugees camped out at our favorite park, waiting to see my father. I was finally able to go outside.

Chiaki and I played with the other children in our toy car. They pushed as we rode, and they rode as we pushed. We chased each other around the big trees. We did not speak the same language, but that didn't stop us.

For about a month, there was always a line leading to the garage. Every day, from early in the morning till late at night, my father tried to write three hundred visas. He watered down the ink to make it last. Gudje and a young Jewish man helped out by stamping my father's name on the visas.

My mother offered to help write the visas, but my father insisted he be the only one, so no one else could get into trouble. So my mother watched the crowd and told my father how many were still in line.

One day, my father pressed down so hard on his fountain pen, the tip broke off. During that month, I only saw him late at night. His eyes were always red and he could hardly talk. While he slept, my mother massaged his arm, stiff and cramped from writing all day.

Soon my father grew so tired, he wanted to quit writing the visas. But my mother encouraged him to continue. "Many people are still waiting," she said. "Let's issue some more visas and save as many lives as we can." H

While the Germans approached from the west, the Soviets came from the east and took over Lithuania. They ordered my

---

G **Literary Focus** **Character Relationships** How does Mr. Sugihara help the refugees? What do his actions tell you about him?

H **Reading Focus** **Making Judgments** What do you think of the relationship between Mr. and Mrs. Sugihara?

father to leave. So did the Japanese government, which reassigned him to Germany. Still, my father wrote the visas until we absolutely had to move out of our home. We stayed at a hotel for two days, where my father still wrote visas for the many refugees who followed him there.

Then it was time to leave Lithuania. Refugees who had slept at the train station crowded around my father. Some refugee men surrounded my father to protect him. He now just issued permission papers—blank pieces of paper with his signature.

As the train pulled away, refugees ran alongside. My father still handed permission papers out the window. As the train picked up speed, he threw them out to waiting hands. The people in the front of the crowd looked into my father's eyes and cried, "We will never forget you! We will see you again!" **I**

I gazed out the train window, watching Lithuania and the crowd of refugees fade away. I wondered if we would ever see them again.

"Where are we going?" I asked my father.

"We are going to Berlin," he replied.

Chiaki and I became very excited about going to the big city. I had so many questions for my father. But he fell asleep as soon as he settled into his seat. My mother and Auntie Setsuko looked really tired, too.

Back then, I did not fully understand what the three of them had done, or why it was so important.

I do now. **J**

Afterword by Hiroki Sugihara

Each time that I think about what my father did at Kaunas, Lithuania, in 1940, my appreciation and understanding of the incident continues to grow. My father remained concerned about the fate of the refugees, and at one point left his address at the Israeli Embassy in Japan. Finally, in the 1960s, he started hearing from "Sugihara survivors," many of whom had kept their visas, and considered the worn pieces of paper to be family treasures.

In 1969, my father was invited to Israel, where he was taken to the famous Holocaust memorial, Yad Vashem. In 1985, he was chosen to receive the "Righteous Among Nations" Award from Yad Vashem. He was the first Japanese person to have been given this great honor.

In 1992, six years after his death, a monument to my father was dedicated in his birthplace of Yaotsu, Japan, on a hill that is now known as the Hill of Humanity. In 1994, a group of Sugihara survivors traveled to Japan to re-dedicate the monument in a ceremony that was attended by several high officials of the Japanese government.

I **Literary Focus** **Character Relationships** Why do you think the refugees say that they will see Mr. Sugihara again?

J **Read and Discuss** How have things turned out for the father?

Vocabulary **fate** (fayt) *n.:* what becomes of someone or something.

Applying Your Skills

RA.L.8.1 Identify and explain various types of characters and how their interactions and conflicts affect the plot. **RA.L.8.3** Explain how authors pace action and use subplots, parallel episodes and climax. **WA.8.6** Produce informal writings.

Passage to Freedom

Respond and Think Critically

Reading Focus

Quick Check

1. Why do the refugees standing outside the Sugiharas' home want to leave Lithuania?
2. How does the Japanese government prevent Mr. Sugihara from helping the refugees?
3. Years later, how is Mr. Sugihara honored?

Read with a Purpose

4. What risks does Mr. Sugihara take to help the refugees?

Reading Skills: Making Judgments

5. Review the chart you made about Mr. Sugihara's relationships with others. Now, write your overall judgment of his character.

Literary Focus

Literary Analysis

6. **Draw Conclusions** What values do Mr. Sugihara's actions teach his son?
7. **Analyze** Re-read the passage in which the narrator and his brother play with the refugee children. What message about life do these lines suggest?

Literary Skills: Character Relationships

8. **Analyze** Everything we learn in this story is told to us by Mr. Sugihara's son. How do you think the father-son relationship affects our view of Mr. Sugihara?
9. **Infer** How do the refugees feel about Mr. Sugihara at the end of the story? How do you know?

Literary Skills Review: Plot

10. **Plot** is a series of events that occur in a story. Use a diagram like the one below to chart the plot of "Passage to Freedom."

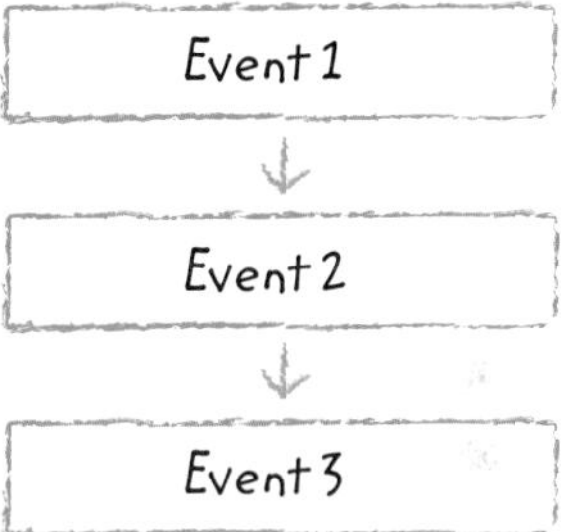

Writing Focus

Think as a Reader/Writer

Use It in Your Writing Look back at the images of eyes that you listed in your *Reader/Writer Notebook*. What do these images tell you about the people being described? Now, try writing some of your own images of eyes. Write sentences to describe the following:

The eyes of someone who is afraid.
The eyes of someone who is happy and excited.
The eyes of someone who is angry.

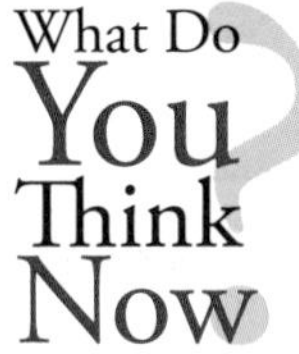

Have your thoughts about helping others versus protecting yourself changed? Why or why not?

Applying Your Skills

Passage to Freedom

Vocabulary Development

Clarifying Word Meanings

Restatements

Writers often help readers understand unfamiliar words by using definitions, examples, contrasts, and **restatements.** When you encounter an unfamiliar word, you can sometimes find a **restatement** in nearby words. For example, read this sentence from "Passage to Freedom."

> "The five men had heard my father could give them visas—official written permission to travel through another country."

In this sentence, the author restates the meaning of the word *visas*.

When you encounter unfamiliar words in your reading, look for such restatements to help you understand the words.

Your Turn

Complete the following sentences with restatements that clarify the meanings of the boldface Vocabulary words.

1. The narrator's father is a **diplomat,** someone who ____________ .
2. The **refugees,** people who ____________ , need his help.
3. Mr. Sugihara asks permission from his **superiors,** or ____________ , several times.
4. The refugees' **fate**— ____________ —is unknown.

Language Coach

Suffixes Adding a "double *e*" (*–ee*) to the ends of some words can transform them into nouns that refer to a person, often someone who has done something or received something. For instance, *refuge* (shelter) can be changed into *refugee* (someone who is seeking shelter or protection). Other examples:

trainee employee escapee

Now, finish the sentences below, adding details that show you understand the boldface words. Look up unfamilar words in a dictionary.

1. The **trainee** felt confident once she ____________ .
2. The **employees** chatted at lunch about ____________ .
3. The police found the **escapee** ____________ .

Academic Vocabulary

Talk About . . .

At the beginning of "Passage to Freedom," we see the way the narrator's father interacts with a young Jewish boy. How did that incident set the stage for the rest of the story?

Learn It Online
Explore suffixes with *WordSharp* at:
go.hrw.com
L8-202
Go

RA.L.8.1 Identify and explain various types of characters and how their interactions and conflicts affect the plot. **WA.8.4.e** Write informational essays or reports, including research, that: document sources and include bibliographies. **WC.8.3** Grammar and Usage: Use all eight parts of speech. *Also covered* **VO.8.6; VO.8.1; WA.8.5.a**

Grammar Link

Conjunctions

A **conjunction** is a word used to join words or groups of words. **Coordinating conjunctions** such as these join words or groups of words used in the same way:

and but or nor for so yet

EXAMPLE: Mr. Sugihara is a diplomat **and** a father. [*and* joins two nouns]

Correlative conjunctions are *pairs* of conjunctions that join words or groups of words used in the same way.

both . . . and either . . . or neither . . . nor
not only . . . but also whether . . . or

EXAMPLE: Mr. Sugihara can obey **either** his government **or** his conscience. [*either . . . or* joins two nouns]

Your Turn

Writing Applications The sentences below contain coordinating conjunctions. Rewrite the sentences using the correlative conjunctions given.

1. **both . . . and** The group of refugees included adults and children.
2. **not only . . . but also** Mr. Sugihara asked his bosses and his family what to do.
3. **either . . . or** He had to decide to help the refugees or to refuse to help them.
4. **neither . . . nor** At the time, the narrator could not understand what his parents had done or why it was so important.

CHOICES

As you respond to the Choices, use these **Academic Vocabulary** words as appropriate: incident, factor, interact, response.

REVIEW

Perform the Story

Group Project With a small group, act out the story. Write a script, making sure that each scene focuses on Mr. Sugihara's relationships with other characters. Choose roles, rehearse your parts, and then act out the story for the class.

CONNECT

Make Character Judgments

Timed Writing Imagine that you are Mr. Sugihara's superior. Do you think Mr. Sugihara should be punished for disobeying orders, or do you think he should be praised for saving lives? Use details from the text to support your position in a short persuasive essay.

EXTEND

Research Refugees

TechFocus Thousands of people live as refugees today. Working with two or three classmates, use credible Internet resources to prepare a report on one group of refugees. Look for answers to these questions using the keywords you collected as you read the story.

- Where are the refugees from?
- Why did they have to leave their homes?
- Where are they living now?
- What action could be taken to help them?

Comparing Characters

CONTENTS

What Do You Think?

How are elderly people a blessing?

QuickTalk

In groups, discuss whether you agree or disagree with the following statements: (1) Friends should be the same age. (2) Adults can't understand how young people feel. Summarize your group's views for the class.

Mother I, Yorkshire Moors, August 1985 (1985) by David Hockney. Photographic Collage. 18 ½" x 13"

Preparing to Read

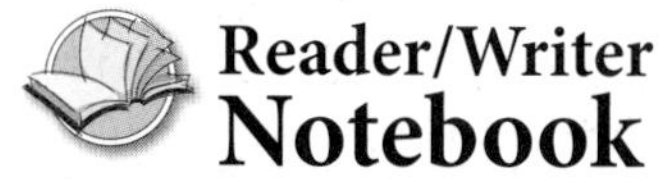

RA.L.8.1 Identify and explain various types of characters and how their interactions and conflicts affect the plot. *Also covered* **RP.8.1**

The Wise Old Woman / Mrs. Flowers

Reader/Writer Notebook

Use your **RWN** to complete the activities for these selections.

Literary Focus

Characters and Genres No matter what kind of story we read, fiction or nonfiction, we are introduced to characters. We learn who the characters are, what battles they face, what actions they take, and their **motivations,** or reasons for behaving as they do. Depending on the **genre,** or type of literature, writers may choose to develop their characters in different ways and for different purposes.

Characters in Nonfiction	Characters in Folk Tales
In an autobiography or biography you learn about real people—their names, ages, and memorable incidents in their lives. The writer is successful if the characters seem true to life and realistic.	In fairy tales and folk tales the characters may not seem as real as those in short stories and in nonfiction because they often symbolize, or represent, aspects of society or such qualities as kindness and cruelty.

Reading Focus

Comparing Characters As you read the selections that follow, take notes about the characters and their situations.

	"The Wise Old Woman" (Folk Tale)	"Mrs. Flowers" (Autobiography)
Main characters	son and mother	Marguerite and Mrs. Flowers
Characters' actions and reactions	Son is upset because of the lord's rule.	

Writing Focus

Think as a Reader/Writer

Find It in Your Reading As you read, note in your *Reader/Writer Notebook* how Uchida and Angelou develop characters through the use of dialogue.

Vocabulary

The Wise Old Woman

arrogant (AR uh guhnt) *adj.:* overly proud. *The new ruler of the town is so arrogant that he believes his rules will solve all the town's problems.*

displeasure (dihs PLEHZH uhr) *n.:* annoyance; dissatisfaction. *The lord showed displeasure when his rules weren't obeyed.*

Mrs. Flowers

benign (bih NYN) *adj.:* kindly; harmless. *Marguerite is comforted by Mrs. Flowers's benign smile.*

intolerant (ihn TAHL uhr uhnt) *adj.:* unwilling to accept something. *Mrs. Flowers was intolerant of rudeness and ignorance.*

Language Coach

Oral Fluency The letter combination /gn/ appears in many English words. When the combination appears at the ends of words such as *sign* and *reign,* the *g* is silent. Which word on the list above follows that rule?

Learn It Online

To get to know these selections better, check out the *PowerNotes* introduction on:

go.hrw.com L8-205 Go

MEET THE WRITERS

Yoshiko Uchida

(1921–1992)

Preserving the Magic

Yoshiko Uchida was born in Alameda, California, and grew up in Berkeley. During World War II, Uchida and her family were imprisoned in one of the camps set up for the 110,000 Japanese Americans living on the West Coast. After the war, Uchida traveled to Japan to rediscover her roots and to collect Japanese folk tales. "The Wise Old Woman" is one of these tales.

Uchida says that she began keeping a journal the day she graduated from elementary school.

> "By putting these special happenings into words . . . I was trying to . . . preserve the magic, as well as the joy and sadness, of certain moments in my life."

Maya Angelou

(1928–)

"When You Get, Give"

Six feet tall, gracious, and commanding, Maya Angelou is as impressive a woman as Mrs. Flowers. She has been an actor, a teacher, a speaker, a civil rights worker and, above all, a writer. Her works include poems, plays, songs, screenplays, and newspaper and magazine articles, as well as four autobiographies. The selection you will read, "Mrs. Flowers," is from *I Know Why the Caged Bird Sings.* On January 20, 1993, Angelou recited one of her poems in honor of Bill Clinton's presidential inauguration.

Angelou has influenced the lives of many young people, both in person and through her writing. She has said,

> "Black people say, when you get, give; when you learn, teach. As soon as that healing takes place, then we have to go out and heal somebody."

Think About the Writers

Based on their biographies, why do you think Uchida is drawn to writing folk tales and Angelou to writing autobiographies?

Preview the Selections

In "The Wise Old Woman" a **mother** and **son** solve some big problems in a small village in Japan.

In "Mrs. Flowers" a remarkable older woman, **Mrs. Flowers,** makes a big impression on a young girl named **Marguerite.**

Opposite: Earthly Paradise of Wuling (detail) (1780s) by Tani Buncho. Handscroll; ink color, and gold on silk, after the Chinese artist Qiu Ying.

The Wise Old Woman

traditional Japanese, retold by **Yoshiko Uchida**

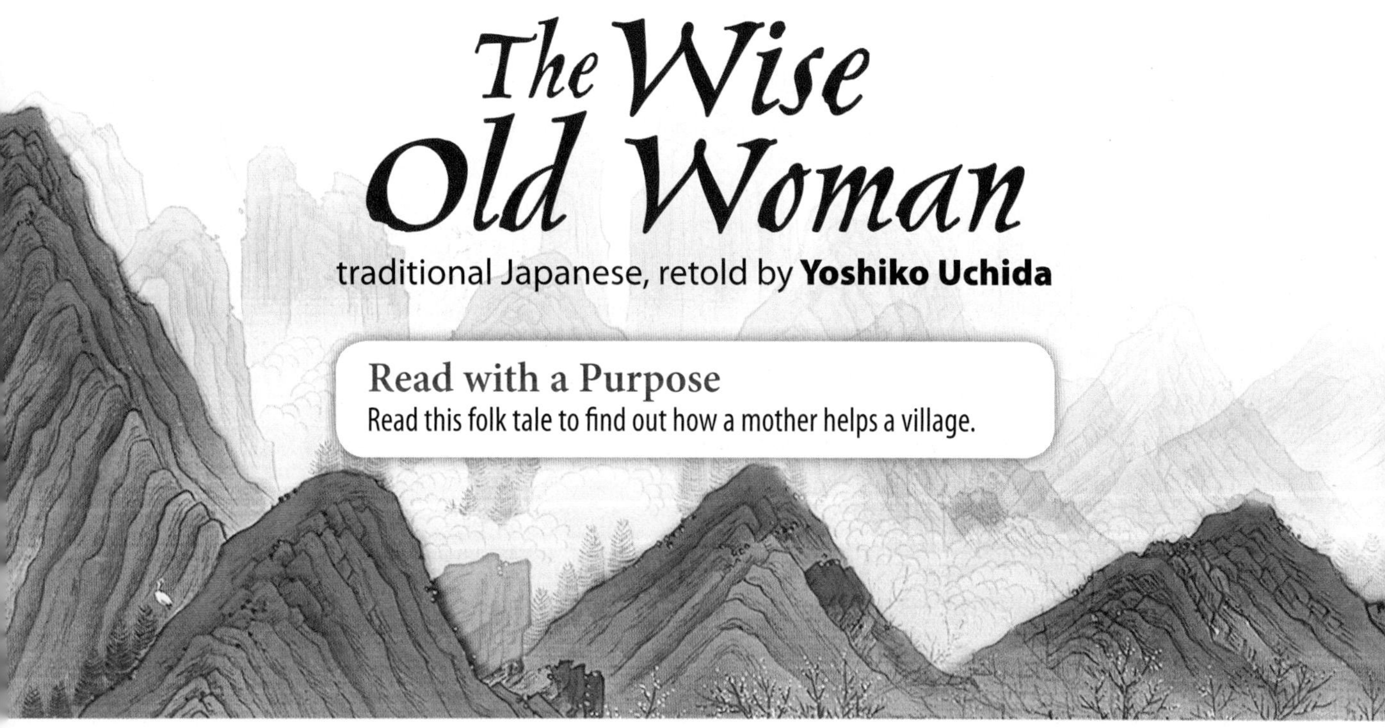

Read with a Purpose
Read this folk tale to find out how a mother helps a village.

Many long years ago, there lived an arrogant and cruel young lord who ruled over a small village in the western hills of Japan.

"I have no use for old people in my village," he said haughtily. "They are neither useful nor able to work for a living. I therefore decree that anyone over seventy-one must be banished from the village and left in the mountains to die."

"What a dreadful decree! What a cruel and unreasonable lord we have," the people of the village murmured. But the lord fearfully punished anyone who disobeyed him, and so villagers who turned seventy-one were tearfully carried into the mountains, never to return. **A**

Gradually there were fewer and fewer old people in the village and soon they disappeared altogether. Then the young lord was pleased.

"What a fine village of young, healthy, and hard-working people I have," he bragged. "Soon it will be the finest village in all of Japan."

Now, there lived in this village a kind young farmer and his aged mother. They were poor, but the farmer was good to his mother, and the two of them lived happily together. However, as the years went by, the mother grew older, and before long she reached the terrible age of seventy-one.

"If only I could somehow deceive the cruel lord," the farmer thought. But there

Vocabulary **arrogant** (AR uh guhnt) *adj.:* overly proud.

A **Read and Discuss** What has the author told us so far? What do the villagers think of the lord's rule?

were records in the village books and everyone knew that his mother had turned seventy-one.

Each day the son put off telling his mother that he must take her into the mountains to die, but the people of the village began to talk. The farmer knew that if he did not take his mother away soon, the lord would send his soldiers and throw them both into a dark dungeon to die a terrible death. **B**

"Mother——" he would begin, as he tried to tell her what he must do, but he could not go on.

Then one day the mother herself spoke of the lord's dread decree. "Well, my son," she said, "the time has come for you to take me to the mountains. We must hurry before the lord sends his soldiers for you." And she did not seem worried at all that she must go to the mountains to die.

"Forgive me, dear mother, for what I must do," the farmer said sadly, and the next morning he lifted his mother to his shoulders and set off on the steep path toward the mountains. Up and up he climbed, until the trees clustered close and the path was gone. There was no longer even the sound of birds, and they heard only the soft wail of the wind in the trees. The son walked slowly, for he could not bear to think of leaving his old mother in the mountains.

B **Literary Focus** **Characters** What difficult situation does the son face?

Earthly Paradise of Wuling (detail) (1780s) by Tani Buncho. Handscroll; ink, color, and gold on silk, after the Chinese artist Qiu Ying.

On and on he climbed, not wanting to stop and leave her behind. Soon, he heard his mother breaking off small twigs from the trees that they passed.

"Mother, what are you doing?" he asked.

"Do not worry, my son," she answered gently. "I am just marking the way so you will not get lost returning to the village."

The son stopped. "Even now you are thinking of me?" he asked, wonderingly.

The mother nodded. "Of course, my son," she replied. "You will always be in my thoughts. How could it be otherwise?"

At that, the young farmer could bear it no longer. "Mother, I cannot leave you in the mountains to die all alone," he said. "We are going home and no matter what the lord does to punish me, I will never desert you again." **C**

So they waited until the sun had set and a lone star crept into the silent sky. Then, in the dark shadows of night, the farmer carried his mother down the hill and they returned quietly to their little house. The farmer dug a deep hole in the floor of his kitchen and made a small room where he could hide his mother. From that day, she spent all her time in the secret room and the farmer carried meals to her there. The rest of the time, he was careful to work in

---

C **Read and Discuss** How do things go on the trip to the mountain?

the fields and act as though he lived alone. In this way, for almost two years he kept his mother safely hidden and no one in the village knew that she was there.

Then one day there was a terrible commotion among the villagers, for Lord Higa of the town beyond the hills threatened to conquer their village and make it his own.

"Only one thing can spare you," Lord Higa announced. "Bring me a box containing one thousand ropes of ash and I will spare your village."

The cruel young lord quickly gathered together all the wise men of his village. "You are men of wisdom," he said. "Surely you can tell me how to meet Lord Higa's demands so our village can be spared."

But the wise men shook their heads. "It is impossible to make even one rope of ash, sire," they answered. "How can we ever make one thousand?"

"Fools!" the lord cried angrily. "What good is your wisdom if you cannot help me now?"

And he posted a notice in the village square offering a great reward of gold to any villager who could help him save their village.

But all the people in the village whispered, "Surely, it is an impossible thing, for ash crumbles at the touch of the finger. How could anyone ever make a rope of ash?" They shook their heads and sighed, "Alas, alas, we must be conquered by yet another cruel lord." **D**

The young farmer, too, supposed that this must be, and he wondered what would happen to his mother if a new lord even more terrible than their own came to rule over them.

When his mother saw the troubled look on his face, she asked, "Why are you so worried, my son?"

So the farmer told her of the impossible demand made by Lord Higa if the village was to be spared, but his mother did not seem troubled at all. Instead she laughed softly and said, "Why, that is not such an impossible task. All one has to do is soak ordinary rope in salt water and dry it well. When it is burned, it will hold its shape and there is your rope of ash! Tell the villagers to hurry and find one thousand pieces of rope." **E**

The farmer shook his head in amazement. "Mother, you are wonderfully wise," he said, and he rushed to tell the young lord what he must do.

"You are wiser than all the wise men of the village," the lord said when he heard the farmer's solution, and he rewarded him with many pieces of gold. The thousand ropes of ash were quickly made and the village was spared.

In a few days, however, there was another great commotion in the village as Lord Higa sent another threat. This time he sent a log with a small hole that curved and bent seven times through its length, and he demanded that a single piece of silk thread be threaded through the hole. "If you cannot perform this task," the lord threatened, "I shall come to conquer your village."

D **Read and Discuss** What is happening in the village now? What do the villagers think of this proposal?

E **Literary Focus** **Characters** Does the mother seem like a realistic character to you? What idea might she symbolize, or represent?

Analyzing Visuals **Viewing and Interpreting** How does this visual match the time, place, and genre of this selection?

Fan bridge by moonlight from *Views of Mount Tempo* by Yashima Gakutei. Color woodblock print.

The young lord hurried once more to his wise men, but they all shook their heads in bewilderment. "A needle cannot bend its way through such curves," they moaned. "Again we are faced with an impossible demand."

"And again you are stupid fools!" the lord said, stamping his foot impatiently. He then posted a second notice in the village square asking the villagers for their help.

Once more the young farmer hurried with the problem to his mother in her secret room.

"Why, that is not so difficult," his mother said with a quick smile. "Put some sugar at one end of the hole. Then tie an ant to a piece of silk thread and put it in at the other end. He will weave his way in and out of the curves to get to the sugar and he will take the silk thread with him."

"Mother, you are remarkable!" the son cried, and he hurried off to the lord with the solution to the second problem.

Once more the lord commended the young farmer and rewarded him with many pieces of gold. "You are a brilliant man and you have saved our village again," he said gratefully. **F**

But the lord's troubles were not over even then, for a few days later Lord Higa

F **Read and Discuss** How have things changed?

sent still another demand. “This time you will undoubtedly fail and then I shall conquer your village,” he threatened. “Bring me a drum that sounds without being beaten.”

“But that is not possible,” sighed the people of the village. “How can anyone make a drum sound without beating it?”

This time the wise men held their heads in their hands and moaned, “It is hopeless. It is hopeless. This time Lord Higa will conquer us all.”

The young farmer hurried home breathlessly. “Mother, Mother, we must solve another terrible problem or Lord Higa will conquer our village!” And he quickly told his mother about the impossible drum.

His mother, however, smiled and answered, “Why, this is the easiest of them all. Make a drum with sides of paper and put a bumblebee inside. As it tries to escape, it will buzz and beat itself against the paper and you will have a drum that sounds without being beaten.”

The young farmer was amazed at his mother's wisdom. “You are far wiser than any of the wise men of the village,” he said, and he hurried to tell the young lord how to meet Lord Higa's third demand.

When the lord heard the answer, he was greatly impressed. “Surely a young man like you cannot be wiser than all my wise men,” he said. “Tell me honestly, who has helped you solve all these difficult problems?” **G**

The young farmer could not lie. “My lord,” he began slowly, “for the past two years I have broken the law of the land. I have kept my aged mother hidden beneath the floor of my house, and it is she who solved each of your problems and saved the village from Lord Higa.”

He trembled as he spoke, for he feared the lord's displeasure and rage. Surely now the soldiers would be summoned to throw him into the dark dungeon. But when he glanced fearfully at the lord, he saw that the young ruler was not angry at all. Instead, he was silent and thoughtful, for at last he realized how much wisdom and knowledge old people possess.

“I have been very wrong,” he said finally. “And I must ask the forgiveness of your mother and of all my people. Never again will I demand that the old people of our village be sent to the mountains to die. Rather, they will be treated with the respect and honor they deserve and share with us the wisdom of their years.”

And so it was. From that day, the villagers were no longer forced to abandon their parents in the mountains, and the village became once more a happy, cheerful place in which to live. The terrible Lord Higa stopped sending his impossible demands and no longer threatened to conquer them, for he too was impressed. “Even in such a small village there is much wisdom,” he declared, “and its people should be allowed to live in peace.”

And that is exactly what the farmer and his mother and all the people of the village did for all the years thereafter.

G **Read and Discuss** What is going on with the evil lord at this point in the story?

Vocabulary **displeasure** (dihs PLEHZH uhr) *n.:* annoyance; dissatisfaction.

AUTOBIOGRAPHY

Mrs. Flowers

from I Know Why the Caged Bird Sings

by **Maya Angelou**

Read with a Purpose

Read this story to find out how a neighbor helps a young girl in need.

Preparing to Read for this story is on page 205.

Build Background

"Mrs. Flowers" is from a volume of Maya Angelou's autobiography. When Angelou (born Marguerite Johnson) was a little girl, her parents separated. In the early 1930s she and her brother, Bailey, were sent to Stamps, Arkansas, to live with their grandmother (called Momma), who owned a general store. A year before meeting Mrs. Flowers, Marguerite had been violently assaulted by a friend of her mother's. Marguerite became depressed and withdrawn, and she stopped speaking.

For nearly a year, I sopped around the house, the Store, the school, and the church, like an old biscuit, dirty and inedible. Then I met, or rather got to know, the lady who threw me my first lifeline.

Mrs. Bertha Flowers was the aristocrat of Black Stamps. She had the grace of control to appear warm in the coldest weather, and on the Arkansas summer days it seemed she had a private breeze which swirled around, cooling her. She was thin without the taut look of wiry people, and her printed voile[1] dresses and flowered hats were as right for her as denim overalls for a farmer. She was our side's answer to the richest white woman in town.

Her skin was a rich black that would have peeled like a plum if snagged, but then no one would have thought of getting close enough to Mrs. Flowers to ruffle her dress, let alone snag her skin. She didn't encourage familiarity. She wore gloves too.

I don't think I ever saw Mrs. Flowers laugh, but she smiled often. A slow widening of her thin black lips to show even, small white teeth, then the slow effortless closing. When she chose to smile on me, I always wanted to thank her. The action was so graceful and inclusively benign.

She was one of the few gentlewomen I have ever known, and has remained throughout my life the measure of what a human being can be. **A**

1. **voile** (voyl): thin, sheer fabric.

A **Read and Discuss** What is the author conveying about Mrs. Flowers?

Vocabulary **benign** (bih NYN) *adj.:* kindly; harmless.

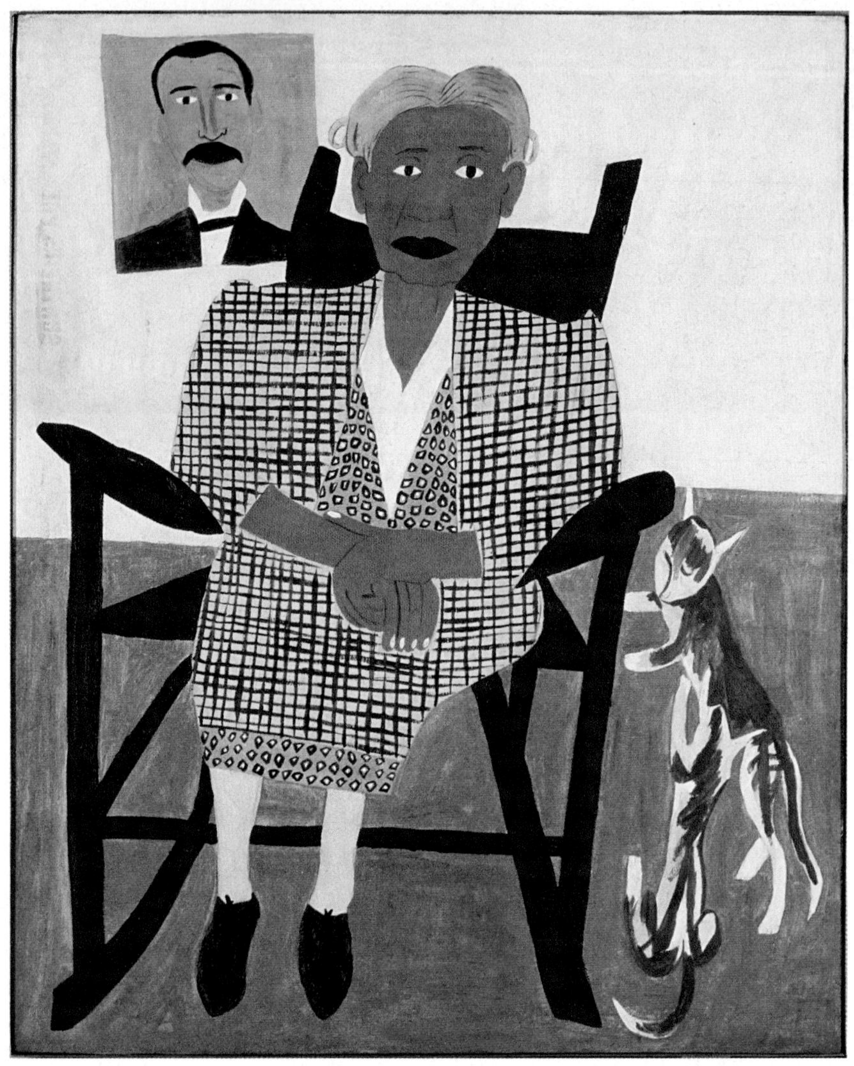

Mom and Dad (1944) by William H. Johnson. Oil on paper board, 31" x 25 ⅜" (78.7 x 64.5 cm).

One summer afternoon, sweet-milk fresh in my memory, she stopped at the Store to buy provisions. Another Negro woman of her health and age would have been expected to carry the paper sacks home in one hand, but Momma said, "Sister Flowers, I'll send Bailey up to your house with these things."

She smiled that slow dragging smile, "Thank you, Mrs. Henderson. I'd prefer Marguerite, though." My name was beautiful when she said it. "I've been meaning to talk to her, anyway." They gave each other age-group looks.

There was a little path beside the rocky road, and Mrs. Flowers walked in front swinging her arms and picking her way over the stones.

She said, without turning her head, to me, "I hear you're doing very good schoolwork, Marguerite, but that it's all written. The teachers report that they have trouble getting you to talk in class." We passed the triangular farm on our left and the path widened to allow us to walk together. I hung back in the separate unasked and unanswerable questions.

"Come and walk along with me, Marguerite." I couldn't have refused even if I wanted to. She pronounced my name so nicely. Or more correctly, she spoke each word with such clarity that I was certain a foreigner who didn't understand English could have understood her.

"Now no one is going to make you talk—possibly no one can. But bear in mind, language is man's way of

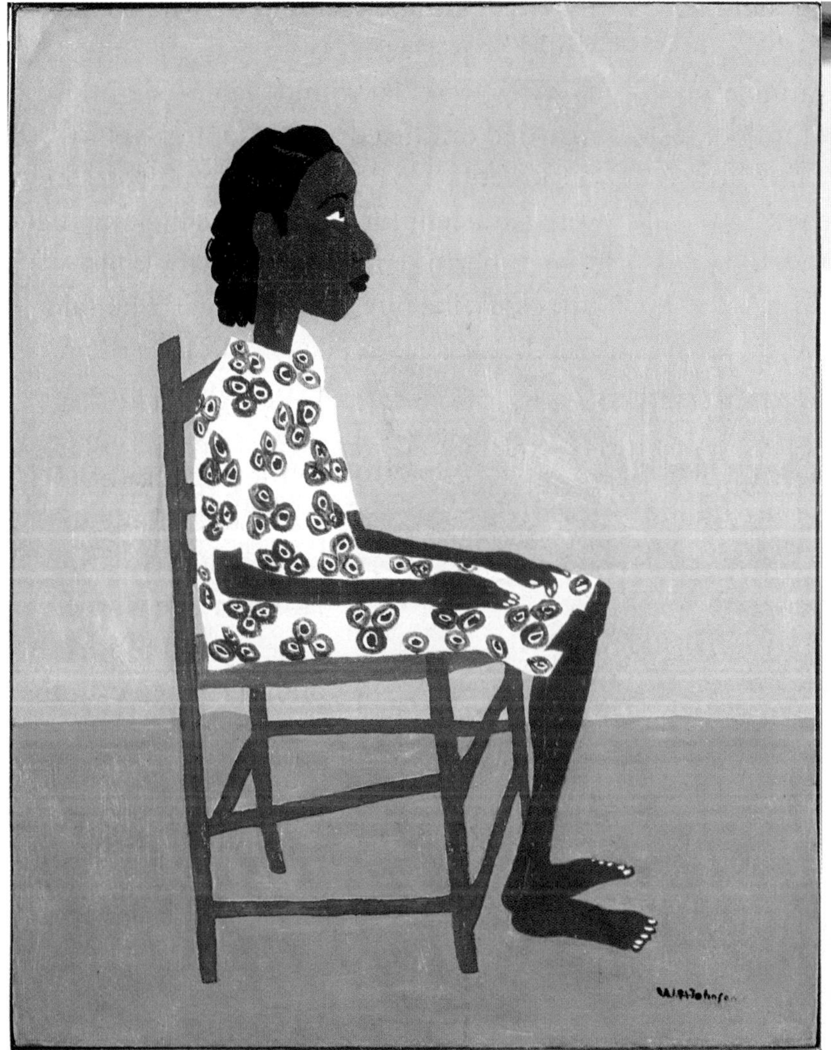

Little Sweet (1944) by William H. Johnson. Oil on paperboard. 28" x 22" (71.1 x 55.8 cm).

Analyzing Visuals

Viewing and Interpreting Are these images similar to how you picture Mrs. Flowers and Marguerite? Why or why not?

communicating with his fellow man and it is language alone which separates him from the lower animals." That was a totally new idea to me, and I would need time to think about it.

"Your grandmother says you read a lot. Every chance you get. That's good, but not good enough. Words mean more than what is set down on paper. It takes the human voice to infuse them with the shades of deeper meaning."

I memorized the part about the human voice infusing words. It seemed so valid and poetic.

She said she was going to give me some books and that I not only must read them, I must read them aloud. She suggested that I try to make a sentence sound in as many different ways as possible.

"I'll accept no excuse if you return a book to me that has been badly handled." My imagination boggled at the punishment I would deserve if in fact I did abuse a book of Mrs. Flowers's. Death would be too kind and brief. **B**

The odors in the house surprised me. Somehow I had never connected Mrs. Flowers with food or eating or any other common experience of common people. There must have been an outhouse, too, but my mind never recorded it.

B **Read and Discuss** What is Mrs. Flowers doing?

The sweet scent of vanilla had met us as she opened the door.

"I made tea cookies this morning. You see, I had planned to invite you for cookies and lemonade so we could have this little chat. The lemonade is in the icebox."

It followed that Mrs. Flowers would have ice on an ordinary day, when most families in our town bought ice late on Saturdays only a few times during the summer to be used in the wooden ice cream freezers.

She took the bags from me and disappeared through the kitchen door. I looked around the room that I had never in my wildest fantasies imagined I would see. Browned photographs leered or threatened from the walls and the white, freshly done curtains pushed against themselves and against the wind. I wanted to gobble up the room entire and take it to Bailey, who would help me analyze and enjoy it.

"Have a seat, Marguerite. Over there by the table." She carried a platter covered with a tea towel. Although she warned that she hadn't tried her hand at baking sweets for some time, I was certain that like everything else about her the cookies would be perfect.

They were flat round wafers, slightly browned on the edges and butter-yellow in the center. With the cold lemonade they were sufficient for childhood's lifelong diet. Remembering my manners, I took nice little ladylike bites off the edges. She said she had made them expressly for me and that she had a few in the kitchen that I could take home to my brother. So I jammed one whole cake in my mouth and the rough crumbs scratched the insides of my jaws, and if I hadn't had to swallow, it would have been a dream come true.

> **"It was the best of times, it was the worst of times. . . ." Her voice slid in and curved down through and over the words. She was nearly singing.**

As I ate she began the first of what we later called "my lessons in living." She said that I must always be intolerant of ignorance but understanding of illiteracy. That some people, unable to go to school, were more educated and even more intelligent than college professors. She encouraged me to listen carefully to what country people called mother wit. That in those homely sayings was couched the collective wisdom of generations. **C**

C **Read and Discuss** What has the author learned from Mrs. Flowers? What, in turn, is the author teaching us?

Vocabulary **intolerant** (ihn TAHL uhr uhnt) *adj.:* unwilling to accept something.

When I finished the cookies she brushed off the table and brought a thick, small book from the bookcase. I had read *A Tale of Two Cities* and found it up to my standards as a romantic novel. She opened the first page and I heard poetry for the first time in my life.

"It was the best of times, it was the worst of times. . . ." Her voice slid in and curved down through and over the words. She was nearly singing. I wanted to look at the pages. Were they the same that I had read? Or were there notes, music, lined on the pages, as in a hymn book? Her sounds began cascading gently. I knew from listening to a thousand preachers that she was nearing the end of her reading, and I hadn't really heard, heard to understand, a single word.

"How do you like that?"

It occurred to me that she expected a response. The sweet vanilla flavor was still on my tongue and her reading was a wonder in my ears. I had to speak.

I said, "Yes, ma'am." It was the least I could do, but it was the most also.

"There's one more thing. Take this book of poems and memorize one for me. Next time you pay me a visit, I want you to recite."

I have tried often to search behind the sophistication of years for the enchantment I so easily found in those gifts. The essence escapes but its aura[2] remains. To be allowed, no, invited, into the private lives of strangers, and to share their joys and fears, was a chance to exchange the Southern bitter wormwood[3] for a cup of mead with Beowulf[4] or a hot cup of tea and milk with Oliver Twist. When I said aloud, "It is a far, far better thing that I do, than I have ever done . . ."[5] tears of love filled my eyes at my selflessness. **D**

On that first day, I ran down the hill and into the road (few cars ever came along it) and had the good sense to stop running before I reached the Store.

I was liked, and what a difference it made. I was respected not as Mrs. Henderson's grandchild or Bailey's sister but for just being Marguerite Johnson.

Childhood's logic never asks to be proved (all conclusions are absolute). I didn't question why Mrs. Flowers had singled me out for attention, nor did it occur to me that Momma might have asked her to give me a little talking-to. All I cared about was that she had made tea cookies for *me* and read to *me* from her favorite book. It was enough to prove that she liked me.

2. **aura** (AWR uh): feeling or mood that seems to surround something like a glow.

3. **wormwood:** bitter-tasting plant. Angelou is referring to the harshness of life for African Americans in the South at that time.

4. **Beowulf** (BAY uh wulf): hero of an Old English epic. During the period portrayed in the epic, people drank **mead,** a drink made with honey.

5. **"It is . . . ever done":** another quotation from Charles Dickens's *A Tale of Two Cities.* One of the characters says these words as he goes voluntarily to die in place of another man.

D **Reading Focus** **Comparing Characters** What similarities can you find between Marguerite and the son in "The Wise Old Woman"?

Applying Your Skills

RA.L.8.1 Identify and explain various types of characters and how their interactions and conflicts affect the plot. RP.8.1 Apply reading comprehension strategies, including making predictions, comparing and contrasting, recalling and summarizing and making inferences and drawing conclusions. *Also covered* WA.8.1.c

The Wise Old Woman / Mrs. Flowers

Respond and Think Critically

Reading Focus

Quick Check

1. In "The Wise Old Woman," how do the mother and son save the village? What is the evil lord's response?
2. Why does Mrs. Flowers have a lasting impression on Marguerite in "Mrs. Flowers"?

Read with a Purpose

3. Describe ways in which the mother in "The Wise Old Woman" and Mrs. Flowers help the people around them.

Reading Skills: Comparing Characters

4. Add a row to your chart as shown below. How are the characters portrayed in each genre?

	"The Wise Old Woman" (Folk Tale)	"Mrs. Flowers" (Autobiography)
Realistic or symbolic characters?		

Vocabulary Check

Complete the following sentences with the appropriate Vocabulary word.

arrogant displeasure benign intolerant

5. The ______ and ______ ruler brushed the townspeople's concerns aside.
6. The angry ruler showed his ______.
7. Mrs. Flowers's ______ manner made Marguerite relax.

Literary Focus

Literary Analysis

8. **Analyze** In "The Wise Old Woman" the lord's opinion of elderly people changes drastically. Describe his original viewpoint, and discuss why he revised his ideas.
9. **Interpret** In "Mrs. Flowers," Marguerite speaks only two words. What do you think Angelou means when she writes, "It was the least I could do, but it was the most also" (p. 217) ?
10. **Compare** Each of these stories involves a relationship between a younger person and an older person. What similarities do you find in these relationships? What differences?
11. **Extend** In what ways might elderly people be considered a community asset?

Literary Skills: Characters and Genre

12. **Compare** Characters in an autobiography are real people. What factors make Marguerite in "Mrs. Flowers" seem more real than the son seems in "The Wise Old Woman"?
13. **Interpret** What "types" do the characters in "The Wise Old Woman" represent?

Writing Focus

Think as a Reader/Writer

Use It in Your Writing Write a character sketch in which you describe a character who has a positive influence on a younger person. Your character may be real or fictional. Like Yoshiko Uchida and Maya Angelou, use dialogue to develop character.

COMPARING TEXTS

Wrap Up

RA.L.8.1 Identify and explain various types of characters and how their interactions and conflicts affect the plot. RA.L.8.5 Identify and explain universal themes across different works by the same author and by different authors. *Also covered* RP.8.2; RP.8.1; WA.8.4.d; WA.8.6

The Wise Old Woman / Mrs. Flowers

Writing Focus

Write a Comparison-and-Contrast Essay

The characters in "The Wise Old Woman" and "Mrs. Flowers" live in different places and different times in history. In both stories, however, a young person learns something important about life from an older person.

Re-examine these two stories, and write a comparison-and-contrast essay that—

- analyzes how the stories' historical settings influence the characters' ideas, motivations, responses, and actions
- looks for ways in which the stories' characters experience similar and different situations
- evaluates the stories' **themes,** or the insights that the stories convey about life

Use the following outline to organize your essay:

I. Introduction and thesis statement
II. Body of essay
  A. Historical settings of the two stories
  B. Similarities and differences in how characters experience conflict
  C. Comparison of story themes
III. Summary and conclusion

Revise your writing to clarify your ideas and to remove unnecessary details. Be sure you have not simply retold the stories. Proofread your essay for errors in spelling, grammar, and punctuation.

Have your opinions about elderly people changed since reading these stories? Explain.

CHOICES

As you respond to the Choices, use the **Academic Vocabulary** words as appropriate: incident, factor, interact, response.

REVIEW

Write in Another Genre

"Mrs. Flowers" comes from Maya Angelou's autobiography. Angelou's descriptions of Mrs. Flowers are warm and vibrant, bringing to life the real-life person who helped Angelou during a difficult period of her life. Maya Angelou is also a poet. Try borrowing some of Angelou's vivid imagery to write a poem that reveals Mrs. Flowers's character to your readers.

CONNECT

Write a Persuasive Letter

In "The Wise Old Woman" the evil lord learns to appreciate the contributions that elderly people can make to society. Think about ways that the elderly have made a difference to you or to society. Then, write a persuasive letter to a local newspaper in which you convince people to volunteer at a home for the elderly.

EXTEND

Design a Web Profile

TechFocus Would you still be essentially the same person if you had grown up in ancient Japan? in 1930s Arkansas? Choose a time and place from history, and put yourself there. Design a Web profile of yourself that describes a day of your life then and there. You may want to include illustrations or other visuals.

INFORMATIONAL TEXT FOCUS

Treatment, Scope, and Organization of Ideas

CONTENTS

What Do You Think? What does it take to be a good citizen?

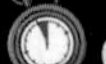

QuickWrite

Imagine that your community is going to give a Citizen of the Year award. Make a list of qualities that you think a good citizen should have.

DOCUMENTS / ARTICLE
Preparing to Read

RP.8.1 Apply reading comprehension strategies, including making predictions, comparing and contrasting, recalling and summarizing and making inferences and drawing conclusions.

Use your **RWN** to complete the activities for these selections.

Preamble to the Constitution / Bill of Rights / Don't Know Much About Liberty

Informational Text Focus

Comparing Texts: Treatment, Scope, and Organization

Two works that discuss the same topic can be very different. Look at the following elements to discover similarities and differences between two or more pieces of informational writing:

- **Treatment** The **treatment** of a topic is the way it is presented. One treatment, for example, might be serious and thorough and include an **objective,** or unbiased, discussion of each key idea. Another treatment might be light and playful and include the writer's **subjective,** or personal, comments.
- **Scope** When the treatment covers many aspects of a topic, the work is said to have a **broad scope.** A treatment that focuses on a narrow aspect of a topic has a **limited scope.**
- **Organization** The order in which ideas are presented varies from work to work. The most common forms of organization are chronological (time) order, sequential (point-by-point) order, order of importance, and organization of related ideas.

Into Action Use this chart to compare the treatment, scope, and organization of works that handle the same or similar topics.

	Preamble and Bill of Rights	Don't Know Much About Liberty
Treatment	serious; direct	
Scope		
Organization		

Writing Focus

Preparing for **Constructed Response**

Very often, test questions require you to show that you understand the main ideas of a work. As you read the following texts, identify the main idea of each section or paragraph. Take notes in your *Reader/Writer Notebook.*

Vocabulary

Preamble to the Constitution

tranquility (trang KWIHL uh tee) *n.:* calm; peace. *We will achieve tranquility if people follow our laws.*

Bill of Rights

excessive (ehk SEHS ihv) *adj.:* too much; too great. *If the punishment is excessive, it is more than the criminal deserves.*

Don't Know Much About Liberty

majority (muh JAWR uh tee) *n.:* larger part of something. *A majority of the voters chose the youngest candidate.*

minority (muh NAWR uh tee) *n.:* smaller part of something. *A minority of the people voted for someone else.*

Language Coach

Antonyms One way to master a word is to take note of what it *isn't.* Antonyms are words that have opposite meanings, such as *warm* and *cold.* Which two Vocabulary words on the list are antonyms?

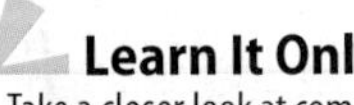

Learn It Online

Take a closer look at comparing texts. Visit the interactive Reading Workshop on:

go.hrw.com L8-221 

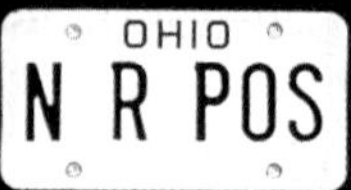

These license plates, read aloud, sound out the Preamble to the Constitution.

Preamble (1987) by Mike Wilkins. Painted metal on vinyl and wood (96" x 96").

PUBLIC DOCUMENT

PREAMBLE TO THE CONSTITUTION OF THE UNITED STATES OF AMERICA

Read with a Purpose

Read the following selections to find out what basic rights are guaranteed by the Constitution and Bill of Rights.

Build Background

A constitution is a written statement of the basic laws and principles by which a country is governed. By 1788 the U.S. Constitution had been ratified by the nine states required for it to go into effect. The Constitution grants important powers to the federal government. It begins with a one-sentence preamble that explains its purpose. The Bill of Rights, which several states demanded be added before they would ratify the Constitution, was ratified in 1791. Some people worried that the Constitution did not do enough to protect people's individual freedoms. In response to these charges, the Bill of Rights—originally written by James Madison—was added to make sure that the new U.S. government protected individual rights.

We the People of the United States, in Order to form a more perfect Union, establish Justice, insure domestic Tranquility, provide for the common defence, promote the general Welfare, and secure the Blessings of Liberty to ourselves and our Posterity, do ordain and establish this Constitution for the United States of America. **A**

A **Read and Discuss** What does the preamble tell us?

Vocabulary **tranquility** (trang KWIHL uh tee) *n.:* calm; peace.

PUBLIC DOCUMENT

BILL *of* RIGHTS

AMENDMENTS 1–10 OF THE CONSTITUTION

The Conventions of a number of the States having, at the time of adopting the Constitution, expressed a desire, in order to prevent misconstruction or abuse of its powers, that further declaratory and restrictive clauses should be added, and as extending the ground of public confidence in the Government will best insure the beneficent ends of its institution;

Resolved, by the Senate and House of Representatives of the United States of America, in Congress assembled, two-thirds of both Houses concurring, that the following articles be proposed to the Legislatures of the several States, as amendments to the Constitution of the United States; all or any of which articles, when ratified by three-fourths of the said Legislatures, to be valid to all intents and purposes as part of the said Constitution, namely: (A)

Amendment I

Congress shall make no law respecting an establishment of religion, or prohibiting the free exercise thereof; or abridging the freedom of speech, or of the press; or the right of the people peaceably to assemble,[1] and to petition the government for a redress[2] of grievances.

1. **assemble:** gather; come together to protest in public.
2. **redress:** compensation for a wrong.

Amendment II

A well regulated militia,[3] being necessary to the security of a free state, the right of the people to keep and bear arms, shall not be infringed.[4]

Amendment III

No soldier shall, in time of peace be quartered[5] in any house, without the consent of the owner, nor in time of war, but in a manner to be prescribed by law.

Amendment IV

The right of the people to be secure in their persons, houses, papers, and effects, against unreasonable searches and seizures, shall not be violated, and no warrants shall issue, but upon probable cause, supported by oath or affirmation, and particularly describing the place to be searched, and the persons or things to be seized.

3. **militia** (muh LIHSH uh): army; armed force.
4. **infringed:** broken, defied.
5. **quartered:** housed. Before the American Revolution, the British military had forced private citizens in colonial America to house British soldiers.

(A) **Informational Focus** **Treatment of Ideas** The Bill of Rights is intended to protect Americans from governmental abuses of power. How does the Bill of Rights treat this idea?

Amendment V

No person shall be held to answer for a capital, or otherwise infamous crime, unless on a presentment or indictment of a grand jury, except in cases arising in the land or naval forces, or in the militia, when in actual service in time of war or public danger; nor shall any person be subject for the same offense to be twice put in jeopardy of life or limb; nor shall be compelled in any criminal case to be a witness against himself, nor be deprived of life, liberty, or property, without due process of law; nor shall private property be taken for public use, without just compensation.

Amendment VI

In all criminal prosecutions, the accused shall enjoy the right to a speedy and public trial, by an impartial jury of the state and district wherein the crime shall have been committed, which district shall have been previously ascertained by law, and to be informed of the nature and cause of the accusation; to be confronted with the witnesses against him; to have compulsory process for obtaining witnesses in his favor, and to have the assistance of counsel for his defense.

Amendment VII

In suits at common law, where the value in controversy shall exceed twenty dollars, the right of trial by jury shall be preserved, and no fact tried by a jury, shall be otherwise reexamined in any court of the United States, than according to the rules of the common law.

Amendment VIII

Excessive bail shall not be required, nor excessive fines imposed, nor cruel and unusual punishments inflicted.

Amendment IX

The enumeration[6] in the Constitution, of certain rights, shall not be construed to deny or disparage others retained by the people.

Amendment X

The powers not delegated to the United States by the Constitution, nor prohibited by it to the states, are reserved to the states respectively, or to the people. **B**

6. **enumeration** (ee noom uh RAY shuhn): listing.

The Liberty Bell.

B **Read and Discuss** Why is the Bill of Rights organized in this way?

Vocabulary **excessive** (ehk SEHS ihv) *adj.:* too much; too great.

MAGAZINE ARTICLE

Don't Know Much About LIBERTY

Americans Are Clueless When It Comes to the First Amendment

from Weekly Reader Senior

Illustrations by Chris Murphy.

When it comes to the First Amendment, most Americans don't know their rights from their wrongs!

Only one in 1,000 Americans can list all five freedoms protected by the First Amendment to the U.S. Constitution, according to a recent survey. (Just in case you're one of those 999 people who can't, the rights are freedom of religion, freedom of speech, freedom of the press, freedom of assembly, and freedom to petition.) **A**

One in seven people could name one of the five First Amendment freedoms, and one in five people could name two, according to the McCormick Tribune Freedom Museum in Chicago, which sponsored the survey.

Although Americans failed the First Amendment pop quiz, they passed the Bart Simpson section of the survey with flying colors. More than half of the respondents could name at least two of the main characters of *The Simpsons*. Twenty-two percent could name all five. **B**

A **Informational Focus** **Scope of Ideas** How does the scope of this article compare to that of the Bill of Rights?

B **Read and Discuss** What does this suggest about the American people?

Those findings made Gene Policinski, executive director of the First Amendment Center, want to eat his shorts (as Bart Simpson would say). "These are such basic freedoms, and they're in our lives every day," he told *Senior Edition.* "All we have to do is look around."

No matter how old you are or what state you live in, you exercise First Amendment freedoms every day, Policinski says. When you turn on the television, you can choose the show you want to watch. If you disagree with a law, you can write a letter to your state representative. If you don't like something the government is doing, you can say so without getting in trouble.

That's exactly what the nation's founders hoped to achieve when they ratified, or approved, the Bill of Rights in 1791. The Bill of Rights is the first 10 amendments to the Constitution. The founders wanted Americans to have control over their daily lives and a say in how the government is run. C

Here's why the founders included each freedom:

1 Freedom of religion

The Colonists came to America in search of religious freedom. They wanted to worship without fear of punishment. The nation's founders included this clause to make sure Congress could neither establish a national religion nor stop people from practicing their chosen religion.

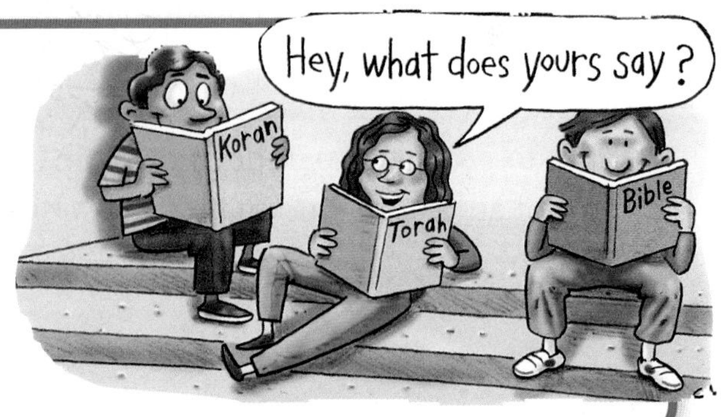

2 Freedom of speech

The Colonists' rocky relationship with Great Britain made them determined to prevent their new government from abusing its power. This clause ensures that the government can't stop people from saying almost anything they want to say—even if it's unpopular or critical of the president.

C **Informational Focus** **Treatment of Ideas** How does this treatment of the First Amendment differ from the original?

3 Freedom of the press

The nation's founders feared that if the government controlled the nation's newspapers, it could violate the Constitution without anyone finding out. This clause allows U.S. newspapers, magazines, and other media to report on whatever they want, as long as they don't print false information or invade people's privacy.

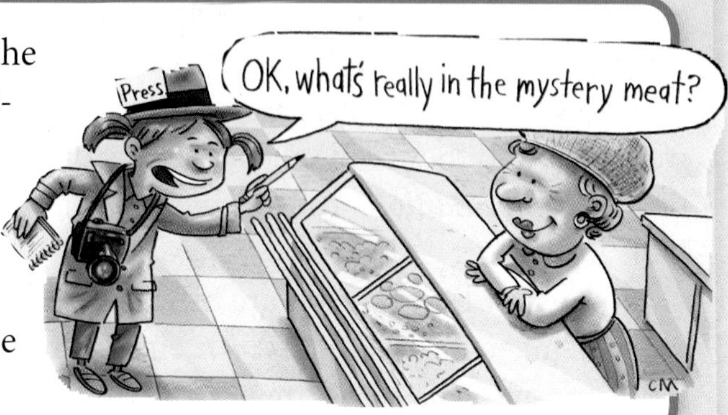

4 Freedom of assembly

Majority may rule in the United States, but the nation's founders wanted to make sure minority voices were still heard. This clause gives Americans the right to protest or parade publicly in support of any cause—no matter how controversial—as long as they do it peacefully.

5 Freedom to petition the government for a redress of grievances

The Colonists started the American Revolution (1775–1783) because they had little voice in Great Britain's government. This clause requires that the government listen to what citizens have to say, whether it be through letter writing or lawsuits. **D**

Read with a Purpose What basic rights are protected by the Constitution and the Bill of Rights?

D **Read and Discuss** What do the reasons behind these freedoms tell us about life without them and how they came about?

Vocabulary **majority** (muh JAWR uh tee) *n.:* larger part of something.
minority (muh NAWR uh tee) *n.:* smaller part of something.

DOCUMENTS/MAGAZINE ARTICLE

Applying Your Skills

OH **RP.8.1** Apply reading comprehension strategies, including making predictions, comparing and contrasting, recalling and summarizing and making inferences and drawing conclusions. **VO.8.4** Infer the literal and figurative meaning of words and phrases and discuss the function of figurative language, including metaphors, similes and idioms.

Preamble to the Constitution / Bill of Rights / Don't Know Much About Liberty

Practicing the Standards

Informational Text and Vocabulary

1. Which of the following *best* describes the **treatment** of the topics in the Bill of Rights?
   A Objective and serious
   B Subjective and biased
   C Humorous and sly
   D Misleading and biased

2. Which text has the broadest **scope**?
   A Preamble to the U.S. Constitution
   B Bill of Rights
   C "Don't Know Much About Liberty"
   D Amendment I of the Bill of Rights

3. How is the final section of "Don't Know Much About Liberty" organized?
   A Time order
   B Point-by-point order
   C Order of importance
   D All of the above

4. Which text has both a humorous and a serious **treatment**?
   A Preamble to the Constitution
   B Bill of Rights
   C "Don't Know Much About Liberty"
   D None of the above

5. *Tranquility* means —
   A concern
   B attitude
   C peace
   D freedom

6. If something is *excessive*, it is —
   A just right
   B too much
   C not enough
   D not necessary

7. What is the opposite of *majority*?
   A multiple
   B mechanism
   C middle
   D minority

8. Which is the *best* definition of *minority*?
   A smaller part
   B young citizens
   C average
   D popular

Writing Focus Constructed Response

Create an outline that shows the main ideas described in the Bill of Rights.

What Do You Think Now?

In what way are the ideas in Amendment I of the Bill of Rights a guide to good citizenship?

Writing Workshop

Short Story

Write with a Purpose

Write a short story for children, teenagers, or adults on the topic of your choice. Your **purpose** for writing is to entertain your readers—the **audience.**

A Good Short Story

- focuses on a conflict that the characters must resolve
- includes a series of related events that lead to a climax
- develops characters through dialogue and action
- provides vivid details of the setting
- ends with a resolution of the conflict
- reveals a theme, a general idea or insight about life

See page 238 for complete rubric.

Reader/Writer Notebook

Use your **RWN** to complete the activities for this workshop.

Think as a Reader/Writer

Just as reading stories can be a lifelong pleasure, writing them can also be fun. When you write a story, you unlock your imagination, letting your ideas flow. In this workshop you will write a short story to share with others. Before you begin writing, read this excerpt from Naomi Shihab Nye's story "Hamadi."

Usually Hamadi was wearing a white shirt, shiny black tie, and a jacket that reminded Susan of the earth's surface just above the treeline on a mountain—thin, somehow purified. He would raise his hands high before giving advice.

← **Details of the character's dress help readers picture him.**

"It is good to drink a tall glass of water every morning upon arising!" If anyone doubted this, he would shake his head. "Oh Susan, Susan, Susan," he would say. . . .

← **The character's formal manner of speaking tells the reader something about him.**

They visited him on the sixth floor of the Traveler's Hotel, where he had lived so long nobody could remember him ever traveling. Susan's father used to remind him of the apartments available over the Victory Cleaners, next to the park with the fizzy pink fountain, but Hamadi would shake his head, pinching kisses at his spartan room. "A white handkerchief spread across a tabletop, my two extra shoes lined by the wall, this spells 'home' to me, this says 'mi casa.' What more do I need?"

← **Details about the character's room give clues to his personality.**

Think About the Professional Model

With a partner, discuss the following questions about the model.

1. How does the writer use dialogue to indicate what Hamadi is like?
2. What do we learn about Hamadi through the description of his apartment?

Prewriting

Choose an Idea for a Story

We write best about things we know well. Although a story is a work of fiction, the characters and events should seem real. Make up a story based on people and places you know. You may want to use the Idea Starters for help.

Plan Your Story's Characters

Think about your characters' appearances. How do they look and move? Think about your characters' personalities. What do they think about? How do they speak? How do other people react to them?

If you plan your characters in advance, you have a better chance of bringing them to life and making them convincing for your audience. Make a list of characters you plan to use in your story. Then, use a chart to outline the traits of each character.

Character	Appearance	Personality	Other's Reactions
Martak	wears futuristic clothing	serious, business-like	Supervisor treats him with respect

Plan Point of View

Who will narrate your story? Will it be the main character, using *I* or *me* as he or she narrates the story? Will it be a secondary character who watches the story unfold? Perhaps you would rather tell the story from the third-person point of view, using the pronouns *he* and *she* when you are discussing the characters.

Decide on a Setting

The setting, where and when the story takes place, can give readers a lot of information. Your setting tells about your characters (a mansion indicates wealth) and can even cause the main conflict in the story (a volcano could erupt and cause problems for everyone). Use these questions to plan your setting:

- When and where does the story happen? Over how much time?
- Is the setting part of the conflict? What mood do you want your setting to evoke?

Idea Starters

- A middle-school student travels back in time.
- A lonely girl discovers a new side of herself.
- A star soccer player tries out for the school play.
- Two former friends compete for a prize.
- A boy and his computer get in trouble.

Peer Review

Share your chart with other students. Talk about whether your characters are believable and what character details might help bring each to life.

Your Turn

Get Started Use your **RWN** to take notes about the **characters** in your story. Also, write down your ideas about the **setting** of the story and the main **conflict** that occurs. Your notes will help you plan your short story.

Learn It Online
To see how one writer met all the assignment criteria visit:

Think About Purpose and Audience

As you plan your story, keep in mind your **purpose** for writing and your **audience.** Do you want simply to entertain, or will your story carry another purpose, such as to inspire your readers to do or feel something? Remember that your audience should dictate the style of writing you use.

Develop a Plot

For your plot, plan four elements.

- A **conflict,** or struggle, which will be the basis of your story.
- A **series of related events** set in motion by the conflict.
- A **climax**, or most exciting point, when something happens that reveals how the conflict will turn out.
- A **resolution,** or outcome showing how things work out.

Outline Your Plot

Here's one writer's **short story action plan**. Use an action plan like this one to outline the plot of your story.

Short Story Action Plan

Beginning

Characters: Martak, a scientist observing an experiment; Johnny, a four-year-old boy building a sand castle; Martak's supervisor; Johnny's parents

Settings: (1) a laboratory in space; (2) the yard of a house in the evening

Introduction to Conflict: Martak, a scientist observing an "experiment," decides the experiment should end.

Middle

1. In lab: Martak observes an experiment and tells his supervisor that they should end it.
2. In yard: Johnny plays in a sandbox, building a sand castle.
3. In lab: Supervisor agrees to end experiment.
4. In yard: Johnny's mother calls him to come in.
5. Climax—on porch: Johnny sees a large star getting bigger. Johnny's parents scream.

End

6. In lab: Martak watches a sphere burning on his monitor.

Your Turn

Plan Your Plot To help you create your plot, make a **short story action plan.** Exchange action plans with a classmate. Think about what he or she says, and then revise your plan. In the "Beginning" section, the writer describes the characters and settings and introduces the conflict. In the "Middle" section, he or she shows the series of related events in time order and includes the climax of the story. In the "End" section, the writer tells how the conflict is resolved.

Drafting

Follow Your Short Story Action Plan

Now that you've completed your action plan, it's time to bring your story to life. Using your outline as a guide, begin drafting. A framework for quick reference appears at the right. As you write, keep in mind the characteristics of a good short story, listed on page 230.

Framework for a Short Story

Introduction

- Use a strong first sentence that grabs the reader's attention.
- Introduce a conflict.

Middle

- Create a series of causes and effects, each leading towards a climax.

End

- Show how the conflict is resolved and how the characters are affected.

Craft a Strong Beginning

Your first sentence should catch the reader's attention. You may want to arouse your reader's curiosity by jumping immediately into the action.

Show Cause and Effect

Remember that a plot is a series of events related by cause and effect. As you write, use transitions to connect the sequence of events leading toward the climax. Use verbs in the active voice to move your plot forward.

Round Out the Ending

Show how characters are affected by the resolution of the conflict. Have they changed or learned something? Does your ending suggest an overall theme?

Grammar Link Using Active Voice

A verb in the **active voice** expresses an action done *by* the subject. A verb in the **passive voice** expresses an action done *to* its subject and always includes a form of the verb *be*. Using the active voice will help make your writing more direct and forceful. Although passive voice can be useful when you do not know (or don't want to say) who performed an action, the overuse of passive voice can make your writing sound weak and awkward. Here is an example from the student model.

Active voice: "I can't support the continued funding of Experiment 023681."
Passive voice: "The funding of this experiment should not be supported." (Who is responsible?)

Reference Note For more on active and passive voice, refer to the *Language Handbook*.

Writing Tip

Unsure about how to craft a strong beginning to your story? Look to the experts: popular authors. Thumb through this textbook, and scan some story openings. Read the first few paragraphs, noting how the author starts the story.

Writing Tip

Remember that realistic dialogue can bring your characters to life.

Your Turn

Write Your Draft Following your **short story action plan,** write a draft of your story. Also, think about

- who tells the story
- how to develop characters and show action through dialogue

Peer Review

As the author of your story, you know it so well that it might be difficult to see what has been left out or left vague. A peer reviewer can tell you whether events in your story are confusing or whether more detail or transitions are needed. When you read someone else's story, first read for enjoyment. Then, re-read to offer the writer suggestions to improve the story. Use the chart to the right as you work with your partner.

Evaluating and Revising

Read the questions in the left column of the chart, and then use the tips in the middle to help you mark where revisions are needed. The right column suggests techniques to use to revise your draft.

Short Story: Guidelines for Content and Organization

Evaluation Questions	Tips	Revision Techniques
1. Does your story contain a well-developed plot? Does the conflict create suspense?	**Place a check mark** next to each element: beginning, conflict, complications, climax, and resolution.	**Add** or **elaborate** on plot elements as necessary. **Delete** details that spoil the suspense.
2. Are main characters complex and convincing?	**Underline** character details, description, and dialogue.	**Add** details about appearance, personality, or background. **Add** dialogue and actions that reveal character, if needed.
3. Does the story establish a clear setting and evoke a mood?	**Highlight** details about the setting and mood.	**Elaborate** on the setting, if necessary, by adding descriptive details.
4. Are events arranged in a coherent order? Are transitions used to show order?	**Number** the major events. **Put a star** next to transitional expressions.	**Rearrange** events that are out of order. **Add** transitional words and phrases, if necessary, to show the order of events.
5. Is the point of view clear and consistent?	**Circle** pronouns that show whether the point of view is first or third person.	**Change** pronouns or details that shift the point of view.
6. Does the story reveal a theme?	**Underline** clues that point to the theme.	**Add** details or sentences that clarify your theme.

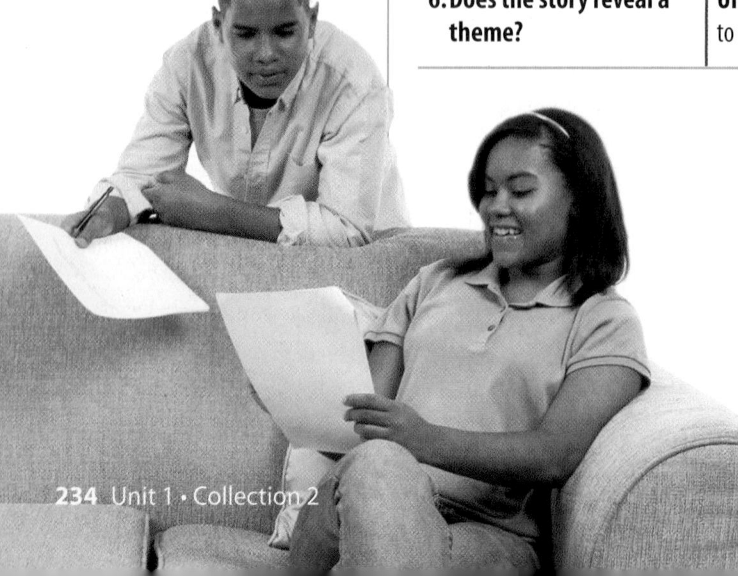

Read this student draft, and notice the comments on its strengths and suggestions for improvement at the right.

Student Draft

Experiment 023681

by Peter Leary, Athens Academy

"They're still regressing," said Martak, as he raised his head from the viewing screen, disappointment shadowing his face. "I can't support the continued funding of Experiment 023681. We have others which work much better."

← The fact that the "experiment" is mysterious creates suspense. Dialogue conveys information about the setting, characters, and conflict.

"Very well," rumbled the deep voice of Martak's supervisor. "It's too bad, though. They seemed so promising."

"I know. Disappointing, isn't it?" commented Martak. "But living conditions are horrible, they insist on killing each other in these petty little things called 'wars,' and look at their life span: on the outside, ninety-five of their 'years'!"

"I agree. Permission granted to terminate Experiment 023681."

Johnny gazed on his mostly finished sand castle, feeling a four-year-old's pride. He knew it was getting dark, so he scooped quickly.

← Suspense grows as another character and scene are introduced.

Martak looked at the small mass of swirling blues, greens, and whites on his monitor.

← The writer returns to the first scene.

MINI-LESSON How to Use Dialogue to Reveal Action and Advance the Plot

Sometimes dialogue is the best way to reveal plot points in a story. Peter can use dialogue to make it clear what is going on in the story. In Peter's draft, Martak looks at his monitor, and then the action returns to Johnny and his mother. In order to spell out what is going on with Martak, Peter adds the following four lines to his revised draft of the story.

Peter's Revision of Paragraph Six

Martak looked at the small mass of swirling blues, greens, and whites on his monitor.

He entered his access code.

"Request?" questioned a tinny voice.

"Terminate Experiment 023681."

"Request confirmed. . . ."

Your Turn

Use Dialogue Read your draft, and then ask yourself,

- "Can I add dialogue that will reveal action?"
- "Does the dialogue that I have included advance the plot?"
- "Does the dialogue that I have included sound natural?"

Once you have answered these questions, make revisions to improve your draft.

Student Draft *continues*

The second setting and characters are further developed.

"John, come in the house!" his mother shouted from the porch.

"I'm coming, Mom, he responded. Ambling to the porch, he glanced behind him at the sky. "Mommy, come look. There's a star that's getting bigger.

His mother screamed to come inside, away from the door and the windows. His dad screamed, "Invaders!" Johnny stood entranced by the light that now seemed to shine on his house.

The climax of the story is reached with its resolution now clear.

Martak watched as the small, perfect sphere was engulfed in yellow flame. The flame slowly turned orange, then red, then finally settled into a black cloud, which died, leaving behind only dust. He sighed and turned to the next experiment.

MINI-LESSON How to Develop Suspense

Peter does a good job of capturing his reader's interest. He can make his story even more interesting by adding suspense. One way that a writer can increase suspense is to emphasize that time is passing and that very soon, something terrible may happen. Notice how the suspense increases when Peter adds the following short scene to his revised draft.

Peter's Revision of Paragraph Seven

"John, come in the house!" his mother shouted from the porch.

Johnny sighed and dropped his shovel as he trudged toward his house. He knew his mother meant it when she said, "John."

He looked up at the darkening sky, and saw the first stars.

"Now, John," said his mother sternly.

"I'm coming, Mom, he responded. Ambling to the porch, he glanced behind him at the sky. "Mommy, come look. There's a star that's getting bigger.

Your Turn

Add Suspense Re-read your short story to see where you could increase suspense by emphasizing the passage of time. Work with a partner to check each other's revisions.

Proofreading and Publishing

Proofreading

Re-read your paper, and correct any errors in spelling, punctuation, capitalization, and grammar before you prepare your final draft.

Grammar Link **Punctuating Dialogue**

Be careful that you use correct punctuation in dialogue, and pay special attention to end punctuation. To make it clear which words are part of the dialogue, or the character's actual words, Peter added punctuation in his final draft.

> "I'm coming, Mom,^" he responded. Ambling to the porch, he glanced behind him at the sky. "Mommy, come look. There's a star that's getting bigger.^"

Notice how the quotation marks make clear just who is saying what. These punctuation marks make the final draft clearer.

Publishing

You might think about submitting your short story to publications like these:

- your school's literary magazine
- an online literary magazine
- short story contests

If you decide to submit your story to a magazine for publication, write a letter to the editor. Include a brief summary of the story that will convince the editor to publish the story. Be sure to address the following points in your letter:

- Why is it important that your short story be published in this particular magazine?
- Why would magazine readers be interested in your short story?

Reflect on the Process As you think about how you wrote your own short story, jot down answers to the following questions in your **RWN.**

1. How did writing a short story help you understand how short stories are put together?
2. How do you think writing your own story will help you in your reading?

Proofreading Tip

It's helpful to have a classmate do a careful proofreading of your story. Ask the classmate to look out for errors in punctuation, especially in dialogue.

Your Turn

Proofread and Publish As you proofread, look closely to make sure that all your sentences have correct end punctuation. Also, make sure that quotation marks are placed correctly. Once you have corrected your draft, you can share it with your classmates or with an even wider audience.

Scoring Rubric

You can use one of the rubrics below to evaluate your short story from the Writing Workshop or your descriptive essay from the activity on the next page. Your teacher will let you know which rubric to use.

6-Point Scale

Score 6 *Demonstrates advanced success*
- focuses consistently on describing a single place
- shows effective spatial organization throughout, with smooth transitions
- offers thoughtful, creative description
- develops the description thoroughly, using precise and vivid sensory details and images
- exhibits mature control of written language

Score 5 *Demonstrates proficient success*
- focuses on describing a single place
- shows effective spatial organization, with transitions
- offers a thoughtful description
- develops the description competently, using sensory details and images
- exhibits sufficient control of written language

Score 4 *Demonstrates competent success*
- focuses on describing a single place, with minor digressions
- shows effective spatial organization, with minor lapses
- offers mostly thoughtful description
- develops the description adequately, with some sensory details and images
- exhibits general control of written language

Score 3 *Demonstrates limited success*
- includes some loosely related material that distracts from the writer's descriptive focus
- shows some spatial organization, with noticeable flaws in the descriptive arrangement
- offers routine, predictable description
- develops the description with uneven use of sensory detail
- exhibits limited control of written language

Score 2 *Demonstrates basic success*
- includes loosely related material that seriously distracts from the writer's descriptive focus
- shows minimal organization, with major gaps in the descriptive arrangement
- offers description that merely skims the surface
- develops the description with inadequate sensory detail
- exhibits significant problems with control of written language

Score 1 *Demonstrates emerging effort*
- shows little awareness of the topic and the descriptive purpose
- lacks organization
- offers unclear and confusing description
- uses sensory detail in only a minimal way, if at all
- exhibits major problems with control of written language

4-Point Scale

Score 4 *Demonstrates advanced success*
- focuses consistently on describing a single place
- shows effective spatial organization throughout, with smooth transitions
- offers thoughtful, creative description
- develops the description thoroughly, using precise and vivid sensory details and images
- exhibits mature control of written language

Score 3 *Demonstrates competent success*
- focuses on describing a single place, with minor digressions
- shows effective spatial organization, with minor lapses
- offers mostly thoughtful description
- develops the description adequately, with some sensory details and images
- exhibits general control of written language

Score 2 *Demonstrates limited success*
- includes some loosely related material that distracts from the writer's descriptive focus
- shows some spatial organization, with noticeable flaws in the descriptive arrangement
- offers a routine, predictable description
- develops the description with uneven use of sensory detail
- exhibits limited control of written language

Score 1 *Demonstrates emerging effort*
- shows little awareness of the topic and the descriptive purpose
- lacks organization
- offers unclear and confusing description
- uses sensory details in only a minimal way, if at all
- exhibits major problems with control of written language

Preparing for Timed Writing

Descriptive Essay

You may encounter a writing prompt for a descriptive essay—an essay giving a detailed description of a particular place, person, or object. Using what you have learned in this collection's stories, your own writings, the rubric on page 238, and the steps below, respond to the following prompt.

Writing Prompt

Write an essay describing a place that is special to you. Use the techniques of fictional writing—metaphors, similes, mood, and the like—to make your description as vivid as possible. Also include sensory details so your readers can picture the place. Conclude with a brief statement of what the place means to you.

Study the Prompt

Re-read the prompt to make sure you understand what the prompt is asking of you. Your essay should be more than just a factual description of a place; it should describe the place in a literary way. You should use as many of the literary techniques you learned about in this collection as you can and apply them to your description.

Tip: Spend about five minutes studying the prompt.

Plan Your Response

First, think of a place that has a special meaning for you. Picture it in your mind in as much detail as possible. Once you have chosen your place, jot down as many details as possible. As you write your notes, keep in mind the following:

- What is your relationship to the place?
- How does being in the place make you feel?
- Why is this place meaningful for you?

You can organize your essay using spatial order, using the words *above, beyond, under*, and so on to guide your reader around the place.

Tip: Spend about fifteen minutes planning your response.

Respond to the Prompt

Using the notes you've just made, draft your descriptive essay. Follow these guidelines:

- State the place you're describing in the introduction.
- In the body of the essay, describe your place for the reader, using as many details as possible to give the reader a clear picture. Use words that make clear how aspects of the place are located.
- In the conclusion, reveal the importance and significance of the place. What is its most important characteristic to you?

Tip: Spend about twenty minutes writing your draft.

Improve Your Response

Revising Go back to the key aspects of the prompt. Did you clearly state what and where your place is? Did you provide enough details? Did you use literary techniques to bring the place to life? Did you state why the place is important to you?

Proofreading Take a few minutes to proofread your essay to correct errors in grammar, spelling, punctuation, and capitalization. Make sure all your edits are neat, and erase any stray marks.

Checking Your Final Copy Before you turn your essay in, read it one more time to catch any errors you may have missed. You'll be glad you took a little extra time to turn in your best work.

Tip: Save ten minutes to improve your paper.

Giving a Speech of Introduction

Speak with a Purpose

Prepare a speech of introduction. After you have practiced delivering your introduction, present it to your class.

Idea Starters

- Introduce a teacher or friend in a school assembly.
- Introduce an author to a book club.
- Introduce a star athlete at an awards banquet.

Use your **RWN** to complete the activities for this workshop.

Think as a Reader/Writer Like writers, speakers want to produce an effect on their audience. Effective speakers, like effective writers, take time to consider who their audience is to develop a message that their listeners will understand and enjoy.

In real life, you may someday be called upon to deliver a speech introducing someone. To do so, you'll need to plan, organize, and draft just as you would if you were writing a story.

Write an Introduction

For the subject of your introduction, choose someone you know or have read about. No matter how well you know the person, though, it is never a good idea simply to get up and "wing it." You need to do careful preparation, even when you want your introduction to seem casual and relaxed.

Learn All You Can

Your first step is to learn about your subject. If you are going to introduce a character you have read about, write down all the details you find in the story. Then, make up extra details that both fit the character and add interest to your introduction. If you are going to introduce a person you know, here are some topics you might want to research or ask your subject about:

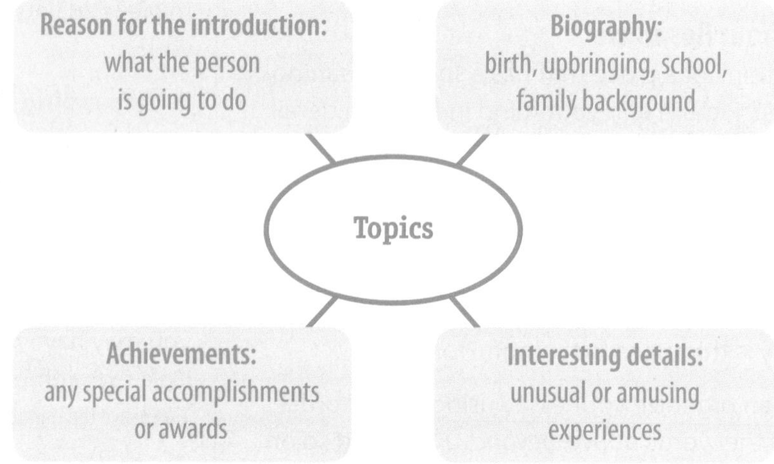

OH C.8.9 Deliver formal and informal descriptive presentations that convey relevant information and descriptive details. C.8.6 Adjust volume, phrasing, enunciation, voice modulation and inflection to stress important ideas and impact audience response.

Organize Your Details

Do you want to tell your listeners who your subject is right away, or would you rather leave that information until the end? Be sure to organize your details in a logical and interesting way. If you want to give a brief history of the person, for example, you might choose chronological order. To build excitement, order of importance might work best.

Draft Your Introduction

Use the information you have gathered to write an interesting introduction. Introductions should not be long and rambling. Be sure to include only important facts and details that will engage your audience's attention. Remember: Your goal is to leave the audience impressed and looking forward to seeing your subject.

A Good Introduction

- states the reason that the subject is being introduced
- tells basic facts about the subject
- lists the subject's major accomplishments
- includes interesting experiences or amusing anecdotes

Practice Your Introduction

Create a neat copy of your introduction. Make sure the type or handwriting is large enough for you to read easily. Highlight words that you plan to emphasize in your introduction. Circle punctuation marks that indicate questions and exclamations. Then, practice your introduction until you can deliver it smoothly. As you practice, keep the following tips in mind:

Verbal Techniques

- Vary the pitch of your voice; avoid speaking in a monotone.
- Don't rush through your presentation. Vary the pace, or speed, of your delivery.
- Adjust the volume of your voice to add effect to what you are saying. Avoid shouting or whispering.

Nonverbal Techniques

- Walk confidently to the stage or the front of the room.
- Remember to breathe, and make eye contact with your listeners.
- Smile, gesture, and move about when it suits your text.
- Pause now and again to allow your listeners to process what you are saying and to react.

Speaking Tip

To improve your speaking, try being a listener. When you practice, use a tape recorder to capture the delivery of your introduction. Take note of where you should speed up or slow down. Also note where you might pause for effect.

PREPARING FOR OHIO ACHIEVEMENT TESTS

Literary Skills Review

Character **Directions:** Read the following selection. Then, read and respond to the questions that follow.

A Nincompoop by **Anton Chekhov**

A few days ago I asked my children's governess, Julia Vassilyevna,[1] to come into my study.

"Sit down, Julia Vassilyevna," I said. "Let's settle our accounts. Although you most likely need some money, you stand on ceremony and won't ask for it yourself. Now then, we agreed on thirty rubles a month. . . ."

"Forty."

"No, thirty. I made a note of it. I always pay the governess thirty. Now then, you've been here two months, so . . ."

"Two months and five days."

"Exactly two months. I made a specific note of it. That means you have sixty rubles coming to you. Subtract nine Sundays . . . you know you didn't work with Kolya[2] on Sundays, you only took walks. And three holidays . . ."

Julia Vassilyevna flushed a deep red and picked at the flounce of her dress, but—not a word.

1. **Vassilyevna** (vah SEHL yehv nah).
2. **Kolya** (KOHL yah): nickname for Nikolai.

"Three holidays, therefore take off twelve rubles. Four days Kolya was sick and there were no lessons, as you were occupied only with Vanya.[3] Three days you had a toothache and my wife gave you permission not to work after lunch. Twelve and seven—nineteen. Subtract . . . that leaves . . . hmm . . . forty-one rubles. Correct?"

Julia Vassilyevna's left eye reddened and filled with moisture. Her chin trembled; she coughed nervously and blew her nose, but—not a word.

"Around New Year's you broke a teacup and saucer: take off two rubles. The cup cost more, it was an heirloom, but—let it go. When didn't I take a loss! Then, due to your neglect, Kolya climbed a tree and tore his jacket: take away ten. Also due to your heedlessness the maid stole Vanya's shoes. You ought to watch everything! You get paid for it. So, that means five more rubles off. The tenth of January I gave you ten rubles. . . ."

3. **Vanya** (VAHN yah): nickname for Ivan.

RA.L.8.1 Identify and explain various types of characters and how their interactions and conflicts affect the plot. *Also covered* **RP.8.2**

"You didn't," whispered Julia Vassilyevna.

"But I made a note of it."

"Well . . . all right."

"Take twenty-seven from forty-one—that leaves fourteen."

Both eyes filled with tears. Perspiration appeared on the thin, pretty little nose. Poor girl!

"Only once was I given any money," she said in a trembling voice, "and that was by your wife. Three rubles, nothing more."

"Really? You see now, and I didn't make a note of it! Take three from fourteen . . . leaves eleven. Here's your money, my dear. Three, three, three, one and one. Here it is!"

I handed her eleven rubles. She took them and with trembling fingers stuffed them into her pocket.

"*Merci,*"[4] she whispered.

I jumped up and started pacing the room. I was overcome with anger.

"For what, this—'*merci*'?" I asked.

"For the money."

"But you know I've cheated you—robbed you! I have actually stolen from you! *Why* this '*merci*'?"

"In my other places they didn't give me anything at all."

"They didn't give you anything? No wonder! I played a little joke on you, a cruel lesson, just to teach you. . . . I'm going to give you the entire eighty rubles! Here they are in an envelope all ready for you. . . . Is it really possible to be so spineless? Why don't you protest? Why be silent? Is it possible in this world to be without teeth and claws—to be such a nincompoop?"

She smiled crookedly and I read in her expression: "It is possible."

I asked her pardon for the cruel lesson and, to her great surprise, gave her the eighty rubles. She murmured her little "*merci*" several times and went out. I looked after her and thought: "How easy it is to crush the weak in this world!"

4. ***Merci*** (mehr SEE): French for "Thank you." During the nineteenth century in czarist Russia, French was spoken by the upper classes.

Literary Skills Review CONTINUED

1. When we read that Julia "flushed a deep red and picked at the flounce of her dress," we infer that she is
   A. mature.
   B. upset.
   C. smart.
   D. shy.

2. When the narrator thinks to himself, "Poor girl," it is an example of what type of characterization?
   A. internal
   B. external
   C. indirect
   D. direct

3. We learn about Julia mostly from
   A. how she dresses.
   B. her inner thoughts.
   C. her actions.
   D. what she says.

4. The narrator's reaction to Julia's thanks ("Merci") reveals that he is
   A. quick to anger.
   B. eager to please.
   C. always busy.
   D. a good listener.

5. When Julia smiles **crookedly,** it probably means that she
   A. is too upset to talk.
   B. does not speak English.
   C. has a toothache.
   D. cannot smile correctly.

6. Which of the following probably does not motivate Julia to stay silent?
   A. She wants to keep her job.
   B. She is too proud to speak.
   C. She is afraid of her boss.
   D. She is very shy.

Short Answer

7. Identify the narrator's motive in talking to Julie. Use information from the passage to support your answer.

Extended Response

8. In the time and place this story takes place, governesses like Julia were little more than servants and were dependent on the goodwill of their employers. If this story were set in the modern-day United States and Julia were the family tutor, do you think Julia would act the same way? Explain, and give reasons to support your ideas.

Informational Skills Review

Treatment, Scope, and Organization of Ideas

Directions: Read the following two documents. Then, answer the questions that follow.

Surrounded by Sound by

A jet takes off from a nearby airport, its dull roar rattling your windows. *Woof!* A dog barks outside. All that noise is driving you crazy! The word *noise* comes from the Latin word *nausea,* meaning "seasickness"—a condition that causes distress. Sources of noise range from pets to construction equipment, stereos to leaf blowers. Noise is considered environmental pollution and is the number-one neighborhood complaint, ahead of crime, litter, and traffic, says a U.S. Census Bureau survey of more than 100 million households.

Hear This!

Long-term exposure to loud sounds harms hearing. Too-loud noise can damage the auditory nerve, which travels between the inner ear and brain. A person's hearing worsens as nerve endings die off. Exposure to loud sounds can also damage or destroy the sensory hair cells of the inner ear. About 28 million Americans have experienced hearing loss of some kind, according to the National Institutes of Health (NIH), and about one-third can blame—at least in part—noise.

How Loud Is Too Loud?

"If you have to raise your voice to be heard, the environment may be too loud for your ears," says researcher Sig Soli of the House Ear Institute. Prolonged exposure to sound above 85 decibels—the level of heavy city traffic—can cause gradual hearing loss, says the National Institute on Deafness and Other Communications Disorders. "The louder the sound, the less time it takes before your hearing is affected," Soli says.

Stressed Out by Sound

Noise pollution impairs concentration, says the World Health Organization. Even low-level noise can cause health problems. How? Loud sounds can signal your body to activate its "fight or flight" response. Your body responds automatically, releasing adrenaline and other stress hormones into the bloodstream. Heart rate, blood pressure, and respiration increase; blood is redirected from the digestive tract to muscles and limbs. Excessive exposure may also contribute to stress-related conditions, such as chronic high blood pressure, ulcers, and migraine headaches, according to the Environmental Protection Agency.

Sound Off on Noise!

Dedicated to preventing noise pollution in our Long Island Sound community

Noise pollution is more than a nuisance—it's hazardous to your health!

Health Effects of Noise Pollution
- hearing loss
- buzzing or ringing in ears (tinnitus)
- impaired concentration
- interrupted sleep, sleep deprivation, fatigue
- high blood pressure, heart disease
- ulcers, migraine headaches

Sound Off on Noise! is a local volunteer organization whose goal is to raise awareness of the problem of noise in our neighborhoods. Its members work to preserve the quality of life on Long Island by

- **educating the public** about noise pollution as a threat to human health and the environment. We display posters, distribute pamphlets, and host informational meetings.
- **raising awareness through the media.** We send press releases to local television and radio outlets as well as to community newspapers.
- **lobbying public officials** about the problem of noise pollution to enlist their support in addressing the issue.
- **contacting agencies** such as local police departments, legislative councils, regulatory agencies, and the federal Department of Environmental Protection.
- **sponsoring free hearing screenings** at community events.

Noise pollution is everyone's problem—and responsibility. If you'd like more information about Sound Off on Noise!, please visit us on the Web at **www.soundoffonnoise.com.**

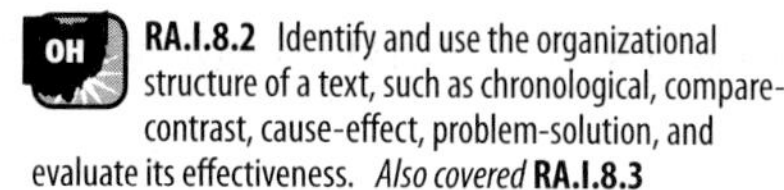

RA.I.8.2 Identify and use the organizational structure of a text, such as chronological, compare-contrast, cause-effect, problem-solution, and evaluate its effectiveness. *Also covered* **RA.I.8.3**

1. The purpose of both passages is to
   A. describe the causes of noise pollution.
   B. praise the quietness of country living.
   C. call attention to the dangers of noise pollution.
   D. list the noise levels of common events.

2. "Surrounded by Sound" is a(n)
   A. article.
   B. brochure.
   C. short story.
   D. manual.

3. The treatment of noise pollution in the two passages is done
   A. humorously.
   B. positively.
   C. angrily.
   D. seriously.

4. A difference between the two passages is that
   A. "Sound Off on Noise!" has a broad scope whereas "Surrounded by Sound" has a more limited scope.
   B. "Surrounded by Sound" has a broad scope whereas "Sound Off on Noise!" has a more limited scope.
   C. one is written about noise problems in New York whereas the other deals with California noise problems.
   D. they disagree about battling noise pollution.

Short Answer

5. Identify and explain the organization of the ideas in "Sound Off on Noise!". Use information from the passage to support your answer.

Extended Response

6. What do you see as the main difference in purpose between the two passages? Do they complement each other, or present differing arguments? Explain, using details to support your ideas.

Vocabulary Skills Review

OH **VO.8.3** Identify the relationships of pairs of words in analogical statements (e. g., synonyms and antonyms) and infer word meanings from these relationships.

Synonyms

Directions: Choose the word or phrase that is the best synonym for each boldfaced word.

1. A leader who grants a prisoner **clemency** offers
   A. weakness.
   B. mercy.
   C. pride.
   D. anger.

2. If something is **archaic,** it is
   A. wooden.
   B. expensive.
   C. outdated.
   D. strong.

3. To feel **anguish** is to feel
   A. bored.
   B. energized.
   C. misery.
   D. amused.

4. A **tedious** story is
   A. confusing.
   B. heartwarming.
   C. boring.
   D. surprising.

5. If a friend is **inquiring** about you, she is
   A. gossiping.
   B. asking.
   C. thinking.
   D. worrying.

6. When you **rehabilitate** something, you
   A. replace it.
   B. research it.
   C. restore it.
   D. remember it.

7. A man's **fate** is his
   A. preference.
   B. destiny.
   C. talent.
   D. belief.

8. At work, your **superiors** are your
   A. coworkers.
   B. assistants.
   C. bosses.
   D. employees.

Academic Vocabulary

Directions: Choose the best synonym for each boldfaced Academic Vocabulary word.

9. An **incident** can also be called
   A. a relationship.
   B. a version.
   C. an event.
   D. a disagreement.

10. Another word for **factor** is
   A. symbol.
   B. machine.
   C. guard.
   D. element.

WA.8.1.a Write narratives that: sustain reader interest by pacing action and developing an engaging plot. *Also covered* **WP.8.10**

Writing Skills Review

Short Story **Directions:** Read the following passage from a short story. Then, answer each question that follows.

(1) Jesse nervously approached the front porch of his house and stopped before climbing the wooden steps to the front door. (2) His mother was probably in the kitchen preparing dinner. (3) His father wouldn't be home for another hour. (4) He knew his family's routine. (5) Wearily, Jesse slipped his backpack off and dropped it on the steps. (6) He froze in terror. (7) Inside the cover of his notebook, there was a letter addressed to his parents. (8) The letter was from the principal. (9) It said that Jesse had been caught plagiarizing a social studies report. (10) How was he going to face his parents?

1. Which words did the writer use to establish **setting**?
   A. "the front porch of his house . . . wooden steps to the front door."
   B. "in the kitchen preparing dinner"
   C. "He froze in terror."
   D. "Inside the cover of his notebook, there was a letter addressed to his parents."

2. Which sentence is unnecessary and can be deleted?
   A. Sentence 4
   B. Sentence 7
   C. Sentence 8
   D. Sentence 9

3. A **cliché** is a phrase or expression that has been used so much that it loses its impact. Which sentence contains a cliché and should be rewritten?
   A. Sentence 2
   B. Sentence 3
   C. Sentence 6
   D. Sentence 8

4. What would be the best way to combine sentences 7 and 8?
   A. Inside the cover of his notebook, there was a letter addressed to his parents and it was from the principal.
   B. A letter that had been addressed to his parents and which was from the principal was inside the cover of his notebook.
   C. A letter sent by the principal and addressed to his parents was inside the cover of his notebook.
   D. Having been signed by the principal, a letter addressed to his parents was inside the cover of his notebook.

5. To develop this story, the writer should do all of the following *except* —
   A. add dialogue between characters
   B. provide a happy ending for all
   C. develop the internal and external conflicts
   D. bring events to a climax and resolution

Read On

Fiction

The Call of the Wild

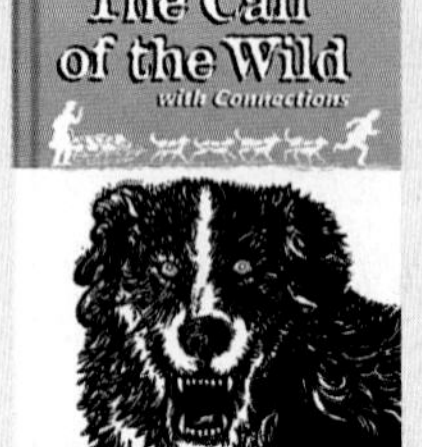

In Jack London's classic adventure story *The Call of the Wild,* Buck is stolen from his comfortable home and forced into service as a sled dog in the Alaskan wilderness. As he struggles to adapt to his new surroundings, Buck learns to draw on his instincts to survive among brutal owners and fierce competition.

The Clay Marble

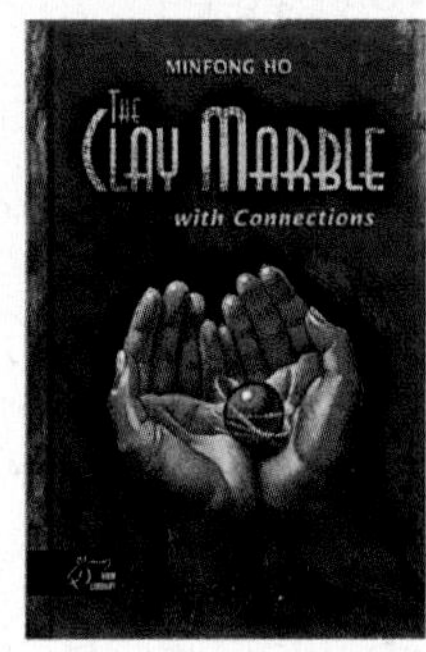

Twelve-year-old Dara and her family flee war-torn Cambodia and find a haven at the refugee camp of Nong Chan. In *The Clay Marble* by Minfong Ho, Dara makes a new friend, Jantu, and for a short while their lives are peaceful. When the war brings chaos to the camp, however, Dara is separated from her family and Jantu. Now she must find the courage to reunite with the people she loves.

Number the Stars

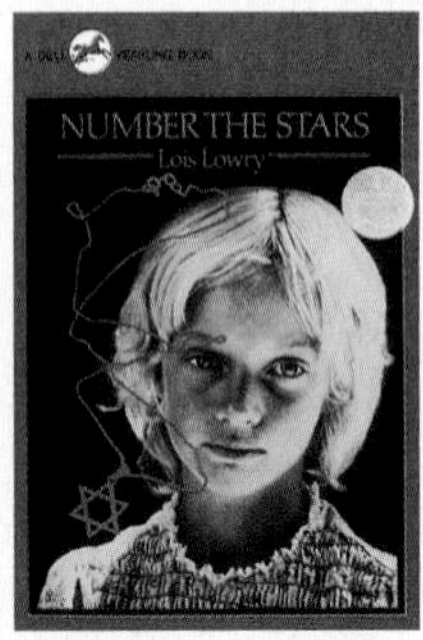

How far would you go to save a friend's life? In the 1990 Newbery Medal winner by Lois Lowry, *Number the Stars,* Annemarie Johansen and Ellen Rosen, best friends living in peaceful Copenhagen, Denmark, don't concern themselves with questions like this—until the Nazis come for Ellen.

Call Me María

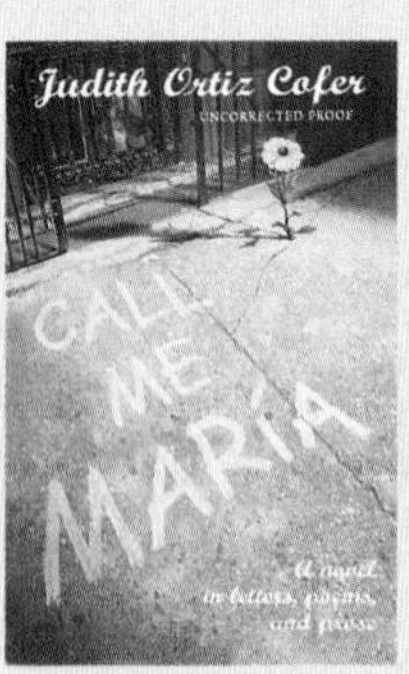

When Maria moves with her father from Puerto Rico to New York, she finds the two worlds couldn't be more different. *Call Me María* by Judith Ortiz Cofer uses a mixture of prose, letters, and poems to describe Maria's experiences adjusting to life in a new country, speaking a new language, and making new friends.

Nonfiction

Freedom's Children

What was it like to walk through angry, violent mobs to integrate an all-white school? to be arrested for refusing to give up a seat on a bus? In *Freedom's Children,* Ellen Levine presents oral histories by African Americans who were involved as children or teenagers in the civil rights movement of the 1950s and 1960s.

Lives of the Musicians

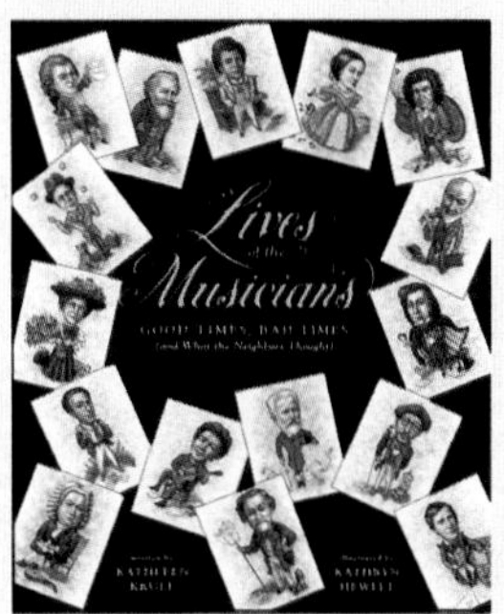

Are you a slob? Well, so was Beethoven. Is your favorite color red? It was also Mozart's favorite. In *Lives of the Musicians,* Kathleen Krull shares fascinating facts and tidbits from the lives of twenty famous musicians. Revealing funny gossip and detailing the musicians' quirky behavior, Krull brings the humanity back to our musical heroes. Hewitt's engaging art provides a perfect counterpoint to the text.

The Story of My Life

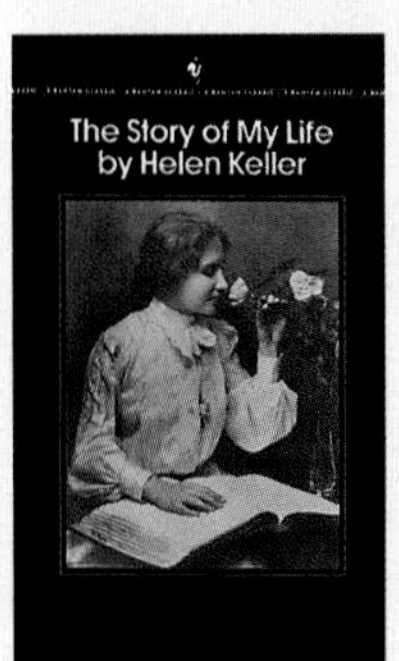

Even though Helen Keller was left blind and deaf by an illness when she was nineteen months old, she was determined to read and write. In *The Story of My Life,* Keller writes about her refusal to give up in the face of unthinkable adversity. The book includes letters and personal records that will lead readers to a greater understanding of her life.

Rescue: The Story of How Gentiles Saved Jews in the Holocaust

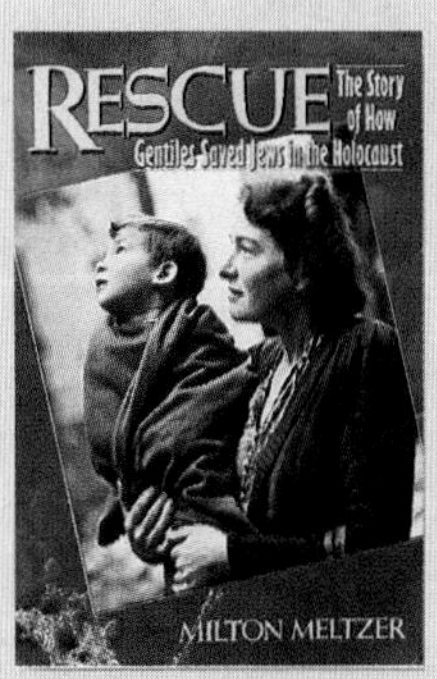

Under Nazi rule, even to be seen talking to a Jew was dangerous—yet all over Europe, non-Jews risked their lives to save neighbors and friends from the death camps. In *Rescue: The Story of How Gentiles Saved Jews in the Holocaust,* Milton Meltzer tells of their heroism.

Learn It Online

Upgrade your understanding of novels. Visit *NovelWise* at:

go.hrw.com L8-251 

BRINLEY
10
16
8
FERON
9

COLLECTION 3

Theme

INFORMATIONAL TEXT FOCUS
Analyzing Text Structures

"You never really understand a person until you consider things from his point of view."

—Harper Lee

What Do You Think? Is it harder to understand others or ourselves?

Learn It Online
Find graphic organizers online to help you as you read:

go.hrw.com L8-253 

Literary Focus

by **Sara Kajder**

What Is a Story's Theme?

You probably enjoy stories—in books, on television, and in the movies—for their excitement, suspense, laughs, exotic settings, and interesting characters. When a story touches you so deeply that you keep thinking about it, however, it has probably taught you something valuable about life. This observation or insight about life is called the theme.

Theme

Theme is the message about life that the reader takes away from a work of literature. Many writers say they don't know their theme when they begin to write. They often start with just a character or a situation. "What would motivate someone to risk everything?" they wonder, or "How would a thirteen-year-old deal with his parents' divorce?" Then they start to write. A theme will often emerge naturally from a story as it progresses and from what the writer believes about life.

What a Theme Is *Not*

A theme is not the subject of a story. Although a subject can usually be described in a single word (for example, *love, war, friendship*) or a phrase (*a boy's survival in the wilderness*), you need a full sentence to explain a theme.

For example, one story in this collection is about a boy's relationship with his grandfather and his heritage. The theme is what you learn about this subject as you read the story.

A theme is not the plot of a story. The plot is a series of related events. When you tell your friends what happened in a movie you saw, you are relating its plot. If you tell them that the movie shows how important it is to be loyal to your country, however, you are describing a theme.

A theme is not a summary of a story. Even if you summarize only the most important events in describing your movie, you will still be retelling the plot, not stating a theme. It is only when you talk about what the movie taught you about life that you are stating the theme. However, summarizing can be a useful step in figuring out the theme. After writing your summary, ask yourself, "What message or truth about life have I gotten from this story?"

> **Summary:** A dog on a bridge wants another dog's bone, but the dog on the bridge doesn't realize that the other dog is his own reflection, so he jumps in to get the other dog's bone and loses his own.

Your answer can be your theme statement.

> **Theme(s):** Greed may get you in trouble.
> Be happy with what you have.

RA.L.8.5 Identify and explain universal themes across different works by the same author and by different authors.

Different Readers, Different Themes

Two readers will rarely state a theme in exactly the same way. In fact, readers may differ on what they see as a story's theme. If you read a story about a man who works hard and achieves great success only to lose all he had gained, such as "Flowers for Algernon" in Collection 1, you might decide the theme is

> It is important to follow your dreams, no matter the outcome.

A classmate, however, might think the theme is

> You cannot change your fate.

And you both could be right. The meaning of a story comes from both the writer and the reader.

Recurring Themes

People all over the world share the same dreams and fears. It is not surprising, then, that all over the world people tell the same stories—more or less. Characters vary and settings differ, but themes recur. These themes—called **universal themes** or **recurring themes**—can be found in ancient myths, in folk tales from around the world, in movies, and even on TV shows.

Examples of Recurring Themes
Never give up on a friend.
Unlimited money and power corrupt.
A good attitude leads to success.
The gift of love can change a person.
Sometimes dreams do come true.

Your Turn Analyze Theme

How many times have you read a story or seen a show with these themes?

- Things may not always be what they seem.
- Wishes can have surprising consequences.
- You should treasure what is good in your life.
- People can have a strong influence over others.

To begin your exploration of themes and recurring themes, look again at the list of themes above. Then, think of novels, stories, poems, and plays you have studied or read on your own. Think also of movies, plays, and TV shows you have seen. With a group of classmates, brainstorm titles of works that reflect those themes. Record your titles in a chart like this:

Theme	Titles
Things may not always be what they seem.	"The Inn of Lost Time" "The Open Window"
Wishes can have surprising consequences.	"Those Three Wishes" "The Monkey's Paw"

Learn It Online

Check out *NovelWise* to learn more about themes. Visit:

Analyzing Visuals

How Can You Determine the Theme of a Painting?

The painter Jackson Pollock (1912–1956) said, "Every good artist paints what he is." Artists engage with themselves and the world. Some may express this engagement in a picture or representational painting. Others may use only color or shape to evoke a feeling. Whatever the approach, most paintings offer an idea or observation about life—that is, a theme.

Analyzing a Painting

Use these guidelines to help you determine a painting's theme.

1. Identify the painting's subject or main focus. Who or what is being depicted?
2. Analyze the setting of the painting. What atmosphere does the setting convey?
3. Examine details that catch your eye—colors, shapes, brushstrokes, and use of light and shadow. What mood do these details help create?
4. Examine the title of the work to see if it reveals the painter's attitude toward his or her subject.
5. Formulate a theme statement based on your analysis of the work.

Your Turn Write About Theme

Look through this textbook to find a piece of artwork that you think offers an insight about life. Describe the theme of that picture.

RA.L.8.5 Identify and explain universal themes across different works by the same author and by different authors.

1. Setting can shape a painting's mood and theme. How does Chepik make the circus setting seem exciting?

2. Observe the positions of the central figures. What attitude do their positions suggest?

3. What atmosphere does the use of light and dark create?

4. Chepik said of this work, "I wanted to paint the beautiful, joyful, colorful, fantasy world of [the] circus." With this in mind, state a theme of this work.

Circus (The Riders) (1991) by Sergei Chepik. Mixed media on canvas (110 cm x 100 cm).

Reading Focus

by **Kylene Beers**

What Skills Help You Understand a Story's Theme?

When asked to find the theme of a story, you may think, "Isn't keeping track of the characters and events enough?" Yet once you are able to state a story's theme in your own words, you will have truly absorbed the meaning of the story—and will be the wiser for it.

Finding the Theme

Like the truths we discover in real life, themes in stories can be complicated, open to interpretation, and sometimes difficult to put into words. So how *do* you put your finger on a story's theme? Try looking at these elements:

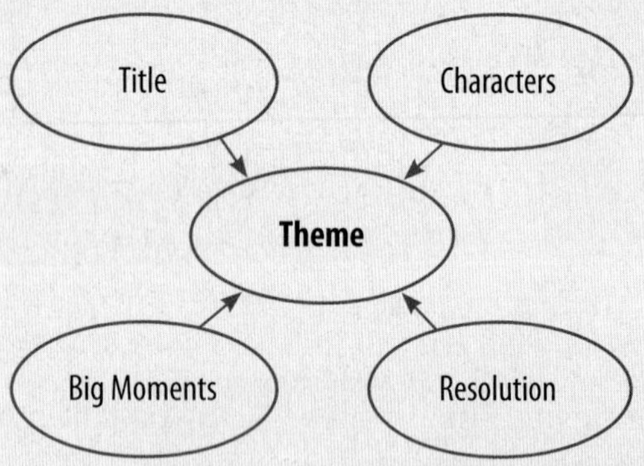

The Title A story's title sometimes hints at the theme. "The Medicine Bag," for example, refers to a Native American tradition, which may be a clue to the story's theme.

The Characters The main characters generally change in the course of the story. What do they discover that could have meaning for other people's lives—including your own? Look in the next column at the example from "Gentleman of Río en Medio" by Juan A. A. Sedillo.

> It took months of negotiation to come to an understanding with the old man. He was in no hurry. What he had the most of was time. He lived up in Río en Medio, where his people had been for hundreds of years.
>
> from "Gentleman of Rio en Medio"
> by Juan A. A. Sedillo

The Big Moments Some scenes or passages in the story seem especially important. What revelation about life might this example suggest to you?

> Don Anselmo stood up. "We have all learned to love these Americans," he said, "because they are good people and good neighbors. I sold them my property because I knew they were good people, but I did not sell them the trees in the orchard."
>
> from "Gentleman of Rio en Medio"
> by Juan A. A. Sedillo

The Resolution Think about how problems or conflicts in the story are settled. How do you feel about the outcome? Does the resolution give you an idea about what the story means? Your answers to these questions will help you to formulate a theme statement.

OH **RA.L.8.5** Identify and explain universal themes across different works by the same author and by different authors. **RP.8.1** Apply reading comprehension strategies, including making predictions, comparing and contrasting, recalling and summarizing and making inferences and drawing conclusions.

Making Generalizations

A **generalization** is a broad statement that extends your observations and experiences to a larger understanding. It is a kind of conclusion you make after considering many specific details. For instance, if your cat and the cats of your friends all purr when being petted, you might generalize: *All cats purr when petted.* However, to be **valid,** a generalization must apply to almost every member of the group. Since there are millions of cats you have not met, to make your generalization valid, you might say: *Many cats purr when petted.*

Making Generalizations About Theme

When you read a story, you note details, connect them to what you already know, and then make a generalization that can apply to all those instances. You can make generalizations about characters, events, and settings. You can also make generalizations about what a story means. This type of generalization is also a **theme statement.** When you state the story's broad meaning, you've generalized from the pages of the book to the world we live in. Here is a diagram that shows the process of making generalizations:

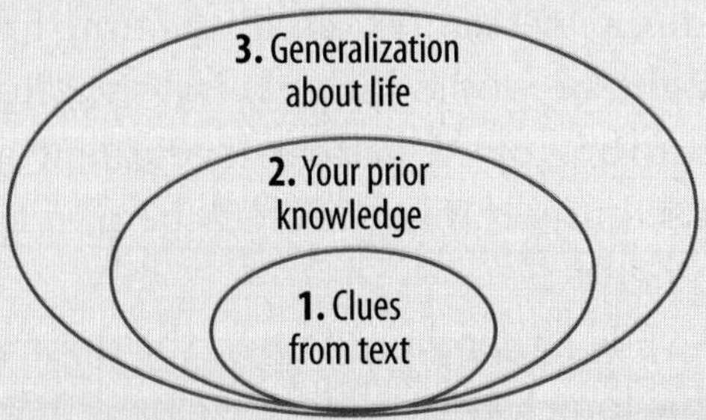

Making Predictions

Have you ever handed someone a tissue *before* the person sneezed? How did you predict that the person would sneeze? You used your knowledge of sneezing and the clues the person was giving you. **Predictions** are guesses about what will happen based on evidence and your prior knowledge.

Making Predictions About Theme When reading a story, you often predict how characters will act or what will happen to them. You can also make predictions about a story's theme. Follow these tips for predicting a story's theme:

- Think about the type of story you are reading and your prior experience with this type.
- Think about how the story's characters and conflicts are similar to those of people you know or have read about.
- Predict the story's end and the insight about life that its characters—and you—will gain.

Your Turn Apply Reading Skills

1. With a partner, brainstorm a short list of movies. Choose three titles, and explain how they hint at the movies' themes.
2. Choose a story you have read from this book, and make a generalization based on what one of the characters learns. Make your generalization in the form of a theme statement.

Now go to the Skills in Action: Reading Model

Learn It Online

For a visual approach to learning, try the *PowerNotes* version of this lesson at:

go.hrw.com L8-259 

SHORT STORY

Read with a Purpose Read to find out what happens to a father and son as the boy grows up.

Reading Focus

Finding the Theme Remember that a story's title can hint at the theme. Think about ideas the title brings to mind, such as the fact that cubs are baby bears—not yet grown up.

The Cub

by **Lois Dykeman Kleihauer**

One of his first memories was of his father bending down from his great height to sweep him into the air. Up he went, gasping and laughing with delight. He could look down on his mother's upturned face as she watched, laughing with them, and at the thick shock of his father's brown hair and at his white teeth.

Then he would come down, shrieking happily, but he was never afraid, not with his father's hands holding him. No one in the world was as strong, or as wise, as his father.

He remembered a time when his father moved the piano across the room for his mother. He watched while she guided it into its new position, and he saw the difference in their hands as they rested, side by side, upon the gleaming walnut. His mother's hands were white and slim and delicate, his father's large and square and strong.

As he grew, he learned to play bear. When it was time for his father to come home at night, he would lurk behind the kitchen door. When he heard the closing of the garage doors, he would hold his breath and squeeze himself into the crack behind the door. Then he would be quiet.

It was always the same. His father would open the door and stand there, the backs of his long legs beguilingly close. "Where's the boy?"

He would glance at the conspiratorial[1] smile on his mother's face, and then he would leap and grab his father about the knees, and his father would look down and shout, "Hey, what's this?

1. **conspiratorial** (kuhn spihr uh TAWR ee uhl): secretive; scheming.

Analyzing Visuals

Viewing and Interpreting How might this picture illustrate a theme of the story?

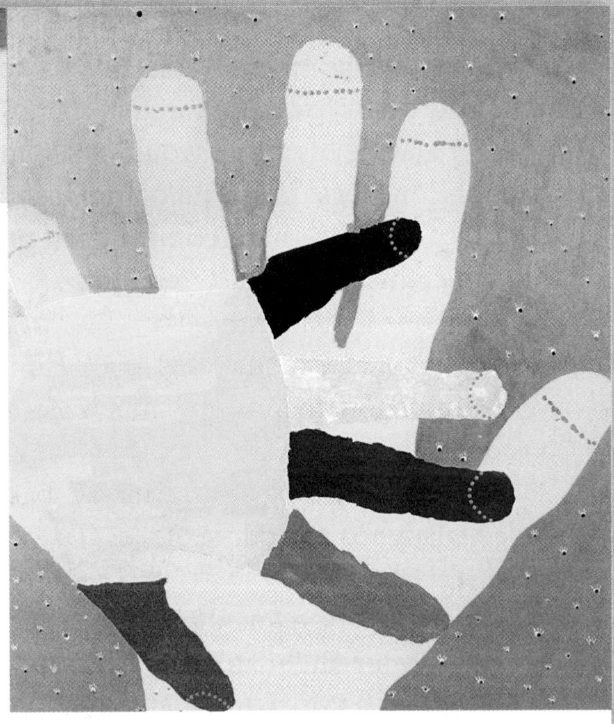

Like Father Like Son (1998) by Gary Hume. Household paint and mixed media on aluminum (200 x 162 cm).

A bear—a young cub!"

Then, no matter how tightly he tried to cling, he was lifted up and perched upon his father's shoulder, and they would march past his mother, and together they would duck their heads beneath the doors.

And then he went to school. And on the playground he learned how to wrestle and shout, how to hold back tears, how to get a half-nelson[2] on the boy who tried to take his football away from him. He came home at night and practiced his new wisdom on his father. Straining and puffing, he tried to pull his father off the lounge chair while his father kept on reading the paper, only glancing up now and then to ask in mild wonderment, "What are you trying to do, boy?"

He would stand and look at his father. "Gee whiz, Dad!" And then he would realize that his father was teasing him, and he would crawl up on his father's lap and pummel him in affectionate frustration.

And still he grew—taller, slimmer, stronger. He was like a young buck, with tiny new horns. He wanted to lock them with any other young buck's, to test them in combat. He measured his biceps with his mother's tape measure. Exultantly, he thrust his arm in front of his father. "Feel that! How's that for muscle?"

His father put his great thumb into the flexed muscle and pressed, and the boy pulled back, protesting, laughing. "Ouch!"

Reading Focus

Making Generalizations Not everyone needs to learn how to wrestle, but what do all children need to learn to do? Consider what generalization you might make based on this passage and on your own experience.

2. **half-nelson:** type of wrestling hold.

Sometimes they wrestled on the floor together, and his mother moved the chairs back. "Be careful, Charles—don't hurt him."

After a while his father would push him aside and sit in his chair, his long legs thrust out before him, and the boy would scramble to his feet, half resentful, half mirthful over the ease with which his father mastered him.

"Doggone it, Dad, someday—" he would say.

He went out for football and track in high school. He surprised even himself now, there was so much more of him. And he could look down on his mother. "Little one," he called her, or "Small fry."

Sometimes he took her wrists and backed her into a chair, while he laughed and she scolded. "I'll—I'll take you across my knee."

"Who will?" he demanded.

"Well—your father still can," she said.

His father—well, that was different.

Reading Focus

Making Predictions The author repeatedly lets us know how the mother feels about the father and son's wrestling. Pay attention to her reactions to help you predict what will happen.

They still wrestled occasionally, but it distressed his mother. She hovered about them, worrying, unable to comprehend the need for their struggling. It always ended the same way, with the boy upon his back, prostrate, and his father grinning down at him. "Give?"

"Give." And he got up, shaking his head.

"I wish you wouldn't," his mother would say, fretting. "There's no point in it. You'll hurt yourselves; don't do it any more."

Reading Focus

Making Generalizations You can connect these details about how the son sees his father to what you know about life—how people and things can seem really large and impressive from a child's point of view.

So for nearly a year they had not wrestled, but he thought about it one night at dinner. He looked at his father closely. It was queer, but his father didn't look nearly as tall or broad-shouldered as he used to. He could even look his father straight in the eyes now.

"How much do you weigh, Dad?" he asked.

His father threw him a mild glance. "About the same; about a hundred and ninety. Why?"

The boy grinned. "Just wondering."

But after a while he went over to his father where he sat reading the paper and took it out of his hands. His father glanced up, his eyes at first questioning and then narrowing to meet the challenge in his son's. "So," he said softly.

"Come on, Dad."

His father took off his coat and began to unbutton his shirt. "You asked for it," he said.

His mother came in from the kitchen, alarmed. "Oh, Charles! Bill! Don't—you'll hurt yourselves!" But they paid no attention to her. They were standing now, their shirts off. They watched each other, intent and purposeful. The boy's teeth gleamed again. They circled for a moment, and then their hands closed upon each other's arms.

They strained against each other, and then the boy went down, taking his father with him. They moved and writhed and turned, in silence seeking an advantage, in silence pressing it to its conclusion. There was the sound of the thumps of their bodies upon the rug and of the quick, hard intake of breath. The boy showed his teeth occasionally in a grimace of pain. His mother stood at one side, both hands pressed against her ears. Occasionally her lips moved, but she did not make a sound.

After a while the boy pinned his father on his back. "Give!" he demanded.

His father said, "Heck no!" And with a great effort he pushed the boy off, and the struggle began again.

But at the end his father lay prostrate, and a look of bewilderment came into his eyes. He struggled desperately against his son's merciless, restraining hands. Finally he lay quiet, only his chest heaving, his breath coming loudly.

Reading Focus

Finding the Theme In the past the father always won the wrestling matches. Think of what it means now that the son has won.

The boy said, "Give!"

The man frowned, shaking his head.

Still the boy knelt on him, pinning him down.

"Give!" he said, and tightened his grip. "Give!"

All at once his father began to laugh, silently, his shoulders shaking. The boy felt his mother's fingers tugging fiercely at his shoulder. "Let him up," she said. "Let him up!"

The boy looked down at his father. "Give up?"

His father stopped laughing, but his eyes were still wet. "Okay," he said. "I give."

The boy stood up and reached a hand to his father to help him up, but his mother was before him, putting an arm about his father's shoulders, helping him to rise. They stood together and looked at him, his father grinning gamely, his mother with baffled pain in her eyes.

The boy started to laugh. "I guess I—" He stopped. "Gosh, Dad, I didn't hurt you, did I?"

"Heck, no, I'm all right. Next time. . . ."

"Yeah, maybe next time. . . ."

And his mother did not contradict what they said, for she knew as well as they that there would never be a next time.

For a moment the three of them stood looking at one another, and then, suddenly, blindly, the boy turned. He ran through the door under which he had ducked so many times when he had ridden on his father's shoulders. He went out the kitchen door, behind which he had hidden, waiting to leap out and pounce upon his father's legs.

It was dark outside. He stood on the steps, feeling the air cool against his sweaty body. He stood with lifted head, looking at the stars, and then he could not see them because of the tears that burned his eyes and ran down his cheeks.

Literary Focus

Theme The son has been deeply moved by the realization that he is now stronger than his father. Think about what the son has learned, and decide what you think the writer is saying about growing up and the cycle of life.

Read with a Purpose How has the relationship between the father and son changed?

A Minnesota neighborhood.

MEET THE WRITER

Lois Dykeman Kleihauer

(1907–1986)

Universal Appeal

Lois Dykeman Kleihauer was born in Argyle, Minnesota. She wrote poems before developing an interest in writing short stories. Most of her work appeared in magazines, including *McCall's, Family Circle,* and *Redbook*. The themes in her stories appeal not only to readers in the United States but also to readers in other countries; her stories have been reprinted in England, Australia, New Zealand, and South Africa.

Think About the Writer Based on the story you just read, why do you think Kleihauer's work is popular with readers all over the world?

SKILLS IN ACTION

Wrap Up

RA.L.8.5 Identify and explain universal themes across different works by the same author and by different authors. *Also covered* **VO.8.7**

Into Action: Finding the Theme

Review "The Cub," and fill in a Theme Map like the one below with information from the story. In the center oval, write your theme statement.

Talk About . . .

1. With a partner, discuss the story's themes. What does the story say about growing up? about being a parent? Try to use each Academic Vocabulary word listed at the right in your discussion.

Write About . . .

Use the underlined Academic Vocabulary words in your answers to the following questions about "The Cub."

2. Why is it significant that the boy is first compared to a cub and later to a young buck? How do the comparisons indicate that the boy is growing up?
3. What is the consequence of the son's winning the wrestling match? How do the results of that match help convey the story's theme?

Writing Focus

Think as a Reader/Writer

Find It in Your Reading In the selections in Collection 3, you will find themes on a topic everyone can relate to: the need to understand others and ourselves. The Writing Focus activities on the Preparing to Read pages will show you ways authors craft their stories. The Applying Your Skills pages will offer opportunities to practice the authors' techniques yourself.

Academic Vocabulary for Collection 3

Talking and Writing About Theme

Academic Vocabulary is the language you use to write and talk about literature. Use these words to discuss the stories you read. The words are underlined throughout the collection.

convey (kuhn VAY) *v.:* communicate; express. *A story's theme is the message about life that the author wants to convey.*

significant (sihg NIHF uh kuhnt) *adj.:* meaningful; important. *Focusing on significant details will help you find the theme.*

indicate (IHN dih kayt) *v.:* point out; suggest. *Important moments in the story may indicate what the story's theme will be.*

consequence (KAHN suh kwehns) *n.:* result of something that happened earlier. *A major consequence that a character suffers—and learns from—can point to a theme.*

Your Turn

Copy these Academic Vocabulary words into your *Reader/Writer Notebook*. Think of a story you know well (such as a fairy tale). Then, write four sentences about the story, using each Academic Vocabulary word.

SHORT STORY

Preparing to Read

STOP THE SUN

by **Gary Paulsen**

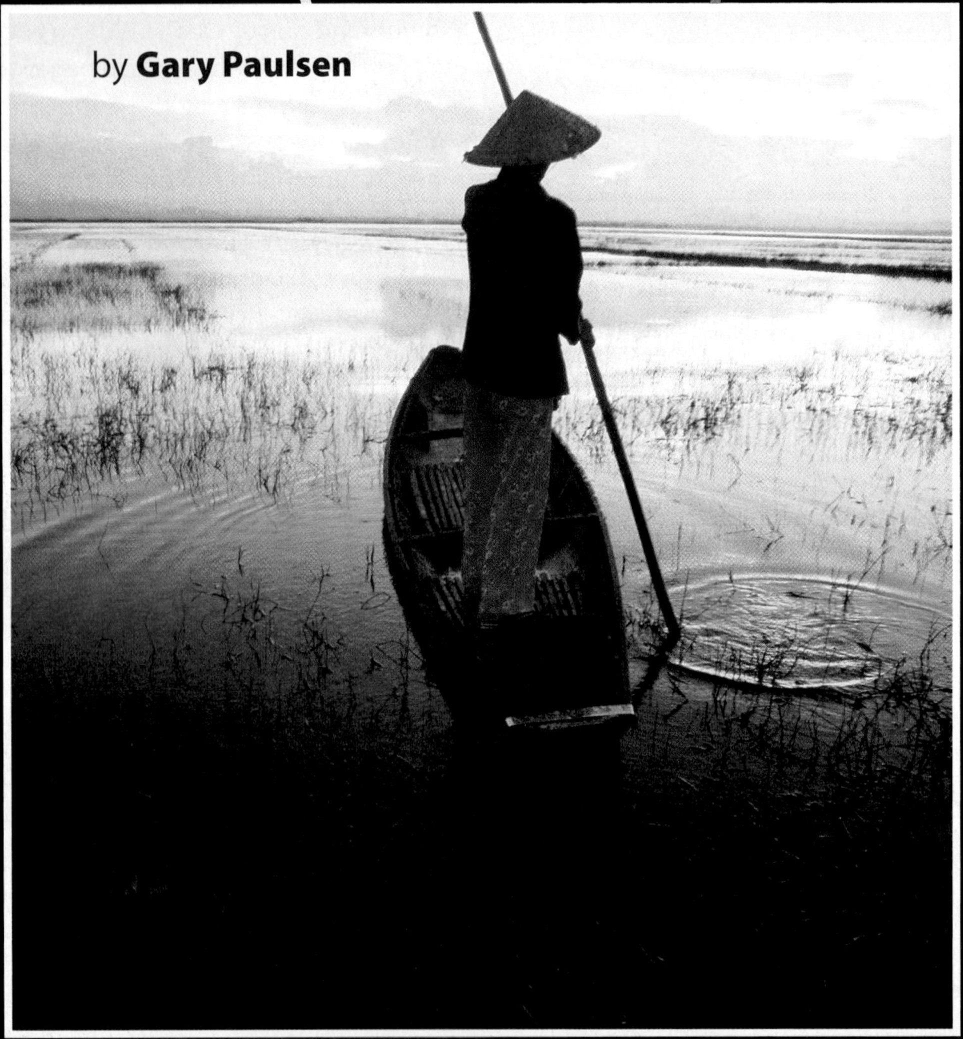

What Do You Think?

How well do you understand others, even those closest to you?

QuickTalk

Discuss why parents might shield a child from what they experienced in wartime. Is withholding information a good idea? Explain

Reader/Writer Notebook

Use your **RWN** to complete the activities for this selection.

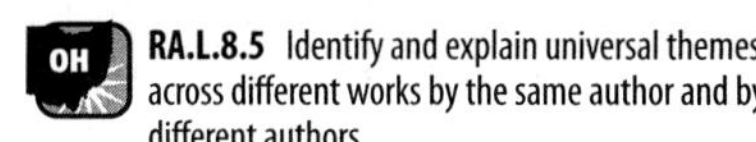

RA.L.8.5 Identify and explain universal themes across different works by the same author and by different authors.

Literary Focus

Theme The **theme** of a story is the idea about life that it conveys. Theme is *not* the same as the subject of a story; the theme is the insight the story expresses *about* the subject. For example, the subject of "Stop the Sun" is a son's effort to understand his father. The theme is what the story says about this subject.

TechFocus As you read, make a list of things a war veteran might want or need when he or she returns home. Examples might be a new job or someone to talk to about the war experience.

Reading Focus

Finding the Theme Most of the time a story's theme is not stated directly. Instead, you must analyze details from the story and consider what you know from real life to formulate a theme statement. Ask yourself, "What idea about life does this story convey?"

Into Action Complete this chart to help you find the theme of "Stop the Sun." Some lines have been filled in to get you started.

Subject: A young man tries to understand his father.		
What you already know about subject: Fathers sometimes don't like to "open up."		
Details about the subject:		
Terry reads books for information about Vietnam.		

Writing Focus

Think as a Reader/Writer

Find It in Your Reading Writers sometimes repeat words and phrases to make a point. In your *Reader/Writer Notebook,* note any such repetitions that Gary Paulsen makes.

Vocabulary

commotion (kuh MOH shuhn) *n.:* noisy confusion; disturbance. *Terry went to see what was causing the commotion.*

foundered (FOWN duhrd) *v.:* broke down; failed. *Terry's speech foundered because it was difficult for him to express his strong feelings.*

ruin (ROO uhn) *n.:* great damage; devastation. *When Terry looks at his father's face, he can see the ruin the war has caused.*

inert (ihn URT) *adj.:* not moving; still. *Terry's father's friends lay on the ground, wounded and inert.*

father's feelings of **ruin** → led to a **commotion** in a hardware store

father's feelings of **ruin** → his ability to return to a normal life **foundered**

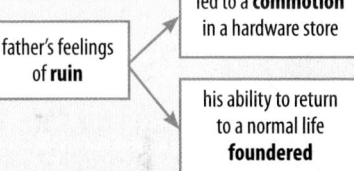

Language Coach

Multiple-Meaning Words Some words have different meanings depending on the context in which they are used. Which word on the list above also means "remains of a decayed building"? How can you tell?

Learn It Online

Augment your vocabulary with Word Watch. Visit:

go.hrw.com L8-267

MEET THE WRITER

Learn It Online
Learn more about the author at:
go.hrw.com L8-268 Go

Gary Paulsen
(1939–)

A "Rough Run"
Because Gary Paulsen's father was an army officer, the family lived all over the United States and in the Philippines. Paulsen calls his boyhood a "rough run." The longest period of time that Paulsen spent in one school was five months. "School was a nightmare," he says, "because I was unbelievably shy and terrible at sports. I had no friends, and teachers ridiculed me."

A Refuge
On a freezing day Paulsen found refuge at the public library. He recounts his experience there as a significant turning point:

"I went in to get warm, and to my absolute astonishment the librarian walked up to me and asked if I wanted a library card. . . . When she handed me the card, she handed me the world. . . . I roared through [every book] she gave me and in the summer read a book a day."

A Run for Fun
As an adult Paulsen has found a sport he enjoys: He races sled dogs in the Iditarod, a grueling race in Alaska.

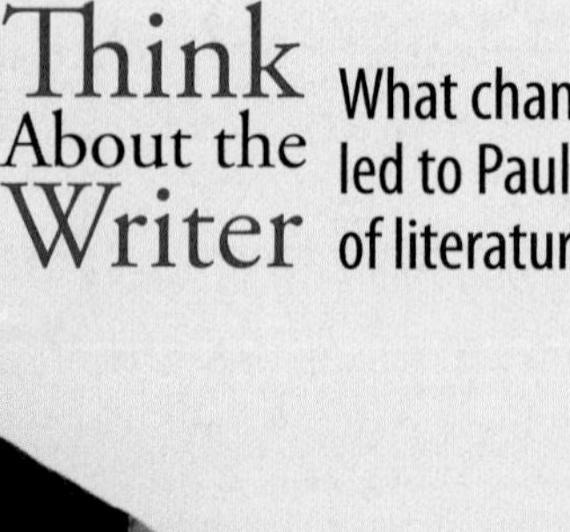

Think About the Writer What chance event led to Paulsen's love of literature?

Build Background
This story centers on a boy whose father suffers from "Vietnam syndrome," a term sometimes used to describe the post-traumatic stress disorder (PTSD) many soldiers who served in Vietnam have. This disorder causes anxiety, depression, nightmares, and intrusive thoughts.

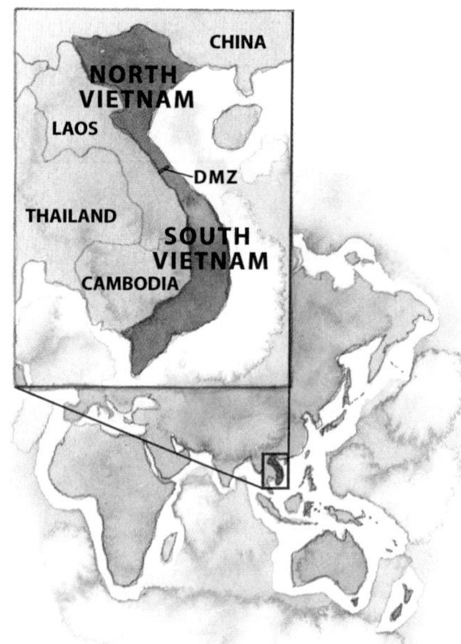

Preview the Selection
Terry Erickson, the main character of this story, struggles to understand and accept his father's unsettling and, at times, embarrassing behavior.

Read with a Purpose Read this story to discover what a son learns about his father.

STOP THE SUN

by **Gary Paulsen**

Terry Erickson was a tall boy, 13, starting to fill out with muscle but still a little awkward. He was on the edge of being a good athlete, which meant a lot to him. He felt it coming too slowly, though, and that bothered him.

But what bothered him even more was when his father's eyes went away.

Usually it happened when it didn't cause any particular trouble. Sometimes during a meal his father's fork would stop halfway to his mouth, just stop, and there would be a long pause while the eyes went away, far away.

After several minutes his mother would reach over and take the fork and put it gently down on his plate, and they would go back to eating—or try to go back to eating—normally. **A**

They knew what caused it. When it first started, Terry had asked his mother in private what it was, what was causing the strange behavior.

"It's from the war," his mother had said. "The doctors at the veterans' hospital call it the Vietnam syndrome."[1]

"Will it go away?"

"They don't know. Sometimes it goes away. Sometimes it doesn't. They are trying to help him."

"But what happened? What actually caused it?"

"I told you. Vietnam."

"But there had to be something," Terry persisted. "Something made him like that. Not just Vietnam. Billy's father was there, and he doesn't act that way."

"That's enough questions," his mother said sternly. "He doesn't talk about it, and I don't ask. Neither will you. Do you understand?"

"But, Mom."

"That's enough."

1. **Vietnam syndrome:** form of post-traumatic stress disorder.

A **Read and Discuss** Why do you think the author has begun the story by describing Terry's problem?

And he stopped pushing it. But it bothered him whenever it happened. When something bothered him, he liked to stay with it until he understood it, and he understood no part of this. **B**

Words. His father had trouble, and they gave him words like Vietnam syndrome. He knew almost nothing of the war, and when he tried to find out about it, he kept hitting walls. Once he went to the school library and asked for anything they might have that could help him understand the war and how it affected his father. They gave him a dry history that described French involvement, Communist involvement, American involvement. But it told him nothing of the war. It was all numbers, cold numbers, and nothing of what had *happened.* There just didn't seem to be anything that could help him.

Another time he stayed after class and tried to talk to Mr. Carlson, who taught history. But some part of Terry was embarrassed. He didn't want to say why he wanted to know about Vietnam, so he couldn't be specific.

"What do you want to know about Vietnam, Terry?" Mr. Carlson had asked. "It was a big war."

Terry had looked at him, and something had started up in his mind, but he didn't let it out. He shrugged. "I just want to know what it was like. I know somebody who was in it."

"A friend?"

"Yessir. A good friend."

Mr. Carlson had studied him, looking into his eyes, but didn't ask any other questions. Instead he mentioned a couple of books Terry had not seen. They turned out to be pretty good. They told about how it felt to be in combat. Still, he couldn't make his father be one of the men he read about. **C**

And it may have gone on and on like that, with Terry never really knowing any more about it except that his father's eyes started going away more and more often. It might have just gone the rest of his life that way except for the shopping mall.

It was easily the most embarrassing thing that ever happened to him.

It started as a normal shopping trip. His father had to go to the hardware store, and he asked Terry to go along.

When they got to the mall they split up. His father went to the hardware store, Terry to a record store to look at albums.

Terry browsed so long that he was late meeting his father at the mall's front door. But his father wasn't there, and Terry looked out to the car to make sure it was still in the parking lot. It was, and he supposed his father had just gotten busy, so he waited.

Still his father didn't come, and he was about to go to the hardware store to find him when he noticed the commotion. Or not a commotion so much as a sudden movement of people.

B **Read and Discuss** What does Terry think about his father's condition? What does he think about the way his mother is dealing with it?

C **Reading Focus** **Finding the Theme** How is Terry trying to understand his father? How successful are his attempts?

Vocabulary **commotion** (kuh MOH shuhn) *n.:* noisy confusion; disturbance.

Later, he thought of it and couldn't remember when the feeling first came to him that there was something wrong. The people were moving toward the hardware store and that might have been what made Terry suspicious.

There was a crowd blocking the entry to the store, and he couldn't see what they were looking at. Some of them were laughing small, nervous laughs that made no sense.

Terry squeezed through the crowd until he got near the front. At first he saw nothing unusual. There were still some people in front of him, so he pushed a crack between them. Then he saw it: His father was squirming along the floor on his stomach. He was crying, looking terrified, his breath coming in short, hot pants like some kind of hurt animal.

It burned into Terry's mind, the picture of his father down on the floor. It burned in and in, and he wanted to walk away, but something made his feet move forward. He knelt next to his father and helped the owner of the store get him up on his feet. His father didn't speak at all but continued to make little whimpering sounds, and they led him back into the owner's office and put him in a chair. Then Terry called his mother and she came in a taxi to take them home. Waiting, Terry sat in a chair next to his father, looking at the floor, wanting only for the earth to open and let him drop in a deep hole. He wanted to disappear. **D**

Words. They gave him words like Vietnam syndrome, and his father was

SOCIAL STUDIES LINK

American soldiers in Vietnam, 1966.

Vietnam War

When Vietnam won its independence from France in 1954, it was split into two halves. When elections to choose a government for a united country did not take place, the communist North tried to unite the whole country under a communist regime. The United States supplied South Vietnam with weapons, troops, and other support, gradually increasing its involvement until by 1969 more than 500,000 U.S. military personnel were in Vietnam. Despite having superior technology and firepower, the United States was unable to defeat a guerrilla army fighting in its home territory. When President Nixon took office in 1969, he began withdrawing U.S. troops. North Vietnam conquered the South, and by 1976, Vietnam had become a reunited country under communist rule.

Ask Yourself

What different insights into the war do this link and the short story offer?

D **Read and Discuss** What is happening with Terry's father?

crawling through a hardware store on his stomach.

When the embarrassment became so bad that he would cross the street when he saw his father coming, when it ate into him as he went to sleep, Terry realized he had to do something. He had to know this thing, had to understand what was wrong with his father.

When it came, it was simple enough at the start. It had taken some courage, more than Terry thought he could find. His father was sitting in the kitchen at the table and his mother had gone shopping. Terry wanted it that way; he wanted his father alone. His mother seemed to try to protect him, as if his father could break.

Terry got a soda out of the refrigerator and popped it open. As an afterthought, he handed it to his father and got another for himself. Then he sat at the table.

His father smiled. "You look serious."

"Well . . ."

It went nowhere for a moment, and Terry was just about to drop it altogether. It may be the wrong time, he thought, but there might never be a better one. He tightened his back, took a sip of pop.

"I was wondering if we could talk about something, Dad," Terry said.

His father shrugged. "We already did the bit about girls. Some time ago, as I remember it."

Analyzing Visuals **Viewing and Interpreting**

In what ways is this scene from Vietnam similar to and different from "the green . . . wet-hot places" that haunt Terry's father?

"No. Not that." It was a standing joke between them. When his father finally got around to explaining things to him, they'd already covered it in school. "It's something else."

"Something pretty heavy, judging by your face."

"Yes."

"Well?"

I still can't do it, Terry thought. Things are bad, but maybe not as bad as they could get. I can still drop this thing.

"Vietnam," Terry blurted out. And he thought, there, it's out. It's out and gone.

"No!" his father said sharply. It was as if he had been struck a blow. A body blow.

"But, Dad."

"No. That's another part of my life. A bad part. A rotten part. It was before I met your mother, long before you. It has nothing to do with this family, nothing. No."

So, Terry thought, so I tried. But it wasn't over yet. It wasn't started yet.

"It just seems to bother you so much," Terry said, "and I thought if I could help or maybe understand it better. . . ." His words ran until he foundered, until he could say no more. He looked at the table, then out the window. It was all wrong to bring it up, he thought. I blew it. I blew it all up. "I'm sorry."

But now his father didn't hear him. Now his father's eyes were gone again, and a shaft of something horrible went through Terry's heart as he thought he had done this thing to his father, caused his eyes to go away.

"You can't know," his father said after a time. "You can't know this thing."

Terry said nothing. He felt he had said too much.

"This thing that you want to know—there is so much of it that you cannot know it all, and to know only a part is . . . is too awful. I can't tell you. I can't tell anybody what it was really like." **E**

It was more than he'd ever said about Vietnam, and his voice was breaking. Terry hated himself and felt he would hate himself until he was an old man. In one second he had caused such ruin. And all because he had been embarrassed. What difference did it make? Now he had done this, and he wanted to hide, to leave. But he sat, waiting, knowing that it wasn't done.

His father looked to him, through him, somewhere into and out of Terry. He wasn't in the kitchen anymore. He wasn't in the house. He was back in the green places, back in the hot places, the wet-hot places. **F**

"You think that because I act strange, that we can talk and it will be all right," his father said. "That we can talk and it will just go away. That's what you think, isn't it?"

Terry started to shake his head, but he knew it wasn't expected.

"That's what the shrinks say," his father continued. "The psychiatrists tell me that if I talk about it, the whole thing will go away.

E **Reading Focus** **Finding the Theme** Why do you think Terry's father "can't tell anybody what it was really like"?

F **Read and Discuss** What is going on with Terry's father? What are the "green places, . . . the wet-hot places"?

Vocabulary **foundered** (FOWN duhrd) *v.:* broke down; failed.
ruin (ROO uhn) *n.:* great damage; devastation.

Analyzing Visuals **Viewing and Interpreting** These pictures of Vietnamese rice paddies look serene, but what might it have been like for a foreign soldier, at night, crossing this terrain?

But they don't know. They weren't there. You weren't there. Nobody was there but me and some other dead people, and they can't talk because they couldn't stop the morning."

Terry pushed his soda can back and forth, looking down, frightened at what was happening. *The other dead people*, he'd said, as if he were dead as well. *Couldn't stop the morning.*

"I don't understand, Dad."

"No. You don't." His voice hardened, then softened again, and broke at the edges. "But see, see how it was. . . ." He trailed off, and Terry thought he was done. His father looked back down to the table, at the can of soda he hadn't touched, at the tablecloth, at his hands, which were folded, inert on the table.

"We were crossing a rice paddy in the dark," he said, and suddenly his voice flowed like a river breaking loose. "We were crossing the paddy, and it was dark, still dark, so black you couldn't see the end of your nose. There was a light rain, a mist, and I was thinking that during the next break I would whisper and tell Petey Kressler how nice the rain felt, but of course I didn't know there wouldn't be a Petey Kressler."

Vocabulary **inert** (ihn URT) *adj.*: not moving; still.

He took a deep, ragged breath. At that moment Terry felt his brain swirl, a kind of whirlpool pulling, and he felt the darkness and the light rain because it was in his father's eyes, in his voice.

"So we were crossing the paddy, and it was a straight sweep, and then we caught it. We began taking fire from three sides, automatic weapons, and everybody went down and tried to get low, but we couldn't. We couldn't get low enough. We could never get low enough, and you could hear the rounds hitting people. It was just a short time before they brought in the mortars and we should have moved, should have run, but nobody got up, and after a time nobody *could* get up. The fire just kept coming and coming, and then incoming mortars, and I heard screams as they hit, but there was nothing to do. Nothing to do."

"Dad?" Terry said. He thought, maybe I can stop him. Maybe I can stop him before . . . before it gets to be too much. Before he breaks. **G**

"Mortars," his father went on, "I hated mortars. You just heard them *wump* as they fired, and you didn't know where they would hit, and you always felt like they would hit your back. They swept back and forth with the mortars, and the automatic weapons kept coming in, and there was no radio, no way to call for artillery. Just the dark to hide in. So I crawled to the side and found Jackson, only he wasn't there, just part of his body, the top part, and I hid under it and waited, and waited, and waited.

"Finally the firing quit. But see, see how it was in the dark with nobody alive but me? I yelled once, but that brought fire again, so I shut up, and there was nothing, not even the screams."

His father cried, and Terry tried to understand, and he thought he could feel part of it. But it was so much, so much and so strange to him.

"You cannot know this," his father repeated. It was almost a chant. "You cannot know the fear. It was almost dark, and I was the only one left alive out of 54 men, all dead but me, and I knew that the Vietcong[2] were just waiting for light. When the dawn came, 'Charley'[3] would come out and finish everybody off, the way they always did. And I thought if I could stop the dawn, just stop the sun from coming up, I could make it."

Terry felt the fear, and he also felt the tears coming down his cheeks. His hand went out across the table, and he took his father's hand and held it. It was shaking. **H**

"I mean I actually thought that if I could stop the sun from coming up, I could live. I made my brain work on that because it was all I had. Through the rest of the night in the rain in the paddy, I thought I could do it. I could stop the dawn." He took a deep breath. "But you can't, you know. You can't stop it from coming, and when I saw the gray light, I knew I was dead. It would just

---

2. **Vietcong:** South Vietnamese guerrillas who fought with support from North Vietnam.
3. **Charley:** term used by American soldiers to refer to the Vietcong.

G **Read and Discuss** Terry's father suddenly provides a lot of detail about his war experience. What point is Paulsen making?

H **Reading Focus** **Finding the Theme** What does Terry's crying indicate? What is he learning from listening to his father?

Infantry Soldiers by Roger Blum.

be minutes, and the light would be full, and I just settled under Jackson's body, and hid."

He stopped, and his face came down into his hands. Terry stood and went around the table to stand in back of him, his hands on his shoulders, rubbing gently.

"They didn't shoot me. They came, one of them poked Jackson's body and went on and they left me. But I was dead. I'm still dead, don't you see? I died because I couldn't stop the sun. I died. Inside where I am—I died."

Terry was still in back of him, and he nodded, but he didn't see. Not that. He understood only that he didn't understand, and that he would probably never understand what had truly happened. And maybe his father would never be truly normal.

But Terry also knew that it didn't matter. He would try to understand, and the trying would have to be enough. He would try hard from now on, and he would not be embarrassed when his father's eyes went away. He would not be embarrassed no matter what his father did. Terry had knowledge now. Maybe not enough and maybe not all that he would need.

But it was a start. **I**

I **Literary Focus** **Theme** What can you infer from the final paragraphs about the theme of this story? What is the story saying about one person's efforts to understand another?

Applying Your Skills

RA.L.8.5 Identify and explain universal themes across different works by the same author and by different authors. RA.L.8.1 Identify and explain various types of characters and how their interactions and conflicts affect the plot. WA.8.4.b

Stop the Sun

Respond and Think Critically

Reading Focus

Quick Check

1. Why is Terry embarrassed by his dad?
2. What steps does Terry take to better understand his father?

Read with a Purpose

3. What has Terry learned about his father's wartime experiences?

Reading Skills: Finding the Theme

4. Review the details you recorded on your chart. Then, add a row and write a sentence stating the story's theme. Be sure the theme applies to the whole story, not just parts of it. Also, refer to this chart as you answer question 9.

Details about the subject: Terry's dad served in Vietnam. Mom won't help Terry. Terry can't find books to help.
Theme of the story:

Literary Focus

Literary Analysis

5. **Compare and Contrast** Terry and his mother support his father in different ways. What do these differences tell us about them?
6. **Interpret** What is the significance of the story's title, "Stop the Sun"?
7. **Make Judgments** Do you think Terry made the right decision about questioning his father on his experiences in Vietnam? Why or why not?

Literary Skills: Theme

8. **Evaluate** A story can have more than one **theme.** Which theme below best states the insight about life this story conveys? Explain. (There is no "right" answer.)
   - War can affect many generations of people.
   - It is hard to walk in another person's shoes.
   - We must try to understand people we love.

Literary Skills Review: Conflict

9. **Identify** Some **conflicts** are **external**—between characters or between a character and some outside force. Other conflicts are **internal**—within a character's mind. Identify one internal and one external conflict that Terry faces in "Stop the Sun."

Writing Focus

Think as a Reader/Writer

Use It in Your Writing Look back through the notes you took about the use of repetition in the story. Describe ways in which Paulsen has used repeated words, phrases, and ideas to help convey the conflicts facing Terry and his family.

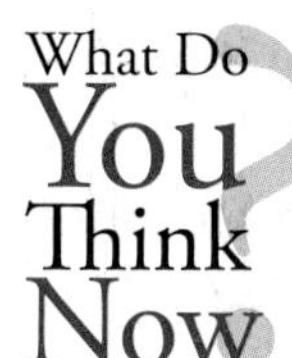

How well does Terry understand his dad at the story's end? Was Terry's effort worth the result? Explain why or why not.

Applying Your Skills

Stop the Sun

Vocabulary Development

Vocabulary Check

Answer the following questions. Be sure to include the boldface Vocabulary word in your answer.

1. What would you do if you heard a **commotion** in the school hallway?
2. If you heard a public speaker whose words **foundered,** what advice might you give?
3. What event might bring **ruin** to a country?
4. What might be the posture of an **inert** person?

Vocabulary Skill: Idioms

An **idiom** is an expression that means something other than the literal meaning of its words. For example, if your friend's "heart was broken," you wouldn't call 911. You would understand that your friend had been disappointed in love.

A language's idioms can be confusing for non-native speakers because they vary from language to language. For example, in English, if someone makes a big deal about a small issue, you might say that person is "making a mountain out of a molehill." In German, however, you might say that person is "making an elephant out of a gnat."

Your Turn

Work in pairs to discuss and clarify the meanings of the following idioms from "Stop the Sun."

1. "When he tried to find out about it, **he kept hitting walls.**"
2. "Terry was just about to **drop it** altogether."
3. "Something pretty **heavy,** judging by your face."

Language Coach

Multiple-Meaning Words Each sentence below contains a boldface word followed by several definitions of that word. Choose the definition that best fits how the word is used in the sentence.

1. "His mother would reach over and take the fork and put it gently down on his **plate,** and they would go back to eating."
   a. dish
   b. illustration
   c. metal coating
2. "He was crying, looking terrified, his breath coming in short, hot **pants.**"
   a. trousers
   b. throbs
   c. gasps

Academic Vocabulary

Talk About . . .

Discuss these questions with a partner, using the underlined Academic Vocabulary words. What information does Terry's father <u>convey</u> about his experiences? What is the <u>significance</u> of Terry's father repeating that Terry "cannot know" his experiences in Vietnam?

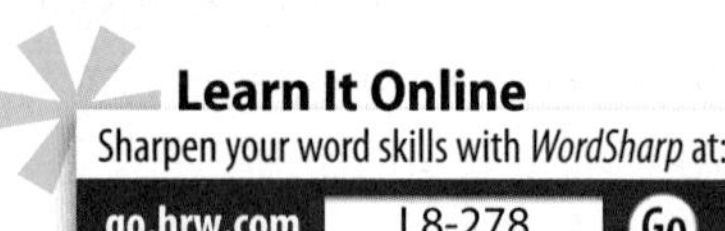

Learn It Online
Sharpen your word skills with *WordSharp* at:
go.hrw.com
L8-278
Go

RA.L.8.5 Identify and explain universal themes across different works by the same author and by different authors. **WA.8.6** Produce informal writings. **C.8.5** Demonstrate an understanding of the rules of the English language and select language appropriate to purpose and audience. *Also covered* **C.8.8.a; WC.8.3; VO.8.4**

Grammar Link

Direct and Indirect Objects

A **direct object** is a noun or pronoun that receives the action of a verb or shows the consequence of the action. A direct object tells *what* or *whom*.

EXAMPLE We read a **story.** (*Story* tells what was read.)

A **direct object** never follows a linking verb, since a linking verb—such as *become* or *is*—does not express action. Also, a direct object is never part of a prepositional phrase.

An **indirect object** is a noun or pronoun that comes between the verb and the direct object and tells *to what* or *to whom* or *for what* or *for whom* the action is performed.

EXAMPLE We read the **children** a story. (The *children* were read to.)

Linking verbs also do not have indirect objects, and indirect objects are never in a prepositional phrase.

Your Turn

Identify each boldface noun or pronoun as a direct or indirect object.

1. His teacher gave **Terry** a book on Vietnam.
2. Then Terry called his **mother,** and she came in a taxi to take them home.
3. Terry handed his **father** a can of soda.
4. Mortar fire killed **Jackson.**
5. "They didn't shoot **me.**"

Writing Application Write one sentence about your school day using a direct object and one using an indirect object.

CHOICES

As you respond to the Choices, use these **Academic Vocabulary** words as appropriate: convey, significant, indicate, consequence.

REVIEW

Discuss a Story's Themes

Listening and Speaking Readers often have different interpretations of the theme of a story. Get together with several classmates to discuss your ideas about the theme of "Stop the Sun." Each person should support his or her interpretation with details from the story and respect one another's points of view.

CONNECT

Write a Personal Essay

Timed Writing Write a brief personal essay about a time when you had difficulty understanding someone's behavior or attitude. Explain what the behavior or attitude was and what you did to try to understand it. Be sure to relate the significance of the experience. Did you learn something about yourself in the process?

EXTEND

Research Veterans' Support

TechFocus "Stop the Sun" deals with the effects of the Vietnam War on a young man's father. How have the veterans of more recent wars been affected by their experiences? Use reliable Internet resources to find out how people and organizations in the United States are supporting veterans and their families. Then, create a PowerPoint® presentation to share the results of your research with your class.

Learn It Online
Turn your personal essay into a digital story. Find out how at:

go.hrw.com L8-279 

SHORT STORY

Preparing to Read

The Medicine Bag

by **Virginia Driving Hawk Sneve**

Descendant of Chief Sitting Bull stands next to his friend and mentor.

What Do You Think?

How can seeing life from someone else's point of view help you understand your own life better?

QuickWrite

What can we learn from others? In what ways do people challenge us to change our values or to take new actions? Explain.

Reader/Writer Notebook

Use your **RWN** to complete the activities for this selection.

RA.L.8.1 Identify and explain various types of characters and how their interactions and conflicts affect the plot. **RA.L.8.5** Identify and explain universal themes across different works by the same author and by different authors.

Literary Focus

Character and Theme A **theme** is the message about life that a work of literature conveys. You can often identify a story's theme by paying attention to how the main character changes in the course of the story. In "The Medicine Bag," for example, Martin's attitude toward his great-grandfather undergoes a major shift. As you read, ask yourself, "What does Martin learn that I could apply to my life?"

Literary Perspectives Apply the literary perspective described on page 283 as you read this story.

Reading Focus

Making Generalizations A theme statement is a type of generalization. A **generalization** is a broad statement based on several particular situations. The generalization is **valid** when it applies to all such situations. You make generalizations by combining evidence in a text with what you already know. For example, when you finish reading "The Medicine Bag," you might make a generalization about how people are affected by their heritage.

Into Action As you read, use details about Martin and your own experiences to make generalizations.

Story Detail	My Experience	Generalization
Martin is embarrassed when Grandpa arrives.	My sister cringes when Mom wears something that is out of style.	

Writing Focus

Think as a Reader/Writer

Find It in Your Reading As you read, note how the author contrasts Grandpa's strength with his weakness. In your *Reader/Writer Notebook,* list details that show both aspects of Grandpa.

Vocabulary

authentic (aw THEHN tihk) *adj.:* genuine. *Martin is proud of his authentic Sioux drum.*

procession (proh SEHSH uhn) *n.:* parade. *The procession of kids and dogs in the street probably looked funny to some people.*

fatigue (fuh TEEG) *n.:* exhaustion; tiredness. *Grandpa was overwhelmed by fatigue after his long trip.*

frail (frayl) *adj.:* weak; fragile. *Although Grandpa's body was frail, he had a strong spirit.*

confines (KAHN fynz) *n.:* borders; boundaries. *Many Sioux continue to live within the confines of the reservation.*

Language Coach

Oral Fluency Many English words have silent letters. Write the words *fatigue, tongue,* and *vaguely* in your *Reader/Writer Notebook.* Which letters are silent in each of these words? Use a dictionary if you need help.

Learn It Online

Take a look at the *PowerNotes* introduction to this story on:

go.hrw.com L8-281 

MEET THE WRITER

Virginia Driving Hawk Sneve

(1933–)

Member of the Sioux

Like Grandpa in "The Medicine Bag," Virginia Driving Hawk Sneve (SNAY vee) was born on the Rosebud Reservation in South Dakota and is a member of the Rosebud Sioux. She taught English for many years. Sneve's children, like the children in the story you are about to read, visited Rosebud on summer vacations.

Passing on the Heritage

Sneve began writing for young readers after she discovered inaccurate references to Native Americans in some of the books she was reading. She explains:

> "When I started writing for children, I did so with the specific purpose of informing my own children about their heritage and trying to correct some misconceptions about how they saw Indian people and how others thought about Indians."

Think About the Writer

Why did Sneve decide to write stories for children?

(below) Custer State Park, South Dakota.

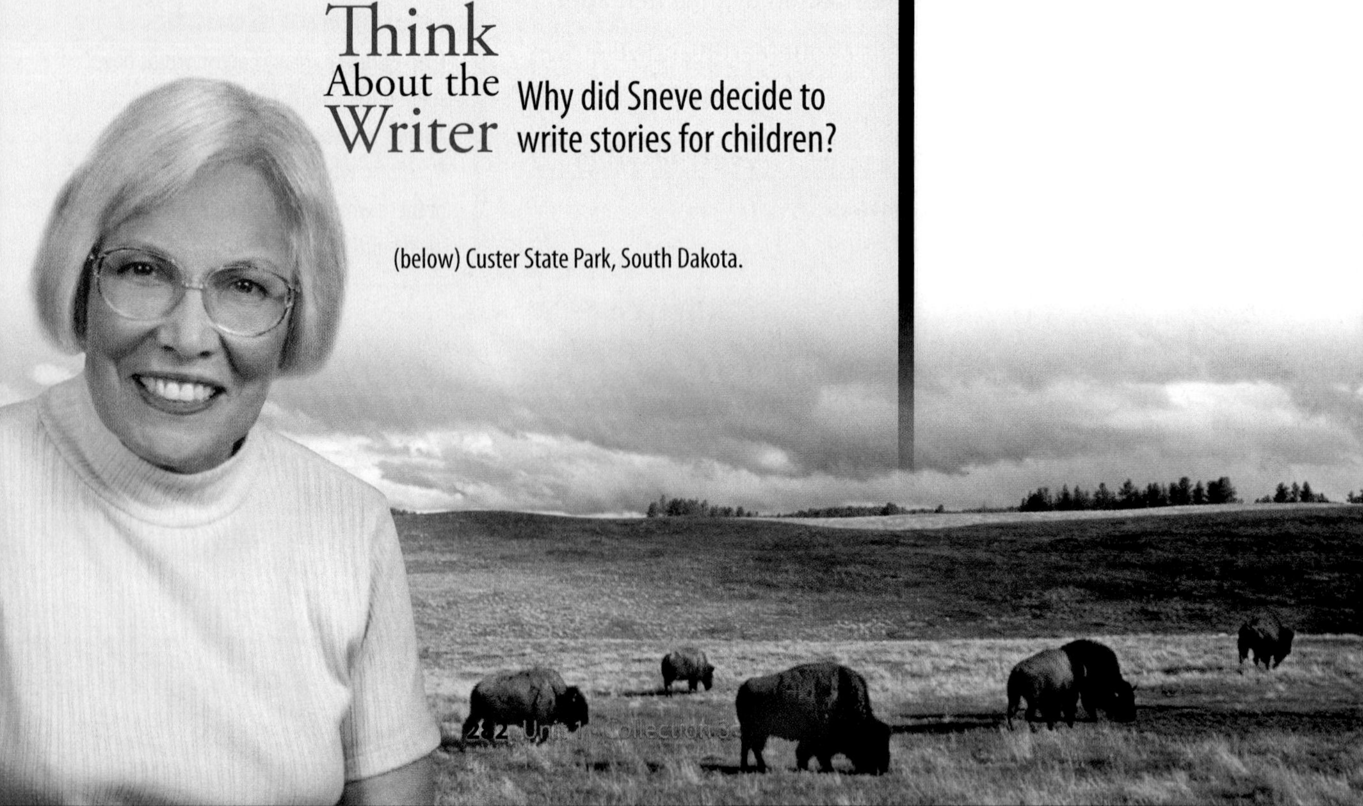

Build Background

Some cultures and families mark the passage into adulthood by a ritual, such as the Jewish bar mitzvah or bat mitzvah ceremony or the Mexican American *quinceañera.* These traditions are known as rites of passage.

In the Sioux tradition a teenage boy becomes a man by making a vision quest—going off alone to find spiritual power and guidance through a dream. Sometimes he also finds an object believed to provide protection or power. This object—referred to as *medicine*—is considered sacred and is passed down from generation to generation.

Preview the Selection

In this story a boy named **Martin** finds a greater appreciation of the traditions of his ancestors when his Sioux great-grandfather, **Joe Iron Shell,** comes to visit.

Read with a Purpose Read to discover what Martin learns from his grandfather.

The Medicine Bag

by **Virginia Driving Hawk Sneve**

My kid sister Cheryl and I always bragged about our Sioux grandpa, Joe Iron Shell. Our friends, who had always lived in the city and only knew about Indians from movies and TV, were impressed by our stories. Maybe we exaggerated and made Grandpa and the reservation sound glamorous, but when we'd return home to Iowa after our yearly summer visit to Grandpa, we always had some exciting tale to tell.

We always had some authentic Sioux article to show our listeners. One year Cheryl had new moccasins that Grandpa had made. On another visit he gave me a small, round, flat rawhide drum which was decorated with a painting of a warrior riding a horse. He taught me a real Sioux chant to sing while I beat the drum with a leather-covered stick that had a feather on the end. Man, that really made an impression.

We never showed our friends Grandpa's picture. Not that we were ashamed of him, but because we knew that the glamorous tales we told didn't go with the real thing. Our friends would have laughed at the picture, because Grandpa wasn't tall and stately like TV Indians. His hair wasn't in braids but hung in stringy gray strands on his neck, and he was old. He was our great-grandfather, and he didn't live in a tepee, but all by himself in a part log, part tar-paper shack on the Rosebud Reservation in South

Literary Perspectives

Use this perspective to help you evaluate the characters and plot of this story.

Analyzing Credibility One way to approach a work of literature is to analyze its **credibility,** or believability. Ask yourself whether the characters act the way people do in real life. Do they seem too good—or bad—to be true? Are their motivations and reactions convincing? Is the situation one that you think is likely to happen, or does it seem too far-fetched? Also ask yourself whether the story's **theme,** or message about life, rings true. Answer these questions based on evidence in the text as well as on your own experience and knowledge of the world around you. As you read this story, use the questions in the text to guide you in using this perspective.

Vocabulary **authentic** (aw THEHN tihk) *adj.:* genuine.

Dakota. So when Grandpa came to visit us, I was so ashamed and embarrassed I could've died. **A**

There are a lot of yippy poodles and other fancy little dogs in our neighborhood, but they usually barked singly at the mailman from the safety of their own yards. Now it sounded as if a whole pack of mutts were barking together in one place.

I got up and walked to the curb to see what the commotion was. About a block away I saw a crowd of little kids yelling, with the dogs yipping and growling around someone who was walking down the middle of the street.

I watched the group as it slowly came closer and saw that in the center of the strange procession was a man wearing a tall black hat. He'd pause now and then to peer at something in his hand and then at the houses on either side of the street. I felt cold and hot at the same time as I recognized the man. "Oh, no!" I whispered. "It's Grandpa!"

I stood on the curb, unable to move even though I wanted to run and hide. Then I got mad when I saw how the yippy dogs were growling and nipping at the old man's baggy pant legs and how wearily he poked them away with his cane. "Stupid mutts," I said as I ran to rescue Grandpa.

When I kicked and hollered at the dogs to get away, they put their tails between their legs and scattered. The kids ran to the curb, where they watched me and the old man. **B**

"Grandpa," I said, and felt pretty dumb when my voice cracked. I reached for his beat-up old tin suitcase, which was tied shut with a rope. But he set it down right in the street and shook my hand.

"Hau, Takoza, Grandchild," he greeted me formally in Sioux.

All I could do was stand there with the whole neighborhood watching and shake the hand of the leather-brown old man. I saw how his gray hair straggled from under his big black hat, which had a drooping feather in its crown. His rumpled black suit hung like a sack over his stooped frame. As he shook my hand, his coat fell open to expose a bright-red satin shirt with a beaded bolo tie[1] under the collar. His get-up wasn't out of place on the reservation, but it sure was here, and I wanted to sink right through the pavement.

"Hi," I muttered with my head down. I tried to pull my hand away when I felt his bony hand trembling, and looked up to see fatigue in his face. I felt like crying. I couldn't think of anything to say, so I picked up Grandpa's suitcase, took his arm, and guided him up the driveway to our house.

1. **bolo tie:** cord with a decorated fastening, worn as a necktie.

A **Reading Focus** **Making Generalizations** A stereotype is an invalid (not valid) generalization because it does not apply to all the people being described. Judging from this paragraph, what stereotypes do some people have about Native Americans?

B **Read and Discuss** What does the narrator's reaction to Grandpa's arrival indicate about his attitude toward him?

Vocabulary **procession** (proh SEHSH uhn) *n.:* parade.
fatigue (fuh TEEG) *n.:* exhaustion; tiredness.

Mom was standing on the steps. I don't know how long she'd been watching, but her hand was over her mouth and she looked as if she couldn't believe what she saw. Then she ran to us.

"Grandpa," she gasped. "How in the world did you get here?"

She checked her move to embrace Grandpa, and I remembered that such a display of affection is unseemly to the Sioux and would embarrass him.

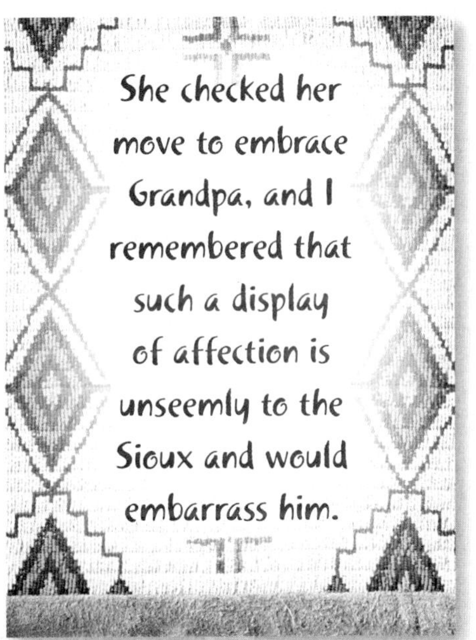
She checked her move to embrace Grandpa, and I remembered that such a display of affection is unseemly to the Sioux and would embarrass him.

"Hau, Marie," he said as he shook Mom's hand. She smiled and took his other arm.

As we supported him up the steps, the door banged open and Cheryl came bursting out of the house. She was all smiles and was so obviously glad to see Grandpa that I was ashamed of how I felt.

"Grandpa!" she yelled happily. "You came to see us!"

Grandpa smiled and Mom and I let go of him as he stretched out his arms to my ten-year-old sister, who was still young enough to be hugged. **C**

"Wicincala, little girl," he greeted her, and then collapsed.

He had fainted. Mom and I carried him into her sewing room, where we had a spare bed.

After we had Grandpa on the bed, Mom stood there helplessly patting his shoulder.

"Shouldn't we call the doctor, Mom?" I suggested, since she didn't seem to know what to do.

"Yes," she agreed, with a sigh. "You make Grandpa comfortable, Martin."

I reluctantly moved to the bed. I knew Grandpa wouldn't want to have Mom undress him, but I didn't want to, either. He was so skinny and frail that his coat slipped off easily. When I loosened his tie and opened his shirt collar, I felt a small leather pouch that hung from a thong[2] around his neck. I left it alone and moved to remove his boots. The scuffed old cowboy boots were tight and he moaned as I put pressure on his legs to jerk them off.

I put the boots on the floor and saw why they fit so tight. Each one was stuffed with money. I looked at the bills that lined the boots and started to ask about them, but Grandpa's eyes were closed again.

Mom came back with a basin of water. "The doctor thinks Grandpa is suffering from heat exhaustion," she explained as she bathed Grandpa's face. Mom gave a big sigh,

2. **thong:** narrow strip of leather.

C **Literary Perspectives** **Analyzing Credibility** How does each family member react to Grandpa's arrival? How believable are their reactions? Explain.

Vocabulary **frail** (frayl) *adj.:* weak; fragile.

"Oh hinh, Martin. How do you suppose he got here?"

We found out after the doctor's visit. Grandpa was angrily sitting up in bed while Mom tried to feed him some soup.

"Tonight you let Marie feed you, Grandpa," spoke my dad, who had gotten home from work just as the doctor was leaving. "You're not really sick," he said as he gently pushed Grandpa back against the pillows. "The doctor said you just got too tired and hot after your long trip." **D**

Soon after our visit to him Grandpa decided that he would like to see where his only living descendants lived and what our home was like.

Grandpa relaxed, and between sips of soup he told us of his journey. Soon after our visit to him Grandpa decided that he would like to see where his only living descendants lived and what our home was like. Besides, he admitted sheepishly, he was lonesome after we left.

I knew everybody felt as guilty as I did—especially Mom. Mom was all Grandpa had left. So even after she married my dad, who's a white man and teaches in the college in our city, and after Cheryl and I were born, Mom made sure that every summer we spent a week with Grandpa.

I never thought that Grandpa would be lonely after our visits, and none of us noticed how old and weak he had become.

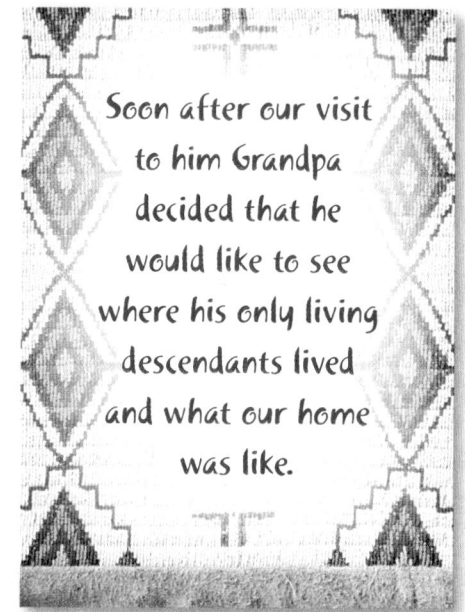

But Grandpa knew and so he came to us. He had ridden on buses for two and a half days. When he arrived in the city, tired and stiff from sitting for so long, he set out, walking, to find us.

He had stopped to rest on the steps of some building downtown and a policeman found him. The cop, according to Grandpa, was a good man who took him to the bus stop and waited until the bus came and told the driver to let Grandpa out at Bell View Drive. After Grandpa got off the bus, he started walking again. But he couldn't see the house numbers on the other side when he walked on the sidewalk, so he walked in the middle of the street. That's when all the little kids and dogs followed him.

I knew everybody felt as bad as I did. Yet I was proud of this eighty-six-year-old man, who had never been away from the reservation, having the courage to travel so far alone. **E**

"You found the money in my boots?" he asked Mom.

"Martin did," she answered, and roused herself to scold. "Grandpa, you shouldn't have carried so much money. What if someone had stolen it from you?"

D **Read and Discuss** What is going on now?

E **Literary Focus** **Character and Theme** How does Grandpa's story of his journey change the way Martin sees him?

Grandpa laughed. "I would've known if anyone tried to take the boots off my feet. The money is what I've saved for a long time—a hundred dollars—for my funeral. But you take it now to buy groceries so that I won't be a burden to you while I am here."

"That won't be necessary, Grandpa," Dad said. "We are honored to have you with us and you will never be a burden. I am only sorry that we never thought to bring you home with us this summer and spare you the discomfort of a long trip."

Grandpa was pleased. "Thank you," he answered. "But do not feel bad that you didn't bring me with you, for I would not have come then. It was not time." He said this in such a way that no one could argue with him. To Grandpa and the Sioux, he once told me, a thing would be done when it was the right time to do it and that's the way it was.

"Also," Grandpa went on, looking at me, "I have come because it is soon time for Martin to have the medicine bag."

We all knew what that meant. Grandpa thought he was going to die and he had to follow the tradition of his family to pass the medicine bag, along with its history, to the oldest male child.

Rawhide beaded pipe bag, Oglala Sioux.

"Even though the boy," he said, still looking at me, "bears a white man's name, the medicine bag will be his."

I didn't know what to say. I had the same hot and cold feeling that I had when I first saw Grandpa in the street. The medicine bag was the dirty leather pouch I had found around his neck. "I could never wear such a thing," I almost said aloud. I thought of having my friends see it in gym class, at the swimming pool, and could imagine the smart things they would say. But I just swallowed hard and took a step toward the bed. I knew I would have to take it. **F**

But Grandpa was tired. "Not now, Martin," he said, waving his hand in dismissal, "it is not time. Now I will sleep."

So that's how Grandpa came to be with us for two months. My friends kept asking to come see the old man, but I put them off. I told myself that I didn't want them laughing at Grandpa. But even as I made excuses, I knew it wasn't Grandpa that I was afraid they'd laugh at.

Nothing bothered Cheryl about bringing her friends to see Grandpa. Every day after school started, there'd be a crew

---

F **Read and Discuss** What is happening with the medicine bag?

of giggling little girls or round-eyed little boys crowded around the old man on the patio, where he'd gotten in the habit of sitting every afternoon.

Grandpa would smile in his gentle way and patiently answer their questions, or he'd tell them stories of brave warriors, ghosts, animals, and the kids listened in awed silence. Those little guys thought Grandpa was great.

Finally, one day after school, my friends came home with me because nothing I said stopped them. "We're going to see the great Indian of Bell View Drive," said Hank, who was supposed to be my best friend. "My brother has seen him three times, so he oughta be well enough to see us."

When we got to my house, Grandpa was sitting on the patio. He had on his red shirt, but today he also wore a fringed leather vest that was decorated with beads. Instead of his usual cowboy boots he had solidly beaded moccasins on his feet that stuck out of his black trousers. Of course, he had his old black hat on—he was seldom without it. But it had been brushed and the feather in the beaded headband

Analyzing Visuals

Viewing and Representing Compare this image with the description of Grandpa on pages 288–289. Why do both of these men command respect?

Sioux medicine man holding a medicine shield and wearing a bearclaw necklace.

was proudly erect, its tip a brighter white. His hair lay in silver strands over the red shirt collar.

I stared just as my friends did and I heard one of them murmur, "Wow!"

Grandpa looked up and when his eyes met mine, they twinkled as if he were laughing inside. He nodded to me and my face got all hot. I could tell that he had known all along I was afraid he'd embarrass me in front of my friends.

"Hau, hoksilas, boys," he greeted, and held out his hand.

My buddies passed in a single file and shook his hand as I introduced them. They were so polite I almost laughed. "How, there, Grandpa," and even a "How do you do, sir."

"You look fine, Grandpa," I said as the guys sat on the lawn chairs or on the patio floor.

"Hanh, yes," he agreed. "When I woke up this morning, it seemed the right time to dress in the good clothes. I knew that my grandson would be bringing his friends."

"You guys want some lemonade or something?" I offered. No one answered. They were listening to Grandpa as he started telling how he'd killed the deer from which his vest was made.

Grandpa did most of the talking while my friends were there. I was so proud of him and amazed at how respectfully quiet my buddies were. Mom had to chase them home at suppertime. As they left, they shook Grandpa's hand again and said to me:

"Martin, he's really great!"

"Yeah, man! Don't blame you for keeping him to yourself." **G**

"Can we come back?"

But after they left, Mom said, "No more visitors for a while, Martin. Grandpa won't admit it, but his strength hasn't returned. He likes having company, but it tires him."

That evening Grandpa called me to his room before he went to sleep. "Tomorrow," he said, "when you come home, it will be time to give you the medicine bag."

I felt a hard squeeze from where my heart is supposed to be and was scared, but I answered, "OK, Grandpa." **H**

All night I had weird dreams about thunder and lightning on a high hill. From a distance I heard the slow beat of a drum. When I woke up in the morning, I felt as if I hadn't slept at all. At school it seemed as if the day would never end and when it finally did, I ran home.

Grandpa was in his room, sitting on the bed. The shades were down and the place was dim and cool. I sat on the floor in front of Grandpa, but he didn't even look at me. After what seemed a long time, he spoke.

"I sent your mother and sister away. What you will hear today is only for a man's ears. What you will receive is only for a man's hands." He fell silent and I felt shivers down my back.

"My father in his early manhood," Grandpa began, "made a vision quest to find a spirit guide for his life. You cannot

---

G **Read and Discuss** What is Martin learning here?

H **Literary Perspectives** **Analyzing Credibility** How believable is Martin's reaction to receiving the medicine bag?

understand how it was in that time, when the great Teton Sioux were first made to stay on the reservation. There was a strong need for guidance from Wakantanka, the Great Spirit. But too many of the young men were filled with despair and hatred. They thought it was hopeless to search for a vision when the glorious life was gone and only the hated confines of a reservation lay ahead. But my father held to the old ways.

"He carefully prepared for his quest with a purifying sweat bath and then he went alone to a high butte[3] top to fast and pray. After three days he received his sacred dream—in which he found, after long searching, the white man's iron. He did not understand his vision of finding something belonging to the white people, for in that time they were the enemy. When he came down from the butte to cleanse himself at the stream below, he found the remains of a campfire and the broken shell of an iron kettle. This was a sign which reinforced his dream. He took a piece of the iron for his medicine bag, which he had made of elk skin years before, to prepare for his quest.

"He returned to his village, where he told his dream to the wise old men of the tribe. They gave him the name Iron Shell, but neither did they understand the meaning of the dream. This first Iron Shell kept the piece of iron with him at all times and believed it gave him protection from the evils of those unhappy days.

"Then a terrible thing happened to Iron Shell. He and several other young men were taken from their homes by the soldiers and sent far away to a white man's boarding school. He was angry and lonesome for his parents and the young girl he had wed before he was taken away. At first Iron Shell resisted the teachers' attempts to change him and he did not try to learn. One day it was his turn to work in the school's blacksmith shop. As he walked into the place, he knew that his medicine had brought him there to learn and work with the white man's iron.

"Iron Shell became a blacksmith and worked at the trade when he returned to the reservation. All of his life he treasured the medicine bag. When he was old and I was a man, he gave it to me, for no one made the vision quest anymore." **I**

Grandpa quit talking and I stared in disbelief as he covered his face with his hands. His shoulders were shaking with quiet sobs and I looked away until he began to speak again.

"I kept the bag until my son, your mother's father, was a man and had to leave us to fight in the war across the ocean. I gave him the bag, for I believed it would protect him in battle, but he did not take it with him. He was afraid that he would lose it. He died in a faraway place."

Again Grandpa was still and I felt his grief around me.

3. **butte** (byoot): steep, flat-topped hill standing alone on a plain.

Vocabulary **confines** (KAHN fynz) *n.:* borders; boundaries.

I **Reading Focus** **Making Generalizations** Based on the details in Grandpa's story of the medicine bag, what generalization can you make about the experience of the Sioux?

"My son," he went on after clearing his throat, "had only a daughter and it is not proper for her to know of these things."

He unbuttoned his shirt, pulled out the leather pouch, and lifted it over his head. He held it in his hand, turning it over and over as if memorizing how it looked.

"In the bag," he said as he opened it and removed two objects, "is the broken shell of the iron kettle, a pebble from the butte, and a piece of the sacred sage."[4] He held the pouch upside down and dust drifted down.

4. **sage:** plant with fragrant leaves.

Analyzing Visuals **Viewing and Interpreting** How does the subject of these portraits compare with your image of Martin's grandfather?

Chief Plenty Coups. Painted portraits of Crow leader Chief Plenty Coups through the years of his life—as a young brave, as a famous chief, and as a tribal elder.

Sioux Horses by Oscar Howe (Mazuha Hokshina, Yanktonai Sioux). Tempera on wove paper (8 ¼" x 10").

"After the bag is yours, you must put a piece of prairie sage within and never open it again until you pass it on to your son." He replaced the pebble and the piece of iron and tied the bag.

I stood up, somehow knowing I should. Grandpa slowly rose from the bed and stood upright in front of me, holding the bag before my face. I closed my eyes and waited for him to slip it over my head. But he spoke.

"No, you need not wear it." He placed the soft leather bag in my right hand and closed my other hand over it. "It would not be right to wear it in this time and place, where no one will understand. Put it safely away until you are again on the reservation. Wear it then, when you replace the sacred sage."

Grandpa turned and sat again on the bed. Wearily he leaned his head against the pillow. "Go," he said, "I will sleep now."

"Thank you, Grandpa," I said softly, and left with the bag in my hands. **J**

That night Mom and Dad took Grandpa to the hospital. Two weeks later I stood alone on the lonely prairie of the reservation and put the sacred sage in my medicine bag. **K**

J **Literary Focus** **Character and Theme** How have Martin's attitudes toward his great-grandfather and his heritage changed since the beginning of the story?

K **Read and Discuss** What does the scene of Martin putting sage in his bag let us know about Grandpa?

Applying Your Skills

OH **RA.L.8.1** Identify and explain various types of characters and how their interactions and conflicts affect the plot. **RA.L.8.5** Identify and explain universal themes across different works by the same author and by different authors. *Also covered* **WA.8.2; WA.8.6**

The Medicine Bag

Respond and Think Critically

Reading Focus

Quick Check

1. Why has Grandpa traveled to see his family?
2. What does Grandpa want to give Martin? Why?
3. What happens at the very end of the story?

Read with a Purpose

4. What has Martin learned from his great-grandfather?

Reading Skills: Making Generalizations

5. Review the generalizations that you wrote in your chart. Combine them into a final, overall generalization about the story.

Story Detail	My Experience	Generalization
Martin is embarrassed when Grandpa arrives.	My sister cringes when Mom wears something that is out of style.	Young people are often embarrassed when their relatives seem odd.

Generalization based on the entire story:

Literary Focus

Literary Analysis

6. **Analyze** Why is Martin ashamed of Grandpa at first? How do Martin's feelings change?
7. **Extend** How might Martin have felt about Grandpa if his friends had not been impressed by him? Explain.
8. **Literary Perspectives** Analyze the credibility of Martin's reactions to Grandpa, citing details from the text and your own experiences.

Literary Skills: Character and Theme

9. **Analyze** What does Martin come to realize about his grandfather and about himself in this story? Turn that realization into a **theme** statement. (Hint: Look at the overall generalization you added to your chart.)

Literary Skills Review: Characterization

10. **Identify** Writers give clues about what characters are like by describing the characters' thoughts, feelings, speech, looks, and actions. Locate and list examples of effective character descriptions from the story.

Writing Focus

Think as a Reader/Writer

Use It in Your Writing Look at the details you noted describing Grandpa's strengths and weaknesses. Think of someone who possesses seemingly opposing traits—perhaps someone who is loud but actually very shy. Write a short description that brings both aspects of that person to life.

What Do You Think Now?

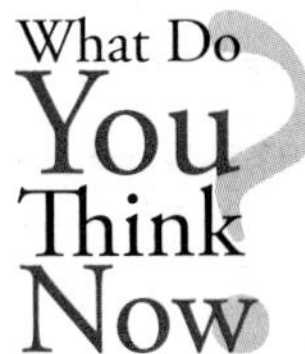

How does hearing Grandpa's story of the medicine bag help Martin understand his own life?

Applying Your Skills

The Medicine Bag

Vocabulary Development

Metaphors and Similes

Have you ever said something like "His room is a pigsty" or "She sleeps like a rock"? In that case, you have used metaphors and similes.

Writers often use metaphors and similes to describe characters, settings, events, and ideas. **Metaphors** directly compare two unlike things without using a specific word of comparison. **Similes,** on the other hand, make direct comparisons between two unlike things by using comparison words such as *like, as, than,* and *resembles.*

EXAMPLES

Simile "His rumpled black suit hung **like a sack** over his stooped frame."

Metaphor His black suit **was a sack** that hung over his stooped frame.

In your reading, you will frequently come across metaphors and similes. Using original metaphors and similes in your own writing will make your writing sparkle and add interest for your readers.

Your Turn

authentic
procession
fatigue
frail
confines

Identify the figure of speech in each sentence as a simile or metaphor. Vocabulary words are boldface.

1. Grandpa was as **frail** as a old stick.
2. From a distance, the **procession** looked like a line of ants.
3. **Fatigue** settled over Grandpa like a soft blanket.
4. Although the medicine bag was as **authentic** as the Hope diamond, it looked old and dirty.
5. The **confines** of the reservation felt like a prison.

Language Coach

Oral Fluency Although the /ue/ letter combination is sometimes silent, as in the Vocabulary word *fatigue,* that letter combination is sometimes pronounced—and not always in the same way! With a partner, study this list of words and sort them into three categories, as shown in the chart. If you are stumped, look them up in a dictionary.

subdue	intrigue	guess	rueful
true	mystique	residue	question
avenue	technique	blue	neutral

/ue/ silent	/ue/ pronounced "oo"	/ue/ pronounced "eh"

Academic Vocabulary

Write About . . .
Write a paragraph explaining Martin's most significant personal characteristics. What do these traits indicate about Martin? Cite evidence from the text to support your assertion, and use the underlined Academic Vocabulary words in your response.

Learn It Online
Explore the vocabulary words further online:
go.hrw.com L8-294 Go

RA.L.8.5 Identify and explain universal themes across different works by the same author and by different authors. R.8.2 Identify appropriate sources and gather relevant information from multiple sources. WA.8.6 Produce informal writings. *Also covered* C.8.9; WC.8.4; VO.8.4

Grammar Link

Phrases

Nearly every sentence you read, write, and speak contains at least one phrase. A **phrase** is a group of related words that is used as a single part of speech and does not contain a verb and the verb's subject. There are many kinds of phrases: **Prepositional phrases** can act as adjectives or adverbs, **participial phrases** act as adjectives, and **appositive phrases** explain or identify key nouns.

PREPOSITIONAL PHRASE We took a trip **to the reservation**.

PARTICIPIAL PHRASE **Chasing away the dogs**, I helped Grandpa.

APPOSITIVE PHRASE Cheryl, **my little sister**, was affectionate with Grandpa.

Using phrases to add information to your writing helps you avoid writing short, choppy sentences. To learn more about phrases, see the Language Handbook.

Your Turn

Writing Applications Combine the pairs of sentences below by adding the boldface phrases to the first sentence of each pair. There may be more than one way to revise the sentences.

1. Grandpa was born many years ago. He was born **on the reservation.**
2. Grandpa sat on the porch. He was **telling fascinating stories.**
3. Grandpa passes on Sioux traditions to the next generation. Grandpa is **a wonderful storyteller.**
4. I was worried about my friends' reactions. I was **fearing embarrassment.**

CHOICES

As you respond to the Choices, use these **Academic Vocabulary** words as appropriate: convey, significant, indicate, consequence.

REVIEW

Add to the Story

Timed Writing What significant lesson about life has Martin learned from his grandfather? Explain the story's main theme, and support your ideas by citing details from the story.

CONNECT

Discuss Traditions

Group Discussion In a small group, discuss ways people mark the passage into adulthood.

- What rites of passage are used in your community today? What is the consequence of undergoing these rites?
- Are rites of passage still important today?

Record your group's opinions, along with examples and reasons that support them. Then, meet with another group to compare your opinions.

EXTEND

Research Sioux History

Use the Internet or library resources to research Sioux history and traditions. Answer these questions as you research: How did the Sioux live before moving onto reservations? What traditions have they maintained? Present your findings to the class.

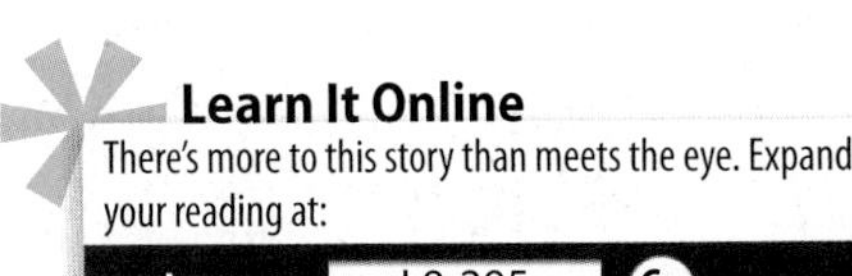

Learn It Online
There's more to this story than meets the eye. Expand your reading at:
go.hrw.com
L8-295
Go

SHORT STORY

Preparing to Read

Gentleman of Río en Medio

by **Juan A. A. Sedillo**

Purchase, Richard H. and Adeline J. Fleischaker Collection, 1996. Fred Jones Jr., Museum of Art, The University of Oklahoma, Norman.

Road to Chimayo (1926) by John Sloan. Oil on canvas (16" x 20").

What Do You Think? What significance do cultural values have in today's world?

QuickTalk

In a small group, share an experience in which someone's actions at first drove you crazy but later made sense once you learned more about the person.

Reader/Writer Notebook

Use your **RWN** to complete the activities for this selection.

RA.L.8.5 Identify and explain universal themes across different works by the same author and by different authors. **RP.8.1** Apply reading comprehension strategies, including making predictions, comparing and contrasting, recalling and summarizing and making inferences and drawing conclusions.

Literary Focus

Recurring Themes Themes such as "True friends are friends forever" can be found in the literature of many times and cultures. Such **recurring themes** explore human experiences common to many settings and circumstances. As you read this story, look for ways in which it shares a theme with other stories in this collection.

TechFocus As you read this story, think about the points you would make to defend one of the parties involved in the conflict.

Reading Focus

Making Predictions One way to discover a story's theme is by making predictions about (1) the meaning of the story's title, (2) the resolution of the main conflict, (3) and the main character's lesson from the experience. Base your predictions on story details and your prior knowledge of other stories' events and themes.

Into Action Use this organizer as you make predictions about "Gentleman of Río en Medio."

Prediction Topic	Text Clue	My Prediction
Story's title	"Gentleman of Río en Medio"	The theme may be about respect.
Conflict's resolution		
Character's lesson		

Writing Focus

Think as a Reader/Writer

Find It in Your Reading Writers use repetition to emphasize important elements in their works. As you read, note in your *Reader/Writer Notebook* how the writer explores the idea of "good people."

Vocabulary

negotiation (nih goh shee AY shuhn) *n.:* process of reaching an agreement. *A negotiation is underway for the property.*

innumerable (ih NOO muhr uh buhl) *adj.:* great many; too many to be counted. *Don Anselmo has innumerable family members.*

boundaries (BOWN duh reez) *n.:* places where one thing ends and another begins. *The property boundaries stretch for miles.*

descendants (dih SEHN duhnts) *n.:* all the generations who come from one person. *Don Anselmo treasures his relatives and descendants.*

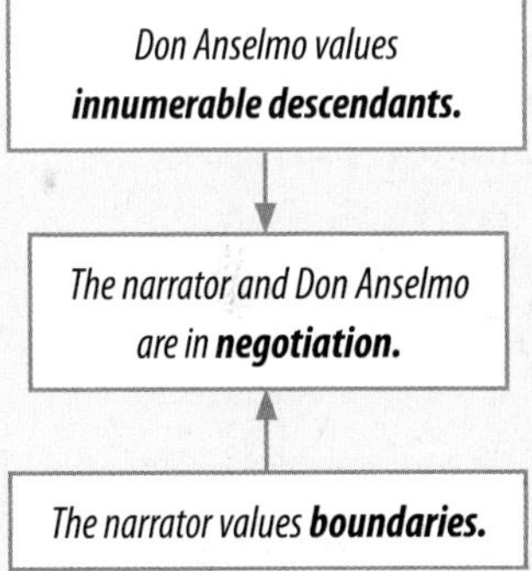

Don Anselmo values innumerable descendants.
The narrator and Don Anselmo are in negotiation.
The narrator values boundaries.

Language Coach

Context Clues In the sentence "It took months of negotiation to come to an understanding with the old man," which word or words best help you guess the definition of *negotiation*?

Learn It Online

Take an in-depth look at vocabulary using Word Watch at:

go.hrw.com L8-297 

MEET THE WRITER

Juan A. A. Sedillo

(1902–1982)

A Long History

Juan Sedillo's family originally came from Spain. In 1769, the king of Spain gave his ancestor, Antonio Sedillo, a land grant in what would become New Mexico. In their new home the Sedillos were active in the law and in public service.

Carrying on the Tradition

Juan A. A. Sedillo was born in New Mexico in 1902. He carried on his family's traditions by becoming an attorney. During and after World War II, Sedillo used his talents in the armed forces, serving as defense counsel in a famous Nazi war crimes trial, the Hadamar case. Sedillo was a distinguished lawyer and judge, serving as law clerk of the New Mexico Supreme Court and as attorney general of New Mexico.

Making His Own Mark

In addition to his legal work, Sedillo wrote a weekly article on Mexico for New Mexico newspapers. "Gentleman of Río en Medio," a short story based on an incident that took place in his law office, is his best-known work.

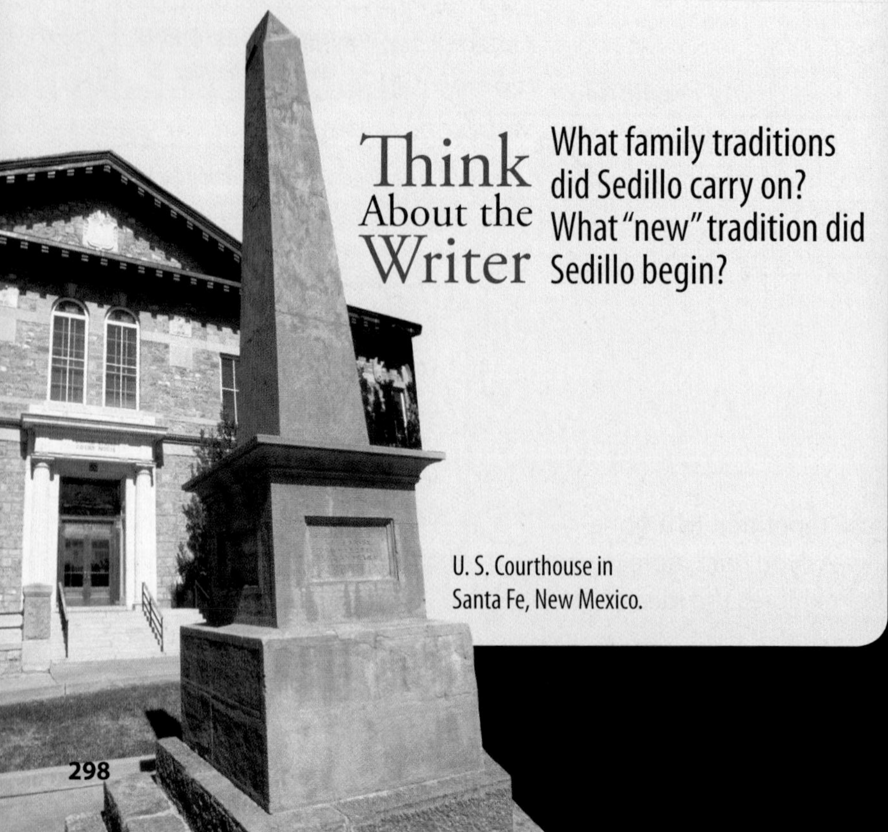

Think About the Writer What family traditions did Sedillo carry on? What "new" tradition did Sedillo begin?

U. S. Courthouse in Santa Fe, New Mexico.

Build Background

The mountains outside New Mexico's capital, Santa Fe, are the setting for "Gentleman of Río en Medio." The land that is now New Mexico was first inhabited by American Indians. Spain claimed the land in the 1600s and 1700s. In 1821, New Mexico became a part of the Republic of Mexico. During the Mexican-American War it was taken by the United States and governed as a territory. New Mexico became the forty-seventh U.S. state in 1912.

Preview the Selection

In this story the narrator represents a couple in a land deal with an old man, **Don Anselmo,** who has his own ideas about money and property.

Read with a Purpose Read this story to find out how people with different values settle a conflict.

Gentleman of Río en Medio

by **Juan A. A. Sedillo**

It took months of negotiation to come to an understanding with the old man. He was in no hurry. What he had the most of was time. He lived up in Río en Medio, where his people had been for hundreds of years. He tilled the same land they had tilled. His house was small and wretched, but quaint. The little creek ran through his land. His orchard was gnarled and beautiful.

The day of the sale he came into the office. His coat was old, green and faded. I thought of Senator Catron,[1] who had been such a power with these people up there in the mountains. Perhaps it was one of his old Prince Alberts.[2] He also wore gloves. They were old and torn and his fingertips showed through them. He carried a cane, but it was only the skeleton of a worn-out umbrella. Behind him walked one of his innumerable kin—a dark young man with eyes like a gazelle.

The old man bowed to all of us in the room. Then he removed his hat and gloves, slowly and carefully. Chaplin[3] once did that in a picture, in a bank—he was the janitor. Then he handed his things to the boy, who stood obediently behind the old man's chair. **A**

There was a great deal of conversation about rain and about his family. He was very proud of his large family. Finally we got down to business. Yes, he would sell, as he had agreed, for twelve hundred

1. **Senator Catron:** Thomas Benton Catron, a Senator from New Mexico (1912–1917).
2. **Prince Alberts:** long coats named after Prince Albert, who later became King Edward VII of Great Britain.
3. **Chaplin:** Charlie Chaplin, a comic star of silent movies.

Vocabulary **negotiation** (nih goh shee AY shuhn) *n.:* process of reaching an agreement.
innumerable (ih NOO muhr uh buhl) *adj.:* great many; too many to be counted.

A **Read and Discuss** What can we say about the story so far?

dollars, in cash. We would buy, and the money was ready. "Don[4] Anselmo," I said to him in Spanish, "we have made a discovery. You remember that we sent that surveyor, that engineer, up there to survey your land so as to make the deed. Well, he finds that you own more than eight acres. He tells us that your land extends across the river and that you own almost twice as much as you thought." He didn't know that. "And now, Don Anselmo," I added, "these Americans are *buena gente,* they are good people, and they are willing to pay you for the additional land as well, at the same rate per acre, so that instead of twelve hundred dollars you will get almost twice as much, and the money is here for you." **B**

The old man hung his head for a moment in thought. Then he stood up and stared at me. "Friend," he said, "I do not like to have you speak to me in that manner." I kept still and let him have his say. "I know these Americans are good people, and that is why I have agreed to sell to them. But I do not care to be insulted. I have agreed to sell my house and land for twelve hundred dollars and that is the price." **C**

I argued with him but it was useless. Finally he signed the deed and took the money but refused to take more than the amount agreed upon. Then he shook hands all around, put on his ragged gloves, took his stick and walked out with the boy behind him.

A month later my friends had moved into Río en Medio. They had replastered the old adobe house, pruned the trees, patched the fence, and moved in for the summer. One day they came back to the office to complain. The children of the village were overrunning their property. They came every day and played under the trees, built little play fences around them, and took blossoms. When they were spoken to, they only laughed and talked back good-naturedly in Spanish.

I sent a messenger up to the mountains for Don Anselmo. It took a week to arrange another meeting. When he arrived he repeated his previous preliminary performance. He wore the same faded cutaway,[5] carried the same stick and was accompanied by the boy again. He shook hands all around, sat down with the boy behind the chair, and talked about the weather. Finally I broached the subject. "Don Anselmo, about the ranch you sold to these people. They are good people and want to be your friends and neighbors always. When you sold to them you signed a document, a deed, and in that deed you agreed to several things. One thing was that they were to have the complete possession of the property. Now, Don Anselmo, it seems that every day the

4. **Don:** a Spanish title of respect, like the English "Sir."

5. **cutaway:** long coat with part of the lower front cut away, used for formal occasions.

B **Read and Discuss** What discovery is the lawyer talking about?

C **Literary Focus** **Recurring Themes** What does Don Anselmo's decision indicate about his values?

Analyzing Visuals **Viewing and Interpreting** Does this image resemble the mental image you have of Don Anselmo? Why or why not?

children of the village overrun the orchard and spend most of their time there. We would like to know if you, as the most respected man in the village, could not stop them from doing so in order that these people may enjoy their new home more in peace." **D**

Don Anselmo stood up. "We have all learned to love these Americans," he said, "because they are good people and good neighbors. I sold them my property because I knew they were good people, but I did not sell them the trees in the orchard."

"The trees in that orchard are not mine, *señor*, they belong to the children of the village."

Purchase, Richard H. and Adeline J. Fleischaker Collection, 1996. Fred Jones Jr., Museum of Art, The University of Oklahoma, Norman.

This was bad. "Don Anselmo," I pleaded, "when one signs a deed and sells real property one sells also everything that grows on the land, and those trees, every one of them, are on the land and inside the boundaries of what you sold."

"Yes, I admit that," he said. "You know," he added, "I am the oldest man in the village. Almost everyone there is my relative and all the children of Río en Medio are my *sobrinos* and *nietos*,[6] my descendants. Every time a child has been born in Río en Medio since I took possession of that house from my mother I have planted a tree for that child. The trees in that orchard are not mine, *señor*, they belong to the children of the village. Every person in Río en Medio born since the railroad came to Santa Fe owns a tree in that orchard. I did not sell the trees because I could not. They are not mine."

There was nothing we could do. Legally we owned the trees but the old man had been so generous, refusing what amounted to a fortune for him. It took most of the following winter to buy the trees, individually, from the descendants of Don Anselmo in the valley of Río en Medio. **E**

6. ***sobrinos*** (soh BREE nohs) **and *nietos*** (nee AY tohs): Spanish for "nephews and nieces" and "grandchildren."

D Reading Focus Making Predictions What is the conflict? What predictions can you make about how the "good people" might resolve the conflict?

E Literary Focus Recurring Themes How do you think the narrator feels about Don Anselmo at the end of the story? How does the narrator's opinion help you identify the story's theme?

Vocabulary **boundaries** (BOWN duh reez) *n.:* places where one thing ends and another begins.
descendants (dih SEHN duhnts) *n.:* all the generations who come from one person.

Applying Your Skills

RA.L.8.5 Identify and explain universal themes across different works by the same author and by different authors. **RA.L.8.4** Compare and contrast different points of view, and explain how voice affects literary text. *Also covered* **RP.8.1; WA.8.4.b**

Gentleman of Río en Medio

Respond and Think Critically

Reading Focus

Quick Check

1. Why does the narrator offer Don Anselmo extra money for his land?
2. Why do the buyers return to the lawyer's office and complain?
3. What is Don Anselmo's reply when the narrator asks him to remedy the problem?

Read with a Purpose

4. How is the story's conflict resolved? Were anyone's values disregarded or tossed aside?

Reading Skills: Making Predictions

5. Add a column to your chart for any revisions you made to your predictions. Review your chart entries, and form a statement about the story's theme.

Prediction Topic	Text Clue	My Prediction	Prediction Revisions
Story's title	"Gentleman of Río en Medio"	The theme may be about respect.	

Literary Focus

Literary Analysis

6. **Infer** Why doesn't Don Anselmo reveal who "owns" the trees on his first visit to the lawyer's office? Was he being clever, or was he unaware of the potential problem? Explain.
7. **Make Judgments** How does Don Anselmo's sense of duty and honor conflict with the narrator's? Who is right? On what basis can you make that decision?

Literary Skills: Recurring Themes

8. **Compare** Refer to the theme statement you wrote for question 5. What other poem, story, or novel do you know that has a similar **theme**? Explain the similarities in themes.

Literary Skills Review: Point of View

9. **Hypothesize** This story is told from the point of view of a narrator who is a character in the story. How might this story differ if Don Anselmo were the narrator?

Writing Focus

Think as a Reader/Writer

Use It in Your Writing In this story both Don Anselmo and the narrator agree that the buyers are "good people," yet they have different ideas about what "good people" do. Write an extended definition of the word *good*. Begin with a definition of the word. Then, give examples of "goodness" in action.

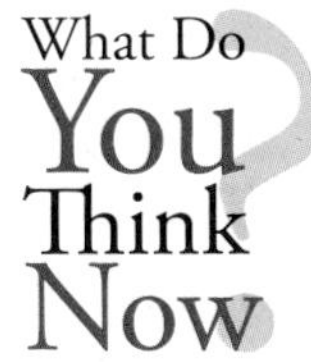

How important do you think it is to respect cultural values that seem out of step with the times? Explain your ideas.

Applying Your Skills

Gentleman of Río en Medio

Vocabulary Development

Synonyms and Shades of Meaning

Good writers sift through many words as they search for exactly the right one to convey their thoughts. Using words precisely gives your writing power. To do this, you need to distinguish **shades of meaning,** slight differences in the words' definitions. For instance, the words below are synonyms, words that have the same basic meaning. These words all mean "great in number."

many innumerable abundant

Each, word, however, has its own special meaning and associations:

- *Many* doesn't give much information; it's a vague word.
- *Innumerable* tells you there were so many, they couldn't be counted.
- *Abundant* implies there is plenty of something.

Before you use a word, look it up to make sure its meaning exactly matches your intention.

Your Turn

negotiation
innumerable
boundaries
descendants

For each set of synonyms below, write two sentences of your own that demonstrate the shades of meaning between the words. Refer to a dictionary if you need help.

1. **negotiation** discussion
2. **innumerable** plentiful
3. **boundaries** edges
4. **descendants** heirs

Language Coach

Context Clues Some stories and texts use words from languages other than English. Non-English words are often set in *italics.* If there is no footnote defining those words, use **context clues**—words surrounding those unknown words—to guess what they mean.

Look at this sentence from "Gentleman of Río en Medio," and use the context to unlock the meaning of the underlined phrase.

> "[T]hese Americans are *buena gente,* they are good people, and they are willing to pay you."

Explain how you arrived at your guess. (If you know Spanish, explain how someone who does not know Spanish could guess the meaning.)

Academic Vocabulary

Write About . . .

Sedillo's story reveals a significant clash between traditional and modern views on property and ownership. In a short paragraph, indicate the consequences this misunderstanding could have had for both parties had they both been inflexible. Use references to the text and the underlined Academic Vocabulary words in your response.

RA.L.8.5 Identify and explain universal themes across different works by the same author and by different authors. **WA.8.5.a** Write persuasive compositions that: establish and develop a controlling idea; **WC.8.4** Grammar and Usage: Use clauses and phrases. *Also covered* **VO.8.7**

Grammar Link

Independent and Subordinate Clauses

Clauses are the main building blocks of sentences. Every clause has a subject and a verb.

Some clauses can stand by themselves as a simple sentence. We call these **independent clauses.**

Other clauses cannot stand alone because they do not express a complete thought. These are called **subordinate clauses,** and they must be combined with other clauses, words, or phrases to make sense.

Don Anselmo sold his property. [The entire sentence is an *independent clause.*]

Because Don Anselmo sold his property [This clause is a *subordinate clause.* Although it has a subject and verb, it cannot stand by itself as a complete sentence.]

Your Turn

Writing Applications Create sentences using the subordinate clauses below as a base. Each new sentence you create should be about "Gentleman of Río en Medio."

1. when the land was surveyed
2. when Don Anselmo sold the land
3. because the new owners wanted
4. that he had given the children

CHOICES

As you respond to the Choices, use these **Academic Vocabulary** words as appropriate: convey, significant, indicate, consequence.

REVIEW

Create a Theme Web

Think of a theme that recurs in many works of literature, or choose one of these: "Love is all you need"; "War can wrench families apart"; or "Effort is more important than talent." Then, create a web that indicates stories or poems that share this theme.

CONNECT

Film Podcast of a Legal Defense

TechFocus With whom did you sympathize more, the buyers or Don Anselmo? Choose a side, and prepare a legal defense. Make a list of at least five points that support your side's case. Then, find a classmate who defended the other side and film a podcast of your arguments for your clients. Post your podcast on a school or class Web site, if possible, and ask your classmates to weigh in on your points.

EXTEND

Perform a Skit

Timed Writing Choose a problem in your community that a lawyer or other negotiator could help solve, such as a neighbor's dog that is tied up outside and barks all night. Write an essay persuading the negotiator to take your side in the dispute. First, choose your position. Then, argue your position respectfully, offering convincing arguments. Finally, suggest a resolution to the issue.

Comparing Themes Across Genres

CONTENTS

What Do You Think?

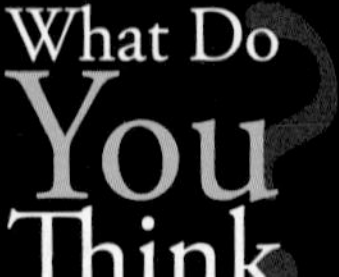

How do people make the transition from one culture to another?

QuickWrite

Imagine arriving in a new country and not speaking the language or knowing the customs. Jot down some thoughts about how you would feel in those first days, weeks, and months.

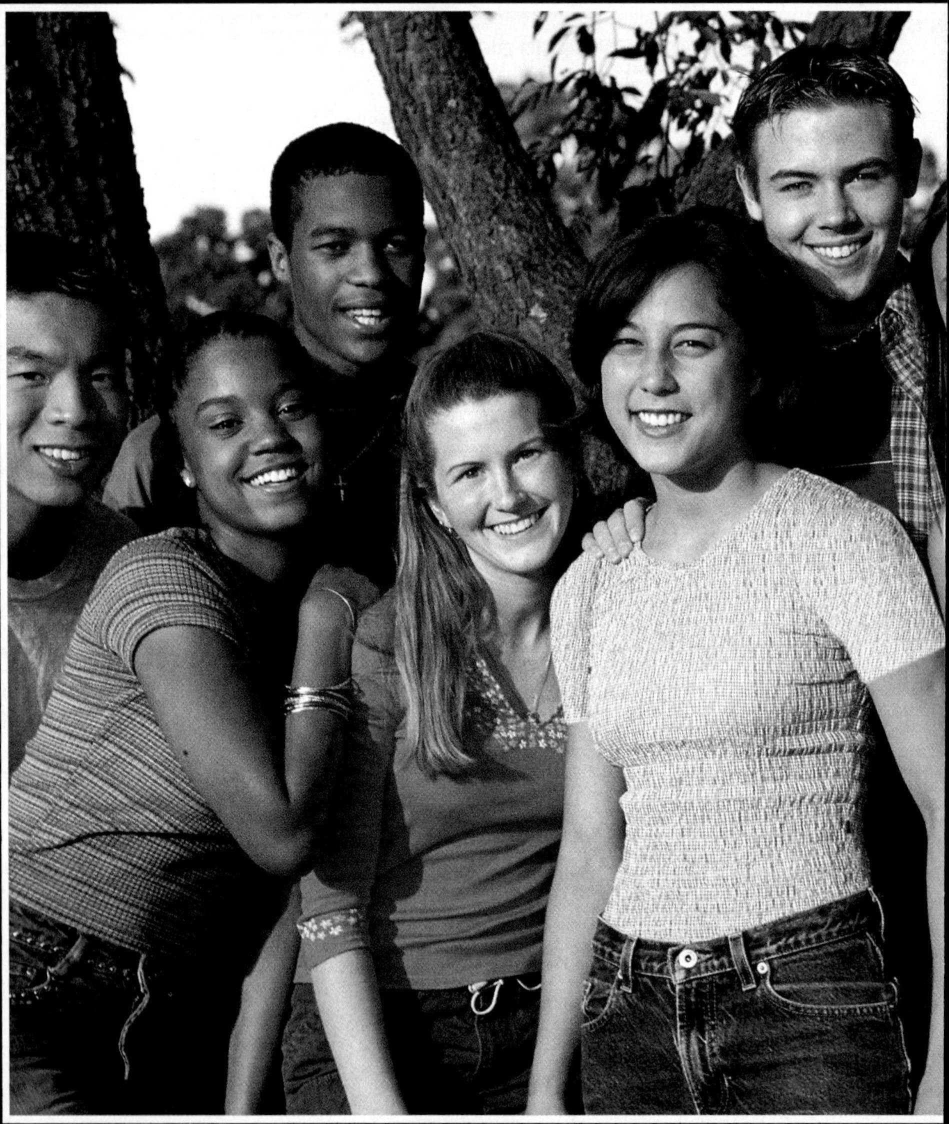

Preparing to Read

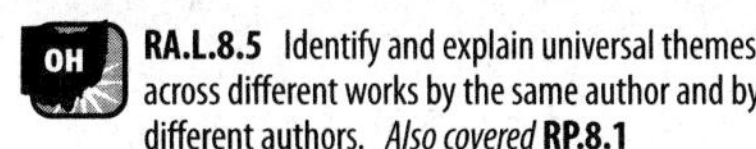

RA.L.8.5 Identify and explain universal themes across different works by the same author and by different authors. *Also covered* **RP.8.1**

A Shot at It / How I Learned English / The Struggle to Be an All-American Girl / Ed McMahon Is Iranian

Literary Focus

Themes Across Genres The selections in this feature deal with the challenges of arriving in a new place, learning a new language, and making new friends, although the selections themselves are written in various **genres,** or types of literature. As you read the autobiography, poem, and essays that follow, you will notice that certain **themes,** or truths about life, emerge. Themes that occur again and again in works from different times, cultures, and genres are called **recurring themes.**

TechFocus As you read, write down questions you might ask in order to learn more about the native culture of a person who has just moved to the United States.

Reading Focus

Comparing Themes To identify a selection's theme, think about its title, the conflicts the characters face, and the moments in which conflicts are resolved. Use the chart below to help you identify the theme of each of the selections.

Title	A Shot at It
Conflicts	getting into the school she wants
Big moment(s)	audition and outcome
Theme	

Writing Focus

Think as a Reader/Writer

Find It in Your Reading Writers sometimes use colorful dialogue to bring characters to life. As you read these selections, note examples of such dialogue in your *Reader/Writer Notebook.*

Reader/Writer Notebook

Use your **RWN** to complete the activities for these selections.

Vocabulary

A Shot at It

mesmerized (MEHS muh ryzd) *v.* used as *adj.:* spellbound; hypnotized. *Mami stared at the TV, mesmerized by the actor's talent.*

impeccably (ihm PEHK uh blee) *adv.:* flawlessly. *The women who interviewed me were impeccably dressed.*

petrified (PEHT ruh fyd) *adj.:* paralyzed with fear. *During the audition, Esmeralda grew petrified and couldn't speak.*

The Struggle to Be an All-American Girl

stoically (STOH ih kuhl lee) *adv.:* here, stubbornly. *Despite changes in the student body, the school stoically stayed the same.*

dissuade (dih SWAYD) *v.:* change someone's mind against; convince not to do. *Offering sound arguments, we tried to dissuade our parents from sending us to school.*

chaotic (kay AHT ihk) *adj.:* confused. *The street scene was disorderly and chaotic.*

Language Coach

Word Origins Franz Mesmer was an Austrian doctor whose studies led to the practice of hypnosis. Which word above is derived from Mesmer's name?

Learn It Online

Explore the vocabulary words with Word Watch online:

go.hrw.com L8-307 

Esmeralda Santiago

(1948–)

Living Two Lives

Born in Puerto Rico, Esmeralda Santiago was thirteen when her mother moved the family to Brooklyn, New York. Although the move from the island to the big city was terrifying at first, Santiago quickly adapted to the new language and way of life. Americanization brought good things to Santiago's life but also made her appreciate her heritage. Her writing allows her to "get back to that feeling of Puertoricanness" she felt before moving to New York.

Gregory Djanikian

(1949–)

Late Bloomer

Living in Egypt for the first few years of his life provided Gregory Djanikian with stories and settings that would later appear in his poetry. When he was six years old, Djanikian moved with his family to Pennsylvania. Although Djanikian is now a writer, he didn't show a strong desire to write until he was a freshman in college. Djanikian's poetry is praised for being lyrical, insightful, and transporting.

Elizabeth Wong

(1958–)

Comments on Life

The playwright Elizabeth Wong uses her work to respond to political and cultural events that are significant to her. Her plays shed light on racial issues and historical events, such as the Tiananmen Square massacre in China. Struggling with both Chinese and American traditions, Wong had a difficult time growing up in Los Angeles's Chinatown. Her life took her to several different places, including New York City, before she settled back in her hometown.

Mariam Salari

(1974–)

Dual Identity

Born in the United States to an Iranian father and a French mother, Mariam Salari grew up in America during the turbulent 1970s. She struggled with the negative ways in which Iranians were portrayed in the media during that time. Still, she developed a fascination with her heritage. She says, "As I learned more about the culture, I began to meet more and more people like me who were very interested in Iranian culture and had a strong familial connection to it."

Think About the Writers

What sort of life experiences do these four writers share? How do you think their heritage and identities affect their writings?

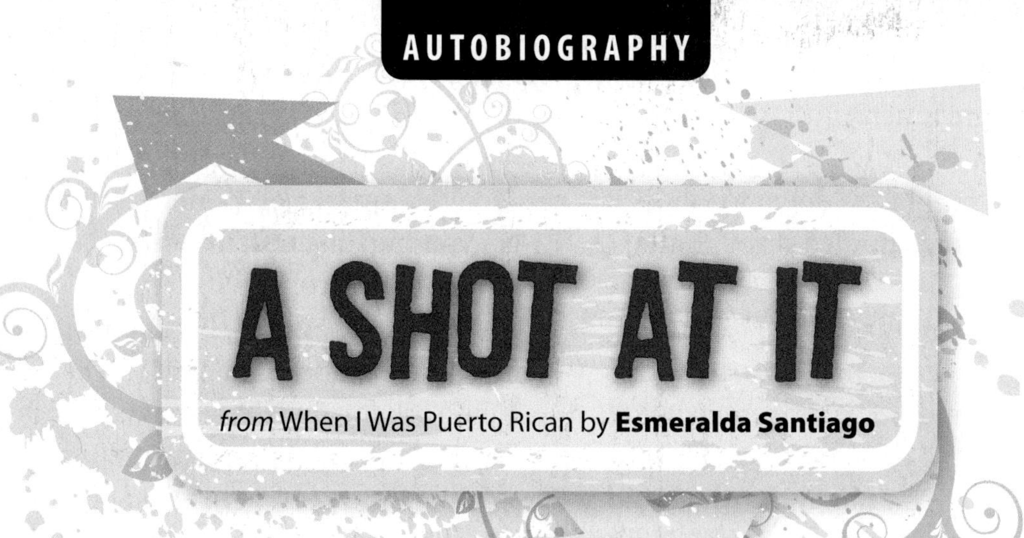

A SHOT AT IT

from When I Was Puerto Rican by **Esmeralda Santiago**

Read with a Purpose

Read this selection to find out if Esmeralda is accepted into the high school she hopes to attend.

Build Background

This selection is an excerpt taken from the final pages of Santiago's memoir *When I Was Puerto Rican*. New York City's High School of Performing Arts is a public school for students who want to pursue careers in theater, music, and dance.

Te conozco bacalao, aunque vengas disfrazao. I recognize you salted codfish, even if you're in disguise.

While Francisco[1] was still alive, we had moved to Ellery Street. That meant I had to change schools, so Mami walked me to P.S. 33, where I would attend ninth grade. The first week I was there I was given a series of tests that showed that even though I couldn't speak English very well, I read and wrote it at the tenth-grade level. So they put me in 9-3, with the smart kids.

One morning, Mr. Barone, a guidance counselor, called me to his office. He was short, with a big head and large hazel eyes under shapely eyebrows. His nose was long and round at the tip. He dressed in browns and yellows and often perched his tortoise-shell glasses on his forehead, as if he had another set of eyes up there.

"So," he pushed his glasses up, "what do you want to be when you grow up?"

"I don't know."

He shuffled through some papers. "Let's see here . . . you're fourteen, is that right?"

"Yes, sir."

"And you've never thought about what you want to be?"

When I was very young, I wanted to be a *jíbara*.[2] When I was older, I wanted to be a cartographer, then a topographer. But

1. **Francisco:** Esmeralda's mother's suitor.

2. ***jíbara*** (HEE bah rah): someone from the mountains of Puerto Rico; a peasant, but in this context it carries with it a certain romanticism.

since we'd come to Brooklyn, I'd not thought about the future much.

"No, sir."

He pulled his glasses down to where they belonged and shuffled through the papers again.

"Do you have any hobbies?" I didn't know what he meant. "Hobbies, hobbies," he flailed his hands, as if he were juggling, "things you like to do after school."

"Ah, yes." I tried to imagine what I did at home that might qualify as a hobby. "I like to read."

He seemed disappointed. "Yes, we know that about you." He pulled out a paper and stared at it. "One of the tests we gave you was an aptitude test. It tells us what kinds of things you might be good at. The tests show that you would be good at helping people. Do you like to help people?"

I was afraid to contradict the tests. "Yes, sir."

"There's a high school we can send you where you can study biology and chemistry which will prepare you for a career in nursing."

I screwed up my face. He consulted the papers again.

"You would also do well in communications. Teaching maybe."

I remembered Miss Brown standing in front of a classroom full of rowdy teenagers, some of them taller than she was.

"I don't like to teach."

Mr. Barone pushed his glasses up again and leaned over the stack of papers on his desk. "Why don't you think about it and get back to me," he said, closing the folder with my name across the top. He put his hand flat on it, as if squeezing something out. "You're a smart girl, Esmeralda. Let's try to get you into an academic school so that you have a shot at college." **A**

On the way home, I walked with another new ninth grader, Yolanda. She had been in New York for three years but knew as little English as I did. We spoke in Spanglish, a combination of English and Spanish in which we hopped from one language to the other depending on which word came first.

"*Te preguntó el* Mr. Barone, you know, *lo que querías hacer* [3] when you grow up?" I asked.

"*Sí, pero,* I didn't know. *¿Y tú?*"[4]

"*Yo tampoco.*[5] He said, *que* I like to help people. *Pero,* you know, *a mí no me gusta la gente.*" When she heard me say I didn't like people much, Yolanda looked at me from the corner of her eye, waiting to become the exception.

By the time I said it, she had dashed up the stairs of her building. She didn't wave as she ducked in, and the next day she wasn't friendly. I walked around the rest of the day in embarrassed isolation, knowing that somehow I had given myself away to the only friend I'd made at Junior High School 33. I had to either take back my words or live with the consequences of stating what was becoming the truth. I'd never

3. ***Te preguntó . . . hacer:*** "He asked you . . . what you wanted to be."
4. ***Sí, pero, . . . ¿Y tú?:*** "Yes, but, . . . And you?"
5. ***Yo tampoco:*** "Me neither."

A **Read and Discuss** What is going on with Esmeralda?

Analyzing Visuals **Viewing and Interpreting** What makes the two sides of the river different? How could this difference represent immigrant life?

View of Lower Manhattan from Brooklyn Heights by James Daugherty.

said that to anyone, not even to myself. It was an added weight, but I wasn't about to trade it for companionship. **B**

A few days later, Mr. Barone called me back to his office.

"Well?" Tiny green flecks burned around the black pupils of his hazel eyes.

The night before, Mami had called us into the living room. On the television "fifty of America's most beautiful girls" paraded in ruffled tulle dresses before a tinsel waterfall.

"Aren't they lovely?" Mami murmured, as the girls, escorted by boys in uniform, floated by the camera, twirled, and disappeared behind a screen to the strains of a waltz and an announcer's dramatic voice calling their names, ages, and states. Mami sat mesmerized through the whole pageant.

B **Literary Focus** **Theme** What challenges does Esmeralda face as a recent immigrant?

Vocabulary **mesmerized** (MEHS muh ryzd) *v.* used as *adj.:* spellbound; hypnotized.

"I'd like to be a model," I said to Mr. Barone.

He stared at me, pulled his glasses down from his forehead, looked at the papers inside the folder with my name on it, and glared. "A model?" His voice was gruff, as if he were more comfortable yelling at people than talking to them.

"I want to be on television."

"Oh, then you want to be an actress," in a tone that said this was only a slight improvement over my first career choice. We stared at one another for a few seconds. He pushed his glasses up to his forehead again and reached for a book on the shelf in back of him. "I only know of one school that trains actresses, but we've never sent them a student from here."

Performing Arts, the write-up said, was an academic, as opposed to a vocational, public school that trained students wishing to pursue a career in theater, music, and dance.

"It says here that you have to audition." He stood up and held the book closer to the faint gray light coming through the narrow window high on his wall. "Have you ever performed in front of an audience?"

"I was announcer in my school show in Puerto Rico," I said. "And I recite poetry. There, not here."

He closed the book and held it against his chest. His right index finger thumped a rhythm on his lower lip. "Let me call them and find out exactly what you need to do. Then we can talk some more."

I left his office strangely happy, confident that something good had just happened, not knowing exactly what. **C**

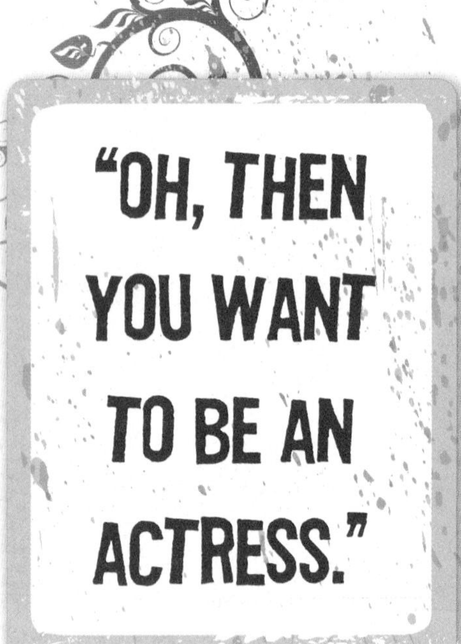
"OH, THEN YOU WANT TO BE AN ACTRESS."

"I'm not afraid . . . I'm not afraid . . . I'm not afraid." Every day I walked home from school repeating those words. The broad streets and sidewalks that had impressed me so on the first day we had arrived had become as familiar as the dirt road from Macún to the highway. Only my curiosity about the people who lived behind these walls ended where the façades of the buildings opened into dark hallways or locked doors. Nothing good, I imagined, could be happening inside if so many locks had to be breached to go in or step out.

It was on these tense walks home from school that I decided I had to get out of Brooklyn. Mami had chosen this as our home, and just like every other time we'd moved, I'd had to go along with her because I was a child who had no choice. But I

C **Read and Discuss** What is happening in the counselor's office now?

wasn't willing to go along with her on this one.

"How can people live like this?" I shrieked once, desperate to run across a field, to feel grass under my feet instead of pavement.

"Like what?" Mami asked, looking around our apartment, the kitchen and living room crisscrossed with sagging lines of drying diapers and bedclothes.

"Everyone on top of each other. No room to do anything. No air."

"Do you want to go back to Macún, to live like savages, with no electricity, no toilets . . ."

"At least you could step outside every day without somebody trying to kill you." **D**

"Ay, Negi,[6] stop exaggerating!"

"I hate my life!" I yelled.

"Then do something about it," she yelled back.

Until Mr. Barone showed me the listing for Performing Arts High School, I hadn't known what to do. **E**

"The auditions are in less than a month. You have to learn a monologue, which you will perform in front of a panel. If you do well, and your grades here are good, you might get into the school."

Mr. Barone took charge of preparing me for my audition to Performing Arts. He selected a speech from *The Silver Cord,* a play by Sidney Howard, first performed in 1926, but whose action took place in a New York drawing room circa 1905.

"Mr. Gatti, the English teacher," he said, "will coach you. . . . And Mrs. Johnson will talk to you about what to wear and things like that."

I was to play Christina, a young married woman confronting her mother-in-law. I learned the monologue phonetically from Mr. Gatti. It opened with "You belong to a type that's very common in this country, Mrs. Phelps—a type of self-centered, self-pitying, son-devouring tigress, with unmentionable proclivities[7] suppressed on the side."

"We don't have time to study the meaning of every word," Mr. Gatti said. "Just make sure you pronounce every word correctly."

Mrs. Johnson, who taught Home Economics, called me to her office.

"Is that how you enter a room?" she asked the minute I came in. "Try again, only this time, don't barge in. Step in slowly, head up, back straight, a nice smile on your face. That's it." I took a deep breath and waited. "Now sit. No, not like that. Don't just plop down. Float down to the chair with your knees together." She demonstrated, and I copied her. "That's better. What do you do with your hands? No, don't hold your chin like that; it's not ladylike. Put your hands on your lap, and leave them there. Don't use them so much when you talk."

I sat stiff as a cutout while Mrs. Johnson and Mr. Barone asked me questions they thought the panel at Performing Arts would ask.

6. **Negi:** Esmeralda's nickname.

7. **proclivities** (pruh KLIHV uh teez): tendencies.

D **Literary Focus** **Theme** What does Esmeralda miss about her previous home?

E **Read and Discuss** What is on Esmeralda's mind?

"Where are you from?"

"Puerto Rico."

"No," Mrs. Johnson said, "Porto Rico. Keep your *r*'s soft. Try again."

"Do you have any hobbies?" Mr. Barone asked. Now I knew what to answer.

"I enjoy dancing and the movies."

"Why do you want to come to this school?"

Mrs. Johnson and Mr. Barone had worked on my answer if this question should come up.

"I would like to study at Performing Arts because of its academic program and so that I may be trained as an actress."

"Very good, very good!" Mr. Barone rubbed his hands together, twinkled his eyes at Mrs. Johnson. "I think we have a shot at this."

"Remember," Mrs. Johnson said, "when you shop for your audition dress, look for something very simple in dark colors."

Mami bought me a red plaid wool jumper with a crisp white shirt, my first pair of stockings, and penny loafers. The night before, she rolled up my hair in pink curlers that cut into my scalp and made it hard to sleep. For the occasion, I was allowed to wear eye makeup and a little lipstick.

"You look so grown up!" Mami said, her voice sad but happy, as I twirled in front of her and Tata.[8]

"*Toda una señorita,*"[9] Tata said, her eyes misty.

8. **Tata:** Esmeralda's grandmother.

9. ***Toda una señorita:*** "All a young lady should be."

We set out for the audition on an overcast January morning heavy with the threat of snow.

"Why couldn't you choose a school close to home?" Mami grumbled as we got on the train to Manhattan. I worried that even if I were accepted, she wouldn't let me go because it was so far from home, one hour each way by subway. But in spite of her complaints, she was proud that I was good enough to be considered for such a famous school. And she actually seemed excited that I would be leaving the neighborhood.

"You'll be exposed to a different class of people," she assured me, and I felt the force of her ambition without knowing exactly what she meant. **F**

Three women sat behind a long table in a classroom where the desks and chairs had been pushed against a wall. As I entered I held my head up and smiled, and then I floated down to the chair in front of them, clasped my hands on my lap, and smiled some more.

"Good morning," said the tall one with hair the color of sand. She was big boned and solid, with intense blue eyes, a generous mouth, and soothing hands with short fingernails. She was dressed in shades of beige from head to toe and wore no makeup and no jewelry except for the gold chain that held her glasses just above her full bosom. Her voice was rich, modulated, each word pronounced as if she were inventing it.

Next to her sat a very small woman with very high heels. Her cropped hair was pouffed around her face, with bangs brushing the tips of her long false lashes, her huge dark brown eyes were thickly lined in black all around, and her small mouth was carefully drawn in and painted cerise. Her suntanned face turned toward me with the innocent curiosity of a lively baby. She was dressed in black, with many gold chains around her neck, big earrings, several bracelets, and large stone rings on the fingers of both hands.

The third woman was tall, small boned, thin, but shapely. Her dark hair was pulled flat against her skull into a knot in back of her head. Her face was all angles and light, with fawnlike dark brown eyes, a straight nose, full lips painted just a shade pinker than their natural color. Silky forest green cuffs peeked out from the sleeves of her burgundy suit. Diamond studs winked from perfect earlobes.

I had dreamed of this moment for several weeks. More than anything, I wanted to impress the panel with my talent, so that I would be accepted into Performing Arts and leave Brooklyn every day. And, I hoped, one day I would never go back.

But the moment I faced these three impeccably groomed women, I forgot my English and Mrs. Johnson's lessons on how to behave like a lady. In the agony of trying to answer their barely comprehensible questions, I jabbed my hands here and there, forming words with my fingers because the words refused to leave my mouth.

"Why don't you let us hear your monologue now?" the woman with the dangling glasses asked softly.

I stood up abruptly, and my chair clattered onto its side two feet from where I

F **Read and Discuss** What is the plan for Esmeralda?

Vocabulary **impeccably** (ihm PEHK uh blee) *adv.:* flawlessly.

stood. I picked it up, wishing with all my strength that a thunderbolt would strike me dead to ashes on the spot.

"It's all right," she said. "Take a breath. We know you're nervous."

I closed my eyes and breathed deeply, walked to the middle of the room, and began my monologue.

"Ju bee lonh 2 a type dats berry cómo in dis kuntree, Meessees Felps. A type off selfcent red self pee tee in sun de boring tie gress wid on men shon ah ball pro klee bee tees on de side."

In spite of Mr. Gatti's reminders that I should speak slowly and enunciate every word, even if I didn't understand it, I recited my three-minute monologue in one minute flat.

The small woman's long lashes seemed to have grown with amazement. The elegant woman's serene face twitched with controlled laughter. The tall one dressed in beige smiled sweetly.

"Thank you, dear," she said. "Could you wait outside for a few moments?"

I resisted the urge to curtsy. The long hallway had narrow wainscotting halfway up to the high ceiling. Single bulb lamps hung from long cords, creating yellow puddles of light on the polished brown linoleum tile. A couple of girls my age sat on straight chairs next to their mothers, waiting their turn. They looked up as I came out and the door shut behind me. Mami stood up from her chair at the end of the hall. She looked as scared as I felt.

"What happened?"

"Nothing," I mumbled, afraid that if I began telling her about it, I would break into tears in front of the other people, whose eyes followed me and Mami as we walked to the EXIT sign. "I have to wait here a minute."

"Did they say anything?"

"No. I'm just supposed to wait."

We leaned against the wall. Across from us there was a bulletin board with newspaper clippings about former students. On the ragged edge, a neat person had printed in blue ink, "P.A." and the year the actor, dancer, or musician had graduated. I closed my eyes and tried to picture myself on that bulletin board, with "P.A. '66" across the top.

The door at the end of the hall opened, and the woman in beige poked her head out.

"Esmeralda?"

"*Sí,* I mean, here." I raised my hand.

She led me into the room. There was another girl in there, whom she introduced as Bonnie, a junior at the school.

"Do you know what a pantomime is?" the woman asked. I nodded. "You and Bonnie are sisters decorating a Christmas tree."

Bonnie looked a lot like Juanita Marín, whom I had last seen in Macún four years earlier. We decided where the invisible Christmas tree would be, and we sat on the floor and pretended we were taking decorations out of boxes and hanging them on the branches.

My family had never had a Christmas tree, but I remembered how once I had helped Papi wind colored lights around the eggplant bush that divided our land from Doña Ana's. We started at the bottom and wound the wire with tiny red bulbs around and around until we ran out; then Papi plugged another cord to it and we kept

going until the branches hung heavy with light and the bush looked like it was on fire.

Before long I had forgotten where I was, and that the tree didn't exist and Bonnie was not my sister. She pretended to hand me a very delicate ball, and just before I took it, she made like it fell to the ground and shattered. I was petrified that Mami would come in and yell at us for breaking her favorite decoration. Just as I began to pick up the tiny fragments of nonexistent crystal, a voice broke in. "Thank you."

Bonnie got up, smiled, and went out.

The elegant woman stretched her hand out for me to shake. "We will notify your school in a few weeks. It was very nice to meet you."

I shook hands all around then backed out of the room in a fog, silent, as if the pantomime had taken my voice and the urge to speak.

On the way home Mami kept asking what had happened, and I kept mumbling, "Nothing. Nothing happened," ashamed that, after all the hours of practice with Mrs. Johnson, Mr. Barone, and Mr. Gatti, after the expense of new clothes and shoes, after Mami had to take a day off from work to take me into Manhattan, after all that, I had failed the audition and would never, ever, get out of Brooklyn. **G**

Epilogue: One of These Days

El mismo jíbaro con diferente caballo.
Same jíbaro, different horse.

A decade after my graduation from Performing Arts, I visited the school. I was by then living in Boston, a scholarship student at Harvard University. The tall, elegant woman of my audition had become my

G **Read and Discuss** What is all of this telling you about the audition?

Vocabulary **petrified** (PEHT ruh fyd) *adj.:* paralyzed with fear.

mentor through my three years there. Since my graduation, she had married the school principal.

"I remember your audition," she said, her chiseled face dreamy, her lips toying with a smile that she seemed, still, to have to control.

I had forgotten the skinny brown girl with the curled hair, wool jumper, and lively hands. But she hadn't. She told me that the panel had had to ask me to leave so that they could laugh, because it was so funny to see a fourteen-year-old Puerto Rican girl jabbering out a monologue about a possessive mother-in-law at the turn of the century, the words incomprehensible because they went by so fast.

"We admired," she said, "the courage it took to stand in front of us and do what you did."

"So you mean I didn't get into the school because of my talent, but because I had chutzpah?"[10] We both laughed.

"Are any of your sisters and brothers in college?"

"No, I'm the only one, so far."

"How many of you are there?"

"By the time I graduated from high school there were eleven of us."

"Eleven!" She looked at me for a long time, until I had to look down. "Do you ever think about how far you've come?" she asked.

"No." I answered. "I never stop to think about it. It might jinx the momentum."

"Let me tell you another story, then," she said. "The first day of your first year, you were absent. We called your house. You said you couldn't come to school because you had nothing to wear. I wasn't sure if you were joking. I asked to speak to your mother, and you translated what she said. She needed you to go somewhere with her to interpret. At first you wouldn't tell me where, but then you admitted you were going to the welfare office. You were crying, and I had to assure you that you were not the only student in this school whose family received public assistance. The next day you were here, bright and eager. And now here you are, about to graduate from Harvard."

"I'm glad you made that phone call," I said.

"And I'm glad you came to see me, but right now I have to teach a class." She stood up, as graceful as I remembered. "Take care."

Her warm embrace, fragrant of expensive perfume, took me by surprise. "Thank you," I said as she went around the corner to her classroom.

I walked the halls of the school, looking for the room where my life had changed. It was across from the science lab, a few doors down from the big bulletin board where someone with neat handwriting still wrote the letters "P.A." followed by the graduating year along the edges of newspaper clippings featuring famous alumni.

"P.A. '66," I said to no one in particular. "One of these days." **H**

10. **chutzpah:** brazenness; daring boldness (Yiddish slang).

H **Read and Discuss** What is the author letting you know in the epilogue?

POEM

How I Learned English

by **Gregory Djanikian**

Sandlot Baseball (1938) by Joe Golinkin (detail).

Read with a Purpose
Read this poem to experience a boy's first baseball game in his new home in America.

Preparing to Read for this selection is on page 307.

It was in an empty lot
Ringed by elms and fir and honeysuckle.
Bill Corson was pitching in his buckskin jacket,
Chuck Keller, fat even as a boy, was on first,
His t-shirt riding up over his gut,
Ron O'Neill, Jim, Dennis, were talking it up
In the field, a blue sky above them
Tipped with cirrus.°

And there I was,
Just off the plane and plopped in the middle
Of Williamsport, Pa. and a neighborhood game,
Unnatural and without any moves,
My notions of baseball and America
Growing fuzzier each time I whiffed. **A**

8. **cirrus:** high, wispy clouds.

A **Read and Discuss** What situation has the author set up for us?

So it was not impossible that I,
Banished to the outfield and daydreaming
Of water, or a hotel in the mountains,
Would suddenly find myself in the path
Of a ball stung by Joe Barone.
I watched it closing in
Clean and untouched, transfixed°
By its easy arc before it hit
My forehead with a thud.

I fell back.
Dazed, clutching my brow,
Groaning, "Oh my shin, oh my shin,"
And everybody peeled away from me
And dropped from laughter, and there we were,
All of us writhing on the ground for one reason
Or another. **B**

Someone said "shin" again,
There was a wild stamping of hands on the ground,
A kicking of feet, and the fit
Of laughter overtook me too,
And that was important, as important
As Joe Barone asking me how I was
Through his tears, picking me up
And dusting me off with hands like swatters,
And though my head felt heavy,
I played on till dusk
Missing flies and pop-ups and grounders
And calling out in desperation things like
"Yours" and "take it," but doing all right,
Tugging at my cap in just the right way,
Crouching low, my feet set,
"Hum baby" sweetly on my lips. **C**

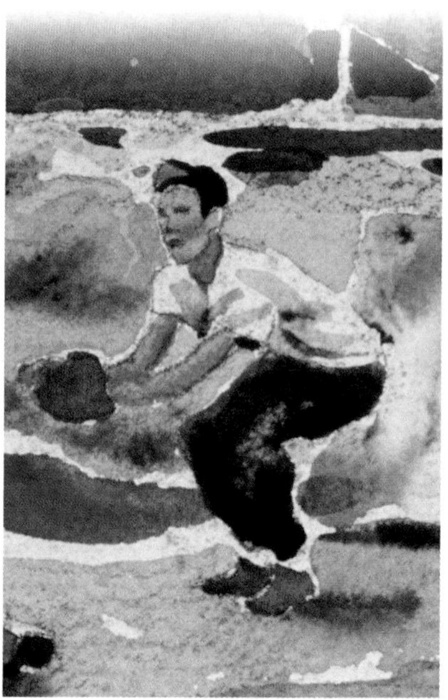

Sandlot Baseball (1938) by Joe Golinkin (detail).

21. transfixed (trans FIHKST): motionless or helpless.

B **Read and Discuss** Why are the boys laughing?

C **Reading Focus** **Contrasting Themes** How does the speaker's first experience of America differ from Santiago's?

Applying Your Skills

RA.L.8.5 Identify and explain universal themes across different works by the same author and by different authors. **WA.8.6** Produce informal writings. **VO.8.4** Infer the literal and figurative meaning of words and phrases and discuss the function of figurative language, including metaphors, similes and idioms.

A Shot at It / How I Learned English

Respond and Think Critically

Reading Focus

Quick Check

1. In "A Shot at It," why does Esmeralda tell Mr. Barone she wants to be an actress?
2. What impression does Esmeralda make on the teacher panel?
3. What amusing mistake does the speaker make in "How I Learned English"?

Read with a Purpose

4. Did Esmeralda get into the school she wanted to in "A Shot at It"? How do you know?
5. In "How I Learned English," what kind of experience did the poem's speaker have in his first baseball game?

Reading Skills: Comparing Themes

6. Once you have found a theme for each selection, formulate a theme statement that fits them both.

	"A Shot at It"	"How I Learned English"
Theme		
Common theme		

Vocabulary Check

Match the Vocabulary words with their definitions.

7. **mesmerized** — a. terrified
8. **impeccably** — b. spellbound
9. **petrified** — c. perfectly

Literary Focus

Literary Analysis

10. **Infer** In "A Shot at It," what motivates Esmeralda to audition for the High School of Performing Arts? Does she really want to be a performer?
11. **Interpret** What does the speaker in "How I Learned English" mean when he describes himself as "unnatural and without any moves" (line 12)?
12. **Compare** What life experience do Esmeralda and the speaker in "How I Learned English" have in common?

Literary Skills: Themes Across Genres

13. **Analyze** In "A Shot at It," what theme is suggested by Esmeralda's success in getting into a highly competitive high school?
14. **Interpret** In "How I Learned English," why does the speaker think his laughter is as important as Joe Barone's helping him up? What does this insight suggest about the poem's theme?

Writing Focus

Think as a Reader/Writer

Use It in Your Writing In your *Reader/Writer Notebook*, look through the notes you took about the ways Santiago and Djanikian use dialogue to enhance their writing. Then, practice using colorful dialogue by writing a description of a student trying out for a sports team or the school orchestra.

ESSAY

The Struggle to Be an All-American Girl

by **Elizabeth Wong**

Read with a Purpose

Read these next two essays to see how a Chinese American girl and an Iranian American girl feel about their heritages.

Preparing to Read for this selection is on page 307.

It's still there, the Chinese school on Yale Street where my brother and I used to go. Despite the new coat of paint and the high wire fence, the school I knew ten years ago remains remarkably, stoically the same.

Every day at 5 P.M., instead of playing with our fourth- and fifth-grade friends or sneaking out to the empty lot to hunt ghosts and animal bones, my brother and I had to go to Chinese school. No amount of kicking, screaming, or pleading could dissuade my mother, who was solidly determined to have us learn the language of our heritage.

Forcibly, she walked us the seven long, hilly blocks from our home to school, depositing our defiant, tearful faces before the stern principal. My only memory of him is that he swayed on his heels like a palm tree, and he always clasped his impatient, twitching hands behind his back. I recognized him as a repressed maniacal child killer and knew that if we ever saw his hands we'd be in big trouble.

We all sat in little chairs in an empty auditorium. The room smelled like Chinese medicine, an imported faraway mustiness. Like ancient mothballs or dirty closets. I hated that smell. I favored crisp new scents. Like the soft French perfume that my American teacher wore in public school.

There was a stage far to the right, flanked by an American flag and the flag of the Nationalist Republic of China,[1] which was also red, white, and blue but not as pretty. **A**

1. **Nationalist Republic of China:** Republic of China, consisting mainly of Taiwan.

Vocabulary **stoically** (STOH ih kuhl lee) *adv.:* here, stubbornly.
dissuade (dih SWAYD) *v.:* change someone's mind against; convince not to do.

A **Read and Discuss** In the narrator's view, how does her Chinese school compare with her American school?

Although the emphasis at the school was mainly language—speaking, reading, writing—the lessons always began with an exercise in politeness. With the entrance of the teacher, the best student would tap a bell and everyone would get up, kowtow,[2] and chant, "Sing san ho," the phonetic for "How are you, teacher?"

Being ten years old, I had better things to learn than ideographs[3] copied painstakingly in lines that ran right to left from the tip of a *moc but,* a real ink pen that had to be held in an awkward way if blotches were to be avoided. After all, I could do the multiplication tables, name the satellites of Mars, and write reports on *Little Women* and *Black Beauty.* Nancy Drew, my favorite book heroine, never spoke Chinese.

2. **kowtow:** show respect by kneeling to touch the ground with the forehead.
3. **ideographs** (IHD ee uh grafs): written symbols representing objects or ideas. Chinese is written with ideographs.

The language was a source of embarrassment. More times than not, I had tried to disassociate myself from the nagging loud voice that followed me wherever I wandered in the nearby American supermarket outside Chinatown. The voice belonged to my grandmother, a fragile woman in her seventies who could outshout the best of the street vendors. Her humor was raunchy, her Chinese rhythmless, patternless. It was quick, it was loud, it was unbeautiful. It was not like the quiet lilting romance of French or the gentle refinement of the American South. Chinese sounded pedestrian. Public.

In Chinatown, the comings and goings of hundreds of Chinese on their daily tasks sounded chaotic and frenzied. I did not want to be thought of as mad, as talking gibberish. When I spoke English, people nodded at me, smiled sweetly, said encouraging words. Even the people in my culture would cluck and say that I'd do well in life. "My, doesn't she move her lips fast," they would say, meaning that I'd be able to keep up with the world outside Chinatown. **B**

My brother was even more fanatical than I about speaking English. He was especially hard on my mother, criticizing her, often cruelly, for her pidgin speech—smatterings of Chinese scattered like chop suey in her conversation. "It's not 'what it is,' Mom," he'd say in exasperation. "It's 'What *is* it, what *is* it, what *is* it!'" Sometimes Mom might leave out an occasional "the" or "a," or perhaps a verb of being. He would stop her in midsentence: "Say it again, Mom. Say it right." When he tripped over his own tongue, he'd blame it on her: "See, Mom, it's all your fault. You set a bad example."

What infuriated my mother most was when my brother cornered her on her consonants, especially "r." My father had played a cruel joke on Mom by assigning her an American name that her tongue wouldn't allow her to say. No matter how hard she tried, "Ruth" always ended up "Luth" or "Roof." **C**

After two years of writing with a *moc but* and reciting words with multiples of meanings, I finally was granted a cultural divorce. I was permitted to stop Chinese school.

I thought of myself as multicultural. I preferred tacos to egg rolls; I enjoyed Cinco de Mayo[4] more than Chinese New Year.

At last, I was one of you; I wasn't one of them.

Sadly, I still am. **D**

4. **Cinco de Mayo:** holiday celebrated by Mexicans and Mexican Americans in honor of a Mexican military victory in 1862. *Cinco de Mayo* is Spanish for "May 5."

B **Reading Focus** **Comparing Themes** How does Wong's experience of learning English compare with Santiago's and Djanikian's?

C **Read and Discuss** What is surprising about the relationship between the children and their mother?

D **Literary Focus** **Theme** What impression does the writer make by using the word *sadly*?

Vocabulary **chaotic** (kay AHT ihk) *adj.*: confused.

ESSAY

ED MCMAHON IS IRANIAN

by **Mariam Salari**

Preparing to Read for this selection is on page 307.

Build Background

In 1979, a group of Iranian students protesting U.S. policy seized a group of American citizens at the U.S. embassy in Tehran, the capital of Iran. After months of negotiations and a failed rescue mission, the fifty-two hostages were released on January 20, 1981. From 1979 to 1981, the Iranian hostage crisis, as it came to be called, was covered widely in the U.S. news media and affected attitudes toward Iranians and Iranian American citizens living in the United States. Says Salari of her confusion at that time, "I remember looking at the images on the television of the Iranians burning the flag, of them taking over the Embassy and the hostages. And I remember my parents being just as against the people who were taking over as all of the Americans were."

It was a typical afternoon. My mother and I were spending time together arranging things in our new Florida home while my little brother was napping.

Then the doorbell rang. As my mom opened the door, a huge explosion occurred. BANG!

With the explosion came a splash of red paint that stained our front door. The scarlet stains on the door branded us: terrorists. My mom slammed the door shut and immediately called my father at work. All I remember is being scared and not knowing what had happened. I could sense that my mom was terrified, which scared me even more. She tried to reassure me that everything was all right and asked me to go to my room and take a nap. Then the police arrived, and she told them what had happened.

Ed McMahon (left) and Johnny Carson (right) on *The Tonight Show Starring Johnny Carson.*

That night when Dad came home, I didn't know what to ask him or what to say; there was an uncomfortable silence and an unspoken tension in the air. After dinner I approached my dad. I curled up next to him in his big brown leather seat, which had become imprinted with the shape of his back. **A**

"So, Daddy, who did that thing today?"

My father looked to my mom for help in answering, but she remained quiet. I could tell that he was scrambling for a suitable answer for his curious five-year-old daughter. "Vell, somevone deed dis because dey vere mad at the Eraniyans who var holding fifty-two American hostages."

"Mad at us? We didn't do anything? Did we?"

"No, ve did not, but dey tink it is our fault."

A **Read and Discuss** What has happened at this point?

"I hate being Iranian. I'm not going to make any friends at my new school because they will all hate me. They will always hate me. I don't want to be Iranian. No one I know is Iranian. I wish I were American."

I was sad and petrified at the same time.

"You are an American, Maryam. You vere born in dis country."

"No, I wish I were a real American. No one here is an Iranian." **B**

My parents looked at each other for a painful second, then my dad looked up at the television—the *Tonight Show with Johnny Carson*[1] was on—desperate for an answer to my bold declaration. "You are wrong," he suddenly blurted out. "Dere are many Eraniyans in de USA."

I looked up at him skeptically. "Like who?" I asked.

Then he pointed to the fat man on the screen. "Heem, Ed Mac MA Hohn is Eraniyan."

Through my tears, I looked at the fat man on the TV. Him? He was an Iranian? Call it naïveté[2] or just childhood ignorance, or maybe it was the fact that I needed to believe my father—whatever it was, I let myself believe it. Of course my dad, with his accent, could have made John F. Kennedy[3] sound like an Iranian name, but that didn't matter to me.

For years I honestly believed that Ed McMahon was Iranian. I would tell my friends, my brothers, everyone, that Ed was Iranian. Every time one of those sweepstakes letters came in the mail, I thought Ed had sent it to us because he knew we were Iranians, too. Of course, every time Ed was on television my dad would say: "Look, dere's Ed Mac MA Hohn, he's Eraniyan."

Now, eighteen years later, Ed Mac MA Hohn is a little joke in our house. My dad still likes to "Iranianize" names of celebrities and try to "trick" us, and I still like to let him do it. **C**

1. **the *Tonight Show with Johnny Carson*:** Johnny Carson (1925–2005) hosted this popular late-night talk show, with Ed McMahon (1923–) as his sidekick, from 1962 to 1992.

2. **naïveté** (nah EEV tay): state of being innocent and childlike; showing lack of worldly experience.

3. **John F. Kennedy:** U.S. president (1961–1963).

B **Literary Focus** **Theme** How does the writer feel about being Iranian American? Why does she feel that way?

C **Read and Discuss** What is the author saying about her father's joke?

Applying Your Skills

RA.L.8.5 Identify and explain universal themes across different works by the same author and by different authors. RA.L.8.8 Explain ways in which the author conveys mood and tone through word choice, figurative language, and syntax. *Also covered* RP.8.1; WA.8.6; VO.8.4

The Struggle to Be an All-American Girl / Ed McMahon Is Iranian

Respond and Think Critically

Reading Focus

Quick Check

1. In "The Struggle to Be an All-American Girl," what does the writer dislike about Chinese school?
2. What happens in "Ed McMahon Is Iranian" to make the writer afraid?

Read with a Purpose

3. How do Wong and Salari regard their heritages? Are their ideas similar or different? Explain.

Reading Skills: Comparing Themes

4. Formulate a theme statement for each selection to complete the chart below. Then, find a theme common to both.

	"The Struggle to Be an All-American Girl"	"Ed McMahon Is Iranian"
Selection theme		
Common theme		

Vocabulary Check

Match the Vocabulary words with their definitions.

5. stoically   **a.** disorderly
6. dissuade   **b.** stubbornly
7. chaotic   **c.** persuade not to

Literary Focus

Literary Analysis

8. **Analyze** Wong describes specific sights and sounds when discussing the Chinese school. Explain how the use of such imagery conveys her feelings about the school.
9. **Interpret** In Salari's essay, do you see the father's statement about Ed McMahon as an intentional lie or as something else? Explain.

Literary Skills: Themes Across Genres

10. **Analyze** At the end of "The Struggle to Be an All-American Girl," Wong states, "At last, I was one of you; I wasn't one of them. Sadly, I still am." What does this ending say about Wong's feelings about her Chinese heritage? What theme is suggested by the statement?
11. **Analyze** At the end of "Ed McMahon Is Iranian," Salari says her father still tries to convince his family that many celebrities are Iranian. Why do you think Salari lets herself believe him? What does her admission suggest about the theme of this selection?

Writing Focus

Think as a Reader/Writer

Use It in Your Writing Review your notes about how each author uses colorful dialogue to convey character. Practice using dialogue in your writing by describing an experience you had learning a second language.

COMPARING TEXTS

Wrap Up

WA.8.4.d Write informational essays or reports, including research, that: support the main ideas with facts, details, examples and explanations from sources **C.8.8.a** Deliver informational presentations that: demonstrate an understanding of the topic and present events or ideas in a logical sequence; *Also covered* **RP.8.1**

A Shot at It / How I Learned English / The Struggle to Be an All-American Girl / Ed McMahon Is Iranian

Writing Focus

Write a Comparison-and-Contrast Essay

Each of these works tells about the childhood experience of being an immigrant in the United States and feeling like an outsider. Re-examine the four selections, and write a comparison-and-contrast essay in which you —

- look for similarities and differences in the ways the narrators adjust to a new culture
- evaluate the selections' themes, the insights that they convey about life
- analyze the adult perspectives of each childhood experience and the ways in which the perspectives are similar and different

Use the following outline to organize your essay:

I. Introduction and thesis statement
II. Body of essay
  A. Similarities and differences in narrators' experiences
  B. Comparison of selection themes; discussion of recurring theme
  C. Adult view of childhood experience
III. Summary and conclusion

Proofread your essay to eliminate errors in spelling, grammar, and punctuation.

What Do You Think Now?

Have your opinions or feelings about what it is like to adapt to a new culture changed? If so, how?

CHOICES

As you respond to the Choices, use the **Academic Vocabulary** words as appropriate: convey, significant, indicate, consequence.

REVIEW

Compare Characters

Timed Writing Santiago, a country girl from Puerto Rico, finds herself in New York City. Wong, who is devoted to being an "American girl," finds herself enrolled in a Chinese school. Write an essay in which you compare and contrast the writers' experiences. Cite details from the selections to support your opinion of how their experiences are alike and different.

CONNECT

Create a Web Site

TechFocus Each of these selections is about a child caught between two cultures. Interview someone you know—a friend, neighbor, or relative—who has a dual cultural heritage. Create a Web profile honoring this person's dual heritage. You may wish to include recipes, cultural facts, and a transcript of the interview on the Web site.

EXTEND

Research a Culture

How much do you know about these authors' places of origin—Puerto Rico, Egypt, China, and Iran? Choose one location, and, with a group, research the location. You may wish to split research subjects into the following categories: culture, food, history, language, political system, and religion. As a group, present your findings to the class.

INFORMATIONAL TEXT FOCUS

Analyzing Text Structures

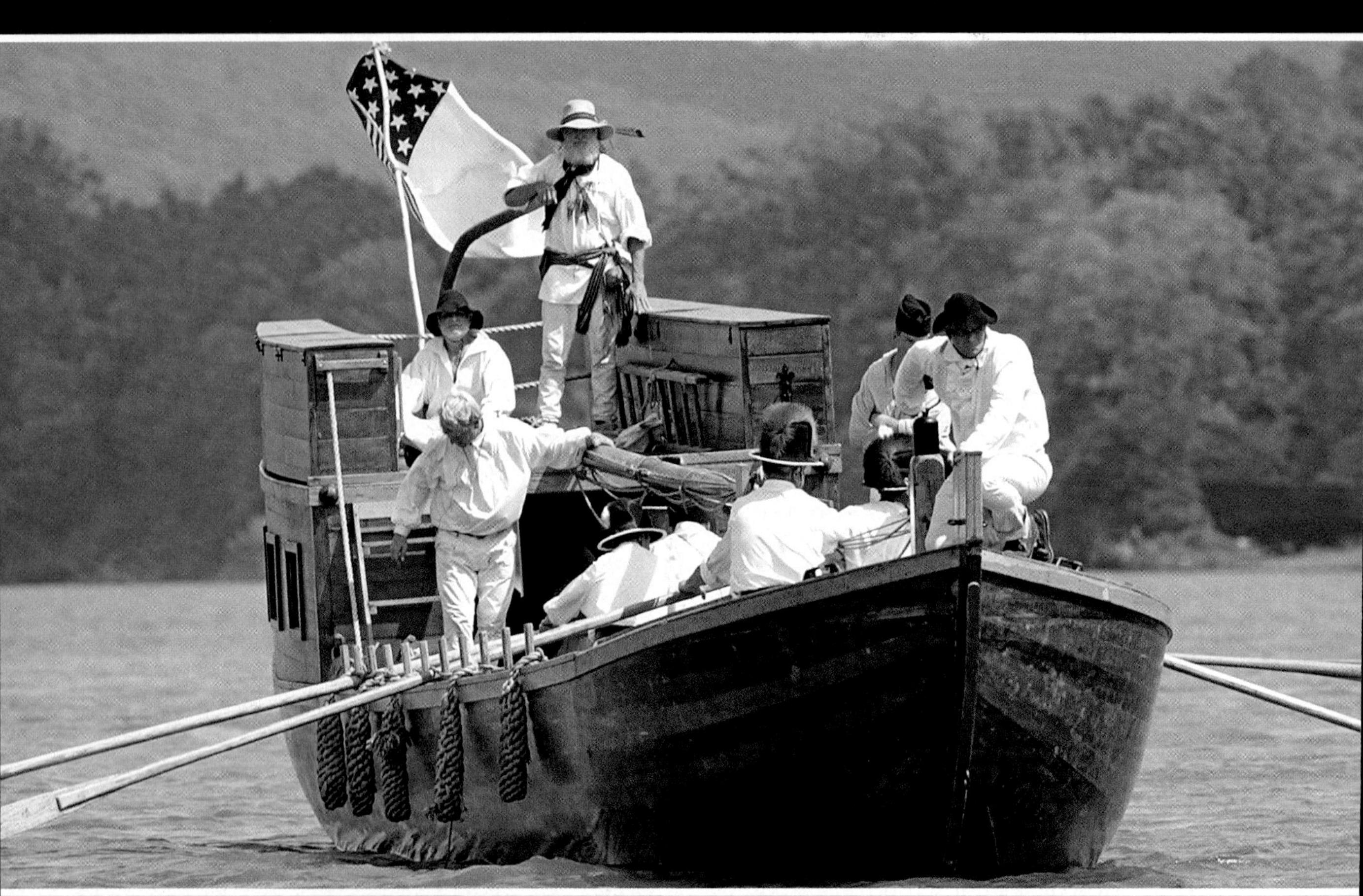

The Discovery Expedition (2003) retraces the route of Lewis and Clark's expedition. The photographs that accompany this selection were taken during the reenactment of Lewis and Clark's historic journey.

CONTENTS

What Do You Think?

How can learning about our country make us better citizens?

QuickWrite

How much do you know about the country you live in? Jot down some facts about the history and geography of the United States.

MAGAZINE ARTICLE

Preparing to Read

Lewis and Clark: Into the Unknown

Informational Text Focus

Cause-and-Effect Organization Writing that follows a cause-and-effect organization explains how or why one thing leads to another. Magazine and news articles often provide information on causes and effects.

- The **cause** is the reason that an action or reaction takes place. To find the causes of an event, ask yourself why it happened.
- The **effect** is the consequence, or result, of a cause. To find the effects of a cause, ask yourself what resulted from the cause.

Into Action A cause often has more than one effect, and an effect may have several causes. As you read, fill in the missing causes and effects in the chart below:

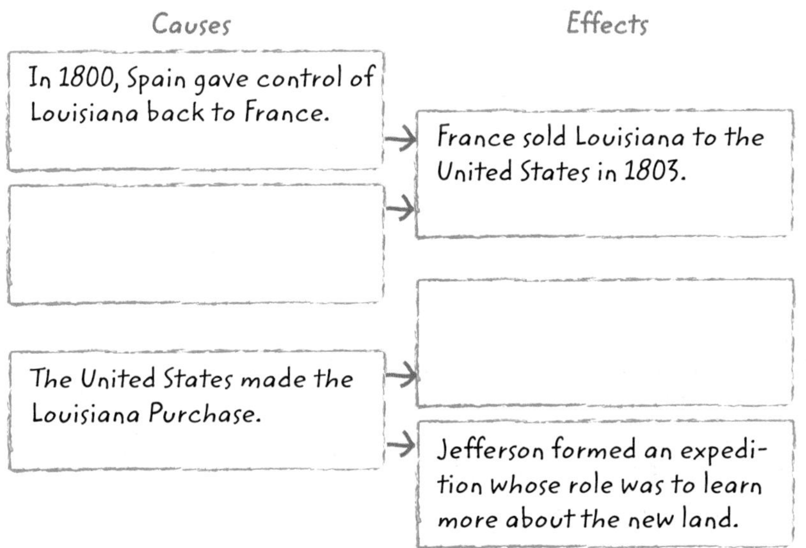
Causes
Effects
In 1800, Spain gave control of Louisiana back to France.
France sold Louisiana to the United States in 1803.
The United States made the Louisiana Purchase.
Jefferson formed an expedition whose role was to learn more about the new land.

Writing Focus

Preparing for **Constructed Response**

Tests often ask you to identify the key causes and effects of an event. As you read this article, list the causes and effects in your *Reader/Writer Notebook*. Weigh them to decide which are most important.

OH **RA.I.8.2** Identify and use the organizational structure of a text, such as chronological, compare-contrast, cause-effect, problem-solution, and evaluate its effectiveness.

Reader/Writer
Notebook

Use your **RWN** to complete the activities for this selection.

Vocabulary

negotiated (nih GOH shee ayt ihd) *v.:* came to an agreement through discussion; talked. *The two countries negotiated until they arrived at an arrangement that they both felt was fair.*

acquisition (ak wuh ZIHSH uhn) *n.:* something purchased or gained. *The land was an acquisition that the United States made from France.*

corps (kawr) *n.:* group of people with special training; a military unit. *The government set up a trained corps of experts to research and explore the new land.*

Language Coach

Word Origins Some words that come from French have silent letters. For example, a *coup* (koo) is an unexpected, brilliant move or action, and a *gourmet* (GUR may) is a food expert. Read aloud the list of Vocabulary words above. Which word do you think comes from French? Explain.

Learn It Online

Reinforce your understanding of this lesson with a multimedia presentation at:

go.hrw.com L8-331 

MAGAZINE ARTICLE

Lewis and Clark: INTO THE UNKNOWN

Meriwether Lewis (1807) by Charles Willson Peale.

William Clark by Charles Willson Peale.

by  

Read with a Purpose

Read this article to learn why the United States put together a team to explore a huge part of the country.

Build Background

In 1800, Spain made a secret agreement giving France control of a huge area of North American land known as the Louisiana Territory. When the United States learned of this arrangement, in 1801, politicians knew that this land was strategically important. It contained the key commercial port of New Orleans as well as the mouth of the Mississippi River. In 1803, the United States decided to buy this land from France, paying about three cents per acre for 828,000 square miles of land. This sale, known as the Louisiana Purchase, doubled the size of the United States.

All the vast, unknown land beyond the great river—what did it look like? What strange animals might be living there? Could prehistoric creatures still exist in such a place? In 1802, these questions were on the mind of America's third president, Thomas Jefferson. At the time, the Mississippi River formed the western boundary of the United States. Little was known about the land beyond.

Jefferson believed westward expansion was in the country's best interest, so the United States negotiated with France for the huge land tract between the Mississippi River and the Rocky Mountains. The president wanted Americans to get excited about this acquisition—the Louisiana Purchase—and about the West. A successful expedition across the continent, he thought, might create that kind of "buzz."

Vocabulary **negotiated** (nih GOH shee ayt ihd) *v.:* came to an agreement through discussion; talked.
acquisition (ak wuh ZIHSH uhn) *n.:* something purchased or gained.

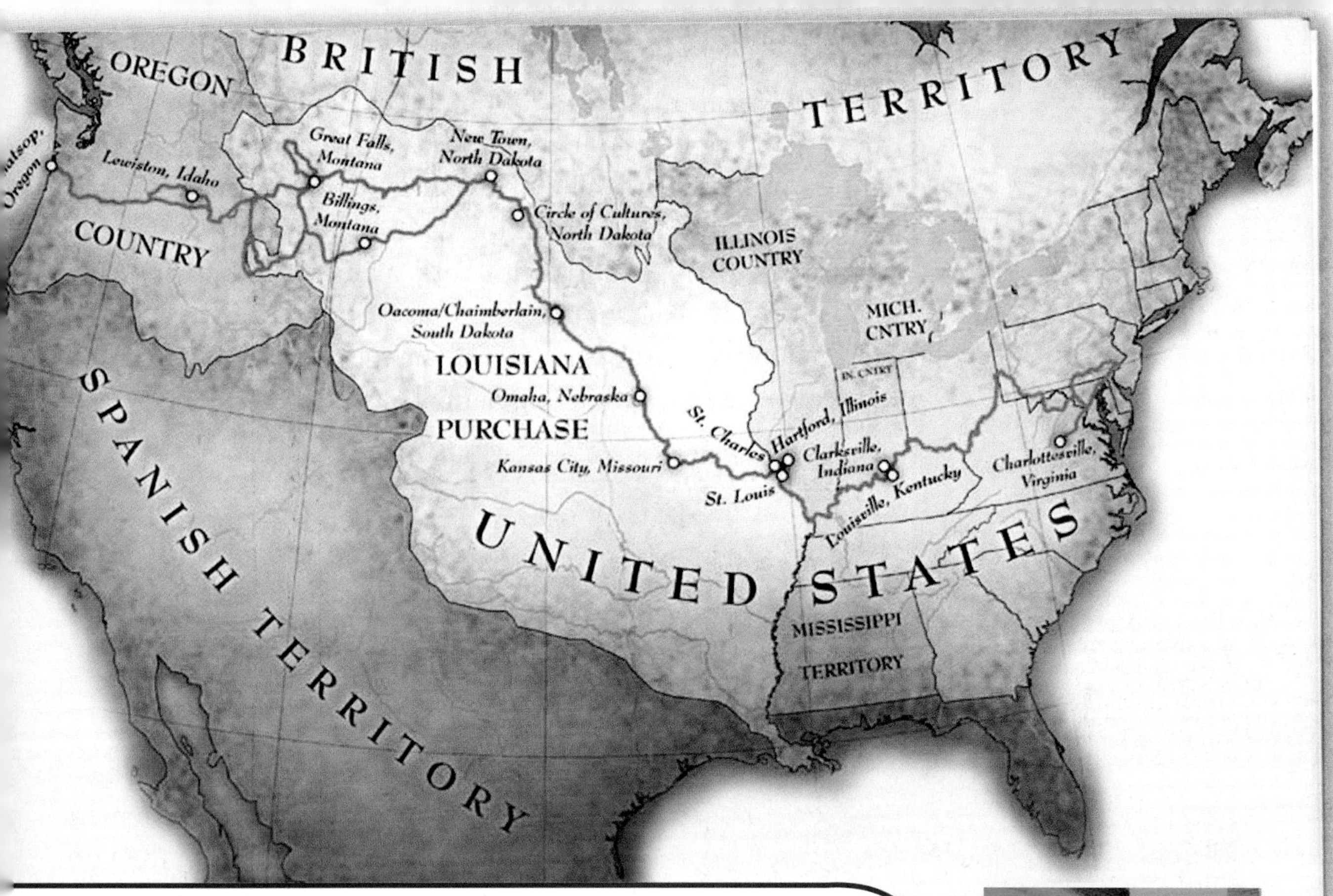

Analyzing Visuals

Viewing and Interpreting Look closely at the map. How is the map of the United States different now?

U.S. explorers would bring back information. They would talk to native peoples, explaining the shift in power and creating goodwill. Most important, they might discover the long-hoped-for Northwest Passage: a continuous water—rather than land—route from the Atlantic to the Pacific oceans. **A**

Forming the Corps

Not only did Jefferson need someone brave and resourceful to lead the expedition, but he also needed to trust him. He chose Meriwether Lewis, his personal secretary. The president sent Lewis to Philadelphia to study with experts to ready him for the trip. Since there would be no doctors in the wilderness, Lewis needed to know medicine. He had to understand celestial navigation (steering by the stars), botany (plant science), and zoology (animal science).

A Informational Focus **Cause and Effect** Why did Jefferson decide to launch an expedition across the continent? Identify the causes of his decision.

Lewis was enthusiastic about the challenge, but knew he did not want to go it alone. He asked his former army comrade and friend William Clark to be co-commander. In 1803, the two headed down the Ohio River toward St. Louis on the Mississippi, along with York, an enslaved person who had been with Clark since childhood. They recruited and trained nearly four dozen men as members of their Corps of Discovery, along with a dog named Seaman.

Strange Places and New Faces

On March 10, 1804, Lewis and Clark attended the St. Louis ceremony that made the Louisiana Purchase official. In late spring, their assembled group started up the Missouri River in boats. As they passed the seven-house cluster of La Charette on May 25, Charles Floyd, one of the corps, noted in his journal that it was "the last settlement of whites on this river." From then on, almost everyone the corps encountered was American Indian.

The explorers knew it would be impossible to get across the continent without help—or at least acceptance—from American Indians. Therefore, Lewis and Clark sought meetings with native peoples along the way. The explorers found many native peoples welcoming but had difficulties with a few.

Contemporary illustration of the original Lewis and Clark expedition.

Welcome Additions

In late October, the explorers began building a winter fort near a large community of Mandan and Hidatsa Indians in what is now North Dakota. During their stay at Fort Mandan, Lewis and Clark learned that horses were needed to cross the mountains. The native peoples told them the Shoshone might provide the animals, if they could strike a bargain.

Vocabulary **corps** (kawr) *n.:* group of people with special training; a military unit.

Lewis and Clark found a Shoshone woman to help with these negotiations: Sacagawea, who had been captured by the Hidatsa years earlier. Lewis and Clark hired her and her husband, Toussaint Charbonneau, a French Canadian fur trapper, as translators. When the corps set out in spring, they and their infant son, Jean Baptiste, went along.

Sacagawea's ability to speak Shoshone was, indeed, a great benefit. She was able to procure horses and provide aid in many ways. The native groups the explorers encountered were sometimes fearful and suspicious of them. When they saw Sacagawea and her little son, however, they felt more at ease. Surely the explorers weren't a war party—not with a young woman and baby. **B**

To the Pacific

The Corps of Discovery faced incredible obstacles. They had run-ins with grizzly bears and shot their canoes through rapids so treacherous that local American Indians stared in disbelief. At one point, they spent a month making a portage° around a waterfall. They lost their way in the Bitterroot Mountains and nearly starved.

The expedition found no Northwest Passage—the dreamed-of water route across the continent. They did discover the new country's rich western assets. They named locations and landmarks and described 178 plants and 122 animals that had been previously unknown. With courage, intelligence, and luck, the Corps of Discovery made it all the way to what is today Oregon—and home again—to tell their remarkable tale. **C**

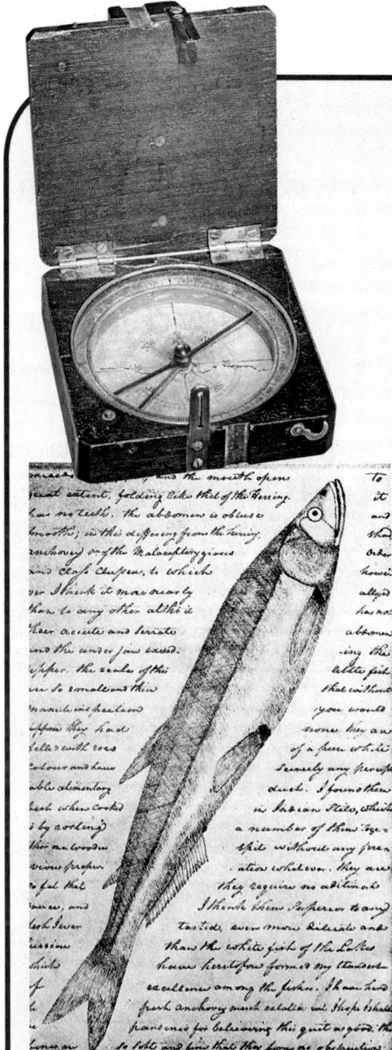

Pocket compass and diary page from Lewis and Clark expedition.

°**portage:** act of carrying boats from one place to another overland in order to bypass sections of a waterway that cannot be navigated.

Read with a Purpose Did Lewis and Clark's expedition accomplish what Jefferson had hoped it would? Why or why not?

B **Informational Focus** **Cause and Effect** What were some of the positive effects of having Sacagawea travel with the corps?

C **Read and Discuss** How did things turn out for the explorers?

MAGAZINE ARTICLE

Applying Your Skills

RA.I.8.2 Identify and use the organizational structure of a text, such as chronological, compare-contrast, cause-effect, problem-solution, and evaluate its effectiveness. **WA.8.4.b** Write informational essays or reports, including research, that: provide a clear and accurate perspective on the subject *Also covered* **VO.8.4**

Lewis and Clark: Into the Unknown

Practicing the Standards

Informational Text and Vocabulary

1. Which of the following sentences *best* displays a **cause-and-effect** organization?

A Sacagawea joined the corps.
B Lewis needed a co-leader, so he hired Clark.
C The United States purchased the territory from France.
D The explorers searched for the Northwest Passage.

2. Because Lewis studied zoology, he was prepared to —

A teach the group to mountain climb
B plot the expedition's directions
C record previously unknown animals
D speak with American Indian groups

3. When the corps needed horses to cross mountains —

A the Mandans grew suspicious of them
B the explorers traveled around a waterfall
C the Hidatsa Indians formed a war party
D Sacagawea was hired as a translator

4. Which of the following is an **effect** of the expedition?

A The nation had information about the western U.S.
B The U.S. sold the territory to Spain at a profit.
C Canals were built, connecting the Atlantic to the Pacific.
D Peace was made with Indians west of the Mississippi.

5. Another term for *acquisition* is —

A territory
B exploration
C addition
D adventure

6. If you have *negotiated* a deal, you have —

A bargained
B purchased
C translated
D argued

7. A *corps* usually includes —

A water that can be navigated
B decisions made by a leader
C traveling equipment
D members with specific skills

Writing Focus Constructed Response

8. Why did Jefferson support the Corps of Discovery? What were the most significant effects of this expedition? Write your answer in the form of a paragraph.

What Do You Think Now?

What new insights into American history does this article offer?

MAGAZINE ARTICLE

Preparing to Read

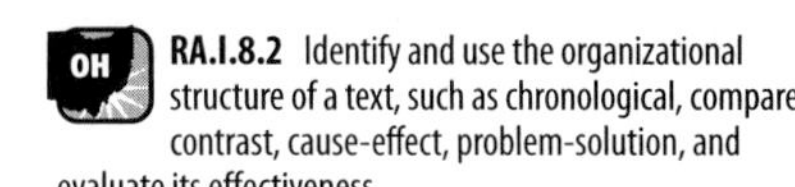

RA.I.8.2 Identify and use the organizational structure of a text, such as chronological, compare-contrast, cause-effect, problem-solution, and evaluate its effectiveness.

Lewis and Clark Revisited

Use your **RWN** to complete the activities for this selection.

Informational Text Focus

Comparison-and-Contrast Organization Comparing involves finding similarities; contrasting involves finding differences. Writers usually organize comparison-and-contrast information in these ways:

- **Block method** First, the writer discusses all the features of one subject. Then, the writer discusses all the features of another subject. For example, a writer comparing Jefferson with Lincoln could write about Jefferson first and then Lincoln.
- **Point-by-point method** The writer discusses one feature at a time, explaining how the feature relates to each subject. For example, to compare Jefferson with Lincoln, a writer might begin by discussing their education. Then, the writer could move on to another topic, such as their political beliefs.

Transition words in either organizational pattern can signal how ideas are related. Words like *both* and *neither* point to similarities; words like *but* and *however* highlight differences.

Into Action This article uses point-by-point organization. Use a chart to keep track of the features being compared and contrasted.

Point Under Discussion	Original Lewis and Clark Expedition	Reenactment of Expedition
Goal of expedition	economic; diplomatic	
U.S. population at the time		
Methods of navigation		

Vocabulary

commemorate (kuh MEHM uh rayt) *v.:* honor the memory of. *This event is planned to commemorate the anniversary of Lewis and Clark's journey.*

mimicking (MIHM ihk ihng) *v.* used as *adj.:* imitating; copying. *The travelers are mimicking the conditions of the original journey.*

resembles (rih ZEHM buhlz) *v.:* looks like. *This modern boat resembles one of the canoes that traveled down the Mississippi two hundred years ago.*

Language Coach

Spelling Patterns For some words that end in *c,* you add a *k* before adding an ending. For example, *panic* becomes *panicked,* and *garlic* becomes *garlicky.* The *k* helps you pronounce these words correctly. How does the word *mimicking* reflect this spelling pattern? What is the base form of this verb?

Writing Focus

Preparing for **Constructed Response**

As you read these selections, record key information about Lewis and Clark in your *Reader/Writer Notebook.*

Delve into vocabulary, using Word Watch at:

go.hrw.com L8-337

MAGAZINE ARTICLE

LEWIS AND CLARK REVISITED

by

Read with a Purpose

Read this article to find out how a modern group of adventurers followed in the footsteps of Lewis and Clark.

Build Background

The following article compares a historical reenactment, or re-creation of a historical event, to the actual historical event. Some reenactments focus on a specific event, such as a battle or an expedition. Other reenactments try to create an accurate portrait of a past period, such as the Middle Ages or Colonial America. All reenactments create a living history, bringing the past to life for both the participants and audiences. A viewing public can enjoy reenactments by visiting them in person, reading about them in magazines, or following Internet updates on them.

Discovery Expedition members David Cain (left) and Payton "Bud" Clark, great-great-great-grandson of William Clark.

President Thomas Jefferson's directions to Meriwether Lewis over 200 years ago were clear: Find and map "the most direct & practicable" waterway to the Pacific, share the country's intentions with people along the way, and record your findings. When Lewis and the rest of the Corps of Discovery stepped forth to explore the Louisiana Territory, however, most details about the terrain[1] and its waterways were murky or unknown.

To commemorate the bicentennial[2] of that courageous expedition, the Army Corps of Engineers facilitated a "journey of rediscovery," named the Discovery Expedition. Starting in 2003, as many as 177 participants, many of them retired military men and women, traveled the well-known Lewis and Clark trail. Around ten reenactors stayed with it from start to finish.

While Lewis and Clark had a diplomatic and economic mission, the reenactors' goals were primarily symbolic and educational. In Lewis and Clark's time, two-thirds of the U.S. population lived within 50 miles of the Atlantic. Now, Americans are spread across the land from sea to sea, details about the trail are available on the Internet, and the "reenactment" was just that, a kind of theater acted out by dedicated history buffs. **A**

STARTING OUT

Organizers of the Discovery Expedition took pains to be authentic but made concessions to time. Lewis, for instance, traversed the Ohio River with a keelboat using oars, poles, sails, or ropes for cordelling (pulling a boat along a waterway from the shore). In the reenactment, "Lewis" had a motor powering his craft. **B**

The bicentennial crew had supplies mimicking the originals'—within reason. Lewis and Clark brought medicines of the day, including "Rush's Pills," which had explosive powder and mercury in the mix. The first explorers smeared themselves with tallow and bear grease to fight mosquitoes.

Lewis and Clark made their first winter camp in Camp Wood, Illinois. Because the Mississippi has moved eastward, reenactors had to place their replica two miles from the original site. The original Corps of Discovery did not spend the cold months in video conferences with schools around the nation, as Discovery Expedition "explorers" did. Those on the modern trek ate venison and salt pork for authenticity but also enjoyed pizza and doughnuts donated by visitors.

1. **terrain:** surface features of land.
2. **bicentennial:** two-hundredth anniversary.

A **Read and Discuss** What has the author told you about the Discovery Expedition?

B **Informational Focus** **Compare and Contrast** What is being contrasted in this paragraph?

Vocabulary **commemorate** (kuh MEHM uh rayt) *v.:* honor the memory of.
mimicking (MIHM ihk ihng) *v.* used as *adj.:* imitating; copying.

ENCOUNTERS ALONG THE WAY

Lewis and Clark met friendly American Indians and adopted some of their ways, including abandoning their military uniforms for buckskin clothing, buffalo robes, and moccasins. The Mandan and Hidatsa peoples helped them pass the winter at Fort Mandan, providing maps for the trek ahead. But other groups threatened the expedition.

The reenactors heard just an echo of that: the Oto and Missouri chiefs welcomed them, for instance, as did the Omaha. The Yankton Sioux held a mock council in Nebraska. However, the Lakota came out in protest, saying that the journey opened "old wounds" about the government's treatment of them after the expedition. C

CHANGES TO THE LAND

The land only vaguely **resembles** the old countryside. The Missouri River stretch called the Missouri Breaks, wrote reporter Anthony Brandt, "still looks almost exactly as Lewis and Clark found it 200 years ago." Other aspects, such as the river system, have changed dramatically. Numerous dams and irrigation projects have left marks, as have agricultural and industrial pollution.

Forests of the Rockies, Cascades, and coastal ranges have been heavily cut and logged. There were 20 million acres of old-growth forest in Oregon and Washington. Now there are 2.3 million, according to Water Planet.

C Informational Focus **Compare and Contrast**
How were the reactions of American Indians to both expeditions similar and different?

Vocabulary **resembles** (rih ZEHM buhlz) *v.:* looks like.

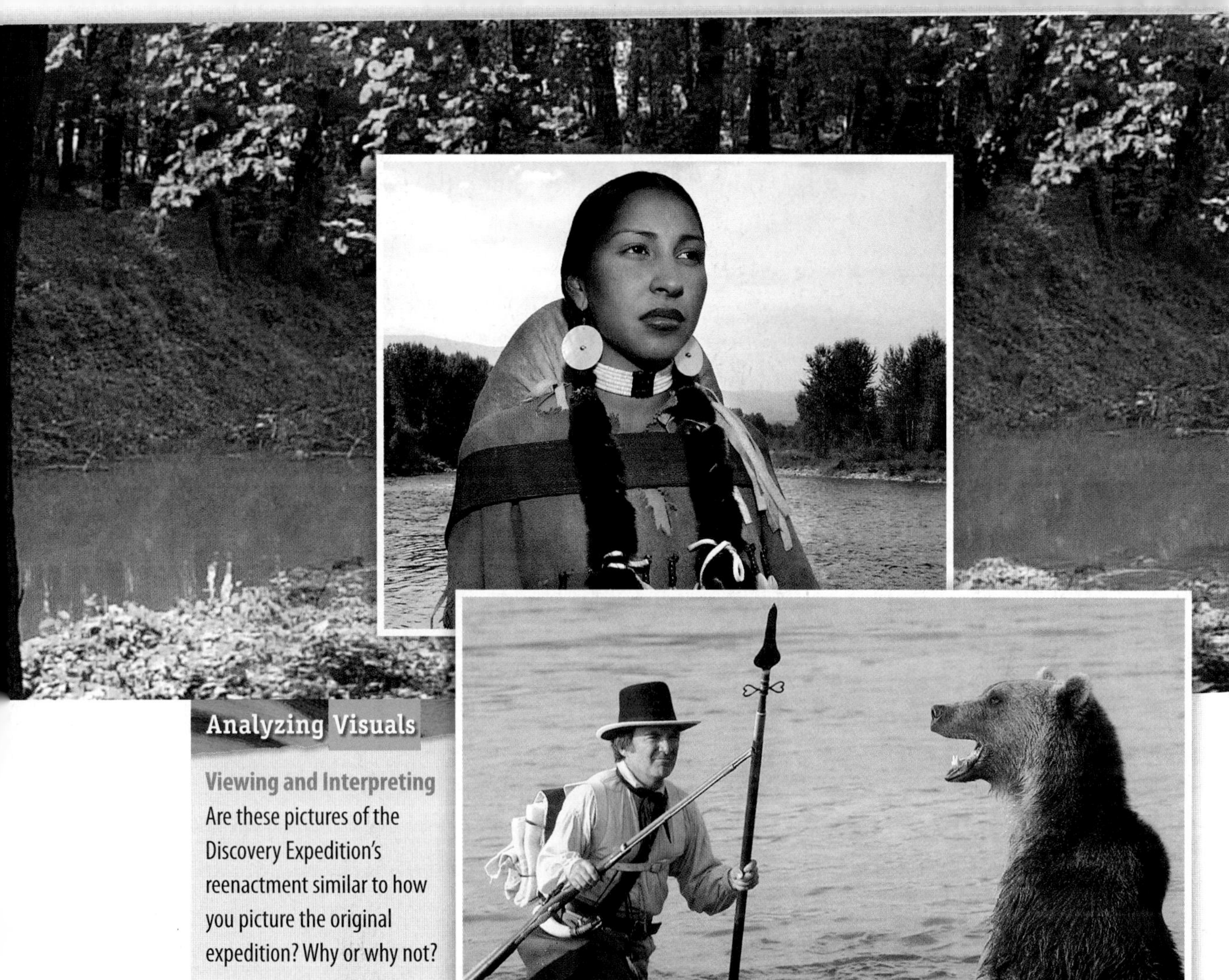

Analyzing Visuals

Viewing and Interpreting Are these pictures of the Discovery Expedition's reenactment similar to how you picture the original expedition? Why or why not?

Lewis and Clark recorded encounters with wildlife, including 40 grizzly kills. Today, these bears are endangered. There were as many as 100,000 from the Great Plains to the Pacific. Now they number about 1,000. **D**

When the original travelers tasted salmon for the first time at the Columbia River, Clark drew a picture of the free-running fish. Estimates place the fishes' population at 30 million then. Today it is closer to 300,000. **E**

D **Informational Focus** **Compare and Contrast** What transition words in this paragraph indicate that the writer is contrasting two different time periods?

E **Read and Discuss** How does this information add to what you have already learned about the two expeditions?

A LONGER HUMAN REACH

The original crew finished in September 1806, in St. Louis. In their day, that city's population was about 1,000. Today, wrote Brandt upon return, "that's fewer than attend a lot of high school football games."

Lewis and Clark returned with crucial knowledge about the United States and its inhabitants. The bicentennial crew, like the originals, accomplished much of what they set out to do—they renewed excitement about this pivotal trek in our country's history.

MAPS THEN AND NOW

The mapmaking tools of Lewis and Clark's time were the octant and the sextant, which determined longitude and latitude when the operator fixed them on the sun, the moon, or a star. Mapmakers marked space by using surveying tools that measured quarter miles. On water, nautical miles were measured by throwing a chain ahead in the water and noting the time taken to meet it.

Today, mapmaking has gone high tech. Satellites photograph sections of the earth, and computers analyze the sections. Maps are created by layering the information digitally. Satellites in global positioning systems can locate a position using beamed signals. **F**

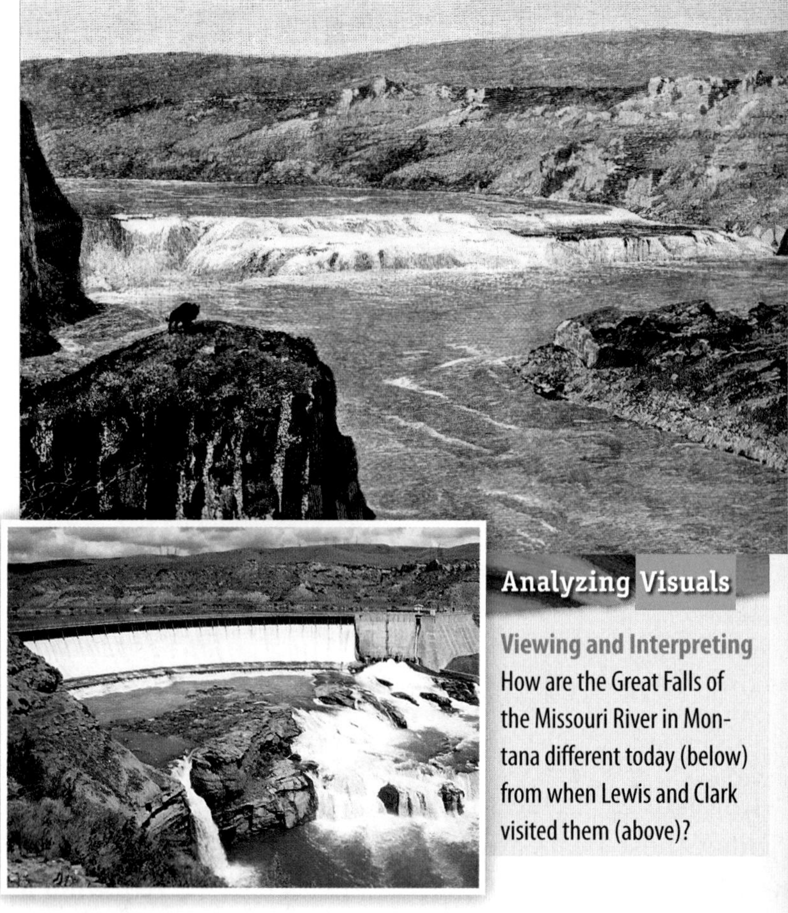

Analyzing Visuals

Viewing and Interpreting How are the Great Falls of the Missouri River in Montana different today (below) from when Lewis and Clark visited them (above)?

F **Read and Discuss** How does this new information change your impression of Lewis and Clark?

Read with a Purpose

How was the modern expedition similar to that of Lewis and Clark?

MAGAZINE ARTICLE
Applying Your Skills

RA.I.8.2 Identify and use the organizational structure of a text, such as chronological, compare-contrast, cause-effect, problem-solution, and evaluate its effectiveness. **WA.8.5.b** Write persuasive compositions that: support arguments with detailed evidence; *Also covered* **VO.8.4**

Lewis and Clark Revisited

Respond and Think Critically

Informational Text and Vocabulary

1. According to the subsection titled "Starting Out," which supplies of the original corps and the reenactors were **similar**?
   A They had medicine called Rush's Pills.
   B They used tallow to fight off mosquitoes.
   C They shared doughnuts and pizza.
   D They ate venison and salt pork.

2. According to the "Encounters Along the Way" subsection, the reenactors were welcomed by some American Indians. In **contrast,** the —
   A Lakota protested the modern explorers
   B Oto and Missouri chiefs greeted them
   C Hidatsa helped them through winter
   D modern men began wearing buckskin

3. According to "Changes to the Land," which aspect of the modern countryside is *most* **similar** to the countryside during Lewis and Clark's time?
   A Industrial changes have left no similarities.
   B Except for dams on rivers, all is the same.
   C Missouri has changed; Oregon is the same.
   D The Missouri Breaks has remained the same.

4. Both expeditions —
   A developed new mapmaking techniques
   B traveled the same route from Missouri to Oregon
   C employed the same amount of people
   D discovered previously unknown plants

5. Another term for *mimicking* is —
   A liking
   B imitating
   C sounding
   D running

6. If a man *resembles* his father, he —
   A is offended by him
   B dislikes him
   C looks like him
   D worries him

7. If a speaker *commemorates* a historical event, he or she —
   A honors the event
   B ignores the event
   C satisfies the event
   D recites at the event

Writing Focus Constructed Response

Do you think modern reenactments can help people appreciate both the past and the present? Share your opinion in an essay. Be sure to use details from the two selections to support your opinion.

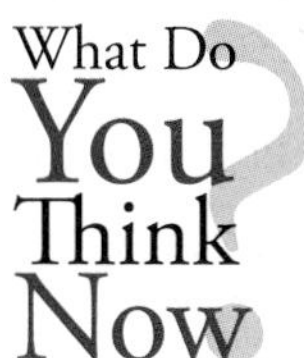

How might participating in a reenactment help you become a more informed citizen?

Writing Workshop

Response to Literature

Write with a Purpose

Write an essay in response to a piece of literature that you have read. Your **purpose** is to provide your reader with the basic information about the work and to share your interpretation and evaluation of it. Your **audience** is your classmates, who may or may not have read the work.

A Good Response to Literature

- engages the reader
- provides necessary background and vital information
- demonstrates careful reading
- includes insightful interpretations
- supports its judgments and opinions with examples
- refers directly to the work
- anticipates an audience's questions

See page 352 for complete rubric.

Think as a Reader/Writer

There are several ways to respond to literature. You could write an analysis of the plot, character, or theme, or you could write a review. Like a movie review, a review of a work of literature provides an analysis and evaluation of the work.

Before you write your own response to literature, read this excerpt from a review of a book entitled *The Best of Ray Bradbury*. The review was written and posted on the Internet by Jason Sacks.

> Ray Bradbury is one of the finest writers of science fiction and fantasy literature. His stories are taught in high school and college literature classes throughout the English-speaking world. He allowed EC Comics to adapt several of his stories in their science fiction comics in the 1950s. That series was unjustly ignored during the comics bust, but now it is back with a collection of some of the finest adaptations from that series.

← The reviewer identifies the author and engages the reader with interesting background facts.

> Mark Chiarello's adaptation of "A Piece of Wood" uses color in a spectacular way to illuminate the story of two men talking about a weapon that could forever end war. And Gibbons's take on "Come Into My Cellar" uses the artist's traditional comics style to great effect, wonderfully conveying the banality of his characters' lives through use of small panels that seem to be just slightly askew.

← Many **details** are provided to support the reviewer's opinion, including specific titles in the collection.

> This book is the ideal gift for a science fiction fan who is interested in comics. The worst of these stories are unmemorable; the best are wonderful examples of what happens when master creators play with each others' ideas.

← The reviewer offers his **recommendation** and anticipates a question, giving reasons to support his **opinions.**

Think About the Professional Model

With a partner, discuss the following questions about the model.

1. What is the overall tone of the review?
2. How does the author summarize his reaction to the collection?

Use your **RWN** to complete the activities for this workshop.

WA.8.2 Write responses to literature that organize an insightful interpretation around several clear ideas, premises or images and support judgments with specific references to the original text, to other texts, authors and to prior knowledge. **WA.8.5.a** Write persuasive compositions that: establish and develop a controlling idea; **WP.8.6** Drafting, Revising and Editing: Organize writing with an effective and engaging introduction, body and a conclusion that summarizes, extends or elaborates on points or ideas in the writing. **WP.8.16** Drafting, Revising and Editing: Apply tools to judge the quality of writing. **WP.8.12** Drafting, Revising and Editing: Add and delete information and details to better elaborate on a stated central idea and to more effectively accomplish purpose. **WP.8.7** Drafting, Revising and Editing: Vary simple, compound and complex sentence structures.

Prewriting

Choose a Literary Work

Which literary work will you be writing about? If your teacher hasn't assigned one, choose a work that you feel strongly about. Once you know which piece of literature you will be writing about, answer these questions:

- What is the title of the work? Carefully record it with the correct spelling, capitalization, and punctuation.
- Who is the author? Record his or her full name.
- What kind of work is it? a short story? a novel? a mystery?
- When was the work published?

Note Your Responses

After jotting down your answers to the questions above, think about how you responded to the work and record your reactions.

- What did you expect before you read the work?
- What kind of reaction did you have? Did you laugh? or cry?
- What did you notice about the style of the writing? Did the writer use vivid descriptive language? What point of view did the author use?
- Why might this work interest your audience?

Think About Audience and Purpose

Before you begin writing, think about who will read your review and what they will need to know. Also, identify your **purpose** for writing and how you want your writing to affect your **audience.**

Details About My Audience	What Is My Purpose?
• students • my age • may not have read work	• give basic information • evaluate work • recommend work

Idea Starters

- Review a story in your textbook.
- Review your favorite novel.
- Review the latest book in a popular series.
- Review a biography of a person you admire.

Writing Tip

As you begin, think about what makes the work special. Start by answering questions like these:

- Is the work like anything else you've read?
- How did the work surprise you?
- What else has the author written?
- Who was your favorite character?
- What kind of reader would enjoy this work?

Your Turn

Get Started Make notes in your **RWN** describing a piece of literature you will write about and your overall response to the work. Then, answer the questions on this page to expand on your response to the literature. Your notes will help you plan your review.

Learn It Online

Need help organizing your essay? Use the interactive graphic organizer at:

Writing Tip

When you write about literature, you should tell your reader what the work is about without retelling the story. Remember that some readers of your essay will have already read the work, but those who have not yet read it will want to discover surprises on their own.

Organize Your Ideas

What should you include in your review? As you plan what you will write, organize your ideas in an outline. A review should include the following:

- **Introduction:** Start with an engaging opening. Make sure to identify the type of work you're covering, the title, and the author. Introduce the main theme of work, and indicate your general reaction.
- **Body:** Here, you can note your interpretations and judgments. Back up your opinions by using examples from the story—such as short quotations.
- **Conclusion:** As you finish the review, try to predict what your readers' questions might be, and answer them here. Explain whether you would recommend this work, and end with a memorable closing statement.

Here's an example of one writer's plan. Use it as a model.

Introduction

Engaging Opening: "The best way to stop arguments is to get people to eat peanut butter sandwiches. They can't talk."
Work and Author: "Scout's Honor" by Avi
Type of Work: short story
Main Theme of Work: Friendship and courage can help people endure difficult circumstances.
My General Reaction: positive

Body

Interpretations and Judgments: The boys learn that admitting they are not as tough as the others takes more courage than going on.
Examples: The umbrella example shows the bonds of friendship.
Short Quotes: Max: "Naw. I wanted to quit but I wasn't tough enough to do it." Horse: "You saying I'm the one who's tough? I hate roughing it!"

Conclusion

Recommendations: I would recommend this story to my classmates and peers.
Closing Statement: Restate the theme of the story—that is, the importance of friendship, courage, and honor.

Your Turn

Plan Your Review Before writing your review, make a plan for its **introduction, body,** and **conclusion.** Share your plan with a classmate, and consider using his or her feedback to make changes to your plan.

Drafting

Follow Your Plan

Using your plan as a guide, draft your response to your chosen piece of literature. As you write, keep in mind the characteristics of a good response to literature, described on page 344. The framework at the right provides a quick reference for you as you draft.

Structure of Response to Literature

Introduction

- Begin with an engaging opening.
- Supply the author's name and the work's title and genre.
- Supply necessary background and main theme.
- Supply your general reaction.

Body

- Give your interpretation and judgments.
- Provide examples and support for each opinion, including quotes.

Conclusion

- Give recommendations.
- Close by restating the theme.

Use Examples

To help your readers understand the points you make, you should cite examples from the text. Notice that in his review of *The Best of Ray Bradbury*, Jason Sacks tells his readers exactly how a particular illustration adds to the story.

> ....Gibbons's take on "Come Into My Cellar" uses the artist's traditional comics style to great effect, wonderfully conveying the banality of his characters' lives through use of small panels that seem to be just slightly askew.

Grammar Link **Pronouns and Referents**

When writing a response to literature, you will be referring to characters, text passages, the author, and so on. Whenever you use a **pronoun** to stand for a **noun,** make sure the pronoun's **referent** (the noun that the pronoun stands for) is clear. Look at the example from the professional model to see how to make referents clear.

> Ray Bradbury is one of the finest writers of science fiction and fantasy literature. His stories are taught in high school and college literature classes throughout the English-speaking world. He allowed EC Comics to adapt several of his stories in their science fiction comics in the 1950s.

Because the writer mentions Bradbury in the first sentence, the *His* in the second sentence and the *he* and *his* in the third sentence are clear.

Writing Tip

You may want to quote passages from the work to help explain your response to the literature. Introduce the quoted material so that your reader knows where the quotation comes from, and enclose any quoted material between quotation marks. Remember to keep your quotations as short as possible. Quote just enough of a passage to illustrate your point, and then explain to your reader why the quote is important.

Your Turn

Write Your Draft Using the plan that you created, write a draft of your review. Think about these questions:

- What **examples** from the literary work can I include?
- What passages, if any, should I quote in the review?
- Are all my **pronoun referents** clear?

Peer Review

Using the chart at the right, you can help your partner give you useful feedback and suggestions by mentioning the kinds of questions you have about your draft.

- Is there a point in your draft that you think might need to be clarified? Direct your partner's attention to that point.
- Do you think you might need to expand your draft? Ask your partner where you might say more about an example or add another point.
- Are there questions on the Evaluating and Revising chart that you are not sure you've addressed in your essay? Point these out to your partner.

Evaluating and Revising

Read the questions in the left column of the chart, and then use the tips in the middle column to help you make revisions to your essay. The right column suggests techniques you can use to revise your draft.

Response to Literature: Guidelines for Content and Organization

Evaluation Questions	Tips	Revision Techniques
1. Does your introduction grab the reader's attention?	**Underline** an attention-getting sentence.	**Add** an interesting fact about the author or a striking quote from the work.
2. Have you given necessary information, including the title of the work and the author's full name?	**Circle** the title and author's name.	**Double-check** the correct spelling of the author's name and the title of the work.
3. Have you mentioned the genre and theme of the work in your introduction?	**Put a star** next to the word or phrase that names the theme.	**Add** a sentence describing what you think is the main theme of the work.
4. Does your draft mention the author's style and how the style does or does not contribute to the work?	**Circle** sentences about the author's style.	**Add** an example of the style and a sentence explaining your reaction to it.
5. Have you referred to the work, choosing quotations from the text that are just long enough to illustrate your point?	**Put wavy lines** under quotations.	**Cut** any part of a quotation that you do not need. **Replace** quotations to illustrate your point better.
6. Have you explained why you feel the way you do about the work, providing details to support your opinions?	**Put a check** beside sentences that explain your opinion.	**Add** a sentence of explanation after a sentence that expresses your opinion.
7. Have you anticipated audience questions and written a satisfying conclusion?	**Draw a box** around your conclusion.	**Add** a recommendation for the reader.

Read this student's draft, and notice the comments on its structure and suggestions for how the response could be improved.

Student Draft

More Than Just Camping

by Jenna Galper, Paradise Canyon Elementary

"The best way to stop arguments is to get people to eat peanut butter sandwiches. They can't talk." The narrator learns this lesson in Avi's short story "Scout's Honor." The narrator and his two friends must go on an overnight hike in the country to progress a level in Boy Scouts. The three boys use friendship, courage, and honor to guide them through their first camping trip.

← In the first paragraph, Jenna opens with an engaging **quote,** identifies the **title, author,** and **genre,** describes the basic **plot** situation, and states her **thesis,** or main idea.

The narrator, Horse, and Max share a special friendship. You can tell that throughout the story. No matter where they are or how bad the circumstances are, the boys still express their friendship and have fun.

← Jenna supports her main idea with an **example** of the characters' friendship.

MINI-LESSON How to Elaborate with Specific Examples

Jenna's second paragraph makes a point about the boys' helping each other, but she offers no evidence from the story. She can use a specific incident from the story to illustrate her point about the boys' friendship. Retelling the anecdote about the umbrella with specific details provides support. She also ends this addition with a comment on how the incident relates to their friendship. Here is how Jenna revised the second paragraph of her response.

Jenna's Revision of Paragraph Two

The narrator, Horse, and Max share a special friendship. ~~You can tell throughout the story.~~ *For example, when they are crossing the George Washington Bridge in the pouring rain, the narrator puts up his umbrella, with him in the middle and Horse and Max on either side. Max and Horse are still getting wet, so the narrator closes his umbrella and they all get equally soaked. If the three boys hadn't had such a great friendship, the narrator would have let his friends get soaked while he stayed dry in the middle.* No matter where they are or how bad the circumstances are, the boys still express their *special bond of* friendship and have fun.

Your Turn

Use Details Read your draft, and then ask yourself, "What details about the work would help to illustrate my points?"

Student Draft *continued*

Jenna adds a second example.

Another example of their outstanding bond is when, despite being cold and tired, the boys still found a way to have fun—FOOD FIGHT! No matter where they are, the narrator, Max, and Horse can always find a way to express their special bond and turn any situation into a celebration.

Jenna supports her main ideas with an **example** of the characters' courage.

Dialogue brings the example to life.

When the boys finally give up on their trip, the narrator is the first to admit that he isn't as tough as the other guys. Max responds by saying, "Naw. I wanted to quit but I wasn't tough enough to do it." Horse makes a fist and demands, "You saying I'm the one who's tough? I hate roughing it!" The boys realize that it takes more courage to admit that they aren't as tough as the others than it does to pretend that they are.

Jenna supports her thesis with an **example** of the characters' sense of honor.

The friends share a great understanding of honor and what it means. The boys promise each other that they won't tell the scout leader that they left early. They clasp hands, and the narrator says two simple words that sum up the whole story: "Scout's Honor."

Jenna sums up by restating her main idea as the **theme** of the story.

The three friends learn much more than just camping. They learn lessons they will never forget.

MINI-LESSON How to Write an Effective Closing Paragraph

In her draft, Jenna ends with a vague closing statement. What lessons do the friends learn? Were these lessons the theme of Avi's story? Jenna decides to improve her draft by restating the theme of the short story in her own words and linking it back to the title and author.

Jenna's Revision of Paragraph Six

In Avi's short story "Scout's Honor," three boys go into the country to learn new skills and earn a badge in Boy Scouts. However, ~~T~~the three friends learn much more than just camping. They learn life lessons they ~~will~~ can take with them forever: friendship, courage, and honor. ~~never forget~~.

Your Turn

Write an Effective Closing Statement With a partner, look over the **conclusion** of your review. If your conclusion is vague or weak, remember that you can improve it by using your own words to restate the **theme** of the work of literature you are reviewing.

Proofreading and Publishing

Proofreading

Re-read your essay for errors in grammar, usage, and punctuation. Pay special attention to the spelling of authors' and characters' names and to the spelling and punctuation in the title of your chosen work. Then, prepare your final copy to share with your audience.

Grammar Link Varying Sentence Structure

Be careful to avoid using the same sentence structure too much. In one of the last paragraphs, Jenna began three sentences with a noun. To vary the sentence structure and add emphasis, Jenna added an introductory phrase to one of the sentences.

> Above all else, the
> ~~The~~ friends share a great understanding of honor and what it means. The boys promise each other that they won't tell the scout leader that they left early. They clasp hands . . . ."

Publishing

Here are some ways to share your response to literature:

- Submit your essay to your school newspaper.
- E-mail your essay to a friend who you think will enjoy the literary work you wrote about.
- Submit your response to an online bookstore that publishes customer reviews.
- Post your work on your personal Web page or the author's Web page.

Reflect on the Process In your **RWN,** note what you learned while writing your response to literature. Then, answer the following questions:

1. How did writing about the literary work lead you to a better understanding or appreciation of it?
2. Was the tone of your response to literature knowledgeable yet friendly? How might you adjust your tone if you were writing this response for a different audience?
3. What new techniques or ideas about literary analysis did you learn in this workshop? How might you apply these techniques to analyzing other forms of literature?

Proofreading Tip

Exchange essays with a classmate, and take time to read each other's reviews carefully. Ask your classmate to read your draft for repetition in sentence structure and for punctuation errors. Is there a place where he or she would change your original sentence structure to add variety?

Your Turn

Proofread and Publish As you are proofreading, look carefully at whether you begin too many sentences in a row with a noun or an article. Where appropriate, add introductory phrases or rearrange word order to make your sentence structure more varied. When your draft is ready, share it with others.

Scoring Rubric

You can use one of the rubrics below to evaluate your response to literature from the Writing Workshop or from the activity on the next page. Your teacher will tell you to use either the four-point or the six-point rubric.

6-Point Scale

Score 6 *Demonstrates advanced success*
- focuses consistently on a clear thesis
- shows effective organization throughout, with smooth transitions
- offers thoughtful, creative ideas
- develops ideas thoroughly, using examples, details, and fully elaborated explanation
- exhibits mature control of written language

Score 5 *Demonstrates proficient success*
- focuses on a clear thesis
- shows effective organization, with transitions
- offers thoughtful ideas
- develops ideas competently, using examples, details, and well-elaborated explanation
- exhibits sufficient control of written language

Score 4 *Demonstrates competent success*
- focuses on a clear thesis, with minor distractions
- shows effective organization, with minor lapses
- offers mostly thoughtful ideas
- develops ideas adequately, with a mixture of general and specific elaboration
- exhibits general control of written language

Score 3 *Demonstrates limited success*
- includes some loosely related ideas that distract from the writer's focus
- shows some organization, with noticeable gaps in the logical flow of ideas
- offers routine, predictable ideas
- develops ideas with uneven elaboration
- exhibits limited control of written language

Score 2 *Demonstrates basic success*
- includes loosely related ideas that seriously distract from the writer's expository/informative purpose
- shows minimal organization, with major gaps in the logical flow of ideas
- offers ideas that merely skim the surface
- develops ideas with inadequate elaboration
- exhibits significant problems with control of written language

Score 1 *Demonstrates emerging effort*
- shows little awareness of the topic and purpose for writing
- lacks organization
- offers unclear and confusing ideas
- develops ideas in only a minimal way, if at all
- exhibits major problems with control of written language

4-Point Scale

Score 4 *Demonstrates advanced success*
- focuses consistently on a clear thesis
- shows effective organization throughout, with smooth transitions
- offers thoughtful, creative ideas
- develops ideas thoroughly, using examples, details, and fully elaborated explanation
- exhibits mature control of written language

Score 3 *Demonstrates competent success*
- focuses on a clear thesis, with minor distractions
- shows effective organization, with minor lapses
- offers mostly thoughtful ideas
- develops ideas adequately, with a mixture of general and specific elaboration
- exhibits general control of written language

Score 2 *Demonstrates limited success*
- includes some loosely related ideas that distract from the writer's focus
- shows some organization, with noticeable gaps in the logical flow of ideas
- offers routine, predictable ideas
- develops ideas with uneven elaboration
- exhibits limited control of written language

Score 1 *Demonstrates emerging effort*
- shows little awareness of the topic and purpose for writing
- lacks organization
- offers unclear, confusing ideas
- develops ideas in only a minimal way, if at all
- exhibits major problems with control of written language

Response to Literature

When responding to a prompt, use what you've learned from your reading, writing your response to literature, and studying the rubric on page 352. Use the steps below to develop a response to the following prompt.

Writing Prompt

Write a response to literature in which you evaluate a book or literary selection that you know well. Your response should encourage your audience—fellow students—to either read or not read the work. Provide details from the literature to support your opinions.

Study the Prompt

Read the prompt carefully, and identify all parts of your task. You must choose a book or other literary selection for your response. Your **response** must make your **opinions** clear. It must also provide several **details** from the work to support your opinions.
Tip: Spend about five minutes studying the prompt.

Plan Your Response

First, think of some books, stories, or poems that you have read recently. Then, choose the piece of literature that you know best. Once you have settled on your subject, jot down the following:

- the work's title, author, genre (novel, short story, poem) and the date of publication
- your reactions to the work
- what your readers need to know about the work

Your response will state your overall opinion of the work, but because your time is limited, you may want to focus on one or two elements that support your opinion. For example, if you thought the selection was depressing, you might focus on the author's use of gloomy images or settings.
Tip: Spend about ten minutes planning your response.

Respond to the Prompt

Using the notes you've just made, draft your response to literature. It may help to follow these guidelines:

- In the introduction, get your readers' attention with an engaging opening. Provide the title, author, and type of work; the basic situation; and your general reaction to the work.
- In the body of your response, use examples and short quotations to support your opinions.
- In the conclusion, anticipate and answer readers' questions and say whether you recommend the work. **Tip:** Spend about twenty minutes writing your draft.

Improve Your Response

Revising Go back to the key aspects of the prompt. Did you identify the work? Did you state your opinion clearly? Did you provide details?

Proofreading Take a few minutes to proofread your response to correct errors in grammar, spelling, punctuation, and capitalization. Make sure all your edits are neat, and erase any stray marks.

Checking Your Final Copy Before you turn in your response, read it one last time to catch any errors you may have missed. You'll be happy you made the extra effort. **Tip:** Save ten minutes to improve your response.

Presenting a Response to Literature

Speak with a Purpose

Adapt your written response to literature into an oral response. After you have rehearsed your response, present it to your class.

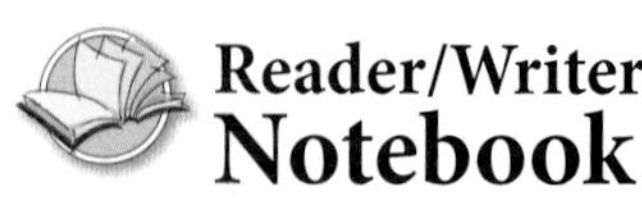

Use your **RWN** to complete the activities for this workshop.

Think as a Reader/Writer Throughout life, people will ask you for your responses to different subjects—perhaps to a musician's new album or to a business strategy at work. You will need to communicate your responses not only through writing but through speaking as well. Just as a writer keeps the readers in mind, you, as an effective speaker, will need to keep your listeners in mind when you present an oral response.

Adapt Your Response

Organize Your Presentation

An effective oral response to a piece of literature includes

- **a well-supported, insightful interpretation of the work.** Show your knowledge, and familiarize your audience with your topic.
- **a description of the writer's technique.** Identify and illustrate how the writer chooses and arranges his or her words.
- **an explanation of the literature's effects.** Describe the work's effects on its intended audience. Provide support for your inference.

As you consider what to include in your speech, think about your audience. What will interest them most? Decide the order in which to present your main ideas, and be sure to follow a coherent pattern of organization.

Organization of an Oral Review	
Introduction	Grab your audience's attention. Introduce the work by title and author, and give a brief preview of your main points. State your thesis in a way that suggests whether you recommend the work.
Body	Support your thesis primarily with references to the text, but also refer to other works of literature, to other authors, or to personal knowledge.
Conclusion	Restate your thesis, and make sure your recommendation is clear. Tell your audience how you believe the work will affect its readers.

OH **C.8.8.a** Deliver informational presentations that: demonstrate an understanding of the topic and present events or ideas in a logical sequence; **C.8.5** Demonstrate an understanding of the rules of the English language and select language appropriate to purpose and audience. **C.8.8.c** Deliver informational presentations that: include an effective introduction and conclusion and use a consistent organizational structure **C.8.9** Deliver formal and informal descriptive presentations that convey relevant information and descriptive details. **C.8.6** Adjust volume, phrasing, enunciation, voice modulation and inflection to stress important ideas and impact audience response. **C.8.7** Vary language choices as appropriate to the context of the speech.

Rehearse and Deliver Your Response

Put Yourself in the Audience's Shoes

One of the most important things you can do to keep your audience engaged is to make sure your presentation is clear and easy to follow. If someone gets confused while reading a review, he or she may take the time to re-read it. If someone gets confused while *listening* to a review, he or she may decide to daydream! As you rehearse your presentation, ask yourself the following questions:

- ✓ Are my **word choices** appropriate for my audience? Are there any technical terms I need to define? Is my vocabulary too simple or too advanced for my listeners?
- ✓ Am I enunciating clearly so that everyone can understand what I am saying? **Enunciation** refers to the distinctness of the sounds you make when you speak. Good enunciation is clear and precise. Poor enunciation often causes words to be slurred or word endings to be left off.
- ✓ Does the **pace** of my delivery sound unhurried, yet not so slow as to lull my listeners to sleep?

A Good Oral Response

- offers a clear interpretation of the piece of literature
- organizes ideas in a way that is easy to follow
- describes the writer's techniques
- explains how the work affects its audience
- includes support for the presenter's opinions
- uses effective words and clear pronunciation

Ask for Feedback

Practice delivering your presentation two or three times in front of your family or friends. As you practice, keep in mind the questions you answered above. After you have rehearsed your presentation, ask for feedback. Was anything you said confusing? Were your examples interesting, and did they support your points well? Use the feedback to rework your presentation as necessary.

Speaking Tip

Believe it or not, the audience may take their cues from you on how to respond to your presentation. Enthusiasm is contagious: The more engaged the audience feels *you* are, the more they will want to pay attention to your presentation.

Be Prepared

Prepare notecards to use as you give your presentation. Make your notes brief and clear so that they help you remember what you need to say but do not tempt you simply to read them to the class. Arrange your notecards in the order in which you want to present your ideas.

Learn It Online
Turn your response into a multimedia presentation. Find out how at MediaScope online:

go.hrw.com L8-355 

Literary Skills Review

Theme **Directions:** Read the two stories. Then, answer each question that follows.

The Dog and the Wolf by **Aesop** (6th cent. B.C.)

One cold and snowy winter the Wolf couldn't find enough to eat. She was almost dead with hunger when a House Dog happened by.

"Ah, cousin," said the Dog, "you are skin and bones. Come, leave your life of roaming and starving in the forest. Come with me to my master and you'll never go hungry again."

"What will I have to do for my food?" said the Wolf.

"Not much," said the House Dog. "Guard the property, keep the Fox from the henhouse, protect the children. It's an easy life."

That sounded good to the Wolf, so the Dog and the Wolf headed to the village. On the way the Wolf noticed a ring around the Dog's neck where the hair had been rubbed off.

"What's that?" she asked.

"Oh, it's nothing," said the Dog. "It's just where the collar is put on at night to keep me chained up. I'm used to it."

"Chained up!" exclaimed the Wolf, as she ran quickly back to the forest.

Better to starve free than to be a well-fed slave.

The Puppy by **Aleksandr Solzhenitsyn** (20th century)

translated by **Michael Glenny**

In our backyard a boy keeps his little dog Sharik chained up, a ball of fluff shackled since he was a puppy.

One day I took him some chicken bones that were still warm and smelt delicious. The boy had just let the poor dog off his lead to have a run round the yard. The snow there was deep and feathery; Sharik was bounding about like a hare, first on his hind legs, then on his front ones, from one corner of the yard to the other, back and forth, burying his muzzle in the snow.

He ran towards me, his coat all shaggy, jumped up at me, sniffed the bones—then off he went again, belly-deep in the snow.

I don't need your bones, he said. Just give me my freedom. . . .

RA.L.8.5 Identify and explain universal themes across different works by the same author and by different authors.

1. In the fable "The Dog and the Wolf," the Wolf decides to go to the village with the House Dog because the Wolf
   A. is cold.
   B. is hungry.
   C. wants an easier life.
   D. likes children.

2. What does the Wolf notice on the way to the village?
   A. children playing happily
   B. well-fed people
   C. a ring on the Dog's neck
   D. a strange smell

3. The Wolf considers the collar to be a symbol of
   A. freedom.
   B. slavery.
   C. honor.
   D. civilization.

4. In the story "The Puppy," the narrator brings Sharik food in order to
   A. steal him from the boy.
   B. teach him to beg.
   C. give him a treat.
   D. keep him from starving.

5. When Sharik rejects the food, the narrator
   A. understands a truth about life.
   B. is sorry for the puppy.
   C. feels angry and sad.
   D. realizes the puppy doesn't like him.

6. What do the House Dog and Sharik have in common?
   A. They both are chained at times.
   B. They both run away from home.
   C. They both are starving.
   D. They both hate their masters.

Short Answer

7. What theme do the fable from ancient Greece and the story from modern-day Russia have in common?

Extended Response

8. What do both the Wolf and Sharik want more than food? Use information from the passage to support your answer.

Informational Skills Review

Text Structures **Directions:** Read the selection. Then, answer each question that follows.

In EXTREME Culture Shock! by

Extreme sports take familiar athletics and give them a new twist or an extra push to the edge. Roller skating becomes aggressive in-line skating. Traditional skiing gives way to speed skiing, at more than 125 miles per hour.

From BMX racing to "up skiing," high-adrenaline sports have gone from obscurity to popularity, exerting influence on popular culture along the way. First, a daring athlete has a will to push the limits. Second, inventiveness is peaked among followers. Marketers sell new concepts inspired by extreme sports, using nontraditional advertising. Then, the mainstream catches on. The energy of X-sports pioneers can influence the larger population, carrying with it new ways of speaking, dressing, and acting.

Sports historians trace this rebel mind-set and its trend-setting ability to the 1950s, when masses of young people on the West Coast became surfers. The creation of smaller, cheaper cars allowed young men and women to chase waves along the coast, flaunting their independence from mainstream culture. Surfing hit the American market like a giant wave. Within a decade, the daring and individualistic extreme sport of surfing was making money not only for those selling boards and baggy shorts, but for people making movies about surfers and for anyone selling a product that could help someone look like a surfer.

In 1965, the "snurfer" was introduced: a surfboard for snow. Ten years later, straps were added—and snowboards filled traditional ski hills. In 1985, less than 10 percent of ski areas allowed snowboarders. Now there are more boarders than skiers.

Compared with traditional athletes, such as basketball players, extreme-sports competitors place less emphasis on team games and group practice. Typically, X-athletes take an individual sport such as skateboarding and apply their ingenuity and defiance to it. These athletes challenge the forces of nature more than one another.

Heroes among extreme-sports fans are athletes like Tony Hawk, a skateboarder who turned pro at 14, is a popular video-game avatar, and has his own clothing

RA.I.8.2 Identify and use the organizational structure of a text, such as chronological, compare-contrast, cause-effect, problem-solution, and evaluate its effectiveness. *Also covered* **RP.8.1; WA.8.4.d**

line. He has a rebel image, as opposed to a conventional baseball or football team player's.

The extreme-sport mind-set has not stopped at the U.S. border. South Africa welcomed a hotel chain that celebrates extreme sports activities, and the first extreme sports club opened in Kyrgyzstan. The X-Games, first held in 1995, attracted competitors from around the world. Like its marketing in the States, global sales around X-sports are *extreme*!

1. According to this article, what is an initial cause in the development of extreme sports?
   A. a love of team play
   B. influence from marketing
   C. a wish to make money
   D. a desire to push limits

2. Which of the following sentences shows a cause-and-effect organization?
   A. The excitement of extreme sports has sparked global sales.
   B. Basketball started out as an extreme sport.
   C. Extreme sports begin as mainstream activities.
   D. Snowboarding is now more popular than snow skiing.

3. The sentence "He has a rebel image, as opposed to a conventional baseball or football team player's" is an example of
   A. a comparison.
   B. a contrast.
   C. a cause.
   D. an effect.

Short Answer

4. Explain how extreme sports differ from conventional sports. Use information from the passage to support your answer.

Extended Response

5. Think about a physical sport that you play or that you know how is played. Is this sport an extreme sport or a traditional sport? Compare and contrast the features of your sport with those of other sports to see which category it belongs in.

OH **VO.8.1** Define unknown words through context clues and the author's use of comparison, contrast and cause and effect. *Also covered* **VO.8.4**

Vocabulary Skills Review

Multiple-Meaning Words

Directions: Choose the answer in which the boldfaced word is used in the same way it is used in the quoted sentences from "Gentleman of Río en Medio" and "The Medicine Bag."

1. "The old man **bowed** to all of us in the room. Then he removed his hat and gloves, slowly and carefully."
   A. The old steps were bowed.
   B. The violin players bowed in rhythm.
   C. After the show, the dancers bowed.
   D. The arches of the ceiling bowed above us.

2. "There was a great **deal** of conversation about rain and about his family."
   A. It was her turn to deal the cards.
   B. She got a deal when she bought that car.
   C. She can't deal with that noisy dog.
   D. The arrangement brought her a good deal of money.

3. "I kept **still** and let him have his say."
   A. In the still of the night, no bird sings.
   B. The mouse stood very still.
   C. I still like that old sweater.
   D. Do you still want to go to the movie?

4. "He was our great-grandfather, and he didn't live in a tepee, but all by himself in a part **log,** part tar-paper shack."
   A. The waitress had to log her work hours.
   B. The lumberjacks log for a living.
   C. Please sign your name in our visitor's log.
   D. I sat down to rest on a log.

5. "I wanted to **sink** right through the pavement."
   A. If you do not swim, you will sink.
   B. Please put your dishes in the sink.
   C. I want my explanation to sink in.
   D. Do not sink your time into that silly project.

6. "Grandpa slowly **rose** from the bed and stood upright in front of me."
   A. This rose smells so sweet!
   B. He rose from his seat when called.
   C. The shoes were a dark rose color.
   D. The leader quickly rose to power.

Academic Vocabulary

Directions: Choose the correct definition for each boldfaced Academic Vocabulary word.

7. Many short stories **convey** a message about life.
   A. reveal
   B. transport
   C. contradict
   D. support

8. The **consequence** of an action is its
   A. cause.
   B. climax.
   C. meaning.
   D. result.

Writing Skills Review

WA.8.2 Write responses to literature that organize an insightful interpretation around several clear ideas, premises or images and support judgments with specific references to the original text, to other texts, authors and to prior knowledge. *Also covered* **WP.8.12; WP.8.13**

Response to Literature

Directions: Read the following passage from a book review. Then, answer each question that follows.

(1) In *Red Scarf Girl,* Ji-li Jiang not only writes a compelling autobiography, she makes the history of the Communist Chinese Cultural Revolution come alive for her readers. (2) The story takes place in Communist China. (3) Her story begins in 1966, when she was twelve years old. (4) Always an excellent student, Ji-li Jiang is shocked to discover that her talent will not be enough for her to get ahead in the new Communist society. (5) She is at a disadvantage because her deceased grandfather had been a wealthy landlord, something that is looked down upon. (6) Many terrible things happen to Ji-li Jiang and her family. (7) Terrible things happen to many innocent people in China at this time. (8) I recommend this book to anyone who would like to meet an interesting girl growing up in difficult times and to anyone who would like to learn about Chinese history.

1. Which transitional word or phrase would add clarity to the first sentence?
   A. but also
   B. because
   C. and so
   D. nevertheless

2. Which sentence is unnecessary for the review and can be deleted?
   A. Sentence 1
   B. Sentence 2
   C. Sentence 5
   D. Sentence 8

3. This passage could be improved by —
   A. providing stronger opinions
   B. adding examples from the story text
   C. combining sentences
   D. giving background information about communism

4. What would be the best way to combine sentences 6 and 7?
   A. Many terrible things happen to Ji-li Jiang's family, and many terrible things happen to other innocent people in China at this time.
   B. Many terrible things happen to innocent people in China at this time, including Ji-li Jiang and her family.
   C. Ji-li Jiang and her family suffered terribly at that time in China, along with other innocent people.
   D. Other innocent people in China at this time had terrible things happen to them and to Ji-li Jiang and her family.

Read On

Fiction

Bud, Not Buddy

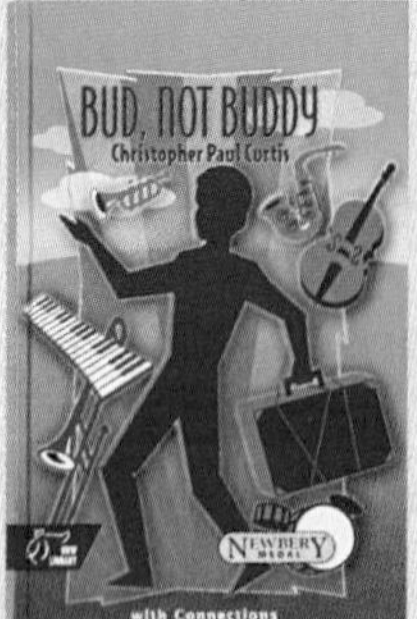

Bud—not Buddy—has gotten bad treatment in orphanages and foster homes, so he runs off in search of his father. Bud does not know his father but suspects that he is a member of the famous jazz band the Dusky Devastators of the Depression! Bud finds both adventure and trouble during his search in *Bud, Not Buddy.* This heartwarming and hilarious novel by Christopher Paul Curtis won a Newbery Medal.

Goodbye, Vietnam

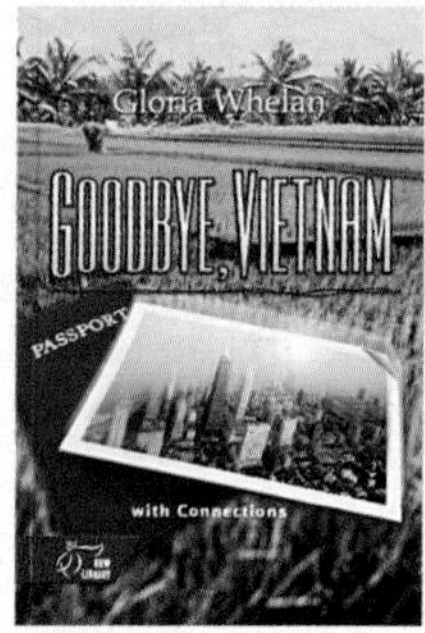

One of the messages in the famous speech by Dr. Martin Luther King, Jr., is that freedom does not come easily for everyone; some people must face injustice and treachery before they can be free. You'll find a character determined to find freedom no matter how dire the situation in Gloria Whelan's *Goodbye, Vietnam.* Thirteen-year-old Mai and her family are forced to leave Vietnam for Hong Kong. The voyage is difficult, but they are determined to persevere so that they can eventually start a new life in the United States.

The Maze

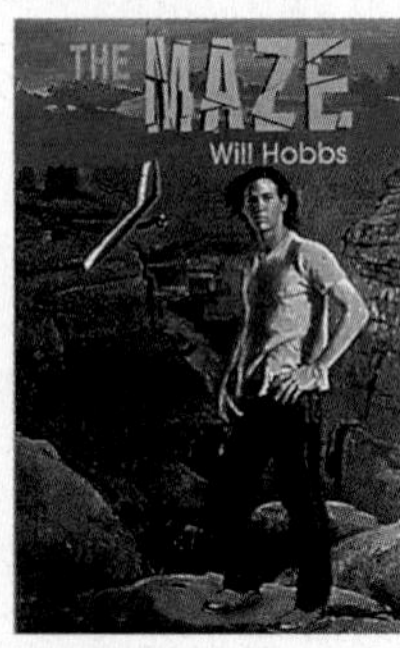

Rick Walker doesn't know where to turn when he is lost and alone. Luckily, a biologist named Lon Peregrino befriends Rick. Lon is dedicated to preserving the nearly extinct California condors that reside by the Maze, a landscape of beautiful, deep canyons. In Will Hobbs's novel *The Maze,* Rick helps Lon protect the condors from extinction while following his own dreams of flight.

The Friends

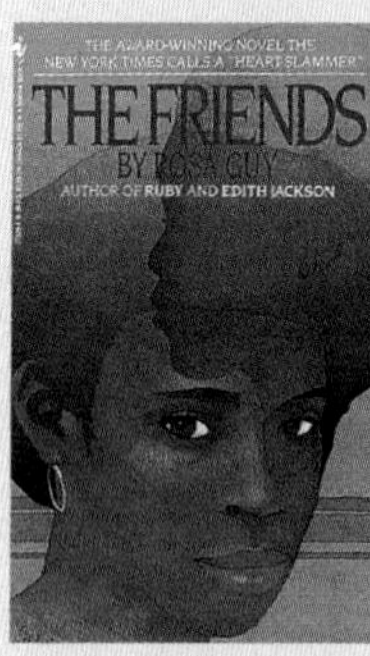

You may know her: the new kid in class whom no one seems to want for a friend. In *The Friends* by Rosa Guy, the new girl is Phyllisia Cathy, and she is from the West Indies. The only person who will befriend her is Edith, a Harlem-born girl who is trying as hard as she can to keep her family together despite facing the hardships of poverty.

Nonfiction

The Captain's Dog: My Journey with the Lewis and Clark Tribe

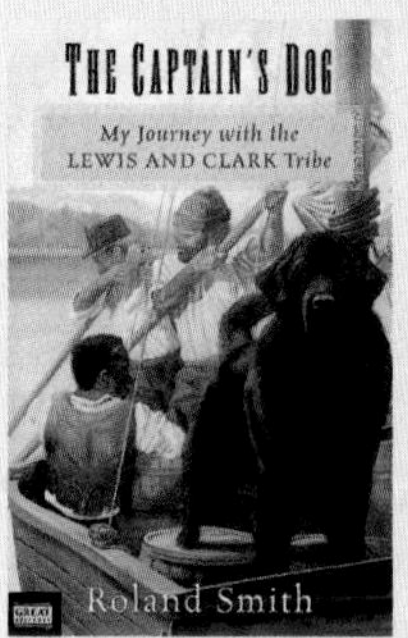

We all have read about history from a human's point of view, but what about a dog's point of view? In *The Captain's Dog,* Roland Smith takes us inside the mind of Captain Lewis's dog, named Seaman. As Lewis and Clark embark on their adventure across America, Seamen shares his own account of the beautiful country, the harsh conditions, and the trailblazing spirit that changed the United States.

The Flight of Red Bird: The Life of Zitkala-Sa

When Gertrude Bonnin was eight years old, she was removed from a Sioux reservation and placed in a boarding school in Indiana. She resisted when her instructors tried to make her renounce her customs. Instead she renamed herself Zitkala-Sa (Red Bird). As an adult, she made people aware of the harsh treatment American Indians were enduring. Doreen Rappaport tells this brave woman's story in *The Flight of Red Bird: The Life of Zitkala-Sa.*

Sacajawea

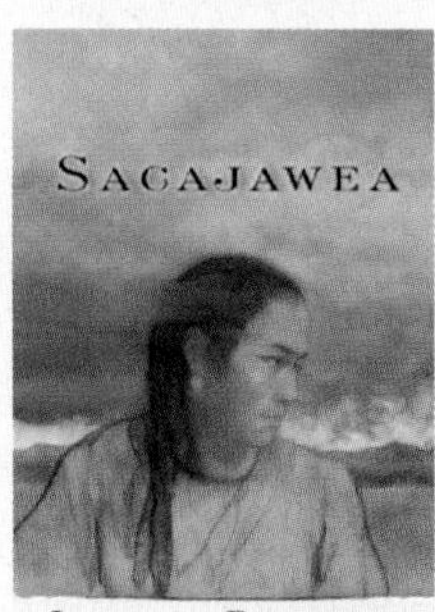

As a translator, peacemaker, caretaker, and guide, Sacajawea was indispensable to the success of the Lewis and Clark expedition. By many accounts, the whole undertaking would have failed without the aid of this famous American Indian. In *Sacajawea,* Joseph Bruchac provides a firsthand look at the journey through the alternating viewpoints of Sacajawea and William Clark.

Immigrant Kids

Today, the only work most children in the United States have to worry about is schoolwork, but this was not always the case. In *Immigrant Kids,* Russell Freedman explores how young people lived in the late nineteenth and early twentieth centuries, when children often had to work under unsafe, exhausting conditions.

Learn It Online
Master your understanding of longer works with *NovelWise* at:
go.hrw.com L8-363 

COLLECTION 4

Style

INFORMATIONAL TEXT FOCUS
Evaluating a Summary

"Could it think, the heart would stop beating."

—Fernando Pessoa

What Do You Think? Is it better to act from the mind or from the heart?

Heart flowers (20th century) by St. Pierre. Haitian art.

Learn It Online
Find out more about the authors in this collection at the Writers' Lives site online:

go.hrw.com L8-365 

Literary Focus

by **Sara Kajder**

How Do You Determine an Author's Style?

When you hear the word *style,* you may immediately think of the way your friends dress or the way a baseball player swings a bat. That's because a person's style is created by *how* he or she does something—such as wear clothes or play a sport. You can determine an author's style by looking at how he or she uses language.

Style

Every writer has a style, though some styles are more easily recognized than others. Dr. Seuss, for example, is known for his regular rhythm, rhyme patterns, and invented words.

Word Choice Most writers do not try to come up with a new style. Rather, their style comes from the choices they make when they put words on a page. A long word or a short one? A simple sentence or one that is long and complex? The decisions they make determine their styles.

Tone and Mood A writer's word choice sets the work's **tone** (or attitude) and **mood** (or feeling). Edgar Allan Poe, for example, chooses scary words that establish an eerie mood in "The Tell-Tale Heart."

> True!—nervous—very, very nervous I had been and am; but why *will* you say that I am mad? The disease had sharpened my senses—not destroyed—not dulled them. Above all was the sense of hearing acute.
>
> from "The Tell-Tale Heart" by Edgar Allan Poe

Literary Devices

Another way to determine an author's style is to examine his or her use of **literary devices.** These include imagery, dialect, and symbols.

Imagery Language that creates word pictures and appeals to our senses is called **imagery.** Images make us feel as if we are seeing (or hearing, touching, tasting, or smelling) what the writer is describing.

Dialect **Dialect** is a way of speaking that is characteristic of a particular place or group of people. Stories written in dialect convey an instant sense of time and place.

Symbols People, places, or events that have meaning in themselves but that also stand for something else are called **symbols.** In Francisco Jiménez's "The Circuit," cardboard boxes are used to carry the family's belongings, but they also symbolize the frequent moves the family makes to earn a living.

RA.L.8.8 Explain ways in which the author conveys mood and tone through word choice, figurative language, and syntax.

Figurative Language

An important part of many writers' style is their use of **figures of speech**—expressions that are not literally true but that suggest similarities between usually unrelated things. **Similes** compare two unlike things using a word of comparison such as *like, than, as,* or *resembles.*

> . . . I'm on my back looking at the sky, trying to pretend I'm in the country, but I can't because even grass in the city feels hard as sidewalk.
>
> from "Raymond's Run" by Toni Cade Bambara

Metaphors compare unlike things directly, without using a specific word of comparison.

> Suddenly I felt the weight of hours, days, weeks, and months of work.
>
> from "The Circuit" by Francisco Jiménez

Personification speaks of a nonhuman or inanimate thing as if it had human or lifelike qualities.

> I saw that dreaming coming into her eyes. I saw the fire that said to practice.
>
> from "Dancer" by Vickie Sears

Idioms are expressions that mean something different from the literal meanings of the words.

> "That new girl should give you a run for your money."
>
> from "Raymond's Run" by Toni Cade Bambara

Irony

Another aspect of writers' style is **irony**—what happens when reality contradicts what we expect.

Verbal irony occurs when we say one thing and mean something else. For example, a friend might say, "That's just great" in a disgusted tone.

Situational irony is a situation that turns out to be the opposite of what we'd expect; for example, a police chief is arrested for burglary.

Dramatic irony occurs when we know something that a character doesn't know; for example, we don't want the heroine to go down the dark hall because we know what she'll find there.

Your Turn

Read this passage, and identify which statement below correctly describes its style.

> But what bothered him even more was when his father's eyes went away.
>
> Usually it happened when it didn't cause any particular trouble. Sometimes during a meal his father's fork would stop halfway to his mouth, just stop, and there would be a long pause while the eyes went away, far away.
>
> from "Stop the Sun" by Gary Paulsen

Style 1	Style 2
The writer uses imagery and idioms to create a light tone about a serious subject.	Repetition and vivid imagery help show a young man's struggle to understand his father.

Learn It Online

To learn how to recognize these literary elements in longer works, visit *NovelWise* at:

go.hrw.com L8-367 

Analyzing Visuals

How Can You Analyze Style in Paintings?

A writer's style is created by elements such as word choice and tone. A painter's style, on the other hand, is created by the use of line, color, shape, and use of light and shadow. As you compare these paintings, consider the elements and effect of each artist's style.

1. Is the subject of this painting depicted in a realistic or an abstract manner?

2. What are the dominant colors of the portrait? What mood do these colors evoke?

3. Gilbert was Washington's official portraitist. How is the style of this painting suited to a historical portrait?

George Washington (*c.* 1797), by Gilbert Stuart (1755–1828). Oil on canvas, (30" x 24").

RA.L.8.8 Explain ways in which the author conveys mood and tone through word choice, figurative language, and syntax.

4. This painting, an example of cubism, breaks subjects into geometrical shapes. Is Washington portrayed realistically or abstractly?

5. What elements of the artist's style are most prominent? What is the effect of the painter's style?

George Washington (1932), by Alfred Maurer (1868–1932). Oil on composition board, (40" x 24"). Gift of Mr. & Mrs. Graaff. Portland Art Museum.

Analyzing a Painting's Style

Use these guidelines to help you analyze style in a painting.

1. Identify the painting's subject. Is the work realistic or abstract?
2. Study the composition. Is the work full of details or more spare? Is the subject close up or at a distance?
3. Observe the artist's color choices. Are the colors bright and vibrant? dark and muted?
4. Look at the lines in the painting. Are there sharp outlines, or do they blur into an image? Are the lines rough or fine? curved or straight?
5. Ask yourself, "How do these style elements help reveal the artist's purpose?"

Your Turn Write About Style

Study the two portraits of George Washington, and compare their styles. What does each painter's style reveal about his purpose? How do the artists' styles affect the mood and tone of each portrait?

Reading Focus

by **Kylene Beers**

What Reading Skills Help You Understand Style?

In order to determine a writer's style, you probably know to look for the literary devices the writer uses—such as word choice, figures of speech, symbols, dialect, and irony. What reading skills will help you find those elements? Try these skills to get started.

Paraphrasing

When you **paraphrase,** you restate a text in your own words. A paraphrase is different from a summary, in which you restate only the most important points. Any time you paraphrase, you should include all the information that is in the original.

Paraphrasing helps you understand difficult lines of poetry and sentences written in an old-fashioned or unfamiliar style. Paraphrasing also helps you appreciate an author's style. When you compare your paraphrase with the original, you will be able to see differences in style.

Look at this passage from Vickie Sears's "Dancer" along with a paraphrase.

Original Text	Paraphrase
"Tell you how it was with her. Took her to a dance not long after she come to live with us. Smartest thing I ever done."	I'll tell you what happened. I took her to a dance soon after she came to live with us. It was the smartest thing I ever did.

You can easily see that the original text is written in dialect and gives us a strong feeling for the narrator's voice. The paraphrase is written in standard English and tells us little about the narrator.

Analyzing Details

Analyzing details can help you understand what you read. Such analyzing helps you follow a plot, visualize a setting, understand characters, and figure out a theme. Analyzing details can also help you appreciate an author's style.

Look at the details in this passage from Francisco Jiménez's "The Circuit." Consider the length and complexity of Jiménez's sentences. Also, look for figures of speech, strong images, and the level of vocabulary he uses.

> The garage was worn out by the years. It had no windows. The walls, eaten by termites, strained to support the roof, full of holes. The dirt floor, populated by earthworms, looked like a gray road map.
>
> from "The Circuit"
> by Francisco Jiménez

Besides giving us a clear picture of the family's new home, the passage also reveals aspects of the author's style. Francisco Jiménez uses both short and long sentences, with occasional figures of speech ("like a gray road map"). He also uses an adult vocabulary ("strained," "populated") as he looks back on a difficult childhood experience.

RP.8.1 Apply reading comprehension strategies, including making predictions, comparing and contrasting, recalling and summarizing and making inferences and drawing conclusions. **RA.I.8.7** Analyze an author's argument, perspective or viewpoint and explain the development of key points.

Reading Aloud

You have probably been asked to **read aloud** by your teacher to demonstrate understanding or fluency—the smoothness with which you read. Reading aloud can also be fun. For example, you may read aloud dialogue from stories to get the flavor of the characters' conversation. Reading aloud can also enable you to hear what the author's style sounds like.

"The Tell-Tale Heart" has no dialogue. The story consists of a long monologue delivered by the narrator to an unspecified "you." But reading some of the story aloud can give you clues to the narrator's personality and to the author's style. What do you learn about Edgar Allan Poe's style from reading this passage aloud?

> Ha! Would a madman have been so wise as this? And then, when my head was well in the room, I undid the lantern cautiously—oh, so cautiously—cautiously (for the hinges creaked)—I undid it just so much that a single thin ray fell upon the vulture eye.
>
> from "The Tell-Tale Heart"
> by Edgar Allan Poe

You might notice, as you gasp for breath, that Poe uses long sentences. By having the narrator repeat himself and throw in parenthetical (or side) comments, Poe also shows that the narrator is—at the very least—highly agitated. You might also notice that Poe uses words that make the passage sound rather weird and scary ("madman," "hinges creaked," and "vulture eye").

Drawing Conclusions

A conclusion is your final thought or judgment about something. To **draw conclusions** about an author's style, consider details from the text and decide how they contribute to the style.

Your Turn

Read the following passage aloud. Then, answer the questions below.

> So I'm strolling down Broadway breathing out and breathing in on counts of seven, which is my lucky number, and here comes Gretchen and her sidekicks: Mary Louise, who used to be a friend of mine when she first moved to Harlem from Baltimore and got beat up by everybody till I took up for her on account of her mother and my mother used to sing in the same choir. . . .
>
> from "Raymond's Run"
> by Toni Cade Bambara

1. What details of Bambara's style do you notice? What conclusions can you draw from them?
2. Paraphrase the passage, and compare your paraphrase with the original.

Now go to the Skills in Action: Reading Model

Learn It Online

Learn with graphics. Use the *PowerNotes* version of this lesson at:

go.hrw.com L8-371 

SKILLS IN ACTION
Reading Model

SHORT STORY

Build Background

The mother in the following story refers to the tragic opera *Madama Butterfly* by Giacomo Puccini. In the opera, a U.S. naval officer stationed in Japan marries a young Japanese woman, Butterfly, and then returns to the United States. She waits faithfully for him, with their child, for years. After he returns to Japan with an American wife, Butterfly commits suicide.

Read with a Purpose Read to discover a mother's advice.

A SMART COOKIE

from
The House on Mango Street

by **Sandra Cisneros**

Reading Focus

Analyzing Details Notice how Cisneros doesn't use quotation marks to set off dialogue. This aspect of Cisneros's style makes the story seem less formal and more intimate.

I could've been somebody, you know? my mother says and sighs. She has lived in this city her whole life. She can speak two languages. She can sing an opera. She knows how to fix a TV. But she doesn't know which subway train to take to get downtown. I hold her hand very tight while we wait for the right train to arrive.

She used to draw when she had time. Now she draws with a needle and thread, little knotted rosebuds, tulips made of silk thread. Someday she would like to go to the ballet. Someday she would like to see a play. She borrows opera records from the public library and sings with velvety lungs powerful as morning glories.

Literary Focus

Symbol Madame Butterfly can be seen as a symbol for women who are overly dependent on men and cannot take care of themselves.

Dialect Read this paragraph aloud to hear the mother's voice and dialect.

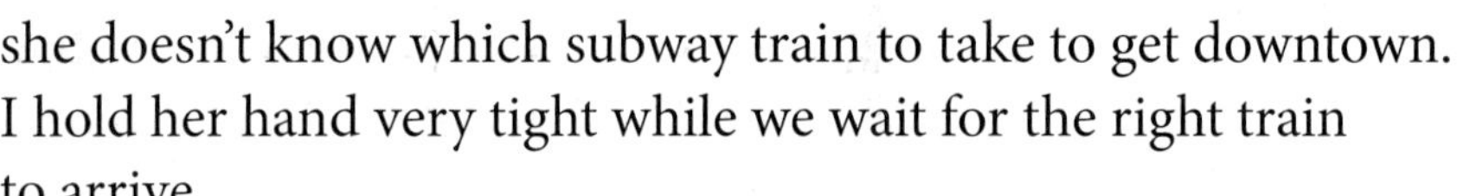

Today while cooking oatmeal she is Madame Butterfly until she sighs and points the wooden spoon at me. I could've been somebody, you know? Esperanza, you go to school. Study hard. That Madame Butterfly was a fool. She stirs the oatmeal. Look

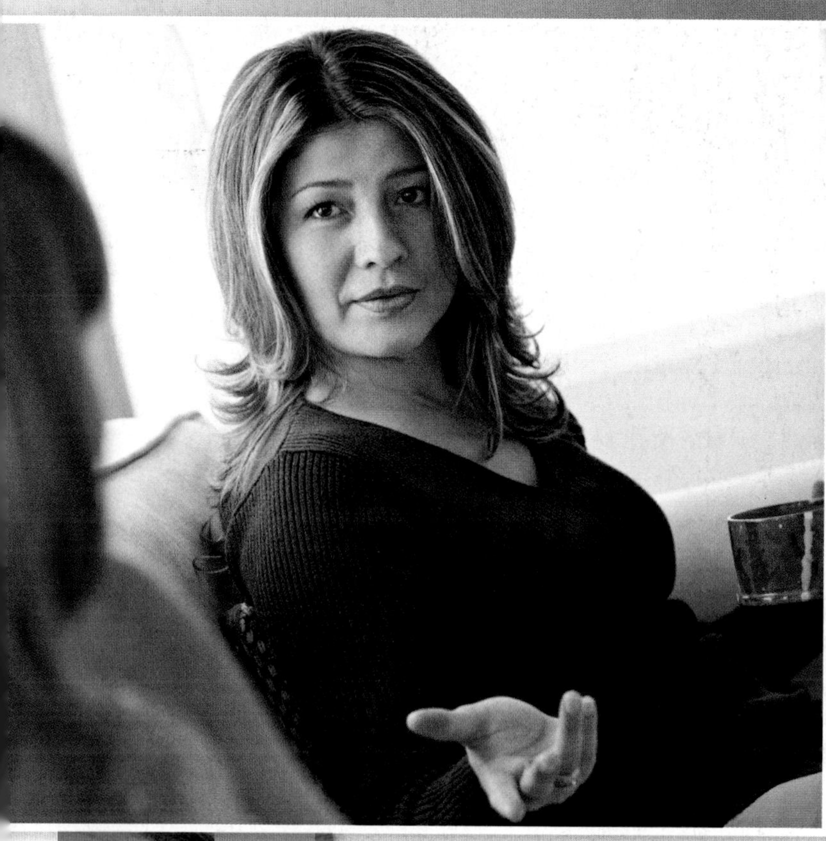

Analyzing Visuals **Viewing and Interpreting** What quote from the story would you choose to go with this photo? Why?

at my comadres.[1] She means Izaura whose husband left and Yolanda whose husband is dead. Got to take care all your own, she says shaking her head.

Then out of nowhere:

Shame is a bad thing, you know. It keeps you down. You want to know why I quit school? Because I didn't have nice clothes. No clothes, but I had brains.

Yup, she says disgusted, stirring again. I was a smart cookie then.

1. **comadres** (koh MAH drays): Spanish for "close female friends" (literally, a child's mother and godmother).

Literary Focus

Irony The last sentence of the story is an example of verbal irony: The mother says the opposite of what she means.

Read with a Purpose What advice does Esperanza's mother give her? Why does she give her this advice?

MEET THE WRITER

Sandra Cisneros

(1954–)

A Daughter's Independence

Like Esperanza, Sandra Cisneros grew up in a Mexican American family in Chicago. The only daughter in a family of seven children, she often felt as if she had "seven fathers." Her father expected her to take on a traditional female role in adult life. Instead, she chose an artist's path, developing a voice that speaks for generations of Mexican American women.

Her Own Style

Cisneros is known for her strong, precise, and colorful style. She often bases her stories on her own experiences and family history. Her bicultural upbringing also heavily influences her style. Cisneros often includes Spanish with her English prose. She writes:

> "I know how much of a role Spanish plays, even when I write in English. If you take [*The House on*] *Mango Street* and translate it, it's Spanish. The syntax, the sensibility, the diminutives, the way of looking at inanimate objects. . . . Incorporating the Spanish, for me, allows me to create new expressions in English. . . ."

Think About the Writer What qualities do you think enabled Cisneros to follow her own path?

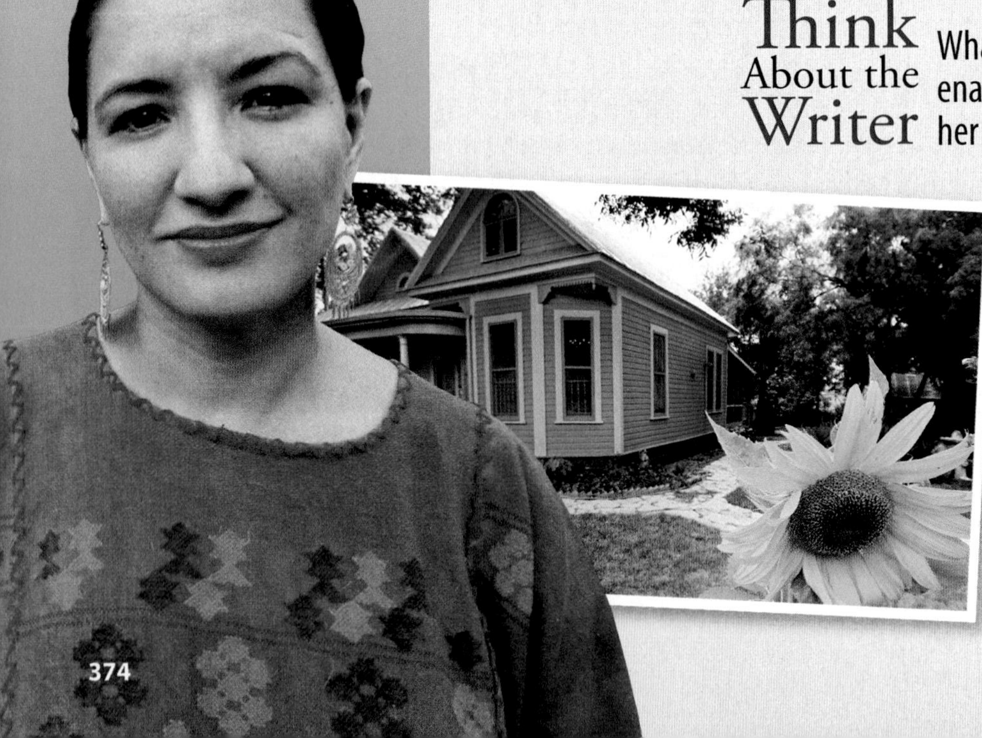

RA.L.8.8 Explain ways in which the author conveys mood and tone through word choice, figurative language, and syntax. RA.L.8.3 Explain how authors pace action and use subplots, parallel episodes and climax. *Also covered* VO.8.7

Into Action: Analyzing Details to Determine Tone

Review "A Smart Cookie," and look for details that set the story's tone. Write the details in the outer circles of a detail map like the one below. In the inner circle, write the word or words that describe the tone.

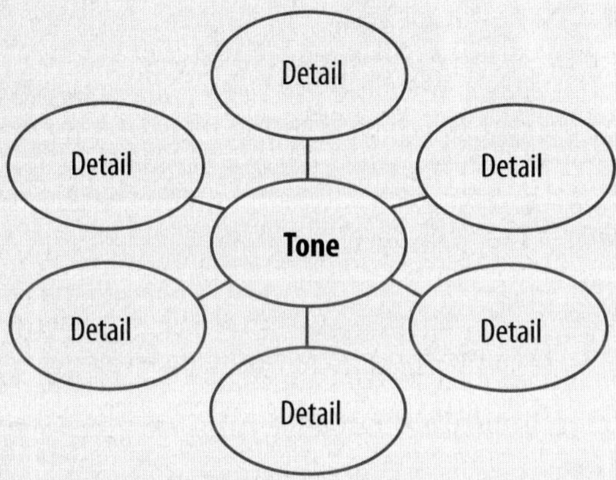

Talk About . . .

1. With a partner, discuss how Cisneros's word choice, figures of speech, and use of irony form her style. Try to use each Academic Vocabulary word listed at the right at least once in your discussion.

Write About . . .

Use the underlined Academic Vocabulary words in your answers to the following questions about "A Smart Cookie."

2. What impact does the idiom *smart cookie* have on the story's message? Who is a smart cookie?
3. Which details from the text give you the impression that Cisneros values education?
4. What is distinctive about the experiences of Esperanza's mother?
5. How does Cisneros establish tone?

Writing Focus

Think as a Reader/Writer

In Collection 4, the Writing Focus activities on the Preparing to Read pages will guide you in observing each writer's unique style. On the Applying Your Skills pages, you will have opportunities to develop similar characteristics in your own writing.

Academic Vocabulary for Collection 4

Talking and Writing About Style

Academic Vocabulary is the language you use to write and talk about literature. Use these words to discuss the short stories you read in this collection. The words are underlined throughout the collection.

distinctive (dihs TIHNGK tihv) *adj.:* special; different from others. *A distinctive style, not one that is bland or clichéd, is an indication of a fine writer.*

establish (ehs TAB lihsh) *v.:* bring about; set up. *Writers establish their own styles by using language in a way that is unique to their own work.*

impact (IHM pakt) *n.:* strong or forceful effect. *A writer's word choice has a critical impact on the story's tone and mood.*

impression (ihm PREHSH uhn) *n.:* idea or notion. *I got the impression the story was serious because of the author's tone.*

Your Turn

Copy these Academic Vocabulary words into your *Reader/Writer Notebook,* and circle any terms you use rarely. Challenge yourself to use those words as you respond to the stories in this collection.

SHORT STORY

Preparing to Read

The Tell-Tale Heart

by **Edgar Allan Poe**

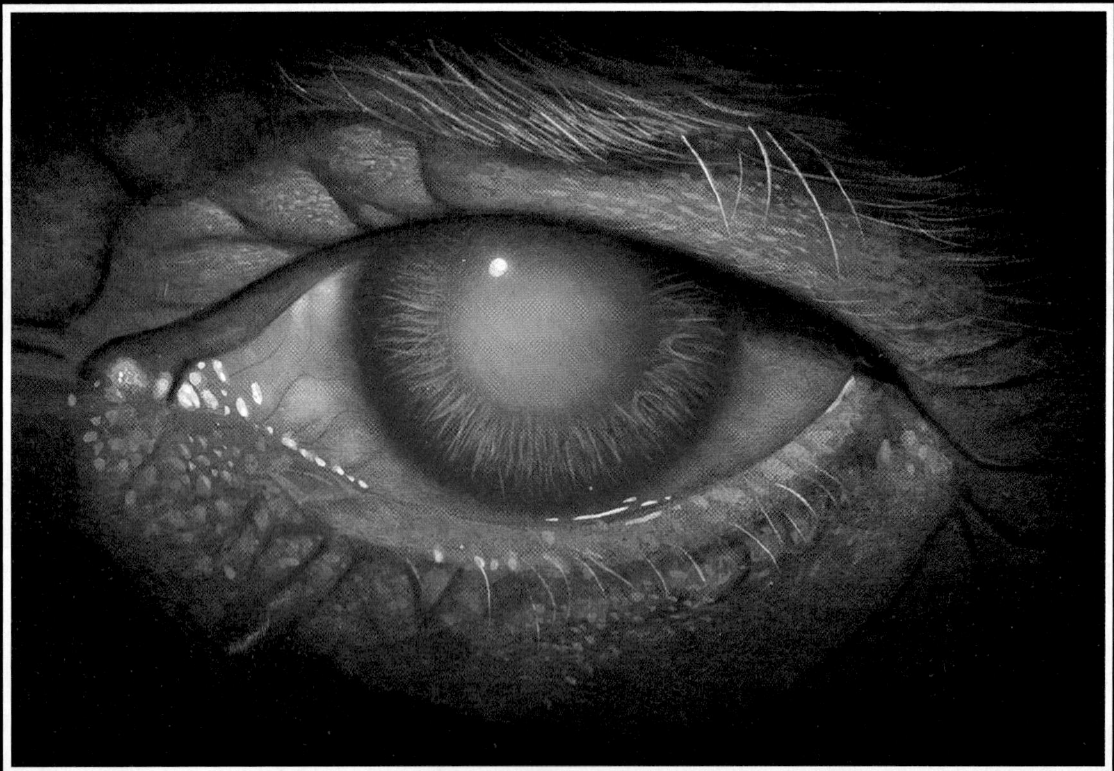

What Do You Think?

When can telling the truth be a lie?

QuickTalk

What is the difference between a lie and a delusion? Share your ideas with a few classmates. Refer to a dictionary, if necessary.

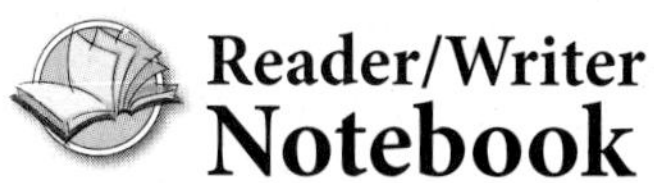

Use your **RWN** to complete the activities for this selection.

RA.L.8.8 Explain ways in which the author conveys mood and tone through word choice, figurative language, and syntax. **RP.8.1** Apply reading comprehension strategies, including making predictions, comparing and contrasting, recalling and summarizing and making inferences and drawing conclusions.

Literary Focus

Irony Much of the horror in "The Tell-Tale Heart" comes from Poe's use of irony. **Irony** is a contrast between expectation and reality. Irony can be tragic, profound, or even funny. There are three kinds of irony:

- **Verbal irony**—we say the opposite of what we mean.
- **Situational irony**—something happens that is opposite from what we expect.
- **Dramatic irony**—we know something a character doesn't know.

Literary Perspectives Apply the literary perspective on page 379 as you read this story.

Reading Focus

Paraphrasing a Text Paraphrasing—restating the text in your own words—can help you unlock the meaning of complicated or confusing text. Paraphrasing can also help you recognize elements of a writer's style, including irony.

Into Action As you read "The Tell-Tale Heart," look for complex sentences to write in a chart like the one below. Paraphrase each sentence, and compare yours with the original. Are any style elements more noticeable? Were any "lost in translation"?

Original Sentence	My Paraphrase
"Hearken! and observe how healthily—how calmly I can tell you the whole story."	Listen and you'll learn how I can tell you my story in a calm and healthy way.

Writing Focus

Think as a Reader/Writer

Find It in Your Reading As you read the following story, notice the impact it has on you. In your *Reader/Writer Notebook,* write down words or phrases that create a deep impression.

Vocabulary

vexed (vehkst) *v.:* disturbed; annoyed. *The old man's eye vexed the narrator.*

audacity (aw DAS uh tee) *n.:* boldness. *Impressed with his own audacity, the narrator smiled.*

vehemently (VEE uh muhnt lee) *adv.:* forcefully; passionately. *He talked more vehemently, but he couldn't drown out the sound.*

gesticulations (jehs TIHK yuh LAY shuhnz) *n.:* energetic gestures. *The narrator's violent gesticulations did not disturb the calm police officers.*

derision (dih RIHZH uhn) *n.:* contempt; ridicule. *Most of all, the narrator hated the smiling derision of the police.*

Language Coach

Oral Fluency All of the words above, except one, have more than one syllable. Which word has only one syllable? Which word has the most syllables? Try saying the words softly and counting the syllables on your fingers.

Learn It Online
See the video introduction of Poe's story at:
go.hrw.com
L8-377
Go

MEET THE WRITER

Learn It Online
Learn more about Poe at:
go.hrw.com L8-378 Go

Edgar Allan Poe

(1809–1849)

Orphaned and Penniless

Born in Boston, Edgar Allan Poe was the son of traveling actors. His father deserted the family when Poe was a baby, and his mother died before his third birthday. Poe was taken in by the wealthy Allan family of Richmond, Virginia, and given a first-class education. At the age of twelve, he had already written enough poems (mainly love poems to girls he knew) to fill a book. By the time he was twenty, he had published two volumes of poetry.

Poe constantly argued with his foster father, John Allan, about money. Allan eventually broke all ties with Poe, leaving him penniless. In 1831, Poe moved in with his aunt, Maria Clemm, and her children in Baltimore. He married his young cousin Virginia Clemm five years later.

Celebrated and Poor

Poe became as celebrated for his tales of horror and mystery as for his poetry. He made very little money from his writing, though—one of his most famous poems, "The Raven," earned him only about fifteen dollars. He seemed to live on the brink of disaster. His wife's death from tuberculosis in 1847 brought on a general decline in his physical and emotional health. He was found very ill in a Baltimore tavern on a rainy day in 1849; he died four days later of unknown causes.

Think About the Writer How might Poe's early life have contributed to his fondness for writing horror stories?

Build Background

Edgar Allan Poe is often credited with having invented the modern horror or suspense story. Many of the familiar elements from today's horror movies are found in this story—fury, murder, blood, and madness.

As both a critic and an author, Poe felt that prose writing should express a focused truth about human existence. He expressed his truths in the horror or suspense genre, but he was also one of the first writers to explore science fiction and detective styles.

Preview the Selection

In this story, an unnamed narrator describes why he is offended by a certain old man and what he plans to do about it.

Read with a Purpose As you read this famous short story, determine whether the narrator is or is not sane.

The Tell-Tale Heart

by **Edgar Allan Poe**

True!—nervous—very, very dreadfully nervous I had been and am; but why *will* you say that I am mad? The disease had sharpened my senses—not destroyed—not dulled them. Above all was the sense of hearing acute. I heard all things in the heaven and in the earth. I heard many things in hell. How, then, am I mad? Hearken! and observe how healthily—how calmly I can tell you the whole story. **A**

It is impossible to say how first the idea entered my brain; but once conceived, it haunted me day and night. Object[1] there was none. Passion there was none. I loved the old man. He had never wronged me. He had never given me insult. For his gold I had no desire. I think it was his eye! Yes, it was this! One of his eyes resembled that of a vulture—a pale blue eye, with a film over it. Whenever it fell upon me, my blood ran cold; and so by degrees—very gradually—I made up my mind to take the life of the old man and thus rid myself of the eye forever. **B**

1. **object** (AHB jihkt): purpose or goal.

Literary Perspectives

Use this perspective to help you analyze Poe's distinctive style.

Analyzing an Author's Techniques To understand an author's style, you analyze his or her techniques. That means that you consider how the word choices contribute to the tone and mood; you appreciate the sensory images; you interpret the figures of speech and their impact; you notice the symbolism of important objects or places; and, especially in a story by Poe, you distinguish the different types of irony in his work. As you read, respond to the notes and questions in the text, which will guide you in using this perspective.

A **Read and Discuss** This paragraph is a bit confusing. What have we learned so far?

B **Reading Focus** **Paraphrasing** Paraphrase the final sentence of this paragraph. What has the narrator decided to do?

Now this is the point. You fancy me mad. Madmen know nothing. But you should have seen *me*. You should have seen how wisely I proceeded—with what caution—with what foresight—with what dissimulation[2] I went to work! I was never kinder to the old man than during the whole week before I killed him. And every night, about midnight, I turned the latch of his door and opened it—oh, so gently! And then, when I had made an opening sufficient for my head, I put in a dark lantern, all closed, closed, so that no light shone out, and then I thrust in my head. Oh, you would have laughed to see how cunningly I thrust it in! I moved it slowly—very, very slowly, so that I might not disturb the old man's sleep. It took me an hour to place my whole head within the opening so far that I could see him as he lay upon his bed. Ha! Would a madman have been so wise as this? And then, when my head was well in the room, I undid the lantern cautiously—oh, so cautiously—cautiously (for the hinges creaked)—I undid it just so much that a single thin ray fell upon the vulture eye. And this I did for seven long nights—every night just at midnight—but I found the eye always closed; and so it was impossible to do the work; for it was not the old man who vexed me, but his Evil Eye. And every morning, when the day broke, I went boldly into the chamber and spoke courageously to him, calling him by name in a hearty tone and inquiring how he had passed the night. So you see he would have been a very profound[3] old man, indeed, to suspect that every night, just at twelve, I looked in upon him while he slept.

Upon the eighth night I was more than usually cautious in opening the door. A watch's minute hand moves more quickly than did mine. Never before that night had I *felt* the extent of my own powers—of my sagacity.[4] I could scarcely contain my feelings of triumph. To think that there I was, opening the door, little by little, and he not even to dream of my secret deeds or thoughts. I fairly chuckled at the idea; and perhaps he heard me; for he moved on the bed suddenly, as if startled. Now you may think that I drew back—but no. His room was as black as pitch with the thick darkness (for the shutters were close fastened, through fear of robbers), and so I knew that he could not see the opening of the door, and I kept pushing it on steadily, steadily. **C**

I had my head in, and was about to open the lantern, when my thumb slipped upon the tin fastening, and the old man sprang up in the bed, crying out—"Who's there?"

I kept quite still and said nothing. For a whole hour I did not move a muscle, and in

2. **dissimulation** (dih sihm yuh LAY shuhn): disguising of intentions or feelings. (Look for a similar word at the end of the story.)

3. **profound** (pruh FOWND): having great intellectual depth and insight.

4. **sagacity** (suh GAS uh tee): intelligence and good judgment.

C **Literary Focus** **Irony** Why is it ironic that the old man feared robbers? What type of irony is this?

Vocabulary **vexed** (vehkst) *v.:* disturbed; annoyed.

The illustrations for this selection are from a short movie based on "The Tell-Tale Heart."

the meantime I did not hear him lie down. He was still sitting up in the bed listening—just as I have done, night after night, hearkening to the deathwatches[5] in the wall. **D**

Presently I heard a slight groan, and I knew it was the groan of mortal terror. It was not a groan of pain or of grief—oh, no!—it was the low, stifled sound that arises from the bottom of the soul when overcharged with awe. I knew the sound well. Many a night, just at midnight, when all the world slept, it has welled up from my own bosom, deepening, with its dreadful echo, the terrors that distracted me. I say I knew it well. I knew what the old man felt, and pitied him, although I chuckled at heart. I knew that he had been lying awake ever since the first slight noise, when he had turned in the bed. His fears had been ever since growing upon him. He had been trying to fancy them causeless but could not. He had been saying to himself—"It is nothing but the wind in the chimney—it is only a mouse crossing the floor," or "It is merely a cricket which has made a single chirp." Yes, he had been trying to comfort himself with these suppositions; but he had found all in vain. *All in vain;* because Death, in approaching him, had stalked with his black shadow before him and enveloped the victim. And it was the mournful influence of the unperceived shadow that caused him to feel—although he neither saw nor heard—to *feel* the presence of my head within the room.

When I had waited a long time, very patiently, without hearing him lie down, I resolved to open a little—a very, very little crevice in the lantern. So I opened it—you cannot imagine how stealthily, stealthily—until, at length, a single dim ray, like the thread of the spider, shot from out the crevice and full upon the vulture eye.

5. **deathwatches:** beetles that burrow into wood and make tapping sounds, which some people believe are a sign of approaching death.

D **Read and Discuss** What mood is the author establishing here?

It was open—wide, wide open—and I grew furious as I gazed upon it. I saw it with perfect distinctness—all a dull blue, with a hideous veil over it that chilled the very marrow in my bones; but I could see nothing else of the old man's face or person, for I had directed the ray, as if by instinct, precisely upon the damned spot. **E**

And now have I not told you that what you mistake for madness is but overacuteness of the senses?—now, I say, there came to my ears a low, dull, quick sound, such as a watch makes when enveloped in cotton. I knew *that* sound well too. It was the beating of the old man's heart. It increased my fury, as the beating of a drum stimulates the soldier into courage.

But even yet I refrained[6] and kept still. I scarcely breathed. I held the lantern motionless. I tried how steadily I could maintain the ray upon the eye. Meantime the hellish tattoo[7] of the heart increased. It grew quicker and quicker and louder and louder every instant. The old man's terror *must* have been extreme! It grew louder, I say, louder every moment!—do you mark me well? I have told you that I am nervous: So I am. And now at the dead hour of the night, amid the dreadful silence of that old house, so strange a noise as this excited me to uncontrollable terror. Yet for some minutes longer I refrained and stood still. But the beating grew louder, louder! I thought the heart must burst. And now a new anxiety seized me—the sound would be heard by a neighbor! The old man's hour had come! With a loud yell, I threw open the lantern and leaped into the room. He shrieked once—once only. In an instant I dragged him to the floor and pulled the heavy bed over him. I then smiled gaily to find the deed so far done. But, for many minutes, the heart beat on with a muffled sound. This, however, did not vex me; it would not be heard through the wall. At length it ceased. The old man was dead. I removed the bed and examined the corpse. Yes, he was stone, stone dead. I placed my hand upon the heart and held it there many minutes. There was no pulsation. He was stone dead. His eye would trouble me no more. **F**

If still you think me mad, you will think so no longer when I describe the wise precautions I took for the concealment of the body. The night waned,[8] and I worked hastily but in silence. First of all I dismembered the corpse. I cut off the head and the arms and the legs.

I then took up three planks from the flooring of the chamber and deposited all between the scantlings.[9] I then replaced the boards so cleverly, so cunningly, that no human eye—not even *his*—could have detected anything wrong. There was nothing to wash out—no stain of any kind—no blood spot whatever. I had been too wary for that. A tub had caught all—ha! ha!

When I had made an end of these labors, it was four o'clock—still dark as midnight.

6. **refrained** (rih FRAYND): held back.
7. **tattoo:** steady beat.
8. **waned** (waynd): gradually drew to a close.
9. **scantlings:** small beams of wood.

E **Reading Focus** **Paraphrasing** Paraphrase this paragraph. Does your paraphrase have the same effect as the original?

F **Read and Discuss** How has the narrator solved his problem?

As the bell sounded the hour, there came a knocking at the street door. I went down to open it with a light heart—for what had I *now* to fear? There entered three men, who introduced themselves, with perfect suavity,[10] as officers of the police. A shriek had been heard by a neighbor during the night; suspicion of foul play had been aroused; information had been lodged at the police office, and they (the officers) had been deputed[11] to search the premises.

I smiled—for *what* had I to fear? I bade the gentlemen welcome. The shriek, I said, was my own in a dream. The old man, I mentioned, was absent in the country.

10. suavity (SWAH vuh tee): smoothness; politeness.

11. deputed (dih PYOOT uhd): appointed.

I took my visitors all over the house. I bade them search—search *well*. I led them, at length, to *his* chamber. I showed them his treasures, secure, undisturbed. In the enthusiasm of my confidence, I brought chairs into the room and desired them *here* to rest from their fatigues, while I myself, in the wild audacity of my perfect triumph, placed my own seat upon the very spot beneath which reposed the corpse of the victim. G

The officers were satisfied. My *manner* had convinced them. I was singularly at ease. They sat, and while I answered cheerily, they chatted of familiar things. But, ere long, I felt myself getting pale and wished them gone. My head ached, and I fancied a ringing in my ears; but still they sat and still chatted. The ringing became more distinct—it

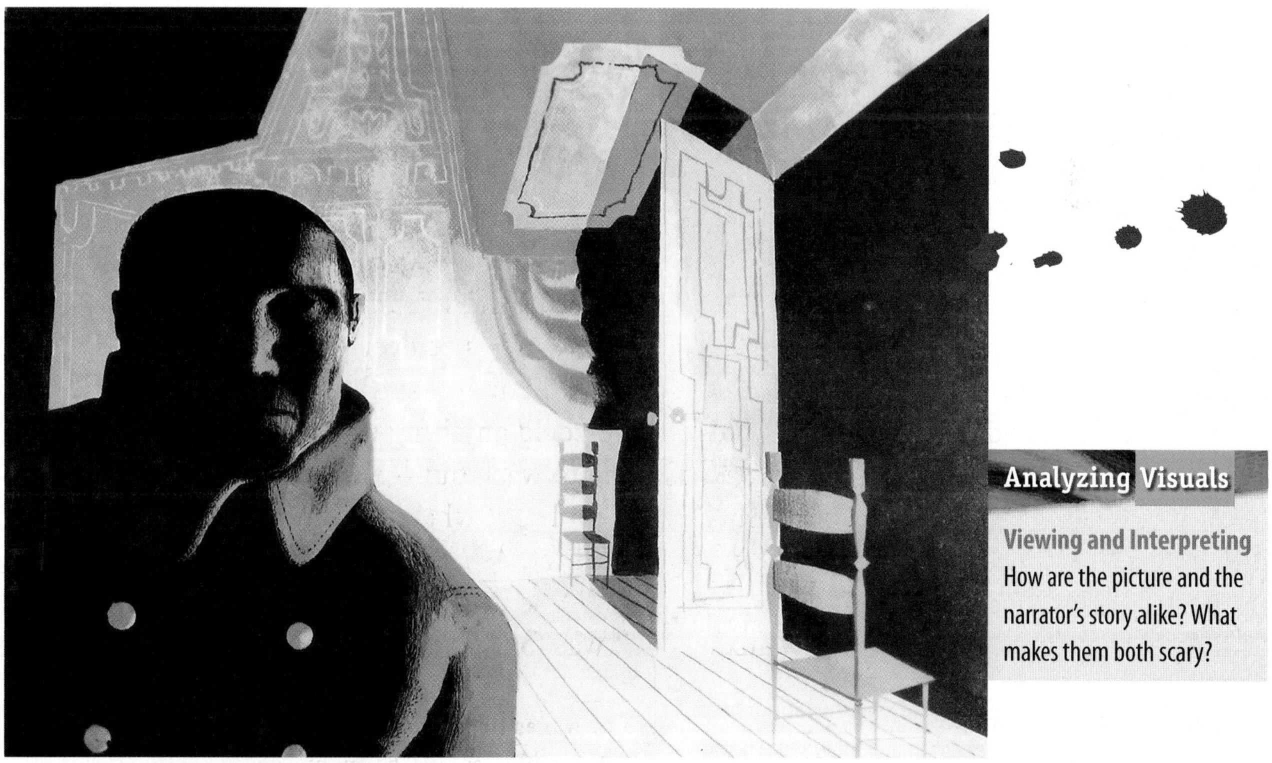

Analyzing Visuals

Viewing and Interpreting How are the picture and the narrator's story alike? What makes them both scary?

G **Literary Perspectives** **Analyzing Techniques** What word choices create the narrator's confident tone in this paragraph?

Vocabulary **audacity** (aw DAS uh tee) *n.:* boldness.

continued and became more distinct: I talked more freely to get rid of the feeling: but it continued and gained definitiveness—until, at length, I found that the noise was *not* within my ears.

No doubt I now grew *very* pale—but I talked more fluently and with a heightened voice. Yet the sound increased—and what could I do? It was *a low, dull, quick sound—much such a sound as a watch makes when enveloped in cotton.* I gasped for breath—and yet the officers heard it not. I talked more quickly—more vehemently; but the noise steadily increased. I arose and argued about trifles, in a high key and with violent gesticulations, but the noise steadily increased. Why *would* they not be gone? I paced the floor to and fro with heavy strides, as if excited to fury by the observation of the men—but the noise steadily increased. Oh God! what *could* I do? I foamed—I raved—I swore! I swung the chair upon which I had been sitting and grated it upon the boards, but the noise arose over all and continually increased. It grew louder—louder—*louder*! And still the men chatted pleasantly, and smiled. Was it possible they heard not? Almighty God!—no, no! They heard!—they suspected!—they *knew!*—they were making a mockery of my horror!—this I thought, and this I think. But anything was better than this agony! Anything was more tolerable than this derision! I could bear those hypocritical smiles no longer! I felt that I must scream or die!—and now—again!—hark! louder! *louder!* louder! louder!— **H**

"Villains!" I shrieked, "dissemble no more! I admit the deed!—tear up the planks!—here, here!—it is the beating of his hideous heart!" **I**

H **Literary Perspectives** **Analyzing Techniques** How does the author's use of language show that the narrator is becoming more and more agitated?

I **Read and Discuss** How do things turn out for the narrator?

Vocabulary **vehemently** (VEE uh muhnt lee) *adv.:* forcefully; passionately.
gesticulations (jehs tihk yuh LAY shuhnz) *n.:* energetic gestures.
derision (dih RIHZH uhn) *n.:* contempt; ridicule.

Applying Your Skills

OH **RA.L.8.8** Explain ways in which the author conveys mood and tone through word choice, figurative language, and syntax. **RA.L.8.3** Explain how authors pace action and use subplots, parallel episodes and climax. *Also covered* **RP.8.1; WA.8.4.b**

The Tell-Tale Heart

Respond and Think Critically

Reading Focus

Quick Check

1. What distinctive quality of the old man's eye makes the narrator hate it so much?
2. How does the narrator kill the old man?
3. Why do the police come to the narrator's house?
4. Why does the narrator finally admit his guilt?

Read with a Purpose

5. Is the narrator mad or very clever? Find support for both theories based on his thoughts and actions.

Reading Skills: Paraphrasing a Text

6. Look back at your paraphrase chart. What did comparing Poe's text with your paraphrases teach you about Poe's style? Write your answer in your chart.

Original Sentence	My Paraphrase

What I learned:

Literary Focus

Literary Analysis

7. **Analyze** How does the opening paragraph **foreshadow,** or hint at, the events of the story?
8. **Speculate** What is your explanation for the "heartbeat" noise that drives the narrator to confess?
9. **Analyze Mood** is the overall feeling in a story. How would you describe the mood of this story? What details does Poe include to create that mood?
10. **Literary Perspectives** What recurring techniques does Poe use to build tension and increase the impact of the story?

Literary Skills: Irony

11. **Infer** We feel a strong sense of dramatic irony in this story. What do we know that the narrator doesn't?
12. **Analyze** How does Poe's use of irony help create a sense of horror and suspense?

Literary Skills Review: Climax

13. **Analyze** The story's final paragraph builds to a kind of mad **climax**, the point of highest emotional tension in a story. How does Poe use words and punctuation to create tension—and even the rhythm of a heartbeat?

Writing Focus

Think as a Reader/Writer

Use It in Your Writing Poe wrote that every word in a story should help create a "single overwhelming impression." How well has he done that in "The Tell-Tale Heart"? In a paragraph, describe the story's impact on you. Mention at least three striking details that help create this impact.

What Do You Think Now

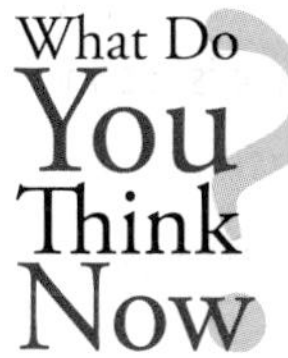

Is the narrator of "The Tell-Tale Heart" telling the truth? Are parts of his story true and parts imagined? How can you tell?

Applying Your Skills

The Tell-Tale Heart

Vocabulary Development

Vocabulary Skills: Synonyms

An important aspect of Poe's style in "The Tell-Tale Heart" is his word choice. The more words you know how to use, the more interesting your own writing will be. A good way to expand your vocabulary is to learn **synonyms**—words with similar meanings—for both familiar and unfamiliar words. To locate synonyms, use a dictionary, a **thesaurus** (a dictionary of synonyms, which can also be found on your computer's software), or a **synonym finder**.

Your Turn

Find synonyms for all of the Vocabulary words in the box. Then, for each Vocabulary word, write two sentences of your own, one using the Vocabulary word, and another using a synonym.

vexed
audacity
vehemently
gesticulations
derision

Vocabulary Skills: Figures of Speech

A **figure of speech** is a word or phrase that describes one thing in terms of another and is not meant to be understood as literally true.

Your Turn

Each boldface phrase below contains a figure of speech from the story. Tell what two things are being compared in each sentence.

1. The narrator says the old man's **eye resembled that of a vulture.**
2. He says the eye makes his **blood run cold.**
3. He is moving in a **room as black as pitch.**
4. The heartbeat causes fury in the narrator the way **the beating of a drum stimulates the soldier into courage.**

Language Coach

Oral Fluency To expand your vocabulary, you should get comfortable pronouncing new words. Answer these questions in your *Reader/Writer Notebook.*

1. Which syllable in *vehemently* gets the most stress? Which consonant is silent?
2. Which syllable in *gesticulations* gets the most stress? Is the *g* pronounced /g/ or /j/?
3. Which syllable in *audacity* gets the most stress? Does the second syllable have a long /a/ or a short /a/ sound?

Academic Vocabulary

Write About . . .

Poe's distinctive style includes his use of italics, dashes, and exclamation points. Read the first sentence from "The Tell-Tale Heart": "True!—nervous—very, very dreadfully nervous I had been and am; but why *will* you say that I am mad?" In a paragraph, explain the impact Poe's use of punctuation has on the feel of the sentence.

RA.L.8.8 Explain ways in which the author conveys mood and tone through word choice, figurative language, and syntax. C.8.9 Deliver formal and informal descriptive presentations that convey relevant information and descriptive details. WC.8.3 Grammar and Usage: Use all eight parts of speech. *Also covered* **VO.8.7; VO.8.4**

Grammar Link

Sentences and Fragments

A **sentence** is a group of words that has a subject and a verb and expresses a complete thought. A sentence begins with a capital letter and ends with a period, a question mark, or an exclamation mark. Here are two examples of complete sentences:

I looked in upon him while he slept.

The officers were making a mockery of my horror!

A **sentence fragment** is a word group that looks like a sentence but does not contain both a subject and a verb or does not express a complete thought. For example:

SENTENCE FRAGMENT Was pale blue and resembled that of a vulture. [What was pale blue and resembled that of a vulture?]

SENTENCE The old man's eye was pale blue and resembled that of a vulture.

Your Turn

Identify the following word groups as sentences or sentence fragments. If the word group is a sentence, add a capital letter and end punctuation. If it is a sentence fragment, correct it by adding words that will make it a complete sentence.

SENTENCE FRAGMENT my head through the door
SENTENCE I poked my head through the door.

1. after he murdered the old man
2. the officers knocked at the door
3. will you ever think about
4. grew louder, louder, louder

Writing Applications Write a paragraph that includes at least one of the corrected sentences.

CHOICES

As you respond to the Choices, use these **Academic Vocabulary** words as appropriate: distinctive, establish, impact, impression.

REVIEW

Analyze the Use of Irony

Timed Writing In "The Tell-Tale Heart," dramatic irony increases the suspense. Identify two examples of dramatic irony in the story, and explain in a brief essay how they create suspense. What would the story be like without this irony?

CONNECT

Prepare Interview Questions

Reporters rely on sources to get the story, but what if their sources are not telling the truth? Imagine you're a journalist reporting on this case. What could you learn from the suspect? from the police? from the neighbors? Whom could you trust? Prepare a list of questions to ask your sources.

EXTEND

Plan a Movie

Group Activity "The Tell-Tale Heart" was made into a movie in 1960. With several classmates, plan a remake. Who would you cast? When would the movie take place? What costumes would the characters wear? Share your ideas with the class.

Learn It Online
Expand your view of this story at:
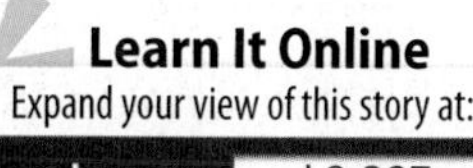
go.hrw.com L8-387

SHORT STORY

Preparing to Read

RAYMOND'S RUN

by **Toni Cade Bambara**

What Do You Think?

What does a person need to do to gain respect?

QuickWrite

Respecting a person means seeing him or her clearly and valuing what you see. Write a paragraph about a time when you gained new respect for someone. What helped you see more clearly?

Reader/Writer Notebook

Use your **RWN** to complete the activities for this selection.

RA.L.8.8 Explain ways in which the author conveys mood and tone through word choice, figurative language, and syntax. **RA.I.8.7** Analyze an author's argument, perspective or viewpoint and explain the development of key points.

Literary Focus

Literary Devices: Dialect Everyone speaks a dialect of some kind. **Dialect** is a way of speaking used by people in a certain area or group. In "Raymond's Run," Toni Cade Bambara captures the voice of her main character by having her speak in a dialect used in 1970s Harlem, a neighborhood in New York City.

Reading Focus

Analyzing Details This story's main character, Squeaky, speaks in dialect and uses **allusions** (references to something in current events, literature, and so on that the writer assumes will be familiar to readers). These and other details help create Squeaky's voice.

Into Action Use a chart to record and analyze details from the text. Identify the types of literary devices (irony, figurative language, slang, dialect) Bambara uses.

Story Details	Literary Device
"And a lot of smart mouths got lots to say about that too. . . . But now, if anybody has anything to say to Raymond, . . . they have to come by me."	dialect; slang
"The big kids call me Mercury. . . ."	

Writing Focus

Think as a Reader/Writer

Find It in Your Reading The story's main character, Squeaky, is quite memorable. As you read, note funny observations that she makes. In your *Reader/Writer Notebook,* write her words and phrases that you find especially engaging.

TechFocus As you read, think about how you might use video and digital technology to flesh out the story's characters.

Vocabulary

mind (mynd) *v.:* take care of. *Squeaky's main responsibility is to mind her brother.*

subject (SUHB jehkt) *adj.:* likely to have; having a tendency. *Raymond is subject to sudden bursts of enthusiasm.*

prodigy (PRAHD uh jee) *n.:* child with exceptional talent. *Cynthia wants to appear as a prodigy who succeeds easily.*

reputation (rehp yuh TAY shuhn) *n.:* the way others see a person. *Squeaky has a reputation as the fastest runner in her neighborhood.*

mastered (MAS tuhrd) *v.:* made oneself the master of; became skillful at. *Squeaky has mastered the fifty-yard dash and always wins.*

Language Coach

Multiple-Meaning Words Scan the Vocabulary words above. Which words are familiar to you? Now, read the definitions. Do those words have the definitions you expected, or are those definitions different? Find these words in a dictionary, and identify additional meanings. Write them in your *Reader/Writer Notebook.*

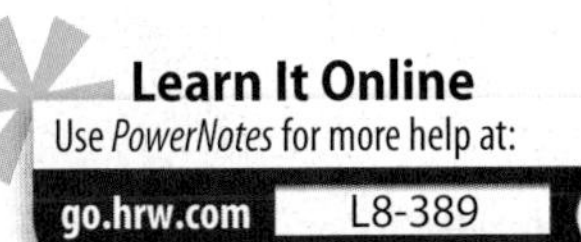

Learn It Online
Use PowerNotes for more help at:
go.hrw.com
L8-389
Go

MEET THE WRITER

Toni Cade Bambara

(1939–1995)

Voices of Her Childhood

Toni Cade Bambara grew up in New York City, where "Raymond's Run" takes place. Her writing drew on the voices of her childhood—the street-corner speechmakers, barbershop storytellers, and performers at Harlem's legendary Apollo Theater.

Stories from the Imagination

The author's stories, however, came from Bambara's imagination.

> "It does no good to write autobiographical fiction, cause the minute the book hits the stand here comes your mama screamin how could you. . . . So I deal in straight-up fiction myself, cause I value my family and friends, and mostly cause I lie a lot anyway."

A New Name

Toni Cade Bambara adopted the name Bambara from a signature on a sketchbook she found in her great-grandmother's trunk. The Bambara are a people of northwestern Africa known for their skill in woodcarving.

Think About the Writer What does Bambara's decision to adopt a new last name suggest about her?

Build Background

"Raymond's Run" is set in Harlem, a neighborhood in New York City. From about 1900 to 1925, many African Americans moved to Harlem from the South. During the 1920s, the neighborhood was the center of an outpouring of writing, music, and art that became known as the Harlem Renaissance. In later decades, economic conditions in Harlem deteriorated. More recently the area has enjoyed revitalization.

Preview the Selection

The main character of this story, a girl called **Squeaky,** has never lost a race. This year, however, she faces stiff competition when a newcomer, **Gretchen,** enters the May Day race.

Read with a Purpose Read this story to learn what surprising discovery a runner makes during a race.

RAYMOND'S RUN

by **Toni Cade Bambara**

I don't have much work to do around the house like some girls. My mother does that. And I don't have to earn my pocket money by hustling; George runs errands for the big boys and sells Christmas cards. And anything else that's got to get done, my father does. All I have to do in life is mind my brother Raymond, which is enough.

Sometimes I slip and say my little brother Raymond. But as any fool can see he's much bigger and he's older too. But a lot of people call him my little brother cause he needs looking after cause he's not quite right. And a lot of smart mouths got lots to say about that too, especially when George was minding him. But now, if anybody has anything to say to Raymond, anything to say about his big head, they have to come by me. And I don't play the dozens[1] or believe in standing around with somebody in my face doing a lot of talking. I much rather just knock you down and take my chances even if I am a little girl with skinny arms and a squeaky voice, which is how I got the name Squeaky. And if things get too rough, I run. And as anybody can tell you, I'm the fastest thing on two feet. **A**

There is no track meet that I don't win the first-place medal. I used to win the twenty-yard dash when I was a little kid in kindergarten. Nowadays, it's the fifty-yard dash. And tomorrow I'm subject to run the quarter-meter relay all by myself and come in first, second, and third. The big kids call me Mercury[2] cause I'm the swiftest thing in the neighborhood. Everybody knows that—except two people who know better, my father and me. He can beat me to Amsterdam Avenue with me having a two-fire-hydrant head start and him running with his hands in his pockets and whistling. But that's private information. Cause

1. **play the dozens:** slang for "trade insults."

2. **Mercury:** in Roman mythology, messenger of the gods, known for his speediness.

A Read and Discuss How does Squeaky's personality fit her job of taking care of her brother Raymond?

Vocabulary **mind** (mynd) *v.:* take care of.
subject (SUHB jehkt) *adj.:* likely to have; having a tendency.

can you imagine some thirty-five-year-old man stuffing himself into PAL[3] shorts to race little kids? So as far as everyone's concerned, I'm the fastest and that goes for Gretchen, too, who has put out the tale that she is going to win the first-place medal this year. Ridiculous. In the second place, she's got short legs. In the third place, she's got freckles. In the first place, no one can beat me and that's all there is to it.

I'm standing on the corner admiring the weather and about to take a stroll down Broadway so I can practice my breathing exercises, and I've got Raymond walking on the inside close to the buildings, cause he's subject to fits of fantasy and starts thinking he's a circus performer and that the curb is a tightrope strung high in the air. And sometimes after a rain he likes to step down off his tightrope right into the gutter and slosh around getting his shoes and cuffs wet. Then I get hit when I get home. Or sometimes if you don't watch him he'll dash across traffic to the island[4] in the middle of Broadway and give the pigeons a fit. Then I have to go behind him apologizing to all the old people sitting around trying to get some sun and getting all upset with the pigeons fluttering around them, scattering their newspapers and upsetting the waxpaper lunches in their laps. So I keep Raymond on the inside of me, and he plays like he's driving a stagecoach which is OK by me so long as he doesn't run me over or interrupt my breathing exercises, which I have to do on account of I'm serious about my running, and I don't care who knows it. **B**

NOW SOME PEOPLE LIKE TO ACT LIKE THINGS COME EASY TO THEM.

Now some people like to act like things come easy to them, won't let on that they practice. Not me. I'll high-prance down 34th Street like a rodeo pony to keep my knees strong even if it does get my mother uptight so that she walks ahead like she's not with me, don't know me, is all by herself on a shopping trip, and I am somebody else's crazy child. Now you take Cynthia Procter for instance. She's just the opposite. If there's a test tomorrow, she'll say something like, "Oh, I guess I'll play handball this afternoon and watch television tonight," just to let you know she ain't thinking about the test.

3. **PAL:** Police Athletic League.

4. **island:** traffic island, a car-free area in the middle of the street.

B **Read and Discuss** What does Squeaky's strategy for managing Raymond show us about both characters?

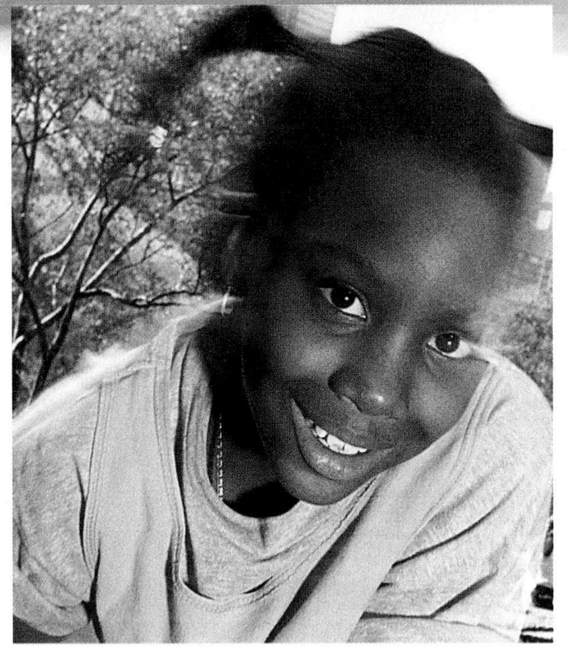

Or like last week when she won the spelling bee for the millionth time, "A good thing you got 'receive,' Squeaky, cause I would have got it wrong. I completely forgot about the spelling bee." And she'll clutch the lace on her blouse like it was a narrow escape. Oh, brother. But of course when I pass her house on my early morning trots around the block, she is practicing the scales on the piano over and over and over and over. Then in music class she always lets herself get bumped around so she falls accidentally on purpose onto the piano stool and is so surprised to find herself sitting there that she decides just for fun to try out the ole keys. And what do you know—Chopin's[5] waltzes just spring out of her fingertips and she's the most surprised thing in the world. A regular prodigy. I could kill people like that. I stay up all night studying the words for the spelling bee. And you can see me any time of day practicing running. I never walk if I can trot, and shame on Raymond if he can't keep up. But of course he does, cause if he hangs back someone's liable to walk up to him and get smart, or take his allowance from him, or ask him where he got that great big pumpkin head. People are so stupid sometimes.

So I'm strolling down Broadway breathing out and breathing in on counts of seven, which is my lucky number, and here comes Gretchen and her sidekicks: Mary Louise, who used to be a friend of mine when she first moved to Harlem from Baltimore and got beat up by everybody till I took up for her on account of her mother and my mother used to sing in the same choir when they were young girls, but people ain't grateful, so now she hangs out with the new girl Gretchen and talks about me like a dog; and Rosie, who is as fat as I am skinny and has a big mouth where Raymond is concerned and is too stupid to know that there is not a big deal of difference between herself and Raymond and that she can't afford to throw stones. So they are steady coming up Broadway and I see right away that it's going to be one of those

5. **Chopin's:** Frédéric François Chopin (SHOH pan) (1810–1849), Polish composer and pianist.

Vocabulary **prodigy** (PRAHD uh jee) *n.:* child with exceptional talent.

Dodge City scenes[6] cause the street ain't that big and they're close to the buildings just as we are. First I think I'll step into the candy store and look over the new comics and let them pass. But that's chicken and I've got a reputation to consider. So then I think I'll just walk straight on through them or even over them if necessary. But as they get to me, they slow down. I'm ready to fight, cause like I said I don't feature a whole lot of chit-chat, I much prefer to just knock you down right from the jump and save everybody a lotta precious time. **C**

6. **Dodge City scenes:** showdowns such as those in the television western *Gunsmoke*, which was set in Dodge City, Kansas. In a typical scene a marshal and an outlaw face off with pistols on an empty street.

"You signing up for the May Day races?" smiles Mary Louise, only it's not a smile at all. A dumb question like that doesn't deserve an answer. Besides, there's just me and Gretchen standing there really, so no use wasting my breath talking to shadows.

"I don't think you're going to win this time," says Rosie, trying to signify[7] with her hands on her hips all salty, completely forgetting that I have whupped her behind many times for less salt than that.

"I always win cause I'm the best," I say straight at Gretchen who is, as far as I'm concerned, the only one talking in this ventriloquist-dummy routine. Gretchen smiles, but it's not a smile, and I'm thinking

7. **signify:** slang for "act boastful or insult someone."

C Reading Focus Analyzing Details Squeaky speaks in dialect and uses allusions ("can't afford to throw stones" and "those Dodge City scenes"). How do these details help you understand and enjoy Squeaky's character?

Vocabulary **reputation** (rehp yuh TAY shuhn) *n.:* the way others see a person.

Analyzing Visuals **Viewing and Interpreting** How does the body language of these girls capture the attitudes of the characters in the story?

that girls never really smile at each other because they don't know how and don't want to know how and there's probably no one to teach us how, cause grown-up girls don't know either. Then they all look at Raymond who has just brought his mule team to a standstill. And they're about to see what trouble they can get into through him.

"What grade you in now, Raymond?"

"You got anything to say to my brother, you say it to me, Mary Louise Williams of Raggedy Town, Baltimore."

"What are you, his mother?" sasses Rosie.

"That's right, Fatso. And the next word out of anybody and I'll be their mother too." So they just stand there and Gretchen shifts from one leg to the other and so do they. Then Gretchen puts her hands on her hips and is about to say something with her freckle-face self but doesn't. Then she walks around me looking me up and down but keeps walking up Broadway, and her sidekicks follow her. So me and Raymond smile at each other and he says, "Gidyap" to his team and I continue with my breathing exercises, strolling down Broadway toward the iceman on 145th with not a care in the world cause I am Miss Quicksilver[8] herself. **D**

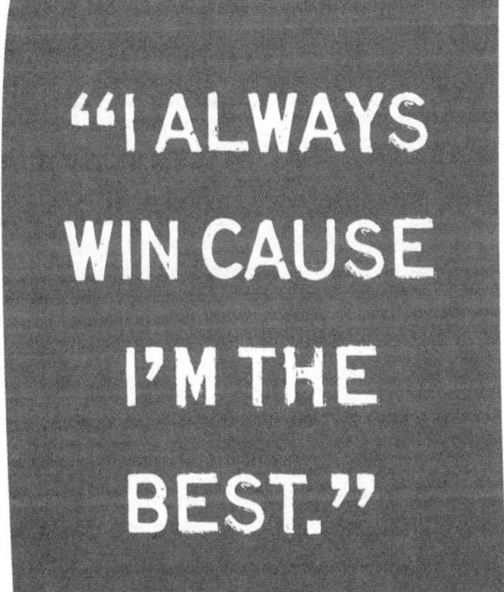
"I ALWAYS WIN CAUSE I'M THE BEST."

I take my time getting to the park on May Day because the track meet is the last thing on the program. The biggest thing on the program is the May Pole dancing, which I can do without, thank you, even if my mother thinks it's a shame I don't take part and act like a girl for a change. You'd think my mother'd be grateful not to have to make me a white organdy dress with a big satin sash and buy me new white baby-doll shoes that can't be taken out of the box till the big day. You'd think she'd be glad her daughter ain't out there prancing around a May Pole getting the new clothes all dirty and sweaty and trying to act like a fairy or a flower or whatever you're supposed to be when you should be trying to be yourself, whatever that is, which is, as far as I am concerned, a poor black girl who really can't afford to buy shoes and a new dress you only wear once a lifetime cause it won't fit next year.

8. **quicksilver:** another name for mercury, a silver-colored liquid metal that flows rapidly.

D **Read and Discuss** How does this scene with the three girls add to what we know about Squeaky?

I was once a strawberry in a Hansel and Gretel pageant when I was in nursery school and didn't have no better sense than to dance on tiptoe with my arms in a circle over my head doing umbrella steps and being a perfect fool just so my mother and father could come dressed up and clap. You'd think they'd know better than to encourage that kind of nonsense. I am not a strawberry. I do not dance on my toes. I run. That is what I am all about. So I always come late to the May Day program, just in time to get my number pinned on and lay in the grass till they announce the fifty-yard dash. **E**

I put Raymond in the little swings, which is a tight squeeze this year and will be impossible next year. Then I look around for Mr. Pearson, who pins the numbers on. I'm really looking for Gretchen if you want to know the truth, but she's not around. The park is jam-packed. Parents in hats and corsages and breast-pocket handkerchiefs peeking up. Kids in white dresses and light-blue suits. The parkees unfolding chairs and chasing the rowdy kids from Lenox[9] as if they had no right to be there. The big guys with their caps on backwards, leaning against the fence swirling the basketballs on the tips of their fingers, waiting for all these crazy people to clear out the park so they can play. Most of the kids in my class are carrying bass drums and glockenspiels[10] and flutes. You'd think they'd put in a few bongos or something for real like that. **F**

Then here comes Mr. Pearson with his clipboard and his cards and pencils and whistles and safety pins and fifty million other things he's always dropping all over the place with his clumsy self. He sticks out in a crowd because he's on stilts. We used to call him Jack and the Beanstalk to get him mad. But I'm the only one that can outrun him and get away, and I'm too grown for that silliness now.

"Well, Squeaky," he says, checking my name off the list and handing me number seven and two pins. And I'm thinking he's got no right to call me Squeaky, if I can't call him Beanstalk.

"Hazel Elizabeth Deborah Parker," I correct him and tell him to write it down on his board.

"Well, Hazel Elizabeth Deborah Parker, going to give someone else a break this year?" I squint at him real hard to see if he is seriously thinking I should lose the race on purpose just to give someone else a break. "Only six girls running this time," he continues, shaking his head sadly like it's my fault all of New York didn't turn out

9. **Lenox:** Lenox Avenue, a major street in Harlem.

10. **glockenspiels** (GLAHK uhn speelz): musical instruments with flat metal bars that are struck with small hammers and produce bell-like sounds. Glockenspiels are often used in marching bands.

E Literary Focus Dialect Why do you think Bambara uses nonstandard grammar in this story, such as "didn't have no better sense" (instead of *didn't have any better sense*)?

F Read and Discuss How do Squeaky's descriptions of May Pole dancing, acting as a strawberry in plays, and commentary on the people in the park on May Day add to our image of her?

in sneakers. "That new girl should give you a run for your money." He looks around the park for Gretchen like a periscope in a submarine movie. "Wouldn't it be a nice gesture if you were . . . to ahhh . . ."

I give him such a look he couldn't finish putting that idea into words. Grown-ups got a lot of nerve sometimes. I pin number seven to myself and stomp away, I'm so burnt. And I go straight for the track and stretch out on the grass while the band winds up with "Oh, the Monkey Wrapped His Tail Around the Flag Pole," which my teacher calls by some other name. The man on the loudspeaker is calling everyone over to the track and I'm on my back looking at the sky, trying to pretend I'm in the country, but I can't, because even grass in the city feels hard as sidewalk, and there's just no pretending you are anywhere but in a "concrete jungle" as my grandfather says. **G**

The twenty-yard dash takes all of two minutes cause most of the little kids don't know no better than to run off the track or run the wrong way or run smack into the fence and fall down and cry. One little kid, though, has got the good sense to run straight for the white ribbon up ahead so he wins. Then the second-graders line up for the thirty-yard dash and I don't even bother to turn my head to watch cause Raphael Perez always wins. He wins before he even begins by psyching the runners, telling them they're going to trip on their shoelaces and fall on their faces or lose their shorts or something, which he doesn't really have to do since he is very fast, almost as fast as I am. After that is the forty-yard dash which I used to run when I was in first grade. Raymond is hollering from the swings cause he knows I'm about to do my thing cause the man on the loudspeaker has just announced the fifty-yard dash, although

G **Read and Discuss** How does Squeaky handle the difficult aspects of her life?

he might just as well be giving a recipe for angel food cake cause you can hardly make out what he's sayin for the static. I get up and slip off my sweat pants and then I see Gretchen standing at the starting line, kicking her legs out like a pro. Then as I get into place I see that ole Raymond is on line on the other side of the fence, bending down with his fingers on the ground just like he knew what he was doing. I was going to yell at him but then I didn't. It burns up your energy to holler.

Every time, just before I take off in a race, I always feel like I'm in a dream, the kind of dream you have when you're sick with fever and feel all hot and weightless. I dream I'm flying over a sandy beach in the early morning sun, kissing the leaves of the trees as I fly by. And there's always the smell of apples, just like in the country when I was little and used to think I was a choo-choo train, running through the fields of corn and chugging up the hill to the orchard. And all the time I'm dreaming this, I get lighter and lighter until I'm flying over the beach again, getting blown through the sky like a feather that weighs nothing at all. But once I spread my fingers in the dirt and crouch over the Get on Your Mark, the dream goes and I am solid again and am telling myself, Squeaky you must win, you must win, you are the fastest thing in the world, you can even beat your father up Amsterdam if you really try. And then I feel my weight coming back just behind my knees then down to my feet then into the earth and the pistol shot explodes in my blood and

I am off and weightless again, flying past the other runners, my arms pumping up and down and the whole world is quiet except for the crunch as I zoom over the gravel in the track. I glance to my left and there is no one. To the right, a blurred Gretchen, who's got her chin jutting out as if it would win the race all by itself. And on the other side of the fence is Raymond with his arms down to his side and the palms tucked up behind him, running in his very own style, and it's the first time I ever saw that and I almost stop to watch my brother Raymond on his first run. But the white ribbon is bouncing toward me and I tear past it, racing into the distance till my feet with a mind of their own start digging up footfuls of dirt and brake me short. Then all the kids standing on the side pile on me, banging me on the back and slapping my head with their May Day programs, for I have won again and everybody on 151st Street can walk tall for another year. **H**

"In first place . . ." the man on the loudspeaker is clear as a bell now. But then he pauses and the loudspeaker starts to whine. Then static. And I lean down to catch my breath and here comes Gretchen walking back, for she's overshot the finish line too, huffing and puffing with her hands on her hips taking it slow, breathing in steady time like a real pro and I sort of like her a little for the first time. "In first place . . ." and then three or four voices get all mixed up on the loudspeaker and I dig my sneaker into the grass and stare at Gretchen who's staring back, we both wondering just who did win. I can hear old Beanstalk arguing with the man on the loudspeaker and then a few others running their mouths about what the stopwatches say. Then I hear Raymond yanking at the fence to call me and I wave to shush him, but he keeps rattling the fence like a gorilla in a cage like in them gorilla movies, but then like a dancer or something he starts climbing up nice and easy but very fast. And it occurs to me, watching how smoothly he climbs hand over hand and remembering how he looked running with his arms down to his side and with the wind pulling his mouth back and his teeth showing and all, it occurred to me that Raymond would make a very fine runner. Doesn't he always keep up with me on my trots? And he surely knows how to breathe in counts of seven cause he's always doing it at the dinner

---

H **Literary Focus** **Dialect** What kind of language does the author use in this paragraph? Why do you think she doesn't use dialect?

table, which drives my brother George up the wall. And I'm smiling to beat the band cause if I've lost this race, or if me and Gretchen tied, or even if I've won, I can always retire as a runner and begin a whole new career as a coach with Raymond as my champion. After all, with a little more study I can beat Cynthia and her phony self at the spelling bee. And if I bugged my mother, I could get piano lessons and become a star. And I have a big rep[11] as the baddest thing around. And I've got a roomful of ribbons and medals and awards. But what has Raymond got to call his own? **I**

So I stand there with my new plans, laughing out loud by this time as Raymond jumps down from the fence and runs over with his teeth showing and his arms down to the side, which no one before him has quite mastered as a running style. And by the time he comes over I'm jumping up and down so glad to see him—my brother Raymond, a great runner in the family tradition. But of course everyone thinks I'm jumping up and down because the men on the loudspeaker have finally gotten themselves together and compared notes and are announcing "In first place—Miss Hazel Elizabeth Deborah Parker." (Dig that.) "In second place—Miss Gretchen P. Lewis." And I look over at Gretchen wondering what the "P" stands for. And I smile. Cause she's good, no doubt about it. Maybe she'd like to help me coach Raymond; she obviously is serious about running, as any fool can see. And she nods to congratulate me and then she smiles. And I smile. We stand there with this big smile of respect between us. It's about as real a smile as girls can do for each other, considering we don't practice real smiling every day, you know, cause maybe we too busy being flowers or fairies or strawberries instead of something honest and worthy of respect . . . you know . . . like being people.

11. **rep:** slang for "reputation." People often create slang by clipping off parts of words.

I **Read and Discuss** How does Squeaky's new plan connect to what we already know about her?

Vocabulary **mastered** (MAS tuhrd) *v.:* made oneself the master of; became skillful at.

Applying Your Skills

RA.L.8.8 Explain ways in which the author conveys mood and tone through word choice, figurative language, and syntax. **RA.L.8.5** Identify and explain universal themes across different works by the same author and by different authors. *Also covered* **RA.I.8.7; WA.8.6**

Raymond's Run

Respond and Think Critically

Reading Focus

Quick Check

1. Explain why taking care of Raymond is not an easy job. How does Squeaky protect him?
2. What does Squeaky decide to do for Raymond?

Read with a Purpose

3. How do you think Squeaky's new discovery will change her life?

Reading Skills: Analyzing Details

4. Review your chart with details about Bambara's writing style. Add a row at the bottom to describe Bambara's overall writing style.

Story Details	Literary Device
"And a lot of smart mouths got lots to say about that too. . . . But now, if anybody has anything to say to Raymond, . . . they have to come by me."	dialect; slang
Bambara's overall writing style:	

Literary Focus

Literary Analysis

5. **Analyze** Is Squeaky very different from the girls she describes in the story? Cite details to support your answer.
6. **Infer** Why do you think Squeaky and Gretchen smile at each other after the race?
7. **Evaluate** Would you have called this story "Raymond's Run"? Defend Bambara's choice, or invent a new title and explain why you think it's better.

Literary Skills: Dialect

8. **Analyze** What does the use of dialect in this story reveal about its narrator and the time and place in which she lives? If this story had been written in standard English, would its impact change? Explain.

Literary Skills Review: Theme

9. **Analyze** Squeaky realizes something important during the race. What does Squeaky's new outlook reveal about the story's **theme,** or insight about life?

Writing Focus

Think as a Reader/Writer

Use It in Your Writing Create a character who has a distinctive way of expressing himself or herself. For example, he or she might speak in a dialect, use exclamations, or exaggerate. Write a paragraph in which your character, in a distinct voice, tells about his or her talent.

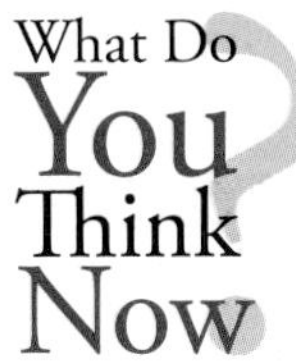

After reading the story, what qualities do you think are most worthy of respect?

Applying Your Skills

Raymond's Run

Vocabulary Development

Vocabulary Check

mind
subject
prodigy
reputation
mastered

Use the Vocabulary words to answer the questions below.

1. When you **mind** a young child, what do you do?
2. What kinds of annoyances are people **subject** to?
3. If you could choose to be a **prodigy** at anything, what would you choose?
4. What skill have you **mastered**?
5. What kind of **reputation** do you strive for?

Vocabulary Skills: Figures of Speech

In "Raymond's Run," Squeaky speaks in a colorful way, using lots of slang. The slang terms she uses are often based on **metaphors,** in which one thing is compared to another. She also sprinkles her language with **similes,** in which she compares one thing to another using words such as *like, as, than,* and *resembles.* In addition, Squeaky uses an **analogy,** or comparison of two things, when she reveals her state of mind before the race by comparing it to a dream about flying.

Your Turn

Identify each boldface figure of speech that follows as a metaphor or a simile. Then, explain the comparison established in each figure of speech.

1. Squeaky prances down the street **like a rodeo pony** to keep her knees strong.
2. Squeaky gets angry when people ask Raymond where he got that great big **pumpkin head.**
3. She says that Mr. Pearson looks around the park **like a periscope in a submarine movie.**

Now, re-read the analogy that Squeaky makes comparing her state of mind before the race to flying (page 398). Then, write an analogy of your own. Open your analogy with words like these: "Playing football is like . . ." or "Reading a good story is like . . ."

Language Coach

Multiple-Meaning Words Become familiar with words that have multiple meanings by completing the following exercises.

1. The verb *mind,* meaning "to look after," can also mean "to obey." Write two sentences—one for each meaning of the word.
2. When used as an adjective, *subject* is followed by the preposition *to* and a noun. For example: *I am subject to allergies.* Another meaning for *subject* is "topic." Create new sentences with the word *subject,* using it both as a noun and an adjective.

Academic Vocabulary

Talk About . . .

Re-read Bambara's biography and quote in the Meet the Writer on page 390. Then, with a partner, discuss your impression of Toni Cade Bambara. Consider how she uses dialect to establish both her own voice and that of her main character, Squeaky.

RA.L.8.8 Explain ways in which the author conveys mood and tone through word choice, figurative language, and syntax. **WC.8.3** Grammar and Usage: Use all eight parts of speech. *Also covered* **VO.8.7; VO.8.4**

Grammar Link

Sentences: Subject and Predicate

A **sentence** is a group of words that has a *subject* and a *predicate* and expresses a complete thought.

The **subject** tells *whom* or *what* the sentence is about. Usually, the subject comes before the predicate, although sometimes it appears someplace else. To find the subject, ask, "Who?" or "What?"

EXAMPLES Squeaky runs faster than anyone else in her neighborhood. [Who runs?] Squeaky's neighborhood is vibrant and colorful. [What is vibrant and colorful?]

The **predicate** tells something about the subject. To find the predicate, ask, "What is the subject doing?" or "What is the subject being?"

EXAMPLES Squeaky runs faster than anyone else in her neighborhood. [What does Squeaky do?] Squeaky's neighborhood is vibrant and colorful. [What is the neighborhood like?]

Your Turn

Copy each sentence. Then, circle the subject and underline the predicate.

1. Raymond runs beside Squeaky.
2. Squeaky realizes that Raymond is pretty fast.
3. The race has been won by Squeaky again.

Writing Applications

Write three sentences about running a race. Label the subjects and predicates in each sentence.

CHOICES

As you respond to the Choices, use these **Academic Vocabulary** words as appropriate: distinctive, establish, impact, impression.

REVIEW

Create a Dialect Dictionary

Group Activity With a few classmates, create a "dictionary" of dialect used in your area. Include words and expressions that people in your neighborhood or group use. For each entry, include the word or expression, with a definition and an example of how it is used in a sentence.

CONNECT

Write a Contrast Essay

Timed Writing In "Raymond's Run," Squeaky does her best to win a race and, as a result of her effort, sees the people around her more clearly. How does she now see Raymond and Gretchen? Write a brief essay contrasting her previous views to her new perceptions.

EXTEND

Portray a Character

TechFocus Plan a digital narrative to develop one or more of the characters in the story—Squeaky, Raymond, and Gretchen. With a partner, begin by choosing a character and then creating a storyboard of your video. What would the character most like to show or explain to a viewer? Feel free to use your imagination, but try to use some of the story's details about the setting and characters.

Learn It Online

Find a storyboard template at the Digital Storytelling site online:

go.hrw.com L8-403 

SHORT STORY

Preparing to Read

The Circuit

by **Francisco Jiménez**

Farmworkers picking strawberries.

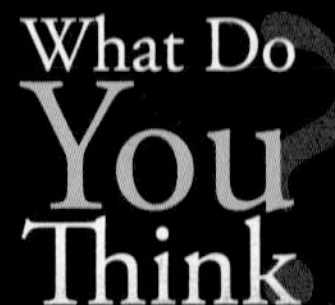

When must you give up what you *want* to do for what you *have* to do?

QuickTalk

Military families, migrant workers, and show-business professionals, among others, must move frequently for their jobs. How might such moves affect children in the family? Discuss your ideas with a partner.

Use your **RWN** to complete the activities for this selection.

RA.L.8.8 Explain ways in which the author conveys mood and tone through word choice, figurative language, and syntax. **RP.8.1** Apply reading comprehension strategies, including making predictions, comparing and contrasting, recalling and summarizing and making inferences and drawing conclusions.

Literary Focus

Tone and Mood **Tone** refers to a writer's attitude about a place, event, or character. Tone is revealed through the writer's use of language. In describing a setting, for example, a writer might use words that reveal his love for the twisting streets of his neighborhood. Words such as *loving*, *sarcastic*, and *angry* describe tone. A writer's word choice also determines a story's **mood,** the overall feeling that a work of literature creates in a reader. Words such as "gloomy," "cheerful," and "eerie" describe mood.

Reading Focus

Reading Aloud If you are having difficulty determining the tone in "The Circuit," try reading a few passages aloud. Fill in a chart like the one below as you read aloud.

Story Passage	Language and Tone
"When I opened the front door to the shack, I stopped. Everything we owned was neatly packed in cardboard boxes. Suddenly I felt even more the weight of hours, days, weeks, and months of work." (page 408)	The narrator's words are simple but meaningful. The tone is sad and reflective.
"The garage was worn out by the years . . . The dirt floor, populated by earthworms, looked like a gray road map." (page 409)	

Writing Focus

Think as a Reader/Writer

Find It in Your Reading As you read, note in your *Reader/Writer Notebook* the words Jiménez uses to describe the places in the story. When you have finished the story, read the words you listed. Then, decide on a word that best sums up how Jiménez feels about each place he describes.

Vocabulary

circuit (SUR kiht) *n.:* regular route of a job. *The family picked crops on a circuit.*

detect (dih TEHKT) *v.:* discover; notice. *He didn't detect any problems with the car.*

populated (PAHP yuh layt ihd) *v.* used as *adj.:* lived in. *The dirt floor, populated by worms, was badly in need of cleaning.*

drone (drohn) *n.:* continuous buzzing sound. *The insects' drone made the day seem hot.*

instinctively (ihn STIHNGK tihv lee) *adv.:* automatically. *Panchito instinctively hid when he saw the school bus.*

Language Coach

Related Words Some words have meanings that give you a clue to the meanings of other words. For example, the word *populated* is related to the word *popular*. Which word on the list above is related to the word *circle*? Use a dictionary to find related words for some of the other Vocabulary words.

Learn It Online
Use Word Watch to improve your vocabulary at:

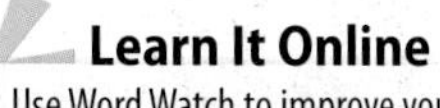 

go.hrw.com L8-405 Go

MEET THE WRITER

Francisco Jiménez

(1943–   )

Growing Up in the Fields

Francisco Jiménez was born in Mexico and came to the United States when he was four years old. At the age of six he started working in the fields. Because he did not know English, he not only failed to pass first grade but also was mistakenly labeled mentally impaired. Later, in the eighth grade, he and his family were deported.

Before he could read English, Jiménez loved looking at books with pictures of butterflies and longed to learn more about them.

> "I knew information was in the words written underneath each picture. . . . I could close my eyes and see the words, but I could not understand what they meant."

Getting an Education

Soon his family was able to return to the United States legally. Jiménez returned to high school and did so well that he earned three college scholarships. He graduated from college with honors and later earned a doctoral degree in Latin American literature. Jiménez, a university professor, has won several awards for his short stories.

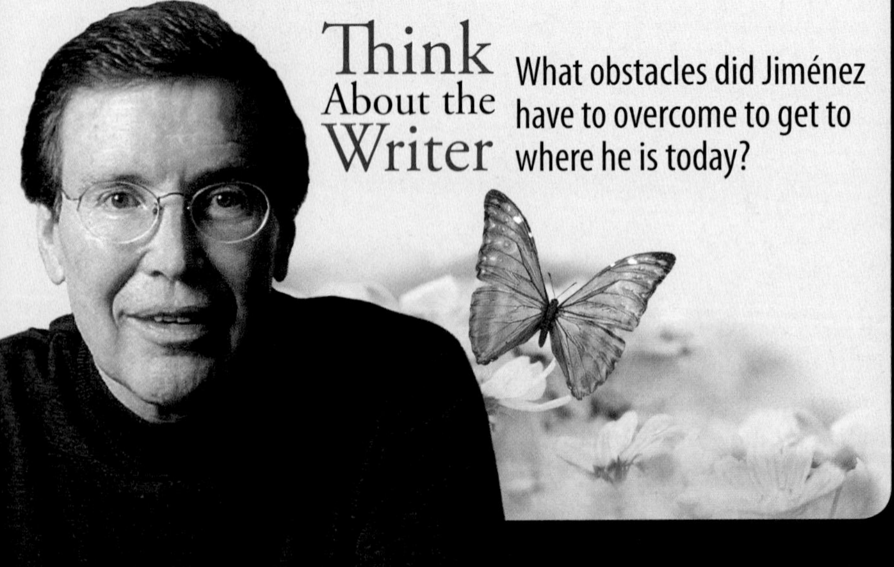

Think About the Writer What obstacles did Jiménez have to overcome to get to where he is today?

Build Background

It was once common for young children to work at difficult, dangerous jobs. In the late 1800s, an international movement to end child labor began. An important step toward restricting child labor in the United States was the Fair Labor Standards Act of 1938. This law made it illegal for children under sixteen to work during school hours in interstate commerce. Despite this and other laws, an estimated 300,000 children still plant, weed, and pick crops on commercial farms in the United States.

Preview the Selection

In this story a young boy named **Panchito** has to make sacrifices in order to help his family survive.

Read with a Purpose Read to discover what effect migrant farm work has on a boy and his family.

The Circuit

CAJAS DE CARTÓN[1]

by **Francisco Jiménez**

It was that time of year again. Ito, the strawberry sharecropper, did not smile. It was natural. The peak of the strawberry season was over, and the last few days the workers, most of them braceros,[2] were not picking as many boxes as they had during the months of June and July.

As the last days of August disappeared, so did the number of braceros. Sunday, only one—the best picker—came to work. I liked him. Sometimes we talked during our half-hour lunch break. That is how I found out he was from Jalisco,[3] the same state in Mexico my family was from. That Sunday was the last time I saw him.

When the sun had tired and sunk behind the mountains, Ito signaled us that it was time to go home. "Ya esora,"[4] he yelled in his broken Spanish. Those were the words I waited for twelve hours a day, every day, seven days a week, week after week. And the thought of not hearing them again saddened me.

As we drove home, Papá did not say a word. With both hands on the wheel, he stared at the dirt road. My older brother, Roberto, was also silent. He leaned his head back and closed his eyes. Once in a while he cleared from his throat the dust that blew in from outside. **A**

1. **Cajas de Cartón** (KAH hahs day kar TOHN): Cardboard Boxes. This is the original title of the story, which Jiménez wrote first in Spanish and later translated into English.
2. **braceros** (bruh SAIR ohs): Mexican farm laborers brought into the United States for limited time periods to harvest crops. *Bracero* comes from the Spanish word *brazo,* meaning "arm."

3. **Jalisco** (hah LEES koh).
4. **Ya esora** (ya ehs OH rah): Spanish for "It's time."

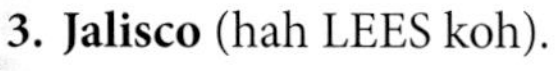

A Literary Focus Mood What mood is evoked in this paragraph? What words create this mood?

Vocabulary **circuit** (SUR kiht) *n.:* regular route of a job.

Yes, it was that time of year. When I opened the front door to the shack, I stopped. Everything we owned was neatly packed in cardboard boxes. Suddenly I felt even more the weight of hours, days, weeks, and months of work. I sat down on a box. The thought of having to move to Fresno and knowing what was in store for me there brought tears to my eyes. **B**

That night I could not sleep. I lay in bed thinking about how much I hated this move.

A little before five o'clock in the morning, Papá woke everyone up. A few minutes later, the yelling and screaming of my little brothers and sisters, for whom the move was a great adventure, broke the silence of dawn. Shortly, the barking of the dogs accompanied them.

While we packed the breakfast dishes, Papá went outside to start the "Carcanchita." That was the name Papá gave his old '38 black Plymouth. He bought it in a used-car lot in Santa Rosa in the winter of 1949. Papá was very proud of his little jalopy. He had a right to be proud of it. He spent a lot of time looking at other cars before buying this one. When he finally chose the Carcanchita, he checked it thoroughly before driving it out of the car lot. He examined every inch of the car. He listened to the motor, tilting his head from side to side like a parrot, trying to detect any noises that spelled car trouble. After being satisfied with the looks and sounds of the car, Papá then insisted on knowing who the original owner was. He never did find out from the car salesman, but he bought the car anyway. Papá figured the original owner must have been an important man, because behind the rear seat of the car he found a blue necktie. **C**

Papá parked the car out in front and left the motor running. "Listo,"[5] he yelled. Without saying a word, Roberto and I began to carry the boxes out to the car. Roberto carried the two big boxes and I carried the two smaller ones. Papá then threw the mattress on top of the car roof and tied it with ropes to the front and rear bumpers.

Everything was packed except Mamá's pot. It was an old, large galvanized pot[6] she had picked up at an army surplus store in Santa María the year I was born. The pot had many dents and nicks, and the more dents and nicks it acquired the more Mamá liked it. "Mi olla,"[7] she used to say proudly.

I held the front door open as Mamá carefully carried out her pot by both handles, making sure not to spill the cooked beans. When she got to the car, Papá reached out to help her with it. Roberto opened the rear car door and Papá gently placed it on the floor behind the front seat. All of us then climbed in. Papá sighed, wiped the sweat off his forehead with his sleeve, and said wearily: "Es todo."[8]

---

5. **listo** (LEES toh): Spanish for "ready."
6. **galvanized pot:** metal pot plated with zinc.
7. **mi olla** (mee OH yah): Spanish for "my pot."
8. **Es todo** (ehs TOH doh): Spanish for "That's all."

B **Read and Discuss** What does this detail tell us about the narrator?

C **Literary Focus** **Tone** What does this description of the car reveal about the writer's feelings for his father?

Vocabulary **detect** (dih TEHKT) *v.:* discover; notice.

As we drove away, I felt a lump in my throat. I turned around and looked at our little shack for the last time.

At sunset we drove into a labor camp near Fresno. Since Papá did not speak English, Mamá asked the camp foreman if he needed any more workers. "We don't need no more," said the foreman, scratching his head. "Check with Sullivan down the road. Can't miss him. He lives in a big white house with a fence around it."

When we got there, Mamá walked up to the house. She went through a white gate, past a row of rosebushes, up the stairs to the front door. She rang the doorbell. The porch light went on and a tall, husky man came out. They exchanged a few words. After the man went in, Mamá clasped her hands and hurried back to the car. "We have work! Mr. Sullivan said we can stay there the whole season," she said, gasping and pointing to an old garage near the stables.

The garage was worn out by the years. It had no windows. The walls, eaten by termites, strained to support the roof, full of holes. The dirt floor, populated by earthworms, looked like a gray road map.

That night, by the light of a kerosene lamp, we unpacked and cleaned our new home. Roberto swept away the loose dirt, leaving the hard ground. Papá plugged the holes in the walls with old newspapers and tin can tops. Mamá fed my little brothers and sisters. Papá and Roberto then brought in the mattress and placed it on the far corner of the garage. "Mamá, you and the little ones sleep on the mattress. Roberto,

Vocabulary **populated** (PAHP yuh layt ihd) *v.* used as *adj.:* lived in.

SOCIAL STUDIES LINK

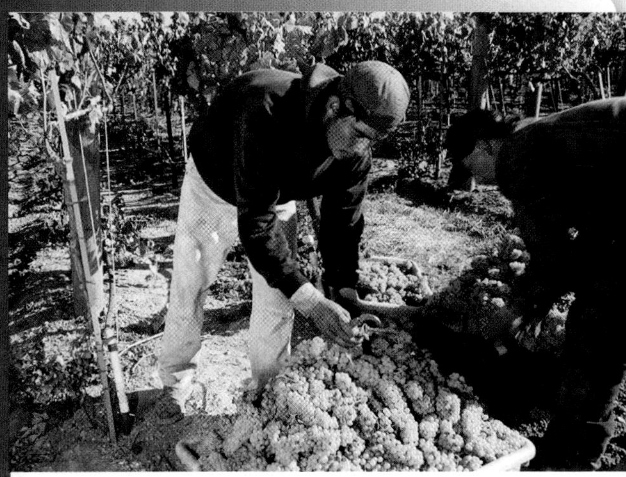

Harvesting grapes.

Migrant Farmworkers

Today when we think of farm work, we often think of machinery. Although machines such as tractors have made farm work easier, over 85 percent of fruits and vegetables still have to be cared for or picked by hand. The bins of apples, peaches, and broccoli at your grocery store would be empty if migrant farmworkers hadn't carefully picked each one of them.

Who are the people picking your food? Most migrant farmworkers or their families come to the United States from Spanish-speaking countries. Every year, as soon as the first crop is ready to harvest, they leave their homes and go to work. When that crop is harvested, they move on to the crop that ripens next. Harvesting is hard and dangerous work, and most migrant farmworkers earn less than $7,500 a year. Today some states, governmental agencies, and other organizations are trying to address the needs of migrant farmworkers.

Ask Yourself

Why does the narrator dread the many moves his family's work demands?

Analyzing Visuals **Viewing and Interpreting** What feelings do you think the narrator has when he sees a bus like this coming down the road?

Panchito, and I will sleep outside under the trees," Papá said. **D**

Early next morning Mr. Sullivan showed us where his crop was, and after breakfast, Papá, Roberto, and I headed for the vineyard to pick.

Around nine o'clock the temperature had risen to almost one hundred degrees. I was completely soaked in sweat and my mouth felt as if I had been chewing on a handkerchief. I walked over to the end of the row, picked up the jug of water we had brought, and began drinking. "Don't drink too much; you'll get sick," Roberto shouted. No sooner had he said that than I felt sick to my stomach. I dropped to my knees and let the jug roll off my hands. I remained motionless with my eyes glued on the hot sandy ground. All I could hear was the drone of insects. Slowly I began to recover. I poured water over my face and neck and watched the dirty water run down my arms to the ground.

I still felt a little dizzy when we took a break to eat lunch. It was past two o'clock, and we sat underneath a large walnut tree that was on the side of the road. While we ate, Papá jotted down the number of boxes we had picked. Roberto drew designs on the ground with a stick. Suddenly I noticed Papá's face turn pale as he looked down the road. "Here comes the school bus," he whispered loudly in alarm. Instinctively, Roberto and I ran and hid in the vineyards. We did not want to get in trouble for not going to school. The neatly dressed boys about my age got off. They carried books under their arms. After they crossed the street, the bus drove away. Roberto and I came out from hiding and joined Papá. "Tienen que tener cuidado,"[9] he warned us.

After lunch we went back to work. The sun kept beating down. The buzzing insects,

9. **Tienen que tener cuidado** (tee EH nehn kay teh NAYR kwee DAH doh): Spanish for "You have to be careful."

D **Read and Discuss** How is the family doing now?

Vocabulary **drone** (drohn) *n.:* continuous buzzing sound.
instinctively (ihn STIHNGK tihv lee) *adv.:* automatically.

the wet sweat, and the hot, dry dust made the afternoon seem to last forever. Finally the mountains around the valley reached out and swallowed the sun. Within an hour it was too dark to continue picking. The vines blanketed the grapes, making it difficult to see the bunches. **E**

"Vámonos,"[10] said Papá, signaling to us that it was time to quit work. Papá then took out a pencil and began to figure out how much we had earned our first day. He wrote down numbers, crossed some out, wrote down some more. "Quince,"[11] he murmured.

When we arrived home, we took a cold shower underneath a water hose. We then sat down to eat dinner around some wooden crates that served as a table. Mamá had cooked a special meal for us. We had rice and tortillas with carne con chile, my favorite dish.

The next morning I could hardly move. My body ached all over. I felt little control over my arms and legs. This feeling went on every morning for days until my muscles finally got used to the work. **F**

It was Monday, the first week of November. The grape season was over and I could now go to school. I woke up early that morning and lay in bed, looking at the stars and savoring[12] the thought of not going to work and of starting sixth grade for the first time that year. Since I could not sleep, I decided to get up and join Papá and Roberto at breakfast. I sat at the table across from Roberto, but I kept my head down. I did not want to look up and face him. I knew he was sad. He was not going to school today. He was not going tomorrow, or next week, or next month. He would not go until the cotton season was over, and that was sometime in February. I rubbed my hands together and watched the dry, acid-stained skin fall to the floor in little rolls.

When Papá and Roberto left for work, I felt relief. I walked to the top of a small grade[13] next to the shack and watched the Carcanchita disappear in the distance in a cloud of dust.

Two hours later, around eight o'clock, I stood by the side of the road waiting for school bus number twenty. When it arrived, I climbed in. Everyone was busy either talking or yelling. I sat in an empty seat in the back.

When the bus stopped in front of the school, I felt very nervous. I looked out the bus window and saw boys and girls carrying books under their arms. I put my hands in my pant pockets and walked to the principal's office. When I entered, I heard a woman's voice say: "May I help you?" I was startled. I had not heard English for months. For a few seconds I remained speechless. I looked at the lady, who waited for an answer. My first instinct was to answer her in Spanish, but I held back. Finally, after struggling for English words, I managed to tell her that I wanted to enroll

10. **Vámonos** (VAH moh nohs): Spanish for "Let's go."
11. **quince** (KEEN say): Spanish for "fifteen."
12. **savoring** (SAY vuhr ihng): enjoying, as if tasting something delicious.
13. **grade:** here, hill.

E **Reading Focus** **Reading Aloud** What is the mood of the paragraph? Read aloud to see, hear, and feel the vineyard.

F **Read and Discuss** What does the narrator reveal about the first day of work at the Sullivans' vineyard?

in the sixth grade. After answering many questions, I was led to my classroom.

Mr. Lema, the sixth-grade teacher, greeted me and assigned me a desk. He then introduced me to the class. I was so nervous and scared at that moment when everyone's eyes were on me that I wished I were with Papá and Roberto picking cotton. After taking roll, Mr. Lema gave the class the assignment for the first hour. "The first thing we have to do this morning is finish reading the story we began yesterday," he said enthusiastically. He walked up to me, handed me an English book, and asked me to read. "We are on page 125," he said politely. When I heard this, I felt my blood rush to my head; I felt dizzy. "Would you like to read?" he asked hesitantly. I opened the book to page 125. My mouth was dry. My eyes began to water. I could not begin. "You can read later," Mr. Lema said understandingly. **G**

For the rest of the reading period I kept getting angrier and angrier with myself. *I should have read,* I thought to myself.

During recess I went into the restroom and opened my English book to page 125. I began to read in a low voice, pretending I was in class. There were many words I did not know. I closed the book and headed back to the classroom.

Mr. Lema was sitting at his desk correcting papers. When I entered he looked up at me and smiled. I felt better. I walked up to him and asked if he could help me with the new words. "Gladly," he said.

The rest of the month I spent my lunch hours working on English with Mr. Lema, my best friend at school.

One Friday, during lunch hour, Mr. Lema asked me to take a walk with him to the music room. "Do you like music?" he asked me as we entered the building.

"Yes, I like corridos,"[14] I answered. He then picked up a trumpet, blew on it, and handed it to me. The sound gave me goose bumps. I knew that sound. I had heard it in many corridos. "How would you like to learn how to play it?" he asked. He must have read my face because before I could answer, he added: "I'll teach you how to play it during our lunch hours."

That day I could hardly wait to get home to tell Papá and Mamá the great news. As I got off the bus, my little brothers and sisters ran up to meet me. They were yelling and screaming. I thought they were happy to see me, but when I opened the door to our shack, I saw that everything we owned was neatly packed in cardboard boxes. **H**

---

14. **corridos** (kor REE dohs): Mexican folk ballads.

G **Reading Focus** **Reading Aloud** Read this paragraph aloud, with expression. How do you think the writer feels about Mr. Lema?

H **Read and Discuss** What has changed for the narrator?

Applying Your Skills

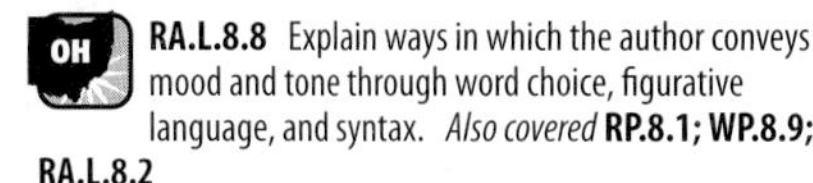

RA.L.8.8 Explain ways in which the author conveys mood and tone through word choice, figurative language, and syntax. *Also covered* **RP.8.1; WP.8.9; RA.L.8.2**

The Circuit

Respond and Think Critically

Reading Focus

Quick Check

1. Why does the family leave the shack near Ito's farm?
2. Why does the narrator, Panchito, consider Mr. Lema his best friend?
3. Why won't Panchito learn to play the trumpet?

Read with a Purpose

4. How do you think Panchito will cope with having to move yet again?

Reading Skills: Reading Aloud

5. Review the notes you took while you read aloud. Then, add a row to the bottom of your chart to describe the story's overall mood. Refer to this chart as you answer questions 10 and 11.

Story Passage	*Language and Tone*
"When I opened the front door to the shack, I stopped. . . ."	*The narrator's words are simple but meaningful. . . .*

Overall mood of the story:

Literary Focus

Literary Analysis

6. **Infer** What can you infer from the story about the family's income and level of education?
7. **Draw Conclusions** What difficulties faced by migrant parents and their children does the text touch on?
8. **Interpret** Is "The Circuit" an effective title? Explain. What idea about life does the title establish and reinforce?
9. **Evaluate** Why do you think Jiménez ends the story so abruptly? Do you think this is an effective choice? Why or why not?

Literary Skills: Tone and Mood

10. **Analyze** What is the story's overall tone? What impact does it have on the story? What other tone might the author have chosen?
11. **Identify** What mood did you sense throughout the story? What words help set the mood?

Literary Skills Review: Setting

12. **Draw Conclusions** Although it is usually defined as the time and place of a story, the **setting** can include other information. What do you learn about migrant workers' customs, foods, and lifestyle from the story's setting?

Writing Focus

Think as a Reader/Writer

Use It in Your Writing In "The Circuit," Jiménez chooses his words carefully to achieve a certain tone. Look back at your answer to question 10. Choose one of the other possible tones you identified, and rewrite a paragraph from the story using that tone.

What Do You Think Now?

Do you think it was more important for Panchito to get an education or to help support his family? Explain.

Applying Your Skills

The Circuit

Vocabulary Development

Vocabulary Check

circuit
detect
populated
drone
instinctively

Answer the following questions.

1. Why might a mail carrier's job be said to follow a **circuit**?
2. If Papá **detects** noises in the car's engine, has he discovered noises or has he repaired them?
3. Is Mr. Sullivan's garage nice enough to be **populated** by a family? Why or why not?
4. What does the **drone** of insects sound like?
5. If people act **instinctively,** are they acting automatically or thoughtfully?

Vocabulary Skills: Spanish and English Words

English is made up of words from different languages. Some of these words became part of English long ago, and others have entered the language recently. Thousands of Spanish words have become part of English. Some of them have changed from the original Spanish form. For instance, *rancho* has become *ranch,* and *la reata* has become *lariat.* Other words, such as *patio* and *plaza,* have undergone slight changes in pronunciation, but not in spelling.

In addition to common nouns, Spanish has also contributed numerous proper nouns. In the sixteenth and seventeenth centuries, Spanish explorers gave Spanish names to mountains, rivers, lakes, and new settlements in North America. If you live in the Southwest, chances are good that some of the place names near you came from Spanish. Many of these names describe distinctive geographical features. For example, if Spanish explorers crossed a very cold river, they might have named it *Frío,* or "Cold."

Your Turn

Copy this chart, and fill in the meanings of the Spanish names. Use a dictionary for reference.

Spanish Name	Meaning
Colorado	
Florida	
Los Angeles	
San Francisco	
Fresno	

Language Coach

Related Words Understanding related words can help you expand your vocabulary. Use a dictionary to find related words for the following words: *migrant, labor,* and *circuit.* Write the related words and their meanings in your *Reader/Writer Notebook.*

Academic Vocabulary

Talk About . . .

In a small group, discuss the impact of hard work and a lack of education on the children of farmworkers. Then, brainstorm a list of services you think might be established to help these children. Present your ideas to the class.

RA.L.8.8 Explain ways in which the author conveys mood and tone through word choice, figurative language, and syntax. **RP.8.1** Apply reading comprehension strategies, including making predictions, comparing and contrasting, recalling and summarizing and making inferences and drawing conclusions. *Also covered* **WC.8.3; WA.8.5.a; VO.8.7**

Grammar Link

Types of Sentences

There is no such thing as an all-purpose sentence. Each sentence is meant to give specific information and provoke a specific response. Sentences are classified according to the following four purposes:

- A **declarative sentence** makes a statement. It is followed by a period.

  Panchito has to work to help feed his family.
- An **interrogative sentence** asks a question. It is followed by a question mark.

  Why can't the family settle in one place?
- An **imperative sentence** gives a command or makes a request. It is followed by a period or an exclamation point.

  Hand me the cardboard box.
- An **exclamatory sentence** shows excitement or expresses strong feeling. It is followed by an exclamation point.

  I can't believe we're moving again!

You can always identify an interrogative sentence by the question mark at the end. End punctuation, however, is not a reliable way to identify other sentence types.

Your Turn

Label each of the following sentences *declarative, interrogative, imperative,* or *exclamatory.*

1. Don't drink too much water.
2. Would you like to learn to play the trumpet?
3. At last we've found work!
4. Migrant farmworkers have a hard life.

Writing Applications Create your own example of each type of sentence.

CHOICES

As you respond to the Choices, use these **Academic Vocabulary** words as appropriate: distinctive, establish, impact, impression.

REVIEW

Rewrite a Passage

Choose a short passage from "The Circuit" and identify its tone. Then, rewrite the passage using a different tone. If the original is sad or nostalgic, for example, you might make it cheerful or humorous. When you have finished, describe the types of changes you had to make in order to change the tone.

CONNECT

Propose a Solution

Timed Writing In the story, Panchito and his siblings do not have the same opportunities for education as most other children in the United States do. Write a brief essay in which you offer a solution to this problem. Support your ideas with details.

EXTEND

Research a Topic

Group Project Panchito has a deep desire for an education. What keeps some children from gaining an education? What percentage of children have to work instead of study? What impact does the limited education of some children have on a country? With a small group of classmates, research one of these issues, and share your findings with the class.

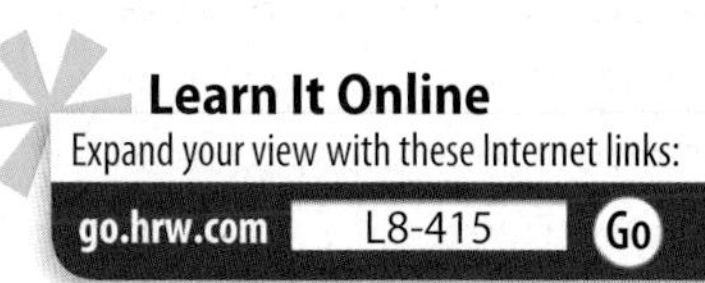

Learn It Online
Expand your view with these Internet links:
go.hrw.com
L8-415
Go

SHORT STORY

Preparing to Read

Dancer

by **Vickie Sears**

Teenager performs shawl dance at powwow.

What Do You Think?

How does belonging to a community satisfy the heart and mind?

QuickWrite

What does it mean to "belong"? How can joining a club, choir, sports or after-school group help someone find fulfillment and happiness?

Reader/Writer Notebook

Use your **RWN** to complete the activities for this selection.

OH **RA.L.8.9** Examine symbols used in literary texts. **RP.8.1** Apply reading comprehension strategies, including making predictions, comparing and contrasting, recalling and summarizing and making inferences and drawing conclusions.

Literary Focus

Symbolism A person, place, thing, or event that has meaning in itself but also stands for something beyond itself is called a **symbol.** A flag, for example, can symbolize patriotism. A desert can symbolize thirst or hopelessness. As you read "Dancer," look for symbols that represent larger ideas or themes.

Reading Focus

Drawing Conclusions A **conclusion** is the final thought or judgment you establish after you have considered all of the evidence. You usually **draw conclusions** about characters, theme, or the author's style after you have finished reading.

Into Action Use a concept map like the one below to draw conclusions about the author's style. As you read, fill in examples of each literary device in the outer circles. Later, you will make a judgment about the style.

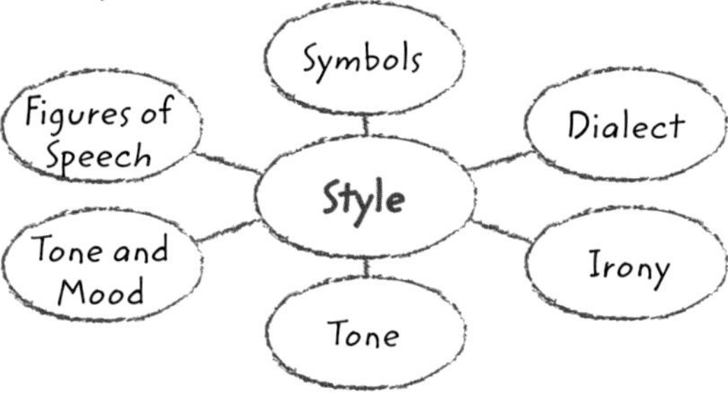

Writing Focus

Think as a Reader/Writer

Find It in Your Reading As you read, watch for **imagery**—words and phrases that appeal to the senses—that the author uses to describe characters and action. Write the images in your *Reader/Writer Notebook.*

TechFocus As you read the story and the Culture Link, think about how you might use the Internet to learn more about the different dances that are mentioned.

Vocabulary

foster (FAWS tuhr) *adj.:* given shelter and care by people other than one's parents. *As a foster child, Clarissa lived in several different homes.*

ferocious (fuh ROH shuhs) *adj.:* brutal; cruel. *The narrator is worried about Clarissa's upsetting, ferocious dreams.*

fixated (FIHK sayt uhd) *adj.:* focused with full attention. *Clarissa is fixated on the dancer's every move and can't look away.*

abnormal (ab NAWR muhl) *adj.:* not normal; unusual. *Clarissa's moods change so rapidly that it seems almost abnormal.*

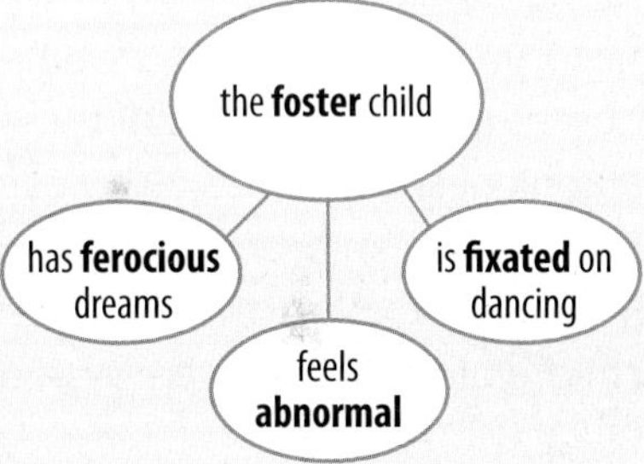

Language Coach

Multiple-Meaning Words The word *foster* is used as an adjective in the Vocabulary list above, but it can also be used as a verb. How does its meaning change when it is a verb? Use a dictionary to help you figure out the answer.

Learn It Online
Build your understanding of terms with Word Watch at:

go.hrw.com L8-417 

MEET THE WRITER

Vickie Sears

(1941–1999)

Finding Identity

Vickie Sears was half-Cherokee, with a Cherokee father. Her father and his family taught her about the Cherokee ways, but he died when Sears was twelve years old. Her mother was not Native American, and she did not allow Sears to visit her father's family after her father's death. Describing this time in her life, Sears said, "I began to sneak off to the Indian Center in downtown Seattle. I became an intertribal person, learning from all the different tribal people who came there. . . . Many things were viewed differently from Father's beliefs, but there were enough comparable attitudes that allowed me not to feel so alone."

Writing from the Heart

Sears was a poet and essayist, but she is perhaps best known for her short stories, many of which reflect her own personal history. Like the characters in her stories, Sears lived in foster homes as a child. In one of the dedications to *Simple Songs,* a book of short stories, she wrote, "To all of the children who ever lived in an orphanage or foster home and had a dream." Her stories explore the unique experience of Native American children in the foster care system.

Think About the Writer What events from her own life does Sears explore in her stories?

(below) A written sample of the Cherokee alphabet.

Build Background

The characters in this story attend Native American powwows. These gatherings vary by location and community, but nearly all include some form of music and dancing. In many regions, powwows are opportunities to visit with members of one's own community or other communities.

Preview the Selection

In this story an angry and frightened five-year-old girl named **Clarissa** comes to live with a foster family. They introduce her to a new community—and her own heritage.

Read with a Purpose Read this story to discover how a lonely girl finds a way to belong.

Dancer

by **Vickie Sears**

Tell you just how it was with her. Took her to a dance not long after she come to live with us. Smartest thing I ever done. Seems like some old Eaglespirit woman saw her living down here and came back just to be with Clarissa.

Five years old she was when she come to us. Some foster kids come with lots of stuff, but she came with everything she had in a paper bag. Some dresses that was too short. A pair of pants barely holding a crotch. A pile of ratty underwear and one new nightgown. Mine was her third foster home in as many months. The agency folks said she was *so-cio-path-ic.*[1] I don't know nothing from that. She just seemed like she was all full up with anger and scaredness like lots of the kids who come to me. Only she was a real loner. Not trusting nobody. But she ran just like any other kid, was quiet when needed. Smiled at all the right times. If you could get her to smile, that is. Didn't talk much, though.

Had these ferocious dreams, too. Real screamer dreams they were. Shake the soul right out of you. She'd be screaming and crying with her little body wriggling on the bed, her hair all matted up on her woody-colored face. One time I got her to tell me what she was seeing, and she told me how she was being chased by a man with a long knife what he was going to kill her with and nobody could hear her calling out for help. She didn't talk too much about them, but they was all bad like that one. Seemed the most fierce dreams I ever remember anybody ever having outside of a vision seek.[2] They said her tribe was Assiniboin,[3] but they weren't for certain. What was for sure was that she was a fine dark-eyed girl just meant for someone to scoop up for loving. **A**

Took her to her first dance in September, like I said, not long after she came. It wasn't like I thought it would be a good thing to do. It was just that we was all going. Me, my own kids, some nieces and nephews and the other children who was living with us. The

1. **sociopathic:** having a personality disorder marked by aggressive antisocial behavior.

2. **vision seek:** vision quest. A journey where a young person goes off alone to find spiritual power and guidance.

3. **Assiniboin** (uh SIHN uh boyn): Native American group from Montana, Alberta, and Saskatchewan.

A **Read and Discuss** What has the author told us about Clarissa so far?

Vocabulary **foster** (FAWS tuhr) *adj.:* given shelter and care by people other than one's parents.
ferocious (fuh ROH shuhs) *adj.:* brutal; cruel.

powwow was just part of what we done all the time. Every month. More often in the summer. But this was the regular first Friday night of the school year. We'd all gather up and go to the school. I was thinking on leaving her home with a sitter cause she'd tried to kill one of the cats a couple of days before. We'd had us a big talk and she was grounded, but, well, it seemed like she ought to be with us. **B**

Harold, that's my oldest boy, he and the other kids was mad with her, but he decided to show her around anyhow. At the school he went through the gym telling people, "This here's my sister, Clarissa." Wasn't no fuss or anything. She was just another one of the kids. When they was done meeting folks, he put her on one of the bleachers near the drum and went to join the men. He was in that place where his voice cracks but was real proud to be drumming. Held his hand up to his ear even, some of the time. Anyhow, Clarissa was sitting there, not all that interested in the dance or drum, when Molly Graybull come out in her button dress. Her arms was all stretched out, and she was slipping around, preening on them spindles of legs that get skinnier with every year. She was well into her seventies, and I might as well admit, Molly had won herself a fair share of dance contests. So it wasn't no surprise how a little girl could get so fixated on Molly. Clarissa watched her move around-around-around. Then all the rest of the dancers after Molly. She sure took in a good eyeful. Fancy dance. Owl dance. Circle dance. Even a hoop dancer was visiting that night. Everything weaving all slow, then fast. Around-around until that child couldn't see nothing else. Seemed like she was struck silent in the night, too. Never had no dreams at all. Well, not the hollering kind anyways. **C**

Next day she was more quiet than usual only I could see she was looking at her picture book and tapping the old one-two, one-two. Tapping her toes on the rug with the inside of her head going around and around. As quiet as she could be, she was.

A few days went on before she asks me, "When's there gonna be another dance?"

I tell her in three weeks. She just smiles and goes on outside, waiting on the older kids to come home from school.

The very next day she asks if she can listen to some singing. I give her the tape recorder and some of Joe Washington from

---

B **Reading Focus** **Drawing Conclusions** The narrator has given you more information about Clarissa. What conclusions can you draw about her character and her foster family so far?

C **Read and Discuss** How do things turn out for Clarissa at her first dance?

Vocabulary **fixated** (FIHK sayt uhd) *adj.:* focused with full attention.

up to the Lummi reservation and the Kicking Woman Singers. Clarissa, she takes them tapes and runs out back behind the chicken shed, staying out all afternoon. I wasn't worried none, though, cause I could hear the music the whole time. Matter of fact, it like to make me sick of them same songs come the end of three weeks. But that kid, she didn't get into no kind of mischief. Almost abnormal how good she was. Worried me some to see her so caught up but it seemed good too. The angry part of her slowed down so's she wasn't hitting the animals or chopping on herself with sticks like she was doing when she first come. She wasn't laughing much either, but she started playing with the other kids when they come home. Seemed like everybody was working hard to be better with each other. **D**

Come March, Clarissa asks, "Can I dance?"

For sure, the best time for teaching is when a kid wants to listen, so we stood side to side with me doing some steps. She followed along fine. I put a tape and started moving faster, and Clarissa just kept up all natural. I could tell she'd been practicing lots. She was doing real good.

Comes the next powwow, which was outside on the track field, I braided Clarissa's hair. Did her up with some ermine[4] and bead ties, then give her a purse to carry. It was all beaded with a rose and leaves. Used to be my aunt's. She held it right next to her side with her chin real high. She joined in a Circle dance. I could see she was watching her feet a little and looking how others do their steps, but mostly she was doing wonderful. When Molly Graybull showed up beside her, Clarissa took to a seat and stared. She didn't dance again that night, but I could see there was dreaming coming into her eyes. I saw that fire that said to practice. And she did. I heard her every day in her room. Finally bought her her very own tape recorder so's the rest of us could listen to music too.

Some months passed on. All the kids was getting bigger. Clarissa, she went into the first grade. Harvey went off to community college up in Seattle, and that left me with Ronnie being the oldest at home. Clarissa was keeping herself busy all the time going over to Molly Graybull's. She was coming home with Spider Woman stories and trickster tales.[5]

4. **ermine:** weasel fur.

5. **Spider Woman stories and trickster tales:** Spider Woman is a character in various Native American creation myths. A trickster tale is the story of a small, less powerful character who outwits a bigger, stronger character.

D **Read and Discuss** How have things changed for Clarissa?

Vocabulary **abnormal** (ab NAWR muhl) *adj.:* not normal; unusual.

CULTURE LINK

Native American Dances

Dance is an important aspect of traditional Native American culture. Held across the country at events called powwows, the dances are often very colorful, with dancers wearing ornate costumes and masks. Dancers move to the beat of drums, other instruments, and singing. A few dances, such as the Owl dance, are performed by couples, but most of the dances are for men only or women only. Of the women's dances, Women's Traditional is one of the oldest and most graceful. It is danced by women of all ages. Fancy Shawl dance (shown at the left) is a newer women's dance that developed in the 1950s and involves quick, light steps.

Ask Yourself

In what way might traditional dances help Clarissa fit into her new community?

One night she speaks up at supper and says, right clear and loud, "I'm an Assiniboin." Clear as it can be, she says it again. Don't nobody have to say nothing to something that proud said. **E**

Next day I started working on a wing dress for Clarissa. She was going to be needing one for sure real soon.

Comes the first school year powwow and everyone was putting on their best. I called for Clarissa to come to my room. I told her, "I think it's time you have something special for yourself." Then I held up the green satin and saw her eyes full up with glitter. She didn't say nothing. Only kisses me and runs off to her room. **F**

Just as we're all getting out of the car, Clarissa whispered to me, "I'm gonna dance with Molly Graybull." I put my hand on her shoulder to say, "You just listen to your spirit. That's where your music is."

We all danced an Owl dance, a Friendship dance, and a couple of Circle dances. Things was feeling real warm and good, and then it was time for the women's traditional. Clarissa joined the circle. She opened her arms to something nobody but her seemed to hear. That's when I saw that old Eagle woman come down and slide right inside of Clarissa, scooping up that child. There Clarissa was, full up with music. All full with that old, old spirit, letting herself dance through Clarissa's feet. Then Molly Graybull come dancing alongside Clarissa, and they was both the same age. **G**

E **Read and Discuss** What do Clarissa's comment, "I'm an Assiniboin," and her foster mother's response tell us?

F **Literary Focus** **Symbol** The new clothes mean more than just new items to wear. What might new clothes symbolize for Clarissa?

G **Literary Focus** **Symbol** What might dancing symbolize in this story?

Applying Your Skills

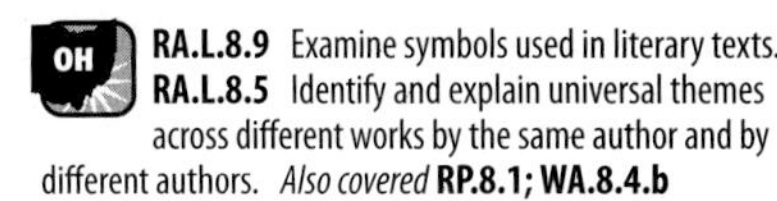
RA.L.8.9 Examine symbols used in literary texts.
RA.L.8.5 Identify and explain universal themes across different works by the same author and by different authors. *Also covered* **RP.8.1; WA.8.4.b**

Dancer

Respond and Think Critically

Reading Focus

Quick Check

1. How does Clarissa behave when she first arrives at the foster home?
2. What does the narrator claim is the smartest thing she ever did? Why?
3. What does Clarissa learn to do?

Read with a Purpose

4. How does Clarissa find a place to belong? Who helps her find this place?

Reading Skills: Drawing Conclusions

5. Review the details you listed in your chart. What conclusions can you draw about the author's style based on these details and your overall impression of the work?

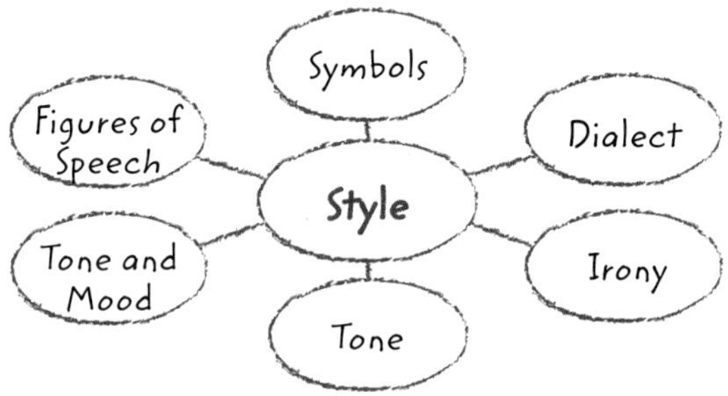

Literary Focus

Literary Analysis

6. **Infer** What can you infer about the narrator's character from the way she thinks about and acts toward Clarissa? Give details.
7. **Summarize** How does Molly Graybull help Clarissa find pride in her heritage?
8. **Cause and Effect** Clarissa changes significantly from the beginning of the story to the end. Discuss these changes and what causes them.

Literary Skills: Symbol

9. **Infer** Molly Graybull and the Eaglespirit woman are not well-rounded characters (they do not change in the course of the story). In fact, the story suggests that they might be symbolic characters. What might these characters symbolize?

Literary Skills Review: Theme

10. **Analyze** A **theme** is an insight about life that a work of literature reveals. Review the symbols in the story, and think about a theme they could reveal. Share your idea in the form of a theme statement.

Writing Focus

Think as a Reader/Writer

Use It in Your Writing Think of a possession or animal that has a strong symbolic meaning for you. What ideas do you associate with it? Write a poem or essay explaining what it symbolizes to you, using strong images to describe your symbol.

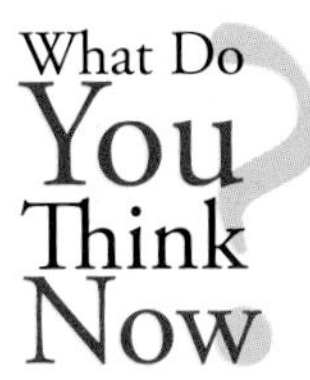

What does Clarissa's experience teach you about the value of community?

Applying Your Skills

Dancer

Vocabulary Development

Vocabulary Check

foster
ferocious
fixated
abnormal

Show that you understand the Vocabulary words by answering the following questions:

1. What qualities make Clarissa's **foster** family a good match for her?
2. Why do you think Clarissa has **ferocious** dreams when she first comes to live with the family?
3. Why is Clarissa **fixated** on Molly Graybull?
4. Why does Clarissa's good behavior seem **abnormal** at first?

Vocabulary Skills: Idioms

An **idiom** is an expression peculiar to a particular language that means something different from the literal (dictionary) meaning of the words. *Put a sock in it* ("Stop talking") is an idiom of American English. If you didn't know this idiom, you might wonder why anyone would want to put a sock in someone's mouth! Every language has its own idioms. When you grow up speaking a language, you understand its idioms without even thinking about them. When you're learning a new language, it can be difficult to figure out what its idioms mean, and it's even harder to use them correctly. Here are some of the idioms in "Dancer":

"Shake the soul right out of you." (page 419)

"meant for someone to scoop up for loving" (page 419)

"She sure took in a good eyeful." (page 420)

"Seemed like she was struck silent. . . ." (page 420)

Your Turn

Review the sentences in which the idioms from the story are found, and write the literal meaning of each idiom. Then, write its figurative meaning.

Language Coach

Multiple-Meaning Words English is full of words that have more than one meaning. Here are some words that are used as nouns in "Dancer": *kids* (page 419), *dresses* (page 419), *pants* (page 419), *rest* (page 420), *fire* (page 421). With a classmate, first check the words' meanings in the story. Then, with the help of a dictionary, decide how the meanings change when the words are used as verbs. You may find more than one meaning.

Academic Vocabulary

Write About . . .

Think about a time when an event in your community had a strong impact on you. Jot down your impressions of the event, and explain why it was important to you. Use the underlined Academic Vocabulary words in your description.

RA.L.8.9 Examine symbols used in literary texts. **RA.L.8.5** Identify and explain universal themes across different works by the same author and by different authors. *Also covered* **WA.8.2; C.8.8.d; WC.8.3; VO.8.4; VO.8.7; WP.8.7**

Grammar Link

Types of Sentences

There are four different types of sentences. Using a variety of sentence types will make your writing more interesting. Here are examples of types of sentences:

A **simple** sentence has one **independent clause** (a clause that expresses a complete thought and can stand by itself as a sentence).
EXAMPLE: Clarissa listened to the music.

A **compound** sentence has two or more independent clauses.
EXAMPLE: Clarissa listened to the music, and she smiled.

A **complex** sentence has one independent clause and at least one subordinate clause. (A **subordinate clause** contains a subject and verb but does not express a complete thought and cannot stand alone as a sentence.)
EXAMPLE: When she listened to music, she smiled.

A **compound-complex** sentence has two or more independent clauses and at least one subordinate clause.
EXAMPLE: When she listened to the music, her eyes lit up, and she began to tap her feet.

More information about clauses can be found in the Language Handbook.

Your Turn

Writing Applications With a partner, study the example sentences above. Then, write a simple sentence about music. Next, add clauses to the sentence in order to form compound, complex, and compound-complex sentences.

CHOICES

As you respond to the Choices, use the **Academic Vocabulary** words as appropriate: distinctive, establish, impact, impression.

REVIEW

Analyze Story Symbols

In "Dancer," numerous things and people appear as themselves and also have symbolic meaning. Describe what each of the following might symbolize in the story: clothing, dances, powwows, Molly Graybull, and Eaglespirit woman.

CONNECT

Write About a Theme

Timed Writing Most short stories reveal an important insight or truth about life. Write a brief essay about the **theme,** or insight about life, which Sears explores in "Dancer." First, state the theme in a full sentence. Then, since stories often have more than one theme, support your choice with details from the text.

EXTEND

Develop a Visual Presentation

TechFocus Sears mentions many dances in her story. Use the Internet and other sources to find information—including videos of performances—about traditional dances from other cultures. Then, create a digital documentary or PowerPoint presentation to present your findings to the class. Use photographs, illustrations, and video segments to establish a vivid impression of what the dances are like.

Learn It Online
Create an eye-popping multimedia presentation!
Visit the *MediaScope* mini-site at:
go.hrw.com L8-425 Go

Author Study: Ray Bradbury

CONTENTS

Ray Bradbury gives keynote address at the grand opening of the Allied Signal Challenger Learning Center, California State Dominguez Hill Campus, California.

What Do You Think?

How can writing fiction help you share your beliefs with others?

QuickWrite

How do people express their ideas about life and the world? Write for a few minutes about the ways in which musicians, writers, and artists share their ideas with others.

Preparing to Read

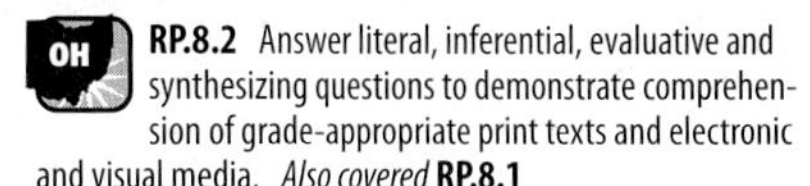

RP.8.2 Answer literal, inferential, evaluative and synthesizing questions to demonstrate comprehension of grade-appropriate print texts and electronic and visual media. *Also covered* **RP.8.1**

from Ray Bradbury Is on Fire! / The Flying Machine / The Dragon / The Fog Horn

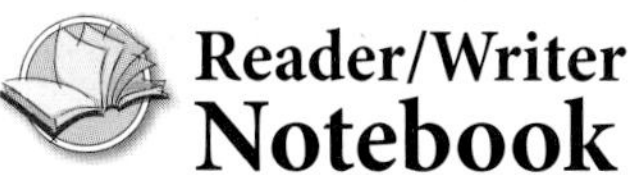

Reader/Writer Notebook

Use your **RWN** to complete the activities for these selections.

Literary Focus

Literary Criticism: Biographical Approach Writers often draw on their own backgrounds to create a story. The setting may be a place they once lived. The characters may be based on people they have known. The themes of an author's work usually involve issues that concern him or her. As you read Ray Bradbury's works, think about how his beliefs and attitudes are reflected in them.

Reading Focus

Drawing Conclusions A **conclusion** is the final idea or judgment you come to after you've considered the evidence. You will be learning about Bradbury's life and reading three of his stories. From this, you will be able to draw conclusions about Bradbury's style and what motivates him to write his stories. As you read, record key biographical information and details from the selections in a chart like the one below.

Biographical Information	Details from Selection
distrusts new technology	

Writing Focus

Think as a Reader/Writer

Find It in Your Reading **Figures of speech** are words or phrases that create an imaginative comparison between two unlike things. Record in your *Reader/Writer Notebook* the **similes** (comparisons using *like, as,* or *resembles*) and **metaphors** (direct comparisons) that help bring Bradbury's fantasies to life.

Vocabulary

from Ray Bradbury Is on Fire!

contradictory (kahn truh DIHK tuhr ee) *adj.:* in disagreement; opposing. *Bradbury is a science fiction writer who is not interested in science—a contradictory position.*

The Flying Machine

writhed (rythd) *v.:* twisted and turned. *The long wall writhed across the land like a snake.*

serene (suh REEN) *adj.:* calm; undisturbed. *The Emperor's face looked serene as he gazed out at his peaceful kingdom.*

solace (SAHL ihs) *n.:* comfort. *The Emperor takes solace from his belief that he is protecting his people.*

Language Coach

Oral Fluency In English words that begin with *wr–*, such as *write,* the initial *w* is silent. Which Vocabulary word above falls into this category? How is it pronounced? Make a list of other words that begin with the letter combination *wr–*.

Learn It Online

Watch the action-packed video introduction at:

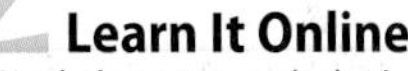

go.hrw.com L8-427

MEET THE WRITER

Learn It Online
Learn more about Bradbury at:
go.hrw.com L8-428 Go

Ray Bradbury
(1920–)

A Writer at Heart

At the age of twelve, Ray Bradbury wrote his first short stories in pencil on brown wrapping paper. He's been writing stories—and novels, poems, plays, and screenplays—ever since. Bradbury is famous for his work ethic. In more than seventy years of writing, he has published more than five hundred works. Bradbury moves effortlessly between past, present, and future. The settings of his works range from Mars and Venus to Ireland and Green Town, a fictional town based on his birthplace, Waukegan, Illinois. Whatever he is writing about, Bradbury's stories are marked by the fantastic, the mysterious, and the magical. They often express his belief that advances in science and technology should never come at the expense of human beings.

Encouraging Others

Bradbury has also explored the realm of nonfiction. One of his notable works of nonfiction is *Zen in the Art of Writing,* a collection of essays that captures the complete joy Bradbury experiences whenever he writes. In this book he encourages aspiring writers to view writing as an exciting venture:

"Writing is supposed to be difficult, agonizing, a dreadful exercise, a terrible occupation. But, you see, my stories have led me through my life. They shout, I follow. They run up and bite me on the leg—I respond by writing down everything that goes on during the bite. When I finish, the idea lets go and runs off."

Think About the Writer

What qualities do you think help to make Ray Bradbury such a successful writer?

Key Elements of Bradbury's Writing

Settings are strange and mysterious places, a combination of fantasy and reality. The past, the present, and the future may blend together in a single story.

Plots are often built around conflicts between characters and powerful forces. Characters may confront monsters, the sinister side of technology, or tyranny.

Messages often focus on our fascination with and our fear of technology. These messages often celebrate heroism and individual freedoms.

INTERVIEW

from RAY BRADBURY IS ON FIRE!

by **James Hibberd**

Read with a Purpose
Read these selections to discover Bradbury's views about technology and its impact on human beings.

Today Bradbury continues to criticize modern innovations, putting him in the seemingly contradictory position of being a sci-fi writer who's also a technophobe.[1] He famously claims to have never driven a car (Bradbury finds accident statistics appallingly unacceptable; he witnessed a deadly car accident as a teen). He is scornful of the Internet (telling one reporter it's "a big scam" by computer companies) and ATMs (asking, "Why go to a machine when you can go to a human being?") and computers ("A computer is a typewriter," he says. "I have two typewriters, I don't need another one"). A

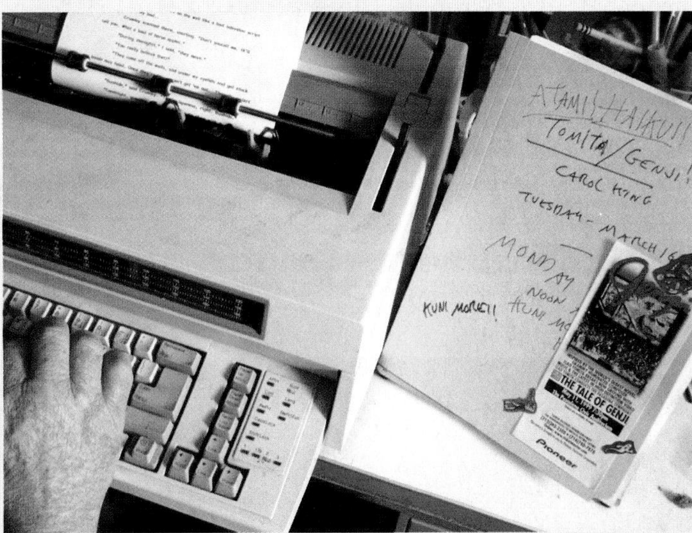
Ray Bradbury typing on a typewriter.

By mocking the electronic shortcuts and distracting entertainment that replace human contact and active thinking, Bradbury shows his science-fiction label is misplaced. He cares little for science or its fictions. The author of more than thirty books, six hundred short stories,

1. **technophobe:** person with a fear or dislike of advanced or complex technology.

A **Literary Focus** **Biographical Approach** What is Bradbury's attitude toward technology?

Vocabulary **contradictory** (kahn truh DIHK tuhr ee) *adj.:* in disagreement; opposing.

and numerous poems, essays, and plays, Bradbury is a consistent champion of things human and real. There is simply no ready label for a writer who mixes poetry and mythology with fantasy and technology to create literate tales of suspense and social criticism; no ideal bookstore section for the author whose stories of rockets and carnivals and Halloween capture the fascination of twelve-year-olds, while also stunning adult readers with his powerful prose and knowing grasp of the human condition.

One secret to Bradbury's lifelong productivity is that his play and his work are the same. When asked, "How often do you write?" Bradbury replies, "Every day of my life—you got to be in love or you shouldn't do it."

. . . When I phoned his Los Angeles home for a 9:00 A.M. interview, Bradbury was thoughtful and cranky, and told me he'd already written a short story.

JAMES HIBBERD. What makes a great story?

RAY BRADBURY. If you're a storyteller, that's what makes a great story. I think the reason my stories have been so successful is that I have a strong sense of metaphor. . . . I grew up on Greek myths, Roman myths, Egyptian myths, and the Norse Eddas. So when you have influences like that, your metaphors are so strong that people can't forget them. (B)

JAMES HIBBERD. You've been critical of computers in the past. But what about programs that aid creativity? Do you think using a word processor handicaps a writer?

(B) **Literary Focus** **Biographical Approach** What are Bradbury's storytelling influences?

A Ray Bradbury Time Line

Born on August 22, 1920, in Waukegan, Illinois.

At age twelve, decides to become a writer.

At age fourteen, moves with his family to Los Angeles, where he develops a love for the movies.

When he is twenty, his first story is accepted by the magazine *Script*.

Publishes stories in pulp magazines such as *Black Mask, Amazing Stories,* and *Weird Tales* throughout the 1940s.

In 1950, publishes *The Martian Chronicles,* which becomes a bestseller.

Wins critical acclaim for his novel *Fahrenheit 451* (1953).

In 1957, publishes *Dandelion Wine,* an autobiographical novel about his boyhood.

1920 1930 1940 1950 1960

RAY BRADBURY. There is no one way of writing. Pad and pencil, wonderful. Typewriter, wonderful. It doesn't matter what you use. In the last month I've written a new screenplay with a pad and pen. There's no one way to be creative. Any old way will work. . . .

JAMES HIBBERD. What's an average workday like for you?

RAY BRADBURY. Well, I've already got my work done. At 7:00 A.M., I wrote a short story.

JAMES HIBBERD. How long does that usually take?

RAY BRADBURY. Usually about a morning. If an idea isn't exciting you shouldn't do it. I usually get an idea around 8 o'clock in the morning, when I'm getting up, and by noon it's finished. And if it isn't done quickly you're going to begin to lie. So as quickly as you can, you emotionally react to an idea. That's how I write short stories. They've all been done in a single morning when I felt passionately about them. . . . **C**

JAMES HIBBERD. There's so much competition for a young person's attention nowadays. For the record, why is reading still important?

RAY BRADBURY. Are you kidding? You can't have a civilization without that, can you? If you can't read and write you can't think. Your thoughts are dispersed if you don't know how to read and write. You've got to be able to look at your thoughts on paper and discover what a fool you were. . . . **D**

C **Read and Discuss** What is Bradbury saying about his manner of working?

D **Reading Focus** **Drawing Conclusions** What is the value of reading for Bradbury?

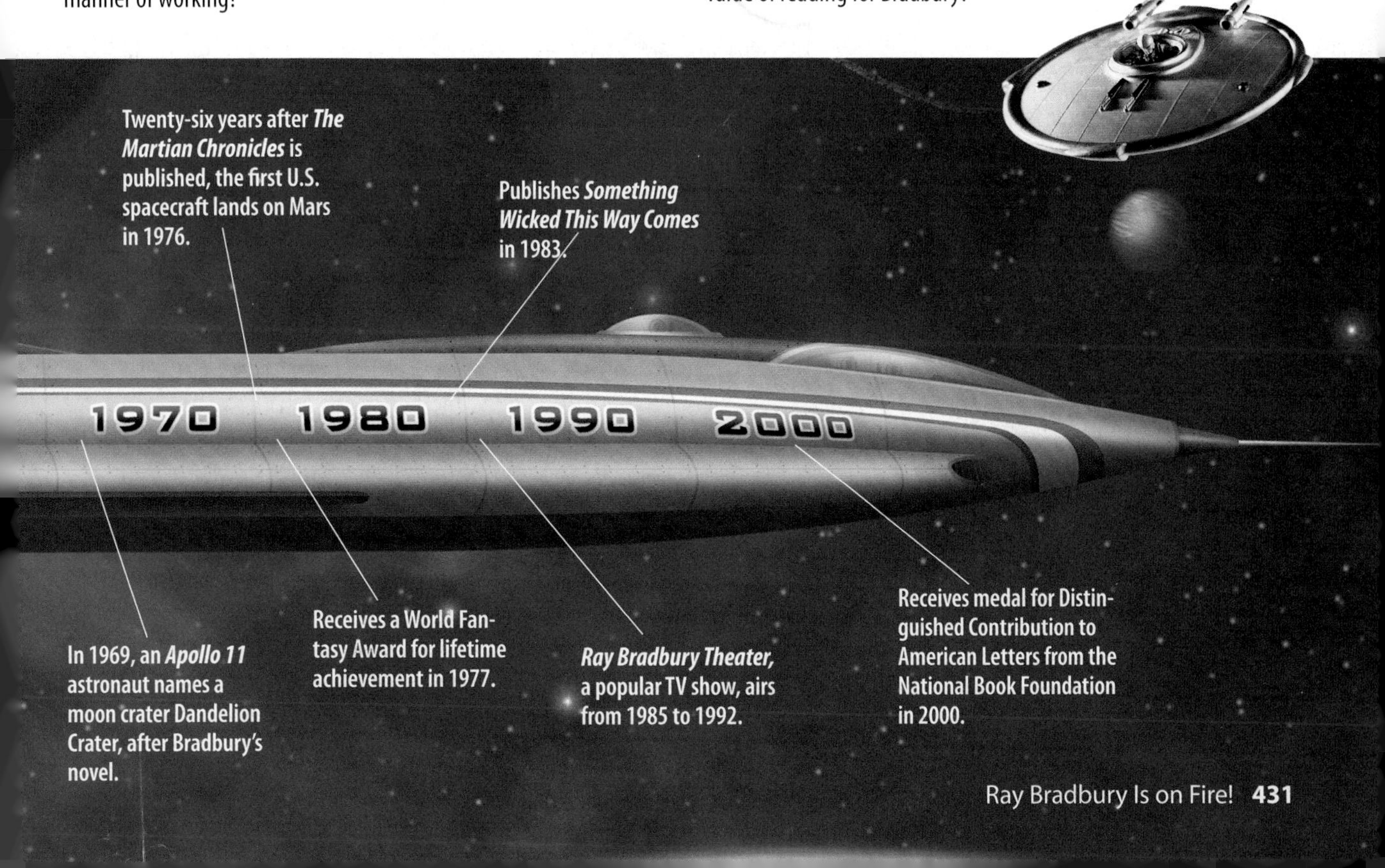

Twenty-six years after *The Martian Chronicles* is published, the first U.S. spacecraft lands on Mars in 1976.

Publishes *Something Wicked This Way Comes* in 1983.

1970 1980 1990 2000

In 1969, an *Apollo 11* astronaut names a moon crater Dandelion Crater, after Bradbury's novel.

Receives a World Fantasy Award for lifetime achievement in 1977.

Ray Bradbury Theater, a popular TV show, airs from 1985 to 1992.

Receives medal for Distinguished Contribution to American Letters from the National Book Foundation in 2000.

SHORT STORY

The Flying Machine

by **Ray Bradbury**

Preparing to Read for this selection is on page 427.

Build Background

Ray Bradbury says he tells tales to warn people about dangers in the world around them. You are about to read a fairy-tale-like story that takes place in the distant past. As you read, think about how this story connects to our world today.

In the year A.D. 400, the Emperor Yuan held his throne by the Great Wall of China, and the land was green with rain, readying itself toward the harvest, at peace, the people in his dominion[1] neither too happy nor too sad.

Early on the morning of the first day of the first week of the second month of the new year, the Emperor Yuan was sipping tea and fanning himself against a warm breeze when a servant ran across the scarlet and blue garden tiles, calling, "Oh, Emperor, Emperor, a miracle!"

"Yes," said the Emperor, "the air *is* sweet this morning."

"No, no, a miracle!" said the servant, bowing quickly.

"And this tea is good in my mouth, surely that is a miracle."

"No, no, Your Excellency."

"Let me guess then—the sun has risen and a new day is upon us. Or the sea is blue. *That* now is the finest of all miracles."

"Excellency, a man is flying!"

"What?" The Emperor stopped his fan.

"I saw him in the air, a man flying with wings. I heard a voice call out of the sky, and when I looked up, there he was, a dragon in the heavens with a man in its mouth, a dragon of paper and bamboo, colored like the sun and the grass."

"It is early," said the Emperor, "and you have just wakened from a dream."

"It is early, but I have seen what I have seen! Come, and you will see it too."

"Sit down with me here," said the Emperor. "Drink some tea. It must be a strange thing, if it is true, to see a man fly. You must have time to think of it, even as I must have time to prepare myself for the sight."

They drank tea.

"Please," said the servant at last, "or he will be gone."

1. **dominion:** country; territory.

The Emperor rose thoughtfully. "Now you may show me what you have seen." **A**

They walked into a garden, across a meadow of grass, over a small bridge, through a grove of trees, and up a tiny hill.

"There!" said the servant.

The Emperor looked into the sky.

And in the sky, laughing so high that you could hardly hear him laugh, was a man; and the man was clothed in bright papers and reeds to make wings and a beautiful yellow tail, and he was soaring all about like the largest bird in a universe of birds, like a new dragon in a land of ancient dragons.

The man called down to them from high in the cool winds of morning. "I fly, I fly!"

The servant waved to him. "Yes, *yes!*"

The Emperor Yuan did not move. Instead he looked at the Great Wall of China now taking shape out of the farthest mist in the green hills, that splendid snake of stones which writhed with majesty across the entire land. That wonderful wall which had protected them for a timeless time from enemy hordes[2] and preserved peace for years without number. He saw the town, nestled to itself by a river and a road and a hill, beginning to waken.

"Tell me," he said to his servant, "has anyone else seen this flying man?"

"I am the only one, Excellency," said the servant, smiling at the sky, waving.

2. **hordes:** moving crowds.

A **Read and Discuss** What is the author suggesting about this emperor and his people?

Vocabulary **writhed** (rythd) *v.:* twisted and turned.

Analyzing Visuals **Viewing and Interpreting**
What qualities of this Chinese nobleman are similar to those of the emperor in the story?

Ancestor Portrait (late 17th or early 18th century) Chinese School. Ink and color on silk.

The Emperor watched the heavens another minute and then said, "Call him down to me."

"Ho, come down, come down! The Emperor wishes to see you!" called the servant, hands cupped to his shouting mouth.

The Emperor glanced in all directions while the flying man soared down the morning wind. He saw a farmer, early in his fields, watching the sky, and he noted where the farmer stood.

The flying man alit with a rustle of paper and a creak of bamboo reeds. He came proudly to the Emperor, clumsy in his rig, at last bowing before the old man.

"What have you done?" demanded the Emperor.

"I have flown in the sky, Your Excellency," replied the man.

"What *have* you done?" said the Emperor again.

"I have just told you!" cried the flier.

"You have told me nothing at all." The Emperor reached out a thin hand to touch the pretty paper and the birdlike keel of the apparatus. It smelled cool, of the wind.

"Is it not beautiful, Excellency?"

"Yes, too beautiful."

"It is the only one in the world!" smiled the man. "And I am the inventor."

"The *only* one in the world?"

"I swear it!"

"Who else knows of this?"

"No one. Not even my wife, who would think me mad with the sun. She thought I was making a kite. I rose in the night and walked to the cliffs far away. And when the morning breezes blew and the sun rose, I gathered my courage, Excellency, and leaped from the cliff. I flew! But my wife does not know of it."

"Well for her, then," said the Emperor. "Come along." **B**

They walked back to the great house. The sun was full in the sky now, and the smell of the grass was refreshing. The Emperor, the servant, and the flier paused within the huge garden.

The Emperor clapped his hands. "Ho, guards!"

The guards came running.

"Hold this man."

The guards seized the flier.

"Call the executioner," said the Emperor.

"What's this!" cried the flier, bewildered. "What have I done?" He began to weep, so that the beautiful paper apparatus rustled.

"Here is the man who has made a certain machine," said the Emperor, "and yet asks us what he has created. He does not know himself. It is only necessary that he create, without knowing why he has done so, or what this thing will do."

The executioner came running with a sharp silver ax. He stood with his naked, large-muscled arms ready, his face covered with a serene white mask.

"One moment," said the Emperor. He turned to a nearby table upon which sat a machine that he himself had created. The Emperor took a tiny golden key from his own neck. He fitted his key to the tiny, delicate machine and wound it up. Then he set the machine going.

B **Read and Discuss** What does the conversation between the emperor and the flying man tell us about the emperor's thoughts?

Vocabulary **serene** (suh REEN) *adj.:* calm; undisturbed.

Blue and Green Landscapes by Li Qing.

The machine was a garden of metal and jewels. Set in motion, the birds sang in tiny metal trees, wolves walked through miniature forests, and tiny people ran in and out of sun and shadow, fanning themselves with miniature fans, listening to tiny emerald birds, and standing by impossibly small but tinkling fountains.

"Is *it* not beautiful?" said the Emperor. "If you asked me what I have done here, I could answer you well. I have made birds sing, I have made forests murmur, I have set people to walking in this woodland, enjoying the leaves and shadows and songs. That is what I have done."

"But, oh, Emperor!" pleaded the flier, on his knees, the tears pouring down his face. "I have done a similar thing! I have found beauty. I have flown on the morning wind. I have looked down on all the sleeping houses and gardens. I have smelled the sea and even *seen* it, beyond the hills, from my high place. And I have soared like a bird; oh, I cannot say how beautiful it is up there, in the sky, with the wind about me, the wind blowing me here like a feather, there like a fan, the way the sky smells in the morning! And how free one feels! *That* is beautiful, Emperor, that is beautiful too!"

"Yes," said the Emperor sadly, "I know it must be true. For I felt my heart move with you in the air and I wondered: What is it like? How does it feel? How do the distant pools look from so high? And how my houses and servants? Like ants? And how the distant towns not yet awake?"

"Then spare me!"

"But there are times," said the Emperor, more sadly still, "when one must lose a little beauty if one is to keep what little beauty one already has. I do not fear you, yourself, but I fear another man."

"What man?"

"Some other man who, seeing you, will build a thing of bright papers and bamboo like this. But the other man will have an evil face and an evil heart, and the beauty will be gone. It is this man I fear."

"Why? Why?"

"Who is to say that someday just such a man, in just such an apparatus of paper and reed, might not fly in the sky and drop huge stones upon the Great Wall of China?" said the Emperor. **C**

No one moved or said a word.

"Off with his head," said the Emperor.

The executioner whirled his silver ax.

"Burn the kite and the inventor's body and bury their ashes together," said the Emperor.

The servants retreated to obey.

The Emperor turned to his hand-servant, who had seen the man flying. "Hold your tongue. It was all a dream, a most sorrowful and beautiful dream. And that farmer in the distant field who also saw, tell him it would pay him to consider it only a vision. If ever the word passes around, you and the farmer die within the hour."

"You are merciful, Emperor."

"No, not merciful," said the old man. Beyond the garden wall he saw the guards burning the beautiful machine of paper and reeds that smelled of the morning wind. He saw the dark smoke climb into the sky. "No, only very much bewildered and afraid." He saw the guards digging a tiny pit wherein to bury the ashes. "What is the life of one man against those of a million others? I must take solace from that thought." **D**

He took the key from its chain about his neck and once more wound up the beautiful miniature garden. He stood looking out across the land at the Great Wall, the peaceful town, the green fields, the rivers and streams. He sighed. The tiny garden whirred its hidden and delicate machinery and set itself in motion; tiny people walked in forests, tiny faces loped through sun-speckled glades in beautiful shining pelts, and among the tiny trees flew little bits of high song and bright blue and yellow color, flying, flying, flying in that small sky.

"Oh," said the Emperor, closing his eyes, "look at the birds, look at the birds!"

C **Literary Focus** **Biographical Approach** Which of Bradbury's concerns do you see reflected in the emperor's words?

D **Read and Discuss** What does the emperor mean by "What is the life of one man against those of a million others?"

Vocabulary **solace** (SAHL ihs) *n.:* comfort.

Applying Your Skills

OH **RP.8.2** Answer literal, inferential, evaluative and synthesizing questions to demonstrate comprehension of grade-appropriate print texts and electronic and visual media. *Also covered* **RP.8.1; WP.8.9; VO.8.4**

from Ray Bradbury Is on Fire! / The Flying Machine

Respond and Think Critically

Reading Focus

Quick Check

1. According to the interview, what does Bradbury believe is necessary for civilization?
2. What does the emperor in "The Flying Machine" say are miracles? What does the servant say is a miracle?

Read with a Purpose

3. Based on these selections, are you surprised at Bradbury's attitudes toward technology?

Reading Skills: Drawing Conclusions

4. You have read a biography, an interview, and one of Bradbury's short stories. Now fill in the third column of your chart. What conclusions can you draw about Bradbury's writing?

Biographical Information	Details from Selection	Conclusions
distrusts new technology	emperor destroys flying machine	

Vocabulary Check

Match the Vocabulary words with their definitions.

5. **serene**
6. **writhed**
7. **contradictory**
8. **solace**

a. opposing
b. comfort
c. peaceful
d. twisted

Literary Focus

Literary Analysis

9. **Explain** In "Ray Bradbury Is on Fire!" what does the interviewer find ironic about calling Bradbury a science fiction writer?
10. **Interpret** Discuss the two inventions in "The Flying Machine." Why does the emperor see beauty only in his own invention?
11. **Analyze** Which of the following messages do you think is more important in the story? Explain your answer.
    - The beauty of nature is a precious resource.
    - New technology can inspire fear.
12. **Extend** Discuss Bradbury's belief that distracting entertainment can interfere with active thinking. What examples from our current society might Bradbury have in mind?

Literary Skills: Biographical Approach

13. **Analyze** Based on the biography and interview, explain which of Bradbury's beliefs and attitudes are reflected in "The Flying Machine."

Writing Focus

Think as a Reader/Writer

Use It in Your Writing Refer to your list of figures of speech that Bradbury uses in this story. Then, write four or five sentences of your own using figurative language to describe an event or an unusual setting.

Chinese lacquered art with dragon representation.

Here is what Ray Bradbury has said about "The Dragon":

It is hard to talk about 'The Dragon' without giving away its secret, telling you the surprise. So all I can talk about is the boy I was that became the young man who thought about, and the older man who wrote, this story. I loved dinosaurs from the age of five, when I saw the film *The Lost World,* filled with prehistoric monsters. I became even more enamored with these beasts when at age thirteen, *King Kong* fell off the Empire State and landed on me in the front row of the Elite Theater. I never recovered. Later, I met and became friends with Ray Harryhausen, who built and film-animated dinosaurs in his garage when we were both eighteen. We dedicated our lives to these monsters, to dragons in all their shapes and forms. Simultaneously, we loved airplanes, rocket ships, trolley cars, and trains. From this amalgam of loves came our lives and careers. We wound up doing *The Beast from 20,000 Fathoms* as our first film. Not very good, but a beginning. He went on to *Mighty Joe Young* and I to *Moby Dick* and its great sea-beast. When I was in my thirties I wrote 'The Dragon' and combined two of these loves. You'll have to read the story to find out which ones. Read on. (A)

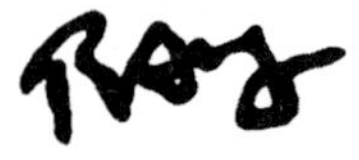

(A) **Literary Focus** **Biographical Approach** What personal interests led Bradbury to write "The Dragon"?

THE DRAGON

by **Ray Bradbury,** adapted by **Vicente Segrelles**

Read with a Purpose Read these selections to see what happens when the past meets the present.

Preparing to Read for this selection is on page 427.

B **Read and Discuss** What information has the author given us in these first four panels?

C

C **Read and Discuss** How do the illustrations help build suspense?

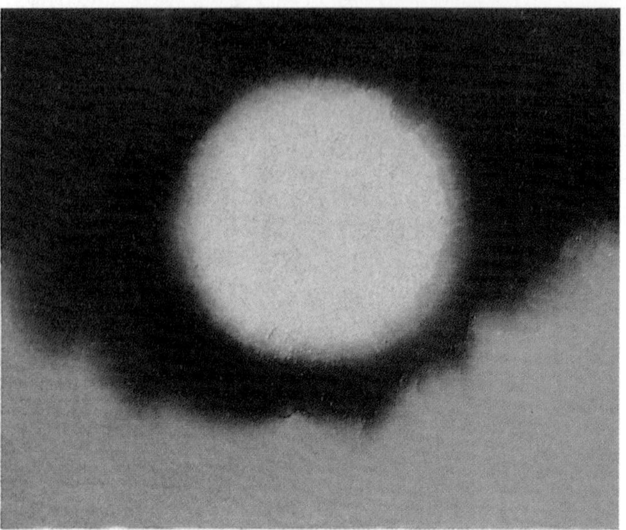

LORD HAVE MERCY!
THE LANCE STRUCK THE UNLIDDED YELLOW EYE, BUCKLED, TOSSED THE MAN THROUGH THE AIR.

THE BLACK BRUNT OF ITS SHOULDER SMASHED THE REMAINING HORSE AND RIDER A HUNDRED FEET AGAINST THE SIDE OF A BOULDER. THE DRAGON'S WAIL BECAME A SHRIEK. THERE WAS FIRE ALL ABOUT.

D

D **Read and Discuss** What has happened to the knights?

E

E **Reading Focus** **Drawing Conclusions** What attitudes and beliefs of Bradbury's are revealed in this story?

The Fog Horn

by **Ray Bradbury**

Preparing to Read for this selection is on page 427.

Out there in the cold water, far from land, we waited every night for the coming of the fog, and it came, and we oiled the brass machinery and lit the fog light up in the stone tower. Feeling like two birds in the gray sky, McDunn and I sent the light touching out, red, then white, then red again, to eye the lonely ships. And if they did not see our light, then there was always our Voice, the great deep cry of our Fog Horn shuddering through the rags of mist to startle the gulls away like decks of scattered cards and make the waves turn high and foam.

"It's a lonely life, but you're used to it now, aren't you?" asked McDunn.

"Yes," I said. "You're a good talker, thank the Lord."

"Well, it's your turn on land tomorrow," he said, smiling, "to dance the ladies and drink gin."

"What do you think, McDunn, when I leave you out here alone?"

"On the mysteries of the sea." McDunn lit his pipe. It was a quarter past seven of a cold November evening, the heat on, the light switching its tail in two hundred directions, the Fog Horn bumbling in the high throat of the tower. There wasn't a town for a hundred miles down the coast, just a road which came lonely through dead country to the sea, with few cars on it, a stretch of two miles of cold water out to our rock, and rare few ships.

"The mysteries of the sea," said McDunn thoughtfully. "You know, the ocean's the most confounded big snowflake ever? It rolls and swells a thousand shapes and colors, no two alike. Strange. One night, years ago, I was here alone, when all of the fish of the sea surfaced out there. Something made them swim in and lie in the bay, sort of trembling and staring up at the tower light going red, white, red, white across them so I could see their funny eyes. I turned cold. They were like a big peacock's tail, moving out there until midnight. Then, without so much as a sound, they slipped away, the million of them was gone. I kind of think maybe, in some sort of way, they came all those miles to worship. Strange. But think how the tower must look to them, standing seventy feet above the water, the God-light flashing out from it, and the tower declaring itself with a monster voice. They never came back, those fish, but don't you think for a while they thought they were in the Presence?"

I shivered. I looked out at the long gray lawn of the sea stretching away into nothing and nowhere.

"Oh, the sea's full." McDunn puffed his pipe nervously, blinking. He had been nervous all day and hadn't said why. "For all our engines and so-called submarines, it'll be ten thousand centuries before we set foot on the real bottom of the sunken lands, in the fairy kingdoms there, and know *real* terror. Think of it, it's still the year 300,000 Before Christ down under there. While we've paraded around with trumpets, lopping off each other's countries and heads, they have been living beneath the sea twelve miles deep and cold in a time as old as the beard of a comet."

"Yes, it's an old world." **A**

"Come on. I got something special I been saving up to tell you."

We ascended the eighty steps, talking and taking our time. At the top, McDunn switched off the room lights so there'd be no reflection in the plate glass. The great eye of the light was humming, turning easily in its oiled socket. The Fog Horn was blowing steadily, once every fifteen seconds.

"Sounds like an animal, don't it?" McDunn nodded to himself. "A big lonely animal crying in the night. Sitting here on the edge of ten billion years called out to the Deeps, I'm here, I'm here, I'm here. And the Deeps do answer, yes, they do. You been here now for three months, Johnny, so I better prepare you. About this time of year," he said, studying the murk and fog, "something comes to visit the lighthouse."

"The swarms of fish like you said?"

"No, this is something else. I've put off telling you because you might think I'm daft. But tonight's the latest I can put it off, for if my calendar's marked right from last year, tonight's the night it comes. I won't go into detail, you'll have to see it yourself. Just sit down there. If you want, tomorrow you can pack your duffel and take the motorboat in to land and get your car parked there at the dinghy pier on the cape and drive on

---

A **Read and Discuss** What is McDunn describing?

back to some little inland town and keep your lights burning nights. I won't question or blame you. It's happened three years now, and this is the only time anyone's been here with me to verify it. You wait and watch." **B**

Half an hour passed with only a few whispers between us. When we grew tired of waiting, McDunn began describing some of his ideas to me. He had some theories about the Fog Horn itself.

"One day many years ago a man walked along and stood in the sound of the ocean on a cold sunless shore and said, "We need a voice to call across the water, to warn ships. I'll make one. I'll make a voice like all of time and all of that fog that ever was; I'll make a voice that is like an empty bed beside you all night long, and like an empty house when you open the door, and like trees in autumn with no leaves. A sound like the birds flying south, crying, and a sound like November wind and the sea on the hard, cold shore. I'll make a sound that's so alone that no one can miss it, that whoever hears it will weep in their souls, and hearths will seem warmer, and being inside will seem better to all who hear it in the distant towns. I'll make me a sound and an apparatus and they'll call it a Fog Horn and whoever hears it will know the sadness of eternity and the briefness of life."

The Fog Horn blew.

"I made up that story," said McDunn quietly, "to try to explain why this thing keeps coming back to the lighthouse every year. The Fog Horn calls it, I think, and it comes. . . ."

"But—" I said.

"Sssst!" said McDunn. "There!" He nodded out to the Deeps.

Something was swimming toward the lighthouse tower.

It was a cold night, as I have said; the high tower was cold, the light coming and going, and the Fog Horn calling and calling through the raveling mist. You couldn't see far and you couldn't see plain, but there was the deep sea moving on its way about the night earth, flat and quiet, the color of gray mud, and here were the two of us alone

---

B **Read and Discuss** What is McDunn saying here?

in the high tower, and there, far out at first, was a ripple, followed by a wave, a rising, a bubble, a bit of froth. And then, from the surface of the cold sea came a head, a large head, dark-colored, with immense eyes, and then a neck. And then—not a body—but more neck and more! The head rose a full forty feet above the water on a slender and beautiful dark neck. Only then did the body, like a little island of black coral and shells and crayfish, drip up from the subterranean.[1] There was a flicker of tail. In all, from head to tip of tail, I estimated the monster at ninety or a hundred feet.

I don't know what I said. I said something.

"Steady, boy, steady," whispered McDunn.

"It's impossible!" I said.

"No, Johnny, *we're* impossible. *It's* like it always was ten million years ago. *It* hasn't changed. It's *us* and the land that've changed, become impossible. *Us!*" **C**

1. **subterranean** (suhb tuh RAY nee uhn): underground.

It swam slowly and with a great dark majesty out in the icy waters, far away. The fog came and went about it, momentarily erasing its shape. One of the monster eyes caught and held and flashed back our immense light, red, white, red, white, like a disk held high and sending a message in primeval[2] code. It was as silent as the fog through which it swam.

"It's a dinosaur of some sort!" I crouched down, holding to the stair rail.

"Yes, one of the tribe."

"But they died out!"

"No, only hid away in the Deeps. Deep, deep down in the deepest Deeps. Isn't *that* a word now, Johnny, a real word, it says so much: the Deeps. There's all the coldness and darkness and deepness in a word like that."

"What'll we do?"

"Do? We got our job, we can't leave. Besides, we're safer here than in any boat trying to

2. **primeval** (pry MEE vuhl): of the earliest times; ancient.

C **Reading Focus** **Drawing Conclusions** What conclusions can you draw about Bradbury's views on humanity?

get to land. That thing's as big as a destroyer and almost as swift."

"But here, why does it come here?"

The next moment I had my answer.

The Fog Horn blew.

And the monster answered.

A cry came across a million years of water and mist. A cry so anguished and alone that it shuddered in my head and my body. The monster cried out at the tower. The Fog Horn blew. The monster roared again. The Fog Horn blew. The monster opened its great toothed mouth and the sound that came from it was the sound of the Fog Horn itself. Lonely and vast and far away. The sound of isolation, a viewless sea, a cold night, apartness. That was the sound. **D**

"Now," whispered McDunn, "do you know why it comes here?"

I nodded.

"All year long, Johnny, that poor monster there lying far out, a thousand miles at sea, and twenty miles deep maybe, biding its time, perhaps it's a million years old, this one creature. Think of it, waiting a million years; could *you* wait that long? Maybe it's the last of its kind. I sort of think that's true. Anyway, here come men on land and build this lighthouse, five years ago. And set up their Fog Horn and sound it and sound it out toward the place where you bury yourself in sleep and sea memories of a world where there were thousands like yourself, but now you're alone, all alone in a world not made for you, a world where you have to hide.

"But the sound of the Fog Horn comes and goes, comes and goes, and you stir from the muddy bottom of the Deeps, and your eyes open like the lenses of two-foot cameras and you move, slow, slow, for you have the ocean sea on your shoulders, heavy. But that Fog Horn comes through a thousand miles of water, faint and familiar, and the furnace in your

---

D **Reading Focus** **Drawing Conclusions** What is distinctive about Bradbury's style in this paragraph?

belly stokes up, and you begin to rise, slow, slow. You feed yourself on great slakes of cod and minnow, on rivers of jellyfish, and you rise slow through the autumn months, through September when the fogs started, through October with more fog and the horn still calling you on, and then, late in November, after pressurizing yourself day by day, a few feet higher every hour, you are near the surface and still alive. You've got to go slow; if you surfaced all at once you'd explode. So it takes you all of three months to surface, and then a number of days to swim through the cold waters to the lighthouse. And there you are, out there, in the night, Johnny, the biggest monster in creation. And here's the lighthouse calling to you, with a long neck like your neck sticking way up out of the water, and a body like your body, and, most important of all, a voice like your voice. Do you understand now, Johnny, do you understand?"

The Fog Horn blew.

The monster answered.

I saw it all, I knew it all—the million years of waiting alone, for someone to come back who never came back. The million years of isolation at the bottom of the sea, the insanity of time there, while the skies cleared of reptile-birds, the swamps dried on the continental lands, the sloths and saber-tooths had their day and sank in tar pits, and men ran like white ants upon the hills. E

The Fog Horn blew.

Last year," said McDunn, "that creature swam round and round, round and round, all night. Not coming too near, puzzled, I'd say. Afraid, maybe. And a bit angry after coming all this way. But the next day, unexpectedly, the fog lifted, the sun came out fresh, the sky was as blue as a painting. And the monster swam off away from the heat and the silence and didn't come back. I suppose it's been brooding on it for a year now, thinking it over from every which way."

The monster was only a hundred yards off now, it and the Fog Horn crying at each other. As the lights hit them, the monster's eyes were fire and ice, fire and ice.

"That's life for you," said McDunn. "Someone always waiting for someone who never comes home. Always someone loving some thing more than that thing loves them. And after a while, you want to destroy whatever that thing is, so it can't hurt you no more." F

The monster was rushing at the lighthouse.

The Fog Horn blew.

"Let's see what happens," said McDunn.

He switched the Fog Horn off.

The ensuing minute of silence was so intense that we could hear our hearts pounding in the glassed area of the tower, could hear the slow greased turn of the light.

The monster stopped and froze. Its great lantern eyes blinked. Its mouth gaped. It gave a sort of rumble, like a volcano. It twitched its head this way and that, as if to

---

E **Literary Focus** **Biographical Approach** What attitudes or beliefs of Bradbury's might be reflected in this interpretation of the monster?

F **Read and Discuss** What is McDunn explaining?

seek the sounds now dwindled off into the fog. It peered at the lighthouse. It rumbled again. Then its eyes caught fire. It reared up, threshed the water, and rushed at the tower, its eyes filled with angry torment.

"McDunn!" I cried. "Switch on the horn!"

McDunn fumbled with the switch. But even as he flicked it on, the monster was rearing up. I had a glimpse of its gigantic paws, fishskin glittering in webs between the finger-like projections, clawing at the tower. The huge eyes on the right side of its anguished head glittered before me like a caldron into which I might drop, screaming. The tower shook. The Fog Horn cried; the monster cried. It seized the tower and gnashed at the glass, which shattered in upon us.

McDunn seized my arm. "Downstairs!"

The tower rocked, trembled, and started to give. The Fog Horn and the monster roared. We stumbled and half fell down the stairs. "Quick!"

We reached the bottom as the tower buckled down toward us. We ducked under the stairs into the small stone cellar. There were a thousand concussions as the rocks rained down; the Fog Horn stopped abruptly. The monster crashed upon the tower. The tower fell. We knelt together, McDunn and I, holding tight, while our world exploded.

Fish swim in Sea-Life Aquarium, Olympic Park, Munich, Germany.

Then it was over, and there was nothing but darkness and the wash of the sea on the raw stones.

That and the other sound.

"Listen," said McDunn quietly. "Listen."

"We waited a moment. And then I began to hear it. First a great vacuumed sucking of air, and then the lament, the bewilderment, the loneliness of the great monster, folded over and upon us, above us, so that the sickening reek of its body filled the air, a stone's thickness away from our cellar. The monster gasped and cried. The tower was gone. The light was gone. The thing that had called to it across a million years was gone. And the monster was opening its mouth and sending out great sounds. The sounds of a Fog Horn, again and again. And ships far at sea, not finding the light, not seeing anything, but passing and hearing late that night, must've thought: There it is, the lonely sound, the Lonesome Bay horn. All's well. We've rounded the cape.

And so it went for the rest of that night.

The sun was hot and yellow the next afternoon when the rescuers came out to dig us from our stoned-under cellar. **G**

"It fell apart, is all," said Mr. McDunn gravely. "We had a few bad knocks from the waves and it just crumbled." He pinched my arm.

There was nothing to see. The ocean was calm, the sky blue. The only thing was a great algaic stink from the green matter that covered the fallen tower stones and the shore rocks. Flies buzzed about. The ocean washed empty on the shore.

The next year they built a new lighthouse, but by that time I had a job in the little town and a wife and a good small warm house that glowed yellow on autumn nights, the doors locked, the chimney puffing smoke. As for McDunn, he was master of the new lighthouse, built to his own specifications, out of steel-reinforced concrete. "Just in case," he said.

The new lighthouse was ready in November. I drove down alone one evening late and parked my car and looked across the gray waters and listened to the new horn sounding, once, twice, three, four times a minute far out there, by itself.

The monster?

It never came back.

"It's gone away," said McDunn. "It's gone back to the Deeps. It's learned you can't love anything too much in this world. It's gone into the deepest Deeps to wait another million years. Ah, the poor thing! Waiting out there, and waiting out there, while man comes and goes on this pitiful little planet. Waiting and waiting."

I sat in my car, listening. I couldn't see the lighthouse or the light standing out in Lonesome Bay. I could only hear the Horn, the Horn, the Horn. It sounded like the monster calling.

I sat there wishing there was something I could say. **H**

G **Read and Discuss** What has happened?

H **Reading Focus** **Drawing Conclusions** Have your impressions about Bradbury's attitude toward technology changed?

Applying Your Skills

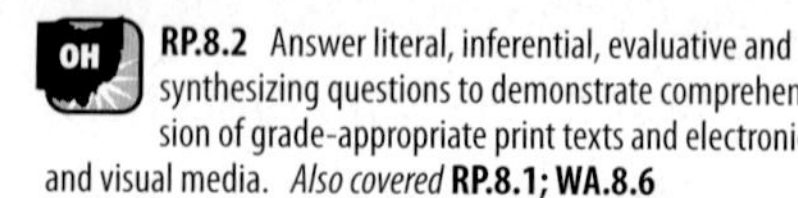
RP.8.2 Answer literal, inferential, evaluative and synthesizing questions to demonstrate comprehension of grade-appropriate print texts and electronic and visual media. *Also covered* **RP.8.1; WA.8.6**

The Dragon / The Fog Horn

Respond and Think Critically

Reading Focus

Quick Check

1. Who are the main characters in "The Dragon"? What problem do they face?
2. In "The Fog Horn," why is the monster drawn to the fog horn?
3. What happens after McDunn switches off the fog horn? Why does it happen?

Read with a Purpose

4. In these selections, what happens when people and creatures from the past encounter modern technology?

Reading Skills: Drawing Conclusions

5. In your chart, fill in more information from the selections. Then, in the third column, draw some conclusions about Bradbury's writing.

Biographical Information	Details from Selection	Conclusions
distrusts new technology	emperor destroys flying machine	

Literary Focus

Literary Analysis

6. **Interpret** Now that you know the dragon's real identity, what do the following descriptions in "The Dragon" refer to: (1) his "unlidded yellow eye"; (2) "his breath like white gas"?
7. **Analyze** Which of these messages do you think Bradbury conveys in "The Dragon"? Explain.
   - Our machines are as powerful as the mythical dragons of old.
   - It is heroic to fight against monsters, even when those monsters are not real.
   - People of earlier times would see our lives as full of terrifying dangers.
8. **Extend** Connect McDunn's statement "the sadness of eternity and the briefness of life" (page 446) to the creature's agony. How does the anguish the monster suffers relate to those who earn their living from the sea and those who wait for the seafarers to return home?

Literary Skills: Biographical Approach

9. In his interview with James Hibberd (page 429), Bradbury expresses his impressions of technology and human civilization. Explain how these concerns are reflected in "The Dragon" and "The Fog Horn." (For help organizing your thoughts, see your responses to question #5.)

Writing Focus

Think as a Reader/Writer

Use It in Your Writing Bradbury uses a string of **similes,** or comparisons using *like* or *as,* to help you imagine the sound of a fog horn (page 446). In a short paragraph, describe a different sound, using as many similes as you can think of. Read your description aloud to a partner, and see if he or she can guess what the sound is.

COMPARING TEXTS

Wrap Up

Author Study: Ray Bradbury

RP.8.2 Answer literal, inferential, evaluative and synthesizing questions to demonstrate comprehension of grade-appropriate print texts and electronic and visual media. **WP.8.6** Drafting, Revising and Editing: Organize writing with an effective and engaging introduction, body and a conclusion that summarizes, extends or elaborates on points or ideas in the writing. *Also covered* **VO.8.7**

Writing Focus

Think as a Reader/Writer

Biographical Analysis After reading the stories in this group, you now know that many of Bradbury's stories reflect his fascination with human society, monsters, and fantasy and reality. His stories also concern the costs and benefits of modern civilization, and the positive and negative effects of technology.

Write a three-paragraph essay in which you consider the messages in Bradbury's stories and how those messages reflect his own attitudes.

- In the essay's first paragraph, introduce your topic and state what you see as Bradbury's main concerns.
- In the second paragraph, write about how Bradbury's concerns are reflected in the short stories you have read. Support your ideas by citing details from the texts.
- In the last paragraph, draw a conclusion about how Bradbury's ideas relate to his fiction.

Evaluation Guidelines	
	An effective essay contains—
✓	a clearly stated topic
✓	main ideas that are supported with details
✓	a clear and logical organization
✓	a thought-provoking conclusion

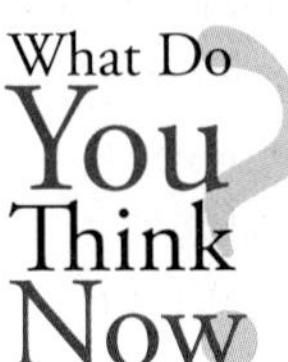

Bradbury shares his ideas through writing. What other ways can we share our ideas and beliefs with the world?

CHOICES

As you respond to the Choices, use these **Academic Vocabulary** words as appropriate: distinctive, establish, impact, impression.

REVIEW

Write an Essay

Timed Writing What do you think about Bradbury's ideas about technology and its impact on human beings and society in general? Do you share his point of view, or do you have a more positive view of the development of technology? Write an essay in which you express your opinion. Include at least two examples from your knowledge or experience that will support your claim.

CONNECT

Create a Graphic Story

Partner Activity Choose another short story by Bradbury or a short story in this book. With a partner, design a graphic version of the story. Most graphic stories are created by a writer and an artist working together. The writer usually divides the story into panels and creates a script. Then, the artist takes over and illustrates the story. You and your partner can share the writing and illustrating or split the tasks.

EXTEND

Paint an Online World

TechFocus Using painting software, create a fantasy world of your own. Will your world exist in the past, future, alternate present, or an imaginary universe? What will your setting look like? Who will live there—people, animals, robots? What impression will it make on visitors? Share your fantasy world with others.

INFORMATIONAL TEXT FOCUS

Evaluating a Summary

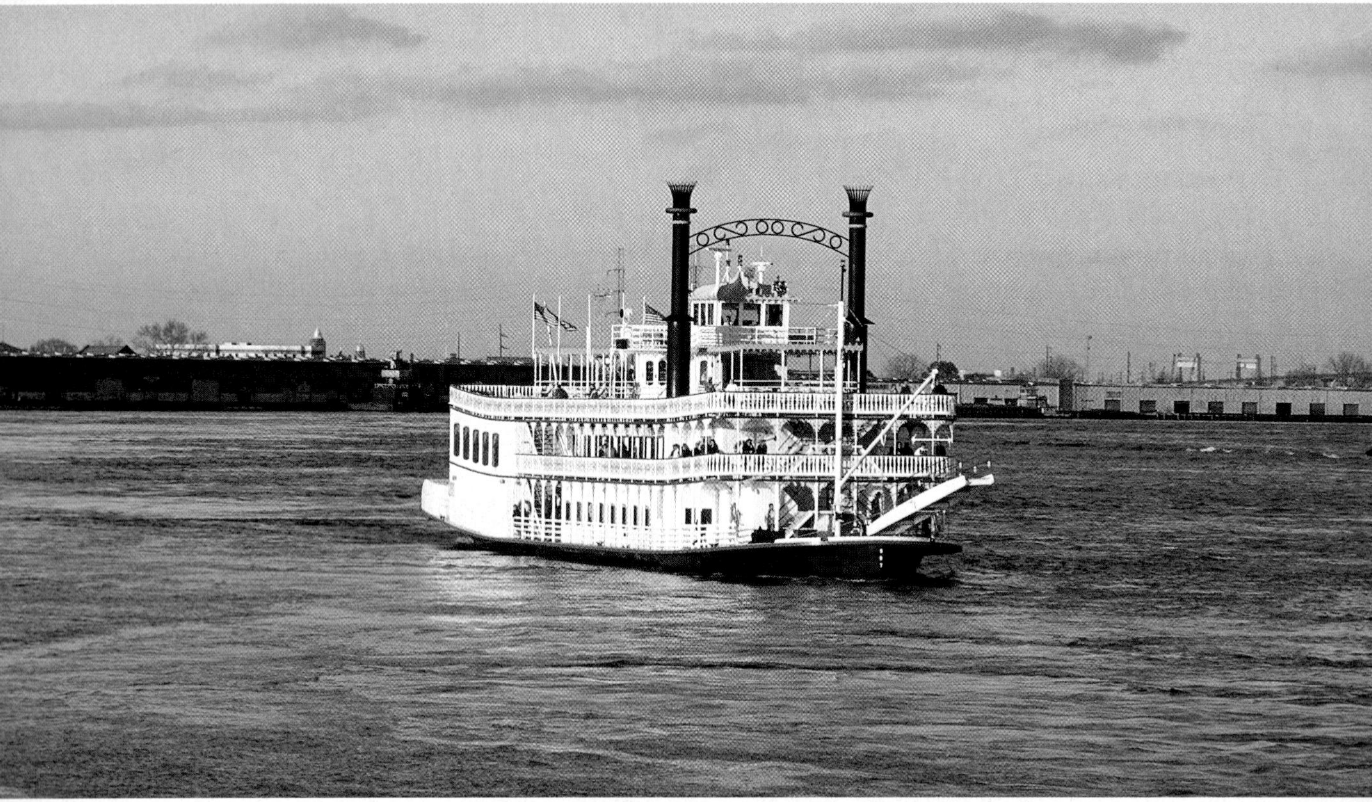

New Orleans paddleboat.

CONTENTS

What Do You Think?

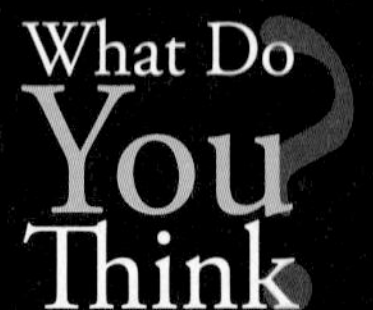

What does it take to make a good idea work?

QuickWrite

Write down a major technological invention developed in your lifetime. What need did it fill? What impact has it had on your life?

ARTICLE/SUMMARIES

Preparing to Read

RA.I.8.3 Compare and contrast the treatment, scope and organization of ideas from different sources on the same topic. **RA.I.8.7** Analyze an author's argument, perspective or viewpoint and explain the development of key points.

Steam Rising: The Revolutionary Power of Paddleboats / Summaries of "Steam Rising"

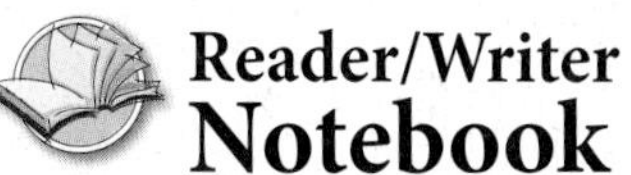

Reader/Writer Notebook

Use your **RWN** to complete the activities for these selections.

Informational Text Focus

Evaluating a Summary A **summary** is a brief recounting of the most important ideas of a work. You may encounter summaries of informational texts in many places. They appear in newspapers, magazines, book reviews, and online. Their purpose is to give you an overview of an article. However, if a summary is not good, you won't understand clearly what the article is about. An effective summary of an informational text should

- cite the article's title and author
- state the topic of the article
- state the main ideas, in the order in which they occur in the article
- include important supporting details (people, places, dates)
- include quotation marks around words from the text that are quoted exactly

Into Action Use a chart like the one below to evaluate the summaries of "Steam Rising: The Revolutionary Power of Paddleboats."

Summary	Title and Author	Topic	Main Ideas in Order	Supporting Details
#1				
#2				

Writing Focus Preparing for Constructed Response

As you read "Steam Rising," note which details are most important for a general understanding of the topic. These details support the main ideas and should be included in an effective summary; less important details should be excluded.

Vocabulary

antiquated (AN tuh kway tihd) *adj.:* old-fashioned. *The steamboat is antiquated technology by today's standards.*

prototype (PROH tuh typ) *n.:* first or original model of something. *After seeing the prototype, the investors were willing to fund the building of steamboats.*

monopoly (muh NAHP uh lee) *n.:* total control over a particular business. *No one else could make money from steamboats because Fulton had a monopoly.*

Language Coach

Context Clues Sometimes writers give clues to a word's meaning within a passage or sentence. Look at this sentence: *Although it was once very popular, the steamboat is an old, antiquated form of travel.* How do the clues shown below help you understand what *antiquated* means?

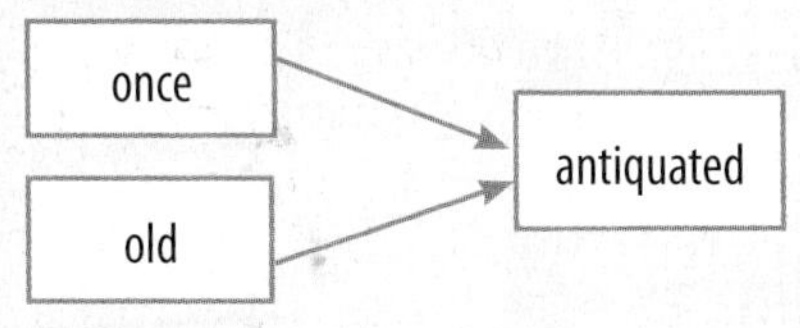

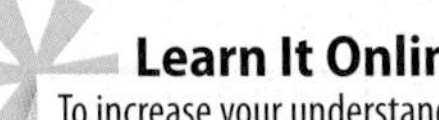

Learn It Online

To increase your understanding of summaries, go to the interactive Reading Workshops at:

go.hrw.com L8-455 

MAGAZINE ARTICLE

STEAM RISING

THE REVOLUTIONARY POWER OF PADDLEBOATS

by THE WORLD ALMANAC®

Read with a Purpose Read this article to learn about the development and impact of a new technology.

"S-t-e-a-m-boat a-comin'!" and the scene changes! . . . all in a twinkling the dead town is alive and moving. Drays, carts, men, boys, all go hurrying from many quarters to a common center, the wharf.

—from *Life on the Mississippi,* by Mark Twain

In the days when paddle steamboats filled the Mississippi River, the famed author Mark Twain served as a cub pilot. He wrote about that experience and his love of steamboats in *Life on the Mississippi.* Today, modern tourists still take these antiquated vessels along U.S. waterways, such as the Columbia River. Travel writers advertise the charms of these trips: the closeness of the riverbank towns, the lull of the running water, and the feeling of time set apart. **A**

ECONOMIC NEED

The steamboat was not invented for pleasure, however. The vessel was developed to help move the country along economically. Before paddle steamboats, travel from Louisville,

A **Read and Discuss** What do we learn about modern-day travelers and the steamboat?

Vocabulary **antiquated** (AN tuh kway tihd) *adj.*: old-fashioned.

Kentucky, to New Orleans, Louisiana, was a four-month project. After their invention, the Industrial Revolution was able to move full steam ahead.

Paddle steamboats are created specifically for inland water runs. A giant paddlewheel is built into the back or side of a flat-bottomed boat, which can navigate shallow waters. Steam rising from wood- or coal-fired boilers turns the wheel. Their design is basic, but their invention revolutionized travel and transport.

Colonial American leaders long recognized the need to power boats with something more predictable than sails, which are at the mercy of the wind. They knew they needed boats capable of traveling upriver. In 1784, the inventor James Rumsey talked with George Washington about such a vessel. John Fitch, of Connecticut, tinkered with the idea of a steamboat as early as 1785. In 1790, he and his partner Henry Voight sent a prototype between Philadelphia and Trenton, Pennsylvania. But they could not raise the funds needed to build a steamboat line. **B**

ROBERT FULTON

Robert Fulton gets credit for creating the first "efficient" steamboat. Fulton hailed from Lancaster, Pennsylvania. As a boy, he spent time in mechanics' shops. There he discovered his talent for drawing. He trained in art in Philadelphia as a teen and then traveled to England, where he was introduced to science and became interested in solving engineering problems. His early ideas included a canal system created on an incline, which would end the need for locks, and a submarine. He had no takers for those ideas, but in 1802, with backing from the U.S. ambassador to France, Robert R. Livingston, Fulton successfully sent a paddle steamboat up a French river. The rest is history.

Along with financial support, Livingston had political steam to offer. The U.S. patent system[1] was not well developed at that point; to profit from their creations, inventors and their backers lobbied[2] politicians for state rights. Livingston was able to obtain a monopoly on New York waterways by promising that Fulton's steamboat could travel at four miles per hour. Fulton sealed the deal by building the *Clermont,* which ran from New York City to Albany at almost five miles per hour. The vessel allowed manufacturers to send raw and finished materials to their destinations more quickly, and Fulton became a rich man.

1. **U.S. patent system:** system that grants an inventor exclusive rights to manufacture an invention for a limited amount of time.
2. **lobbied** (LAHB eed): influenced lawmakers.

B **Read and Discuss** What was so special about paddlewheel steamboats?

Vocabulary **prototype** (PROH tuh typ) *n.:* first or original model of something.
monopoly (muh NAHP uh lee) *n.:* total control over a particular business.

Analyzing Visuals **Viewing and Interpreting** How does the image above capture the feeling of Mark Twain's words at the start of this selection?

The *Baton Rouge*. Illustration from Mark Twain's *Life on the Mississippi*. Boston: James R. Osgood and Company, 1883. Frontispiece image.

Delta Queen riverboat on the Mississippi.

RIVER COMMERCE

Early steamboats were inefficient and sometimes dangerous. But engineers learned from mistakes and improved their design. In addition, Congress authorized funding for major improvements along the Mississippi and Ohio rivers, which encouraged the development of waterway engineering. These factors, along with industrial growth, contributed to the steamboat's rapid rise. In 1814, records show, 21 steamboats visited New Orleans. By 1833, that number had grown to more than 1,200.

By the 1850s, when Twain was working on the river, paddleboats had become fancy affairs. "And the boat IS a rather handsome sight, too," he wrote in *Life on the Mississippi,* going on to describe gingerbread trim atop the pilothouse, shiny white railings, and the flapping flag. These vessels had come to define the Mississippi, the principal U.S. waterway. Until railroads crisscrossed the country in the 1870s, nothing replaced the great U.S. steamboat, and in many ways, nothing ever has. **C**

Read with a Purpose

What important role did steamboats play in U.S. history?

C **Read and Discuss** What is the main idea here?

SUMMARIES OF "STEAM RISING: THE REVOLUTIONARY POWER OF PADDLEBOATS"

Summary #1

"Steam Rising" outlines the development of the U.S. paddle steamboat: its design, its inventors, and the importance of this method of transportation in national history. As steamboats were developed, trade along the country's waterways increased. Fancy steamboats plowed up and down the Mississippi in the 1850s, delivering goods and people to places far and wide. "Steam Rising" is about paddle steamboats and how important they are to people who love boats. Admirers of this unique method of travel and transport still exist today. Mark Twain, the famous U.S. author, said it best: "And the boat is a rather handsome sight, too." D

Summary #2

"Steam Rising: The Revolutionary Power of Paddleboats" by World Almanac describes the invention, development, and impact of the steam-powered paddleboat. Steamboat technology played a major role in America's Industrial Revolution. Colonial Americans understood the importance of using America's waterways for travel and to transport materials in order to make the economy run more efficiently. As early as 1784, inventors were working on ideas for a steamboat that would be able to travel upstream. Building such a vessel was expensive, however, and funds were not easy to find.

Robert Fulton gets credit for making the first working model of a steamboat, paddling up a French river in 1802. Fulton was from Lancaster, Pennsylvania. He discovered a love of drawing early in life, and after studying science, he applied his talents to solving engineering problems. With both financial and political aid from U.S. ambassador Robert R. Livingston, Fulton was able to build and patent his steamboat designs. Fulton's steamboats allowed manufacturers to deliver their products more quickly and ultimately made Fulton rich. E

Steamboat designs evolved, becoming safer and more efficient as well as more attractive. These improvements, along with government improvements to America's rivers, allowed the steamboat to blossom. By 1833, records show that 1,200 steamboats visited New Orleans alone. Until the advent of the railroads, the steamboat played an important role in the U.S. economy. F

D Informational Focus Evaluating a Summary What important information is missing in the first sentence of Summary #1?

E Informational Focus Evaluating a Summary Do all the details in Summary #2 support the article's main idea? Explain.

F Read and Discuss What do these summaries show you?

ARTICLE/SUMMARIES

Applying Your Skills

OH **RA.I.8.3** Compare and contrast the treatment, scope and organization of ideas from different sources on the same topic. **RA.I.8.7** Analyze an author's argument, perspective or viewpoint and explain the development of key points. *Also covered* **WA.8.4.d; VO.8.4**

Steam Rising: The Revolutionary Power of Paddleboats / Summaries of "Steam Rising"

Practicing the Standards

Informational Text and Vocabulary

1. What critical **supporting detail** from the article does the first summary omit?

A James Rumsey talked to George Washington about creating a steamboat.

B Robert Fulton was the creator of the first effective steamboat.

C The *Clermont* paddled from New York City to Albany at almost five miles per hour.

D The Mississippi River was the principal U.S. waterway.

2. The second **summary** differs from the first summary in that it —

A includes a quotation

B provides more supporting details

C states an opinion

D uses Fulton's personal letters as a source

3. Which feature of an effective **summary** is missing from the first summary but included in the second?

A the full title and author

B the main idea

C some supporting details

D a quotation

4. If someone calls a piece of furniture *antiquated,* he or she means that it is —

A attractive

B fancy

C old-fashioned

D historical

5. Which of the following words is a synonym for *prototype?*

A original

B patent

C exclusive

D current

6. A *monopoly* gives a person —

A the right to influence lawmakers

B a guaranteed income

C a portion of profits from an invention

D exclusive control over something

Writing Focus Constructed Response

Which details in the article did you identify as most important? Create an outline of the original article that shows the details you would include in a summary.

What Do You Think Now?

What did you learn from this article about how a new idea can be made to work?

Writing Workshop

Technical Documents

Write with a Purpose

Write a technical document in which you explain how to operate a tool or a machine or how to complete a multistep process. Your **purpose** is to explain how to do something. Your **audience** is classmates or others who are not familiar with the project or process you will explain.

A Good Technical Document

- encourages the reader
- demonstrates the expertise of the author
- provides a clear sequence of steps
- gives all the information necessary for success
- uses formatting, such as bulleted lists and font styles, to help the reader
- anticipates readers' questions or difficulties

See page 470 for complete rubric.

Think as a Reader/Writer

Reading directions can be confusing and frustrating. Why couldn't the writer be clear? If you have ever tried to explain something complicated in writing, you know that it can be difficult to communicate exactly what you want your reader to understand. A good writer can create a technical document that is clear and well organized. Before you write your own technical document, notice how Dennis Coello gives clear information in the opening of his article "Fix a Flat," originally published in *Boys' Life* magazine.

Flat tires are part of bicycling. But fixing a flat is easy. You will need:

- two tire levers (small tools used to pry the tire from the rim)
- a six-inch crescent wrench (if your wheels aren't quick-release)
- a tube repair kit
- an air pump

Most flats are in the rear. Removing the rear wheel from the bike is more difficult than removing the front one, but it's easy once you know how.

First, **shift the chain onto the smallest freewheel cog.** Remove the brake cable by pressing both brake pads toward the wheel so you can easily lift the loose end from its housing in the brake lever.

Next, **put the bike on its back.** Flip the quick-release lever or use the crescent wrench to loosen both axle nuts. Take the derailleur body (the mechanism that moves the chain from sprocket to sprocket) and pull it back toward you. Then, **lift the chain and remove the wheel.**

← The **introduction** encourages the audience to read on.

← Using **a bulleted list** helps the reader to quickly see what tools are needed.

← Using **boldface print** helps the reader understand the basic instruction.

← **Transition words** such as *first, next,* and *then* make the sequence of steps clear.

Think About the Professional Model

With a partner, discuss the following questions about the model.

1. How does Coello encourage readers to think they can fix flats?

2. How does Coello's writing style match his purpose for writing?

Reader/Writer Notebook

Use your **RWN** to complete the activities for this workshop.

WA.8.3.a Write business letters, letters to the editor and job applications that: address audience needs, stated purpose and context in a clear and efficient manner; **WA.8.3.c** Write business letters, letters to the editor and job applications that: include appropriate facts and details; **WA.8.3.b** Write business letters, letters to the editor and job applications that: follow the conventional style appropriate to the text using proper technical terms; **WP.8.15** Drafting, Revising and Editing: Proofread writing, edit to improve conventions and identify and correct fragments and run-ons.

Prewriting

Choose a Topic

A technical document can explain any process, from putting on a play or operating a dishwasher to training a dog to sit and stay. Your teacher might assign a topic for this writing assignment, but if you have a choice of topics, consider projects that you feel confident doing. It might be something that you have taught someone else to do.

Technical documents often focus on a specific tool or machine. You might write about a tool or machine you know how to use well, such as a DVD player, power drill, or MP3 music player. Think about devices you use every day at school or in hobbies and sports.

Note the Details

Concentrate on the details you need to communicate to your audience. The chart below shows specific details that an effective technical document will include.

Details	
Essential Information	What is the task or tool you will explain?
Materials Needed	What does your reader need to have to complete the process successfully?
Steps	What are the steps, in order, that your reader must follow?
Factors	Are there any conditions that might affect the outcome? Do you need to provide any warnings about safety?
Variables	Your reader won't have exactly the same equipment and conditions you have. How can you make sure your technical document will apply to a variety of situations?
Questions	What are some questions your audience will probably have about the project?

Idea Starters

- Is there a tool or machine you use frequently?
- Is there a game that you would like to teach others to play?
- What skill do you have that you would like to explain to others?
- What hobbies or crafts do you enjoy working on?
- What do you think would benefit a friend or family member to learn?

Peer Review

If possible, teach a partner part of the process in person. Notice which steps are difficult, and pay careful attention to questions your partner asks. Take notes about how you will address these questions in your technical document.

Your Turn

Get Started Brainstorm a list of topics for your technical document in your **RWN.** Choose a topic that is interesting and that you feel comfortable explaining. Then, create a detail chart like the one shown on this page. Answer the questions and take notes about each category of detail.

Learn It Online

See how one writer conveyed instructions. Use an interactive writer's model at:

go.hrw.com L8-463 

Technical Documents

Writing Tip

Think about the words your audience may not know that relate to your topic. **Jargon** is specialized vocabulary used in a particular field. For example, a sailor uses the terms *jib, keel,* and *mainstay* to describe parts of a boat.

What jargon might you use in your document? You might decide to eliminate jargon by stating the same information in simpler words. If you must include jargon, be sure to give your readers a clear definition of any unfamiliar terms.

Think About Audience and Purpose

When you have been given the job of writing a technical document, your **purpose** is to give your **audience** the benefit of expert knowledge that you have and they need. Ask yourself these questions to think about who will read your technical document and what they will need to know to be successful.

- Why might someone be reading this document?
- What might readers already know about your topic?
- What will they need to know before they begin this process?
- What kind of format might help them follow your directions?

Technical Document Outline

Use an outline like the one below to plan your technical document. Note that the introduction and conclusion of many technical documents are fairly short. The key information and explanations appear in the body.

Introduction

- What tool or task will I explain? ______________________________
- What results can my readers expect? ______________________________
- What encouragement can I provide to reassure my readers? ______________________________

Body

- What materials are needed? ______________________________
- What are the steps of the process in order? ______________________________
- What possible difficulties do my readers need to anticipate? ______________________________
- How can I help my readers avoid common mistakes? ______________________________

Conclusion

- What can I tell my readers about why the tool or task is important? ______________________________
- What are the possible rewards of the project? ______________________________
- How can I suggest a way to use the tool more efficiently or for another purpose? ______________________________

Your Turn

Create an Organized Outline

In your **RWN,** create an outline like the one on this page. Briefly note the information you will include in the introduction, body, and conclusion of your technical document. Be sure to include any necessary details from your detail chart.

Drafting

Follow Your Plan

Use your outline from page 464 and the framework at the right to draft your technical document.

Framework for a Technical Document

Introduction

- Clearly state your purpose for writing.
- Explain what you will be teaching your readers to do, and then give them an idea of how you will present the information.
- Encourage readers to keep reading.

Body

- Provide a list of tools and supplies your reader will need.
- Provide a sequence of steps or a list of tips, depending on the type of instructions you are giving.
- Give a warning about any difficult part of the process.

Conclusion

- State the end result that your reader will have achieved.

Format Your Document

The way you format your document can make a big difference in how successful your reader is in completing his or her task. Use boldface and italic type to draw your reader's attention to the key words or steps.

When you are writing about a number of steps that must be done in the proper order, it is important to make the sequence of steps clear. One way to help your reader follow the steps correctly is to use a bulleted list. You might also choose to create a numbered list like the one below.

Step 1. Shift the chain onto the smallest freewheel cog.
Step 2. Remove the brake cable.
Step 3. Put the bike on its back.

Grammar Link Using Precise Language

You probably know a lot about the topic you are going to write about and could give a lot of information about it. When you are writing technical documents, however, you want your instructions to be as brief and precise as possible. As you create your draft, try to put yourself in your reader's shoes and identify any steps in your document that might be confusing. One way to avoid confusion is to use precise language. Look at the following examples of vague and precise language.

Vague Language	Precise Language
• Loosen the nuts with the wrench. • Take the wheel off the bike.	• Use the crescent wrench to loosen both axle nuts. • Lift the chain, and remove the wheel.

Writing Tip

Remember that your readers are more likely to pay attention to your instructions if you use a friendly and encouraging tone.

Your Turn

Draft Your Document Using the notes in your detail chart from page 463 and your framework, create your first draft. Also, think about:

- any jargon you'll need to define
- the tone you will use in your writing. Will it be formal or informal? Why?
- how to give your audience the confidence they need to successfully follow your explanation.

Peer Review

Working with a partner, review your drafts and take notes. Imagine yourself performing the steps described. (Ask your partner to read your work in the same way.) Answering each question in this chart can help you figure out where and how your drafts could be improved.

Evaluating and Revising

Read the questions in the left column of the chart, and then use the tips in the middle column to help you make revisions to your document. The right column suggests techniques you can use to revise your draft.

Technical Document: Guidelines for Content and Organization

Evaluation Questions	Tips	Revision Techniques
1. Does your introduction encourage your audience to continue reading?	**Underline** a sentence that encourages your reader.	**Insert** a sentence that puts your audience at ease or will make them curious.
2. Does your document include a list of necessary tools or supplies?	**Put a star** next to each item in the list.	**Indent** your list, and **add** a bullet before each item.
3. Is the sequence of your steps clear? Have you used clear, direct language?	**Circle** all your numbers or transition words. **Highlight** unclear language.	**Add** numbers or words like *first, then,* and *next.* **Revise** confusing or unclear language.
4. Does your draft include important sentences that you want to make sure your reader pays attention to?	**Draw a box** around the most important sentences.	**Use** boldface type to draw your reader's attention to these sentences.
5. Have you included sentences that explain the results of the actions in the process you are writing about?	**Put a check mark** beside sentences that describe the results your reader can expect.	**Add** sentences that tell your reader what to expect.
6. Have you included a warning about any difficult parts of the process?	**Bracket** any sentences that caution your reader.	**Add** a sentence that warns your reader of a possible difficulty.

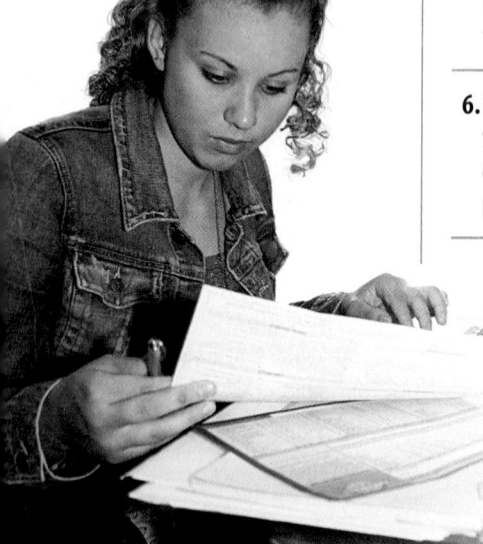

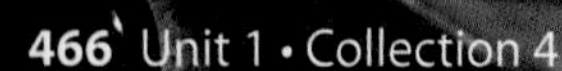

Read this student draft, and notice the comments on its strengths as well as suggestions on how it could be improved.

Student Draft

Guide to Cell Phones

by Sadie Aikman, Abiding Word Lutheran School

Operating a cell phone is a simple task. No matter how many "special features" it has, it serves one purpose: to make and receive calls.

← **Notice that Sadie encourages the reader by saying that using a cell phone is a "simple task."**

Dialing a number is easy. Simply push the corresponding numbers that match the person's phone number and press the green button on either the left or right side of the keypad (depending on which model you own). To hang up, just press the red button on the other side.

← **Sadie uses clear, direct language to explain each step.**

MINI-LESSON How to Write an Engaging Introduction

Sadie has offered encouragement to her readers in the introduction to her technical document. At the same time, she needs to add a more engaging introduction so she can catch her readers' attention and keep them reading. Since cell phones are a part of almost everyone's life, Sadie can draw upon that familiarity to write a more interesting beginning for her technical document.

Sadie's Revision of Paragraph One

Most teens can't wait to get their first cell phone. They deliberate for hours about what cover and color to choose: red, white, and blue American flag, or school colors and mascot, or polka dots. Then they have to choose the all important ring: their favorite song, school fight song, or something silly like a lullaby. These decisions are time-consuming, but actually learning to use a cell phone is not.^ Operating a cell phone is a simple task. No matter how many "special features" it has, it serves one purpose: to make and receive calls.

Your Turn

Read your draft, and then ask yourself:

- Have I engaged my readers with an interesting beginning?
- Have I explained what might happen if a step is skipped or incompletely followed?

Student Draft *continues*

Sadie warns readers that this part of the process might be more difficult.

To add a contact to your phone is a little more complicated. Go to your menu screen and scroll over to "Contacts." Press "OK," and another screen should come up. Scroll down to "Add Contact" and press "OK." It will ask you to insert the name of the person you wish to add; just look down at your keypad and the letters will be listed. You will have to insert the number. Just press "OK," and you're done! You now have a contact in your phone.

Sadie presents the steps in the order they must be followed.

To change your ring tone, volume, wallpaper, etc., you go back to your menu screen and find "settings." Push "OK," and a screen will come up giving the things that you can change. Scroll down to the icon that represents what you want to change. Press "OK" and follow the directions.

Sadie's document has a clear conclusion.

Congratulations! You have successfully programmed your phone to your liking.

MINI-LESSON Using Transition Words to Show Sequence

Sadie's partner became confused when trying to follow the directions for adding a contact. Sadie decided to add **transition words,** such as *first, then, again* and *afterward,* to make the order of the steps clear.

Sadie's Revision of Paragraph Three

To add a contact to your phone is a little more complicated. ^First, go to your menu screen and scroll over to "Contacts." Press "OK," and another screen should come up. ^Then, scroll down to "Add Contact" and press "OK" ^again. It will ask you to insert the name of the person you wish to add; just look down at your keypad and the letters will be listed. ^Afterward you will have to insert the number. Just press "OK," and you're done! You now have a contact in your phone.

Your Turn

Use Transition Words to Show Sequence With a partner, review your draft for steps that must be followed in a specific sequence. Ask your partner to identify areas where a transition might make your document easier to follow.

Proofreading and Publishing

Proofreading

When you have finished your draft, review your document for errors in spelling, grammar, usage, and punctuation. Be sure that the steps in the process you are writing about are in the correct order.

Grammar Link **Using Commas Correctly**

You should make it easy for readers to follow your thoughts as they read your technical document. Using commas correctly will help you show the transition from one step or idea to the next. Look at the following examples:

Example 1

First go to your menu screen and scroll over to "Contacts." Next press "OK" and another screen should come up.

Example 2

First, go to your menu screen and scroll over to "Contacts." Next, press "OK," and another screen should come up.

In the second example, the commas make the sequence clear so that the reader doesn't have to go back and re-read the instructions. When you are proofreading your document, check to see that you have correctly used commas to indicate sequence.

Publishing

Here are some suggestions on how you might share your technical document with a larger audience.

- Compile a class "how-to" manual. Ask writers if they want to add illustrations to their articles. Choose a title and design a cover.
- Post your work on an Internet site.

Reflect on the Process In your **RWN,** write short responses to the following questions:

1. What did you learn about clear writing by creating a technical document? What did you learn about the process you explained?
2. How did your document improve during revision? Which change do you think had the greatest impact?

Proofreading Tip

A small error in a technical document could create serious problems for readers. Double check any numbers, statistics, or specific details to make sure you have given the correct information.

Your Turn

Proofread and Publish

Proofread your draft to eliminate errors. As you proofread, check that you have used correct punctuation. Then, make a final copy of your technical document and publish it.

Scoring Rubric

You can use one of the rubrics below to evaluate your technical document from the Writing Workshop or your response to the on-demand activity on the next page. Your teacher will tell you which rubric to use.

6-Point Scale

Score 6 *Demonstrates advanced success*
- focuses consistently on a process appropriate to the prompt
- shows effective, step-by-step organization throughout, with smooth transitions
- offers a thoughtful, creative explanation of the process
- explains each step of the process thoroughly, using examples and detailed instructions
- exhibits mature control of written language

Score 5 *Demonstrates proficient success*
- focuses on a process appropriate to the prompt
- shows effective, step-by-step organization, with transitions
- offers a thoughtful explanation of the process
- explains each step of the process thoroughly, using examples and detailed instructions
- exhibits sufficient control of written language

Score 4 *Demonstrates competent success*
- focuses on an appropriate process, with minor distractions
- shows effective, step-by-step organization, with minor lapses
- offers a mostly thoughtful explanation of the process
- explains the process adequately, with a mixture of general and specific instructions
- exhibits general control of written language

Score 3 *Demonstrates limited success*
- includes some loosely related material that distracts from the writer's "how-to" focus
- shows some organization, with noticeable gaps in the step-by-step process
- offers a routine, predictable explanation of the process
- explains the process with uneven elaboration
- exhibits limited control of written language

Score 2 *Demonstrates basic success*
- includes loosely related material that seriously distracts from the writer's "how-to" focus
- shows minimal organization, with major gaps in the step-by-step process
- offers explanation that merely skims the surface
- explains the process with inadequate elaboration
- exhibits significant problems with control of written language

Score 1 *Demonstrates emerging effort*
- shows little awareness of the topic and purpose for writing
- lacks organization
- offers unclear and confusing explanation
- develops the explanation in only a minimal way, if at all
- exhibits major problems with control of written language

4-Point Scale

Score 4 *Demonstrates advanced success*
- focuses consistently on a process appropriate to the prompt
- shows effective, step-by-step organization throughout, with smooth transitions
- offers a thoughtful, creative explanation of the process
- explains each step of the process thoroughly, using examples and detailed instructions
- exhibits mature control of written language

Score 3 *Demonstrates competent success*
- focuses on an appropriate process, with minor distractions
- shows effective, step-by-step organization, with minor lapses
- offers a mostly thoughtful explanation of the process
- explains the process adequately, with a mixture of general and specific instructions
- exhibits general control of written language

Score 2 *Demonstrates limited success*
- includes some loosely related material that distracts from the writer's "how-to" focus
- shows some organization, with noticeable gaps in the step-by-step process
- offers a routine, predictable explanation of the process
- explains the process with uneven elaboration
- exhibits limited control of written language

Score 1 *Demonstrates emerging effort*
- shows little awareness of the topic and purpose for writing
- lacks organization
- offers unclear and confusing explanation
- develops the explanation in only a minimal way, if at all
- exhibits major problems with control of written language

Technical Directions

When responding to a prompt, use what you've learned from your reading, writing your technical document, and studying the rubric on page 470. Use the steps below to develop a technical document.

Writing Prompt

Write a technical document in which you explain how to use a tool or machine or how to complete a multistep process. Make sure you explain each step clearly and completely and that you arrange steps in a clear order. Also include any materials needed.

Study the Prompt

Be sure to read the prompt and identify all parts of the task. You must give directions for using a tool or completing a multistep process. It is important that your directions are made for someone who has no experience with the process or the tool. You must also explain each step carefully. **Tip:** Spend about five minutes studying the prompt.

Plan Your Response

Think of a process that you know how to do very well or a tool you use often. Make sure it's something that requires several steps, and try to select a process or tool that will interest your readers. Once you understand your task and have settled on your subject:

- write down what background information your readers will need before they start
- jot down the steps in your process, in the order they will be completed
- think about the best format for presenting your process.
- think about any materials needed for the process

Tip: Spend about twenty minutes planning your response.

Respond to the Prompt

Using the notes you've just made, draft your essay. Follow these guidelines:

- Begin with a brief introduction, explaining to your readers why they might need to follow your directions.
- The main part of your document should list the steps in order for completing the process or using the tool. Make sure that you warn readers of potential problems and also tell them what results to expect. Consider using bulleted or numbered lists to highlight important steps and ideas.
- In the conclusion, point out the usefulness of your process or tool. **Tip:** Spend about twenty minutes writing your draft.

Improve Your Response

Revising Go back to the key aspects of the prompt. Is your essay clearly organized? Are your process steps connected by clear transitional phrases? Have you included all necessary information?

Proofreading Take a few minutes to proofread your essay to correct errors in grammar, spelling, punctuation, and capitalization. Make sure all your edits are neat, and erase any stray marks.

Checking Your Final Copy Before you turn in your essay, read it one more time to catch any errors you may have missed. You'll be glad you give your best effort. **Tip:** Save ten minutes to improve your paper.

Presenting and Responding to an Instructional Speech

Speak and Listen with a Purpose

Adapt your technical document into an instructional speech. Rehearse and present your speech to the class. Listen and respond to a classmate's instructional speech. Participate in a question-and-answer session.

Think as a Reader/Writer Regardless of the career you pursue, one thing is for certain: At some point, you will need to respond to directions or give them yourself. Just as a writer must provide clear instructions to an audience of readers, a speaker must also communicate clearly to a listening audience.

Adapting Your Technical Document into a Presentation

Because you are adapting a technical document, you have a head start on your presentation. Now you will need to change, add to, or clarify your instructions for your listening audience. Follow these suggestions as you review your document:

- **Organization** Make sure your presentation is clear. You may need to add transitional words or strengthen your phrases.
- **Word Choice** Read your instructions aloud. Do your sentences sound natural? Sentences that are appropriate in written text often sound odd when spoken. Revise your wording as necessary.
- **Verbal and Nonverbal Cues** What points do you want to emphasize, both with your tone of voice and with **gestures** or **body language?** Consider the **pacing** of your delivery: You may need to slow down your delivery when you come to a complicated part.
- **Visuals** Think about props, graphics, or other visuals that will help you demonstrate your instructions.

Rehearse and Present Your Instructional Speech

When you rehearse your speech, try presenting it to friends or family members. Ask them whether they had trouble understanding your instructions, and revise as necessary.

When you present your speech in class, remember to pronounce your words clearly, make eye contact with audience members, and show enthusiasm. Watch your audience for signs that they are confused. Try restating your directions in different words to clear up any confusion.

Use your **RWN** to complete the activities for this workshop.

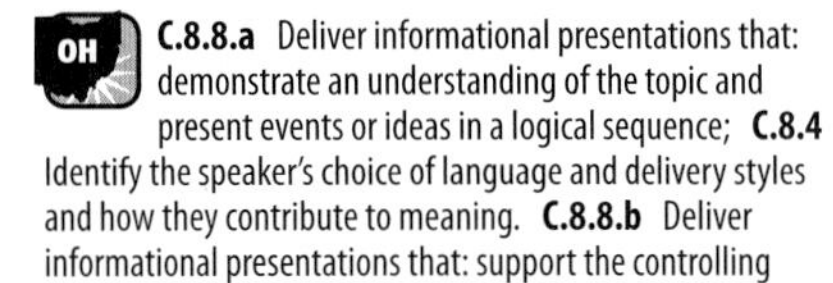

C.8.8.a Deliver informational presentations that: demonstrate an understanding of the topic and present events or ideas in a logical sequence; **C.8.4** Identify the speaker's choice of language and delivery styles and how they contribute to meaning. **C.8.8.b** Deliver informational presentations that: support the controlling idea or thesis with well-chosen and relevant facts, details, examples, quotations, statistics, stories and anecdotes

Listening and Responding to an Instructional Speech

When you give an instructional speech, your effort is obvious for everyone to see. When you listen and respond to an informative speech, your effort isn't as apparent, but is just as important.

Listen Actively

Has anyone ever said to you, "I know you *hear* me—but are you *listening* to me?" Hearing is something you do without thinking about it. Listening involves focus and concentration.

Active-Listening Tips	
Think while you listen.	• Think about similar tasks that you have done. • Imagine yourself completing the steps the speaker is describing.
Take notes.	• Jot down each step in the process. • Write question marks next to instructions you would like to ask the speaker about later.
Give feedback.	• Offer **nonverbal feedback** by looking at the speaker and nodding that you understand. • Ask for clarification if you are confused. • **Summarize** what you think the speaker is saying. Then, ask him or her if that is what was meant.

A Good Instructional Speech

- has clear transitions so that steps are easy for the audience to follow
- includes props or visuals, if possible, to help demonstrate a task
- adjusts wording or explanations as needed if audience seems confused
- uses verbal and nonverbal cues to make instructions clear

Participate in a Question-and-Answer Session

A question-and-answer session is an excellent wrap-up for both the speaker and the audience. The audience has an opportunity to ask for clarification, and the speaker has a chance to clear up misunderstandings.

If you are the speaker in a question-and-answer session, answer the questions as briefly and clearly as possible. Be patient with audience members who are confused.

If you are an audience member, take an active part in the session by asking relevant questions and listening to the speaker's response.

Speaking Tip

If you are the speaker conducting a question-and-answer session, repeat the questions you are asked in your own words. Not only does repeating a question allow you to check your understanding, but it also helps anyone who wasn't able to hear the question the first time.

Learn It Online

Graphics can make your speech more compelling. See how on MediaScope:

go.hrw.com L8-473 Go

Literary Skills Review

Style **Directions:** Read the following selection. Then, read and respond to the questions that follow.

Gil's Furniture Bought and Sold

by **Sandra Cisneros**

There is a junk store. An old man owns it. We bought a used refrigerator from him once, and Carlos sold a box of magazines for a dollar. The store is small with just a dirty window for light. He doesn't turn the lights on unless you got money to buy things with, so in the dark we look and see all kinds of things, me and Nenny. Tables with their feet upside-down and rows and rows of refrigerators with round corners and couches that spin dust in the air when you punch them and a hundred T.V.'s that don't work probably. Everything is on top of everything so the whole store has skinny aisles to walk through. You can get lost easy.

The owner, he is a black man who doesn't talk much and sometimes if you didn't know better you could be in there a long time before your eyes notice a pair of gold glasses floating in the dark. Nenny who thinks she is smart and talks to any old man, asks lots of questions. Me, I never said nothing to him except once when I bought the Statue of Liberty for a dime.

But Nenny, I hear her asking one time how's this here and the man says, This, this is a music box, and I turn around quick thinking he means a *pretty* box with flowers painted on it, with a ballerina inside. Only there's nothing like that where this old man is pointing, just a wood box that's old and got a big brass record in it with holes. Then he starts it up and all sorts of things start happening. It's like all of a sudden he let go a million moths all over the dusty furniture and swan-neck shadows and in our bones. It's like drops of water. Or like marimbas only with a funny little plucked sound to it like if you were running your fingers across the teeth of a metal comb.

And then I don't know why, but I have to turn around and pretend I don't care about the box so Nenny won't see how stupid I am. But Nenny, who is stupider, already is asking how much and I can see her fingers going for the quarters in her pants pocket.

This, the old man says shutting the lid, this ain't for sale.

RA.L.8.8 Explain ways in which the author conveys mood and tone through word choice, figurative language, and syntax. *Also covered* **WA.8.2**

1. The narrator's tone at the beginning of the story can best be described as
   A. scornful.
   B. angry.
   C. bitter.
   D. upbeat.

2. Cisneros uses dialect to do all of the following except
   A. to make the characters believable.
   B. to give the characters a unique voice.
   C. to make fun of the characters.
   D. to show us how the characters speak to one another.

3. The narrator of this story says, "It's like all of a sudden he let go a million moths all over the dusty furniture and swan-neck shadows and in our bones." She uses these figures of speech to describe as
   A. how dirty the store is.
   B. how creepy she thinks insects are.
   C. the animal puppets in the store.
   D. the magical sound of the music box.

4. When the narrator says that the music is "like drops of water," she is using
   A. a simile.
   B. a metaphor.
   C. personification.
   D. irony.

5. In this story the music box might be a symbol for
   A. the unsold furniture.
   B. the power of beauty in our lives.
   C. a child's fear of scary places.
   D. the experience of going shopping.

6. When the narrator says that Nenny is "stupider" than she is, she is using verbal irony. What she really means is that
   A. Nenny is not ashamed to like the music box.
   B. she is angry because Nenny has some money.
   C. Nenny is not as smart as the narrator is.
   D. she is embarrassed to be seen with Nenny.

Short Answer

7. Identify and explain the situational irony in this story. Use information from the story to support your answer.

Extended Response

8. Based on details in this short story, what can you conclude about the author's style? Write a few sentences, citing details from the story to support your response.

Informational Skills Review

Evaluating a Summary

Directions: Read the following selections. Then, read and respond to the questions that follow.

Native Hoops by 

The Native Stars basketball team is part of a year-round athletic program in Arizona for Native American girls in grades 7 through 12. Players from in and around Phoenix take part. From August to October, the girls prepare for their school tryouts. Through March, they play on their school teams, and when the school season ends, they compete together in Native American summer tournaments. The program is designed to build the girls' confidence—and to help talented players break through barriers to achieve national success.

Basketball, known there as "rez ball," has long been part of life on Native American reservations. The problem is that even the best players are not seen much outside the reservation boundaries. Consequently, Native Americans have yet to break into the NBA or WNBA.

To help Native American athletes get past these limitations, people like Coach Everett Largo of the Native Stars are stepping forward with special programs. "I'm just trying to help these young Native Americans who come out here to the city," says the coach. "A lot of times when they come off the reservations, they kind of hold back. On the reservation it's more laid back. It's quiet. The urban world is fast and very competitive."

Professional teams and business leaders have recognized the problem, too. The Native American Basketball Invitational (NABI) tournament was started in 2003 by sponsors that include the Phoenix Suns and the Arizona Diamondbacks. The event draws high-level U.S. and Canadian teams and large crowds.

Another major competition, the Lori Piestewa National Native American Games, was begun in 2003 as well. Piestewa, a Hopi, was killed in Iraq—the first Native American woman to die in the U.S. military. The annual games held in her honor include competitions in basketball, softball, volleyball, and track and field.

The Native Stars attended the Piestewa games for the first time in 2006, earning good reviews all around. This year, as always, the girls are working hard to prepare for summer tournaments like NABI. "It [is] neat to play with the best of the best," says Native Star Paula Martinez, a Pascua Yaqui Indian. "Yeah, we [have] wins and losses, but it [is] great," says teammate Danielle Explain, a Navajo. "You can also get your game better by watching others play."

RA.I.8.3 Compare and contrast the treatment, scope and organization of ideas from different sources on the same topic. **RA.I.8.7** Analyze an author's argument, perspective or viewpoint and explain the development of key points.

Summary

In this article the author describes the importance of basketball to young Native Americans and the programs and tournaments in which they participate. Basketball is a common sport on Native American reservations, but no Native Americans have played in the NBA or WNBA. Because of this, several programs have been developed to raise the confidence of these players and the profile of Native American athletes around the nation and the world. These include training programs, such as the Native Stars girls' basketball team in Phoenix, Arizona, and competitions, such as the Native American Basketball Invitational (NABI) and the Lori Piestewa tournament, which also includes basketball, softball, volleyball, and track and field.

1. Which passage from the summary is not an important supporting detail and could be omitted?
   A. "the author describes the importance of basketball"
   B. "Basketball is a common sport on Native American reservations"
   C. "no Native Americans have played in the NBA or WNBA"
   D. "which also includes basketball, softball, volleyball, and track and field"

2. What missing information would be important to include in the summary?
   A. a list of other sports played on reservations
   B. a quotation from the team's coach
   C. the article's title and source
   D. the ages of the basketball players

Short Answer

3. Identify the main idea of both the article and the summary. Use information from the passage to support your answer.

Extended Response

4. Identify two or three essential elements of a good summary. Cite examples from the summary to support your answer.

Vocabulary Skills Review

OH **VO.8.1** Define unknown words through context clues and the author's use of comparison, contrast and cause and effect.

Context Clues

Directions: Use context clues to identify the meaning of each boldfaced word or phrase in the following sentences.

1. "The **peak** of the strawberry season was over, and the last few days the workers, most of them braceros, were not picking as many boxes as they had during the months of June and July."
   In this sentence, **peak** means
   A. part of a baseball cap.
   B. crest of a hill.
   C. lowest point.
   D. highest point.

2. "The yelling and screaming of my little brothers and sisters . . . broke the silence of dawn. Shortly, the barking of the dogs **accompanied** them."
   In this sentence, **accompanied** means
   A. joined in with.
   B. fought against.
   C. quieted.
   D. awoke.

3. "While we ate, Papá **jotted down** the number of boxes we had picked."
   In this sentence, **jotted down** means
   A. wrote a brief note about.
   B. analyzed thoroughly.
   C. stacked up.
   D. recounted.

4. "The vines **blanketed** the grapes, making it difficult to see the bunches."
   In this sentence, **blanketed** means
   A. revealed.
   B. destroyed.
   C. covered.
   D. exposed.

5. "Papá sighed, wiped the sweat off his forehead with his sleeve, and said **wearily:** 'Es todo [That's all].'"
   In this sentence, **wearily** means
   A. weirdly.
   B. tiredly.
   C. meanly.
   D. angrily.

Academic Vocabulary

Directions: Choose the best synonym for each of the boldfaced Academic Vocabulary words below.

6. Artwork that is **distinctive** is
   A. unique.
   B. required.
   C. agreeable.
   D. common.

7. When you describe the **impact** of a story, you are describing its
   A. ending.
   B. theme.
   C. essence.
   D. effect.

WP.8.12 Add and delete information and details to better elaborate on a stated central idea and to more effectively accomplish purpose. *Also covered* WA.8.4; WP.8.13

Writing Skills Review

Technical Documents

Directions: Read the paragraph below. Then, answer each question that follows.

(1) It's easy to create an electonic file for photographs if you follow a few simple steps. (2) Right-click on your computer's desktop. (3) Scroll down to New Folder. (4) When the folder appears on your desktop, give it a descriptive name such as "Vacation Photos 2009." (5) Now you are ready to copy photo files into your folder. (6) Open your CD containing photo files by double-clicking the icon. (7) Select the files you want to copy by holding down Shift on your keyboard and clicking the file names. (8) Once the files have been selected, click once, and drag those files to your newly created photo folder. (9) Open the folder and check the file names to be sure they are there. (10) Now you are done.

1. The writer's intended **audience** is —
   A. small children
   B. computer experts
   C. everyday people
   D. athletes

2. Which sentence could be deleted as unnecessary?
   A. Sentence 2
   B. Sentence 5
   C. Sentence 7
   D. Sentence 10

3. Which two sentences should be combined into a single sentence?
   A. Sentences 2 and 3
   B. Sentences 4 and 5
   C. Sentences 5 and 6
   D. Sentences 8 and 9

4. Which of the following is the *best* transition to add at the beginning of sentence 1?
   A. Finally,
   B. First,
   C. For example,
   D. Similarly,

5. What detail might be added to these directions to better explain the information in sentence 5?
   A. How to load the photo CD
   B. Where to buy CDs
   C. What type of files are on the CD
   D. The maker of the CD software

Read On

Fiction

River Rats

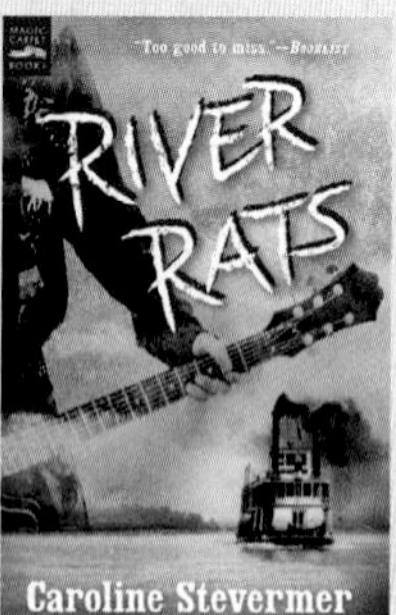

Imagine if paddleboats became as important in the future as they were in the nineteenth century. In *River Rats,* Caroline Stevermer tells the story of a postnuclear future in which a group of orphan kids travels up and down the Mississippi River on a sturdy paddleboat. As tough and challenging as their life on the river is, it's better than trying to survive on the dangerous and savage shore.

Roll of Thunder, Hear My Cry

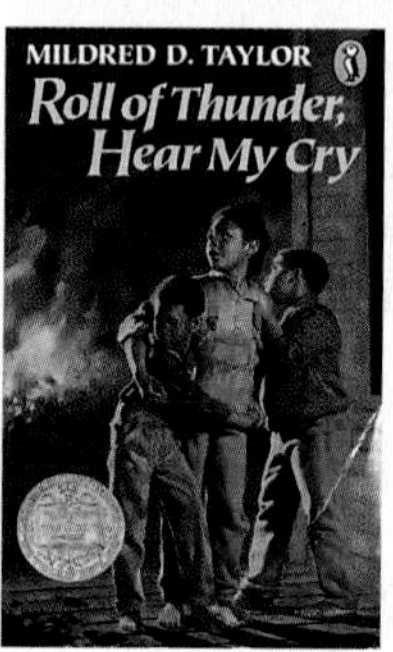

Eight-year-old Cassie Logan does not understand the startling actions of white landowners in Depression-era Mississippi. Over the course of a year, she learns another lesson—why her family is desperately fighting to hold on to the land they call home. In *Roll of Thunder, Hear My Cry,* Mildred Taylor tells a story of pride and courage that all families can learn from.

Out of the Dust

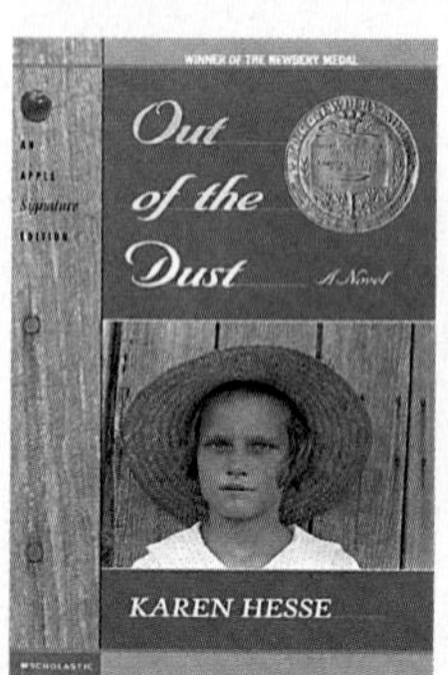

While dust storms are devastating her family's Oklahoma farm in 1934, Billie Jo finds joy only in playing the piano. Then a terrible accident takes that joy away and changes Billie Jo's life forever. *Out of the Dust,* Karen Hesse's Newbery Medal–winning novel, tells the story of Billie Jo's coming to terms with her struggles and misfortunes. The story is told through a series of free-verse poems written in everyday language.

A Christmas Carol

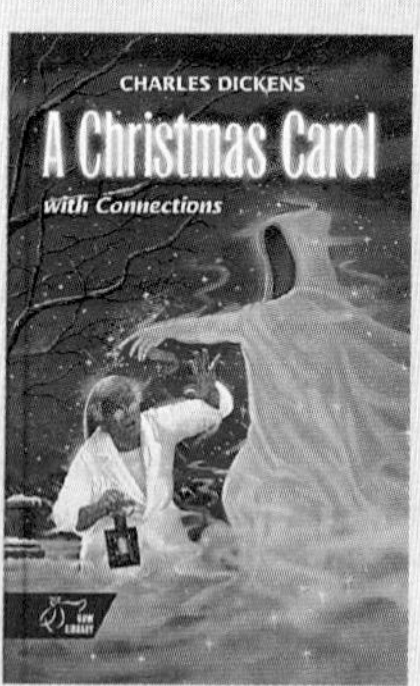

During his lifetime, Charles Dickens was known for his acts of charity. Perhaps that aspect of Dickens's character inspired his holiday classic *A Christmas Carol.* Ebenezer Scrooge, a bitter, selfish old man, is unmoved by the holiday season. With the help of three Christmas spirits, he is able to change the course of his life and discover the joys of giving and receiving.

Nonfiction

There Comes a Time: The Struggle for Civil Rights

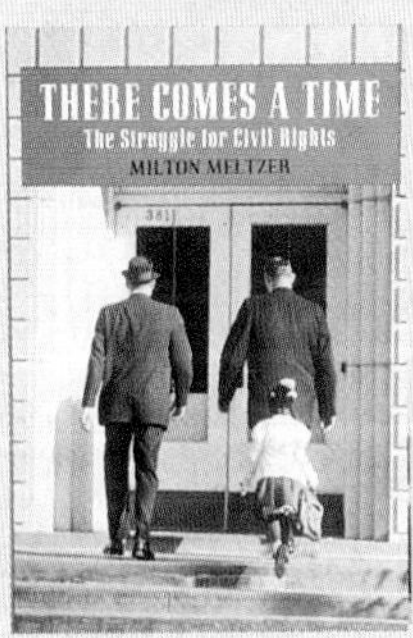

The Civil Rights Movement was one of the most important chapters in American history, yet it is often confusing to people because of its large scale. In *There Comes a Time: The Struggle for Civil Rights,* Milton Meltzer gives an overview of African Americans' struggle for equality. The penetrating writing is accompanied by many riveting photographs, which eloquently capture the energy of the Civil Rights Movement.

Savion: My Life in Tap

A superstar in the world of tap dancing, Savion Glover combines hip style, grace, innovation, and virtuosity. In *Savion: My Life in Tap,* we see the dancer's journey from child prodigy to bona fide tap master. Glover describes his influences, struggles, and triumphs, emphasizing his goal to make tap dancing an art form with worldwide popularity.

Travels with Charley

By the time John Steinbeck turned fifty-eight, he had written the classic American novels *Of Mice and Men* and *The Grapes of Wrath.* He continued his career by writing *Travels with Charley* about his journey across the country. With his French poodle, Charley, by his side, Steinbeck encountered fascinating aspects of America in the 1960s.

Black Hands, White Sails

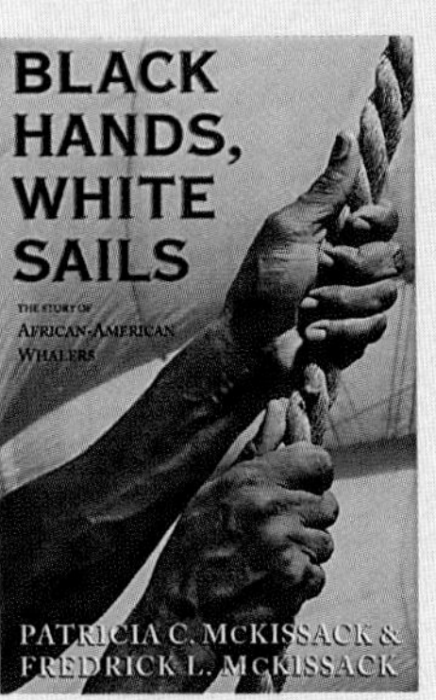

In *Black Hands, White Sails,* Patricia C. and Fredrick L. McKissack bring attention to the African Americans who worked in the whaling industry from colonial times until the nineteenth century. Some became shipowners and captains, while others played key roles in the Civil War and the Underground Railroad.

Learn It Online

Master your knowledge of novels. Learn tips for studying novels with *NovelWise* at:

go.hrw.com L8-481 

UNIT 2

Nonfiction
Writers on Writing

Joseph Bruchac on Nonfiction Joseph Bruchac has traveled the world as a teacher, writer, and storyteller. Known for his award-winning nonfiction and fiction books for young adults, Bruchac often creates works that draw on his Native American heritage. He lives in the foothills of New York.

"One of my first loves was nature writing. I can't remember a time when I wasn't fascinated by the natural world. By the time I was in fifth grade, I was reading every book I could get my hands on that dealt with animals or the outdoors. The thought that what I was reading really happened,

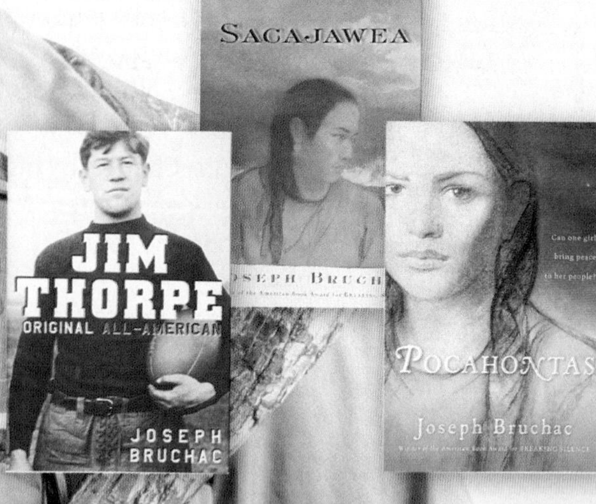

that I might go out and see a robin building its nest or a fox feeding its cubs, excited my imagination. Soon I was writing nonfiction essays about my observations of birds and animals. For many years, right up until I went to college, my aim was to become a naturalist who wrote books—like Roger Tory Peterson, author of the famous guide to American birds.

But by the time I was in eighth grade, I was also reading other kinds of nonfiction, especially history, with the same excitement. Part of that was because my grandmother always pointed out the history around me and gave me books about that history. I grew up near where the Battle of Saratoga was fought during the Revolutionary War. I'd walk the fields and hills and see those events happening once again in my mind's eye. Reading about a battle in a place I knew firsthand made 1775 seem as real as the present day.

To write nonfiction, you can't fake it. You have to know what you are writing about. Because nonfiction is about the real world and not imaginary kingdoms, there are often living people who can help a writer learn more about their subject. When I wrote the book *The Trail of Tears,* I traveled parts of that trail where the Cherokee people suffered, the route through Georgia and Tennessee to Oklahoma. To this day, whenever I write historical nonfiction, I always make it a point to walk the land. While working on *Jim Thorpe,* a story about the life of the famous American Indian athlete, I interviewed Grace Thorpe and Jack Thorpe, two of his children, who shared many interesting stories about their father.

Nonfiction is important for many reasons. Real events can be just as intriguing and dramatic as anything made up. Nonfiction shows us that we live in a world of wonders and infinite possibilities. Nonfiction also reminds us of what might be done (and sometimes what would better not be done) in the future.

When I write nonfiction, my aim is to share with readers stories about people and places that will be as interesting and exciting as the best nonfiction books I read when I was young. I hope I can take readers like you to places you've never been before—and help you see more of the incredible world around us.”

Think as a Writer

When he was growing up, Bruchac was fascinated by nature writing and historical writing. Which of the nonfiction forms interests you most? Why?

46
englandsnorthwest
106
englandsnorthwest

COLLECTION 5

Elements of Nonfiction

INFORMATIONAL TEXT FOCUS

Proposition and Support

"Fall down seven times;
stand up eight times."

—Japanese proverb

What Do You Think?

What qualities help people overcome hard times?

Athletes race to the finish line.

Learn It Online

Explore nonfiction through the Reading Workshops online.

go.hrw.com L8-485 

Literary Focus

by **Sara Kajder**

What Is Nonfiction?

Some people enjoy entering into imaginary worlds. They choose to read fiction. Others prefer to read about the world as it really is. They choose to read nonfiction. Nonfiction is a broad category that could include even the telephone directory. When we talk about nonfiction, though, we usually mean well-written prose that deals with real people, things, events, and places.

Types of Nonfiction

Nonfiction comes in many **genres,** or types. Here are some of the most common.

Biography A **biography** is an account of a person's life written by another person. Biographies usually tell the story of someone famous, such as an athlete, scientist, or writer. They are among the most popular types of literature.

Autobiography An **autobiography** is a person's account of his or her own life. Many are written by famous people, but anyone can write about his or her experiences—surviving difficulties or living during interesting times.

Essay An **essay** is a short piece of prose that examines a single subject. A **personal essay** focuses on the writer's response to an experience. Its tone is usually informal and conversational. A **formal essay** is objective, and it is impersonal in tone. Its purpose is to inform readers about a topic.

Speech A **speech** is similar to an essay but is delivered orally. Its purpose is to bring the audience together and inform them of something.

Elements of Nonfiction

Main Idea When you read nonfiction, you look for the **main idea**—the writer's most important message. A writer's main idea is usually supported with details, such as examples and quotations.

Structural Patterns All text has a structure. Here are some of the **structural patterns** common in nonfiction:

- **Chronological order:** This is when events are listed in the order in which they happened. This type of pattern usually makes **cause-and-effect** relationships clear. In "Camp Harmony," for example, you'll learn what **caused** the family to move and the **effects** of their move.
- **Order of importance:** Some nonfiction is presented with the facts in order, from the most to the least important, or vice versa.
- **Logical order:** Many essays, such as "Americans All," use logical order, in which supporting details are arranged in related groups so that connections are clear.

Repetition Nonfiction texts may also contain other structural patterns. **Repetition** of key ideas and the use of **parallel grammatical forms** both help nonfiction writers make their points clear.

RA.L.8.6 Explain how an author's choice of genre affects the expression of a theme or topic. **RA.I.8.7** Analyze an author's argument, perspective or viewpoint and explain the development of key points. **RA.I.8.5** Assess the adequacy, accuracy and appropriateness of an author's details, identifying persuasive techniques and examples of bias and stereotyping.

Qualities of Nonfiction

Purpose All writing has a **purpose.** It may be to

- provide information
- express personal feelings
- entertain
- influence

Whenever you read nonfiction, ask yourself, "What is the author's purpose for writing this?"

Logic Simply put, **logic** means "accurate reasoning." To be logical, statements must be supported by reasons, evidence, and examples. Ideas that stray from the main topic are kept to a minimum or are eliminated altogether.

Unity and Coherence

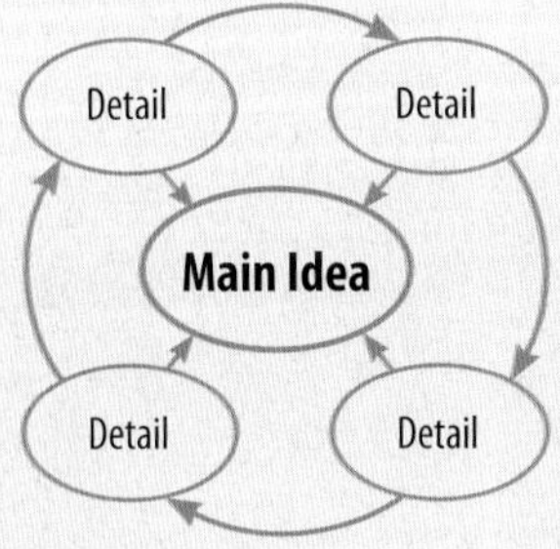

Unity When a nonfiction text has **unity,** all its details support the main idea or topic. It also has **internal consistency**—that is, all its parts are connected and agree with what came before.

Coherence When a text has **coherence** (koh HIHR uhns), one idea flows from another. A text is structured so that it presents information in an order that readers can easily follow. Transition words such as *first*, *next*, and *finally* also help a writer create coherence.

Your Turn Analyze Nonfiction

Read these two responses to "The Treasure of Lemon Brown" by Walter Dean Myers. Then, answer the questions that follow.

Text 1

Lemon Brown is a homeless person; therefore, he could not have been a good blues player. I once knew a person who played the harmonica really well. He had red hair and lived close by. I think homeless people should all be given a place to stay so they don't have to sleep on the sidewalk. Even though Lemon Brown is homeless that doesn't mean he's not human.

Text 2

The character of Lemon Brown reminds us of the humanity of homeless people. They are not just misfits who embarrass us by sleeping on our sidewalks and begging for change. They, too, once had jobs and families. We should always remember that they are human beings with ideas, opinions, and a life history. We should treat them with concern and respect.

1. What type of nonfiction are these texts? Are they essays? biographies? autobiographies?
2. Which response is logical and has unity? How can you tell?

Learn It Online
Use *PowerNotes* as a visual aid to boost your learning at:
go.hrw.com L8-487 Go

Analyzing Visuals

How Can You See Nonfiction Structure in a Photograph?

Nonfiction deals with real people and events. Art can do this, too, especially photography. Photographers often capture scenes from real life that they feel reveal greater truths. They decide what goes into the frame and where. Then, it's up to us as viewers to examine their choices and to "read" the photo's main idea.

Analyzing a Photograph

Use these guidelines to help you analyze a photograph:

1. Identify the subject. What aspect of real life does it capture?
2. Think about the way in which the subject is depicted. Is the subject shown in a realistic or an imaginative way?
3. Examine the lighting. Is it dark or bright? How does light affect the mood? Is it bleak? cheerful?
4. Evaluate the coherence and unity of information within the frame. How do forms and shapes contribute to the whole?
5. Combine your observations to make a reasonable inference about the artist's purpose and main idea.

Your Turn Write About Nonfiction

A critic said, "Struth wants to make people more aware of how to read a picture" and of "the intent of the photographer." How does the coherence of the photograph hint at Struth's purpose? How does the act of viewing the photograph echo its content?

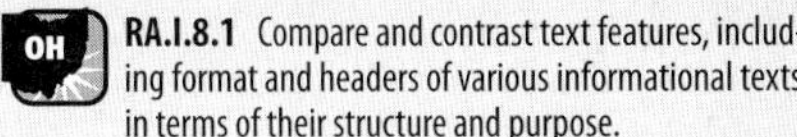
RA.I.8.1 Compare and contrast text features, including format and headers of various informational texts in terms of their structure and purpose.

1. The paintings on the walls are framed. How does Struth create yet another frame with his photograph?

2. How do the figures in the photograph compare to those in the painting? Which look most real? Think of size, color, and placement.

3. How does Struth use color and tone to blur the line between real life and art?

Art Institute 2 (1990), Thomas Struth, German, b. 1954. Chromogenic color print mounted to acrylic, (184.1 x 219 cm). Restricted gift of Susan and Lewis Manilow, 1991.28, The Art Institute of Chicago. Photography © The Art Institute of Chicago.

Reading Focus

by **Kylene Beers**

What Reading Skills Help You Understand Nonfiction?

You may wonder, "Is reading nonfiction different from reading fiction?" Reading narrative nonfiction (biographies, autobiographies) is almost the same as reading fiction: You follow the chain of events, make inferences about characters, and visualize the setting. Here are some additional strategies that can help you when reading all types of nonfiction.

Finding the Main Idea

One of the most important things to discuss about a work of nonfiction is its main idea. The **main idea** is the most important message of the entire text (not just part of the text). At times, the main idea is stated directly; at times, you may have to figure it out. Use these tips to help you figure out the main idea of an essay or article.

Tips for Finding the Main Idea

- Look for key statements made by the writer.
- Look at the details the writer provides. (*Who, what, when, where, why,* and *how* questions will help you identify important details.)
- Think about what the details add up to.
- Use your own words to state the main idea.

For example, you will learn many details about Harriet Tubman in Ann Petry's biography. Think about those details. What they *all* say about Tubman forms Petry's main idea.

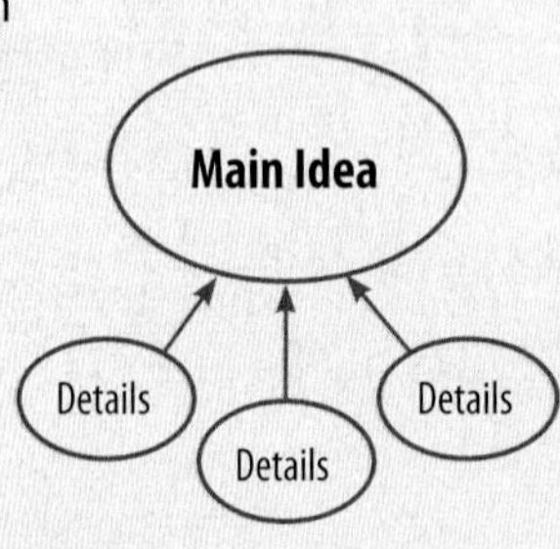

Analyzing Details

You can use the technique of **analyzing details** to help you understand almost any element of literature. For example, analyzing details can help you find the main idea of a nonfiction work. Analyzing details can also help you recognize the structural patterns of a text as well as its unity and coherence.

Transitional Words Paying attention to **transitional words,** which connect sentences and ideas, can make nonfiction text easier to understand. These words can also help you recognize the structural pattern of a text.

Here is a list of some of the ways transitional words are used (as well as some of the words):

- to connect ideas **chronologically,** or in time order—*first, next, before, then, when, while, meanwhile, at last, finally*
- to connect things in **space**—*above, across, among, before, below, here, in, near, there, under, next to*
- to connect ideas in **order of importance**—*first, mainly, more important, to begin with, then, last*

RA.I.8.7 Analyze an author's argument, perspective or viewpoint and explain the development of key points. **RP.8.3** Monitor own comprehension by adjusting speed to fit the purpose, or by skimming, scanning, reading on, looking back, note taking or summarizing what has been read so far in text. **RA.I.8.2** Identify and use the organizational structure of a text, such as chronological, compare-contrast, cause-effect, problem-solution, and evaluate its effectiveness. **RA.I.8.8** Recognize how writers cite facts, draw inferences and present opinions in informational text.

- to **compare** ideas—*also, and, another, just as, like, similarly*
- to **contrast** ideas—*although, but, not, however, still, yet, on the other hand*

Notice the transitional words and phrases in this passage. They have been underlined.

> At ten o'clock, he rapped at the door again, yelling, "Lights out!" and Mother rushed to turn the light off not a second later. . . . As it grew quieter in the barracks, I could hear the light patter of rain. . . . I finally had to get out and haul my cot toward the center of the room. In a short while, Henry was up.
>
> from "Camp Harmony"
> by Monica Sone

Facts and Opinions When you analyze details, look for **facts**—true statements—and **opinions**—statements that cannot be proved true or false. Opinions are an important part of many nonfiction pieces but should not be mistaken for facts.

Allusion Another kind of detail you might notice is an **allusion,** or a reference to aspects of a culture that people share. The allusion might be to literature, religion, history, mythology, sports, or music. The following excerpt from Dr. Martin Luther King, Jr.'s, speech "I Have a Dream" makes an allusion to a passage from the Bible:

> I have a dream that one day every valley shall be exalted, and every mountain and hill shall be made low, the rough places shall be made plain, and the crooked places will be made straight.
>
> from "I Have a Dream"
> by Martin Luther King, Jr.

Outlining

Making an outline can help you organize your ideas for your writing. Outlining a text you are reading, however, can help you keep track of important ideas and their supporting details. As you read, stop at the end of each paragraph and ask, "What is the most important idea?" Some paragraphs will present a new idea, and others will supply supporting details for an earlier idea. Record important ideas and supporting details in an outline form like this one:

I. Topic
A. Important idea: ____________
1. Supporting detail: ____________
2. Supporting detail: ____________
3. Supporting detail: ____________

The number of levels (I, A, 1, and so on) and items (I, II, III or A, B, C or 1, 2, 3, and so on) you need will depend on the information in the text.

Your Turn Apply Reading Skills

Choose a passage from this page. Then, do the following.

1. State its main idea. Then, list at least three details that support the main idea. Are those details facts or opinions?
2. Circle any transitional words you find. What structural pattern does the article follow?
3. Create an outline of the passage. Does the outline cause you to rethink the main idea?

Now go to the Skills in Action: Reading Model

Learn It Online
Learn more about text structures and outlining at:
go.hrw.com L8-491 Go

SKILLS IN ACTION

Reading Model

PERSONAL ESSAY

Read with a Purpose Read to discover one writer's ideas about what it means to be American.

AMERICANS ALL

by **Michael Dorris**

Literary Focus

Personal Essay The title and first sentence give you clues that this nonfiction piece is a personal essay. Using the first-person pronoun *I*, the writer is describing his ideas about people from America.

I recognize them instantly abroad: on the street, in crowded rooms, on airplanes, at restaurants—but how? It's emphatically not skin color, not clothing, not little red-white-and-blues stitched to their breast pockets. They don't have to say anything, to show a passport, or to sing the "Star-Spangled Banner," but nevertheless they're unmistakable in any foreign setting.

Literary Focus

Structural Patterns The writer uses a comparison-and-contrast structural pattern. He shows how Americans are different from one another yet also have things in common.

Americans. We come in all varieties of size, age, and style. We travel singly and in groups. We're alternately loud and disapproving or humble and apologetic. We seek each other out or self-consciously avoid each other's company. We pack our gear in Gucci bags or stuff it into Patagonia backpacks, travel first-class or on Eurailpasses,[1] stay in youth hostels or in luxury hotels, but none of that matters. It's as though we're individually implanted with some invisible beeper, some national homing device, that's activated by the proximity of similar equipment.

This common denominator[2] is manifest[3] in shared knowledge (we all know who Mary Tyler Moore[4] is), topics of mutual interest or dispute (guns, the environment, choice), and popular culture (do we or do we not deserve a thousand-calorie break today?).

1. **Eurailpasses:** inexpensive train tickets for travel in Europe.
2. **common denominator:** common characteristic.
3. **manifest** (MAN uh fehst): shown; revealed.
4. **Mary Tyler Moore:** star of a television show that was popular when this essay was written.

Analyzing Visuals **Viewing and Interpreting** Do you think this picture was taken in the United States? What clues might help you make a guess?

In other words, we take the same things seriously or not seriously, are capable of speaking, when we choose to, not merely a common language, but a common idiom, and know the melodies, if not all the words, to many of the same songs.

Why, then, doesn't any of this count when we're *not* overseas? Why, at home, do we seem so different from each other, so mutually incompatible, so strange and forbidding? Do we have to recognize each other in Tokyo or Cairo in order to see through the distinctions and into the commonalities? How does that "we," so obvious anywhere else in the world, get split into "us" and "them" when we're stuck within our own borders?

The answer is clear: To be Americans means to be not the clone of the people next door. I fly back from any homogeneous country, from a place where every person I see is blond, or black, or belongs to only one religion, and then disembark at JFK.[5]

Reading Focus

Facts and Opinions Here, Dorris is giving his opinion. Do you think it is a valid opinion that is based on facts?

Reading Focus

Main Idea This key statement reveals the writer's main idea.

5. **JFK:** John F. Kennedy International Airport in New York City.

I revel[6] in the cadence of many accents, catch a ride to the city with a Nigerian American or Russian American cabdriver. Eat Thai food at a Greek restaurant next to a table of Chinese American conventioneers from Alabama. Get directions from an Iranian American cop and drink a cup of Turkish coffee served by a Navajo student at Fordham who's majoring in Japanese literature. Argue with everybody about everything. I'm home.

Literary Focus

Unity Placing these examples together creates a unified passage that emphasizes Dorris's main idea—that Americans are a diverse people.

6. **revel** (REHV uhl): delight.

Read with a Purpose According to Michael Dorris, what does it mean to be an American?

MEET THE WRITER

Michael Dorris

(1945–1997)

Professor and Writer

A member of the Modoc, a Native American people originally from the California-Oregon border region, Michael Dorris was a professor of cultural anthropology and Native American studies at Dartmouth College in New Hampshire before taking a leave to devote himself to writing fiction and nonfiction full time.

One of his nonfiction books focuses on his adopted son Adam, who was born with fetal alcohol syndrome (FAS). Dorris adopted Adam and two other children before marrying and collaborating with the poet and novelist Louise Erdrich. The single-father parenting duties didn't faze him: "I have this very rich background of grandmothers and aunts and a mother, a wonderful extended family who made nothing seem impossible or out of reach."

Think About the Writer How might Dorris's background have contributed to his delight in diversity?

SKILLS IN ACTION

Wrap Up

OH **RA.I.8.7** Analyze an author's argument, perspective or viewpoint and explain the development of key points. **VO.8.7** Determine the meanings and pronunciations of unknown words by using dictionaries, thesauruses, glossaries, technology and textual features, such as definitional footnotes or sidebars.

Into Action: Main Idea and Details

Review "Americans All" to find details that show how Americans are different and similar. Write the details in a chart like the one below. Then, review the details and state the author's main idea.

Details Showing Differences	Details Showing Similarities

Main Idea:

Talk About . . .

1. With a partner, discuss what Michael Dorris discovers about Americans both when he is abroad and when he is back home. Try to use each Academic Vocabulary word listed at the right in your discussion.

Write About . . .

Use the underlined Academic Vocabulary words in your answers to the following questions.

2. Why does Dorris make the observation that Americans abroad all seem alike?
3. Which do you think is more important to emphasize: the differences among people or their similarities? Explain your position.
4. Why do Americans have different reactions to each other abroad and at home?
5. How does Dorris define what it means to be American?

Writing Focus

Think as a Reader/Writer

You will find different genres of nonfiction in Collection 5. The Writing Focus activities on the Preparing to Read pages will guide you in recognizing what goes into each type of writing. The activities on the Applying Your Skills pages will give you a chance to use these techniques in your own writing.

Academic Vocabulary for Collection 5

Talking and Writing About Nonfiction

Academic Vocabulary is the language you use to write and talk about literature. Use these words to discuss the texts in this collection. The words are underlined throughout the collection.

observation (ahb zuhr VAY shuhn) *n.:* act of taking notice of something for some special purpose; study. *The observation of human nature is important to writers of personal essays.*

emphasize (EHM fuh syz) *v.:* give importance to; pay special attention to. *A writer can choose to emphasize one thing or another.*

reactions (ree AK shuhnz) *n.:* responses. *We read essays for the writers' interesting reactions to the world around them.*

define (dih FYN) *v.:* make clear the meaning of; explain. *Writers are often able to define situations that others just wonder at.*

Your Turn

Copy these Academic Vocabulary words into your *Reader/Writer Notebook.* Try to use the words when you talk about the selections in this collection.

BIOGRAPHY

Preparing to Read

from *Harriet Tubman*: Conductor on the Underground Railroad

by **Ann Petry**

What Do You Think? How much should a person sacrifice for freedom?

QuickTalk

How important is a person's individual freedom to a healthy society? Discuss with a partner how individual freedom shapes American society.

Harriet Tubman (c. 1945) by William H. Johnson. Oil on paperboard, sheet. 29 3/8" x 23 3/8" (73.5 cm x 59.3 cm)

Use your **RWN** to complete the activities for this selection.

OH **RA.I.8.7** Analyze an author's argument, perspective or viewpoint and explain the development of key points.

Literary Focus

Biography and Coherence A **biography** is the story of someone's life written by another person. We "meet" the people in a biography the same way we get to know people in our own lives. We observe their actions and motivations, learn their values, and see how they interact with others. Soon, we feel we know them.

A good biography has **coherence**—all the details come together in a way that makes the biography easy to understand. In nonfiction a text is coherent if the important details support the main idea and connect to one another in a clear order.

Literary Perspectives Apply the literary perspective described on page 499 as you read this selection.

Reading Focus

Finding the Main Idea The **main idea** is the central idea or message of a nonfiction text. To find the main idea, look for key statements made by the writer and for details that point to an important idea. Then, think about the meaning of *all* the details.

Into Action As you read the biography, write down details that seem important. When you have finished, write the main idea.

Harriet Tubman: Conductor on the Underground Railroad	
Important detail:	"It was the largest group that she had ever conducted."
Important detail:	

Writing Focus

Think as a Reader/Writer

Find It in Your Reading In this biography, Ann Petry turns historical facts into a dramatic story. As you read, record in your *Reader/Writer Notebook* **objective,** or factual, passages and **subjective** passages, which reveal the writer's feelings and opinions.

Vocabulary

fugitives (FYOO juh tihvz) *n.:* people fleeing from danger or oppression. *Traveling by night, the fugitives escaped to the North.*

incomprehensible (ihn kahm prih HEHN suh buhl) *adj.:* impossible to understand. *The code that Harriet Tubman used was incomprehensible to slave owners.*

incentive (ihn SEHN tihv) *n.:* reason to do something; motivation. *The incentive of a warm house and good food kept the fugitives going.*

dispel (dihs PEHL) *v.:* get rid of by driving away. *Harriet tried to dispel the travelers' fear of capture.*

eloquence (EHL uh kwehns) *n.:* ability to write or speak gracefully and convincingly. *Frederick Douglass was known for his eloquence in writing and speaking.*

Language Coach

Roots The Latin root *loqui* means "to speak." What word in the Vocabulary list above comes from this root? How is its meaning the same or different from that of the Latin root?

Learn It Online
Get a sneak peek of this story with a video introduction at:

go.hrw.com L8-497 Go

Learn It Online
Get more on the author's life at:
go.hrw.com L8-498 Go

MEET THE WRITER

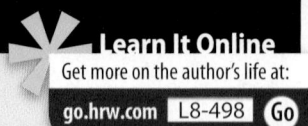

Ann Petry
(1908–1997)

"A Message in the Story"

A native of Old Saybrook, Connecticut, Ann Petry was the granddaughter of a man who escaped from slavery on a Virginia plantation and went north by way of the Underground Railroad. She earned a Ph.D. in 1931 and worked as a pharmacist in her family's drugstore before moving to New York, where she became a writer of books for young people and adults. About her writing she said:

> "My writing has, of course, been influenced by the books I've read but it has been much more influenced by the circumstances of my birth and my growing up, by my family. . . .
>
> "We always had relatives visiting us. They added excitement to our lives. They brought with them the aura and the customs of a very different world. They were all storytellers, spinners of yarns. So were my mother and my father.
>
> "Some of these stories had been handed down from one generation to the next, improved, embellished, embroidered. Usually there was a message in the story, a message for the young, a message that would help a young black child survive, help convince a young black child that black is truly beautiful."

Think About the Writer Petry grew up listening to stories. How might this have shaped the way she wrote?

Build Background

In the Biblical Book of Exodus, Moses is chosen by God to lead the people of Israel out of slavery in Egypt. Moses takes his people on a long, perilous desert journey and leads them to the Promised Land. As you read this biography, look for reasons why Harriet Tubman was called the Moses of her people.

Preview the Selection

This excerpt from a biography relates how **Harriet Tubman** led a group of eleven people out of slavery in 1851. The fugitives traveled by night and slept by day, always on the alert. The risk of capture was constantly on their minds.

Read with a Purpose Read to discover how Harriet Tubman led enslaved people to freedom.

from

Harriet Tubman
CONDUCTOR ON THE UNDERGROUND RAILROAD

by **Ann Petry**

The Railroad Runs to Canada

Along the Eastern Shore of Maryland, in Dorchester County, in Caroline County, the masters kept hearing whispers about the man named Moses, who was running off slaves. At first they did not believe in his existence. The stories about him were fantastic, unbelievable. Yet they watched for him. They offered rewards for his capture.

They never saw him. Now and then they heard whispered rumors to the effect that he was in the neighborhood. The woods were searched. The roads were watched. There was never anything to indicate his whereabouts. But a few days afterward, a goodly number of slaves would be gone from the plantation. Neither the master nor the overseer had heard or seen anything unusual in the quarter.[1] Sometimes one or the other would vaguely remember having heard a whippoorwill call somewhere in the woods, close by, late at night. Though it was the wrong season for whippoorwills.

Sometimes the masters thought they had heard the cry of a hoot owl, repeated, and would remember having thought that the intervals between the low moaning cry were wrong, that it had been repeated four times in succession instead of three. There was never anything more than that to suggest

1. **quarter:** area in a plantation where enslaved blacks lived. It consisted of windowless, one-room cabins made of logs and mud.

Literary Perspectives

Use this perspective to help you explore historical context.

Analyzing Historical Context When applying this perspective, you view a literary text within its historical context. Specifically, you notice historical information about the time in which the author wrote, about the time in which the text is set, and about the ways in which people of the period saw and thought about the world in which they lived. History, in this biography, refers to the social, political, economic and cultural climate of the American South in the time period before the Civil War, when many African Americans were enslaved. As you read, use the notes and questions in the text to guide you in using this perspective.

that all was not well in the quarter. Yet, when morning came, they invariably discovered that a group of the finest slaves had taken to their heels. **A**

Unfortunately, the discovery was almost always made on a Sunday. Thus a whole day was lost before the machinery of pursuit could be set in motion. The posters offering rewards for the fugitives could not be printed until Monday. The men who made a living hunting for runaway slaves were out of reach, off in the woods with their dogs and their guns, in pursuit of four-footed game, or they were in camp meetings saying their prayers with their wives and families beside them.

Harriet Tubman could have told them that there was far more involved in this matter of running off slaves than signaling the would-be runaways by imitating the call of a whippoorwill, or a hoot owl, far more involved than a matter of waiting for a clear night when the North Star was visible.

In December 1851, when she started out with the band of fugitives that she planned to take to Canada, she had been in the vicinity of the plantation for days, planning the trip, carefully selecting the slaves that she would take with her.

She had announced her arrival in the quarter by singing the forbidden spiritual[2]—"Go down, Moses, 'way down to Egypt Land"—singing it softly outside the door of a slave cabin, late at night. The husky voice was beautiful even when it was barely more than a murmur borne on the wind. **B**

Once she had made her presence known, word of her coming spread from cabin to cabin. The slaves whispered to each other, ear to mouth, mouth to ear, "Moses is here." "Moses has come." "Get ready. Moses is back again." The ones who had agreed to go North with her put ashcake[3] and salt herring in an old bandanna, hastily tied it into a bundle, and then waited patiently for the signal that meant it was time to start.

There were eleven in this party, including one of her brothers and his wife. It was the largest group that she had ever conducted,

2. **forbidden spiritual:** Spirituals are religious songs, some of which are based on the biblical story of the Israelites' escape from slavery in Egypt. Plantation owners feared that the singing of certain spirituals might lead to rebellion.

3. **ashcake:** cornmeal bread baked in hot ashes.

A **Read and Discuss** How has the author gotten us interested?

B **Literary Focus** **Biography** Do you think the details about Tubman's voice are factual? Explain.

Vocabulary **fugitives** (FYOO juh tihvz) *n.:* people fleeing from danger or oppression.

but she was determined that more and more slaves should know what freedom was like.

She had to take them all the way to Canada. The Fugitive Slave Law[4] was no longer a great many incomprehensible words written down on the country's law books. The new law had become a reality. It was Thomas Sims, a boy, picked up on the streets of Boston at night and shipped back to Georgia. It was Jerry and Shadrach, arrested and jailed with no warning. C

She had never been in Canada. The route beyond Philadelphia was strange to her. But she could not let the runaways who accompanied her know this. As they walked along, she told them stories of her own first flight; she kept painting vivid word pictures of what it would be like to be free.

But there were so many of them this time. She knew moments of doubt, when she was half afraid and kept looking back over her shoulder, imagining that she heard the sound of pursuit. They would certainly be pursued. Eleven of them. Eleven thousand dollars' worth of flesh and

4. **Fugitive Slave Law:** harsh federal law passed in 1850 stating that fugitives who escaped from slavery to free states could be forced to return to their owners. As a result, those who escaped were safe only in Canada. The law also made it a crime for a free person to help fugitives or to prevent their return.

Harriet Tubman.

C **Literary Perspectives** **Historical Context** What do the names of captured fugitives add to the biography's impact?

Vocabulary **incomprehensible** (ihn kahm prih HEHN suh buhl) *adj.:* impossible to understand.

bone and muscle that belonged to Maryland planters. If they were caught, the eleven runaways would be whipped and sold South, but she—she would probably be hanged. **D**

They tried to sleep during the day but they never could wholly relax into sleep. She could tell by the positions they assumed, by their restless movements. And they walked at night. Their progress was slow. It took them three nights of walking to reach the first stop. She had told them about the place where they would stay, promising warmth and good food, holding these things out to them as an incentive to keep going.

When she knocked on the door of a farmhouse, a place where she and her parties of runaways had always been welcome, always been given shelter and plenty to eat, there was no answer. She knocked again, softly. A voice from within said, "Who is it?" There was fear in the voice.

She knew instantly from the sound of the voice that there was something wrong. She said, "A friend with friends," the password on the Underground Railroad.

The door opened, slowly. The man who stood in the doorway looked at her coldly, looked with unconcealed astonishment and fear at the eleven disheveled runaways who were standing near her. Then he shouted, "Too many, too many. It's not safe. My place was searched last week. It's not safe!" and slammed the door in her face. **E**

She turned away from the house, frowning. She had promised her passengers food and rest and warmth, and instead of that, there would be hunger and cold and more walking over the frozen ground. Somehow she would have to instill courage into these eleven people, most of them strangers, would have to feed them on hope and bright dreams of freedom instead of the fried pork and corn bread and milk she had promised them.

They stumbled along behind her, half dead for sleep, and she urged them on, though she was as tired and as discouraged as they were. She had never been in Canada, but she kept painting wondrous word pictures of what it would be like. She managed to dispel their fear of pursuit so that they would not become hysterical, panic-stricken. Then she had to bring some of the fear back, so that they would stay awake and keep walking though they drooped with sleep.

Yet, during the day, when they lay down deep in a thicket, they never really slept, because if a twig snapped or the wind sighed in the branches of a pine tree, they jumped to their feet, afraid of their own shadows, shivering and shaking. It was very cold, but they dared not make fires because someone would see the smoke and wonder about it.

She kept thinking, eleven of them. Eleven thousand dollars' worth of slaves. And she had to take them all the way to Canada.

D **Reading Focus** **Finding the Main Idea** What important detail do you learn in this paragraph?

E **Read and Discuss** What is happening with Harriet Tubman and her group?

Vocabulary **incentive** (ihn SEHN tihv) *n.:* reason to do something; motivation.
dispel (dihs PEHL) *v.:* get rid of by driving away.

Sometimes she told them about Thomas Garrett, in Wilmington.[5] She said he was their friend even though he did not know them. He was the friend of all fugitives. He called them God's poor. He was a Quaker[6] and his speech was a little different from that of other people. His clothing was different, too. He wore the wide-brimmed hat that the Quakers wear.

She said that he had thick white hair, soft, almost like a baby's, and the kindest eyes she had ever seen. He was a big man and strong, but he had never used his strength to harm anyone, always to help people. He would give all of them a new pair of shoes. Everybody. He always did. Once they reached his house in Wilmington, they would be safe. He would see to it that they were.

She described the house where he lived, told them about the store where he sold shoes. She said he kept a pail of milk and a loaf of bread in the drawer of his desk so that he would have food ready at hand for any of God's poor who should suddenly appear before him, fainting with hunger. There was a hidden room in the store. A whole wall swung open, and behind it was a room where he could hide

5. **Wilmington:** city in Delaware.

6. **Quaker:** member of the Society of Friends, a religious group active in the movement to end slavery.

Harriet Tubman (at left) with a group she helped escape from slavery.

fugitives. On the wall there were shelves filled with small boxes—boxes of shoes—so that you would never guess that the wall actually opened. **F**

While she talked, she kept watching them. They did not believe her. She could tell by their expressions. They were thinking. New shoes, Thomas Garrett, Quaker, Wilmington—what foolishness was this? Who knew if she told the truth? Where was she taking them anyway?

That night they reached the next stop—a farm that belonged to a German. She made the runaways take shelter behind trees at the edge of the fields before she knocked at the door. She hesitated before she approached the door, thinking, suppose that he too should refuse shelter, suppose—Then she thought, *Lord, I'm going to hold steady on to You and You've got to see me through*—and knocked softly.

She heard the familiar guttural voice say, "Who's there?"

She answered quickly, "A friend with friends."

He opened the door and greeted her warmly. "How many this time?" he asked.

"Eleven," she said and waited, doubting, wondering.

He said, "Good. Bring them in."

He and his wife fed them in the lamp-lit kitchen, their faces glowing as they offered food and more food, urging them to eat, saying there was plenty for everybody, have more milk, have more bread, have more meat.

They spent the night in the warm kitchen. They really slept, all that night and until dusk the next day. When they left, it was with reluctance. They had all been warm and safe and well-fed. It was hard to exchange the security offered by that clean, warm kitchen for the darkness and the cold of a December night. **G**

"Go On or Die"

Harriet had found it hard to leave the warmth and friendliness, too. But she urged them on. For a while, as they walked, they seemed to carry in them a measure of contentment; some of the serenity and the cleanliness of that big, warm kitchen lingered on inside them. But as they walked farther and farther away from the warmth and the light, the cold and the darkness entered into them. They fell silent, sullen, suspicious. She waited for the moment when some one of them would turn mutinous. It did not happen that night.

Two nights later, she was aware that the feet behind her were moving slower and slower. She heard the irritability in their voices, knew that soon someone would refuse to go on.

She started talking about William Still and the Philadelphia Vigilance Committee.[7] No one commented. No one asked any questions. She told them the story of William

7. **Philadelphia Vigilance Committee:** group that offered help to people escaping slavery. William Still, a free African American, was chairman of the committee.

F **Read and Discuss** How does Harriet keep her group going even when they are exhausted and afraid?

G **Reading Focus** **Finding the Main Idea** What have you learned about the families who helped the travelers?

and Ellen Craft and how they escaped from Georgia. Ellen was so fair that she looked as though she were white, and so she dressed up in a man's clothing and she looked like a wealthy young planter. Her husband, William, who was dark, played the role of her slave. Thus they traveled from Macon, Georgia, to Philadelphia, riding on the trains, staying at the finest hotels. Ellen pretended to be very ill—her right arm was in a sling and her right hand was bandaged because she was supposed to have rheumatism.[8] Thus she avoided having to sign the register at the hotels, for she could not read or write. They finally arrived safely in Philadelphia and then went on to Boston. **H**

No one said anything. Not one of them seemed to have heard her.

She told them about Frederick Douglass, the most famous of the escaped slaves, of his eloquence, of his magnificent appearance. Then she told them of her own first, vain effort at running away, evoking the memory of that miserable life she had led as a child, reliving it for a moment in the telling.

But they had been tired too long, hungry too long, afraid too long, footsore too long. One of them suddenly cried out in despair,

Analyzing Visuals **Viewing and Interpreting** What details in this picture of Ellen Craft hide her real identity?

"Let me go back. It is better to be a slave than to suffer like this in order to be free."

She carried a gun with her on these trips. She had never used it—except as a threat. Now, as she aimed it, she experienced a feeling of guilt, remembering that time, years ago, when she had prayed for the death of Edward Brodas, the Master, and then, not too long afterward, had heard that

8. **rheumatism** (ROO muh tihz uhm): painful swelling and stiffness of the joints or muscles.

H Literary Focus **Coherence** In what way do the stories Tubman tells the fugitives help create a coherent biography?

Vocabulary **eloquence** (EHL uh kwehns) *n.:* ability to write or speak gracefully and convincingly.

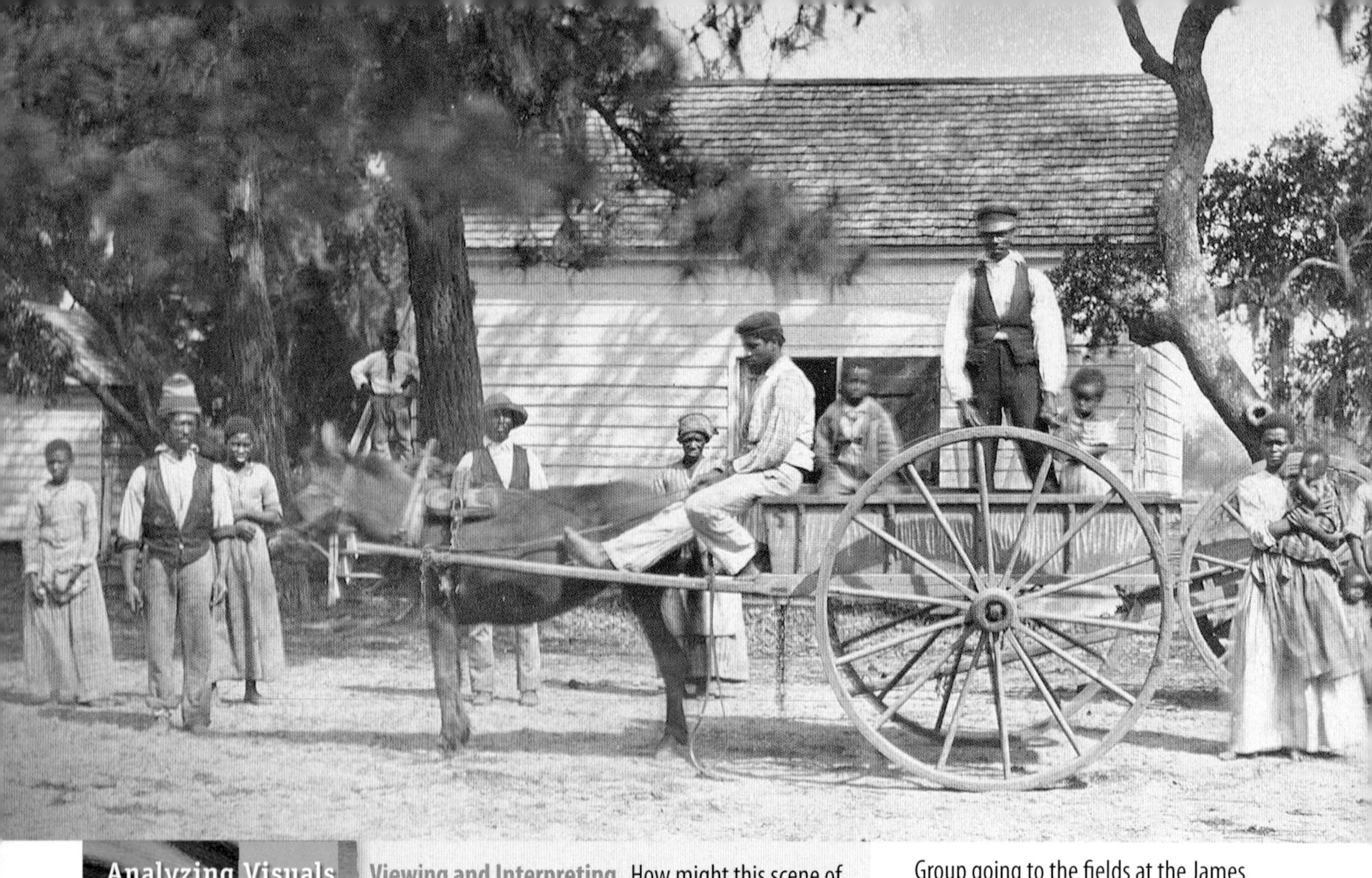

Analyzing Visuals **Viewing and Interpreting** How might this scene of a plantation be like or unlike the plantation from which Harriet Tubman and the fugitives have escaped?

Group going to the fields at the James Hopkinson's plantation, c. 1862. Photographer: Henry P. Moore.

great wailing cry that came from the throats of the field hands, and knew from the sound that the Master was dead.

One of the runaways said again, "Let me go back. Let me go back," and stood still, and then turned around and said, over his shoulder, "I am going back."

She lifted the gun, aimed it at the despairing slave. She said, "Go on with us or die." The husky, low-pitched voice was grim. **I**

He hesitated for a moment and then he joined the others. They started walking again. She tried to explain to them why none of them could go back to the plantation. If a runaway returned, he would turn traitor; the master and the overseer would force him to turn traitor. The returned slave would disclose the stopping places, the hiding places, the corn stacks they had used with the full knowledge of the owner of the farm, the name of the German farmer who had fed them and sheltered them. These people who had risked their own security to help runaways would be ruined, fined, imprisoned.

She said, "We got to go free or die. And freedom's not bought with dust."

I **Read and Discuss** What is going on between Harriet Tubman and the fugitives?

This time she told them about the long agony of the Middle Passage[9] on the old slave ships, about the black horror of the holds, about the chains and the whips. They too knew these stories. But she wanted to remind them of the long, hard way they had come, about the long, hard way they had yet to go. She told them about Thomas Sims, the boy picked up on the streets of Boston and sent back to Georgia. She said when they got him back to Savannah, got him in prison there, they whipped him until a doctor who was standing by watching said, "You will kill him if you strike him again!" His master said, "Let him die!"

Thus she forced them to go on. Sometimes she thought she had become nothing but a voice speaking in the darkness, cajoling, urging, threatening. Sometimes she told them things to make them laugh; sometimes she sang to them and heard the eleven voices behind her blending softly with hers, and then she knew that for the moment all was well with them.

She gave the impression of being a short, muscular, indomitable woman who could never be defeated. Yet at any moment she was liable to be seized by one of those curious fits of sleep,[10] which might last for a few minutes or for hours. **J**

Even on this trip, she suddenly fell asleep in the woods. The runaways, ragged, dirty, hungry, cold, did not steal the gun as they might have and set off by themselves or turn back. They sat on the ground near her and waited patiently until she awakened. They had come to trust her implicitly, totally. They, too, had come to believe her repeated statement, "We got to go free or die." She was leading them into freedom, and so they waited until she was ready to go on. **K**

Finally, they reached Thomas Garrett's house in Wilmington, Delaware. Just as Harriet had promised, Garrett gave them all new shoes, and provided carriages to take them on to the next stop.

By slow stages they reached Philadelphia, where William Still hastily recorded their names, and the plantations whence they had come, and something of the life they had led in slavery. Then he carefully hid what he had written, for fear it might be discovered.

9. **Middle Passage:** route traveled by ships carrying captured Africans across the Atlantic Ocean to the Americas. The captives endured the horrors of the Middle Passage crammed into holds, airless cargo areas below deck.

10. **fits of sleep:** Harriet's losses of consciousness were caused by a serious head injury that she had suffered as a teenager. Harriet had tried to protect someone else from punishment, and an enraged overseer threw a two-pound weight at her head.

J **Literary Focus** **Biography** What factual information about Harriet Tubman does this passage reveal?

K **Read and Discuss** What does this new detail about the gun reveal?

In 1872 he published this record in book form and called it *The Underground Railroad.* In the foreword to his book he said: "While I knew the danger of keeping strict records, and while I did not then dream that in my day slavery would be blotted out, or that the time would come when I could publish these records, it used to afford me great satisfaction to take them down, fresh from the lips of fugitives on the way to freedom, and to preserve them as they had given them." Ⓛ

William Still, who was familiar with all the station stops on the Underground Railroad, supplied Harriet with money and sent her and her eleven fugitives on to Burlington, New Jersey.

Harriet felt safer now, though there were danger spots ahead. But the biggest part of her job was over. As they went farther and farther north, it grew colder; she was aware of the wind on the Jersey ferry and aware of the cold damp in New York. From New York they went on to Syracuse,[11] where the temperature was even lower.

In Syracuse she met the Reverend J. W. Loguen, known as "Jarm" Loguen. This was the beginning of a lifelong friendship. Both Harriet and Jarm Loguen were to become friends and supporters of Old John Brown.[12]

"We got to go free or die."

From Syracuse they went north again, into a colder, snowier city—Rochester. Here they almost certainly stayed with Frederick Douglass, for he wrote in his autobiography:

"On one occasion I had eleven fugitives at the same time under my roof, and it was necessary for them to remain with me until I could collect sufficient money to get them to Canada. It was the largest number I ever had at any one time, and I had some difficulty in providing so many with food and shelter, but, as may well be imagined, they were not very fastidious in either direction, and were well content with very plain food, and a strip of carpet on the floor for a bed, or a place on the straw in the barn loft."

Late in December 1851, Harriet arrived in St. Catharines, Canada West (now Ontario), with the eleven fugitives. It had taken almost a month to complete this journey. Ⓜ

11. **Syracuse:** city in central New York State.

12. **John Brown** (1800–1859): abolitionist (opponent of slavery) who was active in the Underground Railroad. In 1859, Brown led a raid on the federal arsenal at Harpers Ferry, then in Virginia, in hopes of inspiring a slave uprising. Federal troops overpowered Brown and his followers, and Brown was convicted of treason and hanged.

Ⓛ **Literary Focus** **Biography** How might William Still's records have been helpful in the creation of this biography?

Ⓜ **Literary Perspectives** **Historical Context** Does the journey's one-month duration surprise you? Why or why not?

Applying Your Skills

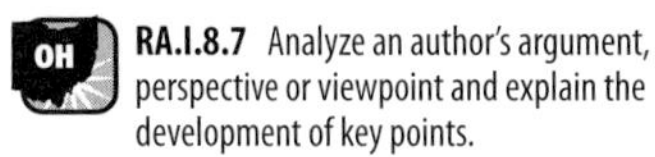

RA.I.8.7 Analyze an author's argument, perspective or viewpoint and explain the development of key points.

from Harriet Tubman: Conductor on the Underground Railroad

Respond and Think Critically

Reading Focus

Quick Check

1. List at least three facts you learned about the Underground Railroad. List at least five facts you learned about Harriet Tubman.

Read with a Purpose

2. What strategies did Harriet Tubman use to get all eleven slaves safely to Canada?

Reading Skills: Finding the Main Idea

3. Review your chart of the story's details. What main idea is supported by these details? Write down this main idea in a new row at the bottom of the chart.

Harriet Tubman: Conductor on the Underground Railroad

Important detail:	"It was the largest group that she had ever conducted."
Important detail:	
Main idea:	

Literary Focus

Literary Analysis

4. **Interpret** How is Tubman like Moses in the Bible? What is *her* Promised Land?

5. **Analyze** You sense **irony** when something happens that is the opposite of what you expect. What is ironic about the fugitive hunters praying with their families on Sundays?

6. **Literary Perspectives** What aspects of life in the 1860s made the fugitives' journey easier than it would be in modern times? What aspects made their journey more difficult?

Literary Skills: Biography and Coherence

7. **Analyze** Petry creates a coherent text by tracking the physical journey that Tubman took. What other methods does Petry use to make Tubman's journey easy to follow?

Literary Skills Review: Character

8. **Compare and Contrast** What is the difference between a leader and a hero? Was Tubman a leader, a hero, or both? Explain.

Writing Focus

Think as a Reader/Writer

Use It in Your Writing Review your notes of objective and subjective passages in the selection. Now, describe a historical figure you admire, including factual details and your feelings about that person.

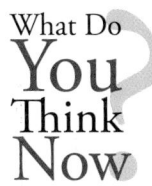

What Do You Think Now?

Has reading this biography changed your mind about the value of freedom? Why or why not?

Applying Your Skills

from Harriet Tubman: Conductor on the Underground Railroad

Vocabulary Development

Vocabulary Check

Answer the following questions. Vocabulary words are in boldface.

1. What are some reasons a person might become a **fugitive**?
2. Is it easy to understand something that is **incomprehensible**?
3. What **incentive** did Harriet Tubman have to lead the slaves to freedom?
4. How did Tubman **dispel** the fears of the fugitives?
5. How did Frederick Douglass's **eloquence** inspire Tubman and the fugitives?

Greek Roots and Affixes

The ancient Greek language helped shape many languages, including English. The Greek alphabet is the source of many of the letters we use today, and our practice of reading from left to right came from the Greek language.

One way Greek words entered the English language was through the Christian Church. English words like *monk, church,* and *prophet* have Greek origins. Another way was through the revival of interest in classical Greek texts during the Renaissance, beginning in the 1300s. Here are some Greek roots and their English derivatives.

Greek Root	Meaning	English Word
–oct–	eight	octagon
–bio–	life	biography
–dem–	people	democracy

Classical Greek is also a source for many English **affixes**—word parts added to a root to alter its meaning. Here are some common Greek affixes and their meanings:

Greek Affix	Meaning	English Word
anti–	opposing	antiwar
–ician	specialist in	technician
hyper–	over; excessive	hyperactive

Your Turn

Knowing the meanings of roots and affixes can help you define new words. Use the roots and affixes from the charts to answer these questions:

1. Does a person who is *antisocial* like being around people?
2. If something is a *biohazard,* would you want to be near it? Why or why not?
3. How might a *hypercritical* person act?
4. When might you need an *electrician*?
5. How many sides does an *octagon* have?
6. What kind of science is *demography*?

Language Coach

Roots Sort the words on the right into groups according to their roots, and write them in a chart like the one below. See if you can think of more words that share these roots.

autobiography
octave
democracy
octet
biosphere
demographics
October
biochemistry
octogenarian

Greek Root		
–oct–	*–bio–*	*–dem–*

RA.I.8.7 Analyze an author's argument, perspective or viewpoint and explain the development of key points. WC.8.3 Grammar and Usage: Use all eight parts of speech. VO.8.4 Infer the literal and figurative meaning of words and phrases and discuss the function of figurative language, including metaphors, similes and idioms. *Also covered* VO.8.7; VO.8.6

Grammar Link

Subject-Verb Agreement

In a sentence the verb should always agree in number with the subject. If the subject is singular, the verb should be singular. If the subject is plural, the verb should be plural.

Singular Verbs	Plural Verbs
comes, helps, does, is	come, help, do, are

EXAMPLES: **He rides** the bicycle. [The singular verb *rides* agrees with the singular subject *He*.]
Most **children love** ice cream. [The plural verb *love* agrees with the plural subject *children*.]

Your Turn

Choose the form of the verb in parentheses that agrees with the subject in the sentence.

EXAMPLE: The thought of bats (*scare, scares*) me. [The singular verb *scares* agrees with the singular subject *thought*.]

1. Many years (*has, have*) passed.
2. The teachers rarely (*gives, give*) high marks.
3. Most airlines (*doesn't, don't*) serve meals.
4. Why (*is, are*) these questions so hard?
5. One of my teeth (*hurts, hurt*) a lot.
6. We (*doesn't, don't*) want to go to the lake.

Writing Applications Write a short paragraph using the following words as subjects: *Harriet Tubman, fugitives,* and *group*. Then, check each sentence to be sure your verbs all agree in number with your subjects.

CHOICES

As you respond to the Choices, use these **Academic Vocabulary** words as appropriate: observation, emphasize, reactions, define.

REVIEW

Make a Time Line

In order to follow the sequence of events in the selection, draw a time line. Start with a straight line. At the left, write "Tubman leaves with eleven fugitives, December 1851." Refer to the text to fill in the time line with other events. Your time line may not be exact, but it should emphasize the most important events in the biography and make the sequence of events clear.

CONNECT

Summarize a Biography

Timed Writing Re-read the excerpt from the biography of Harriet Tubman. Then, write a summary of the biography. In the first paragraph, include the title of the work, the author's name, and a general observation about the work. In the second paragraph, summarize the important events covered in the biography.

EXTEND

Map an Escape

Group Project The fugitives discussed in this biography had an advantage over many others fleeing slavery: They were escaping from the northernmost slave state, Maryland. Work with a group to find out which states allowed slavery in 1851. Then, choose a location in one of those states and draw a map showing a possible route to freedom. Research the Underground Railroad to see if there were any stops along your route.

AUTOBIOGRAPHY

Preparing to Read

Camp Harmony

from Nisei Daughter

by **Monica Sone**

Dust storm at Manzanar War Relocation Authority Center, 1942.
Photographer: Dorothea Lange.

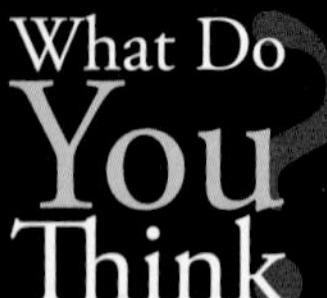

How do people react when they are forced to leave home?

QuickWrite

What would you take if you had to leave home abruptly and you could bring only two suitcases? What would you find hard to leave behind?

Reader/Writer Notebook

Use your **RWN** to complete the activities for this selection.

OH **RA.L.8.6** Explain how an author's choice of genre affects the expression of a theme or topic. **RA.I.8.7** Analyze an author's argument, perspective or viewpoint and explain the development of key points.

Literary Focus

Autobiography and Unity An **autobiography** is a person's account of his or her own life or of part of it. Through autobiography we learn about the events in a person's life as well as the writer's observations about the impact of those experiences. Like all nonfiction, an autobiography should have **unity:** Its details should all support the main idea or topic.

TechFocus As you read the story, think about how you might create a graphic depiction of it by using a storyboard program.

Reading Focus

Analyzing Details One way to evaluate unity in a piece of writing is to analyze the details. Do all of the details contribute to the main idea of the work? Do they draw a clear picture of the subject?

Into Action As you read, look for details that reveal Monica Sone's experiences and observations. Record these details on a chart like the one below, and explain what those details reveal about her life.

Details from the Text	What the Details Reveal
The internment camp housing is primitive.	The family's need for privacy and comfort is disregarded.
Armed guards in towers watch the camp 24/7.	

Writing Focus

Think as a Reader/Writer

Find It in Your Reading As you read, notice how the author uses transitions to move from one part of her story to the next. What transitional words and phrases does she use to show the passage of time and the relationship between ideas? List these transitions in your *Reader/Writer Notebook.*

Vocabulary

tersely (TURS lee) *adv.:* briefly and clearly; without unnecessary words. *The child tersely gave his one-word description of the pigs near the camp.*

breach (breech) *n.:* opening caused by a break, such as in a wall or in a line of defense. *Monica was small enough to wiggle into the breach.*

riveted (RIHV iht ihd) *v.* used as *adj.:* intensely focused on. *The family was riveted by the sight of the burning stove.*

vigil (VIHJ uhl) *n.:* keeping guard; act of staying awake to keep watch. *Armed guards kept a constant vigil over the Japanese Americans.*

Language Coach

Derivations The English word *vigil* derives from the same word in Latin. In Latin, *vigil* means "awake." How does this meaning connect to the English meaning shown in the Vocabulary list above?

Learn It Online
Hear a professional actor read this excerpt at:
go.hrw.com
L8-513
Go

MEET THE WRITER

Monica Sone

(1919–)

A Child of Two Worlds

Born in Seattle, Washington, Monica Sone lived in two worlds. Her parents were from Japan, but she was a native-born American. Growing up, Sone found it challenging to establish her identity. "I found myself switching my personality back and forth daily like a chameleon," she says.

Remembering

While in Camp Harmony, Sone wrote several letters to a friend describing the living conditions in the camp. Her friend saved these and one day showed them to an editor at Little, Brown and Co. The editor was interested in the letters, and he asked Sone if she would consider writing a book about her camp experiences. Sone says,

> "I was eager to do so. This was because after I eventually left camp and moved to the eastern part of the country, I discovered that the general public knew nothing about our evacuation and imprisonment of tens of thousands of Americans. I wanted to tell our story."

Sone's autobiography, *Nisei Daughter,* was published in 1953. It was the first book about the internment camps written by an internee.

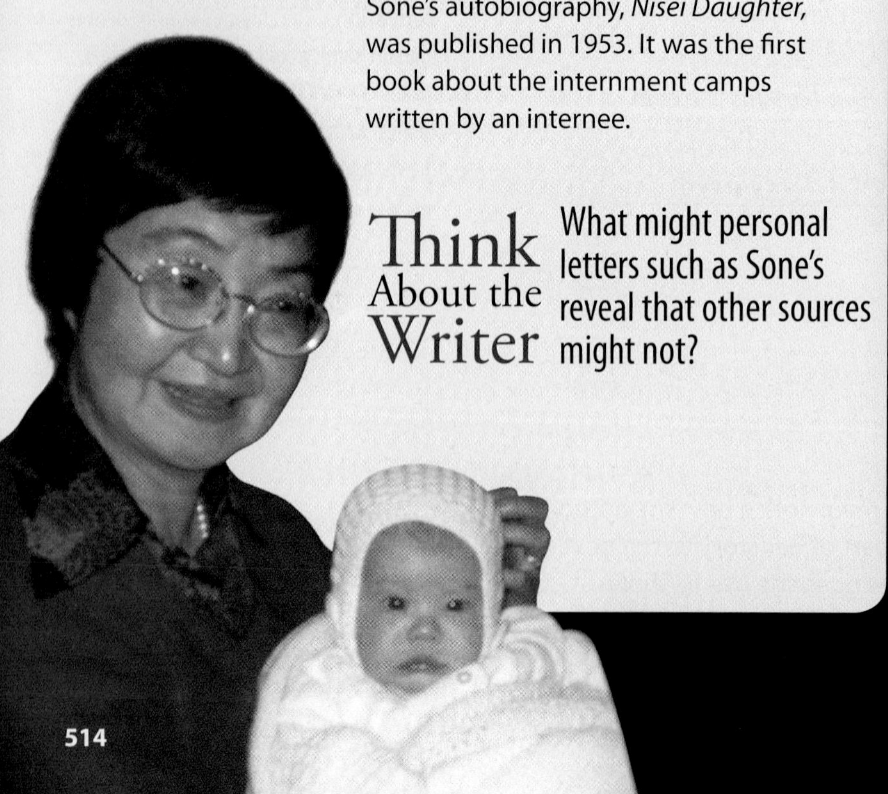

Think About the Writer What might personal letters such as Sone's reveal that other sources might not?

Build Background

In 1942, many thousands of Japanese Americans living on the West Coast were sent to internment camps. They had committed no crime, but the United States had gone to war with Japan. Executive Order 9066 made their confinement legal. Ironically, many of the evacuated families had sons or brothers serving in the U.S. Army in the war overseas. Most of the 120,000 Japanese Americans who were detained spent three years living behind barbed wire.

Preview the Selection

In this excerpt from her autobiography, **Monica Sone** tells about her family's experience in Camp Harmony, an internment camp to which her family, as Japanese Americans, was forced to relocate.

Read with a Purpose Read this story to discover how a girl and her family react when they are forced from their home during wartime.

Camp Harmony

from Nisei Daughter

by **Monica Sone**

When our bus turned a corner and we no longer had to smile and wave, we settled back gravely in our seats. Everyone was quiet except for a chattering group of university students, who soon started singing college songs. A few people turned and glared at them, which only served to increase the volume of their singing. Then suddenly a baby's sharp cry rose indignantly above the hubbub. The singing stopped immediately, followed by a guilty silence. Three seats behind us, a young mother held a wailing red-faced infant in her arms, bouncing it up and down. Its angry little face emerged from multiple layers of kimonos, sweaters, and blankets, and it, too, wore the white pasteboard tag[1] pinned to its blanket. A young man stammered out an apology as the mother gave him a wrathful look. She hunted frantically for a bottle of milk in a shopping bag, and we all relaxed when she had found it.

We sped out of the city southward along beautiful stretches of farmland, with dark, newly turned soil. In the beginning we devoured every bit of scenery which flashed past our window and admired the massive-muscled workhorses plodding along the edge of the highway, the rich burnished copper color of a browsing herd of cattle, the vivid spring green of the pastures, but eventually the sameness of the country landscape palled[2] on us. We tried to sleep to escape from the restless anxiety which kept bobbing up to the surface of our minds. I awoke with a start when the bus filled with excited buzzing. A small group of straw-hatted Japanese farmers stood by the highway, waving at us. I felt a sudden warmth toward them, then a twinge of pity. They would be joining us soon. **A**

1. **white pasteboard tag:** All Japanese American families registering for evacuation were given numbered tags to wear and to attach to their luggage. Monica's family became number 10710.

2. **palled:** became boring or tiresome.

A **Read and Discuss** What has the author told us so far?

About noon we crept into a small town. Someone said, "Looks like Puyallup, all right." Parents of small children babbled excitedly, "Stand up quickly and look over there. See all the chick-chicks and fat little piggies?" One little city boy stared hard at the hogs and said tersely, "They're bachi—dirty!"

Our bus idled a moment at the traffic signal, and we noticed at the left of us an entire block filled with neat rows of low shacks, resembling chicken houses. Someone commented on it with awe, "Just look at those chicken houses. They sure go in for poultry in a big way here." Slowly the bus made a left turn, drove through a wire-fence gate, and to our dismay, we were inside the oversized chicken farm. The bus driver opened the door, the guard stepped out and stationed himself at the door again. Jim, the young man who had shepherded us into the buses, popped his head inside and sang out, "OK, folks, all off at Yokohama, Puyallup."

We stumbled out, stunned, dragging our bundles after us. It must have rained hard the night before in Puyallup, for we sank ankle deep into gray, glutinous[3] mud. The receptionist, a white man, instructed us courteously, "Now, folks, please stay together as family units and line up. You'll be assigned your apartment." **B**

We were standing in Area A, the mammoth parking lot of the state fairgrounds.

3. **glutinous:** sticky; gluey.

B **Read and Discuss** What is happening to Sone's family?

Vocabulary **tersely** (TURS lee) *adv.:* briefly and clearly; without unnecessary words.

A family on the way to a Japanese internment camp.

Analyzing Visuals

Viewing and Interpreting What might these evacuees be thinking? What detail stands out most?

There were three other separate areas, B, C, and D, all built on the fairgrounds proper, near the baseball field and the racetracks. This camp of army barracks was hopefully called Camp Harmony.

We were assigned to apartment 2–I–A, right across from the bachelor quarters. The apartments resembled elongated,[4] low stables about two blocks long. Our home was one room, about eighteen by twenty feet, the size of a living room. There was one small window in the wall opposite the one door. It was bare except for a small, tinny wood-burning stove crouching in the center. The flooring consisted of two-by-fours laid directly on the earth, and dandelions were already pushing their way up through the cracks. Mother was delighted when she saw their shaggy yellow heads. "Don't anyone pick them. I'm going to cultivate them."

Father snorted, "Cultivate them! If we don't watch out, those things will be growing out of our hair."

Just then Henry stomped inside, bringing the rest of our baggage. "What's all the excitement about?"

Sumi replied laconically,[5] "Dandelions."

Henry tore off a fistful. Mother scolded, "Arra! Arra! Stop that. They're the only beautiful things around here. We could have a garden right in here."

"Are you joking, Mama?"

4. **elongated:** lengthened.

5. **laconically:** with few words; briefly.

I chided Henry, "Of course she's not. After all, she has to have some inspiration to write poems, you know, with all the 'nari keri's.'[6] I can think of a poem myself right now:

Oh, Dandelion, Dandelion,
Despised and uprooted by all,
Dance and bob your golden heads
For you've finally found your home
With your yellow fellows, nari keri,
amen!" **C**

Henry said, thrusting the dandelions in Mother's black hair, "I think you can do ten times better than that, Mama."

Sumi reclined on her sea bag[7] and fretted, "Where do we sleep? Not on the floor, I hope."

"Stop worrying," Henry replied disgustedly. **D**

Mother and Father wandered out to see what the other folks were doing and they found people wandering in the mud, wondering what other folks were doing. Mother returned shortly, her face lit up in an ecstatic smile, "We're in luck. The latrine is right nearby. We won't have to walk blocks."

We laughed, marveling at Mother who could be so poetic and yet so practical.

6. **nari keri's:** referring to a phrase used to end many Japanese poems, meant to convey wonder and awe.

7. **sea bag:** large canvas bag like the ones sailors use to carry their personal belongings. Each person was allowed to bring only one sea bag of bedding and two suitcases of clothing to the internment camps.

C **Literary Focus** **Autobiography** What details does Sone include in writing about her own life that a biographer would not know?

D **Read and Discuss** What do we find out about the family's apartment?

SOCIAL STUDIES **LINK**

Family awaiting shipment to Manzanar, 1942 (detail). Photographer: Dorothea Lange.

Japanese Internment Camps

Immediately after the declaration of Executive Order 9066 in February 1942, the U.S. government constructed internment camps in parts of Arkansas, California, Arizona, Colorado, Idaho, Washington, Utah, and Wyoming. By August 1942, most of the Japanese Americans in the western part of the country were imprisoned in these camps. Over half of these internees were children. Internees faced many difficulties. The physical environment was often harsh, the food was bad, and the people had little or no privacy. Traditional family structure and discipline were hard to maintain. Released in 1945, at the end of World War II, internees returned home to find their property stolen and their livelihoods gone. They had to wait more than forty years for an apology and compensation from the U.S. government.

Ask Yourself

What hardships did Sone face while forced to live in an internment camp?

Father came back, bent double like a woodcutter in a fairy tale, with stacks of scrap lumber over his shoulder. His coat and trouser pockets bulged with nails. Father dumped his loot in a corner and explained, "There was a pile of wood left by the carpenters and hundreds of nails scattered loose. Everybody was picking them up, and I hustled right in with them. Now maybe we can live in style, with tables and chairs." **E**

The block leader knocked at our door and announced lunchtime. He instructed us to take our meal at the nearest mess hall. As I untied my sea bag to get out my pie plate, tin cup, spoon, and fork, I realized I was hungry. At the mess hall we found a long line of people. Children darted in and out of the line, skiing in the slithery mud. The young stood impatiently on one foot, then the other, and scowled, "The food had better be good after all this wait." But the issei[8] stood quietly, arms folded, saying very little. A light drizzle began to fall, coating bare black heads with tiny sparkling raindrops. The chow line inched forward.

Lunch consisted of two canned sausages, one lob of boiled potato, and a slab of bread. Our family had to split up, for the hall was too crowded for us to sit together. I wan-

8. **issei:** Japanese who immigrated to North America. Issei were forbidden by law to become U.S. citizens.

E **Read and Discuss** How does this new information connect with what we learned earlier?

dered up and down the aisles, back and forth along the crowded tables and benches, looking for a few inches to squeeze into. A small issei woman finished her meal, stood up, and hoisted her legs modestly over the bench, leaving a space for one. Even as I thrust myself into the breach, the space had shrunk to two inches, but I worked myself into it. My dinner companion, hooked just inside my right elbow, was a baldheaded, gruff-looking issei man who seemed to resent nestling at mealtime. Under my left elbow was a tiny, mud-spattered girl. With busy, runny nose, she was belaboring her sausages, tearing them into shreds and mixing them into the potato gruel which she had made with water. I choked my food down. **F**

We cheered loudly when trucks rolled by, distributing canvas army cots for the young and hardy, and steel cots for the older folks. Henry directed the arrangement of the cots. Father and Mother were to occupy the corner nearest the woodstove. In the other corner, Henry arranged two cots in an L shape and announced that this was the combination living room–bedroom area, to be occupied by Sumi and myself. He fixed a male den for himself in the corner nearest the door. If I had had my way, I would have arranged everyone's cots in one neat row, as in Father's hotel dormitory.

We felt fortunate to be assigned to a room at the end of the barracks, because we had just one neighbor to worry about. The partition wall separating the rooms was only seven feet high, with an opening of four feet at the top, so at night, Mrs. Funai next door could tell when Sumi was still sitting up in bed in the dark, putting her hair up. "Mah, Sumi-chan," Mrs. Funai would say through the plank wall, "are you curling your hair tonight, again? Do you put it up every night?" Sumi would put her hands on her hips and glare defiantly at the wall.

The block monitor, an impressive nisei[9] who looked like a star tackle, with his crouching walk, came around the first night to tell us that we must all be inside our room by nine o'clock every night. At ten o'clock, he rapped at the door again, yelling, "Lights out!" and Mother rushed to turn the light off not a second later.

Throughout the barracks, there was a medley[10] of creaking cots, whimpering infants, and explosive night coughs. Our attention was riveted on the intense little woodstove, which glowed so violently I feared it would melt right down to the floor. We soon learned that this condition lasted for only a short time, after which it suddenly turned into a deep freeze. Henry and Father took turns at the stove to produce the harrowing[11] blast which all but singed our army blankets but did not penetrate through them. As it grew quieter in the barracks, I could hear the light patter of

9. **nisei:** native U.S. or Canadian citizen born of Japanese immigrant parents.

10. **medley:** jumble; mixture.

11. **harrowing:** extremely distressing.

F **Reading Focus** **Analyzing Details** What details does the author use in these two paragraphs to show how the issei differ from the children and young people?

Vocabulary **breach** (breech) *n.:* opening caused by a break, such as in a wall or in a line of defense.
riveted (RIHV iht ihd) *v.* used as *adj.:* intensely focused on.

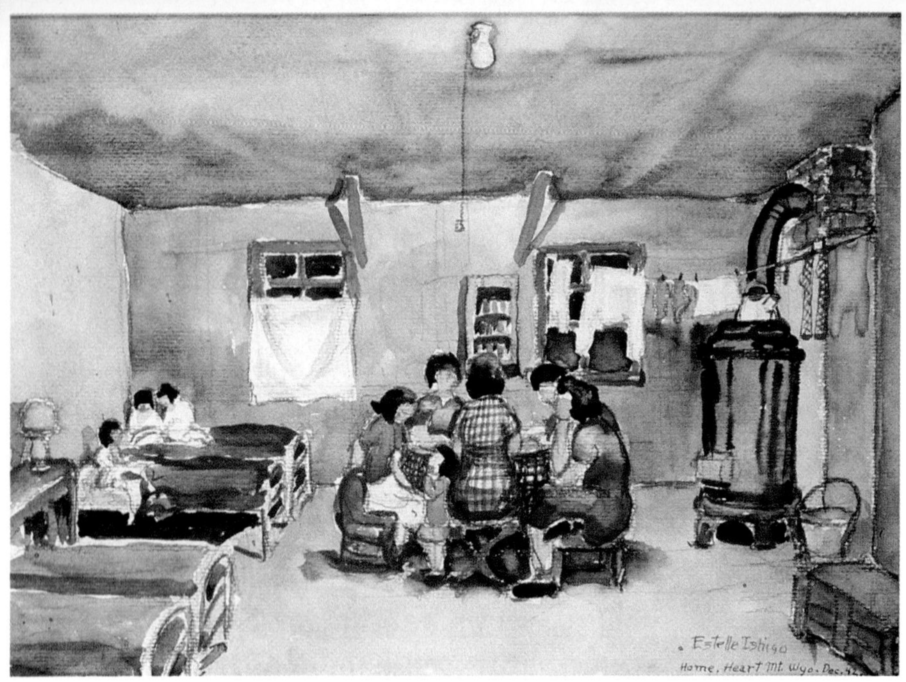

Home, Heart Mountain (December 1942) by Estelle Ishigo. Watercolor painting.

rain. Soon I felt the *splat! splat!* of raindrops digging holes into my face. The dampness on my pillow spread like a mortal bleeding, and I finally had to get out and haul my cot toward the center of the room. In a short while, Henry was up. "I've got multiple leaks, too. Have to complain to the landlord first thing in the morning." **G**

All through the night I heard people getting up, dragging cots around. I stared at our little window, unable to sleep. I was glad Mother had put up a makeshift curtain on the window, for I noticed a powerful beam of light sweeping across it every few seconds. The lights came from high towers placed around the camp, where guards with tommy guns kept a twenty-four-hour vigil. I remembered the wire fence encircling us, and a knot of anger tightened in my breast. What was I doing behind a fence, like a criminal? If there were accusations to be made, why hadn't I been given a fair trial? Maybe I wasn't considered an American anymore. My citizenship wasn't real, after all. Then what was I? I was certainly not a citizen of Japan, as my parents were. On second thought, even Father and Mother were more alien residents of the United States than Japanese nationals, for they had little tie with their mother country. In their twenty-five years in America, they had worked and paid their taxes to their adopted government as any other citizen.

Of one thing I was sure. The wire fence was real. I no longer had the right to walk out of it. It was because I had Japanese ancestors. It was also because some people had little faith in the ideas and ideals of democracy. They said that after all these were but words and could not possibly ensure loyalty. New laws and camps were surer devices. I finally buried my face in my pillow to wipe out burning thoughts and snatch what sleep I could. **H**

G **Read and Discuss** What have we learned about life at Camp Harmony?

Vocabulary **vigil** (VIHJ uhl) *n.:* keeping guard; act of staying awake to keep watch.

H **Literary Focus** **Unity** How has the author's mood changed from the beginning of the selection to this point? Does this change of mood contribute to the work's unity or detract from it? Explain.

Applying Your Skills

RA.L.8.6 Explain how an author's choice of genre affects the expression of a theme or topic. **RA.I.8.7** Analyze an author's argument, perspective or viewpoint and explain the development of key points. *Also covered* **WA.8.1.a**

Camp Harmony

Respond and Think Critically

Reading Focus

Quick Check

1. Summarize, or write a short restatement of, the main events in "Camp Harmony."

Read with a Purpose

2. What are Monica Sone and her family's reactions to their new situation?

Reading Skills: Analyzing Details

3. Review the details you listed as you read, and identify the main idea of the selection. Did any details seem out of place or disrupt the unity of the autobiography? Explain.

Details from the Text	What the Details Reveal
The internment camp housing is primitive.	The family's need for privacy and comfort is disregarded.
Main idea:	

Literary Focus

Literary Analysis

4. **Analyze** Sone describes her mother as "poetic and yet so practical." State one example from the text that illustrates each quality.
5. **Interpret** How would you define the mood of the people on the bus at the beginning of the journey to Camp Harmony? at the end of the journey?
6. **Analyze** Sone says the camp "was hopefully called Camp Harmony." Do you think the name is appropriate, or is it ironic? Support your answer with evidence from the text.

Literary Skills: Autobiography and Unity

7. **Analyze** What time period is covered in this excerpt? How does the use of chronological organization contribute to the work's unity?
8. **Evaluate** Identify at least two personal observations that Sone makes. Why are these observations appropriate in an autobiography but not in another type of nonfiction work, such as an encyclopedia?

Literary Skills Review: Point of View

9. **Extend** "Camp Harmony" is told from the **first-person point of view**—that is, using the word *I*. What information might a third-person account include that Sone's cannot?

Writing Focus

Think as a Reader/Writer

Use It in Your Writing Review the transitions you recorded as you read. Then, write a brief autobiographical essay about an important day in your life. Use transitional words and phrases to show how the details you include are connected to your main idea.

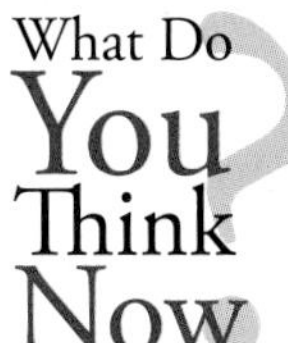

Were you surprised by the internees' reactions to their situation? With whom did you identify the most? Why?

Applying Your Skills

Camp Harmony

Vocabulary Development

Verify Word Meanings Using Restatement

In your reading, you probably come across words whose meanings you think you know, but you are not quite sure about. How can you verify their meanings? One strategy is to look at a word's **context**—the words and sentences that surround it—for clues.

One type of context clue is **restatement,** a rephrasing of a word in more familiar terms. For example, if you were unfamiliar with the word *resourceful,* you could probably make a good guess about its meaning by noting the restatement, which appears in boldface in the following sentence:

> The resourceful internees were **able to think of ways to deal with their situation**. They collected scraps of wood to make furniture.

Your Turn

tersely
breach
riveted
vigil

Rewrite the following sentences to include restatements of the boldface Vocabulary words. Your restatements can be in the same sentence or in an additional sentence. Circle your restatement.

1. One little boy stared at the hogs and said **tersely**, "Dirty."
2. Guards with tommy guns kept a constant **vigil** around the prison camp.
3. The narrator thrust herself into the tiny **breach** between two people sitting on the bench.
4. The family's attention was **riveted** on the burning stove.

Language Coach

Derivations When you learn a new word, pay attention to related words that are **derived** from, or come from, the same root, such as *hazard* and *hazardous.* Write down and define two words that derive from the same root as the following words from the selection:

- emerged (page 515)
- quarters (page 517)
- instructed (page 518)

Referring to a dictionary may be helpful.

Academic Vocabulary

Talk About . . .

In a small group, discuss your reactions to injustice. Then, answer the following questions:

1. How would you define *injustice*?
2. When have you observed injustice in your community or on TV?
3. What do you think can be done to combat injustice?

Use Academic Vocabulary words in your discussion.

Learn It Online
Learn more about words with *WordSharp* at:
go.hrw.com L8-522 Go

RA.L.8.6 Explain how an author's choice of genre affects the expression of a theme or topic. RA.I.8.7 Analyze an author's argument, perspective or viewpoint and explain the development of key points. WC.8.7 Grammar and Usage: Maintain the use of appropriate verb tenses. *Also covered* VO.8.7; VO.8.1

Grammar Link

Using Correct Verb Tenses

A common error in using verbs is switching tenses in the same or nearby sentences. The **tense** of a verb indicates the time of the action—for example, past, present, or future. When describing events that occur at the same time, be sure your verbs are in the same tense.

INCONSISTENT Monica's mother **saw** the dandelion and **is** delighted.

CONSISTENT Monica's mother **saw** the dandelion and **was** delighted.

CONSISTENT Monica's mother **sees** the dandelion and **is** delighted.

Your Turn

Read the following paragraph, and decide whether it should be rewritten in the present or past tense. Then, change the verb forms as necessary to make the tense consistent throughout the paragraph.

[1] Monica Sone's mother sees the best in things and admired the dandelions. [2] She planned a garden of them and is grateful for any type of beauty. [3] She is even happy about the nearness of the latrine, though the others were not so thrilled. [4] Like her mother, Sone's father has been grateful for good things, however small. [5] He finds a pile of lumber and loose nails and envisioned these scraps as the family's furniture.

Writing Applications Now, choose another tense and write a short paragraph of your own, using that tense consistently throughout your paragraph.

CHOICES

As you respond to the Choices, use these **Academic Vocabulary** words as appropriate: observation, emphasize, reactions, define.

REVIEW

Make an Outline

Re-read the selection and create an outline of the author's main ideas and supporting details. Review your outline, and describe ways in which Monica Sone achieves unity in her writing.

CONNECT

Compose a Persuasive Letter

Timed Writing Write a letter to President Franklin D. Roosevelt. Your purpose is to persuade him to cancel Executive Order 9066. State your argument to make your case, supporting it with details from the text as well as from your own observations of life.

EXTEND

Create a Graphic Story

TechFocus Retell a scene from Monica Sone's autobiography as a graphic story. First, think of which event you want to depict. Then, use an online storyboard program to draw the scene in three or four panels, with short descriptions underneath. Include dialogue balloons as needed.

Preparing to Read

The Gettysburg Address

by **Abraham Lincoln**

from I Have a Dream

by **Dr. Martin Luther King, Jr.**

Dr. Martin Luther King, Jr., delivers his I Have a Dream speech on the steps of the Lincoln Memorial in Washington, D.C., during the 1963 March on Washington.

What Do You Think?

What does the idea of freedom mean to you?

QuickTalk

Lincoln and King use the idea of freedom to inspire their listeners. How do you define freedom? Discuss with a partner.

Reader/Writer
Notebook

Use your **RWN** to complete the activities for these selections.

RA.I.8.5 Assess the adequacy, accuracy and appropriateness of an author's details, identifying persuasive techniques and examples of bias and stereotyping. **RA.I.8.7** Analyze an author's argument, perspective or viewpoint and explain the development of key points. **RA.I.8.1** Compare and contrast text features, including format and headers of various informational texts in terms of their structure and purpose.

Literary Focus

Speech and Structural Patterns Speeches are meant to be delivered orally. Good speakers use certain **structural patterns** to emphasize the message of the speech and to make their ideas memorable. Two types of structural patterns are **repetition**—the use of repeated key words and phrases—and **parallelism**—the use of a similar pattern of words, phrases, and sentences.

Keep the faith. In times of hardship, *keep the faith.*
Endeavor *to take* care of yourself and *to be* kind to others.

TechFocus As you read the Gettysburg Address, imagine how you would recite it if you were creating a podcast.

Reading Focus

Analyzing Details Analyzing details will help you gain a deeper understanding of a speaker's message. Ask yourself why the speaker may have included each detail and what idea it emphasizes.

Into Action As you read the following speeches, look for details that convey important ideas and write them in a chart like the one below.

Details from the Text	Idea Emphasized
"we cannot dedicate—we cannot consecrate—we cannot hallow—this ground"	difficulty in adequately honoring the many sacrificed lives

Writing Focus

Think as a Reader/Writer

Find It in Your Reading As you read, list in your *Reader/Writer Notebook* words and phrases that seem important. Place a star next to the words and phrases that are repeated.

Vocabulary

The Gettysburg Address

detract (dih TRAKT) *v.:* take away from; make less important. *Lincoln believes nothing people say can add to or detract from the sacrifices made at Gettysburg.*

nobly (NOH blee) *adv.:* in a manner that is excellent or heroic. *Lincoln honors the brave men who died nobly for freedom and equality.*

I Have a Dream

creed (kreed) *n.:* statement of belief or principles. *Dr. King developed a creed of nonviolence.*

oasis (oh AY sihs) *n.:* place or thing offering relief. *A land of equality for all races would be an oasis after years of racism.*

Language Coach

Related Words The Vocabulary word *creed* comes from the Latin word for "I believe." Related words include *credible* and *credit.* How does the idea of belief come through in each of those words?

Learn It Online
Listen to the speech and improve your own reading skills at:

go.hrw.com L8-525 

Abraham Lincoln

(1809–1865)

A Wartime President

When he was a boy, Abraham Lincoln rarely went to school. He was interested in learning, however, and eventually taught himself law. He entered the field of politics and was elected president in 1860, during a period of crisis that quickly erupted into war between the Northern and Southern states. In 1863, during the Civil War, he issued the Emancipation Proclamation. This proclamation led to the adoption of the Thirteenth Amendment to the Constitution, which outlawed slavery.

When war broke out, Lincoln was determined to keep the Union together. He did not live to see his country reunited, however. He was shot by an assassin in a theater in Washington, D.C.

Dr. Martin Luther King, Jr.

(1929–1968)

A National Leader

Dr. Martin Luther King, Jr., was a Baptist minister from Atlanta, Georgia, and a national leader in the civil rights movement. He faced violence and arrest while spreading his message of nonviolent resistance. He believed that the racism and segregation he witnessed daily could be overcome without using further violence. He became known for his powerful voice and eloquent message.

In 1964, four years before he was assassinated in Memphis, Tennessee, King was awarded the Nobel Peace Prize.

Think About the Writers

What vision did Lincoln and King share?

Preview the Selections

At his address at Gettysburg, **Abraham Lincoln** expresses his vision of American democracy while commemorating the soldiers who were killed in the Battle of Gettysburg during the Civil War.

In "I Have a Dream," a speech delivered in August 1963, **Dr. Martin Luther King, Jr.,** expresses his hopes for the future of race relations and inspires a nation.

Read with a Purpose

Read this speech to learn how Lincoln honored those who sacrificed their lives.

Build Background

The Battle of Gettysburg, which took place in Pennsylvania in 1863, was a turning point in the Civil War. After the bloody three-day battle, 51,000 soldiers on both sides were dead, wounded, or missing. On November 19, 1863, part of the battle-field was dedicated as a military cemetery. President Lincoln gave the following short address at the dedication ceremony.

The Gettysburg Address

by **Abraham Lincoln**

President Abraham Lincoln delivering the Gettysburg Address on the battlefield during the Civil War, 1863.

November 19, 1863

Four score and seven years[1] ago our fathers brought forth on this continent a new nation, conceived[2] in liberty, and dedicated to the proposition that all men are created equal. **A**

Now we are engaged in a great civil war, testing whether that nation, or any nation so conceived and so dedicated, can long endure. We are met on a great battlefield of that war. We have come to dedicate a portion of that field, as a final resting place for those who here gave their lives that that nation might live. It is altogether fitting and proper that we should do this. **B**

1. **four score and seven years:** eighty-seven years.
2. **conceived:** developed.

A **Read and Discuss** What idea is Lincoln expressing at the start of his speech?

B **Reading Focus** **Analyzing Details** What details does Lincoln provide about the war that is being fought and why it is important?

But, in a larger sense, we cannot dedicate—we cannot consecrate[3]—we cannot hallow[4]—this ground. The brave men, living and dead, who struggled here, have consecrated it, far above our poor power to add or detract. The world will little note nor long remember what we say here, but it can never forget what they did here. It is for us the living, rather, to be dedicated here to the unfinished work which they who fought here have thus far so nobly advanced. It is rather for us to be here dedicated to the great task remaining before us—that from these honored dead we take increased devotion to that cause for which they gave the last full measure of devotion—that we here highly resolve that these dead shall not have died in vain—that this nation, under God, shall have a new birth of freedom—and that government of the people, by the people, for the people, shall not perish from the earth. **C**

3. **consecrate:** set apart as sacred or holy.
4. **hallow:** make holy.

C **Literary Focus** **Structural Patterns** How does Lincoln use parallelism to create a clear description of a democratic government?

Vocabulary **detract** (dih TRAKT) *v.:* take away from; make less important.
nobly (NOH blee) *adv.:* in a manner that is excellent or heroic.

A statue in Gettysburg, Pennsylvania.

from

I Have a Dream

by **Dr. Martin Luther King, Jr.**

Read with a Purpose

Read this speech to discover what Dr. Martin Luther King, Jr., envisioned America could and should be.

Build Background

On August 28, 1963, more than 200,000 Americans of all races and from all over the country took part in a march in Washington, D.C., to demand full equality for African Americans. Late in the day, Dr. Martin Luther King, Jr., rose to speak. What follows is a portion of his deeply moving speech.

August 28, 1963

I say to you today, my friends, that in spite of the difficulties and frustrations of the moment I still have a dream. It is a dream deeply rooted in the American Dream. **A**

I have a dream that one day this nation will rise up and live out the true meaning of its creed: "We hold these truths to be self-evident; that all men are created equal."

I have a dream that one day on the red hills of Georgia the sons of former slaves and the sons of former slave owners will be able to sit down together at the table of brotherhood.

I have a dream that one day even the state of Mississippi, a desert state sweltering with the heat of injustice and oppression, will be transformed into an oasis of freedom and justice.

I have a dream that my four little children will one day live in a nation where they will not be judged by the color of their skin but by the content of their character. **B**

I have a dream today.

I have a dream that one day every valley shall be exalted,[1] every hill and mountain shall be made low, the rough places will be made plain, and the crooked places will be made straight, and the glory of the Lord shall be revealed, and all flesh shall see it together.

1. **exalted** (ehg ZAWL tihd): raised; lifted up.

A **Read and Discuss** To what is King referring?

B **Reading Focus** **Analyzing Details** What details does King include to illustrate his ideas?

Vocabulary **creed** (kreed) *n.:* statement of belief or principles.
oasis (oh AY sihs) *n.:* place or thing offering relief.

Analyzing Visuals **Viewing and Interpreting** What does this photograph show you about the way King's message continues to be received?

Annual Martin Luther King, Jr. march in Raleigh, N.C., in 2007.

This is our hope. This is the faith with which I return to the South. With this faith we will be able to hew out of the mountain of despair a stone of hope. With this faith we will be able to transform the jangling discords of our nation into a beautiful symphony of brotherhood. With this faith we will be able to work together, to pray together, to struggle together, to go to jail together, to stand up for freedom together, knowing that we will be free one day. **C**

This will be the day when all of God's children will be able to sing with new meaning "My country 'tis of thee, sweet land of liberty, of thee I sing. Land where my fathers died, land of the pilgrim's pride, from every mountainside, let freedom ring."

And if America is to be a great nation, this must become true. So let freedom ring from the prodigious[2] hilltops of New Hampshire. Let freedom ring from the mighty mountains of New York. Let freedom ring from the heightening Alleghenies of Pennsylvania!

Let freedom ring from the snowcapped Rockies of Colorado!

Let freedom ring from the curvaceous peaks of California!

But not only that; let freedom ring from Stone Mountain of Georgia!

Let freedom ring from Lookout Mountain of Tennessee!

Let freedom ring from every hill and molehill of Mississippi. From every mountainside, let freedom ring.

When we let freedom ring, when we let it ring from every village and every hamlet, from every state and every city, we will be able to speed up that day when all of God's children, black men and white men, Jews and Gentiles, Protestants and Catholics, will be able to join hands and sing in the words of the old Negro spiritual, "Free at last! Free at last! Thank God almighty, we are free at last!" **D**

2. **prodigious** (pruh DIHJ uhs): huge; amazing.

C **Read and Discuss** What does King think about equality as it relates to our country?

D **Literary Focus** **Structural Patterns** How does King's use of repetition in the last sentence strengthen his message?

Applying Your Skills

RA.I.8.5 Assess the adequacy, accuracy and appropriateness of an author's details, identifying persuasive techniques and examples of bias and stereotyping. **RA.I.8.7** Analyze an author's argument, perspective or viewpoint and explain the development of key points. *Also covered* **RA.I.8.1; WP.8.6**

The Gettysburg Address / *from* I Have a Dream

Respond and Think Critically

Reading Focus

Quick Check

1. In Lincoln's speech, what is happening in the present (1863)? How is that related to the past, according to Lincoln?
2. What problem does King's speech address?

Read with a Purpose

3. How does Lincoln honor those who sacrificed their lives?
4. What is King's vision for America?

Reading Skills: Analyzing Details

5. Review the notes you took as you read. Add a column to your chart, and identify those details that contain repetition or parallel structure. Then, put a check mark beside details you found persuasive or moving.

Details from the Text	Idea Emphasized	Structural Pattern
"we cannot dedicate—we cannot consecrate—we cannot hallow—this ground"	difficulty in adequately honoring the many sacrificed lives	

Literary Focus

Literary Analysis

6. **Identify** What two ideals does Abraham Lincoln emphasize in his speech?
7. **Infer** King makes **allusions,** or references, to the Declaration of Independence and to the patriotic hymn "My Country, 'Tis of Thee." Why might King want to remind his audience of these texts?
8. **Compare and Contrast** What do you think is the message of the Gettysburg Address? How is it similar to and different from the message of King's speech?

Literary Skills: Speech and Structural Patterns

9. **Analyze** Lincoln names the steps required in the "great task" that remains. Each step begins with the word *that.* What are the steps? How does the use of parallel structure help Lincoln convey them?
10. **Analyze** Find several examples of repeated words or sentences in King's speech. What important ideas is he emphasizing?

Writing Focus

Think as a Reader/Writer

Use It in Your Writing Review your list of key ideas from the speeches. Write a short paragraph persuading others to support your views on a topic you care about. Use repetition to emphasize your most important ideas.

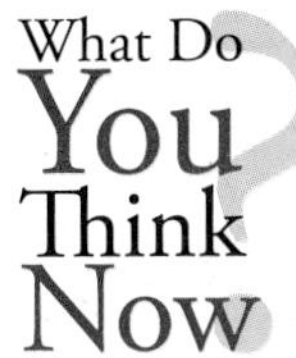

How has reading these speeches changed your ideas about freedom? How can freedom mean different things to different people?

The Gettysburg Address / *from* I Have a Dream

Vocabulary Development

Vocabulary Skills: Word Analogies

A **word analogy** is a puzzle that consists of two pairs of words that have the same relationship. The relationship might involve words that

- have the same meaning or similar meanings: *starving* and *famished*
- have opposite meanings: *adore* and *despise*
- have some other relationship, such as cause and effect: *drought* and *famine*

EXAMPLE *Bright* is to *dark* as *happy* is to ______.

Since *bright* and *dark* are opposites, you should fill the blank with a word that means the opposite of *happy*, such as *sad*.

Your Turn

detract
nobly
creed
oasis

Complete each analogy with the Vocabulary word at right that best fits in the blank. Use each word only once. After you have completed each analogy, explain the relationship between the word pairs.

1. *Wisely* is to *foolishly* as ______ is to *basely*.
2. *Dream* is to *vision* as *belief* is to ______.
3. *Illness* is to *hospital* as *thirst* is to ______.
4. *Congratulate* is to ______ as *admire* is to *dislike*.

Language Coach

Related Words The word *nobly* comes from the Latin word *nobilis*, originally meaning "well known." Related words include *noble*, *nobility*, and *nobleman*. Now use a dictionary to discover how the words *detract*, *tractor*, *contract*, and *retractions* are related. What core meaning do these words share?

Academic Vocabulary

Write About . . .

Write a short paragraph about the way King used repetition to emphasize his main points. Explain your reactions to his speech. Were his techniques successful? Use specific text references and the underlined Academic Vocabulary words in your response.

RA.I.8.5 Assess the adequacy, accuracy and appropriateness of an author's details, identifying persuasive techniques and examples of bias and stereotyping. RA.I.8.7 Analyze an author's argument, perspective or viewpoint and explain the development of key points. *Also covered* WC.8.3; VO.8.3; VO.8.7; VO.8.6; RA.I.8.1

Grammar Link

Pronoun Case

A pronoun's **case** is the form it takes to show its relationship to other words in a sentence. There are three cases of pronouns:

NOMINATIVE The pronoun is used as a subject (*I, you, he, she, it, we, they*). **He** had a dream.

OBJECTIVE The pronoun is used as a direct object, indirect object, or an object of a preposition (*me, you, him, her, it, us, them*). King inspired **her** and **me.**

Note: To choose the correct pronoun for a sentence with a compound object, try each form of the pronoun separately in the sentence.

POSSESSIVE The pronoun shows possession (*my/mine, your/yours, his, her/hers, its, our/ours, their/theirs*). King shared **his** dream.

Your Turn

Complete the following sentences by choosing the correct pronoun in the parentheses. Identify the case of each pronoun.

1. Lincoln told (*they, them, their*) his ideas.
2. (*He, Him, His*) was known for simple speech.
3. King's message spoke directly to my friends and (*I, me, mine*).
4. King's ideas are now (*we, us, ours*).

Writing Applications Write three sentences of your own that contain pronouns. Use each pronoun case—nominative, objective, and possessive—at least once.

CHOICES

As you respond to the Choices, use these **Academic Vocabulary** words as appropriate: observation, emphasize, reactions, define.

REVIEW

Create a Podcast of a Speech

TechFocus To create a podcast of Lincoln's speech, copy the speech and underline words or phrases that seem most important. Highlight structural patterns, such as the use of repetition and parallelism. Then, record yourself reading the speech. Emphasize the underlined words by slowing down, raising your voice, or changing your tone. Evaluate your presentation by listening to your recording. Re-record, if necessary, to improve your delivery.

CONNECT

Discuss a Topic

Timed Writing King argues that having faith in a better future gives people the strength to do what is necessary to achieve that future. In a brief essay, state whether you believe that a positive outlook can affect a person's ability to create change. Use examples to support your assertion.

EXTEND

Research Nonviolent Resistance

Group Project Research the way King used nonviolent means in the struggle for civil rights. How did demonstrations, marches, sit-ins, and boycotts lead to change? Present your findings to the class.

Learn It Online

There's more to these speeches than meets the eye. Learn more at:

go.hrw.com L8-533 

ESSAY

Preparing to Read

THE BORDER
A GLARE OF TRUTH

by **Pat Mora**

Stepping into the American Dream (20th century) by Xavier Cortada. Acrylic on canvas.

What Do You Think?

What do we most appreciate about the places we live?

 **QuickWrite**

What kinds of things do people miss most when they are no longer in familiar surroundings?

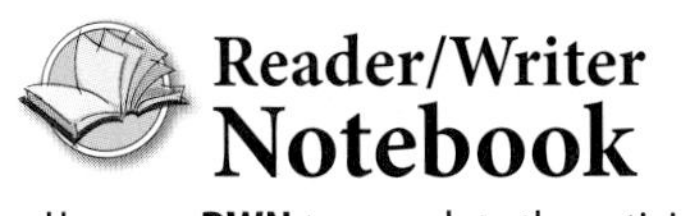

Reader/Writer Notebook

Use your **RWN** to complete the activities for this selection.

OH **RA.L.8.3** Explain how authors pace action and use subplots, parallel episodes and climax. **RA.I.8.7** Analyze an author's argument, perspective or viewpoint and explain the development of key points. **RP.8.3** Monitor own comprehension by adjusting speed to fit the purpose, or by skimming, scanning, reading on, looking back, note taking or summarizing what has been read so far in text.

Literary Focus

Essay and Logic An **essay** is nonfiction writing that examines a single subject. "The Border: A Glare of Truth" is a **personal essay**—one that reveals the writer's insights, ideas, and opinions.

Most essayists rely on logic to make their points. **Logic** is reason—an ordered way of thinking that helps us arrive at truth. For an essay to be logical, its main ideas must be supported by details, facts, examples, and personal observations.

Reading Focus

Making an Outline An **outline** is a record of the important ideas and supporting details in a text. By listing the details beneath the idea they support, you can see how the ideas and details are related. Outlining a piece of writing reveals its logical structure.

Into Action Use the organizer below to outline "The Border: A Glare of Truth." Expand the outline with additional important ideas and supporting details as needed.

I. **First important idea:** Mora misses living close to the border.
  A. Supporting detail: She misses special foods.
  B. Supporting detail: She misses hearing Spanish spoken.
II. **Second important idea:** ________________

TechFocus As you develop your outline on paper, consider how, in an online environment, hyperlinks could provide additional information.

Writing Focus

Think as a Reader/Writer

Find It in Your Reading As you read, notice the way Mora describes people, places, and things. List three of these people, places, or things in your *Reader/Writer Notebook.* Beneath each one, record the descriptive modifiers Mora uses. Remember that modifiers can be words or phrases.

Vocabulary

proximity (prahk SIHM uh tee) *n.:* state of being close by; nearness. *She lived in close proximity to the border.*

versatility (vur suh TIHL uh tee) *n.:* ability to do many things well. *Her versatility in languages enabled her to speak English and Spanish equally well.*

shunning (SHUHN ihng) *v.:* avoiding; having little to do with. *The author is no longer shunning her culture, which she had done as a youth.*

domination (dahm ih NAY shuhn) *n.:* act of controlling; power. *Criminals exert domination over some border towns.*

insulated (IHN suh layt ihd) *v.:* shielded; protected. *Their wealth insulated them from need.*

Language Coach

Word Origins *Dominus* means "master" in Latin. Which Vocabulary word on the list above comes from this word? How can you tell? Now, see if you can list three other words that come from the same origin.

Learn It Online
Hone your understanding of words with Word Watch:

go.hrw.com L8-535 

MEET THE WRITER

Learn It Online
Learn more about Mora at:
go.hrw.com L8-536 Go

Pat Mora

(1942–)

Roots in Mexico

After fleeing Mexico to escape the violence of the Mexican Revolution, both sets of Pat Mora's grandparents settled in Texas. Mora grew up in a bilingual environment: Her parents taught her and her siblings both Spanish and English, and her aunt told the children tales in both languages.

A World of Stories

Mora's early life was filled with words. Mora explains,

> "I always liked reading, and I always liked writing, but I don't think I thought of being a writer. . . . I never saw a writer like me—who was bilingual."

Her Own Voice

Mora did not begin writing seriously until she was a mother with a job. "Evenings and weekends, after dishes were washed and homework questions answered, I wrote," Mora remembers. Today Mora is a distinguished, full-time writer and speaker.

Think About the Writer How might Mora be regarded as a role model for developing writers?

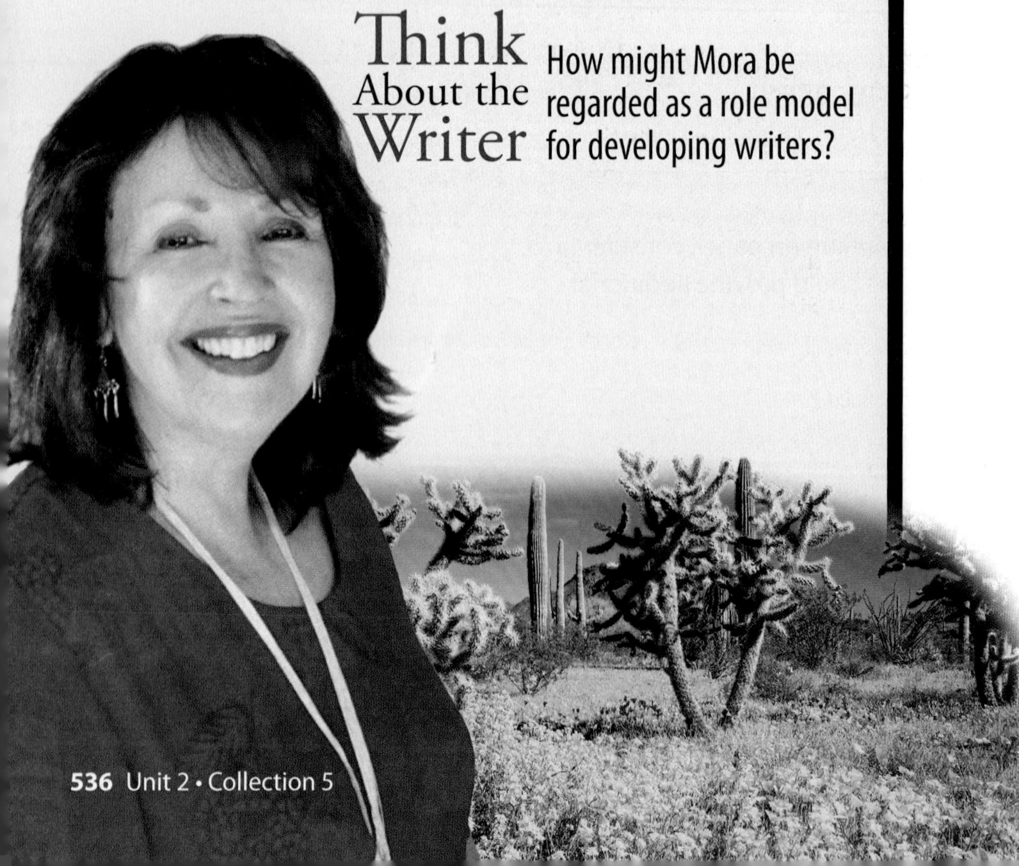

Build Background

Originally, much of the land that is now in the United States was part of Mexico. The border region has always been a place of vibrant cultural blending and exchange. It is also a troubled place. Areas along the border struggle with poverty, pollution, and crime. The United States and Mexico are currently working together to try to solve some of these problems.

Preview the Selection

In this personal essay, **Pat Mora** explores her feelings about moving away from the border area, where she grew up.

Read with a Purpose Read to find out what Mora misses most from the days when she lived near the border.

THE BORDER
A GLARE OF TRUTH

by **Pat Mora**

I moved away for the first time from the U.S.-Mexican border in the fall of 1989. Friends were sure I'd miss the visible evidence of Mexico's proximity found in cities such as my native El Paso. Friends smiled that I'd soon be back for *good* Mexican food, for the delicate taste and smell of *cilantro,*[1] for soft tortillas[2] freshly made. There were jokes about care packages flying to the Midwest. (A)

Although most of my adult home and work life had been spent speaking English, I was prepared to miss the sound of Spanish weaving in and out of my days like the warm aroma from a familiar bakery. I knew I'd miss the pleasure of moving back and forth between two languages—a pleasure that can deepen human understanding and increase our versatility conceptually as well as linguistically.[3]

And indeed, when I hear a phrase in Spanish in a Cincinnati restaurant, my head turns quickly. I listen, silently wishing to be part of that other conversation, if only for a few moments, to feel Spanish in my mouth. I'm reading more poetry in Spanish, sometimes reading the lines aloud to myself, enjoying sounds I don't otherwise hear. Recently I heard a voice on National Public Radio say that learning another language is renaming the world. What an interesting perception. Because language shapes as well as reflects our reality, exploring it allows us to see and to explore our world anew, much as experiencing the world with

1. **cilantro** (sih LAHN troh): herb often used in Mexican cuisine.
2. **tortillas** (tawr TEE yuhz): type of flatbread.
3. **linguistically** (lihng GWIHS tuh klee): relating to words or language.

(A) **Literary Focus** **Essay** A personal essay explores the author's reactions to something. What is Mora's subject?

Vocabulary **proximity** (prahk SIHM uh tee) *n.:* state of being close by; nearness.
versatility (vur suh TIHL uh tee) *n.:* ability to do many things well.

a young child causes us to pause, savor. I smile when my children, who were too busy when they were younger, now inform me that when they visit, they hope we'll be speaking Spanish. They have discovered as I did that languages are channels, sometimes to other people, sometimes to other views of the world, sometimes to other aspects of ourselves. So we struggle with irregular verbs, laughing together. B

Is it my family—children, parents, siblings, niece, nephews—that I miss in this land of leaves so unlike my bare desert? Of course, but my family, although miles away, is with me daily. The huge telephone bills and the steady stream of letters and cards are a long-distance version of the web of caring we once created around kitchen tables. Our family web just happens to stretch across these United States, a sturdy, elastic web steadily maintained by each in his or her own way.

Oh, I miss the meals seasoned with that family phrase, "Remember the time when . . . ?" But I've learned through the years to cherish our gatherings when I'm in the thick of them, to sink into the faces and voices, to store the memories and stories like the industrious Ohio squirrel outside my window stores her treasures.

I've enjoyed this furry, scurrying companion as I've enjoyed the silence of bare tree limbs against an evening sky, updrafts of snow outside our third-floor window,

---

B Reading Focus **Making an Outline** What important idea is the author telling us about Spanish? List her supporting details.

the ivory light of cherry blossoms. I feel fortunate to be experiencing the geographical center of this country, which astutely calls itself the Heartland. If I'm hearing the "heart," its steady, predictable rhythms, what am I missing from this country's southern border, its margin? **C**

Is it other rhythms? I remember my mixed feelings as a young girl whenever my father selected a Mexican station on the radio, feelings my children now experience about me. I wanted so to *be an American,* which in my mind, and perhaps in the minds of many on the border, meant (and means) shunning anything from Mexico.

But as I grew I learned to like dancing to those rhythms. I learned to value not only the rhythms but all that they symbolized. As an adult, such music became associated with celebrations and friends, with warmth and the sharing of emotions. I revel in a certain Mexican passion not for life or about life, but in life—a certain intensity in the daily living of it, a certain abandon in such music, in the hugs, sometimes in the anger. I miss the *chispas,* "sparks," that spring from the willingness, the habit, of allowing the inner self to burst through polite restraints. Sparks can be dangerous but, like risks, are necessary.

I brought cassettes of Mexican and Latin American music with us when we drove to Ohio. I'd roll the car window down and turn the volume up, taking a certain delight in sending such sounds like mischievous imps across fields and into trees. Broadcasting my culture, if you will.

On my first return visit to Texas, I stopped to hear a group of *mariachis* playing their instruments with proud gusto. I was surprised and probably embarrassed when my eyes filled with tears not only at the music, but at the sight of wonderful Mexican faces. The musicians were playing for some senior citizens. The sight of brown, knowing eyes that quickly accepted me with a smile, the stories in those eyes and in the wrinkled faces were more delicious than any *fajitas*[4] or *flan.*[5]

When I lived on the border, I had the privilege accorded to a small percentage of our citizens: I daily saw the native land of my grandparents. I grew up in the Chihuahua desert, as did they, only we grew up on different sides of the Rio Grande. That desert—its firmness, resilience, and fierceness, its whispered chants and tempestuous dance, its wisdom and majesty—shaped us as geography always shapes its inhabitants. The desert persists in me, both inspiring and compelling me to sing about

4. **fajitas** (fah HEE tahz): dish of grilled meat with tortillas.

5. **flan** (flahn): Mexican custard.

C **Read and Discuss** What do Mora's descriptions of things she misses and her mention of the squirrel tell you about the way she sees the world?

Vocabulary **shunning** (SHUHN ihng) *v.:* avoiding; having little to do with.

her and her people, their roots and blooms and thorns.

The desert is harsh, hard as life, no carpet of leaves cushions a walk, no forest conceals the shacks on the other side of the sad river. Although a Midwest winter is hard, it ends, melts into rich soil yielding the yellow trumpeting of daffodils. But the desert in any season can be relentless as poverty and hunger, realities prevalent[6] as scorpions in that stark terrain. Anthropologist Renato Rosaldo, in his provocative challenge to his colleagues, *Culture and Truth,* states that we live in a world "saturated with inequality, power, and domination."

6. prevalent (PREHV uh lehnt) common; in general use.

The culture of the border illustrates this truth daily, glaringly. Children go to sleep hungry and stare at stores filled with toys they'll never touch, with books they'll never read. Oddly, I miss that clear view of the difference between my comfortable life and the lives of so many who also speak Spanish, value family, music, celebration. In a broader sense, I miss the visible reminder of the difference between my insulated, economically privileged life and the life of most of my fellow humans. What I miss about the sights and sounds of the border is, I've finally concluded, its stern honesty. The fierce light of that grand, wide Southwest sky not only filled me with energy, it revealed the glare of truth. **D**

Analyzing Visuals

Viewing and Interpreting
How do these signs reflect Mora's bilingual experience?

D Literary Focus Essay Is it logical that Mora would miss seeing how poor people live? Why or why not?

Vocabulary **domination** (dahm ih NAY shuhn) *n.:* act of controlling; power.
insulated (IHN suh layt ihd) *v.:* shielded; protected.

Applying Your Skills

OH **RA.L.8.3** Explain how authors pace action and use subplots, parallel episodes and climax. **RA.I.8.7** Analyze an author's argument, perspective or viewpoint and explain the development of key points. *Also covered* **RP.8.3; WA.8.6**

The Border: A Glare of Truth

Respond and Think Critically

Reading Focus

Quick Check

1. What ideas about language does Mora offer?
2. Has Mora found happiness living in the "Heartland"? Explain.

Read with a Purpose

3. What does Mora miss most about living on the border? Why does she miss these things?

Reading Skills: Making an Outline

4. Study the outline that you completed while reading the essay. Consider all the important ideas you listed. Then, identify the main idea of the essay as a whole. Write the main idea at the top of your outline as shown below.

   Main Idea ______

   I. **First important idea:** Mora misses living close to the border.
      - A. Supporting detail: She misses special foods.
      - B. Supporting detail: She misses hearing Spanish spoken.

   II. **Second important idea:** ______

Literary Focus

Literary Analysis

5. **Compare and Contrast** Mora compares the desert to poverty. How are they alike, and how are they different?
6. **Infer** What does Mora suggest about communities that are isolated from poverty?
7. **Infer** The author says she heard someone on radio saying that "learning another language is renaming the world." Why is that idea so interesting to the author?

Literary Skills: Essay and Logic

8. **Analyze** Personal essays contain both fact and opinion. Find an example of each in Mora's essay.
9. **Analyze** Has Mora presented the ideas in her essay logically? Explain why or why not.

Literary Skills Review: Description

10. **Analyze** An effective description appeals to the senses and creates a mood, or emotional response. How do Mora's descriptions of the United States–Mexico border and of Ohio strengthen her essay?

Writing Focus

Think as a Reader/Writer

Use It in Your Writing Mora uses vivid, descriptive words to bring her two worlds alive. Think of a place you love, and describe it in a paragraph. Use a variety of modifiers, including phrases. Do not name the place. When you are finished, trade papers with a classmate and try to guess the places you each described.

What Do You Think Now

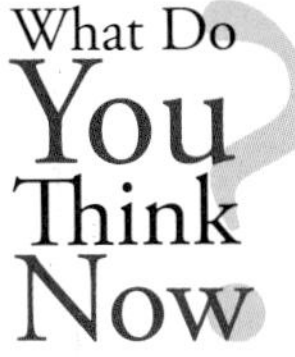

How has reading Mora's essay deepened your appreciation for the place where you live?

Applying Your Skills

The Border: A Glare of Truth

Vocabulary Development

Vocabulary Check

Answer the following questions. Vocabulary words are in boldface.

1. If you are living in **proximity** to the Mexican border, are you close to it or far from it?
2. Should we be **shunning** things that are bad for us? Explain.
3. Would a meek or shy person display **domination** over his or her peers? Why or why not?
4. How might showing **versatility** at a job interview benefit the person looking for a job?
5. In what ways can wealth and location cause one to be **insulated** from life's harsh realities?

Vocabulary Skills: Anglo-Saxon Roots and Affixes

Anglo-Saxon, the language of early settlers of Great Britain, was an important foundation of modern English. Here are some Anglo-Saxon **roots** found in English words.

Root	Meaning	Related English Word
–wit/wis–	know	wise
–haep–	luck	happy
–hieran–	hear	heard

Learning Anglo-Saxon **affixes** will help you guess the meanings of many unfamiliar words. An example is the prefix *un–*, which means "not" or "the opposite of." You can now guess that *unlock* means to "undo the locking." Here are other Anglo-Saxon affixes and their meanings.

Affix	Meaning
mis–	badly
–ness	the state of being

Your Turn

With a partner, explain the meaning of each word below. Use the roots and affixes listed in the charts to help you. Next to each definition, write another word that shares the same root or affix.

1. mishandled
2. witty
3. hearing
4. thoughtfulness
5. happiness

Language Coach

Word Origins The word *domination* is part of a large word family derived from the Latin word *dominus*. Related words include *domineer, dominion, dominant,* and *dominate.* Sort the words from the box into their proper word families, and enter them into a chart like the one below.

insulator
versatile
approximate
reverse
insulation
insular
proxy
adverse

versatility	proximity	insulated

Academic Vocabulary

Write About . . .
Look around you at the place you are now. Jot down your observations of (what you see) and your reactions to (what you think of) the place.

OH **RA.L.8.3** Explain how authors pace action and use subplots, parallel episodes and climax. **RP.8.3** Monitor own comprehension by adjusting speed to fit the purpose, or by skimming, scanning, reading on, looking back, note taking or summarizing what has been read so far in text. *Also covered* **WC.8.6; VO.8.7; VO.8.6; RA.I.8.7**

Grammar Link

Correct Placement of Modifiers

A **modifier** is a word or phrase that describes or limits the meaning of another word or phrase. Always place modifiers as close as possible to what they modify, or tell about. A modifier that is too far from what it modifies is misplaced, and your reader could become confused. Look at this example.

Teary-eyed, music fills the author with joy.

Since the modifier *teary-eyed* is closest to *music,* it appears to modify *music* instead of the word it should modify: *author.* Let's try the sentence again.

Music fills the *teary-eyed* author with joy.

Your Turn

Rewrite each sentence below by placing the misplaced modifier as close as possible to the word it should modify.

1. Far into the night, the mariachis tuned their instruments and performed.
2. When living on the border, the desert seemed beautiful to Mora.
3. Mora came to love the heartland after moving.

Writing Applications Now, write three sentences of your own in which you use correctly placed modifiers.

CHOICES

As you respond to the Choices, use these **Academic Vocabulary** words as appropriate: observation, emphasize, reactions, define.

REVIEW

Discuss Language

Timed Writing Mora says that language shapes as well as reflects our reality. Do you agree or disagree? Write an essay stating your opinion and supporting it with details, facts, examples, and personal observations. Then, look over your work. Did you use order and reason? If not, revise it so that it flows more logically.

CONNECT

Research Regional Dishes

Partner Project Mora writes about missing the foods she used to eat. What kinds of foods are unique to where you live? If you don't know, perform research online or at a library to find out. Share your findings with the class. With your teacher's permission, bring samples to share.

EXTEND

Create an Online Outline

TechFocus Use the Internet to gather information on Mexican culture. Organize the information into an outline. Then, make your outline into a Web page. Hyperlink parts of the outline to pictures, videos, and audio files so that your audience can get a taste of the culture. You can design your Web page on paper, if necessary.

Analyzing Historical Fiction

CONTENTS

The Battle of Shiloh (detail) (1862) by Kurz and Allison. Color litho.

What Do You Think?

How might events from the past affect our lives today?

QuickTalk

Think of a historical event you are curious about. With a partner, discuss what it might have been like to have been alive during this event.

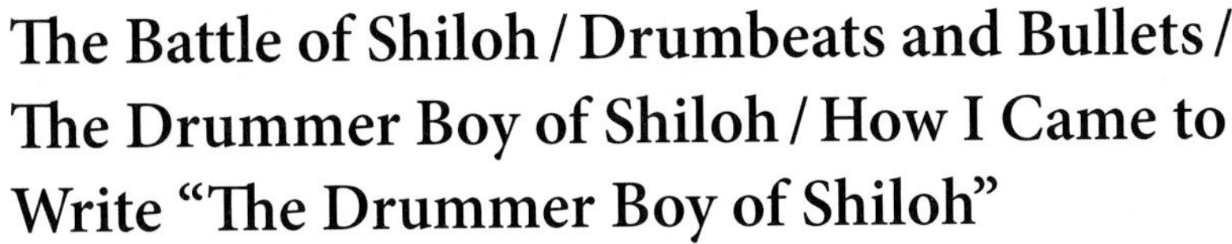

Preparing to Read

RA.L.8.6 Explain how an author's choice of genre affects the expression of a theme or topic. *Also covered* **RP.8.1**

The Battle of Shiloh / Drumbeats and Bullets / The Drummer Boy of Shiloh / How I Came to Write "The Drummer Boy of Shiloh"

Literary Focus

Historical Fact and Historical Fiction **Historical fiction** combines fiction—an imagined story—and history—factual events from the past. When you read historical fiction, look for how the writer combines fact and fiction. "The Battle of Shiloh" and "Drumbeats and Bullets" are nonfiction, providing historical background. Ray Bradbury's story combines historical fact and fiction. In the final selection, he explains how he was inspired to write it.

Reading Focus

Comparing Treatments The selections that follow provide different treatments of a shared topic: the Battle of Shiloh during the U.S. Civil War. To analyze the treatment of a topic, look for the types of details (fact/opinion) that are given, as well as how those details are presented (in lists or charts, in order of importance, in story form). Use a chart like this one to compare the selections.

Selection	Type of Treatment
"The Battle of Shiloh"	Types of details: How details are presented:
"Drumbeats and Bullets"	Types of details: How details are presented:
"The Drummer Boy of Shiloh"	Type of details: How details are presented:

Writing Focus

Think as a Reader/Writer

Pay attention to how each text presents facts. Note in your *Reader/Writer Notebook* how the short story combines fact and fiction.

Reader/Writer Notebook

Use your **RWN** to complete the activities for these selections.

Vocabulary

Drumbeats and Bullets

intensified (ihn TEHN suh fyd) *v.:* increased; strengthened. *As the sound of drumming intensified, the soldiers couldn't hear anything except their marching orders.*

vital (VY tuhl) *adj.:* of great importance or need. *Drummer boys were vital during the Civil War because they communicated orders on the battlefield.*

The Drummer Boy of Shiloh

immortality (ihm awr TAL uh tee) *n.:* endless life. *Believing in their own immortality, the boy soldiers were not afraid to fight.*

legitimate (luh JIHT uh miht) *adj.:* allowed by law. *Many drummer boys were not legitimate members of the army, since they were too young to officially enlist.*

tremor (TREHM uhr) *n.:* shaking movement; vibration. *Joby almost lost his balance as the explosions caused a tremor in the ground.*

Language Coach

Roots One way to guess at the meaning of an unfamiliar word is to look for a familiar word within it. Which Vocabulary words in the list above contain familiar roots?

Learn It Online

There's more to words than just definitions. Get the whole story on:

go.hrw.com L8-545 

MEET THE WRITERS

Jim Murphy
(1947–)

A Sense of Adventure

Jim Murphy grew up in Kearny, New Jersey, a small town where he and his friends played football and baseball when they weren't "roaming around town . . . inventing various 'adventures.'" Murphy has retained that sense of adventure in his many nonfiction books.

A Sense of History

The idea for *The Boys' War,* the book that features "Drumbeats and Bullets," originated while Murphy was researching an unrelated project at the library: "I spotted . . . the Civil War diary of a fifteen-year-old Union soldier named Elisha Stockwell, Jr. Hmmm, I thought, I didn't know kids so young had fought in that war. . . . Why not let him and other young soldiers talk about the war in their own words? This started my search for other Union and Confederate voices."

Ray Bradbury
(1920–)

A Busy Writer

Ray Bradbury has published more than five hundred works. He is most widely known for his fantasy and science fiction short stories and novels. He has also written plays, poetry, and television scripts. From 1985 until 1992 Bradbury hosted a television series called *The Ray Bradbury Theater.*

For more information on Bradbury and his work, see the Author Study on pages 426–453.

Think About the Writers

Based on their biographies and the subjects to which they are drawn, do you think Murphy's and Bradbury's styles of writing will be similar or different?

Preview the Selections

"The Battle of Shiloh" and the Data Bank provide facts about an important battle in the Civil War.

"Drumbeats and Bullets" presents the history of boys who enlisted in the army during the Civil War but were too young to carry a gun.

In "The Drummer Boy of Shiloh," a fictional story set during the Civil War, **Joby** prepares for the next day's battle.

In "Why I Wrote 'The Drummer Boy of Shiloh,'" author **Ray Bradbury** explores the origins of his famous story.

ENCYCLOPEDIA ENTRY

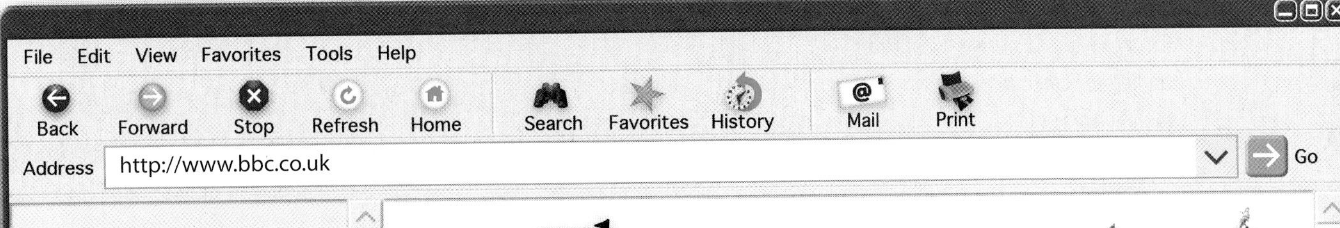

Read with a Purpose
Read these documents to learn about a famous Civil War battle.

The Battle of Shiloh

from Encarta

Shiloh, Battle of, also called the Battle of Pittsburg Landing, engagement of the American Civil War. The name Shiloh was taken from that of a meetinghouse, 5 km (3 mi) from Pittsburg Landing, that is on the Tennessee River, 14 km (9 mi) north of Savannah, Tennessee. Here on April 6, 1862, a Confederate army of 40,000 men under General Albert S. Johnston surprised and attacked a Union army of 45,000 men under General Ulysses S. Grant. During the battle, which lasted from dawn to

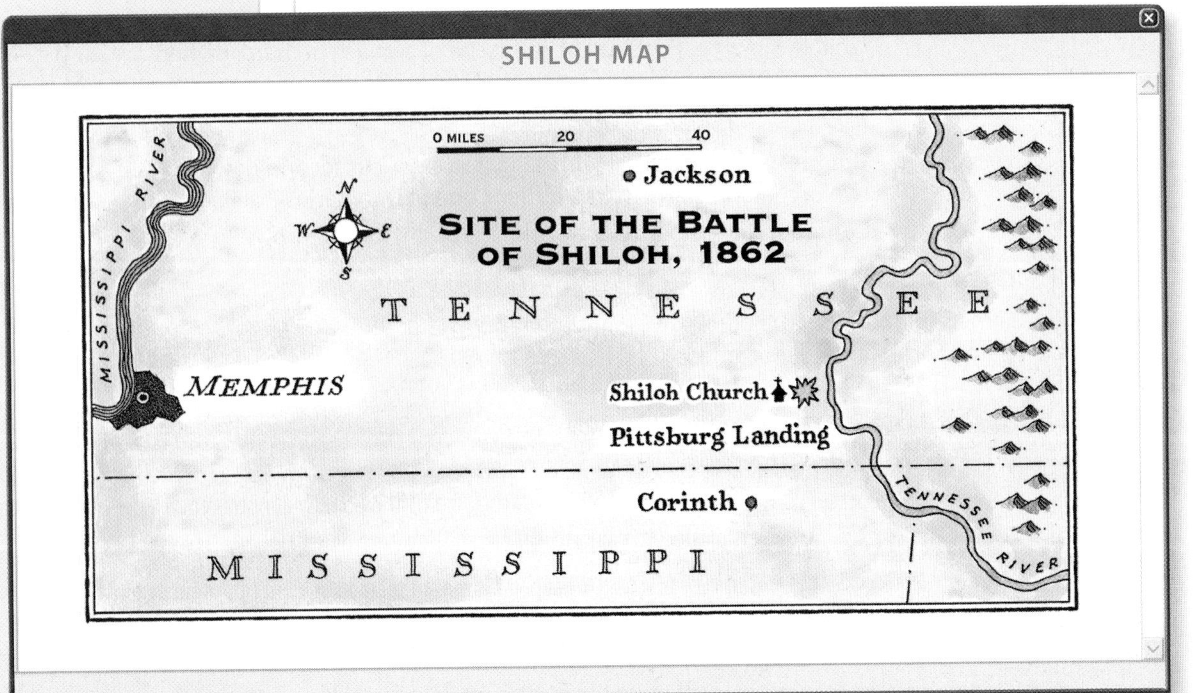

Analyzing Visuals

Viewing and Interpreting Do these soldiers look prepared to fight a major battle? Explain.

Company H, 44th Indiana Volunteers outside a camp in Tennessee, c. 1863.

dusk and was one of the most desperate of the war, the Union troops were steadily driven back, but Johnston was killed, and his successor, General Pierre G. T. Beauregard, ordered operations suspended a few hours later. The following day Grant, with 25,000 reinforcements under General Don Carlos Buell, attacked the Confederates and forced them to withdraw to Corinth, Mississippi. Thus, Grant regained all the ground he had lost, and the two-day battle ended without a conclusive victory for either side. Casualties numbered more than 10,000 in each army. A national military park and cemetery commemorating the battle are located at Shiloh. **A**

Data Bank: The Battle of Shiloh

Date: April 6–7, 1862

Location In Tennessee near the Mississippi border beside the Tennessee River (Shiloh was a nearby church) at the site of a peach orchard, owned by Sarah Bell, in bloom at the time of the battle. (Observers compared peach blossoms cut down by bullets to snow.) **B**

Generals **Union**—Ulysses S. Grant with 45,000 troops. (On second day, 25,000 reinforcements participated under General Don Carlos Buell.)

Confederate—Albert Sidney Johnston with 40,000 troops.

Casualties: 23,746

Largest, bloodiest battle of the Civil War to that point. (Larger battles, like Gettysburg, were still to come.)

close this window

A **Reading Focus** **Comparing Treatments** How does this encyclopedia article treat its subject matter? Is it objective or biased? How can you tell?

B **Read and Discuss** What point is the author making with this comparison?

Internet

HISTORY

DRUMBEATS and BULLETS

by **Jim Murphy**

Read with a Purpose

Read this historical account to learn about the role of drummer boys in the Civil War.

Preparing to Read for this selection is on page 545.

Build Background

Currently, the minimum age for enlistment in the United States Armed Forces is seventeen. During the Civil War, boys as young as twelve enlisted in the army (often lying about their age) and found themselves marching alongside grown men—often as drummers. Many of these drummer boys were runaways or were homeless.

The groggy soldier woke up to a persistent, brain-rattling drumming noise. *Thrump. Thrump. Thrump.* He rolled over in an attempt to ignore the sound and pulled his blanket up over his head. The drumming went on and intensified as drummers all over camp signaled the call to muster.[1] There was no escaping it, and eventually—and usually with a grumble—the soldier got up to start another day.

Soldiers probably came to hate the sound of the drums, especially when they heard them on a drizzly, cold morning. Yet drummer boys who served during the Civil War provided valuable service to the armies of both sides, although some didn't realize it at first.

"I wanted to fight the Rebs," a twelve-year-old boy wrote, "but I was very small and they would not give me a musket. The next day I went back and the man behind the desk said I looked as if I could hold a drum and if I wanted I could join that way. I did, but I was not happy to change a musket for a stick."

This boy was disappointed at being assigned a "nonfighting" and, to him, dull job. Most likely, he saw himself always

1. **muster:** assemble; come together.

Vocabulary **intensified** (ihn TEHN suh fyd) *v.:* increased; strengthened.

drumming in parades or in the safety of camp. He would soon learn differently.

The beat of the drum was one of the most important means of communicating orders to soldiers in the Civil War. Drummers did find themselves in camp sounding the routine calls to muster or meals and providing the beat for marching drills. But more often than not, they were with the troops in the field, not just marching to the site of the battle but in the middle of the fighting. It was the drumbeat that told the soldiers how and when to maneuver[2] as smoke poured over the battlefield. And the sight of a drummer boy showed soldiers where their unit was located, helping to keep them close together. **A**

Drummers were such a vital part of battle communication that they often found themselves the target of enemy fire. "A ball hit my drum and bounced off and I fell over," a Confederate drummer at the Battle of Cedar Creek recalled. "When I got up, another ball tore a hole in the drum and another came so close to my ear that I heard it sing."

Naturally, such killing fire alarmed many drummer boys at first. But like their counterparts with rifles, they soon learned how to face enemy shells without flinching. Fourteen-year-old Orion Howe was struck by several Confederate bullets during the Battle of Vicksburg in 1863. Despite his wounds, he maintained his position and

relayed the orders given him. For his bravery, Howe would later receive the Medal of Honor.

Drumming wasn't the only thing these boys did, either. While in camp, they would carry water, rub down horses, gather wood, or cook for the soldiers. There is even evidence that one was a barber for the troops when he wasn't drumming. After a battle, most drummers helped carry wounded soldiers off the field or assisted in burial details. And many drummer boys even got their wish to fight the enemy.

Fighting in the Civil War was particularly bloody. Of the 900 men in the First

2. **maneuver** (muh NOO vuhr): move as a troop.

A **Read and Discuss** What have we learned so far?

Vocabulary **vital** (VY tuhl) *adj.:* of great importance or need.

Drummer boys of the 61st New York Infantry, March 1863.

Maine Heavy Artillery, 635 became casualties *in just seven minutes* of fighting at the Battle of Petersburg. A North Carolina regiment saw 714 of its 800 soldiers killed at Gettysburg. At such a time, these boys put down their drums and took up whatever rifle was handy. One such drummer was Johnny Clem.

Clem ran away from home in 1861 when he was eleven years old. He enlisted, and the Twenty-second Michigan Regiment took him in as their drummer, paying him thirteen dollars a month for his services. Several months later, at the Battle of Shiloh, Clem earned the nickname of "Johnny Shiloh" when a piece of cannon shell bounced off a tree stump and destroyed his drum. When another drum was shattered in battle, Clem found a musket and fought bravely for the rest of the war, becoming a sergeant[3] in the fall of 1863. **B**

The Civil War would be the last time drummer boys would be used in battle. The roar of big cannons and mortars, the rapid firing of thousands of rifles, and the shouts of tens of thousands of men made hearing a drumbeat difficult. More and

3. **sergeant** (SAHR juhnt): noncommissioned officer in the military.

B **Reading Focus** **Comparing Treatments** How does the treatment of the Battle of Shiloh in this piece compare to its treatment in the encyclopedia entry and Data Bank?

more, bugles were being used to pass along orders. Military tactics were changing, too. Improved weapons made it impractical to have precise lines of soldiers face their enemy at close range. Instead, smaller, fast-moving units and trench warfare, neither of which required drummers, became popular.

Even as their role in the fighting was changing, Civil War drummers stayed at their positions signaling orders to the troops. Hundreds were killed and thousands more wounded. "A cannon ball came bouncing across the corn field," a drummer boy recalled, "kicking up dirt and dust each time it struck the earth. Many of the men in our company took shelter behind a stone wall, but I stood where I was and never stopped drumming. An officer came by on horseback and chastised the men, saying 'this boy puts you all to shame. Get up and move forward.' We all began moving across the cornfield. . . . Even when the fighting was at its fiercest and I was frightened, I stood straight and did as I was ordered. . . . I felt I had to be a good example for the others." **C**

C **Read and Discuss** What is all this saying?

Analyzing Visuals **Viewing and Interpreting** How might these drummers be setting a good example for the troops?

Members of the drum corps of the 93rd New York Infantry Regiment, August 1863.

Applying Your Skills

RA.L.8.6 Explain how an author's choice of genre affects the expression of a theme or topic. RP.8.1 Apply reading comprehension strategies, including making predictions, comparing and contrasting, recalling and summarizing and making inferences and drawing conclusions. WA.8.6 Produce informal writings. *Also covered* VO.8.4

The Battle of Shiloh / Drumbeats and Bullets

Respond and Think Critically

Reading Focus

Quick Check

1. How many died in the Battle of Shiloh? Who won this battle?
2. How did battle tactics change after the Civil War?

Read with a Purpose

3. What information did you learn about the Civil War that was new or surprising?
4. What role did the drummer boys play during battle?

Reading Skills: Comparing Treatments

5. Review your chart comparing the selections. How are they similar and different?

Selections	Treatment of Topic
"The Battle of Shiloh"	Types of details: facts, statistics How details are presented: summary of battle
"Drumbeats and Bullets"	Types of details: How details are presented:

Vocabulary Check

Fill in the blanks with the correct Vocabulary word.

vital intensified

6. As the battle __________, the role of the drummer boys became __________.

Literary Focus

Literary Analysis

7. **Draw Conclusions** The Data Bank entry for the Battle of Shiloh tells us that this battle was the bloodiest to that point in the Civil War. What does this detail suggest about future battles during the Civil War?
8. **Evaluate** Which of the selections gave you a better sense of what the Battle of Shiloh was like? Give your opinion, and support it with details.
9. **Make Judgments** How did these young drummers come to fight in the war? At what age do you think people should be allowed to join the military? Explain your idea.

Literary Skills: Historical Fiction

10. Make a list of five facts about the Civil War that could form the basis for a fictional story. Explain briefly why you chose these facts as inspiration for a piece of **historical fiction.**

Writing Focus

Think as a Reader/Writer

Use It in Your Writing Did you notice that the encyclopedia entry has long sentences packed with information? Jim Murphy, on the other hand, uses short sentences with bite-sized bits of information. Write a paragraph on what you've learned about the Civil War, paying attention to how you impart your facts. Which style will you use?

THE DRUMMER BOY of SHILOH

by **Ray Bradbury**

Read with a Purpose

Read this short story to experience what a drummer boy feels before a Civil War battle.

Preparing to Read for this selection is on page 545.

Build Background

This short story takes place during the American Civil War on the night before the Battle of Shiloh. As you read this story, you might have questions about the story's historical accuracy. Bradbury did his research. You've also done yours—think of all you've learned about the Battle of Shiloh and drummer boys. As you read, consider how your prior reading of historical sources widens your comprehension of this story.

In the April night, more than once, blossoms fell from the orchard trees and lighted with rustling taps on the drumhead. At midnight a peach stone, left miraculously on a branch through winter, flicked by a bird, fell swift and unseen; it struck once, like panic, and jerked the boy upright. In silence he listened to his own heart ruffle away, away—at last gone from his ears and back in his chest again.

After that he turned the drum on its side, where its great lunar face peered at him whenever he opened his eyes.

His face, alert or at rest, was solemn. It was a solemn time and a solemn night for a boy just turned fourteen in the peach orchard near Owl Creek, not far from the church at Shiloh. **A**

". . . thirty-one . . . thirty-two . . . thirty-three." Unable to see, he stopped counting.

Beyond the thirty-three familiar shadows, forty thousand men, exhausted by nervous expectation and unable to sleep for romantic dreams of battles yet unfought, lay crazily askew in their uniforms. A mile farther on, another army was strewn helter-

A **Read and Discuss** How does the story begin?

skelter, turning slowly, basting themselves with the thought of what they would do when the time came—a leap, a yell, a blind plunge their strategy, raw youth their protection and benediction.[1]

Now and again the boy heard a vast wind come up that gently stirred the air. But he knew what it was—the army here, the army there, whispering to itself in the dark. Some men talking to others, others murmuring to themselves, and all so quiet it was like a natural element arisen from South or North with the motion of the earth toward dawn.

What the men whispered the boy could only guess, and he guessed that it was "Me, I'm the one, I'm the one of all the rest who won't die. I'll live through it. I'll go home. The band will play. And I'll be there to hear it."

"Yes," thought the boy, *"that's all very well for them, they can give as good as they get!"*

For with the careless bones of the young men, harvested by night and bindled[2] around campfires, were the similarly strewn steel bones of their rifles with bayonets fixed like eternal lightning lost in the orchard grass.

"Me," thought the boy, *"I got only a drum, two sticks to beat it, and no shield."*

There wasn't a man-boy on this ground tonight who did not have a shield he cast, riveted, or carved himself on his way to his first attack, compounded of remote but nonetheless firm and fiery family devotion, flag-blown patriotism, and cocksure immortality, strengthened by the touchstone of very real gunpowder, ramrod, Minié ball,[3] and flint. But without these last, the boy felt his family move yet farther off in the dark, as if one of those great prairie-burning trains had chanted them away, never to return—leaving him with this drum, which was worse than a toy in the game to be played tomorrow or someday much too soon.

The boy turned on his side. A moth brushed his face, but it was peach blossom. A peach blossom flicked him, but it was a moth. Nothing stayed put. Nothing had a name. Nothing was as it once was.

If he stayed very still when the dawn came up and the soldiers put on their bravery with their caps, perhaps they might go away, the war with them, and not notice him lying small here, no more than a toy himself. **B**

"Well, by thunder now," said a voice. The boy shut his eyes to hide inside himself, but it was too late. Someone, walking by in the night, stood over him. "Well," said the voice quietly, "here's a soldier crying before the fight. Good. Get it over. Won't be time once it all starts."

And the voice was about to move on when the boy, startled, touched the drum at his elbow. The man above, hearing this, stopped. The boy could feel his eyes, sense him slowly bending near. A hand must have

1. **benediction** (behn uh DIHK shuhn): blessing.
2. **bindled:** bundled together.
3. **Minié** (MIHN ee) **ball:** cone-shaped rifle bullet, used in the 1800s.

B **Read and Discuss** What does this passage tell you about the drummer?

Vocabulary **immortality** (ihm awr TAL uh tee) *n.:* endless life.

come down out of the night, for there was a little *rat-tat* as the fingernails brushed and the man's breath fanned the boy's face.

"Why, it's the drummer boy, isn't it?"

The boy nodded, not knowing if his nod was seen. "Sir, is that you?" he said.

"I assume it is." The man's knees cracked as he bent still closer. He smelled as all fathers should smell, of salt-sweat, tobacco, horse and boot leather, and the earth he walked upon. He had many eyes. No, not eyes, brass buttons that watched the boy.

He could only be, and was, the general. "What's your name, boy?" he asked.

"Joby, sir," whispered the boy, starting to sit up.

"All right, Joby, don't stir." A hand pressed his chest gently, and the boy relaxed. "How long you been with us, Joby?"

"Three weeks, sir."

"Run off from home or join legitimate, boy?"

Silence.

"Darn-fool question," said the general. "Do you shave yet, boy? Even more of a fool. There's your cheek, fell right off the tree overhead. And the others here, not much older. Raw, raw, darn raw, the lot of you. You ready for tomorrow or the next day, Joby?"

"I think so, sir."

"You want to cry some more, go on ahead. I did the same last night."

"You, sir?"

"God's truth. Thinking of everything ahead. Both sides figuring the other side will just give up, and soon, and the war done in weeks and us all home. Well, that's not how it's going to be. And maybe that's why I cried."

"Yes, sir," said Joby. **C**

The general must have taken out a cigar now, for the dark was suddenly filled with the Indian smell of tobacco—unlighted yet, but chewed as the man thought what next to say.

"It's going to be a crazy time," said the general. "Counting both sides, there's a hundred thousand men—give or take a few thousand—out there tonight, not one as can spit a sparrow off a tree or knows a horse clod from a Minié ball. Stand up, bare the breast, ask to be a target, thank them, and sit down, that's us, that's them. We should turn tail and train four months; they should do the same. But here we are, taken with spring fever and thinking it blood lust, taking our sulfur with cannons instead of with molasses,[4] as it should be—going to be a hero, going to live forever. And I can see all them over there nodding agreement, save the other way around. It's wrong, boy, it's wrong as a head put on hind-side front and a man marching backward through life.

Analyzing Visuals **Viewing and Interpreting**
How does this painting capture the vulnerability of the drummer boys?

A Study for The Wounded Drummer Boy (19th Century) by Eastman J. Johnson. Oil on board.

4. **molasses:** Sulfur and molasses were used to treat constipation and other discomforts.

C **Read and Discuss** What is conveyed through this conversation?

Vocabulary **legitimate** (luh JIHT uh miht) *adj.:* allowed by law.

Sometime this week more innocents will get shot out of pure Cherokee enthusiasm than ever got shot before. Oil Creek was full of boys splashing around in the noonday sun just a few hours ago. I fear it will be full of boys again, just floating, at sundown tomorrow, not caring where the current takes them." **D**

The general stopped and made a little pile of winter leaves and twigs in the dark, as if he might at any moment strike fire to them to see his way through the coming days when the sun might not show its face because of what was happening here and just beyond.

The boy watched the hand stirring the leaves and opened his lips to say something, but did not say it. The general heard the boy's breath and spoke himself.

"Why am I telling you this? That's what you wanted to ask, eh? Well, when you got a bunch of wild horses on a loose rein somewhere, somehow you got to bring order, rein them in. These lads, fresh out of the milkshed, don't know what I know; and I can't tell them—men actually die in war. So each is his own army. I got to make one army of them. And for that, boy, I need you."

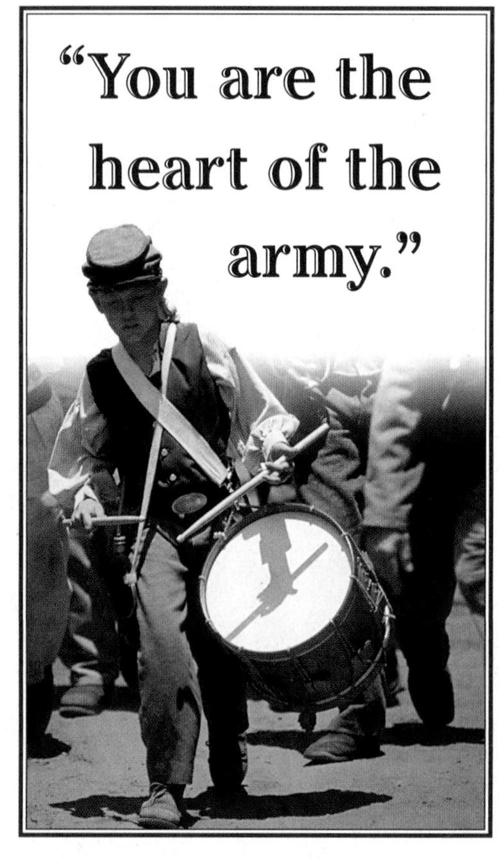
"You are the heart of the army."

"Me!" The boy's lips barely twitched.

"You, boy," said the general quietly. "You are the heart of the army. Think about that. You are the heart of the army. Listen to me, now."

And lying there, Joby listened. And the general spoke. If he, Joby, beat slow tomorrow, the heart would beat slow in the men. They would lag by the wayside. They would drowse in the fields on their muskets. They would sleep forever after that—in those same fields, their hearts slowed by a drummer boy and stopped by enemy lead.

But if he beat a sure, steady, ever-faster rhythm, then, then, their knees would come up in a long line down over that hill, one knee after the other, like a wave on the ocean shore. Had he seen the ocean ever—seen the waves rolling in like a well-ordered cavalry charge to the sand? Well, that was

---

D **Reading Focus** **Comparing Treatments** According to the historical facts you read, is the general's prediction about the coming battle well-founded?

it, that's what he wanted; that's what was needed. Joby was his right hand and his left. He gave the orders, but Joby set the pace.

So bring the right knee up and the right foot out and the left knee up and the left foot out, one following the other in good time, in brisk time. Move the blood up the body, and make the head proud and the spine stiff and the jaw resolute. Focus the eye and set the teeth; flare the nostril and tighten the hands; put steel armor all over the men, for blood moving fast in them does indeed make men feel as if they'd put on steel. He must keep at it, at it! Long and steady, steady and long! Then, even though shot or torn, those wounds got in hot blood—in blood he'd helped stir—would feel less pain. If their blood was cold, it would be more than slaughter: It would be murderous nightmare and pain best not told and no one to guess.

The general spoke and stopped, letting his breath slack off. Then, after a moment, he said, "So there you are, that's it. Will you do that, boy? Do you know now you're general of the army when the general's left behind?"

The boy nodded mutely.

"You'll run them through for me then, boy?"

"Yes, sir."

"Good. And, God willing, many nights from tonight, many years from now, when you're as old or far much older than me, when they ask you what you did in this awful time, you will tell them—one part humble and one part proud—I was the drummer boy at the battle of Owl Creek or of the Tennessee River, or maybe they'll just name it after the church there. I was the drummer boy at Shiloh. Good grief, that has a beat and sound to it fitting for Mr. Longfellow.[5] 'I was the drummer boy at Shiloh.' Who will ever hear those words and not know you, boy, or what you thought this night, or what you'll think tomorrow or the next day when we must get up on our legs and move." **E**

The general stood up. "Well, then, God bless you, boy. Good night."

"Good night, sir." And tobacco, brass, boot polish, salt-sweat, and leather, the man moved away through the grass.

Joby lay for a moment staring, but unable to see where the man had gone. He swallowed. He wiped his eyes. He cleared his throat. He settled himself. Then, at last, very slowly and firmly, he turned the drum so it faced up toward the sky.

He lay next to it, his arm around it, feeling the tremor, the touch, the muted thunder as all the rest of the April night in the year 1862, near the Tennessee River, not far from the Owl Creek, very close to the church named Shiloh, the peach blossoms fell on the drum. **F**

5. **Mr. Longfellow:** Henry Wadsworth Longfellow (1807–1882), popular American poet who was known for writing poems with strong, regular rhythms. (See "Paul Revere's Ride," page 705.)

E **Read and Discuss** What is the general saying?

Vocabulary **tremor** (TREHM uhr) *n.:* shaking movement; vibration.

F **Literary Focus** **Historical Fiction** Which parts of this paragraph are facts, and which are fiction?

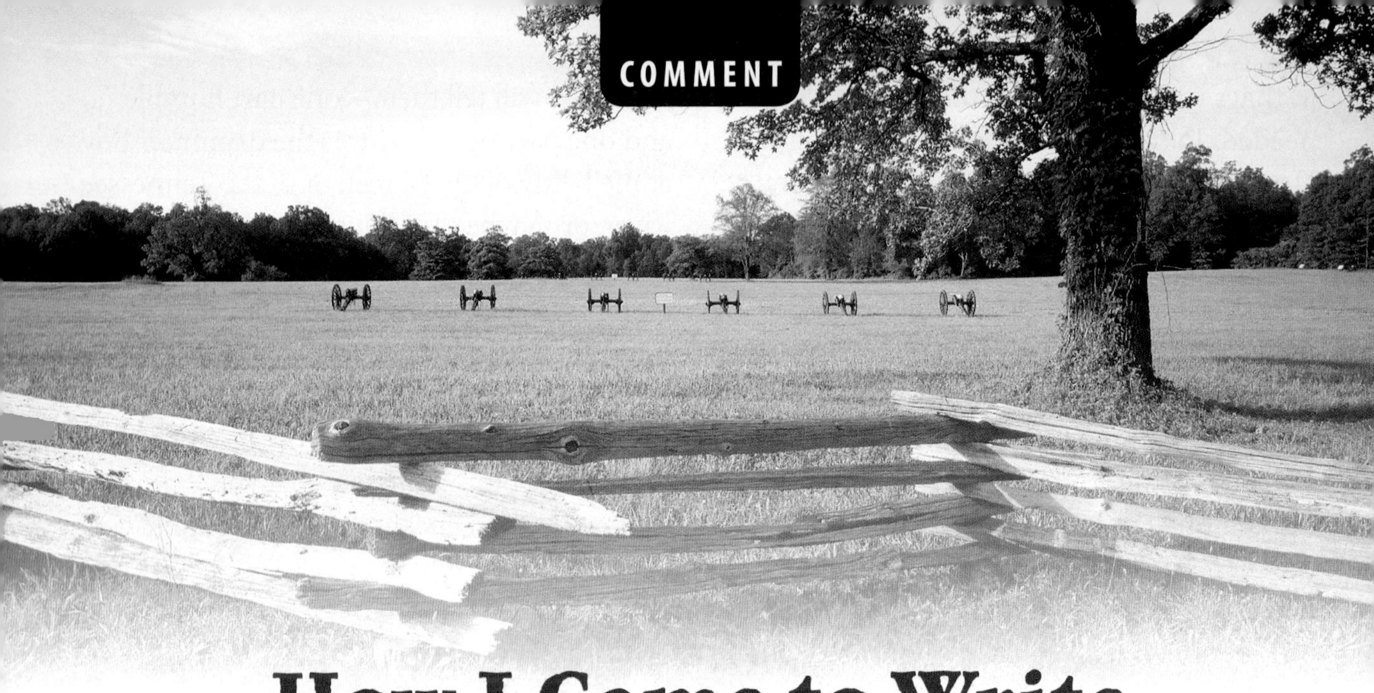

COMMENT

How I Came to Write THE DRUMMER BOY of SHILOH

by **Ray Bradbury**

Read with a Purpose
Read this comment to learn how Bradbury was inspired to write this story.

Preparing to Read for this selection is on page 545.

I was browsing through the morning newspaper forty years ago when I came across an obituary of an actor named Olin Howland who had appeared in dozens of films.

Along with the facts about his sickness and departure, it mentioned the fact that his great-grandfather was the drummer boy at Shiloh.

Peach Orchard at Shiloh National Military Park.

I cannot possibly tell you the impact of those words.

This often happens with me.

On one occasion many years ago my wife quoted "There Will Come Soft Rains" by Sara Teasdale, and the sound of that title caused me to write a story.

So here I was with the drummer boy of Shiloh. The sound of it was so poetic and so haunting that I rushed to the typewriter and, lacking full knowledge about the War between the States, nevertheless, in a white-hot passion wrote the first draft of "The Drummer Boy of Shiloh" in one afternoon. **A**

Johnny Clem, the twelve-year-old drummer boy of Shiloh.

When I finished, I was in tears because something had been waiting in me for many years to be released: my feelings about North and South and the terrible war that ensued between them.

Glancing at the story, I realized how ignorant I was as to the facts surrounding that drummer boy on that particular day so many, many years ago.

I had to go and do some research and make sure there was a peach orchard and that it was the proper time of year for blossoms to fall on the drum and to see which generals were lined up and how many troops there were, even if I didn't use all of the facts.

When I finished doing my research, I went back to the story and applied my knowledge. **B**

In later years I wrote a one-act play about his story and have seen it performed many times. It never ceases to bring me to tears. It is one of the mostly deeply felt stories I have ever written.

I am much pleased that you contain it here in this collection.

A **Read and Discuss** Where does Bradbury get ideas for his stories?

B **Literary Focus** **Historical Fiction** What did Bradbury do to make sure his fictional story was accurate?

Applying Your Skills

RA.L.8.6 Explain how an author's choice of genre affects the expression of a theme or topic. RP.8.1 Apply reading comprehension strategies, including making predictions, comparing and contrasting, recalling and summarizing and making inferences and drawing conclusions. *Also covered* **VO.8.4; WA.8.1.a**

The Drummer Boy of Shiloh / How I Came to Write "The Drummer Boy of Shiloh"

Respond and Think Critically

Reading Focus

Quick Check

1. Why does the general stop to talk to the drummer boy?
2. What observations about battles does the general make to the drummer boy?

Read with a Purpose

3. How do the drummer boy's feelings change over the course of the story?
4. What inspired Bradbury to write the story?

Reading Skills: Comparing Treatments

5. Complete your chart comparing the selections. How is their treatment of information similar or different?

Selections	Type of Treatment
"The Battle of Shiloh"	Types of details: How details are presented:
"Drumbeats and Bullets"	Types of details: How details are presented:
"The Drummer Boy of Shiloh"	Types of details: How details are presented:

Vocabulary Check

Match the Vocabulary words with their definitions.

6. **tremor** a. lawful
7. **immortality** b. quaking movement
8. **legitimate** c. everlasting life

Literary Focus

Literary Analysis

9. **Analyze** Refer to the encyclopedia entry on p. 547. Does Bradbury provide any clues as to who the general could be? Explain.
10. **Interpret** What is the meaning of the statement, "The soldiers put on their bravery with their caps"?
11. **Compare** With a partner, compare the manner in which orders were communicated to soldiers during the Civil War with the communications systems used today.

Literary Skills: Historical Fiction

12. **Compare and Contrast** Look back at the facts of Johnny Clem's life (page 551). How is Joby like and unlike Johnny Clem?
13. **Evaluate** How credible, or believable, is "The Drummer Boy of Shiloh"? Has Bradbury effectively woven together fact and fiction? Explain.

Writing Focus

Think as a Reader/Writer

Use It in Your Writing Re-read your notes on how Bradbury incorporates factual information in his story. Jot down some ideas for a short story to be set during a particular historical period. How would you incorporate factual information about the period into your story? Develop the framework for your story's plot.

COMPARING TEXTS

Wrap Up

RA.L.8.6 Explain how an author's choice of genre affects the expression of a theme or topic. **RP.8.1** Apply reading comprehension strategies, including making predictions, comparing and contrasting, recalling and summarizing and making inferences and drawing conclusions. *Also covered* **WA.8.4.d**

The Battle of Shiloh / Drumbeats and Bullets / The Drummer Boy of Shiloh / How I Came to Write "The Drummer Boy of Shiloh"

Writing Focus

Writing a Comparison-and-Contrast Essay

Re-examine the selections in this feature, and write a comparison-and-contrast essay in which you compare the historical facts to Bradbury's fictional story.

Prewriting

Select a Topic To compare the historical facts to Bradbury's story, first decide what you want to say. Begin your essay with one of these statements:

- Based on the historical facts, Bradbury's story "The Drummer Boy of Shiloh" presents (or does not present) a believable portrait of a Civil War drummer boy.
- Based on the historical facts, Bradbury's story is a believable (or not a believable) account of events on the night before the battle of Shiloh.

Review the Elements of an Essay Now, review the elements of what makes a successful comparison-and-contrast essay before you begin writing. An effective essay—

- conveys a clear main idea
- is organized logically and consistently
- uses details from the texts to support ideas

Gather Details Create a chart like the one that follows to organize your ideas. Fill in details about "The Drummer Boy of Shiloh" and information from the historical sources. Then, compare the two columns to see how they match up—or don't.

Text Elements	"The Drummer Boy of Shiloh"	Historical facts
Setting	a peach orchard the night before the Battle of Shiloh	
Characters	Joby, general	
Events		

Drafting

Organize your essay. Most comparison-and-contrast essays are organized in either of these ways:

Point-by-Point Method	Block Method
Body paragraph: • Subject 1 detail • Subject 2 detail	Body paragraph: • All subject 1 details
Body paragraph: • Subject 1 detail • Subject 2 detail	Body paragraph: • All subject 2 details

Revising and Editing

Re-read your essay to make sure your main idea is clearly stated. Add transitional words to clarify your ideas. Proofread your essay.

What Do You Think Now?

How has learning about the Civil War affected you? What new understanding have you gained?

INFORMATIONAL TEXT FOCUS

Proposition and Support

Amistad, Anthony Hopkins, Dimon Hounsou (1997).

NOTE/SPEECH/EDITORIAL

Preparing to Read

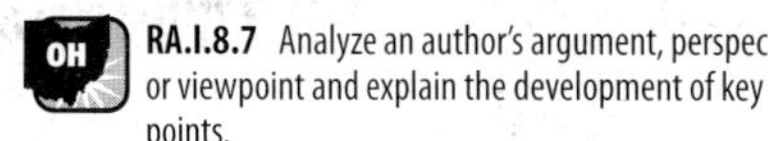

RA.I.8.7 Analyze an author's argument, perspective or viewpoint and explain the development of key points.

Use your **RWN** to complete the activities for these selections.

Fragment on Slavery, 1854 / *from* What to the Slave Is the Fourth of July? / Apologies for Past Actions Are Still Appropriate Today

Informational Text Focus

Proposition and Support Writers constantly try to persuade you to do things—to go somewhere, to buy something, to think a certain way. It's important to read persuasive arguments critically and to evaluate the writers' arguments to determine how credible, or believable, they are.

The writer of a persuasive article usually begins with a **proposition,** or an opinion. Then it is up to you to evaluate each reason that **supports** the proposition. A reason answers the question "Why?" about the proposition statement. Some types of support include **facts,** or true details, including the results of research or surveys; **statistics,** or facts in number form; **examples,** or instances that illustrate reasons or facts; **anecdotes,** or brief stories, such as personal experiences; definitions; and opinions from experts.

Into Action Fill in a chart like this one to help you identify the proposition and support provided in each informational text. Refer to the list above to help you categorize the supporting details.

"Fragment on Slavery"	"What to the Slave . . ."	"Apologies for Past . . ."
Proposition:	Proposition:	Proposition:
Support:	Support:	Support:

Writing Focus

Preparing for **Constructed Response**

On writing tests you are often asked to state an opinion and then support it with relevant details. As you read these selections, look for ways the writers signal that they are providing support. Write down these signals in your *Reader/Writer Notebook*.

Vocabulary

Fragment on Slavery, 1854

denounce (dih NOWNS) *v.:* speak against. *We must denounce all injustice.*

perpetuate (puhr PEHCH oo ayt) *v.:* cause to continue. *We are opposed to anything that can perpetuate injustice.*

conceded (kuhn SEED ihd) *v.:* admitted; acknowledged. *We conceded the point; we do not need to argue.*

hypocrisy (hih PAHK ruh see) *n.:* false show of virtue or goodness. *His hypocrisy is obvious because he says he is honest yet constantly lies.*

Apologies for Past Actions Are Still Appropriate . . .

despicable (DEHS pih kuh buhl) *adj.:* hateful; detested. *The institution of slavery is a despicable part of America's past.*

Language Coach

Word Origins The Latin word *cedere* means "to go." Look for the word in the list above that contains this word root. Many other English words are also built on this root. Here are some examples.

Word	Meaning
recede	go back
antecedent	something that comes before
exceed	go beyond

NOTE

Read with a Purpose

Read the note and speech to understand arguments against slavery.

Build Background

Abraham Lincoln, the U.S. president from 1861 to 1865, presided over the country during the American Civil War, in which Northern states and Southern states fought over the institution of slavery, among other issues. In 1863, Lincoln signed the Emancipation Proclamation, which freed all American slaves in the Southern states. Lincoln struggled with the political reality of slavery throughout his career. Some of his earliest writings on the practice date from the 1830s, years before he became president.

Fragment on Slavery, 1854

by Abraham Lincoln

If A can prove, however conclusively, that he may of right enslave B—why may not B snatch the same argument, and prove equally that he may enslave A? **A**

You say A is white, and B is black. It is color, then, the lighter having the right to enslave the darker? Take care. By this rule you are to be slave to the first man you meet with a fairer skin than your own.

You do not mean color exactly? You mean the whites are intellectually the superior of the blacks and, therefore, have the right to enslave them? Take care again. By this rule, you are to be slave to the first man you meet with an intellect superior to your own.

But, say you, it is a question of interest; and, if you can make it your interest, you have the right to enslave another. Very well. And if he can make it his interest, he has the right to enslave you. **B**

A **Informational Focus** **Proposition and Support** How does Lincoln use a question to present a proposition?

B **Read and Discuss** What is Lincoln doing with all these examples?

Read with a Purpose

Is Lincoln's argument convincing? Why or why not?

Abraham Lincoln (1860) by George Peter Alexander Henly.

SPEECH

from

What to the Slave Is the Fourth of July?

by Frederick Douglass

Build Background

Frederick Douglass was raised as a slave in Maryland. Although it was illegal in Maryland for a slave to be educated, Douglass managed to learn to read. After escaping slavery, Douglass became a passionate speaker against the institution. His speeches were so well written that some people in the audience doubted the story of his past. They did not believe that a former slave could express himself so well. As a result, Douglass decided to write his autobiography in 1845. Because he revealed the name of his former owner in it, Douglass had to leave the country. When he came back from Europe, he bought his freedom and launched a newspaper dedicated to the antislavery cause. He delivered this speech on July 5, 1852, in Rochester, New York.

Frederick Douglas (c. 1844) attributed to Elisha Hammond. Oil on canvas 69.9 x 57.1 cm.

Fellow citizens, pardon me, and allow me to ask, why am I called upon to speak here today? What have I or those I represent to do with your national independence? Are the great principles of political freedom and of natural justice, embodied in that Declaration of Independence, extended to us? And am I, therefore, called upon to bring our humble offering to the national altar, and to confess the benefits, and express devout gratitude for the blessings resulting from your independence to us? . . .

Fellow citizens, above your national, tumultuous joy, I hear the mournful wail of millions, whose chains, heavy and grievous yesterday, are today rendered more intolerable by the jubilant shouts that reach them. . . .

My subject, then, fellow citizens, is "American Slavery." I shall see this day and its popular characteristics from the slave's point of view. Standing here, identified with the American bondman,[1] making his wrongs mine, I do not hesitate to declare, with all my soul, that the character and conduct of this nation never looked blacker to me than on this Fourth of July.

. . . I will, in the name of humanity, which is outraged, in the name of liberty, which is fettered,[2] in the name of the Constitution and the Bible, which are disregarded and trampled upon, dare to call in question and to denounce, with all the emphasis I can command, everything that serves to perpetuate slavery—the

1. **bondman:** someone who is enslaved.
2. **fettered** (FEHT uhrd): in chains.

Vocabulary **denounce** (dih NOWNS) *v.:* speak against.
perpetuate (puhr PEHCH oo ayt) *v.:* cause to continue.

Analyzing Visuals

Viewing and Interpreting What is happening in this image? How does it relate to the ideas in Douglass's speech?

great sin and shame of America! "I will not equivocate[3]—I will not excuse." I will use the severest language I can command, and yet not one word shall escape me that any man, whose judgment is not blinded by prejudice, or who is not at heart a slave-holder, shall not confess to be right and just. . . . **A**

What point in the anti-slavery creed[4] would you have me argue? On what branch of the subject do the people of this country need light? Must I undertake to prove that the slave is a man? That point is conceded already. Nobody doubts it. The slave-holders themselves acknowledge it in the enactment of laws for their government. They acknowledge it when they punish disobedience on the part of the slave. There are seventy-two crimes in the State of Virginia, which, if committed by a black man (no matter how ignorant he be), subject him to the punishment of death; while only two of these same crimes will subject a white man to like punishment. **B**

What is this but the acknowledgment that the slave is a moral, intellectual, and responsible being? The manhood of the slave is conceded. It is admitted in the fact that Southern statute books are covered with enactments, forbidding, under severe fines and penalties, the teaching of the slave to read and write. When you can point to any such laws in reference to the beasts of the field, then I may consent to argue the manhood of the slave. When the dogs in your streets, when the fowls of the air, when the cattle on your hills, when the fish of the sea, and the reptiles that crawl, shall be unable to distinguish the slave from a brute, then I will argue with you that the slave is a man!

For the present it is enough to affirm the equal manhood of the Negro race. Is it not astonishing that, while we are plowing, planting, and reaping, using all kinds of mechanical tools, erecting houses, constructing bridges, building ships, working in metals of brass,

3. **equivocate** (ih KWIHV uh kayt): speak vaguely; try to mislead by speaking indirectly.

4. **creed:** belief.

A Informational Focus Proposition and Support
How does Douglass introduce his proposition? What is his proposition?

B Informational Focus Proposition and Support
What facts does Douglass give to prove that the state of Virginia regards slaves as men?

Vocabulary **conceded** (kuhn SEED ihd) *v.:* admitted; acknowledged.

iron, copper, silver, and gold; that while we are reading, writing, and ciphering,[5] acting as clerks, merchants, and secretaries, having among us lawyers, doctors, ministers, poets, authors, editors, orators, and teachers; that we are engaged in all the enterprises common to other men—digging gold in California, capturing the whale in the Pacific, feeding sheep and cattle on the hillside, living, moving, acting, thinking, planning, living in families as husbands, wives, and children, and above all, confessing and worshipping the Christian God, and looking hopefully for life and immortality beyond the grave—we are called upon to prove that we are men? **C**

Would you have me argue that man is entitled to liberty? That he is the rightful owner of his own body? You have already declared it. Must I argue the wrongfulness of slavery? Is that a question for republicans?[6] Is it to be settled by the rules of logic and argumentation, as a matter beset with great difficulty, involving a doubtful application of the principle of justice, hard to understand? How should I look today in the presence of Americans, dividing and subdividing a discourse, to show that men have a natural right to freedom, speaking of it relatively and positively, negatively and affirmatively? To do so would be to make myself ridiculous, and to offer an insult to your understanding. There is not a man beneath the canopy of heaven who does not know that slavery is wrong for him.

5. **ciphering** (SY fuhr ihng): doing arithmetic.
6. **republicans:** citizens who believe in the elected government, a republic.

What! Am I to argue that it is wrong to make men brutes, to rob them of their liberty, to work them without wages, to keep them ignorant of their relations to their fellow men, to beat them with sticks, to flay their flesh with the lash, to load their limbs with irons, to hunt them with dogs, to sell them at auction, to sunder[7] their families, to knock out their teeth, to burn their flesh, to starve them into obedience and submission to their masters? Must I argue that a system thus marked with blood and stained with pollution is wrong? No—I will not. I have better employment for my time and strength than such arguments would imply. . . . **D**

At a time like this, scorching irony, not convincing argument, is needed. Oh! had I the ability, and could I reach the nation's ear, I would today pour out a fiery stream of biting ridicule, blasting reproach, withering sarcasm, and stern rebuke. For it is not light that is needed, but fire; it is not the gentle shower, but thunder. We need the storm, the whirlwind, and the earthquake. The feeling of the nation must be quickened; the conscience of the nation must be roused; the propriety[8] of the nation must be startled; the hypocrisy of the nation must be exposed; and its crimes against God and man must be denounced. . . . **E**

7. **sunder:** drive apart; separate.
8. **propriety** (pruh PRY uh tee): sense of correct behavior.

Read with a Purpose

What are Douglass's main arguments against slavery?

C Informational Focus Proposition and Support
What support does Douglass provide here?

D Read and Discuss What is Douglass talking about here? Why has Douglass provided such brutal details?

E Informational Focus Proposition and Support
How does the conclusion of Douglass's speech relate to his initial proposition?

Vocabulary **hypocrisy** (hih PAHK ruh see) *n.:* false show of virtue or goodness.

Apologies for Past Actions Are Still Appropriate TODAY

The Macon Telegraph

Read with a Purpose

Read this editorial to see how aspects of slavery continue to be debated.

FEB. 21, 2007, MACON, GEORGIA—The mayor of Macon has issued an executive order apologizing for the city's role in the institution of slavery. According to the 1830 U.S. Census, Bibb County had a population of 7,154, of which 2,988 were slaves. In 1830, Georgia had a population of 516,823, and of those, 217,531 were slaves. Two states, Kentucky and South Carolina, had more slaves than free persons. Mississippi's white population outnumbered the slave population by less than 5,000.

While some will have questions about the mayor's motives or disagree with an apology, there is no question that the despicable institution of slavery is part of our nation's legacy. Slaves were first brought to this country in 1619, one year before the pilgrims landed at Plymouth Rock, and whatever our country's fortunes are, the backbone of those fortunes rested on the economic shoulders of slave labor. **A**

It's easy to wonder in 2007 how this country, founded on freedom, could have stood for such an institution. Certainly, it was a different time. Thankfully, civilization has progressed to the point of recognizing each individual's intrinsic value, and we have come to understand the true meaning of "We hold these truths to be self-evident, that all men are created equal, that they are endowed by their Creator with certain unalienable Rights."

A Informational Focus **Proposition and Support** What is this editorial's proposition? How do statistics support this proposition?

Vocabulary **despicable** (DEHS pih kuh buhl) *adj.:* hateful; detested.

Monument (by sculptor Ed Dwight) to the underground railroad, on Detroit's riverfront.

With that said, why do some Americans have so much trouble dealing with historical records that lead to the conclusion that an apology for slavery is not only warranted but necessary? Though slavery was ended with the 14th and 15th amendments to the Constitution, the effects of hundreds of years of servitude still live on in a race of people who were enslaved simply on the basis of their skin color. Those who feel absolved of responsibility by saying they had nothing to do with slavery should look around. They are enjoying today the white privileges that were etched in law only to be recently erased; the ultimate affirmative action program[1] of which they are beneficiaries. **B**

In the scope of things the mayor's apology may mean little to the city, but it could mean a lot to him. That's OK. Each government entity has to examine its own history before taking such a step. In Maine, Indiana, Massachusetts, New Hampshire and Ohio, the slave population, according to the census, was in the single digits. Vermont didn't have a single slave, but in a city where the African-American population is 62.5 percent, it is more than likely the slaves that inhabited the area are the ancestors of many present-day residents.

Issuing an official apology and recognizing the contributions of slaves can have a cathartic[2] effect, not only for the descendants of slaves, but for the descendants of slave owners—some of whom are still living in the area, too. **C**

1. **affirmative action program:** plan that aims to correct past discrimination by giving preference to members of certain groups, such as African Americans, Native Americans, or women.

2. **cathartic** (kuh THAHR tihk): causing relief from emotional tensions.

Read with a Purpose

How are some aspects of slavery still being debated?

B Informational Focus **Proposition and Support** What argument in this paragraph supports the editorial's proposition?

C Read and Discuss What point is the author making here?

NOTE/SPEECH/EDITORIAL

Applying Your Skills

Fragment on Slavery, 1854 / *from* What to the Slave Is the Fourth of July? / Apologies for Past Actions Are Still Appropriate Today

Practicing the Standards

Informational Text and Vocabulary

1. What is Lincoln's basic **argument** in "Fragment on Slavery"?
   A Slavery can be proven right.
   B Slavery is an oppressive institution.
   C Everybody could become a slave.
   D Arguments for slavery do not hold up.

2. How does Lincoln support his **proposition** in "Fragment on Slavery"?
   A He offers counterarguments to the propositions of others.
   B He poses a series of open-ended questions.
   C He draws conclusions based on predictions.
   D He offers statistics that show slavery is wrong.

3. What **proposition** does Douglass support in his speech?
   A Slavery is immoral and unjust.
   B Virginia is a slave state.
   C It is illegal for slaves to learn to read.
   D The Fourth of July celebrates independence.

4. Which of these **arguments** used by Douglass supports his proposition?
   A The slave is a moral, intellectual, and responsible being.
   B The Constitution and the Bible denounce slavery.
   C Virginia state law holds the slave accountable for seventy-two crimes.
   D All of the above

5. To support its **proposition,** the *Macon Telegraph* editorial uses all of following *except* —
   A facts
   B anecdotes
   C logical reasoning
   D statistics

6. Which of following facts provides support for the **proposition** that an apology for slavery is still relevant today?
   A Vermont didn't have a single slave.
   B In 1830, Georgia had a population of 516,823.
   C Descendants of slaves and slaveholders are still alive.
   D Slavery is a despicable institution.

RA.I.8.7 Analyze an author's argument, perspective or viewpoint and explain the development of key points. **RA.I.8.8** Recognize how writers cite facts, draw inferences and present opinions in informational text. **WA.8.5.a** Write persuasive compositions that: establish and develop a controlling idea; *Also covered* **VO.8.4**

7. Which of the following **propositions** is *not* found in these selections?

A Slavery can't be defended by logic.

B Slaves should be taught to read and write.

C The legacy of slavery is still relevant today.

D Slavery is unfair and inhumane.

8. If you *denounce* a suggested rule, you —

A support it with facts

B speak out against it

C do not understand it

D prove that it is fair

9. When you *perpetuate* something, you —

A explain it

B cease doing it

C ignore it

D keep it going

10. Which of the following sentences uses the word *conceded* correctly?

A I *conceded* the picnic with my friends.

B He *conceded* she had a superior argument.

C She *conceded* because it was her first time doing the task.

D Presented with a gift, she *conceded* her thanks.

11. One example of *hypocrisy* is —

A planning carefully for an important event

B ignoring the advice that people give you

C saying one thing but doing something else

D taking the blame for something you did

12. If something is *despicable,* it is —

A lovely

B dreamlike

C frozen

D horrible

Writing Focus **Constructed Response**

Think about the arguments presented in the *Macon Telegraph* editorial. Then, write a letter to the editor in response to it, either agreeing or disagreeing with the writer's position.

What Do You Think Now?

Has your understanding of how slavery continues to affect the United States changed after reading the selections? Explain.

Writing Workshop

Persuasive Writing

Write with a Purpose

Write a persuasive essay supporting your position on an important issue. Your **purpose** is to explain your point of view and give your audience good reasons to agree with you. Take into account the concerns of your **audience,** which may consist of classmates, teachers, parents, school board members, or local newspaper readers.

A Good Persuasive Essay

- includes a thesis statement that clearly states a position on an issue
- presents at least three strong reasons to support the position
- supports each reason with evidence, logical arguments, and possibly emotional appeals
- is clearly organized and presents a consistent point of view
- anticipates objections and addresses counter arguments
- concludes with a restatement of the writer's position and possibly a call to action

See page 582 for complete rubric.

Use your **RWN** to complete the activities for this workshop.

Think as a Reader/Writer

In your daily conversations you often find yourself explaining and defending your ideas. In this workshop you'll write an essay in which you present an opinion and try to persuade others to agree with you. Before you begin, read these excerpts from Dr. Martin Luther King, Jr.'s, powerful "I Have a Dream" speech (page 529), delivered on August 28, 1963, in Washington, D.C.

I say to you today, my friends, that in spite of the difficulties and frustrations of the moment I still have a dream. It is a dream deeply rooted in the American Dream.

← King acknowledges his **audience's** feelings.

I have a dream that one day this nation will rise up and live out the true meaning of its creed: "We hold these truths to be self-evident; that all men are created equal."

← Quoting a well-known authority, the U.S. Declaration of Independence, **supports** his position.

I have a dream that one day on the red hills of Georgia the sons of former slaves and the sons of former slave owners will be able to sit down together at the table of brotherhood.

I have a dream that one day even the state of Mississippi, a desert state sweltering with the heat of injustice and oppression, will be transformed into an oasis of freedom and justice.

I have a dream that my four little children will one day live in a nation where they will not be judged by the color of their skin but by the content of their character. . . .

← King restates his **main point** in fresh ways, adding more **details.**

When we let freedom ring, . . . we will be able to speed up that day when all God's children . . . will be able to join hands and sing . . . "Free at last! Free at last! Thank God almighty, we are free at last!"

← He makes an **emotional appeal** and a **call to action.**

Think About the Professional Model

With a partner, discuss the following questions about the model.

1. What opinion does King support in this speech? How does he support this opinion in this excerpt?
2. What was King's purpose for writing? Was he successful? Explain.

WA.8.5.a Write persuasive compositions that: establish and develop a controlling idea; **WA.8.5.b** Write persuasive compositions that: support arguments with detailed evidence

Prewriting

Choose an Issue

An **issue** is a subject about which people disagree. When choosing an issue to write about, try to find something that is controversial and important to many people. Brainstorm issues with a partner or small group. Evaluate possible ideas by completing a chart like the one below. If you can answer "yes" to all three of the questions, you may have found a great issue for your essay.

What are some possible issues?	Is the issue debatable?	Do I have strong feelings about the issue?	Would other people have strong feelings about the issue?
leash laws in local parks	Yes. Some people think dogs should always be on leashes.	No. My dog would run away if it was off leash.	Yes. Some dog owners want no-leash hours before 9 AM and after 9 PM.
starting a paper recycling program at our school	Yes. Some people think recycling is too much trouble, but others think it is important.	Yes. I believe that what we do to the planet today will affect it—and us—in the future.	Yes. Some of my friends are worried that we are destroying the planet.

Write a Thesis Statement

Where do you stand on the issue you have chosen? In a persuasive essay, your **thesis statement,** or opinion statement, should identify the issue and make your position clear. A good thesis is focused and consistent; it establishes a tone that will prepare the reader to consider your point of view. Here is a formula you can follow for writing your thesis statement:

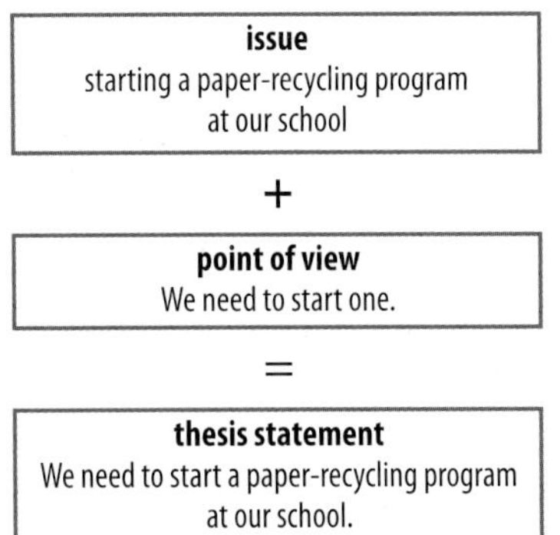

issue
starting a paper-recycling program at our school
+
point of view
We need to start one.
=
thesis statement
We need to start a paper-recycling program at our school.

Idea Starters

Think about current controversies in these areas:

- neighborhood changes, such as a new mall or park
- school dress code
- extended school year
- limits on Internet access
- leash laws for dogs
- making "volunteer" work mandatory

Peer Review

Ask a partner to review your three best ideas. Ask which idea your partner thinks would make the most interesting essay. You might also ask your partner's opinion on each issue. If you find out that you and your partner disagree, consider choosing that topic. Your goal could be to change your partner's mind.

Your Turn

Get Started Brainstorm a list of issues in your **RWN.** Then, make a chart to evaluate the issues. After reviewing the chart, choose the best issue for your essay.

Next, write a **thesis statement.** Make sure your thesis tells both your issue and your point of view.

Learn It Online
An interactive graphic organizer can help you organize your ideas. Try one at:

go.hrw.com L8-575 

Writing Tip

You can use analogies and comparisons to help your audience understand how you see things. An **analogy** compares two seemingly unlike actions, ideas, or things by pointing out a similarity between them: "Recycling paper is like fighting forest fires: both save trees." A **comparison** is more straightforward: "Recycling paper and using public transportation are both effective ways to help the environment."

Think About Audience and Purpose

As you plan, keep your **audience** and **purpose** in mind. Your **audience** may be members of your school community or perhaps the readers of a local newspaper. When you write a persuasive essay, your **purpose** is to convince your readers to agree with you on a controversial issue and, perhaps, to inspire them to action.

Support Your Position

The key to successful persuasion is developing a strong argument. Once you have stated your thesis, your task is to develop at least three strong reasons to support your position. Then, jot down the supporting evidence (examples, statistics, and quotations) that backs up each reason.

Choose Appeals to Reason and to Emotions

In your argument, you'll want to appeal both to your readers' sense of logic and to their emotions. **Appeals to reason,** or logical appeals, are the evidence that will persuade your readers' minds. Appeals to reason include facts, research, and quotations.

Effective persuasive writing also includes **emotional appeals**—reasons and expressions that affect how your audience feels—their hearts. You might choose words that you know are likely to make your audience angry, frustrated, or hopeful. Be sure to select emotional appeals that are right for your audience. Below are examples of each type of appeal.

Appeals to Reason	Appeals to Emotions
• facts and examples • research and survey results • statistics—facts in numerical form • anecdotes—brief true stories • direct quotations	• statements that appeal to an audience's sense of right or responsibility • language that is charged with emotion • anecdotes that create a strong emotional response

Gather Evidence

To be convincing, a persuasive essay needs **evidence** readers can trust. Here are some sources you can use to locate strong evidence:

- Use Web sites, but be sure you use trustworthy sites, such as those for universities, respected magazines and newspapers, or online reference works.
- Contact experts to provide evidence. Expert opinions can strengthen your argument and their credentials will impress readers.
- Search books, magazine and newspaper articles, and encyclopedias for facts and statistics that support your argument.

Your Turn

Plan Your Essay In your **RWN,** list three reasons your reader should support your position. Then, create a two-column chart and gather the evidence—**appeals to reason** and **appeals to emotions**—that you will use in your essay.

Drafting

Organize and Draft Your Essay

Use a framework like the one to the right to organize and draft your essay. Consider arranging your reasons in order of importance. You can present the most important reason first and follow with less important reasons, or you can begin with the least important reason and build up to the most important one.

Framework for a Persuasive Essay

Introduction

- Attention-grabbing beginning
- Thesis statement

Body

- Reason #1 (evidence: appeals to reason and emotion)
- Reason #2 (evidence: appeals to reason and emotion)
- Reason #3 (evidence: appeals to reason and emotion

Conclusion

- Restatement of opinion
- Summary of reasons
- Call to action or closing statement

Elaborate on Your Ideas

You can elaborate on your ideas by defining words that your readers may not know, explaining the way a piece of evidence supports a reason, adding evidence such as an example or a quote from an expert, or using a comparison to illustrate an idea.

End with a Bang

You might end your essay forcefully with a **call to action.** Ask your audience to take a specific action, such as voting a certain way or joining a volunteer group.

Grammar Link **Avoiding Run-on Sentences**

Your persuasive essay will be more effective if your ideas are clearly expressed. Writing about a topic you care about could lead you to create a **run-on sentence**—two or more complete thoughts that are run together as if they were one complete sentence. Avoid this problem while you draft by thinking about the idea you want to express in each sentence. Here are two strategies you can use to avoid run-on sentences.

Write Two Sentences Instead of One

Run-on Sentence: We could save over one hundred trees a year, we should start today.

Correct: We could save over one hundred trees a year**. We** should start today.

Write a Sentence with a Comma and a Conjunction

Run-on Sentence: Our school uses about six tons of paper a year we could reduce that amount.

Correct: Our school uses about six tons of paper a year**, but** we could reduce that amount.

Reference Note For more information on run-on sentences, see the Language Handbook.

Writing Tip

Remember that some of your readers may not agree with your position on the issue. You need to address their concerns, or counterarguments, by showing you understand their views. You don't have to agree with the counterargument; just indicate you're aware of it.

Your Turn

Outline Your Essay Using the notes in your chart, make an outline. Then, using your outline and the basic elements of a persuasive essay, create your first draft. Also think about these questions:

- What tone will you use to appeal to your audience?
- How can your writing style persuade your audience that you know your issue and that they should believe you?
- How can you use conjunctions and punctuation to avoid run-on sentences?

Peer Review

As you read your partner's persuasive essay, think about the issue. Did reading the draft change your opinion about the issue? Why or why not? Are there any important aspects of the topic that the writer left out?

Evaluating and Revising

Read the questions in the left column of the chart, and then use the tips in the middle column to help you make revisions to your essay. The right column suggests techniques you can use to revise your draft.

Persuasive Essay: Guidelines for Content and Organization

Evaluation Questions	Tips	Revision Techniques
1. Does your introduction contain a clear thesis statement?	**Circle** the sentence or sentences that state the issue and your position.	**Add** a thesis statement or **revise** your statement for clarity.
2. Are the paragraphs in the essay arranged in order of importance?	**Number** the paragraphs in order of importance.	**Rearrange** the paragraphs if necessary.
3. Have you provided reasons and evidence to support your opinion?	**Put a star** next to each reason, and **highlight** your evidence.	**Add** reasons, or add an example, statistic, anecdote, comparison, or expert opinion to support a reason, if needed.
4. Does the body of your paper include elaboration to clarify reasons or evidence? Have you addressed counterarguments?	**Draw a box** around anything that needs to be clarified. **List** any counterarguments that have not been addressed.	**Elaborate** by adding explanations and addressing reader concerns.
5. Does your paper present a consistent point of view?	**Draw a wavy line** under any sentence that does not support the position expressed in the thesis statement.	**Cut** any lines of argument that do not support your position.
6. Does your conclusion restate your opinion and summarize your reasons? Is there a call to action?	**Underline** the restatement, the summary, and the call to action.	**Add** a restatement, summary, and call to action if necessary.

Read this student draft, and notice the comments on its strengths as well as suggestions on how it could be improved.

Student Draft

Letter to the School Board

by Teresa Lacey, Franklin Middle School

Distinguished Members of the School Board:

I am in favor of the proposed requirement that eighth-graders spend fifteen hours during the school year volunteering to help the elderly.

One reason this would be a good idea is that it would be a learning experience. Students could learn how to work with and relate to older people.

Another reason I think this rule would be magnificent is that it is a good way to help others. Eighth-graders can help people who cannot do things themselves. Students could do yard work or housework, run errands, or just spend time with the elderly so they would not be alone.

← Teresa's **thesis statement** clearly states the issue and her opinion.

← Teresa's first **reason** is presented and explained.

← Her second **reason** is presented and followed by specific examples.

MINI-LESSON How to Include Logical and Emotional Appeals

In persuasive writing, reasons must be fully supported with **logical evidence** (for instance, **examples, facts,** or **anecdotes**). **Emotional appeals** are also an effective way to persuade your audience. Teresa reviewed her draft and added a personal anecdote that presents logical evidence. She also changed several words to make the project sound more exciting. These changes created emotional appeals. Notice how the new paragraph supports Teresa's **thesis.**

Teresa's Revision of Paragraph Two

One reason this would be a good idea is that it would be a learning experience. Students could learn how to work with and relate to older people. *My mother works at a nursing home, so I have had the opportunity to help her in the summer. I have learned to help with the residents there by playing games or walking with them, or by reading aloud to them. But it's not just a one-way street! The people there have taught me lessons about getting through tough times and about friendship. I love hearing the stories they tell about their lives.*

Your Turn

Include Logical and Emotional Appeals Read your draft and then ask yourself:

- Have I fully supported each of my reasons with logical evidence?
- Have I used language and writing strategies that will get an emotional response from my audience?

Consider adding logical or emotional appeals to strengthen your persuasion.

Student Draft *continues*

Finally, I think just spending at least fifteen hours a school year with the elderly would improve students' people skills. Students would learn to talk to and relate to others. They would learn how to be less shy, too. In a recent *Time* magazine poll, sixty percent of people becoming nurses in care homes said they learned how to talk to residents and their families more confidently.

Teresa includes **statistics** to back up her claim.

For all these reasons, I believe the proposed requirement for volunteering would make a good rule. I hope that you will consider my reasons and vote to accept the proposed requirement.

She concludes with a strong, direct **call to action.**

MINI-LESSON How to Address Counterarguments

Anticipating an objection your audience might raise to your opinion can be very persuasive. When Teresa was reviewing her draft, her partner had one comment: "I already have so much to do, how could I possibly add in volunteering to my busy schedule?"

Teresa thought about the question. She decided to include a **counterargument** and her response in her essay. To do this, Teresa decided on the strongest response to a concern about the time volunteering might take. She argues that volunteering would not be as time-consuming as readers might expect. She added this paragraph immediately before her conclusion.

Teresa's Revision Before the Conclusion

Some students might argue that they already have too much work to do. It's true that we have many obligations, but the proposal is for just fifteen hours per school year. If those hours are spread out over nine months, it works out to less than two hours a month. The benefits to both students and community residents would be worth a little rescheduling.

For all these reasons, I believe the proposed requirement for volunteering would make a good rule. I hope that you will consider my reasons and vote to accept the proposed requirement.

Your Turn

Addressing Counterarguments

Consider how readers might respond to your opinions. Ask yourself the following questions:

- What are some of the objections that readers might raise to your ideas?
- How can you respond to these arguments?

Look for a place in your essay where you might address possible counterarguments. If you have already done so, check that your appeals are as persuasive as possible.

Proofreading and Publishing

Proofreading

Look for errors you may have introduced when cutting and moving material. Also, be sure that you have documented your evidence and double-checked examples, statistics, names, and quotations. When you are done, exchange your essay with a partner. Read your partner's essay once for grammatical errors and then once again for spelling errors.

Grammar Link **Placing Modifiers**

Place modifying words, phrases, and clauses as near as possible to the words they modify.

Misplaced Modifier: When she is on a leash, the owner controls the dog. (Is the owner leashed?)
Revision: The owner controls the dog when she is on the leash. (The clause modifies *dog*.)

Dangling Modifier: Securely fenced and clean, people can let their dogs play freely. (The adjectives cannot logically modify anything in this sentence.)
Revision: People can let their dogs play freely in the securely fenced and clean park. (The missing noun *park* is added.)

Publishing

Here are some suggestions on how you might share your persuasive essay with a larger audience.

- Submit your essay as an editorial to a school or community newspaper.
- Post your essay on an Internet bulletin board where your audience is likely to read it.

Reflect on the Process In your **RWN,** write short responses to the questions below.

1. How do you think your essay could have been more convincing to your audience? Explain.
2. Did your essay achieve your purpose for writing? In what way?
3. How did addressing possible counterarguments help you better understand an opposing viewpoint? Explain.

Proofreading Tip

Take a break before you proofread your essay. If you go right from revising to proofreading, you might be tired and overly familiar with your words. As a result, you might miss some obvious errors. After a short break, your brain will be clear and ready to catch mistakes.

Your Turn

Proofread and Publish

Proofread your essay for grammar, mechanics, and usage mistakes. Pay special attention to placement of modifiers. Publish your essay for your audience.

Scoring Rubric

You can use one of the rubrics below to evaluate your persuasive essay from the Writing Workshop or from the activity on the next page. Your teacher will tell you which rubric to use.

6-Point Scale

Score 6 *Demonstrates advanced success*
- focuses consistently on a clear and reasonable position
- shows effective organization throughout, with smooth transitions
- offers thoughtful, creative ideas and reasons
- supports a position thoroughly, using convincing, fully elaborated reasons and evidence
- exhibits mature control of written language

Score 5 *Demonstrates proficient success*
- focuses on a clear and reasonable position
- shows effective organization, with transitions
- offers thoughtful ideas and reasons
- supports a position competently, using convincing, well-elaborated reasons and evidence
- exhibits sufficient control of written language

Score 4 *Demonstrates competent success*
- focuses on a reasonable position, with minor distractions
- shows effective organization, with minor lapses
- offers mostly thoughtful ideas and reasons
- elaborates reasons and evidence with a mixture of the general and the specific
- exhibits general control of written language

Score 3 *Demonstrates limited success*
- includes some loosely related ideas that distract from the writer's position
- shows some organization, with noticeable gaps in the logical flow of ideas
- offers routine, predictable ideas and reasons
- supports ideas with uneven reasoning and elaboration
- exhibits limited control of written language

Score 2 *Demonstrates basic success*
- includes loosely related ideas that seriously distract from the writer's persuasive purpose
- shows minimal organization, with major gaps in the logical flow of ideas
- offers ideas and reasons that merely skim the surface
- supports ideas with inadequate reasoning and elaboration
- exhibits significant problems with control of written language

Score 1 *Demonstrates emerging effort*
- shows little awareness of the topic and purpose for writing
- lacks organization
- offers unclear and confusing ideas
- demonstrates minimal persuasive reasoning or elaboration
- exhibits major problems with control of written language

4-Point Scale

Score 4 *Demonstrates advanced success*
- focuses consistently on a clear and reasonable position
- shows effective organization throughout, with smooth transitions
- offers thoughtful, creative ideas and reasons
- supports a position thoroughly, using convincing, fully elaborated reasons and evidence
- exhibits mature control of written language

Score 3 *Demonstrates competent success*
- focuses on a reasonable position, with minor distractions
- shows effective organization, with minor lapses
- offers mostly thoughtful ideas and reasons
- elaborates reasons and evidence with a mixture of the general and the specific
- exhibits general control of written language

Score 2 *Demonstrates limited success*
- includes some loosely related ideas that distract from the writer's position
- shows some organization, with noticeable gaps in the logical flow of ideas
- offers routine, predictable ideas and reasons
- supports ideas with uneven reasoning and elaboration
- exhibits limited control of written language

Score 1 *Demonstrates emerging effort*
- shows little awareness of the topic and purpose for writing
- lacks organization
- offers unclear and confusing ideas
- demonstrates minimal persuasive reasoning or elaboration
- exhibits major problems with control of written language

Persuasive Essay

When responding to a prompt, use what you've learned from your reading, writing your persuasive essay, and studying the rubrics on page 582. Use the steps below to develop a response to the following prompt.

Writing Prompt
Students have many choices when deciding how to spend their time after school in extracurricular activities. Write an essay persuading a friend to join the activity that you enjoy the most. Convince your friend with strong reasons and persuasive appeals.

Study the Prompt

Begin by reading the prompt carefully. Circle or underline key words: *extracurricular activities, after school, enjoy.*

The word *convince* tells you to use a *persuasive* approach in your essay. You will explain *why* you enjoy the activity and more importantly, *why* your friend will enjoy it. Your reasons must appeal to your audience. **Tip:** Spend about five minutes studying the prompt.

Plan Your Response

Make a list of your extracurricular activities and think about which one would appeal to your friend. Possible activities might include exercising, working with others, competing on academic or sports teams, volunteering, or tutoring other students.

Ask yourself *why* you enjoy the activity. Then think about the reasons that your friend might also enjoy the activity. They might be the same reasons. Decide on two or three reasons to support the position that your friend should join you in this extracurricular activity. Use examples and anecdotes, or brief stories, to support each reason.

Plan your reasons so that your most persuasive reason is presented last to end the essay as strongly as possible. Emotional language helps make your persuasive appeal more effective. **Tip:** Spend about ten minutes planning your response.

Respond to the Prompt

One way to begin this essay is to describe the extracurricular activity and invite your friend to join. Use one reason for each body paragraph. Remember to appeal to what your friend enjoys and values with specific examples and anecdotes. Conclude your persuasive essay with a brief scenario about the two of you enjoying the activity together. **Tip:** Spend about twenty minutes writing your persuasive essay.

Improve Your Response

Revising Go back to the key aspects of the prompt. Did you fully describe what the activity is and what it involves? Does your essay provide persuasive reasons to convince your reader that joining you in the extracurricular activity is a good idea? Have you added specific examples or anecdotes to make the essay more convincing? If not, add these elements to your essay.

Proofreading Take time to reread and edit your response to correct errors in grammar, spelling, punctuation, and capitalization. Make sure that your edits are neat and the paper is legible.

Checking Your Final Copy Before you turn in your paper, read it one more time to catch any errors you may have missed. You'll be glad you took this extra step. **Tip:** Save five or ten minutes to improve your paper.

Presenting a Persuasive Speech

Speak with a Purpose

Adapt your persuasive essay into a persuasive speech. Rehearse your speech, and then present it to your class.

Think as a Reader/Writer Speaking to persuade and writing to persuade are similar skills. However, to give an effective speech, you will need to do much more than read a persuasive essay directly from the page; you will need to deliver your most important points in a solid presentation that will grab the attention of your audience.

Adapt Your Essay

Consider Your Audience, Message, and Purpose

If your listening **audience** is different from your essay's audience, you will need to reconsider the content of your **message** to make sure that it relates to the listeners' backgrounds and interests. Consider what reasons, examples, and facts would appeal to those who will be listening. For example, if you are giving a speech to convince a group of parents to contribute money for the creation of an art gallery in the school's hallways, you can connect with your audience by stressing that the gallery would display the work of students—their children—not professionals. Making the content of your speech match your audience's backgrounds and interests will help you achieve your **purpose**—to persuade listeners that your opinion is the right one.

Organize Your Speech

Even the best message can get lost in rambling sentences and wandering ideas. To make sure your speech is **coherent,** or easily understood, be certain that all your ideas are clearly related, given in an order that makes sense, and connected with **transitional words** and **phrases.**

Once you have identified which pieces of support from your essay need to be changed to fit your listening audience, you can start organizing your speech notes. The first step in organizing is to identify the most important points and write brief sentences and phrases about those points on notecards or in an **outline.** Once you have your points listed on notecards, you can number them in the order you want to present them.

Use your **RWN** to complete the activities for this workshop.

C.8.2 Identify and analyze the persuasive techniques used in presentations and media messages. **C.8.9** Deliver formal and informal descriptive presentations that convey relevant information and descriptive details. **C.8.5** Demonstrate an understanding of the rules of the English language and select language appropriate to purpose and audience. **C.8.10.b** Deliver persuasive presentations that: include relevant evidence, differentiating between evidence and opinion to support a position and to address counter-arguments or listener bias

Deliver Your Speech

Since the purpose of your speech is to persuade others, your delivery, or the way you give the speech, is critical. To ensure that your speech runs smoothly, practice giving it more than once. Keep the following suggestions in mind as you practice:

- **If possible, practice in front of an audience** so that you can get used to speaking in front of a group.
- **Practice using your notecards** just as you will use them on the day of your speech.
- **Use a timer or watch** to ensure that you stay within the time limit you have been given.
- **Finally, review the evaluation guidelines below.** Knowing how your audience will evaluate your presentation will help you prepare.

Guidelines for Evaluating a Persuasive Speech	
Content	• What is the purpose of the speech? Paraphrase the speaker's purpose. • What is the topic? Paraphrase the speaker's point of view on the topic. Does the speaker clearly state his or her opinion? • Which reasons are convincing and which are not? Are they supported?
Delivery	• Describe the speaker's tone. Is it conversational or does it sound too formal? • Does the speaker speak loudly and slowly enough? • How often does the speaker make eye contact with the audience? • How do the speaker's nonverbal messages (such as gestures and facial expressions) match the verbal message? Are any of the gestures distracting? In what way are they distracting?
Credibility (Believability)	• What is the speaker's bias? How do you know? • What facts has the speaker used to support his or her opinion? • Does the speaker have unsupported opinions? What are they?

A Good Persuasive Speech

- is tailored to listeners' backgrounds and interests
- has a clear message and purpose and convincing support
- is coherent, with clearly connected ideas
- uses transitional words and phrases for clarity
- uses verbal and nonverbal cues to reinforce the message of the speech

Speaking Tip

Remember that you are the creator of your speech, and you can modify it to respond to audience feedback, if necessary. Some modifications you can make are to spend more or less time on a point, add some humor, or speak more loudly.

Learn It Online

Pictures, cartoons, graphs, and charts can make your speech stand out. See how on MediaScope:

go.hrw.com  L8-585 

Literary Skills Review

Nonfiction **Directions:** Read the following selection. Then, read and respond to the questions that follow.

from The Power of Nonviolence

John Lewis,
interviewed by Joan Morrison and Robert K. Morrison

When I was a boy, I would go downtown to the little town of Troy, and I'd see the signs saying "White" and "Colored" on the water fountains. There'd be a beautiful, shining water fountain in one corner of the store marked "White," and in another corner was just a little spigot marked "Colored." I saw the signs saying "White Men," "Colored Men," and "White Women," "Colored Women." And at the theater we had to go upstairs to go to a movie. You bought your ticket at the same window that the white people did, but they could sit downstairs, and you had to go upstairs.

I wondered about that, because it was not in keeping with my religious faith, which taught me that we were all the same in the eyes of God. And I had been taught that all men are created equal.

It really hit me when I was fifteen years old, when I heard about Martin Luther King, Jr., and the Montgomery bus boycott. Black people were walking the streets for more than a year rather than riding segregated buses. To me it was like a great sense of hope, a light. Many of the teachers at the high school that I attended were from Montgomery, and they would tell us about what was happening there. That, more than any other event, was the turning point for me, I think. It gave me a way out. . . .

Lewis went on to college, where he attended workshops and studied the philosophy of nonviolence.

In February, 1960, we planned the first mass lunch-counter sit-in. About five hundred students, black and white, from various colleges showed up and participated in a nonviolent workshop the night before the sit-in. Some of them came from as far away as Pomona College in California and Beloit College in Wisconsin.

We made a list of what we called the "Rules of the Sit-in"—the do's and don'ts—and we mimeographed it on an old machine and passed it out to all the students. I wish I had a copy of this list today. I remember it said things like, "Sit up straight. Don't talk back. Don't Laugh. Don't strike back." And at the end it said,

An African American student sits at a lunch counter reserved for white customers during a March 25, 1960, sit-in.

"Remember the teachings of Jesus, Gandhi, Thoreau, Martin Luther King, Jr."

Then the next day it began. We wanted to make a good impression. The young men put on their coats and ties, and the young ladies their heels and stockings. We selected seven stores to go into, primarily the chain stores—Woolworth's, Kresge's, and the Walgreen drugstore—and we had these well-dressed young people with their books going to the lunch counters. They would sit down in a very orderly, peaceful, nonviolent fashion and wait to be served. They would be reading a book or doing their homework or whatever while they were waiting.

I was a spokesperson for one of these groups. I would ask to be served, and we would be told that we wouldn't be served. The lunch counter would be closed, and they would put up a sign saying "Closed—not serving." Sometimes they would lock the door, leave us in there, and turn out all the lights, and we would continue to sit.

After we had been doing this for a month, it was beginning to bother the business community and other people in Nashville. We heard that the city had decided to allow the police officials to stand by and allow the hoodlum element to come in and attack us—and that the police would arrest us—to try to stop the sit-ins. We had a meeting after we heard that, to decide did we still want to go down on this particular day. And we said yes.

I was with the group that went into the Woolworth's there. The lunch counter was upstairs—just a long row of stools in front of a counter. My group went up to sit there, and after we had been there for half an hour or so, a group of young white men came in and began pulling people off the lunch-counter stools, putting lighted cigarettes out in our hair or faces or down our backs, pouring ketchup and hot sauce all over us, pushing us down to the floor and beating us. Then the police came in and started arresting *us.* They didn't arrest a single person that beat us, but they arrested all of us and charged us with disorderly conduct.

That was the first mass arrest of students in the South for participating in a sit-in. Over one hundred of us were arrested that day. We were sentenced, all of us, to a fifty-dollar fine or thirty days in jail, and since we wouldn't pay the fine, we were put in jail. . . .

Lewis and his fellow students were jailed, but they continued their protests when they were released. In April, 1960, the mayor of Nashville agreed that the lunch counters should be desegregated.

And so Nashville became the first major city in the South to desegregate its downtown lunch counters and restaurants. That was the power of nonviolence. . . .

I think one thing the movement did for all of us in the South, black and white alike, was to have a cleansing effect on our psyche. I think it brought up a great deal of the dirt and a great deal of the guilt from under the rug to the top, so that we could deal with it, so that we could see it in the light. And I think that in a real sense, we are a different people. We are better people. It freed even those of us who didn't participate—black people, white people alike—to be a little more human.

RA.L.8.6 Explain how an author's choice of genre affects the expression of a theme or topic.
Also covered **WA.8.2**

1. Which of the following is the best statement of the main idea of the text?
   A. It is good to be a spokesperson for a protest.
   B. All men and women are created equal.
   C. Police sometimes arrest protesters unfairly.
   D. Injustice can be overcome with nonviolence.

2. The text has unity because it is all about
   A. segregated facilities.
   B. lunch-counter sit-ins.
   C. ending segregation.
   D. the power of nonviolence.

3. Which structural pattern does John Lewis use to describe events?
   A. main idea
   B. order of importance
   C. logical order
   D. chronological order

4. The purpose of this text is to
   A. give some facts about nonviolence.
   B. show that people still struggle with prejudice.
   C. give a personal account of an important protest.
   D. convince readers that protests are common.

Short Answer

5. Explain why this text is logical. Use information from the passage to support your answer.

Extended Response

6. What personal thoughts and details does John Lewis include in his description of the protest? Is his description coherent? Explain.

Informational Skills Review

Proposition and Support

Directions: Read the selection below. Then, answer each question that follows.

Dear Councilman Duane:

More and more minors are smoking. When teens smoke, many problems arise. Something needs to be done to prove to minors that smoking is a bad thing. I am writing this letter to you in hopes that you will take steps to end this big problem.

Many problems develop when teenagers smoke. When teens smoke, laws are broken. Merchants break laws by intentionally selling cigarettes to minors. Teenage smokers damage their bodies permanently by smoking. Cigarettes cause addictions; even when teens want to quit, they often find they can't. Smoking can even affect a teenager's schooling. If a teenager needs a cigarette badly, he or she may ditch school to get one.

To help stop this problem, the city council could start a campaign against teenage smoking. You could make sure that schools with the sixth grade and older have a required class about the hazards of smoking, especially before the legal age. You could sponsor contests in each school for the best "Don't Smoke" posters, poems, essays, and stories. You could put the winners' posters and writing up around New York City. An educational campaign aimed at young teenagers would definitely help solve the problem of smoking by minors.

Some teenagers think, "It's my body; I can do what I want with it." Most smoking teenagers haven't fully matured emotionally. That means that what they believe now can change drastically in the following three to ten years of their lives. Therefore, as adults they may seriously regret decisions they made as teenagers.

Thank you for listening to my thoughts on this matter. I appreciate it and hope that you can do something to end the dilemma. Teenagers need to stop smoking, and you, as a person in power, can help them understand that it isn't all right to smoke.

Hannah Fleury
St. Luke's School
New York, New York

RA.I.8.7 Analyze an author's argument, perspective or viewpoint and explain the development of key points.

1. Which of the following sentences states the letter writer's proposition?
   A. "Even when teens want to quit, they often find they can't."
   B. "Teenagers think, 'It's my body; I can do what I want with it.'"
   C. "Something needs to be done to prove to minors that smoking is a bad thing."
   D. "Most smoking teenagers haven't fully matured emotionally."

2. Which of the following statements from the letter is an opinion?
   A. "Cigarettes cause addictions."
   B. "More and more minors are smoking."
   C. "When teens smoke, many problems arise."
   D. "Something needs to be done to prove to minors that smoking is a bad thing."

3. To keep students from smoking, the author suggests all of the following except a(n)
   A. required class.
   B. fine for smoking.
   C. school contest.
   D. educational campaign.

4. Which of the following sentences does not offer support for the letter writer's main idea?
   A. "When teens smoke, laws are broken."
   B. "Cigarettes cause addictions."
   C. "Smoking can even affect a teenager's schooling."
   D. "Teenagers need to stop smoking."

5. The letter writer uses all of the following supports for her argument except
   A. facts.
   B. opinions.
   C. anecdotes.
   D. statistics.

Short Answer

6. Explain what the conclusion of this letter does. Use the information from the passage to support your answer.

Extended Response

7. What is the letter writer's purpose for writing this letter? Do you think she achieved her purpose? Explain. Support your answer by using information from the passage.

Vocabulary Skills Review

OH **VO.8.3** Identify the relationships of pairs of words in analogical statements (e. g., synonyms and antonyms) and infer word meanings from these relationships.

Synonyms

Directions: Choose the word or phrase that is the best synonym of each boldfaced Vocabulary word.

1. **Proximity** means
   A. simplicity.
   B. closeness.
   C. distance.
   D. difference.

2. Something that is **vital** to life is
   A. dangerous.
   B. special.
   C. similar.
   D. necessary.

3. If a man is **insulated** from cold weather, he is
   A. protected.
   B. surprised.
   C. distracted.
   D. fearful.

4. **Domination** means
   A. energy.
   B. control.
   C. frustration.
   D. expectation.

5. If two countries have **discords,** they have
   A. compacts.
   B. contracts.
   C. confusion.
   D. conflicts.

6. A **creed** is a statement of
   A. arguments.
   B. beliefs.
   C. accusations.
   D. facts.

7. When the sound **intensified,** it became
   A. funnier.
   B. lower.
   C. stronger.
   D. smaller.

8. An **incentive** is a
   A. motivation.
   B. opening.
   C. incident.
   D. protection.

Academic Vocabulary

Directions: Choose the correct definition for each boldfaced Academic Vocabulary word from this collection.

9. When you **emphasize** something, you
   A. ignore it.
   B. repeat it.
   C. stress it.
   D. eliminate it.

10. Your **reactions** are your
    A. desires.
    B. responses.
    C. reasons.
    D. behaviors.

WP.8.16 Drafting, Revising and Editing: Apply tools to judge the quality of writing. **WA.8.4.b** Write informational essays or reports, including research, that: provide a clear and accurate perspective on the subject *Also covered* **WP.8.6; WP.8.13**

Writing Skills Review

Persuasive Essay

Directions: Read the following passage from an essay supporting a position. Then, answer each question that follows.

(1) Although more American students are getting high school diplomas than at any other time in the past, the high school dropout rate is still too high. (2) Various estimates place the dropout rate between 12 and 25 percent. (3) The unemployment rate for high school dropouts is greater than that for graduates. (4) Dropping out of high school reduces one's options for work. (5) Also, the jobs available to a person without a degree may be less stable. (6) People believe students who already have jobs do not need a diploma. (7) However, with a diploma, students can earn more and choose from a greater number of jobs. (8) A diploma gives students a bright, shining future filled with opportunities. (9) To help "at risk" students stay in school, we need to consider a range of proposals. (10) We need to offer career counseling to students. (11) Second, we should provide stimulating, quality education that will give students incentives to complete their schooling. (12) Third, we must get parents more involved in school programs and policies.

1. Which title would *best* fit this persuasive essay?
   A. The Problem of Unemployment
   B. At-Risk High School Students
   C. Decrease the Dropout Rate
   D. Career Counseling Helps

2. In sentence 6, the author provides a —
   A. topic sentence
   B. supporting fact
   C. solution
   D. counterargument

3. Sentence 7 is an example of —
   A. supporting evidence
   B. a detail
   C. an emotional appeal
   D. a call to action

4. Which **transitional word** would make sentence 10 clearer?
   A. First
   B. Finally
   C. Last
   D. Because

5. In this essay, the author includes all of the following *except* a(n) —
   A. thesis
   B. conclusion
   C. argument
   D. body

Read On

Fiction

The Glory Field

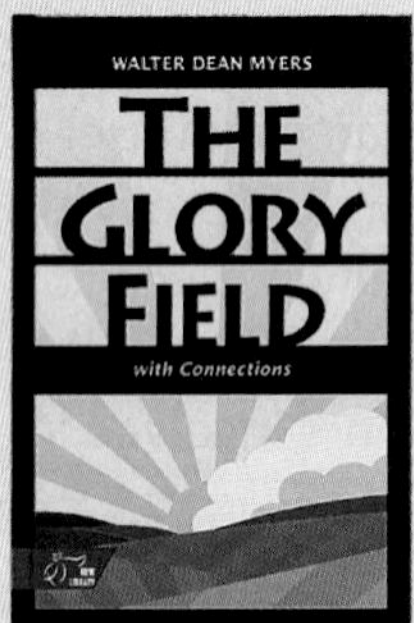

In *The Glory Field,* Walter Dean Myers covers 250 years in the lives of an African American family. From their beginnings in Africa to the end of segregation in America, the members of the Lewis family have always supported one another despite the challenges they faced. Can they persuade one lost relative in modern-day New York City to return to their South Carolina home?

Little Women

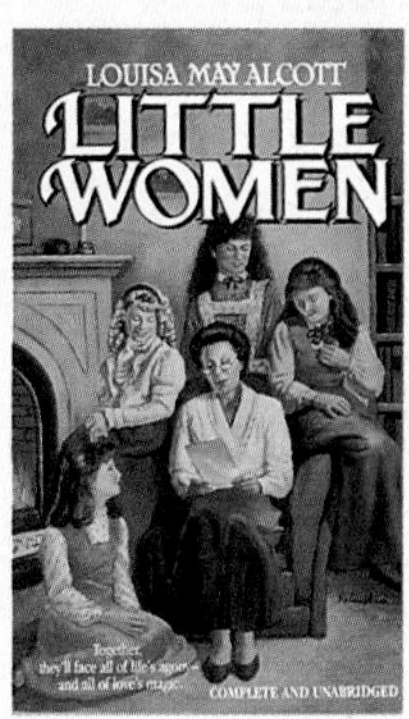

In Louisa May Alcott's *Little Women,* readers are introduced to Meg, Jo, Beth, and Amy March, four sisters, who are growing up in Massachusetts during the Civil War. This classic American story about familial love has been a favorite of readers for more than a century. The book has been adapted into a movie four times.

North by Night: A Story of the Underground Railroad

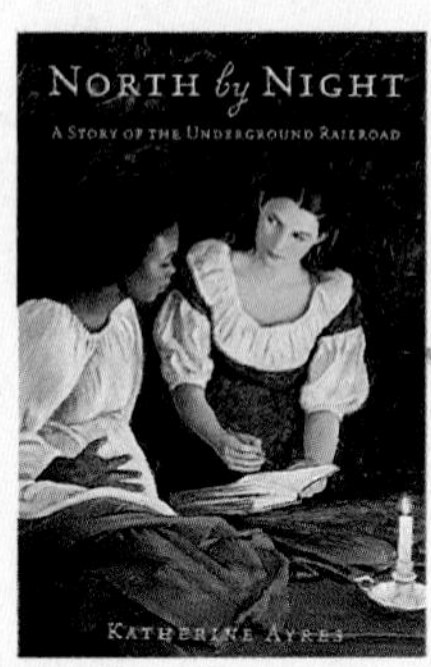

Katherine Ayres's *North by Night: A Story of the Underground Railroad* is composed of fictional journal entries and letters written by sixteen-year-old Lucy Spenser. Lucy has been helping fugitives from slavery reach Canada for four years. When one of the fugitives dies while giving birth to a baby, Lucy is faced with a difficult decision.

Journey Home

As World War II comes to a close, Yuki Sakane and her family are finally released from an internment camp and allowed to return home to Berkeley, California. However, the Sakanes quickly find that Berkeley has changed. Because of the war, former friends and other residents have become suspicious of returning Japanese Americans. Yuki and her family try to overcome this hostility in Yoshiko Uchida's novel *Journey Home.*

Nonfiction

The Boys' War

Grizzled men were not the only soldiers who fought in the American Civil War. Many teenagers signed up to fight for both the Union and the Confederate armies. In *The Boys' War,* Jim Murphy tells of the excitement the young soldiers felt as they embarked on this new experience and the horror they felt when they came face to face with the grim reality of war.

Behind Barbed Wire

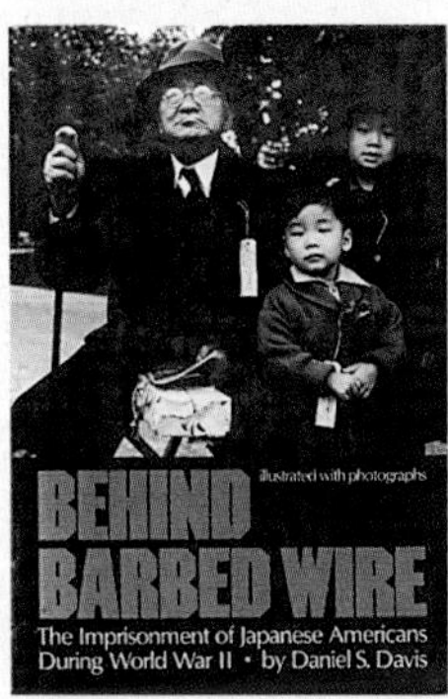

After the bombing of Pearl Harbor, Japanese Americans were forced to abandon their homes and businesses and live in internment camps. Families were crowded into long barracks behind fences and guarded by armed soldiers twenty-four hours a day. In *Behind Barbed Wire,* Daniel S. Davis describes the many difficulties Japanese Americans faced during World War II and the courage they showed in making a fresh start when they were finally released from the camps.

Behind Rebel Lines

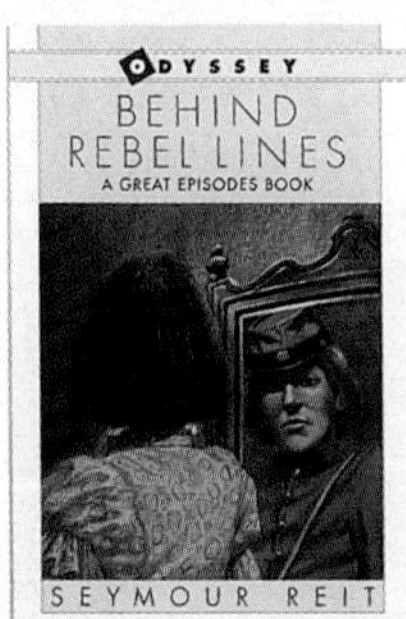

Determined to be a member of the Union army, Emma Edmonds presents herself as a man named Franklin Thompson and enlists as a private. Seymour Reit details her adventures in *Behind Rebel Lines.* When Edmonds is sent across Confederate lines to spy, she learns military secrets and how hard it is to be a soldier, no matter what side you are fighting for.

To Be a Slave

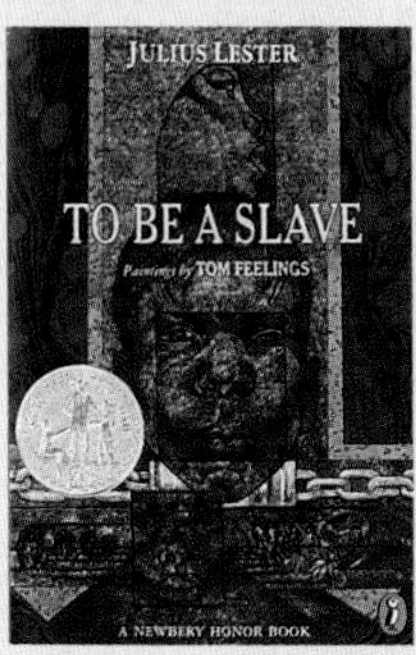

In *To Be a Slave,* a Newbery Honor book written by Julius Lester, men and women who lived through slavery tell their stories in their own words. Readers who want to learn more about this subject should also read Lester's *Long Journey Home,* an uplifting sequel that details six true stories of freedom.

Learn It Online

Explore other novels and find tips for choosing, reading, and studying works using *NovelWise*:

go.hrw.com L8-595 

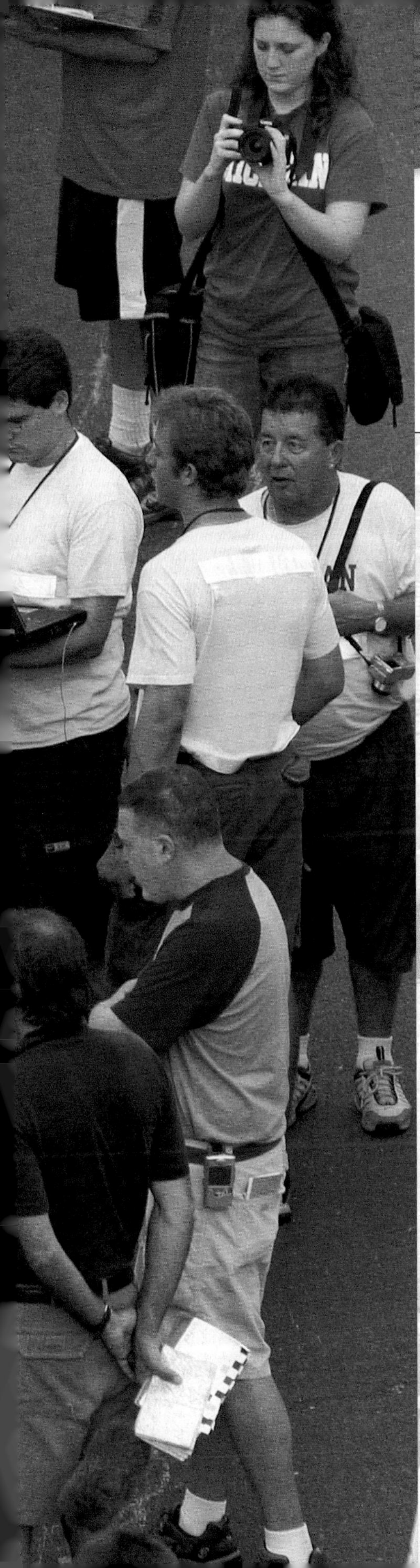

COLLECTION 6

Reading for Life

"Problems can become opportunities when the right people come together."

—**Robert Redford**

What Do You Think?

How can we solve the problems we face in daily life?

The start of a 2,500 mile solar-powered car race between Austin, Texas, and Calgary, Canada, in 2005.

Learn It Online

Find graphic organizers online to help you as you read:

go.hrw.com L8-597 Go 

by **Carol Jago**

What Kinds of Documents Will I Read in Real Life?

Let's say you want to see a movie. Besides finding out the time and place, you might want to read reviews, get information about the cast and director, and reserve seats. You'll be reading many types of informational documents, such as the ones below.

Workplace Documents

The odds are good that in the next thirty years you will hold a variety of jobs. The job you volunteer for at age thirteen will probably be very different from the one you accept at age forty. Whether you are taking orders at a restaurant or giving orders to a staff of a thousand, your job will likely require you to read for information. When earning a living is involved, that information is important. The **workplace documents** you will read serve two basic functions: communication and instruction.

Communication E-mails, memorandums (memos), and reports will tell you about upcoming meetings, changes in policy, and other important information you need to know in order to do your job. Letters of application and résumés will help you find a job.

Instruction
Employee manuals tell what is expected of you on the job. User guides teach you how to operate the equipment you use.

Public Documents

Public documents contain information about public agencies and community groups. They can be about voting issues, health concerns, and many other subjects. They tell about situations, decisions, responsibilities, schedules, occasions, and interesting events. You'll use public documents if you work with a government agency, school, park, or library. Public documents inform people what is happening in their community, city, state, nation, and even on the planet.

THE REAL-LIFE READING AND COMPREHENSION TEST...
CAUTION
DRY PAINT
8-20 Ucomics.com/nonsequitur

RA.I.8.9 Distinguish the characteristics of consumer materials, functional or workplace documents and public documents.

Consumer Documents

A **consumer** is someone who buys something or uses what someone else buys. That covers just about everyone: you, your friends—even a baby. The things consumers buy fall into two basic categories: goods (stuff) and services (help).

Many goods are simple to use. You don't need an instruction manual to figure out what to do with a candy bar! More complicated goods may not be so easy to use. Let's say you buy a computer. Now what? You'll need some information to get your computer up and running. Therefore, the computer package will include **consumer documents** to give you the information you need to set up and operate your computer. The documents also define legal rights and responsibilities—yours, those of the company that made the computer, and those of the company that sold it.

- **Product information** on the box or label will tell you if an item is what you want. Is the shirt washable? Does the CD player have the features you want? Read to find out.
- **Contracts** spell out exactly what services will and will not be provided. Contracts are generally binding once you or your parent or guardian sign them. So read carefully before you do.
- **Warranties** guarantee that a product will work for a specified period of time. They also spell out what happens if it doesn't work properly and what you have to do to receive service.
- **Instruction manuals** tell how to set up and use a product. If you break the product because you didn't read the instructions carefully, you'll be responsible for the damage.
- **Technical directions** give precise technical information about installing and assembling a product.

Technical Directions

Directions are important for many activities. You may need to follow them when you cook, dance, exercise, play sports, sing, or play music. **Technical directions** are the kind you follow when you assemble or operate any kind of scientific, mechanical, or electronic device. If you skip a step or perform one out of order, the device may not work or may even break, so read the directions carefully. When following technical directions, it is a good idea to

- read the directions all the way through before you begin
- check off the steps one by one as you complete them
- compare your work with the diagrams and drawings for each step

Your Turn Analyze Documents

In your *Reader/Writer Notebook,* write four headings at the top of two pages: Workplace Documents and Public Documents on one page, and Consumer Documents and Technical Directions on the other page. Under each heading, list all the documents of that type you think you might need to use sometime soon. Put check marks next to any you have already used or can find in your home or classroom. Add items (and check marks) as you think of them and as you read the documents in this collection.

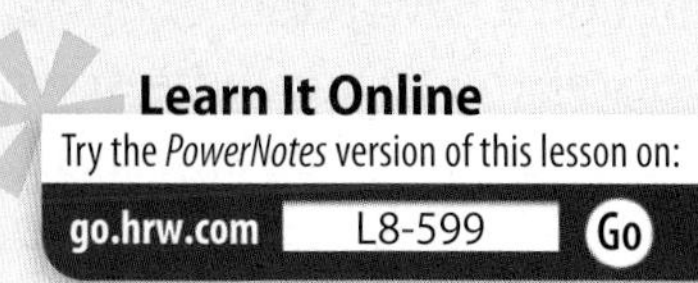

Learn It Online
Try the PowerNotes version of this lesson on:
go.hrw.com
L8-599
Go

Analyzing Visuals

How Can You Analyze Information in a Poster?

A common form of visual information in our society is advertising. Savvy consumers know how to analyze a visual advertisement, such as a poster. They read the small print and interpret the intent of the poster. Analyzing the information in a poster can help you generate an informed opinion about its subject.

Analyzing a Poster

Answer these questions when analyzing the information in a poster.

1. Preview the text and image to find the subject and purpose. Does the poster suggest that you buy something? support a cause?
2. Scan the small print to identify the company or group responsible for creating the poster.
3. Examine the style of the headings. Do the headings seize your attention, or are they more subtle?
4. View and interpret the image. Is the ad trying to dazzle you with color? entice you with glamour?
5. Analyze the persuasive makeup of the advertisement. To what feelings or interests is it trying to appeal?

Your Turn Write About Purpose

Flip through a newspaper or magazine to find a full-page advertisement. Study the ad and write down its intent. Then, describe how the designer has used color, layout, and style to get the message across.

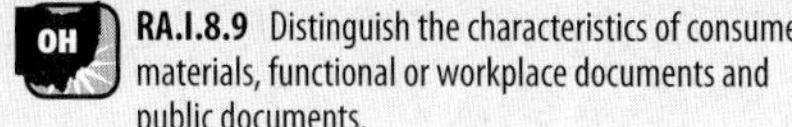

RA.I.8.9 Distinguish the characteristics of consumer materials, functional or workplace documents and public documents.

1. What is the subject of this advertisement? What are the poster's creators trying to get you to do?

2. Notice the placement of the blocks of text. What elements do they share with the photograph of the dancer?

3. What mood does the poster create? How does color contribute to this mood?

ALVIN AILEY®

AMERICAN DANCE THEATER

JUDITH JAMISON ARTISTIC DIRECTOR

Masazumi Chaya ASSOCIATE ARTISTIC DIRECTOR

DEC 4 2002–JAN 5 2003

CITYTIX® 1-212-581-1212

CITY CENTER
West 55th Street between
6th and 7th Avenues

www.alvinailey.org

Reading Focus

by **Kylene Beers**

What Skills Help You Read Informational Texts?

What do you do when you want to see your favorite team play a game? You look up the schedule, ticket prices, and routes to the stadium. In short, you read informational documents. Since your life is probably pretty busy, you'll want to find the information you need quickly. Here are some skills that will help you navigate informational texts.

Previewing

Before you start to read an informational document, you want to be sure it has the information you need. A good way to find out is by previewing the text. To **preview** a text, first glance over the document quickly, without reading every word. Pay attention only to heads and subheads. They give important information, as do charts, lists, and illustrations. Follow these tips for previewing a text:

Tips for Previewing Informational Texts

1. If the text has numbered steps, think of someone telling you, "First, do this. Next, do that."
2. Look for heads and subheads. They are like someone saying, "Look here! This is a new topic."
3. Watch for boldface and italic type. They signal key words and ideas.
4. You can often find what you are looking for in bulleted or numbered lists.
5. Look at graphics such as maps or charts. They give you additional information.

Skimming and Scanning

Skimming and scanning can also help you find the information you need in a document. To skim and scan, you read quickly through the text. Then, when you find what you need, you can slow down and read carefully.

Skimming is looking at a document quickly. You read the title, heads, and subheads. Then, you read the first line or two of each paragraph.

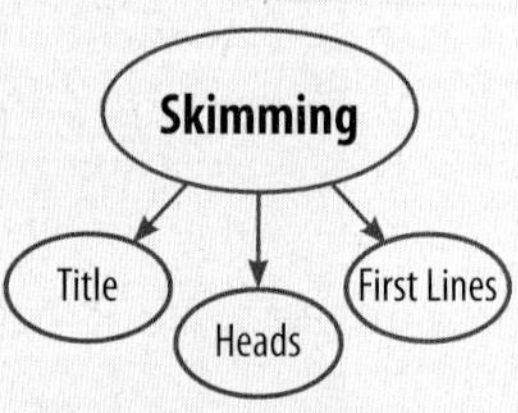

Scanning is looking for the particular information you want. You search for boldface key words and phrases or other important details that relate to your topic.

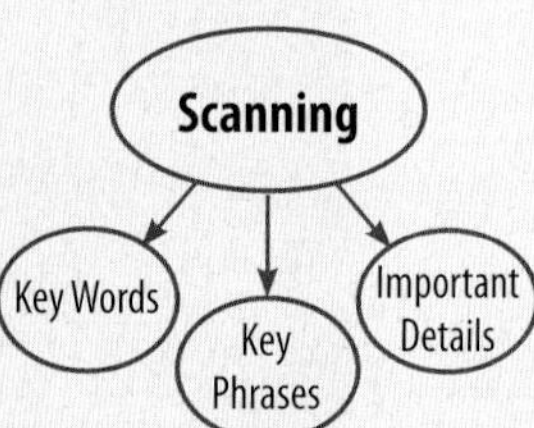

RP.8.1 Apply reading comprehension strategies, including making predictions, comparing and contrasting, recalling and summarizing and making inferences and drawing conclusions. RP.8.3 Monitor own comprehension by adjusting speed to fit the purpose, or by skimming, scanning, reading on, looking back, note taking or summarizing what has been read so far in text. RA.I.8.4 Analyze information found in maps, charts, tables, graphs, diagrams, cutaways and overlays.

Understanding Graphics

A good place to find information quickly in a text is in its graphics. **Graphics** include graphs, tables, maps, cartoons, and illustrations. The titles or captions to these graphics can often point you to information you need.

Tables list information in categories. Facts are put in horizontal rows and vertical columns. You choose a category at the top or on the left side that interests you and read down or across to find the information. Here is an example of a table:

Types of Graphics	
Tables	put information into categories
Graphs	show relationships
Illustrations	show what is being described
Maps	show geographical areas

Graphs show relationships between things. Two common types are line graphs and bar graphs. You have probably seen line graphs showing how the economy is doing in cartoons like this one:

"At times like this, I wish I were a poet"

Illustrations are often included to provide visual interest and to make directions more clear. We can usually understand a process better when we can see what is being described. **Cartoons** are a type of illustration that adds humor to a presentation. They may present useful information from an unusual point of view.

Your Turn Apply Reading Skills

1. What strategy would you use if you were looking for key statements in an informational text?
2. What type of graphic aid would help you install a printer for your computer?
3. Preview the text below. Then, describe what you think the text will be about.

Did You Know?

- In our city there are 165,000 licensed dogs.
- The city devotes a total of 10 acres to leash-free dog areas.
- The city devotes 1,050 acres to softball, 1,040 acres to golf, and 287 acres to tennis.
- Eastside Leash-Free Dog Park accommodates 2,000 dogs per week on its 1-acre site.

Now go to the Skills in Action: Reading Model

Learn It Online
Need help reading informational text? Check out the interactive Reading Workshops on:

go.hrw.com L8-603 

Build Background

The Global Positioning System (GPS) uses satellite signals to find the location, speed, and direction of a receiver. GPS was first developed by the United States Department of Defense for military use. But GPS is now used in a wide range of consumer products, from cell phones to cars.

Read with a Purpose Read to learn what documents you might use in acquiring a GPS device.

GPS DOCUMENTS

from 

The Browns recently vacationed in New York and rented a car with a Global Positioning System (GPS) receiver. They found the device to be very useful, so when they returned home to Indiana, they discussed buying one for their daughter, Nidia. She was attending college in California and had an internship that required extensive traveling. Soon after, their son Eric, an eighth grader, saw the following advertisement in a newspaper and pointed it out to his parents.

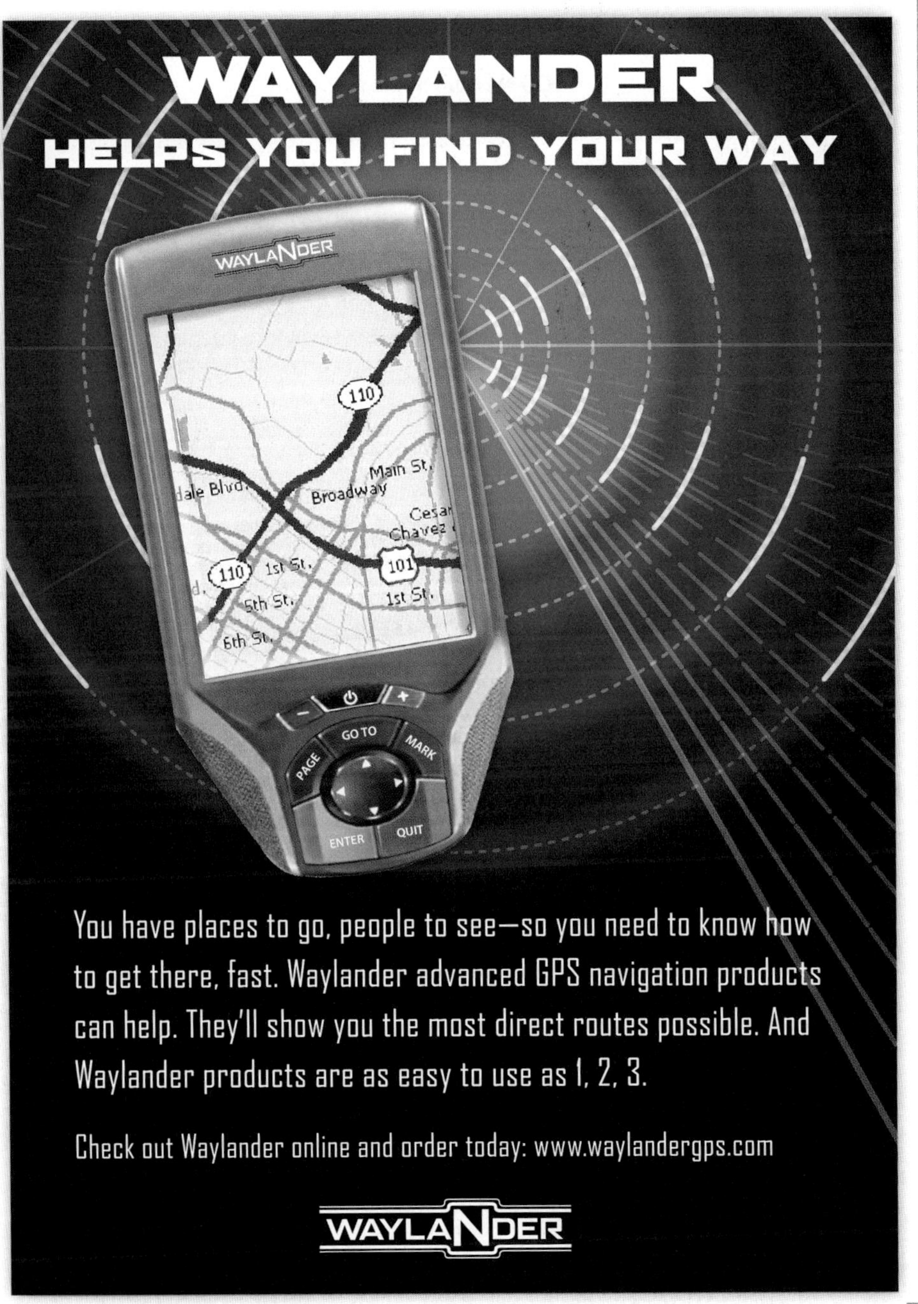
WAYLANDER
HELPS YOU FIND YOUR WAY
WAYLANDER
110
Main St.
Broadway
Cesar Chavez
101
1st St.
5th St.
6th St.
1st St.
GO TO
MARK
PAGE
ENTER
QUIT
You have places to go, people to see—so you need to know how to get there, fast. Waylander advanced GPS navigation products can help. They'll show you the most direct routes possible. And Waylander products are as easy to use as 1, 2, 3.
Check out Waylander online and order today: www.waylandergps.com
WAYLANDER

Informational Text Focus

Consumer Documents This advertisement praises the Waylander GPS product and tells where to get more information.

The Browns did their homework, comparing several GPS products. In the end, they did decide to buy a Waylander for Nidia, based on the price and consumer reports. They ordered the unit over the Internet and had it delivered to her directly. When it arrived, Nidia excitedly looked over the instructions, beginning with the table of contents.

Reading Focus

Previewing By previewing the table of contents, you learn about the topics covered in the instruction manual.

HOW TO USE YOUR WAYLANDER

CONTENTS

Reading Focus

Scanning If you have problems with your GPS device, scan the table of contents to find troubleshooting advice (on page 130).

Nidia had a basic idea about the way GPS units work, but the list of unfamiliar terms in the table of contents made her realize there was plenty she needed to learn. So she sat down in her favorite chair to read through the instructions. The introduction discussed satellite systems and gave an overview. Nidia then zeroed in on the instructions for operation. After reading "How Does It Work?" she moved on to the chapter called "The Keypad."

Nidia activated her unit and tried to use it while viewing the manual. She was all thumbs at first—or at least she felt that way. She hit MARK when she meant to hit PAGE. Then she got the hang of it. After a little practice, she put the unit down and continued reading. But when she shifted in her chair, some papers fell out of the manual. One of them was an extended warranty.

THE KEYPAD

Your keypad is not much larger than the face of a watch. Smaller buttons surround the bigger key button in the center, which provides four directions, displayed by arrows. When your unit has been activated, the display below the buttons shows a series of screens, called pages. On each page are specific functions.

To cycle through the pages, use POWER, PAGE, and QUIT:

1. ***Power.*** Press the POWER button. Hold for two seconds.
2. ***Status.*** A welcome will appear, followed by the status page.
3. ***Location.*** Press PAGE. Information about your location will appear.
4. ***Map Data.*** Press PAGE again to see map data.
5. ***Navigation Information.*** Press PAGE again for navigation information.
6. ***Menu Commands.*** Press PAGE again to see the menu commands.
7. ***Return.*** Hit QUIT when you want to rotate pages backward.
8. ***End.*** Press the POWER button again to turn the unit off.

Informational Text Focus

Technical Directions These technical directions include a numbered list of steps to follow.

The buttons on your keypad help you perform various functions:

POWER turns the unit on and off.

ARROWS on the center key button help you change selections on the screens.

PAGE provides map and navigation information.

ENTER confirms entries and allows you to enter data in highlighted screens.

GO TO sets a course for a destination you select.

MARK stores a current location in a log for later reference.

QUIT sends you back to a previous page. It will back you out of functions. It clears data entry or restores a data field's previous value.

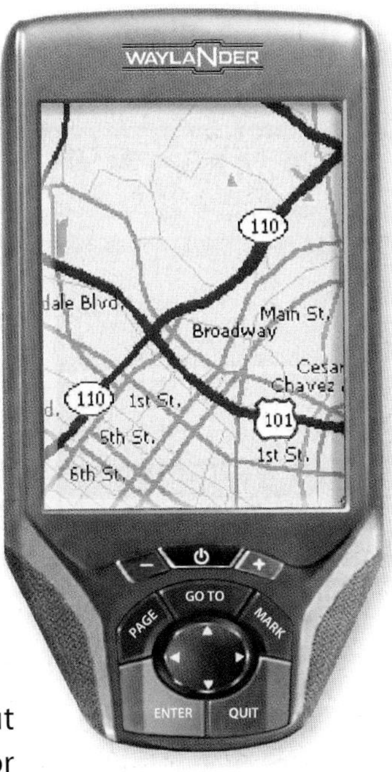

Reading Focus

Understanding Graphics These illustrations of the GPS device and its buttons help you understand the technical directions that follow.

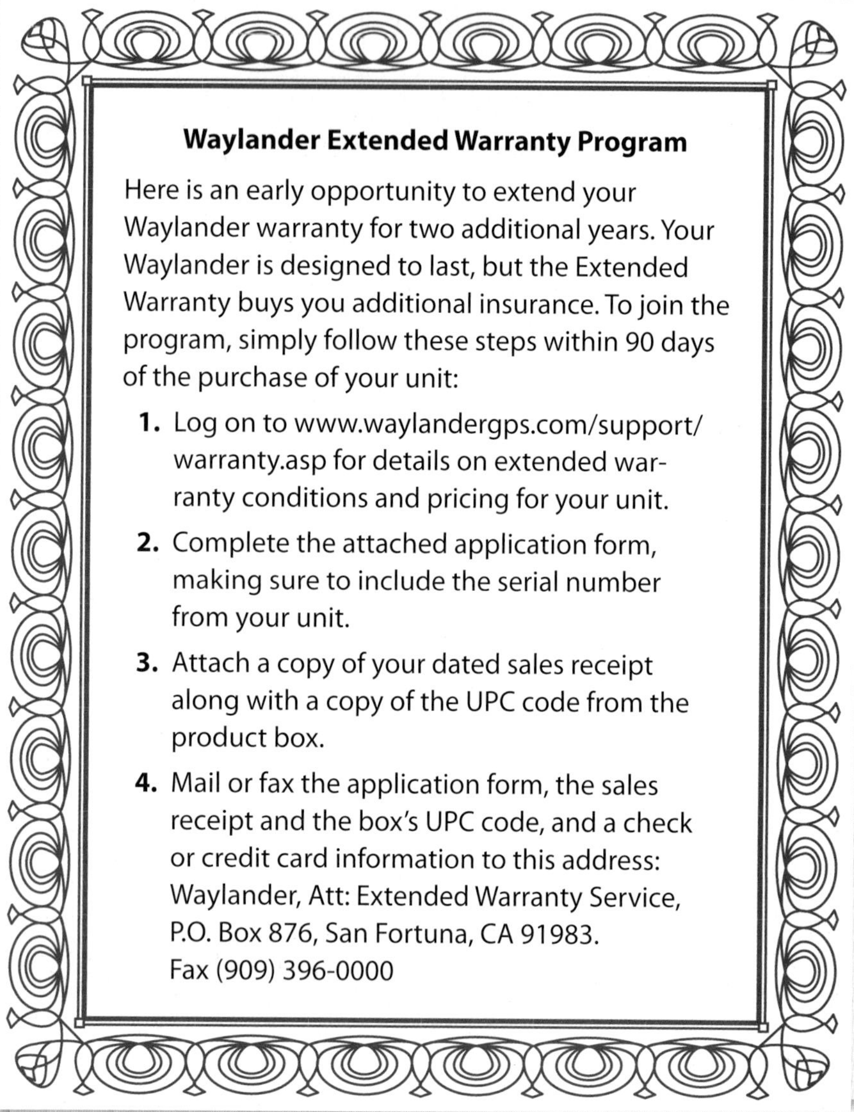

Waylander Extended Warranty Program

Here is an early opportunity to extend your Waylander warranty for two additional years. Your Waylander is designed to last, but the Extended Warranty buys you additional insurance. To join the program, simply follow these steps within 90 days of the purchase of your unit:

1. Log on to www.waylandergps.com/support/warranty.asp for details on extended warranty conditions and pricing for your unit.
2. Complete the attached application form, making sure to include the serial number from your unit.
3. Attach a copy of your dated sales receipt along with a copy of the UPC code from the product box.
4. Mail or fax the application form, the sales receipt and the box's UPC code, and a check or credit card information to this address: Waylander, Att: Extended Warranty Service, P.O. Box 876, San Fortuna, CA 91983. Fax (909) 396-0000

Informational Text Focus

Consumer Document When reading a consumer document like a warranty, it is important to read it very carefully and follow the directions exactly.

Nidia knew she would have to balance the likelihood of needing a repair against the cost of the extended warranty and the cost of the unit. Because she didn't know the cost of the extended warranty, she wasn't sure if it made sense to purchase it. Nidia called her parents, who told her that an extended warranty has been offered free as part of a promotion. She had done the right thing by calling. It always makes sense to have as much information as possible before making an important decision.

Read with a Purpose What did you learn about the documents you use when you acquire a GPS device?

SKILLS IN ACTION

Wrap Up

RA.I.8.9 Distinguish the characteristics of consumer materials, functional or workplace documents and public documents. *Also covered* **VO.8.7; VO.8.4**

Into Action: Reading for Information

In a chart like the one below, give examples and explain how you were able to use each text feature to help you understand the GPS documents.

Informational Text Feature	Examples and Explanations
Headings	
Graphics	
Numbered lists	

Talk About . . .

1. With a partner, discuss how easy—or difficult—it was to understand the GPS documents. Try to use each Academic Vocabulary word listed at the right at least once in your discussion.

Write About . . .

Use the Academic Vocabulary words to answer these questions about the GPS documents.

2. How can you tell the sequence of the steps to follow in operating the GPS device?
3. What kind of information is specified in a warranty?
4. Why is it critical to follow technical directions carefully?
5. What fundamental information does the keypad chapter give you?

Writing Focus

Think as a Reader/Writer

Find It In Your Reading The Writing Focus activities on the Preparing to Read pages guide you to recognize how each type of document delivers information. On the Applying Your Skills pages, you will check your understanding of these document types.

Academic Vocabulary for Collection 6

Talking and Writing About Informational Documents

Academic Vocabulary is the language you use to write and talk about what you read. Use these words to discuss the informational documents you read in this collection. The words are underlined throughout the collection.

specify (SPEHS uh fy) *v.:* mention or describe in detail; give as a condition. *When signing up with an Internet provider, be sure to specify which service you are choosing.*

sequence (SEE kwuhns) *n.:* order. *With technical directions, you must follow each step in the correct sequence.*

fundamental (fuhn duh MEHN tuhl) *adj.:* basic; essential. *Manuals provide fundamental information, so read them carefully.*

critical (KRIHT ih kuhl) *adj.:* vital; very important. *It is critical to read technical directions carefully in order to avoid making mistakes.*

Your Turn

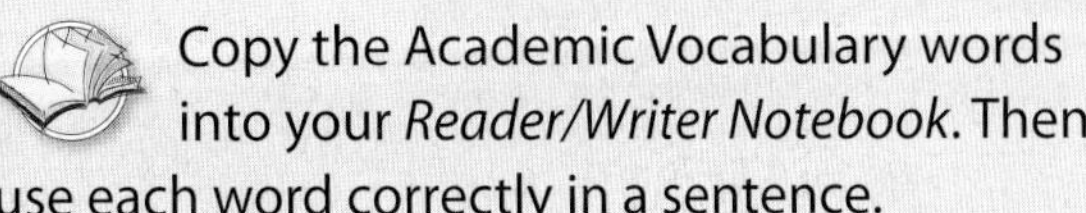

Copy the Academic Vocabulary words into your *Reader/Writer Notebook*. Then, use each word correctly in a sentence.

Solve a Problem

CONTENTS

What Do You Think?

How do we solve problems that affect an entire community?

QuickWrite

What improvements would you like to see in your community? You might consider a town pool or new traffic signs, for example. Jot down your ideas.

DOCUMENTS

Preparing to Read

RA.I.8.9 Distinguish the characteristics of consumer materials, functional or workplace documents and public documents. *Also covered* **RP.8.1**

Skateboard Park Documents / Leash-Free Dog Run Documents

Reader/Writer Notebook

Use your **RWN** to complete the activities for these selections.

Informational Text Focus

Using Information to Solve Problems Getting accurate information is critical when you need to find a solution to a problem. You may gather information from different sources, including **workplace documents,** such as memos, e-mails, and reports; **public documents,** such as schedules, government publications, and Web sites; and **consumer documents,** such as contracts, advertisements, and manuals. When you have gathered your information, judge its reliability by evaluating its sources. You may also find that you need more information to solve the problem.

Reading Focus

Previewing When you **preview,** you look over text you are about to read to see what lies ahead. You may begin by noticing titles, headings, subheadings, boldface terms, and illustrations. You can also read opening sentences or paragraphs.

Into Action To complete a preview chart, list each document you will read, explain what it is, and describe the topic it covers:

Title/Description	Kind of Document	Topic
Memorandum	memo from the Parks Department	issues regarding the new skateboard park: need, liability, cost, location
The City Beat	newspaper article	

Writing Focus

Preparing for **Constructed Response**

Imagine that you are trying to solve the problems described in these documents. Use the information provided to form opinions about the skateboard park and the dog run.

Vocabulary

Skateboard Park Documents

potentially (poh TEHN shuh lee) *adv.:* possibly. *The situation is potentially dangerous because people could be hurt.*

proposal (pruh POHZ uhl) *n.:* suggestion. *We presented our proposal for the new park at the city council meeting.*

hazards (HAZ uhrdz) *n.:* dangers; things that can cause danger. *Broken glass and sharp nails are two street hazards.*

Leash-Free Dog Run Documents

empowered (ehm POW uhrd) *adj.:* given the power to do something. *The police are empowered to fine lawbreakers.*

ample (AM puhl) *adj.:* as much as is needed; enough. *We need to give people ample opportunities to speak.*

Language Coach

Prefixes A **prefix** is a word part added to the front of a word. The prefixes *–en* and *–em* mean "to cause to be." Which Vocabulary word has one of these prefixes? What does it mean without the prefix?

Learn It Online

To learn more about analyzing various forms of writing, visit *MediaScope* at:

go.hrw.com L8-611 

MEMORANDUM

Skateboard Park Documents

Read with a Purpose Read these workplace, public, and consumer documents to solve a skateboarding problem.

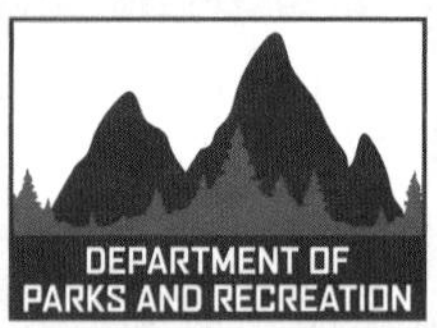

From: A. Longboard, Assistant Director of Parks and Recreation
To: J. Cool, Director of Parks and Recreation
Re: Establishment of a Permanent Skateboard Park

CRITICAL ISSUES

A. Need. Ten percent of the families in this city, about seven thousand households, include at least one skateboarder. The city provides no designated space for skateboarding. Police reports show that citations for illegal skating are rising every month. This problem is particularly acute in downtown areas, leading to complaints from businesses. The nearest public skateboard park is twenty miles to the east in Mogul, where illegal skating dropped sharply when its park opened last year.

B. Liability.[1] California AB 1296 states that persons who skateboard on public property are expected to know that it is a potentially dangerous sport. They cannot sue the city, county, or state for their injuries as long as the city has passed an ordinance[2] requiring

- helmet, kneepads, and elbow pads for skaters
- clear and visible signs warning citizens of this requirement
- citations for skaters who violate the ordinance

Such an ordinance was enacted by our city council on July 15, 2000. Therefore, building a skateboard park would not pose a liability risk.

C. Cost. Local groups have raised half the necessary $140,000. The Parks and Recreation Department's budget can fund the other half. Costs will be minimal—only inspection for damage and yearly maintenance. **A**

D. Location. The city already owns two sites:

- 1.3 acres of the park area between 180th Avenue and 360th Drive, bordered by Drab Street and Grinding Drive, two heavily used thoroughfares. On two sides of the park are neighborhood houses.
- 2.1 acres in the 15-acre sports park at Ramp and Spin avenues. This site is set back from heavily traveled roads but still offers excellent access and visibility from service roads within the park. It is also three-tenths of a mile from the fire station and paramedic aid. There are no residential neighborhoods bordering the complex. **B**

1. **liability** (ly uh BIHL uh tee): legal responsibility.
2. **ordinance** (AWR duh nuhns): law; rule.

A **Read and Discuss** Given the information presented here, how could we describe the need for establishing a skateboard park?

B **Informational Focus** **Using Information** How do the two proposed sites compare?

Vocabulary **potentially** (poh TEHN shuh lee) *adv.:* possibly.

The City Beat

by N. PARKER

A lively debate occurred at last Tuesday's packed city council meeting on the subject of whether to establish a skateboard park. Mayor Gridlock made a few opening remarks and then turned the microphone over to J. Cool, Director of Parks and Recreation. Mr. Cool read from portions of a report prepared by his staff, who had investigated the need for and the liability, risks, cost, and possible location of a park. Several members of the community spoke.

K. Skater said, "Skateboarding is a challenging sport. It's good for us. But right now we have no place to skate, and so kids are getting tickets for illegal skating. Lots of people say it's too dangerous, but that's not true. Kids get hurt in every sport, but you can make it a lot less dangerous for us if you give us a smooth place to practice. Still, we skaters have to be responsible and only take risks we can handle. That teaches us a lot."

D. T. Merchant remarked, "I am a store owner downtown. These skaters use our curbs and handrails as their personal skating ramps. They threaten pedestrians and scare people. If we build them an alternative, I believe most will use it. Then the police can concentrate on the few who break the rules."

G. Homeowner had this to say: "Skaters are illiterate bums. They think safety gear means thick hair gel. They have no respect. They will disturb my neighborhood all night long with their subhuman noise. I would like to remind the city council—I pay taxes and I vote. A skateboard park? Not in my backyard!"

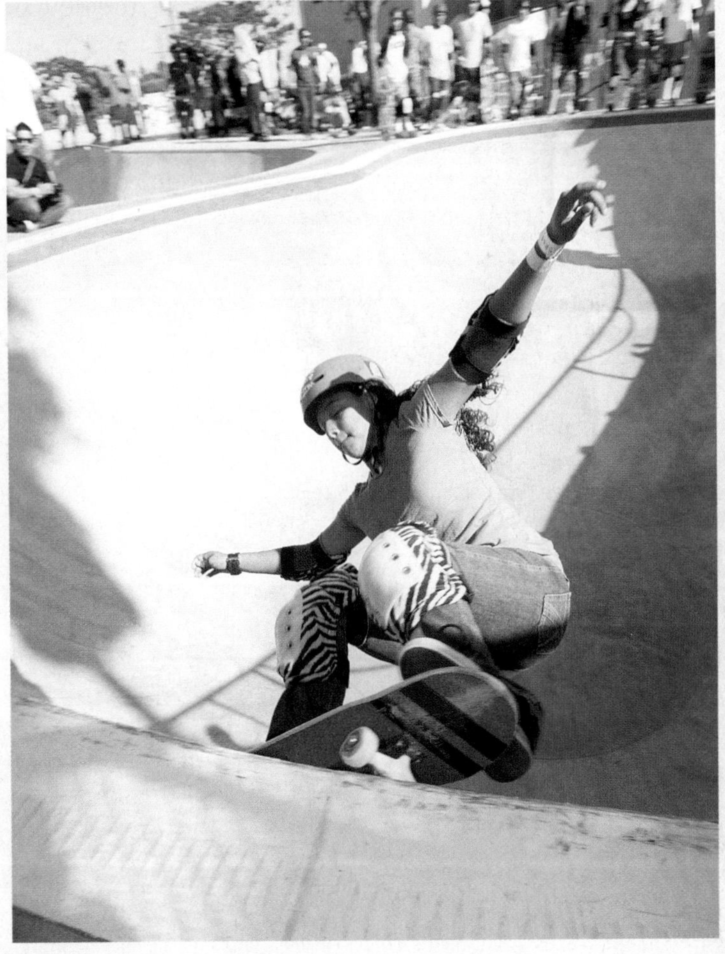

F. Parent: "My son is an outstanding citizen. He is respectful and well behaved. He also lives to skateboard. This city has placed my son at risk by failing to give him a safe place to skate. If we were talking about building a basketball court, nobody would think twice before agreeing. I'm a voter too, and I expect the city council to be responsive to the needs of *all* citizens."

Finally, S. B. Owner said, "I am the owner of the Skate Bowl. Skateboarding is not a fad. It is here to stay. You may not like the way some skaters act or look, but I know them all. They're great kids. Seems like most of the good folks here tonight are worried about safety. So here's what I propose: I will sell all safety gear at my store at 50 percent off. That's less than it costs me, folks. All that you parents have to do is fill out the emergency information card for your skater and return it to me. I'll see that the information is entered in a database that paramedics, hospital workers, and police officers can access. I'll also make sure that everyone who comes to my store knows what the Consumer Product Safety Commission says: "'Kids who want to skate are going to skate. Let's help them skate safely.'" **C**

Mr. Owner's proposal was met with a standing ovation. Plans to move ahead with the new skateboard park project will be put to a formal vote at next month's regular session.

C **Read and Discuss** How do the various citizens' comments add to the debate?

Vocabulary **proposal** (pruh POHZ uhl) *n.:* suggestion.

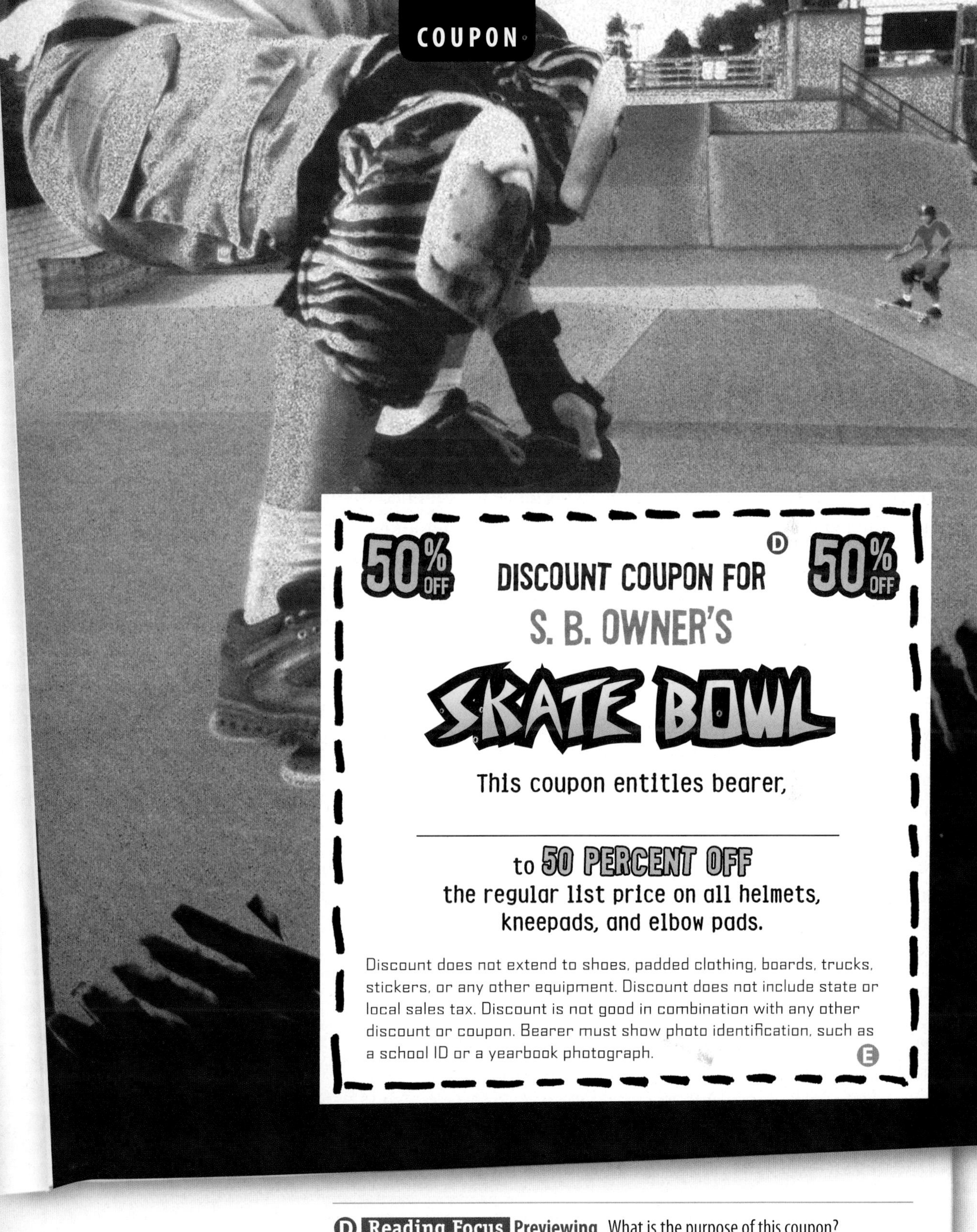

50% OFF
DISCOUNT COUPON FOR
50% OFF
S. B. OWNER'S
SKATE BOWL
This coupon entitles bearer,
to 50 PERCENT OFF
the regular list price on all helmets, kneepads, and elbow pads.
Discount does not extend to shoes, padded clothing, boards, trucks, stickers, or any other equipment. Discount does not include state or local sales tax. Discount is not good in combination with any other discount or coupon. Bearer must show photo identification, such as a school ID or a yearbook photograph.

D Reading Focus Previewing What is the purpose of this coupon?

E Informational Focus Using Information Why is it important to read the fine print on this coupon?

DOCUMENT

Excerpts from

Consumer Product Safety Commission: Document 93

Approximately 26,000 persons go to hospital emergency rooms each year for skateboarding-related injuries. Several factors—lack of protective equipment, poor board maintenance, and irregular riding surfaces—are involved in these accidents.

Who gets injured. Six of every ten skateboard injuries happen to children under fifteen years of age. Skateboarders who have been skating for less than a week suffer one third of the injuries; riders with a year or more of skating experience have the next highest number of injuries.

Injuries to first-time skateboarders are, for the most part, caused by falls. Experienced riders suffer injuries mostly when they fall after their skateboards strike rocks and other irregularities in the riding surface, or when they attempt difficult stunts. F

Environmental hazards. Irregular surfaces account for more than half the skateboarding injuries caused by falls. Before riding, skateboarders should check the surface for holes, bumps, rocks, and debris. Areas set aside for skateboarding generally have smoother riding surfaces. Skateboarding in the street can result in collisions with cars, causing serious injury or even death. G

The skateboard. Before using their boards, riders should check them for hazards, such as loose, broken, or cracked parts; sharp edges; slippery top surfaces; and wheels with nicks and cracks. Serious defects should be corrected by a qualified repair person.

Protective gear. Protective gear—such as slip-resistant, closed shoes, helmets, and specially designed padding—may not fully protect skateboarders from fractures, but its use is recommended because such gear can reduce the number and severity of injuries.

The protective gear currently on the market is not subject to federal performance standards, and so careful selection by consumers is necessary. In a helmet, look for proper fit and a chin strap; make sure the helmet does not block the rider's vision and hearing. Body padding should fit comfortably. If it is tight, it can restrict circulation and reduce the skater's ability to move freely. Loose-fitting padding, on the other hand, can slip off or slide out of position.

Source: U.S. Consumer Product Safety Commission, Washington, D.C. 20207

F **Informational Focus** **Using Information** What ideas or opinions from the other documents can be supported with these statistics?

G **Read and Discuss** What does the information in the Consumer Safety Commission document add to the argument?

Vocabulary **hazards** (HAZ uhrdz) *n.:* dangers; things that can cause danger.

Read with a Purpose Now that you've read these documents, how would you solve the skateboarding problem?

DOCUMENTS

Applying Your Skills

OH **RA.I.8.9** Distinguish the characteristics of consumer materials, functional or workplace documents and public documents. **VO.8.4** Infer the literal and figurative meaning of words and phrases and discuss the function of figurative language, including metaphors, similes and idioms.

Skateboard Park Documents

Practicing the Standards

Informational Text and Vocabulary

1. The **memorandum** gives information about —
   - **A** the benefits of opening a skateboard park
   - **B** the reasons against building a skateboard park
   - **C** a proposal for developing a skateboard park
   - **D** a history of the old skateboard park

2. Which statement is supported by information in all the documents?
   - **A** Many skateboarding injuries are caused by dangerous surfaces.
   - **B** Skateboarding is the most dangerous sport practiced in cities today.
   - **C** More students skateboard than play any other sport or activity.
   - **D** Most citizens believe that skateboarding should be outlawed.

3. Which document would you read to learn about all sides of the issue?
   - **A** The advertisement
   - **B** The memorandum
   - **C** The Consumer Product Safety Commission document
   - **D** The newspaper article

4. Another word for *hazards* is —
   - **A** faults
   - **B** dangers
   - **C** arguments
   - **D** worries

5. If a problem is *potentially* serious, it is —
   - **A** very serious
   - **B** not at all serious
   - **C** definitely serious
   - **D** possibly serious

6. Someone who presents a *proposal* gives a —
   - **A** suggestion
   - **B** summary
   - **C** reaction
   - **D** prediction

Writing Focus Constructed Response

7. If you lived in this community, would you support the new skateboard park? Write a letter to the city council explaining your opinion. Cite information from the skateboard park documents to support your position. If you support the park, be sure to specify which site you prefer and explain why.

What Do You Think Now?

What do these documents suggest about how we can solve community problems?

WEB SITE

Leash-Free Dog Run Documents

Read with a Purpose Read these workplace, public, and consumer documents to learn what is involved in creating a dog run.

Welcome to the SouthPaws Web site. SouthPaws is a not-for-profit group dedicated to creating and maintaining a leash-free space on the south side of our city for its 165,000 canine (that's dog) citizens. Please consider joining our 3,300+ members. Your membership fees are tax-deductible and will help give our dogs their own space! If you are interested in volunteering, please check out Volunteer Want Ads. Finally, you might want to consider SouthPaws T-shirts, sweats, caps, or leashes as a gift or for yourself. All proceeds support SouthPaws. **A**

What's New?

Congratulations and thank you to the hundreds of volunteers who gathered signatures on the SouthPaws petition. All that hard work last spring paid off! The residents of our city have voted to establish a park or a beach where our dogs can run unleashed. This space will be jointly funded by the city and SouthPaws donations. SouthPaws volunteers will supervise the space during daylight hours and will be empowered to ticket dog owners who do not observe cleanup and safety rules. We will have one trial year after the space officially opens to prove that the idea works. Now we need your help more than ever. **B**

A **Read and Discuss** What problem has the writer introduced to us?

B **Informational Focus** **Using Information** Where will the money for the proposed dog run come from?

Vocabulary **empowered** (ehm POW uhrd) *adj.:* given the power to do something.

	PRO	CON
CAMEO PARK	• is centrally located • has convenient access roads • has street parking	• will incur high maintenance costs • is smallest, at 1.2 residential acres • is now a popular family park • may lead nearby residents to object to noise, nuisances
ROCKY POINT BEACH	• is little used • consists of 5 nonresidential acres • has ample parking • will incur low start-up and maintenance costs	• is inconveniently located • has non-sand beach; smooth but potentially slippery rocks
MAIN BEACH	• is centrally located • consists of 7.3 nonresidential acres • has sand beach	• is heavily used all year • may cause conflicts with businesses • has limited, costly parking • will require 24-hour security and maintenance staffing • will incur high maintenance costs

Ⓒ

The most likely locations for the dog run are described above. Click **here** to cast your vote in our survey. Ⓓ

Ⓒ **Reading Focus** **Previewing** What information is summarized in these bulleted lists?

Ⓓ **Read and Discuss** Is the design of this page clear and effective? Why or why not?

Internet

LETTER

1111 South P Street · South City, CA 90123

December 12, 2010

Ms. T. Wagger
Director of Parks and Recreation
2222 Central Avenue
South City, CA 90123

Dear Ms. Wagger,

SouthPaws members would like you to take their concerns into account when choosing the site of the proposed dog run. Here they are, in order of importance:

1. Space. Healthy dogs need ample space in which to run. The park needs to be large enough for a fair number of dogs to run around in it without colliding with one another. Ample size will minimize the possibility of dogfights.

2. Conflicts. A site that is already popular for sports, family activities, or tourism will likely be a problem.

3. Site. Our research shows that dog beaches are preferable to dog parks. Dogs are hard on park grass, which quickly turns to mud in rainy weather. Sand or shells can be brushed off a dog, but mud requires a bath. Dog beaches are also easier to supervise and clean.

Thank you for working with us to find a solution that is in the best interests of the most people. We are looking forward to meeting with you next week. **E**

Sincerely,

A. K. Nine

A. K. Nine
Chairperson, SouthPaws Site Committee **F**

E **Read and Discuss** What is the purpose of the chairperson's letter?

F **Informational Focus** **Using Information** How might the writer's connection with the SouthPaws Site Committee affect the information presented in this letter?

Vocabulary **ample** (AM puhl) *adj.*: as much as is needed; enough.

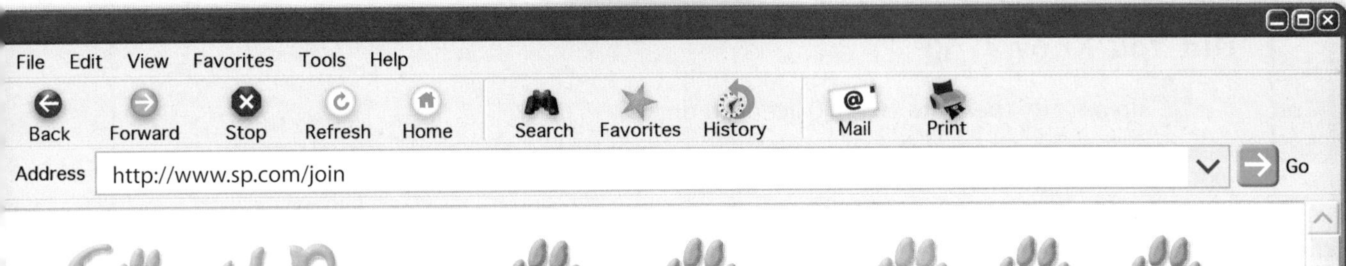

SouthPaws Membership Information

Annual Tax-Deductible Membership Fees

Basic: $15 per year; entitles you to newsletter and voting rights
Deluxe: $25 per year; entitles you to the above plus one T-shirt or cap
Sponsor: $100 per year; entitles you to all of the above plus discounted dog-obedience classes and merchandise from local merchants
Angel: $250 per year; entitles you to all of the above plus your name on our Dog Walk of Fame G

Membership in SouthPaws makes a great gift. Print out a membership application, complete it, and mail it with your donation.

Don't want to join? Then how about making a donation? We appreciate contributions in any amount.

> G **Informational Focus** Using Information
> How does the information about membership fees add to your understanding of the situation?

SouthPaws

Did You Know? (H)

 In our city there are 165,000 licensed dogs.

 The city devotes a total of 10 acres to leash-free dog areas.

 The city devotes 1,050 acres to softball, 1,040 acres to golf, and 287 acres to tennis.

 Eastside Leash-Free Dog Park accommodates 2,000 dogs per week on its 1-acre site. (I)

New!

Help SouthPaws while you tell the world about your best friend. Buy a brick in the new Dog Walk of Fame. Your pet's name and a short message will be inscribed. Be sure to provide your pet's name, your name, and your message (up to 45 characters). (Available to SouthPaws members only; $50 per pet's name.)

(H) **Reading Focus** **Previewing** What kinds of information do you find here? What is the purpose of this list?

(I) **Read and Discuss** The writer has given us a number of facts here. What point is being made?

Read with a Purpose What have you learned about the issues related to dog runs?

Internet

Applying Your Skills

RA.I.8.9 Distinguish the characteristics of consumer materials, functional or workplace documents and public documents. VO.8.4 Infer the literal and figurative meaning of words and phrases and discuss the function of figurative language, including metaphors, similes and idioms.

Leash-Free Dog Run Documents

Practicing the Standards

Informational Text and Vocabulary

1. The decision to build the dog run was made by —
   - **A** the city council
   - **B** Parks and Recreation
   - **C** SouthPaws
   - **D** voters

2. On the **Web site,** the list of the pros and cons of each potential dog run site offers —
   - **A** an opinion on which site is best
   - **B** a comparison of the sites
   - **C** the site most voters chose
   - **D** all possible locations in town

3. The purpose of the **business letter** is to —
   - **A** convince the Parks Department to build a dog run
   - **B** tell the Parks Department which site is best
   - **C** share concerns about a dog run site
   - **D** state the requirements for choosing a site

4. The site that best meets the needs and concerns of SouthPaws members is —
   - **A** Cameo Park
   - **B** Rocky Point Beach
   - **C** Main Beach
   - **D** none of the above

5. If someone is *empowered* to make a decision, he or she is —
   - **A** guaranteed to make the best decision
   - **B** able to make a decision by asking for help
   - **C** unable to make a decision based on the evidence
   - **D** given the power to make the decision

6. Another word for *ample* is —
   - **A** controversial
   - **B** narrow
   - **C** lacking
   - **D** enough

Writing Focus Constructed Response

7. What decision did you make about the location of the dog run? Write a brief opinion statement that expresses your decision. Cite information from the Leash-Free Dog Run documents to support your position.

What Do You Think Now?

What do these documents say about effective ways to solve problems affecting an entire community?

INFORMATIONAL TEXT FOCUS

Reading Consumer Documents

CONTENTS

What Do You Think?

What questions should you ask when you are shopping for a product?

QuickWrite

Think of something you might want to purchase, such as a bicycle or cell phone. How do you decide which kind to buy? Jot down your ideas.

CONSUMER DOCUMENTS
Preparing to Read

RA.I.8.9 Distinguish the characteristics of consumer materials, functional or workplace documents and public documents. *Also covered* **RP.8.3; RA.I.8.1**

WarpSpeedNet Documents / SweetPlayer Documents

Informational Text Focus

Consumer Documents Consumer documents give you information that is fundamental for making smart buying decisions. The **elements** that make up consumer materials define what the document is—warranty, contract, product, information, or instruction manual. The **features** are what make consumer documents unique. For example, every contract tells what you get and what you give. Without those elements, a contract isn't a contract. Features are found in the details. Some features may be to your advantage; others may not.

Reading Focus

Skimming and Scanning These techniques can help you get the information you need from consumer documents.

- **Skimming** is reading quickly. When you skim, you get a general idea of the information included.
- **Scanning** is looking for specific information. You can use chapter titles, headings, subheadings, terms in italics or boldface, and graphics to help you locate the information you need.

Into Action Use a chart like this one as you skim and scan.

Document	Skimming	Scanning
Advertisement	It's an ad for an Internet service provider.	The ad does not give exact prices.
Service Agreement		

Writing Focus

Preparing for **Constructed Response**

You will be reading an advertisement. In your *Reader/Writer Notebook,* note which details are the most clear and helpful.

Reader/Writer Notebook

Use your **RWN** to complete the activities for these selections.

Vocabulary

WarpSpeedNet Documents

disconnected (dihs kuh NEHK tihd) *v.* used as *adj.:* not connected; cut off; separated. *Our phone call was disconnected when the cord was unplugged.*

discontinued (dihs kuhn TIHN yood) *v.* used as *adj.:* not continued; stopped; ended. *Service will be discontinued if you do not pay your bills.*

authorization (aw thuhr uh ZAY shuhn) *n.:* official permission. *You must receive authorization to use the computer lab.*

SweetPlayer Documents

abide (uh BYD) (with *by*) *v.:* accept and follow. *I agree to abide by all of the conditions of this contract.*

liable (LY uh buhl) *adj.:* legally responsible. *The company is liable for replacing a faulty product.*

Language Coach

Prefixes Which two Vocabulary words share a prefix? What is it, and what does it mean? (For a clue, look at the definitions.) List five other words that begin with this prefix. Use a dictionary if you need help.

Learn It Online

Take another look at consumer documents using the interactive Reading Workshops at:

go.hrw.com L8-625 

ADVERTISEMENT

WarpSpeedNet Documents

Read with a Purpose Read these consumer documents to learn what purchasing high-speed internet service involves.

Choosing a High-Speed Internet Service Provider

Juan's family's phone line is always busy because everyone uses the Internet. They decide it is time to purchase high-speed Internet access. They see this advertisement for cable service:

Element—description of selling points. ***Features***—*no equipment to buy, speedy, convenient.*

Element—enticements to buy. ***Features***—*free installation, money-back guarantee, short-term offer.*

Element—contact information.

Element—limitations. ***Features***—*is not available everywhere, does not work with all computers, has expiration date.*

WarpSpeedNet

You Get What You Want—Now.

Only WarpSpeedNet provides all the cable equipment and services you need for a lightning-fast Internet connection through your home computer. Never wait again to dial in, log on, or connect. WarpSpeedNet is always on, always ready to go. You'll never be disconnected in the middle of a download again! **A**

WarpSpeedNet is point-and-click easy to use. Get weather reports now, news now, Web shopping now, music now, games now. Anything the World Wide Web offers, WarpSpeedNet brings to you—now!

CALL DURING THE NEXT TWO WEEKS TO RECEIVE FREE INSTALLATION AND A RISK-FREE 30-DAY MONEY-BACK GUARANTEE

Call now and mention priority code RIW.
1-555-WarpNet

Service subject to availability in your area. Offer good in South and North County areas only. Minimum computer system requirements apply. Offer expires 12/31/10. **B**

A Reading Focus Skimming How can skimming—reading quickly—help you learn what this ad is selling?

B Informational Focus Consumer Documents Why do you think product limitations, an element of some ads, are usually presented in tiny type?

Vocabulary **disconnected** (dihs kuh NEHK tihd) *v.* used as *adj.:* not connected; cut off; separated.

Reading a Service Agreement Juan's family decides to give WarpSpeedNet a try. They live in South County, meet the minimum computer system requirements, and call within the two-week deadline. They are now entitled to everything the company promised: free installation, thirty-day money-back trial, and all the necessary cable equipment. They also receive some important consumer documents. Let's take a look at some of those documents.

WarpSpeedNet

Service Agreement (C)

1. Equipment

A. Equipment includes rental of cable modem and necessary connections to permit use of one (1) computer with WarpSpeedNet service.

B. WarpSpeedNet will install equipment. Subscriber will grant company reasonable access to install, inspect, repair, maintain, or disconnect the equipment. Refusal to do so may result in discontinued service.

C. Cable equipment remains the property of WarpSpeedNet. Upon termination of service, equipment shall be returned in original condition, ordinary wear and tear excepted.

2. Charges

A. Subscriber agrees to pay for the monthly service subscribed to, including charges for installation, in advance. Monthly charges are set forth on a separate price list and are subject to change.

B. Subscribers who discontinue service will be required to pay all due and past-due charges. If the subscriber reconnects service, a charge will apply. (D)

C. If cable equipment is lost, damaged, or stolen, subscriber must pay $300 to WarpSpeedNet for replacement.

____
Company representative signature and date

____
Subscriber signature and date

Element*—*services (what Juan's family gets).* *Features*—*equipment for one computer, installation, and setup.

Element*—*costs (what Juan's family pays).* *Features*—*payments per agreement, including all fees, charges, and replacement costs.

Element*—*signatures (no contract is valid without them).

(C) **Read and Discuss** How does the information in the contract connect with the advertisement Juan's family received?

(D) **Informational Focus** **Consumer Documents** What feature in Clause 2B is not spelled out exactly? Why might this be a problem?

Vocabulary **discontinued** (dihs kuhn TIHN yood) *v.* used as *adj.:* not continued; stopped; ended.

Reading an Instruction Manual Juan's family also receives an instruction manual. Let's take a look.

Welcome to

WarpSpeedNet E

Element—table of contents.

E Reading Focus Scanning How does scanning, or looking for specific information, help you locate information in this instruction manual?

Cable Modem Lights

There are four lights on the front of your cable modem.

1. POWER ● **POWER**	**STEADY GREEN:** Power is on.
2. CABLE ○ POWER ● **CABLE** ○ PC ○ DATA	**STEADY GREEN:** Cable is ready to use. **FLASHING RED-GREEN:** Cable is setting up connection. Wait. **FLASHING RED:** Connection has a problem. See Troubleshooting, page 33. **NO LIGHT:** There is no cable connection. Call for service.
3. COMPUTER LINK ○ POWER ○ CABLE ● **PC** ○ DATA	**STEADY GREEN:** Connection is working. **FLASHING RED:** There is a connection problem. See Troubleshooting, page 33. **NO LIGHT:** Computer has been turned off or disconnected.
4. DATA ● **DATA**	**FLASHING LIGHT:** Modem is sending or receiving data. **F**

Element—explanation of product.
Features—specific meaning of each light.

F **Read and Discuss** How do the table of contents and the page on cable modem lights help Juan's family understand the equipment?

Reading a Warranty If the cable modem doesn't work, what can Juan's family do? Let's check the warranty. A warranty tells you when, how, and for how long you can get your money back. WarpSpeedNet's warranty offers a refund if the equipment fails during the first year. But that doesn't really apply to Juan's family. Can you figure out why? (Hint: Go back and read the contract.)

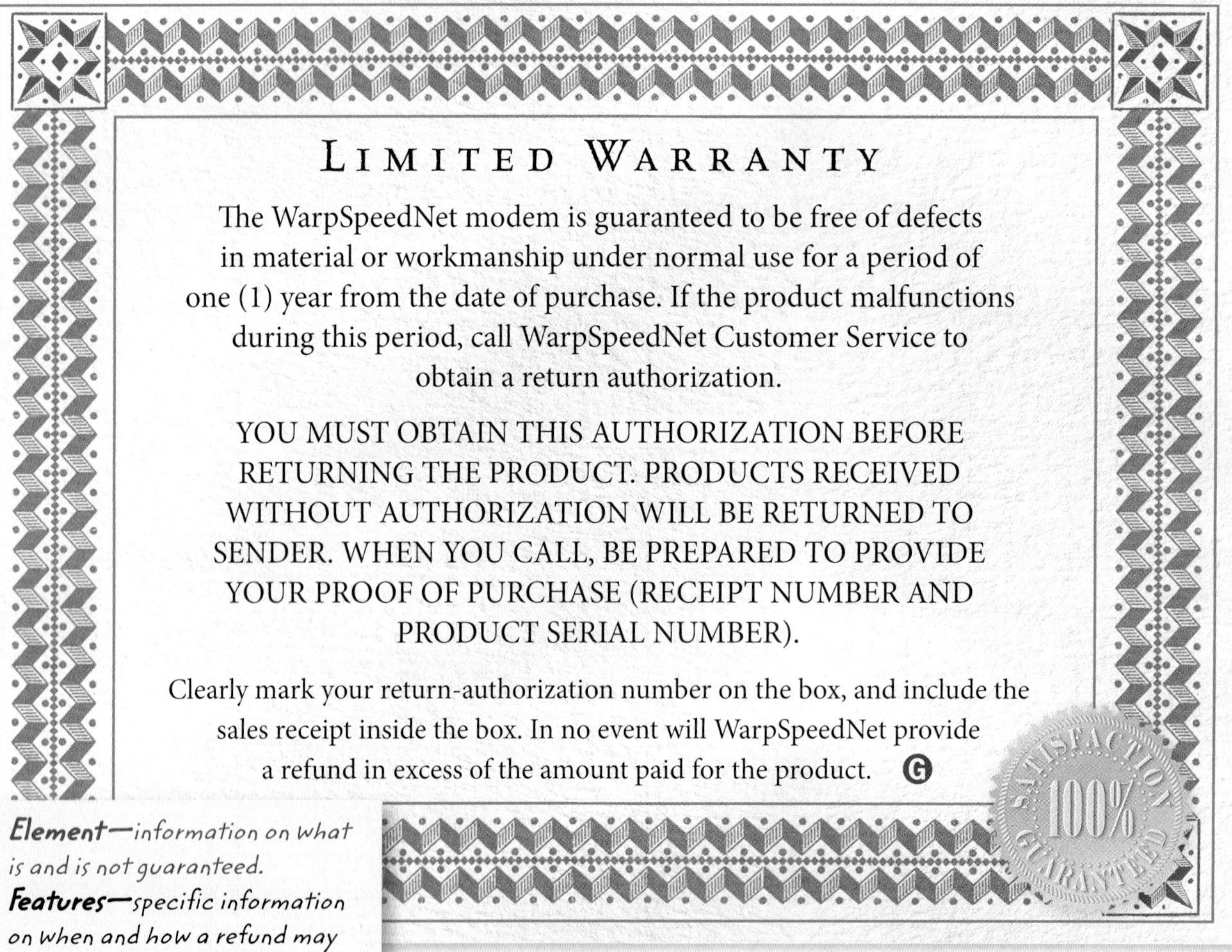

LIMITED WARRANTY

The WarpSpeedNet modem is guaranteed to be free of defects in material or workmanship under normal use for a period of one (1) year from the date of purchase. If the product malfunctions during this period, call WarpSpeedNet Customer Service to obtain a return authorization.

YOU MUST OBTAIN THIS AUTHORIZATION BEFORE RETURNING THE PRODUCT. PRODUCTS RECEIVED WITHOUT AUTHORIZATION WILL BE RETURNED TO SENDER. WHEN YOU CALL, BE PREPARED TO PROVIDE YOUR PROOF OF PURCHASE (RECEIPT NUMBER AND PRODUCT SERIAL NUMBER).

Clearly mark your return-authorization number on the box, and include the sales receipt inside the box. In no event will WarpSpeedNet provide a refund in excess of the amount paid for the product. G

Element—*information on what is and is not guaranteed.*
Features—*specific information on when and how a refund may be obtained.*

G **Read and Discuss** How does the warranty connect with the equipment deal laid out in the service agreement?

Vocabulary **authorization** (aw thuhr uh ZAY shuhn) *n.:* official permission.

Read with a Purpose What did the family learn about their high-speed internet service?

CONSUMER DOCUMENTS
Applying Your Skills

OH RA.I.8.9 Distinguish the characteristics of consumer materials, functional or workplace documents and public documents. **RP.8.3** Monitor own comprehension by adjusting speed to fit the purpose, or by skimming, scanning, reading on, looking back, note taking or summarizing what has been read so far in text. *Also covered* **WA.8.5.b; VO.8.4; RA.I.8.1**

WarpSpeedNet Documents

Practicing the Standards

Informational Text and Vocabulary

1. In which document would you look to find out how to operate the cable equipment?

A Warranty
B Instructional manual
C Advertisement
D Service agreement

2. Important elements of the WarpSpeedNet and all **advertisements** include —

A an enticement to buy and contact information
B a discount offer for the first individuals to call
C an Internet address and a toll-free phone number
D a description of how to use the product

3. The purpose of the **instruction manual** is to —

A lay out the responsibilities of the WarpSpeedNet company
B describe how to install, use, and maintain the cable equipment
C explain why you should buy the cable service
D provide all the information you need to make your purchasing decision

4. If you have *authorization*, you have —

A an error in your understanding
B curiosity about an issue
C official permission to do something
D the ability to write clearly

5. Something that has been *disconnected* is —

A cut off
B not appropriate
C thrown away
D acted upon

6. If a project is *discontinued*, it is —

A reduced
B not perfect
C not easy
D stopped

Writing Focus Constructed Response

7. In a paragraph, critique the advertisement you read. Specify which elements are most helpful and which are least helpful. Which features do you think are fair, unfair, or misleading? Support your opinion with examples from the document.

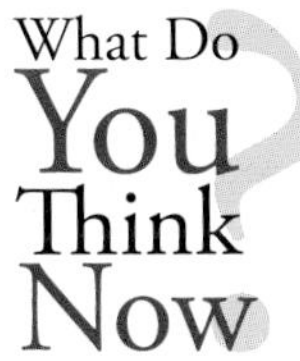

What have you learned about making smart consumer decisions?

SweetPlayer Documents

Read with a Purpose Read these consumer documents to determine their purpose.

Choosing an MP3 Player Now Juan is ready to use that high-speed modem. His first stop? MP3s and fast downloads! MP3 is an audio format, a software code that turns sounds into information a computer can understand. MP3 squeezes good sound quality into a small package. The sound-size combination makes MP3 the most popular audio format used today. Juan checks out the rules for downloading MP3s on the Internet.

IS IT LEGAL?

The Internet is full of music. You can get your favorite hit in MP3 format with a single click. It's easy, it's free—and it could be illegal. Many music sites contain music that someone has digitally copied from a CD and then placed where other people can download it. It's a convenient and popular practice, but it is not legal. So what is legal?

1. You may rip tracks from a CD you own to a computer as long as they are for your own use and not for the use of other people.
2. You may download free promotional tracks. This is an increasingly popular way for artists to introduce their work to you. Free and promotional tracks are clearly marked, usually under the heading "Free Music." There are often CDs for sale by the artist, too. Watch out, though. If a friend wants the same track, he or she will have to download it. It is not legal for you to copy a CD you downloaded from the Internet.
3. You may buy the track for your own use. Many sites, including those of more and more record companies, are now offering songs for sale in this manner.

Rule of thumb: If the way in which music is to be downloaded doesn't fit any of the three situations described above, the process probably isn't legal. When in doubt, check the copyright notice on the site. **A**

A **Read and Discuss** What does this box say about downloading music?

Internet

Juan can't wait to start listening to music on the family's computer. He needs the right software and has narrowed his search to a product called SweetPlayer—but which version should he get? Let's look at the Internet advertisement.

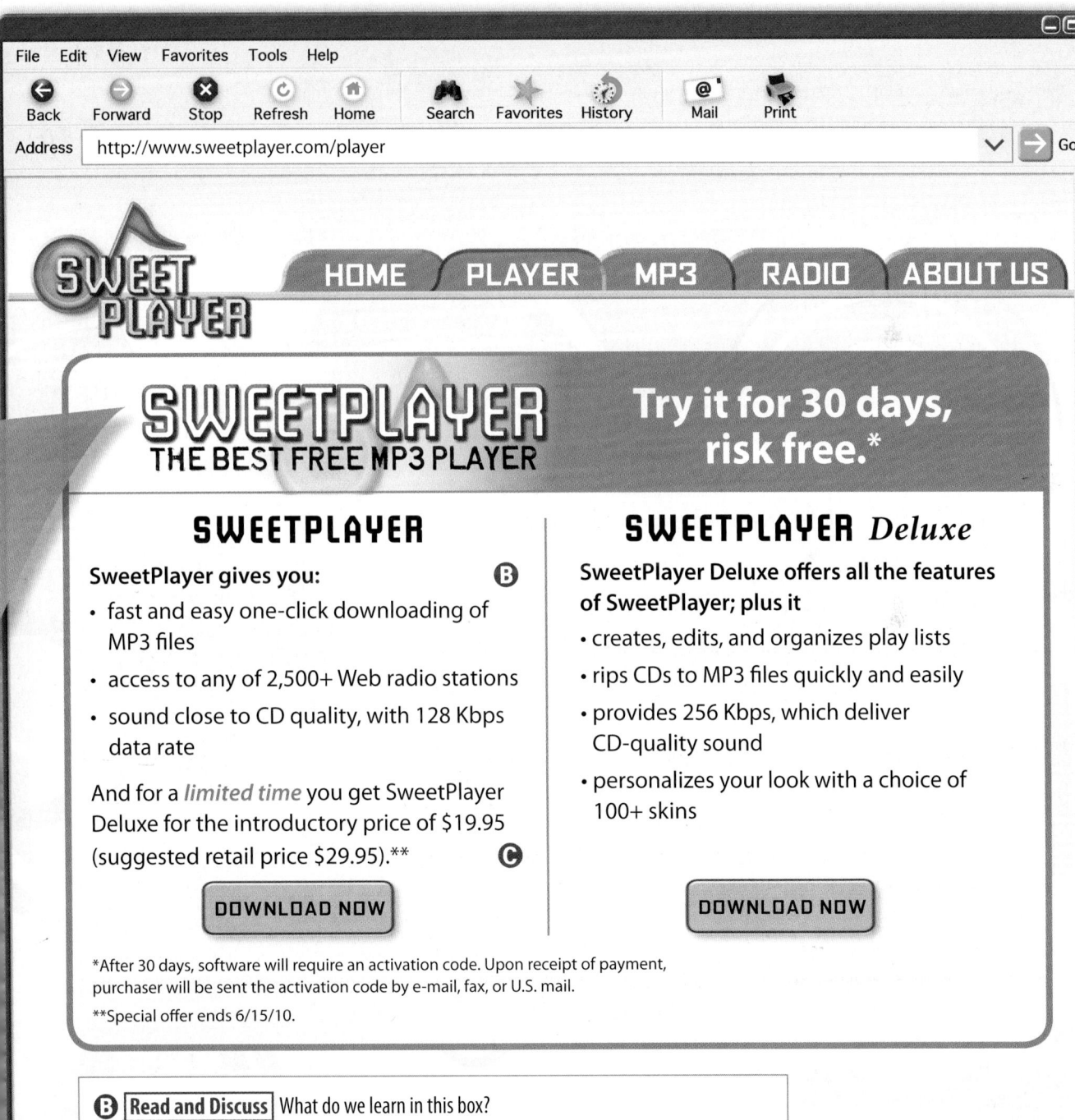

SWEETPLAYER

SweetPlayer gives you: **B**

- fast and easy one-click downloading of MP3 files
- access to any of 2,500+ Web radio stations
- sound close to CD quality, with 128 Kbps data rate

And for a *limited time* you get SweetPlayer Deluxe for the introductory price of $19.95 (suggested retail price $29.95).** **C**

DOWNLOAD NOW

SWEETPLAYER *Deluxe*

SweetPlayer Deluxe offers all the features of SweetPlayer; plus it

- creates, edits, and organizes play lists
- rips CDs to MP3 files quickly and easily
- provides 256 Kbps, which deliver CD-quality sound
- personalizes your look with a choice of 100+ skins

DOWNLOAD NOW

*After 30 days, software will require an activation code. Upon receipt of payment, purchaser will be sent the activation code by e-mail, fax, or U.S. mail.

**Special offer ends 6/15/10.

B **Read and Discuss** What do we learn in this box?

C **Reading Focus Scanning** Scan this advertisement to find out how much SweetPlayer costs. How about SweetPlayer Deluxe?

Following Download Directions Juan clicks on the button to download SweetPlayer Deluxe. The following downloading directions appear on the screen:

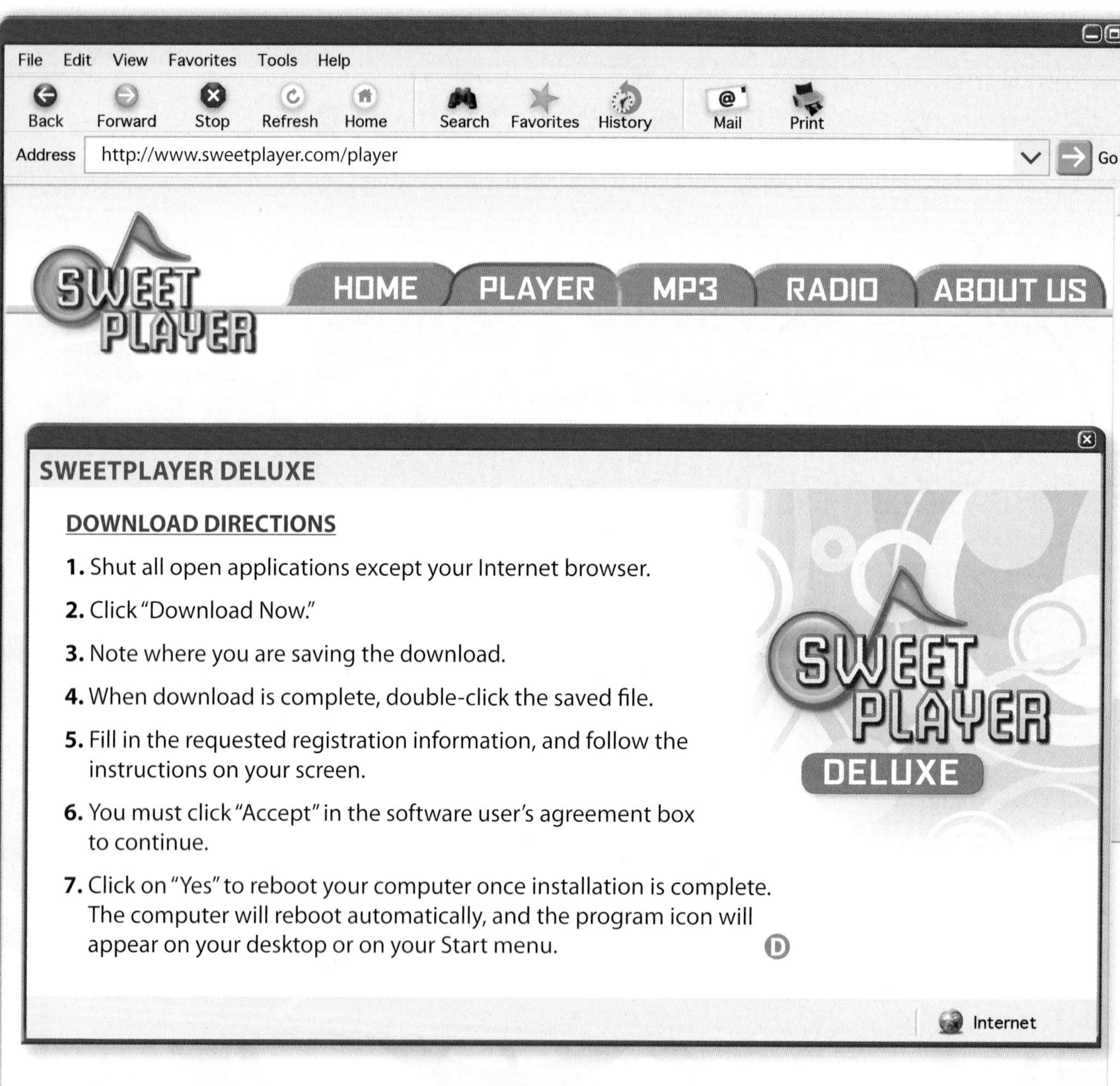

File Edit View Favorites Tools Help
Back Forward Stop Refresh Home Search Favorites History Mail Print
Address http://www.sweetplayer.com/player
Go
SWEET PLAYER
HOME PLAYER MP3 RADIO ABOUT US
SWEETPLAYER DELUXE
DOWNLOAD DIRECTIONS
1. Shut all open applications except your Internet browser.
2. Click "Download Now."
3. Note where you are saving the download.
4. When download is complete, double-click the saved file.
5. Fill in the requested registration information, and follow the instructions on your screen.
6. You must click "Accept" in the software user's agreement box to continue.
7. Click on "Yes" to reboot your computer once installation is complete. The computer will reboot automatically, and the program icon will appear on your desktop or on your Start menu. D
SWEET PLAYER DELUXE
Internet

D **Informational Focus** **Consumer Documents** Which common elements of technical directions do you see here?

Reading a Software User's Agreement Even though he plans to click "Accept," Juan reads the software user's agreement carefully. (Remember that a user agreement is a form of contract.) It is long and complicated. Here are the parts that grab Juan's attention.

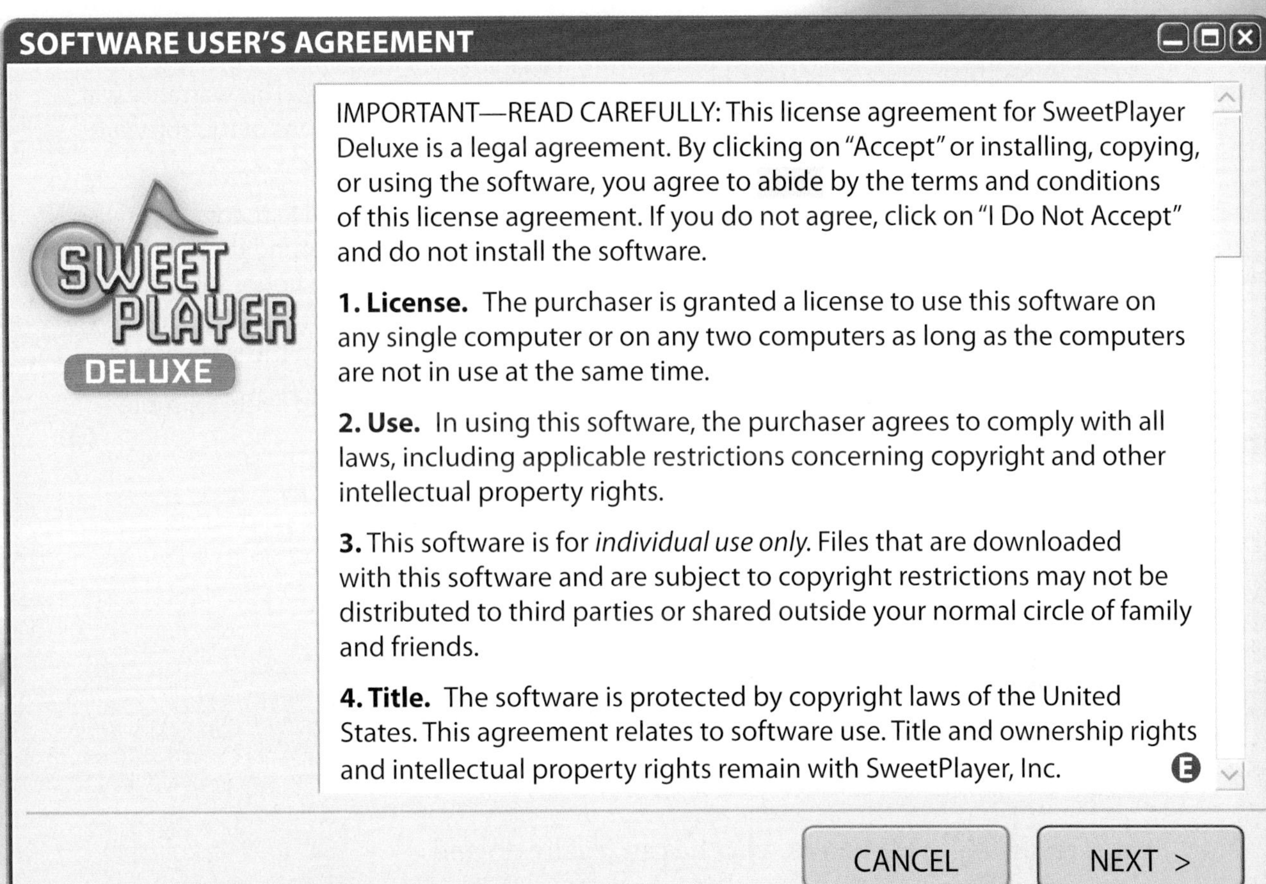
SOFTWARE USER'S AGREEMENT

IMPORTANT—READ CAREFULLY: This license agreement for SweetPlayer Deluxe is a legal agreement. By clicking on "Accept" or installing, copying, or using the software, you agree to abide by the terms and conditions of this license agreement. If you do not agree, click on "I Do Not Accept" and do not install the software.

1. License. The purchaser is granted a license to use this software on any single computer or on any two computers as long as the computers are not in use at the same time.

2. Use. In using this software, the purchaser agrees to comply with all laws, including applicable restrictions concerning copyright and other intellectual property rights.

3. This software is for *individual use only.* Files that are downloaded with this software and are subject to copyright restrictions may not be distributed to third parties or shared outside your normal circle of family and friends.

4. Title. The software is protected by copyright laws of the United States. This agreement relates to software use. Title and ownership rights and intellectual property rights remain with SweetPlayer, Inc. E

E **Reading Focus** **Skimming** Why would it be a mistake just to skim a software user's agreement before you accept it?

Vocabulary **abide** (uh BYD) (with *by*) *v.*: accept and follow.

Reading a Limited Warranty Before clicking on "Accept," Juan also reads the warranty. (F)

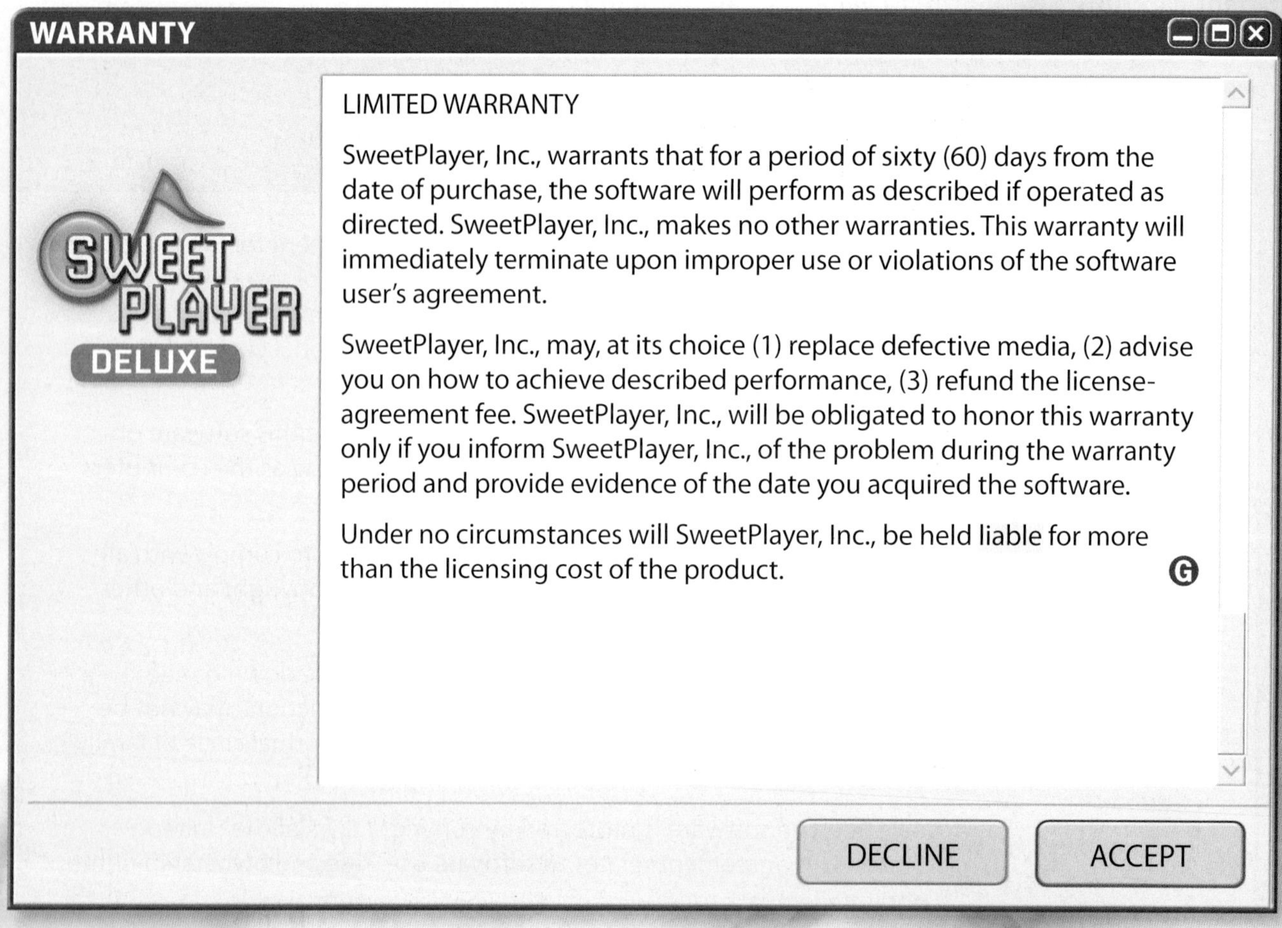
WARRANTY

LIMITED WARRANTY

SweetPlayer, Inc., warrants that for a period of sixty (60) days from the date of purchase, the software will perform as described if operated as directed. SweetPlayer, Inc., makes no other warranties. This warranty will immediately terminate upon improper use or violations of the software user's agreement.

SweetPlayer, Inc., may, at its choice (1) replace defective media, (2) advise you on how to achieve described performance, (3) refund the license-agreement fee. SweetPlayer, Inc., will be obligated to honor this warranty only if you inform SweetPlayer, Inc., of the problem during the warranty period and provide evidence of the date you acquired the software.

Under no circumstances will SweetPlayer, Inc., be held liable for more than the licensing cost of the product. (G)

Now Juan is ready to go! He knows what he can legally do and what the company must legally provide. He clicks "Accept."

(F) **Informational Focus** **Consumer Documents** Identify four specific features of the SweetPlayer warranty.

(G) **Read and Discuss** When Juan accepts the user's agreement, what does that mean?

Vocabulary **liable** (LY uh buhl) *adj.:* legally responsible.

Read with a Purpose What is the purpose of these consumer documents?

CONSUMER DOCUMENTS

Applying Your Skills

RA.I.8.9 Distinguish the characteristics of consumer materials, functional or workplace documents and public documents. WA.8.4.b Write informational essays or reports, including research, that: provide a clear and accurate perspective on the subject *Also covered* VO.8.4; RP.8.3

SweetPlayer Documents

Practicing the Standards

Informational Text and Vocabulary

1. The SweetPlayer **download directions** are most like —
   A a warranty
   B a contract
   C an instruction manual
   D product information

2. The "Accept" button on the **software user's agreement** takes the place of a —
   A description of services
   B catalog of equipment
   C feature of a warranty
   D signature on a contract

3. The **advertisement** and the **software user's agreement** are alike in that they both —
   A offer important information about the product
   B entice the reader to buy the product
   C discuss legal terms and conditions of use
   D tell the buyer how to get a refund

4. The **software user's agreement** and the **warranty** are different in that the first —
   A describes the product, while the second describes the company
   B is a legal document, while the second is not
   C outlines mainly what the seller must do, while the second outlines mainly what the buyer must do
   D outlines mainly what the buyer must do, while the second outlines mainly what the seller must do

5. If you are *liable* for something, you are —
   A responsible for it
   B unhappy with it
   C not connected with it
   D limited by it

6. When a writer encourages people to *abide* by a law, she wants readers to —
   A challenge the law
   B rewrite the law
   C follow the law
   D shorten the law

Writing Focus Constructed Response

7. In a short essay, explain the benefits and risks of skimming these consumer documents. List two examples of how skimming is helpful and two examples of how it can be harmful.

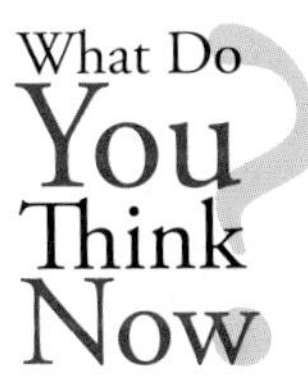

After reading these documents, what specific questions would you ask before making a major purchase?

INFORMATIONAL TEXT FOCUS

Following Technical Directions

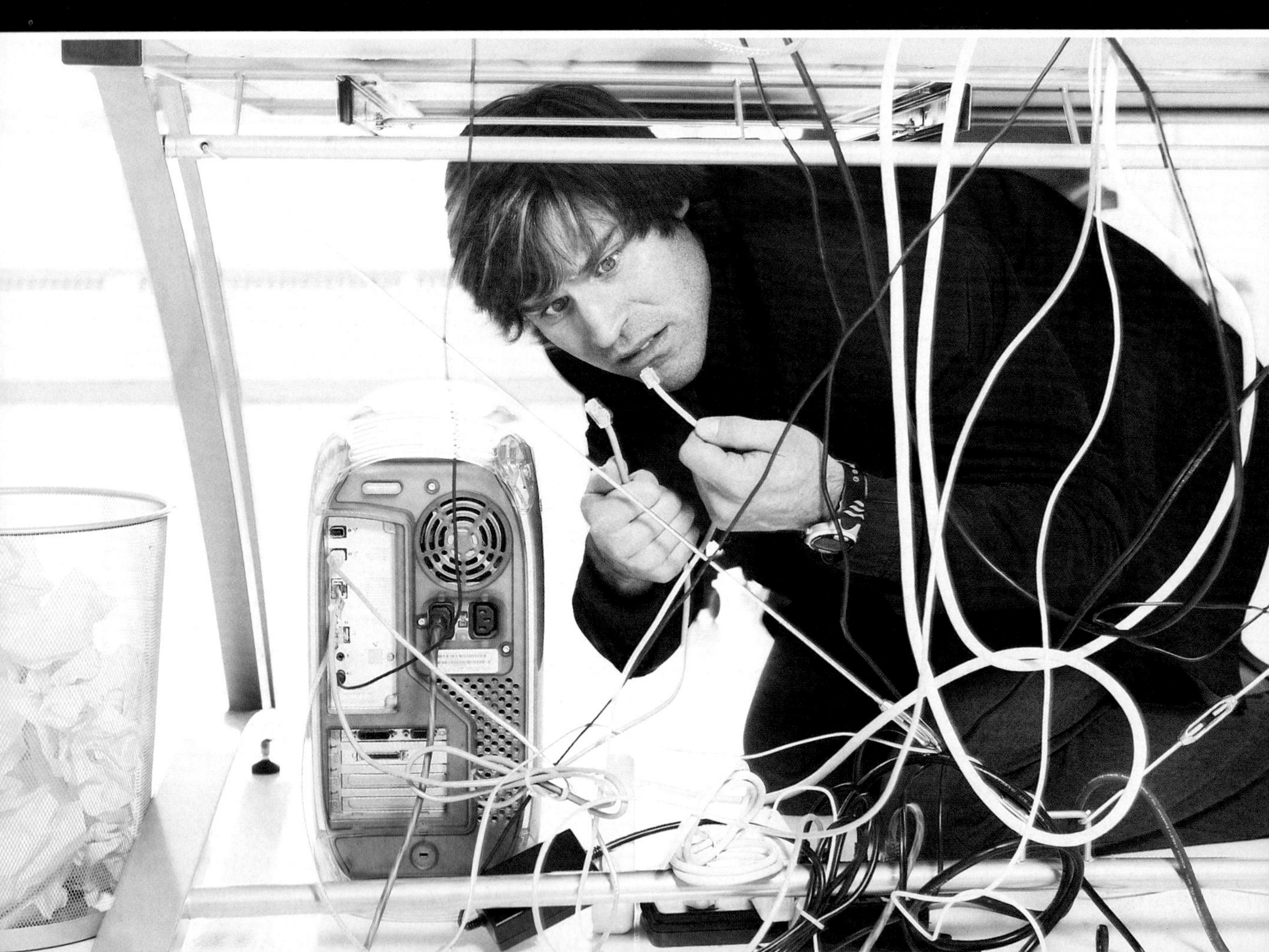

CONTENTS

What Do You Think?

How can following instructions help us in our daily life?

QuickWrite

List some tasks that instructions helped you complete. Which directions did you follow exactly? Which did you follow more loosely?

TECHNICAL DIRECTIONS
Preparing to Read

RA.I.8.9 Distinguish the characteristics of consumer materials, functional or workplace documents and public documents. **RA.I.8.4** Analyze information found in maps, charts, tables, graphs, diagrams, cutaways and overlays.

Guide to Computers

Use your **RWN** to complete the activities for this selection.

Informational Text Focus

Technical Directions Many products come with instruction manuals that explain how the product works. The manuals also outline basic parts and functions and specify the steps you must follow to assemble or operate the product. When the product is a scientific, electronic, or mechanical device, these instructions are called **technical directions.** If you skip steps or perform them out of order, the device may not work. Technical directions usually contain

- a parts list or glossary of key terms that you'll need to know
- illustrations, diagrams, and photos that show key steps
- clearly labeled instructions that appear in a logical sequence

Vocabulary

functions (FUHNGK shuhnz) *n.:* uses; purposes. *A computer's many functions include calculating data and storing information.*

corresponding (kawr uh SPAHN dihng) *adj.:* matching; equivalent. *Be careful to plug the cable into the corresponding outlet.*

secure (sih KYUR) *v.:* fix firmly in place. *Be sure to secure the cord firmly in the port on the back of the computer.*

Reading Focus

Understanding Graphics Instruction manuals may include illustrations, diagrams, and photos. These visual elements—often called *figures*—can help you understand what is being described.

Into Action As you read the following texts, note what types of figures are provided and what type of information they convey.

	What the Figures Tell Me
Photos	
Diagrams	
Illustrations	

Language Coach

Multiple-Meaning Words Some words look familiar but when used in technical documents have meanings that differ from their familiar meanings. For example, *functions* can be a noun meaning "events" and a verb meaning "works." What is another meaning of *functions*? How about the Vocabulary word *secure*? What other meanings does this word have?

Writing Focus

Preparing for **Constructed Response**

As you read, notice how the steps in the technical directions follow a logical progression. In your *Reader/Writer Notebook,* write any questions you have about steps that are unclear or steps that seem to be missing or out of sequence.

Learn It Online
Do pictures help you learn? Try the *PowerNotes* lesson at:

go.hrw.com L8-639 

GUIDE TO COMPUTERS

Figure 1 *Believe it or not, this MP3 player contains a computer!*

Read with a Purpose

Read to figure out the purpose of this set of technical directions.

WHAT IS A COMPUTER?

Did a computer help you wake up this morning? You might think of a computer as something you use to send e-mails or surf the Internet, but computers are around you all of the time. Computers are in alarm clocks, cars, phones, and even MP3 players. An MP3 player, like the one in **Figure 1,** allows you to build your own music lists and carry thousands of songs with you wherever you go.

A **computer** is an electronic device that performs tasks by processing and storing information. A computer performs a task when it is given a command and has the instructions necessary to carry out that command. Computers do not operate by themselves, or "think."

Basic Functions

The basic functions a computer performs are shown in **Figure 2.** The information you give to a computer is called *input.* Downloading songs onto your MP3 player or setting your alarm clock is a type of input. To perform a task, a computer processes the input, changing it to a desired form. Processing could mean adding a list of numbers, executing a drawing, or even moving a piece of equipment. Input doesn't have to be processed immediately; it can be stored until it is needed. Computers store information in their *memory.* For example, your MP3 player stores the songs you have chosen to input. It can then process this stored information by playing the songs you request. *Output* is the final result of the task performed by the computer. The output of an MP3 player is the music you hear when you put on your headphones! **A**

A **Read and Discuss** What point is the author trying to make here?

Vocabulary **functions** (FUHNGK shuhnz) *n.:* uses; purposes.

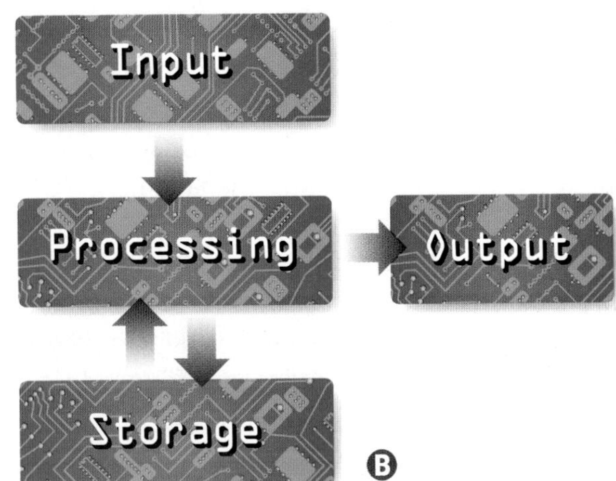

Figure 2 *The Functions of a Computer*

COMPUTER HARDWARE

For each function of a computer, there is a corresponding part of the computer where that function occurs. *Hardware* refers to the parts, or equipment, that make up a computer. As you read about each piece of hardware, refer to **Figure 3.**

Input Devices

An *input device* is a piece of hardware that feeds information to the computer. You can enter information into a computer by using a keyboard, mouse, scanner, digitizing pad and pen, or digitizing camera—or even your own voice!

Central Processing Unit

A computer performs tasks within an area called the *central processing unit,* or CPU. In a personal computer, the CPU is a microprocessor. Input goes through the CPU for immediate processing or for storage in memory. The CPU is where the computer does calculations, solves problems, and executes the instructions given to it. Some computers now come with two—or more—CPUs to process information more effectively.

B Reading Focus Graphics What do the arrows in this diagram indicate?

Vocabulary **corresponding** (kawr uh SPAHN dihng) *adj.:* matching; equivalent.

Memory

Information can be stored in the computer's memory until it is needed. CD-ROMs, DVDs, and flash drives inserted into a computer and hard disks inside a computer have memory to store information. Two other types of memory are *ROM* (read-only memory) and *RAM* (random-access memory).

ROM is permanent. It handles functions such as computer start-up, maintenance, and hardware management. ROM normally cannot be added to or changed, and it cannot be lost when the computer is turned off. On the other hand, RAM is temporary. It stores information only while that information is being used. RAM is sometimes called working memory. The more RAM a computer has, the more information can be input and the more powerful the computer is.

Figure 3 *Computer Hardware* Ⓒ

Ⓒ **Reading Focus Graphics** How does this graphic help you understand the functions of a computer?

Output Devices

Once a computer performs a task, it shows the results of the task on an *output device.* Monitors, printers, and speaker systems are all examples of output devices.

Modems

One piece of computer hardware that serves as an input device as well as an output device is a *modem.* Modems allow computers to communicate. One computer can input information into another computer over a telephone or cable line as long as each computer has its own network connection. In this way, modems permit computers to "talk" with other computers. **D**

D **Read and Discuss** What does this part say about the computer's hardware?

THE INTERNET—A GLOBAL NETWORK

Thanks to high-speed connections and computer software, it is possible to connect many computers and allow them to communicate with one another. That's what the **Internet** is—a huge computer network consisting of millions of computers that can all share information with one another. **E**

How the Internet Works

Computers can connect to one another on the Internet by using a modem to dial into an Internet service provider, or ISP. A home computer connects to an ISP over a phone or cable line. A school, business, or other group can connect all of its computers to form a local area network (LAN). Then, a single network connection can be used to connect the LAN to an ISP. As depicted in **Figure 4,** ISPs are connected globally by satellite. And that's how computers go global!

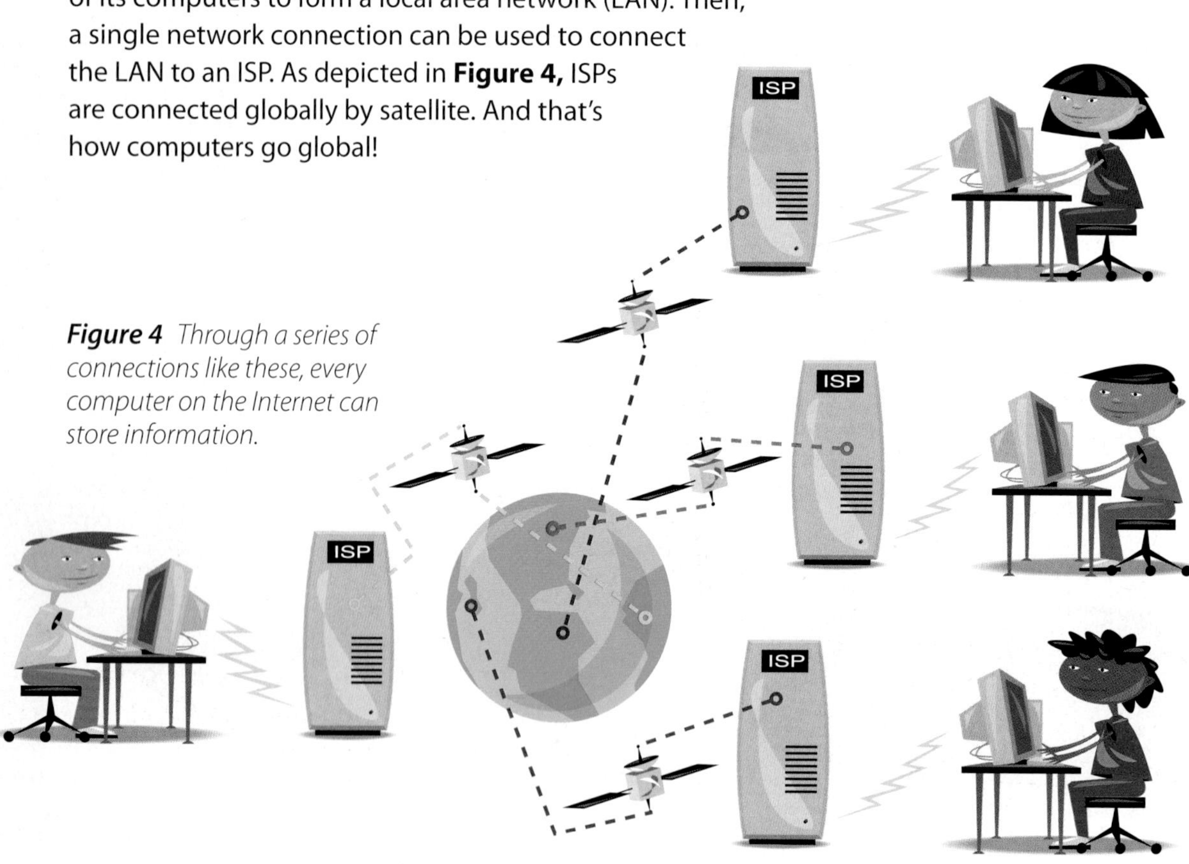

Figure 4 *Through a series of connections like these, every computer on the Internet can store information.*

E **Read and Discuss** What is the purpose of the Internet?

HOW TO SET UP A DESKTOP COMPUTER

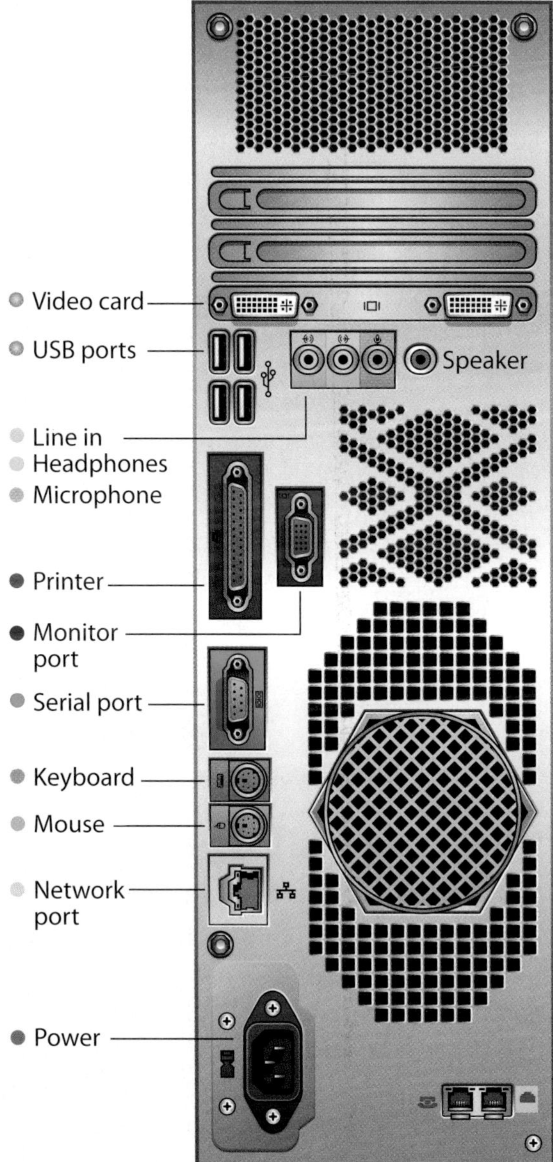

Figure 5 *Computer Connections*

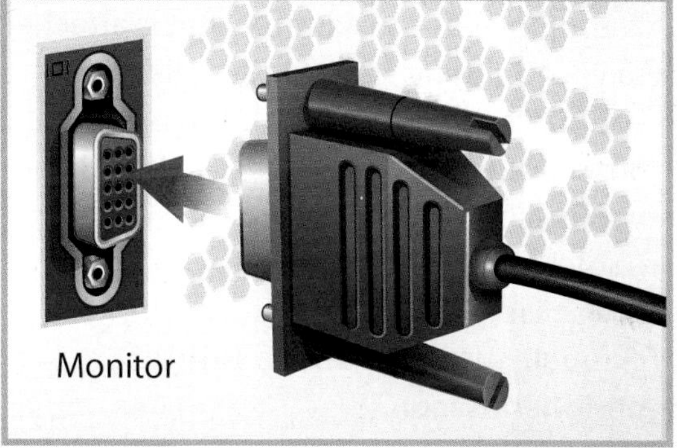

F

STEP 1 Connect the monitor to the computer.

The monitor has two cords. One cord, the **monitor interface cable,** lets the computer communicate with the monitor. The monitor cable connects to the video port (the port designated for monitors) at the back of the computer. The connector on this cord is a plug with pins in it; the pins correspond to holes in the video port on the computer. This cable probably has screws to secure the connection. The other cord is the **monitor's power cord,** which plugs into the wall outlet or **surge protector,** a plug-in device that protects electronic equipment from high-voltage electrical surges (see Step 5).

F Reading Focus Graphics How are the two graphics on this page different? What is the purpose of each?

Vocabulary secure (sih KYUR) *v.:* fix firmly in place.

STEP 2 Connect the printer to the computer.

The connector on the cable that is attached to your printer is most likely a USB cable. USB ports (USB stands for Universal Serial Bus) can accept any device with a USB connector. Connect one end to the back of your printer. Then connect the other end to an available USB port on the back of your computer where you see a **printer** or **peripherals icon.**

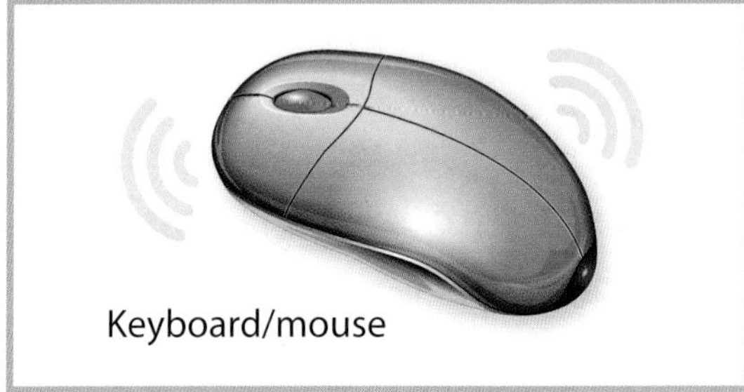

STEP 3 Connect the keyboard and mouse.

Look at the **connector** on the cord that is attached to the keyboard or mouse. If this connector is round, plug the cord into a matching port on the back of the computer. (See Figure 5 illustration on page 645.) If the connector on the cord is flat, plug it into any available USB port. (See Step 2 illustration.) If you are using a cordless keyboard or mouse, connect it to the computer using the manufacturer's technical directions.

STEP 4 Connect the modem to the computer by using a network cable.

Connect the **network cable** to the network port on the back of your computer. Connect the other end of the network cable to your modem. As long as you have an active Internet connection, the software should automatically detect that you are connected to the Internet when your computer starts.

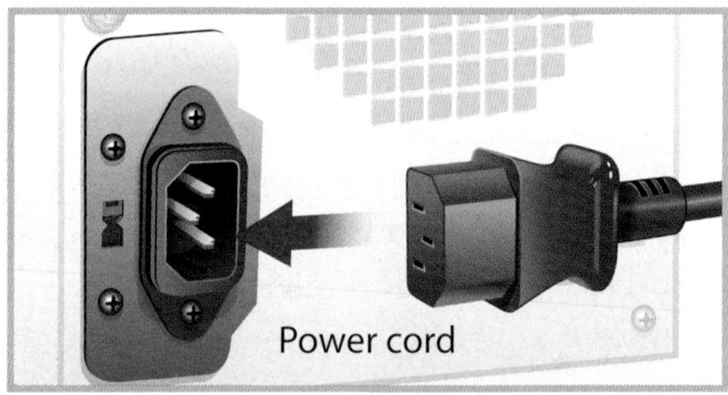

STEP 5 Connect the power cords.

The **power cord** is a three-pronged, grounded cord that you attach to your computer. First, attach one end of the power cord to the computer; then, plug the other end of the cord into a **surge protector**. Plug the surge protector into a grounded wall outlet. Turn on the monitor and then the computer, and you are ready to go! G

G **Informational Focus** Technical Directions
Why are diagrams and text both included in these directions?

Read with a Purpose What is the purpose of this document?

TECHNICAL DIRECTIONS
Applying Your Skills

RA.I.8.9 Distinguish the characteristics of consumer materials, functional or workplace documents and public documents. RA.I.8.4 Analyze information found in maps, charts, tables, graphs, diagrams, cutaways and overlays. WA.8.3.c Write business letters, letters to the editor and job applications that: include appropriate facts and details

Guide to Computers

Practicing the Standards

Informational Text and Vocabulary

1. The purpose of these **technical directions** is to —
   A convince you to buy a new computer
   B establish legal responsibility for a computer
   C describe how to install a computer
   D explain the possible uses of a computer

2. Figure 3 gives information about —
   A MP3 setups
   B a computer's hardware
   C steps to avoid
   D output devices

3. According to these directions, when should you connect the **modem** to your computer?
   A Before you connect anything else
   B After you hook up the monitor
   C Before you connect the power cords
   D After you connect the keyboard and mouse

4. Another word for *functions* is —
   A breakdowns
   B circuits
   C purposes
   D reasons

5. What are *corresponding* parts?
   A Parts that match or fit together
   B Parts that use electrical current
   C Parts that are connected to the Internet
   D Parts that are broken or not working

6. If a plug is *secure*, it is —
   A connected to the Internet
   B firmly attached
   C waterproof
   D very powerful

Writing Focus Constructed Response

7. Think of something you know how to do well. Write a list of instructions that explain how to do it. The task could be that of operating a familiar technical device, such as a DVD or MP3 player, or it could be a nontechnical task, such as playing a game or cooking according to a recipe you enjoy. Make sure to include all of the steps in the correct sequence.

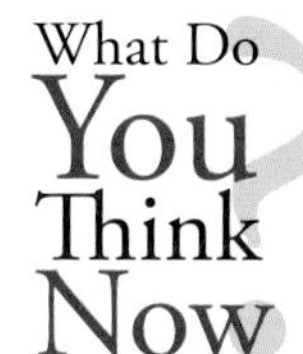

What new ideas do you have about the role of directions in daily life?

Writing Workshop

Business Letter and Memo

Write with a Purpose

Write a letter addressed to someone who is in charge of a business, a school, or another organization or institution. Your **purpose** is to communicate a clear, important message. Your **audience** is the person who will receive the letter.

Then, write a memorandum with the **purpose** of following up on the information in the business letter.

A Good Business Letter

- follows the format for business letters
- is purposeful and brief
- maintains a friendly but formal tone
- uses the addressee's official title and is suited to its audience
- states the purpose, or main idea, early in the letter
- is grammatically correct and free of spelling errors

A Good Memo

- follows the format for a memo
- is brief and to the point

Reader/Writer Notebook

Use your **RWN** to complete the activities for this workshop.

Think as a Reader/Writer

We all have to write business letters and memos (short for "memorandums") at some point in life. To succeed, you will need to know how to write them well. Here is a sample business letter and a follow-up memo:

4804 Homestead Drive
Rancho Dominguez, CA 90220 ← Heading

February 6, 2009 ← Date

Robert Toms, Customer Service Manager ← Inside address
BookLand Company
5602 Greene Avenue
Rosewood, NY 22310

Dear Mr. Toms: ← Salutation and addressee's official title

I am writing to request that BookLand exchange my copy of the novel The New Land for a new one because my copy contains pages on which the print is illegible. ← First paragraph includes the purpose for writing

Enclosed is my flawed copy and the receipt from the store. Please send a new copy to the above address. Thank you.

Sincerely, ← Closing

Susan Flores

Susan Flores ← Signature

Memo ← Heading
Date: February 18, 2009
To: Gil Forey, Shipping Dept.
From: Bob Toms, Customer Service Dept.
Subject: Book Exchange

Gil, please send a new copy of The New Land to Ms. Flores at the address on the attached letter. ← Body is brief and to the point

Think About the Professional Model

With a partner, discuss the following questions about the model:

1. What was the purpose of this letter? Did this letter fulfill that purpose?
2. How would you describe the tone of the letter?
3. What makes the tone of the memo slightly different?

Prewriting

Choose a Topic

Think about the kinds of situations that might call for a business letter. Usually, the topic of a business letter is of some importance and is treated seriously. Read the Idea Starters at the right, and use your imagination to supply the details for each situation.

Think About Your Audience and Purpose

Take some time to think about the **purpose** for writing your letter. Are you making a request? suggesting something new? expressing your satisfaction—or dissatisfaction—with a product or a situation? What do you want to see happen? Before you begin writing your letter, draft a simple statement of purpose in your **RWN.**

Considering your **audience** when you are writing a business letter is also important. Remember that you are writing to this person because you think that he or she has the power or ability to give you a job, produce your new invention, financially support your team, refund your money, or change the way something happens. Fill in a chart like the one below to help you think about your audience.

What are the values and interests of the audience?	What are the audience's worries and concerns?	What concerns do you have in common?	What questions will your audience have?

Addresses and Titles

Before you send a business letter, you should be sure that the addresses—your address and your recipient's address—are correct. You also need to be sure that you use the correct title for the person you are writing to.

Idea Starters

Here are some situations that might call for a business letter:

- applying for a job
- expressing your opinion about a product
- proposing a new program for an organization
- requesting information about a company
- asking a business to sponsor your baseball team

Your Turn

Get Started Choose a topic for your business letter, and draft a **statement of purpose.** Then, to help you think about your **audience,** fill in a chart like the one at the left in your **RWN**. You'll also need to confirm that you have the proper title and address for the recipient of your letter.

Learn It Online

To see how one writer structured a business letter, use the interactive writer's model at:

go.hrw.com L8-649 

Kinds of Business Letters

Business letters generally fall into five categories. Determining the kind of letter you are writing will help clarify your purpose in writing. Which category does your letter fall into?

- **Letters of inquiry** request information or an answer.
- **Job application letters** express your interest in a particular job and tell an employer why you are suited to that job.
- **Letters of complaint** explain a problem and request a response that will solve the problem.
- **Letters of commendation** are usually written to let an employee's supervisor know that the employee has done a good job.
- **Thank-you letters** are written directly to the person who has done something you appreciate.

Outline and Format Your Letter

Use the outline below to help you format and organize the information in your business letter.

Business Letter Outline
Heading sender's address and date, with month spelled out
Inside Address or recipient's address
Salutation or greeting, followed by a colon
Body Paragraph 1: Purpose (why you are writing the letter). Paragraph 2: Information relevant to your goal, including questions and information about your background. Paragraph 3: Express appreciation to the recipient in advance for taking the time to take action on your request.
Closing followed by a comma
Signature handwritten sender's name, typed out

Your Turn

Create an Outline In your **RWN,** prepare an outline for your business letter. Think carefully about the body of your letter. Make sure you include all the necessary background information and ask any questions that are necessary for achieving your goal. Identify what you want the recipient to do.

Drafting

Draft Your Letter

Use the outline on page 650 and the framework at the right as guides for drafting your letter. Remember to stay focused on what you want your letter to accomplish—your purpose in writing the letter. Also, keep in mind your audience's values and concerns.

Framework for a Business Letter

Introduction

- State your purpose for writing.

Middle

- Include background information.
- Ask questions.

Conclusion

- Express appreciation to the recipient.

Consider Your Tone

When you speak to a person who is in a position of authority—your school principal, for instance—you are careful to maintain a respectful tone and speak more formally than you do with your friends. Your tone of voice when you speak reflects your attitude. When you write, your choice of words and the way you write about your subject gives your writing its tone. The tone of your business letter reflects your attitude toward the subject you are writing about and the person you are writing to. All business letters should be written in a formal style and tone. They should not include sentence fragments or slang.

The Memo

The term *memo* comes from the longer word *memorandum*. Both terms come from the same root as the word *memory*. In general, the purpose of a business memo is to remind the audience of something or to point something out quickly and simply. Memos are generally sent to people who work with the writer. Because the sender and the receiver know each other, a memo might be slightly less formal than a business letter.

Grammar Link Use Formal Language

In both business letters and memos, replace slang and informal language with a formal style to maintain a respectful tone.

Informal Language	Revision
Hi, Ms. Santoro! (The informality is not appropriate in a business letter.)	Dear Ms. Santoro: (Replace the informal greeting with the standard salutation.)
Thanks! (Avoid using exclamation points in business letters.)	Thanks for your help. (Slight informality can be appropriate for some audiences.)
I think your new product is really cool. (The slang term "cool" is not appropriate.)	I think your new product works remarkably well. (Replace slang with formal language.)

Writing Tip

Here are a few things to keep in mind when you are writing a business letter:

- Use a formal form of address.
- If you do not know the name of the person to whom you are writing, you may use the salutation "To Whom It May Concern," followed by a colon.
- Use a standard complimentary close such as "Sincerely."
- Sign your full name.
- Type your full name below your signature.

Your Turn

Write Your Draft Following the Writer's Framework, write a draft of your letter. Be sure your letter

- clearly states your purpose for writing
- is written in a formal tone
- contains all the elements of a business letter (including the date, both your and the recipient's addresses, a salutation, and a closing)
- includes a clear statement of purpose

Peer Review

Exchange letters with a writing partner. Ask your partner to read the letter as if it were addressed to him or her. Ask how well he or she thinks your audience will receive the letter.

Then, ask your writing partner if your memo is clear and to the point. Use the chart at the right as a guide.

Evaluating and Revising

Read the questions in the left-hand column of the chart and then use the tips in the middle column to help you make revisions to your letter or memo. In the right-hand column you'll find techniques you can use to revise your draft.

Business Letter and Memo: Guidelines for Content and Organization

Evaluation Questions	Tips	Revision Techniques
1. Is your message clear and brief?	**Underline** the sentence or sentences that state your main point.	**Add** a statement that makes clear your purpose for writing.
2. Have you chosen a tone that is appropriate for your audience?	**Put a star** next to instances of casual phrasing or slang.	**Replace** overly informal word choices with more formal words.
3. Have you included all the necessary back-ground information?	**Draw a box** around the part of your letter that includes background information.	**Elaborate** by adding explanations and addressing reader's concerns.
4. Have you followed the standard business let-ter or memo format?	**Label** each section of your letter and memo, and **circle** the correct punctuation.	**Add** any missing parts of the letter and memo, and **cor-rect** punctuation.
5. Have you checked your letter for grammar, punctuation, and spelling errors?	**Circle** any problems that you find.	**Correct** any problems you find.

Read this student's draft, and note the comments about its strengths and suggestions on how it could be improved.

Student Draft

March 2, 2009

Henry Diaz, Director
Camp Sunset
10902 Sunset Road
Tampa, FL 33601

Dear Mr. Diaz:

For the last five years, I have attended Camp Sunset as a camper, moving from Novice status when I was eight years old to my current rank as Camper II. Now at age 13, I am ready to use my experience to serve as a counselor for boys age 8-10 in the Pioneer section of Camp Sunset. My completed application for the position is attached.

I have learned the routines and programs of Camp Sunset: the safety procedures for swimming and hiking, the opportunities for public service, and the creativity of the crafts programs. In addition, my five years as a Boy Scout have prepared me for the job as a counselor at Camp Sunset. I have earned badges in Leadership and Community Service involving supervision of younger scouts. A letter of recommendation from my Scout Master, Gerald Fisher, is attached.

I would make a totally awesome counselor! Take a look at my application!

Yours truly,

Cedric Kinney

Cedric Kinney

← Cedric has included the proper information in the **header.**

← Here, Cedric **introduces** himself to his audience.

The **body** of Cedric's letter provides **support** for his application for the position of camp counselor.

← For most of the letter, Cedric maintains a **serious tone** that is suitable for an application for a position of responsibility.

MINI-LESSON How to Keep Your Tone Consistent

When Cedric reviewed the draft of his letter, he noticed a shift in tone in his last paragraph. Here is his revision:

Cedric's Revision of the Last Paragraph

~~I would make a totally awesome counselor! Take a look at my application!~~ *I am eager to apply my experiences as a camper and as a Scout to the job of camp counselor. Please consider my application.*

Your Turn

Maintain a Serious Tone

Review your letter to be sure that you have not slipped into language that is too informal for the situation. Eliminate slang that you might use in writing to a close friend but that is not appropriate here.

Student Draft *continues*

Cedric is missing information from the **heading** of his memo.

Cedric strays from the **main point** of his memo here.

Memo
To: Phil Stevens
From: Cedric Kinney, Counselor

Hey, Phil!
In response to your request for an RSVP: 20 campers from my group will attend the Bon Voyage party. I hope that we will have good weather on that day. Some campers have expressed concern about the possibility of rain.

MINI-LESSON How to Revise and Format Your Memo

The person or people who receive a memo expect the information in the heading to be presented in a specific order so that they can read it quickly. Cedric needed to reformat the head of his memo and eliminate the unnecessary—and too informal—salutation.

The body of a memo should be brief and to the point. Cedric added non-essential information about his hopes for good weather and neglected essential information about the total number of people attending the party. He corrected both problems in his revision.

Cedric's Revision

Memo
Date: August 22, 2009
To: Phil Stevens, Camp Coordinator
From: Cedric Kinney, Counselor
Subject: RSVP for Bon Voyage Party

~~Hey, Phil!~~
In response to your request for an RSVP: 20 campers from my group will attend the Bon Voyage party. ~~I hope that we will have good weather on that day. Some campers have expressed concern about the possibility of rain.~~
In addition, 14 parents will also be coming to the festivities.

Your Turn

Be Brief but Complete Keep your memo brief, but do not neglect to include important information. Ask yourself these questions as you edit your memo:

- Have I included all of the essential information?
- Have I eliminated unnecessary and distracting details?

Proofreading and Publishing

Proofreading

You have revised your business letter and your memo. Now it is time to polish them, eliminating any errors that might distract your readers. Edit your letter and your memo to correct any misspellings, punctuation errors, and problems in sentence structure.

Grammar Link Formatting Your Letter Properly

If you format your letter in a standard way, your reader will take the letter more seriously. Use one of the following styles to format your business letter:

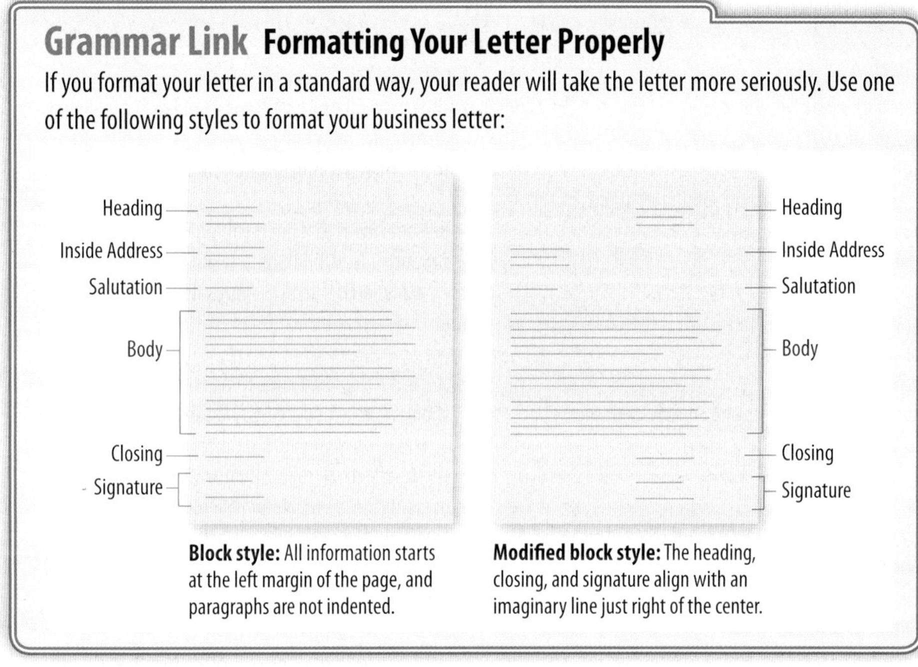

Block style: All information starts at the left margin of the page, and paragraphs are not indented.

Modified block style: The heading, closing, and signature align with an imaginary line just right of the center.

Publishing

Now it is time to publish your letter and memo to a wider audience. Here are some ways to share your documents:

- Do you know someone who writes and reads business letters and memos in his or her work? Give your documents to that person and ask for feedback.
- E-mail your documents to a friend, and ask your friend to reply as if he or she were the person addressed in the letter and memo.

Reflect on the Process In your **RWN,** write a short response to the following questions:

1. Why do you think it is important to proofread business letters and memos?
2. What might a carefully prepared document suggest to you, as the recipient, about the writer?

Proofreading Tip

Producing an error-free business letter or memo is very important. Ask three peers to join a proofreading circle with you. Circulate your letters and memos so that three readers will review each letter and memo for errors.

Writing Tip

When writing a business letter, use only one side of unlined, full-size (8½" x 11") white paper. Type or word-process your letter, or use your best handwriting, using blue or black ink; single-space your letter. If the body contains more than one paragraph, leave a blank line between paragraphs.

Your Turn

Proofread and Publish

Proofread your letter and your memo, eliminating all errors in word choice, grammar, punctuation, and spelling. Be sure that you have followed carefully the format for business letters and memos.

Scoring Rubric

You can use one of the rubrics below to evaluate your business letter from the Writing Workshop or from the activity on the next page. Your teacher will tell you which rubric to use.

6-Point Scale

Score 6 ***Demonstrates advanced success***
- shows a clear sense of purpose and focused engagement with the topic
- shows effective organization throughout, with smooth transitions
- presents ideas that are meaningful and insightful
- supports ideas thoroughly, using fully elaborated explanations and specific examples
- displays a mature control of written language

Score 5 ***Demonstrates proficient success***
- shows a clear sense of purpose and focus on the topic
- shows effective organization, with transitions
- presents ideas that are meaningful
- supports ideas competently, using well-elaborated explanations and specific examples
- displays sufficient control of written language

Score 4 ***Demonstrates competent success***
- shows a sense of purpose and topic, but may include some loosely related ideas
- shows effective organization, with minor lapses
- presents ideas that are mostly meaningful
- elaborates on ideas with a mixture of the general and the specific
- displays general control of written language

Score 3 ***Demonstrates limited success***
- includes some loosely related ideas that distract from the writer's ideas
- shows some organization, with noticeable gaps in the logical flow of ideas
- presents ideas that may be routine and predictable
- supports ideas with uneven elaboration
- displays limited control of written language

Score 2 ***Demonstrates basic success***
- includes loosely related ideas that seriously distract from the writer's ideas
- shows minimal organization, with major gaps in the logical flow of ideas
- presents ideas that are mostly simplistic and superficial
- supports ideas with inadequate elaboration
- displays significant problems with control of written language

Score 1 ***Demonstrates emerging effort***
- shows little awareness of the topic and purpose for writing
- lacks organization and a logical plan
- presents ideas that are mostly simplistic or that may be unclear or illogical
- develops ideas in only a minimal way, if at all
- displays major problems with control of written language

4-Point Scale

Score 4 ***Demonstrates advanced success***
- shows a clear sense of purpose and focused engagement with the topic
- shows effective organization throughout, with smooth transitions
- presents ideas that are meaningful and insightful
- supports ideas thoroughly, using fully elaborated explanations and specific examples
- displays a mature control of written language

Score 3 ***Demonstrates competent success***
- shows a sense of purpose and topic, but may include some loosely related ideas
- shows effective organization, with minor lapses
- presents ideas that are mostly meaningful
- elaborates on ideas with a mixture of the general and the specific
- displays general control of written language

Score 2 ***Demonstrates limited success***
- includes some loosely related ideas that distract from the writer's ideas
- shows some organization, with noticeable gaps in the logical flow of ideas
- presents ideas that may be routine and predictable
- supports ideas with uneven elaboration
- displays limited control of written language

Score 1 ***Demonstrates emerging effort***
- shows little awareness of the topic and purpose for writing
- lacks organization and a logical plan
- presents ideas that are mostly simplistic or that may be unclear or illogical
- develops ideas in only a minimal way, if at all
- displays major problems with control of written language

Business Letter

When responding to a prompt, use what you have learned from your reading, writing your business letter, and studying the rubric on page 656. Use the steps below to develop a response to the following prompt.

Writing Prompt

Write a business letter in which you express an opinion or make a formal request to a business or organization about a product or service. Make sure you use standard business letter format.

Study the Prompt

Begin by reading the prompt carefully. Circle or underline key instructional words: *opinion, formal request, business, organization, format*. Re-read the prompt to make sure you understand your task.

Remember that a business letter is different from a personal letter in both content and style. The prompt is reminding you to use the business letter format. You must think back to what you have learned to use the correct style. **Tip:** Spend about five minutes studying the prompt.

Plan Your Response

Think of a reason you might write to a business or organization. Make sure you think of a product or service that you can write about easily. Once you understand your task and have settled on your topic,

- identify the business or organization you'll be addressing
- write down your main point
- jot down several ideas that support your main idea about the product or service
- list the parts of a standard business letter that you'll need to include

Tip: Spend about fifteen minutes planning your response to the prompt.

Respond to the Prompt

Begin writing your letter using the notes you've just made. You can start with the actual body of the letter and add the other elements (date, addresses, salutation) later. It may help to follow these guidelines:

- In the heading of your letter, include the date and recipient's address. If you choose to include your address, list it above that of the recipient.
- In the body, include a formal salutation, introduction and statement of purpose, support, and conclusion.
- In the closing, include a complimentary close (such as *Sincerely*), your signature, and your typed full name.

As you are writing, remember to use formal language and a respectful tone. **Tip:** Spend about twenty minutes writing your draft.

Improve Your Response

Revising Go back to the key aspects of the prompt. Did you use the standard business letter format? Does your letter make a clear point?

Proofreading Take a few minutes to proofread your letter to correct errors in grammar, spelling, punctuation, and capitalization. Make sure all your edits are neat, and erase any stray marks.

Checking Your Final Copy Before you turn your letter in, read it one more time to catch any errors you may have missed. **Tip:** Save ten minutes to improve your paper.

Interviewing

Speak with a Purpose

With a partner, take turns interviewing each other. Prepare appropriate interview questions in advance, and then participate in two interviews, once as an interviewer and once as an interviewee. Prepare a summary of the main points of the interview you conducted.

Tips for Professional Situations

In this workshop, you may not need to conduct background research. For a formal interview, however, knowing as much as possible about a topic is critical. For instance, during a job interview you will want to show that you are knowledgeable about the company and the position for which you are applying.

Reader/Writer Notebook

Use your **RWN** to complete the activities for this workshop.

Think as a Reader/Writer Writers thoughtfully compose and edit their text to create top-notch works. Interviewers, too, must carefully prepare their questions in order to conduct first-rate interviews.

Interviews—conversations in which one person asks questions to obtain information—are more common than you might think. You've probably been interviewed—by a teacher, the school nurse, or a neighbor wanting you to baby-sit or mow the lawn. In this workshop, you will work with a partner to learn both how to conduct an interview and how to be interviewed yourself.

Prepare for the Interview

First Things First

A good interviewer is well prepared. Before you take out your pencil and notepad, follow these steps:

- **Decide on your topic.** With your partner, brainstorm ideas for your interview. Think about interests your partner has that you would like to know more about, such as his or her hobbies or sports. Consider, too, interviewing each other about your career aspirations: What jobs interest you? Why?
- **Research your topic.** If appropriate, go to a library or search the Internet to find out all you can about your topic. The more you know, the better your questions will be.
- **Make a list of questions.** Ask obvious questions rather than assuming that you know the answers. Don't ask questions that can be answered with a simple yes or no. Avoid questions that might influence your subject, such as "You hate losing, don't you?"
- **Organize your list of questions.** Begin with easier questions that will break the ice. Then, progress to questions that will provide specific information about the topic. These questions often will take longer for the interviewee to answer.
- **Gather your materials.** Before beginning your interview, be sure you have sufficient paper and pens or pencils. If you are planning to use a recording device, check to see that it is in working order.

Conduct the Interview

Showtime!

How do you make the most of your opportunity as an interviewer? Follow these guidelines:

- **Set the ground rules.** If you want to record the interview or quote your interviewee's exact words, ask permission first.
- **Be courteous and patient.** Allow your interviewee plenty of time to answer your questions. Try not to interrupt. Respect the person's ideas and opinions, even if you disagree with them.
- **Listen carefully.** Don't rush on to your next question. If you are confused, ask for an explanation. If an answer reminds you of a related question, ask that question—even if it isn't on your list.
- **Focus on the interviewee—not on yourself.** Avoid going off on tangents, such as "something like that happened to me. . . ."
- **Wrap things up.** A good interview is leisurely but doesn't go on forever. Know when to stop. Be sure to thank your interviewee, and give him or her a chance to add any comments.

Following Up the Interview

Use these steps to help get your thoughts in order after an interview:

- **Review your notes.** As soon as possible, read through your notes, and make sure your information is complete and clear.
- **Write a summary.** To make sure you understand what was said, write a summary of the main points of the interview.
- **Check your facts.** If you can, check the spelling of all names and technical facts.

Turning the Tables: Being Interviewed

Remember these tips when you are on the other side of the interview:

- **Stay relaxed.** Listen carefully to each question before you answer. If a question confuses you, ask the interviewer to reword it or repeat it. Take your time. Long, thoughtful answers are better than short, curt ones.
- **Be accurate.** If you're not sure of something, say so.
- **Keep a sense of humor.**

A Good Interviewer

- comes prepared with an organized list of questions
- listens carefully, asking for clarification when needed
- is polite and respectful

A Good Interviewee

- offers thoughtful, clear answers
- is poised and relaxed

Tip for Professional Situations

If you run out of time during a face-to-face interview, remember that you can always phone or e-mail later to check a fact or ask a final question.

Informational Skills Review

Analyzing Documents

Directions: Read the following documents. Then, read and respond to the questions that follow.

All Channels Newsletter

April 20, 2007, Vol. 6, Issue 4

Going Digital: What's Your IQ on DTV?

"What transition to DTV?" In a recent consumer survey, participants were asked if they had heard of the upcoming switch to digital television (DTV) broadcasting. More than half reported that they had seen, read, or heard no information about the changeover. Yet this major change is scheduled for February 17, 2009.

After that date, digital broadcasting will replace the less efficient analog method. DTV signals will be sent from local transmitters to homes. Analog TVs will no longer receive signals. To continue broadcast service, analog households have three options:

- Buy a TV with an HDTV (high definition television) tuner, which receives programming in several digital formats.
- Buy a converter box for each analog TV in the home. Such devices convert digital signals into analog form.
- Pay for cable or satellite services. Cable and satellite companies provide signal conversion.

Nearly 20 million U.S. households rely on over-the-air television signals, so if they do not make plans beforehand, their TVs will go dark. Given this scenario, an immediate, national educational program is needed. Toward that end, legislation on consumer education has been proposed in the House of Representatives.

Instructions for Using Your New HDTV Cable Converter Box

To view HDTV, follow these steps.
The first includes an important safety precaution:

1. Read all steps before connecting to the power source. DO NOT plug the converter box into the power outlet right away.
2. Connect the cable from the wall into the connector marked CABLE IN on the back of your converter box.
3. Connect the HDTV set to your VCR, following specific diagrams for stereo and nonstereo models. If there is no VCR, connect the set directly to the cable box.
4. Now plug the converter into the wall outlet. Wait until the clock on the converter box shows the correct time.
5. Press POWER on the converter box. Wait until the cable signal loads. This can take up to 10 minutes.
6. Turn to channel 99 for remote control programming. Select "Video Input" to view HDTV programming on the set.

RA.I.8.9 Distinguish the characteristics of consumer materials, functional or workplace documents and public documents.

LIMITED WARRANTY

Grant's TVs warrants this Product against defects in material or workmanship as follows:

LABOR: For a period of one (1) year from the date of purchase, if this Product is determined to be defective, Grant's TVs will repair or replace the Product.

PARTS: Grant's TVs will supply, at no charge, new or rebuilt replacements in exchange for defective parts for a period of one (1) year.

ACCESSORIES: Parts and labor for all accessories are for one (1) year.

1. These HDTV documents are intended primarily to assist a
   A. consumer.
   B. politician.
   C. manufacturer.
   D. salesperson.

2. The topic of the newsletter article is
   A. the efficiency of DTV.
   B. the 2009 switch to DTV.
   C. buying converter boxes.
   D. paying for satellite service.

3. The HDTV warranty will cover only
   A. damage due to an accident.
   B. damage due to adjustments.
   C. damage due to defective parts.
   D. damage due to misuse.

4. The newsletter article and the instructions are alike because both
   A. explain how to install HDTV.
   B. are legal documents.
   C. explain terms and conditions.
   D. give information about a product.

Short Answer

5. Identify and explain what document you should consult if you open the box and your new HDTV unit is broken. Use information from the passage to support your answer.

Extended Response

6. Imagine that your job is to teach people how to switch to digital television. What types of documents would you use? How might you make the information easily available? Use information from the passage to support your answer.

Vocabulary Skills Review

Context Clues

Directions: Use context clues to determine the meaning of each boldfaced word or phrase in the following sentences.

1. "By clicking on the Accept button, you agree to **abide** by the rules explained in this license agreement."
   In this sentence, **abide** by means to
   A. understand.
   B. read.
   C. share.
   D. follow.

2. "According to the legal agreement, the company is not **liable** if a person gets hurt while using the product."
   In this sentence, **liable** means
   A. sympathetic.
   B. responsible.
   C. happy.
   D. flexible.

3. "Avalanches occasionally happen; people who ski in the wilderness are **potentially** making a dangerous choice."
   In this sentence, **potentially** means
   A. definitely.
   B. possibly.
   C. suddenly.
   D. rarely.

4. "The students took a **proposal** to the principal to offer free ice cream in the lunchroom next year."
   In this sentence, a **proposal** is a(n)
   A. argument.
   B. invitation.
   C. problem.
   D. suggestion.

5. "Uneven or broken sidewalks can be safety **hazards** for skateboarders."
   In this sentence, **hazards** are
   A. dangers.
   B. inconveniences.
   C. challenges.
   D. skills.

6. "'Input' and 'Output' are two **functions** that make the computer run smoothly."
   In this sentence, **functions** means
   A. names.
   B. uses.
   C. bugs.
   D. plans.

Academic Vocabulary

Directions: Use context clues to determine the meaning of the boldfaced Academic Vocabulary.

7. "It is **critical** to follow directions when assembling a product so that it will work properly."
   In this sentence, **critical** means
   A. helpful.
   B. unhelpful.
   C. important.
   D. unnecessary.

8. "It is important to follow directions in the correct **sequence.**"
   In this sentence, **sequence** means
   A. order.
   B. style.
   C. method.
   D. organization.

WA.8.3.b Write business letters, letters to the editor and job applications that: follow the conventional style appropriate to the text using proper technical terms;

Writing Skills Review

Business Documents **Directions:** Read the following memo. Then, answer each question that follows.

(1) To: John Kilas, Varsity Basketball Coach
(2) From: Fred Williams, Headmaster
(3) Re: Awards Ceremony

(4) John, congratulations on another winning season! (5) You and the team have made this school extremely proud. (6) You have led one of the city's best basketball teams to another championship. (7) You've also nurtured another group of student athletes who understand the importance of an education. (8) My son, Toby, especially enjoyed the game against Wooter in which our team came back from 25 points down to win. (9) In honor of all these accomplishments, the school would like to host a celebratory awards ceremony, honoring all of the players and coaches. (10) At your earliest convenience, would you please send me a list of all the players with their names correctly spelled so we can order the awards? (11) Congratulations again!

1. Which of the following should be included in the **heading** of this memorandum?
   A. A return address
   B. A signature
   C. The date
   D. The sender's country

2. Which sentence could be deleted as unnecessary?
   A. Sentence 2
   B. Sentence 7
   C. Sentence 8
   D. Sentence 9

3. Which sentences could be combined by adding the transitions *not only* and *but*?
   A. Sentences 4 and 5
   B. Sentences 6 and 7
   C. Sentences 8 and 9
   D. Sentences 10 and 11

4. The memo's use of repetition in sentences 4 and 11 —
   A. is unnecessary
   B. should be eliminated
   C. clarifies a point
   D. adds emphasis

Read On

Magazines

Cobblestone

Each issue of *Cobblestone* focuses on an important aspect of the history of the United States. You might read about a historic figure such as Robert E. Lee, a famous event such as the California gold rush, or a document such as the Bill of Rights. There has even been an issue dedicated to American cartoons! *Cobblestone* brings history to life with informative feature stories, engaging activities, and riveting photographs.

National Geographic Kids

In *National Geographic Kids* magazine you will read reports on developments in technology and features on exotic animals. You'll find Kids Did It!, profiles of young people who are making impressive achievements in science, sports, and music. Also, check out the Web site at www.nationalgeographic.com/kids.

Cricket

Cricket magazine has been capturing the imagination of kids for more than twenty-five years. In a typical issue you'll find folk tales, poetry, biographies, and just about any other style of writing you can think of. *Cricket* also features word games, story contests, and plenty of compelling illustrations.

Muse

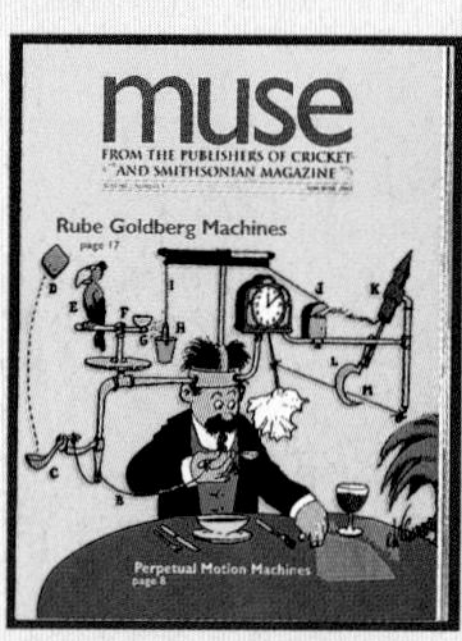

Muse gets you to question the world around you and to wonder how and why things work the way they do. The articles (many of which are written by experts) cover a range of topics having to do with art, science, and history. There are also nine cartoon Muses (like the nine Muses in Greek mythology) who appear in the margins of each issue and add a little humor by making comments and cracking jokes.

Web Sites

4Kids

The team of teachers, artists, writers, students, and technology experts at *4Kids* has put together an award-winning Web site that provides an easy, fun, and totally unique learning environment. The Web site points the way to some of the best sites in all subjects for learning on the Internet. *4Kids* also has a section that answers your questions about technology and even a page with online video games. To see all these features and more, visit www.4kids.org.

Kids' Castle

Kids' Castle is an online magazine developed by *Smithsonian* magazine. You will discover a variety of worlds inside: air and space, history, the arts, animals, science, and personalities. Click on the history link, and you might learn the story behind postage stamps. Follow the sports links, and you could learn about vintage baseball leagues, where the rules of the game were different from those of today. That's just the beginning. For more, log on to www.kidscastle.si.edu.

MidLink

MidLink, an online magazine, fosters creativity in students around the globe through international poetry exchanges. Kids also build Web sites on topics such as favorite authors, historic landmarks, and camping experiences. With its links to sites on social studies, science, and more, *MidLink* can also serve as a research tool. You'll find *MidLink* at www.ncsu.edu/midlink.

NASA Kids

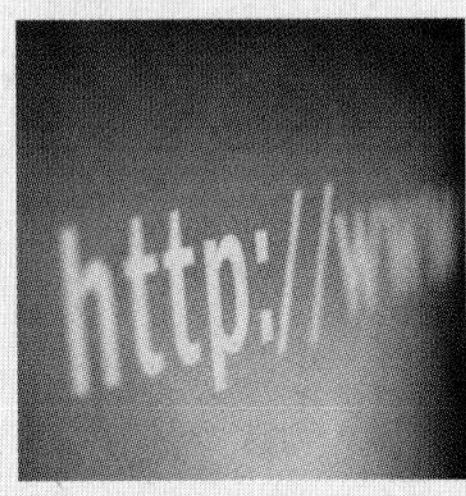

Have you ever wanted the inside scoop on outer space? Now you can find it on the Web at kids.msfc.nasa.gov. You'll discover a three-dimensional map of the solar system, biographical pieces about astronauts, and information on how NASA keeps track of all of its spacecraft. The site is also loaded with games, and it even features an art gallery.

UNIT 3

Poetry
Writers on Writing

Aimee Nezhukumatathil on Poetry Aimee Nezhukumatathil (neh ZOO KOO mah tah tihl) was born in Chicago to a Filipina mother and a South Indian father. This interesting heritage has found its way into her poetry along with themes of love and loss. She currently teaches creative writing at the State University of New York, Fredonia.

"You should have seen the look of confusion and even disgust on my friends' faces when I told them we would be having fish for breakfast. Fried fish: the size of our pinky fingers and with heads and eyeballs still intact! This was the morning after a slumber party during my junior high years—wasn't there supposed to be 'fun' foods like jelly-filled donuts or fresh baked muffins? Clean, sweet foods. Nothing with *eyeballs.* It was hard for me to explain to my friends that this was considered normal in the Philippines (where my mother is from) and in fact, a sign of great respect for your guests to be served hot crispy fish and rice for breakfast. Seeing my friends' faces twisted in disapproval made me, at first, disappointed that they wouldn't try something new, but second, mad at *myself* for not describing the delicious fish in such a way as to make it more appetizing and exciting.

Poetry is like one of those bullion/chicken broth cubes that you use to make a giant pot of soup. If you've ever unwrapped the cube and tasted it, you know that it is extremely concentrated with flavor and salt. These pungent cubes can color and flavor the description of something ordinary (water) into the most vibrant and alive way of communicating (a tasty soup). Poetry writing fills in the gaps of understanding an event, a place, a relationship, and even unusual foods. By just *talking* to my friends in junior high, I was not able to describe the delicious and savory fish breakfast. But years later, with *poetry,* I could highlight the sharp-tasty crunch of each bite, the warm and satisfying fullness of the rice—all washed down with a glass of ice cold mango juice: the taste of sunrise.

Even now, when I try to describe, for example, a recent trip to India—how magical it was to shop for saris (the South Indian women's dress) with my grandmother—all the luminous bolts of glossy silks and sateen fabrics from the stacks of cloth on the store's shelves thrown at our feet—I know I can't possibly do it justice. But in a *poem,* when I am compacting/concentrating an experience into thin lines and stanzas, I can be choosy and select all the 'important' and sensory details like the sly winking eye of the shop owner: an asterisk on his face. Or I could describe the gold threads and glass beadwork on silken fabric colored like a robin's egg. These rich details bring that sari shopping experience alive—even to people who have never seen that type of dress before.

If your writing is seasoned with concrete and specific details, no matter how different you think your experience is from someone else's, you will find your way to a tasty connection. And ultimately for me, connection, communicating—that's what writing poetry is all about. ”

Think as a Writer

Nezhukumatathil says that poetry allows her to connect and communicate with others. How do you make that kind of connection?

COLLECTION 7

Poetry

"The poetry and the songs that you are supposed to write, I believe are in your heart. You just have to open up your heart and not be afraid to get them out."

—**Judy Collins**

What Do **You** Think

How important is it that we express our feelings?

Learn It Online

Listen to the poems in this collection online at:

go.hrw.com L8-669 

Literary Focus

by **Sara Kajder**

What Do You Need to Know About Poetry?

Did you ever read the song lyrics before playing a new CD? Sometimes the words don't seem all that special. It takes music to bring them to life. Poetry is different. Poets use words to create music. To learn how poets do this, read on!

Sounds of Poetry

Word Choice One way poets create music in their poems is through the words they choose. The English poet Samuel Taylor Coleridge once defined poetry as "the best words in their best order." Listen to to these opening lines from a famous poem:

> Listen my children, and you shall hear
> Of the midnight ride of Paul Revere,
> On the eighteenth of April, in Seventy-five;
> Hardly a man is now alive
> Who remembers that famous day and year.
>
> from "Paul Revere's Ride"
> by Henry Wadsworth Longfellow

All Longfellow gave us were words on a page, and yet more than a century after he wrote them down, the music still comes through.

"I think that I shall never see, a poem as lovely as a ~~bee~~, ~~flea~~, ~~sea~~, ~~ski~~, ~~plea~~, ~~key~~ . . ."

Rhythm If words can create the haunting music of a poem, **rhythm**—the repetition of stressed and unstressed syllables—provides the poem's beat. Like many other languages, English is accented. Certain syllables get a stronger beat then other syllables. The beat of a poem comes from the patterns made by the stressed and unstressed syllables. If you say a few English words aloud, you'll hear the beat built into them: MOUN-tain, be-CAUSE, Cin-cin-NAT-i.

Read aloud this little **elegy**—a poem for someone who has died. Listen to the way your voice rises and falls as you read.

> This lovely flower fell to seed;
> Work gently, sun and rain;
> She held it as her dying creed
> That she would grow again.
>
> "For My Grandmother"
> by Countee Cullen

A regular pattern of stressed and unstressed syllables is called **meter.** Cullen's simple meter, along with the short, plain words and few, short lines, helps us share the simple loveliness and faith Cullen saw in his grandmother.

RA.L.8.6 Explain how an author's choice of genre affects the expression of a theme or topic.

Rhyme The chiming effect of **rhyme** adds to the music of a poem. Most rhymes in poetry are **end rhymes.** In "For My Grandmother" the end rhymes are *seed* and *creed,* and *rain* and *again* (pronounced the old-fashioned way: uh GAYN). When the two rhyming lines are consecutive, they're called a **couplet.** Here is a couplet with end rhymes that are spelled differently—*moan* and *bone*—but they rhyme:

> Well, he seemed so low that I couldn't say
> no; then he says with a sort of moan:
> "It's the cursèd cold, and it's got right hold
> till I'm chilled clean through to the
> bone."
>
> from "The Cremation of Sam McGee"
> by Robert W. Service

Rhymes can also occur within lines; these are called **internal rhymes.** In the two lines above, *low* and *no,* and *cold* and *hold* are internal rhymes.

These rhymes are all **exact rhymes.** Many modern poets prefer **approximate rhymes** (also called *near rhymes, off rhymes, imperfect rhymes,* or *slant rhymes*). Approximate rhymes are sounds that are similar but not exactly the same, like *fellow* and *follow* or *cat* and *catch.* In this example, *staff* and *scarf* are approximate rhymes:

> Quick, as it fell, from the broken staff
> Dame Barbara snatched the silken scarf.
>
> from "Barbara Frietchie"
> by John Greenleaf Whittier

Some people think approximate rhymes sound less artificial than exact rhymes, more like everyday speech. Some poets use approximate rhymes because they feel that all the good exact rhymes have already been used too many times.

Repetition Poets also make music in their poems by using repetition. The repeated beginnings and structures of the lines create the rhythm in the following example.

> oh mother you plunged me sobbing and
> laughing
> into our past
> into the river crossing at five
> into the spinach fields
> into the plainview cotton rows
> into tuberculosis wards
> into braids and muslin dresses
>
> from "My Mother Pieced Quilts"
> by Teresa Palomo Acosta

Poets also use repetition of sounds. Note all the *s* sounds as you read aloud these lines:

> and weightless suspended on a line
> in space
>
> from "The Word"
> by Manuel Ulacia

This is **alliteration** (uh lit uhr AY shun), the repetition of consonant sounds in several words that are close together. Repeated vowel sounds, as in *weightless* and *space,* are called **assonance** (AS uh nuhns).

Onomatopoeia The line from Service's poem, quoted in the first column, also includes an example of **onomatopoeia** (ahn oh maht oh PEE uh), which is the use of words with sounds that imitate or suggest their meaning—such as *moan.* Doesn't *sizzle* sound like bacon frying on the grill? How about *snap, crackle, pop*? Words like these help poets bring sound and sense together.

Literary Focus

Poetic Devices

Poems appeal to our emotions and imagination as well as to our sense of reason. Very often, poets use poetic devices such as these:

Imagery We are drawn into the experience of the poem through the poet's use of **imagery,** or language that appeals to our senses. The following example appeals to our senses of touch, sight, and hearing:

> If our eyes we'd close, then the lashes froze
> till sometimes we couldn't see;
> It wasn't much fun, but the only one to
> whimper was Sam McGee.
>
> from "The Cremation of Sam McGee"
> by Robert W. Service

Symbols A **symbol** is something that has meaning in itself and also stands for something else. In "For My Grandmother," the flower has meaning as a plant that blooms and produces seed, but it also represents Countee Cullen's grandmother. Some symbols in literature are obvious, and some are fresh and subtle. Here are some common, or universal, symbols you will probably recognize:

flag / country

dove / peace

4-leaf clover / good luck

Figures of Speech **Figures of speech** are words or phrases that describe one thing in terms of another and are not meant literally. **Similes** compare two unlike things using words such as *like, as, than,* and *resembles.* When you say, "He is as stubborn as a mule," you are using a simile. In this simile, the cold weather is compared to a nail:

> Talk of your cold! through the parka's fold
> it stabbed like a driven nail.
>
> from "The Cremation of Sam McGee"
> by Robert W. Service

A **metaphor** makes a comparison without using a connecting word. If you said, "He is such a stubborn mule," you'd be using a metaphor. When poets carry a metaphor over several lines, it is called an **extended metaphor.** Here's an example:

> A word is dead
> When it is said,
> Some say.
>
> I say it just
> Begins to live
> That day.
>
> by Emily Dickinson

A special kind of metaphor in which a nonhuman or inanimate thing is described as if it had human or lifelike qualities is called **personification**. In this example, grim melancholy, or sadness, sits on a large group of people watching a ballgame.

> So upon that stricken multitude grim
> melancholy sat,
>
> from "Casey at the Bat"
> by Ernest Lawrence Thayer

RA.L.8.6 Explain how an author's choice of genre affects the expression of a theme or topic.

Types of Poetry

Most people can recognize a poem when they see it. Poems usually come in **lines** instead of sentences and present ideas in **stanzas** instead of paragraphs. But there are exceptions to every rule, and poems come in many varieties.

Narrative Poems Simply put, **narrative poems** tell stories. "Paul Revere's Ride" tells of a famous incident that took place during the American Revolution. "Barbara Frietchie" tells of a woman's courageous actions during the Civil War.

Ballads A **ballad** is a song or songlike poem that tells a story. The story is often about love, betrayal, or death. Ballads usually have a regular, steady rhythm, a simple rhyme pattern, and a refrain, all of which make them easy to memorize. "The Dying Cowboy" is a traditional ballad.

Epics **Epics** are long narrative poems, originally passed down by word of mouth, that tell about heroes who embody the values of the culture recounting the tale. *Beowulf* is an ancient epic from England. "Casey at the Bat" is a humorous poem that imitates the epic form.

Lyric Poems **Lyric poems** usually do not tell a story. Instead, they express personal thoughts and feelings of the poet or the **speaker** (the poem's narrator). "Birdfoot's Grampa" expresses feelings about people and nature.

Sonnets A **sonnet** is a specific type of lyric poem that is always fourteen lines long and usually has a particular type of meter. There are two main forms of sonnets: Elizabethan and Italian. "On the Grasshopper and the Cricket" is written in the Italian form by a famous English poet.

Odes **Odes** are long, lyric poems that were traditionally written to celebrate a famous person or a lofty idea. Today many odes, such as "Ode to Thanks," are written to celebrate ordinary things.

Elegies An **elegy** is a poem of mourning, usually for someone who has died. "O Captain! My Captain!" is an elegy for the slain president Abraham Lincoln.

Free-Verse Poems **Free-verse poems** do not follow a regular meter or rhyme scheme, but they do include other elements of poetry, such as rhythm, imagery, figures of speech, and alliteration. The free-verse poem "I Hear America Singing" is answered by another free-verse poem, "I, Too."

Your Turn Analyze Poetry

Read this little poem by W. S. Merwin, and answer the questions below.

Your absence has gone through me
Like thread through a needle.
Everything I do is stitched with its color.

"Separation" by W. S. Merwin

1. What type of poem is "Separation"?
2. What figures of speech does it contain?
3. What examples of alliteration can you find in the poem?

Learn It Online

To find out more about poetic devices and types of poetry, use *PowerNotes* at:

go.hrw.com L8-673 Go

Analyzing Visuals

How Can You Find Poetic Elements in a Painting?

You have just learned some of the elements that go into creating a poem. While poetry and painting are very different media, they use some of the same elements, although in different ways. Poems create **imagery** through words, while paintings use color, line, shape, and perspective. Both may include **symbols**—things that have meaning in themselves but also stand for something else beyond—and **repetition**. They both also use these elements to present their subject in an original way.

Analyzing a Painting

Use these guidelines to analyze poetic elements in a painting.

1. Focus on the subject of the painting. Is the representation realistic or fanciful? somber or cheerful? What is the artist trying to convey by showing the subject in this way?
2. Consider the "language" of the painting—that is, its color, line, imagery, and perspective. What tone and mood are suggested by this "language"?
3. What details does the artist include or repeat? Are any details in the painting symbolic of something else?
4. How do the artist's visual choices relate to the subject? How do visual and poetic elements combine to create a fresh idea about the painting's subject?

Your Turn Write About Poetic Elements in Art

Find a piece of art in this textbook that appeals to you. Then, write a description of the artwork's poetic elements. Do you find any symbolism in its subject matter? What senses do its images appeal to? How does repetition of color, shape, line, or pattern contribute to the work's mood? How do all these elements contribute to the message of the piece?

1. Malcah Zeldis has painted historic subjects as well as domestic scenes. What might this painting be saying about daily life?

2. What does Zeldis's use of repetition of color, shape, and other details add to the meaning of this painting?

3. Think of the size and placement of the cat. What do you think this cat may symbolize?

Black Cat (1981) by Malcah Zeldis (1931–).

Reading Focus

by **Kylene Beers**

Which Reading Skills Help You Understand Poetry?

Robert Frost said that a poem "begins in delight and ends in wisdom." As we read a poem, we delight in its rhythms, rhymes, images, and comparisons and in the story or experience it shares. Yet by the end we often find wisdom that touches us.

Reading a Poem

Poems are meant to be enjoyed as well as analyzed. Here are some tips for reading poems.

Read the poem for pleasure. Then, ask yourself why you liked it. Perhaps you liked the story or the feelings expressed. If you enjoyed the sounds, you've probably picked up on **rhyme.** If you liked the beat of the lines, you responded to the **rhythm.** If you liked the poet's unusual comparisons, you've noticed **figures of speech.** These elements of the poem help you enjoy the poem.

Notice the rhymes, rhythm, and rich **imagery**—language that appeals to the senses—in these opening lines from "Barbara Frietchie."

> Up from the meadows rich with corn,
> Clear in the cool September morn,
>
> The clustered spires of Frederick stand
> Green-walled by the hills of Maryland.
>
> Round about them orchards sweep,
> Apple and peach tree fruited deep,
>
> from "Barbara Frietchie"
> by John Greenleaf Whittier

Read the poem aloud. After you've read the poem silently a few times, read it aloud. Each poem has its own sound, which you can hear more distinctly by reading it aloud. Pay special attention to punctuation. Don't stop just because you've come to the end of a line. Stop only when there is a punctuation mark. Pause briefly at commas and dashes, and a little longer at periods.

Pay attention to each word. Poets often use few words, so each word is important. Look up any unfamiliar words. The shorter the poem, the more important each word is likely to be—like in this short poem by Alberto Forcada:

> Grandmother,
> I'm cold;
> can you knit me
> some wrinkles?
>
> "Sweater" by Alberto Forcada

Pay attention to the title. Did you notice how important the title "Sweater" is to understanding that poem? Sometimes the meaning of the poem is stated or hinted at in the title.

RP.8.1 Apply reading comprehension strategies, including making predictions, comparing and contrasting, recalling and summarizing and making inferences and drawing conclusions. **RP.8.3** Monitor own comprehension by adjusting speed to fit the purpose, or by skimming, scanning, reading on, looking back, note taking or summarizing what has been read so far in text. **RA.L.8.6** Explain how an author's choice of genre affects the expression of a theme or topic.

Re-reading

One of the most important strategies for understanding—and enjoying—a poem is **re-reading.** You will understand some poems right away, but you will want to re-read them to enjoy their music. You will probably have no trouble following the story of "Paul Revere's Ride," but reading it over a few times, especially out loud, will help you enjoy its rhymes and rollicking rhythm.

When you re-read a poem that confuses you, think about each word and the feelings it brings up. Those feelings will be important clues to the poem's meaning.

Paraphrasing

Another useful strategy for understanding a poem is paraphrasing. You restate a line, sentence, or stanza in your own words. You also explain the figures of speech. Poets sometimes use **inversion**—that is, they put parts of their sentences in reverse order from what you are used to. When you paraphrase, you put the sentence into a familiar order. For instance, in "On the Grasshopper and the Cricket," John Keats writes

> The poetry of earth is ceasing never:
>
> from "On the Cricket and the Grasshopper" by John Keats

You might paraphrase the line as "The earth's poetry never ends." But you'll have to read the poem to understand what "the poetry of earth" is.

Using Form to Find Meaning

A poem's form can help you understand its meaning. A sonnet, like "On the Grasshopper and the Cricket," has a strict form. When you have learned the rules (as you will see on page 737), you will have a clue to figuring out the sonnet's meaning.

Other aspects of form can also help you understand a poem's meaning. In free-verse poems, such as "Ode to Thanks," the poet may use long lines as well as lines of only one word. Ask yourself why. It could be for the rhythm or the meaning—or, most likely, for both.

Your Turn Apply Reading Skills

Read this opening stanza from "Ode to Thanks":

> Thanks to the word
> that says *thanks!*
> Thanks to *thanks,*
> word
> that melts
> iron and snow!
>
> from "Ode to Thanks"
> by Pablo Neruda

1. Read the stanza aloud several times. Then, paraphrase it.
2. What does the figure of speech "word that melts iron and snow" mean?
3. Why do you think the poet puts the word *word* on its own line?

Now go to the Skills in Action: Reading Model

Learn It Online
Try the *PowerNotes* version of this lesson:
go.hrw.com L8-677 Go

Reading Model

Read with a Purpose Read these two poems to discover the writers' messages.

Reading Focus

Reading a Poem The title gives us a clue that this poem will be about learning some kind of lesson.

Riding Lesson

by **Henry Taylor**

I learned two things
from an early riding teacher.
He held a nervous filly°
in one hand and gestured
with the other, saying, "Listen.
Keep one leg on one side,
the other leg on the other side,
and your mind in the middle."
He turned and mounted.
She took two steps, then left
the ground, I thought for good.
But she came down hard, humped
her back, swallowed her neck,
and threw her rider as you'd
throw a rock. He rose, brushed
his pants and caught his breath,
and said, "See that's the way
to do it. When you see
they're gonna throw you, get off."

3. **filly:** young female horse.

Literary Focus

Forms of Poetry Because the poem does not rhyme or have a regular meter, it is a free-verse poem. Because it expresses an idea rather than tells a story, it is a lyric poem.

Reading Focus

Re-reading Re-read the riding instructor's comment to the speaker, and think about what broader lesson, or message, the poet might intend.

Introduction to Poetry

by **Billy Collins**

I ask them to take a poem
and hold it up to the light
like a color slide

or press an ear against its hive.

I say drop a mouse into a poem
and watch him probe his way out,

or walk inside the poem's room
and feel the walls for a light switch.

I want them to water-ski
across the surface of a poem
waving at the author's name on the shore.

But all they want to do
is tie the poem to a chair with rope
and torture a confession out of it.

They begin beating it with a hose
to find out what it really means.

Read with a Purpose What might each author want you to learn from his poem?

Reading Focus

Reading a Poem The title and first line will give you clues that the speaker is giving a lesson on poetry.

Literary Focus

Figures of Speech The poet uses a simile to compare reading a poem to examining a color slide. In later lines, the poem is also compared, through metaphor, to a hive, a maze, a room, and a body of water.

Literary Focus

Figures of Speech In the last two stanzas, the poet contrasts his pleasant suggestions for how to read a poem with the way his students go about it by using an extended metaphor in which the poem is seen as a prisoner who is brutalized.

MEET THE WRITERS

Henry Taylor

(1942–)

A Lover of Horses

A Pulitzer Prize–winning poet, Henry Taylor grew up in rural Virginia, where his father was a dairy farmer. Although Taylor decided at an early age not to follow in his father's footsteps, he was strongly influenced by his surroundings. He says,

> "Horses, in fact, were central to my life until I was in my early twenties; my sisters and I had various ponies and horses around the place, showing in small local horse and pony shows, and generally being as horsy as we could be. . . . Many of my poems draw heavily on that experience."

Billy Collins

(1941–)

A "Lifter of Chalk"

When Billy Collins was named poet laureate of the United States in 2001, he said,

> "It came completely out of the blue, like a soft-wrecking ball from outer space."

Surprising and playful images are typical of Collins's poetry. Collins was born in New York City. For more than thirty years, he has been a professor of English at the City University of New York—or, as he modestly puts it, a "lifter of chalk in the Bronx." His poetry has brought him many awards as well as wide popularity. Some have called him the most popular poet in America.

Think About the Writers

How have the poets' interests in real life been translated into their poems?

SKILLS IN ACTION

Wrap Up

RA.L.8.6 Explain how an author's choice of genre affects the expression of a theme or topic. **RP.8.1** Apply reading comprehension strategies, including making predictions, comparing and contrasting, recalling and summarizing and making inferences and drawing conclusions. *Also covered* **VO.8.7**

Into Action: Reading a Poem

Choose either "Riding Lesson" or "Introduction to Poetry." Fill in a chart like the one below to demonstrate your skills at reading a poem. Describe in the right-hand column what the items in the left-hand column contributed to your understanding or enjoyment of the poem.

Title of Poem: ______	My Comments
Re-reading/ reading aloud	
Paraphrasing	
Using form to find meaning	

Talk About . . .

1. With a partner who has chosen the same poem as you, talk about what you learned from the poem. Refer to the chart you filled in above for ideas, and try to use the Academic Vocabulary words listed at the right in your discussion.

Write About . . .

Use the underlined Academic Vocabulary words in your answers to the following questions. Definitions of the terms appear to the right.

2. What associations are evoked in your mind when the speaker in "Riding Lesson" says that the horse "threw her rider as you'd / throw a rock"?
3. What do you think is Billy Collins's intent in suggesting that his students "walk inside the poem's room / and feel the walls for a light switch"?
4. What is your interpretation of the meaning of each poem?

Writing Focus

Think as a Reader/Writer

You will find many types of poems in Collection 7. The Writing Focus activities on the Preparing to Read pages will guide you in understanding each poet's techniques. On the Applying Your Skills pages, you will have opportunities to practice these techniques in your own writing.

Academic Vocabulary for Collection 7

Talking and Writing About Poetry

Academic Vocabulary is the language you use to write and talk about literature. Use these words to discuss the poetry in this collection. The words are underlined throughout the collection.

intent (ihn TEHNT) *n.:* purpose; plan; aim. *The intent of a lyric poem is to share an idea or emotion.*

evoke (ih VOHK) *v.:* draw out; elicit. *A good poem will often evoke strong feelings in a reader.*

associations (uh soh see AY shuhnz) *n.:* connections in the mind between different things. *To understand a poem, you may have to consider your own associations to the words and images.*

interpretation (ihn tur pruh TAY shuhn) *n.:* explanation of the meaning. *Each reader may have a different interpretation of a poem.*

Your Turn

Copy these Academic Vocabulary words into your *Reader/Writer Notebook*. Now, think of one of your favorite songs. Use each Academic Vocabulary word in a sentence that explains why the song appeals to you.

Poetry and Feeling

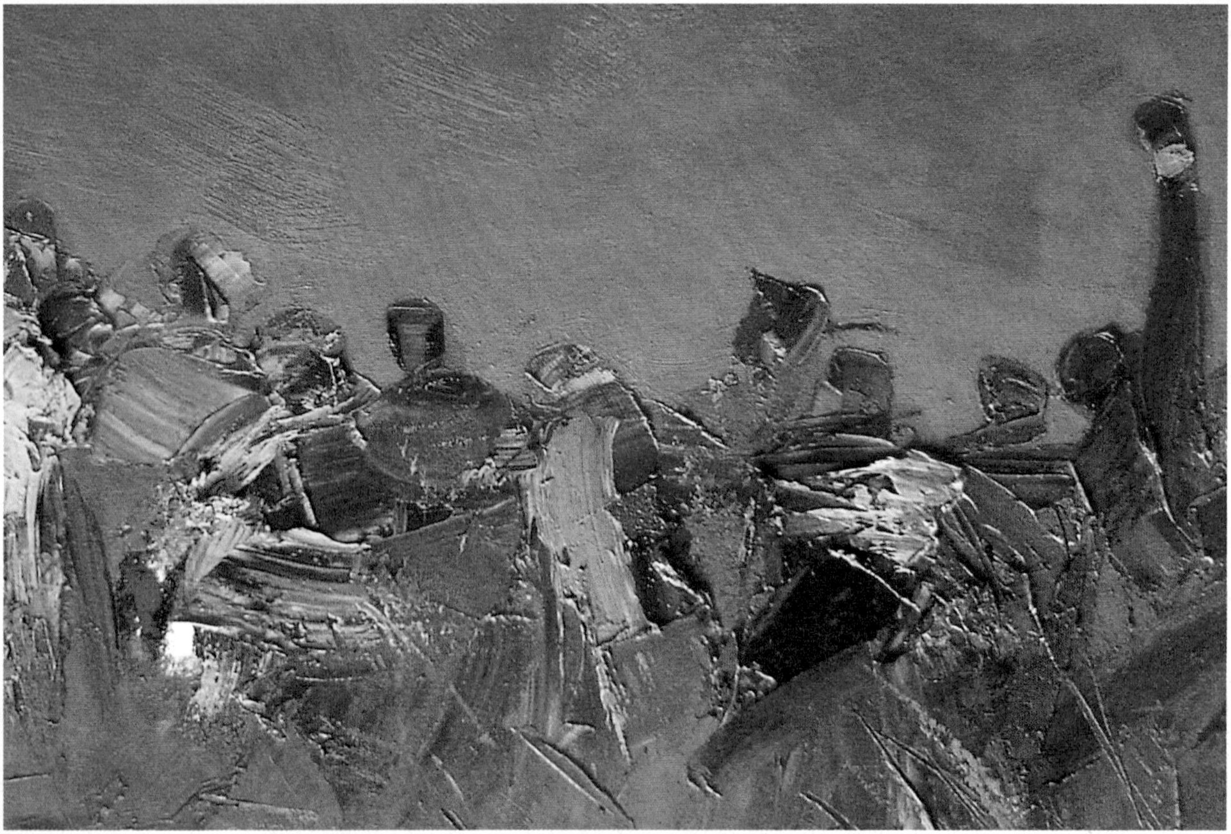

Blue Riot (detail) by TAFA. Oil on canvas (30" x 40"). Courtesy of the artist.

CONTENTS

What makes something beautiful? meaningful? important?

QuickWrite

What do you find beautiful? Is there something that gives special meaning to your life? Is there an object that is especially important to you? Write down your ideas.

Preparing to Read

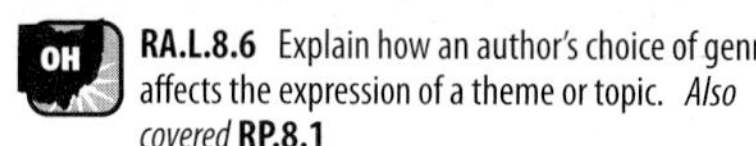

RA.L.8.6 Explain how an author's choice of genre affects the expression of a theme or topic. *Also covered* **RP.8.1**

Birdfoot's Grampa / Valentine for Ernest Mann

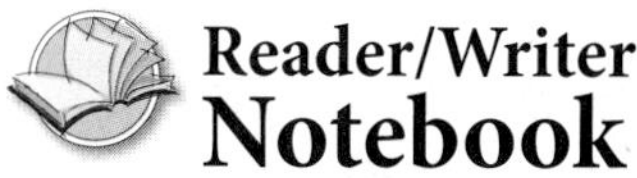

Reader/Writer Notebook

Use your **RWN** to complete the activities for these selections.

Literary Focus

Lyric Poems Some poems tell stories, while others vividly express the thoughts and feelings of the speaker. Poems that express thoughts and feelings are called **lyric poems.** Lyric poems are usually short, and they evoke—rather than state directly—a single, strong emotion.

Reading Focus

Reading a Poem The first time you read a poem, don't worry about identifying literary elements; just enjoy! Then, read the poem again, paying closer attention to its individual parts, such as its title, the writer's word choice, and punctuation.

Into Action As you read the poem, keep track of what you get out of the poem each time you read it by filling in a chart like this one.

Birdfoot's Grampa	Valentine for Ernest Mann
First reading:	First reading: I like the way the speaker talks directly to me. I think the part about the skunks is funny.
Second reading:	Second reading:

Vocabulary

Valentine for Ernest Mann

spirit (SPIHR iht) *n.:* courage; liveliness. *Asking a famous poet to write you a poem shows spirit.*

drifting (DRIHF tihng) *v.* used as *adj.:* being carried along as if by a current of air or water. *We can catch beautiful, poetic images drifting throughout our lives.*

re-invented (ree ihn VEHN tihd) *v.:* created again, or made new. *Poets have re-invented ordinary things to help readers see them in a new way.*

Language Coach

Connotations Words have two kinds of meanings: **denotations** you find in a dictionary, and **connotations** are the feelings and associations the words bring forth. Think about the word *spirit,* listed above. What connotations does that word evoke?

Writing Focus

Think as a Reader/Writer

Find It in Your Reading Both of these poems use imagery to help the reader see ordinary things in a new light. **Images** appeal to the reader's sense of sight, smell, touch, hearing, or taste. As you read these poems, list at least three sensory images from each poem in your *Reader/Writer Notebook.*

Learn It Online

To observe a good reader in action visit:

go.hrw.com L8-683 

MEET THE WRITERS

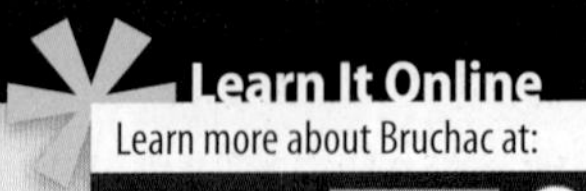

Learn It Online
Learn more about Bruchac at:
go.hrw.com L8-684 Go

Joseph Bruchac

(1942–)

When You Least Expect Them

Joseph Bruchac was born in Saratoga Springs, New York, and raised there by his grandmother and grandfather, who was a member of the Abenaki people. Bruchac studied wildlife conservation in college. Today he is a well-known editor, publisher, poet, and collector of folk tales. He says that "Birdfoot's Grampa" describes a lesson he was taught "in the way most good lessons come to you—when you least expect them."

Naomi Shihab Nye

(1952–)

Finding Poetry in the Familiar

Naomi Shihab Nye often runs workshops in schools to help students find the poetry hidden in their imagination. She is inspired by everyday activities and tasks. In her poems, Nye makes the tiniest, most mundane details exceptional and wonderful. She once said:

> "Familiar sights, sounds, smells have always been my necessities. Let someone else think about future goals and professional lives! I will keep track of the bucket and the hoe . . . and clouds drifting in from the horizon."

For more information about Naomi Shihab Nye, see page 164.

Think About the Writers

What does each of the poets believe poetry can express?

Preview the Selections

The speaker of "Birdfoot's Grampa" is frustrated when his grandfather stops their car again and again to move small toads out of the way.

In "Valentine for Ernest Mann," the speaker responds to someone who has asked for a poem.

Read with a Purpose Read this poem to find out what is important to the speaker's grandfather.

BIRDFOOT'S GRAMPA

by **Joseph Bruchac**

The old man
must have stopped our car
two dozen times to climb out
and gather into his hands
the small toads blinded
by our lights and leaping,
live drops of rain. **A**

The rain was falling,
a mist about his white hair
and I kept saying
you can't save them all
accept it, get back in
we've got places to go.

But, leathery hands full
of wet brown life,
knee deep in the summer
roadside grass,
he just smiled and said
they have places to go to
too. **B**

A **Read and Discuss** What is Grampa doing?

B **Literary Focus** **Lyric Poem** The speaker and Grampa have different ideas about what is important. What idea do you think the poem is expressing?

Read with a Purpose Read this poem to find out where poems hide.

Valentine for Ernest Mann

by **Naomi Shihab Nye**

You can't order a poem like you order a taco.
Walk up to the counter, say, "I'll take two"
and expect it to be handed back to you
on a shiny plate.

Still, I like your spirit.
Anyone who says, "Here's my address,
write me a poem," deserves something in reply.
So I'll tell a secret instead:
poems hide. In the bottoms of our shoes,
they are sleeping. They are the shadows
drifting across our ceilings the moment
before we wake up. What we have to do
is live in a way that lets us find them. **A**

A **Literary Focus** **Lyric Poem** What idea is the poet exploring?

Vocabulary **spirit** (SPIHR iht) *n.:* courage; liveliness.
drifting (DRIHF tihng) *v.* used as *adj.:* being carried along as if by a current of air or water.

Once I knew a man who gave his wife
two skunks for a valentine.
He couldn't understand why she was crying.
"I thought they had such beautiful eyes."
And he was serious. He was a serious man
who lived in a serious way. Nothing was ugly
just because the world said so. He really
liked those skunks. So, he re-invented them
as valentines and they became beautiful.
At least, to him. And the poems that had been hiding
in the eyes of skunks for centuries
crawled out and curled up at his feet.

Maybe if we re-invent whatever our lives give us
we find poems. Check your garage, the odd sock
in your drawer, the person you almost like, but not quite.
And let me know. **B**

B **Read and Discuss** How does the skunk story connect to the way the poet views the origins and development of poetry?

Vocabulary **re-invented** (ree ihn VEHN tihd) *v.:* created again, or made new.

Applying Your Skills

RA.L.8.6 Explain how an author's choice of genre affects the expression of a theme or topic. RP.8.1 Apply reading comprehension strategies, including making predictions, comparing and contrasting, recalling and summarizing and making inferences and drawing conclusions. *Also covered* **WA.8.1.b; WP.8.9**

Birdfoot's Grampa / Valentine for Ernest Mann

Respond and Think Critically

Reading Focus

Read with a Purpose

1. What is important to Birdfoot's Grampa? What does "Valentine for Ernest Mann" say about where poems hide? What do both poems suggest is important in life?

Reading Skills: Reading a Poem

2. Complete the chart below if you haven't done so already. Then, describe what you noticed about each poem the second time you read it that you hadn't noticed in the first reading.

Birdfoot's Grampa	Valentine for Ernest Mann
First reading:	First reading:
Second reading:	Second reading:

Vocabulary Check

Match each Vocabulary word with its definition.

3. **spirit** — **a.** floating
4. **drifting** — **b.** created again
5. **re-invented** — **c.** liveliness

Literary Focus

Literary Analysis

6. **Analyze** To what is the speaker comparing the toads in the poem's first stanza? What figure of speech does Bruchac use to create that comparison?
7. **Interpret** What point is Grampa trying to convey to his passenger concerning the toads?
8. **Interpret** In the second stanza of "Valentine for Ernest Mann," what human things does the poet say poems do? What is the poet telling us by using this figure of speech?
9. **Analyze** What comparison is Nye making in the first stanza? the second stanza? What is she saying about poems by using these comparisons?
10. **Analyze** Why does the speaker tell us about the man and the skunks? (What do skunks have to do with poetry?)
11. **Extend** Many people, like Birdfoot's Grampa, believe that their actions can make a difference. Think of someone who has acted on that belief. What was the intent of the person's actions? Were the actions worth doing? Explain.

Literary Skills: Lyric Poems

12. **Classify** How do these poems fit the definition of lyric poetry? (See page 683.) Support your answer with details from the poem.

Writing Focus

Think as a Reader/Writer

Use It in Your Writing Follow Nye's advice, and try to find a lyric poem in your life. Write a lyric poem that uses sensory images to help readers view something apparently ordinary in a new way.

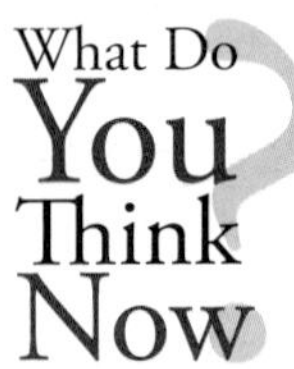

Have the poems changed your idea of beauty? Do you see skunks and toads in the same way? Why, or why not?

Preparing to Read

My Mother Pieced Quilts / Sweater/Suéter

Literary Focus

Symbolism A **symbol** is a person, a place, a thing, or an event that stands for something beyond itself. Some symbols are traditional and common to a culture. We understand them because people have agreed on their meaning. For example, in this country a blindfolded woman holding scales has come to symbolize justice. In literature, however, symbols are created by the writers, and the meanings of the symbols are open to interpretation by readers.

Reading Focus

Reading Poetry Poetry is written in lines—some long and some very short. Some poets use punctuation in their lines, while others do not. When you read a poem that does not use punctuation, you have to look for the thought units. That means that you do not come to a stop at the end of every line. You have to see if the sense of the line carries over to the next line.

Into Action As you read each poem, fill in a chart like the one below with thought units. Add rows to your charts as needed.

My Mother Pieced Quilts	
1st thought unit	they were meant as covers in winter
2nd thought unit	

Writing Focus

Think as a Reader/Writer

Find It in Your Reading Teresa Palomo Acosta, the writer of "My Mother Pieced Quilts," includes lists of things—especially types of fabrics—in her poem. As you read the poem, note in your *Reader/Writer Notebook* the lists of objects or images that are grouped together.

OH **RA.L.8.9** Examine symbols used in literary texts. **RP.8.1** Apply reading comprehension strategies, including making predictions, comparing and contrasting, recalling and summarizing and making inferences and drawing conclusions.

Reader/Writer Notebook

Use your **RWN** to complete the activities for these selections.

Vocabulary

My Mother Pieced Quilts

frayed (frayd) *adj.:* worn away; unraveled. *Frayed pieces of fabric are finished into a quilt.*

somber (SAHM buhr) *adj.* dark; melancholy. *She grew somber, thinking about the funeral.*

taut (tawt) *adj.:* pulled tight. *The taut thread holds the quilt together.*

Language Coach

Language Conventions Proper nouns name specific people, places, and things. In English, proper nouns are capitalized. Teresa Palomo Acosta, however, deliberately begins proper nouns, such as *January, October, Michigan, Santa Fe,* and *Easter,* with lowercase letters in her poem. After you've read the poem, stop to think why she made that choice.

Learn It Online
Develop your vocabulary with Word Watch:

go.hrw.com L8-689 Go

MEET THE WRITERS

Teresa Palomo Acosta

(1949–)

A Love of Poetry

Teresa Acosta grew up in McGregor, Texas, and began writing poetry when she was just sixteen. As a teenager she enjoyed European and Early American poetry. Later she was inspired by African American and Mexican American poetry, when it became available to her. She has been involved in various projects to promote Latino literature and is the co-author of the book *Las Tejanas: 300 Years of History.*

Alberto Forcada

(1969–)

The Dreams of Children

The poems of Alberto Forcada that appear in *Despertar (Awaking)*—"Suéter" is one of them—describe the dreams and fantasies of children. Forcada has a degree in philosophy from the National University of Mexico. His poems have been collected in three books and have been published in magazines such as *De Polanco para Polanco,* which serves a neighborhood in Mexico City.

Think About the Writers

Based on the information above, what do you think Teresa Palomo Acosta and Alberto Forcado find important?

Build Background

"My Mother Pieced Quilts"

Piecing a quilt means sewing together pieces of fabric to create a bed cover. Usually the scraps of fabric are stitched together to form a pattern. Some quilts follow a traditional pattern, while others are unique.

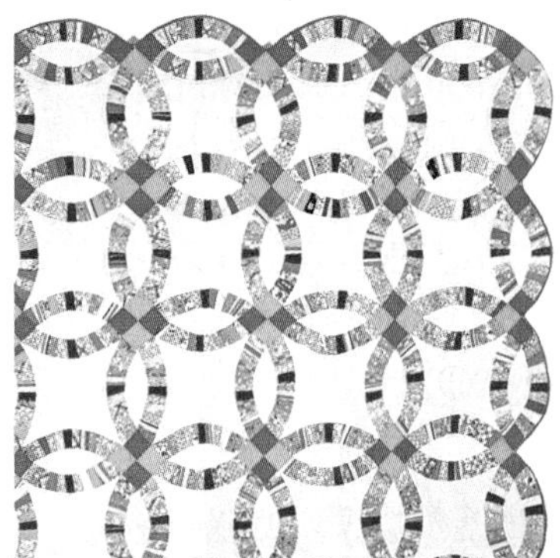

Wedding Ring, American quilt (detail) (c. 1930) Cotton patchwork.

Preview the Selections

In "My Mother Pieced Quilts," the speaker tells us about the associations she makes with the patchwork in her mother's quilts.

In "Sweater," the speaker asks his grandmother for more than a garment to keep himself warm.

Read with a Purpose Read these poems to discover how objects made by the hands of a loved one can take on special meaning.

they were just meant as covers
in winters
as weapons
against pounding january winds

but it was just that every morning I awoke to these
october ripened canvases
passed my hand across their cloth faces
and began to wonder how you pieced
all these together
these strips of gentle communion cotton and flannel nightgowns
wedding organdies
dime store velvets **A**

A **Literary Focus** **Symbolism** What might the different types of fabric listed here symbolize?

how you shaped patterns square and oblong and round
positioned
balanced
then cemented them
with your thread
a steel needle
a thimble
how the thread darted in and out
galloping along the frayed edges, tucking them in
as you did us at night
oh how you stretched and turned and rearranged
your michigan spring faded curtain pieces
my father's santa fe work shirt
the summer denims, the tweeds of fall **B**

B **Read and Discuss** What is Acosta illustrating for us as she lists different fabrics, shapes, and clothing types?

Vocabulary **frayed** (frayd) *adj.:* worn away; unraveled.

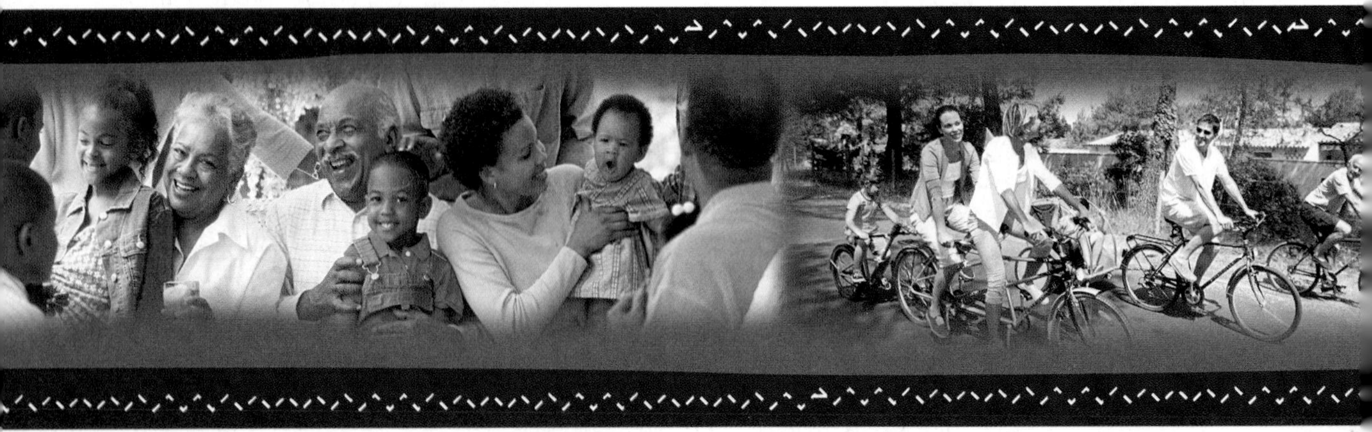

in the evening you sat at your canvas
—our cracked linoleum floor the drawing board
me lounging on your arm
and you staking out the plan:
whether to put the lilac purple of easter against the red
plaid of winter-going-
into-spring
whether to mix a yellow with blue and white and
paint the
corpus christi noon when my father held your hand
whether to shape a five-point star from the
somber black silk you wore to grandmother's funeral

Vocabulary **somber** (SAHM buhr) *adj.:* dark; melancholy.

Crazy patchwork quilt (c. 1875).

Analyzing Visuals

Viewing and Interpreting Do you think the mother's quilts looked like this one, or the ones on pages 690 and 691? Why or why not?

you were the river current
carrying the roaring notes . . .
forming them into pictures of a little boy reclining
a swallow flying
you were the caravan master at the reins
driving your threaded needle artillery across the
    mosaic cloth bridges
delivering yourself in separate testimonies°

oh mother you plunged me sobbing and laughing
into our past
into the river crossing at five
into the spinach fields
into the plainview cotton rows
into tuberculosis wards
into braids and muslin dresses
sewn hard and taut to withstand the thrashing of
    twenty-five years

stretched out they lay
armed/ready/shouting/celebrating

knotted with love
the quilts sing on **C**

---

43. testimonies: declarations. For example, people make testimonies of faith or of love.

C **Read and Discuss** Acosta uses phrases such as "river current," "caravan master," "driving your needle," to describe her mother's quilting activities. What do these phrases tell us about the mother and the way Acosta views her?

Vocabulary **taut** (tawt) *adj.:* pulled tight.

Sweater

by **Alberto Forcada**
translated by **Judith Infante**

Grandmother,
I'm cold;
can you knit me
some wrinkles? **A**

A Read and Discuss What is the speaker really saying here?

Suéter

por **Alberto Forcada**

Abuela,
tengo frío;
téjeme a mí también
unas arrugas.

Applying Your Skills

RA.L.8.9 Examine symbols used in literary texts. **RP.8.1** Apply reading comprehension strategies, including making predictions, comparing and contrasting, recalling and summarizing and making inferences and drawing conclusions. **WA.8.6** Produce informal writings.

My Mother Pieced Quilts / Sweater/Suéter

Respond and Think Critically

Reading Focus

Read with a Purpose

1. Why are the quilts in "My Mother Pieced Quilts" more than just "covers"? Why does the speaker of "Sweater" want wrinkles?

Reading Skills: Reading Poetry

2. Review your charts, and think about the ideas each poem expresses. Then, decide what **theme,** or insight about life, comes through in each poem. Add a theme statement to each chart.

My Mother Pieced Quilts

1st thought unit	they were meant as covers in winter
2nd thought unit	

Poem's theme:

Vocabulary Check

Match each Vocabulary word with its definition.

3. **frayed** — **a.** pulled tight
4. **somber** — **b.** worn away; unravelled
5. **taut** — **c.** dark; melancholy

Literary Focus

Literary Analysis

6. **Identify** A figure of speech that gives something nonhuman human qualities is called **personification**. List three or more examples of personification in Acosta's poem.

7. **Hypothesize** To what does the speaker of "Sweater" compare the sweater? Would he have used this comparison if the poem had been addressed to his sister? Why or why not?

8. **Compare** In line 6 of "My Mother Pieced Quilts," the speaker refers to the quilts as "ripened canvases." What associations can you make between what her mother does and what a painter of pictures might do?

Literary Skills: Symbolism

9. **Interpret** What do you think the quilts symbolize for the speaker of "My Mother Pieced Quilts"?

10. **Interpret** Why do you think Forcado titled his poem "Sweater"? What might the sweater symbolize?

Literary Skills Review: Diction

11. **Analyze** A writer's choice of words is called **diction.** In "Sweater," how is the writer's choice of very simple words appropriate?

Writing Focus

Think as a Reader/Writer

Use It in Your Writing Look back at your lists in your **RWN**. Now, write a paragraph about an object that is significant to you. Like Acosta, use the form of a list to create a rich description.

Why do some ordinary objects, such as quilts and sweaters, evoke strong meanings?

Preparing to Read

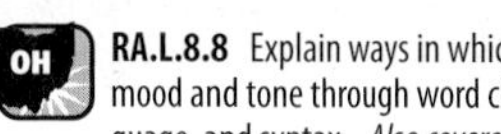

RA.L.8.8 Explain ways in which the author conveys mood and tone through word choice, figurative language, and syntax. *Also covered* **RP.8.3**

A word is dead / The Word/La palabra

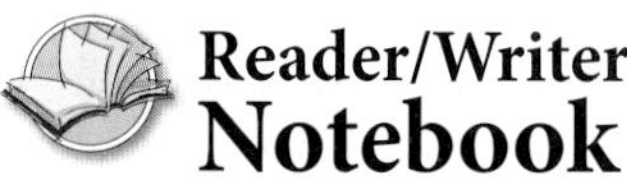

Reader/Writer Notebook

Use your **RWN** to complete the activities for these selections.

Literary Focus

Figures of Speech Important elements of poetry, **figures of speech** are comparisons that are not literally true.

- A **simile** compares two things using a word such as *like, as,* or *than. The moon looked like a golden coin high in the sky.*
- A **metaphor** directly compares two very different things. *The moon was a golden coin high in the sky.*
- **Personification** describes a nonhuman thing as if it were human. *The moon smiled down from high in the sky.*

TechFocus As you read, think about sounds and images to use for a multimedia presentation of a similar poem of your own.

Reading Focus

Re-reading Almost no one can read a poem once and understand it fully. Read poems several times to understand and appreciate the artistry that went into writing them.

Into Action As you read each poem, use a chart like the one below to track what you discover on each reading.

	A word is dead
1st reading (for pleasure)	This is a simple poem about words.
2nd reading (study word choices)	
3rd reading (my analysis)	

Language Coach

Language Conventions When reading poetry, be aware that poets often leave out punctuation marks from their poems. Look at the following stanza from "A word is dead."

A word is dead
When it is said,
Some say.

When you read the stanza, think of it as if it had the following punctuation:

"A word is dead
when it is said,"
some say.

As you read the poems that follow, try re-punctuating them to help you understand their meaning. Also look for any words the poets may have deliberately left out of their poems, and mentally fill them in.

Writing Focus

Think as a Reader/Writer

Find It in Your Reading As you read the poems, note in your *Reader/Writer Notebook* the figures of speech the poets use.

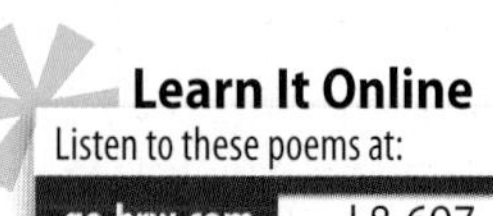

Learn It Online
Listen to these poems at:
go.hrw.com L8-697 Go

Learn It Online
Examine Dickinson's life at:
go.hrw.com L8-698 Go

Emily Dickinson

(1830–1886)

"Letter to the World"

Although today Emily Dickinson is one of the most respected poets in the world, her work was almost completely unknown during her lifetime. Dickinson led an extremely private life in her family home in Amherst, Massachusetts. After she died, her sister Lavinia discovered the poems—almost eighteen hundred of them—that Dickinson had gathered into handmade booklets. Dickinson said that her poems were her "letter to the world" that never wrote to her.

Manuel Ulacia

(1954–2001)

Professor and Poet

Manuel Ulacia studied both architecture and literature. He went on to become a professor at Yale University and also taught at Mexico City's Universidad Autónoma. In addition to his own poetry, Ulacia studied and wrote about the work of his mentor, Octavio Paz, a Nobel Prize–winning Latin American poet and essayist.

Think About the Writers

Dickinson led a private life; Ulacia taught at universities. What did they have in common?

Preview the Selections

In a "A word is dead" the speaker contrasts her beliefs about language with what other people think.

In "The Word" the speaker uses comparisons to tell readers what a word is like.

Read with a Purpose Read these poems to discover new ideas about words.

A word is dead

by **Emily Dickinson**

A word is dead
When it is said,
Some say.

I say it just
Begins to live
That day. **A**

A **Read and Discuss** What point is the poet making?

The Word

by **Manuel Ulacia**
translated **by Jennifer Clement**

comes out from the pen
like a rabbit from a magician's hat
astronaut who knows itself alone
and weightless suspended on a line
in space **B**

B **Literary Focus** **Figures of Speech**
To what does the speaker compare words? What do these comparisons tell us about words?

La palabra

por **Manuel Ulacia**

sale de la pluma
como el conejo del sombrero de un mago
astronauta que se sabe sola y sin peso
suspendida en una línea
en el espacio

Sketch of a Rabbit (c. 1900–1925) by Seiho Takeuchi.

Applying Your Skills

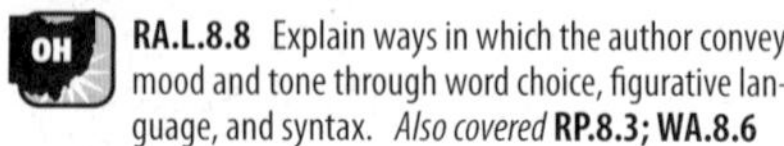
RA.L.8.8 Explain ways in which the author conveys mood and tone through word choice, figurative language, and syntax. *Also covered* **RP.8.3; WA.8.6**

A word is dead / The Word/La palabra

Respond and Think Critically

Reading Focus

Read with a Purpose

1. What ideas do these poems convey about words?

Reading Skills: Re-reading

2. Review the charts you completed as you read the poems. Now, add a row to each chart with your final impression of each poem.

	A word is dead	The Word
1st Reading	This is a simple poem about words.	
2nd Reading		
3rd Reading		
My Final Impression		

Literary Focus

Literary Analysis

3. **Interpret** In Dickinson's poem, what do people mean when they say "A word is dead/ When it is said"?
4. **Interpret** In "The Word," how can a word be like an astronaut in space?
5. **Make Judgments** Do you agree with either Dickinson's or Ulacia's point of view about words? Explain.
6. **Extend** Name a word that seems "alive" to you. Why does it seem so?
7. **Extend** A children's rhyme goes, "Sticks and stones / Can break my bones / But names can never hurt me." How would Dickinson feel about that saying? How do you feel about it?

Literary Skills: Figures of Speech

8. **Interpret** Dickinson uses personification when she says that a word "begins to live." How do you think a word might begin to "live" after it is spoken?
9. **Interpret** What do the images in lines 2–4 of Ulacia's poem make you see?

Literary Skills Review: Imagery

10. **Analyze** **Imagery** appeals to the senses of sight, hearing, touch, taste, and smell. In Ulacia's poem, to which sense does the image of a rabbit coming from a magician's hat appeal? To which senses does the image of an astronaut "weightless suspended on a line in space" appeal?

Writing Focus

Think as a Reader/Writer

Use It in Your Writing Look back at the figures of speech you jotted down in your *Reader/Writer Notebook*. Now, write a paragraph expressing your views on words. Like these poets, use figures of speech to get your ideas across. You might start the same way that Dickinson did: "A word is. . . ."

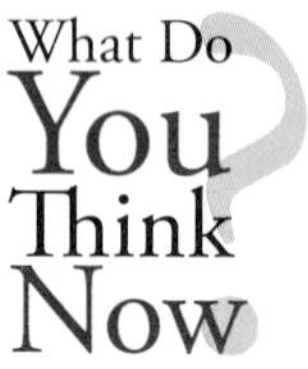

How have these poems changed your thoughts about the importance of words? Explain.

Wrap Up

Poetry and Feeling

WA.8.1.b Write narratives that: use literary devices to enhance style and tone; and **WA.8.6** Produce informal writings. **C.8.9** Deliver formal and informal descriptive presentations that convey relevant information and descriptive details. *Also covered* **VO.8.2**

Vocabulary Development

Connotations

Connotations are the meanings, associations, or emotions suggested by a word. A word's connotations can be different from its **denotation,** or dictionary definition. For example, imagine that "Birdfoot's Grampa" had instead been titled "Birdfoot's Grandfather." The title's connotations would have been very different, even though the basic meanings of *grandfather* and *grampa* are the same.

Often, a word's connotations affect shades of meaning or intensity. For example, in line 44 of "My Mother Pieced Quilts," Acosta uses the word *sobbing,* rather than *crying.* While *sobbing* basically means the same as *crying,* it is associated with greater intensity. Here are more examples.

Word	Words with Stronger Connotations	
talk	chatter	slander
thin	skinny	skeletal

Your Turn

For each word in the left-hand column below, write a word or two in the right-hand column that has a similar denotation but different connotations.

1. afraid	
2. happy	
3. relaxed	
4. careful	
5. house	

CHOICES

As you respond to the Choices, use these **Academic Vocabulary** words as appropriate: intent, evoke, associations, interpretation.

REVIEW

Create a Multimedia Presentation

TechFocus Ulacia and Dickinson offered clever interpretations of words; now write your own poem about thoughts. Use figures of speech to portray what thoughts do and how they are created and grow. Use presentation software to present your poem to the class, and be sure to incorporate sound files and images.

CONNECT

Write a Personal Essay

Timed Writing Some poems you have just read celebrate the wisdom and nurturing offered by older relatives. Write a personal essay about your relationship with an older relative or friend. What gift has this person passed along? Did he or she give you something tangible, tell you a story, give you advice, or teach you by example?

EXTEND

Analyze a Translation of a Poem

"Sweater" and "The Word" were originally written in Spanish and then translated into English. If you know Spanish, read each poem in both languages. How are the original Spanish versions different from the English translations? Has anything been lost in translation? Explain.

Learn It Online
Find action-packed vocabulary lessons online:
go.hrw.com
L8-701
Go

Poetry and Storytelling

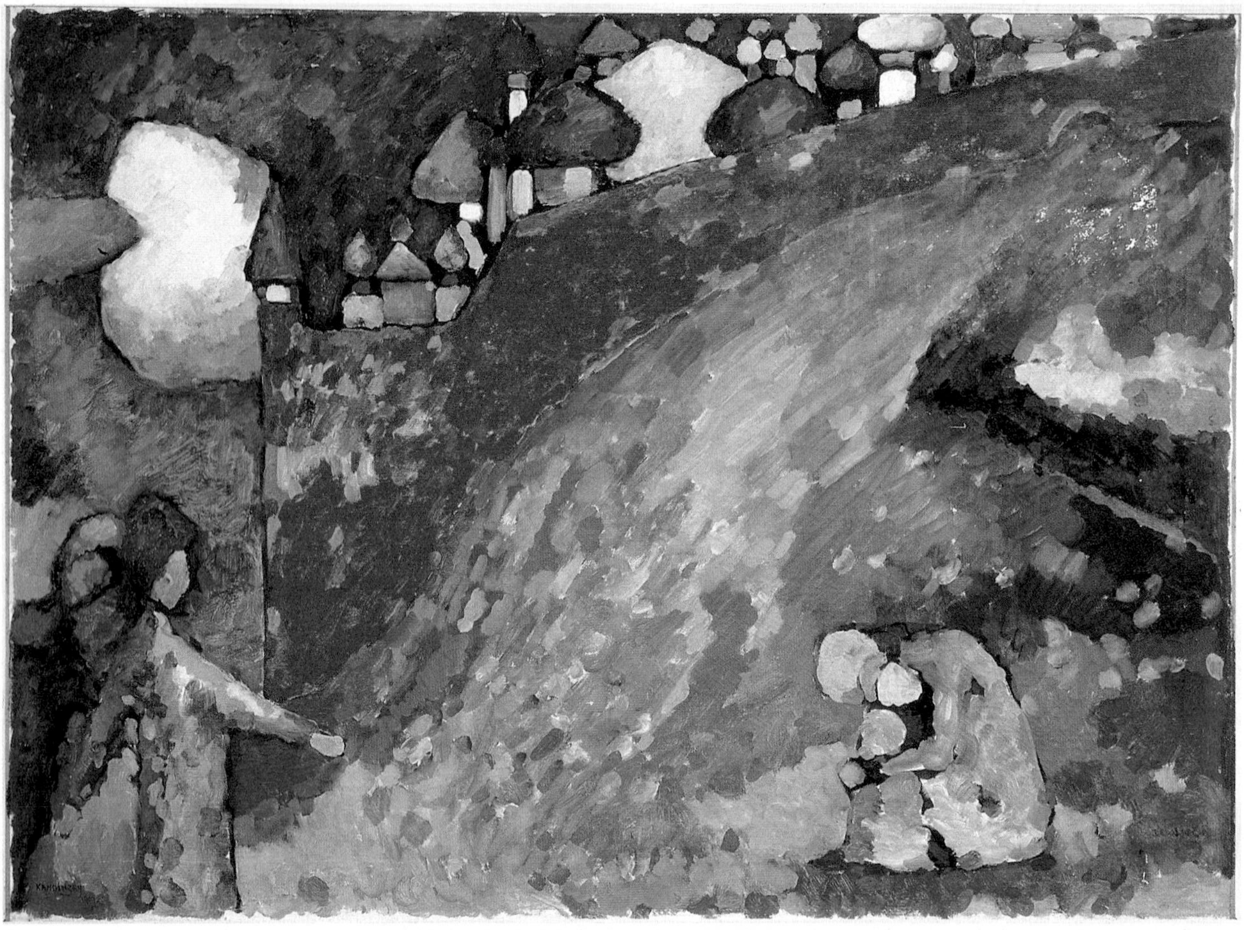

Cupolas (1909) by Wassily Kandinsky. Oil on cardboard (33 ½" x 45 ¹¹⁄₁₆").

CONTENTS

How do people express their beliefs and emotions?

QuickTalk

In a small group, discuss ways that people express themselves. For example, how do they stand up to authority, make requests, demonstrate their skills?

Preparing to Read

Paul Revere's Ride / Barbara Frietchie

Literary Focus

Narrative Poetry: Rhythm and Meter A **narrative poem** tells a story, complete with characters, setting, and plot. Many narrative poems use a strong rhythm and meter. In language, **rhythm** is the rise and fall of the voice, produced by stressed and unstressed syllables. When the stresses occur in a regular pattern, we call it **meter.**

"Paul Revere's Ride" is written with a strong meter. Notice, when you read it aloud, how the meter sounds like a galloping horse: da da DUM da da DUM da da DUM.

Reading Focus

Paraphrasing To paraphrase, restate a text in your own words. A paraphrase restates all the information in the original, unlike a summary, which retells only the most important points.

Into Action Stop to paraphrase difficult lines of poems. Keep track of your paraphrases in a chart like this one.

Paul Revere's Ride	My Paraphrase
lines 1-3	Listen, and I will tell you all about Paul Revere's famous midnight ride that took place on April 18, 1775.
lines	

Writing Focus

Think as a Reader/Writer

Find It in Your Reading As you read these poems, notice the poets' use of end rhyme—rhyming words that are at the ends of lines. Note in your *Reader/Writer Notebook* the pattern of the rhymes.

RA.L.8.6 Explain how an author's choice of genre affects the expression of a theme or topic.
RA.L.8.8 Explain ways in which the author conveys mood and tone through word choice, figurative language, and syntax. *Also covered* **RP.8.1**

Reader/Writer Notebook

Use your **RWN** to complete the activities for these selections.

Vocabulary

Paul Revere

impetuous (ihm PEHCH oo uhs) *adj.:* impulsive; eager. *The impetuous soldier rushed into battle.*

aghast (uh GAST) *adj.:* shocked; horrified. *The citizens were aghast at the sight of the invading troops.*

Barbara Frietchie

stirred (sturd) *v.:* moved; roused. *One woman's actions stirred the general's emotions.*

host (hohst) *n:* army; large number. *An enemy host flooded the streets.*

The approaching British **host**
↓
left the people **aghast** and
↓
stirred the group to take action.

Language Coach

Multiple-Meaning Words Many English words have more than one meaning. For example, *stirred* most often means "mixed together," as in "He stirred the cake batter." How is the word *stirred* used in the definition and example sentence above?

Learn It Online

Find out more about "Paul Revere's Ride" through the *PowerNotes* introduction at:

go.hrw.com L8-703 

MEET THE WRITERS

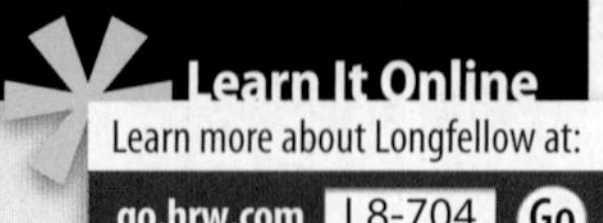
Learn It Online
Learn more about Longfellow at:
go.hrw.com L8-704 Go

Henry Wadsworth Longfellow

(1807–1882)

A Poet of American History

If you had gone to school a hundred years ago, you and all your friends would probably be able to recite by heart several of the poems of Henry Wadsworth Longfellow. Born in Portland, Maine, Longfellow became the most popular poet of his day. Many of his poems, such as *Evangeline* (1847), *The Song of Hiawatha* (1855), and *The Courtship of Miles Standish* (1858), were inspired by people and events in American history. As "Paul Revere's Ride" shows, Longfellow believed that one person's actions could make a difference.

John Greenleaf Whittier

(1807–1892)

The Granger Collection, New York.

Dedicated to Freedom

John Greenleaf Whittier was born and raised on a farm in Haverhill, Massachusetts, where his Quaker family had lived since 1688. Whittier devoted most of his life to the antislavery movement. His poems reflect his dedication to freedom and justice and his deep religious faith. Whittier was one of the hugely popular Fireside Poets, whose works sold the way best-selling novels do today.

Think About the Writers

What values do you think Longfellow and Whittier held in common?

Preview the Selections

In "Paul Revere's Ride," you will read Longfellow's account of how **Paul Revere** warned his fellow citizens that the British forces were coming.

In "Barbara Frietchie," you will meet a woman named **Barbara Frietchie,** who bravely challenged an enemy general in order to show support for her country.

Paul Revere's Ride

by **Henry Wadsworth Longfellow**

Read with a Purpose

Read the following poems to learn about Paul Revere's and Barbara Frietchie's memorable actions.

Build Background

This poem is based loosely on historical events. On the night of April 18, 1775, Paul Revere, William Dawes, and Samuel Prescott set out from Boston to warn American colonists of a planned British raid on Concord, Massachusetts.

Listen, my children, and you shall hear
Of the midnight ride of Paul Revere, **A**
On the eighteenth of April, in Seventy-five;
Hardly a man is now alive
Who remembers that famous day and year.

He said to his friend, "If the British march
By land or sea from the town tonight,
Hang a lantern aloft in the belfry° arch
Of the North Church tower as a signal light—
One, if by land, and two, if by sea;
And I on the opposite shore will be,
Ready to ride and spread the alarm
Through every Middlesex village and farm,
For the country folk to be up and to arm." **B**

Then he said, "Good night!" and with muffled oar
Silently rowed to the Charlestown shore,

8. **belfry** (BEHL free): steeple of a church where bells are hung.

A **Literary Focus** **Rhythm** The rhythm of this poem reflects its subject—a long, fast ride on horseback. Clap out the first two lines of the stanza. What feeling does the rhythm evoke?

B **Read and Discuss** What is Revere's plan?

Just as the moon rose over the bay,
Where swinging wide at her moorings° lay
The Somerset, British man-of-war;
A phantom ship, with each mast and spar°
Across the moon like a prison bar,
And a huge black hulk, that was magnified
By its own reflection in the tide.

Meanwhile, his friend, through alley and street, **C**
Wanders and watches with eager ears,
Till in the silence around him he hears
The muster° of men at the barrack door,
The sound of arms, and the tramp of feet,
And the measured tread of the grenadiers,°
Marching down to their boats on the shore.

Then he climbed the tower of the Old North Church,
By the wooden stairs, with stealthy tread,
To the belfry chamber overhead, **D**
And startled the pigeons from their perch
On the somber rafters, that round him made
Masses and moving shapes of shade—
By the trembling ladder, steep and tall,
To the highest window in the wall,
Where he paused to listen and look down
A moment on the roofs of the town,
And the moonlight flowing over all.

Beneath, in the churchyard, lay the dead,
In their night encampment on the hill,
Wrapped in silence so deep and still
That he could hear, like a sentinel's° tread,

18. moorings: cables holding a ship in place so that it doesn't float away.

20. mast and spar: poles supporting a ship's sails.

27. muster: assembly; gathering.

29. grenadiers (grehn uh DIHRZ): foot soldiers who carry and throw grenades.

45. sentinel's (SEHN tuh nuhlz): guard's.

C Literary Focus **Narrative Poetry** The author begins this stanza with the transitional word *Meanwhile*. The stanza before begins with *Then*. Why might transitions be important in a narrative poem?

D Reading Focus **Paraphrasing** Paraphrase what Revere's friend did at the church tower (lines 31–33).

SOCIAL STUDIES LINK

A statue of a minuteman in Lexington, Massachusetts.

Revere's Ride and the American Revolution

Paul Revere's famous ride succeeded in forestalling the planned raid on Boston by the British. One reason the British planned to raid Concord was to arrest two Americans who were calling for armed resistance to England. The British also wanted to destroy a supply of arms in Concord. The day after Revere's ride, armed volunteers known as minutemen confronted the British at Lexington and Concord. These were the first battles of the American Revolution. The war lasted for eight years until September 3, 1783, when the Treaty of Paris was signed and the United States was recognized as an independent country.

Ask Yourself

What might have happened had Revere and his friends not warned people of the British advance?

The watchful night wind, as it went
Creeping along from tent to tent,
And seeming to whisper, "All is well!"
A moment only he feels the spell
Of the place and the hour, and the secret dread
Of the lonely belfry and the dead;
For suddenly all his thoughts are bent
On a shadowy something far away,
Where the river widens to meet the bay—
A line of black that bends and floats
On the rising tide, like a bridge of boats. **E**

Meanwhile, impatient to mount and ride,
Booted and spurred, with a heavy stride
On the opposite shore walked Paul Revere.
Now he patted his horse's side,
Now gazed at the landscape far and near,
Then, impetuous, stamped the earth,

E **Read and Discuss** What is the speaker letting us know?

Vocabulary **impetuous** (ihm PEHCH u uhs) *adj.:* impulsive; eager.

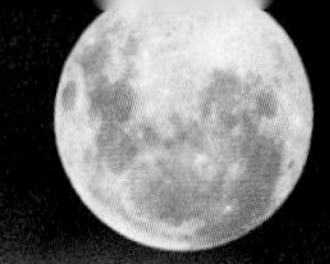

And turned and tightened his saddle girth;
But mostly he watched with eager search
The belfry tower of the Old North Church,
As it rose above the graves on the hill,
Lonely and spectral° and somber and still.
And lo! as he looks, on the belfry's height
A glimmer, and then a gleam of light!
He springs to the saddle, the bridle he turns,
But lingers and gazes, till full on his sight
A second lamp in the belfry burns! **F**

A hurry of hoofs in a village street,
A shape in the moonlight, a bulk in the dark,
And beneath, from the pebbles, in passing, a spark
Struck out by a steed flying fearless and fleet:
That was all! And yet, through the gloom and the light,
The fate of a nation was riding that night;
And the spark struck out by that steed, in his flight,
Kindled the land into flame with its heat. **G**

He has left the village and mounted the steep,
And beneath him, tranquil and broad and deep,
Is the Mystic, meeting the ocean tides;
And under the alders° that skirt its edge,
Now soft on the sand, now loud on the ledge,
Is heard the tramp of his steed as he rides.

It was twelve by the village clock,
When he crossed the bridge into Medford town.
He heard the crowing of the cock,
And the barking of the farmer's dog,
And felt the damp of the river fog,
That rises after the sun goes down.

67. spectral: ghostly.

84. alders (AWL duhrz): shrubs and trees of the birch family.

F **Read and Discuss** What has happened?

G **Literary Focus** **Rhythm** Re-read lines 73–80. Here, the action is at full speed. What association can you make between the rhythm and the action?

Analyzing Visuals **Viewing and Interpreting** This is a foreboding depiction of Paul Revere's ride. Is it how you picture the ride? Why or why not?

It was one by the village clock,
When he galloped into Lexington.
He saw the gilded weathercock°
Swim in the moonlight as he passed,
And the meetinghouse windows, blank and bare,
Gaze at him with a spectral glare,
As if they already stood aghast
At the bloody work they would look upon.

95. weathercock: weathervane made to look like a rooster (cock). Weathervanes indicate the direction in which the wind is blowing.

Vocabulary **aghast** (uh GAST) *adj.*: shocked; horrified.

It was two by the village clock,
When he came to the bridge in Concord town.
He heard the bleating of the flock,
And the twitter of birds among the trees,
And felt the breath of the morning breeze
Blowing over the meadows brown.
And one was safe and asleep in his bed
Who at the bridge would be first to fall,
Who that day would be lying dead,
Pierced by a British musket ball.

You know the rest. In the books you have read,
How the British Regulars fired and fled—
How the farmers gave them ball for ball,
From behind each fence and farmyard wall,
Chasing the redcoats down the lane,
Then crossing the fields to emerge again
Under the trees at the turn of the road,
And only pausing to fire and load. **H**

So through the night rode Paul Revere;
And so through the night went his cry of alarm
To every Middlesex village and farm—
A cry of defiance and not of fear,
A voice in the darkness, a knock at the door,
And a word that shall echo forevermore!
For, borne on the night wind of the Past,
Through all our history, to the last,
In the hour of darkness and peril and need,
The people will waken and listen to hear
The hurrying hoofbeats of that steed,
And the midnight message of Paul Revere. **I**

H **Literary Focus** **Narrative Poem** Retell the story this poem has recounted.

I **Read and Discuss** What is Longfellow trying to get across to his readers?

Build Background

This poem is set during the Civil War. In 1862, after defeating Union forces at the Second Battle of Bull Run, Confederate troops moved north into Maryland. Led by generals Robert E. Lee and "Stonewall" Jackson, the troops marched into the town of Frederick. Lee and his men were expecting a warm welcome, but the people of Frederick were loyal to the Union. Whittier based "Barbara Frietchie" on these events.

Barbara Frietchie

by **John Greenleaf Whittier**

Up from the meadows rich with corn,
Clear in the cool September morn,

The clustered spires of Frederick stand
Green-walled by the hills of Maryland. **A**

Round about them orchards sweep,
Apple and peach tree fruited deep,

Fair as the garden of the Lord
To the eyes of the famished rebel horde,°

On that pleasant morn of the early fall
When Lee marched over the mountain wall;

Over the mountains winding down,
Horse and foot, into Frederick town. **B**

Forty flags with their silver stars,
Forty flags with their crimson bars,

8. horde: crowd.

A **Literary Focus** **Rhythm** The first two lines have a regular meter, which is varied in the next two. What might the poet's intent be in varying the beat of the lines?

B **Read and Discuss** What have we learned about the time and place of the story?

Flapped in the morning wind: the sun
Of noon looked down, and saw not one.

Up rose old Barbara Frietchie then,
Bowed with her fourscore years and ten;

Bravest of all in Frederick town,
She took up the flag the men hauled down

In her attic window the staff° she set,
To show that one heart was loyal yet.

Up the street came the rebel tread,°
Stonewall Jackson riding ahead.

Under his slouched hat left and right
He glanced; the old flag met his sight.

"Halt!"—the dust-brown ranks stood fast.
"Fire!"—out blazed the rifle blast.

It shivered the window, pane and sash;
It rent° the banner with seam and gash.

Quick, as it fell, from the broken staff
Dame Barbara snatched the silken scarf.

She leaned far out on the windowsill,
And shook it forth with a royal will.

"Shoot, if you must, this old gray head,
But spare your country's flag," she said. **C**

A shade of sadness, a blush of shame,
Over the face of the leader came;

21. staff: pole; stick.

23. tread: footstep.

30. rent (past tense of *rend,* meaning "tear"): tore; ripped.

C **Read and Discuss** What has happened?

The nobler nature within him stirred
To life at that woman's deed and word;

"Who touches a hair of yon gray head
Dies like a dog! March on!" he said. **D**

All day long through Frederick street
Sounded the tread of marching feet:

All day long that free flag tossed
Over the heads of the rebel host.

Ever its torn folds rose and fell
On the loyal winds that loved it well;

And through the hill gaps sunset light
Shone over it with a warm good night.

Barbara Frietchie's work is o'er,
And the Rebel rides on his raids no more.

Honor to her! and let a tear
Fall, for her sake, on Stonewall's bier.°

Over Barbara Frietchie's grave,
Flag of Freedom and Union, wave!

Peace and order and beauty draw
Round thy symbol of light and law;

And ever the stars above look down
On thy stars below in Frederick town! **E**

Barbara Frietchie (detail) (1876) by Dennis Malone Carter (1827–1881). Oil on canvas (36 ¼" x 46 ¼"). Kirby Collection of Historical Paintings, Lafayette College, Easton Pennsylvania. Photo by Thomas Kosa.

54. bier (bihr): coffin and the platform on which it rests. Stonewall Jackson died in 1863 after being wounded in battle.

D Reading Focus Paraphrasing What happens in lines 37–42? Paraphrase that passage.

E Read and Discuss Now what do we know?

Vocabulary **stirred** (sturd) *v.:* moved; roused.
host (hohst) *n.:* army; large number.

Applying Your Skills

RA.L.8.6 Explain how an author's choice of genre affects the expression of a theme or topic. RA.L.8.8 Explain ways in which the author conveys mood and tone through word choice, figurative language, and syntax. *Also covered* **RP.8.1; VO.8.4; WA.8.1.b**

Paul Revere's Ride / Barbara Frietchie

Respond and Think Critically

Reading Focus

Read with a Purpose

1. Why is it important that people remember what Paul Revere and Barbara Frietchie did?

Reading Skills: Paraphrasing

2. If you haven't done so already, paraphrase the final lines of "Paul Revere's Ride" and "Barbara Frietchie" to learn each poem's message.

	My Paraphrase
Paul Revere's Ride lines 125–130	
Barbara Frietchie lines 55–60	

Vocabulary Check

Fill in the blanks with the correct Vocabulary words.

impetuous aghast stirred host

3. The townspeople were ________ that a British ________ was coming. Revere, always ________, was ready to act. His bravery was ________ by the desire to protect his people.

Literary Focus

Literary Analysis

4. **Interpret** What is your interpretation of Longfellow's words "The fate of a nation was riding that night"?
5. **Infer** Why does Longfellow believe that Americans will remember Revere's ride "In the hour of darkness and peril and need"?
6. **Make Judgments** Discuss the bravery or folly of Barbara Frietchie's response, "Shoot, if you must, this old gray head, /but spare your country's flag."

Literary Skills: Narrative Poetry: Rhythm and Meter

7. **Analyze** Summarize the events of "Paul Revere's Ride." How does the poem's strong rhythm enhance the story it tells?
8. **Analyze** Narrative poems contain characters. What do Frietchie's actions reveal about her?

Literary Skills Review: Rhyme

9. **Analyze** A **rhyme scheme** is the pattern of rhymes in a poem. What are the rhyme schemes of "Paul Revere's Ride" and "Barbara Frietchie"? For what purpose might the poets have chosen to use regular rhyming patterns?

Writing Focus

Think as a Reader/Writer

Use It in Your Writing Create an outline for a short narrative poem about an event that took place at your school. Next to narrative details, list word pairs you would use as end rhymes.

What Do You Think Now

How did the poems clarify your ideas about when it might be important to express your beliefs?

Preparing to Read

The Cremation of Sam McGee / The Dying Cowboy

RA.L.8.6 Explain how an author's choice of genre affects the expression of a theme or topic.
RA.L.8.8 Explain ways in which the author conveys mood and tone through word choice, figurative language, and syntax.

Literary Focus

Ballads and Hyperbole A **ballad** is a song or a songlike poem that tells a story, usually about lost love, betrayal, or death. Ballads usually use simple language and much repetition. Most ballads have **refrains,** repeated words, phrases, lines, or group of lines. Some ballads, such as "The Cremation of Sam McGee" use **hyperbole,** or exaggeration, to make a point.

Literary Perspectives Apply the literary perspective described on page 723 as you read "The Dying Cowboy."

Reading Focus

Using Form to Find Meaning Many poems are in the form of **stanzas**—groups of consecutive lines that form a single unit. Determining the main idea or the events described in each stanza can help you understand the ballads you will read.

Into Action Use a chart to record the main idea of each stanza of the following poems. Add a row for each stanza.

Poem: The Cremation of Sam McGee

Stanza Number	Main Idea or Events
1	The speaker tells us that the poem will be about the night he cremated Sam McGee.
2	

Writing Focus

Think as a Reader/Writer

Find It in Your Reading As you read, note in your *Reader/Writer Notebook* the poets' use of **imagery,** language that appeals to the senses. How does the imagery enliven the stories?

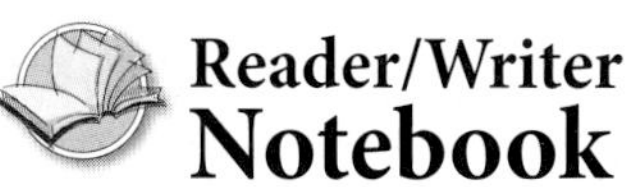

Use your **RWN** to complete the activities for these selections.

Vocabulary

The Cremation of Sam McGee

tax (taks) *v.:* here, burden; strain. *Sam's request will tax his friend, emotionally and physically.*

loathed (lohthd) *v.:* hated. *Sam loathed the cold.*

spent (spehnt) *adj.:* worn-out. *Sam McGee was spent from trying to stay warm.*

The Dying Cowboy

comrade (KAHM rad) *n.:* companion; friend; associate. *The cowboy and Sam McGee both ask favors of their comrades.*

Language Coach

Multiple-Meaning Words In day-to-day life, you might say you **spent** money to pay a **tax** you owed. Both *spent* and *tax,* however, have very different meanings as used in "The Cremation of Sam McGee." What meanings do those words have in the poem? Look at the definitions above to find out.

Learn It Online
Use Word Watch to investigate these words at:

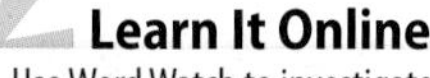

go.hrw.com L8-715

MEET THE WRITER

Robert W. Service

(1874–1958)

"A Story Jack London Never Got"

Born in Lancashire, England, Robert W. Service immigrated to Canada in his early twenties. After traveling along the Canadian Pacific coast, he took a job with a bank and was transferred to the Yukon Territory. He wrote his most popular poems there, including "The Cremation of Sam McGee." The poem was inspired by a story Service heard at a party where he was feeling awkward and out of place:

> "I was staring gloomily at a fat fellow across the table. . . . Suddenly he said, 'I'll tell you a story Jack London never got.' Then he spun a yarn of a man who cremated his pal. It had a surprise climax which occasioned much laughter. I did not join, for I had a feeling that here was a decisive moment of destiny. I still remember how a great excitement usurped me. Here was a perfect ballad subject. The fat man who ignored me went his way to bankruptcy, but he had pointed me the road to fortune."

Service left the party and spent the next six hours wandering through the frozen woods, verses in his head. When he went to bed, the poem was complete; he didn't even put it on paper until the next day.

Think About the Writer What do the details of Service's background suggest about him?

Build Background

The Cremation of Sam McGee

In the 1890s, thousands of fortune hunters rushed north, braving bitter cold and deep snow. Gold had been found in northwestern Canada, in the Klondike region of the Yukon Territory. The town of Dawson, at the center of the region, became the Yukon's capital. (Cremation is the burning of a body to ashes.)

The Dying Cowboy

Ballads like this one were sung by cowboys in the American West. This ballad is based on an eighteenth-century Irish tune, and it gave rise to the famous blues song "St. James Infirmary." The ballad also provided the title and the haunting theme music for *Bang the Drum Slowly,* a movie about the death of a young baseball player.

Preview the Selections

The two ballads you are about to read are both about a man dying before his time who asks a friend to honor his last request. The main characters of the poems are **Sam McGee** in "The Cremation of Sam McGee" and simply **a handsome young cowboy** in "The Dying Cowboy."

Read with a Purpose Read the poems to learn what last requests the speakers have been asked to honor.

The Cremation of Sam McGee

by **Robert W. Service**

There are strange things done in the midnight sun
By the men who moil° for gold;
The Arctic trails have their secret tales
That would make your blood run cold;
The Northern Lights have seen queer sights,
But the queerest they ever did see
Was that night on the marge° of Lake Lebarge
I cremated Sam McGee. **A**

2. **moil:** labor.

7. **marge:** edge.

Now Sam McGee was from Tennessee, where the cotton blooms and blows.
Why he left his home in the South to roam 'round the Pole, God only knows.
He was always cold, but the land of gold seemed to hold him like a spell;
Though he'd often say in his homely way that he'd "sooner live in hell." **B**

On a Christmas Day we were mushing our way over the Dawson trail.
Talk of your cold! through the parka's fold it stabbed like a driven nail.

A **Read and Discuss** What has the poet told us so far?

B **Reading Focus** **Using Form to Find Meaning** What do we learn about McGee in this stanza?

If our eyes we'd close, then the lashes froze till sometimes
we couldn't see;
It wasn't much fun, but the only one to whimper was
Sam McGee.

And that very night, as we lay packed tight in our robes
beneath the snow,
And the dogs were fed, and the stars o'erhead were
dancing heel and toe,
He turned to me, and "Cap," says he, "I'll cash in this
trip, I guess;
And if I do, I'm asking that you won't refuse my last
request."

Well, he seemed so low that I couldn't say no; then he
says with a sort of moan:
"It's the cursèd cold, and it's got right hold till I'm chilled
clean through to the bone.
Yet 'tain't being dead—it's my awful dread of the icy
grave that pains;
So I want you to swear that, foul or fair, you'll cremate
my last remains." **C**

A pal's last need is a thing to heed, so I swore I would
not fail;
And we started on at the streak of dawn; but God! he
looked ghastly pale.
He crouched on the sleigh, and he raved all day of his
home in Tennessee;
And before nightfall a corpse was all that was left of Sam
McGee.

C **Read and Discuss** Why is cremation so important to Sam McGee?

There wasn't a breath in that land of death, and
I hurried, horror-driven,
With a corpse half hid that I couldn't get rid, because of
a promise given;
It was lashed to the sleigh, and it seemed to say: "You
may tax your brawn and brains,
But you promised true, and it's up to you to cremate
those last remains." **D**

Now a promise made is a debt unpaid, and the trail has
its own stern code.
In the days to come, though my lips were dumb, in my
heart how I cursed that load.
In the long, long night, by the lone firelight, while the
huskies, round in a ring,
Howled out their woes to the homeless snows—O God!
how I loathed the thing.

D Literary Focus Hyperbole How do the exaggerations in this stanza convey the way the speaker feels about the corpse?

Vocabulary **tax** (taks) *v.:* here, burden; strain.
loathed (lohthd) *v.:* hated.

And every day that quiet clay seemed to heavy and
heavier grow;
And on I went, though the dogs were spent and the grub
was getting low;
The trail was bad, and I felt half mad, but I swore I
would not give in;
And I'd often sing to the hateful thing, and it hearkened°
with a grin.

Till I came to the marge of Lake Lebarge, and a derelict°
there lay;
It was jammed in the ice, but I saw in a trice it was called
the "Alice May."
And I looked at it, and I thought a bit, and I looked at
my frozen chum;
Then "Here," said I, with a sudden cry, "is my cre-ma-
tor-ium." **E**

Some planks I tore from the cabin floor, and I lit the
boiler fire;
Some coal I found that was lying around, and I heaped
the fuel higher;
The flames just soared, and the furnace roared—such a
blaze you seldom see;
And I burrowed a hole in the glowing coal, and I stuffed
in Sam McGee.

Then I made a hike, for I didn't like to hear him sizzle so;
And the heavens scowled, and the huskies howled, and
the wind began to blow.
It was icy cold, but the hot sweat rolled down my cheeks,
and I don't know why;
And the greasy smoke in an inky cloak went streaking
down the sky.

40. hearkened (HAHR kuhnd): listened carefully.

41. derelict (DEHR uh lihkt): abandoned ship.

E **Read and Discuss** How is the speaker handling McGee's death?

Vocabulary **spent** (spehnt) *adj.:* worn-out.

I do not know how long in the snow I wrestled with grisly° fear;
But the stars came out and they danced about ere again I ventured near;
I was sick with dread, but I bravely said: "I'll just take a peep inside.
I guess he's cooked, and it's time I looked"; . . . then the door I opened wide.

And there sat Sam, looking cool and calm, in the heart of the furnace roar;
And he wore a smile you could see a mile, and he said: "Please close that door.
It's fine in here, but I greatly fear you'll let in the cold and storm—
Since I left Plumtree, down in Tennessee, it's the first time I've been warm." **F**

There are strange things done in the midnight sun
By the men who moil for gold;
The Arctic trails have their secret tales
That would make your blood run cold;
The Northern Lights have seen queer sights,
But the queerest they ever did see
Was that night on the marge of Lake Lebarge
I cremated Sam McGee. **G**

F **Literary Focus** **Ballad** What is the climax of this story?

G **Read and Discuss** Why has the poet chosen to end the poem by repeating its beginning?

53. **grisly** (GRIHZ lee): here, caused by something horrible.

The Dying Cowboy

traditional American ballad

The Bronco Buster (1910) by Frederic Remington.

As I rode out by Tom Sherman's barroom,
As I rode out so early one day,
'Twas there I espied a handsome young cowboy,
All dressed in white linen, all clothed for the grave.

"I see by your outfit that you are a cowboy,"
These words he did say as I boldly stepped by.
"Come sit down beside me and hear my sad story,
For I'm shot in the breast and I know I must die. **A**

"Then beat your drum slowly and play your fife lowly,
And play the dead march as you carry me along,
And take me to the graveyard and throw the sod o'er me,
For I'm a young cowboy and I know I've done wrong.

"'Twas once in the saddle I used to go dashing,
'Twas once in the saddle I used to go gay,
But I first took to drinking and then to card playing,
Got shot in the body and I'm dying today. **B**

"Let sixteen gamblers come handle my coffin,
Let sixteen young cowboys come sing me a song,

A **Read and Discuss** What have we learned so far?

B **Reading Focus** **Using Form to Find Meaning** What is the main idea of this stanza? What information does it offer readers?

Take me to the green valley and lay the sod o'er me,
For I'm a poor cowboy and I know I've done wrong.

"Go bring me back a cup of cool water
To cool my parched lips," this cowboy then said.
Before I returned, his soul had departed
And gone to his Maker—the cowboy lay dead.

We swung our ropes slowly and rattled our spurs lowly,
And gave a wild whoop as we carried him on,
For we all loved our comrade, so brave, young and handsome,
We all loved our comrade, although he'd done wrong. C

C **Literary Perspectives** **Analyzing Archetypes** What might the cowboy represent? What elements of his character are common in other stories?

Vocabulary **comrade** (KAHM rad) *n.:* companion; friend; associate.

Literary Perspectives

The following perspective will help you analyze the archetypes in this ballad.

Analyzing Archetypes Patterns that appear in literature across cultures and are repeated through the ages are called **archetypes.** An archetype can be a character, plot, image, or setting. For example, there are stories about heroes on quests in both ancient myths and in modern movies. In this ballad, concentrate on the character of the dying cowboy. How is he like other characters you know? Notice the question above that guides you in using this perspective.

Applying Your Skills

RA.L.8.6 Explain how an author's choice of genre affects the expression of a theme or topic. **RA.L.8.8** Explain ways in which the author conveys mood and tone through word choice, figurative language, and syntax. *Also covered* **WA.8.2**

The Cremation of Sam McGee / The Dying Cowboy

Respond and Think Critically

Reading Focus

Read with a Purpose

1. What last request does each speaker fulfill?

Reading Skills: Using Form to Find Meaning

2. Complete the charts you began while reading. Then, add a row to each chart and write a short summary of each ballad.

Poem: The Cremation of Sam McGee

Stanza Number	Main Idea or Events
1	
2	

My Summary:

Vocabulary Check

Match each Vocabulary word with its synonym.

3. **loathed** — **a.** tired
4. **tax** — **b.** friend
5. **spent** — **c.** hated
6. **comrade** — **d.** burden

Literary Focus

Literary Analysis

7. **Identify** List two or three details from "The Cremation of Sam McGee" that help you picture the frozen landscape or feel the cold.
8. **Infer** Based on the language he uses to describe Sam McGee and his actions, what does the speaker think of Sam?
9. **Analyze** How does Service's writing style make a dire event—death—come across as light and odd instead of sad and dreary?
10. **Analyze** What details about his life help us understand what has happened to cause the dying cowboy's death?
11. **Literary Perspectives** In what ways is the dying cowboy timeless? How might the archetype of the lone cowboy be represented in a modern story?

Literary Skills: Ballad and Hyperbole

12. **Analyze** How does the use of hyperbole contribute to the humor of "The Cremation of Sam McGee"? Use examples in your response.
13. **Analyze** "The Dying Cowboy" is a ballad, typical of the ballads sung by cowboys to help time pass more quickly. What characteristics of ballads does this poem have?

Writing Focus

Think as a Reader/Writer

Use It in Your Writing How does the use of imagery bring the ballads to life? What feelings do the images evoke? Explain, and give examples.

What Do You Think Now

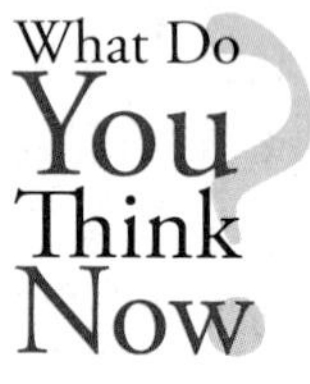

What ideas about life are these poems expressing?

Preparing to Read

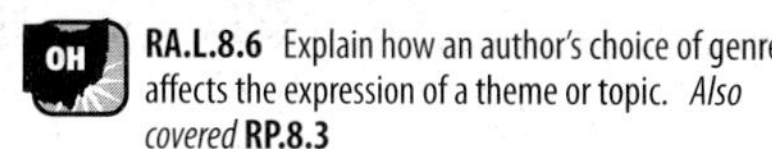

from Beowulf / Casey at the Bat

Literary Focus

Epic and Mock-Heroic Poems An **epic** is a long narrative poem written in formal, elegant language that tells about a series of quests undertaken by a great hero. In ancient epics, such as *Beowulf,* this hero is a warrior who embodies the values cherished by the hero's culture. "Casey at the Bat" is a **mock-heroic poem** that imitates the old epic tales, but in a comical way. For example, instead of a warrior, we have a small-town baseball player, and instead of the epic poet's elegant similes, metaphors, and alliteration, we have sports slang.

TechFocus As you read, write down heroic qualities that Beowulf and Casey both exhibit. Also, list qualities you look for in a hero.

Reading Focus

Re-reading Poetry is meant to be read and re-read. Each time you read a poem, you unlock layers of meaning.

Into Action Use a chart to record what you learn from these poems each time you read them. Read each poem at least twice.

Beowulf	My Comments
First reading	I'm not sure what a mead-hall is.
Second reading	Now I understand what a mead-hall is and why the warriors would miss it.
Third reading	

Writing Focus

Think as a Reader/Writer

Find It in Your Reading Heroic actions call for strong active verbs to describe them. As you read, write in your *Reader/Writer Notebook* the verbs that tell about Beowulf's and Casey's actions.

Use your **RWN** to complete the activities for these selections.

Vocabulary

from Beowulf

purge (purj) *v.:* get rid of something harmful. *Beowulf wanted to purge the monsters from the kingdom.*

scorn (skawrn) *n.:* obvious disrespect or dislike for someone or something. *The monsters feel scorn for the Danes.*

Casey at the Bat

defiance (dih FY uhns) *n.:* willingness to fight; rebellious feelings. *Filled with defiance, Casey sneered at the pitcher.*

our hero	
wants victory; wants to **purge** his enemy	feels **scorn** and **defiance** for his enemy

Language Coach

Language Conventions: Spelling Note the suffix *–ance* in the Vocabulary word *defiance.* You might be tempted to spell the word with *–ence.* Think of a way to help you remember the *–ance* spelling for the ending for this word, and write it in your *Reader/Writer Notebook.*

Learn It Online

Dig deeper into poetry with audio recordings at:

MEET THE WRITER

Ernest Lawrence Thayer

(1863–1940)

Secret Author

When the journalist Ernest Lawrence Thayer submitted "Casey at the Bat" to the *San Francisco Examiner* in 1888, he had no idea it would become the most famous baseball poem ever written. In fact, he didn't even sign his own name to his work, choosing instead to use a nickname, Phin.

Surprise Success

Shortly after the poem appeared in the California newspaper, a copy was given to a vaudeville entertainer named William De Wolf Hopper, who was about to appear in a Baseball Night performance in New York. He went onstage and recited it; the audience went wild. Hopper went on to make a successful career of touring the country reciting "Casey at the Bat."

Undesired Attention

Despite the poem's popularity, Thayer considered it badly written and for years would not admit authorship. When he was finally identified as the author, he refused to take money for the poem's many reprintings.

"All I ask is never to be reminded of it again."

Think About the Writer What can you infer about the author from his reaction to his poem's success?

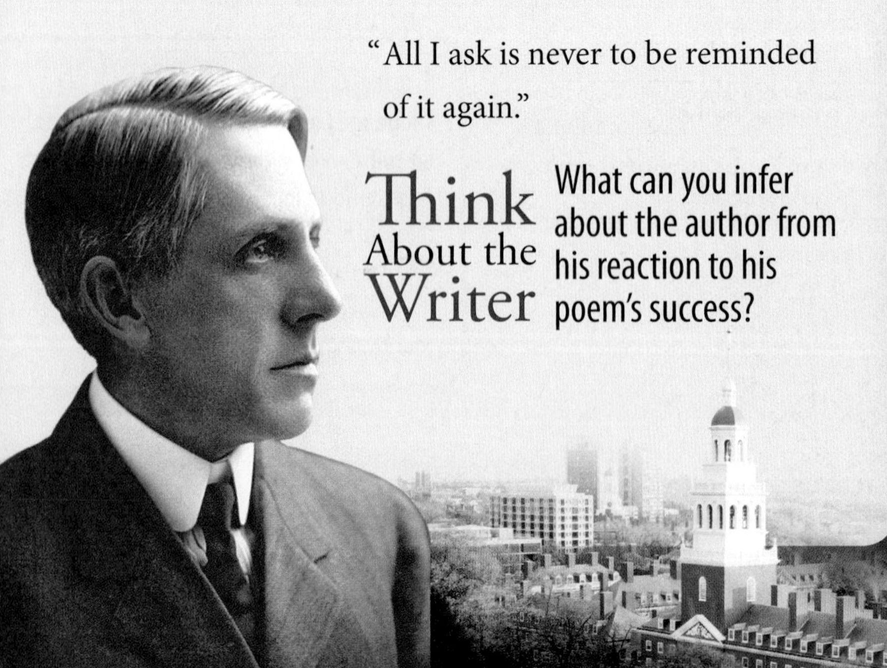

Build Background

Beowulf is considered the first great work of English literature. The poem was handed down orally for many generations and has an unknown author. Since it was originally written in Old English, which is very different from the English used today, the epic has been translated into Modern English many times.

First page of *Beowulf* (10th century). Old English vernacular poem.

Preview the Selections

In the excerpt from the epic poem, **Beowulf**, a warrior from the land of the Geats (in Scandinavia), has arrived at the court of **Hrothgar**, a Danish king. Beowulf gives his credentials; that is, he tells the king why he should be chosen to face **Grendel**, a huge monster who has been devouring Hrothgar's followers.

In "Casey at the Bat" by Ernest Lawrence Thayer, you will meet **Casey**—the star baseball player of Mudville—who plans to turn around the game for his losing team.

Read with a Purpose Read these poems to find out how their heroes plan to save the day.

from Beowulf

translated by
Burton Raffel

"Hail, Hrothgar!
Higlac is my cousin° and my king; the days
Of my youth have been filled with glory. Now Grendel's
Name has echoed in our land: Sailors
Have brought us stories of Herot, the best
Of all mead-halls,° deserted and useless when the moon
Hangs in skies the sun had lit,
Light and life fleeing together. **A**
My people have said, the wisest, most knowing
And best of them, that my duty was to go to the Danes'
Great King. They have seen my strength for themselves,
Have watched me rise from the darkness of war,
Dripping with my enemies' blood. I drove
Five great giants into chains, chased
All of that race from the earth. I swam

2. cousin: any relative. Higlac is Beowulf's uncle and his king.

6. mead-halls: Mead is a drink made from honey, water, yeast, and malt. The hall was a central gathering place where warriors could feast, listen to a bard's stories, and sleep in safety.

A **Reading Focus** **Re-reading** What do you learn from re-reading lines 1–8?

Gundestrup caldron (1st century B.C.E.).

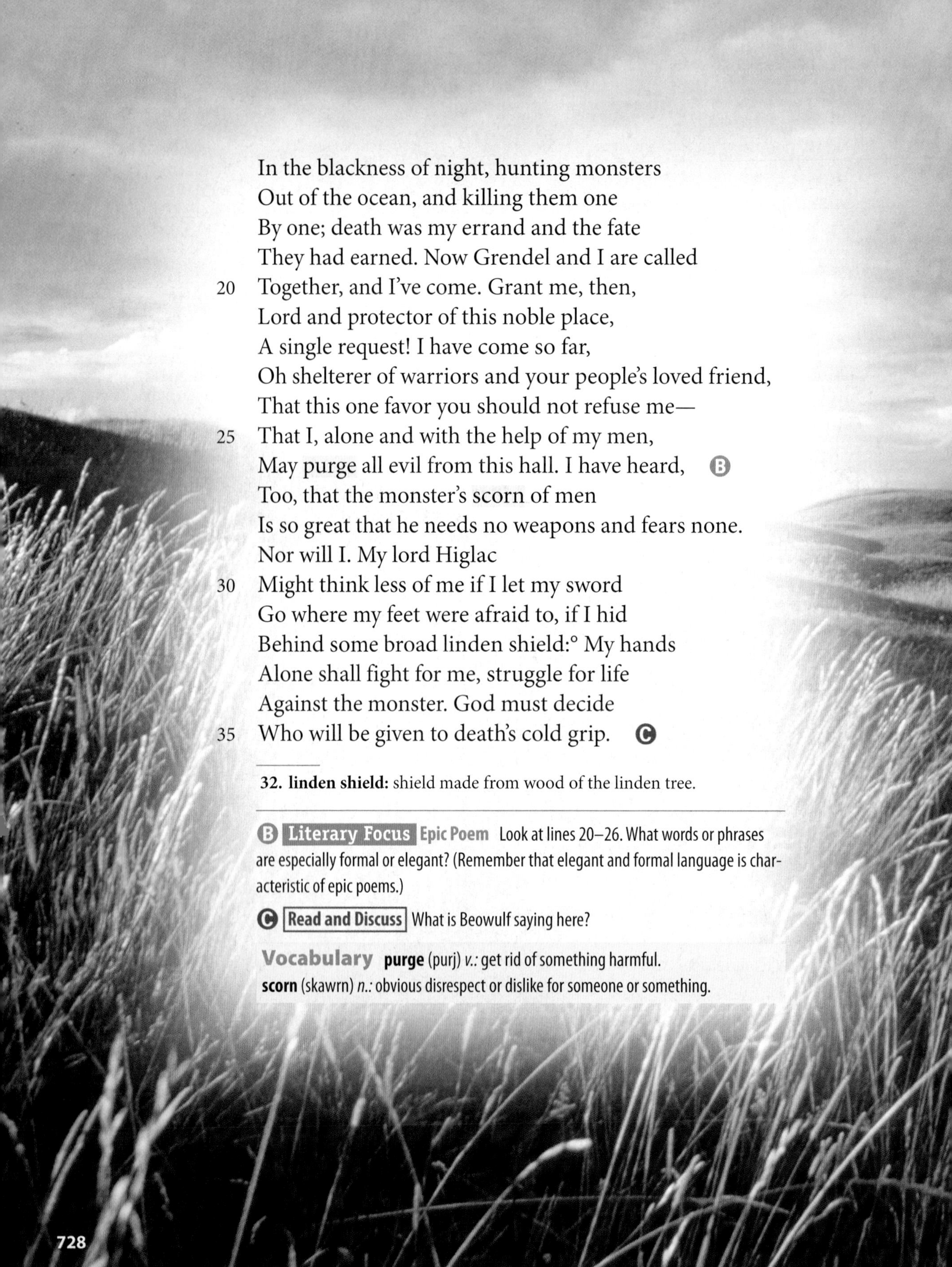

In the blackness of night, hunting monsters
Out of the ocean, and killing them one
By one; death was my errand and the fate
They had earned. Now Grendel and I are called
Together, and I've come. Grant me, then,
Lord and protector of this noble place,
A single request! I have come so far,
Oh shelterer of warriors and your people's loved friend,
That this one favor you should not refuse me—
That I, alone and with the help of my men,
May purge all evil from this hall. I have heard, **B**
Too, that the monster's scorn of men
Is so great that he needs no weapons and fears none.
Nor will I. My lord Higlac
Might think less of me if I let my sword
Go where my feet were afraid to, if I hid
Behind some broad linden shield:° My hands
Alone shall fight for me, struggle for life
Against the monster. God must decide
Who will be given to death's cold grip. **C**

---

32. linden shield: shield made from wood of the linden tree.

B **Literary Focus** **Epic Poem** Look at lines 20–26. What words or phrases are especially formal or elegant? (Remember that elegant and formal language is characteristic of epic poems.)

C **Read and Discuss** What is Beowulf saying here?

Vocabulary **purge** (purj) *v.:* get rid of something harmful.
scorn (skawrn) *n.:* obvious disrespect or dislike for someone or something.

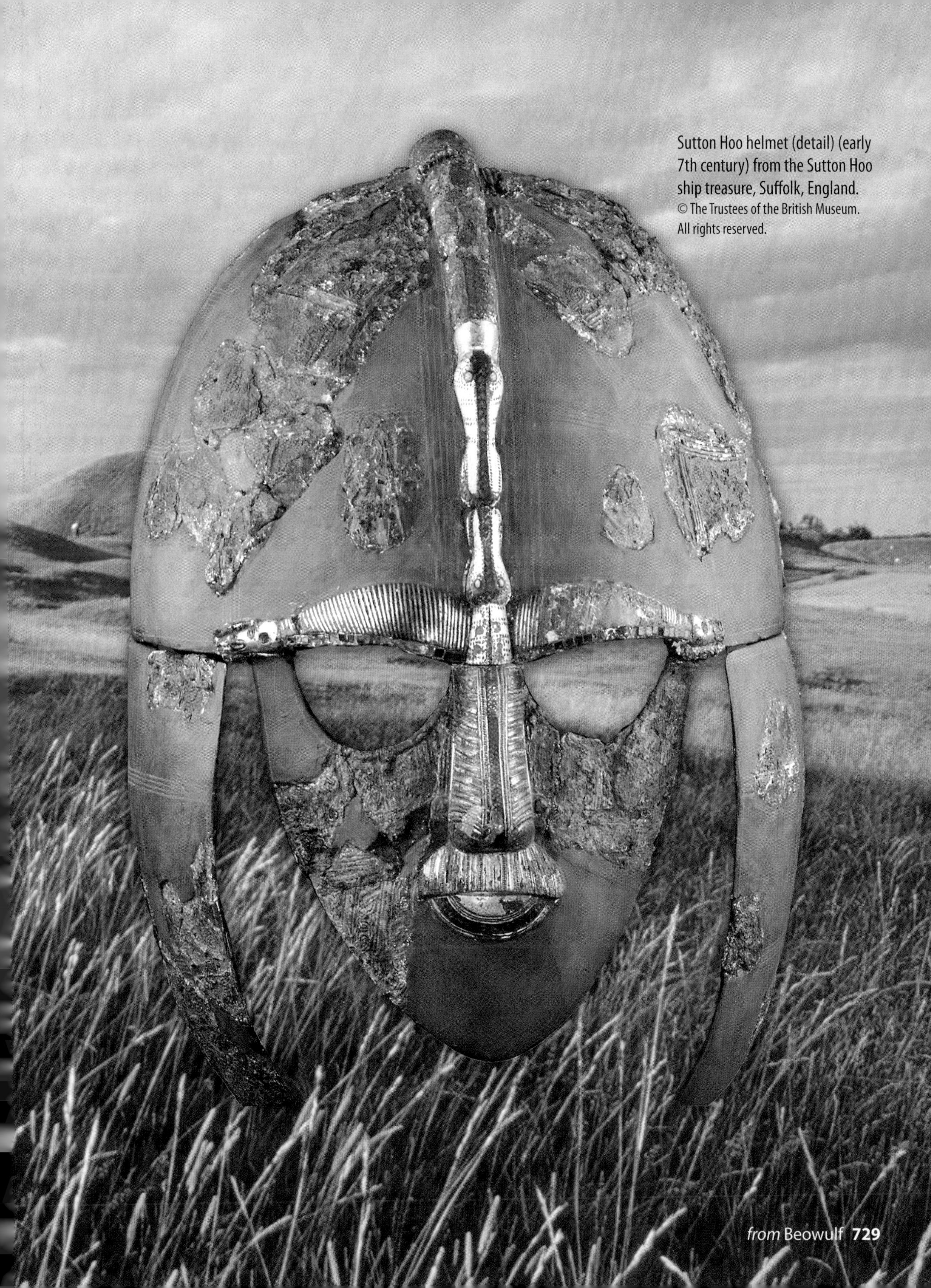

Sutton Hoo helmet (detail) (early 7th century) from the Sutton Hoo ship treasure, Suffolk, England.

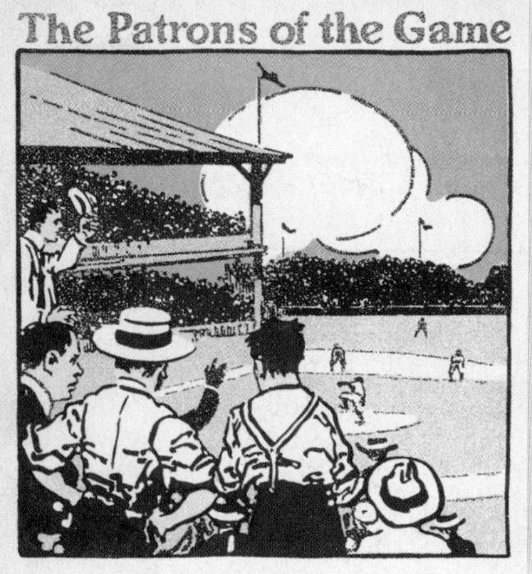

Illustrations by Dan Sayre Groesbeck (1912).

The outlook wasn't brilliant for the Mudville nine that day;
The score stood four to two, with but one inning more to play;
And so, when Cooney died at first, and Burrows did the same,
A sickly silence fell upon the patrons of the game.

A straggling few got up to go in deep despair. The rest
Clung to the hope which springs eternal in the human breast;
They thought, if only Casey could but get a whack, at that,
They'd put up even money now, with Casey at the bat.

But Flynn preceded Casey, as did also Jimmy Blake,
And the former was a pudding, and the latter was a fake;
So upon that stricken multitude grim melancholy sat,
For there seemed but little chance of Casey's getting to the bat. **A**

But Flynn let drive a single, to the wonderment of all,
And Blake, the much-despised, tore the cover off the ball;
And when the dust had lifted, and they saw what had occurred,
There was Jimmy safe on second, and Flynn a-hugging third.

A **Read and Discuss** What is happening so far? What is the crowd thinking?

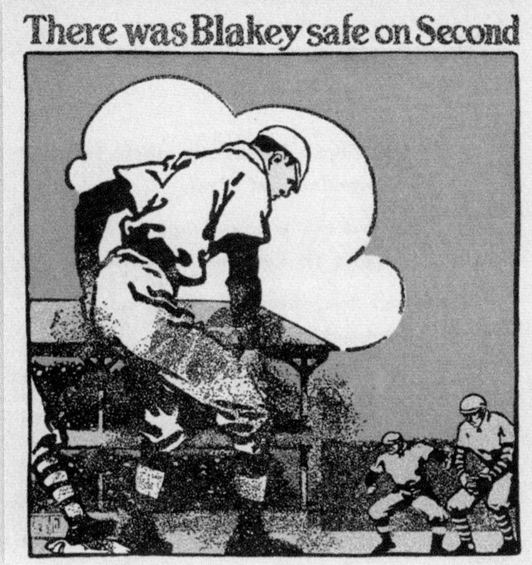
There was Blakey safe on Second

Mighty Casey was Advancing to the Bat

Then from the gladdened multitude went up a joyous yell;
It bounded from the mountaintop, and rattled in the dell;
It struck upon the hillside, and recoiled upon the flat;
For Casey, mighty Casey, was advancing to the bat. **B**

There was ease in Casey's manner as he stepped into his place;
There was pride in Casey's bearing, and a smile on Casey's face;
And when, responding to the cheers, he lightly doffed his hat,
No stranger in the crowd could doubt 'twas Casey at the bat.

Ten thousand eyes were on him as he rubbed his hands with dirt;
Five thousand tongues applauded when he wiped them on his shirt;
Then while the writhing pitcher ground the ball into his hip,
Defiance gleamed in Casey's eye, a sneer curled Casey's lip. **C**

B **Read and Discuss** How have things changed?

C **Reading Focus Re-reading** Re-read this stanza. What impression of Casey do you get?

Vocabulary **defiance** (dih FY uhns) *n.:* willingness to fight; rebellious feelings.

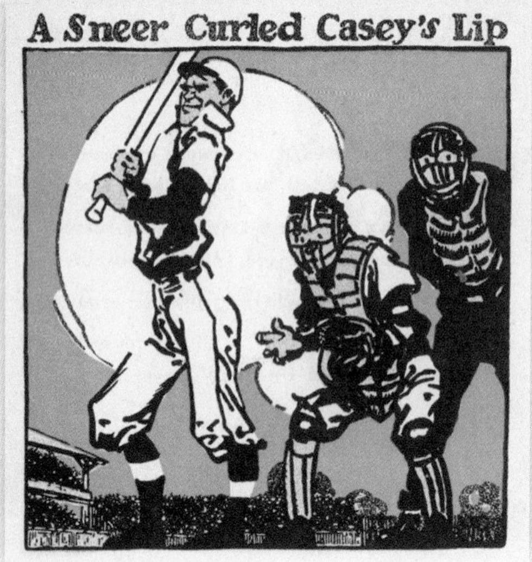
A Sneer Curled Casey's Lip

"Strike one" the Umpire Said

And now the leather-covered sphere came hurtling through the air,
And Casey stood a-watching it in haughty grandeur there;
Close by the sturdy batsman the ball unheeded sped.
"That ain't my style," said Casey. "Strike one," the umpire said.

From the benches, black with people, there went up a muffled roar,
Like the beating of the storm waves on a stern and distant shore;
"Kill him! Kill the umpire!" shouted someone on the stand;
And it's likely they'd have killed him had not Casey raised his hand.

With a smile of Christian charity great Casey's visage shone;
He stilled the rising tumult; he bade the game go on; **D**
He signaled to the pitcher, and once more the spheroid flew;
But Casey still ignored it, and the umpire said, "Strike two."

"Fraud!" cried the maddened thousands, and the echo answered, "Fraud!"

D **Read and Discuss** What does this information tell us about Casey as a person and a player?

But a scornful look from Casey, and the audience was awed;
They saw his face grow stern and cold, they saw his muscles strain,
And they knew that Casey wouldn't let that ball go by again.

The sneer is gone from Casey's lips, his teeth are clenched in hate,
He pounds with cruel violence his bat upon the plate;
And now the pitcher holds the ball, and now he lets it go,
And now the air is shattered by the force of Casey's blow. **E**

Oh! somewhere in this favored land the sun is shining bright;
The band is playing somewhere, and somewhere hearts are light;
And somewhere men are laughing, and somewhere children shout,
But there is no joy in Mudville—mighty Casey has struck out! **F**

E **Literary Focus** **Epic Poem** How are Casey's actions similar to those of a hero in an epic like *Beowulf*?

F **Read and Discuss** What just happened? Discuss the irony—the unexpected outcome—of the poem's ending.

Applying Your Skills

RA.L.8.6 Explain how an author's choice of genre affects the expression of a theme or topic. RP.8.3 Monitor own comprehension by adjusting speed to fit the purpose, or by skimming, scanning, reading on, looking back, note taking or summarizing what has been read so far in text. *Also covered* WP.8.9

from Beowulf / Casey at the Bat

Respond and Think Critically

Reading Focus

Read with a Purpose

1. How well do Beowulf and Casey fill the role of a hero? Explain.

Reading Skills: Re-reading

2. Once you've finished these poems, add a final comment about each to your chart.

Poem Title	My Comments
First Reading	
Second Reading	
Third Reading	

My Final Comments:

Vocabulary Check

Match the Vocabulary words with their definitions.

3. purge	**a.** obvious disrespect or dislike
4. scorn	**b.** rebellious feelings
5. defiance	**c.** get rid of

Literary Focus

Literary Analysis

6. **Infer** What can you infer about Hrothgar's warriors in *Beowulf*?
7. **Hypothesize** Why does Beowulf want to fight Grendel without a sword or shield? What would defeating Grendel prove?
8. **Draw Conclusions** In "Casey at the Bat" what can you conclude about Casey's usual performance at the plate?
9. **Evaluate** "Casey at the Bat" is often cited as the most famous baseball poem ever written. Do you feel it deserves such an honor? Explain.
10. **Compare** What associations can you make between Casey and sports stars of today? Support your ideas with details from the poem.

Literary Skills: Epic and Mock-Epic Poems

11. **Analyze** List three characteristics of epic poetry that you find in *Beowulf.*
12. **Compare and Contrast** What similarities can you find between *Beowulf* and "Casey at the Bat"? What key differences do you see?

Literary Skills Review: Diction

13. **Classify** A writer's or speaker's choice of words is called **diction.** Which words in "Casey at the Bat" are appropriate for describing a baseball game? Which words are formal and more appropriate for an epic?

Writing Focus

Think as a Reader/Writer

Use It in Your Writing Using strong, active verbs, write a short paragraph about a heroic action you have witnessed, heard about, or performed yourself.

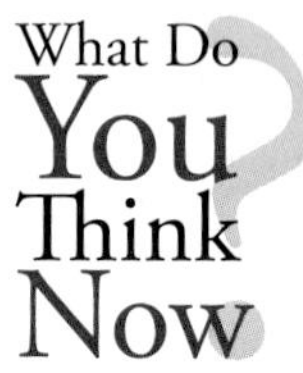

How do you feel about people who express great confidence in themselves?

Wrap Up

Poetry and Storytelling

OH **RP.8.1** Apply reading comprehension strategies, including making predictions, comparing and contrasting, recalling and summarizing and making inferences and drawing conclusions. *Also covered* **WA.8.4.b; WP.8.1; VO.8.4**

Vocabulary Development

Precise Meanings

A poet's words must sound right in the poem and convey an exact—precise—meaning. Notice the words Thayer uses in "Casey at the Bat":

> "A straggling few got up to go in deep despair."

If Thayer had instead used the words a *few sad fans left* instead of "a straggling few" and "deep despair," the reader would have much less information about the fans' emotions.

Your Turn

Use a dictionary to find a more precise word or phrase to replace each boldface word below.

1. Paul Revere's friend **goes** through town toward the Old North Church.
2. Stonewall Jackson **strongly** commands his troops not to shoot Barbara Frietchie.
3. Sam McGee **dislikes** the **cold** Yukon weather.
4. The fans are **sad** when Casey strikes out.

Language Coach

Language Conventions: Spelling The sound /uh/ in English can be spelled in different ways. Note the spellings in these words: *cousin, blood, hunting.*

Now, use a dictionary to help you fill in the blanks with the correct vowels for the following words:

__cquire (uh KWYR)
strenu__s (STREN yoo uhs)
dang__r (DAYN juhr)
weap__n (WEHP uhn)

CHOICES

As you respond to the Choices, use these **Academic Vocabulary** words as appropriate: intent, evoke, associations, interpretation.

REVIEW

Paraphrase a Well-Known Poem

Partner Work With a partner, choose a short poem in this collection. Each of you should paraphrase it in your own words. Exchange your paraphrase with your partner's. Note the differences in your paraphrases, and discuss the reasons for your word choices.

CONNECT

Write About Leaders

Timed Writing Are there any other people like Paul Revere, in history or in the present, who have rallied their people with cries "of defiance and not of fear"? Choose a leader, and explain the intent of his or her message. How did he or she evoke in people a desire for action? Give examples to support your ideas.

EXTEND

Discuss What Makes a Hero

TechFocus Using an online discussion board, collaborate with classmates to define the qualities of a hero. Start by discussing Beowulf's and Casey's qualities. Then, add your interpretations about what makes a hero. Ask classmates to contribute their opinions. Review all of the responses, and use them to create a set of criteria, or standards, for heroism. Share your completed list with the class.

Poetry and Form

CONTENTS

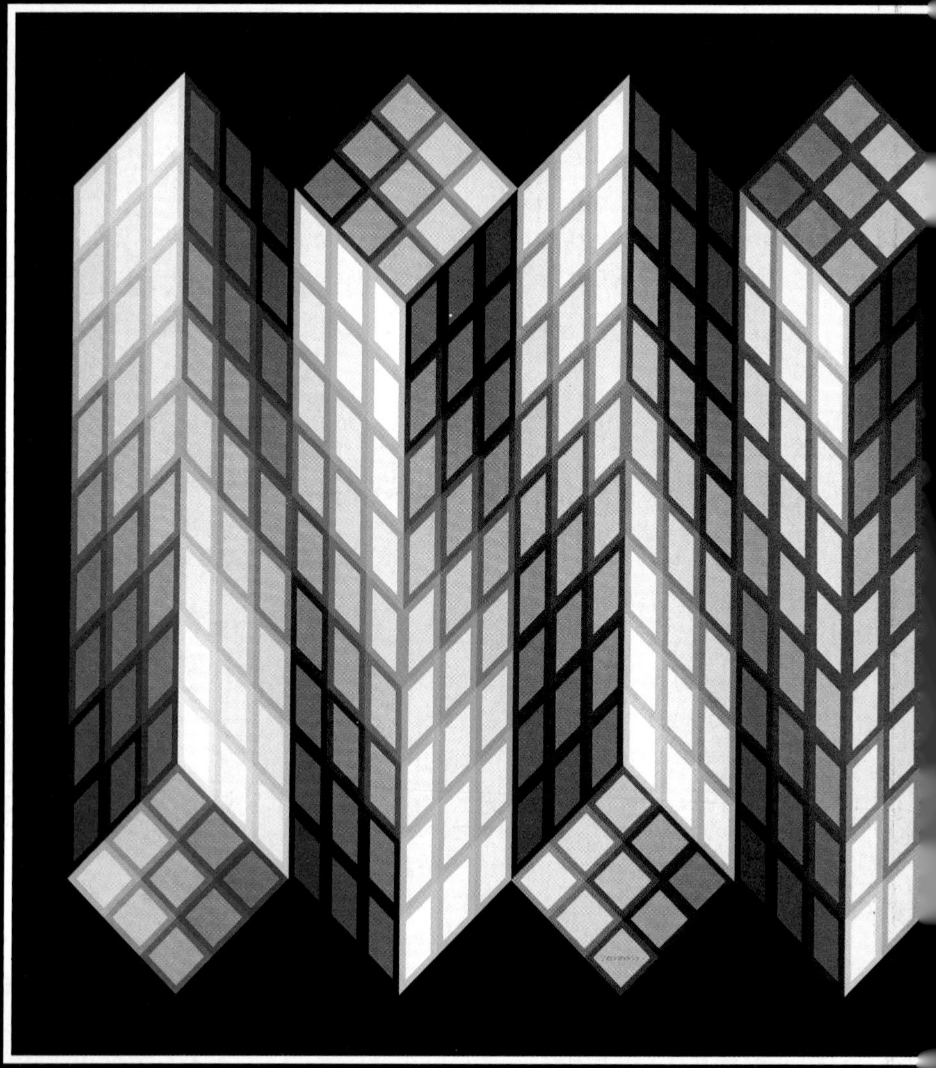

Toroni-Nagy (1969) by Victor Vasarely.

What Do You Think?

Why are poems such a useful form for expressing emotions such as joy, grief, and wonder?

QuickTalk

Discuss times when the form of an activity—such as writing, playing sports, or celebrating—helped you express feelings.

Preparing to Read

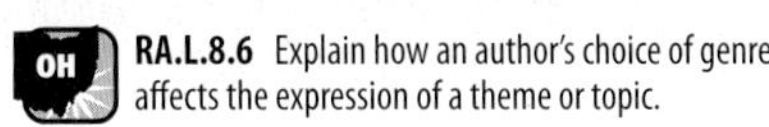
RA.L.8.6 Explain how an author's choice of genre affects the expression of a theme or topic.

On the Grasshopper and the Cricket

Literary Focus

Sonnet A **sonnet** is a fourteen-line poem that is usually written in **iambic pentameter. Iambic** refers to verse in which an unstressed syllable is followed by a stressed syllable. **Pentameter** is verse with five stressed beats in every line.

˘ / ˘ / ˘ / ˘ / ˘ /
The poetry of earth is never dead

Keats's poem is written in the **Italian sonnet** form, in which he makes a main point in the first eight lines and responds to the point in the last six lines.

Reading Focus

Using Form to Find Meaning Examining the form of a poem can help you figure out the poem's meaning.

Into Action Use a chart like the one below to help you use form to find meaning in "On the Grasshopper and the Cricket."

Sonnet's Structure	What I Find in the Poem
Octave (first eight lines) Problem, questions, or idea presented	
Sestet (final six lines) Solution, answer, or comment	

Writing Focus

Think as a Reader/Writer

Find It in Your Reading This poem is filled with imagery that appeals to the senses of sight, touch, and hearing. As you read, make a list of these images in your *Reader/Writer Notebook*.

Reader/Writer Notebook

Use your **RWN** to complete the activities for this selection.

Language Coach

Inverted Word Order Why do poets sometimes order words in a way that doesn't seem natural? Take "increasing ever" in line 12 of "On the Grasshopper and the Cricket." "Ever increasing" might be the word order you would expect.

When poets write in iambic pentameter, they alternate unstressed and stressed syllables in each line. Changing "increasing ever" to "ever increasing" would destroy the rhythm of iambic pentameter.

Look at line 9 for similar wording. Why might the poet have chosen to order the words as he did?

Learn It Online

Use *PowerNotes* as a visual aid to boost your learning:

go.hrw.com L8-737 

MEET THE WRITER

John Keats
(1795–1821)

From Medical School to Poetry
When Keats wrote "On the Grasshopper and the Cricket," he had only begun to write sonnets. He had trained to be a doctor for six years and had passed his examinations to practice medicine, but he disliked surgery. What he really wanted to do was become a poet. Keats did indeed become a poet, one of the greatest in the English language.

A Short, Tragic Life
Keats's short life was filled with tragedy. When he was eight, his father died in an accident. His mother died of tuberculosis when Keats was fourteen. Keats's beloved brother Tom died of tuberculosis in 1818. Shortly afterward, Keats himself began to show signs of the disease. He had fallen in love with a young woman named Fanny Brawne, but he knew that his illness would keep them from marrying. Even though he was dying, Keats continued to write poems of such beauty and depth of meaning that they are still read and admired today.

"Beauty is truth, truth beauty,"—that is all
Ye know on earth, and all ye need to know.

Think About the Writer How might appreciating the beauty in life have helped Keats during difficult times?

John Keats (detail) (c. 1822)
by William Hinton, after Joseph Severn.
Oil on canvas (30" x 25").
National Portrait Gallery, London.

Build Background
"On the Grasshopper and the Cricket" was written as the result of a sonnet-writing contest that John Keats had with another poet, his friend Leigh Hunt. Snug indoors on a winter's night in 1816, the two poets heard the chirping of a cricket. Hunt challenged Keats to see which of them could write the better sonnet on the subject of the grasshopper and the cricket—within fifteen minutes.

Preview the Selection
This sonnet compares the songs of the grasshopper and the cricket. Notice when each insect sings.

Read with a Purpose Read this poem to learn what "poetic" insects contribute to the earth.

ON THE Grasshopper AND THE Cricket

by **John Keats**

Huts at Walberswick, Suffolk by Christine McKechnie. Collage and watercolor on paper.

The poetry of earth is never dead:
When all the birds are faint with the hot sun,
And hide in cooling trees, a voice will run (A)
From hedge to hedge about the new-mown mead;°
That is the Grasshopper's—he takes the lead
In summer luxury—he has never done
With his delights; for when tired out with fun
He rests at ease beneath some pleasant weed.
The poetry of earth is ceasing never:
On a lone winter evening, when the frost
Has wrought a silence, from the stove there shrills
The Cricket's song, in warmth increasing ever,
And seems to one in drowsiness half lost,
The Grasshopper's among some grassy hills. (B)

4. mead: meadow.

(A) **Literary Focus** **Sonnet** Which syllables in line 3 are stressed? Is this line iambic pentameter? How do you know?

(B) **Read and Discuss** How does the poem explain the line "The poetry of earth is never dead?"

Applying Your Skills

RA.L.8.6 Explain how an author's choice of genre affects the expression of a theme or topic.
RA.L.8.8 Explain ways in which the author conveys mood and tone through word choice, figurative language, and syntax. *Also covered* **WP.8.9**

On the Grasshopper and the Cricket

Respond and Think Critically

Reading Focus

Read with a Purpose

1. How do the grasshopper and the cricket keep the poetry of the earth alive?

Reading Skills: Using Form to Find Meaning

Review the chart you completed, and answer the questions that follow.

Sonnet's Structure	What I Find in the Poem
Octave (first eight lines) Problem, questions, or idea presented	
Sestet (final six lines) Solution, answer, or comment	

2. What season is described in the first eight lines of the poem? Who is the poet of that season?
3. What season is described in the final six lines? Who is the poet of that season?
4. What observation about nature does the poem's speaker convey?

Literary Focus

Literary Analysis

5. **Interpret** Which line of the poem echoes the first line? How do the changed words affect the meaning?
6. **Analyze** Poets often describe things in unexpected ways. What is unexpected about Keats's description of the weed in line 8?
7. **Analyze** Read Keats's poem aloud. Apart from the regular meter, what else do you notice about the poem's sound? What do you notice about its pattern of end rhymes?
8. **Infer** Think about Keats's view of nature and the way it plays out in the poem. How might you characterize Keats's view of the world?

Literary Skills: Sonnet

9. **Evaluate** Review the definition of a sonnet on page 737. What elements make "On the Grasshopper and the Cricket" a sonnet?

Literary Skills Review: Tone

10. **Analyze** The attitude a writer takes toward the subject, characters, and audience—**tone**—is revealed through the writer's use of language. How would you describe the tone of "On the Grasshopper and the Cricket"? Use evidence from the poem in your answer.

Writing Focus

Think as a Reader/Writer

Use It in Your Writing Look back at the images you listed in your *Reader/Writer Notebook*. Then, write a four-line description of your classroom. Be sure to include an image that appeals to each of the senses of sight, hearing, and touch. Share your writing with a partner.

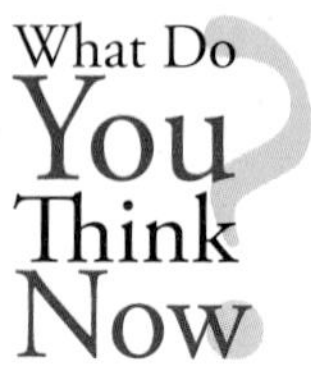

What feelings about life does Keats express through the sonnet?

Preparing to Read

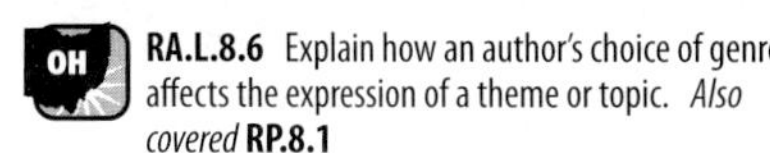

RA.L.8.6 Explain how an author's choice of genre affects the expression of a theme or topic. *Also covered* **RP.8.1**

Ode to Thanks

Literary Focus

Ode The **ode** originated in ancient Greece. For centuries, poets imitated these long, complex poems, which celebrated, in elegant language, one person or thing. Over the centuries, odes have been written to nightingales, Greek vases, autumn, melancholy, joy, solitude, and winners in the Olympic Games. Although today's odes are looser in form, they still celebrate a particular person or thing.

Reading Focus

Reading a Poem Many poems are written in **stanzas,** groups of lines or sentences that function much as paragraphs do in prose. Sentences, or units of thought, in poems often extend over several lines of poetry. As you read this poem, identify its units of thought. Then, consider what each stanza has to say.

Into Action Use a chart like the one below to help you find meaning in this poem.

"Ode to Thanks"	What it means to me
Stanza 1 Unit of thought: lines 1-6	Say thanks to thanks; the word thanks has special power.
Stanza 2 Unit of thought:	

Writing Focus

Think as a Reader/Writer

Find It in Your Reading In this poem, Neruda uses many **metaphors**—comparisons between two unlike things that do not use connecting words, such as *like* or *as.* In your *Reader/Writer Notebook,* list three metaphors Neruda uses in the poem. Note what he is comparing and what the comparison might mean.

Reader/Writer Notebook

Use your **RWN** to complete the activities for this selection.

Language Coach

Language Conventions: Text Styles

Note that in this poem, italic type—*type that is slanted like this*—means that Neruda is talking about the word *thanks* rather than actually thanking something (in which case, he uses regular type).

Skim the poem. What other words are in italic type? Why do you think they are italicized?

MEETTHE WRITER

Learn It Online
Delve into Neruda's life at:
go.hrw.com L8-742 Go

Pablo Neruda
(1904–1973)

A Man of the World

Pablo Neruda was born and died in his beloved Chile, but he lived many years of his life abroad. Sometimes he was a diplomat representing his country, and sometimes he lived in political exile. In 1971, Neruda won the Nobel Prize in literature. Today, Neruda is considered by many to be the most influential Latin American poet of the twentieth century.

A Poet for Everyone

Neruda was only in his twenties when he first became famous for his love poems. In his odes, Pablo Neruda gave up a complex, formal style and adopted a plainer one, using simple words and short lines so that his poems could be enjoyed by all people.

> "I wanted to describe many things that had been sung and said over and over again. My intention was to start like the boy chewing on his pencil, setting to work on his composition assignment about the sun, the blackboard, the clock, or the family."

Think About the Writer From the information above, what can you infer about Neruda's attitude toward life?

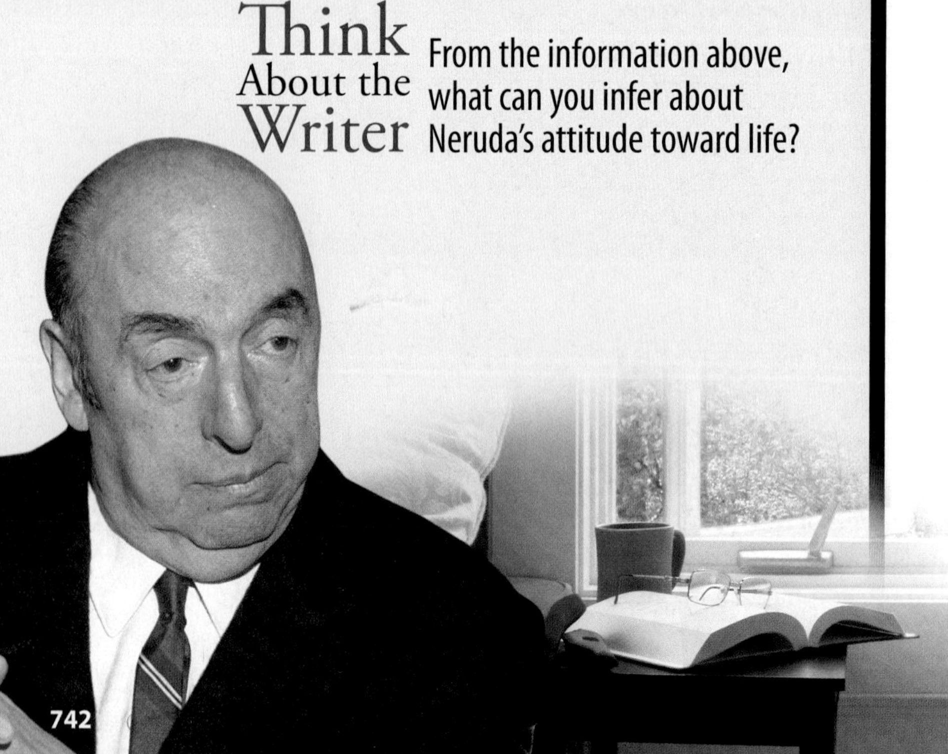

Preview the Selection

The speaker in "Ode to Thanks" expresses his gratitude for the word *thanks,* while reflecting on all the good that this one simple word produces.

Read with a Purpose Read this poem to discover the importance of one little word.

Ode to Thanks

by **Pablo Neruda**

translated by **Ken Krabbenhoft**

Thanks to the word
that says *thanks!*
Thanks to *thanks,*
word
that melts
iron and snow!

The world is a threatening place
until
thanks
makes the rounds
from one pair of lips to another,
soft as a bright
feather
and sweet as a petal of sugar,
filling the mouth with its sound
or else a mumbled
whisper. **A**
Life becomes human again:
it's no longer an open window.
A bit of brightness
strikes into the forest,
and we can sing again beneath the leaves. **B**
Thanks, you're the medicine we take
to save us from
the bite of scorn.

A **Read and Discuss** What point is the poet making about the word *thanks?*

B **Reading Focus** **Reading a Poem** What thought is expressed in lines 20–22?

Your light brightens the altar of harshness.
Or maybe
a tapestry
known
to far distant peoples.
Travelers
fan out
into the wilds,
and in that jungle
of strangers,
merci°
rings out
while the hustling train
changes countries,
sweeping away borders,
then *spasibo*°
clinging to pointy
volcanoes, to fire and freezing cold,
or *danke,*° yes! and *gracias,*° and
the world turns into a table:
a single word has wiped it clean,
plates and glasses gleam,
silverware tinkles,
and the tablecloth is as broad as a plain. **C**

Thank you, *thanks,*
for going out and returning,
for rising up
and settling down.
We know, *thanks,*
that you don't fill every space—
you're only a word—
but
where your little petal
appears
the daggers of pride take cover,
and there's a penny's worth of smiles.

36. *merci* (mehr SEE): French for "thanks."

41. *spasibo* (spa SEE buh): Russian for "thanks."

44. *danke* (DAHNG kuh): German for "thanks." ***gracias*** (GRAH see ahs): Spanish for "thanks."

C **Read and Discuss** Now what is the poet saying?

Applying Your Skills

OH **RA.L.8.6** Explain how an author's choice of genre affects the expression of a theme or topic. **RA.L.8.8** Explain ways in which the author conveys mood and tone through word choice, figurative language, and syntax. *Also covered* **RP.8.1; WP.8.9**

Ode to Thanks

Respond and Think Critically

Reading Focus

Read with a Purpose

1. Why is the word *thanks* so important?

Reading Skills: Reading a Poem

2. Review the chart you began on page 741. Then, add a row to the chart and write down what insight about life Neruda conveys in this poem.

"Ode to Thanks"	What it means to me
Stanza 1 Unit of thought: lines 1-6	"Say thanks to thanks"; The word thanks has special power.

Insight about life:

Literary Focus

Literary Analysis

3. **Interpret** In what way is the word *thanks* like medicine (lines 23–25)?
4. **Draw Conclusions** According to Neruda, how can the word *thanks* affect people all over the world? What might have been his intent in choosing to include the word *thanks* in other languages in lines 36–44?
5. **Analyze** How does the image of a table (lines 45–49) convey an additional idea about *thanks?* To what senses does the image appeal?
6. **Interpret** The last line of "Ode to Thanks" is "and there's a penny's worth of smiles." What interpretation can you offer for this line?
7. **Extend** Neruda makes a point that a small word, *thanks,* sends a powerful message. What other "simple" words carry powerful messages and associations?

Literary Skills: Ode

8. **Compare and Contrast** Review the definition of an ode on page 741. How is "Ode to Thanks" similar to classical odes? How is it different? Cite details to support your answer.

Literary Skills Review: Repetition

9. **Analyze** Free-verse poets often use repetition for both sound and sense. How do the many uses of the word *thanks* add to the meaning of the poem? How do the repeated structures of the phrases create rhythm in lines 12–14 and 51–53?

Writing Focus

Think as a Reader/Writer

Use It in Your Writing Review the metaphors Neruda uses in his ode. Now, choose a person, place, or thing you would like to celebrate, and write an ode. Your purpose is to express strong, positive feelings about many aspects of your subject. Like Neruda, strive to include interesting metaphors in your ode.

What Do You Think Now?

How could writing an ode help you express your feelings?

Preparing to Read

O Captain! My Captain!

RA.L.8.6 Explain how an author's choice of genre affects the expression of a theme or topic. **RA.L.8.8** Explain ways in which the author conveys mood and tone through word choice, figurative language, and syntax. *Also covered* **RP.8.1**

Reader/Writer Notebook

Use your **RWN** to complete the activities for this selection.

Literary Focus

Elegy and Extended Metaphor An **elegy** (EHL uh jee) is a poem of mourning. Most elegies are about someone who has died. "O Captain! My Captain!" mourns the tragic death of President Abraham Lincoln. Whitman's elegy includes an **extended metaphor**, a comparison that is extended through several lines or even an entire poem. As you read, decide who the captain really is and what the ship represents.

Reading Focus

Paraphrasing When you **paraphrase,** you restate all of the text in your own words. A paraphrase is unlike a summary, which covers only major points. Paraphrasing can help you understand difficult poems, especially ones that use **inversion,** the reversal of the normal word order of a sentence. Look for the subject and verb to help you paraphrase sentences with inversion.

Into Action Use a chart to paraphrase complicated sentences or phrases. An example that includes inversion is shown below.

Text from Poem	My Paraphrase
"O the bleeding drops of red, / Where on the deck my Captain lies, / Fallen cold and dead."	Oh, the blood that is on the deck where my dead captain lies.

Vocabulary

weathered (WEHTH uhrd) *v.:* survived; came through safely. *The crew weathered the storm and returned to port.*

mass (mas) *n.:* large group, in this case, of people. *The mass gathers to welcome the captain and his ship.*

mournful (MAWRN fuhl) *adj.:* full of deep sadness. *The mournful speaker is upset about his fallen captain.*

poem's speaker

- **weathered** the storm with the captain as leader
- is **mournful** as he sees the welcoming **mass** on the shore

Language Coach

Word Forms and Origins Which word on the Vocabulary list also appears in two other forms in the Literary Focus section? If you chose *mournful*, you're right. The word *mourn*, built on the Indo-European root *mer*, means "remember." In what way is mourning a remembrance?

Writing Focus

Think as a Reader/Writer

Find It in Your Reading Many poets use repetition to add emphasis and rhythm to their writing. Look for instances of repeated words and phrases in "O Captain! My Captain!" Note them in your *Reader/Writer Notebook*.

Learn It Online

Increase your word knowledge with Word Watch at:

go.hrw.com L8-746 

MEET THE WRITER

Learn It Online
Explore Whitman's life at:
go.hrw.com L8-747 Go

Walt Whitman
(1819–1892)

A Colorful Character
Walt Whitman, who was born in Long Island, New York, was never interested in being like everyone else. He dressed and behaved in a manner all his own. According to one story, Whitman once drove a horse-drawn carriage along Broadway in New York City, reciting Shakespeare at the top of his lungs.

Leaves of Grass
Whitman was a determined and talented writer. When he couldn't find a publisher for his book of poems, *Leaves of Grass*, he published the book himself in 1855. He even wrote his own reviews. The poems in the book embrace and celebrate all aspects of the United States and its people.

A Criticized Masterpiece
Leaves of Grass is now recognized as a masterpiece, but that wasn't always so. Many readers criticized Whitman's poems because they were about common people and experiences and because they were written in free verse instead of in rhyme and meter. Undeterred, Whitman continued adding poems to *Leaves of Grass* and publishing new editions of the book until he died. It is now one of the best-loved books in American literature.

"An American bard at last!"

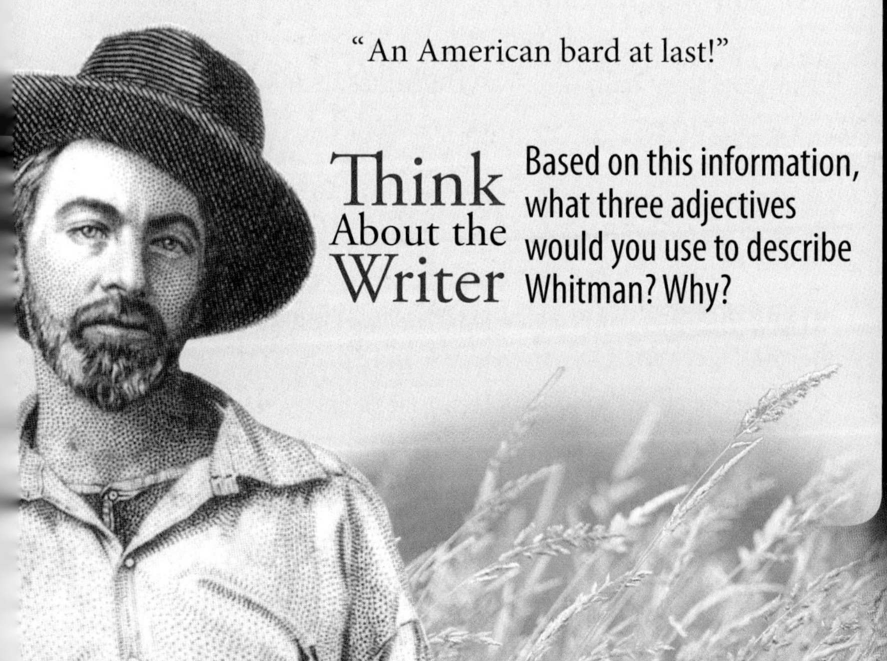

Think About the Writer Based on this information, what three adjectives would you use to describe Whitman? Why?

Build Background
Walt Whitman lived in Washington, D.C., during the Civil War, where he worked as a government clerk and war correspondent and also served as a volunteer nurse. He cared for thousands of wounded soldiers who filled the nearby military hospitals. The Saturday before Abraham Lincoln's second inauguration, Whitman attended a reception at the White House. On inauguration day, March 4, 1865, Whitman twice saw Lincoln pass by in his carriage. He commented that the president "looked very much worn and tired; the lines, indeed, of vast responsibilities, intricate questions, and demands of life and death, cut deeper than ever upon his dark brown face; yet all the old goodness, tenderness, sadness, and canny shrewdness, underneath the furrows." Lincoln was assassinated on April 14, 1865, just a month after Whitman saw him on inauguration day. Although the Civil War was over, the difficult job of healing the country had just begun.

Preview the Selection
In this poem, the speaker—a sailor in a ship returning after a perilous journey—tries to encourage his captain to rise up and see the adoring crowds that are celebrating and waiting for him at the port.

Read with a Purpose Read this poem to discover how the speaker in the poem feels about his captain.

O Captain! My Captain!

by **Walt Whitman**

O Captain! my Captain! our fearful trip is done,
The ship has weathered every rack,° the prize we sought
is won, **A**
The port is near, the bells I hear, the people all exulting,°
While follow eyes the steady keel, the vessel grim and
daring;
But O heart! heart! heart!
O the bleeding drops of red,
Where on the deck my Captain lies,
Fallen cold and dead. **B**

O Captain! my Captain! rise up and hear the bells;
Rise up—for you the flag is flung—for you the bugle
trills,
For you bouquets and ribboned wreaths—for you the
shores a-crowding,
For you they call, the swaying mass, their eager faces
turning;

---

2. **rack:** here, violent change or disorder, like that caused by a storm.
3. **exulting** (ehg ZUHLT ihng): rejoicing.

A **Reading Focus** **Paraphrasing** Paraphrase these first two lines. Be sure to use normal word order.

B **Read and Discuss** What are we hearing the speaker say?

Vocabulary **weathered** (WEHTH uhrd) *v.:* survived; came through safely.
mass (mas) *n.:* large group, in this case, of people.

Here Captain! dear father!
The arm beneath your head!
It is some dream that on the deck,
You've fallen cold and dead.

My Captain does not answer, his lips are pale and still,
My father does not feel my arm, he has no pulse nor will,
The ship is anchored safe and sound, its voyage closed
and done,
From fearful trip the victor° ship comes in with object
won:
Exult O shores, and ring O bells!
But I with mournful tread,
Walk the deck my Captain lies,
Fallen cold and dead. **C**

---

20. victor: winning; triumphant.

C **Read and Discuss** What does this stanza tell us about the captain?

Vocabulary **mournful** (MAWRN fuhl) *adj.:* full of deep sadness.

Applying Your Skills

RA.L.8.6 Explain how an author's choice of genre affects the expression of a theme or topic. **RA.L.8.8** Explain ways in which the author conveys mood and tone through word choice, figurative language, and syntax. *Also covered* **RP.8.1; WA.8.2; VO.8.4**

O Captain! My Captain!

Respond and Think Critically

Reading Focus

Read with a Purpose

1. How does the speaker feel about his captain?

Reading Skills: Paraphrasing

2. Review your paraphrases on the chart you began on page 746. Then, use a chart like the one below to explain what each stanza means. Finally, sum up the meaning of the poem as a whole.

Stanza 1 Meaning	Stanza 2 Meaning	Stanza 3 Meaning	Meaning of Poem

Vocabulary Check

Match each Vocabulary word with its definition.

3. **mass** — **a.** full of sorrow
4. **mournful** — **b.** large group
5. **weathered** — **c.** survived

Literary Focus

Literary Analysis

6. **Analyze** What line is repeated at the end of each stanza? Why is the situation it describes **ironic;** that is, not what one would expect for the victorious return of a ship's captain?

7. **Interpret** The poet uses a metaphor in lines 13 and 18. What is the metaphor, and how does it enhance the sadness of the poem?

8. **Interpret** In line 20, the poet says, "From fearful trip the victor ship comes in with object won." If the ship is a metaphor for the country, what "trip" has the country made? What "object" has it won?

Literary Skills: Elegy and Extended Metaphor

9. **Analyze** "O Captain! My Captain!" is built on an extended metaphor. What clues tell you that the captain is Abraham Lincoln and that the ship stands for the United States?

10. **Analyze** Whitman's elegy mourns the death of Lincoln. How does it reflect both Whitman's and the nation's grief over Lincoln's death?

Literary Review Skills: Rhyme and Meter

11. **Analyze** How does the use of a strong meter and regular rhyme (or near-rhyme) scheme affect the poem's power and meaning? What emotions do these sound effects evoke?

Writing Focus

Think as a Reader/Writer

Use It in Your Writing Look back at your list of examples of repetition. How does Whitman use repetition to emphasize his point and convey the emotions he is feeling? Write a short analysis of how Whitman uses repetition in the poem.

How might Whitman's poetic expression of sadness have helped others who read or heard his poem?

Preparing to Read

I Hear America Singing / I, Too

RA.L.8.6 Explain how an author's choice of genre affects the expression of a theme or topic. **RA.L.8.8** Explain ways in which the author conveys mood and tone through word choice, figurative language, and syntax. *Also covered* **RP.8.1**

Literary Focus

Free Verse A **free-verse** poem does not follow a regular rhyme scheme or meter. Without a strict pattern to follow, poets writing free verse rely on their own sense of **rhythm** to make their poems "musical." They may also use the following poetic devices:

- **Alliteration:** repetition of consonant sounds (**s**now **s**piraling)
- **Onomatopoeia** (ahn uh maht uh PEE uh): the use of words whose sounds echo their meanings (the chain saw's *buzz*)
- **Imagery:** language that appeals to the five senses
- **Figures of speech:** language based on comparisons, such as metaphors, similes, and personification

Reading Focus

Reading Aloud One way to fully understand and appreciate the poetic devices in a poem is to read it aloud.

Into Action As you read these poems aloud, record instances of the following poetic devices. Then, add your impressions of them.

Alliteration	Onomatopoeia	Imagery	Figures of Speech	Rhythm
			America is singing	

TechFocus In "I, Too," notice how Hughes gives a voice to a group of people. Think about a group you know who needs to be heard.

Writing Focus

Think as a Reader/Writer

Find It in Your Reading Record in your *Reader/Writer Notebook* images from the poems that evoke a strong emotional response.

Use your **RWN** to complete the activities for these selections.

Language Coach

Multiple-Meaning Words The speakers in the poems that follow both talk about "singing."

The word *sing* has many meanings, some of which appear in the dictionary entry below. Read through these definitions of the verb *sing*.

sing (sihng) *v.:* **1.** to make music with the voice. **2.** to make pleasant musical sounds (Birds were *singing* in the trees.) **3.** to make a humming, whistling, or buzzing sound (I heard the kettle sing.) **4.** to shout out or proclaim. **5.** slang: to inform about or tell on.

As you read the poems, think about the ways the poets talk about singing. What differences, if any, do you find in the meaning of the word as it is used in those poems?

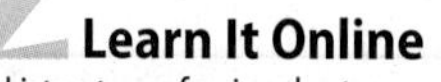

Learn It Online

Listen to professional actors read these poems at:

go.hrw.com L8-751 

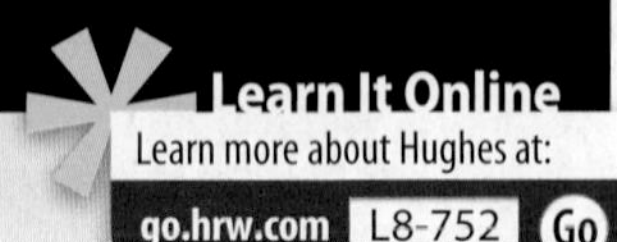

Learn It Online
Learn more about Hughes at:
go.hrw.com L8-752 Go

Walt Whitman

(1819–1892)

For a biography of Walt Whitman, see page 747.

Langston Hughes

(1902–1967)

A Chance Meeting of Poets

Born in Joplin, Missouri, Langston Hughes began writing poetry in his early teens. As a young man, he traveled around the world and held many jobs, including teacher, clerk, deckhand, and flower salesman. One day in 1925, Hughes discovered that the famous poet Vachel Lindsay was staying at the Washington, D.C., hotel where Hughes was working as a busboy. Hughes left some of his poems beside Lindsay's dinner plate. That night, Lindsay read them aloud at a poetry reading, announcing that he had discovered a great new poet. The next day, Hughes received national publicity.

A Commitment to Justice and Strength

Hughes believed in writing for everyday people, those who "are not too important to themselves or the community, or too well fed, or too learned to watch the lazy world go round." From his grandmother, he learned strength and determination. In his autobiography, he wrote:

> "Nobody cried in my grandmother's stories. They worked, or schemed, or fought. . . . Something about my grandmother's stories (without her ever having said so) taught me the uselessness of crying about anything."

Think About the Writers

How might Hughes's varied jobs and experiences have helped him write poems?

Build Background

"I Hear America Singing"

Walt Whitman was the first American poet to use free verse. Today many poets write in free verse, so we take it for granted. In Whitman's day, however, people were used to poems written in "poetic" language, which used strict rhyme schemes and meters. These people were shocked by Whitman's sprawling lines and use of slang. In time many critics came to feel that Walt Whitman was the first and greatest poet to "give voice" to America. "I Hear America Singing" offers a good example of why they came to think so.

Preview the Selections

"I, Too" was written by Langston Hughes in response to "I Hear America Singing" by Walt Whitman. While Whitman's poem is a celebration of the American worker, Hughes's poem points out the injustices felt by African Americans.

Read with a Purpose Read these poems to see how diverse people sing America's "songs," in their own ways.

I HEAR AMERICA SINGING

by **Walt Whitman**

I hear America singing, the varied carols I hear,
Those of mechanics, each one singing his as it should be blithe and strong,
The carpenter singing his as he measures his plank or beam,
The mason singing his as he makes ready for work, or leaves off work, **A**
The boatman singing what belongs to him in his boat, the deckhand singing on the steamboat deck,
The shoemaker singing as he sits on his bench, the hatter singing as he stands,
The woodcutter's song, the plowboy's on his way in the morning, or at noon intermission or at sundown,
The delicious singing of the mother, or of the young wife at work, or of the girl sewing or washing,
Each singing what belongs to him or her and to none else,
The day what belongs to the day—at night the party of young fellows, robust, friendly,
Singing with open mouths their strong melodious songs. **B**

A **Literary Focus** **Free Verse** What does Whitman do in these lines to create a sense of rhythm?

B **Read and Discuss** What picture is Whitman painting for us?

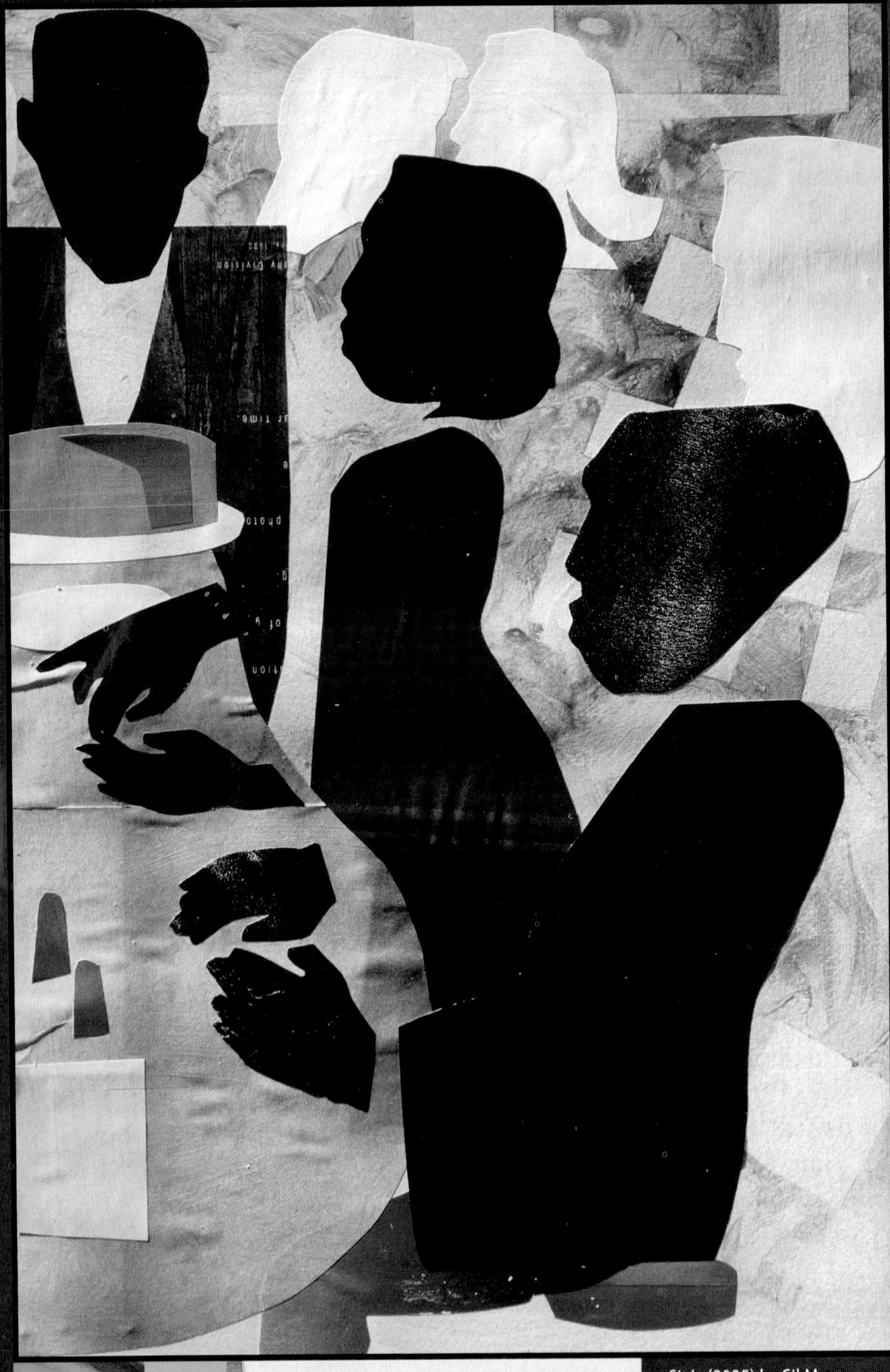

Analyzing Visuals **Viewing and Interpreting** How well does this image match your interpretation of Hughes's poem?

Sit In (2005) by Gil Mayers. Collage.

I, TOO

by **Langston Hughes**

I, too, sing America.

I am the darker brother.
They send me to eat in the kitchen
When company comes,
But I laugh,
And eat well,
And grow strong. **A**

Tomorrow,
I'll sit at the table
When company comes.
Nobody'll dare
Say to me,
"Eat in the kitchen,"
Then.

Besides,
They'll see how beautiful I am
And be ashamed—

I, too, am America. **B**

A **Read and Discuss** What have we learned about the speaker?

B **Literary Focus** **Free Verse** What metaphor appears in the poem's last line? What two things are being compared?

Applying Your Skills

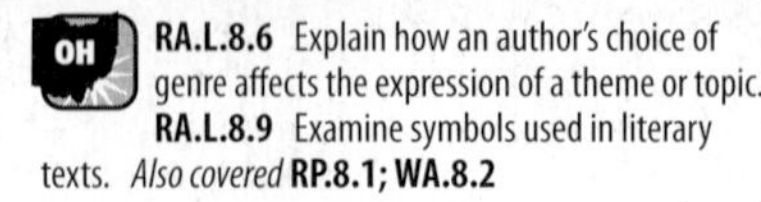

RA.L.8.6 Explain how an author's choice of genre affects the expression of a theme or topic. **RA.L.8.9** Examine symbols used in literary texts. *Also covered* **RP.8.1; WA.8.2**

I Hear America Singing / I, Too

Respond and Think Critically

Reading Focus

Read with a Purpose

1. What might Whitman mean when he talks of "Each [person] singing what belongs to him or her and to none else?" What does Hughes mean when he says "I, too, sing America"?

Reading Skills: Reading Aloud

2. Review the entries in the chart you began on page 751. Then, write a statement that describes how reading aloud helped you identify sound devices and appreciate each poem.

Literary Focus

Literary Analysis

3. **Analyze** Discuss the examples of working people in "I Hear America Singing." How do all those descriptions connect to the title?
4. **Make Judgments** Based on his poem, how do you think Whitman regarded America and its growth?
5. **Interpret** "I, Too" was written in response to "I Hear America Singing." Whitman's poem is a celebration of the American worker. What does Hughes's poem celebrate?
6. **Extend** Has Hughes's prediction in "I, Too" (written in 1922) in any way come true? In what ways, if any, has it not come true?

Literary Skills: Free Verse

7. **Evaluate** How well does the imagery from "I Hear America Singing" help you "see" or "hear" an American worker? Explain.
8. **Analyze** The poems you just read are **free-verse** poems—without a regular rhyme scheme or meter. They do, however, use repetition to create rhythm. In each poem, find examples of repeated words, lines, and sentence patterns. You may want to use a chart like this one to help you gather details.

Examples of Repetition	My Notes
"singing his as he"	

Literary Skills Review: Symbol

9. **Interpret** A **symbol** is a person, place, thing, or event that stands for something beyond itself. What do you think the kitchen and the table symbolize in Hughes's poem? Explain your response.

Writing Focus

Think as a Reader/Writer

Use It in Your Writing Look back at the images you noted in your *Reader/Writer Notebook*. How did these images evoke a mood, or overall emotional effect? Try to capture the mood of each poem with a single word such as *joyful* or *angry*. Then, describe the different moods of the poems, using the images you noted to support your interpretations.

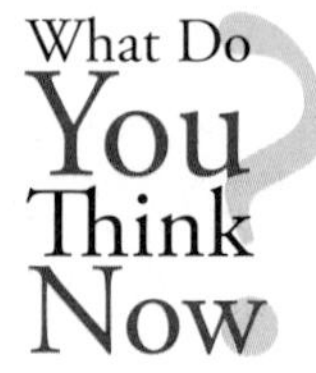

What different attitudes do the two poets express in these poems?

Wrap Up

Poetry and Form

RA.L.8.8 Explain ways in which the author conveys mood and tone through word choice, figurative language, and syntax. WA.8.6 Produce informal writings. *Also covered* C.8.9; VO.8.1; VO.8.7; WP.8.17

Vocabulary Development

Multiple-Meaning Words

Many English words have more than one meaning. Some words can even be used as different parts of speech. Look at the following example:

The **cycle** of semesters continues every year.
The author wrote a **cycle** of poems.
The stars **cycle** through the heavens.
The riders **cycle** madly to the finish line.

Cycle is used as a noun in the first two sentences; in the final two, *cycle* is used as a verb. To be a good reader, learn the common meanings of multiple-meaning words and use context to determine which meaning applies.

Your Turn

The first three words below are from "I Hear America Singing"; the last word is from "I, Too." Write down each word's meaning in the poem. Then, use a dictionary to determine the word's other possible meanings.

	Meaning in Poem	Other Meanings
leaves (line 4)		
intermission(line 7)		
company (line 4)		

CHOICES

As you respond to the Choices, use these **Academic Vocabulary** words as appropriate: intent, evoke, associations, interpretation.

REVIEW

Write About Media Imagery

Timed Writing Advertising, like poetry, is full of images. Think about ads you have seen from television or magazines. In two paragraphs, give your opinion: What associations do companies want people to make with their products? When is imagery deceptive rather than just creative?

CONNECT

Create a Web Page

TechFocus Think of a group you believe is not being heard (perhaps endangered animals or an oppressed people). Write a poem with a similar structure to Langston Hughes's "I, Too." Make a Web page for your poem, with critical words hyperlinked to images, sound files, or Web sites.

EXTEND

Recite a Poem

Listening and Speaking Which poet's work did you enjoy most from the "Poetry and Form" section of this collection? Choose a poet, and check out a collection of his or her poems from a library. Find another work from the poet, and recite it for your class. Introduce your poem first, explaining your interpretation of its meaning.

Learn It Online
Sharpen your knowledge of multiple-meaning words with *WordSharp* at:

go.hrw.com L8-757 Go

COMPARING TEXTS

Analyzing Biographical Context

CONTENTS

What Do You Think?

How much do our surroundings affect our feelings and attitudes?

QuickWrite

Make a list of places where you have lived, traveled, or spent time. Briefly describe how each of these places influenced your outlook on life.

Preparing to Read

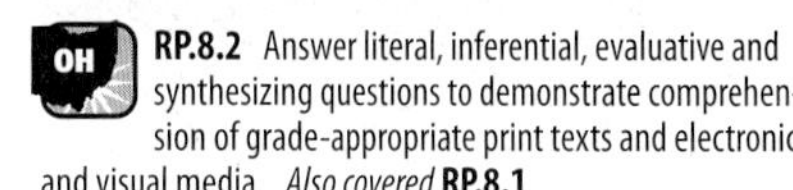
RP.8.2 Answer literal, inferential, evaluative and synthesizing questions to demonstrate comprehension of grade-appropriate print texts and electronic and visual media. *Also covered* RP.8.1

Robert Frost: The New England Poet/ Out, Out—

Literary Focus

Biographical Context Writers are often influenced by their surroundings—the people, events, and environments around them. For example, the settings in their works may reflect places they have lived. Their characters may be based on people they know or have heard about. A biographical approach to literary criticism looks at the connections between a writer's life and his or her work:

- How might events in the writer's life have affected the work?
- What effect did the writer's surroundings have on the work?
- To what extent do the writer's beliefs affect the work?

Reading Focus

Making Connections In the pages that follow, you will connect what you learn from reading a short biography of Robert Frost to a poem written by Frost.

Into Action As you read Meet the Writer and "Robert Frost: The New England Poet," use the chart below to record key details about Frost's life. After you read the poem, record the ways you see Frost's biography reflected in the piece.

	Biography	Poem
Work	farmer, poet	
Family	two sons died	
Environment		
Beliefs		

Writing Focus

Think as a Reader/Writer

Find It in Your Reading Note in your *Reader/Writer Notebook* the instances of dialogue Frost uses in "Out, Out—."

Reader/Writer Notebook

Use your **RWN** to complete the activities for these selections.

Vocabulary

Robert Frost: The New England Poet

summoned (SUHM uhnd) *v.:* called; requested to come. *During the medical emergency, we summoned a doctor.*

recite (rih SYT) *v.:* present a memorized text orally, often in a formal manner. *When you recite a poem, speak up so that others can hear you.*

Out, Out—

rueful (ROO fuhl) *adj.:* regretful. *When he understood the grave situation, the boy's expression became rueful.*

appeal (uh PEEL) *n.:* plea or call for help or sympathy. *He turned to us in appeal, but there was nothing we could do to help.*

Language Coach

Word Forms Many words can be used as either a noun or a verb. For example, the Vocabulary word *summoned* is a verb meaning "called; requested to come." A *summons,* however, is a written order telling someone to appear in court. What other word on the list above can be used as a noun or a verb? Use a dictionary if you need help.

Learn It Online

There's more to words than just definitions. Get the whole story at:

go.hrw.com L8-759 

MEET THE WRITER

Learn It Online
Get more on Frost's life and work at:
go.hrw.com L8-760 Go

Robert Frost

(1874–1963)

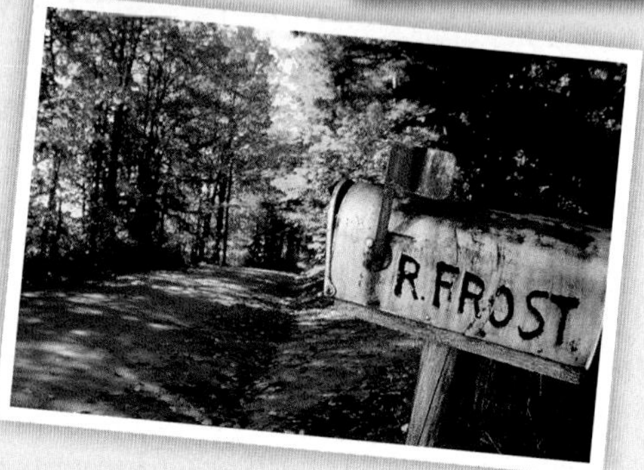

From Farmer to Poet

Winner of four Pulitzer Prizes for Poetry, Robert Frost was for years the best-known poet in the United States. Frost was born in San Francisco, but he was raised in New England, which became the setting for almost all of his poetry. As a young man, Frost had tried raising chickens on a farm that his grandfather had given him, but he was unsuccessful. He also had a difficult time selling his poems. In 1912, after the deaths of two of his children, he and his family moved to England. There, Frost met with success: He found a publisher for his first two collections of poems (*A Boy's Will* and *North of Boston*). The books were immediately popular, and by the time Frost returned to the United States, publishers were interested in his work.

"A poem begins as a lump in the throat,
a sense of wrong, a homesickness,
a lovesickness."

An American Icon

Frost spent the rest of his long life farming, writing poetry, giving lectures, and reading his poems to audiences. By the end of his life, he had become a kind of national poet. On Frost's seventy-fifth birthday, the U.S. Senate passed a resolution in his honor. It stated, "His poems have helped to guide American thought and humor and wisdom, setting forth to our minds a reliable representation of ourselves and of all men." When he read his poem "The Gift Outright" at John F. Kennedy's inauguration in 1961, Frost became the first poet to read a poem at a presidential inauguration.

Key Elements of Frost's Poetry

Meter Frost remained committed to writing poetry in traditional meter at a time when many poets were trading metered forms for free verse.

Rhythm Frost tried to capture the sound of speech—especially the spoken rhythms of the farmers and other people he encountered every day.

Messages Frost's messages often reflect a tragic view of life. However, his attention to detail—especially that of nature—offers a possibility of hope and redemption.

Think About the Writer What aspects of Frost's life or work do you think helped him become an American icon?

BIOGRAPHY

ROBERT FROST: The New England Poet

Read with a Purpose Read this biography to find out what inspired Robert Frost's poem, "Out, Out—."

Robert Frost lived in New England for most of his life and found his subjects in the landscapes and people of that area, especially in New Hampshire and Vermont. The plain speech and everyday subjects of his poems disguise their complex thoughts.

Frost once wrote that a subject for poetry "should be common in experience and uncommon in books. . . . It should have happened to everyone but it should have occurred to no one before as material."

He drew on the events that occurred around him for his subjects. For example, Frost based the poem "Out, Out—" on an article in the *Littleton Courier,* a New Hampshire newspaper. The article, entitled "Sad Tragedy at Bethlehem," appeared in the March 31, 1901, issue. It read as follows:

Raymond Fitzgerald a Victim of Fatal Accident

Raymond Tracy Fitzgerald, one of the twin sons of Michael G. and Margaret Fitzgerald of Bethlehem, died at his home Thursday afternoon, March 24, as the result of an accident by which one of his hands was badly hurt in a sawing machine. The young man was assisting in sawing up some wood in his own dooryard [yard] with a sawing machine and accidentally hit the loose pulley, causing the saw to descend upon his hand, cutting and lacerating it badly. Raymond was taken into the house and a physician was immediately summoned, but he died very suddenly from the effects of the shock, which produced heart failure. . . . **A**

In his poems, Frost tried to depict the sounds of New Englanders' speech. He deliberately used the everyday language he heard in conversations with farmers. Frost wrote about his fascination with speech:

"I have sought only those words I had met up with as a boy in New Hampshire, working on farms during the summer vacations. I listened to the men with whom I worked and found that I could make out their conversation as they talked together out of earshot, even when I had not plainly heard the words they spoke. When I started to carry their conversation over into poetry, I could hear their voices." **B**

Given Frost's feelings about the importance of the spoken word, it is not surprising that he liked to "say" rather than to recite his poetry. However, Frost never read "Out, Out—" (page 762) in public because he felt it was "too cruel."

A **Read and Discuss** What do you think the poem "Out, Out—" will be about?

B **Literary Focus** **Biographical Context** How does Frost describe the dialogue in his poems? What can you infer about the poet from that description?

Vocabulary **summoned** (SUHM uhnd) *v.:* called; requested to come.

recite (rih SYT) *v.:* present a memorized text orally, often in a formal manner.

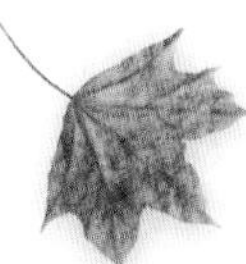

OUT, OUT—

by **Robert Frost**

Read with a Purpose

Read this poem to discover how suddenly something unexpected can happen.

Preparing to Read for this selection is on page 759.

Build Background

The title of this poem is an **allusion**—a reference to another literary work or a work in another field, such as history, mythology, or science. This title's allusion is to a famous speech by Macbeth in Shakespeare's play of that name. Macbeth has just heard of his wife's death, and he speaks bitterly of the shortness of life:

"Out, out, brief candle!
Life's but a walking shadow, a poor player
That struts and frets his hour upon the stage,
And then is heard no more. It is a tale
Told by an idiot, full of sound and fury,
Signifying nothing."

The buzz saw snarled and rattled in the yard
And made dust and dropped stove-length sticks of wood,
Sweet-scented stuff when the breeze drew across it.
And from there those that lifted eyes could count
Five mountain ranges one behind the other
Under the sunset far into Vermont. **A**
And the saw snarled and rattled, snarled and rattled,
As it ran light, or had to bear a load.
And nothing happened: day was all but done.
Call it a day, I wish they might have said
To please the boy by giving him the half hour
That a boy counts so much when saved from work.

A **Literary Focus** **Biographical Context** What is the setting of this poem? Did Frost live somewhere similar? Explain.

His sister stood beside them in her apron
To tell them "Supper." At the word, the saw,
As if to prove saws knew what supper meant,
Leaped out at the boy's hand, or seemed to leap—
He must have given the hand. However it was,
Neither refused the meeting. But the hand!
The boy's first outcry was a rueful laugh,
As he swung toward them holding up the hand,
Half in appeal, but half as if to keep
The life from spilling. Then the boy saw all—
Since he was old enough to know, big boy
Doing a man's work, though a child at heart—
He saw all spoiled. "Don't let him cut my hand off—
The doctor, when he comes. Don't let him, sister!" **B**
So. But the hand was gone already.
The doctor put him in the dark of ether.°
He lay and puffed his lips out with his breath.
And then—the watcher at his pulse took fright.
No one believed. They listened at his heart.
Little—less—nothing!—and that ended it.
No more to build on there. And they, since they
Were not the one dead, turned to their affairs. **C**

---

28. ether (EE thuhr): chemical compound used as an anesthetic.

B **Read and Discuss** What has happened?

C **Reading Focus** **Making Connections** What connections do you see between this poem and Frost's biography?

Vocabulary **rueful** (ROO fuhl) *adj.:* regretful.
appeal (uh PEEL) *n.:* plea or call for help or sympathy.

Applying Your Skills

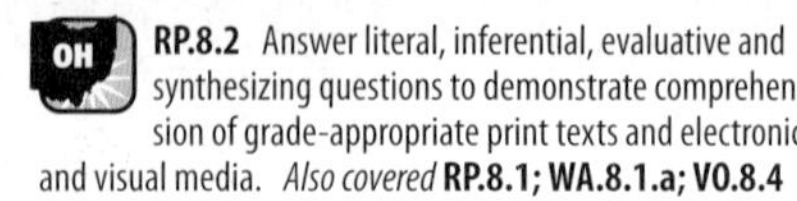
RP.8.2 Answer literal, inferential, evaluative and synthesizing questions to demonstrate comprehension of grade-appropriate print texts and electronic and visual media. *Also covered* RP.8.1; WA.8.1.a; VO.8.4

Robert Frost: The New England Poet / Out, Out—

Respond and Think Critically

Reading Focus

Quick Check

1. Why is Frost considered "the New England Poet"?
2. In the poem "Out, Out—," what causes the boy's death? How do the others respond?

Read with a Purpose

3. In Frost's biography, what real-life event inspired the poem "Out, Out—"?
4. In "Out, Out—" what was so unexpected about the boy's death?

Reading Skills: Making Connections

5. Complete the chart you began on page 759. Then, formulate a statement in which you show a connection between Frost's life and "Out, Out—." Also use this chart as you respond to item 13.

	Biography	Poem
Work	farmer, poet	about a farming family
Family	two sons died	about boy's death
Environment		
Beliefs		

Vocabulary Check

Match the Vocabulary words with their definitions.

6. appeal	**a.** regretful
7. recite	**b.** called
8. rueful	**c.** plea
9. summoned	**d.** speak aloud

Literary Focus

Literary Analysis

10. **Interpret** Re-read the background information for "Out, Out—." How does the literary **allusion,** or reference, in the poem's title affect your interpretation?
11. **Infer** Re-read lines 10–12 of "Out, Out—." What do these details suggest about the poem's speaker? What is his or her wish?
12. **Analyze** Who or what does the poem suggest is to blame for the tragedy? (See lines 14–18.)

Literary Skills: Biographical Context

13. **Draw Conclusions** "Out, Out—" ends with a surprising observation told in a matter-of-fact tone. Why do you think no one shows signs of grief or horror? Could this reaction be based on Frost's knowledge of rural life? Explain.

Literary Skills Review: Sound Devices

14. **Analyze** "Out, Out—" opens with **onomatopoeia**—words whose sounds imitate their meaning. What do you think is Frost's intent in opening with these sinister sounds?

Writing Focus

Think as a Reader/Writer

Use It in Your Writing Did you notice how Frost uses everyday spoken dialogue to create the sense of real-life tragedy in this poem? Write a brief narrative about an actual event that you have heard about or witnessed. Use dialogue to help re-create the event.

COMPARING TEXTS

Wrap Up

RP.8.2 Answer literal, inferential, evaluative and synthesizing questions to demonstrate comprehension of grade-appropriate print texts and electronic and visual media. **RP.8.1** Apply reading comprehension strategies, including making predictions, comparing and contrasting, recalling and summarizing and making inferences and drawing conclusions. *Also covered* **WA.8.1.b; WP.8.2; WA.8.2**

Robert Frost: The New England Poet / Out, Out—

Writing Focus

Write an Analytic Essay

Biographical Context By reading Frost's biography and poem, you have had a chance to examine how a writer's life and surroundings may have influenced his or her work.

Assignment Write an essay in which you consider the connections between Frost's life and his poetry.

- In the essay's first paragraph, introduce your topic and state what general associations you see between Frost's life and work.
- In the body of the essay, write in detail about how Frost's life affected his work. Support your analysis by citing details from the biographies and "Out, Out—." Refer to your connections chart for specifics.
- Finally, in the last paragraph, draw a conclusion about the relationship between Frost's life and this poem.

Evaluation Guidelines

An effective essay contains
✓ a clearly stated topic
✓ main ideas that are supported with details
✓ a clear and logical organization
✓ a thought-provoking conclusion

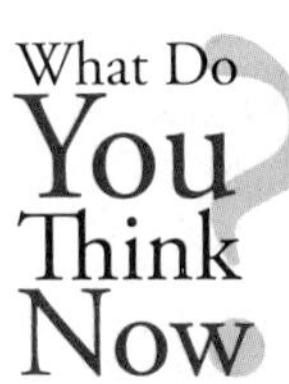

How did Robert Frost's environment affect his feelings and attitudes?

CHOICES

As you respond to the Choices, use these **Academic Vocabulary** words as appropriate: intent, evoke, associations, interpretation.

REVIEW

Compare Two Texts

Timed Writing Re-read the 1901 news article that inspired "Out, Out—" (page 761). Then, re-read the poem. In a short essay, describe the similarities and differences in the accounts of the two events. What information in the newspaper article is missing from the poem? What insights in the poem are missing from the newspaper account?

CONNECT

Write a Poem

Choose a real-life event you have read about or witnessed. It can be amusing or tragic. Then, write a short poem based on this event. Which real-life details will you use? Will you make up details? What feelings will you try to evoke? Share your poem—and its source—with the class.

EXTEND

Storyboard a Writer's Life

TechFocus Think of a writer whose work you enjoy. Then, use online sources to research this writer's life. Once you know the basics, storyboard a scene that you would use in a film version of this writer's life.

Learn It Online
Expand your view of this poem with these Internet links:

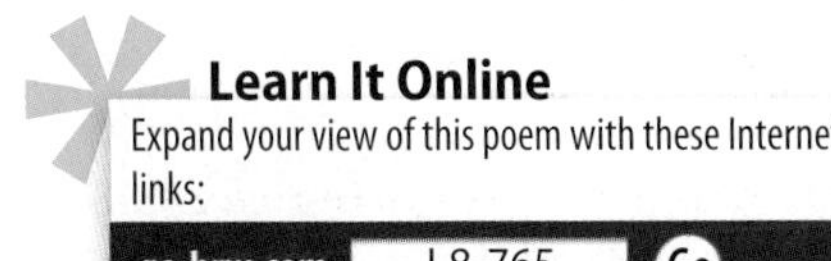

COMPARING TEXTS

Analyzing Symbol and Theme

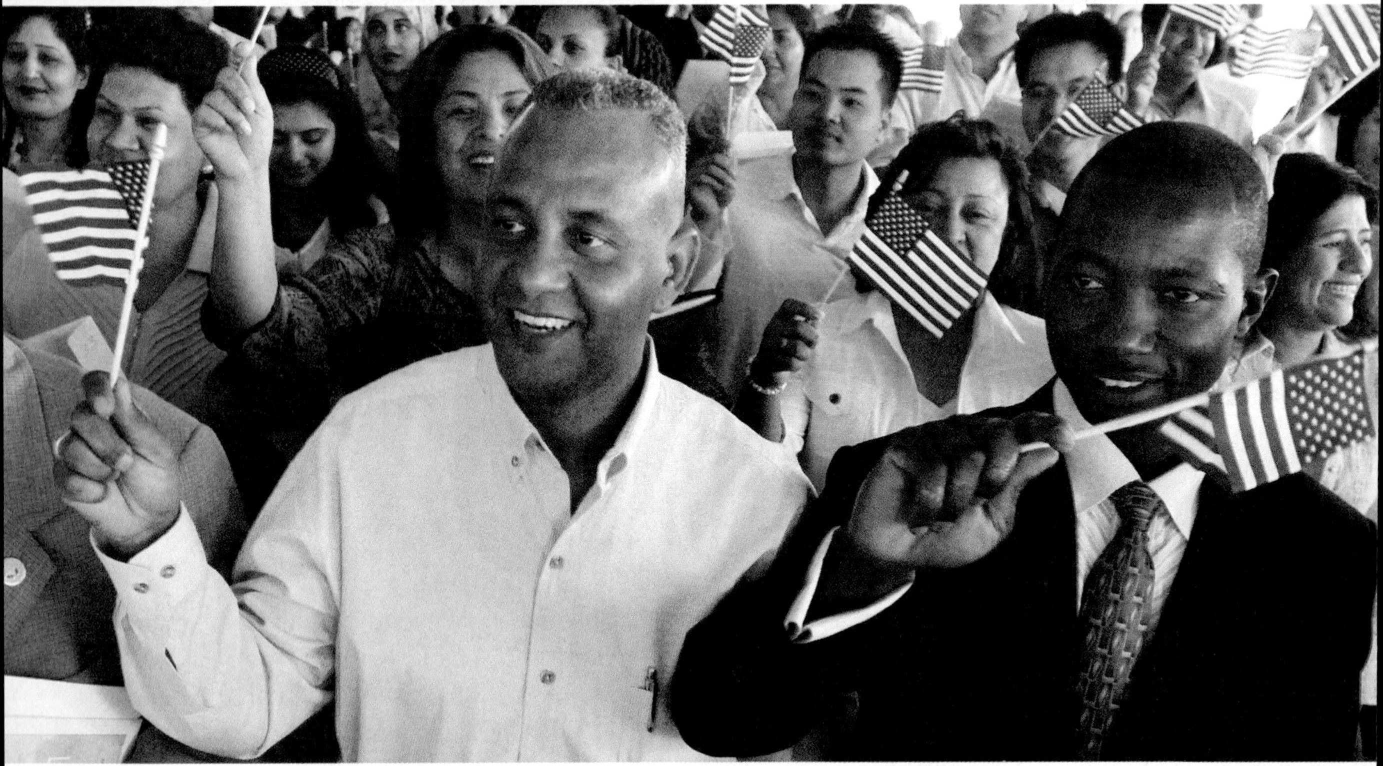

Newly sworn-in U.S. citizens during a naturalization ceremony on May 21, 2007.

CONTENTS

What do the concepts of freedom and liberty mean? How do we express these ideas?

QuickWrite

Why do many people move to the United States? Discuss your ideas with a small group of classmates, and write down your group's top three reasons.

Preparing to Read

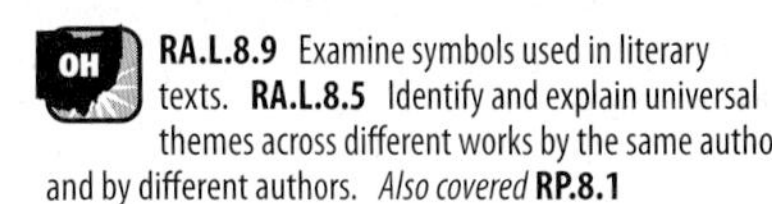

RA.L.8.9 Examine symbols used in literary texts. **RA.L.8.5** Identify and explain universal themes across different works by the same author and by different authors. *Also covered* **RP.8.1**

The New Colossus / First Stop: Ellis Island / Refugee in America / Saying Yes / The First Americans

Literary Focus

Symbol and Theme In literature, a **symbol** is a person, place, thing, or event that stands for something beyond itself. For example, an abandoned toy may symbolize a character's passage into adulthood. Often, analyzing a literary symbol can lead you to recognize the work's **theme,** or insight about life. As you read the following works, look for symbols with associations that help you understand the writers' ideas about what it means to be American.

Reading Focus

Comparing and Contrasting Themes The following selections were written at different times and by different members of American society. To uncover each selection's theme, analyze selection details and consider your own knowledge. As you read, use a chart like this to help you identify each selection's theme. Later, you will compare and contrast these themes across the selections.

Title	"The New Colossus"
Important Details	unlike conquering Colossus; Mother of Exiles
Symbols	Statue of Liberty
My Knowledge	
Theme Statement	

Writing Focus

Think as a Reader/Writer

Find It in Your Reading Writers can affect how a reader feels simply by choosing the right words. As you read each selection, note in your *Reader/Writer Notebook* examples of words and phrases that evoke a strong emotional response.

Reader/Writer Notebook

Use your **RWN** to complete the activities for these selections.

Vocabulary

The New Colossus

yearning (YURN ihng) *v.:* longing for; wanting badly. *The immigrants, yearning for a better life, took a risk and moved to the United States.*

teeming (TEEM ihng) *adj.:* full (in this case, of people); crowded. *The lower deck of the ship was teeming with people.*

The First Americans

patriots (PAY tree uhts) *n.:* people who love and support their country. *Patriots will often fly a flag to show their love of country.*

wholesome (HOHL suhm) *adj.:* good for the mind and spirit. *The authors want wholesome legends of American Indian life taught in school.*

Language Coach

Word Origins *Whole* in *wholesome* comes from the Old English word *hál,* meaning "whole." Other words with this same origin are *holy*, *healthy*, and *heal*. With a partner, discuss how the idea of wholeness exists in these other words.

Learn It Online

Elevate your vocabulary skills with Word Watch:

go.hrw.com L8-767 

Learn It Online
Learn more about Hughes at:
go.hrw.com L8-768 Go

MEET THE WRITERS

Emma Lazarus
(1849–1887)

"Mother of Exiles"

Emma Lazarus was born into a wealthy family in New York City. From an early age, Lazarus studied the classics and foreign languages. Her first collection of poetry was published when she was a teenager. After reading an article by Lazarus in support of Jewish refugees from Russia, the Statue of Liberty committee asked her to write a poem for the statue's pedestal. The result was the powerful sonnet "The New Colossus."

Langston Hughes
(1902–1967)

For a biography of Langston Hughes, see page 752.

Diana Chang
(1934–)

Advice for Young Writers

Born in the United States to a Eurasian mother and a Chinese father, Diana Chang has taught creative writing at Barnard College in New York City. In an interview, Chang gave the following advice:

> "First of all, you cannot 'decide' to become a serious writer. . . . But you can write. If you have it in you to write, you will write and you will continue to write and send things out and eventually some will be taken. After your work starts to be published, other people will say to you, 'You are a writer.'"

Think About the Writers

What quality or qualities do Lazarus and Chang appear to possess?

POEM

The New Colossus

by **Emma Lazarus**

Read with a Purpose

Read this poem to discover how one writer compares the Statue of Liberty with the ancient statue of the Colossus.

Build Background

In 1886, the Statue of Liberty, a gift from France to the United States, was erected in New York Harbor. In 1903, a poem by Emma Lazarus called "The New Colossus" was engraved on a bronze plaque that was placed inside the pedestal of the statue. The title of the poem refers to the Colossus, a huge bronze (or brazen) statue of the Greek god Helios that towered over the harbor of the Greek city of Rhodes from 280 to 225 B.C.

Not like the brazen giant of Greek fame,
With conquering limbs astride from land to land;
Here at our sea-washed, sunset gates shall stand
A mighty woman with a torch, whose flame
Is the imprisoned lightning, and her name
Mother of Exiles. From her beacon-hand **A**
Glows world-wide welcome; her mild eyes command
The air-bridged harbor that twin cities frame.
"Keep, ancient lands, your storied pomp°!" cries she
With silent lips. "Give me your tired, your poor,
Your huddled masses yearning to breathe free,
The wretched refuse° of your teeming shore.
Send these, the homeless, tempest-tost° to me.
I lift my lamp beside the golden door!" **B**

9. **pomp:** splendor; magnificence.
12. **refuse** (REHF yoos): something useless or unwanted.
13. **tempest-tost:** upset by storm. *Tempest* here refers to other hardships as well.

A **Read and Discuss** What is the poet talking about here? What is she saying about the two statues?

B **Literary Focus Theme** What theme is suggested by the words Lazarus gives the Statue of Liberty?

Vocabulary **yearning** (YURN ihng) *v.:* longing for; wanting badly.
teeming (TEEM ihng) *adj.:* full (in this case, of people); crowded.

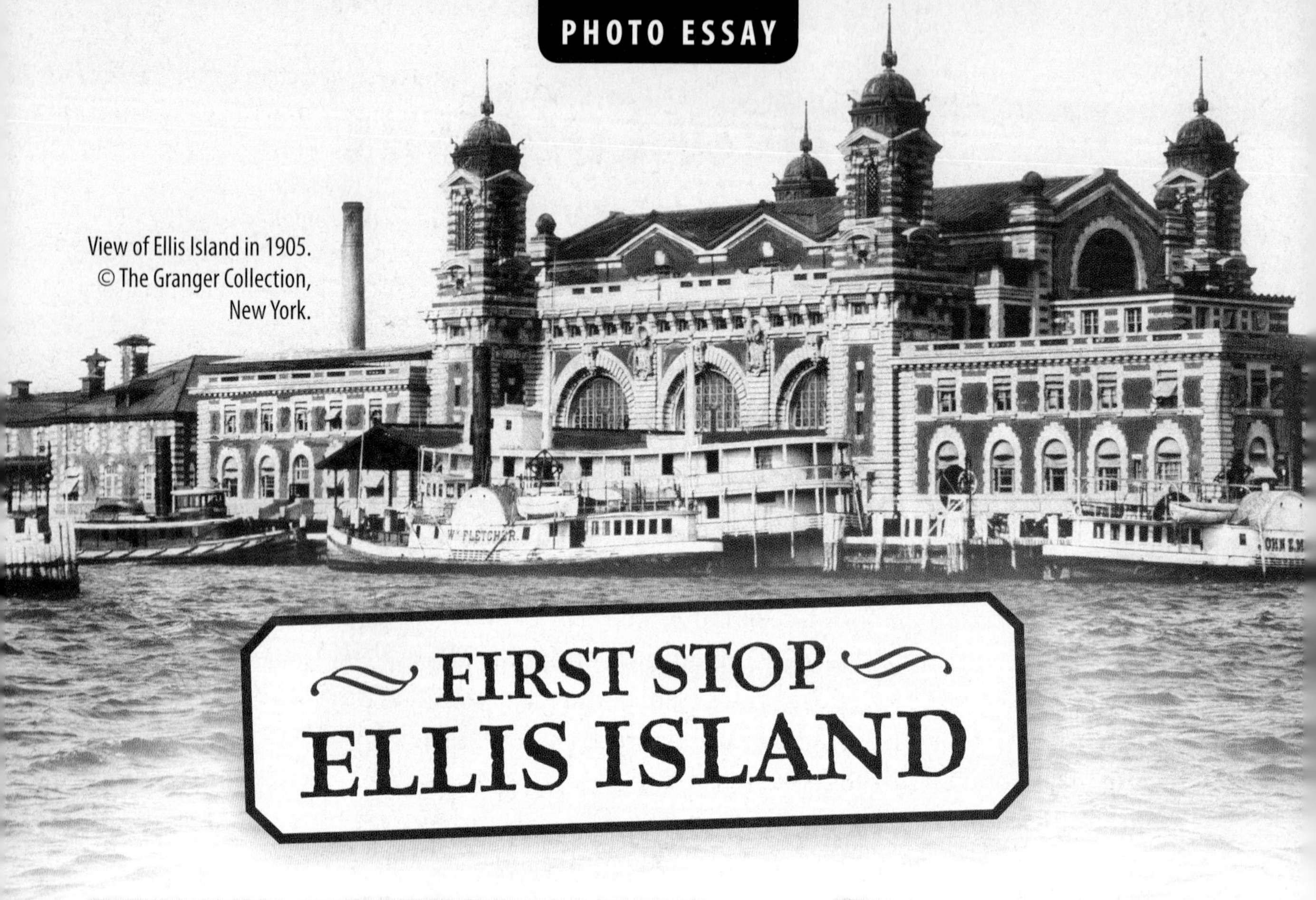

View of Ellis Island in 1905. © The Granger Collection, New York.

FIRST STOP ELLIS ISLAND

Read with a Purpose

View this photo essay to see the faces of immigrants who came to the United States and to learn what their journeys involved.

As they sailed into New York Harbor, immigrants spotted the Statue of Liberty in the distance and, nearby, Ellis Island. Ellis Island was their first stop in the United States. There they were given medical examinations and officially permitted to enter the country. More than twelve million people arrived through this gateway between 1892 and 1954. The peak year was 1907—when more than one million newcomers entered through the "Golden Door." **A**

A **Read and Discuss** What have we learned about Ellis Island?

Women from Guadeloupe, French West Indies, at Ellis Island on April 6, 1911.

"Well, I came to America because I heard the streets were paved with gold. When I got here, I found out three things: first, the streets weren't paved with gold; second, they weren't paved at all; and third, I was expected to pave them." **B**

—Old Italian Story

Jewish war orphans arriving from Eastern Europe in 1921.

"We naturally were in steerage. Everyone had smelly food, and the atmosphere was so thick and dense with smoke and bodily odors that your head itched, and when you went to scratch your head you got lice in your hands. We had six weeks of that."

—Sophia Kreitzberg, a Russian Jewish immigrant in 1908

Children's playground, Ellis Island roof garden.

"I can remember only the hustle and bustle of those last weeks in Pinsk, the farewells from the family, the embraces and the tears. Going to America then was almost like going to the moon."

—Golda Meir, a Russian Jewish immigrant in 1906 **C**

A Slovakian mother and daughter wait to be admitted to Ellis Island, about 1915.

"Those who are loudest in their cry of 'America for Americans' do not have to look very far back to find an ancestor who was an immigrant."

—New Immigrants' Protective League, 1906 **D**

B **Literary Focus** **Symbol** What does this immigrant's story tell us about the power of symbols?

C **Read and Discuss** What do Sophia's and Golda's comments tell us about the immigrants' journeys?

D **Literary Focus** **Theme** What idea about life does this quote from the New Immigrants' Protective League convey?

Applying Your Skills

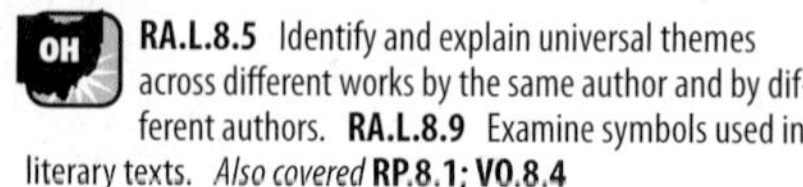
RA.L.8.5 Identify and explain universal themes across different works by the same author and by different authors. RA.L.8.9 Examine symbols used in literary texts. *Also covered* RP.8.1; VO.8.4

The New Colossus / First Stop: Ellis Island

Respond and Think Critically

Reading Focus

Quick Check

1. In "The New Colossus," how does the speaker describe the statue that stands at New York's "gates"?
2. Why was it required for immigrants to stop at Ellis Island first?

Read with a Purpose

3. What do you think is Lazarus's intent in comparing the "old Colossus" and the new one?
4. What did you learn from the photo essay about the immigrants' experiences?

Reading Skills: Comparing and Contrasting Themes

5. Review the charts you created, and compare the themes of the two selections you have just read. Are the themes similar or different?

	"The New Colossus"	"First Stop: Ellis Island"
Theme		

Vocabulary Check

Fill in the blanks with the correct Vocabulary word.

yearning teeming

6. The Statue of Liberty welcomes the _______ masses from other lands, those who are _______ to find a better life.

Literary Focus

Literary Analysis

7. **Interpret** In the late 1800s, immigrants from Europe poured into America. What do you think the statue in "The New Colossus" means when she tells these countries to keep their "storied pomp"? Explain your interpretation.
8. **Analyze** How does Lazarus's use of **personification** (giving human traits to something nonhuman) affect our understanding of what the Statue of Liberty represents?
9. **Extend** What qualities might help immigrants as they make their difficult journeys?

Literary Skills: Symbol and Theme

10. **Interpret** What do the statue's words to people coming to the United States reveal about the American dream? What do the words suggest about the poem's theme? What symbols does Lazarus use to emphasize her message?
11. **Analyze** How might the immigrants in the photographs be considered symbols of America?

Writing Focus

Think as a Reader/Writer

Use It in Your Writing Look back at your notes in your *Reader/Writer Notebook*. What words and phrases evoked the strongest emotions in you? Write a paragraph in which you explain why you find these examples so gripping. What ideas do you connect with the words? How does the language make you feel?

POEM

REFUGEE IN AMERICA

by **Langston Hughes**

Read with a Purpose

Read this poem to see how its speaker feels about the American dream of freedom and liberty.

Preparing to Read for this selection is on page 767.

Build Background

This poem about the American dream was written around 1943, before the civil rights movement of the 1950s and 1960s. The civil rights movement led to increased liberties for African Americans. For example, the Civil Rights Act of 1964 made discrimination based on race, religion, or national origin illegal. The Voting Rights Act of 1965 was designed to stop tactics used to keep African Americans from voting.

There are words like *Freedom*
Sweet and wonderful to say.
On my heart-strings freedom sings
All day everyday.

There are words like *Liberty*
That almost make me cry.
If you had known what I knew
You would know why. **B**

A **Literary Focus** **Theme** What is a refugee? What does the title suggest about this poem's theme?

B **Read and Discuss** What is the speaker trying to help us understand?

POEM

Saying Yes by **Diana Chang**

Read with a Purpose

Read this poem to see how the speaker struggles for the right words to describe herself.

Preparing to Read for this selection is on page 767.

"Are you Chinese?"
"Yes."

"American?"
"Yes."

"*Really* Chinese?"
"No . . . not quite."

"*Really* American?"
"Well, actually, you see . . ." Ⓐ

But I would rather say
yes

Not neither-nor,
not maybe,
but both, and not only

The homes I've had,
the ways I am

I'd rather say it
twice,
yes Ⓑ

Ⓐ **Read and Discuss** What problem does the speaker face?

Ⓑ **Literary Focus Theme** What idea about life does this speaker convey?

Applying Your Skills

RA.L.8.9 Examine symbols used in literary texts. RA.L.8.5 Identify and explain universal themes across different works by the same author and by different authors. *Also covered* RP.8.1; WA.8.1.b; RA.L.8.8

Refugee in America / Saying Yes

Respond and Think Critically

Reading Focus

Read with a Purpose

1. After reading "Refugee in America," do you see any differences in meaning between the words *freedom* and *liberty*? Explain.
2. In "Saying Yes," how does the speaker describe herself when asked a series of questions about her nationality? Why does she respond that way?

Reading Skills: Comparing and Contrasting Themes

3. Review the charts you created to help you identify each selection's theme (page 767). Then, compare the themes of the poems you have just read. In what ways are the themes similar or different? Use your responses to help you answer question 8.

	"Refugee in America"	"Saying Yes"
Theme		
Similarities		
Differences		

Literary Focus

Literary Analysis

4. **Interpret** The word *refugee* typically refers to a displaced person or someone without a country. Since Hughes was born in the United States, why do you think he chose to title his poem "Refugee in America"?
5. **Analyze** Chang uses dialogue in the first eight lines of "Saying Yes." What does the use of dialogue add to the poem'?
6. **Extend** When describing the confusion that accompanies one's ancestry, the speaker in "Saying Yes" says, "Not neither-nor, / not maybe, / but both, and not only. . . ." Can this confusion apply to anyone? Why or why not?

Literary Skills: Symbol and Theme

7. **Compare and Contrast** Describe the similarities and differences in what these poems have to say about the power of words. Which words in these poems are symbolic? Explain.
8. **Interpret** One aspect of the American dream is a belief in freedom, equality, and respect for all Americans. What theme do these poems convey about the American dream?

Literary Skills Review: Repetition

9. **Analyze** The use of repeated words, phrases, and structures helps emphasize key ideas and gives poems rhythm. Find examples of repetition in these two poems, and explain how its use helps the poets achieve their purpose.

Writing Focus

Think as a Reader/Writer

Use It in Your Writing The two short poems you just read explore the power of language. Which words or phrases made an impression on you? Choose a word or phrase from the poems, and write your own poem that explores some ideas you associate with that word or phrase.

SPEECH

THE FIRST AMERICANS

The Grand Council Fire of American Indians

December 1, 1927

Read with a Purpose

Read this speech to find out how some Native Americans felt about the portrayal of Native Americans in textbooks.

Preparing to Read for this selection is on page 767.

Build Background

In 1927, an organization called the Grand Council Fire of American Indians sent a group of representatives from the Chippewa, Ottawa, Navajo, Sioux, and Winnebago peoples to address the mayor of Chicago. Their goal was to persuade him that Native Americans should be more fairly and accurately represented in textbooks and classrooms. Mayor William Hale Thompson, who had been re-elected just a month before the council met with him, had campaigned on the slogan "America First." (Thompson opposed U.S. involvement in world affairs and claimed that the British government influenced the U.S. government's policies.) "The First Americans" comments on this and other patriotic slogans of the time, which excluded many Americans from the American dream.

To the mayor of Chicago:

You tell all white men "America First." We believe in that. We are the only ones, truly, that are one hundred percent. We therefore ask you, while you are teaching schoolchildren about America First, teach them truth about the First Americans. **A**

We do not know if school histories are pro-British, but we do know that they are unjust to the life of our people—the American Indian. They call all white victories battles and all Indian victories massacres. The battle with Custer[1] has been taught to schoolchildren as a fearful massacre on our part. We ask that this, as well as other incidents, be told fairly. If the Custer battle was a massacre, what was Wounded Knee?[2]

1. **battle with Custer:** the Battle of the Little Bighorn, which took place in 1876 in what is now Montana. General George A. Custer (1839–1876) led an attack on a Native American village and was killed along with all of his troops by Sioux and Cheyenne forces.
2. **Wounded Knee:** Wounded Knee Creek, in South Dakota, was the site of a battle in 1890 between U.S. soldiers and Sioux whom they had captured. The U.S. soldiers killed about two hundred Sioux men, women, and children.

A **Read and Discuss** What are we being told here?

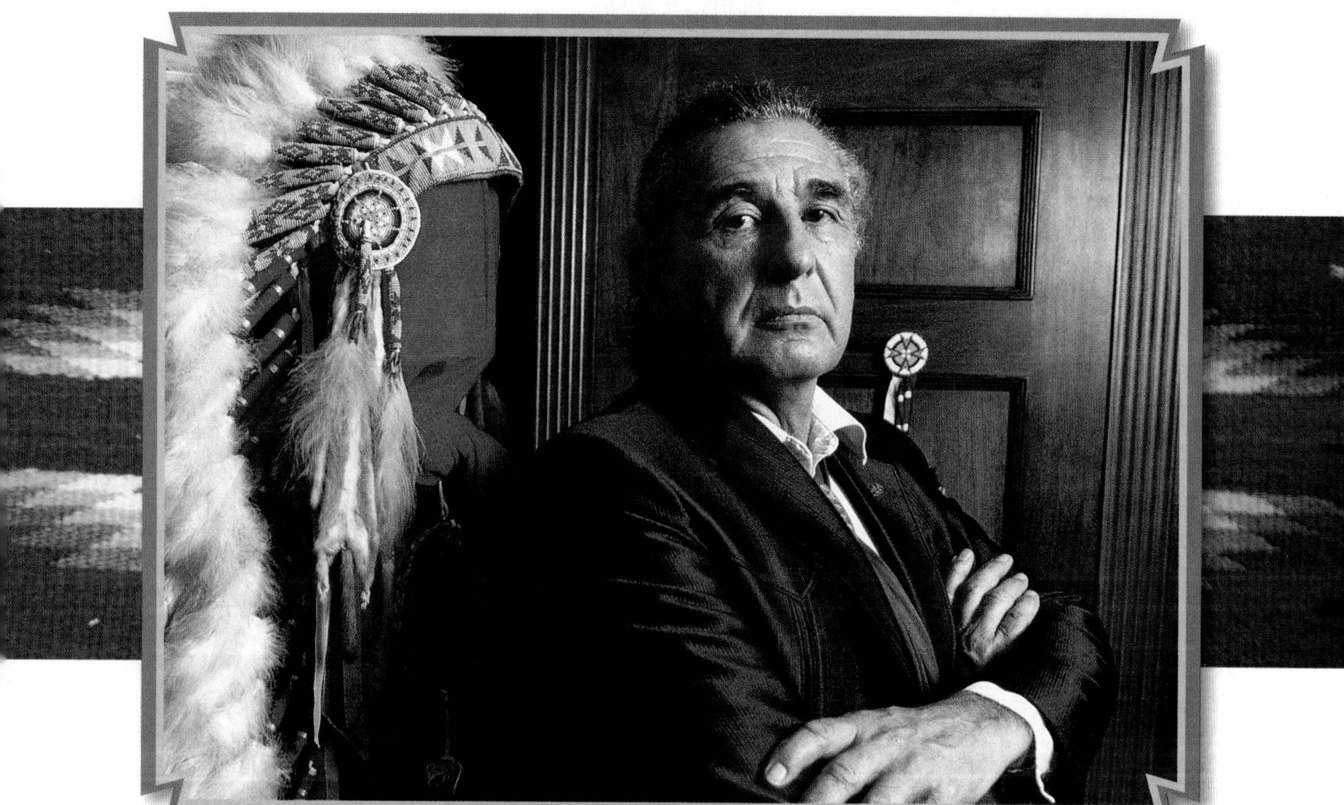

Ben Nighthorse Campbell, a Colorado congressman (1992–2004) and a Northern Cheyenne chief.

History books teach that Indians were murderers—is it murder to fight in self-defense? Indians killed white men because white men took their lands, ruined their hunting grounds, burned their forests, destroyed their buffalo. White men penned[3] our people on reservations, then took away the reservations. White men who rise to protect their property are called patriots—Indians who do the same are called murderers.

3. **penned:** confined or enclosed. (A pen is a fenced area where animals are kept.)

White men call Indians treacherous—but no mention is made of broken treaties on the part of the white man. White men say that Indians were always fighting. It was only our lack of skill in white man's warfare that led to our defeat. An Indian mother prayed that her boy be a great medicine man rather than a great warrior. It is true that we had our own small battles, but in the main we were peace loving and home loving. **B**

White men called Indians thieves—and yet we lived in frail skin lodges and needed no locks or iron bars. White men

Vocabulary **patriots** (PAY tree uhts) *n.:* people who love and support their country.

B **Reading Focus** **Comparing and Contrasting Themes** Compare this speaker's concerns with those of the speakers in Hughes's and Chang's poems. How are their situations different? How are they similar?

call Indians savages. What is civilization? Its marks are a noble religion and philosophy, original arts, stirring music, rich story and legend. We had these. Then we were not savages, but a civilized race.

We made blankets that were beautiful, that the white man with all his machinery has never been able to duplicate. We made baskets that were beautiful. We wove in beads and colored quills designs that were not just decorative motifs but were the outward expression of our very thoughts. We made pottery—pottery that was useful, and beautiful as well. Why not make schoolchildren acquainted with the beautiful handicrafts in which we were skilled? Put in every school Indian blankets, baskets, pottery.

We sang songs that carried in their melodies all the sounds of nature—the running of waters, the sighing of winds, and the calls of the animals. Teach these to your children that they may come to love nature as we love it.

We had our statesmen—and their oratory[4] has never been equaled. Teach the children some of these speeches of our people, remarkable for their brilliant oratory.

We played games—games that brought good health and sound bodies. Why not put these in your schools? We told stories. Why not teach schoolchildren more of the wholesome proverbs and legends of our people? Tell them how we loved all that was beautiful. That we killed game only for food, not for fun. Indians think white men who kill for fun are murderers. **C**

Tell your children of the friendly acts of Indians to the white people who first settled here. Tell them of our leaders and heroes and their deeds. Tell them of Indians such as Black Partridge, Shabbona, and others who many times saved the people of Chicago at great danger to themselves. Put in your history books the Indian's part in the World War. Tell how the Indian fought for a country of which he was not a citizen, for a flag to which he had no claim, and for a people that have treated him unjustly.

The Indian has long been hurt by these unfair books. We ask only that our story be told in fairness. We do not ask you to overlook what we did, but we do ask you to understand it. A true program of America First will give a generous place to the culture and history of the American Indian.

We ask this, Chief, to keep sacred the memory of our people.

4. **oratory** (AWR uh tawr ee): skill in public speaking; the art of public speaking.

C **Read and Discuss** What would history books including examples of Native American weavings, baskets, songs, speeches, games, and heroic actions show readers?

Vocabulary **wholesome** (HOHL suhm) *adj.:* good for the mind and spirit.

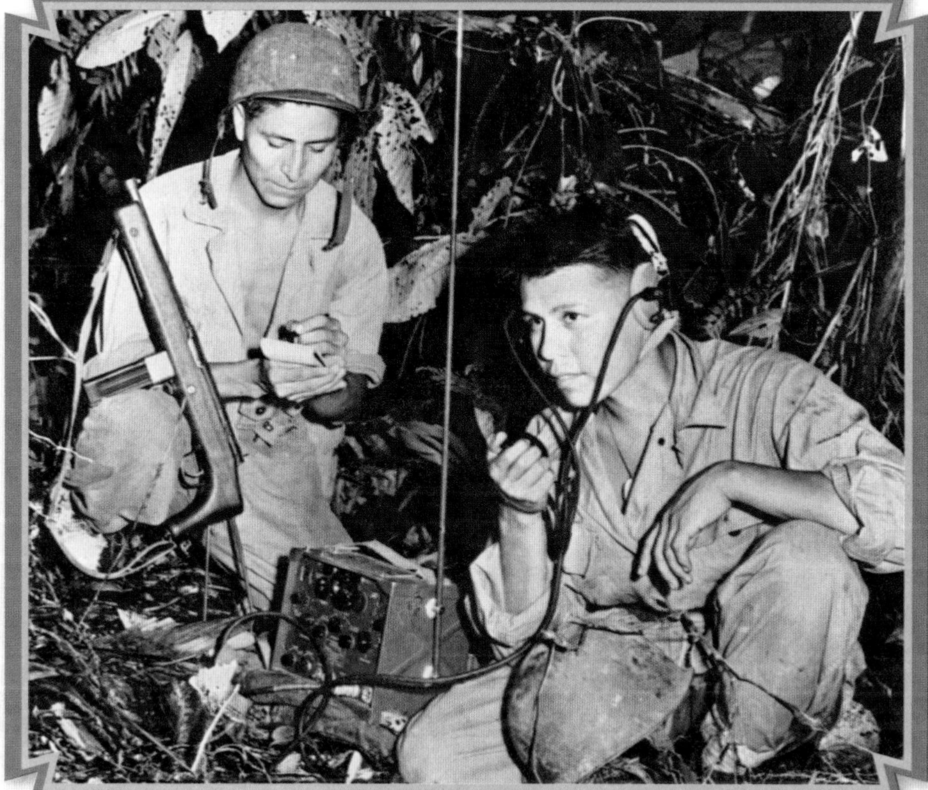

Analyzing Visuals

Viewing and Interpreting
How do these photographs of Native American accomplishments illustrate the point of the speech?

Navajo "code talkers" attached to a Marine regiment in the Pacific during World War II relay orders using a code based on their native language. The code was particularly effective because few non-Navajos understood the complex language.

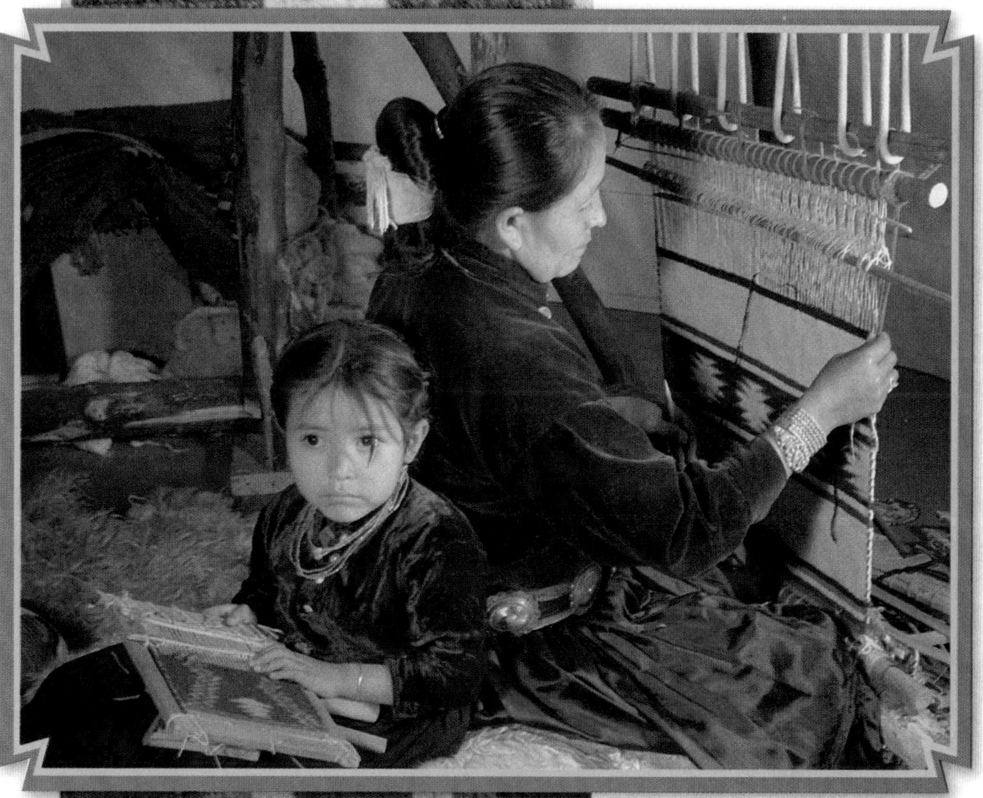

A Native American woman and child demonstrate weaving techniques at the Golden Gate International Exposition, held in San Francisco in 1939 and 1940.

Applying Your Skills

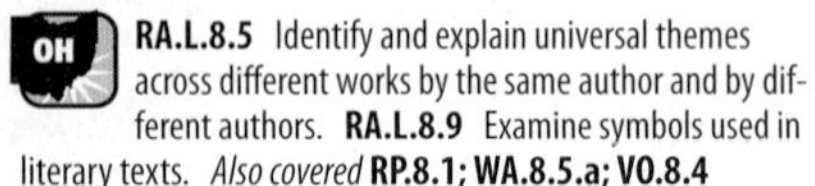

RA.L.8.5 Identify and explain universal themes across different works by the same author and by different authors. **RA.L.8.9** Examine symbols used in literary texts. *Also covered* **RP.8.1; WA.8.5.a; VO.8.4**

The First Americans

Respond and Think Critically

Reading Focus

Quick Check

1. What is the intent of this speech?
2. What does the council recommend that children should be taught? Why?

Read with a Purpose

3. How do the speakers feel about their portrayal in textbooks?

Reading Skills: Comparing and Contrasting Themes

4. Finish filling in the themes of the selections in a chart like the one below. Then, identify a universal theme that applies to them all.

Selection	Theme
"The New Colossus"	
"First Stop: Ellis Island"	
"Refugee in America"	
"Saying Yes"	
"The First Americans"	

Universal Theme:

Vocabulary Check

Include the boldface Vocabulary words in your answers to the questions below. Refer to a dictionary if you need help.

5. What actions might **patriots** take?
6. How does one decide what is or isn't **wholesome?**

Literary Focus

Literary Analysis

7. **Analyze** A **stereotype** is a fixed idea about a group of people; for example, the statement "Athletes are not intellectual" reflects a stereotype. Stereotypes are often offensive. What stereotypes about Native Americans does the speaker address in this speech?
8. **Infer** What can you infer from the fact that a council had to be formed to request that positive aspects of Native American life be included in history books?
9. **Extend** How might teaching unbiased accounts of historical events change how a group is viewed?

Literary Skills: Symbol and Theme

10. **Connect** The writers of the speech mention the importance of appreciating their peoples' blankets, pottery, and other handicrafts. How can art be a symbol of a culture?
11. **Analyze** In a nonfiction text, we generally refer to themes as main ideas. In this speech, what main idea is conveyed about history? about education? about citizenship?

Writing Focus

Think as a Reader/Writer

Use It in Your Writing Review the notes in your *Reader/Writer Notebook*. Now, think of an issue you feel strongly about. Write a short persuasive essay to convince others to agree with your view. Try to include language that will evoke an emotional response from your readers.

COMPARING TEXTS
Wrap Up

RA.L.8.9 Examine symbols used in literary texts. C.8.9 Deliver formal and informal descriptive presentations that convey relevant information and descriptive details. VO.8.7 Determine the meanings and pronunciations of unknown words by using dictionaries, thesauruses, glossaries, technology and textual features, such as definitional footnotes or sidebars. *Also covered* WA.8.4.d

The New Colossus / First Stop: Ellis Island / Refugee in America / Saying Yes / The First Americans

Writing Focus

Writing a Comparison-and-Contrast Essay

Each of the selections in this feature presents an idea of the American dream. Some also explore how the American dream can fall short for certain individuals or groups. Choose two selections from this section, and write an essay comparing their views of the American dream.

To find points of comparison for your essay, review the charts you filled in for the selections. You can organize your essay this way:

Paragraph 1: Present an introduction and thesis statement.

Paragraph 2: Explain how selection 1 reflects the hopes and realities of the American dream.

Paragraph 3: Explain how selection 2 reflects the hopes and realities of the American dream.

Paragraph 4: Draw a conclusion about the similarities and differences in how each selection treats the American dream.

Revision Questions:

- Did I state my main idea clearly?
- Did I include details and examples that support my main points?
- Is the organization of my essay easy to follow, with transitional words or phrases for clarity?

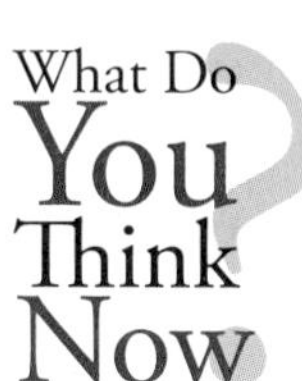

How have these selections expanded your ideas about the concepts of freedom and liberty?

CHOICES

As you respond to the Choices, use these **Academic Vocabulary** words as appropriate: intent, evoke, associations, interpretation.

REVIEW

Find Symbols

Timed Writing What makes people yearn to come to America? Think of two or three things—people, places, foods, songs, sports—that you associate with the American dream. Then, describe each symbol and explain how it relates to the American dream.

CONNECT

Present an Oral Reading

Listening and Speaking Prepare "The New Colossus," "Refugee in America," or "Saying Yes" for an oral presentation. Before you begin, copy the selection onto a piece of paper. Note the punctuation marks that indicate where you should pause briefly and where you should come to a complete stop. Use your voice to express your interpretation of the poem.

EXTEND

Create a Web Site

TechFocus Using history texts and reliable Internet sites, research the Statue of Liberty's history. Then, create a Web site for your findings. Along with your text, include pictures—and sound files, if possible—to evoke what the times were like when the statue was new.

Media Workshop

Multimedia Presentation: Poetry

Write with a Purpose

Select three or four poems to be used in a poetry presentation using multimedia. They can be poems you read in this anthology or other poems. Create a script for your presentation. As you develop your script, think about your **audience.** Who will view your presentation? Think about your **purpose.** Are you hoping to entertain your audience or to make them think differently about a subject?

A Good Poetry Presentation

- has a unifying topic or theme
- captures the audience's attention in the introduction
- includes a variety of selections
- is made expressive through voice modulation and tone as well as gestures
- uses different media, such as sound effects, visuals, and music, to enhance the reading
- has a thoughtful conclusion

Reader/Writer Notebook

Use your **RWN** to complete the activities for this workshop.

Think as a Reader/Writer

Before you plan your own poetry presentation, read this presentation of "On the Grasshopper and the Cricket" by John Keats. Then, read the notes in the margin that offer suggestions on how to present a poem orally.

Some poems take us to surprising places. John Keats's "On the Grasshopper and the Cricket" gives me a feeling of being present in nature, listening to its music. ← Grab your audience's attention with a brief introduction.

On the Grasshopper and the Cricket by **John Keats** ← Pause briefly after reading the title.

The poetry of earth is never dead
When all the birds are faint with the hot sun,
And hide in cooling trees, a voice will run ← Don't stop at the ends of lines unless there is punctuation indicating a pause.
From hedge to hedge about the new-mown mead;
That is the Grasshopper's—he takes the lead
In summer luxury—he has never done
With his delights; for when tired out with fun
He rests at ease beneath some pleasant weed.
The poetry of earth is ceasing never; ← Enunciate, or carefully pronounce, all your words.
On a lone winter evening, when the frost
Has wrought a silence, from the stove there shrills
The Cricket's song, in warmth increasing ever
And seems to one in drowsiness half lost,
The Grasshopper's among some grassy hills.

This poem emphasizes Keats's belief that poetry is everywhere in nature and that if we listen carefully enough, we can hear it. ← Point out a key feature of the poem that you find interesting.

Think About the Model

With a partner, discuss the following questions about the model:

1. How effective is the speaker's introduction? How might it be improved?
2. How well does the speaker help you understand the poem's theme?

OH **WA.8.2** Write responses to literature that organize an insightful interpretation around several clear ideas, premises or images and support judgments with specific references to the original text, to other texts, authors and to prior knowledge. **WP.8.6** Drafting, Revising and Editing: Organize writing with an effective and engaging introduction, body and a conclusion that summarizes, extends or elaborates on points or ideas in the writing. **C.8.9** Deliver formal and informal descriptive presentations that convey relevant information and descriptive details. **C.8.9** Deliver formal and informal descriptive presentations that convey relevant information and descriptive details. **C.8.8.e** Deliver informational presentations that: draw from multiple sources, including both primary and secondary sources, and identify sources used. **WP.8.4** Prewriting: Determine a purpose and audience and plan strategies to address purpose and audience.

Prewriting

Select Poems

Before you select poems for your reading, decide on a topic or theme for your performance. To hold your audience's attention, choose a group of poems that will create suspense, elicit a variety of moods, or appeal to your audience's sense of humor. Like any form of theater, a poetry reading should be dramatic. Here are some suggestions for grouping poems that appear in this anthology:

Theme or Topic	Poems
Famous characters in poetry	"Barbara Frietchie" (page 711) "Paul Revere's Ride" (page 705) "Casey at the Bat" (page 730)
America the beautiful	"The New Colossus" (page 769) "I Hear America Singing" (page 753)
Poems to make you laugh	"The Cremation of Sam McGee" (page 717) "Casey at the Bat" (page 730)
Short and sweet	"A word is dead" (page 699) "Sweater" (page 695) "For My Grandmother" (page 670)

Consider reading some of your own poetry as well.

Think About Purpose and Audience

As you begin planning your presentation, think about your **purpose.** Are you hoping to make your audience laugh? Do you want them to think seriously about a topic? Or do you just want to entertain them with a dramatic oral presentation of a beautifully written poem? As you think about your **audience,** decide who they are and what they are likely to respond to. Picture them in your mind as you plan your presentation.

Prepare Background Material

Learn as much as you can about the poems you are presenting. Find out if there are special circumstances surrounding the composition of the poems. See if anything in the poet's own life gives you clues to a poem's meaning. You may want to share this information with your audience.

Ask Yourself

Do the poems

- have a common topic or theme?
- sound interesting when read aloud?
- lend themselves to a dramatic presentation?
- have possibilities for the use of different media?

Your Turn

Get Started Read different poems, from this anthology or from other sources, and make a list of candidates in your **RWN.** Then, narrow the list until you find three or four poems that would work well together in an oral presentation.

Learn It Online

Learn to create an attention-grabbing multimedia presentation. Visit MediaScope at:

go.hrw.com L8-783 

Multimedia Presentation: Poetry

Research Tip

- Search for sources using the library's online catalog.
- Use electronic databases for information.
- Find CDs of poetry readings.
- Search for reliable sites on the Internet.
- Ask a librarian for help with your research.

For more guidance in doing research, see the Communications Handbook.

Preparing Your Presentation

Interpret and Read Poems

After you choose a theme or topic and the poems to read, prepare your oral interpretation following these steps:

- Read and reread each poem aloud, concentrating on its meaning. Jot down ideas on ways to communicate your thoughts and feelings to an audience.
- Copy the poems, and add notes and marks to guide you in your reading. Underline words or phrases to be emphasized. Use slashes to represent pauses.
- Aim for a natural reading of the lines. Follow the punctuation of the poem, varying your pauses, volume, tone, and the emphasis you put on certain words.
- Practice reading the poems aloud in front of a small audience. Identify the vocal effects that work best.
- Tape-record or videotape your practice reading. Analyze the recording to see whether you need to make any changes.

Plan Your Use of Media

Look at the list below to help you brainstorm different ways in which you can make your poetry presentation, a multimedia event.

Visual Aids	Audio Aids	Audiovisual Aids
• illustrations from books and magazines • posters • photographs • images from Web sites	• audiotapes or CDs of voices or sound effects • recordings from Web sites • recordings of music on CD or tape	• clips from movies or TV programs

Remember that your goal is to enhance, or add to, your presentation with the kinds of media that are just right for the poems you have selected. As you think about media for your poetry presentation, ask yourself the following questions:

- What will using this medium add to my presentation?
- How will the visual or audio aid help my audience to grasp the meaning of the poems?
- What visual and audio aids are available to me?
- What special equipment will I need? How will I obtain it?

Your Turn

Plan Your Presentation Make notes in your **RWN** as you plan how to present the poems. Then, work on your plan. Create an outline that will include basic information on the poems, poets, and background as well as ideas about media to accompany your presentation of the poems.

Drafting

Follow the Writer's Framework

Now that you have planned your use of media, you are ready to plan your overall presentation. Use the writer's framework to the right to help you draft a script for an effective multimedia poetry presentation. Be sure to think about where media will have the most impact in your presentation. Is there a way that media can help grab the attention of your audience in your introduction? Perhaps media can also help make your conclusion more dramatic and interesting.

Framework for a Poetry Performance Script

Introduction
- an attention-getting opener
- titles and authors of poems
- a theme or topic

Body
- a presentation of each poem
- any special media effects

Conclusion
- a dramatic conclusion
- a summary of the theme or topic

Develop a Script

Remember that an effective presentation makes poetry come alive for the listeners. Your insights into the poems you have chosen can help your audience appreciate the poets' skills.

Grammar Link Using Clear Pronoun References

In your presentation, you will be talking about several poems and authors. You will probably be referring to various aspects of the poems, such as theme, sound effects, and figurative language. Your audience will more easily follow your presentation if you use pronouns correctly. (Pronouns are words that stand for nouns or other pronouns; for example, ***he*** */ Harry,* ***hers*** */ Mary's,* ***its*** */ the dog's.*) Below are some examples of clear and unclear pronoun references. You can find more information about the correct use of pronouns in the Language Handbook.

UNCLEAR: The book contains my favorite poem. I have read **it** several times.	CLEAR: I have read the book several times because **it** contains my favorite poem.
UNCLEAR: My dad talked to my brother before **he** left for work.	CLEAR: Before my dad left for work, **he** talked to my brother.
UNCLEAR: When the students in the choir sang for the hospital patients, **they** were happy and excited.	CLEAR: When **they** sang for the hospital patients, the students in the choir were happy and excited.

Writing Tip

As you draft your script, picture your audience. Have you included details that will pique their interest and keep them engaged throughout your presentation? For example, perhaps you need to add more interesting background information about the poets' lives and work.

Your Turn

Write Your Draft Following the framework, write a draft of the script for your poetry presentation. Think about ways in which you can make this presentation exciting for your audience. Once you have completed your draft, look for examples of vague pronoun reference in your script, and correct them.

Peer Review

Working with a peer, review your scripts. Answer each question in the chart at the right to locate where and how your presentations could be improved. As you discuss your scripts, be sure to take notes in your **RWN** about each other's suggestions. You can refer to your notes as you revise your poetry presentation.

Evaluating and Revising

Read the questions in the left-hand column of the chart. Then, use the tips in the middle column to help you make revisions to your script. The right-hand column suggests techniques you can use to revise your draft.

Poetry Presentation: Guidelines for Content and Organization

Evaluation Questions	Tips	Revision Techniques
1. Does your introduction grab your listeners' attention?	**Put stars** next to interesting or surprising details.	**Add** attention-getting details.
2. Does your introduction clearly present the theme or topic?	**Underline** the theme or topic.	**Insert** a statement of theme or topic, if needed.
3. Do you develop the theme or topic in the body of your script?	**Put a check mark** next to the paragraphs that develop your theme or topic.	**Add** details that develop your theme in more depth.
4. Have you planned to use different media in your presentation?	**Number** each form of media.	**Add** another form of media, if possible.
5. Do you provide a dramatic conclusion?	**Highlight** the dramatic element in your conclusion.	**Find** media that will add drama to your conclusion.
6. When you read the poems, do you pause at punctuation marks rather than at line breaks?	**Circle** each punctuation mark in the poetry.	**Rehearse** a clear and expressive reading of the poetry.
7. Have you practiced maintaining a good pace—not too fast or too slow? Have you practiced using gestures?	**Practice** your entire presentation.	**Use** a watch or timer to check your pacing. **Plan** any gestures you will use.

Read this draft of a poetry presentation script; note the comments on its strengths and suggestions on how it could be improved.

Draft

Walt Whitman: An American Original

Today Walt Whitman is recognized as one of America's great poets. His work has been translated into many languages. In my presentation, I'm going to focus on two well-known poems that show his individuality and genius.

← **Topic** of poetry presentation (Walt Whitman's originality) is presented at beginning.

When Whitman published the first edition of his volume of poetry, *Leaves of Grass,* in 1855, many readers didn't know what to make of it. No one had ever written poetry like it before. Some readers did recognize its worth, though, and in the years since then, Whitman has found his place as a great original poet.

← **Background information** is introduced to give the audience context for the poems in the presentation.

What was so new about Whitman's poetry? Most American poets of the time wrote in a fairly formal style, using rhyme and a set meter. Whitman used rhyme and meter in some of his poems, but he also wrote free verse. Poetry written in this style mimics the sound of natural speech: It lacks a regular meter and rhyme scheme. Whitman's subject matter was also unconventional: He wrote about himself and about Americans from all walks of life. Listen to "I Hear America Singing."

← Paragraph **elaborates** on Whitman's original style.

MINI-LESSON How to Enunciate

When you present something orally, it's important to keep in mind that your audience has to understand every word. You need to **enunciate;** that is, speak each word clearly, or misinterpretations or misunderstandings are bound to follow. The author of the script above highlighted places in his script where he wanted to make sure his enunciation was very clear.

Example

When Whitman published the first edition of his volume of poetry, *Leaves of Grass,* in 1855, many readers didn't know what to make of it. No one had ever written poetry like it before. Some readers did recognize its worth, though, and in the years since then, Whitman has found his place as a great original poet.

Your Turn

Read your draft. Where do you need to make notes about **enunciation**? Are there any words or phrases that might be misunderstood or misinterpreted if they're not pronounced clearly? Add notes as needed to help you as you deliver your oral presentation effectively.

Multimedia Presentation: Poetry

Writing Tip

As you revise your script, picture your presentation in your mind. Are there any places where you could add visual or audio effects? What kinds of transitions can you develop between the script and the presentation of media? Think about what would make your audience truly pay attention.

MINI-LESSON How to Use Media Elements Effectively

Your script should indicate the use of any special media, such as sound effects, music, and visuals. Look at this addition to the script on page 787. The author has added notes to indicate when to use which media to make the poetry presentation more effective.

Revision

Visuals: photograph of Walt Whitman by Mathew Brady (c. 1866); title page of *Leaves of Grass* (1855); painting *The Jolly Flatboatmen in Port* (1857) by George Caleb Bingham; photograph of Lincoln's funeral (1882)
Music: "O Captain! My Captain!" excerpt from *Memories of Lincoln* by John Church (available on CD)
Recordings: wax cylinder recording by Thomas Edison of Whitman reading his own poetry (available on CD or Web site)
Texts by Whitman: "I Hear America Singing;" "O Captain! My Captain!"; excerpt from preface of *Leaves of Grass*; excerpt from *Specimen Days*

Walt Whitman: An American Original

[Present visual: Photograph by Mathew Brady]

Today Walt Whitman is recognized as one of America's great poets. His work has been translated into many languages. In my presentation, I'm going to focus on two well-known poems that show his individuality and genius.

[Present visual: Title page of Leaves of Grass]

When Whitman published the first edition of his volume of poetry, *Leaves of Grass,* in 1855, many readers didn't know what to make of it. No one had ever written poetry like it before. Some readers did recognize its worth, though, and in the years since then, Whitman has found his place as a great original poet.

What was so new about Whitman's poetry? Most American poets of the time wrote in a fairly formal style, using rhyme and a set meter. Whitman also used rhyme and meter in some of this poems, but he also wrote free verse. Poetry written in this style mimics the sound of natural speech: It lacks a regular meter and rhyme scheme. Whitman's subject matter was also unconventional: He wrote about himself and about Americans from all walks of life. Listen to "I Hear America Singing."

[Text by Whitman: "I Hear America Singing"]

Your Turn

Using Different Media Review your presentation script. Have you used media effectively? Is there any way you could make your presentation more appealing through the use of auditory or visual effects? Do you need to add anything to make the presentation more exciting for your audience?

Proofreading and Presenting

Proofreading

Check your final version of the script to make sure it is free from any errors in spelling, punctuation, and sentence structure. Even though you may be the only person who reads the script, you don't want errors to get in the way of a good presentation. Proofread your writing carefully, using proofreading marks to make the necessary corrections. Use a dictionary and the Language Handbook in the Resource Center to look up any words you're not sure of or style questions you may have.

Grammar Link Marking Up Your Script

Your audience can't see your script while you're speaking, of course, but you will depend on it to cue you when it is time to present a new form of media or change something about your delivery. Think about the following ways to mark up your script:

- Write notes in the margin to remind you where to make gestures you have planned.
- Add slashes to indicate pauses you wish to make.
- Highlight parts of your script in different colors to indicate where you should change volume, tone, or emphasis.

Presenting

Here are some poetry presentation ideas:

- Stage your presentation for your class or for the whole school.
- Record your oral presentation, and share it on the school public address system or even as part of a local radio show.
- Videotape the presentation, and archive it in the school library.

Reflect on the Process As you think about your presentation, write a short response in your **RWN** to the following questions:

1. What was the biggest challenge in choosing poems to present?
2. How did you choose your topic or theme? Do you think the topic or theme worked? Why or why not?
3. What strategies did you use to keep your audience interested? Which ones worked the best? Why?
4. What would you do differently the next time you do a poetry presentation? Explain.

Proofreading Tip

There are three main areas to focus on when proofreading: spelling, punctuation, and sentence structure. It makes sense to focus on just one area at a time while proofreading. Ask two peers to help you, assigning each person just one area to check.

Presentation Tip

- Check the pronunciations of poets' names and of any unfamiliar words in the poems.
- Do not pause automatically at the end of each line, even if the poem contains rhyme.
- Let the punctuation guide your pauses. Pause at commas and semicolons; pause a little longer at dashes and periods.

Your Turn

Proofread and Present

Proofread your script, making sure you have corrected any errors. Have you included all the directions necessary for your poetry presentation? Are you happy with the script, or are there any changes you still want to make? Are you ready to deliver your presentation?

Literary Skills Review

Poetry **Directions:** Answer each question that follows.

1. Homer's great stories of the heroes of the Trojan War, the *Iliad* and the *Odyssey;* the ancient Mesopotamian story of the hero-king Gilgamesh; and the story of the warrior Beowulf, who saves a people from monsters—all of these are called

   A. ballads.

   B. epics.

   C. lyrics.

   D. elegies.

2. Read this short poem by Langston Hughes, and answer the questions that follow.

   O God of dust and rainbows help
   us see
   That without dust the rainbow
   would not be.

   This poem could best be described as

   A. a ballad.

   B. a sonnet.

   C. a lyric.

   D. an epic.

3. In the poem above, the rhyme could best be described as

   A. free verse.

   B. a couplet.

   C. meter.

   D. approximate rhyme.

4. An old song of love, betrayal, or death that rhymes and has a refrain is called

   A. a ballad.

   B. a sonnet.

   C. an epic.

   D. a stanza.

5. If you were reading a serious poem written to mourn someone who has died, you would be reading

   A. an ode.

   B. an epic.

   C. a lyric.

   D. an elegy.

6. A regular pattern of stressed and unstressed syllables in a poem is called

   A. meter.

   B. couplet.

   C. simile.

   D. metaphor.

7. The sentence "People are like snowflakes, no two are alike" uses a

   A. metaphor.

   B. simile.

   C. couplet.

   D. symbol.

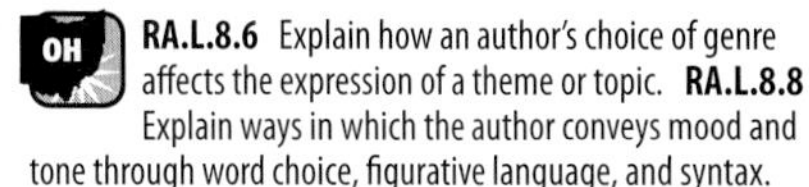

OH
RA.L.8.6 Explain how an author's choice of genre affects the expression of a theme or topic. **RA.L.8.8** Explain ways in which the author conveys mood and tone through word choice, figurative language, and syntax.

8. If you read a poem called "Ode to the North Wind," you could expect a
   A. poem that was lighthearted and humorous.
   B. mournful song with a refrain.
   C. sad poem about someone who died.
   D. serious poem written in formal language.

9. Read these famous lines from the Bible, and answer the questions that follow.

   To every thing there is a season,
   And a time to every purpose under the heaven:
   A time to be born, and a time to die;
   A time to plant, and a time to pluck up that which is planted.
   —Ecclesiastes 3:1–2

   Which of the following comments about these lines is correct?
   A. The lines are in free verse.
   B. The lines are in couplets.
   C. The lines are a ballad.
   D. The lines are written in strict meter.

10. In the lines from the Bible, above, the words *season* and *heaven* could be considered
    A. exact rhymes.
    B. approximate rhymes.
    C. internal rhymes.
    D. repetition.

11. Read the following poem, and answer the questions that follow. (Be sure to count the number of lines in the poem. Also, note that "*D.R.*" in line 6 means "Dominican Republic.")

    I've heard said that among the eskimos
    there are over a hundred words for snow:
    the soft kind, the hard-driving kind, the roll
    a snowball kind: snow being such a force
    in their lives, it needs a blizzard of words.
    In my own D.R. we have many rains:
    the sprinkle, the shower, the hurricane,
    the tears, the many tears for our many dead.
    I've asked around and find that in all tongues
    there are at least a dozen words for talk:
    the heart-to-heart, the chat, the confession,
    the juicy gossip, the quip, the harangue—
    no matter where we're from we need to talk
    about snow, rain, about being human.
    —Julia Alvarez

    This poem is an example of
    A. an elegy.
    B. an ode.
    C. a ballad.
    D. a sonnet.

Literary Skills Review CONTINUED

12. In line 3, Alvarez uses imagery to appeal to the reader's sense of
    A. taste.
    B. touch.
    C. smell.
    D. hearing.

13. In line 5, the phrase "a blizzard of words" is an example of
    A. metaphor.
    B. simile.
    C. alliteration.
    D. personification.

14. In lines 7, 8, 11, and 12, what does Alvarez use to create rhythm in the poem?
    A. repetition.
    B. balance.
    C. onomatopoeia.
    D. symbols.

Short Answer

15. Identify the theme of Alvarez's poem. Use information from her poem to support your answer.

Extended Response

16. List at least four elements of poetry. Then, describe what all poems have in common. Use information from the questions above to support your answer.

OH **VO.8.1** Define unknown words through context clues and the author's use of comparison, contrast and cause and effect. *Also covered* **VO.8.3**

Vocabulary Skills Review

Multiple-Meaning Words

Directions: Choose the answer in which the boldfaced word is used the same way as in the quoted passages.

1. "You can't order a poem like you **order** a taco."
   A. He put the pages in order.
   B. Will you order me a spinach salad?
   C. Don't order me around like that.
   D. Pick up your clothes—and that's an order!

2. "Walk up to the counter, say, 'I'll **take** two.'"
   A. The director wanted a sixth take of the scene.
   B. What is your take on this controversy?
   C. Can you take the stress of your new job?
   D. You may take the puppy you like most.

3. "Still, I like your **spirit**."
   A. The cheerleader has a strong spirit.
   B. A book can spirit you away to an imaginary place.
   C. In the spirit of the holiday, I gave away the best seat.
   D. He always follows the spirit, if not the letter, of the law.

4. "Check your garage, the odd sock / in your drawer, the person you almost **like**, but not quite."
   A. Your friend looks like my cousin.
   B. Do you like chocolate ice cream?
   C. My brother is afraid of spiders, roaches, and the like.
   D. My old house looks something like this photograph.

5. "filling the mouth with its **sound** / or else a mumbled / whisper"
   A. I like the sound of the violin.
   B. We spent the day sailing on the sound.
   C. At boot camp, we all had to sound off.
   D. I think your argument is sound.

6. "Travelers / **fan** out / into the wilds."
   A. The spinning fan cooled the room.
   B. If you fan the fire, it will burn faster.
   C. The dogs will fan out to hunt the fox.
   D. I am not a big fan of that singer.

Academic Vocabulary

Directions: Choose the correct synonym for each boldfaced Academic Vocabulary word.

7. It is the **intent** of many lyric poets to arouse strong feelings in their readers.
   A. plan
   B. aim
   C. dream
   D. act

8. Readers' **associations** contribute to their understanding of poems.
   A. connections
   B. acquaintances
   C. relatives
   D. interpretations

Read On

Poetry

In the Eyes of the Cat

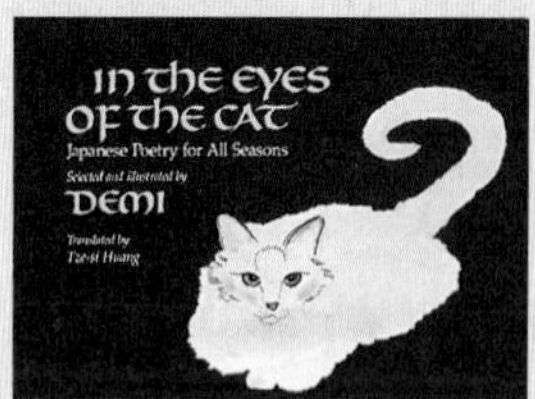

You will gain an appreciation of Japanese poetry in *In the Eyes of the Cat.* The editor and illustrator Demi has selected short poems about animals, from the gnat to the monkey, and has arranged them according to the seasons. The illustrations, which are as important as the poems, at times burst with colors and at other times are subdued with the pastel colors of fall and winter. The intricate artwork, along with the fine translations, help make this a thoroughly enjoyable book for all readers.

You Come Too

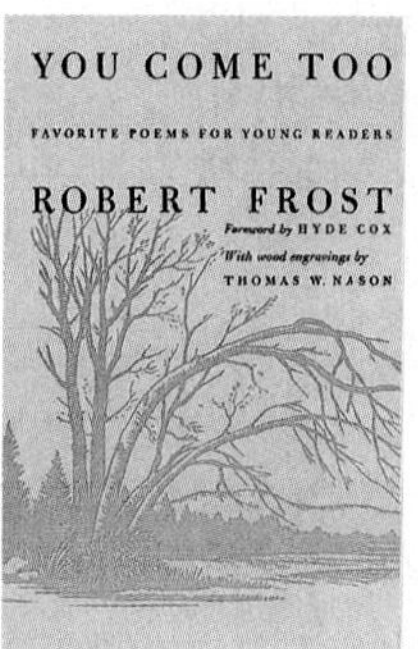

Discover some of the best of Robert Frost's poetry in *You Come Too.* In this collection for readers of all ages, you'll encounter poems such as "Christmas Tree," "Hyla Brook," and his famous, inviting title poem. Frost brings to life the trees, mountains, cliffs, dirt roads, old fences, grassy fields, and abandoned houses of his beloved New England. Reading his work, you'll have the sense that you are there—deep in the woods or at the edge of a babbling brook.

Canto Familiar

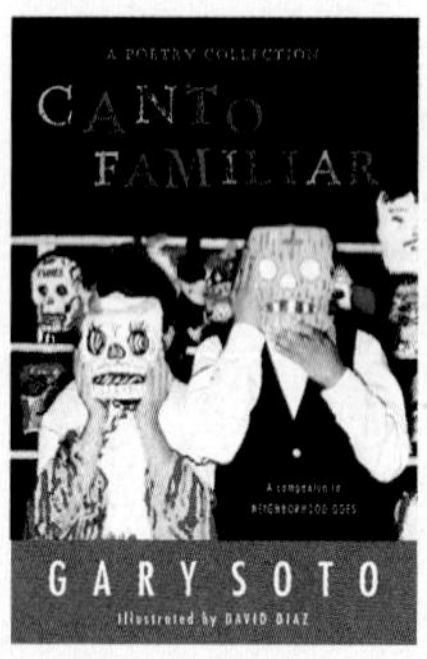

Gary Soto, the well-known writer for young adults, celebrates the experience of growing up in a Mexican American community in *Canto Familiar.* Many of these touching poems focus on everyday tasks, such as washing dishes or ironing clothes. Soto lovingly and humorously captures childhood in this collection. Artist Annika Nelson supplements the writing with original and beautiful woodcut illustrations.

This Same Sky: A Collection of Poems from Around the World

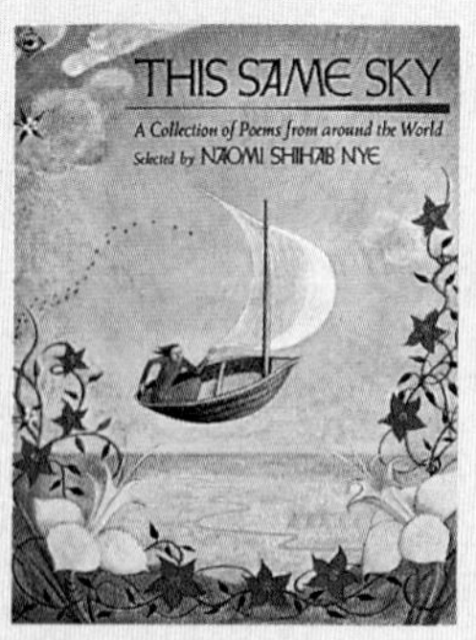

In her anthology, *This Same Sky: A Collection of Poems from Around the World,* Naomi Shihab Nye offers up a large assortment of poems from countries in the Middle East, Asia, Africa, India, and South and Central America. Like the variety of the poem's origins, the subject matter varies greatly and includes musings on language, nature, childhood, and politics. The collection is a great resource for kids and parents alike.

Nonfiction

Island of Hope: The Story of Ellis Island and the Journey to America

Dramatic firsthand stories and evocative archival photographs combine to bring the Ellis Island experience to life in Martin Sandler's *Island of Hope: The Story of Ellis Island and the Journey to America*. Both the joys and miseries of the immigration process are captured in this historic account. Sandler also gives an overview of the immigrants' lives after they were finally settled in America.

Lincoln: A Photobiography

Russell Freedman's *Lincoln: A Photobiography* takes an intimate look at the man who has been called our greatest president. Freedman writes about Abraham Lincoln's childhood, his legendary debates with Stephen Douglas, and his struggles as president during the years of the Civil War. The photographs and text of this Newbery Medal winner are complemented by illustrations and historical documents.

A Great and Glorious Game

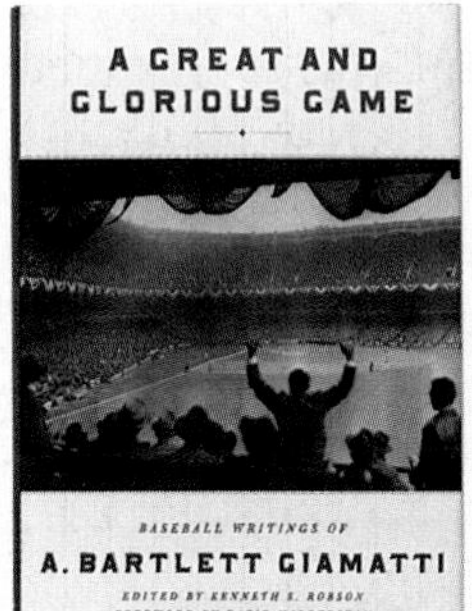

Baseball was more than a game to A. Bartlett Giamatti; each game was a drama that gave insight into the American character. *A Great and Glorious Game* collects some of Giamatti's writings about the game he loved, from the time he was a literature professor at Yale University through the period when he served as commissioner of baseball.

The Harlem Renaissance

In *The Harlem Renaissance,* Veronica Chambers looks back at a special time in American history. During the 1920s, African American musicians such as Duke Ellington, writers such as Zora Neale Hurston, and painters such as William H. Johnson produced visionary art. Their work continues to influence American culture and society to this day.

UNIT 4

Drama

Writers on Writing

Cassandra Medley on Drama Award-winning playwright and teacher Cassandra Medley was born in Detroit. Many of her acclaimed works, including her play *Relativity,* explore family relationships and issues surrounding race and identity in the United States.

"I was blessed to be born in a family of natural storytellers; my father, his mother, and several aunts had the ability to hold an audience spellbound by a story 'acted out' through tone of voice, facial expression, pauses to create tension, suspense, and surprise. A steady pastime was to sit quietly

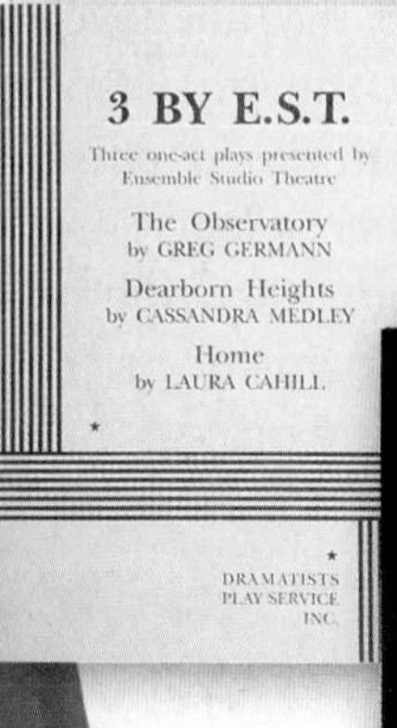

while listening to family members tell or retell family lore, gossip, and relived memories—some passed down through generations. There is the story of the great-grandmother who lived into the 20th century, and could, as a very old woman, recall the day she was freed from slavery. There is the story of my mother's refusal to leave a Detroit restaurant when they "refused to serve Negroes," and the memory I have of the day my father drove two hundred miles back to his hometown to finally play golf at the golf course where he was once refused entry as a boy.

Now I write stories that "come alive" in front of an audience—stories that depend on actors who make my characters live and breathe on the spot. Plays are written to be performed in front of onlookers, for the dialogue to be spoken out into the air, with live bodies moving around in three-dimensional space. We write plays in order to create a back-and-forth communion, an exchange, or a response with the audience. They laugh at a gesture or joke an actor may make. They may cry at a moment of hope, irony, or tragedy. They may be visibly bored with a scene, or intensely frightened, and jump in their seats at a scary moment. Hopefully at the end, they clap, and at times they stand on their feet and yell "bravo." It is this direct, flesh-and-blood experience that makes theater so thrilling.

The word *playwright* originates from the word *wright*—meaning a worker who makes structures and objects. We dramatists construct stories intended to live "off" of the page, with events happening in front of your very eyes. This is the challenge of writing for the stage, but the crucial factor is to have a strong, vibrant story. All of us have the potential to create and retell stories—we all gossip, tell lies, retell favorite stories, and re-create versions of our own and other people's lives.

The text of a play is just the blueprint. Think of how a music score needs the conductor and musicians to play the sounds in order to bring the music to life. In the same way, dramatic text needs the lights, sounds, and actors, all shaped by a director to give the full experience of theater. Drama is one of the earliest forms of storytelling; try and see as much live theater as you possibly can!"

Think as a Writer

In her essay, Medley says we all "have the potential to create and retell stories." What are some of your favorite stories that you might like to retell?

di Garanzia

COLLECTION 8

Elements of Drama

INFORMATIONAL TEXT FOCUS

Treatment, Scope, and Organization of Ideas

"There is a thin line that separates laughter and pain, comedy and tragedy, humor and hurt. And how do you know laughter if there is no pain to compare it with?"

—Erma Bombeck

What Do You Think? How can we do the best with what we've been given?

Learn It Online

Find more drama on *NovelWise* online:

go.hrw.com L8-799 Go

Literary Focus

by **Sara Kajder**

What Do You Need to Know About Drama?

Long before television, radios, and even books were invented, people gathered to watch dramas. This enduring form of entertainment lives on today through television, film, and in theaters. Read on to learn more about the types and elements of drama.

Types of Drama

Play A **play,** or drama, is a story acted out by live people in front of other live people. Plays are generally written in script form and can be read as well as viewed. Plays can be serious, funny, sad, mysterious, or scary. They might tell the story of kings and queens, of great battles, or of the doings of ordinary people.

Tragedy The oldest plays we have scripts for come from ancient Greece. There, two kinds of plays were performed: tragedies and comedies. A **tragedy** presents serious and important situations that end unhappily—usually with the death of one or more main characters.

Comedy The ancient Greek tragedies were about kings and queens and other nobility, but the comedies could be about anyone: noble folk, ordinary folk, and servants. A **comedy** is any play that ends happily. You may think of a comedy as a funny play, and indeed, many comedies are designed to make us laugh. But comedies often have other purposes as well, such as to make us think about important topics.

Some of the **elements of humor** that make us laugh in a play are listed below with examples from William Shakespeare's *Pyramus and Thisbe*:

- **wordplay**—puns or other clever or silly exchanges of words

> What dreadful dole is here?
>   Eyes, do you see?
>   How can it be?
> O dainty duck, O dear!

- **misstatements**—using the wrong words or saying the opposite of what is meant

> I see a voice; now will I to the chink,
> To spy and I can hear my Thisbe's face.

- **exaggeration**—overstatements

> Whereat, with blade, with bloody blameful blade,
> He bravely broached his boiling bloody breast.

- **comic actions**—unexpected behavior and exaggerated facial expressions

RA.L.8.6 Explain how an author's choice of genre affects the expression of a theme or topic.

Elements of Drama

Dramatic Structure Like stories, plays consist of **characters** who have a **conflict** of some kind. They want something and struggle to achieve it, overcoming various obstacles along the way. The action rises to a **climax** and ends with a **resolution.**

Dialogue Most plays have no narrator to describe for us what is happening and why. Instead, we learn about characters and their situations primarily through **dialogue**—conversations that take place between two or more actors.

In addition to dialogue, some plays contain other types of lines, or spoken words.

- A **monologue** is a long speech by one actor to one or more other actors onstage. Through monologues playwrights can more fully reveal character.
- A **soliloquy** is a long speech by a character alone on the stage, speaking to himself or herself. Soliloquies help to reveal characters more fully, allowing us to listen in on a character's emotional struggles, learn of an important event from the character's past, or witness a character's decision-making process. The soliloquy was especially popular in the Shakepearean era.
- An **aside** is a comment or line that is spoken aloud by a character to the audience, but is not heard by other characters onstage. By using asides, playwrights help the audience understand a character's true feelings yet mask those feelings from other characters in the play.

Stage Directions Stage directions describe what is happening onstage. They may give information about the setting, props, and characters' actions and emotions. They are usually printed in italic type and appear at the beginning of a scene or in parentheses next to dialogue.

The *Diary of Anne Frank* opens with a long description of the set, which includes this:

> *The curtains rise on an empty stage.*
> *It is late afternoon, November 1945.*
> *The rooms are dusty, the curtains in rags.*
> *Chairs and tables are overturned.*

In this passage, the stage directions that appear in parentheses describe Mr. Frank's emotions.

> **Miep.** Are you all right, Mr. Frank?
> **Mr. Frank.** (*quickly controlling himself*).
> Yes, Miep, yes.

Your Turn Analyzing Drama

Choose a play or movie you have seen recently and answer the following questions.

1. Was the play or movie a comedy or tragedy? How could you tell?
2. What conflict did the main character face? How was the conflict resolved?
3. What did you learn about the main character through the play's dialogue?

Learn It Online
Do pictures help you learn? Try the *PowerNotes* version of this lesson at:
go.hrw.com L8-801 

Analyzing Visuals

What Dramatic Elements Can You Find in Photographs?

Most visual art exhibits some elements of drama. Paintings, sculptures, and photographs may be tragic or comic, for example. They may present characters in conflict. They may include action and emotion. Look for the dramatic elements in these photographs of a rehearsal and production of the Broadway play *Wicked,* a musical adaptation of *The Wizard of Oz.*

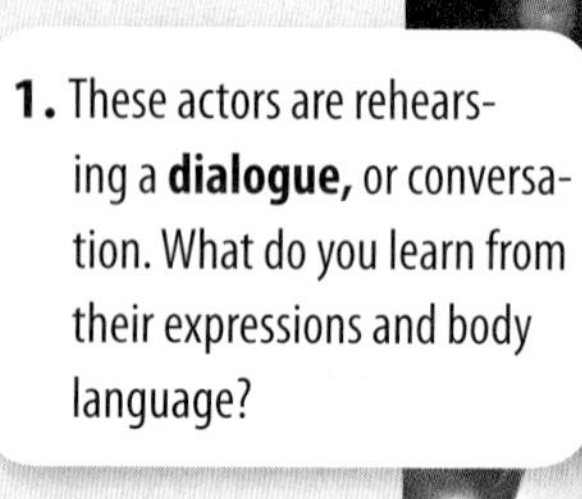

1. These actors are rehearsing a **dialogue,** or conversation. What do you learn from their expressions and body language?

2. Why do you think one of the actors is wearing a hat and bag? (The photograph on the next page will give you a clue.)

Kristin Chenoweth and Idina Menzel in a rehearsal of *Wicked.* © Joan Marcus.

RA.L.8.6 Explain how an author's choice of genre affects the expression of a theme or topic.

3. Here, the same two actors are on stage with other actors. What effect is created by the lights, costumes, and makeup?

4. What do the actors' facial expressions suggest about what is happening on stage?

5. Do you think this scene is from a tragedy, comedy, or serious drama? What makes you think so?

Broadway production of *Wicked.*

Analyzing Photographs

Use these guidelines to analyze dramatic elements in photographs.

1. Who is in the photograph? What can you infer about the people from their facial expressions, clothing, and actions?
2. Study the colors and use of light. What tone or mood is set?
3. Take note of the background. What setting is depicted?
4. Think about the overall impact of the photograph. Is its subject comic, tragic, or both?

Your Turn Write About Dramatic Elements in Photographs

Choose two photographs shown from the production of *The Diary of Anne Frank* on pages 839–912, and describe the dramatic elements you see.

Reading Focus

by **Kylene Beers**

What Reading Skills Can Help You Understand Drama?

When you watch a play, the sets, actors, lighting, music, and costumes all help you understand what is happening. Reading a play takes a little more effort, however. You have to use reading skills, such as those described below, to understand what is happening.

Visualizing

A script is a framework—it conveys the basics of a play, but it doesn't bring the play to life for you. Instead, you must use clues in the script to **visualize,** to picture in your mind, what is happening.

In these stage directions from Act One of *The Diary of Anne Frank,* we are given a great deal of information about what is happening on stage:

> *The door at the foot of the small stairwell swings open.* MR. FRANK *comes up the steps into view. He is a gentle, cultured European in his middle years. There is still a trace of a German accent in his speech.*
> *He stands looking slowly around, making a supreme effort at self-control. He is weak, ill. His clothes are threadbare.*

As you read, use a chart like this one to help you visualize a play's action, sets, and characters.

	What the Text Reveals
Setting	stairwell, doorway
Character's Appearance	thin, ill, weak, poorly dressed
Character's Actions	looking, controlling emotions
What I Visualize Mr. Frank is brave but helpless as he stands alone in a place full of painful memories.	

Analyzing Dialogue and Reading Aloud

Playwrights use dialogue to develop their characters and further the action. As you read drama, look carefully at the dialogue to understand characters' conflicts and emotions. Also read passages of dialogue aloud to step into the world of the play. We can learn a lot about the characters from this short dialogue from *The Diary of Anne Frank.*

> **Mrs. Van Daan.** *(rising, nervous, excited).* Something's happened to them! I know it!
> **Mr. Van Daan.** Now Kerli!
> **Mrs. Van Daan.** Mr. Frank said they'd be here at seven o'clock. He said . . .
> **Mr. Van Daan.** They have two miles to walk. You can't expect . . .

Ask these questions as you analyze dialogue:

- What words do the characters use to express themselves? Do they deliberately use overly formal or informal language?
- What emotions are expressed in the dialogue?
- How are the characters' relationships with others in the play revealed in the dialogue?
- What critical decisions of the characters are revealed in the dialogue?
- How does the dialogue advance the plot?

RA.L.8.8 Explain ways in which the author conveys mood and tone through word choice, figurative language, and syntax. **RP.8.1** Apply reading comprehension strategies, including making predictions, comparing and contrasting, recalling and summarizing and making inferences and drawing conclusions.

Making Inferences

In most plays there is no narrator to tell us what a character is like. Instead, we make **inferences,** guesses based on clues in the text, to figure out a character's personality and why he or she acts in a certain way.

Read this passage from *The Diary of Anne Frank.* Then, look at the chart below to see how you can make inferences based on text clues within this passage.

Mrs. Frank (*to* ANNE). Would you like some water? (ANNE *shakes her head.*) Was it a very bad dream? Perhaps if you told me . . . ?
Anne. I'd rather not talk about it.
Mrs. Frank. Poor darling. Try to sleep, then. I'll sit right here beside you until you fall asleep. (*She brings a stool over, sitting there.*)
Anne. You don't have to.
Mrs. Frank. But I'd like to stay with you . . . very much. Really.
Anne. I'd rather you didn't.

Text Clue	Sample Inferences
Anne has had a bad dream.	Anne is afraid of something.
Anne's mother tries to comfort her.	Mrs. Frank is kind and loving.
Anne tells her mother that she wants to be left alone.	Anne doesn't want to tell her mother what's bothering her. Anne may not trust her mother.

Your Turn Applying Reading Skills

Read the following excerpt from a scene in *The Diary of Anne Frank* silently to yourself, paying careful attention to both dialogue and stage directions.

Peter (*to* ANNE). Have you seen my shoes?
Anne (*innocently*). Your shoes?
Peter. You've taken them, haven't you?
Anne. I don't know what you're talking about.
Peter. You're going to be sorry!
Anne. Am I?

[PETER *goes after her.* ANNE, *with his shoes in her hand, runs from him, dodging behind her mother.*]

Mrs. Frank (*protesting*). Anne, dear!
Peter. Wait till I get you!

1. Which stage direction describes the way Anne speaks a line of dialogue?
2. What conflict is revealed in these lines of dialogue?
3. What inference can you make about Anne's personality based on her actions?
4. Which details help you to visualize the action in this scene?

Now go to the Skills in Action: Reading Model

Learn It Online
Try the *PowerNotes* version of this lesson at:

COMEDY

Build Background

Alice in Wonderland is a classic tale that has been translated into film and drama over and over again. Alice, the story's heroine, has a series of adventures in which she meets fantastical creatures such as the Mad Hatter, a Dormouse, and a Caterpillar.

Preview the Selection

In this scene, **Alice** is running from a pack of cards when she encounters the Red Queen.

Read with a Purpose Read this scene to find out what happens when Alice meets the Red Queen and plays a bizarre game of chess.

from

by **Lewis Carroll,** adapted for the stage by **Eva Le Gallienne and Florida Friebus**

Act II, Scene 1

ALICE, THE RED QUEEN

At rise, ALICE *is seen still running, but now she is facing left. She slows down wearily and comes to a stop. As lights come up, she finds herself in a land that is marked out in squares, like a huge chessboard, with a large tree at the right. Presently, from the left, with a thump, thump of footsteps, the* RED QUEEN *enters and comes face to face with* ALICE.

Red Queen. Where do you come from and where are you going? Look up, speak nicely, and don't twiddle your fingers.

Alice (*attending to all these directions as well as she can*). You see I've lost my way.

Red Queen. I don't know what you mean by *your* way, all the ways about here belong to *me*—but why did you come out here at all? Curtsey while you're thinking what to say. It saves time.

Literary Focus

Types of Drama Comedies are usually full of **humor.** Note, in particular, the **wordplay** here. Alice uses the expression "I've lost my way," and the Red Queen takes the expression literally by insisting that it's *her* way, not Alice's.

Alice in Profile by Lesley Fotherby. Watercolor on paper.

Alice (*aside*). I'll try it when I go home the next time I'm a little late for dinner.

Red Queen (*looking at her watch*). It's time for you to answer now. Open your mouth a *little* wider when you speak and always say "Your Majesty."

Alice. I only wanted to see what the garden was like, Your Majesty—

Red Queen (*patting* ALICE *on the head which she doesn't like at all*). That's right, though when you say "garden"—*I've* seen gardens, compared with which this would be a wilderness.

Alice (*going right on*).—and I thought I'd try and find my way to the top of that hill.

Red Queen. When you say "hill"—*I* could show you hills in comparison with which you'd call that a valley.

Alice. No, I shouldn't, a hill *can't* be a valley, you know. That would be nonsense—

Red Queen. You call it "nonsense" if you like, but *I've* heard nonsense, compared with which that would be as sensible as a dictionary! (ALICE *curtsies again as she is afraid by the* QUEEN'S *tone that she is a little offended.*)

Alice (*surveying the view*). I declare it's marked out just like a large chessboard. It's a great huge game of chess that's being played—all over the world—if this *is* the world at all, you know. Oh, what fun it is! How I *wish* I was part of it. I wouldn't mind being a Pawn, if only I might join—though of course I should *like* to be a queen, best. (*She glances shyly at the* QUEEN *who smiles pleasantly.*)

Literary Focus

Elements of Drama This stage direction tells us the dialogue is an **aside,** in which the audience hears these words, but the characters on stage do not.

Reading Focus

Analyzing Dialogue Look at the Red Queen's "know-it-all," boastful interruptions to Alice's explanation. Her choice of words gives the reader insight into what she is like.

Red Queen. That's easily managed. You can be the White Queen's Pawn, if you like, as Lily's too young to play; and you're in the Second Square to begin with: when you get to the Eighth Square, you'll be a Queen. (*They begin to run hand in hand—the scene does not change—the* QUEEN *runs so fast* ALICE *can scarcely keep up with her and still the* QUEEN *keeps crying.*) *Faster, faster!*

Reading Focus

Visualizing As you read the stage directions, visualize the two characters running yet not moving ahead and not passing anything ("the scene does not change").

Alice (*to herself*). I wonder if all the things move along with us?

Red Queen. Faster! Don't try to talk! (ALICE *falters and falls back a little.*) Faster! Faster!

Alice (*at last getting her breath*). Are we nearly there?

Red Queen. Nearly there! Why, we passed it ten minutes ago! Faster! (*They run on in silence for awhile.*) Now! Now! Faster, Faster! (*The* QUEEN *pulls* ALICE *up in line with herself again. They run on . . . then slowly come to a stop.* ALICE *drops to ground. The* QUEEN *seats* ALICE *under the tree. Kindly*) You may rest a little now.

Alice (*looking around in surprise*). Why, I do believe we've been under this tree the whole time! Everything's just as it was!

Red Queen. Of course it is. What would you have it?

Alice. Well, in *our* country, you'd generally get to somewhere else—if you ran very fast for a long time as we've been doing.

Red Queen. A slow sort of country! Now, *here,* you see, it takes all the running *you* can do to keep in the same place. If you want to get somewhere else, you must run at least twice as fast as that!

Reading Focus

Making Inferences You can already tell that the queen is—at the very least —"unique." From what she has just said, you can infer that this place where she lives is indeed a strange "wonderland," where things work the opposite of what one would expect.

Alice. I'd rather not try, please! I'm quite content to stay here—only I *am* so hot and thirsty!

Red Queen. I know what you'd like. (*Takes a large, hard-wafer biscuit out of her pocket.*) Have a biscuit? (ALICE *takes it but finds it very dry. She chokes and puts remainder of biscuit in her pocket.*) While you're refreshing yourself, I'll just take the measurements. (*She marches to a point downstage, right, in front of the tree, where she begins to measure with a tape measure, taking little sidesteps from right to left, and marking the end of each "square" with a bounce in her knees, and a gesture of her hand, as though placing a peg.*) At the end of two yards . . . (*She takes two sidesteps left. Bounce.*) I shall give you your directions —Have another biscuit?

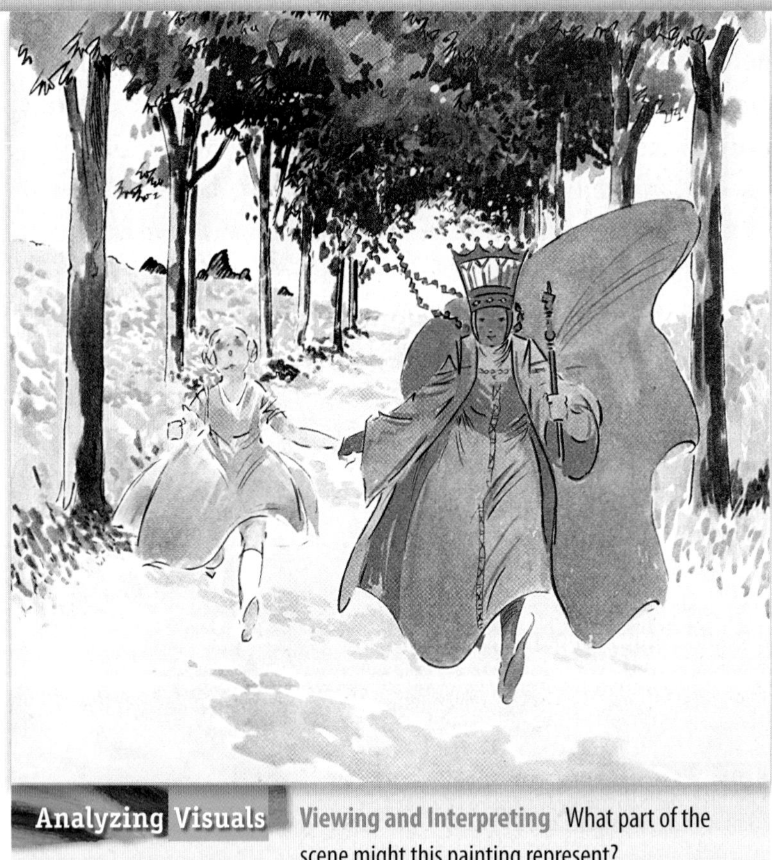

Analyzing Visuals **Viewing and Interpreting** What part of the scene might this painting represent?

Alice and the Red Queen (detail) by Pecoud. Illustration from *Alice in Wonderland* by Lewis Carroll. Color lithograph.

Alice. No, thank you, one's *quite* enough.

Red Queen. Thirst quenched, I hope? At the end of three yards . . . (*Business*°) I shall repeat them for fear of your forgetting them. At the end of four. . . (*Business*) I shall say goodbye. And at the end of *five* . . . (*Business*) I shall go! (*She marches back to her starting point and begins walking slowly along the line that she has measured, describing each square with suitable gestures.*) A pawn goes two squares in its first move, you know. So you'll go *very* quickly through the Third Square . . . by railway, I should think . . . and you'll find yourself in the Fourth Square in no time. Well, *that* square belongs to Tweedledum and Tweedledee . . . the Fifth is mostly water . . . the Sixth belongs to Humpty Dumpty . . . But you make no remark?

Alice. I . . . I didn't know I had to make one just then.

° **business:** In the context of drama, *business* refers to movements an actor makes to make a scene more realistic.

Red Queen. You *should* have said, "It's extremely kind of you to tell me all this," . . . however, we'll suppose it said . . . the Seventh Square is all forest . . . however, one of the Knights will show you the way . . . and in the Eighth square we shall be Queens together, and it's all feasting and fun! (*She turns to* ALICE. ALICE *gets up and curtsies.*) Speak in French when you can't think of the English for a thing. Turn out your toes when you walk, and remember who you are! (*She turns left and starts running.*)

Alice. She *can* run very fast!

Red Queen. Good-bye. (*She exits, left. Blackout. Shrill whistle of a steam engine*)

Reading Focus

Reading Aloud To appreciate the silliness of the Red Queen's character, read this paragraph of dialogue aloud. What would her commands to Alice sound like?

Read with a Purpose How does the bizarre nature of the Red Queen's game of chess add to the humor of this work?

MEET THE WRITER

Lewis Carroll

(1832–1898)

"A Very Uncommon Share of Genius"

Lewis Carroll, the author of *Alice's Adventures in Wonderland* and *Through the Looking Glass,* had so many talents that he worked under two names. Born Charles Lutwidge Dodgson, he was both creative and successful in his studies. One teacher even remarked that he had "a very uncommon share of genius."

As Dodgson, he got a degree in mathematics from Oxford University and became a priest in the Church of England. He published mathematics papers under this name, but when he began to publish poems and stories, he chose the pen name Lewis Carroll.

Think About the Writer Which of his many talents do you think Carroll enjoyed most? Why?

SKILLS IN ACTION

Wrap Up

RA.L.8.6 Explain how an author's choice of genre affects the expression of a theme or topic. RA.L.8.8 Explain ways in which the author conveys mood and tone through word choice, figurative language, and syntax. *Also covered* RP.8.1

Into Action: Dialogue

Use an organizer like the one below to analyze how dialogue reflects what the characters are like. In the boxes on the left, list qualities of Alice or the Red Queen. In the boxes on the right, find two examples that reflect each character's qualities.

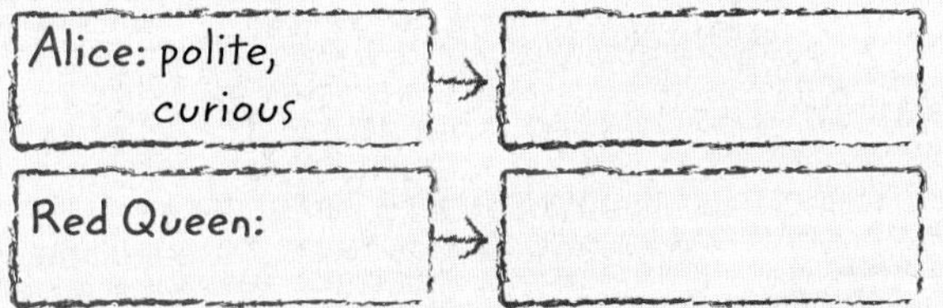

Talk About . . .

1. In a small group, discuss the scene you read from *Alice in Wonderland*. To begin, select a portion of text that you find the most entertaining or interesting. Then, support your opinion by citing the text's use of dialogue, action, stage directions, or humor. Try to use the Academic Vocabulary listed to the right in your discussion.

Write About . . .

Use the underlined Academic Vocabulary words in your answers to the questions below. The words' definitions are in the box to the right.

2. How do the stage directions contribute to the play's humor?
3. What insight do the queen's words give into her personality? What "queenly" attributes does she have? What are her flaws?
4. How would you describe Alice's way of expressing herself? Explain.
5. What is evident about the relationship between Alice and the queen?

Writing Focus

Think as a Reader/Writer

Use the Writing Focus activities on the Preparing to Read pages to analyze aspects of writer's craft in dramas. On the Applying Your Skills pages, you will get a chance to practice some techniques in your own writing.

Academic Vocabulary for Collection 8

Talking and Writing About Drama

The following Academic Vocabulary terms will help you as you write about and discuss dramas. These terms are underlined throughout this collection.

contribute to (kuhn TRIHB yoot too) *v.:* play a part in; bring about. *Quirky wordplay and exaggeration are two elements that contribute to the humor of a drama.*

insight (IHN syt) *n.:* understanding of how things work or how people think or act. *Descriptive stage directions give insight into the characters' personalities and lives.*

evident (EHV uh duhnt) *adj.:* plain; clear; obvious. *Her actions made it evident that she was not happy.*

express (ehk SPREHS) *v.:* show; put into words. *Discover characters' personalities by studying how they express themselves.*

Your Turn

Copy the words from the Academic Vocabulary list into your *Reader/Writer Notebook*. Put a star next to words you've never used in your writing and classroom discussions. Make a point of trying to use those words as you answer questions about the plays in the collection that follows.

GRAPHIC PLAY

Preparing to Read

Pyramus and Thisbe

from A Midsummer Night's Dream
by **William Shakespeare**

Globe Theater. © Donald Cooper/PhotoStage.

What Do You Think? Should we appreciate an unskilled but sincere effort?

QuickWrite

When have you enjoyed watching athletes or performers do their very best, even though it is not very good? Jot down your ideas about what made it enjoyable.

Reader/Writer Notebook

Use your **RWN** to complete the activities for this selection.

OH **RP.8.1** Apply reading comprehension strategies, including making predictions, comparing and contrasting, recalling and summarizing and making inferences and drawing conclusions. **RA.L.8.6** Explain how an author's choice of genre affects the expression of a theme or topic.

Literary Focus

Comedy A comedy is a play that has a happy ending. The main characters in a comedy encounter problems and obstacles before getting what they want. A comedy doesn't have to be humorous, but most are. Much of the humor in *Pyramus and Thisbe* comes from clever and silly **wordplay,** confused **misstatements,** verbal or behavioral **exaggeration,** and other **comic actions.**

TechFocus As you read the graphic version of the play, think of how you might illustrate a scene from your favorite comedy.

Reading Focus

Visualizing and Reading Aloud A play is meant to be acted. The sound of the words, as well as the actors' behavior, contribute to the play's meaning and delight. To appreciate reading a play, visualize the action as you read both silently and aloud.

Into Action As you read, use a chart like the one below to note how you picture the action in *Pyramus and Thisbe.*

Lines from the Play	What I Visualize
O, kiss me through the hole of this vile wall!	The two lovers awkwardly try to push their faces through the small hole in the wall.

Writing Focus

Think as a Reader/Writer

Find It in Your Reading **Doggerel** is a term that refers to poorly written, even laughably bad, poetic verse. Bad rhymes, clichés, overly sentimental imagery, and overused alliteration are all characteristics of doggerel. As you read *Pyramus and Thisbe,* a short play within Shakespeare's comedy *A Midsummer Night's Dream,* look for examples of bad poetry, which were actually written by the famous playwright himself in order to provoke laughter.

Vocabulary

tedious (TEE dee uhs) *adj.:* long and boring. *Philostrate discourages Theseus from watching a tedious play.*

merit (MEHR iht) *n.:* worth. *Although he's been warned that it has little merit, Theseus wants to see the play.*

vile (vyl) *adj.:* very unpleasant. *The source of a deadly misunderstanding, the vile lion scares Thisbe away.*

amend (uh MEHND) *v:* make better. *Maybe those watching the awful play can use their imaginations to amend it.*

Expectation of the play:
- professionally done—no need to **amend**

Reality:
- is **tedious**
- has no **merit**
- **vile** acting

Language Coach

Archaic Language As you read the play, you will encounter the pronoun *thou,* meaning "you," which is seldom used today. Verbs commonly used with *thou* include *art* ("are"), *hast* ("have"), and *wilt* ("will").

Learn It Online
Use Word Watch to explore vocabulary words at:

go.hrw.com 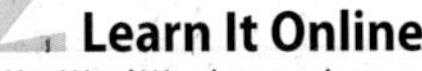 L8-813  Go

MEET THE WRITER

William Shakespeare
(1564–1616)

Globe Theater in London, 2006.

Most people consider William Shakespeare the greatest writer in the English language. He is even more famous today than he was during his life, but little is known about his personal life.

A Hometown Boy

We do know that Shakespeare was born in the town of Stratford-upon-Avon into a middle-class family. His father was a successful glove-maker who also served as mayor. Young William probably attended the local grammar school, where subjects were taught in Latin. Shakespeare was only eighteen years old when he married Anne Hathaway. The couple had three children. Even when Shakespeare was working in London, Anne and the children remained in Stratford, where Shakespeare visited, made investments, and participated in the life of the town.

Poet and Playwright

From 1592 to 1594, theaters in England were often closed because authorities feared that the plague would spread through the audience. During this time, Shakespeare turned to forms of poetry other than dramatic verse. He dedicated a long poem to the Earl of Southampton, who became his patron. Shakespeare's 154 sonnets, some of which he probably composed while waiting for the theaters to reopen, are considered among the best ever written.

A Life in the Theater

By 1594, once fear of the plague was past, Shakespeare was the principal writer, a regular actor, and a stockholder in The Lord Chamberlain's Men, a popular theater company that often performed for Queen Elizabeth I. In 1599, Shakespeare and a group of friends built the Globe Theater just outside of London. In 1603, James I became king. In return for entertaining at court, The Lord Chamberlain's Men were allowed to change their name to The King's Men. By the time of Shakespeare's death at age 52, he had written more than 37 plays in verse—plays that are performed to this day.

All the world's a stage,
And all the men and women merely players . . .

from As You Like It (II, vii, 139–140)

Think About the Writer Do you think Shakespeare would be surprised to know that his plays and poems are still so popular? Why or why not?

Theater in Shakespeare's Day

Entertainment for Everyone

In Shakespeare's time, people of all classes went to the theater. For a penny, you could stand in the yard around the stage. The people in this part of the audience were called groundlings. If you were able to pay a little more, you could sit in one of the galleries. Those who wanted to show off their wealth paid extra to have chairs set up on the stage itself. Plays were performed in the afternoon, and people ate, drank, moved around, and visited during the performance. With up to 3,000 people in theaters such as the Globe, attending plays probably was more like attending modern sports events than today's theater. Acting styles of the time were often exaggerated—after all, the actor's first job was to get the audience's attention.

If you were able to ignore the bustle around you and really focus on the play's leading lady, you'd be in for another surprise—all the young female characters were played by boys specially trained to impersonate women. Older female characters were played by grown men. Women were strictly forbidden to act on the stage.

Model of Globe Theater.

Theater Under the Sun

Before Shakespeare's time, plays were rarely performed under a roof. Traveling troupes of players often performed in the courtyards of inns. People stood on the ground around the stage or sat on chairs set up in the galleries that connected the inns' rooms. When James Burbage built the first permanent theater (called The Theater), he designed it much like the courtyard of an inn. Unfortunately, The Theater didn't make enough money. Burbage fell behind on his rent. To escape the landlord, Burbage and his company tore The Theater down under cover of night and rowed the pieces across the river. Shakespeare's company used these pieces to build The Globe Theater.

The Globe was a three-story polygonal (many sided—no one knows exactly how many sides the Globe had) building that looked like a circle. This outer building where people sat in galleries enclosed an open, unroofed yard. The stage extended halfway into the yard, so people could watch the play from three sides. Behind the main stage was a curtained inner stage with a small balcony above it. Behind the inner stage was the two-story tiring, or changing, room. This room had doors leading to the stage.

A Spectacular Show

The arrangement of the stage allowed for great spectacle. Without much scenery to move around, the action was almost continuous. Actors appeared from the tiring room in elaborate costumes, seemed to disappear through trapdoors in the floor of the stage, flew from wires, or were carried up to heaven through trapdoors in the ceiling of the rear part of the stage, which was beautifully painted with suns, moons, and stars. Live musicians played from the gallery, and the actors were accomplished singers and dancers. No wonder people looked eagerly for the flag flying from the tiring room that signaled there would be a performance that day.

Scene with Pyramus, Thisbe, and Wall from a production of *A Midsummer Night's Dream,* performed by members of the Royal Shakespeare Company.

Preview the Selection

Pyramus and Thisbe is a play in its own right, but it is also a part of another play called *A Midsummer Night's Dream*. In order to appreciate the selection, it helps to know how the two plays fit together.

A Romantic Comedy

A Midsummer Night's Dream is a romantic comedy—a play about the humorous ways in which one or more couples overcome obstacles to be together. Shakespeare's play has a complicated plot that involves four couples.

- **Theseus and Hippolyta**
  Theseus is the duke of Athens. He is about to marry Hippolyta, the queen of the Amazons.
- **Lysander and Hermia**
  Lysander and Hermia are in love, but Hermia's father wants her to marry Demetrius instead. He appeals to Theseus, who rules that by Athenian law Hermia must marry Demetrius, be sent to a nunnery, or be put to death.
- **Demetrius and Helena**
  Helena, Hermia's best friend, loves Demetrius, who once loved her but now prefers Hermia.
- **Oberon and Titania**
  Oberon is the king of the fairies, and Titania is his queen. Throughout much of the play they are involved in a feud.

The complications begin when Lysander and Hermia flee Athens into the forest. Demetrius follows Hermia, and Helena follows Demetrius. There the fairy king Oberon instructs his servant Puck to sort out the lovers' problems with the aid of magic drops from a flower. However, a case of mistaken identity causes Lysander and Demetrius both to love Helena instead of Hermia. Oberon then has Puck remove the spell from Lysander, who once again loves Hermia. Demetrius now loves Helena, as he once had before. Theseus and Hermia's father agree to let the young people marry their sweethearts, and everyone is happy.

The Play Within the Play

How does *Pyramus and Thisbe* fit into the plot? A group of local tradespeople decide to put on the play for Theseus and Hippolyta's wedding. They rehearse in the forest, where they, too, are swept up in Oberon and Titania's quarrel. At the end, when all is right again, they perform the play for the duke, his new wife, and the happy couples. The tradespeople are awful actors, and their rehearsals and performance provide much of the play's humor.

Reading the Selection

Take a look at the selection. You'll see that the play has been converted into a graphic story. The pictures will help you to understand what is happening. You'll also notice that each frame has two colors of text. Shakespeare's original text is in black. The green text is a modern English translation, or paraphrase. Use the green text to help you understand the original—not to replace it. If you don't read the original text, you'll miss both the beauty and humor of Shakespeare's language. Finally, remember that Theseus's, Hippolyta's, and their guests' remarks are also an important part of the play.

Read with a Purpose Read to enjoy a performance given for a duke named Theseus. Shakespeare's original verse appears in black type. A paraphrase of the lines appears in green type.

Pyramus and Thisbe

from A Midsummer Night's Dream, Act 5, Scene 1

by **William Shakespeare**

edited, with a modern English translation and illustrated by **Simon Greaves**

Characters (in the order in which they speak)

THESEUS
duke of Athens, now married to Hippolyta

PHILOSTRATE
master of revels to the Athenian court

HIPPOLYTA
queen of the Amazons, now married to Theseus

PETER QUINCE
a carpenter who speaks the prologue

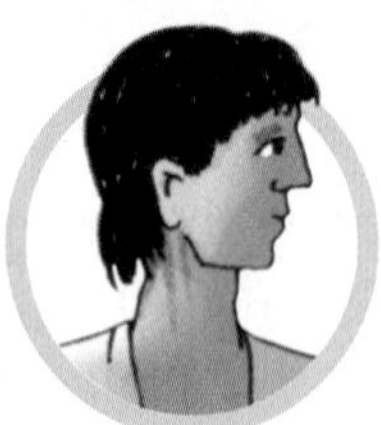

LYSANDER
an Athenian lord, now married to Hermia

DEMETRIUS
an Athenian lord, now married to Helena

FRANCIS FLUTE
a bellows-mender who plays Thisbe

NICK BOTTOM
a weaver who plays Pyramus

TOM SNOUT
a tinker who plays Wall

SNUG
a joiner who plays Lion

ROBIN STARVELING
a tailor who plays Moonshine

It is the evening after the weddings of Theseus and Hippolyta, Lysander and Hermia, and Demetrius and Helena. Theseus asks Philostrate what entertainments have been arranged.

The four lovers arrive and Theseus calls Philostrate to find out what entertainments have been arranged.

Say, what abridgment have you for this evening?
What masque? What music? How shall we beguile
The lazy time, if not with some delight?

Tell me what you have to pass the time this evening. What play? What music? How shall we spend our spare time, if not with something pleasant?

There is a brief how many sports are ripe:
Make choice of which your Highness will see first.

Here is a list of the entertainments ready for you. Please choose which you'd like to see first.

Theseus reads through the list of acts, but doesn't like any of them. Then he comes across the play about Pyramus and Thisbe.

'A tedious brief scene of young Pyramus
And his love Thisbe; very tragical mirth.'
Merry and tragical? Tedious and brief?
This is hot ice and wondrous strange snow!
How shall we find the concord of this discord?

'An over-long, short play about Pyramus and his love Thisbe: a very funny tragedy.'
Funny and tragic? Long and short? This is like hot ice or snow in midsummer! Is it possible to find sanity in this insanity?

A

 **Read and Discuss** What is Theseus doing here?

Vocabulary **tedious** (TEE dee uhs) *adj.:* long and boring.

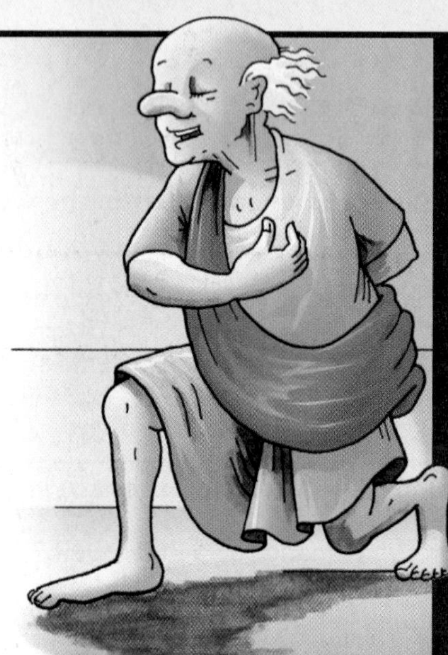

A play there is, my lord, some ten words long,
Which is as brief as I have known a play:
But by ten words, my lord, it is too long,
Which makes it tedious. For in all the play
There is not one word apt, one player fitted.
And tragical, my noble lord, it is,
For Pyramus doth therein kill himself.
Which, when I saw rehearsed, I must confess,
Made mine eyes water; but more merry tears
The passion of loud laughter never shed.
The play, my lord, is about ten words long - which is as short a play as I've come across, but that's still ten words too many, making it way too long. There's not a single good word in the play, or one actor suited to his part.
It's called a tragedy, my lord, in that Pyramus kills himself. And when I saw the play in rehearsal, I have to say I cried - but no-one has ever cried tears of such helpless laughter.

We will hear it.
We'll have it.
No, my noble lord;
It is not for you. I have heard it over,
And it is nothing, nothing in the world;
Unless you can find sport in their intents,
Extremely stretched, and conned with cruel pain,
To do you service.
No, my lord, it's not for you. I've heard it read and it's useless, complete rubbish - unless you find funny all the hard work they've put into the play to please you.

I will hear that play;
For never anything can be amiss,
When simpleness and duty tender it.
Go, bring them in.
I'll watch that play. For nothing can ever be too bad, when done without fuss and a wish to please. Go and fetch them.
Philostrate leaves to find the actors.
I love not to see wretchedness o'ercharged,
And duty in his service perishing.
I hate to see people made fools of, when they're trying to do their best.
Why, gentle sweet, you shall see no such thing.
Why, my love, you'll see no such thing.

B Reading Focus Reading Aloud First, read Shakespeare's text in black. Then, read the paraphrase in green type to be sure you understand what is being said. Finally, read the original version aloud. How does reading aloud add to your appreciation of the passage?

He says they can do nothing in this kind.
He says they're hopeless.
The kinder we, to give them thanks for nothing.
Our sport shall be to take what they mistake;
And what poor duty cannot do, noble respect
Takes it in might, not merit.
That makes us all the kinder, then, for thanking them for nothing. We'll enjoy what they attempt, even if they mess it up. And if it's awful, despite their wish to please, we'll respect their efforts.
Peter Quince arrives with the introduction.
If we offend, it is with our good will.
That you should think, we come not to offend,
But with good will. To show our simple skill,
That is the true beginning of our end.
Consider, then, we come but in despite.
We do not come, as minding to content you,
Our true intent is. All for your delight,
We are not here. That you should here repent you,
The actors are at hand; and, by their show,
You shall know all, that you are like to know.
If we upset you, we mean to. To tell you that we don't want to upset, but please you. All we really want to do, is show off. To show off our simple skills. We're here to cause pain. We haven't come to please you. What we want to do is. For your pleasure, we are not here. That you should take pity on yourselves, because the actors are now here. You'll find out all you need to know about the play.

C

This fellow doth not stand upon points.[1]
This man doesn't have any idea about full stops.
He hath rid his prologue like a rough colt; he knows not the stop.
He's read through his introduction like a man on a wild young horse - he doesn't have any control.

1. **points / full stops:** periods (the punctuation marks).

C **Read and Discuss** What does this conversation between Hippolyta and Theseus show us?

Vocabulary **merit** (MEHR iht) *n.:* worth.

Bottom and the other actors arrive. They act the whole play in mime, as Peter reads aloud.

Gentles, perchance you wonder at this show;
But wonder on, till truth make all things plain.
This man is Pyramus, if you would know;
This beauteous lady Thisbe is certain.
This man, with lime and roughcast, doth present
Wall, that vile wall which did these lovers sunder;
And through Wall's chink, poor souls, they are content
To whisper. At the which let no man wonder.
This man, with lanthorn, dog, and bush of thorn,
Presenteth Moonshine; for, if you will know,
By moonshine did these lovers think no scorn
To meet at Ninus' tomb, there, there to woo.
This grisly beast, which Lion hight by name,
The trusty Thisbe, coming first by night,
Did scare away, or rather did affright;
And, as she fled, her mantle she did fall,
Which Lion vile with bloody mouth did stain.
Anon comes Pyramus, sweet youth and tall,
And finds his trusty Thisbe's mantle slain:
Whereat, with blade, with bloody blameful blade,
He bravely broached his boiling bloody breast;
And Thisbe, tarrying in mulberry shade,
His dagger drew, and died. For all the rest,
Let Lion, Moonshine, Wall, and lovers twain
At large discourse, while here they do remain. D

It maybe you're wondering what this show's about - but keep guessing until all's been explained. This man is Pyramus, and this beautiful lady is Thisbe. This man, covered in plaster stands for the wall - that horrible wall that kept the lovers apart. All they can do is whisper to each other through a hole in the wall. Which shouldn't surprise anyone. This man, with the lantern, dog and thorn bush is the moon - for it was by moonlight that the two lovers were brave enough to meet one another at a tomb. This frightening animal, called Lion, scared Thisbe (who arrived first, at night). As she ran away, she dropped her shawl, which the lion stained with its bloody mouth. Pyramus, a tall, sweet young man, comes along later. He finds Thisbe's bloody shawl, and thinking her dead, bravely kills himself with a blade to his bloody breast. Thisbe had been waiting in a wood. On Pyramus' death, she takes his knife and stabs herself to death. Let Lion, Moonshine, Wall and the two lovers tell you the rest, while here on stage.

I wonder if the lion be to speak?

I wonder if the lion gets to say anything?

No wonder, my lord. One lion may, when many asses do.

Don't be surprised if it does, my lord. Why shouldn't one lion speak, when so many asses do?

D **Reading Focus** **Reading Aloud** Read aloud the original text beginning with, "Anon comes Pyramus." What is the effect of Shakespeare's language—especially the alliteration—as you read aloud?

Vocabulary **vile** (vyl) *adj.:* very unpleasant.

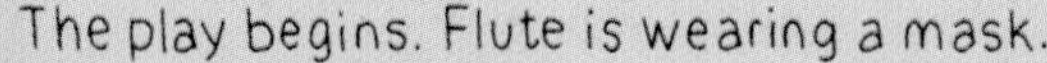
The play begins. Flute is wearing a mask.

O wall, full often hast thou heard my moans,
 For parting my fair Pyramus and me!
My cherry lips have often kissed thy stones,
 Thy stones with lime and hair knit up in thee.

O wall, you've often heard me complain at you for keeping me from my love, Pyramus. My red lips have often kissed your stones - stones held together with lime and hair.

I see a voice; now will I to the chink,
To spy and I can hear my Thisbe's face.
Thisbe!

I see a voice. I'll go to the gap in the wall and look through, so I can hear Thisbe's face. Thisbe!

Bottom looks through a gap in the wall made by Snout's two fingers.

My love thou art, my love I think.

My love? You are my love, I think.

Think what thou wilt, I am thy lover's grace.

You can think what you like. I am your lover.

O, kiss me through the hole of this vile wall!

Kiss me through the hole in this horrible wall.

I kiss the wall's hole, not your lips at all.

I'm kissing the wall's hole, not your lips! **E**

E **Literary Focus** **Comedy** How do the text and the illustrations contribute to your appreciation of this comic scene?

F

F Reading Focus **Reading Aloud** Read aloud the text in this and the previous frame, beginning with, "This is the silliest stuff." Use one voice for Hippolyta, and another for Theseus. What does Theseus think of the play? What point is he expressing?

Vocabulary **amend** (uh MEHND) *v.:* make better.

G **Read and Discuss** What is happening in the play within a play? How are Theseus, Hippolyta, and their guests enjoying the performance?

Lion leaves. Pyramus arrives. He finds Thisbe's shawl.
Sweet moon, I thank thee for thy sunny beams...
But mark, poor Knight,
What dreadful dole is here?
Eyes, do you see?
How can it be?
O dainty duck, O dear!
Thy mantle good -
What stained with blood?
Sweet moon, I thank you
for your sunny beams. -
But what's this, poor knight,
What terrible, sad thing is this?
Eyes do you see?
How can this be?
Oh my love! Oh dear!
Your lovely shawl -
What, stained with blood?
Thinking Thisbe eaten by
a lion, Pyramus takes his
sword and stabs himself
in the heart.
Thus die I, thus, thus, thus!
Now am I dead,
Now am I fled...
Tongue, lose thy light;
Moon, take thy flight.
Now die, die, die, die, die.
And so I die.
Now I'm dead,
Now I'm gone.
Tongue, stop talking.
Moon, fly away.
I die, I die, I die!
As Pyramus dies,
the moon leaves.
How chance Moonshine
is gone before Thisbe
comes back and finds
her lover?
How is it the moon has
gone before Thisbe
comes back to find her
lover?
She will find him
by starlight. Here
she comes; and
her passion ends
the play.
She'll find him by
starlight. Here
she comes. Her
big speech will
end the play.
Methinks she
should not use
a long one for
such a Pyramus.
I hope she will
be brief.
I don't think this
Pyramus is worth
a long speech.
I hope it's short.

H **Literary Focus** **Comedy** In this scene, Pyramus kills himself. What makes the scene seem humorous instead of tragic?

Thisbe finds Pyramus.

Dead, dead? A tomb
Must cover thy sweet eyes.
These lily lips,
This cherry nose,
These yellow cowslip cheeks,
Are gone, are gone.
Lovers, make moan.
His eyes were green as leeks.
O Sisters Three,
Come, come to me,
With hands as pale as milk;
Lay them in gore,
Since you have shore
With shears his thread of silk.

Dead? Dead? A tomb
Must cover your sweet eyes.
Your white lips,
Your red nose,
Your bright yellow cheeks,
Are gone, are gone.
Lovers cry out.
His eyes were as green
as leeks.
Sisters of Death
Come to me,
Lay your milky white hands
In his blood,
Since it's you who have cut
The silk thread of his life
with your scissors.

Tongue, not a word.
Come, trusty sword.
Come, blade, my breast imbrue!
And farewell, friends.
Thus Thisbe ends.
Adieu, adieu, adieu.
No more words.
Come, my good sword.
Come, blade -
Stab my breast.
Goodbye, my friends.
My life is at an end.
Goodbye, goodbye.
Moonshine and Lion are left to bury the dead.
Only Moonshine and Lion are left to bury the dead.
Aye, and Wall too.
And there's Wall too.
No, I assure you; the wall is down that parted their fathers. Will it please you to see the epilogue, or to hear a Bergomask dance between two of our company?
No, you're quite wrong. The wall that kept their fathers apart has been pulled down. Would you like to see a few last words, or hear a country dance put on by two of us?

No epilogue, I pray you; for your play needs no excuse. Never excuse; for when the players are all dead, there need none to be blamed. Marry, if he that writ it had played Pyramus and hanged himself in Thisbe's garter, it would have been a fine tragedy: and so it is truly, and very notably discharged... Let your epilogue alone. I

No closing words, please, for your play needs no apologies - when all the actors are dead, there's no-one left to blame anyway. If the writer of it had also played Pyramus and then hanged himself with Thisbe's garter, that would have been a fine tragedy - as of course it was. And very well acted - so don't worry about final words.

I **Read and Discuss** What does Theseus mean when he says, "No epilogue, I pray you, for your play needs no excuse"?

CULTURE LINK

Illustration (detail) from Ovid's *Metamorphosis* (1479).

A Tale Told Time and Again

Shakespeare did not invent the story of Pyramus and Thisbe. Instead, he based his play within a play on an ancient Greek Myth, which he probably read in *Metamorphosis,* a book by the Roman writer Ovid. In fact, there are many versions of this tale. Shakespeare himself told the tale again, in *Romeo and Juliet,* which became the basis for other new plays. *The Fantasticks* and *West Side Story* are popular musical adaptations. Artists throughout the years have also depicted the story. The painting you see here dates from the fifteenth century—even before Shakespeare wrote his plays.

Ask Yourself

How are the details in this painting of Pyramus and Thisbe like or unlike those in the play you have just read?

Applying Your Skills

RA.L.8.6 Explain how an author's choice of genre affects the expression of a theme or topic. RP.8.1 Apply reading comprehension strategies, including making predictions, comparing and contrasting, recalling and summarizing and making inferences and drawing conclusions. *Also covered* **WA.8.1.a; WA.8.1.b**

Pyramus and Thisbe

Respond and Think Critically

Reading Focus

Quick Check

1. Why does Thisbe run away at Ninus's Tomb?
2. Why does Pyramus kill himself?

Read with a Purpose

3. How well did you enjoy the play within a play? Give details from *Pyramus and Thisbe* along with the reasons for your opinion.

Reading Skills: Visualizing and Reading Aloud

4. Review your visualizing chart. Choose the image you find most humorous, and make a sketch of what you visualized.

Lines from the Play	What I Visualize
O, kiss me through the hole of this vile wall!	The two lovers awkwardly try to push their faces through the small hole in the wall.

5. Which part of the play do you find the most fun to read aloud? Explain your choice.

Literary Focus

Literary Analysis

6. **Infer** Why do you think Theseus insists on seeing the play, even when he is warned that it is bad?
7. **Interpret** Do you think Peter Quince expresses what he means to say in his introduction on page 821? Why or why not?
8. **Make Judgments** Do you think that the actors are trying to be funny? Explain.
9. **Evaluate** What do you think of the dramatic device of a play within a play? Did you find the back and forth between the action of the play, explanations by the actors, and commentary by the onstage audience to be humorous or merely confusing? Explain.

Literary Skills: Comedy

10. **Analyze** How does Shakespeare bring humor to what should be such a sad story? Give details from the play in your response.

Literary Skills Review: Plot

11. **Analyze** *Pyramus and Thisbe* is a play within a play; it tells a story separate from the story of the main play, *A Midsummer Night's Dream.* Trace the plot events of *Pyramus and Thisbe* to be sure you understand what story it tells.

Writing Focus

Think as a Reader/Writer

Use It in Your Writing Review the notes you took about **doggerel,** bad poetic verse. Follow the example of the great bard, and write four to six lines of doggerel yourself.

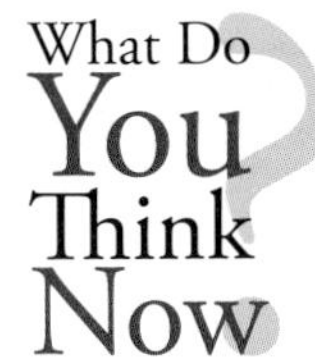

How has Theseus's reaction to *Pyramus and Thisbe* affected your appreciation of a sincere effort?

Applying Your Skills

Pyramus and Thisbe

Vocabulary Development

Vocabulary Check

Complete each sentence using one of the Vocabulary words below.

tedious merit vile amend

1. Kiera played a ________ character who betrays her friends.
2. Though not long, the play was still ________.
3. The play was too boring, so the producer asked the writer to ________ it.
4. It is a reviewer's job to decide whether a play has ________.

Vocabulary Skills: The History of English

Shakespeare wrote his plays more than four hundred years ago, using what is now called Early Modern English. Although this form of the language is similar to ours, it uses many words that are today considered **archaic**—words that are rarely used or whose meanings have changed.

Your Turn

Find the location of these archaic words in the play and use the adapted text in green to infer their meanings. For more help, use a dictionary.

Archaic Word	Location in Play	Meaning
amiss	p. 820, frame 3	wrong
sunder	p. 822, line 6	
hight	p. 822, line 13	
twain	p. 822, line 24	

Language Coach

Archaic Language Along with the verb forms that go with the second-person pronoun *thou,* Early Modern English contains other forms that are no longer used.

For example, many third-person verbs in the present tense end in *–th.* Look at the following examples. Then, write the modern form of each italicized archaic word.

1. Pyramus *doth* go to meet Thisbe at Ninus's Tomb.
2. Thisbe *hath* a shawl that the lion bloodies.
3. Snout *presenteth* a hole in the wall between his two fingers.

Academic Vocabulary

Talk About . . .

With a partner, discuss how Shakespeare's use of language contributes to the humor of the scene. How does the use of language affect the ways the characters express themselves?

C.8.9 Deliver formal and informal descriptive presentations that convey relevant information and descriptive details. **WC.8.3** Grammar and Usage: Use all eight parts of speech. *Also covered* **VO.8.7; VO.8.5**

Grammar Link

Sentence Structure: Inversion

Typically, the parts of a sentence come in a certain order.

Subject	Verb	Object
Snug	took	the part.

Shakespeare doesn't always follow this rule. Sometimes he uses **inversion**—in which some elements of a sentence are inverted, or switched around. One reason he uses inversion is for effect. For instance, instead of having Hippolyta say, "I don't love to see wretchedness o'ercharged," Shakespeare highlights her distaste by inverting the verb and adverb: "I love not to see wretchedness o'ercharged." The inversion puts the stress on the word *not*. Another reason for Shakespeare's inversions is to make his sentences fit the rhythm of his verse or to make lines rhyme.

Your Turn

Writing Applications Each of the following sentences from the play includes inversion. First identify the inverted words or phrases in each sentence. Then, rewrite the sentences using standard sentence structure.

1. "A play there is, my lord, some ten words long."
2. "The kinder we, to give them thanks for nothing."
3. "This beauteous lady Thisbe is certain."
4. "Thus have I, Wall, my part discharged so."
5. "This is the silliest stuff that ever I heard."

CHOICES

As you respond to the Choices, use these **Academic Vocabulary** words as appropriate: contribute to, insight, evident, and express.

REVIEW

Write a Review

Timed Writing Write a review of *Pyramus and Thisbe* as if you were Theseus telling a friend who was not there about the performance. Comment on both the acting and the writing. End your review with Theseus's recommendation about whether or not his friend should see the play.

CONNECT

Design a Graphic Story

TechFocus Using storyboard software, design a graphic version of a scene from your favorite comedy. Plan how many panels you will need. Then, draw the cartoons, putting the words in thought bubbles. You can also add descriptions of the action in text below the panels.

EXTEND

View and Review the Play

Listening and Speaking With a group of classmates, arrange to view one of the movie adaptations of *A Midsummer Night's Dream*. After you watch the film, discuss how well the *Pyramus and Thisbe* segment worked in the film version. Was the humor of the play more evident in the film or in the graphic version you just read? Support your ideas.

DRAMA

Preparing to Read

The Diary of Anne Frank

by **Frances Goodrich** and **Albert Hackett**

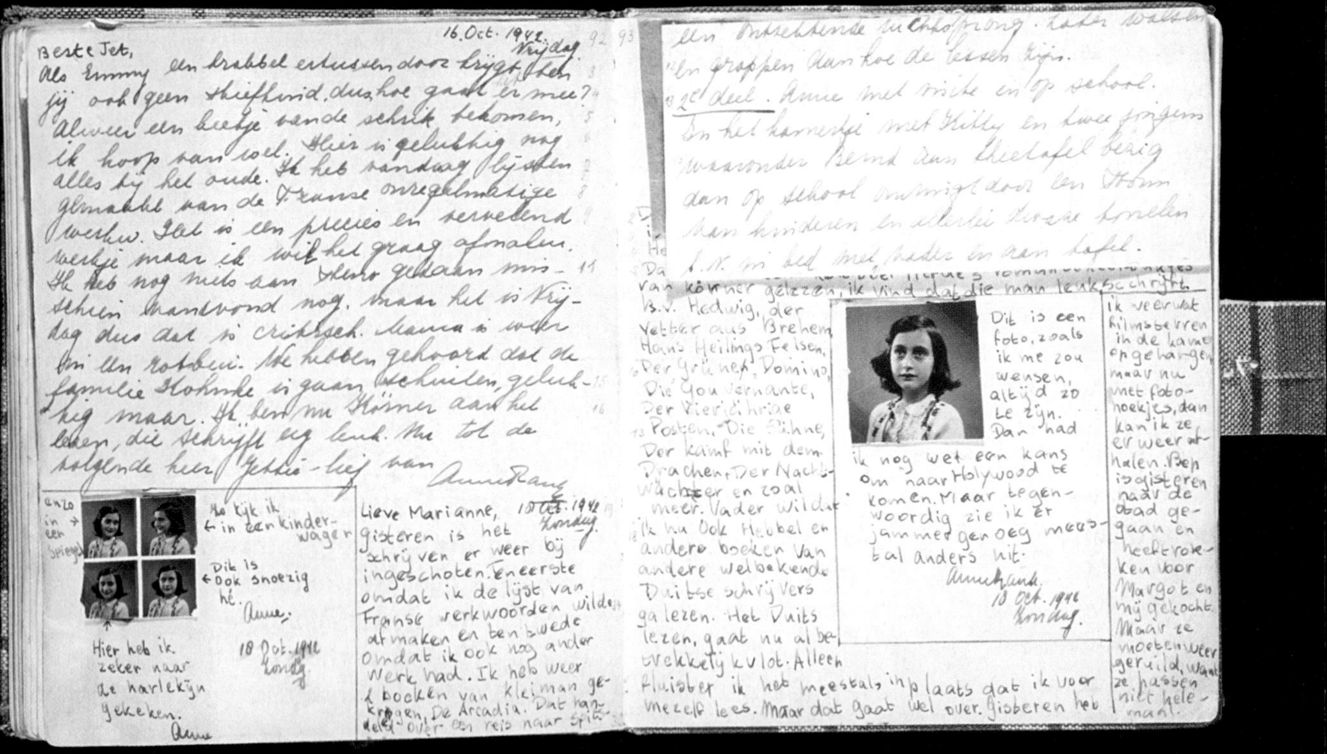

Pages from Anne Frank's diary, written in 1942.

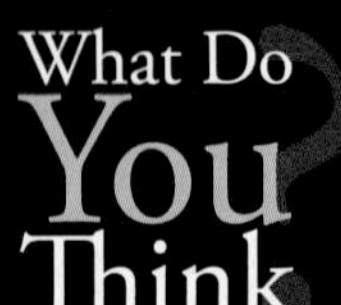

How can you make the best of a bad situation?

QuickTalk

In a small group, discuss times when you each had to do something you didn't want to do, yet "rose to the occasion" and made the best of it. What skills did you draw on to make your situation tolerable?

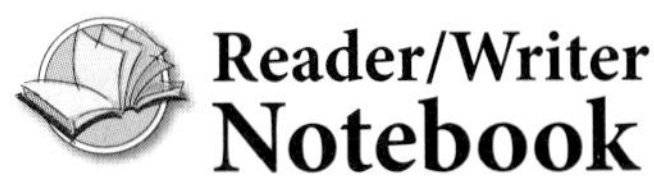

Reader/Writer Notebook

Use your **RWN** to complete the activities for this selection.

RA.L.8.6 Explain how an author's choice of genre affects the expression of a theme or topic. **RP.8.1** Apply reading comprehension strategies, including making predictions, comparing and contrasting, recalling and summarizing and making inferences and drawing conclusions.

Literary Focus

Elements of Drama A **drama** is a work of literature that is performed by actors for an audience. Key features of a dramatic script include **dialogue,** the lines the characters speak, and **stage directions,** which describe what is happening on stage. Like most literature, drama focuses on a set of characters that have problems, or **conflicts.** Over the course of the play, the characters try to solve those problems. The main parts of a drama are **exposition** (characters and setting are established), **complications** (conflicts arise), **climax** (the conflict reaches its most suspenseful moment), and **resolution** (the conflict is resolved).

Literary Perspective Apply the literary perspective described on page 841 as you read this play.

Reading Focus

Making Inferences When you read dramas, you **make inferences**, or informed guesses, about the characters' personalities and why they act as they do. To make an inference, look for text clues and connect what the text says to what you know about life.

Into Action Use a chart like this one to record the inferences you make as you read *The Diary of Anne Frank.*

What the Text Says	My Connections	My Inferences
Miep tries to comfort Mr. Frank.	Friends often try to help in times of suffering.	Miep is a good friend to Mr. Frank.

Writing Focus

Think as a Reader/Writer

Find It in Your Reading A play consists of **dialogue,** or conversations between two or more characters. As you read, make notes in your *Reader/Writer Notebook* about what the dialogue reveals about the characters.

Vocabulary

conspicuous (kuhn SPIHK yoo uhs) *adj.:* noticeable. *The Nazis required Jews to wear a conspicuous yellow Star of David.*

indignantly (ihn DIHG nuhnt lee) *adv.:* with anger caused by something felt to be unjust. *Anne indignantly claimed that she had not been rude.*

tyranny (TIHR uh nee) *n.:* absolute power used unjustly. *The tyranny of the Nazis caused many Jewish families to flee.*

ostentatiously (ahs tehn TAY shuhs lee) *adv.:* in a showy way. *Mrs. Van Daan ostentatiously wore a fur coat in July.*

forlorn (fawr LAWRN) *adj.:* abandoned and lonely. *Without her friends, Anne felt forlorn.*

Language Coach

Suffixes The suffix *–ly* usually signals that a word is an adverb. Adverbs describe how, where, when, or to what extent. Which two Vocabulary words above are adverbs? Use each one in a sentence.

Learn It Online

For a preview of this play, see the video introduction on:

go.hrw.com L8-833 

MEET THE WRITER

Frances Goodrich
(1890–1984)

Albert Hackett
(1900–1995)

Together Onstage and Off

Authors Frances Goodrich and Albert Hackett both started out as actors. They began writing plays and screenplays together and were married soon after. Working at desks facing in opposite directions in the same room, they would each write a version of a scene, then read and comment on the other's version before revising. In this way, Goodrich and Hackett created the scripts for many hit movies, including *Easter Parade, Father of the Bride,* and *It's a Wonderful Life.*

The Making of a Masterpiece

The Diary of Anne Frank, a work totally different from Goodrich and Hackett's other writing, is considered their masterpiece. Before they wrote the play, they spent ten days in Amsterdam visiting the Secret Annex and questioning Otto Frank on his memories. It took them two years and eight drafts to complete the play, which opened on Broadway in 1955 to great acclaim. The play won a Pulitzer Prize in 1956 and has since been performed countless times in countries around the world.

Think About the Writers Why do you think the writers put so much effort into this play?

Preview the Selection

Anne Frank and her family fled the Nazis in 1942 and went into hiding. Each day they lived in fear of being discovered and deported to a concentration camp. During her time in hiding, Anne Frank kept a diary in which she described the events of daily life and expressed her feelings and ideas. Her once-private words became public after the end of World War II and have since inspired millions of readers and audiences around the world.

This play is based on the events Anne described, and even includes some passages from the diary.

Build Background

I hope I shall be able to confide in you completely, as I have never been able to do in anyone before, and I hope that you will be a great support and comfort to me.

So begins the diary of a thirteen-year-old Jewish girl named Anne Frank. Anne's diary opens in 1942 with stories of boyfriends, parties, and school life. It closes two years later, just days before Anne is captured and imprisoned in a Nazi concentration camp.

Anne Frank was born in Frankfurt, Germany, in 1929. When she was four years old, her family immigrated to Amsterdam, the Netherlands, to escape the anti-Jewish measures being introduced in Germany. In Amsterdam, Otto Frank, Anne's father, managed a company that sold pectin, a substance used in making jams and jellies. Anne and her older sister, Margot, enjoyed a happy, carefree childhood until May 1940, when the Netherlands capitulated (surrendered) to the invading German army. Anne wrote in her diary about the Nazi occupation that followed:

After May 1940, good times rapidly fled: first the war, then the capitulation, followed by the arrival of the Germans, which is when the sufferings of us Jews really began. Anti-Jewish decrees followed each other in quick succession. Jews must wear a yellow star, Jews must hand in their bicycles, Jews are banned from trains and are forbidden to drive. Jews are only allowed to do their shopping between three and five o'clock and then only in shops which bear the placard "Jewish shop." Jews must be indoors by eight o'clock and cannot even sit in their own gardens after that hour. Jews are forbidden to visit theaters, cinemas, and other places of entertainment. Jews may not take part in public sports. Swimming baths, tennis courts, hockey fields, and other sports grounds are all prohibited to them. Jews may not visit Christians. Jews must go to Jewish schools, and many more restrictions of a similar kind.

So we could not do this and were forbidden to do that. But life went on in spite of it all.

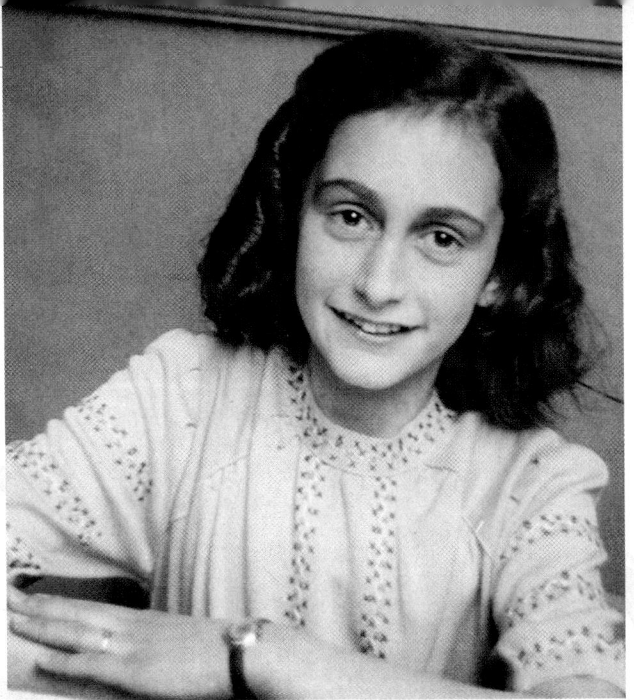

Anne Frank, 1942.

Soon, however, the situation in the Netherlands grew worse. As in other German-occupied countries, the Nazis began rounding up Jews and transporting them to concentration camps and death camps, where prisoners died from overwork, starvation, or disease, or were murdered in gas chambers. Escaping Nazi-occupied territory became nearly impossible. Like many

Analyzing Visuals **Viewing and Interpreting** What do the photo and map reveal about the Franks' situation?

Nazis arresting Jewish families in the Warsaw Ghetto, Poland, 1943.

other Jews trapped in Europe at the time, Anne and her family went into hiding to avoid capture. Others were not so lucky, as Anne knew:

> *Countless friends and acquaintances have gone to a terrible fate. Evening after evening the green and gray army lorries [trucks] trundle past. The Germans ring at every front door to inquire if there are any Jews living in the house. If there are, then the whole family has to go at once. If they don't find any, they go on to the next house. No one has a chance of evading them unless one goes into hiding. Often they go around with lists and only ring when they know they can get a good haul. Sometimes they let them off for cash—so much per head. It seems like the slave hunts of olden times. . . . In the evenings when it's dark, I often see rows of good, innocent people accompanied by crying children, walking on and on, in the charge of a couple of these chaps, bullied and knocked about until they almost drop. No one is spared—old people, babies, expectant mothers, the sick—each and all join in the march of death.*

The Frank family and four other Jews lived for more than two years hidden in a few cramped rooms (now known as the Secret Annex) behind Mr. Frank's office and warehouse. In August 1944, the Nazi police raided their hiding place and sent all eight of its occupants to concentration camps. Of the eight, only Otto Frank survived. Anne died of typhus in a camp in Germany called Bergen-Belsen. She was fifteen years old.

When she began her diary, Anne didn't intend to show it to anyone unless she found a "real friend." Through its dozens of translations and the stage adaptation you are about to read, Anne's diary has found her generations of friends all over the world.

ANNE FRANK'S LIFE / WORLD EVENTS

1929

Anne Frank's Life — June 12: Anne Frank is born in Frankfurt, Germany.

1930 to 1932

World Events: The National Socialist German Workers' (Nazi) party begins its rise to power. The Nazis proclaim the superiority of the German "master race" and blame Jews for the German defeat in World War I and for the troubled economy.

Adolf Hitler

1933

Anne Frank's Life: The Franks decide to leave Germany to escape Nazi persecution. While Mr. Frank looks for a new home in Amsterdam, the Netherlands, the rest of the family stays with relatives in Aachen, Germany.

World Events:

January 30: The Nazi party leader, Adolf Hitler, becomes chancellor (head of the government) of Germany.

March 10: The first concentration camp is established by the Nazis at Dachau, Germany.

April: The Nazis pass their first anti-Jewish law, banning the public employment of Jews.

Anne with her father at Miep Santrouschitz and Jan Gies's wedding.

1934

1935

World Events — September 15: The Nuremberg Laws are passed, denying Jews German citizenship and forbidding marriage between Jews and non-Jews.

1936

World Events — October 25: Germany and Italy form an alliance (the Axis).

1937

Anne Frank's Life — Summer: The Van Pels family (called the Van Daans in Anne's diary) flee Germany for the Netherlands.

1938

Anne Frank's Life — December 8: Fritz Pfeffer (called Albert Dussel in Anne's diary) flees Germany for the Netherlands.

Anne playing with her friend Sanne Ledermann in Amsterdam The Granger Collection, New York.

World Events:

March 12–13: The German army invades and annexes Austria.

September 29: The Munich Agreement, granting Germany the right to annex part of Czechoslovakia, is drafted and signed by representatives of France, Great Britain, Italy, and Germany.

November 9–10: Kristallnacht (Night of the Broken Glass). Led by the SS, the Nazi special police, Germans beat and kill Jews, loot Jewish stores, and burn synagogues.

ANNE FRANK'S LIFE

WORLD EVENTS

Anne, second from left, with friends on her tenth birthday.
The Granger Collection, New York.

1939

World Events

March: Germany invades and occupies most of Czechoslovakia.

September 1: Germany invades Poland; World War II begins. France and Great Britain declare war on Germany two days later.

1940

World Events

Spring: Germany invades Denmark, Norway, the Netherlands, Belgium, Luxembourg, and France.

September 27: Japan joins the Axis.

1941

World Events

June 22: Germany invades the Soviet Union.

December: The United States enters the war on the side of the Allied nations (including Great Britain, the Soviet Union, and other countries) after Japan attacks the U.S. naval base at Pearl Harbor in Hawaii.

1942

Anne Frank's Life

June 12: Anne receives a diary for her thirteenth birthday.

July 6: The Franks go into hiding after Margot receives an order to appear for deportation to a labor camp in Germany. The Van Pels family joins them one week later.

November 16: Fritz Pfeffer becomes the eighth occupant of the Secret Annex.

World Events

January: The "Final Solution" is secretly announced at a conference of Nazi officials: Europe's Jews are to be "exterminated," or murdered. Construction of death camps begins in Poland. Millions of people (Jews and non-Jews) will die in those camps.

1943

1944

Anne Frank's Life

August 4: Nazi police raid the Secret Annex; the occupants are sent to concentration camps.

September: Mr. Van Pels dies in Auschwitz.

December 20: Fritz Pfeffer dies in Neuengamme.

World Events

June 6: D-day. Allied forces land in Normandy, in northern France, and launch an invasion of western Europe.

1945

Anne Frank's Life

Anne's mother, Edith Frank, dies in Auschwitz. Three weeks later Otto Frank is freed when Auschwitz is liberated by the Soviet army. Anne and Margot die in Bergen-Belsen a few weeks before British soldiers liberate the camp. Peter Van Pels dies in Mauthausen. Mrs. Van Pels dies in Theresienstadt.

World Events

May 8: The war in Europe ends with Germany's unconditional surrender to the Allies.

September 2: Japan surrenders after the United States drops atomic bombs on the Japanese cities of Hiroshima and Nagasaki. World War II ends one week later.

Bombing of Nagasaki.

Read with a Purpose Read this play to discover how Anne Frank's wartime experiences affect her view of the world.

The Diary of Anne Frank

by **Frances Goodrich** and **Albert Hackett**

CHARACTERS

Occupants of the Secret Annex:		Workers in Mr. Frank's Business:
Anne Frank	**Peter Van Daan**	**Miep Gies,**[1] a young Dutchwoman
Margot Frank, her older sister	**Mr. Van Daan,** his father	**Mr. Kraler,**[2] a Dutchman
Mr. Frank, their father	**Mrs. Van Daan,** his mother	
Mrs. Frank, their mother	**Mr. Dussel,** a dentist	

Setting: Amsterdam, the Netherlands, July 1942 to August 1944; November 1945.

ACT ONE

SCENE 1

The scene remains the same throughout the play. It is the top floor of a warehouse and office building in Amsterdam, Holland. The sharply peaked roof of the building is outlined against a sea of other roof-tops stretching away into the distance. Nearby is the belfry of a church tower, the Westertoren, whose carillon[3] *rings out the hours. Occasionally faint sounds float up from below: the voices of children playing in the street, the tramp of marching feet, a boat whistle from the canal.*[4]

1. **Miep Gies** (meep khees).
2. **Kraler** (KRAH luhr).
3. **carillon** (KAR uh lahn): set of bells, each of which produces a single tone.
4. **canal:** artificial waterway. Amsterdam, which was built on soggy ground, has more than one hundred canals, built to help drain the land. The canals are used like streets.

Analyzing Visuals **Viewing and Interpreting** How can this view of the stage help you visualize the play?

Stage scene showing the Secret Annex in a 1997 stage production of *The Diary of Anne Frank*.

The three rooms of the top floor and a small attic space above are exposed to our view. The largest of the rooms is in the center, with two small rooms, slightly raised, on either side. On the right is a bathroom, out of sight. A narrow, steep flight of stairs at the back leads up to the attic. The rooms are sparsely furnished, with a few chairs, cots, a table or two. The windows are painted over or covered with makeshift blackout curtains. In the main room there is a sink, a gas ring for cooking, and a wood-burning stove for warmth.

The room on the left is hardly more than a closet. There is a skylight in the sloping ceiling. Directly under this room is a small, steep stairwell, with steps leading down to a door. This is the only entrance from the building below. When the door is opened, we see that it has been concealed on the outer side by a bookcase attached to it.

The curtain rises on an empty stage. It is late afternoon, November 1945.

The rooms are dusty, the curtains in rags. Chairs and tables are overturned. **A**

The door at the foot of the small stairwell swings open. MR. FRANK *comes up the steps into view. He is a gentle, cultured European in his middle years. There is still a trace of a German accent in his speech.*

He stands looking slowly around, making a supreme effort at self-control. He is weak, ill. His clothes are threadbare.

A **Literary Focus** **Drama** Stage directions are unique to written plays. They provide information to readers, actors, and directors. What key information about the setting do these stage directions provide?

After a second he drops his rucksack on the couch and moves slowly about. He opens the door to one of the smaller rooms and then abruptly closes it again, turning away. He goes to the window at the back, looking off at the Westertoren as its carillon strikes the hour of six; then he moves restlessly on.

From the street below we hear the sound of a barrel organ and children's voices at play. There is a many-colored scarf hanging from a nail. MR. FRANK *takes it, putting it around his neck. As he starts back for his rucksack, his eye is caught by something lying on the floor. It is a woman's white glove. He holds it in his hand and suddenly all of his self-control is gone. He breaks down crying.*

We hear footsteps on the stairs. MIEP GIES *comes up, looking for* MR. FRANK. MIEP *is a Dutchwoman of about twenty-two. She wears a coat and hat, ready to go home. She is pregnant. Her attitude toward* MR. FRANK *is protective, compassionate.*

Miep. Are you all right, Mr. Frank?
Mr. Frank (*quickly controlling himself*). Yes, Miep, yes.
Miep. Everyone in the office has gone home. . . . It's after six. (*Then, pleading*) Don't stay up here, Mr. Frank. What's the use of torturing yourself like this?
Mr. Frank. I've come to say goodbye. . . . I'm leaving here, Miep.
Miep. What do you mean? Where are you going? Where?
Mr. Frank. I don't know yet. I haven't decided.
Miep. Mr. Frank, you can't leave here! This is your home! Amsterdam is your home. Your business is here, waiting for you. . . . You're needed here. . . . Now that the war is over, there are things that . . .
Mr. Frank. I can't stay in Amsterdam, Miep. It has too many memories for me. Everywhere, there's something . . . the house we lived in . . . the school . . . that street organ playing out there. . . . I'm not the person you used to know, Miep. I'm a bitter old man. (*Breaking off*) Forgive me. I shouldn't speak to you like this . . . after all that you did for us . . . the suffering . . .
Miep. No. No. It wasn't suffering. You can't say we suffered. (*As she speaks, she straightens a chair which is overturned.*)
Mr. Frank. I know what you went through, you and Mr. Kraler. I'll remember it as long as I live. (*He gives one last look around.*) Come, Miep. (*He starts for the steps, then remembers his rucksack, going back to get it.*)

Literary Perspectives

The following perspective will help you relate to and understand this play.

Analyzing Responses to Literature One way to find meaning in what you read is to relate it to your own experiences and knowledge. In addition, you should pay attention to any associations the text brings up in your mind. These connections will add richness and depth to your interpretation of what you read.

As you read *The Diary of Anne Frank,* combine what you already know about World War II, Nazism, and the Holocaust with details presented in the play to better appreciate the seriousness of the Franks' and Van Daans' situation. Also use your knowledge of human nature to enrich your understanding of the characters' motivations and behaviors. As you read, notice the notes and questions in the text, which will guide you in using this perspective.

Miep (*hurrying up to a cupboard*). Mr. Frank, did you see? There are some of your papers here. (*She brings a bundle of papers to him.*) We found them in a heap of rubbish on the floor after . . . after you left.
Mr. Frank. Burn them. (*He opens his rucksack to put the glove in it.*)
Miep. But, Mr. Frank, there are letters, notes . . .
Mr. Frank. Burn them. All of them.
Miep. Burn this? (*She hands him a paperbound notebook.*)
Mr. Frank (*quietly*). Anne's diary. (*He opens the diary and begins to read.*) "Monday, the sixth of July, nineteen forty-two." (*To* MIEP) Nineteen forty-two. Is it possible, Miep? . . .

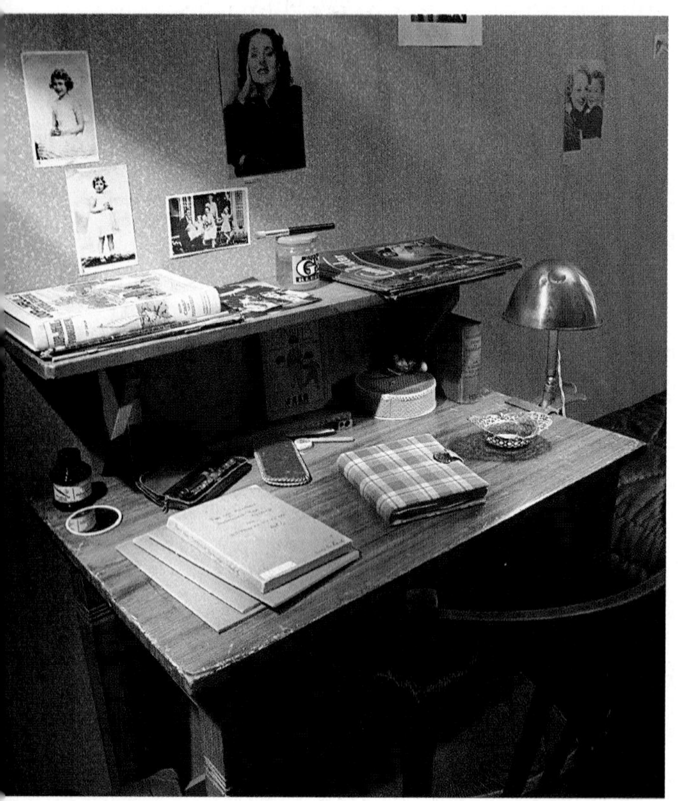

Anne's desk in the Anne Frank House Museum in Amsterdam, set up to look as it did when she and her family hid in the house.

Only three years ago. (*As he continues his reading, he sits down on the couch.*) "Dear Diary, since you and I are going to be great friends, I will start by telling you about myself. My name is Anne Frank. I am thirteen years old. I was born in Germany the twelfth of June, nineteen twenty-nine. As my family is Jewish, we emigrated to Holland when Hitler came to power."

[*As* MR. FRANK *reads on, another voice joins his, as if coming from the air. It is* ANNE*'s voice.*] **B**

Mr. Frank and Anne's Voice. "My father started a business, importing spice and herbs. Things went well for us until nineteen forty. Then the war came, and the Dutch capitulation, followed by the arrival of the Germans. Then things got very bad for the Jews."

[MR. FRANK*'s voice dies out.* ANNE*'s voice continues alone. The lights dim slowly to darkness. The curtain falls on the scene.*]

Anne's Voice. You could not do this and you could not do that. They forced Father out of his business. We had to wear yellow stars.[5] I had to turn in my bike. I couldn't go to a Dutch school anymore. I couldn't go to the movies or ride in an automobile or even on a streetcar, and a million other things. But somehow we children still managed to have

5. **yellow stars:** The Nazis ordered all Jews to sew a large Star of David (a six-pointed star) on their outer clothing so that they could be easily recognized as Jews.

B Literary Focus Drama A voiceover occurs when a character's voice is heard without the character being on stage. How might hearing Anne without seeing her affect an audience watching the play?

fun. Yesterday Father told me we were going into hiding. Where, he wouldn't say. At five o'clock this morning Mother woke me and told me to hurry and get dressed. I was to put on as many clothes as I could. It would look too suspicious if we walked along carrying suitcases. It wasn't until we were on our way that I learned where we were going. Our hiding place was to be upstairs in the building where Father used to have his business. Three other people were coming in with us . . . the Van Daans and their son Peter . . . Father knew the Van Daans but we had never met them . . . **C**

[*During the last lines the curtain rises on the scene. The lights dim on.* ANNE'S *voice fades out.*]

SCENE 2

It is early morning, July 1942. The rooms are bare, as before, but they are now clean and orderly. **D**

MR. VAN DAAN, *a tall, portly man in his late forties, is in the main room, pacing up and down, nervously smoking a cigarette. His clothes and overcoat are expensive and well cut.*

MRS. VAN DAAN *sits on the couch, clutching her possessions: a hatbox, bags, etc. She is a pretty woman in her early forties. She wears a fur coat over her other clothes.*

PETER VAN DAAN *is standing at the window of the room on the right, looking down at the street below. He is a shy, awkward boy of sixteen. He wears a cap, a raincoat, and long Dutch trousers, like plus fours.*[6] *At his feet is a black case, a carrier for his cat.*

The yellow Star of David is conspicuous *on all of their clothes.*

Mrs. Van Daan (rising, nervous, excited). Something's happened to them! I know it!

Mr. Van Daan. Now, Kerli!

Mrs. Van Daan. Mr. Frank said they'd be here at seven o'clock. He said . . .

Mr. Van Daan. They have two miles to walk. You can't expect . . .

Mrs. Van Daan. They've been picked up. That's what's happened. They've been taken . . .

[MR. VAN DAAN *indicates that he hears someone coming.*]

Mr. Van Daan. You see?

[PETER *takes up his carrier and his school bag, etc., and goes into the main room as* MR. FRANK *comes up the stairwell from below.* MR. FRANK *looks much younger now. His movements are brisk, his manner confident. He wears an overcoat and carries his hat and a small cardboard box. He crosses to the* VAN DAANS, *shaking hands with each of them.*]

6. **plus fours:** baggy trousers that end in cuffs just below the knees.

C **Read and Discuss** How have the writers captured our interest in what will happen next?

D **Literary Focus** **Drama** A flashback shows events that happened earlier. What clue in the stage directions tells you that a flashback has begun?

Vocabulary **conspicuous** (kuhn SPIHK yoo uhs) *adj.:* noticeable.

Mr. Frank. Mrs. Van Daan, Mr. Van Daan, Peter. (*Then, in explanation of their lateness*) There were too many of the Green Police[7] on the streets . . . we had to take the long way around.

[*Up the steps come* MARGOT FRANK, MRS. FRANK, MIEP *(not pregnant now), and* MR. KRALER. *All of them carry bags, packages, and so forth. The Star of David is conspicuous on all of the* FRANKS' *clothing.* MARGOT *is eighteen, beautiful, quiet, shy.* MRS. FRANK *is a young mother, gently bred, reserved. She, like* MR. FRANK, *has a slight German accent.* MR. KRALER *is a Dutchman, dependable, kindly.*

As MR. KRALER *and* MIEP *go upstage to put down their parcels,* MRS. FRANK *turns back to call* ANNE.]

Mrs. Frank. Anne?

[ANNE *comes running up the stairs. She is thirteen, quick in her movements, interested in everything, mercurial*[8] *in her emotions. She wears a cape and long wool socks and carries a school bag.*]

Mr. Frank (*introducing them*). My wife, Edith. Mr. and Mrs. Van Daan (MRS. FRANK *hurries over, shaking hands with them.*) . . . their son, Peter . . . my daughters, Margot and Anne.

[ANNE *gives a polite little curtsy as she shakes* MR. VAN DAAN'*s hand. Then she immediately starts off on a tour of investigation of her new home, going upstairs to the attic room.*

MIEP *and* MR. KRALER *are putting the various things they have brought on the shelves.*]

Mr. Kraler. I'm sorry there is still so much confusion.

Mr. Frank. Please. Don't think of it. After all, we'll have plenty of leisure to arrange everything ourselves.

Miep (*to* MRS. FRANK). We put the stores of food you sent in here. Your drugs are here . . . soap, linen here.

Mrs. Frank. Thank you, Miep.

Miep. I made up the beds . . . the way Mr. Frank and Mr. Kraler said. (*She starts out.*) Forgive me. I have to hurry. I've got to go to the other side of town to get some ration books[9] for you.

Mrs. Van Daan. Ration books? If they see our names on ration books, they'll know we're here.

Mr. Kraler. There isn't anything . . .

Miep. Don't worry. Your names won't be on them. (*As she hurries out*) I'll be up later.

} *Together*

Mr. Frank. Thank you, Miep.

Mrs. Frank (*to* MR. KRALER). It's illegal, then, the ration books? We've never done anything illegal.

Mr. Frank. We won't be living here exactly according to regulations.

[*As* MR. KRALER *reassures* MRS. FRANK, *he takes various small things, such as matches and soap, from his pockets, handing them to her.*]

---

7. **Green Police:** Nazi police, who wore green uniforms.
8. **mercurial** (muhr KYOOR ee uhl): changeable.
9. **ration books:** books of stamps or coupons issued by the government during wartime. People could purchase scarce items, such as food, clothing, and gasoline, only with these coupons.

Mr. Kraler. This isn't the black market,[10] Mrs. Frank. This is what we call the white market . . . helping all of the hundreds and hundreds who are hiding out in Amsterdam.

[*The carillon is heard playing the quarter-hour before eight.* MR. KRALER *looks at his watch.* ANNE *stops at the window as she comes down the stairs.*]

Anne. It's the Westertoren!

Mr. Kraler. I must go. I must be out of here and downstairs in the office before the workmen get here. (*He starts for the stairs leading out.*) Miep or I, or both of us, will be up each day to bring you food and news and find out what your needs are. Tomorrow I'll get you a better bolt for the door at the foot of the stairs. It needs a bolt that you can throw yourself and open only at our signal. (*To* MR. FRANK) Oh . . . You'll tell them about the noise?

Mr. Frank. I'll tell them.

Mr. Kraler. Goodbye, then, for the moment. I'll come up again, after the workmen leave.

Mr. Frank. Goodbye, Mr. Kraler.

Mrs. Frank (*shaking his hand*). How can we thank you?

[*The others murmur their goodbyes.*]

Mr. Kraler. I never thought I'd live to see the day when a man like Mr. Frank would have to go into hiding. When you think—

[*He breaks off, going out.* MR. FRANK *follows him down the steps, bolting the door after him. In the interval before he returns,* PETER *goes over to* MARGOT, *shaking hands with her. As* MR. FRANK *comes back up the steps,* MRS. FRANK *questions him anxiously.*]

Mrs. Frank. What did he mean, about the noise?

Mr. Frank. First let us take off some of these clothes.

[*They all start to take off garment after garment. On each of their coats, sweaters, blouses, suits, dresses is another yellow Star of David.* MR. *and* MRS. FRANK *are underdressed quite simply. The others wear several things: sweaters, extra dresses, bathrobes, aprons, nightgowns, etc.*]

Mr. Van Daan. It's a wonder we weren't arrested, walking along the streets . . .

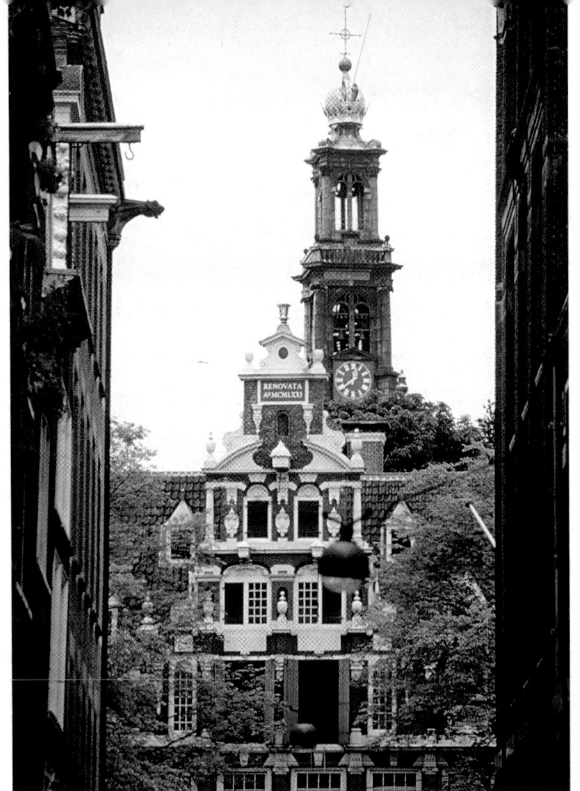

Westerkerk, the church in Amsterdam whose bells Anne hears.

10. **black market:** place or system for buying and selling goods illegally, without ration stamps.

Petronella with a fur coat in July . . . and that cat of Peter's crying all the way.

Anne (*as she is removing a pair of panties*). A cat?

Mrs. Frank (*shocked*). Anne, please!

Anne. It's all right. I've got on three more.

[*She pulls off two more. Finally, as they have all removed their surplus clothes, they look to* MR. FRANK, *waiting for him to speak.*] **E**

Mr. Frank. Now. About the noise. While the men are in the building below, we must have complete quiet. Every sound can be heard down there, not only in the workrooms but in the offices too. The men come at about eight-thirty and leave at about five-thirty. So, to be perfectly safe, from eight in the morning until six in the evening we must move only when it is necessary, and then in stockinged feet. We must not speak above a whisper. We must not run any water. We cannot use the sink or even, forgive me, the w.c.[11] The pipes go down through the workrooms. It would be heard. No trash . . . (MR. FRANK *stops abruptly as he hears the sound of marching feet from the street below. Everyone is motionless, paralyzed with fear.* MR. FRANK *goes quietly into the room on the right to look down out of the window.* ANNE *runs after him, peering out with him. The tramping feet pass without stopping. The tension is relieved.* MR. FRANK, *followed by* ANNE, *returns to the main room and resumes his instructions to the group.*) . . . No trash must ever be thrown out which might reveal that someone is living up here . . . not even a potato paring. We must burn everything in the stove at night. This is the way we must live until it is over, if we are to survive. **F**

[*There is silence for a second.*]

Mrs. Frank. Until it is over.

Mr. Frank (*reassuringly*). After six we can move about . . . we can talk and laugh and have our supper and read and play games . . . just as we would at home. (*He looks at his watch.*) And now I think it would be wise if we all went to our rooms, and we settled before eight o'clock. Mrs. Van Daan, you and your husband will be upstairs. I regret that there's no room for Peter. But he will be here, near us. This will be our common room, where we'll meet to talk and eat and read like one family.

Mr. Van Daan. And where do you and Mrs. Frank sleep?

Mr. Frank. This room is also our bedroom.

Mrs. Van Daan. That isn't right. We'll sleep here and you take the room upstairs. } *Together*

Mr. Van Daan. It's your place. } *Together*

Mr. Frank. Please. I've thought this out for weeks. It's the best arrangement. The only arrangement.

Mrs. Van Daan (*to* MR. FRANK). Never, never can we thank you. (*Then, to* MRS. FRANK) I don't know what would have happened to us, if it hadn't been for Mr. Frank.

11. **w.c.:** short for "water closet," or toilet.

E **Reading Focus** **Making Inferences** Characters in a drama reveal themselves through their actions as well as words. What do Anne's actions reveal about her?

F **Literary Perspectives** **Analyzing Responses** What do your reactions to Mr. Frank's rules tell you about the characters' situation?

Mr. Frank. You don't know how your husband helped me when I came to this country . . . knowing no one . . . not able to speak the language. I can never repay him for that. (*Going to* MR. VAN DAAN) May I help you with your things? **G**

Mr. Van Daan. No. No. (*To* MRS. VAN DAAN) Come along, liefje.[12]

Mrs. Van Daan. You'll be all right, Peter? You're not afraid?

Peter (*embarrassed*). Please, Mother.

[*They start up the stairs to the attic room above.* MR. FRANK *turns to* MRS. FRANK.]

Mr. Frank. You too must have some rest, Edith. You didn't close your eyes last night. Nor you, Margot.

Anne. I slept, Father. Wasn't that funny? I knew it was the last night in my own bed, and yet I slept soundly.

Mr. Frank. I'm glad, Anne. Now you'll be able to help me straighten things in here. (*To* MRS. FRANK *and* MARGOT) Come with me. . . . You and Margot rest in this room for the time being. (*He picks up their clothes, starting for the room on the right.*)

Mrs. Frank. You're sure . . . ? I could help. . . . And Anne hasn't had her milk . . .

Mr. Frank. I'll give it to her. (*To* ANNE *and* PETER) Anne, Peter . . . it's best that you take off your shoes now, before you forget. (*He leads the way to the room, followed by* MARGOT.)

12. **liefje** (LEEF hyuh): Dutch for "little dear one."

Margot and Anne in the stage production. © Joan Marcus.

Mrs. Frank. You're sure you're not tired, Anne?

Anne. I feel fine. I'm going to help Father.

Mrs. Frank. Peter, I'm glad you are to be with us.

Peter. Yes, Mrs. Frank.

[MRS. FRANK *goes to join* MR. FRANK *and* MARGOT.

During the following scene MR. FRANK *helps* MARGOT *and* MRS. FRANK *to hang up their clothes. Then he persuades them both to lie down and rest. The* VAN DAANS, *in their room above, settle themselves. In the main room* ANNE *and* PETER *remove their shoes.* PETER *takes his cat out of the carrier.*]

G **Reading Focus** **Making Inferences** What do these details about Mr. Frank and the Van Daans tell you about them?

Anne. What's your cat's name?
Peter. Mouschi.[13]
Anne. Mouschi! Mouschi! Mouschi! (*She picks up the cat, walking away with it. To* PETER) I love cats. I have one . . . a darling little cat. But they made me leave her behind. I left some food and a note for the neighbors to take care of her. . . . I'm going to miss her terribly. What is yours? A him or a her?
Peter. He's a tom. He doesn't like strangers. (*He takes the cat from her, putting it back in its carrier.*)
Anne (*unabashed*). Then I'll have to stop being a stranger, won't I? Is he fixed?
Peter (*startled*). Huh?
Anne. Did you have him fixed?
Peter. No.
Anne. Oh, you ought to have him fixed—to keep him from—you know, fighting. Where did you go to school?
Peter. Jewish Secondary.
Anne. But that's where Margot and I go! I never saw you around.
Peter. I used to see you . . . sometimes . . .
Anne. You did?
Peter. . . . in the schoolyard. You were always in the middle of a bunch of kids. (*He takes a penknife from his pocket.*)
Anne. Why didn't you ever come over?
Peter. I'm sort of a lone wolf. (*He starts to rip off his Star of David.*)
Anne. What are you doing?
Peter. Taking it off.
Anne. But you can't do that. They'll arrest you if you go out without your star.

[*He tosses his knife on the table.*]

Peter. Who's going out? **H**
Anne. Why, of course! You're right! Of course we don't need them anymore. (*She picks up his knife and starts to take her star off.*) I wonder what our friends will think when we don't show up today?
Peter. I didn't have any dates with anyone.
Anne. Oh, I did. I had a date with Jopie to go and play ping-pong at her house. Do you know Jopie de Waal?[14]
Peter. No.
Anne. Jopie's my best friend. I wonder what she'll think when she telephones and there's no answer? . . . Probably she'll go over to the house. . . . I wonder what she'll think . . . we left everything as if we'd suddenly been called away . . . breakfast dishes in the sink . . . beds not made . . . (*As she pulls off her star, the cloth underneath shows clearly the color and form of the star.*) Look! It's still there! (PETER *goes over to the stove with his star.*) What're you going to do with yours?
Peter. Burn it.
Anne (*she starts to throw hers in, and cannot*). It's funny, I can't throw mine away. I don't know why. **I**
Peter. You can't throw . . . ? Something they

13. **Mouschi** (MOO shee).

14. **Jopie de Waal** (YOH pee duh VAHL).

H **Reading Focus** **Making Inferences** What do Peter's words and actions tell you about him?

I **Literary Focus** **Drama** Conflict in a drama may occur between two characters or within a character's mind. What conflict does Anne feel here?

branded you with . . . ? That they made you wear so they could spit on you?

Anne. I know. I know. But after all, it is the Star of David, isn't it?

[*In the bedroom, right,* MARGOT *and* MRS. FRANK *are lying down.* MR. FRANK *starts quietly out.*]

Peter. Maybe it's different for a girl.

[MR. FRANK *comes into the main room.*]

Mr. Frank. Forgive me, Peter. Now let me see. We must find a bed for your cat. (*He goes to a cupboard.*) I'm glad you brought your cat. Anne was feeling so badly about hers. (*Getting a used small washtub*) Here we are. Will it be comfortable in that?

Peter (*gathering up his things*). Thanks.

Mr. Frank (*opening the door of the room on the left*). And here is your room. But I warn you, Peter, you can't grow anymore. Not an inch, or you'll have to sleep with your feet out of the skylight. Are you hungry?

Peter. No.

Mr. Frank. We have some bread and butter.

Peter. No, thank you.

Mr. Frank. You can have it for luncheon then. And tonight we will have a real supper . . . our first supper together.

Peter. Thanks. Thanks. (*He goes into his room. During the following scene he arranges his possessions in his new room.*)

I've never had a diary. And I've always longed for one.

Mr. Frank. That's a nice boy, Peter.

Anne. He's awfully shy, isn't he?

Mr. Frank. You'll like him, I know.

Anne. I certainly hope so, since he's the only boy I'm likely to see for months and months.

[MR. FRANK *sits down, taking off his shoes.*]

Mr. Frank. Annele,[15] there's a box there. Will you open it?

[*He indicates a carton on the couch.* ANNE *brings it to the center table. In the street below, there is the sound of children playing.*]

Anne (*as she opens the carton*). You know the way I'm going to think of it here? I'm going to think of it as a boardinghouse. A very peculiar summer boardinghouse, like the one that we— (*She breaks off as she pulls out some photographs.*) Father! My movie stars! I was wondering where they were! I was looking for them this morning . . . and Queen Wilhelmina![16] How wonderful!

Mr. Frank. There's something more. Go on. Look further. (*He goes over to the sink, pouring a glass of milk from a thermos bottle.*)

Anne (*pulling out a pasteboard-bound book*). A diary! (*She throws her arms around her father.*) I've never had a diary. And I've

15. **Annele** (AHN uh luh): Yiddish for "little Anne" (like "Annie").

16. **Queen Wilhelmina** (vihl hehl MEE nah) (1880–1962): queen of the Netherlands from 1890 to 1948.

Anne and her father: in the stage production. © Joan Marcus.

Anne (*sobered*). Never . . . ? Not even at nighttime, when everyone is gone? Or on Sundays? Can't I go down to listen to the radio?
Mr. Frank. Never. I am sorry, Anneke.[17] It isn't safe. No, you must never go beyond that door.

[*For the first time* ANNE *realizes what "going into hiding" means.*]

Anne. I see.
Mr. Frank. It'll be hard, I know. But always remember this, Anneke. There are no walls, there are no bolts, no locks that anyone can put on your mind. Miep will bring us books. We will read history, poetry, mythology. (*He gives her the glass of milk.*) Here's your milk. (*With his arm about her, they go over to the couch, sitting down side by side.*) As a matter of fact, between us, Anne, being here has certain advantages for you. For instance, you remember the battle you had with your mother the other day on the subject of overshoes? You said you'd rather die than wear overshoes? But in the end you had to wear them? Well now, you see, for as long as we are here, you will never have to wear overshoes! Isn't that good? And the coat that you inherited from Margot, you won't have to wear that anymore. And the piano! You won't have to practice on the piano. I tell you, this is going to be a fine life for you!

always longed for one. (*She looks around the room.*) Pencil, pencil, pencil, pencil. (*She starts down the stairs.*) I'm going down to the office to get a pencil.
Mr. Frank. Anne! No! (*He goes after her, catching her by the arm and pulling her back.*)
Anne (*startled*). But there's no one in the building now.
Mr. Frank. It doesn't matter. I don't want you ever to go beyond that door.

17. **Anneke** (AHN uh kuh): another affectionate nickname for Anne.

[ANNE's *panic is gone.* PETER *appears in the doorway of his room, with a saucer in his hand. He is carrying his cat.*]

Peter. I . . . I . . . I thought I'd better get some water for Mouschi before . . .

Mr. Frank. Of course.

[*As he starts toward the sink, the carillon begins to chime the hour of eight. He tiptoes to the window at the back and looks down at the street below. He turns to* PETER, *indicating in pantomime that it is too late.* PETER *starts back for his room. He steps on a creaking board. The three of them are frozen for a minute in fear. As* PETER *starts away again,* ANNE *tiptoes over to him and pours some of the milk from her glass into the saucer for the cat.* PETER *squats on the floor, putting the milk before the cat.* MR. FRANK *gives* ANNE *his fountain pen and then goes into the room at the right. For a second* ANNE *watches the cat; then she goes over to the center table and opens her diary.*

In the room at the right, MRS. FRANK *has sat up quickly at the sound of the carillon.* MR. FRANK *comes in and sits down beside her on the settee,*[18] *his arm comfortingly around her.* **J**

Upstairs, in the attic room, MR. *and* MRS. VAN DAAN *have hung their clothes in the closet and are now seated on the iron bed.* MRS. VAN DAAN *leans back, exhausted.* MR. VAN DAAN *fans her with a newspaper.*

ANNE *starts to write in her diary. The lights dim out; the curtain falls.*

In the darkness ANNE's *voice comes to us again, faintly at first and then with growing strength.*]

Anne's Voice. I expect I should be describing what it feels like to go into hiding. But I really don't know yet myself. I only know it's funny never to be able to go outdoors . . . never to breathe fresh air . . . never to run and shout and jump. It's the silence in the nights that frightens me most. Every time I hear a creak in the house or a step on the street outside, I'm sure they're coming for us. The days aren't so bad. At least we know that Miep and Mr. Kraler are down there below us in the office. Our protectors, we call them. I asked Father what would happen to them if the Nazis found out they were hiding us. Pim[19] said that they would suffer the same fate that we would. . . . Imagine! They know this, and yet when they come up here, they're always cheerful and gay, as if there were nothing in the world to bother them. . . . Friday, the twenty-first of August, nineteen forty-two. Today I'm going to tell you our general news. Mother is unbearable. She insists on treating me like a baby, which I loathe. Otherwise things are going better. The weather is . . . **K**

---

18. settee (seh TEE): small couch.

19. Pim: family nickname for Mr. Frank.

J **Literary Focus** **Drama** At this point the family is in hiding and must stay silent during the daytime hours. What actions does this extended stage direction describe?

K **Read and Discuss** What do we learn in this scene?

[As ANNE*'s voice is fading out, the curtain rises on the scene.]*

SCENE 3

It is a little after six o'clock in the evening, two months later.

MARGOT *is in the bedroom at the right, studying.* MR. VAN DAAN *is lying down in the attic room above.*

The rest of the "family" is in the main room. ANNE *and* PETER *sit opposite each other at the center table, where they have been doing their lessons.* MRS. FRANK *is on the couch.* MRS. VAN DAAN *is seated with her fur coat, on which she has been sewing, in her lap. None of them are wearing their shoes.*

Their eyes are on MR. FRANK, *waiting for him to give them the signal which will release them from their day-long quiet.* MR. FRANK, *his shoes in his hand, stands looking down out of the window at the back, watching to be sure that all of the workmen have left the building below.*

After a few seconds of motionless silence, MR. FRANK *turns from the window.*

Mr. Frank (*quietly, to the group*). It's safe now. The last workman has left.

[There is an immediate stir of relief.]

Anne (her pent-up energy explodes). WHEE!
Mrs. Frank (*startled, amused*). Anne!
Mrs. Van Daan. I'm first for the w.c.

[She hurries off to the bathroom. MRS. FRANK *puts on her shoes and starts up to the sink to prepare supper.* ANNE *sneaks* PETER*'s shoes from under the table and hides them behind her back.* MR. FRANK *goes into* MARGOT'S *room.]*

Mr. Frank (*to* MARGOT). Six o'clock. School's over.

*[*MARGOT *gets up, stretching.* MR. FRANK *sits down to put on his shoes. In the main room* PETER *tries to find his.]*

Peter (*to* ANNE). Have you seen my shoes?
Anne (*innocently*). Your shoes?
Peter. You've taken them, haven't you?
Anne. I don't know what you're talking about.
Peter. You're going to be sorry!
Anne. Am I?

*[*PETER *goes after her.* ANNE, *with his shoes in her hand, runs from him, dodging behind her mother.]*

Mrs. Frank (*protesting*). Anne, dear!
Peter. Wait till I get you!
Anne. I'm waiting! (PETER *makes a lunge for her. They both fall to the floor.* PETER *pins her down, wrestling with her to get the shoes.*) Don't! Don't! Peter, stop it. Ouch!
Mrs. Frank. Anne! . . . Peter!

[Suddenly PETER *becomes self-conscious. He grabs his shoes roughly and starts for his room.]*

Anne (*following him*). Peter, where are you going? Come dance with me.

Peter. I tell you I don't know how.
Anne. I'll teach you.
Peter. I'm going to give Mouschi his dinner.
Anne. Can I watch?
Peter. He doesn't like people around while he eats.
Anne. Peter, please.
Peter. No!

[*He goes into his room.* ANNE *slams his door after him.*] Ⓛ

Mrs. Frank. Anne, dear, I think you shouldn't play like that with Peter. It's not dignified.
Anne. Who cares if it's dignified? I don't want to be dignified.

[MR. FRANK *and* MARGOT *come from the room on the right.* MARGOT *goes to help her mother.* MR. FRANK *starts for the center table to correct* MARGOT'S *school papers.*]

Mrs. Frank (*to* ANNE). You complain that I don't treat you like a grown-up. But when I do, you resent it.
Anne. I only want some fun . . . someone to laugh and clown with. . . . After you've sat still all day and hardly moved, you've got to have some fun. I don't know what's the matter with that boy.
Mr. Frank. He isn't used to girls. Give him a little time.
Anne. Time? Isn't two months time? I could cry. (*Catching hold of* MARGOT) Come on, Margot . . . dance with me. Come on, please.
Margot. I have to help with supper.
Anne. You know we're going to forget how to dance. . . . When we get out, we won't remember a thing.

[*She starts to sing and dance by herself.* MR. FRANK *takes her in his arms, waltzing with her.* MRS. VAN DAAN *comes in from the bathroom.*]

Mrs. Van Daan. Next? (*She looks around as she starts putting on her shoes.*) Where's Peter?
Anne (*as they are dancing*). Where would he be!
Mrs. Van Daan. He hasn't finished his lessons, has he? His father'll kill him if he catches him in there with that cat and his work not done. (MR. FRANK *and* ANNE *finish their dance. They bow to each other with extravagant formality.*) Anne, get him out of there, will you?
Anne (*at* PETER'S *door*). Peter? Peter?
Peter (*opening the door a crack*). What is it?
Anne. Your mother says to come out.
Peter. I'm giving Mouschi his dinner.
Mrs. Van Daan. You know what your father says. (*She sits on the couch, sewing on the lining of her fur coat.*)
Peter. For heaven's sake, I haven't even looked at him since lunch.
Mrs. Van Daan. I'm just telling you, that's all.
Anne. I'll feed him.
Peter. I don't want you in there.
Mrs. Van Daan. Peter!
Peter (*to* ANNE). Then give him his dinner and come right out, you hear?

Ⓛ **Literary Focus** **Drama** What is the cause of the conflict between Anne and Peter?

[*He comes back to the table.* ANNE *shuts the door of* PETER*'s room after her and disappears behind the curtain covering his closet.*]

Mrs. Van Daan (*to* PETER). Now is that any way to talk to your little girlfriend?
Peter. Mother . . . for heaven's sake . . . will you please stop saying that?
Mrs. Van Daan. Look at him blush! Look at him!
Peter. Please! I'm not . . . anyway . . . let me alone, will you? M
Mrs. Van Daan. He acts like it was something to be ashamed of. It's nothing to be ashamed of, to have a little girlfriend.
Peter. You're crazy. She's only thirteen.
Mrs. Van Daan. So what? And you're sixteen. Just perfect. Your father's ten years older than I am. (*To* MR. FRANK) I warn you, Mr. Frank, if this war lasts much longer, we're going to be related and then . . .
Mr. Frank. Mazel tov![20]
Mrs. Frank (*deliberately changing the conversation*). I wonder where Miep is. She's usually so prompt.

[*Suddenly everything else is forgotten as they hear the sound of an automobile coming to a screeching stop in the street below. They are tense, motionless in their terror. The car starts away. A wave of relief sweeps over them. They pick up their occupations again.* ANNE *flings open the door of* PETER*'s room, making a dramatic entrance. She is dressed in* PETER*'s clothes.* PETER *looks at her in fury. The others are amused.*]

Anne. Good evening, everyone. Forgive me if I don't stay. (*She jumps up on a chair.*) I have a friend waiting for me in there. My friend Tom. Tom Cat. Some people say that we look alike. But Tom has the most beautiful whiskers, and I have only a little fuzz. I am hoping . . . in time . . .
Peter. All right, Mrs. Quack Quack!
Anne (*outraged—jumping down*). Peter! N
Peter. I heard about you . . . how you talked so much in class they called you Mrs. Quack Quack. How Mr. Smitter made you write a composition . . . "'Quack, quack,' said Mrs. Quack Quack."
Anne. Well, go on. Tell them the rest. How it was so good he read it out loud to the class and then read it to all his other classes!
Peter. Quack! Quack! Quack . . . Quack . . . Quack . . .

[ANNE *pulls off the coat and trousers.*]

Anne. You are the most intolerable, insufferable boy I've ever met!

[*She throws the clothes down the stairwell.* PETER *goes down after them.*]

Peter. Quack, quack, quack!
Mrs. Van Daan (*to* ANNE). That's right, Anneke! Give it to him!
Anne. With all the boys in the world . . . why I had to get locked up with one like you! . . .

20. **mazel tov** (MAH zuhl tohv): Yiddish expression meaning "congratulations."

M Literary Perspectives **Analyzing Responses** What do you know about teenagers that helps you "get" Peter's reaction?

N Reading Focus **Making Inferences** What do Anne's actions suggest about her character? Why is Peter so upset with her?

Peter. Quack, quack, quack, and from now on stay out of my room!

[*As* PETER *passes her,* ANNE *puts out her foot, tripping him. He picks himself up and goes on into his room.*]

Mrs. Frank (*quietly*). Anne, dear . . . your hair. (*She feels* ANNE*'s forehead.*) You're warm. Are you feeling all right?

Anne. Please, Mother. (*She goes over to the center table, slipping into her shoes.*)

Mrs. Frank (*following her*). You haven't a fever, have you?

Anne (*pulling away*). No. No.

Mrs. Frank. You know we can't call a doctor here, ever. There's only one thing to do . . . watch carefully. Prevent an illness before it comes. Let me see your tongue.

Anne. Mother, this is perfectly absurd.

Mrs. Frank. Anne, dear, don't be such a baby. Let me see your tongue. (*As* ANNE *refuses,* MRS. FRANK *appeals to* MR. FRANK.) Otto . . . ?

Mr. Frank. You hear your mother, Anne.

[ANNE *flicks out her tongue for a second, then turns away.*]

Mrs. Frank. Come on—open up! (*As* ANNE *opens her mouth very wide*) You seem all right . . . but perhaps an aspirin . . .

Mrs. Van Daan. For heaven's sake, don't give that child any pills. I waited for fifteen minutes this morning for her to come out of the w.c.

Anne. I was washing my hair!

Peter in the stage production. © Joan Marcus.

Mr. Frank. I think there's nothing the matter with our Anne that a ride on her bike or a visit with her friend Jopie de Waal wouldn't cure. Isn't that so, Anne?

[MR. VAN DAAN *comes down into the room. From outside we hear faint sounds of bombers going over and a burst of ack-ack.*][21] **O**

Mr. Van Daan. Miep not come yet?

Mrs. Van Daan. The workmen just left, a little while ago.

Mr. Van Daan. What's for dinner tonight?

21. **ack-ack:** slang for "antiaircraft gunfire."

O **Literary Focus** **Drama** How do the sound effects remind audiences of a larger conflict that affects the characters?

Mrs. Van Daan. Beans.

Mr. Van Daan. Not again!

Mrs. Van Daan. Poor Putti! I know. But what can we do? That's all that Miep brought us.

[MR. VAN DAAN *starts to pace, his hands behind his back.* ANNE *follows behind him, imitating him.*]

Anne. We are now in what is known as the "bean cycle." Beans boiled, beans en casserole, beans with strings, beans without strings . . .

[PETER *has come out of his room. He slides into his place at the table, becoming immediately absorbed in his studies.*]

Mr. Van Daan (*to* PETER). I saw you . . . in there, playing with your cat.

Mrs. Van Daan. He just went in for a second, putting his coat away. He's been out here all the time, doing his lessons.

Mr. Frank (*looking up from the papers*). Anne, you got an "excellent" in your history paper today . . . and "very good" in Latin.

Anne (*sitting beside him*). How about algebra?

Mr. Frank. I'll have to make a confession. Up until now I've managed to stay ahead of you in algebra. Today you caught up with me. We'll leave it to Margot to correct.

Anne. Isn't algebra vile, Pim!

Mr. Frank. Vile!

Margot (*to* MR. FRANK). How did I do?

Anne (*getting up*). Excellent, excellent, excellent, excellent!

Mr. Frank (*to* MARGOT). You should have used the subjunctive here . . .

Margot. Should I? . . . I thought . . . look here . . . I didn't use it here . . .

[*The two become absorbed in the papers.*]

Anne. Mrs. Van Daan, may I try on your coat?

Mrs. Frank. No, Anne.

Mrs. Van Daan (*giving it to* ANNE). It's all right . . . but careful with it. (ANNE *puts it on and struts with it.*) My father gave me that the year before he died. He always bought the best that money could buy.

Anne. Mrs. Van Daan, did you have a lot of boyfriends before you were married?

Mrs. Frank. Anne, that's a personal question. It's not courteous to ask personal questions.

Mrs. Van Daan. Oh, I don't mind. (*To* ANNE) Our house was always swarming with boys. When I was a girl, we had . . .

Mr. Van Daan. Oh, God. Not again!

Mrs. Van Daan (*good-humored*). Shut up! (*Without a pause, to* ANNE. MR. VAN DAAN *mimics* MRS. VAN DAAN, *speaking the first few words in unison with her.*) One summer we had a big house in Hilversum. The boys came buzzing round like bees around a jam pot. And when I was sixteen! . . . We were wearing our skirts very short those days and I had good-looking legs. (*She pulls up her skirt, going to* MR. FRANK.) I still have 'em. I may not be as pretty as I used to be, but I still have my legs. How about it, Mr. Frank? P

P **Literary Focus** **Drama** What do you learn about Mrs. Van Daan's character from these lines of dialogue?

Mr. Van Daan. All right. All right. We see them.

Mrs. Van Daan. I'm not asking you. I'm asking Mr. Frank.

Peter. Mother, for heaven's sake.

Mrs. Van Daan. Oh, I embarrass you, do I? Well, I just hope the girl you marry has as good. (*Then, to* ANNE) My father used to worry about me, with so many boys hanging round. He told me, if any of them gets fresh, you say to him . . . "Remember, Mr. So-and-So, remember I'm a lady."

Anne. "Remember, Mr. So-and-So, remember I'm a lady." (*She gives* MRS. VAN DAAN *her coat.*)

Mr. Van Daan. Look at you, talking that way in front of her! Don't you know she puts it all down in that diary?

Mrs. Van Daan. So, if she does? I'm only telling the truth!

[ANNE *stretches out, putting her ear to the floor, listening to what is going on below. The sound of the bombers fades away.*]

Mrs. Frank (*setting the table*). Would you mind, Peter, if I moved you over to the couch?

Anne (*listening*). Miep must have the radio on.

[PETER *picks up his papers, going over to the couch beside* MRS. VAN DAAN.]

Mr. Van Daan (*accusingly, to* PETER). Haven't you finished yet?

Peter. No.

Mr. Van Daan. You ought to be ashamed of yourself.

Peter. All right. All right. I'm a dunce. I'm a hopeless case. Why do I go on?

Mrs. Van Daan. You're not hopeless. Don't talk that way. It's just that you haven't anyone to help you, like the girls have. (*To* MR. FRANK) Maybe you could help him, Mr. Frank?

Mr. Frank. I'm sure that his father . . . ?

Mr. Van Daan. Not me. I can't do anything with him. He won't listen to me. You go ahead . . . if you want.

Mr. Frank (*going to* PETER). What about it, Peter? Shall we make our school coeducational?

Mrs. Van Daan (*kissing* MR. FRANK). You're an angel, Mr. Frank. An angel. I don't know why I didn't meet you before I met that one there. Here, sit down, Mr. Frank . . . (*She forces him down on the couch beside* PETER.) Now, Peter, you listen to Mr. Frank.

Mr. Frank. It might be better for us to go into Peter's room.

[PETER *jumps up eagerly, leading the way.*]

Mrs. Van Daan. That's right. You go in there, Peter. You listen to Mr. Frank. Mr. Frank is a highly educated man.

[*As* MR. FRANK *is about to follow* PETER *into his room,* MRS. FRANK *stops him and wipes the lipstick from his lips. Then she closes the door after them.*]

All right. All right. I'm a dunce. I'm a hopeless case.

Anne (*on the floor, listening*). Shh! I can hear a man's voice talking.

Mr. Van Daan (*to* ANNE). Isn't it bad enough here without your sprawling all over the place?

[ANNE *sits up.*]

Mrs. Van Daan (*to* MR. VAN DAAN). If you didn't smoke so much, you wouldn't be so bad-tempered.

Mr. Van Daan. Am I smoking? Do you see me smoking?

Mrs. Van Daan. Don't tell me you've used up all those cigarettes.

Mr. Van Daan. One package. Miep only brought me one package.

Mrs. Van Daan. It's a filthy habit anyway. It's a good time to break yourself.

Mr. Van Daan. Oh, stop it, please.

Mrs. Van Daan. You're smoking up all our money. You know that, don't you? Q

Mr. Van Daan. Will you shut up? (*During this,* MRS. FRANK *and* MARGOT *have studiously kept their eyes down. But* ANNE, *seated on the floor, has been following the discussion interestedly.* MR. VAN DAAN *turns to see her staring up at him.*) And what are you staring at?

Anne. I never heard grown-ups quarrel before. I thought only children quarreled.

Mr. Van Daan. This isn't a quarrel! It's a discussion. And I never heard children so rude before.

Anne (*rising,* indignantly). *I,* rude!

Mr. Van Daan. Yes!

Mrs. Frank (*quickly*). Anne, will you get me my knitting? (ANNE *goes to get it.*) I must remember, when Miep comes, to ask her to bring me some more wool.

Margot (*going to her room*). I need some hairpins and some soap. I made a list. (*She goes into her bedroom to get the list.*)

Mrs. Frank (*to* ANNE). Have you some library books for Miep when she comes?

Q Literary Focus Drama Based on this exchange and others from earlier in the play, how would you describe the Van Daans' relationship?

Vocabulary **indignantly** (ihn DIHG nuhnt lee) *adv.:* with anger caused by something felt to be unjust.

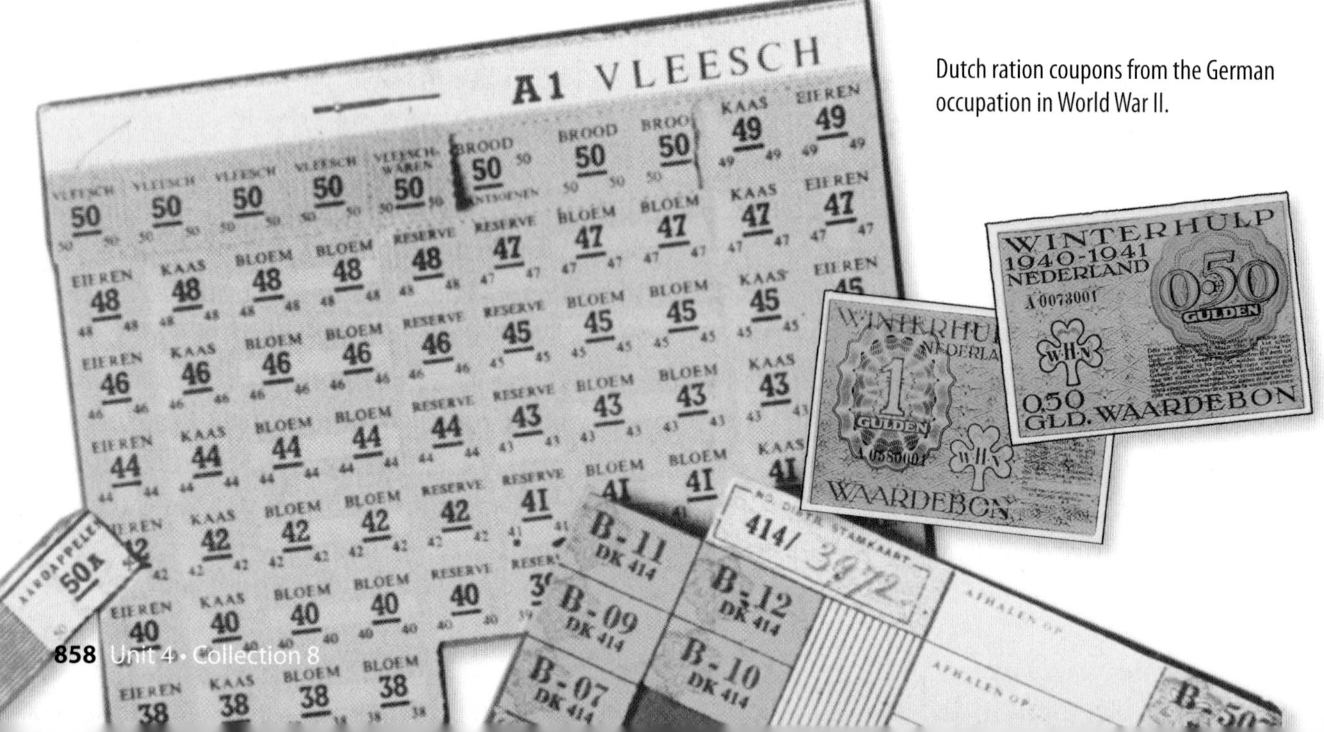

Dutch ration coupons from the German occupation in World War II.

Anne. It's a wonder that Miep has a life of her own, the way we make her run errands for us. Please, Miep, get me some starch. Please take my hair out and have it cut. Tell me all the latest news, Miep. (*She goes over, kneeling on the couch beside* MRS. VAN DAAN.) Did you know she was engaged? His name is Dirk, and Miep's afraid the Nazis will ship him off to Germany to work in one of their war plants. That's what they're doing with some of the young Dutchmen . . . they pick them up off the streets—

Mr. Van Daan (*interrupting*). Don't you ever get tired of talking? Suppose you try keeping still for five minutes. Just five minutes.

[*He starts to pace again. Again* ANNE *follows him, mimicking him.* MRS. FRANK *jumps up and takes her by the arm up to the sink and gives her a glass of milk.*]

Mrs. Frank. Come here, Anne. It's time for your glass of milk.

Mr. Van Daan. Talk, talk, talk. I never heard such a child. Where is my . . . ? Every evening it's the same, talk, talk, talk. (*He looks around.*) Where is my . . . ?

Mrs. Van Daan. What're you looking for?

Mr. Van Daan. My pipe. Have you seen my pipe?

Mrs. Van Daan. What good's a pipe? You haven't got any tobacco.

Mr. Van Daan. At least I'll have something to hold in my mouth! (*Opening* MARGOT'S *bedroom door*) Margot, have you seen my pipe?

Margot. It was on the table last night.

[ANNE *puts her glass of milk on the table and picks up his pipe, hiding it behind her back.*]

Mr. Van Daan. I know. I know. Anne, did you see my pipe? . . . Anne!

Mrs. Frank. Anne, Mr. Van Daan is speaking to you.

Anne. Am I allowed to talk now?

Mr. Van Daan. You're the most aggravating. . . . The trouble with you is, you've been spoiled. What you need is a good old-fashioned spanking.

Anne (*mimicking* MRS. VAN DAAN). "Remember, Mr. So-and-So, remember I'm a lady." (*She thrusts the pipe into his mouth, then picks up her glass of milk.*)

Mr. Van Daan (*restraining himself with difficulty*). Why aren't you nice and quiet like your sister Margot? Why do you have to show off all the time? Let me give you a little advice, young lady. Men don't like that kind of thing in a girl. You know that? A man likes a girl who'll listen to him once in a while . . . a domestic girl, who'll keep her house shining for her husband . . . who loves to cook and sew and . . . R

Anne. I'd cut my throat first! I'd open my veins! I'm going to be remarkable! I'm going to Paris . . .

Mr. Van Daan (*scoffingly*). Paris!

Anne. . . . to study music and art.

Mr. Van Daan. Yeah! Yeah!

Anne. I'm going to be a famous dancer or singer . . . or something wonderful.

R Literary Perspectives Analyzing Responses What do you know about people that explains the conflict between Anne and Mr. Van Daan?

[*She makes a wide gesture, spilling the glass of milk on the fur coat in* MRS. VAN DAAN'S *lap.* MARGOT *rushes quickly over with a towel.* ANNE *tries to brush the milk off with her skirt.*]

Mrs. Van Daan. Now look what you've done . . . you clumsy little fool! My beautiful fur coat my father gave me . . .
Anne. I'm so sorry.
Mrs. Van Daan. What do you care? It isn't yours. . . . So go on, ruin it! Do you know what that coat cost? Do you? And now look at it! Look at it!
Anne. I'm very, very sorry.
Mrs. Van Daan. I could kill you for this. I could just kill you!

[MRS. VAN DAAN *goes up the stairs, clutching the coat.* MR. VAN DAAN *starts after her.*]

Mr. Van Daan. Petronella . . . liefje! Liefje! . . . Come back . . . the supper . . . come back!
Mrs. Frank. Anne, you must not behave in that way.
Anne. It was an accident. Anyone can have an accident.
Mrs. Frank. I don't mean that. I mean the answering back. You must not answer back. They are our guests. We must always show the greatest courtesy to them. We're all living under terrible tension. (*She stops as* MARGOT *indicates that* MR. VAN DAAN *can hear. When he is gone, she continues.*) That's why we must control ourselves. . . . You don't hear Margot getting into arguments with them, do you? Watch Margot. She's always courteous with them. Never familiar. She keeps her distance. And they respect her for it. Try to be like Margot. Ⓢ
Anne. And have them walk all over me, the way they do her? No, thanks!
Mrs. Frank. I'm not afraid that anyone is going to walk all over you, Anne. I'm afraid for other people, that you'll walk on them. I don't know what happens to you, Anne. You are wild, self-willed. If I had ever talked to my mother as you talk to me . . .
Anne. Things have changed. People aren't like that anymore. "Yes, Mother." "No, Mother." "Anything you say, Mother." I've got to fight things out for myself! Make something of myself!
Mrs. Frank. It isn't necessary to fight to do it. Margot doesn't fight, and isn't she . . . ?
Anne (*violently rebellious*). Margot! Margot! Margot! That's all I hear from everyone . . . how wonderful Margot is . . . "Why aren't you like Margot?"
Margot (*protesting*). Oh, come on, Anne, don't be so . . .
Anne (*paying no attention*). Everything she does is right, and everything I do is wrong! I'm the goat around here! . . . You're all against me! . . . And you worst of all!

[*She rushes off into her room and throws herself down on the settee, stifling her sobs.* MRS. FRANK *sighs and starts toward the stove.*]

Mrs. Frank (*to* MARGOT). Let's put the soup on the stove . . . if there's anyone who cares to eat. Margot, will you take the bread out?

Ⓢ **Literary Focus** **Drama** What is the difference between the way Margot handles conflict and the way Anne does?

(MARGOT *gets the bread from the cupboard.*) I don't know how we can go on living this way. . . . I can't say a word to Anne . . . she flies at me . . .

Margot. You know Anne. In half an hour she'll be out here, laughing and joking.

Mrs. Frank. And . . . (*She makes a motion upward, indicating the* VAN DAANS.) . . . I told your father it wouldn't work . . . but no . . . no . . . he had to ask them, he said . . . he owed it to him, he said. Well, he knows now that I was right! These quarrels! . . . This bickering!

Margot (*with a warning look*). Shush. Shush.

[*The buzzer for the door sounds.* MRS. FRANK *gasps, startled.*]

Mrs. Frank. Every time I hear that sound, my heart stops!

Margot (*starting for* PETER'S *door*). It's Miep. (*She knocks at the door.*) Father?

Anne and Mrs. Van Daan in the stage production. © Joan Marcus.

[MR. FRANK *comes quickly from* PETER'S *room.*]

Mr. Frank. Thank you, Margot. (*As he goes down the steps to open the outer door*) Has everyone his list?

Margot. I'll get my books. (*Giving her mother a list*) Here's your list. (MARGOT *goes into her and* ANNE'S *bedroom on the right.* ANNE *sits up, hiding her tears, as* MARGOT *comes in.*) Miep's here.

[MARGOT *picks up her books and goes back.* ANNE *hurries over to the mirror, smoothing her hair.*]

Mr. Van Daan (*coming down the stairs*). Is it Miep?

Margot. Yes. Father's gone down to let her in.

Mr. Van Daan. At last I'll have some cigarettes!

Mrs. Frank (*to* MR. VAN DAAN). I can't tell you how unhappy I am about Mrs.

Van Daan's coat. Anne should never have touched it.

Mr. Van Daan. She'll be all right.

Mrs. Frank. Is there anything I can do?

Mr. Van Daan. Don't worry.

[*He turns to meet* MIEP. *But it is not* MIEP *who comes up the steps. It is* MR. KRALER, *followed by* MR. FRANK. *Their faces are grave.* ANNE *comes from the bedroom.* PETER *comes from his room.*]

Mrs. Frank. Mr. Kraler!

Mr. Van Daan. How are you, Mr. Kraler?

Margot. This is a surprise.

Mrs. Frank. When Mr. Kraler comes, the sun begins to shine.

Mr. Van Daan. Miep is coming?

Mr. Kraler. Not tonight. (MR. KRALER *goes to* MARGOT *and* MRS. FRANK *and* ANNE, *shaking hands with them.*)

Mrs. Frank. Wouldn't you like a cup of coffee? . . . Or, better still, will you have supper with us?

Mr. Frank. Mr. Kraler has something to talk over with us. Something has happened, he says, which demands an immediate decision.

Mrs. Frank (*fearful*). What is it?

[MR. KRALER *sits down on the couch. As he talks he takes bread, cabbages, milk, etc., from his briefcase, giving them to* MARGOT *and* ANNE *to put away.*]

Mr. Kraler. Usually, when I come up here, I try to bring you some bit of good news. What's the use of telling you the bad news when there's nothing that you can do about it? But today something has happened. . . . Dirk . . . Miep's Dirk, you know, came to me just now. He tells me that he has a Jewish friend living near him. A dentist. He says he's in trouble. He begged me, could I do anything for this man? Could I find him a hiding place? . . . So I've come to you. . . . I know it's a terrible thing to ask of you, living as you are, but would you take him in with you?

Mr. Kraler has something to talk over with us. Something has happened.

Mr. Frank. Of course we will.

Mr. Kraler (*rising*). It'll be just for a night or two . . . until I find some other place. This happened so suddenly that I didn't know where to turn.

Mr. Frank. Where is he?

Mr. Kraler. Downstairs in the office.

Mr. Frank. Good. Bring him up.

Mr. Kraler. His name is Dussel[22] . . .

Mr. Frank. Dussel. . . . I think I know him.

Mr. Kraler. I'll get him.

[*He goes quickly down the steps and out.* MR. FRANK *suddenly becomes conscious of the others.*]

Mr. Frank. Forgive me. I spoke without consulting you. But I knew you'd feel as I do.

Mr. Van Daan. There's no reason for you to consult anyone. This is your place. You have a right to do exactly as you please. The only thing I feel . . . there's so little food as it is . . . and to take in another person . . .

---

22. **Dussel** (DOOS uhl).

[PETER *turns away, ashamed of his father.*]

Mr. Frank. We can stretch the food a little. It's only for a few days.
Mr. Van Daan. You want to make a bet?
Mrs. Frank. I think it's fine to have him. But, Otto, where are you going to put him? Where?
Peter. He can have my bed. I can sleep on the floor. I wouldn't mind.
Mr. Frank. That's good of you, Peter. But your room's too small . . . even for you.
Anne. I have a much better idea. I'll come in here with you and Mother, and Margot can take Peter's room and Peter can go in our room with Mr. Dussel.
Margot. That's right. We could do that.
Mr. Frank. No, Margot. You mustn't sleep in that room . . . neither you nor Anne. Mouschi has caught some rats in there. Peter's brave. He doesn't mind.
Anne. Then how about *this?* I'll come in here with you and Mother, and Mr. Dussel can have my bed.
Mrs. Frank. No. No. *No!* Margot will come in here with us and he can have her bed. It's the only way. Margot, bring your things in here. Help her, Anne.

[MARGOT *hurries into her room to get her things.*]

Anne (*to her mother*). Why Margot? Why can't I come in here?
Mrs. Frank. Because it wouldn't be proper for Margot to sleep with a. . . . Please, Anne. Don't argue. Please.

[ANNE *starts slowly away.*]

Mr. Frank (*to* ANNE). You don't mind sharing your room with Mr. Dussel, do you, Anne?
Anne. No. No, of course not.
Mr. Frank. Good. (ANNE *goes off into her bedroom, helping* MARGOT. MR. FRANK *starts to search in the cupboards.*) Where's the cognac?[23]
Mrs. Frank. It's there. But, Otto, I was saving it in case of illness.
Mr. Frank. I think we couldn't find a better time to use it. Peter, will you get five glasses for me?

[PETER *goes for the glasses.* MARGOT *comes out of her bedroom, carrying her possessions, which she hangs behind a curtain in the main room.* MR. FRANK *finds the cognac and pours it into the five glasses that* PETER *brings him.* MR. VAN DAAN *stands looking on sourly.* MRS. VAN DAAN *comes downstairs and looks around at all the bustle.*]

Mrs. Van Daan. What's happening? What's going on?
Mr. Van Daan. Someone's moving in with us.
Mrs. Van Daan. In here? You're joking.
Margot. It's only for a night or two . . . until Mr. Kraler finds him another place.
Mr. Van Daan. Yeah! Yeah! **T**

23. **cognac** (KOHN yak): type of brandy (distilled wine).

T **Reading Focus** **Making Inferences** How do you think Mr. Van Daan feels about another person coming to live in the Annex?

[MR. FRANK *hurries over as* MR. KRALER *and* DUSSEL *come up.* DUSSEL *is a man in his late fifties, meticulous, finicky . . . bewildered now. He wears a raincoat. He carries a briefcase, stuffed full, and a small medicine case.*]

Mr. Frank. Come in, Mr. Dussel.
Mr. Kraler. This is Mr. Frank.
Dussel. Mr. Otto Frank?
Mr. Frank. Yes. Let me take your things. (*He takes the hat and briefcase, but* DUSSEL *clings to his medicine case.*) This is my wife, Edith . . . Mr. and Mrs. Van Daan . . . their son, Peter . . . and my daughters, Margot and Anne.

[DUSSEL *shakes hands with everyone.*]

Mr. Kraler. Thank you, Mr. Frank. Thank you all. Mr. Dussel, I leave you in good hands. Oh . . . Dirk's coat.

[DUSSEL *hurriedly takes off the raincoat, giving it to* MR. KRALER. *Underneath is his white dentist's jacket, with a yellow Star of David on it.*]

Dussel (*to* MR. KRALER). What can I say to thank you . . . ?
Mrs. Frank (*to* DUSSEL). Mr. Kraler and Miep. . . . They're our lifeline. Without them we couldn't live.
Mr. Kraler. Please. Please. You make us seem very heroic. It isn't that at all. We simply don't like the Nazis. (*To* MR. FRANK, *who offers him a drink*) No, thanks. (*Then, going on*) We don't like their methods. We don't like . . .
Mr. Frank (*smiling*). I know. I know. "No one's going to tell us Dutchmen what to do with our damn Jews!"
Mr. Kraler (*to* DUSSEL). Pay no attention to Mr. Frank. I'll be up tomorrow to see that they're treating you right. (*To* MR. FRANK) Don't trouble to come down again. Peter will bolt the door after me, won't you, Peter?
Peter. Yes, sir.
Mr. Frank. Thank you, Peter. I'll do it.
Mr. Kraler. Good night. Good night.
Group. Good night, Mr. Kraler. We'll see you tomorrow. (*Etc., etc.*)

[MR. KRALER *goes out with* MR. FRANK. MRS. FRANK *gives each one of the "grown-ups" a glass of cognac.*]

Mrs. Frank. Please, Mr. Dussel, sit down.

[DUSSEL *sinks into a chair.* MRS. FRANK *gives him a glass of cognac.*]

Dussel. I'm dreaming. I know it. I can't believe my eyes. Mr. Otto Frank here! (*To* MRS. FRANK) You're not in Switzerland, then? A woman told me. . . . She said she'd gone to your house . . . the door was open, everything was in disorder, dishes in the sink. She said she found a piece of paper in the wastebasket with an address scribbled on it . . . an address in Zurich.[24] She said you must have escaped to Zurich.
Anne. Father put that there purposely . . . just so people would think that very thing!
Dussel. And you've been *here* all the time?
Mrs. Frank. All the time . . . ever since July.

---

24. Zurich (ZUR ihk): Switzerland's largest city. Because Switzerland remained neutral during World War II, many refugees sought safety there.

[ANNE *speaks to her father as he comes back.*]

Anne. It worked, Pim . . . the address you left! Mr. Dussel says that people believe we escaped to Switzerland.

Mr. Frank. I'm glad. . . . And now let's have a little drink to welcome Mr. Dussel. (*Before they can drink,* DUSSEL *bolts his drink.* MR. FRANK *smiles and raises his glass.*) To Mr. Dussel. Welcome. We're very honored to have you with us.

Mrs. Frank. To Mr. Dussel, welcome.

[*The* VAN DAANS *murmur a welcome. The "grown-ups" drink.*]

Mrs. Van Daan. Um. That was good.

Mr. Van Daan. Did Mr. Kraler warn you that you won't get much to eat here? You can imagine . . . three ration books among the seven of us . . . and now you make eight.

[PETER *walks away, humiliated. Outside, a street organ is heard dimly.*]

Dussel (*rising*). Mr. Van Daan, you don't realize what is happening outside that you should warn me of a thing like that. You don't realize what's going on. . . . (*As* MR. VAN DAAN *starts his characteristic pacing,* DUSSEL *turns to speak to the others.*) Right here in Amsterdam every day hundreds of Jews disappear. . . . They surround a block and search house by house. Children come home from school to find their parents gone. Hundreds are being deported[25] . . . people that you and I know . . . the Hallensteins . . . the Wessels . . .

Mrs. Frank (*in tears*). Oh, no. No!

Dussel. They get their call-up notice . . . come to the Jewish theater on such and such a day and hour . . . bring only what you can carry in a rucksack. And if you refuse the call-up notice, then they come and drag you from your home and ship you off to Mauthausen. The death camp!

Mrs. Frank. We didn't know that things had got so much worse.

Dussel. Forgive me for speaking so.

Anne (*coming to* DUSSEL). Do you know the de Waals? . . . What's become of them? Their

25. **deported:** forcibly sent away (here, to concentration camps and death camps).

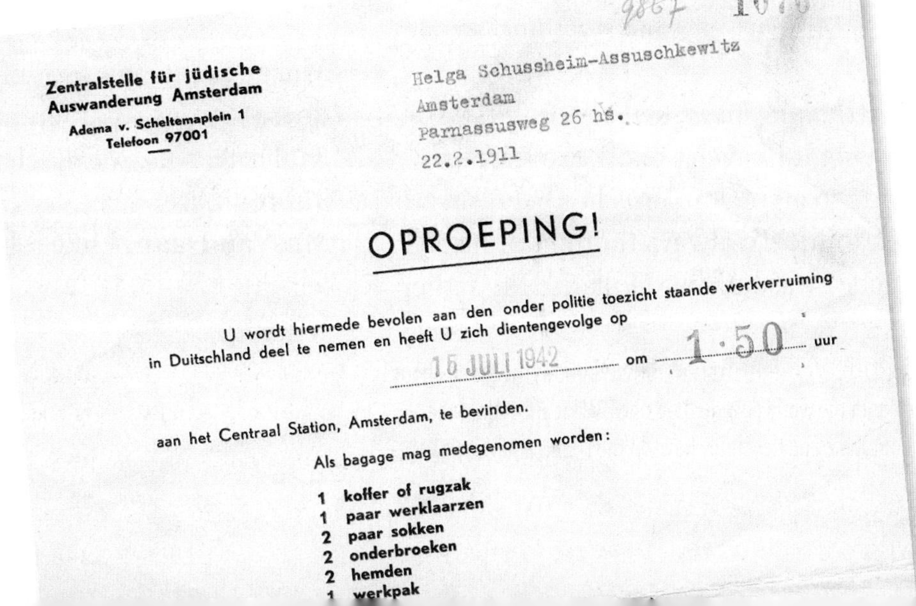

9867 1076

Zentralstelle für jüdische Auswanderung Amsterdam
Adema v. Scheltemaplein 1
Telefoon 97001

Helga Schussheim-Assuschkewitz
Amsterdam
Parnassusweg 26 hs.
22.2.1911

OPROEPING!

U wordt hiermede bevolen aan den onder politie toezicht staande werkverruiming in Duitschland deel te nemen en heeft U zich dientengevolge op 15 JULI 1942 om 1·50 uur aan het Centraal Station, Amsterdam, te bevinden.

Als bagage mag medegenomen worden:

1 koffer of rugzak
1 paar werklaarzen
2 paar sokken
2 onderbroeken
2 hemden
1 werkpak

The call-up document that was issued when Jews in Amsterdam were ordered to depart for work or concentration camps. It states what they can bring and when they must leave.

daughter Jopie and I are in the same class. Jopie's my best friend.
Dussel. They are gone.
Anne. Gone?
Dussel. With all the others.
Anne. Oh, no. Not Jopie! U

[*She turns away, in tears.* MRS. FRANK *motions to* MARGOT *to comfort her.* MARGOT *goes to* ANNE, *putting her arms comfortingly around her.*]

Mrs. Van Daan. There were some people called Wagner. They lived near us . . . ?
Mr. Frank (*interrupting, with a glance at* ANNE). I think we should put this off until later. We all have many questions we want to ask. . . . But I'm sure that Mr. Dussel would like to get settled before supper.
Dussel. Thank you. I would. I brought very little with me.
Mr. Frank (*giving him his hat and briefcase*). I'm sorry we can't give you a room alone. But I hope you won't be too uncomfortable. We've had to make strict rules here . . . a schedule of hours . . . We'll tell you after supper. Anne, would you like to take Mr. Dussel to his room?
Anne (*controlling her tears*). If you'll come with me, Mr. Dussel? (*She starts for her room.*)
Dussel (*shaking hands with each in turn*). Forgive me if I haven't really expressed my gratitude to all of you. This has been such a shock to me. I'd always thought of myself as Dutch. I was born in Holland. My father

was born in Holland, and my grandfather. And now . . . after all these years . . . (*He breaks off.*) If you'll excuse me.

[DUSSEL *gives a little bow and hurries off after* ANNE. MR. FRANK *and the others are subdued.*]

Anne (*turning on the light*). Well, here we are.

[DUSSEL *looks around the room. In the main room* MARGOT *speaks to her mother.*]

Margot. The news sounds pretty bad, doesn't it? It's so different from what Mr. Kraler tells us. Mr. Kraler says things are improving.
Mr. Van Daan. I like it better the way Kraler tells it.

U Literary Focus Drama Dussel informs the group about happenings in the world outside the Annex. What effect does the news about Jopie and her family have on the Franks and Van Daans?

Anne and Mr. Dussel in the stage production. © Joan Marcus.

[*They resume their occupations, quietly.* PETER *goes off into his room. In* ANNE'S *room,* ANNE *turns to* DUSSEL.]

Anne. You're going to share the room with me.

Dussel. I'm a man who's always lived alone. I haven't had to adjust myself to others. I hope you'll bear with me until I learn.

Anne. Let me help you. (*She takes his brief-case.*) Do you always live all alone? Have you no family at all?

Dussel. No one. (*He opens his medicine case and spreads his bottles on the dressing table.*)

Anne. How dreadful. You must be terribly lonely.

Dussel. I'm used to it.

Anne. I don't think I could ever get used to it. Didn't you even have a pet? A cat, or a dog?

Dussel. I have an allergy for fur-bearing animals. They give me asthma.

Anne. Oh, dear. Peter has a cat.

Dussel. Here? He has it here?

Anne. Yes. But we hardly ever see it. He keeps it in his room all the time. I'm sure it will be all right.

Dussel. Let us hope so. (*He takes some pills to fortify himself.*)

Anne. That's Margot's bed, where you're going to sleep. I sleep on the sofa there. (*Indicating the clothes hooks on the wall*) We cleared these off for your things. (She goes over to the window.) The best part about this room . . . you can look down and see a bit of the street and the canal. There's a houseboat . . . you can see the end of it . . . a bargeman lives there with his family. . . . They have a baby and he's just beginning to walk and I'm so afraid he's going to fall into the canal someday. I watch him . . .

Dussel (*interrupting*). Your father spoke of a schedule.

Anne (*coming away from the window*). Oh, yes. It's mostly about the times we have to be quiet. And times for the w.c. You can use it now if you like.

Dussel (*stiffly*). No, thank you.
Anne. I suppose you think it's awful, my talking about a thing like that. But you don't know how important it can get to be, especially when you're frightened. . . . About this room, the way Margot and I did . . . she had it to herself in the afternoons for studying, reading . . . lessons, you know . . . and I took the mornings. Would that be all right with you?
Dussel. I'm not at my best in the morning.
Anne. You stay here in the mornings, then. I'll take the room in the afternoons.
Dussel. Tell me, when you're in here, what happens to me? Where am I spending my time? In there, with all the people?
Anne. Yes.
Dussel. I see. I see.
Anne. We have supper at half past six.
Dussel (*going over to the sofa*). Then, if you don't mind . . . I like to lie down quietly for ten minutes before eating. I find it helps the digestion.
Anne. Of course. I hope I'm not going to be too much of a bother to you. I seem to be able to get everyone's back up.

[DUSSEL *lies down on the sofa, curled up, his back to her.*]

Dussel. I always get along very well with children. My patients all bring their children to me, because they know I get on well with them. So don't you worry about that.

[ANNE *leans over him, taking his hand and shaking it gratefully.*]

Anne. Thank you. Thank you, Mr. Dussel.

[*The lights dim to darkness. The curtain falls on the scene.* ANNE'S *voice comes to us, faintly at first and then with increasing power.*]

Anne's Voice. . . . And yesterday I finished Cissy Van Marxvelt's latest book. I think she is a first-class writer. I shall definitely let my children read her. Monday, the twenty-first of September, nineteen forty-two. Mr. Dussel and I had another battle yesterday. Yes, Mr. Dussel! According to him, nothing, I repeat . . . nothing is right about me . . . my appearance, my character, my manners. While he was going on at me, I thought . . . sometime I'll give you such a smack that you'll fly right up to the ceiling! Why is it that every grown-up thinks he knows the way to bring up children? Particularly the grown-ups that never had any. I keep wishing that Peter was a girl instead of a boy. Then I would have someone to talk to. Margot's a darling, but she takes everything too seriously. To pause for a moment on the subject of Mrs. Van Daan. I must tell you that her attempts to flirt with Father are getting her nowhere. Pim, thank goodness, won't play. **V**

[*As she is saying the last lines, the curtain rises on the darkened scene.* ANNE'S *voice fades out.*]

V **Read and Discuss** How is the group responding to their new circumstances?

Applying Your Skills

RA.L.8.6 Explain how an author's choice of genre affects the expression of a theme or topic. **RA.L.8.7** Identify examples of foreshadowing and flashback in a literary text. *Also covered* **RP.8.1**

The Diary of Anne Frank, Act One, Scenes 1–3

Respond and Think Critically

Reading Focus

Quick Check

1. Why do the two families go into hiding?
2. Describe Anne Frank. What is she like? What is her attitude toward hiding at first?

Read with a Purpose

3. When does Anne begin to understand what going into hiding means? How is life in the Secret Annex different from life outside?

Reading Skills: Making Inferences

4. Review the inferences you have made so far. Then make an inference based on this text clue:

What the Text Says	My Connections	My Inferences
Peter tells Anne, "... in the schoolyard. You were always in the middle of a bunch of kids."		

Literary Focus

Literary Analysis

5. **Compare and Contrast** Describe Mr. Frank's and Mr. Van Daan's different reactions to the news of Mr. Dussel's arrival.
6. **Interpret** Mr. Frank tells Anne, "There are no walls, there are no bolts, no locks that anyone can put on your mind" (page 850). What does he mean?
7. **Literary Perspectives** Do Anne and Peter seem to have typical teenage attitudes toward their families? Support your response with examples from the text and from your own experiences.
8. **Literary Perspectives** Based on your own reactions, what do you think would be the hardest part of life in the Secret Annex? Explain.

Literary Skills: Elements of Drama

9. **Identify** By the end of Scene 3, we have met all ten characters who appear in the play. List those characters and choose two or three adjectives to describe each one.
10. **Analyze** List the conflicts that have developed among the characters by the end of Scene 3. Why are these conflicts dangerous for the characters?
11. **Analyze** Sounds from outside the Secret Annex play an important part in the play. Some remind us of ordinary life in the city. Others punctuate the scene with reminders of the danger outside. List four of the sounds heard so far. Which sounds are pleasant? Which are threatening?

Literary Skills Review: Flashback

12. **Analyze** A **flashback** interrupts a story to take you back to earlier times and events. Most of this play is told in an extended flashback, framed by the opening and closing scenes. Where in Scene 1 does the flashback begin? What do we learn about the characters and their basic situation before the flashback begins?

SCENE 4

It is the middle of the night, several months later. The stage is dark except for a little light which comes through the skylight in PETER'S *room.*

Everyone is in bed. MR. *and* MRS. FRANK *lie on the couch in the main room, which has been pulled out to serve as a makeshift double bed.*

MARGOT *is sleeping on a mattress on the floor in the main room, behind a curtain stretched across for privacy. The others are all in their accustomed rooms.*

From outside we hear two drunken soldiers singing "Lili Marlene." A girl's high giggle is heard. The sound of running feet is heard coming closer and then fading in the distance. Throughout the scene there is the distant sound of airplanes passing overhead.

A match suddenly flares up in the attic. We dimly see MR. VAN DAAN. *He is getting his bearings. He comes quickly down the stairs and goes to the cupboard where the food is stored. Again the match flares up, and is as quickly blown out. The dim figure is seen to steal back up the stairs.* **A**

There is quiet for a second or two, broken only by the sound of airplanes and running feet on the street below. Suddenly, out of the silence and the dark, we hear ANNE *scream.*

Anne (*screaming*). No! No! Don't . . . don't take me!

[*She moans, tossing and crying in her sleep. The other people wake, terrified.* DUSSEL *sits up in bed, furious.*]

Dussel. Shush! Anne! Anne, for God's sake, shush!

Anne (*still in her nightmare*). Save me! Save me!

[*She screams and screams.* DUSSEL *gets out of bed, going over to her, trying to wake her.*]

Dussel. For God's sake! Quiet! Quiet! You want someone to hear?

[*In the main room* MRS. FRANK *grabs a shawl and pulls it around her. She rushes in to* ANNE, *taking her in her arms.* MR. FRANK *hurriedly gets up, putting on his overcoat.* MARGOT *sits up, terrified.* PETER'S *light goes on in his room.*]

Mrs. Frank (*to* ANNE, *in her room*). Hush, darling, hush. It's all right. It's all right. (*Over her shoulder, to* DUSSEL) Will you be kind enough to turn on the light, Mr. Dussel? (*Back to* ANNE) It's nothing, my darling. It was just a dream.

[DUSSEL *turns on the light in the bedroom.* MRS. FRANK *holds* ANNE *in her arms. Gradually* ANNE *comes out of her nightmare, still trembling with horror.* MR. FRANK *comes into the room, and goes quickly to the window, looking out to be sure that no one outside has heard* ANNE'S *screams.* MRS. FRANK *holds* ANNE, *talking softly to her. In the main room*

A **Literary Focus** **Drama** What is Mr. Van Daan doing in the first few moments of the scene? How might his actions create complications later?

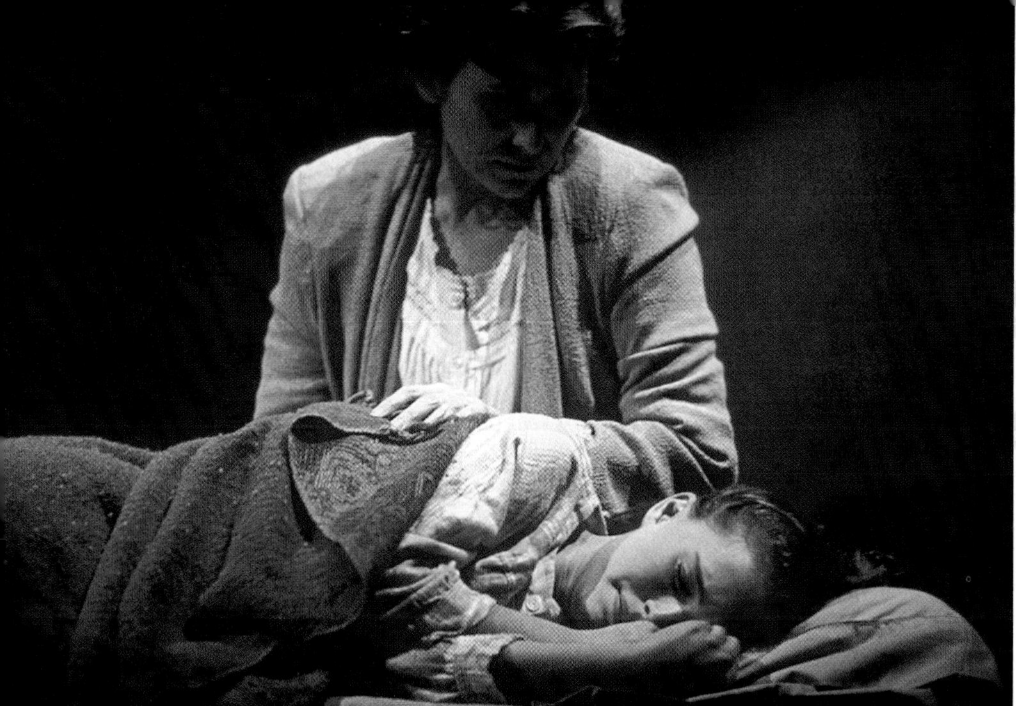

Anne and her mother in the stage production. ©Joan Marcus.

MARGOT *stands on a chair, turning on the center hanging lamp. A light goes on in the* VAN DAANS' *room overhead.* PETER *puts his robe on, coming out of his room.*] **B**

Dussel (*to* MRS. FRANK, *blowing his nose*). Something must be done about that child, Mrs. Frank. Yelling like that! Who knows but there's somebody on the streets? She's endangering all our lives.
Mrs. Frank. Anne, darling.
Dussel. Every night she twists and turns. I don't sleep. I spend half my night shushing her. And now it's nightmares!

[MARGOT *comes to the door of* ANNE'S *room, followed by* PETER. MR. FRANK *goes to them, indicating that everything is all right.* PETER *takes* MARGOT *back.*]

Mrs. Frank (*to* ANNE). You're here, safe, you see? Nothing has happened. (*To* DUSSEL) Please, Mr. Dussel, go back to bed. She'll be herself in a minute or two. Won't you, Anne?
Dussel (*picking up a book and a pillow*). Thank you, but I'm going to the w.c. The one place where there's peace!

[*He stalks out.* MR. VAN DAAN, *in underwear and trousers, comes down the stairs.*]

Mr. Van Daan (*to* DUSSEL). What is it? What happened?
Dussel. A nightmare. She was having a nightmare!
Mr. Van Daan. I thought someone was murdering her.
Dussel. Unfortunately, no.

B **Reading Focus** **Making Inferences** How do the other characters respond to Anne's cries? What does each character's reaction suggest about him or her?

[*He goes into the bathroom.* MR. VAN DAAN *goes back up the stairs.* MR. FRANK, *in the main room, sends* PETER *back to his own bedroom.*]

Mr. Frank. Thank you, Peter. Go back to bed.

[PETER *goes back to his room.* MR. FRANK *follows him, turning out the light and looking out the window. Then he goes back to the main room, and gets up on a chair, turning out the center hanging lamp.*]

Mrs. Frank (*to* ANNE). Would you like some water? (ANNE *shakes her head.*) Was it a very bad dream? Perhaps if you told me . . . ?
Anne. I'd rather not talk about it.
Mrs. Frank. Poor darling. Try to sleep, then. I'll sit right here beside you until you fall asleep. (*She brings a stool over, sitting there.*)
Anne. You don't have to.
Mrs. Frank. But I'd like to stay with you . . . very much. Really.
Anne. I'd rather you didn't.
Mrs. Frank. Good night, then. (*She leans down to kiss* ANNE. ANNE *throws her arm up over her face, turning away.* MRS. FRANK, *hiding her hurt, kisses* ANNE'*s arm.*) You'll be all right? There's nothing that you want?
Anne. Will you please ask Father to come.
Mrs. Frank (*after a second*). Of course, Anne dear. (*She hurries out into the other room.* MR. FRANK *comes to her as she comes in.*) Sie verlangt nach Dir![1]
Mr. Frank (*sensing her hurt*). Edith, Liebe, schau . . .[2]

1. **Sie . . . Dir:** German for "She's asking for you."
2. **Liebe, schau:** "Dear, look."

Mrs. Frank. Es macht nichts! Ich danke dem lieben Herrgott, dass sie sich wenigstens an Dich wendet, wenn sie Trost braucht! Geh hinein, Otto, sie ist ganz hysterisch vor Angst.[3] (*As* MR. FRANK *hesitates*) Geh zu ihr.[4] (*He looks at her for a second and then goes to get a cup of water for* ANNE. MRS. FRANK *sinks down on the bed, her face in her hands, trying to keep from sobbing aloud.* MARGOT *comes over to her, putting her arms around her.*) She wants nothing of me. She pulled away when I leaned down to kiss her.
Margot. It's a phase. . . . You heard Father. . . . Most girls go through it . . . they turn to their

3. **Es . . . Angst:** "It doesn't matter! I thank the dear Lord that she turns at least to you when she needs comfort! Go to her, Otto, she's completely hysterical with fear."
4. **Geh zu ihr:** "Go to her."

Anne and her father in the stage production. ©Joan Marcus.

fathers at this age . . . they give all their love to their fathers.

Mrs. Frank. You weren't like this. You didn't shut me out.

Margot. She'll get over it. . . .

[She smoothes the bed for MRS. FRANK *and sits beside her a moment as* MRS. FRANK *lies down. In* ANNE'S *room* MR. FRANK *comes in, sitting down by* ANNE. ANNE *flings her arms around him, clinging to him. In the distance we hear the sound of ack-ack.]*

Anne. Oh, Pim. I dreamed that they came to get us! The Green Police! They broke down the door and grabbed me and started to drag me out the way they did Jopie.

Mr. Frank. I want you to take this pill.

Anne. What is it?

Mr. Frank. Something to quiet you.

[She takes it and drinks the water. In the main room MARGOT *turns out the light and goes back to her bed.]*

Mr. Frank (*to* ANNE). Do you want me to read to you for a while?

Anne. No. Just sit with me for a minute. Was I awful? Did I yell terribly loud? Do you think anyone outside could have heard?

Mr. Frank. No. No. Lie quietly now. Try to sleep.

Anne. I'm a terrible coward. I'm so disappointed in myself. I think I've conquered my fear . . . I think I'm really grown-up . . . and then something happens . . . and I run to you like a baby. . . . I love you, Father. I don't love anyone but you.

Mr. Frank (*reproachfully*). Annele!

Anne. It's true. I've been thinking about it for a long time. You're the only one I love.

Mr. Frank. It's fine to hear you tell me that you love me. But I'd be happier if you said you loved your mother as well. . . . She needs your help so much . . . your love . . .

Anne. We have nothing in common. She doesn't understand me. Whenever I try to explain my views on life to her, she asks me if I'm constipated. **C**

Mr. Frank. You hurt her very much just now. She's crying. She's in there crying.

C **Reading Focus** **Making Inferences** What do Anne's words suggest about the way she feels about her mother?

Anne. I can't help it. I only told the truth. I didn't want her here . . . (*Then, with sudden change*) Oh, Pim, I was horrible, wasn't I? And the worst of it is, I can stand off and look at myself doing it and know it's cruel and yet I can't stop doing it. What's the matter with me? Tell me. Don't say it's just a phase! Help me.

Mr. Frank. There is so little that we parents can do to help our children. We can only try to set a good example . . . point the way. The rest you must do yourself. You must build your own character.

Anne. I'm trying. Really I am. Every night I think back over all of the things I did that day that were wrong . . . like putting the wet mop in Mr. Dussel's bed . . . and this thing now with Mother. I say to myself, that was wrong. I make up my mind, I'm never going to do that again. Never! Of course, I may do something worse . . . but at least I'll never do *that* again! . . . I have a nicer side, Father . . . a sweeter, nicer side. But I'm scared to show it. I'm afraid that people are going to laugh at me if I'm serious. So the mean Anne comes to the outside and the good Anne stays on the inside, and I keep on trying to switch them around and have the good Anne outside and the bad Anne inside and be what I'd like to be . . . and might be . . . if only . . . only . . .

[*She is asleep.* MR. FRANK *watches her for a moment and then turns off the light, and starts out. The lights dim out. The curtain falls on the scene.* ANNE*'s voice is heard, dimly at first and then with growing strength.*]

Anne's Voice. . . . The air raids[5] are getting worse. They come over day and night. The noise is terrifying. Pim says it should be music to our ears. The more planes, the sooner will come the end of the war. Mrs. Van Daan pretends to be a fatalist.[6] What will be, will be. But when the planes come over, who is the most frightened? No one else but Petronella! . . . Monday, the ninth of November, nineteen forty-two. Wonderful news! The Allies have landed in Africa. Pim says that we can look for an early finish to the war. Just for fun, he asked each of us what was the first thing we wanted to do when we got out of here. Mrs. Van Daan longs to be home with her own things, her needlepoint chairs, the Bechstein piano her father gave her . . . the best that money could buy. Peter would like to go to a movie. Mr. Dussel wants to get back to his dentist's drill. He's afraid he is losing his touch. For myself, there are so many things . . . to ride a bike again . . . to laugh till my belly aches . . . to have new clothes from the skin out . . . to have a hot tub filled to overflowing and wallow in it for hours . . . to be back in school with my friends . . . **D**

[*As the last lines are being said, the curtain rises on the scene. The lights dim on as* ANNE*'s voice fades away.*]

5. **air raids:** Allied aircraft conducted air raids, or bombing attacks on ground targets, in the Netherlands because the country was occupied by the Germans.
6. **fatalist** (FAY tuh lihst): person who believes that all events are determined by fate and therefore cannot be prevented or affected by people's actions.

D **Read and Discuss** What is Anne talking about?

SCENE 5

It is the first night of the Hanukkah[7] celebration. MR. FRANK *is standing at the head of the table on which is the menorah.[8] He lights the shamas, or servant candle, and holds it as he says the blessing. Seated, listening, are all of the "family," dressed in their best. The men wear hats;* PETER wears *his cap.*

Mr. Frank (*reading from a prayer book*). "Praised be Thou, oh Lord our God, Ruler of the universe, who has sanctified us with Thy commandments and bidden us kindle the Hanukkah lights. Praised be Thou, oh Lord our God, Ruler of the universe, who has wrought wondrous deliverances for our fathers in days of old. Praised be Thou, oh Lord our God, Ruler of the universe, that Thou has given us life and sustenance and brought us to this happy season." (MR. FRANK *lights the one candle of the menorah as he continues.*) "We kindle this Hanukkah light to celebrate the great and wonderful deeds wrought through the zeal with which God filled the hearts of the heroic Maccabees, two thousand years ago. They fought against indifference, against tyranny and oppression, and they restored our Temple to us. May these lights remind us that we should ever look to God, whence cometh our help." Amen. (*Pronounced "oh-mayn"*)

All. Amen.

[MR. FRANK *hands* MRS. FRANK *the prayer book.*]

Mrs. Frank (*reading*). "I lift up mine eyes unto the mountains, from whence cometh my help. My help cometh from the Lord who made heaven and earth. He will not suffer thy foot to be moved. He that keepeth thee will not slumber. He that keepeth Israel doth neither slumber nor sleep. The Lord is thy keeper. The Lord is thy shade upon thy right hand. The sun shall not smite thee by day, nor the moon by night. The Lord shall keep thee from all evil. He shall keep thy soul. The Lord shall guard thy going out and thy coming in, from this time forth and forevermore."[9] Amen.

All. Amen.

[MRS. FRANK *puts down the prayer book and goes to get the food and wine.* MARGOT *helps her.* MR. FRANK *takes the men's hats and puts them aside.*]

Dussel (*rising*). That was very moving.

Anne (*pulling him back*). It isn't over yet!

Mrs. Van Daan. Sit down! Sit down!

---

7. **Hanukkah** (HAH noo kah): joyous eight-day Jewish holiday, usually falling in December, celebrating the rededication of the holy Temple in Jerusalem in 164 B.C. The Temple had been taken over by the Syrians, who had conquered Jerusalem. The Maccabee family led the Jews in a successful rebellion against the Syrians and retook the Temple.
8. **menorah** (muh NOH ruh): Hebrew for "lamp." Mr. Frank is lighting a menorah that holds nine candles: eight candles, one for each of the eight nights of Hanukkah, and the shamas, the candle used to light the others.
9. Mrs. Frank is reading Psalm 121 from the Bible.

Vocabulary **tyranny** (TIHR uh nee) *n.:* absolute power used unjustly.

Anne distributing presents in the stage production. ©Joan Marcus.

Anne. There's a lot more, songs and presents.
Dussel. Presents?
Mrs. Frank. Not this year, unfortunately.
Mrs. Van Daan. But always on Hanukkah everyone gives presents . . . everyone!
Dussel. Like our St. Nicholas's Day.[10]

[*There is a chorus of no's from the group.*]

Mrs. Van Daan. No! Not like St. Nicholas! What kind of a Jew are you that you don't know Hanukkah?
Mrs. Frank (*as she brings the food*). I remember particularly the candles. . . . First, one, as we have tonight. Then, the second night, you light two candles, the next night three . . . and so on until you have eight candles burning. When there are eight candles, it is truly beautiful.
Mrs. Van Daan. And the potato pancakes.
Mr. Van Daan. Don't talk about them!
Mrs. Van Daan. I make the best latkes[11] you ever tasted!
Mrs. Frank. Invite us all next year . . . in your own home.
Mr. Frank. God willing!
Mrs. Van Daan. God willing.
Margot. What I remember best is the presents we used to get when we were little . . . eight days of presents . . . and each day they got better and better.
Mrs. Frank (*sitting down*). We are all here, alive. That is present enough. **E**

10. **St. Nicholas's Day:** Christian holiday celebrated in the Netherlands and other European countries on December 5, on which small gifts are given.

11. **latkes** (LAHT kuhz): potato pancakes, a traditional Hanukkah food.

E Literary Focus **Drama** What **mood,** or overall feeling, does the dialogue in this scene create? In what way is the mood of this scene different from the mood in Scene 4?

Anne. No, it isn't. I've got something. . . . (*She rushes into her room, hurriedly puts on a little hat improvised from the lampshade, grabs a satchel bulging with parcels, and comes running back.*)
Mrs. Frank. What is it?
Anne. Presents!
Mrs. Van Daan. Presents!
Dussel. Look!
Mr. Van Daan. What's she got on her head?
Peter. A lampshade!
Anne (*she picks out one at random*). This is for Margot. (*She hands it to* MARGOT, *pulling her to her feet.*) Read it out loud.
Margot (*reading*).

You have never lost your temper.
You never will, I fear,
You are so good.
But if you should,
Put all your cross words here.

(*She tears open the package.*) A new crossword puzzle book! Where did you get it?
Anne. It isn't new. It's one that you've done. But I rubbed it all out, and if you wait a little and forget, you can do it all over again.
Margot (*sitting*). It's wonderful, Anne. Thank you. You'd never know it wasn't new.

[*From outside we hear the sound of a streetcar passing.*]

Anne (*with another gift*). Mrs. Van Daan.
Mrs. Van Daan (*taking it*). This is awful . . . I haven't anything for anyone . . . I never thought . . .
Mr. Frank. This is all Anne's idea.
Mrs. Van Daan (*holding up a bottle*). What is it?
Anne. It's hair shampoo. I took all the odds and ends of soap and mixed them with the last of my toilet water.[12]
Mrs. Van Daan. Oh, Anneke!
Anne. I wanted to write a poem for all of them, but I didn't have time. (*Offering a large box to* MR. VAN DAAN) Yours, Mr. Van Daan, is *really* something . . . something you want more than anything. (*As she waits for him to open it*) Look! Cigarettes!
Mr. Van Daan. Cigarettes!
Anne. Two of them! Pim found some old pipe tobacco in the pocket lining of his coat . . . and we made them . . . or rather, Pim did.
Mrs. Van Daan. Let me see . . . Well, look at that! Light it, Putti! Light it.

[MR. VAN DAAN *hesitates.*]

Anne. It's tobacco, really it is! There's a little fluff in it, but not much.

[*Everyone watches intently as* MR. VAN DAAN *cautiously lights it. The cigarette flares up. Everyone laughs.*]

Peter. It works!
Mrs. Van Daan. Look at him.
Mr. Van Daan (*spluttering*). Thank you, Anne. Thank you.

[ANNE *rushes back to her satchel for another present.*]

Anne (*handing her mother a piece of paper*). For Mother, Hanukkah greeting. (*She pulls her mother to her feet.*)

12. **toilet water:** cologne.

Mrs. Frank (*she reads*).

> Here's an IOU that I promise to pay.
> Ten hours of doing whatever you say.
> Signed, Anne Frank.

(MRS. FRANK, *touched, takes* ANNE *in her arms, holding her close.*)

Dussel (*to* ANNE). Ten hours of doing what you're told? *Anything* you're told?

Anne. That's right.

Dussel. You wouldn't want to sell that, Mrs. Frank?

Mrs. Frank. Never! This is the most precious gift I've ever had! F

[*She sits, showing her present to the others.* ANNE *hurries back to the satchel and pulls out a scarf, the scarf that* MR. FRANK *found in the first scene.*]

Anne (*offering it to her father*). For Pim.

Mr. Frank. Anneke . . . I wasn't supposed to have a present! (*He takes it, unfolding it and showing it to the others.*)

Anne. It's a muffler . . . to put round your neck . . . like an ascot, you know. I made it myself out of odds and ends. . . . I knitted it in the dark each night, after I'd gone to bed. I'm afraid it looks better in the dark!

Mr. Frank (*putting it on*). It's fine. It fits me perfectly. Thank you, Annele.

[ANNE *hands* PETER *a ball of paper with a string attached to it.*]

Anne. That's for Mouschi.

Peter (*rising to bow*). On behalf of Mouschi, I thank you.

Anne (*hesitant, handing him a gift*). And . . . this is yours . . . from Mrs. Quack Quack. (*As he holds it gingerly in his hands*) Well . . . open it. . . . Aren't you going to open it?

Peter. I'm scared to. I know something's going to jump out and hit me.

Anne. No. It's nothing like that, really.

Mrs. Van Daan (*as he is opening it*). What is it, Peter? Go on. Show it.

Anne (*excitedly*). It's a safety razor!

Dussel. A what?

Anne. A razor!

Mrs. Van Daan (*looking at it*). You didn't make that out of odds and ends.

Anne (*to* PETER). Miep got it for me. It's not new. It's secondhand. But you really do need a razor now.

Dussel. For what?

Anne. Look on his upper lip . . . you can see the beginning of a moustache.

Dussel. He wants to get rid of that? Put a little milk on it and let the cat lick it off.

Peter (*starting for his room*). Think you're funny, don't you.

Dussel. Look! He can't wait! He's going in to try it!

Peter. I'm going to give Mouschi his present! (*He goes into his room, slamming the door behind him.*)

Mr. Van Daan (*disgustedly*). Mouschi, Mouschi, Mouschi.

[*In the distance we hear a dog persistently barking.* ANNE *brings a gift to* DUSSEL.]

F **Literary Focus** **Drama** Which lines of dialogue show that Anne has changed her attitude toward her mother?

Anne. And last but never least, my roommate, Mr. Dussel.

Dussel. For me? You have something for me? (*He opens the small box she gives him.*)

Anne. I made them myself.

Dussel (*puzzled*). Capsules! Two capsules!

Anne. They're earplugs!

Dussel. Earplugs?

Anne. To put in your ears so you won't hear me when I thrash around at night. I saw them advertised in a magazine. They're not real ones. . . . I made them out of cotton and candle wax. Try them. . . . See if they don't work. . . . See if you can hear me talk . . .

Dussel (*putting them in his ears*). Wait now until I get them in . . . so.

Anne. Are you ready?

Dussel. Huh?

Anne. Are you ready?

Dussel. Good God! They've gone inside! I can't get them out! (*They laugh as* DUSSEL *jumps about, trying to shake the plugs out of his ears. Finally he gets them out. Putting them away*) Thank you, Anne! Thank you!

Mr. Van Daan. A real Hanukkah!
Mrs. Van Daan. Wasn't it cute of her?
Mrs. Frank. I don't know when she did it.
Margot. I love my present.
} *Together*

Anne (*sitting at the table*). And now let's have the song, Father . . . please . . . (*To* DUSSEL) Have you heard the Hanukkah song, Mr. Dussel? The song is the whole thing! (*She sings*) "Oh, Hanukkah! Oh, Hanukkah! The sweet celebration . . ."

Menorah lit for Hanukkah.

Mr. Frank (*quieting her*). I'm afraid, Anne, we shouldn't sing that song tonight. (*To* DUSSEL) It's a song of jubilation, of rejoicing. One is apt to become too enthusiastic.

Anne. Oh, please, please. Let's sing the song. I promise not to shout!

Mr. Frank. Very well. But quietly, now . . . I'll keep an eye on you and when . . .

[*As* ANNE *starts to sing, she is interrupted by* DUSSEL, *who is snorting and wheezing.*]

Dussel (*pointing to* PETER). You . . . You! (PETER *is coming from his bedroom, ostentatiously holding a bulge in his coat as if he were holding his cat, and dangling* ANNE'*s present before it.*) How many times . . . I told you . . . Out! Out!

Mr. Van Daan (*going to* PETER). What's the matter with you? Haven't you any sense? Get that cat out of here.

Peter (*innocently*). Cat?

Mr. Van Daan. You heard me. Get it out of here!

Peter. I have no cat.

Vocabulary **ostentatiously** (ahs tehn TAY shuhs lee) *adv.:* in a showy way.

[*Delighted with his joke, he opens his coat and pulls out a bath towel. The group at the table laugh, enjoying the joke.*]

Dussel (*still wheezing*). It doesn't need to be the cat . . . his clothes are enough . . . when he comes out of that room . . .

Mr. Van Daan. Don't worry. You won't be bothered anymore. We're getting rid of it.

Dussel. At last you listen to me. (He goes off into his bedroom.)

Mr. Van Daan (*calling after him*). I'm not doing it for you. That's all in your mind . . . all of it! (*He starts back to his place at the table.*) I'm doing it because I'm sick of seeing that cat eat all our food.

Peter. That's not true! I only give him bones . . . scraps . . .

Mr. Van Daan. Don't tell me! He gets fatter every day! Damn cat looks better than any of us. Out he goes tonight!

Peter. No! No!

Anne. Mr. Van Daan, you can't do that! That's Peter's cat. Peter loves that cat.

Mrs. Frank (*quietly*). Anne.

Peter (*to* MR. VAN DAAN). If he goes, I go.

Mr. Van Daan. Go! Go! G

Mrs. Van Daan. You're not going and the cat's not going! Now please . . . this is Hanukkah . . . Hanukkah . . . this is the time to celebrate. . . . What's the matter with all of you? Come on, Anne. Let's have the song.

Anne (*singing*).

Oh, Hanukkah!
Oh, Hanukkah!
The sweet celebration.

Mr. Frank (*rising*). I think we should first blow out the candle . . . then we'll have something for tomorrow night.

Margot. But, Father, you're supposed to let it burn itself out.

Mr. Frank. I'm sure that God understands shortages. (*Before blowing it out*) "Praised be Thou, oh Lord our God, who hast sustained us and permitted us to celebrate this joyous festival."

[*He is about to blow out the candle when suddenly there is a crash of something falling below. They all freeze in horror, motionless. For a few seconds there is complete silence.* MR. FRANK *slips off his shoes. The others noiselessly follow his example.* MR. FRANK *turns out a light near him. He motions to* PETER *to turn off the center lamp.* PETER *tries to reach it, realizes he cannot, and gets up on a chair. Just as he is touching the lamp, he loses his balance. The chair goes out from under him. He falls. The iron lampshade crashes to the floor. There is a sound of feet below running down the stairs.*] H

Mr. Van Daan (*under his breath*). God Almighty! (*The only light left comes from the Hanukkah candle.* DUSSEL *comes from his room.* MR. FRANK *creeps over to the stairwell and stands listening. The dog is heard barking excitedly.*) Do you hear anything?

Mr. Frank (*in a whisper*). No. I think they've gone.

Mrs. Van Daan. It's the Green Police. They've found us.

Mr. Frank. If they had, they wouldn't have left. They'd be up here by now.

G Literary Perspectives Analyzing Responses How do your own feelings about conflicts affect your response to this scene?

H Literary Focus Drama What complication is introduced here?

Mrs. Van Daan. I know it's the Green Police. They've gone to get help. That's all. They'll be back!
Mr. Van Daan. Or it may have been the Gestapo,[13] looking for papers . . .
Mr. Frank (*interrupting*). Or a thief, looking for money.
Mrs. Van Daan. We've got to do something. . . . Quick! Quick! Before they come back.
Mr. Van Daan. There isn't anything to do. Just wait.

[MR. FRANK *holds up his hand for them to be quiet. He is listening intently. There is complete silence as they all strain to hear any sound from below. Suddenly* ANNE *begins to sway. With a low cry she falls to the floor in a faint.* MRS. FRANK *goes to her quickly, sitting beside her on the floor and taking her in her arms.*]

Mrs. Frank. Get some water, please! Get some water!

[MARGOT *starts for the sink.*]

Mr. Van Daan (*grabbing* MARGOT). No! No! No one's going to run water!
Mr. Frank. If they've found us, they've found us. Get the water. (MARGOT *starts again for the sink.* MR. FRANK, *getting a flashlight*) I'm going down.

[MARGOT *rushes to him, clinging to him.* ANNE *struggles to consciousness.*]

Margot. No, Father, no! There may be someone there, waiting. . . . It may be a trap!

13. **Gestapo** (guh STAH poh): Nazi secret police.

Mr. Frank. This is Saturday. There is no way for us to know what has happened until Miep or Mr. Kraler comes on Monday morning. We cannot live with this uncertainty.
Margot. Don't go, Father!
Mrs. Frank. Hush, darling, hush. (MR. FRANK *slips quietly out, down the steps, and out through the door below.*) Margot! Stay close to me.

[MARGOT *goes to her mother.*]

Mr. Van Daan. Shush! Shush!

[MRS. FRANK *whispers to* MARGOT *to get the water.* MARGOT *goes for it.*]

Mrs. Van Daan. Putti, where's our money? Get our money. I hear you can buy the Green Police off, so much a head. Go upstairs quick! Get the money!
Mr. Van Daan. Keep still!
Mrs. Van Daan (*kneeling before him, pleading*). Do you want to be dragged off to a concentration camp? Are you going to stand there and wait for them to come up and get you? Do something, I tell you!
Mr. Van Daan (*pushing her aside*). Will you keep still!

[*He goes over to the stairwell to listen.* PETER *goes to his mother, helping her up onto the sofa. There is a second of silence; then* ANNE *can stand it no longer.*]

Anne. Someone go after Father! Make Father come back!
Peter (*starting for the door*). I'll go.
Mr. Van Daan. Haven't you done enough?

[*He pushes* PETER *roughly away. In his anger against his father* PETER *grabs a chair as if to hit him with it, then puts it down, burying his face in his hands.* MRS. FRANK *begins to pray softly.*]

Anne. Please, please, Mr. Van Daan. Get Father.

Mr. Van Daan. Quiet! Quiet! I

[ANNE *is shocked into silence.* MRS. FRANK *pulls her closer, holding her protectively in her arms.*]

Mrs. Frank (*softly, praying*). "I lift up mine eyes unto the mountains, from whence cometh my help. My help cometh from the Lord who made heaven and earth. He will not suffer thy foot to be moved. . . . He that keepeth thee will not slumber . . ."

[*She stops as she hears someone coming. They all watch the door tensely.* MR. FRANK *comes quietly in.* ANNE *rushes to him, holding him tight.*]

Mr. Frank. It was a thief. That noise must have scared him away.

Mrs. Van Daan. Thank God.

Mr. Frank. He took the cash box. And the radio. He ran away in such a hurry that he didn't stop to shut the street door. It was swinging wide open. (*A breath of relief sweeps over them.*) I think it would be good to have some light.

Margot. Are you sure it's all right?

Mr. Frank. The danger has passed. (MARGOT *goes to light the small lamp.*) Don't be so terrified, Anne. We're safe.

Dussel. Who says the danger has passed? Don't you realize we are in greater danger than ever?

Mr. Frank. Mr. Dussel, will you be still! (MR. FRANK *takes* ANNE *back to the table, making her sit down with him, trying to calm her.*)

Dussel (*pointing to* PETER). Thanks to this clumsy fool, there's someone now who knows we're up here! Someone now knows we're up here, hiding!

Mrs. Van Daan (*going to* DUSSEL). Someone knows we're here, yes. But who is the someone? A thief! A thief! You think a thief is going to go to the Green Police and say . . . "I was robbing a place the other night and I heard a noise up over my head?" You think a thief is going to do that?

Dussel. Yes. I think he will.

Mrs. Van Daan (*hysterically*). You're crazy! (*She stumbles back to her seat at the table.* PETER *follows protectively, pushing* DUSSEL *aside.*)

Dussel. I think someday he'll be caught and then he'll make a bargain with the Green Police . . . if they'll let him off, he'll tell them where some Jews are hiding!

[*He goes off into the bedroom. There is a second of appalled silence.*]

Mr. Van Daan. He's right.

Anne. Father, let's get out of here! We can't stay here now. . . . Let's go . . .

Mr. Van Daan. Go! Where?

Mrs. Frank (*sinking into her chair at the table*). Yes. Where?

Mr. Frank (*rising, to them all*). Have we lost all faith? All courage? A moment ago we

---

I **Literary Focus** **Drama** How does this part of the scene create suspense?

thought that they'd come for us. We were sure it was the end. But it wasn't the end. We're alive, safe. (MR. VAN DAAN *goes to the table and sits.* MR. FRANK *prays*) "We thank Thee, oh Lord our God, that in Thy infinite mercy Thou hast again seen fit to spare us." (*He blows out the candle, then turns to* ANNE.) Come on, Anne. The song! Let's have the song! (*He starts to sing.* ANNE *finally starts falteringly to sing, as* MR. FRANK *urges her on. Her voice is hardly audible at first.*) **J**

Anne (*singing*).

Oh, Hanukkah! Oh, Hanukkah!
The sweet . . . celebration . . .

[*As she goes on singing, the others gradually join in, their voices still shaking with fear.* MRS. VAN DAAN *sobs as she sings.*]

Group.

Around the feast . . . we . . . gather
In complete . . . jubilation . . .
Happiest of sea . . . sons
Now is here.
Many are the reasons for good cheer.

[DUSSEL *comes from the bedroom. He comes over to the table, standing beside* MARGOT, *listening to them as they sing.*]

Together
We'll weather
Whatever tomorrow may bring.

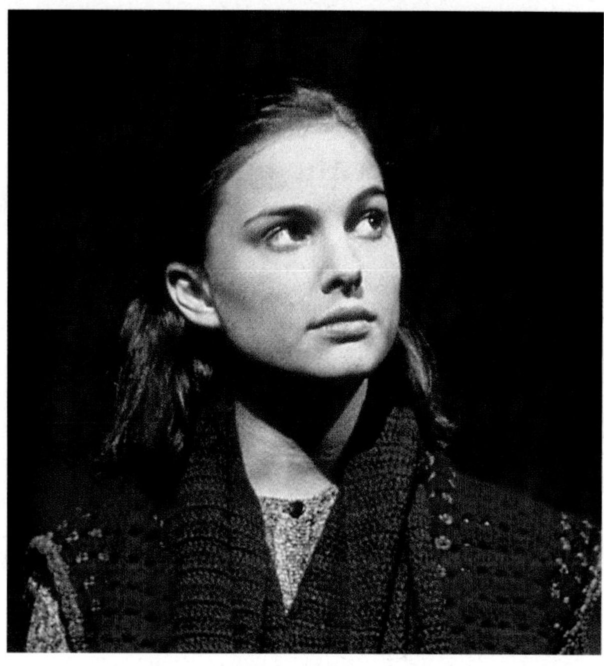

Anne in the stage production. ©Joan Marcus.

[*As they sing on with growing courage, the lights start to dim.*]

So hear us rejoicing
And merrily voicing
The Hanukkah song that we sing.
Hoy!

[*The lights are out. The curtain starts slowly to fall.*]

Hear us rejoicing
And merrily voicing
The Hanukkah song that we sing.

[*They are still singing as the curtain falls.*] **K**

Curtain

J Literary Focus Drama Think about each character's response to the latest plot development. Whose view of the situation is the most realistic, the most hopeful?

K Read and Discuss What does this scene reveal about the characters' situation?

Applying Your Skills

RA.L.8.6 Explain how an author's choice of genre affects the expression of a theme or topic. RA.L.8.5 Identify and explain universal themes across different works by the same author and by different authors. *Also covered* RP.8.1

The Diary of Anne Frank, Act One, Scenes 4–5

Respond and Think Critically

Reading Focus

Quick Check

1. What tensions does Anne's nightmare reveal?
2. What are the characters doing in Scene 5?
3. What happens at the end of Scene 5?

Read with a Purpose

4. How has Anne's view of the world changed in Scenes 4–5? Support your answer with examples from the play.

Reading Skills: Making Inferences

5. Continue working on your inferences chart. What inference can you make from the text clue given below?

What the Text Says	My Connections	My Inferences
Peter threatens to leave if his cat has to leave.		

Literary Focus

Literary Analysis

6. **Speculate** Imagine that you are watching this play in a theater. What questions do you have as the curtain comes down on Act One? What do you predict will happen in Act Two?
7. **Compare and Contrast** How does the Hanukkah celebration contrast with the harsh reality outside the hiding place? What is the **mood,** or emotional effect, in the beginning of the Hanukkah scene? What happens to change that mood?
8. **Extend** Characters in literature, like people in real life, sometimes take courage from a speech or a song. How do the families take courage at the end of Scene 5? Can you think of other episodes in plays or movies (or real life) in which people facing danger summon up courage from a speech or a song? Explain.
9. **Literary Perspectives** How do your experiences with holiday celebrations contribute to your responses to Scene 5?

Literary Skills: Elements of Drama

10. **Evaluate** Go back to the list of characters you made after you read Scenes 1–3. What adjectives, if any, would you change now? Why?
11. **Analyze** Anne is a dynamic character who changes during the play. How do her gifts to Peter and Mrs. Frank show that she has changed?
12. **Analyze** Describe the reversal—the sudden change in the characters' fortunes—that occurs in Scene 5. What impact does that plot event have on the audience?

Literary Skills Review: Theme

13. **Interpret** A **theme** is a general idea or insight about life as revealed in a work of literature. In drama, the theme can often be discovered in the characters' actions or dialogue. What theme is revealed in Anne's conversation with her father at the end of Scene 4?

ACT TWO

SCENE 1

In the darkness we hear ANNE*'s voice, again reading from the diary.*

Anne's Voice. Saturday, the first of January, nineteen forty-four. Another new year has begun and we find ourselves still in our hiding place. We have been here now for one year, five months, and twenty-five days. It seems that our life is at a standstill. Ⓐ

[*The curtain rises on the scene. It is late afternoon. Everyone is bundled up against the cold. In the main room* MRS. FRANK *is taking down the laundry, which is hung across the back.* MR. FRANK *sits in the chair down left, reading.* MARGOT *is lying on the couch with a blanket over her and the many-colored knitted scarf around her throat.* ANNE *is seated at the center table, writing in her diary.* PETER, MR. *and* MRS. VAN DAAN, *and* DUSSEL *are all in their own rooms, reading or lying down.*

As the lights dim on, ANNE*'s voice continues, without a break.*]

Anne's Voice. We are all a little thinner. The Van Daans' "discussions" are as violent as ever. Mother still does not understand me. But then I don't understand her either. There is one great change, however. A change in myself. I read somewhere that girls of my age don't feel quite certain of themselves. That they become quiet within and begin to think of the miracle that is taking place in their bodies. I think that what is happening to me is so wonderful . . . not only what can be seen, but what is taking place inside. Each time it has happened, I have a feeling that I have a sweet secret. (*We hear the chimes and then a hymn being played on the carillon outside.*) And in spite of any pain, I long for the time when I shall feel that secret within me again.

[*The buzzer of the door below suddenly sounds. Everyone is startled.* MR. FRANK *tiptoes cautiously to the top of the steps and listens. Again the buzzer sounds, in* MIEP*'s V-for-victory signal.*[1]]

Mr. Frank. It's Miep!

[*He goes quickly down the steps to unbolt the door.* MRS. FRANK *calls upstairs to the* VAN DAANS *and then to* PETER.]

Mrs. Frank. Wake up, everyone! Miep is here! (ANNE *quickly puts her diary away.* MARGOT *sits up, pulling the blanket around her shoulders.* DUSSEL *sits on the edge of his bed, listening, disgruntled.* MIEP *comes up*

1. **V-for-victory signal:** three short rings and one long ring, Morse code for the letter *V*, the Allied symbol for victory.

Ⓐ **Literary Focus Drama** More than a year has elapsed since the end of Act One. What is life like now for the characters in the Annex, according to the voiceover?

the steps, followed by MR. KRALER. *They bring flowers, books, newspapers, etc.* ANNE *rushes to* MIEP, *throwing her arms affectionately around her.*) Miep . . . *and* Mr. Kraler. . . . What a delightful surprise!

Mr. Kraler. We came to bring you New Year's greetings.

Mrs. Frank. You shouldn't . . . you should have at least one day to yourselves. (*She goes quickly to the stove and brings down teacups and tea for all of them.*)

Anne. Don't say that, it's so wonderful to see them! (*Sniffing at* MIEP'*s coat*) I can smell the wind and the cold on your clothes.

Miep (*giving her the flowers*). There you are. (*Then to* MARGOT, *feeling her forehead*) How are you, Margot? . . . Feeling any better?

Margot. I'm all right.

Anne. We filled her full of every kind of pill so she won't cough and make a noise.

[*She runs into her room to put the flowers in water.* MR. *and* MRS. VAN DAAN *come from upstairs. Outside there is the sound of a band playing.*]

Mrs. Van Daan. Well, hello, Miep. Mr. Kraler.

Mr. Kraler (*giving a bouquet of flowers to* MRS. VAN DAAN). With my hope for peace in the New Year.

Peter (*anxiously*). Miep, have you seen Mouschi? Have you seen him anywhere around? **B**

Miep. I'm sorry, Peter. I asked everyone in the neighborhood had they seen a gray cat. But they said no.

[MRS. FRANK *gives* MIEP *a cup of tea.* MR. FRANK *comes up the steps, carrying a small cake on a plate.*]

Mr. Frank. Look what Miep's brought for us!

Mrs. Frank (*taking it*). A cake!

Mr. Van Daan. A cake! (*He pinches* MIEP'*s cheeks gaily and hurries up to the cupboard.*) I'll get some plates.

[DUSSEL, *in his room, hastily puts a coat on and starts out to join the others.*]

Mrs. Frank. Thank you, Miepia. You shouldn't have done it. You must have used all of your sugar ration for weeks. (*Giving it to* MRS. VAN DAAN) It's beautiful, isn't it?

Mrs. Van Daan. It's been ages since I even saw a cake. Not since you brought us one last year. (*Without looking at the cake, to* MIEP) Remember? Don't you remember, you gave us one on New Year's Day? Just this time last year? I'll never forget it because you had "Peace in nineteen forty-three" on it. (*She looks at the cake and reads*) "Peace in nineteen forty-four!"

Miep. Well, it has to come sometime, you know. (*As* DUSSEL *comes from his room*) Hello, Mr. Dussel.

Mr. Kraler. How are you?

Mr. Van Daan (*bringing plates and a knife*). Here's the knife, liefje. Now, how many of us are there?

Miep. None for me, thank you.

Mr. Frank. Oh, please. You must.

Miep. I couldn't.

B **Reading Focus** **Making Inferences** What can you infer happened to Mouschi based on the events of the previous scene of the play?

Mr. Kraler and Mr. Frank converse in stage production. ©Joan Marcus.

Mr. Van Daan. Good! That leaves one . . . two . . . three . . . seven of us.

Dussel. Eight! Eight! It's the same number as it always is!

Mr. Van Daan. I left Margot out. I take it for granted Margot won't eat any.

Anne. Why wouldn't she!

Mrs. Frank. I think it won't harm her.

Mr. Van Daan. All right! All right! I just didn't want her to start coughing again, that's all.

Dussel. And please, Mrs. Frank should cut the cake.

Mr. Van Daan. What's the difference?

Mrs. Van Daan. It's not Mrs. Frank's cake, is it, Miep? It's for all of us.

} *Together*

Dussel. Mrs. Frank divides things better.

Mrs. Van Daan (*going to* DUSSEL). What are you trying to say?

Mr. Van Daan. Oh, come on! Stop wasting time!

} *Together*

Mrs. Van Daan (*to* DUSSEL). Don't I always give everybody exactly the same? Don't I?

Mr. Van Daan. Forget it, Kerli.

Mrs. Van Daan. No. I want an answer! Don't I?

Dussel. Yes. Yes. Everybody gets exactly the same . . . except Mr. Van Daan always gets a little bit more.

[MR. VAN DAAN *advances on* DUSSEL, *the knife still in his hand.*]

Mr. Van Daan. That's a lie!

[DUSSEL *retreats before the onslaught of the* VAN DAANS.] C

Mr. Frank. Please, please! (*Then, to* MIEP) You see what a little sugar cake does to us? It goes right to our heads!
Mr. Van Daan (*handing* MRS. FRANK *the knife*). Here you are, Mrs. Frank.
Mrs. Frank. Thank you. (*Then, to* MIEP, *as she goes to the table to cut the cake*) Are you sure you won't have some?
Miep (*drinking her tea*). No, really, I have to go in a minute.

[*The sound of the band fades out in the distance.*]

Peter (*to* MIEP). Maybe Mouschi went back to our house . . . they say that cats . . . Do you ever get over there . . . ? I mean . . . do you suppose you could . . . ?
Miep. I'll try, Peter. The first minute I get, I'll try. But I'm afraid, with him gone a week . . .
Dussel. Make up your mind, already someone has had a nice big dinner from that cat!

[PETER *is furious, inarticulate. He starts toward* DUSSEL *as if to hit him.* MR. FRANK *stops him.* MRS. FRANK *speaks quickly to ease the situation.*]

Mrs. Frank (*to* MIEP). This is delicious, Miep!
Mrs. Van Daan (*eating hers*). Delicious!
Mr. Van Daan (*finishing it in one gulp*). Dirk's in luck to get a girl who can bake like this!
Miep (*putting down her empty teacup*). I have to run. Dirk's taking me to a party tonight.
Anne. How heavenly! Remember now what everyone is wearing and what you have to eat and everything, so you can tell us tomorrow.
Miep. I'll give you a full report! Goodbye, everyone!
Mr. Van Daan (*to* MIEP). Just a minute. There's something I'd like you to do for me. (*He hurries off up the stairs to his room.*)
Mrs. Van Daan (*sharply*). Putti, where are you going? (*She rushes up the stairs after him, calling hysterically.*) What do you want? Putti, what are you going to do?
Miep (*to* PETER). What's wrong?
Peter (*his sympathy is with his mother*). Father says he's going to sell her fur coat. She's crazy about that old fur coat.
Dussel. Is it possible? Is it possible that anyone is so silly as to worry about a fur coat in times like this?
Peter. It's none of your darn business . . . and if you say one more thing . . . I'll, I'll take you and I'll . . . I mean it . . . I'll . . .

[*There is a piercing scream from* MRS. VAN DAAN, *above. She grabs at the fur coat as* MR. VAN DAAN *is starting downstairs with it.*]

Mrs. Van Daan. No! No! No! Don't you dare take that! You hear? It's mine! (*Downstairs* PETER *turns away, embarrassed, miserable.*) My father gave me that! You didn't give it to me. You have no right. Let go of it . . . you hear?

C **Literary Focus** **Drama** Have the conflicts among the characters increased or decreased since the end of Act One? How can you tell?

[MR. VAN DAAN *pulls the coat from her hands and hurries downstairs.* MRS. VAN DAAN *sinks to the floor, sobbing. As* MR. VAN DAAN *comes into the main room, the others look away, embarrassed for him.*]

Mr. Van Daan (*to* MR. KRALER). Just a little—discussion over the advisability of selling this coat. As I have often reminded Mrs. Van Daan, it's very selfish of her to keep it when people outside are in such desperate need of clothing. . . . (*He gives the coat to* MIEP.) So if you will please to sell it for us? It should fetch a good price. And by the way, will you get me cigarettes. I don't care what kind they are . . . get all you can. D

My father gave me that! You didn't give it to me. You have no right.

Miep. It's terribly difficult to get them, Mr. Van Daan. But I'll try. Goodbye.

[*She goes.* MR. FRANK *follows her down the steps to bolt the door after her.* MRS. FRANK *gives* MR. KRALER *a cup of tea.*]

Mrs. Frank. Are you sure you won't have some cake, Mr. Kraler?
Mr. Kraler. I'd better not.
Mr. Van Daan. You're still feeling badly? What does your doctor say?
Mr. Kraler. I haven't been to him.
Mrs. Frank. Now, Mr. Kraler! . . .
Mr. Kraler (*sitting at the table*). Oh, I tried. But you can't get near a doctor these days . . . they're so busy. After weeks I finally managed to get one on the telephone. I told him I'd like an appointment . . . I wasn't feeling very well. You know what he answers . . . over the telephone . . . "Stick out your tongue!" (*They laugh. He turns to* MR. FRANK *as* MR. FRANK *comes back.*) I have some contracts here . . . I wonder if you'd look over them with me . . .
Mr. Frank (*putting out his hand*). Of course.
Mr. Kraler (*he rises*). If we could go downstairs . . . (MR. FRANK *starts ahead;* MR. KRALER *speaks to the others.*) Will you forgive us? I won't keep him but a minute. (*He starts to follow* MR. FRANK *down the steps.*)
Margot (*with sudden foreboding*). What's happened? Something's happened! Hasn't it, Mr. Kraler?

[MR. KRALER *stops and comes back, trying to reassure* MARGOT *with a pretense of casualness.*]

Mr. Kraler. No, really. I want your father's advice . . .
Margot. Something's gone wrong! I know it!
Mr. Frank (*coming back, to* MR. KRALER). If it's something that concerns us here, it's better that we all hear it.
Mr. Kraler (*turning to him, quietly*). But . . . the children . . . ?

D **Literary Perspectives** **Analyzing Responses** What does your experience with people tell you about Mr. Van Daan's desire to sell his wife's coat?

Mr. Frank. What they'd imagine would be worse than any reality.

[*As* MR. KRALER *speaks, they all listen with intense apprehension.* MRS. VAN DAAN *comes down the stairs and sits on the bottom step.*]

Mr. Kraler. It's a man in the storeroom . . . I don't know whether or not you remember him . . . Carl, about fifty, heavyset, near-sighted. . . . He came with us just before you left.

Mr. Frank. He was from Utrecht?

Mr. Kraler. That's the man. A couple of weeks ago, when I was in the storeroom, he closed the door and asked me . . . "How's Mr. Frank? What do you hear from Mr. Frank?" I told him I only knew there was a rumor that you were in Switzerland. He said he'd heard that rumor too, but he thought I might know something more. I didn't pay any attention to it . . . but then a thing happened yesterday . . . He'd brought some invoices to the office for me to sign. As I was going through them, I looked up. He was standing staring at the bookcase . . . your bookcase. He said he thought he remembered a door there . . . Wasn't there a door there that used to go up to the loft? Then he told me he wanted more money. Twenty guilders[2] more a week. E

Mr. Van Daan. Blackmail!

Mr. Frank. Twenty guilders? Very modest blackmail.

Mr. Van Daan. That's just the beginning.

Dussel (*coming to* MR. FRANK). You know what I think? He was the thief who was down there that night. That's how he knows we're here.

Mr. Frank (*to* MR. KRALER). How was it left? What did you tell him?

Mr. Kraler. I said I had to think about it. What shall I do? Pay him the money? . . . Take a chance on firing him . . . or what? I don't know.

Dussel (*frantic*). For God's sake, don't fire him! Pay him what he asks . . . keep him here where you can have your eye on him.

Mr. Frank. Is it so much that he's asking? What are they paying nowadays?

Mr. Kraler. He could get it in a war plant. But this isn't a war plant. Mind you, I don't know if he really knows . . . or if he doesn't know.

Mr. Frank. Offer him half. Then we'll soon find out if it's blackmail or not.

Dussel. And if it is? We've got to pay it, haven't we? Anything he asks we've got to pay!

Mr. Frank. Let's decide that when the time comes.

Mr. Kraler. This may be all my imagination. You get to a point, these days, where you suspect everyone and everything. Again and again . . . on some simple look or word, I've found myself . . .

[*The telephone rings in the office below.*]

Mrs. Van Daan (*hurrying to* MR. KRALER). There's the telephone! What does that mean,

2. **guilders** (GIHL duhrz): Dutch money.

E **Literary Focus** **Drama** What complication does Mr. Kraler introduce? How does it contribute to the suspense?

CULTURE LINK

The United States Holocaust Memorial Museum

In 1978, more than thirty years after the end of World War II, President Jimmy Carter asked a committee led by Holocaust survivor and author Elie Wiesel to suggest ways in which the victims of the Holocaust could be honored. The committee called for the construction of a memorial museum in Washington, D.C. In 1985, participants in a ground-breaking ceremony for the United States Holocaust Memorial Museum buried on the National Mall, near the Lincoln Memorial and the Washington Monument, two small containers of ashes and dirt from concentration camps. Opened in 1993, the museum serves both as a memorial to the Holocaust's victims and a reminder of the dangers of genocide—the mass killing of a people—and threats to democracy that still exist in the world today. Since 1993, more than 25 million people have visited the museum.

Ask Yourself

What quotations from Anne Frank's diary would you include in an exhibit in the Holocaust Museum?

the telephone ringing on a holiday?

Mr. Kraler. That's my wife. I told her I had to go over some papers in my office . . . to call me there when she got out of church. (*He starts out.*) I'll offer him half, then. Goodbye . . . we'll hope for the best!

[*The group call their goodbyes halfheartedly.* MR. FRANK *follows* MR. KRALER *to bolt the door below. During the following scene,* MR. FRANK *comes back up and stands listening, disturbed.*]

Dussel (*to* MR. VAN DAAN). You can thank your son for this . . . smashing the light! I tell you, it's just a question of time now. (*He goes to the window at the back and stands looking out.*)

Margot. Sometimes I wish the end would come . . . whatever it is.

Mrs. Frank (*shocked*). Margot!

[ANNE *goes to* MARGOT, *sitting beside her on the couch with her arms around her.*]

Margot. Then at least we'd know where we were.

Mrs. Frank. You should be ashamed of yourself! Talking that way! Think how lucky we are! Think of the thousands dying in the war, every day. Think of the people in concentration camps.

Anne (*interrupting*). What's the good of that? What's the good of thinking of misery when you're already miserable? That's stupid!

Mrs. Frank. Anne! **F**

[*As* ANNE *goes on raging at her mother,* MRS. FRANK *tries to break in, in an effort to quiet her.*]

Anne. We're young, Margot and Peter and I! You grown-ups have had your chance! But look at us. . . . If we begin thinking of all the horror in the world, we're lost! We're trying to hold on to some kind of ideals . . . when everything . . . ideals, hopes . . . everything is being destroyed! It isn't our fault that the world is in such a mess! We weren't around when all this started! So don't try to take it out on us! (*She rushes off to her room, slamming the door after her. She picks up a brush from the chest and hurls it to the floor. Then she sits on the settee, trying to control her anger.*)

Mr. Van Daan. She talks as if we started the war! Did we start the war? (*He spots* ANNE'S *cake. As he starts to take it,* PETER *anticipates him.*)

Peter. She left her cake. (*He starts for* ANNE'S *room with the cake. There is silence in the main room.* MRS. VAN DAAN *goes up to her room, followed by* MR. VAN DAAN. DUSSEL *stays looking out the window.* MR. FRANK *brings* MRS. FRANK *her cake. She eats it slowly, without relish.* MR. FRANK *takes his cake to* MARGOT *and sits quietly on the sofa beside her.* PETER *stands in the doorway of* ANNE'S *darkened room, looking at her, then makes a little movement to let her know he is there.* ANNE *sits up quickly, trying to hide the signs of her tears.* PETER *holds out the cake to her.*) You left this.

Anne (*dully*). Thanks.

[PETER *starts to go out, then comes back.*]

Peter. I thought you were fine just now. You know just how to talk to them. You know

F **Reading Focus** **Making Inferences** Why do you think Margot and Anne's views differ from their mother's?

Anne's room in the Anne Frank House Museum, Amsterdam.

just how to say it. I'm no good . . . I never can think . . . especially when I'm mad. . . . That Dussel . . . when he said that about Mouschi . . . someone eating him . . . all I could think is . . . I wanted to hit him. I wanted to give him such a . . . a . . . that he'd. . . . That's what I used to do when there was an argument at school. . . . That's the way I . . . but here. . . . And an old man like that . . . it wouldn't be so good.

Anne. You're making a big mistake about me. I do it all wrong. I say too much. I go too far. I hurt people's feelings. . . .

[DUSSEL *leaves the window, going to his room.*]

Peter. I think you're just fine. . . . What I want to say . . . if it wasn't for you around here, I don't know. What I mean . . .

[PETER *is interrupted by* DUSSEL*'s turning on the light.* DUSSEL *stands in the doorway, startled to see* PETER. PETER *advances toward him forbiddingly.* DUSSEL *backs out of the room.* PETER *closes the door on him.*]

Anne. Do you mean it, Peter? Do you really mean it?

Peter. I said it, didn't I?

Anne. Thank you, Peter! G

[*In the main room* MR. *and* MRS. FRANK *collect the dishes and take them to the sink, washing them.* MARGOT *lies down again on the couch.* DUSSEL, *lost, wanders into* PETER*'s room and takes up a book, starting to read.*]

Peter (*looking at the photographs on the wall*). You've got quite a collection.

Anne. Wouldn't you like some in your room? I could give you some. Heaven knows you spend enough time in there . . . doing heaven knows what . . .

Peter. It's easier. A fight starts, or an argument . . . I duck in there.

Anne. You're lucky, having a room to go to. His Lordship is always here. . . . I hardly ever get a minute alone. When they start in on me, I can't duck away. I have to stand there and take it.

Peter. You gave some of it back just now.

Anne. I get so mad. They've formed their opinions . . . about everything . . . but we . . . we're still trying to find out. . . . We have problems here that no other people our age have ever had. And just as you think you've solved them, something comes along and bang! You have to start all over again.

Peter. At least you've got someone you can talk to.

Anne. Not really. Mother . . . I never discuss anything serious with her. She doesn't understand. Father's all right. We can talk about everything . . . everything but one thing. Mother. He simply won't talk about her. I don't think you can be really intimate with anyone if he holds something back, do you?

Peter. I think your father's fine.

Anne. Oh, he is, Peter! He is! He's the only one who's ever given me the feeling that I have any sense. But anyway, nothing can take the place of school and play and friends of your own age . . . or near your age . . . can it?

G Literary Focus Drama How has Anne and Peter's relationship changed since Act One?

Peter. I suppose you miss your friends and all.

Anne. It isn't just . . . (*She breaks off, staring up at him for a second.*) Isn't it funny, you and I? Here we've been seeing each other every minute for almost a year and a half, and this is the first time we've ever really talked. It helps a lot to have someone to talk to, don't you think? It helps you to let off steam.

Peter (*going to the door*). Well, any time you want to let off steam, you can come into my room.

Anne (*following him*). I can get up an awful lot of steam. You'll have to be careful how you say that.

Peter. It's all right with me.

Anne. Do you mean it?

Peter. I said it, didn't I?

[*He goes out.* ANNE *stands in her doorway looking after him. As* PETER *gets to his door, he stands for a minute looking back at her. Then he goes into his room.* DUSSEL *rises as he comes in, and quickly passes him, going out. He starts across for his room.* ANNE *sees him coming and pulls her door shut.* DUSSEL *turns back toward* PETER*'s room.* PETER *pulls his door shut.* DUSSEL *stands there, bewildered, forlorn.*

The scene slowly dims out. The curtain falls on the scene. ANNE*'s voice comes over in the darkness . . . faintly at first and then with growing strength.*]

Anne's Voice. We've had bad news. The people from whom Miep got our ration books have been arrested. So we have had to cut down on our food. Our stomachs are so empty that they rumble and make strange noises, all in different keys. Mr. Van Daan's is deep and low, like a bass fiddle. Mine is high, whistling like a flute. As we all sit around waiting for supper, it's like an orchestra tuning up. It only needs Toscanini[3] to raise his baton and we'd be off in the "Ride of the Valkyries."[4] Monday, the sixth of March, nineteen forty-four. Mr. Kraler is in the hospital. It seems he has ulcers. Pim says we are his ulcers. Miep has to run the business and us too. The Americans have landed on the southern tip of Italy. Father looks for a quick finish to the war. Mr. Dussel is waiting every day for the warehouse man to demand more money. Have I been skipping too much from one subject to another? I can't help it. I feel that spring is coming. I feel it in my whole body and soul. I feel utterly confused. I am longing . . . so longing . . . for everything . . . for friends . . . for someone to talk to . . . someone who understands . . . someone young, who feels as I do . . . **H**

[*As these last lines are being said, the curtain rises on the scene. The lights dim on.* ANNE*'s voice fades out.*]

3. **Toscanini** (tahs kuh NEE nee): Arturo Toscanini (1867–1957), a famous orchestra conductor.
4. **"Ride of the Valkyries"** (val KIHR eez): lively piece of music from an opera by the German composer Richard Wagner (1813–1883).

H **Read and Discuss** How is the new year developing for the families?

Vocabulary **forlorn** (fawr LAWRN) *adj.:* abandoned and lonely.

SCENE 2

It is evening, after supper. From outside we hear the sound of children playing. The "grown-ups," with the exception of MR. VAN DAAN, *are all in the main room.* MRS. FRANK *is doing some mending.* MRS. VAN DAAN *is reading a fashion magazine.* MR. FRANK *is going over business accounts.* DUSSEL, *in his dentist's jacket, is pacing up and down, impatient to get into his bedroom.* MR. VAN DAAN *is upstairs working on a piece of embroidery in an embroidery frame.*

In his room PETER *is sitting before the mirror, smoothing his hair. As the scene goes on, he puts on his tie, brushes his coat and puts it on, preparing himself meticulously for a visit from* ANNE. *On his wall are now hung some of* ANNE'*s motion picture stars.*

In her room ANNE *too is getting dressed. She stands before the mirror in her slip, trying various ways of dressing her hair.* MARGOT *is seated on the sofa, hemming a skirt for* ANNE *to wear.*

In the main room DUSSEL *can stand it no longer. He comes over, rapping sharply on the door of his and* ANNE'*s bedroom.*

Anne (*calling to him*). No, no, Mr. Dussel! I am not dressed yet. (DUSSEL *walks away, furious, sitting down and burying his head in his hands.* ANNE *turns to* MARGOT.) How is that? How does that look?
Margot (*glancing at her briefly*). Fine.
Anne. You didn't even look.
Margot. Of course I did. It's fine.
Anne. Margot, tell me, am I terribly ugly?
Margot. Oh, stop fishing.
Anne. No. No. Tell me.
Margot. Of course you're not. You've got nice eyes . . . and a lot of animation, and . . .
Anne. A little vague, aren't you?

[*She reaches over and takes a brassiere out of* MARGOT'*s sewing basket. She holds it up to herself, studying the effect in the mirror. Outside,* MRS. FRANK, *feeling sorry for* DUSSEL, *comes over, knocking at the girls' door.*]

Mrs. Frank (*outside*). May I come in?
Margot. Come in, Mother.
Mrs. Frank (*shutting the door behind her*). Mr. Dussel's impatient to get in here.
Anne (*still with the brassiere*). Heavens, he takes the room for himself the entire day.
Mrs. Frank (*gently*). Anne, dear, you're not going in again tonight to see Peter?
Anne (*dignified*). That is my intention.
Mrs. Frank. But you've already spent a great deal of time in there today.
Anne. I was in there exactly twice. Once to get the dictionary, and then three quarters of an hour before supper.
Mrs. Frank. Aren't you afraid you're disturbing him?
Anne. Mother, I have some intuition.
Mrs. Frank. Then may I ask you this much, Anne. Please don't shut the door when you go in.
Anne. You sound like Mrs. Van Daan! (*She throws the brassiere back in* MARGOT'*s sewing basket and picks up her blouse, putting it on.*)
Mrs. Frank. No. No. I don't mean to suggest anything wrong. I only wish that you wouldn't expose yourself to criticism . . . that

you wouldn't give Mrs. Van Daan the opportunity to be unpleasant.

Anne. Mrs. Van Daan doesn't need an opportunity to be unpleasant!

Mrs. Frank. Everyone's on edge, worried about Mr. Kraler. This is one more thing . . .

Anne. I'm sorry, Mother. I'm going to Peter's room. I'm not going to let Petronella Van Daan spoil our friendship.

[MRS. FRANK *hesitates for a second, then goes out, closing the door after her. She gets a pack of playing cards and sits at the center table, playing solitaire. In* ANNE'S *room* MARGOT *hands the finished skirt to* ANNE. *As* ANNE *is putting it on,* MARGOT *takes off her high-heeled shoes and stuffs paper in the toes so that* ANNE *can wear them.*]

Margot (*to* ANNE). Why don't you two talk in the main room? It'd save a lot of trouble. It's hard on Mother, having to listen to those remarks from Mrs. Van Daan and not say a word.

Anne. Why doesn't she say a word? I think it's ridiculous to take it and take it.

Margot. You don't understand Mother at all, do you? She can't talk back. She's not like you. It's just not in her nature to fight back.

Anne. Anyway . . . the only one I worry about is you. I feel awfully guilty about you. (*She sits on the stool near* MARGOT, *putting on* MARGOT'S *high-heeled shoes.*)

Margot. What about?

Anne. I mean, every time I go into Peter's room, I have a feeling I may be hurting you. (MARGOT *shakes her head.*) I know if it were me, I'd be wild. I'd be desperately jealous, if it were me.

Margot. Well, I'm not.

Anne. You don't feel badly? Really? Truly? You're not jealous?

Margot. Of course I'm jealous . . . jealous that you've got something to get up in the morning for. . . . But jealous of you and Peter? No. **I**

[ANNE *goes back to the mirror.*]

Anne. Maybe there's nothing to be jealous of. Maybe he doesn't really like me. Maybe I'm just taking the place of his cat . . . (*She picks up a pair of short white gloves, putting them on.*) Wouldn't you like to come in with us?

Margot. I have a book.

[*The sound of the children playing outside fades out. In the main room* DUSSEL *can stand it no longer. He jumps up, going to the bedroom door and knocking sharply.*]

Dussel. Will you please let me in my room!

Anne. Just a minute, dear, dear Mr. Dussel. (*She picks up her mother's pink stole and adjusts it elegantly over her shoulders, then gives a last look in the mirror.*) Well, here I go . . . to run the gantlet.[5] (*She starts out, followed by* MARGOT.)

5. **run the gantlet** (GAWNT liht): proceed while under attack from both sides.

I **Literary Focus** **Drama** What does this scene reveal about the relationship between the two sisters? How are their characters similar or different?

Dussel (*as she appears—sarcastic*). Thank you so much.

[DUSSEL *goes into his room.* ANNE *goes toward* PETER*'s* room, *passing* MRS. VAN DAAN *and her parents at the center table.*]

Mrs. Van Daan. My God, look at her! (ANNE *pays no attention. She knocks at* PETER*'s door.*) I don't know what good it is to have a son. I never see him. He wouldn't care if I killed myself. (PETER *opens the door and stands aside for* ANNE *to come in.*) Just a minute, Anne. (*She goes to them at the door.*) I'd like to say a few words to my son. Do you mind? (PETER *and* ANNE *stand waiting.*) Peter, I don't want you staying up till all hours tonight. You've got to have your sleep. You're a growing boy. You hear?

They don't realize how much more advanced we are.

Mrs. Frank. Anne won't stay late. She's going to bed promptly at nine. Aren't you, Anne?
Anne. Yes, Mother . . . (*To* MRS. VAN DAAN) May we go now?
Mrs. Van Daan. Are you asking me? I didn't know I had anything to say about it.
Mrs. Frank. Listen for the chimes, Anne dear.

[*The two young people go off into* PETER*'s room, shutting the door after them.*]

Mrs. Van Daan (*to* MRS. FRANK). In my day it was the boys who called on the girls. Not the girls on the boys.
Mrs. Frank. You know how young people like to feel that they have secrets. Peter's room is the only place where they can talk.
Mrs. Van Daan. Talk! That's not what they called it when I was young.

[MRS. VAN DAAN *goes off to the bathroom.* MARGOT *settles down to read her book.* MR. FRANK *puts his papers away and brings a chess game to the center table. He and* MRS. FRANK *start to play. In* PETER*'s room,* ANNE *speaks to* PETER, *indignant, humiliated.*]

Anne. Aren't they awful? Aren't they impossible? Treating us as if we were still in the nursery.

[*She sits on the cot.* PETER *gets a bottle of pop and two glasses.*]

Peter. Don't let it bother you. It doesn't bother me.
Anne. I suppose you can't really blame them . . . they think back to what *they* were like at our age. They don't realize how much more advanced we are. . . . When you think what wonderful discussions we've had! . . . Oh, I forgot. I was going to bring you some more pictures.
Peter. Oh, these are fine, thanks.
Anne. Don't you want some more? Miep just brought me some new ones.
Peter. Maybe later. (*He gives her a glass of pop and, taking some for himself, sits down facing her.*)
Anne (*looking up at one of the photographs*). I remember when I got that. . . . I won it. I bet Jopie that I could eat five ice-cream cones.

We'd all been playing ping-pong. . . . We used to have heavenly times . . . we'd finish up with ice cream at the Delphi or the Oasis, where Jews were allowed . . . there'd always be a lot of boys . . . we'd laugh and joke. . . . I'd like to go back to it for a few days or a week. But after that I know I'd be bored to death. I think more seriously about life now. I want to be a journalist . . . or something. I love to write. What do you want to do?

Peter. I thought I might go off someplace . . . work on a farm or something . . . some job that doesn't take much brains.

Anne. You shouldn't talk that way. You've got the most awful inferiority complex.

Peter. I know I'm not smart.

Anne. That isn't true. You're much better than I am in dozens of things . . . arithmetic and algebra and . . . well, you're a million times better than I am in algebra. (*With sudden directness*) You like Margot, don't you? Right from the start you liked her, liked her much better than me.

Peter (*uncomfortably*). Oh, I don't know.

[*In the main room* MRS. VAN DAAN *comes from the bathroom and goes over to the sink, polishing a coffeepot.*]

Anne. It's all right. Everyone feels that way. Margot's so good. She's sweet and bright and beautiful and I'm not.

Peter. I wouldn't say that. **J**

Anne. Oh, no, I'm not. I know that. I know quite well that I'm not a beauty. I never have been and never shall be.

Peter. I don't agree at all. I think you're pretty.

Anne. That's not true!

Peter. And another thing. You've changed . . . from at first, I mean.

Anne. I have?

Peter. I used to think you were awful noisy.

Anne. And what do you think now, Peter? How have I changed?

Peter. Well . . . er . . . you're . . . quieter.

[*In his room* DUSSEL *takes his pajamas and toilet articles and goes into the bathroom to change.*]

Anne. I'm glad you don't just hate me.

Peter. I never said that.

Anne. I bet when you get out of here, you'll never think of me again.

Peter. That's crazy.

Anne. When you get back with all of your friends, you're going to say . . . now what did I ever see in that Mrs. Quack Quack.

Peter. I haven't got any friends.

Anne. Oh, Peter, of course you have. Everyone has friends.

Peter. Not me. I don't want any. I get along all right without them.

Anne. Does that mean you can get along without me? I think of myself as your friend.

Peter. No. If they were all like you, it'd be different.

[*He takes the glasses and the bottle and puts them away. There is a second's silence and then* ANNE *speaks, hesitantly, shyly.*]

J **Reading Focus** **Making Inferences** Why do you think Anne asks Peter about his feelings for Margot?

Anne. Peter, did you ever kiss a girl?
Peter. Yes. Once.
Anne (*to cover her feelings*). That picture's crooked. (PETER *goes over, straightening the photograph.*) Was she pretty?
Peter. Huh?
Anne. The girl that you kissed.
Peter. I don't know. I was blindfolded. (*He comes back and sits down again.*) It was at a party. One of those kissing games.
Anne (*relieved*). Oh. I don't suppose that really counts, does it?
Peter. It didn't with me.
Anne. I've been kissed twice. Once a man I'd never seen before kissed me on the cheek when he picked me up off the ice and I was crying. And the other was Mr. Koophuis, a friend of Father's, who kissed my hand. You wouldn't say those counted, would you?
Peter. I wouldn't say so.
Anne. I know almost for certain that Margot would never kiss anyone unless she was engaged to them. And I'm sure too that Mother never touched a man before Pim. But I don't know . . . things are so different now. . . . What do you think? Do you think a girl shouldn't kiss anyone except if she's engaged or something? It's so hard to try to think what to do, when here we are with the whole world falling around our ears and you think . . . well . . . you don't know what's going to happen tomorrow and. . . . What do you think?
Peter. I suppose it'd depend on the girl. Some girls, anything they do's wrong. But others . . . well . . . it wouldn't necessarily be wrong with them. (*The carillon starts to strike nine o'clock.*) I've always thought that when two people . . .

Anne and Peter in the stage production. ©Joan Marcus.

Anne. Nine o'clock. I have to go.
Peter. That's right.
Anne (*without moving*). Good night.

[*There is a second's pause; then* PETER *gets up and moves toward the door.*]

Peter. You won't let them stop you coming?
Anne. No. (*She rises and starts for the door.*) Sometime I might bring my diary. There are so many things in it that I want to talk over with you. There's a lot about you.
Peter. What kind of thing?

Anne. I wouldn't want you to see some of it. I thought you were a nothing, just the way you thought about me.
Peter. Did you change your mind, the way I changed my mind about you?
Anne. Well. . . . You'll see . . .

[*For a second* ANNE *stands looking up at* PETER, *longing for him to kiss her. As he makes no move, she turns away. Then suddenly* PETER *grabs her awkwardly in his arms, kissing her on the cheek.* ANNE *walks out dazed. She stands for a minute, her back to the people in the main room. As she regains her poise, she goes to her mother and father and* MARGOT, *silently kissing them. They murmur their good nights to her. As she is about to open her bedroom door, she catches sight of* MRS. VAN DAAN. *She goes quickly to her, taking her face in her hands and kissing her, first on one cheek and then on the other. Then she hurries off into her room.* MRS. VAN DAAN *looks after her and then looks over at* PETER*'s room. Her suspicions are confirmed.*]

Mrs. Van Daan (*she knows*). Ah hah!

[*The lights dim out. The curtain falls on the scene. In the darkness* ANNE*'s voice comes, faintly at first and then with growing strength.*]

Anne's Voice. By this time we all know each other so well that if anyone starts to tell a story, the rest can finish it for him. We're having to cut down still further on our meals. What makes it worse, the rats have been at work again. They've carried off some of our precious food. Even Mr. Dussel wishes now that Mouschi was here. Thursday, the twentieth of April, nineteen forty-four. Invasion fever is mounting every day. Miep tells us that people outside talk of nothing else. For myself, life has become much more pleasant. I often go to Peter's room after supper. Oh, don't think I'm in love, because I'm not. But it does make life more bearable to have someone with whom you can exchange views. No more tonight. P.S. . . . I must be honest. I must confess that I actually live for the next meeting. Is there anything lovelier than to sit under the skylight and feel the sun on your cheeks and have a darling boy in your arms? I admit now that I'm glad the Van Daans had a son and not a daughter. I've outgrown another dress. That's the third. I'm having to wear Margot's clothes after all. I'm working hard on my French and am now reading *La Belle Nivernaise.*[6] **K**

[*As she is saying the last lines, the curtain rises on the scene. The lights dim on as* ANNE*'s voice fades out.*]

SCENE 3

It is night, a few weeks later. Everyone is in bed. There is complete quiet. In the VAN DAANS' *room a match flares up for a moment and then is quickly put out.* MR. VAN DAAN, *in bare feet, dressed in underwear and trousers, is dimly seen coming stealthily down the stairs and into the main room, where* MR. *and* MRS.

6. ***La Belle Nivernaise*** (nee VEHR nehz): children's story by Alphonse Daudet (1840–1897).

K **Read and Discuss** What has changed within the household?

FRANK *and* MARGOT *are sleeping. He goes to the food safe and again lights a match. Then he cautiously opens the safe, taking out a half loaf of bread. As he closes the safe, it creaks. He stands rigid.* MRS. FRANK *sits up in bed. She sees him.* L

Mrs. Frank (*screaming*). Otto! Otto! Komme schnell![7]

[*The rest of the people wake, hurriedly getting up.*]

Mr. Frank. Was ist los? Was ist passiert?[8]

[DUSSEL, *followed by* ANNE, *comes from his room.*]

Mrs. Frank (*as she rushes over to* MR. VAN DAAN). Er stiehlt das Essen![9]
Dussel (*grabbing* MR. VAN DAAN). You! You! Give me that.
Mrs. Van Daan (*coming down the stairs*). Putti . . . Putti . . . what is it?
Dussel (*his hands on* MR. VAN DAAN*'s neck*). You dirty thief . . . stealing food . . . you good-for-nothing . . .
Mr. Frank. Mr. Dussel! For God's sake! Help me, Peter!

[PETER *comes over, trying, with* MR. FRANK, *to separate the two struggling men.*]

Peter. Let him go! Let go!

7. **Komme schnell:** German for "Come quickly."
8. **Was . . . passiert:** "What's going on? What happened?"
9. **Er . . . Essen:** "He is stealing the food."

[DUSSEL *drops* MR. VAN DAAN, *pushing him away. He shows them the end of a loaf of bread that he has taken from* MR. VAN DAAN.]

Dussel. You greedy, selfish . . . !

[MARGOT *turns on the lights.*]

Mrs. Van Daan. Putti . . . what is it?

[*All of* MRS. FRANK*'s gentleness, her self-control, is gone. She is outraged, in a frenzy of indignation.*]

Mrs. Frank. The bread! He was stealing the bread!
Dussel. It was you, and all the time we thought it was the rats!
Mr. Frank. Mr. Van Daan, how could you!
Mr. Van Daan. I'm hungry.
Mrs. Frank. We're all of us hungry! I see the children getting thinner and thinner. Your own son Peter . . . I've heard him moan in his sleep, he's so hungry. And you come in the night and steal food that should go to them . . . to the children!
Mrs. Van Daan (*going to* MR. VAN DAAN *protectively*). He needs more food than the rest of us. He's used to more. He's a big man.

[MR. VAN DAAN *breaks away, going over and sitting on the couch.*]

Mrs. Frank (*turning on* MRS. VAN DAAN). And you . . . you're worse than he is! You're a mother, and yet you sacrifice your child to this man . . . this . . . this . . .
Mr. Frank. Edith! Edith!

L **Literary Focus** **Drama** What new conflict has arisen?

[MARGOT *picks up the pink woolen stole, putting it over her mother's shoulders.*]

Mrs. Frank (*paying no attention, going on to* MRS. VAN DAAN). Don't think I haven't seen you! Always saving the choicest bits for him! I've watched you day after day and I've held my tongue. But not any longer! Not after this! Now I want him to go! I want him to get out of here!

Mr. Frank. Edith!
Mr. Van Daan. Get out of here?
Mrs. Van Daan. What do you mean?
} *Together*

Mrs. Frank. Just that! Take your things and get out! M

Mr. Frank (*to* MRS. FRANK). You're speaking in anger. You cannot mean what you are saying.

Mrs. Frank. I mean exactly that!

[MRS. VAN DAAN *takes a cover from the* FRANKS' *bed, pulling it about her.*]

Mr. Frank. For two long years we have lived here, side by side. We have respected each other's rights . . . we have managed to live in peace. Are we now going to throw it all away? I know this will never happen again, will it, Mr. Van Daan?

Mr. Van Daan. No. No.

Mrs. Frank. He steals once! He'll steal again!

[MR. VAN DAAN, *holding his stomach, starts for the bathroom.* ANNE *puts her arms around him, helping him up the step.*]

Mr. Frank. Edith, please. Let us be calm. We'll all go to our rooms . . . and afterwards we'll sit down quietly and talk this out . . . we'll find some way . . .

Mrs. Frank. No! No! No more talk! I want them to leave!

Mrs. Van Daan. You'd put us out, on the streets?

Mrs. Frank. There are other hiding places.

Mrs. Van Daan. A cellar . . . a closet. I know. And we have no money left even to pay for that.

Mrs. Frank. I'll give you money. Out of my own pocket I'll give it gladly. (*She gets her purse from a shelf and comes back with it.*)

Mrs. Van Daan. Mr. Frank, you told Putti you'd never forget what he'd done for you when you came to Amsterdam. You said you could never repay him, that you . . .

Mrs. Frank (*counting out money*). If my husband had any obligation to you, he's paid it, over and over.

Mr. Frank. Edith, I've never seen you like this before. I don't know you.

Mrs. Frank. I should have spoken out long ago.

Dussel. You can't be nice to some people.

Mrs. Van Daan (*turning on* DUSSEL). There would have been plenty for all of us, if *you* hadn't come in here!

Mr. Frank. We don't need the Nazis to destroy us. We're destroying ourselves. N

[*He sits down, with his head in his hands.* MRS. FRANK *goes to* MRS. VAN DAAN.]

M **Reading Focus** **Making Inferences** What does this sudden change in attitude suggest about Mrs. Frank's character? What might Anne and the audience learn about her from her outburst?

N **Read and Discuss** How does Mr. Frank's comment connect to the events in the scene?

Analyzing Visuals **Viewing and Interpreting** What scene from the play does this photo capture?

Scene from the stage production. ©Joan Marcus.

Mrs. Frank (*giving* MRS. VAN DAAN *some money*). Give this to Miep. She'll find you a place.
Anne. Mother, you're not putting *Peter* out. Peter hasn't done anything.
Mrs. Frank. He'll stay, of course. When I say I must protect the children, I mean Peter too.

[PETER *rises from the steps where he has been sitting.*]

Peter. I'd have to go if Father goes.

[MR. VAN DAAN *comes from the bathroom.* MRS. VAN DAAN *hurries to him and takes him to the couch. Then she gets water from the sink to bathe his face.*]

Mrs. Frank (*while this is going on*). He's no father to you . . . that man! He doesn't know what it is to be a father!
Peter (*starting for his room*). I wouldn't feel right. I couldn't stay.
Mrs. Frank. Very well, then. I'm sorry.
Anne (*rushing over to* PETER). No, Peter! No! (PETER *goes into his room, closing the door after him.* ANNE *turns back to her mother, crying.*) I don't care about the food. They can have mine! I don't want it! Only don't send them away. It'll be daylight soon. They'll be caught . . .

Margot (*putting her arms comfortingly around* ANNE). Please, Mother!

Mrs. Frank. They're not going now. They'll stay here until Miep finds them a place. (*To* MRS. VAN DAAN) But one thing I insist on! He must never come down here again! He must never come to this room where the food is stored! We'll divide what we have . . . an equal share for each! (DUSSEL *hurries over to get a sack of potatoes from the food safe.* MRS. FRANK *goes on, to* MRS. VAN DAAN) You can cook it here and take it up to him.

[DUSSEL *brings the sack of potatoes back to the center table.*]

Margot. Oh, no. No. We haven't sunk so far that we're going to fight over a handful of rotten potatoes.

Dussel (*dividing the potatoes into piles*). Mrs. Frank, Mr. Frank, Margot, Anne, Peter, Mrs. Van Daan, Mr. Van Daan, myself . . . Mrs. Frank . . . O

[*The buzzer sounds in* MIEP*'s signal.*]

Mr. Frank. It's Miep! (*He hurries over, getting his overcoat and putting it on.*)

Margot. At this hour?

Mrs. Frank. It is trouble.

Mr. Frank (*as he starts down to unbolt the door*). I beg you, don't let her see a thing like this!

Dussel (*counting without stopping*) . . . Anne, Peter, Mrs. Van Daan, Mr. Van Daan, myself . . .

Margot (*to* DUSSEL). Stop it! Stop it!

Dussel. . . . Mr. Frank, Margot, Anne, Peter, Mrs. Van Daan, Mr. Van Daan, myself, Mrs. Frank . . .

Mrs. Van Daan. You're keeping the big ones for yourself! All the big ones. . . . Look at the size of that! . . . And that! . . .

[DUSSEL *continues with his dividing.* PETER, *with his shirt and trousers on, comes from his room.*]

Margot. Stop it! Stop it!

[*We hear* MIEP*'s excited voice speaking to* MR. FRANK *below.*]

Miep. Mr. Frank . . . the most wonderful news! . . . The invasion[10] has begun!

Mr. Frank. Go on, tell them! Tell them!

[MIEP *comes running up the steps, ahead of* MR. FRANK. *She has a man's raincoat on over her nightclothes and a bunch of orange-colored flowers in her hand.*]

Miep. Did you hear that, everybody? Did you hear what I said? The invasion has begun! The invasion!

[*They all stare at* MIEP, *unable to grasp what she is telling them.* PETER *is the first to recover his wits.*]

10. **the invasion:** On June 6, 1944, Allied forces landed in Normandy, a region of northern France, to launch a military campaign against the Germans.

O **Literary Focus** **Drama** How would you compare this conflict to others that have flared up among the characters throughout the play? Explain.

Peter. Where?
Mrs. Van Daan. When? When, Miep?
Miep. It began early this morning . . .

[*As she talks on, the realization of what she has said begins to dawn on them. Everyone goes crazy. A wild demonstration takes place.* MRS. FRANK *hugs* MR. VAN DAAN.]

Did you hear what I said? The invasion has begun!

Mrs. Frank. Oh, Mr. Van Daan, did you hear that?

[DUSSEL *embraces* MRS. VAN DAAN. PETER *grabs a frying pan and parades around the room, beating on it, singing the Dutch national anthem.* ANNE *and* MARGOT *follow him, singing, weaving in and out among the excited grown-ups.* MARGOT *breaks away to take the flowers from* MIEP *and distribute them to everyone. While this pandemonium is going on,* MRS. FRANK *tries to make herself heard above the excitement.*]

Mrs. Frank (*to* MIEP). How do you know?
Miep. The radio . . . The BBC![11] They said they landed on the coast of Normandy! (P)
Peter. The British?
Miep. British, Americans, French, Dutch, Poles, Norwegians . . . all of them! More than four thousand ships! Churchill[12] spoke, and General Eisenhower![13] D-day, they call it!
Mr. Frank. Thank God, it's come!
Mrs. Van Daan. At last!
Miep (*starting out*). I'm going to tell Mr. Kraler. This'll be better than any blood transfusion.
Mr. Frank (*stopping her*). What part of Normandy did they land, did they say?
Miep. Normandy . . . that's all I know now . . . I'll be up the minute I hear some more! (*She goes hurriedly out.*)
Mr. Frank (*to* MRS. FRANK). What did I tell you? What did I tell you?

[MRS. FRANK *indicates that he has forgotten to bolt the door after* MIEP. *He hurries down the steps.* MR. VAN DAAN, *sitting on the couch, suddenly breaks into a convulsive sob. Everybody looks at him, bewildered.*]

Mrs. Van Daan (*hurrying to him*). Putti! Putti! What is it? What happened?
Mr. Van Daan. Please. I'm so ashamed.

[MR. FRANK *comes back up the steps.*]

Dussel. Oh, for God's sake!

11. **BBC:** British Broadcasting Corporation. People listened to the BBC, illegally, for news of the war that was more accurate than what German-controlled broadcasters offered.

12. **Churchill:** Sir Winston Churchill (1874–1965), British prime minister during World War II.

13. **General Eisenhower:** Dwight D. Eisenhower (1890–1969), commander of the Allied forces in western Europe. He later became president of the United States (1953–1961).

(P) **Literary Perspectives** **Analyzing Responses** What does your knowledge of World War II tell you about this news?

Mrs. Van Daan. Don't, Putti.
Margot. It doesn't matter now!
Mr. Frank (*going to* MR. VAN DAAN). Didn't you hear what Miep said? The invasion has come! We're going to be liberated! This is a time to celebrate! (*He embraces* MRS. FRANK *and then hurries to the cupboard and gets the cognac and a glass.*)
Mr. Van Daan. To steal bread from children!
Mrs. Frank. We've all done things that we're ashamed of.
Anne. Look at me, the way I've treated Mother . . . so mean and horrid to her.
Mrs. Frank. No, Anneke, no.

[ANNE *runs to her mother, putting her arms around her.*]

Anne. Oh, Mother, I was. I was awful.
Mr. Van Daan. Not like me. No one is as bad as me!
Dussel (*to* MR. VAN DAAN). Stop it now! Let's be happy!
Mr. Frank (*giving* MR. VAN DAAN *a glass of cognac*). Here! Here! Schnapps![14] L'chaim![15]

[MR. VAN DAAN *takes the cognac. They all watch him. He gives them a feeble smile.* ANNE *puts up her fingers in a V-for-victory sign. As* MR. VAN DAAN *gives an answering V sign, they are startled to hear a loud sob from behind them. It is* MRS. FRANK, *stricken with remorse. She is sitting on the other side of the room.*]

Mrs. Frank (*through her sobs*). When I think of the terrible things I said . . .

[MR. FRANK, ANNE, *and* MARGOT *hurry to her, trying to comfort her.* MR. VAN DAAN *brings her his glass of cognac.*]

Mr. Van Daan. No! No! You were right!
Mrs. Frank. That I should speak that way to you! . . . Our friends! . . . Our guests! (*She starts to cry again.*)
Dussel. Stop it, you're spoiling the whole invasion!

[*As they are comforting her, the lights dim out. The curtain falls.*]

Anne's Voice (*faintly at first and then with growing strength*). We're all in much better spirits these days. There's still excellent news of the invasion. The best part about it is that I have a feeling that friends are coming. Who knows? Maybe I'll be back in school by fall. Ha, ha! The joke is on us! The warehouse man doesn't know a thing and we are paying him all that money! . . . Wednesday, the second of July, nineteen forty-four. The invasion seems temporarily to be bogged down. Mr. Kraler has to have an operation, which looks bad. The Gestapo have found the radio that was stolen. Mr. Dussel says they'll trace it back and back to the thief, and then, it's just a matter of time till they get to us. Everyone is low. Even poor Pim can't raise their spirits. I have often been downcast myself . . . but never in despair. I can shake off everything if I write. But . . . and that is the great question . . . will I ever be able to write well? I want to so much. I want to go on living even after

14. **schnapps** (shnahps) *n.*: strong liquor.
15. **l'chaim** (luh HAH yihm): Hebrew toast meaning "to life."

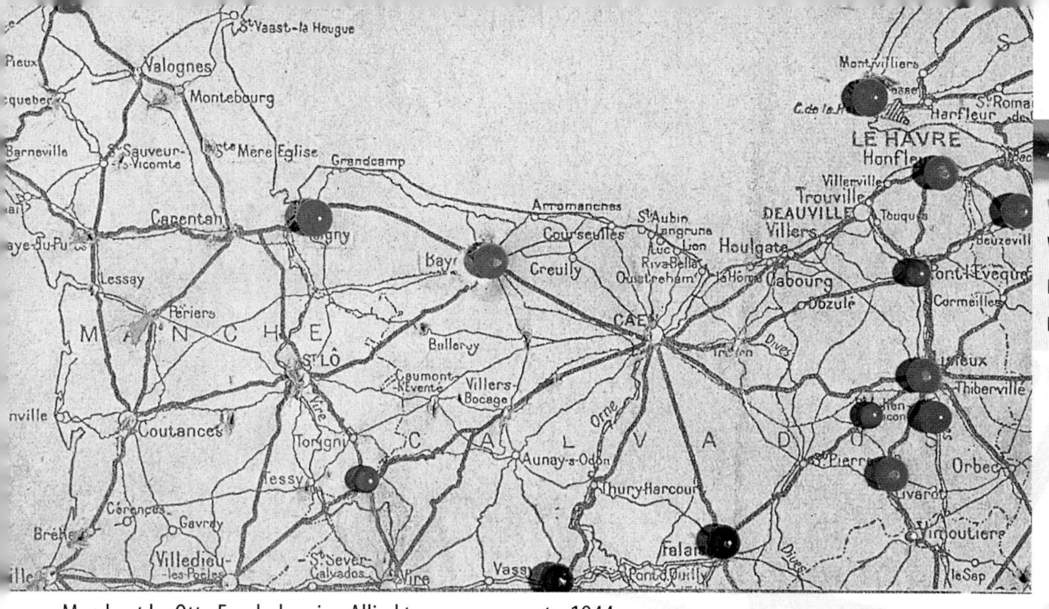

Map kept by Otto Frank showing Allied troop movements, 1944.

Analyzing Visuals

Viewing and Interpreting Why might Mr. Frank keep a map showing troop movements during the war?

my death. Another birthday has gone by, so now I am fifteen. Already I know what I want. I have a goal, an opinion. **Q**

[*As this is being said, the curtain rises on the scene, the lights dim on, and* ANNE*'s voice fades out.*]

SCENE 4

It is an afternoon a few weeks later. . . . Everyone but MARGOT *is in the main room. There is a sense of great tension.*

Both MRS. FRANK *and* MR. VAN DAAN *are nervously pacing back and forth.* DUSSEL *is standing at the window, looking down fixedly at the street below.* PETER *is at the center table, trying to do his lessons.* ANNE *sits opposite him, writing in her diary.* MRS. VAN DAAN *is seated on the couch, her eyes on* MR. FRANK *as he sits reading.*

The sound of a telephone ringing comes from the office below. They all are rigid, listening tensely. DUSSEL *rushes down to* MR. FRANK.

Dussel. There it goes again, the telephone! Mr. Frank, do you hear?

Mr. Frank (*quietly*). Yes. I hear.

Dussel (*pleading, insistent*). But this is the third time, Mr. Frank! The third time in quick succession! It's a signal! I tell you it's Miep, trying to get us! For some reason she can't come to us and she's trying to warn us of something!

Mr. Frank. Please. Please.

Mr. Van Daan (*to* DUSSEL). You're wasting your breath.

Dussel. Something has happened, Mr. Frank. For three days now Miep hasn't been

---

Q **Reading Focus** **Making Inferences** What do Anne's comments about Pim suggest about her father's mood?

Moveable bookcase, which hid the stairs to the Secret Annex. (left) with one of the Franks' Dutch helpers.

to see us! And today not a man has come to work. There hasn't been a sound in the building!

Mrs. Frank. Perhaps it's Sunday. We may have lost track of the days.

Mr. Van Daan (*to* ANNE). You with the diary there. What day is it?

Dussel (*going to* MRS. FRANK). I don't lose track of the days! I know exactly what day it is! It's Friday, the fourth of August. Friday, and not a man at work. (*He rushes back to* MR. FRANK, *pleading with him, almost in tears.*) I tell you Mr. Kraler's dead. That's the only explanation. He's dead and they've closed down the building, and Miep's trying to tell us!

Mr. Frank. She'd never telephone us.

Dussel (*frantic*). Mr. Frank, answer that! I beg you, answer it!

Mr. Frank. No.

Mr. Van Daan. Just pick it up and listen. You don't have to speak. Just listen and see if it's Miep.

Dussel (*speaking at the same time*). For God's sake . . . I ask you.

Mr. Frank. No. I've told you, no. I'll do nothing that might let anyone know we're in the building.

Peter. Mr. Frank's right.

Mr. Van Daan. There's no need to tell us what side you're on.

Mr. Frank. If we wait patiently, quietly, I believe that help will come.

[*There is silence for a minute as they all listen to the telephone ringing.*]

Dussel. I'm going down. (*He rushes down the steps.* MR. FRANK *tries ineffectually to hold him.* DUSSEL *runs to the lower door, unbolting it. The telephone stops ringing.* DUSSEL *bolts the door and comes slowly back up the steps.*) Too late. R

[MR. FRANK *goes to* MARGOT *in* ANNE'S *bedroom.*]

R **Literary Focus** **Drama** How is Anne's reaction to this complication different from the reactions of other characters? How has Anne changed over the course of the play?

Mr. Van Daan. So we just wait here until we die.

Mrs. Van Daan (*hysterically*). I can't stand it! I'll kill myself! I'll kill myself!

Mr. Van Daan. For God's sake, stop it!

[*In the distance, a German military band is heard playing a Viennese waltz.*]

Mrs. Van Daan. I think you'd be glad if I did! I think you want me to die!

Mr. Van Daan. Whose fault is it we're here? (MRS. VAN DAAN starts for her room. He follows, talking at her.) We could've been safe somewhere . . . in America or Switzerland. But no! No! You wouldn't leave when I wanted to. You couldn't leave your things. You couldn't leave your precious furniture.

Mrs. Van Daan. Don't touch me!

[*She hurries up the stairs, followed by* MR. VAN DAAN. PETER, *unable to bear it, goes to his room.* ANNE *looks after him, deeply concerned.* DUSSEL *returns to his post at the window.* MR. FRANK *comes back into the main room and takes a book, trying to read.* MRS. FRANK *sits near the sink, starting to peel some potatoes.* ANNE *quietly goes to* PETER*'s room, closing the door after her.* PETER *is lying face down on the cot.* ANNE *leans over him, holding him in her arms, trying to bring him out of his despair.*]

Anne. Look, Peter, the sky. (*She looks up through the skylight.*) What a lovely, lovely day! Aren't the clouds beautiful? You know what I do when it seems as if I couldn't stand being cooped up for one more minute? I *think* myself out. I think myself on a walk in the park where I used to go with Pim. Where the jonquils and the crocuses and the violets grow down the slopes. You know the most wonderful part about *thinking* yourself out? You can have it any way you like. You can have roses and violets and chrysanthemums all blooming at the same time. . . . It's funny . . . I used to take it all for granted . . . and now I've gone crazy about everything to do with nature. Haven't you?

Peter. I've just gone crazy. I think if something doesn't happen soon . . . if we don't get out of here . . . I can't stand much more of it!

Anne (*softly*). I wish you had a religion, Peter.

Peter. No, thanks! Not me!

Anne. Oh, I don't mean you have to be Orthodox[16] . . . or believe in Heaven and Hell and Purgatory and things . . . I just mean some religion . . . it doesn't matter what. Just to believe in something! When I think of all that's out there . . . the trees . . . and flowers . . . and sea gulls . . . When I think of the dearness of you, Peter . . . and the goodness of the people we know . . . Mr. Kraler, Miep, Dirk, the vegetable man, all risking their lives for us every day. . . . When I think of these good things, I'm not afraid anymore . . . I find myself, and God, and I . . .

[PETER *interrupts, getting up and walking away.*]

Peter. That's fine! But when I begin to think, I get mad! Look at us, hiding out for two years. Not able to move! Caught here like . . .

---

16. Orthodox: Orthodox Jews strictly observe Jewish law.

The Frank family in the stage production, ready to depart. ©Joan Marcus.

waiting for them to come and get us . . . and all for what?

Anne. We're not the only people that've had to suffer. There've always been people that've had to . . . sometimes one race . . . sometimes another . . . and yet . . .

Peter. That doesn't make me feel any better!

Anne (*going to him*). I know it's terrible, trying to have any faith . . . when people are doing such horrible. . . . But you know what I sometimes think? I think the world may be going through a phase, the way I was with Mother. It'll pass, maybe not for hundreds of years, but someday. . . . I still believe, in spite of everything, that people are really good at heart.

Peter. I want to see something now . . . not a thousand years from now! (*He goes over, sitting down again on the cot.*)

Anne. But, Peter, if you'd only look at it as part of a great pattern . . . that we're just a little minute in the life . . . (*She breaks off.*) Listen to us, going at each other like a couple of stupid grown-ups! Look at the sky now. Isn't it lovely? (*She holds out her hand to him.* PETER *takes it and rises, standing with her at the window looking out, his arms around her.*) Someday, when we're outside again, I'm going to . . .

[*She breaks off as she hears the sound of a car, its brakes squealing as it comes to a sudden stop. The people in the other rooms also become aware of the sound. They listen tensely. Another car roars up to a screeching stop.* ANNE *and* PETER *come from* PETER'S *room.* MR. *and* MRS. VAN DAAN *creep down the stairs.* DUSSEL *comes out from his room. Everyone is listening, hardly breathing. A doorbell clangs again and again in the building below.* MR. FRANK *starts quietly down the steps to the door.* DUSSEL *and* PETER *follow him. The others stand rigid, waiting, terrified.*

In a few seconds DUSSEL *comes stumbling back up the steps. He shakes off* PETER'S *help and goes to his room.* MR. FRANK *bolts the door below and comes slowly back up the steps. Their eyes are all on him as he stands there for a minute. They realize that what they feared has happened.* MRS. VAN DAAN starts to whimper. MR. VAN DAAN *puts her gently in a chair and then hurries off up the stairs to their room to collect their things.* PETER *goes to comfort his mother. There is a sound of violent pounding on a door below.*] S

Mr. Frank (*quietly*). For the past two years we have lived in fear. Now we can live in hope.

[*The pounding below becomes more insistent. There are muffled sounds of voices, shouting commands.*]

Men's Voices. Aufmachen! Da drinnen! Aufmachen! Schnell! Schnell! Schnell![17] (*Etc., etc.*)

17. **Aufmachen . . . Schnell:** German for "Open up! You in there! Open up! Quickly! Quickly! Quickly!"

[*The street door below is forced open. We hear the heavy tread of footsteps coming up.* MR. FRANK *gets two school bags from the shelves and gives one to* ANNE *and the other to* MARGOT. *He goes to get a bag for* MRS. FRANK. *The sound of feet coming up grows louder.* PETER *comes to* ANNE, *kissing her goodbye; then he goes to his room to collect his things. The buzzer of their door starts to ring.* MR. FRANK *brings* MRS. FRANK *a bag. They stand together, waiting. We hear the thud of gun butts on the door, trying to break it down.*

ANNE *stands, holding her school satchel, looking over at her father and mother with a soft, reassuring smile. She is no longer a child, but a woman with courage to meet whatever lies ahead.*

The lights dim out. The curtain falls on the scene. We hear a mighty crash as the door is shattered. After a second ANNE'S *voice is heard.*]

Anne's Voice. And so it seems our stay here is over. They are waiting for us now. They've allowed us five minutes to get our things. We can each take a bag and whatever it will hold of clothing. Nothing else. So, dear Diary, that means I must leave you behind. Goodbye for a while. P.S. Please, please, Miep, or Mr. Kraler, or anyone else. If you should find this diary, will you please keep it safe for me, because someday I hope . . . T

[*Her voice stops abruptly. There is silence. After a second the curtain rises.*]

S **Literary Focus** **Drama** Throughout the play, there have been "false alarms" as the characters feared the end was near. Do you think that this complication is another false alarm? Why or why not?

T **Read and Discuss** What has happened?

SCENE 5

It is again the afternoon in November 1945. The rooms are as we saw them in the first scene. MR. KRALER *has joined* MIEP *and* MR. FRANK. *There are coffee cups on the table. We see a great change in* MR. FRANK. *He is calm now. His bitterness is gone. He slowly turns a few pages of the diary. They are blank.*

Mr. Frank. No more. (*He closes the diary and puts it down on the couch beside him.*)
Miep. I'd gone to the country to find food. When I got back, the block was surrounded by police . . .
Mr. Kraler. We made it our business to learn how they knew. It was the thief . . . the thief who told them.

[MIEP *goes up to the gas burner, bringing back a pot of coffee.*]

Mr. Frank (*after a pause*). It seems strange to say this, that anyone could be happy in a concentration camp. But Anne was happy in the camp in Holland where they first took us. After two years of being shut up in these rooms, she could be out . . . out in the sunshine and the fresh air that she loved.
Miep (*offering the coffee to* MR. FRANK). A little more?
Mr. Frank (*holding out his cup to her*). The news of the war was good. The British and Americans were sweeping through France. We felt sure that they would get to us in time. In September we were told that we were to be shipped to Poland. . . . The men to one camp. The women to another. I was sent to Auschwitz. They went to Belsen. In January we were freed, the few of us who were left. The war wasn't yet over, so it took us a long time to get home. We'd be sent here and there behind the lines where we'd be safe. Each time our train would stop . . . at a siding or a crossing . . . we'd all get out and go from group to group . . . Where were you? Were you at Belsen? At Buchenwald? At Mauthausen? Is it possible that you knew my wife? Did you ever see my husband? My son? My daughter? That's how I found out about my wife's death . . . of Margot, the Van Daans . . . Dussel. But Anne . . . I still hoped. . . . Yesterday I went to Rotterdam. I'd heard of a woman there. . . . She'd been in Belsen with Anne. . . . I know now. **U**

[*He picks up the diary again and turns the pages back to find a certain passage. As he finds it, we hear* ANNE*'s voice.*]

Anne's Voice. In spite of everything, I still believe that people are really good at heart.

[MR. FRANK *slowly closes the diary.*]

Mr. Frank. She puts me to shame.

[*They are silent.*]

Curtain

U **Literary Focus** **Drama** The part of a play that tells what happens to all the characters is called the **resolution.** According to Mr. Frank, what has happened to them all?

Applying Your Skills

OH **RA.L.8.6** Explain how an author's choice of genre affects the expression of a theme or topic. **RP.8.1** Apply reading comprehension strategies, including making predictions, comparing and contrasting, recalling and summarizing and making inferences and drawing conclusions. *Also covered* **WA.8.6; RA.L.8.8**

The Diary of Anne Frank, Act Two, Scenes 1–5

Respond and Think Critically

Reading Focus

Quick Check

1. What does Mr. Van Daan do in Act Two, Scene 3 that increases tension in the Secret Annex?
2. How does Miep's news in Act Two, Scene 3 affect the characters?

Read with a Purpose

3. What is Anne's view of the world at the end of Act Two? Support your response with examples from the play.

Reading Skills: Making Inferences

4. Review your completed inferences chart. Which inferences were on target? Which inferences about characters did you need to revise as you read further?

Literary Focus

Literary Analysis

5. **Evaluate** In Act One, Scene 4, Mr. Frank tells Anne, "You must build your own character." Has Anne done this by the end of the play? Explain.
6. **Interpret** During the crisis in Act Two, Scene 3, Mr. Frank says, "We don't need the Nazis to destroy us. We're destroying ourselves." What does Mr. Frank mean by that remark?
7. **Make Judgments** Comment on Anne's statement, "In spite of everything, I still believe that people are really good at heart." Do you agree with her statement, in light of what happened to her and her family? Explain.
8. **Literary Perspectives** How did you respond to Anne's wish to go on living after her death (page 907)? How has her wish come true?

Literary Skills: Elements of Drama

9. **Analyze** What is the main conflict of the play? Is it the external conflict between the characters and the Nazis or something else? Give reasons that support your response.
10. **Analyze** The **climax** of a play is its moment of greatest tension, the point at which the conflict is about to be resolved. What is the play's climax? How did you feel at that moment?

Literary Skills Review: Dramatic Irony

11. **Analyze** **Dramatic irony** occurs when the audience or reader knows something a character does not. Identify at least one instance of dramatic irony in Act Two and explain what makes it ironic.

Writing Focus

Think as a Reader/Writer

Use It in Your Writing Look back at your notes on what the dialogue in the play reveals about the characters. Choose a character from the play and write a brief description of him or her based on what you learned from the dialogue.

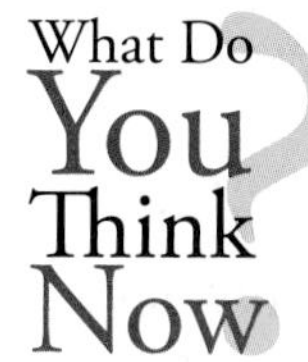

How has the characters' behavior affected your ideas on how to make the best of a difficult situation?

Applying Your Skills

The Diary of Anne Frank

Vocabulary Development

Clarifying Word Meaning: Contrast

One way to discover the meaning of an unfamiliar word is to look for **contrast clues** that show how a word is unlike another word. Words that signal contrast include *although, but, yet, however, in contrast, instead, not,* and *unlike.*

For example, you can guess that the meaning of the word *inarticulate* is "unable to speak" from the contrast clue in the following sentence:

> Peter became *inarticulate* when he was angry, **but** Anne always **found plenty to say**.

Your Turn

conspicuous
forlorn
indignantly
ostentatiously
tyranny

Fill in the blanks in the following sentences with the correct Vocabulary word. Contrast clues are boldface in the passages.

1. Mr. Van Daan's desire for food was ________, **but** the other characters kept their hunger pangs **well hidden**.
2. The Nazis exercised great ________, over the Dutch people; **however,** in the Secret Annex, the characters demonstrated great **tolerance and respect** toward each other.
3. Mrs. Van Daan ________ showed off her fur; **in contrast**, Mrs. Frank **modestly** covered herself with a shawl.
4. Anne often left the room ________ after hearing critical comments from Mr. Van Daan, **unlike** Margot, who responded **calmly** to criticism.
5. **Instead** of feeling ________ in the concentration camp, Anne at first felt **overjoyed** at being outside after so many months indoors.

Language Coach

Suffixes Notice the suffix *–ly* that appears in the Vocabulary words *indignantly* and *ostentatiously*. This suffix indicates the words are adverbs. When you remove the suffix, you create adjectives.

Write two sentences using the adjectives *indignant* and *ostentatious*. For additional practice with the suffix *–ly,* add it to the adjectives *conspicuous* and *forlorn*. Then, use these newly formed adverbs in sentences of your own.

Academic Vocabulary

Talk About ...

With a partner, discuss how the realities of World War II and the Holocaust contribute to the events in *The Diary of Anne Frank*.

- Which historic events are evident during the play?
- How do the characters express their reactions to these events?
- What insight about life can you draw from these details concerning the connection of world history and personal lives?

Learn It Online
Focus on vocabulary with *WordSharp:*
go.hrw.com
L8-914
Go

WA.8.4.e Write informational essays or reports, including research, that: document sources and include bibliographies. **WC.8.2** Use correct punctuation and capitalization. *Also covered* **VO.8.7; VO.8.6; RP.8.3; WA.8.6; VO.8.1**

Grammar Link

Capitalization and Punctuation

Capitalization and punctuation help readers make sense of sentences. To help your readers, follow the capitalization and punctuation rules below.

CAPITALIZATION Capitalize the first word in every sentence and all proper nouns—including names of people, pets, historical and geographical places, nationalities, religions, organizations, monuments, and businesses.

> **B**illie went to **W**ashington, **D.C.**, where she visited the **L**incoln **M**emorial and **A**unt **L**ulu's house.

PUNCTUATION An **end mark** is a mark of punctuation placed at the end of a sentence. Use a **period** at the end of a statement, request, or command. Use a **question mark** at the end of a direct question. Place an **exclamation point** at the end of an exclamation or urgent command.

> Leila handed me the salt**.** (statement)
> Hand me the salt, please**.** (request)
> Will you hand me the salt, Leila**?** (question)
> Hey, Leila**!** (exclamation) Watch out**!** (command)

Your Turn

Correct the capitalization errors and supply the appropriate punctuation for each sentence below.

1. The play is about two families that hide in amsterdam during wartime
2. don't you dare tell me how the play ends
3. which character is your favorite
4. i wonder what happened to miep after the end of the play

CHOICES

As you respond to the Choices, use these **Academic Vocabulary** words as appropriate: contribute to, insight, evident, express.

REVIEW

Create a Time Line

Map out the events of the play on a time line. Use the time line on pages 837–838 as an inspiration. First, review the play and jot down all the major events. Look for clues in the stage directions and Anne's voice-overs. Place events on the time line in the order in which they took place.

CONNECT

Describe a Tradition

Timed Writing In Act One, Scene 4, the characters take comfort in celebrating Hanukkah, the Jewish festival of lights. What traditions or celebrations bring you and your loved ones together? Write a brief description of one tradition or celebration.

EXTEND

Report on the Holocaust

Research Project How do memories of the Holocaust continue to affect the world today? Using Internet and print sources in a library, research one of these topics: (1) the work of the Anne Frank Foundation, or (2) the creation of the U.S. Holocaust Memorial Museum in Washington, D.C. Write a brief report on what

COMPARING TEXTS

Comparing Characters and Conflicts

CONTENTS

Children play soccer in front of a burned-out building in Sarajevo, Bosnia and Herzegovina, 1992.

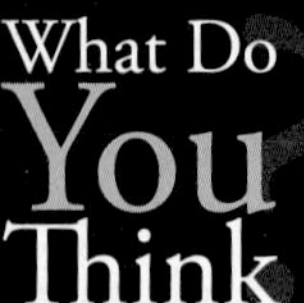

How might a person's diary help him or her cope in a time of war?

QuickWrite

How do you think keeping a diary or a blog—an online diary—might help you deal with the events in your life? Jot down your ideas.

Preparing to Read

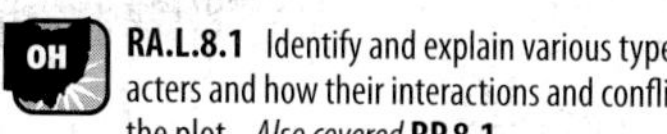
RA.L.8.1 Identify and explain various types of characters and how their interactions and conflicts affect the plot. *Also covered* **RP.8.1**

from The Diary of a Young Girl / *from* My Childhood Under Fire: A Sarajevo Diary

Literary Focus

Conflict and Character Narratives, whether fiction, nonfiction, or dramatic, revolve around **conflict,** a character's struggle to achieve a goal. As characters face conflict and take steps to resolve it, we in turn gain insight into their hopes, fears, strengths, and weaknesses. The diary entries that follow are accounts of how two young girls faced conflict in times of war. As you read, consider what the diary entries reveal about the writers.

TechFocus As you read these diary entries, think about what you might want to say in a modern form of a diary: a blog.

Reading Focus

Comparing Characters As you read these selections, observe the similarities and differences in the ways that two girls react to the historical conflicts they live through.

Into Action Create a chart like the one below to record each character's reactions.

Character/ Writer	Historical Conflict	Character's Opinions	Character's Emotions
Anne			
Nadja			

Writing Focus

Think as a Reader/Writer

Find It in Your Reading Diaries are usually written for personal use, but they can also be works of literature. Note in your *Reader/Writer Notebook* how the writers use specific, carefully chosen words to express themselves, their feelings, and their opinions.

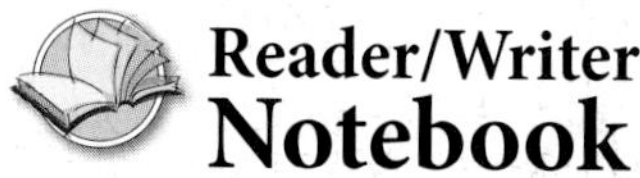
Reader/Writer Notebook

Use your **RWN** to complete the activities for these selections.

Vocabulary

from The Diary of a Young Girl

liberation (lihb uh RAY shuhn) *n.:* release from imprisonment or enemy occupation. *When the troops withdrew, the city celebrated its liberation.*

cherished (CHEHR ihsht) *v.* used as *adj.:* valued; well loved. *Her ideals are her most cherished possession because they give meaning to her life.*

from My Childhood Under Fire: A Sarajevo Diary

invasion (ihn VAY zhuhn) *n.:* act of entering by force. *When soldiers entered the city, our citizens protested the invasion.*

reigns (raynz) *v.:* predominates; is widespread. *When war ends, peace reigns.*

Language Coach

Oral Fluency What do *eight* and *sleigh* have in common? These words contain the letters *ei,* pronounced "ay," and the *g* that follows is silent. Which of the Vocabulary words above follows that pattern? With a partner, list three other words that contain that letter combination and pronunciation.

Learn It Online

Master these words. Visit Word Watch at:

go.hrw.com L8-917 

MEET THE WRITERS

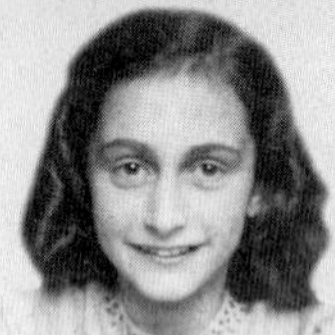

Anne Frank

(1929–1945)

A Lasting Voice

Anne Frank was born to a Jewish family in Frankfurt, Germany, in 1929. Her family immigrated to Amsterdam, the Netherlands, when she was four. Anne had a happy childhood until 1940, when German forces invaded and occupied the Netherlands. Jewish citizens began to be deported and killed. Anne and her family went into hiding in an attic, where she began her diary, which served as the basis for the play *The Diary of Anne Frank.*

For more information on Anne Frank, see Build Background (pages 835–838) and "A Tragedy Revealed: A Heroine's Last Days" (pages 932–948).

Nadja Halilbegovich

(1979–)

The Power of a Diary

Nadja Halilbegovich was born in Bosnia and Herzegovina, a part of the former Yugoslavia in southeastern Europe. She grew up in a middle-class family in Sarajevo, the capital of Bosnia and Herzegovina. "We owned a comfortable apartment in Sarajevo and a cottage in the countryside, where we spent our weekends," Nadja writes.

In 1992, when Nadja was twelve, civil war broke out in Yugoslavia. The streets of Sarajevo became filled with soldiers. Bombings were frequent, and many innocent civilians died. The war lasted three years. Nadja writes, "On May 31, 1992, I opened my notebook and began to write. Instantly this diary became a friend who listened to all that I desperately needed to share."

Nadja survived the war and is now a peace activist and a singer.

Think About the Writers

What similarities do you see in the lives of these two girls? What common experiences led them to start diaries?

Build Background

In this feature, you will read two diaries written by girls from different countries and times. *The Diary of a Young Girl* was written by Anne Frank in the 1940s, during the Nazi occupation of the Netherlands in World War II. *My Childhood Under Fire* was written by Nadja Halilbegovich in the 1990s, during the Yugoslavian civil war.

Preview the Selections

The excerpts you will read from *The Diary of a Young Girl* are from the actual diary of **Anne Frank,** which her father published after World War II. The authors of the play *The Diary of Anne Frank* (page 839) based their character of Anne on the person revealed in this diary.

In *My Childhood Under Fire: A Sarajevo Diary,* a thirteen-year-old girl, **Nadja Halilbegovich,** starts a diary as her home city is caught up in the larger Yugoslavian civil war of the 1990s.

from

The Diary of a Young Girl

by **Anne Frank**

Read with a Purpose

Read these diary pages to discover the real-life voice of Anne Frank.

Wednesday, 3 May, 1944

. . . Since Saturday we've changed over, and have lunch at half past eleven in the mornings, so we have to last out with one cupful of porridge; this saves us a meal. Vegetables are still very difficult to obtain; we had rotten boiled lettuce this afternoon. Ordinary lettuce, spinach, and boiled lettuce, there's nothing else. With these we eat rotten potatoes, so it's a delicious combination! **A**

As you can easily imagine, we often ask ourselves here despairingly: "What, oh, what is the use of the war? Why can't people live peacefully together? Why all this destruction?"

The question is very understandable, but no one has found a satisfactory answer to it so far. Yes, why do they make still more gigantic planes, still heavier bombs, and, at the same time, prefabricated[1] houses for reconstruction? Why should millions be spent daily on the war and yet there's

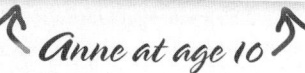

A **Read and Discuss** Anne provides a lot of detail in this first paragraph. What picture is she creating for us?

1. **prefabricated:** constructed in pieces for easy shipment and assembly.

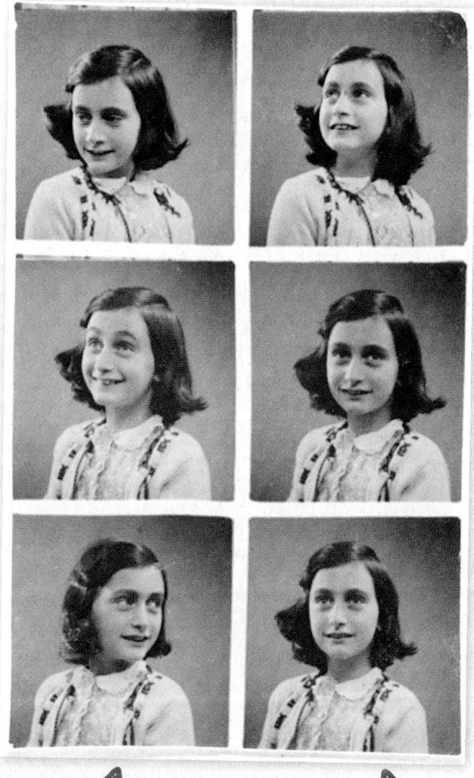

Anne at age 10

not a penny available for medical services, artists, or poor people?

Why do some people have to starve while there are surpluses rotting in other parts of the world? Oh, why are people so crazy?

I don't believe that the big men, the politicians and the capitalists alone, are guilty of the war. Oh no, the little man is just as guilty; otherwise the peoples of the world would have risen in revolt long ago! There's in people simply an urge to destroy, an urge to kill, to murder and rage, and until all mankind, without exception, undergoes a great change, wars will be waged, everything that has been built up, cultivated, and grown will be destroyed and disfigured, after which mankind will have to begin all over again. **B**

I have often been downcast, but never in despair; I regard our hiding as a dangerous adventure, romantic and interesting at the same time. In my diary I treat all the privations[2] as amusing. I have made up my mind now to lead a different life from other girls and, later on, different from ordinary housewives. My start has been so very full of interest, and that is the sole reason why I have to laugh at the humorous side of the most dangerous moments.

Anne in 1939

I am young and I possess many buried qualities; I am young and strong and am living a great adventure; I am still in the midst of it and can't grumble the whole day long. I have been given a lot: a happy nature, a great deal of cheerfulness and strength. Every day I feel that I am developing inwardly, that the liberation is drawing nearer,

2. **privations:** lack of necessities.

B Literary Focus **Conflict and Character** What do Anne's thoughts reveal about how the war is affecting her?

Vocabulary **liberation** (lihb uh RAY shuhn) *n.:* release from imprisonment or enemy occupation.

and how beautiful nature is, how good the people are about me, how interesting this adventure is! Why, then, should I be in despair?

Yours,

Anne

Saturday, 15 July, 1944

. . . "For in its innermost depths youth is lonelier than old age." I read this saying in some book and I've always remembered it, and found it to be true. Is it true, then, that grown-ups have a more difficult time here than we do? No. I know it isn't. Older people have formed their opinions about everything and don't waver before they act. It's twice as hard for us young ones to hold our ground and maintain our opinions in a time when all ideals are being shattered and destroyed, when people are showing their worst side and do not know whether to believe in truth and right and God.

Anyone who claims that the older ones have a more difficult time here certainly doesn't realize to what extent our problems weigh down on us, problems for which we are probably much too young but which thrust themselves upon us continually, until, after a long time, we think we've found a solution, but the solution doesn't seem able to resist the facts which reduce it to nothing again. That's the difficulty in these times: Ideals, dreams, and cherished hopes rise within us, only to meet the horrible truth and be shattered. **C**

It's really a wonder that I haven't dropped all my ideals, because they seem so absurd and impossible to carry out. Yet I keep them, because in spite of everything I still believe that people are really good at heart. I simply can't build up my hopes on a foundation consisting of confusion, misery, and death. I see the world gradually being turned into a wilderness, I hear the ever approaching thunder, which will destroy us too, I can feel the sufferings of millions, and yet, if I look up into the heavens, I think that it will all come right, that this cruelty too will end, and that peace and tranquility will return again.

In the meantime, I must uphold my ideals, for perhaps the time will come when I shall be able to carry them out. **D**

Yours,

Anne

C **Reading Focus** **Comparing and Contrasting Characters** How is Anne's attitude in this entry different from that in the previous entry?

D **Read and Discuss** How does this passage fit in with what we know about Anne?

Vocabulary **cherished** (CHEHR ihsht) *v.* used as *adj.:* valued; well loved.

Applying Your Skills

RA.L.8.1 Identify and explain various types of characters and how their interactions and conflicts affect the plot. **RP.8.1** Apply reading comprehension strategies, including making predictions, comparing and contrasting, recalling and summarizing and making inferences and drawing conclusions. **WA.8.6** Produce informal writings. *Also covered* **VO.8.4**

from The Diary of a Young Girl

Respond and Think Critically

Reading Focus

Quick Check

1. How does Anne describe herself in the first entry?
2. In the second entry, what reasons does Anne give for keeping her ideals?

Read with a Purpose

3. Does the character revealed in the excerpts from Anne's diary surprise you? If so, in what ways? If not, why not?

Reading Skills: Comparing Characters

4. Fill in the chart you made on the Preparing to Read page with your observations about Anne. As you read the next selection, fill in the row for Nadja. Then you will be able to compare two characters.

Character/ Writer	Historical Conflict	Character's Opinions	Character's Emotions
Anne			
Nadja			

Vocabulary Check

Fill in each blank with the correct Vocabulary word.

liberation cherished

5. The end of war brought ________ and the return of our ________ freedoms.

Literary Focus

Literary Analysis

6. **Interpret** What internal conflict does Anne express in the second diary entry? How does she resolve this conflict?
7. **Analyze** In the first entry, Anne writes, "There's in people simply an urge to destroy, an urge to kill, to murder and rage. . . ." In the second entry, she says that "in spite of everything I still believe that people are really good at heart." How do you think Anne was able to reconcile these seemingly contradictory opinions?
8. **Connect** **Dramatic irony** is created when the reader knows something a character does not know. What do we know as we read Anne's diary that Anne does not know? How does having this insight make you feel?

Literary Skills: Conflict and Character

9. **Analyze** Look over the chart you filled in for item 4. Now, write a short paragraph about Anne's character as it is revealed in her diary. Consider the opinions Anne expresses, the way she describes herself, and the way she deals with conflict.

Writing Focus

Think as a Reader/Writer

Use It in Your Writing Review the words Anne uses to describe herself. Write a profile of yourself or someone else. Like Anne, choose your words and phrases carefully to give the reader a clear picture of the person you are describing.

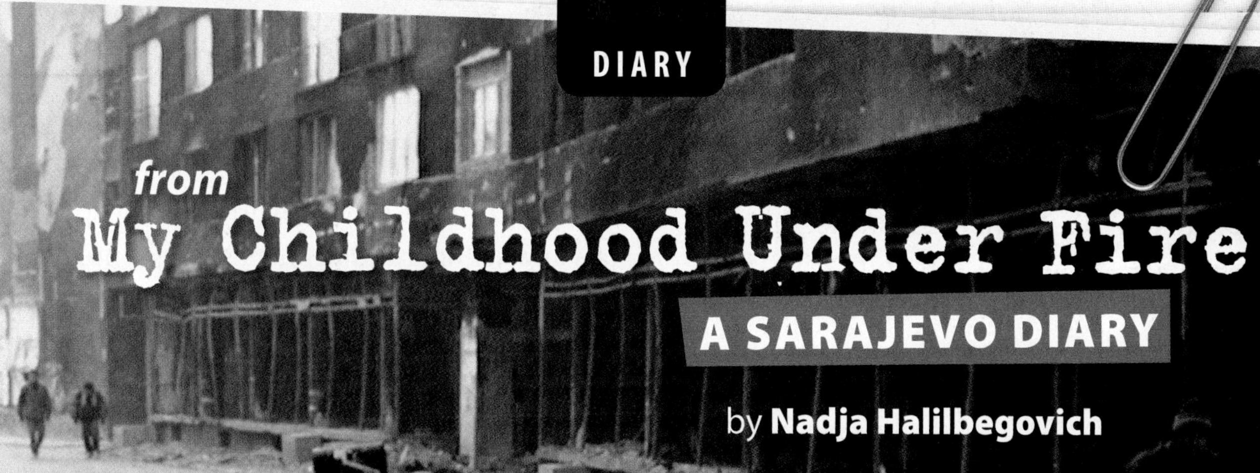

DIARY

from
My Childhood Under Fire
A SARAJEVO DIARY

by **Nadja Halilbegovich**

Read with a Purpose
Read these diary entries to understand how it felt to grow up during a war in the 1990s.

Preparing to Read for this selection is on page 917.

Build Background
The former Yugoslavia—located between Italy and Greece, in Europe—was made up of many different ethnic and religious groups. In the early 1990s, Yugoslavia fell into civil war. In 1992, fighting broke out in Bosnia and Herzegovina between Serbs who wanted to remain part of Yugoslavia and Bosnian Muslims and Croatians who wanted independence from Yugoslavia. Three years of war followed. Much of the fighting took place in Sarajevo, the region's capital city. In 1995, a peace plan dividing Bosnia and Herzegovina into two parts was signed between the warring parties.

May 31, 1992

The war is furiously raging through Sarajevo and my homeland. Its first victim was Suada Dilberovic, a medical student from Dubrovnik. Her young life was cut off by a sniper at the Vrabanja Bridge. A great crowd had gathered in front of the presidential building to protest the invasion. From the roof of the Holiday Inn, snipers shot at unarmed citizens who had come to demonstrate their desire to live in peace and unity.

I watched these war images on television and kept all my sadness inside. Now, after nearly two months, I can no longer bear all my piled-up feelings. This is why I write to you, dear diary.

Even at this moment, the deafening explosions jolt me back to this cruel reality. Seeing my city being destroyed, I feel a sharp pain in my soul. I don't understand why this is happening to us. I desperately want to wake up from this nightmare, but instead every dawn moans with the sounds of air-raid sirens, and I head to the filthy basement. To wait. **A**

Vocabulary **invasion** (ihn VAY zhuhn) *n.:* act of entering by force.

A **Read and Discuss** What is happening in Nadja's life?

January 1, 1993

I WISH YOU A HAPPY NEW YEAR! We spent New Year's Eve with our neighbors. We made soy sandwiches, mint cake, rice pastry, rice pie, rice wine and chocolate rice cake—there was rice in almost everything! We played music and danced. There were tears in our eyes when we wished each other a peaceful year. It is horrible to think like this, but not all of us may live to see peace.

May the old year be the last one of the war!

And may these pages reflect the happiness and peace in my soul.

June 27, 1993

Today is my dad's fifty-first birthday. I made a card and some war-recipe cookies and put them in a cute box. I wanted to surprise him, so I set the box outside our apartment door, rang the doorbell and quickly hid inside. Dad asked me to open the door, but I said I was too busy. He thought this was pretty strange since I always rush to the door when anyone visits. He opened the door himself and was very touched to find his present. After he read my card, we shared the cookies.

August 12, 1993

Some people call the murderers in the hills "beasts" or "animals." I think that even though animals are not human, in many ways they are humane. Animals are often more sensitive and loving than humans. They are devoted friends. Those who kill children and the elderly, who bomb hospitals and schools and orphanages are entirely inhumane.

December 27, 1993

How can anyone survive? In the last five days, over twenty thousand shells have landed on the suburb of Zuc Hill. Do they know that they are killing not only Bosnians but Croats, Serbs and all the others who consider this country their homeland? Do they know that we help each other, that we love each other? Do they know that young people are getting married, paying no attention to religious differences, only to their hearts and character? I can't write about this anymore! It hurts too much. B

December 31, 1993

This last day of 1993 goes by with intensified shelling. Four shells hit the very center of the city. As usual, the victims are civilians. Five were killed and thirty were wounded. Poor people! They only wanted a slice of bread or a piece of tomato to bring hope into the last hours of the old year and the start of the new. Instead the last moans of this bloody year are the deafening sounds of explosions.

Another war-infected year has passed. My wish is that peace **reigns** throughout

---

B **Literary Focus** **Conflict and Character** What is Nadja's reaction to the war around her?

Vocabulary **reigns** (raynz) *v.:* predominates; is widespread.

the whole planet, that there are no wars anywhere and that I will live my life freely again. I wish that people will love each other and be loved. Finally, I wish the words I write will become more cheerful.

HAPPY NEW YEAR! **C**

August 5, 1995

I don't know if this is very typical among people living through a war, but before I fall asleep, dreadful images of bloody bodies appear before my eyes. In the morning I remember nothing in detail, but the horror remains. Sometimes at night, like a child, I call my mom to come and talk to me. Her voice comforts me and dispels the darkness and heavy thoughts.

August 6, 1995

Sometimes I wonder if this is really me—the cheerful girl who went to sixth grade and loved shopping and going to the theater. That girl of twelve is infinitely different than this crushed sixteen year old in her worn-out clothes who aimlessly stares out the window. I ask myself, Why am I sitting at my desk when the sun is shining outside? Where are my suitcases packed for summer vacation? My questions mock me. I give too much freedom to my thoughts! I want to force them down, tie them, enslave and control them. But I can't. I can't even control my eyes that aimlessly stare at nothing. The only things left are my emotions, and I must keep hold of them. If I let them loose, they will flood everything around me: this notebook, this desk and even the sun, which mercilessly burns my cheeks through the window.

I wonder if I will always exist in some middle space between the painful memories of my past and the reality of my present—searching for the future. **D**

Nadja Halilbegovich on her first visit to post-war Sarajevo, where she visited the tunnel she had escaped through (now a museum).

C Reading Focus Comparing and Contrasting Characters How are Nadja's wishes similar to Anne's?

D Read and Discuss What do the final diary entries suggest about Nadja's state of mind?

Applying Your Skills

OH **RA.L.8.1** Identify and explain various types of characters and how their interactions and conflicts affect the plot. *Also covered* **VO.8.4; RP.8.1; WA.8.6**

from My Childhood Under Fire: A Sarajevo Diary

Respond and Think Critically

Reading Focus

Quick Check

1. What situation does Nadja face at the beginning of her diary?
2. What does Nadja wish for on New Year's Eve of 1993?

Read with a Purpose

3. What did you learn from Nadja's diary about growing up during a war?

Reading Skills: Comparing Characters

4. Review the Comparing Characters chart you filled in for Anne. Now, complete the row for Nadja. What comparisons can you draw about these two people?

Character/ Writer	Historical Conflict	Character's Opinions	Character's Emotions
Anne			
Nadja			

Vocabulary Check

Fill in each blank with the correct Vocabulary word.

invasion reigns

5. Due to the _______ and occupation, war _______ for three years.

Literary Focus

Literary Analysis

6. **Infer** Look back at Nadja's entries from 1993. What do the entries tell us about how that year affects her?
7. **Interpret** What insight does Nadja express when she writes "though animals are not human, in many ways they are humane"?
8. **Extend** Nadja survived the civil war physically. However, how might she still suffer from her experience? Use examples from the text to explain your answer.
9. **Analyze** Nadja was thirteen when she began the diary and sixteen at the time of the final entry. Discuss how Nadja's age might contribute to the content and tone of her entries.

Literary Skills: Conflict and Character

10. **Compare and Contrast** How does Nadja's experience affect her ideas about human nature? Compare her ideas with Anne's.
11. **Analyze** Look over the chart you made for item 4. Write a short paragraph comparing Anne's and Nadja's responses to war. Consider each character's hopes, fears, and opinions.

Writing Focus

Think as a Reader/Writer

Use It in Your Writing Review your notes on the words and phrases Nadja uses to describe her ideas and experiences. Using equally specific words and phrases, write a short paragraph describing an experience of your own.

Wrap Up

RA.L.8.1 Identify and explain various types of characters and how their interactions and conflicts affect the plot. **RP.8.1** Apply reading comprehension strategies, including making predictions, comparing and contrasting, recalling and summarizing and making inferences and drawing conclusions. *Also covered* **WA.8.4.d; WA.8.6; C.8.8.e; VO.8.7**

from The Diary of a Young Girl/ *from* My Childhood Under Fire: A Sarajevo Diary

Writing Focus

Write a Comparison-and-Contrast Essay

This feature contains two diaries written by girls who are from different historical eras but who faced similar conflicts. From their words, it is evident that each young woman responded in her own way. Write an essay comparing Anne and Nadja. Consider the insights you have gained into each character's feelings and opinions and into the way she describes herself and deals with conflict. Be sure to review the charts you filled in after each selection.

You can organize your essay this way:

Paragraph 1: In an introduction and thesis statement, briefly explain the historical conditions faced by each character.
Paragraph 2: Explain Anne Frank's feelings, opinions, and reactions.
Paragraph 3: Explain Nadja Halilbegovich's feelings, opinions, and reactions.
Paragraph 4: Draw a conclusion about the similarities and differences of each character's response to the historical conflict at hand.

Before you turn in your essay, review it carefully to be sure it is free from errors in grammar, spelling, and punctuation.

What Do You Think Now? What have these selections revealed to you about how a diary can help someone in a time of war?

CHOICES

As you respond to the Choices, use these **Academic Vocabulary** words as appropriate: contribute to, insight, evident, express.

REVIEW

Write an Essay

Timed Writing The writers of *The Diary of Anne Frank* based their play (page 839) on Anne Frank's actual diary. Some critics have felt that the playwrights did not capture the real Anne. Re-read Anne's diary entries. Then, write a short essay giving your opinion on how well you think the playwrights captured Anne's personality.

CONNECT

Create a Blog

TechFocus People are fascinated by the diary form, including the online form: blogs. Diaries and blogs may contribute valuable records of human lives to future historians. Consider how you would create a blog that would tell the story of your daily life. What events would you describe? What feelings would you express?

EXTEND

Present a Research Report

Group Project With a group, research the history of the Yugoslavian war of the early 1990s. Examine the causes, the effects on people of different regions, and the resolutions. Then, prepare an oral presentation to share your findings. If possible, include photographs and maps.

INFORMATIONAL TEXT FOCUS

Text Structures: Treatment, Scope, and Organization

Visitors to the Auschwitz Museum in Poland view photographs of people who were victims of the Nazis.

CONTENTS

What Do You Think?

How do historical tragedies continue to shape the world we live in?

QuickTalk

With a small group of classmates, discuss a recent large-scale tragedy that you've seen on the news or read about. How did it affect you? How will memories of it affect future generations?

MAGAZINE ARTICLE
Preparing to Read

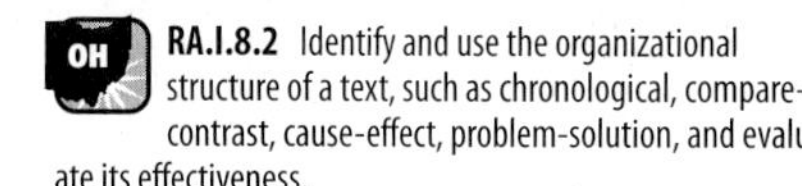
RA.I.8.2 Identify and use the organizational structure of a text, such as chronological, compare-contrast, cause-effect, problem-solution, and evaluate its effectiveness.

A Tragedy Revealed: A Heroine's Last Days

Use your **RWN** to complete the activities for this selection.

Informational Text Focus

Text Structure and Organization For any text to be clear, it requires structure and organization. Three of the most common structural patterns are:

- **Chronological order:** Events are described in the order in which they happen. This pattern is often used in historical writing. Usually, when a text uses chronological order, it makes **cause-and-effect relationships** clear. A text about World War II, for example, might explain the causes of the war and the war's effect on a country.
- **Order of importance:** Details that support the author's argument are presented from least to most important or from most to least important.
- **Logical order:** Details are arranged into related groups so that their connections are clear. For example, a review of a movie may discuss its plot, characters, and soundtrack.

Into Action "A Tragedy Revealed" uses all three structural patterns listed above. Use this chart to identify the organization of the article's supporting details.

Structural Pattern	Details from the Text That Fit That Pattern
Chronological order	1. "In the summer of 1942 . . . during the Nazi occupation of Holland." (page 931)
Order of importance	
Logical order	

Writing Focus

Preparing for **Constructed Response**

As you read, take note of the main ideas presented by Ernst Schnabel. Record the main ideas in your *Reader/Writer Notebook.* This will make the essay's structure more evident.

Vocabulary

annihilation (uh ny uh LAY shuhn) *n.:* complete destruction. *We still mourn the Nazi's annihilation of six million Jews.*

inexplicable (ihn ihk SPLIHK uh buhl) *adj.:* unable to be explained. *There were inexplicable sounds coming from below.*

premonition (prehm uh NIHSH uhn) *n.:* feeling that something, usually bad, will happen. *The residents had a premonition their hiding place would be found.*

emaciated (ih MAY shee ay tihd) *v.* used as *adj.:* extremely thin, as from starvation. *Anne's eyes still shined brightly in her thin, emaciated face.*

raucous (RAW kuhs) *adj.:* loud and rough. *They were frightened by the raucous shouting outside the window.*

Language Coach

Oral Fluency Because most of the Vocabulary words above have many syllables, they may seem hard to pronounce. Use the pronunciation guide in parentheses to sound out each word. The capital letters indicate which syllable gets the most stress. Then, read aloud the sentences following the definitions to practice using the words in conversation.

Learn It Online
Learn more about text structures online at:
go.hrw.com L8-929 

MAGAZINE ARTICLE

A TRAGEDY REVEALED

A Heroine's Last Days

by Ernst Schnabel

Close-up of the barbed-wire fence at the Auschwitz-Birkenau Concentration Camp.

Read with a Purpose

Read this article to find out what happened to Anne Frank after she was taken prisoner.

Last year in Amsterdam I found an old reel of movie film on which Anne Frank appears. She is seen for only ten seconds and it is an accident that she is there at all.

The film was taken for a wedding in 1941, the year before Anne Frank and seven others went into hiding in their "Secret Annex." It has a flickering, Chaplinesque[1] quality, with people popping suddenly in and out of doorways, the nervous smiles and hurried waves of the departing bride and groom.

Then, for just a moment, the camera seems uncertain where to look. It darts to the right, then to the left, then whisks up a wall, and into view comes a window crowded with people waving after the departing automobiles. The camera swings

1. **Chaplinesque** (chap lih NEHSK): like the old silent movies starring Charlie Chaplin (1889–1977).

farther to the left, to another window. There a girl stands alone, looking out into space. It is Anne Frank.

Just as the camera is about to pass on, the child moves her head a trifle. Her face flits more into focus, her hair shimmers in the sun. At this moment she discovers the camera, discovers the photographer, discovers us watching seventeen years later, and laughs at all of us, laughs with sudden merriment and surprise and embarrassment all at the same time.

I asked the projectionist to stop the film for a moment so that we could stand up to examine her face more closely. The smile stood still, just above our heads. But when I walked forward close to the screen, the smile ceased to be a smile. The face ceased to be a face, for the canvas screen was granular and the beam of light split into a multitude of tiny shadows, as if it had been scattered on a sandy plain. **A**

Anne Frank, of course, is gone too, but her spirit has remained to stir the conscience of the world. Her remarkable diary has been read in almost every language. I have seen a letter from a teenaged girl in Japan who says she thinks of Anne's Secret Annex as her second home. And the play based on the diary has been a great success wherever it is produced. German audiences, who invariably greet the final curtain of *The Diary of Anne Frank* in stricken silence, have jammed the theaters in what seems almost a national act of penance. **B**

Last year I set out to follow the fading trail of this girl who has become a legend. The trail led from Holland to Poland and back to Germany, where I visited the moss-grown site of the old Bergen-Belsen concentration camp at the village of Belsen and saw the common graves shared by Anne Frank and thirty thousand others. I interviewed forty-two people who knew Anne or who survived the ordeal that killed her. Some had known her intimately in those last tragic months. In the recollections of others she appears only for a moment. But even these fragments fulfill a promise. They make explicit a truth implied in the diary. As we somehow knew she must be, Anne Frank, even in the most frightful extremity, was indomitable.

The known story contained in the diary is a simple one of human relationships, of the poignant maturing of a perceptive girl who is thirteen when her diary begins and only fifteen when it ends. It is a story without violence, though its background is the most dreadful act of violence in the history of man, Hitler's annihilation of six million European Jews.

In the summer of 1942, Anne Frank, her father, her mother, her older sister, Margot, and four others were forced into hiding during the Nazi occupation of Holland. Their

---

A **Informational Focus** **Text Structure** How are the text's details organized up to this point?

B **Read and Discuss** What point is the author making?

Vocabulary **annihilation** (uh ny uh LAY shuhn) *n.:* complete destruction.

refuge was a tiny apartment they called the Secret Annex, in the back of an Amsterdam office building. For twenty-five months the Franks, the Van Daan family, and later a dentist, Albert Dussel,[2] lived in the Secret Annex, protected from the Gestapo[3] only by a swinging bookcase which masked the entrance to their hiding place and by the heroism of a few Christians who knew they were there. Anne Frank's diary recounts the daily pressures of their cramped existence: the hushed silences when strangers were in the building, the diminishing food supply, the fear of fire from the incessant Allied air raids, the hopes for an early invasion, above all the dread of capture by the pitiless men who were hunting Jews from house to house and sending them to concentration camps. Anne's diary also describes with sharp insight and youthful humor the bickerings, the wounded pride, the tearful reconciliations of the eight human beings in the Secret Annex. It tells of Anne's wishes for the understanding of her adored father, of her despair at the gulf between her mother and herself, of her tremulous and growing love for young Peter Van Daan. **C**

The actual diary ends with an entry for August 1, 1944, in which Anne Frank, addressing her imaginary friend Kitty, talks of her impatience with her own unpredictable personality. The stage version goes further: It attempts to reconstruct something of the events of August 4, 1944, the day the Secret Annex was violated and its occupants finally taken into a captivity from which only one returned.

What really happened on that August day fourteen years ago was far less dramatic than what is now depicted on the stage. The automobiles did not approach with howling sirens, did not stop with screaming brakes in front of the house on the Prinsengracht canal in Amsterdam. No rifle butt pounded against the door until it reverberated, as it now does in the theater every night somewhere in the world. The truth was, at first, that no one heard a sound.

It was midmorning on a bright summer day. In the hidden apartment behind the secret bookcase there was a scene of relaxed domesticity. The Franks, the Van Daans, and Mr. Dussel had finished a poor breakfast of ersatz[4] coffee and bread. Mrs. Frank and Mrs. Van Daan were about to clear the table. Mr. Van Daan, Margot Frank, and Mr. Dussel were resting or reading. Anne Frank was very likely at work on one of the short stories she often wrote when she was not busy with her diary or her novel. In Peter Van Daan's tiny attic room Otto Frank was

2. **Van Daan . . . Dussel:** In her diary, Anne made up names. The Van Daans were really named Van Pels, and Albert Dussel was really Fritz Pfeffer.

3. **Gestapo** (guh STAH poh): Nazi secret police force, known for its use of terror.

4. **ersatz** (ehr ZAHTS): artificial. Regular coffee beans were unavailable because of severe wartime shortages.

C **Read and Discuss** What have we learned about Anne Frank and her diary?

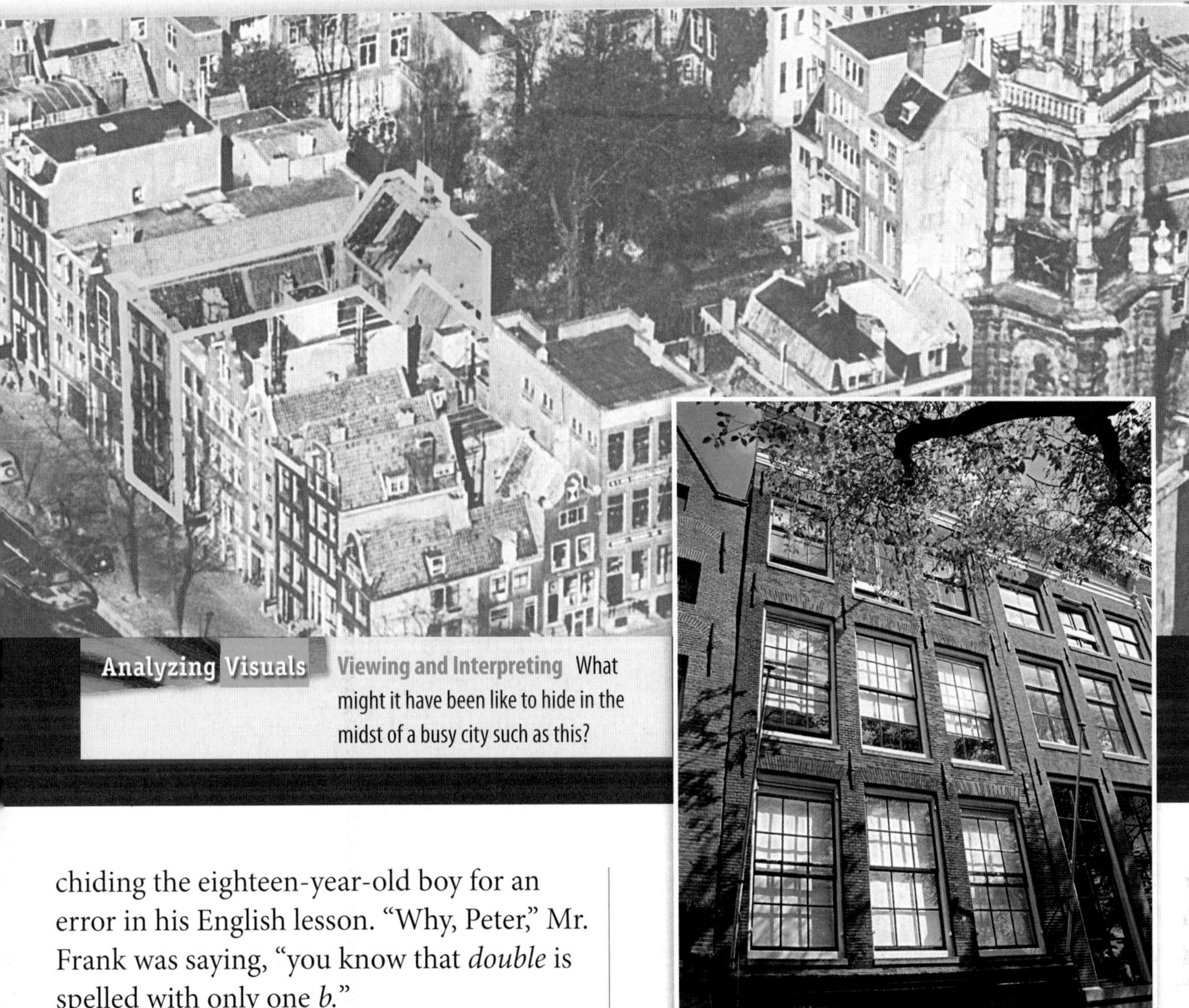

Analyzing Visuals **Viewing and Interpreting** What might it have been like to hide in the midst of a busy city such as this?

Front of Anne Frank House, Amsterdam, The Netherlands.

chiding the eighteen-year-old boy for an error in his English lesson. "Why, Peter," Mr. Frank was saying, "you know that *double* is spelled with only one *b*."

In the main part of the building four other people, two men and two women, were working at their regular jobs. For more than two years these four had risked their lives to protect their friends in the hide-out, supplied them with food, and brought them news of a world from which they had disappeared. One of the women was Miep, who had just got married a few months earlier. The other was Elli, a pretty typist of twenty-three. The men were Kraler and Koophuis,[5] middle-aged spice merchants who had been business associates of Otto Frank's before the occupation. Mr. Kraler was working in one office by himself. Koophuis and the two women were in another.

I spoke to Miep, Elli, and Mr. Koophuis in Amsterdam. The two women had not been arrested after the raid on the Secret Annex. Koophuis had been released in poor health after a few weeks in prison, and

5. **Kraler and Koophuis:** The author continues to use Anne's made-up names. Kraler and Koophuis were really named Victor Kugler and Johannes Kleiman.

Kraler, who now lives in Canada, had eventually escaped from a forced labor camp. **D**

Elli, now a mother, whose coloring and plump good looks are startlingly like those of the young women painted by the Dutch masters,[6] recalled: "I was posting entries in the receipts book when a car drove up in front of the house. But cars often stopped, after all. Then the front door opened, and someone came up the stairs. I wondered who it could be. We often had callers. Only this time I could hear that there were several men. . . ."

Miep, a delicate, intelligent, still young-looking woman, said: "The footsteps moved along the corridor. Then a door creaked, and a moment later the connecting door to Mr. Kraler's office opened, and a fat man thrust his head in and said in Dutch: 'Quiet. Stay in your seats.' I started and at first did not know what was happening. But then, suddenly, I knew."

Mr. Koophuis is now in very poor health, a gaunt, white-haired man in his sixties. He added: "I suppose I did not hear them because of the rumbling of the spice mills in the warehouse. The fat man's head was the first thing I knew. He came in and planted himself in front of us. 'You three stay here, understand?' he barked. So we stayed in the office and listened as someone else went upstairs, and doors rattled, and then there were footsteps everywhere. They searched the whole building."

Mr. Kraler wrote me this account from Toronto: "A uniformed staff sergeant of the Occupation Police[7] and three men in civilian clothes entered my office. They wanted to see the storerooms in the front part of the building. All will be well, I thought, if they don't want to see anything else. But after the sergeant had looked at everything, he went out into the corridor, ordering me again to come along. At the end of the corridor they drew their revolvers all at once and the sergeant ordered me to push aside the bookcase and open the door behind it. I said: 'But there's only a bookcase there!' At that he turned nasty, for he knew everything. He took hold of the bookcase and pulled. It yielded and the secret door was exposed. Perhaps the hooks had not been properly fastened. They opened the door and I had to precede them up the steps. The policemen followed me. I could feel their pistols in my back. I was the first to enter the Franks' room. Mrs. Frank was standing at the table. I made a great effort and managed to say: 'The Gestapo is here.'" **E**

Otto Frank, now sixty-eight, has remarried and lives in Switzerland. Of the eight who lived in the Secret Annex, he is the

6. **Dutch masters:** seventeenth-century painters, including Rembrandt, Frans Hals (frahns hahls), and Jan Vermeer (yahn vuhr MEHR).

7. **Occupation Police:** police organized by the German forces while they occupied the Netherlands.

D Informational Focus **Text Structure** How has the structural pattern of the article changed?

E Read and Discuss What is happening here? What mood has been created by these accounts?

only survivor. A handsome, soft-spoken man of obviously great intelligence, he regularly answers correspondence that comes to him about his daughter from all over the world. He recently went to Hollywood for consultation on the movie version of *The Diary of Anne Frank*. About the events of that August morning in 1944 Mr. Frank told me: "I was showing Peter Van Daan his spelling mistakes when suddenly someone came running up the stairs. The steps creaked, and I started to my feet, for it was morning, when everyone was supposed to be quiet. But then the door flew open and a man stood before us holding his pistol aimed at my chest.

"In the main room the others were already assembled. My wife and the children and Van Daans were standing there with raised hands. Then Albert Dussel came in, followed by another stranger. In the middle of the room stood a uniformed policeman. He stared into our faces.

"'Where are your valuables?' he asked. I pointed to the cupboard where my cash box was kept. The policeman took it out. Then he looked around and his eye fell on the leather briefcase where Anne kept her diary and all her papers. He opened it and shook everything out, dumped the contents on the floor so that Anne's papers and notebooks and loose sheets lay scattered at our feet. No one spoke, and the policeman didn't even glance at the mess on the floor as he put our valuables into the briefcase and closed it. He asked us whether we had

The common living room, dining room, and room of the Van Pels family in the Anne Frank House.

any weapons. But we had none, of course. Then he said, 'Get ready.'"

Who betrayed the occupants of the Secret Annex? No one is sure, but some suspicion centers on a man I can only call M., whom the living remember as a crafty and disagreeable sneak. He was a warehouse clerk hired after the Franks moved into the building, and he was never told of their presence. M. used to come to work early in the mornings, and he once found a locked briefcase which Mr. Van Daan had carelessly left in the office, where he sometimes worked in the dead of night. Though Kraler claimed it was his own briefcase, it is possible the clerk suspected. Little signs lead to bigger conclusions. In the course of the months he had worked in the building, M. might have gathered many such signs: the dial on the office radio left at BBC[8] by nocturnal listeners, slight rearrangements in the office furniture, and, of course, small inexplicable sounds from the back of the building.

M. was tried later by a war crimes court, denied everything, and was acquitted. No one knows where he is now. I made no effort to find him. Neither did I search out Silberthaler, the German police sergeant who made the arrest. The betrayers would have told me nothing.

8. **BBC:** British Broadcasting Corporation.

Ironically enough, the occupants of the Secret Annex had grown optimistic in the last weeks of their self-imposed confinement. The terrors of those first nights had largely faded. Even the German army communiqués[9] made clear that the war was approaching an end. The Russians were well into Poland. On the Western front Americans had broken through at Avranches and were pouring into the heart of France. Holland must be liberated soon. In her diary Anne Frank wrote that she thought she might be back in school by fall.

Now they were all packing. Of the capture Otto Frank recalled: "No one wept. Anne was very quiet and composed, only just as dispirited as the rest of us. Perhaps that was why she did not think to take along her notebooks, which lay scattered about on the floor. But maybe she too had the premonition that all was lost now, everything, and so she walked back and forth and did not even glance at her diary." **F**

As the captives filed out of the building, Miep sat listening. "I heard them going," she said, "first in the corridor and then down the stairs. I could hear the heavy boots and the footsteps, and then the very light footsteps of Anne. Through the years she had taught herself to walk so softly that you

9. **communiqués** (kuh myoo nih KAYZ): official bulletins.

F **Read and Discuss** What have we learned about the day of the capture?

Vocabulary **inexplicable** (ihn ihk SPLIHK uh buhl) *adj.:* unable to be explained.
premonition (prehm uh NIHSH uhn) *n.:* feeling that something, usually bad, will happen.

could hear her only if you knew what to listen for. I did not see her, for the office door was closed as they all passed by."

At Gestapo headquarters the prisoners were interrogated only briefly. As Otto Frank pointed out to his questioners, it was unlikely, after twenty-five months in the Secret Annex, that he would know the whereabouts of any other Jews who were hiding in Amsterdam.

The Franks, the Van Daans, and Dussel were kept at police headquarters for several days, the men in one cell, the women in the other. They were relatively comfortable there. The food was better than the food they had had in the Secret Annex and the guards left them alone.

Suddenly, all eight were taken to the railroad station and put on a train. The guards named their destination: Westerbork, a concentration camp for Jews in Holland, about eighty miles from Amsterdam. Mr. Frank said: "We rode in a regular passenger train. The fact that the door was bolted did not matter very much. We were together and had been given a little food for the journey. We were actually cheerful. Cheerful, at least, when I compare that journey to our next. We had already anticipated the possibility that we might not remain in Westerbork to the end. We knew what was happening to Jews in Auschwitz. But weren't the Russians already deep into Poland? We hoped our luck would hold.

"As we rode, Anne would not move from the window. It was summer outside. Meadows, stubble fields, and villages flew by. The telephone wires along the right of way curved up and down along the windows. After two years it was like freedom for her. Can you understand that?"

"Anne was very quiet and composed, only just as dispirited as the rest of us."

Among the names given me of survivors who had known the Franks at Westerbork was that of a Mrs. de Wiek, who lives in Apeldoorn, Holland. I visited Mrs. de Wiek in her home. A lovely, gracious woman, she told me that her family, like the Franks, had been in hiding for months before their capture. She said: "We had been at Westerbork three or four weeks when the word went around that there were new arrivals. News of that kind ran like wildfire through the camp, and my daughter Judy came running to me, calling, 'New people are coming, Mama!'

"The newcomers were standing in a long row in the mustering square,[10] and one of the clerks was entering their names on a list. We looked at them, and Judy pressed close against me. Most of the people in the camp were adults, and I had often wished for a

10. **mustering square:** place of assembly for inspection and roll call.

young friend for Judy, who was only fifteen. As I looked along the line, fearing I might see someone I knew, I suddenly exclaimed, 'Judy, see!'

"In the long line stood eight people whose faces, white as paper, told you at once that they had been hiding and had not been in the open air for years. Among them was this girl. And I said to Judy, 'Look, there is a friend for you.'

"I saw Anne Frank and Peter Van Daan every day in Westerbork. They were always together, and I often said to my husband, 'Look at those two beautiful young people.'

"Anne was so radiant that her beauty flowed over into Peter. Her eyes glowed and her movements had a lilt to them. She was very pallid at first, but there was some-

(above)The women's barracks in the Auschwitz-Birkenau Concentration Camp. (right) The personal effects of the people deported to Auschwitz around 1945 litter the train tracks leading to the camp's entrance.

Analyzing Visuals

Viewing and Interpreting How do you think Anne and Peter were able to be happy in such oppressive conditions?

thing so attractive about her frailty and her expressive face that at first Judy was too shy to make friends.

"Anne was happy there, incredible as it seems. Things were hard for us in the camp. We 'convict Jews' who had been arrested in hiding places had to wear blue overalls with a red bib and wooden shoes. Our men had their heads shaved. Three hundred people lived in each barracks. We were sent to work at five in the morning, the children to a cable workshop and the grown-ups to a shed where we had to break up old batteries and salvage the metal and the carbon rods. The food was bad, we were always kept on the run, and the guards all screamed 'Faster, faster!' But Anne was happy. It was as if she had been liberated. Now she could see new people and talk to them and could laugh. She could laugh while the rest of us thought nothing but: Will they send us to the camps in Poland? Will we live through it?

"Edith Frank, Anne's mother, seemed numbed by the experience. She could have been a mute. Anne's sister Margot spoke little and Otto Frank was quiet too, but his was a reassuring quietness that helped Anne and all of us. He lived in the men's barracks, but once when Anne was sick, he came over to visit her every evening and would stand beside her bed for hours, telling her stories. Anne was so like him. When another child, a twelve-year-old boy named David, fell ill, Anne stood by his bed and talked to him. David came from an Orthodox family, and he and Anne always talked about God." **G**

Anne Frank stayed at Westerbork only three weeks. Early in September a thousand of the "convict Jews" were put on a freight train, seventy-five people to a car. Brussels fell to the Allies, then Antwerp, then the Americans reached Aachen. But the victories were coming too late. The Franks and their friends were already on the way to Auschwitz, the camp in Poland where four million Jews died.

Mrs. de Wiek was in the same freight car as the Franks on that journey from Westerbork to Auschwitz. "Now and then when the train stopped," she told me, "the SS guards[11] came to the door and held out their caps and we had to toss our money and valuables into the caps. Anne and Judy sometimes pulled themselves up to the small barred window of the car and described the villages we were passing through. We made the children repeat the addresses where we could meet after the war if we became separated in the camp. I remember that the Franks chose a meeting place in Switzerland.

"I sat beside my husband on a small box. On the third day in the train, my husband suddenly took my hand and said, 'I want to thank you for the wonderful life we have had together.'

"I snatched my hand away from his, crying, 'What are you thinking about? It's not over!'

11. **SS guards:** Nazi special police, who ran the concentration camps.

G **Read and Discuss** What information has Mrs. de Wiek given us about the Franks?

"But he calmly reached for my hand again and took it and repeated several times, 'Thank you. Thank you for the life we have had together.' Then I left my hand in his and did not try to draw it away."

On the third night, the train stopped, the doors of the car slid violently open, and the first the exhausted passengers saw of Auschwitz was the glaring searchlights fixed on the train. On the platform, kapos (criminal convicts who were assigned to positions of authority over the other prisoners) were running back and forth shouting orders. Behind them, seen distinctly against the light, stood the SS officers, trimly built and smartly uniformed, many of them with huge dogs at their sides. As the people poured out of the train, a loudspeaker roared, "Women to the left! Men to the right!"

"Thank you. Thank you for the life we have had together."

Mrs. de Wiek went on calmly: "I saw them all as they went away, Mr. Van Daan and Mr. Dussel and Peter and Mr. Frank. But I saw no sign of my husband. He had vanished. I never saw him again.

"'Listen!' the loudspeaker bawled again. 'It is an hour's march to the women's camp. For the children and the sick there are trucks waiting at the end of the platform.'

"We could see the trucks," Mrs. de Wiek said. "They were painted with big red crosses. We all made a rush for them. Who among us was not sick after those days on the train? But we did not reach them. People were still hanging on to the backs of the trucks as they started off. Not one person who went along on that ride ever arrived at the women's camp, and no one has ever found any trace of them."

Mrs. de Wiek, her daughter, Mrs. Van Daan, Mrs. Frank, Margot, and Anne survived the brutal pace of the night march to the women's camp at Auschwitz. Next day their heads were shaved; they learned that the hair was useful as packing for pipe joints in U-boats.[12] Then the women were put to work digging sods of grass, which they placed in great piles. As they labored each day, thousands of others were dispatched with maniacal efficiency in the gas chambers, and smoke rising from the stacks of the huge crematoriums[13] blackened the sky.

Mrs. de Wiek saw Anne Frank every day at Auschwitz. "Anne seemed even more beautiful there," Mrs. de Wiek said, "than she had at Westerbork. Of course her long hair was gone, but now you could see that her beauty was in her eyes, which seemed to grow bigger as she grew thinner. Her gaiety had vanished, but she was still alert and

12. **U-boats:** submarines.

13. **crematoriums** (kree muh TAWR ee uhmz): furnaces in which prisoners' bodies were cremated (burned to ashes).

Analyzing Visuals

Viewing and Interpreting What do you think was the artist's intent in documenting the daily life of prisoners at the Theresienstadt Concentration Camp?

The Blind of Theresienstadt by Leo Haas. Watercolor.

sweet, and with her charm she sometimes secured things that the rest of us had long since given up hoping for.

"For example, we each had only a gray sack to wear. But when the weather turned cold, Anne came in one day wearing a suit of men's long underwear. She had begged it somewhere. She looked screamingly funny with those long white legs but somehow still delightful.

"Though she was the youngest, Anne was the leader in her group of five people. She also gave out the bread to everyone in the barracks and she did it so fairly there was none of the usual grumbling.

"We were always thirsty at Auschwitz, so thirsty that at roll call we would stick out our tongues if it happened to be raining or snowing, and many became sick from bad water. Once, when I was almost dead because there was nothing to drink, Anne suddenly came to me with a cup of coffee. To this day I don't know where she got it.

"In the barracks many people were dying, some of starvation, others of weakness and despair. It was almost impossible not to give up hope, and when a person gave up, his face became empty and dead. The Polish woman doctor who had been caring for the sick said to me, 'You will pull through. You still have your face.'

"Anne Frank, too, still had her face, up to the very last. To the last also she was moved by the dreadful things the rest of us had somehow become hardened to. Who bothered to look when the flames shot up into the sky at night from the crematoriums? Who was troubled that every day new people were being selected and gassed? Most of us were beyond feeling. But not Anne. I can still see her standing at the door and looking down the camp street as a group of naked Gypsy girls were driven by on their way to the crematorium. Anne watched them going and cried. And she also cried when we marched past the Hungarian children who had been waiting half a day in the rain in front of the gas chambers. And Anne nudged me and said, 'Look, look! Their eyes!' Anne cried. And you cannot imagine how soon most of us came to the end of our tears." **H**

Late in October the SS selected the healthiest of the women prisoners for work in a munitions factory in Czechoslovakia. Judy de Wiek was taken from her mother, but Anne and her sister Margot were rejected because they had contracted scabies.[14] A few days later there was another selection for shipment from Auschwitz. Stripped, the women waited naked for hours on the mustering ground outside the barracks. Then, one by one, they filed into the barracks, where a battery of powerful lights had been set up and an SS doctor waited to check them over. Only those able to stand a trip and do hard work were being chosen for this new shipment, and many of the women lied about their age and condition in the hope that they would escape the almost certain death of Auschwitz. Mrs. de Wiek was rejected and so was Mrs. Frank. They waited, looking on.

"Next it was the turn of the two girls, Anne and Margot," Mrs. de Wiek recalled. "Even under the glare of that light Anne still had her face, and she encouraged Margot, and Margot walked erect into the light. There they stood for a moment, naked and shaven-headed, and Anne looked at us with her unclouded face, looked straight and stood straight, and then they were approved and passed along. We could not see what was on the other side of the light. Mrs. Frank screamed, 'The children! Oh, God!'"

The chronicle of most of the other occupants of the Secret Annex ends at Auschwitz. Mrs. Frank died there of malnutrition two months later. Mr. Frank saw Mr. Van Daan marched to the gas chambers. When the SS fled Auschwitz before the approaching Russians in January 1945, they took Peter Van Daan with them. It was bitter cold and the roads were covered with ice and Peter Van Daan, Anne Frank's shy beloved, was never heard of again.

From Auschwitz, Mr. Dussel, the dentist, was shipped to a camp in Germany, where he died. Only Otto Frank remained there alive until liberation. Anne Frank and Mrs. Van Daan and Margot had been selected for shipment to Bergen-Belsen.

14. **scabies:** skin disease that causes severe itching.

H **Read and Discuss** What does Mrs. de Wiek mean when she says that Anne "still had her face"?

Last year I drove the 225 miles from Amsterdam to Belsen and spent a day there walking over the heath.[15] The site of the old camp is near the city of Hannover, in the state of Lower Saxony. It was June when I arrived, and lupine was in flower in the scrubland.

My guide first showed me the cemetery where fifty thousand Russian prisoners of war, captured in one of Hitler's great early offensives, were buried in 1941. Next to them is a cemetery for Italians. No one knows exactly whether there are three hundred or three thousand in that mass grave.

About a mile farther we came to the main site of the Bergen-Belsen camp. Amid the low growth of pine and birches many large rectangular patches can be seen on the heath. The barracks stood on these, and between them the worn tracks of thousands of bare feet are still visible. There are more mass graves nearby, low mounds overgrown with heath grass or new-planted dwarf pines. Boards bearing the numbers of the dead stand beside some mounds, but others are unmarked and barely discernible. Anne Frank lies there. **I**

The train that carried Anne from Auschwitz to Belsen stopped at every second station because of air raids. At Bergen-Belsen there were no roll calls, no

15. **heath (heeth):** area of open wasteland covered with low-growing plants.

I **Read and Discuss** What picture is the author giving us of Bergen-Belsen as it is today?

A memorial stands at one of the several mass graves at the site of the former Nazi concentration camp, Bergen-Belsen, in Belsen, Germany. The inscription reads 'Here Rest 1,000 Dead, April 1945.'

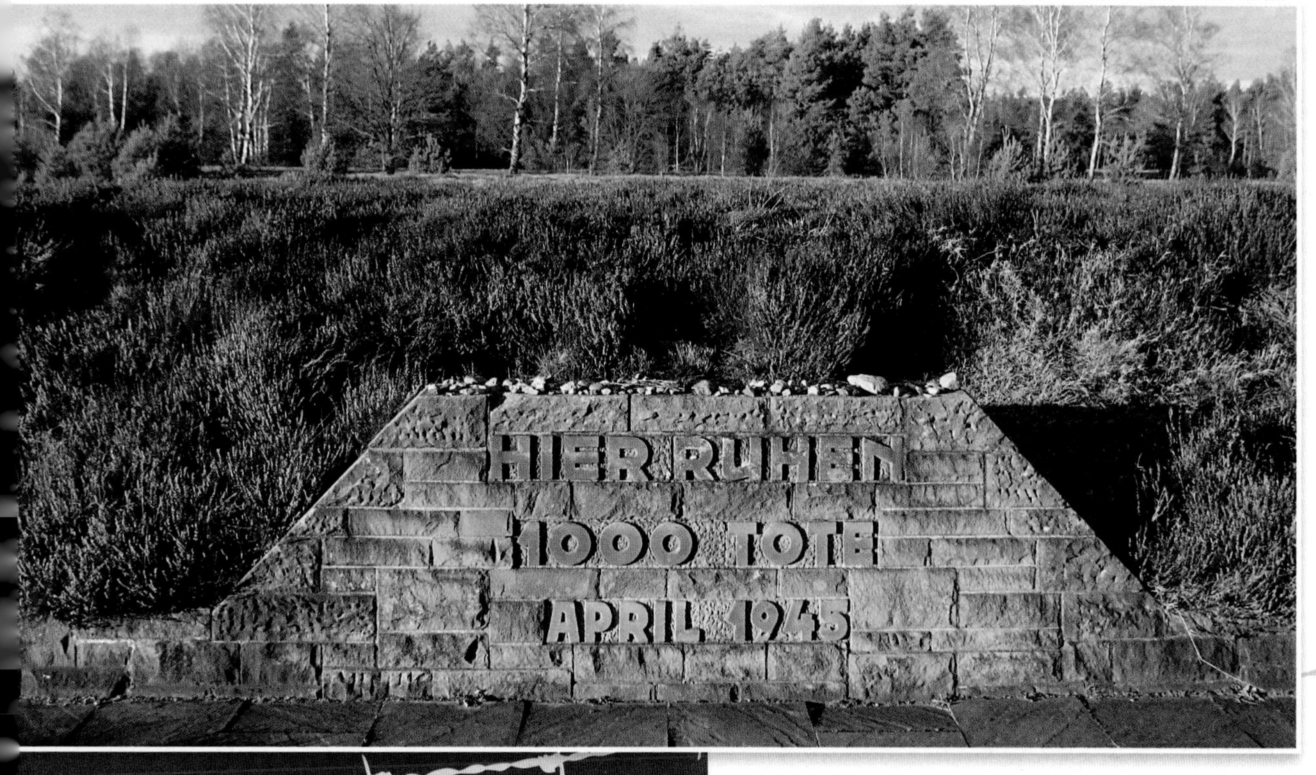
HIER RUHEN
1000 TOTE
APRIL 1945

Anne Frank (second from left) with a group of friends. The Granger Collection, New York.

organization, almost no sign of the SS. Prisoners lived on the heath without hope. The fact that the Allies had reached the Rhine encouraged no one. Prisoners died daily—of hunger, thirst, sickness.

The Auschwitz group had at first been assigned to tents on the Bergen-Belsen heath, tents which, one survivor recalls, gave an oddly gay, carnival aspect to the camp. One night that fall a great windstorm brought the tents crashing down, and their occupants were then put in wooden barracks. Mrs. B. of Amsterdam remembered about Anne: "We lived in the same block and saw each other often. In fact, we had a party together at Christmastime. We had saved up some stale bread, and we cut this up and put onions and boiled cabbage on the pieces. Over our feast we nearly forgot our misery for a few hours. We were almost happy. I know that it sounds ghastly now, but we really were a little happy in spite of everything."

One of Anne Frank's dearest childhood friends in Amsterdam was a girl named Lies Goosens.[16] Lies is repeatedly mentioned in the diary. She was captured before the Franks were found in the Secret Annex, and Anne wrote of her great fears for the safety of her friend. Now the slim and attractive wife of an Israeli army officer, Lies lives in Jerusalem. But she was in Bergen-Belsen in February 1945, when she heard that a group of Dutch Jews had been moved into the next compound.

Lies said, "I waited until night. Then I stole out of the barracks and went over to the barbed wire which separated us from the newcomers. I called softly into the darkness, 'Is anyone there?'

"A voice answered, 'I am here. I am Mrs. Van Daan.'

"We had known the Van Daans in Amsterdam. I told her who I was and asked whether Margot or Anne could come to the fence. Mrs. Van Daan answered in a breathless voice that Margot was sick but that Anne could probably come and that she would go look for her.

"I waited, shivering in the darkness. It took a long time. But suddenly I heard a voice: 'Lies? Lies? Where are you?'

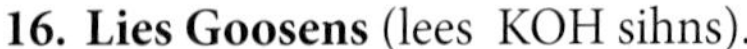

16. Lies Goosens (lees KOH sihns).

"I ran in the direction of the voice, and then I saw Anne beyond the barbed wire. She was in rags. I saw her emaciated, sunken face in the darkness. Her eyes were very large. We cried and cried as we told each other our sad news, for now there was only the barbed wire between us, nothing more, and no longer any difference in our fates.

"But there was a difference after all. My block still had food and clothing. Anne had nothing. She was freezing and starving. I called to her in a whisper, 'Come back tomorrow. I'll bring you something.'

"And Anne called across, 'Yes, tomorrow. I'll come.'

"I saw Anne again when she came to the fence on the following night," Lies continued. "I had packed up a woolen jacket and some zwieback[17] and sugar and a tin of sardines for her. I called out, 'Anne, watch now!' Then I threw the bundle across the barbed wire.

"But I heard only screams and Anne crying. I shouted, 'What's happened?' And she called back, weeping, 'A woman caught it and won't give it to me.' Then I heard rapid footsteps as the woman ran away. Next night I had only a pair of stockings and zwieback, but this time Anne caught it."

In the last weeks at Bergen-Belsen, as Germany was strangled between the Russians and the Western Allies, there was almost no food at all. The roads were blocked, the railroads had been bombed, and the SS commander of the camp drove around the district trying unsuccessfully to requisition supplies. Still, the crematoriums worked night and day. And in the midst of the starvation and the murder there was a great epidemic of typhus.

Both Anne and Margot Frank contracted the disease in late February or early March of 1945. Margot lay in a coma for several days. Then, while unconscious, she somehow rolled from her bed and died. Mrs. Van Daan also died in the epidemic.

The death of Anne Frank passed almost without notice. For Anne, as for millions of others, it was only the final anonymity, and I met no one who remembers being with her in that moment. So many were dying. One woman said, "I feel certain she died because of her sister's death. Dying is easy for anyone left alone in a concentration camp." Mrs. B., who had shared the pitiful Christmastide feast with Anne, knows a little more: "Anne, who was very sick at the time, was not informed of her sister's death. But a few days later she sensed it and soon afterward she died, peacefully."

Three weeks later British troops liberated Bergen-Belsen. **J**

Miep and Elli, the heroic young women who had shielded the Franks for two years, found Anne's papers during the week after

17. **zwieback** (ZWEE bahk): sweetened bread that is sliced and toasted after it is baked.

Vocabulary **emaciated** (ih MAY shee ay tihd) *v.* used as *adj.:* extremely thin, as from starvation.

J **Read and Discuss** Now what has happened?

the police raid on the Secret Annex. "It was terrible when I went up there," Miep recalled. "Everything had been turned upside down. On the floor lay clothes, papers, letters, and school notebooks. Anne's little wrapper hung from a hook on the wall. And among the clutter on the floor lay a notebook with a red-checked cover. I picked it up, looked at the pages, and recognized Anne's handwriting."

Elli wept as she spoke to me: "The table was still set. There were plates, cups, and spoons, but the plates were empty, and I was so frightened I scarcely dared take a step. We sat down on the floor and leafed through all the papers. They were all Anne's, the notebooks and the colored duplicate paper from the office too. We gathered all of them and locked them up in the main office.

Anne Frank, about age 12, c. 1941.

Thus Anne Frank's voice was preserved out of the millions that were silenced.

"A few days later M. came into the office, M. who now had the keys to the building. He said to me, 'I found some more stuff upstairs,' and he handed me another sheaf of Anne's papers. How strange, I thought, that *he* should be the one to give these to me. But I took them and locked them up with the others." **K**

Miep and Elli did not read the papers they had saved. The red-checked diary, the office account books into which it overflowed, the 312 tissue-thin sheets of colored paper filled with Anne's short stories and the beginnings of a novel about a young girl who was to live in freedom—all these were kept in the safe until Otto Frank finally returned to Amsterdam alone. Thus Anne Frank's voice was preserved out of the millions that were silenced. No louder than a child's whisper, it speaks for those millions and has outlasted the raucous shouts of the murderers, soaring above the clamorous voices of passing time. **L**

Read with a Purpose

What did you learn about Anne's final days?

K **Read and Discuss** Elli says that she thought it strange that M. should be the one to give her some of Anne's papers. Why would that be strange?

L **Informational Focus** **Text Structure** What order of importance do the details in the final paragraph reflect?

Vocabulary **raucous** (RAW kuhs) *adj.:* loud and rough.

MAGAZINE ARTICLE

Applying Your Skills

VO.8.4 Infer the literal and figurative meaning of words and phrases and discuss the function of figurative language, including metaphors, similes and idioms. **RA.I.8.1** Compare and contrast text features, including format and headers of various informational texts in terms of their structure and purpose.

A Tragedy Revealed: A Heroine's Last Days

Practicing the Standards

Informational Text and Vocabulary

1. What overall **organizational structure** does the article use?

A Chronological order

B Logical order

C Order of importance

D Question and answer

2. According to the author, what may have been a **cause** in the discovery of the Secret Annex?

A Mr. Koophuis was a traitor and reported the Annex occupants to the police.

B Mr. Van Daan was discovered listening to a radio in the downstairs office.

C There were small telltale signs, such as rearranged furniture and muffled sounds.

D The occupants of the Secret Annex were spotted entering the building.

3. What happened to Anne soon after her sister Margot died?

A Anne died of typhus.

B Anne was taken to Bergen-Belsen.

C Anne found an old friend, named Lies.

D Anne received a letter from her father.

4. What important role did Miep and Elli play after the capture of the people in the Annex?

A They published Anne's story in the local paper.

B They found and preserved the artifacts left behind in the Annex.

C They helped to assist another Jewish family.

D They turned M. in to the police.

5. If a newspaper article reports that a city was *annihilated,* it means that the city was —

A liberated

B founded

C destroyed

D evacuated

6. Which of the following words means the opposite of *emaciated*?

A hungry

B satisfied

C skinny

D fat

7. A *raucous* person is —

A loud

B crazy

C timid

D fast

Writing Focus **Constructed Response**

Write a brief outline of the essay to show how the author uses the different structural patterns. How do these different text structures interact?

What Do You Think Now?

Why is it important to keep memories of the Holocaust alive?

ESSAY

Preparing to Read

RP.8.1 Apply reading comprehension strategies, including making predictions, comparing and contrasting, recalling and summarizing and making inferences and drawing conclusions.

Reader/Writer Notebook

Use your **RWN** to complete the activities for this selection.

Walking with Living Feet

Informational Text Focus

Treatment and Scope Writings on the Holocaust take many forms. The **treatment** of their ideas is also varied. For example, writings such as memoirs are **subjective,** containing opinions and personal biases. Subjective details allow us to more fully understand the emotional experiences of the writers. Other writings, such as histories, are usually **objective,** based on fact. Objective writing usually serves to report or instruct.

Texts about the Holocaust also have different **scopes,** or coverage of topics and ideas. For example, a history of the Nazi's treatment of the Jewish people might have a **broad** scope, whereas an essay about a specific prison camp will have a more **narrow** scope.

Into Action Use a chart like the one below to help you identify the treatment and scope of the two informational pieces.

A Tragedy Revealed	Walking with Living Feet
Treatment: both subjective and objective	Treatment:
Subjective detail: "... her spirit remained to stir the conscience of the world."	Detail:
Objective detail:	Detail:
Scope:	Scope:

Writing Focus

Preparing for **Constructed Response**

As you read this text, jot down your ideas about whether the details the writer includes are subjective or objective and whether the scope is broad or narrow.

Vocabulary

hysterically (hihs TEHR uh klee) *adv.:* in an uncontrolled or wild manner. *When she thought about the horrors of the Holocaust, she began crying hysterically.*

barracks (BAR ehks) *n.:* large buildings or groups of buildings in which many people live. *At the Nazi concentration camps, Jews were forced to live in crowded barracks.*

compressed (kuhm PREHST) *v.:* constricted; stifled, as if squeezed. *The gas chamber compressed the visitor until she felt she could no longer breathe.*

Language Coach

Affixes The word *press* has many meanings, such as "push," "squeeze," "force," "urge," and "emphasize." When you add a prefix, as in *compress,* you create a word with a new meaning. Think about how these prefixes change the meaning of *press* in the words *depression, impress, oppressive,* and *repression.* How do the different suffixes change the meanings? Consult a dictionary if you need help.

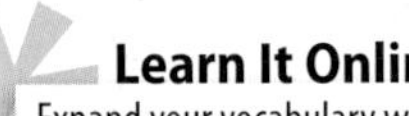

Learn It Online

Expand your vocabulary with Word Watch at:

go.hrw.com L8-948 

PERSONAL ESSAY

Walking with Living Feet

by **Dara Horn,** Millburn High School
Millburn, New Jersey

Read with a Purpose

Read this selection to learn more about the effects of the Holocaust.

I had a very unusual fifteenth birthday. During my birthday week, at the end of April, I was traveling with five thousand high school students from around the world, visiting concentration camps in Poland. I learned more there than I learned during my entire life in school; once I stepped out of a gas chamber, I became a different person. When I turned fifteen, I discovered that no matter how much you read about the Holocaust, nothing can ever be like seeing it with your own eyes. The day after my fifteenth birthday was the turning point of my life. I was at Majdanek, one of the largest Nazi concentration camps. And I will never forget it. **A**

Majdanek has been left exactly as it was when it was in use, so intact that if it were to be "plugged in," it could start gassing people tomorrow.

I stood in a gas chamber there, at Majdanek. I saw the blue stains of Zyklon B streaking the ceilings and walls, the poison used to kill the people who were crushed into this tiny, gray cement room. I could see how their fingers had scraped off the white paint, trying to escape. The cement floor that I sat on was cold and clammy; the air in the room seemed made of chills. When I first sat down, I did not notice, but soon those chilling waves were seeping into my skin, like so many tiny fingers trying to pull at my nerves and make my bones quiver. All around me, kids were crying hysterically, yet the chills that rankled the air around me hadn't reached my mind, and I could not

A Informational Focus Treatment Does this first paragraph indicate a subjective or an objective treatment?

Vocabulary **hysterically** (hihs TEHR uh klee) *adv.:* in an uncontrolled or wild manner.

feel. I hated myself for it. Anger, fear, pain, and shock—I could have felt all of those and more, but instead I felt nothing. That void was far worse: All the other emotions around me showed the presence of human hearts, but I was almost not there at all. I wanted to feel; I hated the guilt I had at my lack of reaction as much as I hated what happened there. Only my squirming skin could attest to my surroundings, and the crawling air made my lungs tighten. I wished I could cry, but I couldn't break down my mental blockade. Why? **B**

The camp of Majdanek extends for miles, but one of the worst things about it is that it's right in a town, almost a city, called Lublin. There are actually houses right next to the barbed wire, the fence with its thorns that stabbed my frightened eyes, enough to separate a universe. The people of that city would have had to be dead not to notice the death which struck daily, right behind their backyards, where I saw children playing. People marched through Lublin from the train station, entered through the same barbed wire gate that I did, and left through the chimney. Nobody in Lublin noticed, because if they had, their fate would have been the same. And today the camp's long gray, barnlike barracks still extend forever, in endless rows, the sky a leaden weight blocking the colors that grace free life. Gray is the color of hell.

Inside each of the barracks is a new horror. Some are museum exhibits, with collections of people's toothbrushes (they were told that they were being "relocated" and to bring one suitcase, the contents of which were confiscated) and people's hair. All of the walls in one barracks are covered with people's hats, hanging in rows. But the worst were the shoes.

About five of the barracks are filled with nothing but the shoes of some of the people who were killed there—over 850,000 pairs. In one barracks, I sat on a platform about five feet off the ground, and surrounding it was an ocean of shoes, five feet deep. In the gas chamber I could not feel, but in that room filled with shoes, my mental blockade cracked. The photographs meant nothing to me, the history lessons and names and numbers were never strong enough. But here each shoe is different, a different size and shape: a high heel, a sandal, a baby's shoe

B **Read and Discuss** What is going on here?

Vocabulary **barracks** (BAR ehks) *n.:* large buildings or groups of buildings in which many people live.

so tiny that its owner couldn't have been old enough to walk, and shoes like mine. Each pair of those shoes walked a path all its own, guided its owner through his or her life and to all of their deaths. Thousands and thousands of shoes, each pair different, each pair silently screaming someone's murdered dreams. No book can teach me what I saw there with my own eyes!

Shoes taken from prisoners at the Auschwitz Concentration Camp.

I glanced at my own shoe, expecting it to be far different from those in that ocean of death, and my breath caught in my throat as I saw that my shoe seemed to be almost the same style as one, no, two, three, of the shoes I saw; it seemed as if every shoe there was my shoe. I touched the toe of one nearby and felt its dusty texture, certain that mine would be different. But as I touched my own toe, tears welled in my eyes as my fingers traced the edges of my dusty, living shoes. Eight hundred and fifty thousand pairs of shoes, but now I understood: They weren't numbers; they were people.

Soon I was crying, but for someone else: for the child whose mother's sandals rested on that pile, for the woman whose husband's shoes swam motionless in that sea, like the tears that streaked my face, for the girl whose best friend's slippers were buried in that ocean of grayness and silence. I was lost to the shoes there. I wished I could throw my shoes into that pile, to grasp and feel each shoe, to jump into the sea of shoes, to become a part of it, to take it with me. I wanted to add my own shoes to that ocean, but all I could leave there were my salty tears. My feet clumped on the wooden platform as I left, and

I had never been more conscious of how my shoes fit my living feet. **C**

At the very end of the camp was another gas chamber and the crematorium, its smokestack jutting through the leaden sky. This gas chamber did not have the blue poison stains that streaked the walls in the one I saw first, or maybe it did: The only light in that cement room was from dozens of memorial candles. It was too dark to see. The air inside was damp and suffocating, like a burial cave, and yet the air was savagely alive. It crawled down my neck and compressed me as the walls and ceiling seemed to move closer. No words can express how it felt to step out of that gas chamber alive, wearing my living shoes.

And I saw the crematorium where the corpses were burned, ovens shaped to fit a person. As I touched the brick furnaces with trembling fingers, my tears froze in my eyes and I could not cry. It was here that I felt my soul go up in flames, leaving me an empty shell.

Majdanek reeks of death everywhere. Even the reminders and signs of life that exist in a cemetery, like a footprint or rustling leaves, are absent here, every image of life erased. Even the wind does not ruffle the grass, which never used to grow here because the prisoners would eat it. But in the crematorium, I felt something I cannot express. No words exist to describe how I felt. It was someone else's nightmare, a nightmare that turned real before I even noticed it. It was a stark and chilling reality that struck me there, standing where people were slaughtered and burned, and my mind simply stopped. Have you ever been to Planet Hell? My people are numbers here, struck from a list and sent out the chimney, their children's bodies roasting. And I was there. You cannot visit this planet through any film or book; photographs cannot bring you here. Planet Hell is beyond the realm of tears. This is why I could not cry.

I left the camp. How many people, who had walked in those 850,000 pairs of shoes, once dreamed of doing what I had just done? And did they, too, forget how to cry?

In Israel I planted a tree with soil I had taken from concentration camps. In the soil were white specks, human bone ash. I am fifteen years old, and I know I can never forget.

C **Informational Focus** **Scope** What does the author's focus on shoes say about the scope of the essay?

Vocabulary **compressed** (kuhm PREHST) *v.:* constricted; stifled, as if squeezed.

MAGAZINE ARTICLE/ESSAY

Applying Your Skills

OH **RP.8.1** Apply reading comprehension strategies, including making predictions, comparing and contrasting, recalling and summarizing and making inferences and drawing conclusions. **VO.8.4** Infer the literal and figurative meaning of words and phrases and discuss the function of figurative language, including metaphors, similes and idioms.

A Tragedy Revealed / Walking with Living Feet

Practicing the Standards

Informational Text and Vocabulary

1. Which of the following statements about the **scope** of the two selections is *not* true?

A "Walking with Living Feet" has a broader scope than "A Tragedy Revealed."

B "A Tragedy Revealed" has a broader scope than "Walking with Living Feet."

C The scope of "A Tragedy Revealed" is broad because it describes many events.

D "Walking with Living Feet" has a narrow scope because it describes one event.

2. What is the main difference in the **treatment** of the two pieces?

A "Walking with Living Feet" is more detailed than "A Tragedy Revealed."

B "Walking with Living Feet" discusses a more painful event than "A Tragedy Revealed."

C "Walking with Living Feet" is objective, whereas "A Tragedy Revealed" is subjective.

D "Walking with Living Feet" is subjective, whereas "A Tragedy Revealed" is both subjective and objective.

3. Which statement accurately describes a similarity between the texts?

A Both texts focus on the causes of World War II.

B Both texts focus on a girl's experiences.

C Both texts call for changes in society.

D Both texts present details about the operation of gas chambers.

4. When a person is laughing *hysterically,* it means that he or she is laughing —

A rudely

B softly

C uncontrollably

D meanly

5. People are *compressed* in a small space when they are —

A crowded together

B spread out

C good friends

D comfortable

6. If you lived in a *barracks,* your building would be —

A large

B small

C dirty

D clean

Writing Focus Constructed Response

Write two paragraphs describing the same event from your life. Write one paragraph with a subjective treatment, and make the other one objective.

What Do You Think Now?

How do historical tragedies continue to shape our world view?

Writing Workshop

Research Report

Write with a Purpose

Write a research report about a historical subject. Your **audience** will include your teacher, classmates, and other students at your school. Your **purpose** is to convey unbiased factual information on your chosen subject.

A Good Research Report

- conveys factual information, not the writer's feelings
- includes documented information gathered from several reliable sources
- presents clearly organized information, providing background where necessary
- presents a thesis, or main idea, supported by examples and explanations
- ends by summarizing ideas or drawing an overall conclusion

See page 962 for complete rubric.

Think as a Reader/Writer

Research often begins with a question about a subject that interests you. The success of your **research report** depends on carefully selecting evidence from sources to support your **thesis,** or main idea. Read the following excerpt from a report that began with a question the writer had about African American soldiers in World War II.

World War II brings many heroic images to mind. People may think of Rosie the Riveter or the Iwo Jima statue of six Marines. One lesser-known story, though, is the heroism of African American soldiers in World War II. The 761st Tank Battalion proved that African Americans could serve their country with excellence and bravery.

← The controlling idea, or **thesis,** of the report is stated clearly.

When the war began in the late 1930s, African Americans made up only a small part of the army. The armed forces were segregated, or separated, by race. . . . In 1940, the U.S. Congress passed the Selective Training and Service Act, which included these words, "there shall be no discrimination against any person on account of race or color" (qtd. in Pfeifer 13–14).The act led to the creation of black combat units, including the 761st Tank Battalion (Pfeifer 22).

← Background on the topic is presented.

← A historical document is quoted and and the source cited.

In October 1944, the battalion joined General George S. Patton's Third Army in Europe. According to the writer Catherine Reef, Patton told the soldiers, "I would never have asked for you if you weren't good. I have nothing but the best in my Army" (qtd. in Reef 51).

← A phrase signals the introduction of a quote from a source.

Think About the Professional Model

With a partner, discuss the following questions about the model:

1. How would you describe the organization of the first paragraph?
2. How does the quote in the last paragraph support the writer's thesis?

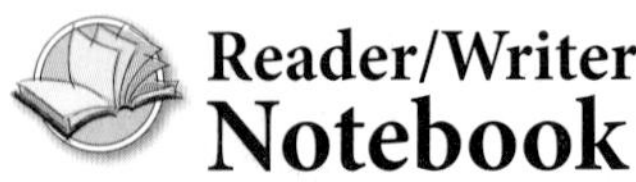

Use your **RWN** to complete the activities for this workshop.

WA.8.4.e Write informational essays or reports, including research, that: document sources and include bibliographies. **WA.8.4.b** Write informational essays or reports, including research, that: provide a clear and accurate perspective on the subject **WP.8.4** Prewriting: Determine a purpose and audience and plan strategies to address purpose and audience.

Prewriting

Choose a Subject

Brainstorm a list of possible historical figures or events to research. Perhaps you are considering the history of basketball as your subject. You cannot hope to cover the entire history of the sport in your report. You need to narrow your broad subject to a manageable one, one that you can research and then say something significant about in the time you have for the assignment.

Broad Subject	Narrow Subject	Narrower Subject
history of basketball	important basketball players	Michael Jordan

Narrow Your Research

To keep your research focused—not too broad—choose an aspect of your subject to research. Posing a question will help guide your work. For example, if you chose the basketball player Michael Jordan as your subject, you couldn't cover everything about him. You might ask this question, however: *What made Michael Jordan an important player in basketball history?*

Think About Purpose and Audience

When planning your research report, keep your purpose and audience in mind. Your **purpose** in expository, or informative, writing is to present factual information about your subject. Your **audience** includes your teacher, classmates, and other students at your school who will read your report.

Gather Sources

Plan to use at least three sources of information for your report. Whenever possible, use **primary sources** (first-hand accounts), such as diaries and letters. **Secondary sources** are interpretations of primary materials. They include encyclopedia entries, newspaper articles, and documentaries.

Idea Starters

Here are some examples of the kinds of people or events that you might research and write about:

- a great musician of the past
- an early governor of your state
- early space exploration
- an important discovery in medicine
- the history of your favorite game
- a major weather event, such as a flood, hurricane, or blizzard

Writing Tip

Use your answers to the following questions to help limit the scope of your research:

- How did an individual or event change the world?
- How did the individual contribute to or affect a moment in history?
- Why is the historical event important and memorable?
- Why should we continue to think about this historical person or event?

Your Turn

Get Started Making notes in your **RWN,** choose a subject and a focused topic. Then, begin gathering information about your topic.

Learn It Online

Use an interactive writer's model to take another look at writing reports. Visit:

go.hrw.com L8-955 

Evaluate Sources

Before you begin taking notes from your sources, evaluate each source to determine whether it is factual, up-to-date, and trustworthy. Answer these questions:

- Is the source nonfiction?
- Is the information current? Does it include recent thinking or research on this historical subject?
- Is the source trustworthy? Is the author an expert in the field? If the source is a Web site, does the address end in *.org, .edu,* or *.gov*?

Prepare a notecard for each source. Accurately record the title of the source, the author, the city in which it was published, the name of the publisher, and the year of publication. Give each source a number.

#1

Lovitt, Chip. Michael Jordan: Basketball's Best. New York: Scholastic, Inc., 2002.

Take Notes

Record each fact or idea on a separate index card. If the idea or fact is from a source, label every note with its source number and the number of the page on which the information is located. As you take notes, you may summarize or paraphrase information by restating it in your own words. If you copy material word for word, be sure to put quotation marks around it in your notes. Remember that you will need to cite your sources.

Writing Tip

Remember the different ways you can take notes from your sources:

- **paraphrase**: restate the information in your own words
- **summarize**: state the main ideas in the source
- **quote**: write down the information word-for-word, using quotation marks

Write a Thesis Statement

Your **thesis statement** tells what the point of the research report will be. It usually appears in your introductory paragraph. Your thesis should state both the topic of your paper and the most important conclusion you've drawn from your research. What do you want your audience to understand about your topic after they have read your report? The answer to this question is your thesis.

Outline Your Report

Organize important information and supporting details in an outline. Sort your notes into several major categories; then, divide them further into subtopics, each to be developed into a full paragraph. Decide how you will organize the information in your report—by order of importance or in chronological (time) order—and record your plan.

Your Turn

Organize Information Finish gathering and evaluating your sources. Decide which facts and ideas you will use in your report, and take notes on the source of each. Then, outline your report in your **RWN** in preparation for drafting.

Drafting

Follow the Writer's Framework

The Framework of a Research Report to the right outlines how to plan your draft to create an effective report. As you write, keep in mind the characteristics of a good research report (page 954). You may need to rearrange your ideas, take out information, or add new information. Keep referring to your notes, and go back to your sources if you need more information. You can expand your draft by interpreting the information you have gathered. Ask yourself, "Why is the information important?"

Framework of a Research Report

Introduction

- Arouses reader's interest, clearly identifies the subject of report, and states the thesis

Body

- Discusses each main idea in one or more paragraphs and supports each main idea with facts, examples, and quotations
  - Idea #1
  - Idea #2
  - Idea #3

Conclusion

- Summarizes or restates main idea(s) and draws conclusions

Works Cited List

- Lists sources alphabetically

Write an Introduction

The main purpose of the research report's introduction is to introduce the subject and to state the thesis, but a good introduction will also entice your audience. Some writers like to begin by drafting their introduction, whereas others prefer to write the introduction after the rest of the paper. Do what works best for you.

Grammar Link Using Transitional Words and Phrases

When you use chronological order to talk about an event or a person's life, you organize the information according to the order in which things happened in time. You can help your reader stay oriented by using **transitional words** and **phrases** to connect ideas chronologically. Here is a list of common words and phrases that indicate sequence in time:

first	next	before	then	when	while	meanwhile	at last	finally

Unclear	Clear
The musicians play a tune. The pianist plays it in double time. The bass player changes the harmony. The musicians come together in a return to the original tune.	*First,* the musicians play a tune. *Then,* the pianist plays it in double time. *Meanwhile,* the bass player changes the harmony. *Finally,* the musicians come together in a return to the original tune.

Reference Note For more transitional words and phrases, see the Language Handbook.

Writing Tip

When you use sources in your writing, you need to guard against plagiarism. Using another writer's words without crediting the source or presenting another writer's ideas as your own is **plagiarism,** or literary theft. Taking careful notes as you research will help you avoid this serious problem.

Writing Tip

For a complete version of a research paper, log on to the Interactive Student Edition at go.hrw.com and go to page 954.

Your Turn

Draft Your Report Using your framework and source notes, create your first draft. Consider writing your introduction after you've drafted the rest of your paper. When writing a chronological report, use transitional words and phrases in your writing to help your reader understand the order in which events occurred.

Peer Review

Working with a partner, review your draft. Answer each question in the chart to the right to locate where and how your drafts could be improved. As you discuss your papers, be sure to take notes about each other's suggestions.

Evaluating and Revising

Read the questions in the left-hand column of the chart, and then use the tips in the middle column to help you make revisions to your research report. The right-hand column suggests techniques you can use to revise your draft.

Reasearch Report: Guidelines for Content and Organization

Evaluation Questions	Tips	Revision Techniques
1. Does your introduction contain a clear statement of your topic and your thesis?	**Put a star** next to your statement of the report's topic and your thesis.	**Add** a thesis statement, if necessary.
2. Does each paragraph in the body of your paper develop one subtopic?	**Label** the margin of each paragraph with the subtopic it develops.	**Delete** unrelated ideas, or **rearrange** information into separate paragraphs. **Link** ideas and information with transitions.
3. Does each paragraph contain supporting evidence?	**Highlight** the facts, examples, and quotations that elaborate on the subtopic.	**Elaborate,** if necessary, with additional facts and explanations from your notes.
4. Does your final paragraph adequately sum up your overall findings, or conclusions?	**Put a check mark** next to the conclusion, or final statement.	If your final statement is unclear, **revise** it for clarity.
5. Have you used material from each source?	**Highlight** material from each source with a different color.	**Add** any missing source material.
6. Have you included all the necessary information on your Works Cited list?	**Put a check mark** beside each piece of information necessary in a citation.	To learn the proper format for a Works Cited list, **consult** the Communications Handbook.

Read this student draft; note the comments on its strengths as well as suggestions on how the draft could be improved.

Student Draft

The Greatest Basketball Player in U.S. History

by Tito Onesto, Talent Middle School

Michael "Air" Jordan is the greatest basketball player of all time because he's a phenomenal athlete with a unique combination of grace, speed, power, and an unquenchable competitive desire. Michael Jordan single-handedly redefined the words "NBA superstar."

← Tito states his **thesis:** Jordan was a uniquely great player.

Players like Robert Parish and Larry Bird played for the Boston Celtics. They are big names in basketball too. Michael Jordan wasn't always a big name. He was cut from his high school varsity team as a sophomore, which made him practice for hours, day after day. Jordan eventually made the varsity team and led the Lanley High School Buccaneers to the North Carolina State Championship.

← He begins by giving **background** in **chronological order.**

He accepted a basketball scholarship to the University of North Carolina. As a freshman, Jordan made the winning shot in the 1982 NCAA Championship game against the Georgetown Hoyas and future NBA rival Patrick Ewing. "That made Mike Jordan into Michael Jordan," stated James and Delores Jordan after the game-winning shot (Lovitt 68).

← Tito **quotes** experts on Jordan's playing.

MINI-LESSON How to Keep Your Focus

At the beginning of his second paragraph, Tito strays too far from his topic. He simply deletes the first two sentences in that paragraph and improves the focus of his report. He then decides to add a quote from the subject of the report in order to support his point that Jordan had an "unquenchable competitive desire."

Tito's Revision of Paragraph Two

~~Players like Robert Parish and Larry Bird played for the Boston Celtics. They are big names in basketball too.~~ Michael Jordan wasn't always a big name. He was cut from his high school varsity team as a sophomore, which made him practice for hours, day after day. "When I was working out and I got tired and figured I ought to stop, I'd close my eyes and see that list without my name on it," Jordan said, "and it usually got me going again" (Lovitt 68). Jordan eventually made the varsity team and led the Lanley High School Buccaneers to the North Carolina State Championship.

Your Turn

Edit Distracting Material As you review your draft, ask yourself whether each point is relevant to your thesis. If you have included information that may distract your reader from your main point, cross out the unnecessary material.

Student Draft *continues*

Jordan was drafted third overall in the 1984 draft by the Chicago Bulls. He averaged 28.8 points, 6.5 rebounds, 5.9 assists, and 2.4 steals per game that rookie season, but it was cut short because of a foot injury in the third game. Michael Jordan's team, the Bulls of Chicago, managed to make the NBA playoffs, but they didn't win, eventually losing to the eventual NBA championship winning team, the Celtics of Boston. Even though the Chicago Bulls got killed in that series, it is remembered because Michael Jordan dropped 63 points, setting an NBA record. "He was God disguised as Michael Jordan," stated Larry Bird after Jordan's 63-point performance (Lovitt 82). After that season, Michael Jordan was considered among the best in the league.

Tito **quotes** another expert in the field. →

Michael Jordan is considered the greatest basketball player in NBA history because of his career accomplishments: six NBA Championships, five-time NBA Most Valuable Player, ten-time Scoring Champ, ten-time All-NBA first team, Rookie of the Year, All-Star Dunk Contest Champion, NCAA National Champion with North Carolina in 1982, and two-time Olympic Gold Medalist. Surely, there will never be another basketball player like Michael Jordan.

He closes with a fresh restatement of his **thesis.** →

Tito includes a **list of cited works** and properly formats each of his sources. →

Works Cited

Lovitt, Chip. Michael Jordan: Basketball's Best. New York: Scholastic, Inc., 2002.

"Michael Jordan's Biography." 23Jordan (2006): 1–4. Online. Internet. 26 February 2006. Available <http://www.23jordan.com/bio1.htm>.

Reed, William F. "Jordan, Michael." World Book Online Reference Center. 2007. Online. Internet. 26 February 2007. <http://worldbookonline.com/wb/Article?id=ar290875&st=michael+jordan>.

MINI-LESSON **How to Eliminate Wordiness**

When Tito read an earlier draft, he realized that he was using far too many words that did not add any information, interest, or elegance to his report. He edited his work for wordiness.

Tito's Revision of Paragraph Four

~~Michael Jordan's team, the~~ *The* Bulls ~~of Chicago,~~ managed to make the ~~NBA~~ playoffs, but they ~~didn't win, eventually losing~~ *lost* to the eventual NBA ~~championship winning~~ *championship* team, the ~~Celtics of Boston~~ *Boston Celtics*.

Your Turn

Eliminate Wordiness Read your draft, and ask yourself if there are places where you have used several words when you could have used one. Edit your draft by taking out any redundancies and unnecessary repetitions of words or ideas.

Proofreading and Publishing

Proofreading

You have revised your research report, and now it is time to polish it, eliminating any errors that might distract your readers. Edit your work to correct any misspellings and errors in punctuation or sentence structure.

Grammar Link **Using Capitalization and Punctuation**

Following the rules for **capitalization** and **punctuation** will help make your report more readable for your audience. Use capital letters to mark the beginnings of sentences, proper nouns, and the most important words in titles. Use end mark punctuation to indicate the end of a sentence.

Incorrect:	Correct:
The popular magazine time contains an article about the history of Basketball did you know that the Sport was first played in springfield, a city in massachusetts	The popular magazine *Time* contains an article about the history of basketball. Did you know that the sport was first played in Springfield, a city in Massachusetts?

Reference Note For more on punctuation, see the Language Handbook.

Publishing

Now it is time to publish your research report. Here are some ways to share your work:

- Is there a team or club at your school that might be interested in your subject? Give the coach or club president a copy.
- Did you write your research report because you became interested in something you learned in another class? Ask the teacher of that class if you can give a multimedia presentation on your research. Use presentation software to prepare, and include audio and visual materials where appropriate.

Reflect on the Process In your **RWN,** write a short response to each of the following questions:

1. What was the most interesting fact you learned from your research?
2. Which part of the process went well for you, and where did you have trouble? What would you do differently the next time you write a report?
3. Did your ideas about the topic change? What else would you like to learn about the topic?

Proofreading Tip

Take the time to carefully proofread the Works Cited section of your report. Remember that all the required punctuation marks help your reader access this information. After you have proofread your own work, exchange reports with a peer, and ask him or her to pay special attention to the punctuation in your Works Cited section. Use the examples of Works Cited in the Communications Handbook.

Your Turn

Proofread and Publish

Proofread your report for instances of wordiness. Make every sentence convey its idea in as concise a manner as possible. Also, be sure that you have followed the rules of capitalization and punctuation throughout your report, including the Works Cited section. Finally, share your work with others.

Scoring Rubric

You can use one of the rubrics below to evaluate your research report and the activity on the next page. Your teacher will tell you to use either the four-point or the six-point rubric.

6-Point Scale

Score 6 *Demonstrates advanced success*
- focuses consistently on a clear thesis
- shows effective organization throughout, with smooth transitions
- offers thoughtful, creative ideas
- develops ideas thoroughly, using examples, details and fully elaborated explanation
- exhibits mature control of written language

Score 5 *Demonstrates proficient success*
- focuses on a clear thesis
- shows effective organization, with transitions
- offers thoughtful ideas
- develops ideas competently, using examples, details, and well-elaborated explanation
- exhibits sufficient control of written language

Score 4 *Demonstrates competent success*
- focuses on a clear thesis, with minor distractions
- shows effective organization, with minor lapses
- offers mostly thoughtful ideas
- develops ideas adequately, with a mixture of general and specific elaboration
- exhibits general control of written language

Score 3 *Demonstrates limited success*
- includes some loosely related ideas that distract from the writer's expository/informative focus
- shows some organization, with noticeable gaps in the logical flow of ideas
- offers routine, predictable ideas
- develops ideas with uneven elaboration
- exhibits limited control of written language

Score 2 *Demonstrates basic success*
- includes loosely related ideas that seriously distract from the writer's expository/informative focus
- shows minimal organization, with major gaps in the logical flow of ideas
- offers ideas that merely skim the surface
- develops ideas with inadequate elaboration
- exhibits significant problems with control of written language

Score 1 *Demonstrates emerging effort*
- shows little awareness of the topic and purpose for writing
- lacks organization
- offers unclear and confusing ideas
- develops ideas in only a minimal way, if at all
- exhibits major problems with control of written language

4-Point Scale

Score 4 *Demonstrates advanced success*
- focuses consistently on a clear thesis
- shows effective organization throughout, with smooth transitions
- offers thoughtful, creative ideas
- develops ideas thoroughly, using examples, details, and fully elaborated explanation
- exhibits mature control of written language

Score 3 *Demonstrates competent success*
- focuses on a clear thesis, with minor distractions
- shows effective organization, with minor lapses
- offers mostly thoughtful ideas
- develops ideas adequately, with a mixture of general and specific elaboration
- exhibits general control of written language

Score 2 *Demonstrates limited success*
- includes some loosely related ideas that distract from the writer's expository/informative focus
- shows some organization, with noticeable gaps in the logical flow of ideas
- offers routine, predictable ideas
- develops ideas with uneven elaboration
- exhibits limited control of written language

Score 1 *Demonstrates emerging effort*
- shows little awareness of the topic and purpose for writing
- lacks organization
- offers unclear and confusing ideas
- develops ideas in only a minimal way, if at all
- exhibits major problems with control of written language

Expository Essay

When responding to an expository, or informative, prompt, use what you've learned from your reading, writing your research report, and studying the rubric on page 962. Use the steps below to develop a response to the following prompt.

Writing Prompt

Being respected is a quality that most of us would like to earn. In an essay, explain how a person gains the respect of others. Be sure to use supporting evidence to back up your points. You may use examples from your own experience or from people you have observed.

Study the Prompt

Begin by reading the prompt carefully. Circle or underline key words: *explain*, *respect*, *earn*, and *quality*. Your purpose is to explain how you think a person earns the respect of other people. What have you observed or experienced that leads to respect? Make a list of actions or aspects that you can illustrate with examples. **Tip:** *Spend about five minutes studying the prompt.*

Plan Your Response

Review your list and be sure that you have specific examples for the actions or aspects listed. Choose two to four aspects or actions that you can explain with examples. "Always sticks with me" can become a specific supporting detail if you clarify what the person did to demonstrate loyalty and earn respect.

Look at your list of points. What do these points have in common? Think about a common idea that you can use to connect your ideas about how respect is earned. That idea becomes the **thesis statement** you will explain in your essay. **Tip:** *Spend about ten minutes planning your response.*

Respond to the Prompt

Using your thesis and your notes, draft your essay. Follow these guidelines:

- Begin your essay with an introduction that catches your reader's attention and includes your thesis.
- The body of the essay should address each aspect or action in a logical order, possibly ending with the point you consider most important. Be sure to support or explain each point with specific examples.
- In the conclusion, restate your thesis and reflect on the way a person earns respect. **Tip:** *Spend about twenty minutes writing your draft.*

Improve Your Response

Revising Go back to the key aspects of the prompt. Does your essay explain how you think a person earns respect? Have you used specific examples? Are the aspects and actions and your thesis connected?

Proofreading Take a few minutes to proofread to correct errors in grammar, spelling, punctuation, and capitalization. Make sure your edits are neat and your paper is legible.

Checking Your Final Copy Before you turn your paper in, read it one more time to catch any errors you may have missed and to make any finishing touches. Taking this one extra step ill help you to turn in your best work. **Tip:** *Save five or ten minutes to improve your paper.*

Giving and Listening to an Informative Speech

Speak and Listen with a Purpose

Adapt your informative report for an informative presentation. Listen actively to a classmate's informative speech.

A Good Informative Speech

- is tailored to listeners' needs
- is appropriate for the audience and purpose
- covers the most important ideas of a research report
- provides sources for facts and evidence
- uses verbal and nonverbal techniques to make the speech clear and interesting

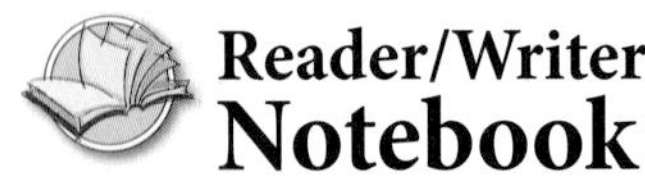

Use your **RWN** to complete the activities for this workshop.

Think as a Reader/Writer When preparing a written informative, or expository, report, you develop your thesis and decide on the best way to convey your research findings to your reader. When preparing an informative speech, you keep the same focus in mind; however, you also need to consider the specific needs of the listening audience.

Adapt Your Informative Report

All of the work you put into writing your report will put you a step ahead when preparing your oral presentation. You will, however, need to adjust the information for your listeners.

- **Think about the purpose and occasion as you make decisions about word choice and delivery.** Are you giving an informal speech, or is your speech part of a formal evaluation? The tone of a formal speech should be serious. Avoid casual language. On the other hand, if you are speaking at an informal occasion, it's a good idea to make sure your speech doesn't sound overly academic. Choose words and phrases that will put your listeners at ease.
- **Limit your speech to your report's major ideas and to the evidence you need to clarify and support those ideas.** Read through a copy of your original report and highlight the most important points you made. Be sure to highlight those major points in your speech. As you adapt your report, remember to keep information that tells your audience where you found your information.
- **Adjust your word choice.** Think about who will be listening to your presentation. Your audience should be able to easily understand your ideas and learn from your speech. Define terms with which your audience will be unfamiliar.
- **Use a simple outline to deliver your speech.** Avoid simply reading your report aloud. Speaking from an outline will make your speech sound more conversational and natural.

C.8.8.a Deliver informational presentations that: demonstrate an understanding of the topic and present events or ideas in a logical sequence; **C.8.5** Demonstrate an understanding of the rules of the English language and select language appropriate to purpose and audience. **C.8.2** Identify and analyze the persuasive techniques used in presentations and media messages. **C.8.4** Identify the speaker's choice of language and delivery styles and how they contribute to meaning.

Deliver Your Informative Speech

Use Verbal Techniques

Use an effective **rate** and **volume** for your audience—avoid speaking too fast, too slowly, too loudly, or too softly. Use your voice to emphasize key points, and be sure not to rush through your presentation.

Use Nonverbal Techniques

Pay attention to the wordless communication you are sending—use natural facial expressions and gestures. Also, add clarity and interest to your presentation by using well-chosen visuals (such as charts, graphs, presentation software, audio clips, and the like).

Evaluate an Informative Speech

An informative speech often contains so much information that you might have trouble absorbing it all. To make the most of the informative speeches you hear, follow the steps listed in the chart below.

Steps for Evaluating an Informative Speech
Content
Determine your purpose for listening. What do you want to learn from the speech? **Make predictions.** Identify two or three points you expect the speaker to cover. **Get ready.** Have a pen or pencil ready for taking notes.
Delivery
Devote your full attention to the speaker. Looking around the room or doing another assignment will prevent you from learning all you can. **Listen for cues that signal main points.** Cues can include words and phrases such as *first, second,* and *finally; there are many reasons or causes; the most important thing is*; and *in conclusion.* Hearing these cues is the key to understanding, interpreting, and organizing the information you hear in the speech. **Summarize the main points of the speech.** As you listen, take notes by summarizing the speaker's main points and supporting details.
Credibility (Believability)
Monitor your understanding. Ask yourself if the speaker covered all of the points you expected. If not, what did he or she leave out? Ask the speaker to clarify.

Speaking Tip

Use the pitch, or the highs and lows, of your voice to create an enthusiastic tone. If the tone of your voice suggests that you do not care about your speech, your audience is likely to feel the same.

Speaking Tip

In order to deliver a strong presentation, practice it until you feel you know it backward and forward. If possible, rehearse your presentation in the same location that you will be giving it.

Listening Tip

Sometimes you may find a speaker's mannerisms or personality distracting or even a little off-putting. Even so, try to focus harder on what the speaker is saying—if you don't pay attention, you may miss something truly interesting.

Literary Skills Review

Drama **Directions:** Read the following excerpt from a play. Then, respond to the questions that follow.

from The Glass Menagerie

by **Tennessee Williams**

Build Background This scene takes place in the Wingfield apartment, in the rear of a large building. The apartment faces an alley and is entered by a fire escape. Laura's brother, Tom, has invited Jim, a friend from work, to dinner as a "gentleman caller" for Laura. The electricity has just gone out, and candles have been lit. Tom and his mother have gone into the kitchen to do the dishes, leaving Laura and Jim to get acquainted. They have just decided to sit on the floor.

from Scene 7

Characters:

Laura Wingfield. A childhood illness has left her crippled, one leg slightly shorter than the other, and held in a brace.
Jim O'Connor. A nice, ordinary, young man.

Jim. Take a pillow!

[LAURA *does. She sits on the floor on the other side of the candelabrum.* JIM *crosses his legs and smiles engagingly at her.*]

I can hardly see you sitting way over there.
Laura. I can—see you.
Jim. I know, but that's not fair, I'm in the limelight.

[LAURA *moves her pillow closer.*]

Good! Now I can see you! Comfortable?
Laura. Yes.
Jim. So am I. Comfortable as a cow! Will you have some gum?
Laura. No, thank you.
Jim. I think that I will indulge, with your permission. (*He musingly unwraps a stick of gum and holds it up.*) Think of the fortune made by the guy that invented the first piece of chewing gum. Amazing, huh? The Wrigley Building is one of the sights of Chicago—I saw it when I went up to the Century of Progress. Did you take in the Century of Progress?
Laura. No, I didn't.
Jim. Well, it was quite a wonderful exposition. What impressed me most was the Hall of Science. Gives you an idea of what the future will be in America, even more wonderful than the present time is! (*There is a pause.* JIM *smiles at her.*) Your brother tells me you're shy. Is that right, Laura?

RA.L.8.6 Explain how an author's choice of genre affects the expression of a theme or topic.

Laura. I—don't know.
Jim. I judge you to be an old-fashioned type of girl. Well, I think that's a pretty good type to be. Hope you don't think I'm being too personal—do you?
Laura *(hastily, out of embarrassment).* I believe I *will* take a piece of gum, if you—don't mind. *(Clearing her throat)* Mr. O'Connor, have you—kept up with your singing?
Jim. Singing? Me?
Laura. Yes. I remember what a beautiful voice you had.
Jim. When did you hear me sing?

[LAURA *does not answer, and in the long pause which follows a man's voice is heard singing off-stage.*]

Voice:
"Oh blow, ye winds, heigh-ho,
A-roving I will go!
    I'm off to my love
    With a boxing glove—
Ten thousand miles away!"

Jim. You say you've heard me sing?
Laura. Oh, yes! Yes, very often . . . I don't suppose—you remember me—at all?
Jim *(smiling doubtfully).* You know I have an idea I've seen you before. I had that idea soon as you opened the door. It seemed almost like I was about to remember your name. But the name that I started to call you—wasn't a name! And so I stopped myself before I said it.
Laura. Wasn't it—Blue Roses?
Jim *(springing up, grinning).* Blue Roses! My gosh, yes—Blue Roses! That's what I had on my tongue when you opened the door! Isn't it funny what tricks your memory plays? I didn't connect you with high school somehow or other. But that's where it was; it was high school. I didn't even know you were Shakespeare's sister! Gosh, I'm sorry.
Laura. I didn't expect you to. You—barely knew me!
Jim. But we did have a speaking acquaintance, huh?
Laura. Yes, we—spoke to each other.
Jim. When did you recognize me?
Laura. Oh, right away!
Jim. Soon as I came in the door?
Laura. When I heard your name I thought it was probably you. I knew that Tom used to know you a little in high school. So when you came in the door—well, then I was—sure.
Jim. Why didn't you *say* something, then?
Laura *(breathlessly).* I didn't know what to say, I was—too surprised!
Jim. For goodness' sakes! You know, this sure is funny!

Literary Skills Review CONTINUED

Laura. Yes! Yes, isn't it, though...
Jim. Didn't we have a class in something together?
Laura. Yes, we did.
Jim. What class was that?
Laura. It was—singing—chorus!
Jim. Aw!
Laura. I sat across the aisle from you in the Aud.
Jim. Aw.
Laura. Mondays, Wednesdays, and Fridays.
Jim. Now I remember—you always came in late.
Laura. Yes, it was so hard for me, getting upstairs. I had that brace on my leg—it clumped so loud!
Jim. I never heard any clumping.
Laura *(wincing at the recollection).* To me it sounded like—thunder!
Jim. Well, well, well, I never even noticed.
Laura. And everybody was seated before I came in. I had to walk in front of all those people. My seat was in the back row. I had to go clumping all the way up the aisle with everyone watching!
Jim. You shouldn't have been self-conscious.
Laura. I know, but I was. It was always such a relief when the singing started.
Jim. Aw, yes, I've placed you now! I used to call you Blue Roses. How was it that I got started calling you that?
Laura. I was out of school a little while with pleurosis. When I came back you asked me what was the matter. I said I had pleurosis—you thought I said *Blue Roses.* That's what you always called me after that!
Jim. I hope you didn't mind.
Laura. Oh, no—I liked it. You see, I wasn't acquainted with many—people. . . .
Jim. As I remember you sort of stuck by yourself.
Laura. I—I—never have had much luck at—making friends.
Jim. I don't see why you wouldn't.
Laura. Well, I—started out badly.
Jim. You mean being—
Laura. Yes, it sort of—stood between me—
Jim. You shouldn't have let it!
Laura. I know, but it did, and—
Jim. You were shy with people!
Laura. I tried not to be but never could—
Jim. Overcome it?
Laura. No, I—I never could!
Jim. I guess being shy is something you have to work out of kind of gradually.
Laura *(sorrowfully).* Yes—I guess it—

RA.L.8.6 Explain how an author's choice of genre affects the expression of a theme or topic. *Also covered* **WA.8.2**

Jim. Takes time!
Laura. Yes—
Jim. People are not so dreadful when you know them. That's what you have to remember! And everybody has problems, not just you, but practically everybody has got some problems. You think of yourself as having the only problems, as being the only one who is disappointed. But just look around you and you will see lots of people as disappointed as you are.

1. This excerpt from the play consists mostly of
   A. monologues.
   B. narration.
   C. dialogue.
   D. asides.

2. From the dialogue in this excerpt, we learn that
   A. Jim and Laura knew each other in high school.
   B. Jim has often thought about Laura.
   C. Laura collects little glass animals.
   D. Laura and Jim have been dating each other.

3. Laura's lines in the play indicate that
   A. she never liked Jim much.
   B. she has always remembered Jim.
   C. Jim was mean to her in school.
   D. she and Jim were once close friends.

4. Which statement accurately sums up these two characters in this excerpt?
   A. They enjoy a lively clash of wits.
   B. They are both falling in love.
   C. Jim is more confident than Laura.
   D. Laura is much wiser than Jim.

Short Answer

5. Explain what kind of information the stage directions for this scene mostly provide. Use examples from the scene to support your explanation.

Extended Response

6. Using the dialogue and the stage directions as clues, describe the characters of Laura and Jim. Support your ideas by citing text passages.

Informational Skills Review

Treatment, Scope, and Organization of Ideas

Directions: Read the following article. Then, respond to the questions that follow.

Blasting Through Bedrock: The Central Pacific Railroad Workers

by **Flo Ota De Lange**

In the winter of 1866–1867, blizzards gripped the Sierra Nevada. Dwellings were buried in blowing, shifting, drifting, driving snow. Men who were building the western portion of the country's first transcontinental railroad had to tunnel from their camp to the mountainside, where they spent long, cold days digging out rock so tracks could be laid. The Central Pacific Railroad was building east from California to meet the Union Pacific Railroad, which was working west from Omaha, Nebraska.

Who were these hard workers who survived the blizzards and helped build the nation's first transcontinental railroad? Most of them were immigrants from China. When other railroad hands saw the newly hired Chinese workers, they were scornful. How could these young men, averaging about four feet ten inches in height, heave a large shovelful of rock? The other workers either didn't know or had forgotten that the ancestors of these men had built one of the Seven Wonders of the World—the Great Wall of China—which was begun in 221 B.C. The wall extends more than four thousand miles and averages about twenty-six feet high and twenty feet wide!

At the start the Central Pacific Railroad hired fifty Chinese laborers. These men knew little about railroad grading, but they learned quickly. Eventually the Chinese labor force grew to between ten thousand and twelve thousand workers. These men dug, blasted tunnels, and laid track up the Sierra Nevada, over the Donner Pass, and down through the deserts of Nevada.

People often credit the transcontinental railroad to men of vision—engineers, financiers, and politicians—without acknowledging the way their vision became a reality. As the president of the Central Pacific Railroad and former governor of California, Leland Stanford, wrote to President Andrew Johnson on October 19, 1865, "The greater portion of the laborers employed by us are Chinese . . . . Without them it would be impossible to complete the western portion of this great national enterprise within the time required by the Acts of Congress."

Complete it these workers did! Cannons roared in New York City and San Francisco when the telegraph lines carried the news: The Union Pacific and the Central Pacific Railroad lines had met at Promontory, Utah, on May 10, 1869.

---

1. The structural pattern of this article is that of logical order because
   A. events are described in the order in which they occurred.
   B. related details are grouped together .
   C. the most important idea comes first.
   D. the most important idea comes last.

2. The treatment of this article is mainly objective because the author
   A. tells about her own experiences.
   B. presents accurate historical facts.
   C. has done a great deal of research.
   D. tells a very interesting story.

3. Of the people responsible for building the railroad, the author's sympathies lie with the
   A. engineers.
   B. financiers.
   C. politicians.
   D. workers.

Short Answer

4. Explain why the scope of this article is narrow. Use information from the passage to support your answer.

Extended Response

5. Do you think the author treated this material subjectively or objectively? Explain your answer, providing examples from the text as support.

Vocabulary Skills Review

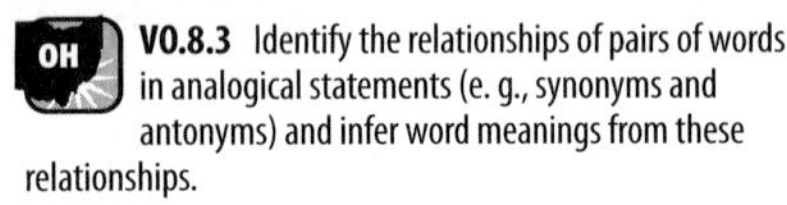

VO.8.3 Identify the relationships of pairs of words in analogical statements (e. g., synonyms and antonyms) and infer word meanings from these relationships.

Synonyms

Directions: Choose the best synonym for the boldfaced word in each sentence.

1. When a sentence is **amended,** it is
   A. extended.
   B. simplified.
   C. corrected.
   D. lengthened.

2. People who oppose **tyranny** fight against
   A. justice.
   B. oppression.
   C. poverty.
   D. racism.

3. If something has **merit,** it has
   A. worth.
   B. beauty.
   C. happiness.
   D. authenticity.

4. A person who speaks **indignantly** speaks
   A. shyly.
   B. humorously.
   C. playfully.
   D. angrily.

5. When someone is **forlorn,** he or she feels
   A. weary.
   B. unhappy.
   C. satisfied.
   D. peaceful.

6. When you celebrate **liberation,** you celebrate
   A. creation.
   B. destruction.
   C. intelligence.
   D. freedom.

7. When an emotion **reigns,** it
   A. predominates.
   B. escapes.
   C. regulates.
   D. submits.

Academic Vocabulary

Directions: Choose the word that is the best synonym for each Academic Vocabulary word below.

8. When a book gives you **insight,** it gives you
   A. understanding.
   B. time.
   C. energy.
   D. confusion.

9. A fact that is **evident** is
   A. clear.
   B. related.
   C. uncertain.
   D. false.

Writing Skills

OH **WA.8.4.d** Write informational essays or reports, including research, that: support the main ideas with facts, details, examples and explanations from sources *Also covered* **WP.8.13**

Research Report

Directions: Read this passage from a research report. Then, answer each question that follows.

(1) Some parasites make their hosts behave strangely. (2) A kind of wasp can make a spider build a home for its larva. (3) According to *Nature* magazine,[1] the wasp stings the spider to paralyze it and then lays an egg on the spider's abdomen. (4) After the larva hatches, it feeds on the living spider's blood. (5) Then, the larva injects a chemical into the spider that makes the spider spin a special kind of web, one very different from its usual web. (6) In a BBC News Online article,[2] Dr. William Eberhard, a scientist who studies these insects, calls it "the ideal web from the wasp-larva point of view" because it provides "a very solid and durable support." (7) When the web is finished, the larva kills and eats the spider, and then builds its cocoon in the spider's last web. (8) As scientist Fritz Vollrath comments in a Discovery.com article,[3] "The irony is that the poor thing that fed this larva builds it a little shelter as its last act. (9) It makes a gruesome fairy tale."

1. Watson, Isabelle. "Hymenoptera and Parasitism." *Nature*, 65. (12) 2006: 78-92.
2. Hidalgo, Roberto. "Surprising Behavior in the Insect World." *BBC News Online* 25 June 2007. 20 Jan. 2008. <http://www.bbc.org/news/2007/June25/hidalgo.html>.
3. "Taking Over: Parasites and Their Hosts." *Discovery* 29 Mar. 2007: 1-4. 22 Jan. 2007. <http://www.discovery.com/creatures/parasites.html>.

---

1. Which of the following would be the *best* **thesis statement** for this research report?
   A. There are many types of parasites found all over the world.
   B. A parasite is an organism that can provide some benefits to its host.
   C. After the larva hatches, it feeds on the living spider's blood.
   D. Some parasites make their hosts behave in surprising ways.

2. Which **transition** might be added to the beginning of sentence 2 to improve clarity?
   A. By the way,
   B. On the other hand,
   C. For example,
   D. As a result,

3. The **sources** mentioned in this passage come from —
   A. print and online media
   B. radio and television news
   C. the Internet
   D. scientific journals

4. The **references** for this report include —
   A. every source written on the topic
   B. sources the writer considered important
   C. all sources cited in the report
   D. all sources the writer could find

Read On

Fiction

Famous Stories for Performance

If you and your friends like to act and want to practice the craft, *Famous Stories for Performance* provides eleven classic scenes for you to choose from. From the lively "Robin Hood and Little John" to the creepy "The Legend of Sleepy Hollow" to the zany "A Mad Tea Party," this collection offers a great introduction to the world of theater.

Tunes for Bears to Dance To

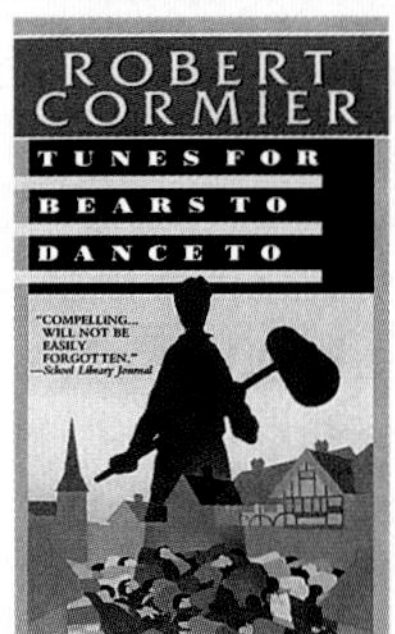

The Holocaust continues to affect people strongly. In Robert Cormier's novel *Tunes for Bears to Dance To,* a lonely boy named Henry meets and befriends Mr. Levine, a Holocaust survivor who is working to build a miniature re-creation of his old village. The two take comfort in one another. Then Mr. Hairston, Henry's racist employer, presents Henry with a difficult choice.

A Gathering of Days

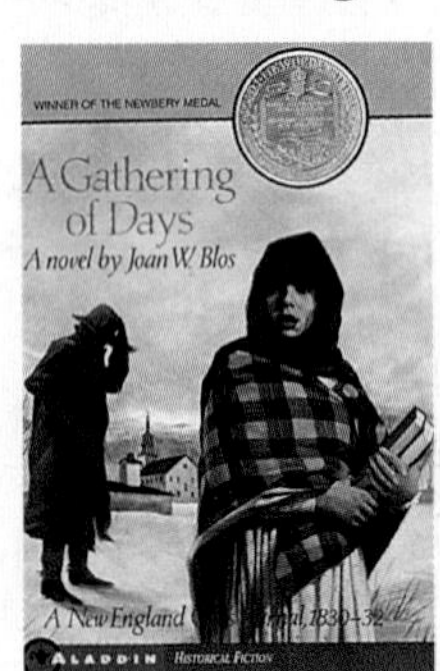

In Joan W. Blos's *A Gathering of Days,* teenaged Catherine Hall receives a journal in which she chronicles an eventful time of her life. Beginning in 1830, Catherine learns about racial prejudice from a man fleeing slavery, loses a close friend, and assumes greater responsibility on her family's New Hampshire farm as she journeys toward adulthood.

King of Shadows

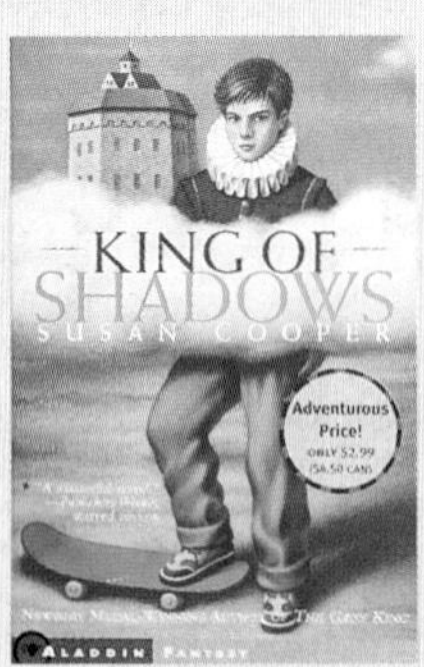

Nat Field is thrilled when he is picked to be in a production of Shakespeare's *A Midsummer Night's Dream.* The drama troupe travels to London to perform at a re-creation of the famous Globe Theatre. In London, Nat falls ill, sleeps fitfully, and awakens to find himself transported back 400 years to Shakespeare's time! Not only that, but he still must act in the play, which is now directed by the famous bard himself.

Nonfiction

I Am David

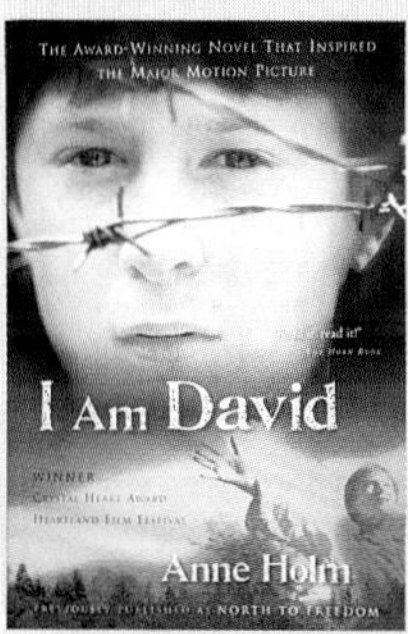

I Am David, by Anne Holm, is a fictional account of a boy's incredible journey. Imprisoned in a prison camp since infancy, David, now twelve, is given a chance to escape with the help of a prison guard. Once free from the camp, David follows the guard's instructions and travels through Greece, Italy, and Switzerland, finally ending up in Denmark, where he is reunited with the mother he has never really known.

Hitler Youth: Growing Up in Hitler's Shadow

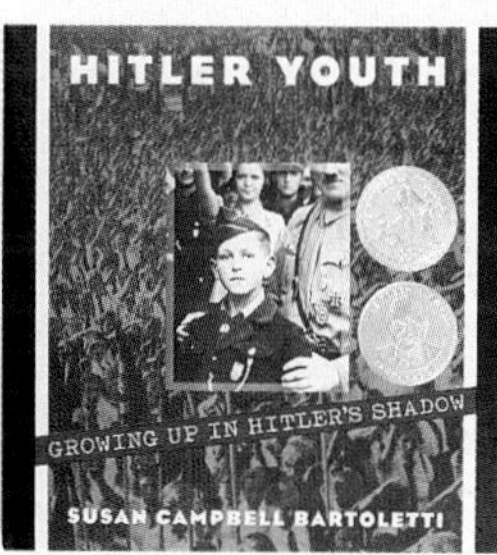

Young people in Germany were heavily influenced by Hitler's racist ideas. In *Hitler Youth: Growing Up in Hitler's Shadow,* Susan Campbell Bartoletti presents several accounts by former members of the Hitler Youth. These people, teenagers during Hitler's reign, tell how Hitler recruited them and earned their loyalty and why they executed so many of his appalling orders.

Zlata's Diary: A Child's Life in Wartime Sarajevo

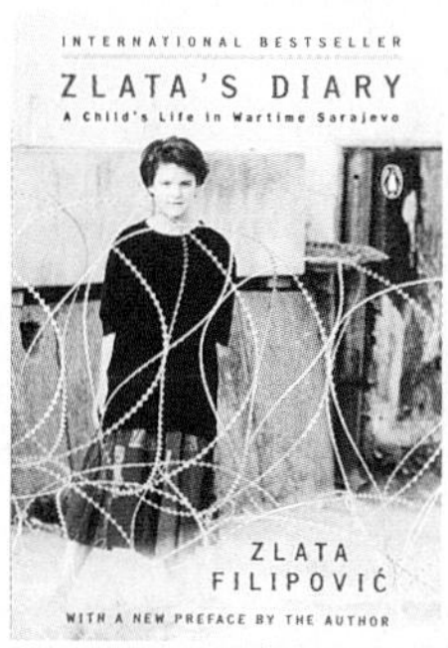

Zlata Filipović was just a young girl when the war in Bosnia started. Her diary chronicles this terrible ethnic conflict with a unique voice and poetic sensibility. An international bestseller when it was first released, *Zlata's Diary: A Child's Life in Wartime Sarajevo* has been compared to Anne Frank's diary in its poignancy and portrayal of a childhood lost to war.

The Upstairs Room and *The Journey Back*

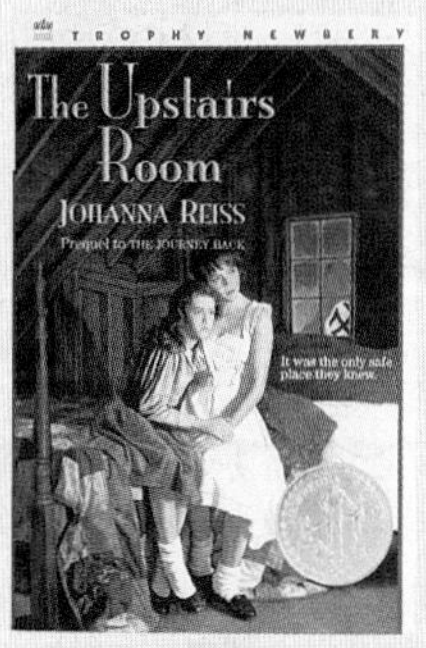

In the Netherlands during World War II, Anne and Margot Frank went into hiding with their parents. At the same time, another pair of sisters escaped to the country to live with a Dutch family in the family's farmhouse during the war. *The Upstairs Room* and its sequel, *The Journey Back,* tell the true story of Johanna Reiss and her sister Sini.

Learn It Online

Explore other novels—and find tips for choosing, reading, and studying works—at:

go.hrw.com L8-975 

Resource Center

Handbook of Literary Terms

For more information about a topic, turn to the page(s) in this book indicated on a separate line at the end of the entries. On another line are cross-references to entries in the handbook that provide closely related information. For instance, at the end of *Autobiography* are cross-references to *Biography* and *Nonfiction*.

ALLITERATION **The repetition of consonant sounds in words that are close together.** Alliteration occurs mostly in poetry, though prose writers use it from time to time. Although alliteration usually occurs at the beginning of words, it can also occur within or at the end of words. In the following stanza, notice the repeated *s*, *m*, and *b* sounds:

> The sun was shining on the sea,
> Shining with all his might:
> He did his very best to make
> The billows smooth and bright—
> And this was odd, because it was
> The middle of the night.
>
> —Lewis Carroll, from "The Walrus and the Carpenter"

The repetition of vowel sounds in words that are close together is called **assonance.**

See pages 671, 751.

See also *Poetry*.

ALLUSION **A reference to a statement, a person, a place, or an event from literature, the arts, history, religion, mythology, politics, sports, or science.** Allusions enrich the reading experience. Writers expect readers to recognize allusions and to think about the literary work and the allusions contained in it almost at the same time. For example, "I Have a Dream" (page 529) alludes to the song "My Country, 'Tis of Thee." A reader who is not familiar with that song will miss some of the speech's intended meaning.

See page 389.

See also *Literary Devices*.

ANALOGY **A comparison made between two things to show how they are alike.** Writers often make analogies to show how something unfamiliar is like something well known or widely experienced. In "Raymond's Run" (page 391), the main character, Squeaky, uses an analogy that compares her feelings before a race to a dream of flying.

See pages 402, 532.

See also *Literary Devices, Metaphor, Simile*.

ANECDOTE **A brief story told to illustrate a point.** Anecdotes are frequently found in memoirs, biographies, autobiographies, and personal essays. In "The Border: A Glare of Truth" (page 537), for example, Pat Mora uses anecdotes from her life to illustrate the bi-cultural experience.

See also *Proposition and Support* in the Handbook of Reading and Informational Terms.

ANTAGONIST See *Protagonist.*

ASSONANCE See *Alliteration.*

ATMOSPHERE See *Mood.*

AUTHOR **The writer of a literary work or document.** Toni Cade Bambara is the author of "Raymond's Run" (page 391); Abraham Lincoln is the author of the Gettysburg Address (page 527).

See page 759.

AUTOBIOGRAPHY **A person's account of his or her own life or of part of it.** "Camp Harmony" (page 515) is an example of autobiographical writing.

See pages 486, 513.

See also *Biography, Nonfiction*.

BALLAD **A song or songlike poem that tells a story.** Ballads usually tell stories of tragedy, love, or adventure, using simple language and a great deal of repetition. They generally have regular rhythm and rhyme patterns that make them easy to memorize. "The Dying Cowboy" (page 722) and "The Cremation of Sam McGee" (page 717) are both ballads.

See pages 673, 715.
See also *Narrative Poem, Poetry*.

BIOGRAPHY **An account of a person's life or of part of it, written or told by another person.** The excerpt from *Harriet Tubman* (page 499) is part of a longer biography.

See pages 486, 497.
See also *Autobiography, Nonfiction*.

CHARACTER **A person or an animal in a story, a play, or another literary work.** Characters can be classified according to the changes they undergo. A **static character** does not change much in the course of a work. The old woman in "Aunty Misery" (page 103) is a static character. In contrast, a **dynamic character** changes as a result of a story's events. Squeaky in "Raymond's Run" (page 391) is a dynamic character.

A character's **motivation** is any force (such as love or fear or jealousy) that drives the character to behave in a particular way.

See pages 150–151, 205, 281, 917.
See also *Characterization, Motivation, Protagonist*.

CHARACTERIZATION **The way a writer reveals the personality of a character.** A writer may simply tell readers that a character is amusing or evil or dull or brave. This method is called **direct characterization.** Most often, though, writers use **indirect characterization,** revealing personality in one or more of the following ways:

1. through the words of the character
2. through description of the character's looks and clothing
3. through description of the character's thoughts and feelings
4. through comments made about the character by other characters in the story
5. through the character's behavior

When a writer uses indirect characterization, we must use our own judgment and the evidence the writer gives to infer the character's **traits.**

See pages 150–151, 163.
See also *Character*.

CHRONOLOGICAL ORDER **The arrangement of events in the order in which they occurred.** Most stories are told in chronological order. Sometimes, however, a writer interrupts the chronological order to flash back to a past event or to flash forward to a future event. *The Diary of Anne Frank* (page 839), for example, begins in 1945, when Mr. Frank arrives at the hiding place. The main story, however, takes place from 1942 to 1944.

See page 929.
See also *Flashback*.

CLIMAX **The point in a story that creates the greatest suspense or interest.** At the climax something happens that reveals how the conflict will turn out.

See page 4.
See also *Drama, Plot, Short Story*.

COMEDY **In general, a story that ends happily for its main characters.** The hero or heroine usually overcomes a series of obstacles to get what he or she wants. (In contrast, the main character in a **tragedy** comes to an unhappy end.) The word *comedy* is not always a synonym for *humor*. Some comedies are humorous; others are not.

See page 800.
See also *Tragedy*.

CONFLICT **A struggle between opposing characters or opposing forces.** In an **external conflict** a character struggles with an outside force, which may be another character, society as a whole, or a natural force. In contrast, an **internal conflict** takes place within a character's own mind. It is a struggle between opposing needs, desires, or emotions. Greg in "The Treasure of Lemon Brown" (page 17) has an external conflict with neighborhood thugs and an internal conflict over his relationship with his father.

See pages 5, 15, 801, 917.
See also *Plot*.

CONNOTATION **A meaning, association, or emotion suggested by a word, in addition to its dictionary definition, or denotation.** Words that have similar denotations may have different connotations. For example, suppose you wanted to describe someone who rarely changes plans in the face of opposition. You could use either *determined* or *pigheaded* to describe the person. The two words have similar denotations, but *determined* has positive connotations and *pigheaded* has negative connotations.

See page 701.
See also *Diction, Style, Tone*.

COUPLET **Two consecutive lines of poetry that rhyme.** Couplets are often used in humorous poems because they pack a quick punch. "Casey at the Bat" (page 730) and "The Cremation of Sam McGee" (page 717) are both written in four-line stanzas consisting of two couplets in each stanza. Shakespeare uses couplets in many of his plays, often for a more serious purpose, to give closure to a speech or an act.

See page 671.
See also *Poetry, Rhyme, Stanza*.

DENOTATION See *Connotation*.

DESCRIPTION **Writing intended to re-create a person, a place, a thing, an event, or an experience.** Description uses images that appeal to the senses of sight, smell, taste, hearing, or touch. It is often used to create a mood or emotion. Writers use description in all forms of fiction, nonfiction, and poetry. This description of the effect of extreme cold on a dog and its owner may make you feel cold, too:

> The frozen moisture of its breathing had settled on its fur in a fine powder of frost, and expecially were its jowls, muzzle, and eyelashes whitened by its crystaled breath. The man's red beard and moustache were likewise frosted, but more solidly, the deposit taking the form of ice and increasing with every warm, moist breath he exhaled. Also, the man was chewing tobacco, and the muzzle of ice held his lips so rigidly that he was unable to clear his chin when he expelled the juice. The result was that a crystal beard of the color and solidity of amber was increasing its length on his chin. If he fell down, it would shatter itself, like glass, into brittle fragments.
>
> —Jack London,
> from "To Build a Fire"

See also *Imagery*.

DIALECT **A way of speaking that is characteristic of a certain geographical area or a certain group of people.** A dialect may have a distinct vocabulary, pronunciation system, and grammar. In a sense, we all speak a dialect. One dialect usually becomes dominant in a country or culture, however, and is accepted as the standard way of speaking and writing. In the United States, for example, the formal language is known as **standard English.** (It's the kind of English taught in schools, used in national newspapers and magazines, and spoken by newscasters on television.)

Writers often reproduce regional dialects or speech to bring a character to life and to give a story color. For example, the dialect Squeaky speaks in "Raymond's Run" (page 391) helps us see and hear her as a real person.

See pages 366, 389.
See also *Literary Devices*.

DIALOGUE **Conversation between two or more characters.** Most stage dramas consist entirely of dialogue together with stage directions. The dialogue in a drama must move the plot along and reveal character. Dialogue is also an important element in most stories and novels, as well as in some poems and nonfiction. By using dialogue, a writer can show what a character is like.

In the written form of a play, dialogue appears without quotation marks. In prose or poetry, however, dialogue is usually enclosed in quotation marks.

A **monologue** is a long speech by an actor to one or more other characters onstage. A **soliloquy** is a part of a drama in which one character who is alone onstage speaks aloud his or her thoughts and feelings. An **aside** is a comment spoken aloud by a character that is heard by the audience but not by the other characters onstage.

See page 801.
See also *Drama*.

DICTION **A writer's or speaker's choice of words.** People use different types of words, depending on the audience they are addressing, the subject they are discussing, and the effect they are trying to produce. For example, slang words that would be suitable for a humorous piece like "Casey at the Bat" (page 730) would not be appropriate for a serious essay like "A Tragedy Revealed: A Heroine's Last Days" (page 930). Diction is an essential element of a writer's style and has a major effect on the tone of a piece of writing.

See also *Connotation, Style, Tone*.

DRAMA **A work of literature meant to be performed for an audience by actors.** (A drama, or **lay,** can also be enjoyed in its written form.) The actors work from the **playwright's** script, which includes dialogue and stage directions. The script of a drama written for the screen is called a **screenplay** (if it's for TV, it's a **teleplay**), and it also includes camera directions.

The action of a drama is usually driven by a character who wants something and takes steps to get it. The main stages of a drama are often described as **exposition, complications, climax,** and **resolution.** Most dramas are divided into **acts** and **scenes.**

See page 801.
See also *Comedy, Tragedy*.

ELEGY **A poem of mourning, usually about someone who has died.** "O Captain! My Captain!" (page 748) is an elegy on the death of President Abraham Lincoln.

See pages 670, 741.
See also *Poetry*.

EPIC **A long narrative poem that is written in heightened language and tells stories of the deeds of a heroic character who embodies the values of a society.** One of the oldest surviving epics is *Gilgamesh,* which was written down around 2000 B.C. in ancient Mesopotamia. Homer's *Iliad* and *Odyssey,* dating from around 500 B.C. in Greece, are two of the best-known Western epics. *Beowulf* (page 727), from around A.D. 700, is the oldest surviving Anglo-Saxon epic. A **mock epic,** such as "Casey at the Bat" (page 730), imitates the epic style in a comical way in order to poke fun at its topic.

See pages 673, 725.
See also *Poetry*.

EPILOGUE **A brief closing section to a piece of literature.** Shakespeare's plays often have an epilogue spoken by an actor directly to the audience (see page 986, under *Meter,* for an example). In *Pyramus and Thisbe* (page 818) the duke tells the actors that their play needs no epilogue.

ESSAY **A short piece of nonfiction prose that examines a single subject.** Most essays can be categorized as either personal or formal.

The **personal essay** generally reveals a great deal about the writer's personality and tastes. Its tone is often conversational, sometimes even humorous, and there may be no attempt to be objective. In fact, in a personal essay the focus is the writer's feelings and response to an experience. Personal essays are also called **informal** or **familiar** essays. "The Struggle to Be an All-American Girl" (page 322) and "Ed McMahon Is Iranian" (page 325) are personal essays.

The **formal essay** is usually serious, objective, and impersonal in tone. Its purpose is to inform readers about a topic or to persuade them to accept the writer's views. The statements in a formal essay should be supported by facts and logic.

See pages 486, 535.
See also *Nonfiction, Objective Writing*.

EXAGGERATION **Overstating something, usually for the purpose of creating a comic effect.** *He's so thin that if he turned sideways, he'd disappear* is an example of exaggeration. Much of the humor in "The Cremation of Sam McGee" (page 717) comes from exaggeration. Exaggeration is also called **hyperbole.**

See pages 715, 800.
See also *Literary Devices, Understatement*.

EXPOSITION **The kind of writing that explains or gives information.** You'll find exposition in newspaper and magazine articles, encyclopedias and dictionaries, and textbooks and other nonfiction books. In fact, what you're reading right now is exposition.

In fiction and drama, **exposition** refers to the part of a plot that gives information about the characters and their problems or conflicts.

See pages 4–5, 833.
See also *Drama, Nonfiction, Plot, Short Story*.

FABLE **A brief story told in prose or poetry that contains a moral, a practical lesson about how to get along in life.** The characters of most fables are animals that speak and behave like people. Some of the most popular fables, such as "The Dog and The Wolf" (page 356), are attributed to Aesop, a storyteller of ancient Greece. Often a moral is stated at the end of a fable.

FICTION **A prose account that is made up rather than true.** The term *fiction* usually refers to **novels** and **short stories.** Fiction is often based on a writer's experiences or on historical events, but a writer may add or alter characters, events, and other details to create a desired effect. "The Inn of Lost Time" (page 33) is entirely made up. "The Circuit" (page 407), on the other hand, is based to some extent on the writer's experiences.

See also *Historical Fiction, Nonfiction*.

FIGURE OF SPEECH **A word or phrase that describes one thing in terms of another and is not meant to be understood as literally true.** Figures of speech always involve some sort of imaginative comparison between seemingly unlike things.

The most common figures of speech are the **simile** (*The sun was shining like a new penny*), the **metaphor** (*The sun was a huge, unblinking eye*), and **personification** (*The sun smiled down on the bathers*).

See pages 367, 672, 751.
See also *Literary Devices, Metaphor, Personification, Simile*.

FLASHBACK Interruption in the present action of a plot to show events that happened at an earlier time. A flashback breaks the normal forward movement of a narrative. Although flashbacks often appear in the middle of a work, they can also be placed at the beginning. They usually give background information the audience needs in order to understand the present action. The first scene of *The Diary of Anne Frank* (page 839) takes place about one year after the main action of the play. Almost the entire play, then, is a flashback to an earlier time. Flashbacks are common in stories, novels, and movies and sometimes appear in stage plays and poems as well.

See also *Plot*.

FOLK TALE A story that has no known author and was originally passed on from one generation to another by word of mouth. Unlike myths, which are about gods and heroes, folk tales are usually about ordinary people—or animals that act like people. Folk tales tend to travel, and you'll often find the same **motifs**—elements such as characters, images, or story lines—in the tales of different cultures. Cinderella, for example, appears as Aschenputtel in Germany, Yeh-Shen in China, Tam in Vietnam, and Little Burned Face among the Algonquin people of North America. "Aunty Misery" (page 103) is a modern retelling of an old folk tale.

See pages 32, 205.
See also *Fable, Legend, Myth, Tall Tale*.

FORESHADOWING The use of clues or hints to suggest events that will occur later in the plot. Foreshadowing is used to build suspense or anxiety in the reader or viewer. A gun found in a bureau drawer in Act One of a drama may foreshadow violence later in the play. In the early part of "The Monkey's Paw" (page 91), details that hint at mystery and danger suggest what later happens to the main character, Herbert.

See also *Suspense*.

FREE VERSE Poetry without a regular meter or rhyme scheme. Poets writing in free verse try to capture the natural rhythms of ordinary conversation—or, as in this free-verse poem, a very unusual conversation:

Love in the Middle of the Air

CATCH ME!
I love you, I trust you,
I love you
CATCH ME!
catch my left foot, my right
foot, my hand!
here I am hanging by my teeth
300 feet up in the air and
CATCH ME!
here I come, flying without wings,
no parachute, doing a double triple
super flip-flop somersault
RIGHT UP HERE WITHOUT A
SAFETY NET AND
CATCH ME!
you caught me!
I love you!

now it's *your* turn

—Lenore Kandel, from "Circus"

Poets writing in free verse may use **internal rhyme, repetition, alliteration, onomatopoeia,** and other sound effects. They also frequently use vivid imagery and striking metaphors and similes. "I Hear America Singing" by Walt Whitman (page 753) is a famous poem written in free verse.

See pages 673, 751.
See also *Meter, Poetry, Repetition, Rhyme, Rhythm*.

HISTORICAL FICTION A novel, story, or play set during a real historical era. Historical events (such as battles that really happened) and historically accurate details give us an idea of what life was like during a particular period and in a specific setting. "The Drummer Boy of Shiloh" (page 554) is an example of historical fiction.

See page 545.
See also *Fiction*.

HUMOR **The quality that makes something seem funny, amusing, or hilarious.** All kinds of writing include **humor,** including poetry, short stories, essays, and plays. In literature as in real life, humor consists of the unexpected. We might laugh with surprise when we see someone slip on a banana peel, for example, or get a pie thrown in his or her face. Besides comic actions like these, humor comes in many verbal forms, such as wordplay, misstatements, and exaggeration.

See page 801.
See also *Comedy*.

HYPERBOLE See *Exaggeration*.

IAMBIC PENTAMETER **A line of poetry that contains five beats consisting of an unstressed syllable followed by a stressed syllable.** The iambic pentameter line is the most common in English poetry. Shakespeare's plays are written in iambic pentameter, and so is "On the Grasshopper and the Cricket" (page 739), as can be seen in the first line:

˘ ˊ ˘ ˊ ˘ ˊ ˘ ˊ ˘ ˊ
The poetry of earth is never dead

See page 737.
See also *Meter, Poetry, Sonnet*.

IDIOM **An expression peculiar to a particular language that means something different from the literal meaning of the words.** *Hold your tongue* (Don't speak) and *Bury your head in the sand* (Ignore a difficult situation) are idioms of American English, as is the title "A Smart Cookie" (page 372).

See page 367.

IMAGERY **Language that appeals to the senses.** Most images are visual—that is, they create pictures in the reader's mind by appealing to the sense of sight. In "Mrs. Flowers" (page 213), Maya Angelou uses words to paint a picture of a smile: "A slow widening of her thin black lips to show even, small white teeth, then the slow effortless closing."

Images can also appeal to the senses of hearing, touch, taste, and smell, or even to several senses at once.

See pages 366, 672, 751.
See also *Description*.

INVERSION **The reversal of the normal word order of a sentence.** For example, a writer might change *Her hair was long* to *Long was her hair,* inverting the sentence to emphasize the word *long* or to fit a poem's rhyme scheme (*Long was her hair—she had plenty to spare*). In "On the Grasshopper and the Cricket" (page 739), Keats uses inversion in the line "The poetry of earth is ceasing never."

See page 677.

IRONY **A contrast between expectation and reality.** Irony can create powerful effects, ranging from humor to strong emotion. The following terms refer to three common types of irony:

1. **Verbal irony** involves a contrast between what is said or written and what is really meant. If you were to call a baseball player who has just struck out "slugger," you would be using verbal irony.
2. **Situational irony** occurs when what happens is very different from what we expected would happen. When Casey strikes out after we've been led to believe he will save the day in "Casey at the Bat" (page 730), the poet is using situational irony.
3. **Dramatic irony** occurs when the audience or the reader knows something a character does not know. *The Diary of Anne Frank* (page 839) is filled with dramatic irony. We know about the tragic fate of the people in the Secret Annex, but they do not. Note the irony in the following words spoken by Mr. Frank to Mr. Van Daan. "Didn't you hear what Miep said? The invasion has come! We're going to be liberated! This is a time to celebrate!" (Act Two, Scene 3)

See pages 367, 377.
See also *Style*.

LEGEND **A story of extraordinary deeds that is handed down from one generation to the next.** Legends are based to some extent on fact. For example, George Washington did exist, but he did not chop down his father's cherry tree when he was a boy.

See also *Fable, Folk Tale, Myth, Tall Tale*.

LIMERICK **A very short humorous or nonsensical poem.** A limerick has five lines, a definite rhythm, and an *aabba* **rhyme scheme.** It tells a brief story. President Woodrow Wilson is said to have written this limerick:

> I sat next to the Duchess at tea;
> It was just as I feared it would be;
> Her rumblings abdominal
> Were truly phenomenal,
> And everyone thought it was me!

See also *Poetry, Rhyme.*

LITERARY DEVICES **The devices a writer uses to develop style and convey meaning.** Literary devices are a writer's tricks of the trade. They include allusion, analogy, dialect, exaggeration, figures of speech, imagery, irony, repetition, symbolism, and understatement. Literary devices that are used mostly in poetry include alliteration, assonance, meter, onomatopoeia, rhyme, and rhythm.

See pages 366, 389, 670, 689.
See also *Dialect, Diction, Figure of Speech, Irony, Style, Symbol.*

LITERARY PERSPECTIVE **The viewpoint from which literature is analyzed.** In analyzing a work of literature, you might consider its credibility, biographical context, or historical context, for example. You might also analyze the archetypes represented, the author's techniques, or even your own responses. Such perspectives are frequently used as a basis for literary criticism.

See pages 55, 165, 283, 841.

LYRIC POEM **A poem that expresses the feelings or thoughts of a speaker rather than telling a story.** Lyric poems can express a wide range of feelings or thoughts. Both "A word is dead" and "The Word" (page 699) explore the speaker's feelings about words. Lyric poems are usually short and imply, rather than directly state, a single strong emotion or idea.

See pages 673, 683.
See also *Poetry.*

METAMORPHOSIS **A miraculous change from one shape or form to another one.** In myths and other stories, the change is usually from human or god to animal, from animal to human, or from human to plant. Greek and Roman myths contain many examples of metamorphosis. The myth of Narcissus, for example, tells how the vain youth Narcissus pines away for love of his own reflection and is finally changed into a flower.

METAPHOR **An imaginative comparison between two unlike things in which one thing is said to be another thing.** The metaphor is an important type of figure of speech. Metaphors are used in all forms of writing and are common in ordinary speech. When you say someone has a heart of stone, you do not mean that the person's heart is made of rock. You mean that the person is cold and uncaring.

Metaphors differ from **similes,** which use words such as *like, as, than,* and *resembles* to make comparisons. William Wordsworth's famous comparison "I wandered lonely as a cloud" is a simile because it uses *as.* If Wordsworth had written "I was a lonely, wandering cloud," he would have been using a metaphor.

"I'm running a loose ship."

Sometimes a writer hints at a connection instead of stating it directly. T. S. Eliot uses an **implied metaphor** in one of his poems when he describes fog as rubbing its back on windows, making a sudden leap, and curling around a house to fall asleep. By using words that we associate with a cat's behavior, Eliot implies a comparison without stating "The fog is a cat."

An **extended metaphor** is a metaphor that is extended, or developed, over several lines of writing or even throughout an entire work. "O Captain! My Captain!" (page 748) contains an extended metaphor in which the United States is compared to a ship and President Abraham Lincoln is compared to the captain of the ship.

See pages 367, 672, 746.
See also *Figure of Speech*, *Simile*.

METER **A pattern of stressed and unstressed syllables in poetry.** It is common practice to show this pattern in writing by using two symbols. The symbol ´ indicates a stressed syllable. The symbol ˘ indicates an unstressed syllable. Indicating the metrical pattern of a poem in this way is called **scanning** the poem. The following lines by William Shakespeare have been scanned in part. (The lines make up an epilogue, or speech at the end of the the play, of the mischief-maker Puck, or Robin Goodfellow, in *A Midsummer Night's Dream. Reprehend* means "criticize"; *serpent's tongue* means "hissing"; *Give me your hands* means "Clap.")

/∪ /∪ / ∪/∪
If we shadows have offended,
/ ∪ / ∪/∪ / ∪
Think but this, and all is mended,
/ ∪ / ∪ / ∪ /
That you have but slumbered here
/ ∪ /∪ /∪/
While these visions did appear,
And this weak and idle theme,
No more yielding but a dream,
Gentles, do not reprehend.
If you pardon, we will mend.
And, as I am an honest Puck,
If we have unearned luck
Now to scape the serpent's tongue,
We will make amends ere long,
Else the Puck a liar call.
So, good night unto you all.
Give me your hands, if we be friends,
And Robin shall restore amends.

—William Shakespeare, from *A Midsummer Night's Dream*

See page 670.
See also *Poetry*, *Rhythm*.

MOOD **The overall feeling or atmosphere of a work of literature.** A work's mood can often be described in one or two adjectives, such as *scary, happy, sad,* or *nostalgic*. A writer produces a mood by creating images and using sounds that convey a particular feeling. "The Tell-Tale Heart" (page 379) is noted for its eerie atmosphere. The setting of a story can also contribute to its mood. For example, the hot sun beating down on the farmworkers in "The Circuit" (page 407) contributes to a mood of oppression.

See pages 5, 31, 405.
See also Tone.

MOTIF See *Folk Tale.*

MOTIVATION **The reasons a character behaves in a certain way.** Among the many reasons for a person's behavior are feelings, experiences, and commands by others. In "Passage to Freedom: The Sugihara Story" (page 195), Mr. Sugihara risks his career to issue visas to fleeing refugees despite his government's refusal. His motivation is his concern for their safety.

See pages 151, 179, 205.
See also *Character.*

MYTH **A story that explains something about the world and typically involves gods or other supernatural forces.** Myths reflect the traditions and beliefs of the culture that produced them. Almost every culture has **creation myths,** stories that explain how the world came to exist or how human beings were created. Other myths explain different aspects of life and the natural world. One of the ancient Greek myths, for instance, tells how Prometheus gave humans the gift of fire. Most myths are very old and were handed down orally before being put in written form. The exact origin of most myths is not known.

See also *Fable, Folk Tale, Legend, Tall Tale.*

NARRATION **The kind of writing that tells a story.** Narration is the main tool of writers of fiction. It is also used in any piece of nonfiction that relates a series of events in the order in which they happened (for example, in historical writing and science articles).

See also *Exposition, Fiction, Nonfiction.*

NARRATIVE POEM **A poem that tells a story.** "Paul Revere's Ride" (page 705) and "Casey at the Bat" (page 730) are narrative poems.

See pages 673, 703.
See also *Poetry.*

NONFICTION **Prose writing that deals with real people, things, events, and places.** Popular forms of nonfiction are autobiography, biography, essay, and speech. "Mrs. Flowers" (page 213) is an excerpt from Maya Angelou's autobiography. Other examples of nonfiction are newspaper stories, magazine articles, historical writing, science reports, and even diaries and letters.

The purpose of nonfiction writing may be to provide information, express personal feelings, entertain, or influence. Some elements of nonfiction texts include main idea, or the writer's most important message, and repetition. Structural patterns include chronolgocial order, order of importance, and logical order. Nonfiction texts also have logic, unity, consistency, and coherence.

See pages 486–487.
See also *Autobiography, Biography, Essay, Fiction, Speech.*

NOVEL **A long fictional story, usually longer than one hundred book pages.** A novel uses all the elements of storytelling—plot, character, setting, theme, and point of view. It usually has more characters, settings, and themes and a more complex plot than a short story. A **novella** is a fictional story that is shorter than a novel and longer than a short story.

See also *Plot, Short Story.*

OBJECTIVE WRITING **Writing that presents facts without revealing the writer's feelings and opinions.** Most news reports in newspapers are objective writing.

See pages 221, 948.
See also *Essay, Subjective Writing.*

ODE **A lyric poem, rhymed or unrhymed, on a serious subject.** Odes are usually addressed to one person or thing. In "Ode to Thanks" (page 743), Pablo Neruda praises the word *thanks.*

See pages 673, 741.
See also *Poetry.*

ONOMATOPOEIA The use of words whose sounds imitate or suggest their meaning. *Buzz, rustle, boom, ticktock, tweet,* and *bark* are all onomatopoeic words. In the following lines the poet suggests the sound of sleigh bells in the cold night air by using onomatopoeia:

> Hear the sledges with the bells—
> Silver bells!
> What a world of merriment their melody
> foretells!
> How they tinkle, tinkle, tinkle,
> In the icy air of night!
> While the stars that oversprinkle
> All the Heavens, seem to twinkle
> With a crystalline delight.
>
> —Edgar Allan Poe,
> from "The Bells"

See pages 671, 751.

PARALLEL EPISODES Repeated elements of the plot. Three times the Big Bad Wolf goes to a little pig's house and says, "I'll huff and I'll puff and I'll blow your house in." Each time this happens, we have a parallel episode. Each of Melinda Alice's wishes in "Those Three Wishes" (page 10) is a parallel episode.

See pages 4, 53, 89.
See also *Plot*.

PERSONIFICATION A figure of speech in which an object or animal is spoken of as if it had human feelings, thoughts, or attitudes. This poet writes about the moon as if it were a woman wearing silver shoes ("shoon"):

> Slowly, silently, now the moon
> Walks the night in her silver shoon;
> This way, and that, she peers, and sees
> Silver fruit upon silver trees.
>
> —Walter de la Mare, from "Silver"

See pages 367, 697.
See also *Figure of Speech*.

PERSUASION A kind of writing intended to convince a reader to think or act in a certain way. Examples of persuasive writing are found in newspaper editorials, in speeches, and in many essays and articles. The techniques of persuasion are widely used in advertising. Persuasion can use language that appeals to the emotions, or it can use logic to appeal to reason. When persuasive writing appeals to reason and not to the emotions, it is called **argument.** The "Gettysburg Address" (page 527) and "I Have a Dream" (page 529) are examples of persuasive writing.

See page 565.
See also *Proposition and Support* in the Handbook of Reading and Informational Terms.

PLAYWRIGHT The author of a play, or drama. Playwrights Frances Goodrich and Albert Hackett wrote *The Diary of Anne Frank* (page 839), which they based on Anne Frank's diary and life story.

See also *Author, Drama*.

PLOT The series of related events that make up a story. Plot is what happens in a short story, novel, play, or narrative poem. Most plots are built from these basic elements: An **introduction,** or **exposition,** tells us who the characters are and usually what their conflict is. **Complications** arise when the characters take steps to resolve the conflict. Eventually the plot reaches a **climax,** the most exciting moment in the story, when the outcome is decided one way or another. The final part of the story is the **resolution,** in which the conflict is resolved and the story is brought to a close.

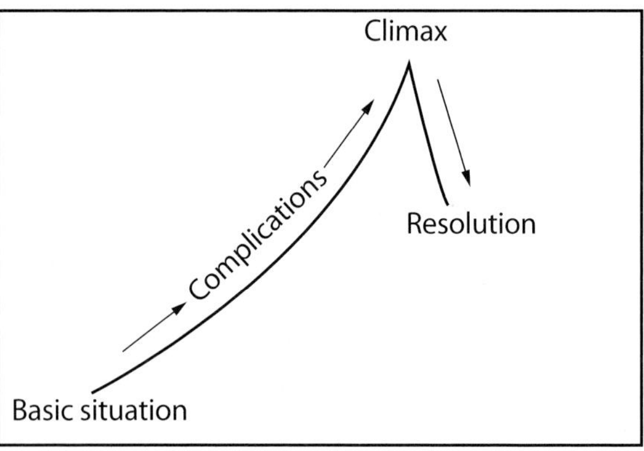

Not all works of fiction or drama have a traditional plot structure. Modern writers often experiment with plot. At times they eliminate some or almost all of the parts of a traditional plot in order to focus on other elements, such as character, point of view, or mood. In "Those Three Wishes" (page 10), the story ends with the climax. The reader infers the resolution.

See pages 4–5, 8.
See also *Climax, Drama, Exposition, Parallel Episodes, Subplot*.

POETRY **A kind of rhythmic, compressed language that uses figures of speech and imagery designed to appeal to our emotions and imagination.** Poetry is usually arranged in lines. It often has a regular pattern of rhythm and may have a regular rhyme scheme. **Free verse** is poetry that has no regular pattern of rhythm or rhyme, though it is generally arranged in lines. Major forms of poetry include the **lyric,** the **narrative,** the **epic,** and the **ballad.**

See also *Ballad, Elegy, Epic, Figure of Speech, Free Verse, Imagery, Lyric Poem, Meter, Narrative Poem, Ode, Prose, Refrain, Rhyme, Rhythm, Sonnet, Speaker*.

POINT OF VIEW **The vantage point from which a story is told.** The most common points of view are the omniscient, the third-person limited, and the first person.

1. In the **omniscient** (all-knowing) **point of view,** the narrator knows everything about the characters and their problems. This all-knowing narrator can tell us about the past, the present, and the future of the characters. The narrator can also tell us what the characters are thinking and what is happening in several places at the same time. But the narrator does not take part in the story's action. Rather, the narrator stands above the action like a god. The omniscient is a familiar point of view; we have heard it in fairy tales since we were very young. "The Monkey's Paw" (page 91) has an omniscient narrator, one who does not tell us everything.
2. In the **third-person-limited point of view,** the narrator focuses on the thoughts and feelings of only one character. From this point of view, we observe the action through the eyes of only one of the characters in the story. "The Treasure of Lemon Brown" (page 17) is told from the third-person-limited point of view.
3. In the **first-person point of view,** one of the characters, using the personal pronoun *I*, tells the story. We become familiar with the narrator, but we can know only what this person knows and observe only what this person observes. All of our information about the story comes from this narrator, who may be unreliable. "The Circuit" (page 407) is told from the first-person point of view.

See page 303.

PROSE **Any writing that is not poetry.** Essays, short stories, novels, newspaper articles, and letters are all written in prose. Unlike poetry, prose is usually composed in paragraphs.

See also *Fiction, Nonfiction, Poetry*.

PROTAGONIST **The main character in a work of literature.** The protagonist is involved in the work's central conflict. If there is another character opposing the protagonist, that character is called the **antagonist.** In "Flowers for Algernon" (page 55), Charlie is the protagonist. In a subplot of the story, Joe Carp and Frank Reilly are his antagonists.

See also *Character*.

PUN **A play on the multiple meanings of a word or on two words that sound alike but have different meanings.** Most often puns are used for humor; they turn up in jokes all the time. *Where does an elephant put suitcases?* Answer: *In its trunk.* This pun is called a **homographic pun;** it is a play on a word (*trunk*) that has two meanings ("proboscis of an elephant" and "compartment in an automobile"). *Is Swiss cheese good for you?* Answer: *Yes, it is holesome.* This pun is called a **homophonic pun;** it is a play on words that sound alike but are spelled differently and have different meanings (*hole* and *whole*). In *Pyramus and Thisbe* (page 818), the duke and his guest use puns in their comments on the play within a play.

REFRAIN A repeated sound, word, phrase, line, or group of lines. Refrains are usually associated with songs and poems but are also used in speeches and other forms of literature. Refrains are most often used to build rhythm, but they may also provide emphasis or commentary, create suspense, or help hold a work together. Refrains may be repeated with small variations in a work to fit a particular context or to create a special effect. "Fallen cold and dead" is a refrain in the poem "O Captain! My Captain!" (page 748).

REPETITION A literary techniques used in many kinds of writing. The repetition might be of words or phrases (as in a refrain), of sounds (as in alliteration and assonance), of grammatical structures, or of events (as in parallel episodes). Speeches such as "I Have a Dream" (page 529), and free-verse poems, such as "I Hear America Singing" (page 753), especially, use repetition to emphasize their points and to create rhythm.

See pages 486, 525.
See also Nonfiction, Poetry.

RESOLUTION See *Plot.*

RHYME The repetition of accented vowel sounds and all sounds following them in words that are close together in a poem. *Mean* and *screen* are rhymes, as are *crumble* and *tumble*. The many purposes of rhyme in poetry include building rhythm, lending a songlike quality, emphasizing ideas, organizing poems (for instance, into stanzas or couplets), providing humor or pleasure for the reader, and aiding memory.

End rhymes are rhymes at the ends of lines. In the following poem, *ought* and *thought* form end rhymes, as do *afternoon* and *soon*:

Condition
I have to speak—I must—I should
—I ought . . .
I'd tell you how I love you if I thought
The world would end tomorrow afternoon.
But short of that . . . well, it might be
too soon.

—Vikram Seth

Internal rhymes are rhymes within lines. The following line has an internal rhyme (*turning/burning*):

Back into the chamber turning, all my soul
within me burning

—Edgar Allan Poe,
from "The Raven"

Rhyming sounds need not be spelled the same way: *Gear/here*, for instance, is a rhyme. Rhymes can involve more than one syllable or more than one word; *poet/know it* is an example. Rhymes involving sounds that are similar but not exactly the same are called **approximate rhymes** (or **near rhymes** or **slant rhymes**). *Leave/live* is an example of an approximate rhyme. Poets writing in English often use this kind of rhyme because they believe it sounds less artificial and more like real speech than exact rhymes do. Also, it is difficult to come up with fresh, original exact rhymes. Poets interested in how a poem looks on the printed page sometimes use **eye rhymes,** or **visual rhymes**—"rhymes" involving words that are spelled similarly but pronounced differently. *Tough/cough* is an eye rhyme. (*Tough/rough* is a "real" rhyme.)

The pattern of end rhymes in a poem is called a **rhyme scheme.** To indicate the rhyme scheme of a poem, use a separate letter of the alphabet for each end rhyme. For example, the rhyme scheme of the opening stanza of "Paul Revere's Ride" (page 705) is *aabba*.

See page 671.
See also *Free Verse, Poetry.*

RHYTHM A musical quality produced by the repetition of stressed and unstressed syllables or by the repetition of certain other sound patterns. Rhythm occurs in all forms of language, both written and spoken, but is particularly important in poetry.

The most obvious kind of rhythm is the regular repetition of stressed and unstressed syllables found in some poetry. In the following lines, which describe a cavalry charge, the rhythm echoes the galloping of the attackers' horses:

> The Assyrian came down like the wolf on the fold,
> And his cohorts were gleaming in purple and gold;
> And the sheen of their spears was like stars on the sea,
> When the blue wave rolls nightly on deep Galilee.
>
> —George Gordon, Lord Byron, from "The Destruction of Sennacherib"

Writers also create rhythm by repeating words and phrases or even by repeating whole lines and sentences. The following passage by Walt Whitman is written in free verse and does not have a regular pattern of rhythm or rhyme. Yet the lines are rhythmical because of Whitman's use of repetition.

> I hear the sound I love, the sound of the human voice,
> I hear all sounds running together, combined,
> fused, or following,
> Sounds of the city and sounds out of the city, sounds of the day and night,
> Talkative young ones to those that like them, the loud laugh of work-people at their meals . . .
>
> —Walt Whitman, from "Song of Myself"

See pages 670, 676, 703, 751.
See also *Meter.*

RISING ACTION See *Plot.*

SATIRE **Writing that ridicules something, often in order to bring about change.** Satire may poke fun at a person, a group of people, an attitude, a social institution, even all of humanity. Writers use satire to convince us of a point of view or to persuade us to follow a course of action.

SETTING **The time and place of a story, play, or narrative poem.** Most often the setting is described early in the story. For example, "The Treasure of Lemon Brown" (page 17) begins, "The dark sky, filled with angry, swirling clouds, reflected Greg Ridley's mood as he sat on the stoop of his building." Setting often contributes to a work's emotional effect. It may also play an important role in the plot, especially in stories involving a conflict between a character and nature such as in "The Cremation of Sam McGee" (page 717).

See pages 5, 31.
See also *Mood, Plot.*

SHORT STORY **A short fictional prose narrative.** The first short stories were written in the nineteenth century. Early short story writers include Sir Walter Scott and Edgar Allan Poe. A short story's plot usually consists of these basic elements: the **introduction (basic situation** or **exposition), complications, climax,** and **resolution.** Short stories are more limited than novels. They usually have only one or two major characters and one important setting.

See pages 4–5.
See also *Fiction, Novel, Plot.*

SIMILE **A comparison between two unlike things, using a word such as *like, as, than,* or *resembles.*** *Her face was as round as a pumpkin* and *This steak is tougher than an old shoe* are similes.

See pages 367, 697.
See also *Figure of Speech, Metaphor.*

SONNET **A fourteen-line poem, usually written in iambic pentameter.** There are two kinds of sonnets: The **English,** or **Shakespearean, sonnet** has three four-line units and ends with a couplet. The **Italian,** or **Petrarchan, sonnet** (named after the fourteenth-century Italian poet Petrarch) poses a question or makes a point in the first eight lines. The last six lines respond to that question or point. "On the Grasshopper and the Cricket" (page 739) is in the form of an Italian sonnet.

See pages 673, 737.
See also *Iambic Pentameter, Poetry.*

SPEAKER The voice talking to us in a poem. The speaker is sometimes, but not always, the poet. It is best to think of the voice in the poem as belonging to a character the poet has created. The character may be a child, a woman, a man, an animal, or even an object.

See page 673.
See also *Poetry*.

SPEECH A speech is similar to an essay, but it is delivered orally. Its purpose is to unite an audience, inform them of something, or persuade them to do something. Speeches often include allusions that the audience will recognize and repetition. We can also read speeches, such as Lincoln's "Gettysburg Address" (page 527) and King's "I Have a Dream" (page 529).

See page 486.
See also *Allusion, Nonfiction, Repetition*.

STANZA A group of consecutive lines in a poem that form a single unit. A stanza in a poem is something like a paragraph in prose: It often expresses a unit of thought. A stanza may consist of any number of lines; it may even consist of a single line. The word *stanza* is an Italian word for "stopping place" or "place to rest." In some poems, such as "Casey at the Bat" (page 730), each stanza has the same rhyme scheme.

STEREOTYPE A fixed idea about the members of a particular group of people that does not allow for any individuality. Stereotypes are often based on misconceptions about racial, social, religious, gender, or ethnic groups. Some common stereotypes are the ideas that all football players are stupid, that all New Yorkers are rude, and that all politicians are dishonest.

STYLE The way a writer uses language. Style results from **diction** (word choice), sentence structure, tone, and the use of **literary devices.** One writer may use many figures of speech, for example; another writer may prefer straightforward language with few figures of speech.

See pages 366–367.
See also *Diction, Literary Devices, Tone*.

SUBJECTIVE WRITING Writing in which the feelings and opinions of the writer are revealed. Editorials, personal essays, and autobiographies are examples of subjective writing, as are many poems.

See also *Objective Writing*.

SUBPLOT A minor plot that relates in some way to the main story. In "Flowers for Algernon" (page 55), Charlie's relationship with Miss Kinnian and his problems at his job are subplots of the main plot, involving the surgery to make Charlie more intelligent.

See pages 4–5, 53.
See also *Plot*.

SUSPENSE The uncertainty or anxiety that a reader feels about what will happen next in a story, novel, or drama. In "The Tell-Tale Heart" (page 379), the suspense builds as the insane narrator describes his long vigil at his victim's door.

See page 49.
See also *Plot*.

SYMBOL A person, a place, a thing, or an event that has meaning in itself and stands for something beyond itself as well. Some symbols are so well known that we sometimes forget they are symbols. The bald eagle, for example, is a symbol of the United States; the Star of David is a symbol of Judaism; and the cross is a symbol of Christianity. In literature, symbols are often personal and surprising. In "Suéter / Sweater" (page 695), for example, a sweater symbolizes the grandmother's love and caring.

See pages 366, 672, 767.
See also *Literary Devices*.

TALL TALE An exaggerated, far-fetched story that is obviously untrue but is told as though it should be believed. Almost all tall tales are humorous. "The Cremation of Sam McGee" (page 717) is a tall tale told in the form of a poem.

See also *Exaggeration, Folk Tale*.

THEME **The general idea or insight about life that a work of literature reveals.** A theme is not the same as a subject. The subject of a work can usually be expressed in a word or two: *love, childhood, death.* A theme is an idea or message that the writer wishes to convey *about* that subject. For example, one theme of "Camp Harmony" (page 515) might be stated as *Innocent people often suffer in times of conflict.* The same themes, such as *Good will triumph over evil,* that appear in works from different cultures and times, are called **recurring themes** or **universal themes.**

"If you were to boil your book down to a few words, what would be its message?

A work's themes (there may be more than one) are usually not stated directly. Most often the reader has to think about all the elements of the work and use them to make an **inference,** or educated guess, about what the themes are.

See pages 254–255, 258–259, 267, 281, 767.

TONE **The attitude a writer takes toward his or her subject, characters, and audience.** For example, a writer's tone might be humorous, as in "Those Three Wishes" (page 10), or passionate and sincere, as in "I Have a Dream" (page 529). When people speak, their tone of voice gives added meaning to what they say. Writers use written language to create effects similar to those that people create with their voices.

See pages 366, 405.
See also *Connotation, Diction, Style.*

TRAGEDY **A play, novel, or other narrative in which the main character comes to an unhappy end.** A tragedy depicts serious and important events. Its hero achieves wisdom or self-knowledge but suffers a great deal—perhaps even dies. A tragic hero is usually dignified and courageous and often high ranking. The hero's downfall may be caused by a **tragic flaw** (a serious character weakness) or by external forces beyond his or her control. *The Diary of Anne Frank* and Shakespeare's *Romeo and Juliet* are tragedies.

See also *Comedy, Drama.*

UNDERSTATEMENT **A statement that says less than what is meant.** Understatement is the opposite of exaggeration. It is usually used for comic effect. If you were to say that the Grand Canyon is a nice little hole in the ground, you would be using understatement.

See also *Exaggeration, Literary Devices.*

WORD CHOICE See *Diction.*

WORD PLAY See *Humor.*

Handbook of Reading and Informational Terms

For more information about a topic, turn to the page(s) in this book indicated on a separate line at the end of the entries. On another line there are cross-references to entries in this Handbook that provide closely related information. For instance, *Chronological Order* contains a cross-reference to *Structural Patterns*.

ANALOGY An **analogy** (uh NAL uh jee) compares one thing with another thing to show, point by point, how they are alike. Writers often use analogies to show how something unfamiliar is like something well-known. Writers of scientific and technical texts often use analogies to explain difficult concepts.

Another kind of analogy is a **word analogy.** This kind of analogy is sometimes used in tests. It asks you to compare two words and figure out how they are related to each other. To complete a word analogy,

1. figure out the relationship between the two words; then,
2. identify another pair of words that are related to each other in the same way.

In a word analogy, the symbol : means "is to." The symbol : : means "as." Once you get the hang of it, completing analogies is fun. Here's an example:

> Select the pair of words that best completes the analogy.
>
> STANZA : POEM : : ____________
>
> **A** metaphor : simile
> **B** chapter : book
> **C** fiction : nonfiction
> **D** words : music

The correct answer is B. The completed analogy should read: Stanza is to poem as chapter is to book. The relationship between stanza and poem is one of *part* to *whole*. Just as a stanza is part of a poem, a chapter is part of a book.

In another kind of word analogy, the words might be opposites:

> DRY : WET : : cold : hot
> Dry is to wet as cold is to hot.

See pages 402, 532.

ANECDOTE See *Proposition and Support*.

CAUSE AND EFFECT The **cause-effect pattern** is a text structure that writers use to explain how or why one thing leads to another. The **cause** is the reason that an action or reaction takes place. The **effect** is the result or consequence of the cause. A cause can have more than one effect, and an effect may have several causes. Writers may explain causes only or effects only. Sometimes a text is organized in a cause-and-effect chain. One cause leads to an effect, which causes another effect, and so on. Notice the cause-and-effect chain in the following paragraph from an interview with John Lewis in *The Power of Nonviolence* (another excerpt of which appears on page 586):

> In April, unknown people bombed the house of our attorney. It shook the whole area, and it shook us. How could we respond to the bombing and do something that would channel the frustration of the students in a nonviolent manner? We decided to have a march, and we sent the mayor a telegram letting him know that by noon we would march on city hall. And the next day, more than five thousand of us marched in twos in an orderly line to the city hall.

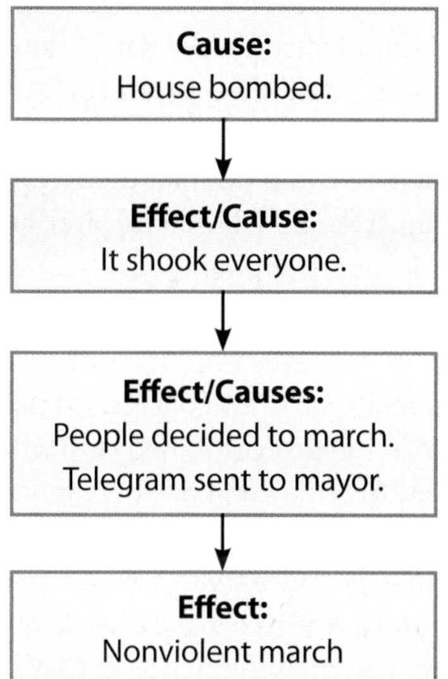

Cause:
House bombed.
Effect/Cause:
It shook everyone.
Effect/Causes:
People decided to march.
Telegram sent to mayor.
Effect:
Nonviolent march

Writers use the cause-effect pattern in both narrative and informational texts. In many stories, events in the plot are connected in a cause-and-effect chain. Some words and phrases that are clues to the cause-effect pattern are *because, depended on, inspired, produced, resulting in, led to,* and *outcome*. Never assume, either in your reading or in real life, that one event causes another just because it happens before it.

See page 331.
See also *Coherence, Organizational Patterns, Structural Patterns*.

CHRONOLOGICAL ORDER Writers use **chronological order,** or time order, when they put events in the sequence in which they happened, one after the other. Chronological order is a common text structure in narratives, both fictional and nonfictional. Chronological order is very important in history texts and in science texts. You will also find chronological order in directions, from directions for a simple process, such as making hot chocolate, to technical directions for using a complex mechanical device, such as an electric generator. Some words and phrases that signal the chronological-order pattern are *first, after, finally, in the meantime, as soon as,* and *at this point*.

See pages 490, 929.
See also *Coherence, Organizational Patterns, Structural Patterns*.

COHERENCE The word *cohere* means "stick together." A text has **coherence** (koh HIHR uhns) when ideas stick together because they're arranged in an order that makes sense to the reader. To aid in coherence, writers often help you follow a text by using **transitions,** words and phrases that show how ideas are connected.

See page 487.
See also *Cause and Effect, Chronological Order, Comparison and Contrast, Order of Importance, Spatial Order*.

COMPARISON AND CONTRAST When you **compare,** you look at how two or more things are similar, that is, alike. When you **contrast,** you look at how things are different. Comparison and contrast is a text structure that discusses similarities and differences. There are two basic ways to organize a comparison-and-contrast text.

1. **Block method.** Discuss all the features (sometimes called **points of comparison**) of Subject 1 first; then, all the features of Subject 2. For each subject, discuss the same features in the same order. A block comparison and contrast of the two subjects Earth and Mars could be organized by subject.

Subject	Features
Earth	• planet surface • weather • length of day and year
Mars	• planet surface • weather • length of day and year

2. **Point-by-point method.** Discuss one feature at a time. First, talk about a feature in Subject 1; then, discuss the same feature in Subject 2.

Features	Subject
planet surface	• Earth • Mars
weather	• Earth • Mars
length of day and year	• Earth • Mars

Expect to see transitions that help you follow the ideas in both block structure and point-by-point structure. The transitions *both* and *neither* help you find similarities. Transitions such as *but* and *however* help you pinpoint differences.

A graphic organizer such as a Venn diagram, which uses overlapping circles to show relationships, can help you keep track of similarities and differences.

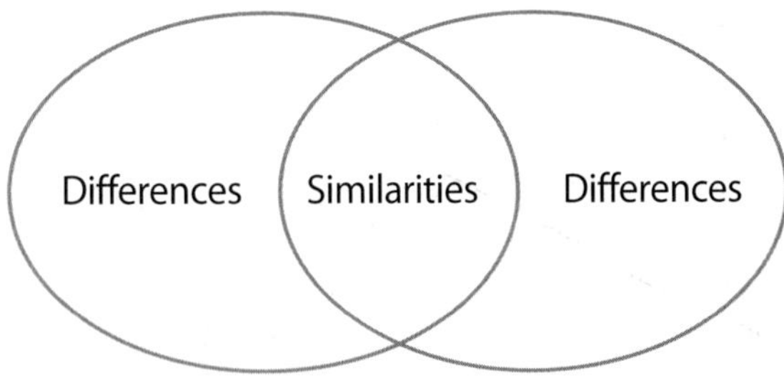

See pages 221, 337.
See also *Coherence, Organizational Patterns, Structural Patterns*.

CONCLUSION A **conclusion** is a final idea or judgment that you draw, or come to, after you've considered all the evidence. In his memoir *Woodsong,* Gary Paulsen tells how he observed his dog Columbia playing a joke on another dog. That observation leads him to a chain of reasoning based on what he knows about other animals. After he considers the evidence, he draws a conclusion.

> If Columbia could do that, I thought, if a dog could do that, then a wolf could do that. If a wolf could do that, then a deer could do that. If a deer could do that, then a beaver, and a squirrel, and a bird, and, and, and . . .
> And I quit trapping then.
> It was wrong for me to kill.

As you read, you draw conclusions based on information in the text combined with what you already know. You may or may not agree with Paulsen's reasoning and the conclusion it leads him to. Your own experiences with animals may tell you that a dog and a wolf may have a sense of humor—but that other animals might not. In that case, you might conclude that Paulsen's conclusion is valid (true and logical) for him, but not for you.

See pages 371, 417, 427.

CONNECTIONS As you read you **make connections** between what is in the text and what you already know from your own experience. This helps you both to understand and to evaluate what you read.

See pages 154, 179, 759.

CONSISTENCY A text is **consistent** when its details focus on the main idea and are in agreement with it. Consistency is important because details that have little or nothing to do with the main idea of the text distract and confuse the reader. Why is the second sentence in the following passage inconsistent with the point of the passage?

> In the winter of 1866–1867 blizzards gripped the Sierra Nevada. Spring came early, and the weather was unusually warm on the East Coast. Dwellings were buried in blowing, shifting, drifting, driving snow.

A sentence about weather on the East Coast is inconsistent with a passage on conditions in the mountains of California.

See page 487.

CONSUMER DOCUMENTS See *Informational Texts.*

CONTEXT CLUE If you don't know the meaning of a word, **context clues,** the words and sentences surrounding it, can sometimes help you guess its meaning. The following chart gives you four types of context clues. In the examples the unfamiliar word appears in boldface (dark type). The context clue is underlined.

Definition: Look for words that define the unfamiliar word, often by giving a **synonym** for it.

> She peeled onions and grated potatoes for the **latkes,** the potato pancakes.

Restatement: Find words that restate the unfamiliar word's meaning.

> Ballet dancers perform on the **pointe** of their toeshoes—a platform about the size of a silver dollar.

Example: Look for examples that reveal the meaning of the unfamiliar word.

> Street vendors offered their **wares:** goods of all kinds were piled in their stalls.

Contrast: Find words that contrast the unfamiliar word with a word or phrase you already know.

> The land was **arid,** in contrast to the rich, fertile land we had left behind.

See pages 297, 304.

DETAIL It is important to **analyze details** in a text to help you understand elements of literature such a plot, setting, characters, theme, and style. For instance, the details in "The Inn of Lost Time" (page 33) reveal that the story takes place in a sixteenth-century Japanese farmhouse.

Useful details that help you follow both fiction and nonfiction are **transitional words.**

Common Transitional Words and Phrases	
Comparing Ideas also, and, moreover, too, similarly, another	**Contrasting Ideas** although, still, yet, but, on the other hand
Showing Cause-Effect for, since, as a result, therefore, so that	**Showing Importance** first, last, to begin with, mainly, more important
Showing Location above, across, over, there, inside, behind	**Showing Time** before, at last, when, eventually, at once

The details that are most important in a text are called **critical details.** If you e-mail a faraway friend about a film you've seen, you have to make decisions about which details to include and which to leave out. A critical detail is one that you must include for the text to make sense. Being able to separate critical details from minor ones is especially important in writing a summary.

See pages 8, 31, 370, 389, 525.
See also *Proposition and Support, Summarizing.*

DOCUMENTS See *Informational Texts.*

ENUMERATION **Enumeration** (ih noo muh RAY shuhn) is a kind of text structure that organizes information into a list. The facts or events on the list may be cited in the order of size, location, importance, or any other order that will make sense to the reader. Some of the words and phrases that signal the enumeration text pattern are *to begin with, second, most important, for instance, another, for example,* and *in fact.* Social studies textbooks and science textbooks often use the enumeration text pattern. For an example of the enumeration pattern, see "The Bill of Rights" (page 224).

See page 221.
See also *Coherence, Logic.*

FACT A **fact** is something that can be verified, or proved. It can be proved by direct observation or by checking a reliable reference source. The following statement is a fact:

> In 1860, Abraham Lincoln was elected president despite winning only 40 percent of the popular vote.

You can verify this fact by looking it up in a history book or in an encyclopedia. In fields where discoveries are still being made, you need to check facts in a recently published source. A Web site on the Internet may be current, but it may not be reliable. Remember that anybody can post a statement on the Internet. If you suspect that a statement given as a fact is not true, try to find the same fact in several sources.

See pages 491, 565.
See also *Opinion.*

FALLACIOUS REASONING Statements that seem reasonable at first may, if examined closely, prove to be based on **fallacious** (fuh LAY shuhs) **reasoning,** faulty reasoning, or mistakes in logic. (The word *fallacious* comes from a Latin word meaning "deceptive" or "tricky." The word *false* comes from the same root, as does the word *fallacy.*) Fallacious reasoning leads to false or incorrect conclusions. Here are some types of fallacious reasoning:

1. **Begging the question,** also called **circular reasoning,** assumes the truth of a statement before it has been proved. You appear to be giving a reason to support your opinion, but all you're doing is restating the same thing in different words.

> Everyone should be required to attend school sports events because mandatory attendance at such events is important.
>
> We can't control worldwide air pollution because every country in the world is guilty of polluting the air.

2. **Name-calling** uses labels to attack the person on the other side of the argument, instead of giving reasons or evidence to support the opposing point of view. This fallacy includes attacking the person's character, situation, or background.

> You're not seriously considering Latisha's childish ideas for the school dance, are you?
>
> Of course, Allen's not going to say that doctors make too much money. His mother's a doctor.

3. **Stereotyping** gives all members of a group the same (usually undesirable) characteristics. It assumes that everyone (or everything) in that group is alike. (The word *stereotype* comes from the word for a metal plate that was used to print the same image over and over.) Stereotypes are often based on misconceptions about racial, social, religious, gender, or ethnic groups.

> Smart kids are poor athletes.
> Actors are conceited.
> Big cities are dirty and dangerous.

4. **Hasty generalization** is a broad, general statement or conclusion that is made without sufficient evidence to back it up. A hasty generalization is often made on the basis of one or two experiences or observations.

> My brother is left-handed, and he's an artist. My aunt is left-handed, and she writes songs. I'm right-handed, and I have no artistic or musical talent at all.
> **Hasty generalization:** Left-handed people are more creative than right-handed people.

If any exceptions to the conclusion can be found, the generalization is not true.

5. **Either/or fallacy** assumes that there is only one correct choice or one solution, even though there may be many.

> Either we have free trade, or we return to the cold war.
> If you don't get good grades this year, you're not college material.

6. **False cause and effect** occurs when one event is said to be the cause of another event just because the two events happened in sequence. You cannot assume that an event caused whatever happened afterward.

> We got new uniforms, and our team won four straight games. The uniforms helped us win.
> Our mayor should be reelected. During her first term the crime rate in our city fell almost 10 percent.

GENERALIZATION A **generalization** is a broad statement that applies to many individuals, experiences, situations, or observations. A generalization is a type of conclusion that is drawn after considering as many of the facts as possible. A valid generalization is based on evidence, specific data, or facts. Here are some specific facts and a generalization based on them. Notice that each fact is one piece of evidence. The generalization then states what the evidence adds up to, drawing a conclusion that applies to all members of the group.

> **Specific Facts:** My dog wags her tail when she's happy. Kathy's dog, Soot, wags his tail when he is happy.
> **Generalization:** All dogs I've seen wag their tails when they're happy.

A generalization jumps from your own specific experiences and observations to a larger, general understanding. To be **valid,** or true, a generalization must apply to every specific individual or instance within the group—including the millions in the group that are not mentioned or listed in arriving at the generalization.

See pages 259, 281.

GRAPHICS Many types of texts can be enhanced by graphics, especially informational texts. **Graphics** include graphs, tables, charts, maps, cartoons, and illustrations.

See page 603.
See also *Informational Texts.*

IDIOM An **idiom** (IHD ee uhm) is an expression peculiar to a particular language that means something different from the literal (dictionary) meaning of the words. If your brother tells you he's fallen for Angela, you know that he means he likes her a lot. Despite what the words say, you know he hasn't fallen down. Every language has its own idioms. When you grow up speaking a language, you understand its idioms without even thinking about them. When you're learning a new language, it's hard to figure out what its idioms mean, and it's even harder to use them correctly.

See pages 278, 424.

INFERENCE An **inference** is a guess based on clues. When you read, you make inferences based on clues that the writer provides. For example, you guess what will happen next in a story based on what the writer has already told you. You change your inferences as the writer gives you more information. Sometimes a writer will deliberately drop a clue that leads you, for a short time, to an incorrect inference about what is going to happen next. That's part of the fun of reading. Until you get to the end of a suspenseful story, you can never be sure about what will happen next.

When you're writing about a story or an informational text, you must be sure your inferences are supported by details in the text.

Supported inferences are based directly on evidence in the writer's text that you can point to and on reasonable prior knowledge. Some interpretation of the evidence is possible, but you cannot ignore or contradict facts in the text that the writer has given you.

Unsupported inferences are conclusions that are not logical. They ignore the facts in the text, or misinterpret them. Whenever you're asked to write an essay about a text, it's a good idea to re-read the text before and after you write your essay. Check each inference you make against the text to make sure you can find evidence for it. For example, if you write an analysis of a character in a story and you say that the character is self-centered, you should cite details from the text to support your inference.

See pages 154, 163, 805, 833.

INFORMATIONAL TEXTS When you're reading for your own enjoyment, a mystery story, for instance, you can read at your own pace. You can speed up to see what happens next. If you get bored, you can move on to another story. When you're **reading for information,** you need to read slowly, looking for main ideas and important details. Slow and careful reading is especially important when you're trying to get meaning from consumer, workplace, and public documents. These documents are often not written by professional writers, so they may be difficult to read.

Consumer documents are texts like warranties, contracts, product information, and instructional manuals. Here are some points to keep in mind when you read consumer documents:

1. Try to read the consumer document before you buy the product. Then you can ask the clerk to explain anything you don't understand.
2. Read all of the pages in whatever language comes most easily to you. (Many documents are printed in two or three languages.) You will often find important information where you least expect it, such as at the very end of the document.
3. Read the fine print; *fine*, here, means "tiny and barely readable." Some fine-print statements in documents are required by law. They are designed to protect you, the consumer, not the company that makes the product, so the company may not be interested in emphasizing these points.
4. Don't expect the document to be interesting or easy to read. If you don't understand a statement and you can't ask someone at the store that sold you the product, send an e-mail to the company that made it. It's OK to complain to the company if you find their consumer document confusing.
5. Before you sign anything, read everything on the page and be sure you understand what you're agreeing to. Ask to take the document home, and have your parent or guardian read it. If you are not of legal age in your state, an adult may be responsible for whatever you've signed. Make a copy of any document that you've put your signature to—and keep it in a place where you can find it.

Workplace documents include items like job applications, memos, instructional manuals, and employee handbooks. In addition to the points about reading consumer documents, you might want to keep these points in mind:

1. Take all the time you need to read and understand the document. Don't let anyone rush you or tell you that a document is not important, that it's just a formality.

2. Read instructions carefully, even if they're just posted on the side of a device you're supposed to operate. Read all of the directions before you start. Ask questions if you're not sure how to proceed. Don't try anything out before you know what will happen next.
3. An employee handbook contains the "rules of the game" at a particular business. It tells you about holidays, work hours, break times, and vacations, as well as other important company policies. Read an employee handbook from cover to cover. Pay special attention to information about health benefits, probationary periods, and policies on sexual harassment.

Public documents are texts put out by public agencies and not-for-profit groups such as community-action organizations and church groups. They might inform readers about matters like health concerns, schedules, and records. As you get older, this type of document will become increasingly important to you. Practice reading public documents now, and talk about your understanding of them with your family.

Technical directions are instructions for assembling, installing, or operating mechanical or electronic devices or machines. As with workplace instructions, read technical directions very carefully before you try to carry out the task described.

Question Sheet for Informational Texts

1. What is the topic? ____________
2. Do I understand what I'm reading? ________
3. What parts should I re-read? ____________

   ____
4. What are the main ideas and details?

   Main idea: ________ Main idea: ________

   Details: ________ Details: ________

   Main idea: ________ Main idea: ________

   Details: ________ Details: ________
5. Summary of what I learned:

   ____

   ____

See pages 598–599.

JUDGMENT When you make **judgments,** you form opinions. As you read a text or watch TV, you're constantly making judgments about what you read and see. When you express your opinions in writing, it's important to support your judgments with evidence. If you're writing about a story's plot or characters, you should support your judgments with references to the text, to other works, or to your own experiences. Before you make judgments about a TV show or a movie, here are some points to keep in mind:

1. Identify the purpose of the program or film. You need to know the writer's goal before you say to what extent the goal was reached. If the writer's purpose was humor, you should judge it for its humor, not for the credibility of its characters and plot.
2. Think about the beliefs and assumptions that the work represents. For example, is violence considered funny? tragic? ordinary? Does the program attack or ignore stereotypes?
3. Evaluate the information presented, especially in a nonfiction TV program. What are the program's sources? How reliable are they? What biases or prejudices do you notice? Be sure to distinguish between provable facts and someone's opinions.
4. Make your own judgment. After you've observed the work critically, draw your own conclusions and support them with references to the work itself, to other works of the same type and purpose, and to your personal knowledge.

See pages 155, 193.

See also *Fallacious Reasoning, Opinion, Purposes of Texts.*

KWL CHART Before you start reading a text, it's a good idea to review what you already know about the subject. As you think about the subject, you'll come up with questions that the text may answer. Making a **KWL chart** can help you focus on a text. The following chart is based on the text from *Harriet Tubman: Conductor on the Underground Railroad* (page 499):

- In the **K** column, jot down what you already know about Harriet Tubman.
- In the **W** column, write any questions you have that the text might answer. Glancing through the text, looking at the pictures, if any, and reading subtitles and captions will help you come up with questions.
- As you read, note in the **L** column what you learn that supplements, answers, or contradicts what you wrote in the other two columns.

K	W	L
What I Know	What I Want to Know	What I Learned
She was African American.	What underground railroad?	

LOGIC is correct reasoning. A **logical text** supports statements with reasons and evidence. A text is illogical when it does not provide reasons backed by evidence (facts and examples). Notice how each sentence in the following text, from "Blasting Through Bedrock: The Central Pacific Railroad Workers" (page 970), gives evidence that supports the sentence before it:

> In the winter of 1866–1867, blizzards gripped the Sierra Nevada. Dwellings were buried in blowing, shifting, drifting, driving snow. Men who were building the western portion of the country's first transcontinental railroad had to tunnel from their camp to the mountainside, where they spent long, cold days digging out rock so tracks could be laid. The Central Pacific Railroad was building east from California to meet the Union Pacific Railroad, which was working west from Omaha, Nebraska.

See pages 535, 487.
See also *Logical Order*.

LOGICAL ORDER is a method of organization used in informational texts. In **logical order,** details are classified into related groups. Writers who use this order may use the **comparison-and-contrast** pattern to show similarities and differences among various groups. For an example of logical order, see "Apologies for Past Actions Are Still Appropriate Today" (page 570), an article about slavery.

See page 929.
See also *Comparison and Contrast, Structural Patterns.*

MAGAZINE A **magazine** is a publication, usually in paperback, that comes out at regular intervals, such as weekly, monthly, or even annually. There are all kinds of magazines that appeal to general or special interests—from groups that love dogs (the magazine *Bark*) to people who enjoy reading about celebrities (the magazine *People*). A growing number of magazines are written especially for teenagers. Magazines may seek to entertain, to inform, or to persuade readers. Most have certain structural features in common:

- An attractive cover gives you the title, price, and date of the magazine and usually some idea of what's inside. A brightly colored illustration is usually included on the cover to grab your attention.

- The table of contents page appears close to the beginning of the magazine. You may also find a list of contributors and letters to the editor in the opening pages.
- Most magazines contain photographs and other kinds of illustrations. Many include cartoons. Graphic features such as color and headings and subheadings in different sizes and fonts (printing styles), along with charts and maps, organize the text visually and often highlight information. You'll often find stories and articles printed in columns, but each page is designed for maximum appeal to the reader. Sidebars, short articles set off within the article, develop a topic related in some way to the main story.
- Many magazines are supported financially not by the price of the publication but by advertising revenues. Advertisers choose to sell their products in magazines that appeal to the kind of buyer they are looking for. Some readers think the splashy ads in some magazines are almost as entertaining as the magazine's features; whereas, others find that the ads interfere with the magazine's contents.

See page 117.
See also *Purposes of Texts*.

MAIN IDEA The **main idea** of a nonfiction text is the writer's most important point, opinion, or message. The main idea may be stated directly, or it may be only suggested or implied. If the idea is not stated directly, it's up to you to look at the details and decide on the idea they all seem to support. Try to restate the writer's main idea in your own words.

See pages 486, 490, 497.
See also *Note Taking, Outlining, Proposition and Support, Summarizing*.

MAPS Maps show the natural landscape of an area. Shading may be used to show physical features, such as mountains and valleys. Colors are often used to show elevation (height above or below sea level). **Political maps** show political units, such as states and nations. The map of Europe in 1942 on page 836 is a political map. **Special-purpose maps** present information that is related to geography, such as the route that refugees escaping the Nazis took from Lithuania to Japan (page 197).

How to Read a Map

1. **Identify the map's focus.** The map's title and labels tell you its focus—its subject and the geographical area it covers.
2. **Study the legend.** The **legend,** or key, explains the symbols, lines, colors, and shading used in the map.
3. **Check directions and distances.** Maps often include a **compass rose,** a diagram that shows north, south, east, and west. If you're looking at a map that doesn't have one, assume that north is at the top, west is to the left, and so on. Many maps also include a **scale** to help you relate distances on the map to actual distances. One inch on a map may equal one, ten, or fifty miles or more.
4. **Look at the larger context.** The **absolute location** of any place on earth is given by its **latitude** (the number of degrees north or south of the equator) and **longitude** (the number of degrees east or west of the **prime meridian,** or zero degrees longitude). Some maps also include **locator maps,** which show the area depicted in relation to a larger area. Notice the locator map in the upper right corner of the map shown here:

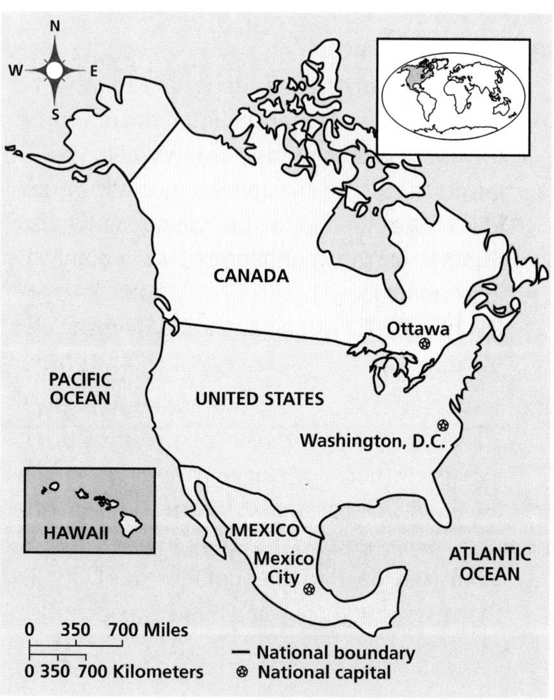

See page 603.

MEANING The most important idea or message of an informational text is called its **underlying meaning.** When you're reading or summarizing a text, to find the underlying meaning, you need to ask yourself the following questions:

- What is the writer's point? What is his or her reason for writing this text?
- What idea do all the critical details add up to?
- What connection can I make between the meaning of this text and the meaning of other texts I have read?
- What connection can I make between this text and my own life? What special meaning does this text have for me? How do I feel about what the writer is saying? Do I agree or disagree? What reasons can I give for my opinion?

See pages 677, 715.

NOTE TAKING Taking notes is a good way to remember a writer's major ideas and interesting details. Notes are especially useful when you read an informational text such as a history or science assignment. You can jot down notes in a notebook such as the kind you might use for a reading log. Many students like to use three-by-five-inch note cards, which can be clipped together or filed in a small file box.

Tips for Taking Notes

1. **Your own words.** Notes don't have to be written in complete sentences. Put them in your own words, using phrases that will help you recall the text. When you take notes, it's a good idea to use either of the following techniques:
   - **Summarize** the information by writing only the important ideas.
   - **Paraphrase** by writing all the ideas in your own words.

   Taking notes in either of these ways will help you avoid using another writer's words. Copying information word for word and presenting it as your own is called **plagiarism** (PLAY juh rihz uhm). When you want to copy another writer's words, you need to put quotation marks around the passage you copy and be sure to identify the writer.
2. **Main ideas.** Jot down each main idea at the top of its own page or note card. As you keep reading, add details that relate to that idea page or to the note card.
3. **Write clearly.** Even though no one but you may ever see your notes (unless you become famous), try to write clearly for your own sake. You'll want to read your notes later, and decoding your own mysterious handwriting can take a lot of time. When you finish taking notes for the day, review them to make sure they make sense to you.

See page 491.
See also *Detail, Main Idea.*

OPINION An **opinion** is a belief or an attitude. An opinion cannot be proved to be true or false. The following statement is an opinion:

> Lincoln was the best president the United States has ever had.

People have different opinions about who was the best president.

A **valid opinion** is an opinion that is supported by facts. The following opinion is valid. It is supported by two verifiable facts.

> Lincoln was a great president because he freed the slaves and led our country through the Civil War.

When you read a persuasive text, remember that statements of opinion can't be proved, but they can and should be supported by facts.

See page 491.
See also *Fact.*

ORDER OF IMPORTANCE is a method of organization often used in informational texts. Writers of persuasive texts have to decide whether to give the strongest reason first or to present the weakest reason first and end with the strongest point. News articles always begin with the most important details because they want to grab the readers' attention immediately. The structure of a news article looks like an upside-down triangle, with the least important details at the bottom.

See also *Detail, Structural Patterns*.

ORGANIZATIONAL PATTERNS Writers of informational texts use a pattern of organization that will make their meaning clear. There are several ways writers can organize information. Don't expect a writer to use the same pattern throughout an entire text. Many writers switch from one pattern to another and may even combine patterns. Recognizing how a writer has organized a text— and noticing where and why the pattern changes—will help you understand what you read. Here are some of the organizational patterns you will find:

- **enumeration** (ih noo muh RAY shuhn), also called **list**—citing a list of details: first, second, and so on
- **chronology,** time order, or sequence—putting events or steps in the order in which they occur
- **comparison-contrast**—pointing out and explaining similarities and differences
- **cause and effect**—showing how events happen as a result of other events
- **problem-solution**—explaining how a problem may be solved
- **question-answer**—asking questions, then giving the answers
- **spatial order**—showing how things relate to each other in space

See pages 221, 486, 929.
See also *Cause and Effect, Chronological Order, Comparison and Contrast, Enumeration, Structural Patterns*.

OUTLINING If you've taken notes on a text, you may want to organize your notes into an outline. Outlining puts main ideas and details in a form that you can review quickly. An **informal outline,** sometimes called a working outline, should have at least three main ideas. You put supporting details under each main idea, like this:

Informal Outline

First main idea
  Detail supporting first main idea
  Another detail supporting first main idea
  Third detail supporting first main idea

Second main idea
  [etc.]

A **formal outline** is especially useful if you're writing a research paper. You might start with a working outline and then revise it into a formal one. Your teacher may ask you to submit a formal outline with your completed research paper, so you have to be sure that it has the correct form. When you create a formal outline, you revise it, making changes as you revise your paper.

Formal outlines use Roman numerals (I, II, III), capital letters (A, B, C), and Arabic numerals (1, 2, 3) to show order, relationship, and relative importance of ideas. The headings in a formal outline should have the same grammatical structure, and you must be consistent in your use of either phrases or sentences (you can't move back and forth between them). There are always at least two divisions under each heading or none at all.

Here is the beginning of a formal outline of "The Scientific Method" (page 122):

Formal Outline

I. Basic Steps
  A. State the Problem
    1. Make an observation
    2. Come up with a research question
  B. Gather Information
    1. Search in books and journals

See also *Main Idea*.

PARAPHRASING Paraphrasing is usually used to restate a poem. In a **paraphrase,** you restate every line in your own words. A paraphrase is longer than a summary. In some cases, it may even be longer than the original text! A paraphrase can help you understand a difficult text. Here is a paraphrase of the poem "A word is dead" by Emily Dickinson (page 699):

> In the first three-line stanza, the speaker says that some people claim that a word is "dead," that is, it no longer has meaning or importance, after it is spoken. In the second three-line stanza the speaker states an opposing opinion, that a word only begins to "live" after it is spoken. This means that a word, especially a loving or hateful word, is like a living thing—it can hurt or bring hope or happiness to people.

See pages 370, 377, 677, 746.

PREDICTIONS As you read a story, you may keep guessing about what will happen next. That means you're already using a reading strategy called **making predictions.** To make predictions, look for clues that the writer gives you. Try to connect those clues with other stories you've read and with experiences in your own life. As you continue to read and more information comes in from the writer, you'll change, or adjust, your guesses. Making predictions as you read helps you become involved with the story and its characters and their conflicts.

See pages 259, 297.

PREVIEWING When you **preview** a text, you look over the material to see what lies ahead. **Scan** (look specifically for) chapter titles, headings, subheadings, and terms printed in boldface or italics. Glance at the illustrations and graphics (such as charts, maps, and time lines), and **skim** (read quickly) a paragraph or two to check the vocabulary level and writing style.

See page 602.

PRIOR KNOWLEDGE The knowledge you already have about a topic before you read a text is called your **prior knowledge.** (*Prior* means "before.")

PROPOSITION AND SUPPORT In a **persuasive text,** the writer's main idea, or thesis, is called a **proposition.** It is usually presented as a positive statement of opinion.

> Middle-school students should be required to wear uniforms.
> The sale of junk food should be prohibited in public schools.
> Every kid should get an allowance.

A proposition should be supported by reasons that explain the writer's opinion. Each reason should be supported, in turn, by details and evidence. The evidence may include **facts** and **figures (statistics), examples, anecdotes** (especially those that tell about personal experiences), and statements or direct **quotations by experts** on the subject.

See page 565.

PUBLIC DOCUMENTS See *Informational Texts.*

PURPOSES OF TEXTS Texts are written for different purposes. The writer may want to

- provide information
- influence the way you think or act
- express personal feelings
- entertain you

Readers also have different purposes: You read to get information, to enjoy a good story, to share an experience. Being aware of why you are reading helps you to **establish a purpose for reading,** which helps you to decide how you will read the text. If you are reading a science fiction novel just for fun, you might read quickly and eagerly to find out what happens next. If you decide to read that same novel for a book report, however, you would read more slowly and carefully.

You might even re-read some parts of the book to decide how you will evaluate it. Sometimes you read to find an answer to a particular question, such as "Where do penguins live?" To find the answer, you may need to use an index or table of contents first and then skim a text (read quickly) to locate the information you want.

See pages 109, 117.
See also *Magazine*.

QUESTIONS One way to monitor your understanding is to ask **questions** as you read. Get in the habit of carrying on a dialogue (in your head or in a reading notebook) with the writer. Make comments, ask questions, and note what puzzles you. Jot down facts that you might want to look up and verify. Experiment with ways of noting questions, such as using sticky notes that you place by paragraphs. If you find yourself confused by a passage, try one of the following strategies:

- Re-read the passage more slowly.
- Read the passage aloud.
- Put the ideas into your own words.
- Look for context clues that might help you figure out the meaning of an unfamiliar word.
- Use a graphic organizer to jot down the text's ideas.

See also *Detail, Fallacious Reasoning*.

RETELLING A reading strategy called **retelling** helps you understand and recall what you read. As you're reading a text, stop often to retell the important events that have happened up to that point. You might want to tell a partner what has happened, or you can jot down notes in a reading notebook or journal. Retelling can be used in reading fiction and in reading historical and scientific texts.

See page 15.
See also *Detail*.

SCANNING When you want to find particular information in a text, you quickly **scan** through it, searching for boldface keywords and phrases and any other details that relate to your topic.

See page 602.
See also *Skimming*.

SCOPE OF TEXT A text is said to have a **broad scope** when it covers many aspects of a topic. When it focuses on one or only a few aspects of a topic, the text is said to have a **narrow** or a **limited scope.**

See pages 221, 948.
See also *Organizational Patterns, Treatment of Text*.

SKIMMING When you want to quickly get the general idea of what a text is about, you **skim** through it, looking at the titles, heads, subheads, and the first lines of paragraphs.

See page 602.
See also *Scanning*.

SOMEBODY WANTED BUT SO Stories are built on conflict. A good way to summarize a story's plot is to reduce it to the following formula:

Somebody (name the main character):

____

Wanted (tell what the main character wants):

____

But (tell what complications develop that get between the main character and what he or she wants):

____

So (tell how it all comes out in the end):

____

____

See page 15.

SPATIAL ORDER Spatial (SPAY shuhl) order is one of the patterns writers use to organize their texts. **Spatial order** shows where things are located. (The word *spatial* is related to the word *space.* Spatial order shows where things are located in space.) Spatial order is often used in descriptive writing. Here is an example from "Camp Harmony" (page 515):

> Our home was one room, about eighteen by twenty feet, the size of a living room. There was one small window in the wall opposite the one door. It was bare except for a small, tinny wood-burning stove crouching in the center.

See also Organizational Patterns.

STATISTICS See *Proposition and Support.*

See page 565.

STORY MAP A graphic organizer like the following one can help you map the plot structure of a story:

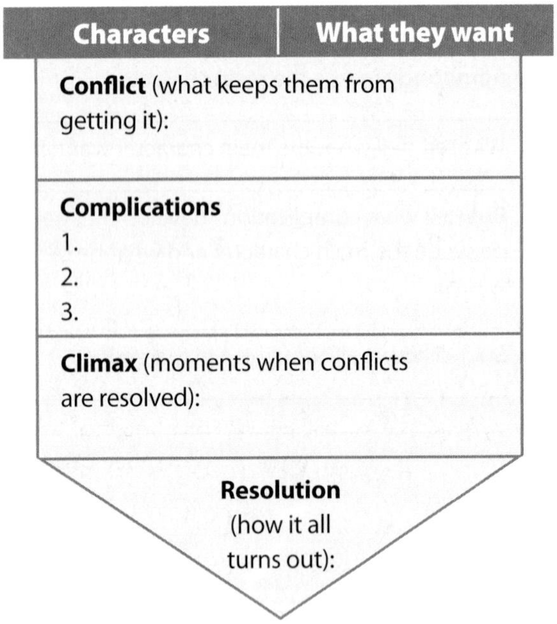

Characters	What they want
Conflict (what keeps them from getting it):	
Complications 1. 2. 3.	
Climax (moments when conflicts are resolved):	
Resolution (how it all turns out):	

See page 4.

STRUCTURAL PATTERNS All texts have a structure. Without structure a piece of writing would fall apart—just as a house would fall down if its basic structure were faulty. The structure that holds a story together is called its **plot.** The structures that support the details in informative texts can be **chronology, order of importance, comparison and contrast,** or **cause and effect.**

Structural features, such as headings, graphics, captions, and boldface type, may be common to many types of texts. Other features may apply only to specific types of text. For example, only newspaper articles such as "Hawaiian Teen Named Top Young Scientist" (page 118) include datelines.

See pages 4, 109, 117, 121, 486, 525, 801.

See also *Cause and Effect, Chronological Order, Comparison and Contrast, Order of Importance, Organizational Patterns, Plot.*

SUMMARIZING When you **summarize**, you mention and explain only the most important ideas of a work. Because a summary is much shorter than the original text, you have to decide which ideas to include and which ones to leave out. To summarize an informational text, start by naming the title, the author, and the subject. Then, go on to state the main ideas and the **key details**, those that support the main idea or underlying meaning. Follow the same order that the writer used. If you quote any of the writer's words, be sure to put quotation marks around them.

If you are summarizing a short story, you cite the story's title and author and the main events of the plot. You should mention the story's main characters, the conflict, and, of course, the resolution of the conflict.

See pages 8, 15, 703.

See also *Main Idea.*

SUPPORT See *Proposition and Support.*

TECHNICAL DIRECTIONS See *Informational Texts.*

TIME LINE Use a **time line** to find out when events happened.

A time line may show a vast span of time, such as thousands or millions of years.

Events on a time line are arranged in chronological order, with long-ago events at one end and more recent events at the other. The approximate date (year or century) of each event appears above, below, or beside the line.

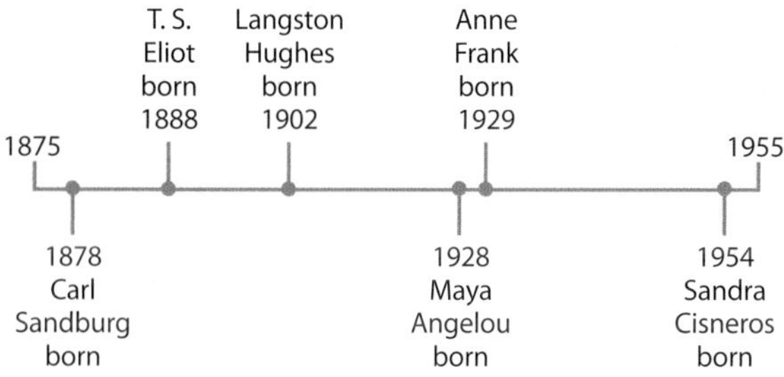

TRANSITIONAL WORDS See *Detail.*

TREATMENT OF TEXT The treatment of a text is the way it is presented. The treatment may be objective, that is, serious, fair, and unbiased, or it may be subjective, that is, from the writer's personal point of view.

See page 221.
See also *Organizational Patterns, Scope of Text.*

UNITY When a text has unity, all its details support the main idea or topic. It also has coherence and internal consistency, that is, all the parts are connected and agree with one another.

See pages 487, 513.
See also *Coherence, Nonfiction.*

VISUALIZING When you visualize a text, you picture it in your own mind. You may visualize a character's appearance, the setting, the action, or any other details described in the text.

See pages 8, 804, 813.

WORKPLACE DOCUMENTS See *Informational Texts.*

Spelling Handbook

Commonly Misspelled Words

No matter how many spelling rules you learn, you will find that it is helpful to learn to spell certain common words from memory. The fifty "demons" in the first list are words that you should be able to spell without any hesitation, even though they all contain spelling challenges. Study them in groups of five until you are sure you know them.

The second, longer list contains words that you should learn if you do not already know them. They are grouped by tens so that you study them ten at a time. In studying each list, pay particular attention to the underlined letters. These letters are generally the ones that pose problems for students.

For more on spelling, see spelling rules in the Language Handbook.

Fifty Spelling Demons				
ache	cough	guess	ready	though
again	could	half	said	through
always	country	hour	says	tired
answer	doctor	instead	seems	tonight
blue	does	knew	shoes	trouble
built	don't	know	since	wear
busy	early	laid	straight	where
buy	easy	minute	sugar	women
can't	every	often	sure	won't
color	friend	once	tear	write

Two Hundred Spelling Words

absence
absolutely
acceptance
accommodate
accumulate
achieve
acquire
across
advertisement
against

aisles
among
announce
anxiety
apology
apparent
appreciation
arctic
arguing
argument

arithmetic
assistance
associate
attacked
attendance
attitude
attorney
basis
beginning
believe

benefit
bicycle
bough
bouquet
brief
brilliant
bureau
business
candidate
career

careless
carrying
ceased
ceiling
choice
college
committee
completely
conceive
conscience

conscious
control
correspondence
courteous
criticize
curiosity
decision
definite
describe
description

desirable
divide
divine
efficiency
eighth
eliminate
embarrass
equipment
especially
exactly

excellent
execute
existence
experience
experiment
explanation
extremely
familiar
favorite
February

field
fierce
finally
foliage
foreign
fortunately
forty
fourth
genius
genuine

government
governor
grammar
guarantee
height
heir
heroes
humorous
hungrily
icicles

imaginary
immediately
independent
inoculate
intelligence
interest
interpret
judgment
knowledge
laboratory

leisure
license
liquor
loneliness
luxury
magazine
marriage
mathematics
meant
medicine

mischief
muscle
museum
necessary
nervous
nineteen
ninety
occasion
occur
occurrence

opinion
opportunity
originally
particularly
patience
perceive
performance
permanent
personal
physical

picnic
possess
preferred
privilege
probably
professor
pursue
realize
receive
recommend

referred
religion
repetition
rhythm
safety
satisfy
scene
schedule
seize
sense

separate
shining
similar
society
speech
strength
studying
stupefy
succeed
success

surprise
suspicion
sympathy
technique
temperament
temporary
theory
thorough
tongue
tragedy

transferred
treasury
tries
university
unnecessary
unusually
useful
using
vacuum
vague

various
veil
vicinity
villain
violence
warrior
wholly
whose
writing
yield

Communications Handbook

Research Strategies

Using a Media Center or Library

To find a book, audiotape, film, or video in a library, start by looking in the **catalog.** Most libraries use an **online,** or computer, **catalog.**

Online catalogs vary from library to library. With some you begin searching for resources by **title, author,** or **subject.** With others you simply enter **keywords** for the subject you're researching. With either system, you enter information into the computer and a new screen will show you a list of materials or subject headings relating to your request. When you find an item you want, write down the title, author, and **call number,** the code of numbers and letters that shows you where to find the item on the library's shelves.

Some libraries still use card catalogs. A **card catalog** is a collection of index cards arranged in alphabetical order by title and author. Nonfiction is also cataloged by subject.

ELECTRONIC DATABASES

Electronic databases are collections of information you can access by computer. You can use these databases to find such resources as encyclopedias, almanacs, and museum art collections.

There are two kinds of electronic databases: **Online databases** are found on the Web. **Portable databases** are available on CD-ROM.

A **CD-ROM** (compact disc–read only memory) is played on a computer equipped with a CD-ROM player. If you were to look up *Maya Angelou* on a CD-ROM guide to literature, for example, you could see and hear her reading passages from her books and also read critical analyses of her work.

PERIODICALS

Most libraries have a collection of magazines and newspapers. To find up-to-date magazine or newspaper articles on a topic, use a computerized index, such as *InfoTrac* or *EBSCO.* Some of these indices provide a summary of each article. Others provide the entire text, which you can read on-screen or print. The *Readers' Guide to Periodical Literature* is a print index of articles that have appeared in hundreds of magazines.

The Reference Section

Every library has materials you can use only in the library. Some examples are listed below. (Some reference works are available in both print and electronic form.)

Encyclopedias

Collier's Encyclopedia
The World Book Encyclopedia

General Biographical References

Current Biography Yearbook
The International Who's Who
Webster's New Biographical Dictionary

Special Biographical References

American Men & Women of Science
Biographical Dictionary of American Sports
Mexican American Biographies

Atlases

Atlas of World Cultures
National Geographic Atlas of the World

Almanacs

Information Please Almanac
The World Almanac and Book of Facts

Books of Quotations

Bartlett's Familiar Quotations

Books of Synonyms

Roget's International Thesaurus
Webster's New Dictionary of Synonyms

Using the Internet

The **Internet** is a huge network of computers. Libraries, news services, government agencies, researchers, and organizations communicate and share information on the Net. The Net also lets you chat online with students around the world. For help in using the Internet to do research or to communicate with someone by computer, explore the options that follow.

THE WORLD WIDE WEB

The easiest way to do research on the Internet is on the World Wide Web. On the Web, information is stored in colorful, easy-to-access files called **Web pages.** Web pages usually have text, graphics, photographs, sound, and even video clips.

■ **Using a Web Browser.** You look at Web pages with a **Web browser,** a program for accessing information on the Web. Every page on the Web has its own address, called a **URL,** or Uniform Resource Locator. If you know the address of a Web page you want to go to, just enter it in the location field on your browser.

Hundreds of millions of Web pages are connected by **hyperlinks,** which let you jump from one page to another. These links usually appear as underlined or colored words or images, or both, on your computer screen. With hundreds of millions of linked Web pages, how can you find the information you want?

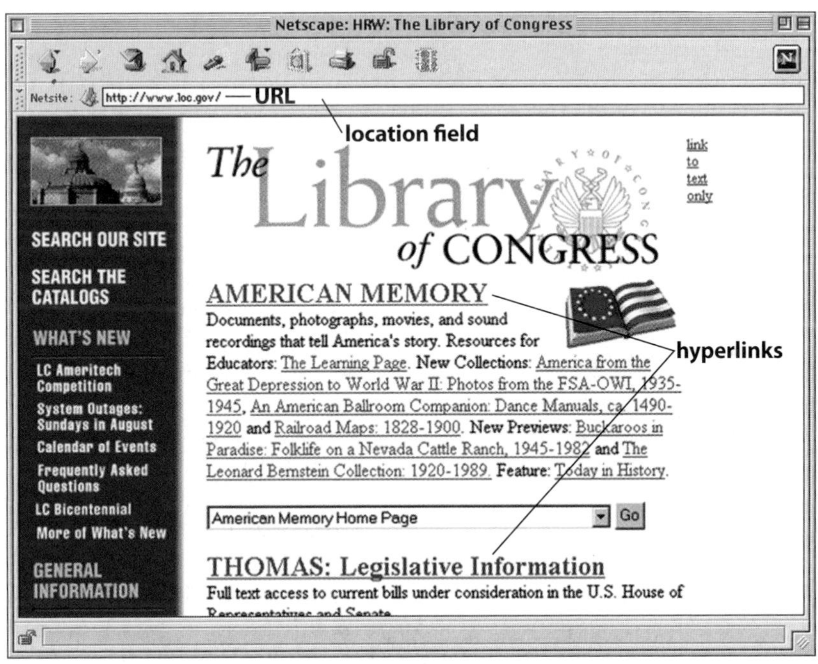

COMMON TOP-LEVEL DOMAINS AND WHAT THEY STAND FOR	
.edu	Educational institution. Site may publish scholarly work or the work of elementary or high school students.
.gov	Government body. Information should be reliable.
.org	Usually a nonprofit organization. If the organization promotes culture (as a museum does), information is generally reliable; if it advocates a cause, information may be biased.
.com	Commercial enterprise. Information should be evaluated carefully.
.net	Organization offering Internet services.

COMMON SEARCH OPERATORS AND WHAT THEY DO	
AND	Demands that both terms appear on the page; narrows search
+	Demands that both terms appear on the page; narrows search
OR	Yields pages that contain either term; widens search
NOT	Excludes a word from consideration; narrows search
–	Excludes a word from consideration; narrows search
NEAR	Demands that two words be close together; narrows search
ADJ	Demands that two words be close together; narrows search
" "	Demands an exact phrase; narrows search

- **Using a Web Directory.** If you're just beginning to look for a research topic, click on a **Web directory,** a list of topics and subtopics created by experts to help users find Web sites. Think of the directory as a giant index. Start by choosing a broad category, such as Literature. Then, work your way down through the subtopics, perhaps from Poetry to Poets. Under Poets, choose a Web page that looks interesting, perhaps one on Robert Frost.
- **Using a Search Engine.** If you already have a topic and need information about it, try using a **search engine,** a software tool that finds information on the Web. To use a search engine, just go to an online search form and enter a **search term,** or keyword. The search engine will return a list of Web pages containing your search term. The list will also show you the first few lines of each page. A search term such as *Frost* may produce thousands of results, or **hits,** including weather data on frost. If you're doing a search on the poet Robert Frost, most of these thousands of hits will be of no use. To find useful material, you have to narrow your search.
- **Refining a Keyword Search.** To focus your research, use **search operators,** such as the words AND or NOT, to create a string of keywords. If you're looking for material on Robert Frost and his life in Vermont, for example, you might enter the following search term:

  Frost AND Vermont NOT weather

  The more focused search term yields pages that contain both *Frost* and *Vermont* and nothing about weather. The chart on the left explains how several search operators work.

Evaluating Web Sources

Since anyone—you, for example—can publish a Web page, it's important to evaluate your sources. Use these criteria to evaluate a source:

AUTHORITY

Who is the author? What is his or her knowledge or experience? Trust respected sources, such as the Smithsonian Institution, not a person's newsletter or home page.

ACCURACY

How trustworthy is the information? Does the author give his or her sources? Check information from one site against information from at least two other sites or print sources.

OBJECTIVITY

What is the author's **perspective,** or point of view? Find out whether the information provider has a bias or a hidden purpose.

CURRENCY

Is the information up-to-date? For a print source, check the copyright date. For a Web source, look for the date on which the page was created or revised. (This date appears at the bottom of the site's home page.)

COVERAGE

How well does the source cover the topic? Could you find better information in a book? Compare the source with several others.

Listing Sources and Taking Notes

When you write a research paper, you must **document,** or identify, your sources so that readers will know where you found your material. You must avoid **plagiarism,** or presenting another writer's words or ideas as if they were your own.

LISTING SOURCES

List each source, and give it a number. (You'll use these source numbers later, when you take notes.) Here's where to find the publication information (such as the name of the publisher and the copyright date) you'll need for different types of sources:

- **Print sources.** Look at the title and copyright pages of the book or periodical.
- **Online sources.** Look at the beginning or end of the document or in a separate electronic file. For a Web page, look for a link containing the word *About.*
- **Portable electronic databases.** Look at the start-up screen, the packaging, or the disc itself.

There are several ways to list sources. The chart on page 1016 shows the style created by the Modern Language Association.

Sample Source Card

Reuben, Paul P. "Chapter 4: Early Nineteenth Century—Emily Dickinson." 3
PAL: Perspectives in American Literature—A Research and Reference Guide.
<http://www.csustan.edu/english/reuben/pal/chap4/dickinson.html>.

TAKING NOTES

Here are some tips for taking notes:

- Put notes from different sources on separate index cards or sheets of paper or in separate computer files.
- At the top of each card, sheet of paper, or file, write a label that briefly gives the subject of the note.
- At the bottom, write the numbers of the pages on which you found the information.
- Use short phrases, and make lists of details and ideas. You don't have to write full sentences.
- Use your own words unless you find material you want to quote. If you quote an author's exact words, put quotation marks around them.

The sample note card below shows how to take notes.

Sample Note Card

Dickinson's definition of poetry 3
In letter to Thomas W. Higginson, editor Atlantic Monthly: "If I read a book and it makes my whole body so cold no fire can ever warm me, I know that is poetry."
online source

PREPARING A LIST OF SOURCES

Use your source cards to make a **works cited** list at the end of your report. List your sources in alphabetical order, following the MLA guidelines for citing sources (see the chart below). Note the sample that follows.

Works Cited

"Emily Dickinson." The Academy of American Poets. 2003. <http://www.poets.org/poets/poets.cfm?prmID=156>.

Johnson, Thomas H., ed. Complete Poems of Emily Dickinson. Boston: Little, Brown, 1960.

Knapp, Bettina Liebowitz. Emily Dickinson. New York: Continuum, 1989.

The chart below shows citations of print, audiovisual, and electronic sources:

MLA GUIDELINES FOR CITING SOURCES	
Books	Give the author, title, city of publication, publisher, and copyright year. Knapp, Bettina Liebowitz. Emily Dickinson. New York: Continuum, 1989.
Magazine and newspaper articles	Give the author, title of article, name of the magazine or newspaper, date, and page numbers. Markiewicz, B. S. "Poets and Friends." American History Nov./Dec. 1995: 42-47.
Encyclopedia articles	Give the author (if named), title of the article, name of the encyclopedia, and edition (year). "Dickinson, Emily." Collier's Encyclopedia. 1996 ed.
Interviews	Give the expert's name, the words *Personal interview* or *Telephone interview,* and the date. Randy Souther. Telephone interview. 2 Jan. 2004.
Films, videotapes, and audiotapes	Give the title, producer or director, medium, distributor, and year of release. Emily Dickinson. Directed by Veronica Young. Annenberg/CPB project, 1988.
CD-ROMs and DVDs	In many cases, not all the information is available. Fill in what you can. Give the author, title of document or article; database title; publication medium (use the term *CD-ROM* or *DVD*); city of publication; publisher; date. "Dickinson, Emily." Microsoft Encarta 2003 Encyclopedia Deluxe Edition. CD-ROM. Redmond, WA: Microsoft Corporation, 1999–2003.
Online Sources	In many cases, not all the information is available. Fill in what you can. Give the author, title of document or article; title of complete work or database; name of editor; publication date or date last revised; name of sponsoring organization; date you accessed the site; the full URL in angle brackets. "Emily Dickinson." The Academy of American Poets. 2003. <http://www.poets.org/poets.cfm?prmID=156>.

Proofreaders' Marks		
Symbol	**Example**	**Meaning**
≡	New mexico (≡ under m)	Capitalize lowercase letter.
/	next Spring (/ through S)	Lowercase capital letter.
∧	a book ∧ quotations (of inserted)	Insert.
℘	a good ~~good~~ idea	Delete.
⁀ ‿	a grape fruit tree	Close up space.
∽	does'nt	Change order (of letters or words).
¶	¶ "Who's there?" she asked.	Begin a new paragraph.
⊙	Please don't forget⊙	Add a period.
∧,	Maya ∧, did you call me?	Add a comma.
∧:	Dear Mrs. Mills ∧:	Add a colon.
∧;	Columbus, Ohio ∧; Dallas, Texas	Add a semicolon
∨" ∨"	∨" Are you OK? ∨" he asked.	Add quotation marks.

Media Handbook

Evaluating Persuasive Images in the Media

Persuasive Images

When you look at a photograph of yourself, what do you see? You see yourself, right? Actually, the person in the picture is not the *real* you, but a representation of you. In fact, all media images are representations of reality that can shape people's ideas about the world. That is why you need to be a critical viewer of media images.

To view images critically, remember that an image is one person's version of reality. An image reflects the point of view of the person who created it. When you see an image, consider other points of view people might have about the image's subject. Image makers, from illustrators to photographers to graphic designers, make conscious choices about what an image will show and how it will show it. People who create all sorts of media images can use *content, color, light and shadow,* and *point of view* to make their images more persuasive.

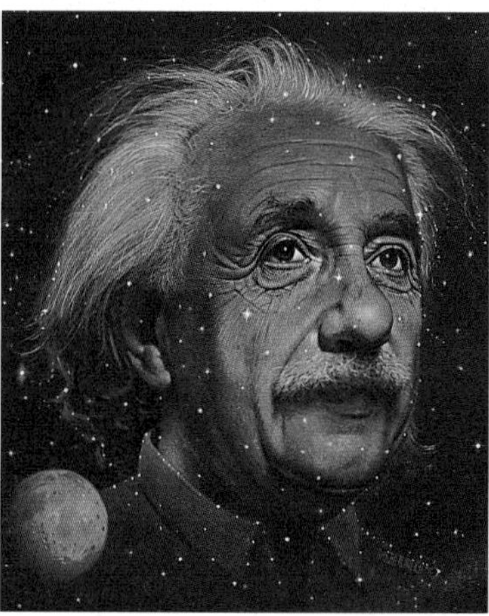

CONTENT The **content** of an image is what it shows—everything included in the image. The way an image maker chooses to portray a subject is the most important persuasive choice he or she will make.

Look, for example, at the two images of the scientist Albert Einstein shown to the right. The image on the top is a caricature of Einstein that presents him as a comical figure. The oil painting below, on the other hand, portrays Einstein as wise, not humorous. The two images reflect the different purposes of the artists who created them. If you had seen only one of these portraits, how would you feel about Einstein? What opinion would you have of this scientist and of his life's work?

The other items in an image are also carefully chosen. An image maker may choose to include **persuasive symbols,** such as a bald eagle or an American flag. He or she may also add to a persuasive message by choosing to leave out certain things. For example, although President Franklin Roosevelt used a wheelchair, many portraits depict him from the waist up in order to depict the president as healthy.

COLOR, LIGHT, AND SHADOW Image makers use **color** to create interest or to establish a mood. To create interest, an illustrator may use color to highlight the most important part of the image—by using a brighter color in that part of the image, for example. A photographer may use a computer, colored pencils, or paints to color one part of a black-and-white photograph to make it stand out.

Image makers can choose to create areas of **light** and **shadow** in their work. An image maker may carefully place shadows to make a subject look frightening or dramatic or romantic. Using plenty of even light with few or no shadows can make the subject look real and approachable. Sometimes photographers simply work with the light they have.

POINT OF VIEW, OR ANGLE The **angle** at which you see the subject of an image can affect your impression of the subject. For example, seeing a subject straight on may create a feeling of connection, but seeing it from above or below can change your impression.

Look at the examples on the right. In the picture on the top, the photographer stood on a ladder and shot the picture looking down at the boy. Do you see how the boy looks small and vulnerable? Now, look at the picture below, taken from a low angle looking up at the same boy. From this angle the boy looks big and powerful, even a little intimidating.

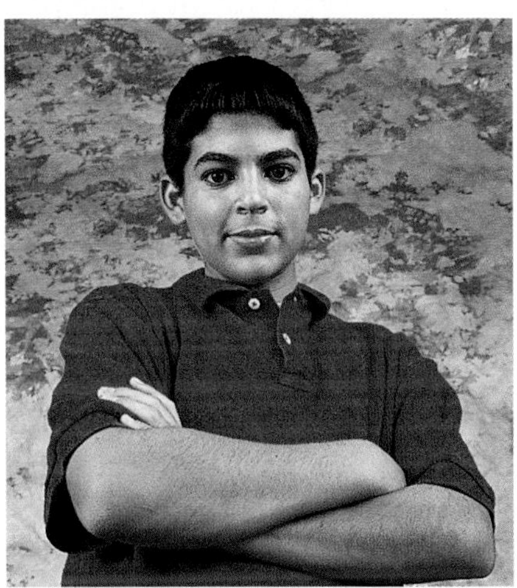

Medium

A **medium** is the means by which an image is created. All image makers use the techniques described above, but still media, such as illustration and photography, have their own unique characteristics and techniques. (The plural of *medium* is **media,** a term often applied to television, radio, newspapers, and the Internet.)

ILLUSTRATION An **illustration** is a picture created to explain something or to share a point of view. Drawings, cartoons, paintings, and computer-generated art are examples of illustrations. Each type of illustration lends itself to a different type of persuasive message.

PHOTOGRAPHY Photographs are powerful partners to the written and spoken word. In a newspaper, for instance, you might read about an erupting volcano. Only when you see the picture that accompanies the article would you fully understand the massive destruction the volcano caused. Because photographs are so powerful and easy to reproduce, they are a popular medium.

The persuasive power of photographs is found in our belief that "photographs do not lie"—that they show reality. However, like illustrations, photographs only *resemble* an actual person, place, thing, or event. You should be aware that people can change or influence the information a photograph provides. As a photograph is being taken, a photographer can, under the right circumstances, use camera angle or lighting to alter the reality of a situation to suit his or her persuasive purposes. Even after developing a photo, a photographer can **crop,** or cut out, an unwanted part of a scene to make the image more persuasive. New computer techniques make it easy to alter photographs in many ways, so today photographs may, indeed, lie.

Evaluating Media Images

To interpret and evaluate a media image, either still or moving, consider the following questions.

QUESTIONS FOR EVALUATING MEDIA IMAGES	
General Questions	• Who created the image? Do I know of a bias this source has—either positive or negative feelings toward the subject? Does this bias affect the message? • For what purpose was this image created?
Questions About Content	• What impression do I get from the image about its subject? Why? • How is this version of reality similar to or different from what I know from my own experience? • Does the image include any persuasive symbols? • What may have been left out of the image?
Questions About Color	• Is the image black-and-white, color, or both? What mood do the color choices create? • What parts of the image stand out because of color? Why might these parts be important?
Questions About Light and Shadow	• Is the light in the image even, or are there shadows? • What mood do the light and shadows create? Do shadows make the subject seem frightening or dramatic? What message does this send?
Questions About Point of View	• At what angle do you see the subject? a normal, direct angle? an angle above the subject? a low angle? • What impression of the subject does the angle give you? Does the subject seem powerful? vulnerable?
Questions About Medium	• What medium carries the image? • How do the characteristics of the medium add to the image's persuasive power?

Creating Graphics for Technical Documents

No matter how clear the text of your technical document is, visuals such as flowcharts and diagrams can make an explanation even clearer to your readers. Providing such graphics helps readers create sharper mental pictures of the information you present.

Effective Graphics

An effective graphic in a technical document should be useful, not merely decorative. Useful graphics

- **add** to the information in the document or **clarify** something difficult to explain in words
- **focus** on a particularly important or potentially confusing part of an object or a process
- are **simple, clear,** and **uncluttered**

Features and Types of Graphics

For clarity, graphics need *titles* and often require *captions* and *labels*.

- **Titles** tell in just a few words exactly what the graphic shows.
- **Captions** explain the graphic using sentences placed near it.
- **Labels** briefly identify different parts of the graphic.

Study the use of titles, captions, and labels in the following graphics.

Three types of graphics are often used in technical documents to summarize information, to make complex information clearer, or to emphasize important points.

- **Illustrations,** such as digital photographs and computer drawings, show readers objects or events that are difficult to understand. For example, the computer-generated drawing below shows the pattern of a quilt.

Water Wheel Variation 2

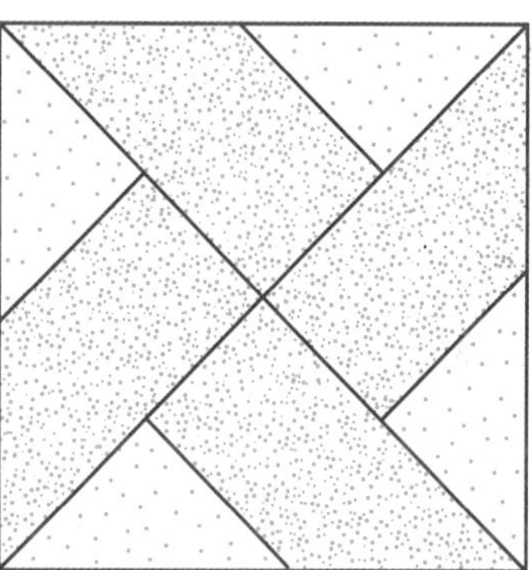

- **Diagrams** use symbols, such as arrows, to illustrate how to do something or how something works. The following diagram shows how a canal lock works.

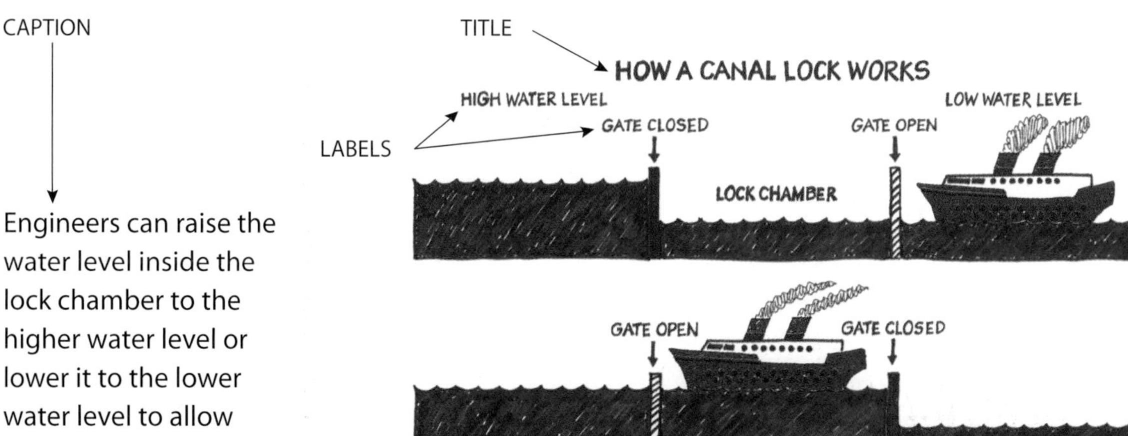

Engineers can raise the water level inside the lock chamber to the higher water level or lower it to the lower water level to allow ships to pass.

- **Charts and graphs** offer a visual way to arrange ideas, showing trends or relationships. **Flowcharts,** such as the one below, show an order of events and can be particularly helpful in summarizing the information in a technical document.

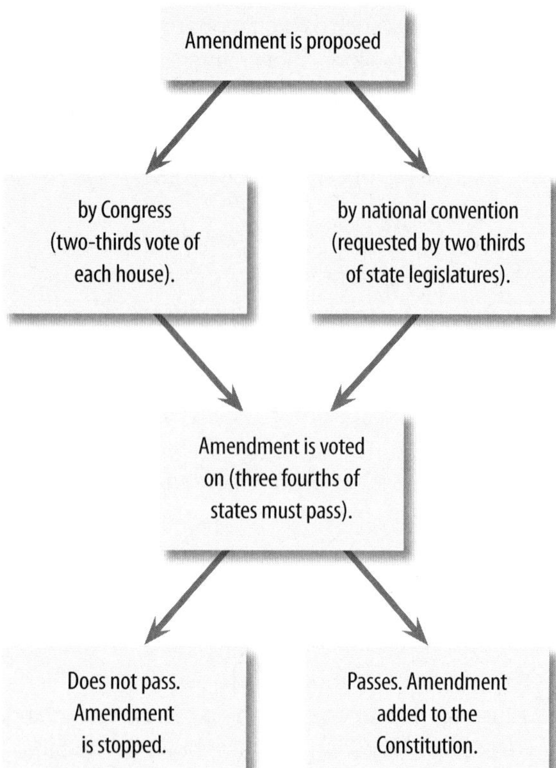
Amendment is proposed
by Congress (two-thirds vote of each house).
by national convention (requested by two thirds of state legislatures).
Amendment is voted on (three fourths of states must pass).
Does not pass. Amendment is stopped.
Passes. Amendment added to the Constitution.

Planning and Creating Graphics

Use the following steps to create computer-generated graphics for your technical document. To familiarize yourself with the variety of programs that are available, consult your computer lab instructor or browse the Internet for information.

1. **Decide what part of your report could be made clearer with the help of a graphic.** This decision is often made during the prewriting stage. A peer editor—someone who is unfamiliar with your topic—could also offer suggestions about where a graphic might be helpful.
2. **Select the best way to illustrate the part you have chosen.** Explore the software that is available to you. Options include scanning existing graphics, importing copyright-free digital photographs, or creating original tables, charts, graphs, and drawings. For example, you might create a table by entering information into a spreadsheet, using a word-processing program to paste certain shapes into a document, or using a drawing program to create a line drawing.
3. **By hand, make a rough sketch of your ideas to make sure the form you have chosen will work.** You may have to make several tries before you figure out the sizes and shapes of items that will work best in your graphic.
4. **Use a software tool to create the graphic.** Make your graphics bold and clear, not cluttered with unnecessary information or decorations. Use color only if it will make your message clearer. If you are working with an unfamiliar program, check any available self-tutoring functions or Help menus.
5. **Add an identifying title, labels, and captions to your graphic where needed.** Also, check the text of your document to be sure you have discussed the graphic. Remember to indicate the source of any information you have borrowed, even if you have created an original graphic using the information.

Language Handbook

1. Parts of Speech

Part of Speech	Definition	Examples
NOUN	**1a.** A *noun* is a word used to name a person, a place, a thing, or an idea.	PERSONS Maya Angelou, children, man PLACES desert, outer space, New York THINGS money, wind, Brooklyn Bridge IDEA courage, love, freedom, equality
Compound Noun	A ***compound noun*** is two or more words used together as a single noun. A compound noun may be written as one word, as separate words, or as a hyphenated word.	ONE WORD seafood, footsteps, Iceland SEPARATE WORDS compact disc, John F. Kennedy HYPHENATED WORD great-grandparents, fourteen-year-old
Collective Noun	A ***collective noun*** is a word that names a group.	faculty, family, herd, team, crew
Common Noun and Proper Noun	A ***common noun*** is a general name for a person, a place, a thing, or an idea. A ***proper noun*** names a particular person, place, thing, or idea. Proper nouns always begin with a capital letter. Common nouns begin with a capital letter in titles and when they begin sentences.	**COMMON** — **PROPER** poem — "Paul Revere's Ride" nation — Mexico athlete — Venus Williams river — Rio Grande
PRONOUN	**1b.** A *pronoun* is a word used in place of one or more nouns or pronouns.	After Bill fed the dogs, Bill let the dogs out. After Bill fed the dogs, **he** let **them** out.
	The word that a pronoun stands for is called its ***antecedent.*** Sometimes the antecedent is not stated.	STATED Jan opened the **book** and began reading **it.** UNSTATED **Who** wrote the book?

Part of Speech	Definition	Examples
Personal Pronouns	A ***personal pronoun*** refers to the one speaking (*first person*), the one spoken to (*second person*), or the one spoken about (*third person*).	**SINGULAR** / **PLURAL** **First Person** I, me, my, mine / we, us, our, ours **Second Person** you, your, yours / you, your, yours **Third Person** he, him, his, she, her, hers, it, its / they, them, their, theirs **He** and **his** friends caught several frogs and put **them** in a bag.
	The possessive pronouns *my, your, his, her, its, our,* and *their* are sometimes called *possessive adjectives.*	
Reflexive and Intensive Pronoun	A ***reflexive pronoun*** refers to the subject and directs the action of the verb back to the subject. An ***intensive pronoun*** emphasizes a noun or another pronoun. Reflexive and intensive pronouns have the same form.	**First Person** myself, ourselves **Second Person** yourself, yourselves **Third Person** himself, herself, itself, themselves REFLEXIVE Alfonso asked **himself** why. INTENSIVE Flo made the cookies **herself**.
	If you are not sure whether a pronoun is reflexive or intensive, read the sentence aloud, omitting the pronoun. If the meaning stays the same, the pronoun is intensive. If it changes, the pronoun is reflexive.	She painted it **herself**. [Intensive: Without *herself*, the meaning stays the same.] They treated **themselves** to a picnic. [Reflexive: Without *themselves*, the sentence doesn't make sense.]
Demonstrative Pronoun	A ***demonstrative pronoun*** (*this, that, these, those*) points out a person, a place, a thing, or an idea.	**This** is Ernie's bike.
Interrogative Pronoun	An ***interrogative pronoun*** (*what, which, who, whom, whose*) introduces a question.	**Who** is the author of "Caroliny Trail"?
Relative Pronoun	A ***relative pronoun*** (*that, what, which, who, whom, whose*) introduces a subordinate clause.	Moe received the gift **that** he had asked for.

Part of Speech	Definition	Examples
Indefinite Pronoun	An ***indefinite pronoun*** refers to a person, a place, or a thing that is not specifically named.	**Common Indefinite Pronouns** all any anyone both each either everybody few many neither no one none one several some something **All** of them wanted to hear the story. The travelers saw **something.**
	Many indefinite pronouns can also serve as adjectives.	INDEFINITE PRONOUN **Both** of the men regretted kidnapping Johnny. ADJECTIVE **Both** men regretted kidnapping Johnny.
ADJECTIVE	**1c. An *adjective* is a word used to modify a noun or a pronoun.**	
	To ***modify*** a word means to describe the word or to make its meaning more definite. An adjective modifies a word by telling ***what kind, which one, how much,*** or ***how many***.	**What Kind?** **tall** woman, **steep** mountain **Which One?** **this** year, **middle** row **How Much?** or **How Many?** **less** time, **many** mistakes
	An adjective may come before or after the word it modifies.	The **old** soldier offered them **three** wishes. The map, although **old,** was **useful** to him.
Articles	The most frequently used adjectives are *a, an,* and *the.* The adjectives *a* and *an* are called ***indefinite articles.*** They indicate that the noun refers to someone or something in general. *A* is used before a word beginning with a consonant sound. *An* is used before a word beginning with a vowel sound.	He gave the clerk **a** nickel and **an** orange.
	The adjective *the* is a ***definite article***. It indicates that the noun refers to someone or something in particular.	Smiley went to **the** swamp to find **the** frog.
Proper Adjective	A ***proper adjective*** is formed from a proper noun and begins with a capital letter.	**Proper Nouns** Africa, Shakespeare **Proper Adjectives** **African** nations, **Shakespearean** drama

Part of Speech	Definition	Examples
Demonstrative Adjective	*This, that, these,* and *those* can be used as adjectives and as pronouns. When they modify a noun or a pronoun, they are called ***demonstrative adjectives.*** When used alone, they are called ***demonstrative pronouns.***	**This** poem was written by Amy Ling. [demonstrative adjective] **This** is an example of personification. [demonstrative pronoun]
VERB	**1d. A *verb* is a word used to express action or a state of being. The verb says something about the subject of a sentence.**	Gary Soto **wrote** "Broken Chain." "Oranges" **is** one of my favorite poems.
Action Verb	**1e. An *action verb* may express physical action or mental action.**	PHYSICAL ACTION jump, shout, scrape MENTAL ACTION worry, imagine, think
Transitive and Intransitive Verb	A ***transitive verb*** is a verb that expresses an action directed toward a person or thing.	Alfonso **borrowed** Ernie's bike. [The action of *borrowed* is directed toward *bike.*]
	With transitive verbs, the action passes from the doer—the subject—to the receiver of the action. Words that receive the action of a transitive verb are called ***objects.***	Mr. White made three **wishes.** [*Wishes* is the object of the verb *made.*]
	An ***intransitive verb*** expresses action (or tells something about the subject) without passing the action to a receiver.	The rake **lay** beside the fence. [The action of *lay* is not directed toward a receiver.]
	A verb may be transitive in one sentence and intransitive in another.	TRANSITIVE The teacher **read** "A Time to Talk." INTRANSITIVE The teacher **read** aloud from the letter.

Part of Speech	Definition	Examples
Linking Verb	**1f. A *linking verb* links, or connects, the subject with a noun, a pronoun, or an adjective in the predicate.**	The winner of the race **is** Squeaky. [winner = Squeaky] Gretchen **is** one of her opponents. [Gretchen = one] Squeaky's brother **looks** happy. [brother = happy] **Common Linking Verbs** Forms of *Be* am, are, be, been, being, is, was, were Other Linking Verbs appear, become, feel, grow, look, remain, seem, smell, sound, stay, taste, turn
	All linking verbs except forms of *be* and *seem* may also be used as action verbs. Whether a verb is used to link words or to express action depends on its meaning in a sentence.	The tiger **looked** tame. [linking] The tiger **looked** for food. [action]
Helping Verb	**1g. A *helping verb* (*auxiliary verb*) helps the main verb to express an action or a state of being.**	**should** be, **might have** won, **will be** seen
	A ***verb phrase*** consists of a main verb preceded by at least one helping verb.	Dr. Strauss and Dr. Nemur **are studying** Charlie. [The main verb is *studying*.] **Commonly Used Helping Verbs** Forms of *Be* am, are, be, been, being, is, was, were Forms of *Do* do, does, did Forms of *Have* have, has, had Other Helping Verbs can, could, may, might, must, shall, should, will, would
	Sometimes the verb phrase is interrupted by other words.	They **may** someday **visit** us. The narrator **could** not [or **could**n't] **see** the old man's "vulture eye."

Part of Speech	Definition	Examples
ADVERB	**1h. An *adverb* is a word used to modify a verb, an adjective, or another adverb. An adverb tells *where, when, how,* or *to what extent* (*how much* or *how long*).**	**Quite stealthily,** the narrator opens the door. [*Quite* modifies the adverb *stealthily*, telling *to what extent; stealthily* modifies the verb *opens*, telling *how*.] He is **extremely** cautious because he buried it **there.** [*Extremely* modifies the adjective *cautious*, telling *to what extent; there* modifies the verb *buries*, telling *where*.] Police officers arrive **soon**. [*Soon* modifies the verb *arrive*, telling *when*.] Note in the examples above that adverbs may come before, after, or between the words they modify.
	The word *not* is an adverb. When *not* is part of a contraction like *hadn't*, the *-n't* is an adverb.	The officers do **not** hear its beating. [*Not* modifies *do hear*, telling *to what extent*.]
PREPOSITION	**1i. A *preposition* is a word used to show the relationship of a noun or a pronoun to another word in the sentence.**	Notice how a change in the preposition changes the relationship between the cat and the house in the following examples. The dog chased the cat **under** the house. The dog chased the cat **around** the house. The dog chased the cat **through** the house. The dog chased the cat **out of** the house. **Commonly Used Prepositions** about above after against at around before between by during for from in inside into like near of on out of through to under with
Prepositional Phrase	A preposition is generally followed by a noun or a pronoun, called the ***object of the preposition.*** All together, the preposition, its object, and any modifiers of the object are called a ***prepositional phrase.***	The wagon traveled **across the prairie.**
	A preposition may have more than one object.	Look closely **at its rhyme and rhythm.**

Part of Speech	Definition	Examples
	Do not to confuse a prepositional phrase that begins with *to* (*to town*) with a verb form that begins with *to* (*to run*).	
CONJUNCTION	**1j.** **A *conjunction* is a word used to join words or groups of words.**	
	Coordinating conjunctions connect words or groups of words used in the same way.	and but or nor for so yet Gretchen **or** Squeaky [two nouns] down the track **and** across the finish line [two prepositional phrases]
	Correlative conjunctions are pairs of conjunctions that connect words or groups of words used in the same way.	both . . . and, either . . . or, neither . . . nor, not only . . . but also, whether . . . or **Neither** Jill **nor** Bill has a bike. [two nouns] **Either** leave a message, **or** call me after 7:00 P.M. [two independent clauses]
INTERJECTION	**1k.** **An *interjection* is a word used to express emotion. It has no grammatical relation to other words in the sentence. Usually an interjection is followed by an exclamation point. Sometimes an interjection is set off by a comma.**	**Common Interjections** aha hey oh oops ouch well whew wow **Wow!** What an exciting race that was! **Well,** he did his best.
Determining Parts of Speech	Part of speech is determined by the way a word is used in a sentence. Many words can be used as more than one part of speech.	The **well** has gone dry. [noun] **Well,** that's a bummer. [interjection] He doesn't look **well** to me. [adjective] He does ride **well,** however. [adverb]

Your Turn Using Parts of Speech

Rewrite the following paragraph about "Jack and the Beanstalk," replacing the vague nouns with specific nouns. Also rewrite each sentence to eliminate the adverb *very* and use a more vivid adjective.

[1] Have you read the story about the boy who traded an animal for some very special seeds? [2] A very large vine grew from the seeds, and the boy climbed it. [3] At the top, he discovered a very large man as well as a bird that laid golden eggs. [4] The boy stole the man's things and very quickly returned home. [5] The boy's parent forgave him for the very silly trade that he had made.

2. Agreement

Number

Number is the form of a word that indicates whether the word is singular or plural.

2a. **When a word refers to one person, place, thing, or idea, it is *singular*. When a word refers to more than one, it is *plural*.**

SINGULAR	book	woman	one	I
PLURAL	books	women	many	we

AGREEMENT OF SUBJECT AND VERB

2b. **A verb agrees with its subject in number. A subject and verb *agree* when they have the same number.**

(1) Singular subjects take singular verbs.
Johnny calls himself Red Chief.

(2) Plural subjects take plural verbs.
Six **girls compete** in the race.

The first auxiliary (helping) verb in a verb phrase must agree with its subject.

She is helping Charlie.
They are helping Charlie.

PROBLEMS IN AGREEMENT

2c. **The number of a subject is not changed by a prepositional phrase following the subject.**

The **book is** on the shelf.
The **book** of fairy tales **is** on the shelf.

2d. **The following indefinite pronouns are singular: *anybody, anyone, each, either, everybody, everyone, neither, nobody, no one, one, somebody, someone.***

Each of them **was sent** a bouquet.

2e. **The following indefinite pronouns are plural: *both, few, many, several.***

Both of the stories **were** written by her.

2f. **The following indefinite pronouns may be either singular or plural: *all, any, most, none, some.***

The number of *all, any, most, none,* or *some* is often determined by the object in a prepositional phrase following the subject. If the subject refers to a singular object, the subject is singular. If the subject refers to a plural object, the subject is plural.

All of the **action occurs** in a warehouse.
[*All* refers to the singular object *action*.]

All of the **events occur** in a warehouse.
[*All* refers to the plural object *events*.]

2g. **Subjects joined by *and* usually take a plural verb.**

Sam and **Bill kidnap** Johnny.

A compound subject that names a single person or thing takes a singular verb. In most cases a compound noun used as a subject also takes a singular verb.

The **captain** and **quarterback** of the team **was** Lyle. [One person, *Lyle*, was both the captain and the quarterback.]

Rock and Roll is my favorite kind of music. [*Rock and roll* is a compound noun naming one kind of music.]

2h. **When subjects are joined by *or* or *nor*, the verb agrees with the subject closest to the verb.**

Neither the **boys** nor the **girls were** on time.
Neither the **boys** nor **Leila was** on time.

2i. **Collective nouns (such as *crowd, family*, and *team*) may be either singular or plural.**

A collective noun takes a singular verb when the noun refers to the group as a unit. A collective noun takes a plural verb when the noun refers to the individual parts or members of the group.

The Frank **family goes** into hiding. [The family as a unit goes into hiding.]

The Frank **family pack** their bags. [The individual members of the family pack bags.]

2j. **When the subject follows all or part of the verb, find the subject and make sure the verb agrees with it. The subject usually follows the verb in questions and in sentences beginning with *here* or *there*.**

Have any other **frogs jumped** on?

There **is** a **frog** on that lily pad.

The contractions *here's*, *there's*, and *where's* contain the verb *is* and are used only with singular subjects.

NONSTANDARD There's the books.

STANDARD There **are** the **books.**

When the subject of a sentence follows a part of the verb, the word order is ***inverted.*** To find the subject of a sentence with inverted order, restate the sentence in normal word order.

INVERTED **Did Frost write** these poems?

NORMAL **Frost did write** these poems.

2k. **Use the contraction *don't* with plural subjects and with the pronouns *I* and *you*. Use the contraction *doesn't* with other singular subjects.**

The **police officers don't** hear the noise.

I don't like that song, and **Tim doesn't** either.

2l. **Words stating amounts are usually singular.**

A word or phrase stating a weight, a measurement, or an amount of money or time is usually considered one item and takes a singular verb.

Twenty-five months is too long to wait.

2m. **The title of a book or the name of an organization or country, even when plural in form, usually takes a singular verb.**

Flowers for Algernon **was made** into a movie.

2n. **A few nouns, though plural in form, are singular and take singular verbs.**

Mathematics is my best subject.

AGREEMENT OF PRONOUN AND ANTECEDENT

A pronoun usually refers to a noun or another pronoun, called its ***antecedent.***

2o. **A pronoun agrees with its antecedent in number and gender.**

Some singular personal pronouns have forms that indicate gender. Masculine pronouns (*he, him, his*) refer to males. Feminine pronouns (*she, her, hers*) refer to females. Neuter pronouns (*it, its*) refer to things (neither male nor female) and sometimes to animals.

Ernie lent **his** bike to Alfonso.

Squeaky protects **her** brother.

He took the girl's **ball** and threw **it.**

Some antecedents may be either masculine or feminine. When referring to such antecedents, use both the masculine and the feminine forms.

No one there gave **his or her** approval.

PROBLEMS IN AGREEMENT

2p. **A singular pronoun is used to refer to *anybody, anyone, each, either, everybody, everyone, neither, nobody, no one, one, someone,* or *somebody*.**

Everybody may express **his** or **her** opinion.

2q. **A plural pronoun is used to refer to *both, few, many,* or *several*.**

Both of the novels were on **their** shelf.

2r. **Either a singular or a plural pronoun may be used to refer to *all, any, most, none,* and *some*.**

The number of the pronoun *all, any, most, none,* or *some* is determined by the number of the object in the preposition in the prepositional phrase following the pronoun.

Only **some** of the paint spilled, but **it** made a big mess. [*Some* refers to *paint*.]

Some of the children are ready for **their** naps. [*Some* refers to *children*.]

2s. **A plural pronoun is used to refer to two or more antecedents joined by *and*.**

When **Bill and Sam** wrote the ransom note, **they** asked for fifteen hundred dollars.

2t. **A singular pronoun is used to refer to two or more singular antecedents joined by *or* or *nor*.**

Julio or Van will bring **his** football.

A singular and a plural antecedent joined by *or* or *nor* can create an awkward sentence. Revise such a sentence to avoid the problem.

AWKWARD Either he or the Wilsons will bring their net.

REVISED Either **he** will bring his net, or the **Wilsons** will bring **theirs.**

Sentences with singular antecedents joined by *or* or *nor* also can sound awkward if the antecedents are of different genders. If the sentence sounds awkward, revise it to avoid the problem.

AWKWARD Either Lori or Tony will read her or his poem about the Holocaust.

REVISED Either **Lori** will read **her** poem about the Holocaust, or **Tony** will read **his**.

2u. Either a singular or a plural pronoun may be used with a collective noun (such as *committee, flock,* and *jury*.)

The **committee** has prepared **its** recommendation. [The committee as a unit has prepared the recommendation.]

The **committee** are sharing **their** ideas for the new campaign. [The separate members of the committee have various ideas.]

2v. A few nouns, though plural in form, are singular and take singular pronouns.

The **news** came, and **it** wasn't bad.

2w. Words stating amounts usually take singular pronouns.

Although they charged **five dollars** a turn, **it** was less than he had expected to pay.

The title of a creative work or the name of an organization or a country, even when plural in form, usually takes a singular pronoun.

I enjoyed reading ***The Outsiders*** because **it** had interesting characters.

Your Turn Correcting Agreement

Revise the following sentences to eliminate the awkward use of *his* or *her*.

1. Each character had his or her own motives.
2. One of the stagehands had forgotten his or her tools.
3. Every actor knew his or her lines.
4. Either Anna or Fred will drive his or her van to the rehearsal.
5. Nobody forgot his or her costume.

3. Using Verbs

The Principal Parts of a Verb

The four basic forms of a verb are called the ***principal parts*** of a verb.

3a. The principal parts of a verb are the *base form*, the *present participle*, the *past*, and the *past participle*.

BASE FORM	return
PRESENT PARTICIPLE	(is) returning
PAST	returned
PAST PARTICIPLE	(have) returned

Notice that the present participle and the past participle require helping verbs (forms of *be* and *have*).

REGULAR VERBS

3b. A *regular verb* forms its past and past participle by adding *-d* or *-ed* to the base form.

BASE FORM	attack
PRESENT PARTICIPLE	(is) attacking
PAST	attacked
PAST PARTICIPLE	(have) attacked

Avoid the following common errors when forming the past or past participle of regular verbs:

(1) leaving off the *-d* or *-ed* ending
The owner used [*not* use] to be a samurai.

(2) adding unnecessary letters
No one drowned [*not* drownded].

IRREGULAR VERBS

3c. An *irregular verb* forms its past and past participle in some other way than by adding *-d* or *-ed* to the base form.

An irregular verb forms its past and past participle by

(1) changing vowels or consonants

BASE FORM	sing
PAST	sang
PAST PARTICIPLE	(have) sung

(2) changing vowels *and* consonants

BASE FORM	see
PAST	saw
PAST PARTICIPLE	(have) seen

(3) making no changes

BASE FORM	cut
PAST	cut
PAST PARTICIPLE	(have) cut

Avoid the following common errors when forming the past or past participle of irregular verbs:

(1) using the past form with a helping verb

NONSTANDARD	Coyote had stole them.
STANDARD	Coyote had **stolen** them.

(2) using the past participle form without a helping verb

NONSTANDARD	They drunk the tea.
STANDARD	They **have drunk** the tea.

(3) adding *-d* or *-ed* to the base form

NONSTANDARD	Possum knowed better.
STANDARD	Possum **knew** better.

Common Irregular Verbs

GROUP I: Each of these irregular verbs has the same form for its past and past participle

BASE FORM	PRESENT PARTICIPLE	PAST	PAST PARTICIPLE
bring	(is) bringing	brought	(have) brought
hold	(is) holding	held	(have) held
keep	(is) keeping	kept	(have) kept
lead	(is) leading	led	(have) led
make	(is) making	made	(have) made
send	(is) sending	sent	(have) sent

Common Irregular Verbs

GROUP II: Each of these irregular verbs has a different form for its past and past participle.

BASE FORM	PRESENT PARTICIPLE	PAST	PAST PARTICIPLE
begin	(is) beginning	began	(have) begun
break	(is) breaking	broke	(have) broken
choose	(is) choosing	chose	(have) chosen
drink	(is) drinking	drank	(have) drunk
eat	(is) eating	ate	(have) eaten
fly	(is) flying	flew	(have) flown
go	(is) going	went	(have) gone
ring	(is) ringing	rang	(have) rung
take	(is) taking	took	(have) taken

Common Irregular Verbs

GROUP III: Each of these irregular verbs has the same form for its base form, past, and past participle.

BASE FORM	PRESENT PARTICIPLE	PAST	PAST PARTICIPLE
burst	(is) bursting	burst	(have) burst
hit	(is) hitting	hit	(have) hit
hurt	(is) hurting	hurt	(have) hurt
let	(is) letting	let	(have) let
put	(is) putting	put	(have) put
read	(is) reading	read	(have) read
set	(is) set	set	(have) set
spread	(is) spreading	spread	(have) spread

Consult a dictionary for the principal parts of an irregular verb.

Verb Tense

3d. **The *tense* of a verb indicates the time of the action or state of being that is expressed by the verb.**

Every verb has six tenses: present, past, future, present perfect, past perfect, and future perfect. The following list shows how the six tenses are related to one another.

- ***Past Perfect***—existing or happening before a specific time in the past
- ***Past***—existing or happening in the past
- ***Present Perfect***—existing or happening before now or starting in the past and continuing now
- ***Present***—existing or happening now
- ***Future Perfect***—existing or happening before a specific time in the future
- ***Future***—existing or happening in the future

Listing all forms of a verb in the six tenses is called ***conjugating*** a verb.

Conjugation of The Verb *Go*

SINGULAR	PLURAL
Present Tense	
I go	we go
you go	you go
he, she, or it goes	they go
Past Tense	
I went	we went
you went	you went
he, she, or it went	they went
Future Tense	
I will go	we will go
you will go	you will go
he, she, or it will go	they will go
Present Perfect Tense	
I have gone	we have gone
you have gone	you have gone
he, she, or it has gone	they have gone
Past Perfect Tense	
I had gone	we had gone
you had gone	you had gone
he, she, or it had gone	they had gone
Future Perfect Tense	
I will have gone	we will have gone
you will have gone	you will have gone
he, she, or it will have gone	they will have gone

This time line shows how the six tenses are related to one another.

The present tense is used to express an action or a state of being occurring now. It can also be used to express a customary action, a general truth, or a future time.

On Fridays, we **play** ball. [customary]

Jupiter **rotates** in space. [general truth]

The new theater **opens** two weeks from today. [future time]

CONSISTENCY OF TENSE

3e. **Do not change needlessly from one tense to another.**

INCONSISTENT Billy pressed the bell, and a man opens the door.

CONSISTENT Billy **pressed** the bell, and a man **opened** the door.

Billy **presses** the bell, and a man **opens** the door.

Sometimes, changing tenses is needed to show the order of events that occur at different times.

Tomorrow I **will read** aloud the story I **wrote** last week. [The action of reading will take place in the future; the action of writing took place in the past.]

VOICE

3f. ***Voice*** **is the form a verb takes to indicate whether the subject of the verb performs or receives the action.**

When the subject performs the action, the verb is in the ***active voice*** and has an object. When the subject receives the action, the verb is in the ***passive voice*** and does not have an object.

ACTIVE Saki **wrote** "The Open Window." ["*The Open Window*" is the direct object.]

PASSIVE "The Open Window" **was written** by Saki. [no object]

Special Problems with Verbs

SIT AND *SET*

(1) The verb *sit* means "rest in an upright, seated position." *Sit* seldom takes an object.

(2) The verb *set* means "put (something) in a place." *Set* usually takes an object.

Base Form	Present Participle	Past	Past Participle
sit (rest)	(is) sitting	sat	(have) sat
set (put)	(is) setting	set	(have) set

Billy **sits** on the sofa. [no object]

Billy **sets** his suitcase in the chair. [Billy sets what? *Suitcase* is the object.]

LIE AND *LAY*

(1) The verb *lie* means "rest," "recline," or "be in a place." *Lie* never takes an object.

(2) The verb *lay* means "put (something) in a place." *Lay* usually takes an object.

Base Form	Present Participle	Past	Past Participle
lie (rest)	(is) lying	lay	(have) lain
lay (put)	(is) laying	laid	(have) laid

Zenta and Tokubei thought they **had lain** asleep for fifty years. [no object]

The boy **had laid** a dime on the counter. [The boy had laid what? *Dime* is the object.]

RISE AND *RAISE*

(1) The verb *rise* means "go up" or "get up." *Rise* never takes an object.

(2) The verb *raise* means "lift up" or "cause (something) to rise." *Raise* usually takes an object.

Base Form	Present Participle	Past	Past Participle
rise (go up)	(is) rising	rose	(have) risen
raise (lift up)	(is) raising	raised	(have) raised

The full moon **rose** slowly through the clouds last night. [no object]

The crowd **raised** signs over their heads. [The crowd raised what? *Signs* is the object.]

Your Turn Using the Active Voice

Revise each of the following sentences by changing verbs in the passive voice to the active voice.

1. The Gettysburg Address was delivered by Abraham Lincoln.
2. It has been admired by writers and imitated by speakers for more than one hundred years.
3. Those who died in the Civil War are honored by this short, eloquent speech.
4. The living are reminded of their "great task" by the address.
5. Freedom must be embraced and guarded by people.

4. Using Pronouns

Case

Case is the form that a noun or a pronoun takes to show its use in a sentence. There are three cases: *nominative, objective*, and *possessive*. Most personal pronouns have different forms for all three cases.

Personal Pronouns		
SINGULAR		
Nominative	**Objective**	**Possessive**
I	me	my, mine
you	you	your, yours
he, she, it	him, her, it	his, her, hers, its
PLURAL		
Nominative	**Objective**	**Possessive**
we	us	our, ours
you	you	your, yours
they	them	their, theirs

Many possessive pronouns (*my, your, his, her, its, our,* and *their*) are also called adjectives.

THE NOMINATIVE FORM

4a. A subject of a verb is in the nominative case.

I enjoy his stories. [*I* is the subject of *enjoy*.]

To choose the correct pronoun in a compound subject, try each form of the pronoun separately.

(*He, Him*) and (*I, me*) read "Paul Revere's Ride."
He read "Paul Revere's Ride."
Him read "Paul Revere's Ride."
I read "Paul Revere's Ride."
Me read "Paul Revere's Ride."

ANSWER **He** and **I** read "Paul Revere's Ride."

4b. A *predicate nominative* is in the nominative case.

The last one to leave was **he.** [*He* identifies the subject *one*.]

To choose the correct form of a pronoun used as a predicate nominative, remember that the pronoun could be used as the subject.

The fastest runners are **she** and **I.** [predicate nominatives]
She and **I** are the fastest runners. [subjects]

THE OBJECTIVE FORM

4c. A direct object is in the objective case.

Ernie surprised **him.** [*Him* tells *whom* Ernie surprised.]

To choose the correct pronoun in a compound direct object, try each form of the pronoun separately after the verb.

Beth met Joe and (*he, him*) at school.
Beth met *he* at school.
Beth met *him* at school.

ANSWER Beth met Joe and **him** at school.

4d. An *indirect object* is in the objective case.

Sandra lent **her** a book of poems. [*Her* tells to *whom* Sandra lent a book.]

To choose the correct pronoun in a compound indirect object, try each form of the pronoun separately.

Ebe sent Bill and (*he, him*) a note.
Ebe sent *he* a note.
Ebe sent *him* a note.

ANSWER Ebe sent Bill and **him** a note.

4e. An *object of a preposition* is in the objective case.

Johnny wanted to stay with **them.** [object of the preposition *with*]

To choose the correct pronoun when the object of a preposition is compound, try each form of the pronoun separately.

Anne stood behind (*he, him*) and (*she, her*).
Anne stood behind *he*.
Anne stood behind *him*.
Anne stood behind *she*.
Anne stood behind *her*.

ANSWER Anne stood behind **him** and **her.**

Special Pronoun Problems

WHO AND *WHOM*

The pronoun *who* has different forms in the nominative and objective cases. *Who* is the nominative form; *whom* is the objective form. When deciding whether to use *who* or *whom* in a question, follow these steps:

(1) Rephrase the question as a statement;
(2) Decide how the pronoun is used in the statement—as subject, predicate nominative, object of the verb, or object of a preposition;
(3) Determine the case of the pronoun;
(4) Select the correct form of the pronoun.

(*Who, Whom*) is that girl with Alfonso?

STEP 1: The statement is *That girl with Alfonso is* (*who, whom*).

STEP 2: The subject is *girl*, the verb is *is*, and the pronoun is a predicate nominative.

STEP 3: A pronoun used as a predicate nominative should be in the nominative case.

STEP 4: The nominative form is *who*.

ANSWER **Who** is that girl with Alfonso?

When you are choosing between *who* or *whom* in a subordinate clause, follow these steps:

(1) Find the subordinate clause;
(2) Decide how the pronoun is used in the clause—as subject, predicate nominative, object of the verb, or object of a preposition;
(3) Determine the case of the pronoun;
(4) Select the correct form of the pronoun.

Mark Twain, (*who, whom*) I admire, wrote funny stories.

STEP 1: The subordinate clause is (*who, whom*) I *admire*.

STEP 2: In this clause, the subject is *I*, and the verb is *admire*. The pronoun is the direct object of the verb.

STEP 3: A pronoun used as a direct object should be in the objective case.

STEP 4: The objective form is *whom*.

ANSWER Mark Twain, **whom** I admire, wrote funny stories.

PRONOUNS WITH APPOSITIVES

To help you choose which pronoun to use before an appositive, omit the appositive and try each form of the pronoun separately.

(*We, Us*) actors memorized the lines. [*Actors* is the appositive.]

We memorized the lines.

Us memorized the lines.

ANSWER **We** actors memorized the lines.

REFLEXIVE PRONOUNS

Reflexive pronouns (such as *myself, himself,* and *yourselves*) can be used as objects.

Brer Possum found **himself** in a dilemma. [*Himself* is the direct object and tells *whom* Brer Possum found in a dilemma.]

Do not use the nonstandard forms *hisself* and *theirself* or *theirselves* in place of *himself* and *themselves.*

Zenta figured it out by **himself** [*not* hisself].

Do not use a reflexive pronoun where a personal pronoun is needed.

Leon and **I** [*not* myself] enjoy rock climbing.

The girls laughed at how they [*not* themselves] looked in the funhouse mirror.

Your Turn Using Pronouns Correctly

Rewrite the following sentences using the correct pronoun case. If a pronoun is used correctly, leave it as is.

1. Do you think it was them whom took the cookies?
2. Yes, I'm certain it was him and her who took they.
3. Us kids saw Joe and she leave the kitchen in a hurry.
4. On the way out, her picked up the cookies and then stuffed they in her purse.
5. Later Joe and her felt guilty and asked theirselves if them should admit their "crime."

5. Using Modifiers

Comparison of Modifiers

A ***modifier*** is a word, a phrase, or a clause that describes or limits the meaning of another word. Two kinds of modifiers—*adjectives* and *adverbs*—take different forms when used to compare things.

5a. **The three degrees of comparison of modifiers are *positive, comparative,* and *superlative*.**

POSITIVE	weak, proudly
COMPARATIVE	weaker, more proudly
SUPERLATIVE	weakest, most proudly

REGULAR COMPARISON

(1) Most one-syllable modifiers form their comparative and superlative degrees by adding *-er* and *-est*.

POSITIVE	near, bright
COMPARATIVE	nearer, brighter
SUPERLATIVE	nearest, brightest

(2) Some two-syllable modifiers form their comparative and superlative degrees by adding *-er* and *-est*. Others form their comparative and superlative degrees by using *more* and *most*.

POSITIVE	gentle, clearly
COMPARATIVE	gentler, more clearly
SUPERLATIVE	gentlest, most clearly

(3) Modifiers that have three or more syllables form their comparative and superlative degrees by using *more* and *most*.

POSITIVE	portable, accurately
COMPARATIVE	more portable, more accurately
SUPERLATIVE	most portable, most accurately

IRREGULAR COMPARISON

Some modifiers do not form their comparative and superlative degrees by using the regular methods.

POSITIVE	bad	good/well	many/much
COMPARATIVE	worse	better	more
SUPERLATIVE	worst	worst	most

To show decreasing comparisons, all modifiers form their comparative and superlative degrees with *less* and *least*.

USES of COMPARATIVE AND SUPERLATIVE FORMS

5b. **Use the comparative degree when comparing two things. Use the superlative degree when comparing more than two things.**

COMPARATIVE	Squeaky is **faster** than Gretchen.
	Luisa performs **more gracefully** than I.
SUPERLATIVE	Mount Everest is the **highest** mountain.
	Of all the children, Charles behaves the **most aggressively.**

Avoid the mistake of using the superlative degree to compare two things.

Of the two stories, I think "The Landlady" is the **more** [*not* most] interesting.

5c. **Use the word *other* or *else* when comparing a member of a group with the rest of the group.**

NONSTANDARD	Smiley's frog can jump farther than any frog in the county. [Smiley's frog is one of the frogs in the county and cannot jump farther than itself.]
STANDARD	Smiley's frog can jump farther than any **other** frog in the county.

5d. **Avoid using double comparisons and double negatives.**

A ***double comparison*** is the use of both *-er* and *more* (*less*) or both *-est* and *most* (*least*) to form a comparison. A comparison should be formed in only one way or the other.

Matt is **younger** [*not* more younger] than Ben.

A ***double negative*** is the use of two negative words to express one negative idea.

I ca**n't** ever [*not* can't never] remember that.

Common Negative Words			
barely	never	none	nothing
hardly	no	no one	nowhere
neither	nobody	not (-n't)	scarcely

Placement of Modifiers

5e. **Place modifying words, phrases, and clauses as close as possible to the word they modify so they clearly modify only one word.**

PREPOSITIONAL PHRASES

MISPLACED Gabriela said **in the morning** she was leaving. [Does the phrase modify *said* or *was leaving*?]

CLEAR Gabriela said she was leaving **in the morning.** [The phase modifies *was leaving*.] **In the morning** Gabriela said she was leaving. [The phrase modifies *said.*]

PARTICIPIAL PHRASES

MISPLACED The narrator visits the old man **obsessed with the "vulture eye."**

CLEAR **Obsessed with the "vulture eye,"** the narrator visits the old man.

A participial phrase that does not modify any word in the sentence is a ***dangling participial phrase.*** To correct a dangling phrase, supply a word that the phrase can modify, or add a subject and verb to the phrase.

DANGLING **Wishing for the money,** the monkey's paw twisted in his hands.

CLEAR Wishing for the money, **he** felt the monkey's paw twist in his hands. **When he wished** for the money, the monkey's paw twisted in his hands.

CLAUSES

MISPLACED My brother saw a hawk circling as he looked up.

CLEAR **As my brother looked up,** he saw a hawk circling.

Your Turn Using Modifiers Correctly

Correct the use of modifiers in the following sentences either by choosing a different degree of comparison or by placing the modifier closer to the word it modifies.

1. Between Sarah and Erin, Sarah is fastest.
2. Sarah is the more talented athlete on the team.
3. Sarah said in the morning she would have to practice for the race.
4. Erin vowed to practice too obsessed with beating Sarah just once.

6. Phrases

6a. **A *phrase* is a group of related words that is used as a single part of speech and does not contain a verb and its subject.**

should have been told [verb phrase, no subject]
for my sister and me [prepositional phrase, no subject or verb]

The Prepositional Phrase

6b. **A *prepositional phrase* includes a preposition, a noun or a pronoun called the *object of the preposition*, and any modifiers of that object.**

Robert Frost was born **in San Francisco.**
The note **from John** surprised Sam and Bill.

ADJECTIVE PHRASE

6c. **An *adjective phrase* is a prepositional phrase that modifies a noun or a pronoun. An adjective phrase tells *what kind* or *which one*.**

Wang Wei was a talented painter **of nature.** [What kind of painter?]

Mike is the one **with the beard.** [Which one?]

An adjective phrase always follows the word it modifies. That word may be the object of another prepositional phrase.

It is a poem **about a boy and a girl on their first date.** [The phrase *about a boy and a girl* modifies the noun *poem*. The phrase *on their first date* modifies the objects *boy* and *girl*.]

More than one adjective phrase may modify the same word.

The box **of old magazines in the closet** is full. [The phrases *of old magazines* and *in the closet* modify the noun *box*.]

ADVERB PHRASE

6d. **An *adverb phrase* is a prepositional phrase that modifies a verb, an adjective, or an adverb. An adverb phrase tells *how, when, where, why,* or *to what extent* (that is, *how long, how many,* or *how far*).**

She treated him **with respect.** [How?]

The painting hangs **on the wall.** [Where?]

They arrived **in the morning.** [When?]

He had been a skier **for years.** [How long?]

An adverb phrase may come before or after the word it modifies.

The Sneves lived in Iowa **for many years.**

For many years the Sneves lived in Iowa.

An adverb phrase may be followed by an adjective phrase that modifies the object in the adverb phrase.

In her poems about the Southwest, Silko uses images that appeal to the senses. [*In her poems* modifies the verb *uses*; *about the Southwest* modifies the noun *poems*.]

More than one adverb phrase may modify the same word or words.

Uchida was born **in Alameda, California, in 1921.** [Both *in Alameda, California*, and *in 1921* modify the verb phrase *was born*.]

Verbals and Verbal Phrases

A ***verbal*** is a form of a verb used as a noun, an adjective, or an adverb. There are three kinds of verbals: the *participle*, the *gerund*, and the *infinitive*.

THE PARTICIPLE

6e. **A *participle* is a verb form that can be used as an adjective.**

(1) ***Present participles*** end in *-ing*.
The **creaking** floorboard bothered Anne.

(2) Most ***past participles*** end in *-d* or *-ed*. Others are irregularly formed.
The **oiled** hinge works smoothly.
Parker, **known** as Bird, was talented.

THE PARTICIPIAL PHRASE

6f. **A *participial phrase* consists of a participle and all of the words related to the participle. The entire phrase is used as an adjective.**

A participle may be modified by an adverb and may also have a complement.

Defending Jabez Stone, Webster proved again that he was a persuasive speaker. [The participial phrase modifies *Webster*. The noun *Jabez Stone* is the direct object of the present participle *defending*.]

Squeaky noticed him **running swiftly alongside the fence.** [The participial phrase modifies *him*. The adverb *swiftly* and the adverb phrase *alongside the fence* modify the participle *running*.]

THE GERUND

6g. **A *gerund* is a verb form ending in *-ing* that is used as a noun.**

Skating can be good exercise. [subject]
My hobby is **writing.** [predicate nominative]
Lock the door before **leaving.** [object of the preposition]
Do they enjoy **singing**? [direct object]

THE GERUND PHRASE

6h. **A *gerund phrase* consists of a gerund and all the words related to it.**

A gerund may be modified by an adverb and may have a complement. Because a gerund functions as a noun, it may also be modified by an adjective.

Minding Raymond is Squeaky's only responsibility. [The gerund phrase is the subject of the verb *is*. The noun *Raymond* is the direct object of the gerund *minding*.]

The murderer heard **the beating of the old man's heart.** [The gerund phrase is the direct object of the verb *heard*. The adjective *the* and the adjective phrase *of the old man's heart* modify the gerund *beating*.]

THE INFINITIVE

6i. **An *infinitive* is a verb form that can be used as a noun, an adjective, or an adverb. An infinitive usually begins with *to*.**

NOUN	**To learn** is a gift. [*To learn* is the subject of *is*.]
ADJECTIVE	He always has time **to talk.** [*To talk* modifies the pronoun *time*.]
ADVERB	Zenta stops at the inn **to rest.** [To *rest* modifies the verb *stops*.]

THE INFINITIVE PHRASE

6j. **An *infinitive phrase* consists of an infinitive and its modifiers and complements.**

An infinitive may be modified by an adjective or an adverb and may also have a complement. The entire infinitive phrase may act as a noun, an adjective, or an adverb.

To escape without a trace was impossible. [The infinitive phrase is a noun used as the subject of the verb *was*. The prepositional phrase *without a trace* modifies the infinitive.]

Singing to them was one way **to boost their spirits.** [The infinitive phrase is an adjective modifying *way*. The noun phrase *their spirits* is the direct object of the infinitive *to boost*.]

Be careful not to confuse infinitives with prepositional phrases beginning with *to*.

Matthew wants **to talk** [infinitive] **to Kim** [prepositional phrase].

Appositives and Appositive Phrases

6k. **An *appositive* is a noun or a pronoun placed beside another noun or pronoun to identify or explain it.**

The poet **Langston Hughes** wrote "Refugee in America." [The noun *Langston Hughes* identifies the noun *poet*.]

Two or more nouns or pronouns may be used as a compound appositive.

He, as both an **artist** and a **naturalist,** particularly admired birds. [The nouns *artist* and *naturalist* explain the pronoun *He*.]

6l. **An *appositive phrase* consists of an appositive and its modifiers.**

Black Hawk, **a chief of the Sauk,** fought hard for the freedom of his people. [The article *a* and the adjective phrase *of the Sauk* modify the appositive *chief*.]

Your Turn Using Phrases

The following pairs of sentences are choppy. Revise each pair by turning one sentence into a phrase and then insert that phrase into the other sentence.

1. Casey had not been at bat that day. Casey was known to all as a strong player.
2. Jimmy Blake was up first. Blake was not a strong hitter.
3. He hit the ball hard. He ripped the hide from it.
4. The crowd roared. The crowd was in the bleachers.
5. Casey behaved arrogantly. He let two good balls go by.

7. Clauses

7a. A *clause* is a group of words that contains a verb and its subject and is used as a part of a sentence.

The two kinds of clauses are the ***independent clause*** and the ***subordinate clause***.

The Independent Clause

7b. An *independent* (or *main*) *clause* expresses a complete thought and can stand by itself as a sentence.

S V
Amy Ling moved to the United States.

The Subordinate Clause

7c. A *subordinate* (or *dependent*) *clause* does not express a complete thought and cannot stand alone as a sentence.

S V
when she was six years old

The meaning of a subordinate clause is complete only when the clause is attached to an independent clause.

Amy Ling moved to the United States **when she was six years old.**

THE ADJECTIVE CLAUSE

7d. An *adjective clause* is a subordinate clause that modifies a noun or a pronoun.

ADJECTIVE	an **intelligent** man
ADJECTIVE PHRASE	a man **of intelligence**
ADJECTIVE CLAUSE	a man **who is intelligent**

An adjective clause usually follows the word it modifies and tells *which one* or *what kind.*

Cheryl showed them the moccasins **that her father had made.** [Which moccasins?]

Helen Keller was a remarkable woman **who could neither see nor hear.** [What kind of woman?]

An adjective clause is usually introduced by a ***relative pronoun,*** a word that relates an adjective clause to the word the clause modifies.

"The Tell-Tale Heart," **which tells the story of a murderer's guilt,** is great to read aloud. [The relative pronoun *which* begins the adjective clause and relates it to the compound noun *"The Tell-Tale Heart."*]

In addition to relating a subordinate clause to the rest of the sentence, a relative pronoun also has a function in the subordinate clause.

Is he the one **who wrote "The Moustache"**? [*Who* functions as subject of the verb *wrote*.]

She is a friend **in whom you can trust.** [*Whom* functions as object of the preposition *on*.]

The relative pronouns *who* and *whom* are used to refer to people only. The relative pronoun *that* is used to refer both to people and to things. The relative pronoun *which* is used to refer to things only.

An adjective clause may be introduced by a relative adverb such as *when* or *where*.

He finally returned to the cabin **where he had left Mary in charge of his children.**

The time period **when dinosaurs ruled** lasted millions of years.

THE ADVERB CLAUSE

7e. An *adverb clause* is a subordinate clause that modifies a verb, an adjective, or an adverb.

ADVERB	You may sit **anywhere.**
ADVERB PHRASE	You may sit **in any chair.**
ADVERB CLAUSE	You may sit **wherever you wish.**

An adverb clause tells *where, when, how, why, to what extent,* or *under what condition.*

Put that box **wherever you can.** [Where?]

Toby got angry **when he saw it.** [When?]

My new friend and I talk **as if we've known each other for a long time.** [How?]

Because she was very hungry, Marisol couldn't wait to eat her lunch. [Why?]

Johnny caused Sam and Bill more trouble **than they had expected.** [To what extent?]

Notice in these examples that an adverb clause does not always follow the word it modifies. When an adverb clause begins a sentence, the clause is followed by a comma.

An adverb clause is introduced by a ***subordinating conjunction***—a word that shows the relationship between the adverb clause and the word or words that the clause modifies.

Common Subordinating Conjunctions			
after	although	as	as if
because	before	how	if
once	since	so that	than
though	unless	until	when
whenever	where	whether	while

THE NOUN CLAUSE

7f. **A *noun clause* is a subordinate clause used as a noun.**

A noun clause may be used as a subject, a complement (predicate nominative, direct object, indirect object), or an object of a preposition.

That Jabez is unlucky is evident. [subject]

A three-year extension was **what the stranger offered Jabez.** [predicate nominative]

The judges ruled **who won.** [direct object]

The sheriff gave **whoever volunteered in the search** a flashlight. [indirect object]

He did not agree to **what the kidnappers demanded.** [object of a preposition]

Common Introductory Words for Noun Clauses		
that	what	whatever
which	whichever	who
whoever	whom	whomever

In many cases, the word that introduces a noun clause has another function within the clause.

The trophy goes to **whoever wins the race.** [*Whoever* introduces the noun clause and is the subject of the verb *wins*.]

Their complaint was **that he had changed.** [The word *that* introduces the noun clause but has no other function in the clause.]

Your Turn Using Clauses

Combine each of these pairs of sentences into one sentence by turning a sentence into a subordinate clause.

1. Mrs. Johnson's husband moved to Oklahoma. He studied religion.
2. The cotton gin would not hire her. Neither would the lumber mill.
3. She didn't want to become a servant. She saw another possibility.
4. The cotton gin and lumber workers walked to her stand. They bought lunch.
5. In time, Mrs. Johnson sold syrup and canned goods at the store. It did good business.

8. Sentences

The Sentence

8a. **A *sentence* is a group of words that has a subject and a verb and expresses a complete thought.**

A sentence begins with a capital letter and ends with a period, a question mark, or an exclamation point.

He told a story about Urashima Taro**.**

Have you read the novel *Shane***?**

What a dangerous mission it must have been**!**

SENTENCE OR SENTENCE FRAGMENT?

When a group of words either does not have a subject and a verb or does not express a complete thought, it is a ***sentence fragment.***

SENTENCE FRAGMENT	After reading the poem. [Who read the poem? What happened afterward?]
SENTENCE	After reading the poem, we asked the teacher several questions.

The Subject and the Predicate

A sentence consists of two parts: a ***subject*** and a ***predicate.***

8b. **A *subject* tells whom or what the sentence is about. The *predicate* tells something about the subject.**

SUBJECT PREDICATE
Helen Callaghan / played baseball.

FINDING THE SUBJECT

Usually, the subject comes before the predicate. Sometimes, however, the subject may appear elsewhere in the sentence. To find the subject of a sentence, ask *Who?* or *What?* before the predicate.

At the top of the tree, **a bird's nest** sat. [What sat? a bird's nest]

Does **Casey** strike out? [Who does strike out? Casey]

The subject of a sentence is never part of a prepositional phrase.

The **tips** of the rabbit's ears were sticking up behind the large cabbage. [*Tips,* not *ears,* is the subject.]

THE SIMPLE SUBJECT

8c. **A *simple subject* is the main word or group of words in the complete subject.**

A ***complete subject*** consists of all the words that name and describe whom or what the sentence is about.

The long **trip** across the desert was finally over. [The complete subject is *the long trip across the desert. Trip* is the simple subject.]

"The Cremation of Sam McGee" is a poem written by Robert W. Service. [*"The Cremation of Sam McGee"* is both the simple subject and the complete subject.]

In this book, the term *subject* refers to the simple subject unless otherwise indicated.

THE SIMPLE PREDICATE, OR VERB

8d. **A *simple predicate,* or *verb,* is the main word or group of words in the complete predicate.**

A ***complete predicate*** consists of a verb and all the words that describe the verb and complete its meaning.

The trees **sagged** beneath the weight of the ice. [The complete predicate is *sagged beneath the weight of the ice.*]

After the race, everyone **congratulated** Squeaky. [The complete predicate is *after the race . . . congratulated Squeaky.*]

THE VERB PHRASE

A simple predicate may be a one-word verb, or it may be a verb phrase. A ***verb phrase*** consists of a main verb and its helping verbs.

Our class **is reading** Anne Frank's diary.

THE COMPOUND SUBJECT

8e. **A *compound subject* consists of two or more connected subjects that have the same verb. The usual connecting word is *and, or,* or *nor.***

Traveling together were **Zeta** and **Matt.**

Smoked **turkey,** baked **ham,** or roast **goose** will be on the Thanksgiving menu.

Neither the **trousers** nor the **shoes** fit.

THE COMPOUND VERB

8f. A *compound verb* consists of two or more verbs that have the same subject. A connecting word—usually *and, or,* or *but*—is used between the verbs.

Mr. Nuttel **sat** down and **waited** for her.
We **can go** forward, **go** back, or **stay** here.

Both the subject and the verb of a sentence may be compound.

The **captain** (S) and the **crew** (S) **battled** (V) the storm and **hoped** (V) for the best. [The captain battled and hoped, and the crew battled and hoped.]

Your Turn Varying Sentence Structure

Use a compound subject or a compound verb to combine each of the following sets of short sentences.

1. Grandmother greets her grandson. She thinks he is someone else.
2. According to Grandmother, blue jays come to the bird feeder. Chickadees come there, too.
3. A nurse enters the room. She offers Grandmother some juice.
4. Orange juice does not interest her. Neither does cranberry juice nor grape juice.
5. Mike should tell Grandmother the truth. He cannot.

9. Complements

Recognizing Complements

9a. A *complement* is a word or a group of words that completes the meaning of a verb.

INCOMPLETE	Mr. White held [*what?*]
COMPLETE	Mr. White held the **paw.**
INCOMPLETE	Marga thanked [*whom?*]
COMPLETE	Marga thanked **her.**
INCOMPLETE	Squeaky is [*what?*]
COMPLETE	Squeaky is **confident.**

A complement may be a noun, a pronoun, or an adjective. A complement is never an adverb or in a prepositional phrase.

ADVERB	Benjamin is studying **hard**.
OBJECT OF A PREPOSITION	Benjamin is studying for his math **test.**
COMPLEMENT	Benjamin is studying his math **notes.**

Direct Objects

9b. A *direct object* is a noun or a pronoun that receives the action of the verb or that shows the result of the action. A direct object tells *what* or *whom* after a transitive verb.

We watched the **movie.** [The noun *movie* receives the action of the transitive verb *watched* and tells *what* we watched.]

A direct object never follows a linking verb nor is it ever part of a prepositional phrase.

William Wordsworth **became** poet laureate. [The linking verb *became* does not express action; therefore, it has no direct object.]

They walked for **miles** in the woods. [*Miles* is not the direct object of the verb *walked;* it is the object of the preposition *for*.]

Indirect Objects

9c. An *indirect object* is a noun or a pronoun that comes between the verb and the direct object and tells *to what* or *to whom* or *for what* or *for whom* the action of the verb is done.

Smiley gave the **stranger** a frog. [The noun *stranger* tells *to whom* Smiley gave a frog.]

Linking verbs do not have indirect objects. Also, an indirect object is never in a prepositional phrase.

Her mother **was** a collector of rare books. [linking verb]
She sent her **mother** a rare book. [indirect object]
She sent a rare book to her **mother.** [object of a preposition]

Direct objects and indirect objects may be compound.

Mrs. Flowers served **cookies** and **lemonade.** [compound direct objects]
He showed **Mr. White** and his **family** the monkey's paw. [compound indirect objects]

Subject Complements

A ***subject complement*** completes the meaning of a linking verb and identifies or describes the subject.

Common Linking Verbs			
appear	be	become	feel
grow	look	remain	seem
smell	sound	stay	taste

The two kinds of subject complements are the ***predicate nominative*** and the ***predicate adjective.***

PREDICATE NOMINATIVES

9d. A *predicate nominative* is a noun or a pronoun that follows a linking verb and identifies or refers to the subject.

Denise is a good **friend.** [*Friend* is a predicate nominative that identifies the subject *Denise.*]
Eva is **one** of my friends. [*One* is a predicate nominative that refers to the subject *Eva.*]

Predicate nominatives never appear in prepositional phrases.

The prize was a **pair** of tickets. [*Pair* is a predicate nominative that identifies the subject *prize. Tickets* is the object of the preposition *of.*]

A predicate nominative may be compound.

Ms. Kinnian was Charlie's **teacher** and **friend.**

Expressions such as *It is I* and *That was he* may sound awkward because in conversation people more frequently say *It's me* and *That was him.* While these nonstandard expressions may be acceptable in speech, it is best to follow the rules of standard English in your writing.

PREDICATE ADJECTIVES

9e. A *predicate adjective* is an adjective that follows a linking verb and describes the subject.

This ground is **swampy.** [*Swampy* follows the linking verb *is* and describes the subject *ground.*]

Some verbs, such as *look, grow,* and *feel,* may be used as either linking verbs or action verbs.

The fieldworker **felt** tired. [*Felt* is a linking verb that links the adjective *tired* to the subject *fieldworker.*]
The fieldworker **felt** the hot wind on his face. [*Felt* is an action verb because it is followed by the direct object *wind,* which tells what the fieldworker felt.]

A predicate adjective may be compound.

A computer can be **helpful** but **frustrating.**

Your Turn Recognizing Linking Verbs

In each of the following sentences, change the *be* verb to an action verb. Then, revise the sentence to read smoothly.

1. Grandfather was all by himself on his journey.
2. He had never been so far from the reservation before.
3. His stories were about warriors and excitement.
4. Children were all around him each day.
5. Moccasins were on his feet.

10. Kinds of Sentences

Sentences Classified by Structure

Sentences may be classified according to **structure**—the kinds and the number of clauses they contain. The four kinds of sentences are ***simple, compound, complex,*** and ***compound-complex.***

THE SIMPLE SENTENCE

10a. **A *simple sentence* has one independent clause and no subordinate clauses.**

Mr. Lema showed him the trumpet.

A simple sentence may contain a compound subject, a compound verb, or both.

(S) **Dr. Nemur** and (S) **Dr. Strauss** (V) **tested** Charlie and (V) **monitored** his progress.

THE COMPOUND SENTENCE

10b. **A *compound sentence* has two or more independent clauses but no subordinate clauses.**

The independent clauses are usually joined by a comma and a coordinating conjunction (*and, but, for, nor, or, so, yet*). Sometimes the clauses are joined by only a semicolon.

It was a lot of money, but **Tokubei paid it.**
Zenta noticed the hand; it had six fingers.

THE COMPLEX SENTENCE

10c. **A *complex sentence* has one independent clause and at least one subordinate clause.**

Mary ate some of the mushrooms before she gave any to the children.

INDEPENDENT CLAUSE	**Mary ate** some of the mushrooms
SUBORDINATE CLAUSE	before **she gave** any to the children

THE COMPOUND-COMPLEX SENTENCE

10d. **A *compound-complex sentence* has two or more independent clauses and at least one subordinate clause.**

I have read several stories in which the main characters are animals, but the story that I like best is "Brer Possum's Dilemma."

INDEPENDENT CLAUSE	**I have read** several stories
INDEPENDENT CLAUSE	the **story is** "Brer Possum's Dilemma"
SUBORDINATE CLAUSE	in which the main **characters are** animals
SUBORDINATE CLAUSE	that **I like** best

Sentences Classified by Purpose

Sentences may be classified according to **purpose.** The four kinds of sentences are ***declarative, interrogative, imperative,*** and ***exclamatory.***

10e. **A *declarative sentence* makes a statement. It is followed by a period.**

According to Lee, Chas caused the trouble by cutting in line**.**

10f. **An *interrogative sentence* asks a question. It is followed by a question mark.**

Did Ariel finish designing the invitations for the costume party**?**

10g. **An *imperative sentence* gives a command or makes a request. It is followed by a period. However, a strong command is followed by an exclamation point.**

Watch them while I'm gone. [mild command]
Father, tell us a story. [request]
Watch out! [strong command]

The "understood" subject of an imperative sentence is always *you*.

Father, (you) tell us a story.
(You) Watch out!

10h. **An *exclamatory sentence* shows excitement or expresses strong feeling. It is followed by an exclamation point.**

What a sad day in Mudville that was!

Your Turn Varying Sentence Structure

Decide whether the information in each numbered item would be best expressed by a simple, compound, complex, or compound-complex sentence. Then, revise each item.

1. They took off their wings. There was not enough room on the ships.
2. The people had been able to fly. They had forgotten how.
3. The Master was a hard man. The Overseer was, too.
4. A slave collapsed in the heat. The Overseer whipped him.
5. She flew awkwardly at first. She soon soared freely. Everyone looked up to her.

11. Writing Effective Sentences

Writing Clear Sentences

One of the easiest ways to make your writing clear is to use complete sentences. A **complete sentence** is a word group that has a subject, has a verb, and expresses a complete thought. *Sentence fragments* and *run-on sentences* are stumbling blocks to the development of clear sentences.

RUN-ON SENTENCES

11a. **Avoid using *run-on sentences*—two complete sentences run together as if they were one.**

Chinese people usually use kites for sport, they use some in religious ceremonies.

You can correct a run-on sentence

(1) by making two sentences
Chinese people usually use kites for sport. They use some in religious ceremonies.

(2) by using a comma and the coordinating conjunction *and, but*, or *or*
Chinese people usually use kites for sport, **but** they use some in religious ceremonies.

To spot run-ons, read your writing aloud. A natural pause in your voice often marks the end of one thought and the beginning of another. If you don't have any end punctuation at this place, you may have found a run-on sentence.

Combining Sentences

11b. **Improve short, choppy sentences by combining them into longer, smoother sentences.**

You can combine sentences

(1) by inserting words

CHOPPY Mrs. Flowers was an intelligent woman. She was generous, too.
COMBINED Mrs. Flowers was an **intelligent, generous** woman.

(2) by inserting phrases

CHOPPY Henry David Thoreau lived at Walden Pond. He lived there for two years. He lived in a simple hut.
COMBINED **For two years** Henry David Thoreau lived **in a simple hut at Walden Pond.** [prepositional phrases]

CHOPPY	Harriet Tubman made the long journey to Philadelphia. She traveled at night.
COMBINED	**Traveling at night**, Harriet Tubman made the long journey to Philadelphia. [participial phrase]

(3) by using *and, but,* or *or*

CHOPPY	Eagle went hunting. Coyote went with him.
COMBINED	Eagle **and** Coyote went hunting.

(4) by using a subordinate clause

CHOPPY	Harriet Tubman believed no person should be a slave. She decided to escape.
COMBINED	Harriet Tubman, **who believed no person should be a slave**, decided to escape. [adjective clause]
CHOPPY	Billy signed the guest book. He saw two other names.
COMBINED	**When Billy signed the guest book**, he saw two other names. [adverb clause]

Improving Sentence Style

11c. **Improve *stringy* and *wordy* sentences by making them shorter and more precise.**

Stringy sentences have too many independent clauses strung together with words like *and* or *but.*

Harriet Ross grew up as a slave in Maryland, and she worked on a plantation there, but in 1844, she married John Tubman, and he was a free man.

You can revise a stringy sentence

(1) by breaking the sentence into two or more sentences

Harriet Ross grew up as a slave in Maryland and worked on a plantation there. In 1844, she married John Tubman, a free man.

(2) by turning some of the independent clauses into phrases or subordinate clauses

Harriet Ross grew up as a slave in Maryland. She worked on a plantation there until, in 1844, she married John Tubman, who was a free man. [Notice that this revision includes changing independent clauses into subordinate clauses.]

Wordy sentences tend to sound awkward and unnatural. You can revise a wordy sentence

(1) by replacing a group of words with one word

WORDY	With great suddenness, the bicycle chain snapped.
REVISED	**Suddenly**, the bicycle chain snapped.

(2) by replacing a clause with a phrase

WORDY	After the play had come to an end, we walked over to a restaurant and treated ourselves to pizza.
REVISED	**After the play**, we walked to a restaurant and treated ourselves to pizza.

(3) by taking out a whole group of unnecessary words

WORDY	Webster was a persuasive orator whose speeches were very convincing.
REVISED	Webster was a persuasive orator.

Your Turn Revising Sentences

Combine the following pairs of sentences so that each revised sentence reads smoothly and shows the intended relationship. If a pair of sentences should not be combined, write *C.*

1. Lemon Brown went to the window. Greg followed him.
2. The men were sitting down. They probably would not come back.
3. Greg asked about Lemon's injury. Lemon handed Greg the flashlight.
4. Lemon revealed his treasure. Greg stared at the strange package.
5. Greg was worried about Lemon. Lemon said that he would be fine.

12. Capital Letters

12a. Capitalize the first word in every sentence.

She has written a report on Harriet Tubman.

The first word of a sentence that is a direct quotation is capitalized even if the quotation begins within a sentence.

In her diary, Anne Frank wrote, "**I**n spite of everything, I still believe that people are really good at heart."

Traditionally, the first word in a line of poetry, including song lyrics, is capitalized.

Go down, Moses,
Way down in Egypt land.
Tell old Pharaoh
To let my people go.
—Traditional spiritual, "Go Down, Moses"

Some poets and songwriters do not follow this style. When you are quoting, follow the capitalization used in the source of the quotation.

12b. Capitalize the pronoun *I*.

"What should **I** do," **I** asked.

12c. Capitalize the interjection *O*.

The interjection *O* is most often used on solemn or formal occasions. It is usually followed by a word in direct address.

Exult **O** shores! and ring **O** bells!
—Walt Whitman, "O Captain! My Captain!"

The interjection *oh* requires a capital letter only at the beginning of a sentence.

Oh, that's all right!
I can't go, but, **oh**, I wish I could.

12d. Capitalize proper nouns.

A **common noun** is a general name for a person, a place, a thing, or an idea. A common noun is capitalized only when it begins a sentence or is part of a title. A **proper noun** is a particular person, place, thing, or idea. A proper noun is always capitalized. Some proper nouns consist of more than one word. In these names, short prepositions (those of fewer than five letters) and articles (*a, an, the*) are not capitalized.

COMMON NOUNS queen, holiday
PROPER NOUNS **Q**ueen **E**lizabeth, **T**hanksgiving

(1) Capitalize the names of persons and animals.
Sandra **C**isneros, **J**ohn **M**c**E**nroe, **K**ermit

(2) Capitalize geographical names.

Type of Name	Examples
Towns, Cities	**G**rover's **C**orners, **S**t. **L**ouis
Counties, States	**O**range **C**ounty, **G**eorgia
Countries	**M**exico, **J**apan
Islands	**L**ong **I**sland, **M**olokai
Bodies of Water	**C**rystal **R**iver, **D**ead **S**ea
Forests, Parks	**A**rgonne **F**orest, **P**almetto **S**tate **P**ark
Streets, Highways	**E**uclid **A**venue, **R**oute 66
Mountains	**M**ount **E**verest, **P**ikes **P**eak
Continents, Regions	**E**urope, the **M**iddle **E**ast

In a hyphenated street number, the second part of the number is not capitalized.
East Fifty-**t**hird Street

Words such as *north, east,* and *southwest* are not capitalized when they indicate direction.
traveling **n**orth, **s**outhwest of Austin

(3) Capitalize the names of planets, stars, and other heavenly bodies.
Saturn, **C**anopus, **U**rsa **M**ajor

The word *earth* is not capitalized unless used with the names of other heavenly bodies. The words *sun* and *moon* are not capitalized.

Water covers more than seventy percent of the surface of the **e**arth.

Mercury, Venus, and **E**arth are planets.

(4) Capitalize the names of teams, organizations, businesses, institutions, and government bodies.

Type of Name	Examples
Teams	**C**hicago **B**ulls, **P**ittsburgh **P**irates
Organizations, Businesses	**G**irl **S**couts, **G**eneral **M**otors
Institutions, Government Bodies	**B**lake **H**ospital, **D**epartment of **L**abor

(5) Capitalize the names of historical events and periods, special events, and calendar items.

Type of Name	Examples
Historical Events, Historical Periods	**P**ersian **G**ulf **C**onflict, **R**enaissance
Special Events, Calendar Items	**K**entucky **S**tate **F**air, **M**emorial **D**ay

The name of a season is not capitalized unless it is part of a proper name.
first day of spring, **B**luegrass **S**pring **F**estival

(6) Capitalize the names of nationalities, races, and peoples.
Italian, **J**apanese, **A**frican **A**merican

(7) Capitalize the names of religions and their followers, holy days, sacred writings, and specific deities.

Type of Name	Examples
Religions and Followers	**C**hristianity, **H**indu, **J**udaism
Holy Days	**R**amadan, **E**aster, **P**assover
Sacred Writings	**K**oran, **T**almud, **B**ible
Specific Deities	**G**od, **A**llah, **V**ishnu

The word *god* is not capitalized when it refers to a god of mythology. The names of specific gods, however, are capitalized.
The Egyptian sun **g**od was **R**a.

(8) Capitalize the names of buildings and other structures.
Plaza **H**otel, **E**iffel **T**ower

(9) Capitalize the names of monuments and awards.
Washington **M**onument, **P**ulitzer **P**rize

(10) Capitalize the names of trains, ships, aircraft, and spacecraft.

Type of Name	Examples
Trains and Ships	***C**alifornia **Z**ephyr*, ***S**anta **M**aria*
Aircraft and Spacecraft	***A**ir **F**orce **O**ne*, ***V**oyager 2*

(11) Capitalize the brand names of business products.
Reebok shoes, **F**ord station wagon

Notice that the names of the types of products are not capitalized.

12e. **Capitalize proper adjectives.**

A ***proper adjective*** is formed from a proper noun and is almost always capitalized.

Proper Noun	Proper Adjective
France	**F**rench cuisine
William **S**hakespeare	**S**hakespearean actor

12f. **Do *not* capitalize the names of school subjects, except names of languages and of courses followed by a number.**

history, **S**panish, **B**iology I

12g. **Capitalize titles.**

(1) Capitalize the title of a person when it comes before a name.
They spoke to **G**overnor Adam and **D**r. Chang.

(2) Capitalize a title used alone or following a person's name only when you want to emphasize the position of someone holding a high office.
Will the **S**ecretary of **E**nergy speak?
The **s**ecretary of our scout troop spoke.
A title used alone in direct address is usually capitalized.
Is everyone here, **R**everend?
May I help you, **S**ir [*or* **s**ir]?

(3) Capitalize a word showing a family relationship when the word is used before or in place of a person's name.

Did **M**om invite **A**unt Frances?

Do not capitalize a word showing a family relationship if a possessive comes before the word.

Barbara's **f**ather knows my **u**ncle.

(4) Capitalize the first and last words and all important words in titles of books, magazines, newspapers, poems, short stories, historical documents, movies, television programs, works of art, and musical compositions.

Unimportant words in titles include prepositions of fewer than five letters (such as *at, of, for, from, with*); coordinating conjunctions (*and, but, for, nor, or, so, yet*); and articles (*a, an, the*).

Type of Name	Examples
Books	*__L__ittle __W__omen*
Magazines	*__F__ield and __S__tream, __S__eventeen*
Newspapers	*__B__oston __H__erald, __USA T__oday*
Poems	"**A T**ime to **T**alk", "**O**ranges"
Short Stories	"**T**he **M**onkey's **P**aw"
Historical Documents	**B**ill of **R**ights, **T**reaty of **G**hent

Type of Name	Examples
Movies	*__T__he __L__ion __K__ing, __S__tar __W__ars*
Television Programs	*__F__ull __H__ouse, __M__urder, __S__he __W__rote*
Works of Art	*__M__ona __L__isa, __I__ and the __V__illage*
Musical Compositions	*__W__est __S__ide __S__tory, __R__hapsody in __B__lue*

The article *the* before a title is not capitalized unless it is the first word of the title.

Is that **t**he *Chicago Sun-Times*?

I am reading "**T**he Tell-Tale Heart."

Your Turn Using Capitalization Correctly

Revise the following sentences by correcting the errors in capitalization.

1. Is that the man who bought the House on fifty-fifth street?
2. Yes, he's our Mayor, mr. Joseph.
3. When they met, mom asked him if he came from new england.
4. He said, "good grief, no, i'm from denver."
5. There was an Article about him in last month's *times herald.*

13. Punctuation

End Marks

An ***end mark*** is a mark of punctuation placed at the end of a sentence. The three kinds of end marks are the *period,* the *question mark,* and the *exclamation point.*

13a. **Use a period at the end of a statement.**

Jabez sought the help of Daniel**.**

13b. **Use a question mark at the end of a question.**

Did Zindel write *Let Me Hear You Whisper***?**

13c. **Use an exclamation point at the end of an exclamation.**

What an exciting race that was**!**

13d. **Use a period or an exclamation point at the end of a request or a command.**

Please read the part**.** [request]

Watch out**!** [command]

13e. **Use a period after most abbreviations.**

Type of Abbreviation	Examples	
Addresses	St. Rd.	Blvd. P.O. Box
Organizations and Companies	Co. Inc.	Corp. Assn.
Personal Names	O. Henry	W. W. Jacobs
Titles Used with Names	Mr. Mrs.	Jr. Dr.
States	Ky. Fla.	Tenn. Calif.
Times	A.M. P.M.	B.C. A.D.

When an abbreviation with a period ends a sentence, another period is not needed. However, a question mark or an exclamation point is used as needed.

This is my friend J. R.
Have you met Nguyen, J. R.**?**

A two-letter state abbreviation without periods is used only when it is followed by a ZIP Code.

Lodi, **CA** 95240

Place the abbreviations A.D. (*anno Domini,* in the year of the Lord) before the number; place B.C. (before Christ) after the number.

A.D. 540, 31 B.C.

Abbreviations for government agencies and other widely used abbreviations are often written without periods. Each letter of the abbreviation is capitalized.

UN, FBI, PTA, NAACP, PBS, CNN, VHF

Commas

ITEMS IN A SERIES

13f. Use commas to separate items in a series.

Words, phrases, and clauses in a series are separated by commas to show where one item in the series ends and the next begins. Make sure there are three or more items in a series; two items often do not need a comma.

WORDS IN A SERIES	In fall, the lake looks cold, gray, and calm.
PHRASES IN A SERIES	Tightening the spokes, checking the tires, and oiling the gears, Carlos prepared his bike for the race.
CLAUSES IN A SERIES	I was late because the car wouldn't start, my dad lost his wallet, and I forgot my lunch.

If all items in a series are joined by *and* or *or,* do not use commas to separate them.

Read *The Friends* **or** *Summer of my German Soldier* **or** *Bridge to Terabithia.*

13g. Use a comma to separate two or more adjectives that come before a noun.

Many ranchers depended on the small, tough, sure-footed mustang.

Sometimes the final adjective in a series is so closely linked to the noun that a comma is not used before it. To test whether the final adjective and the noun are linked, insert the word *and* between the adjectives. If *and* makes sense, use a comma.

Training a frisky colt to become a gentle, **dependable riding** horse takes patience. [*And* makes no sense between *dependable* and *riding*. A comma is not necessary.]

A comma should never be used between an adjective and the noun immediately following it.

Mary O'Hara wrote a tender, **suspenseful story** about a young boy and his cold.

COMPOUND SENTENCES

13h. Use a comma before *and, but, or, nor, for, so,* or *yet* when it joins independent clauses.

Outside, the wind was higher than ever**, and** the old man started nervously at the sound of a door banging upstairs.
—W. W. Jacobs, "The Monkey's Paw"

When the independent clauses are very short, the comma before *and, but,* or *or* may sometimes be omitted.

They were hungry **but** they had no food.

INTERRUPTERS

13i. Use commas to set off an expression that interrupts a sentence.

(1) Use commas to set off a nonessential participial phrase or a nonessential subordinate clause.

A ***nonessential*** (or ***nonrestrictive***) phrase or clause adds information that can be omitted without changing the main idea of the sentence.

NONESSENTIAL PHRASE	The spider web, **shining in the early light,** looked like sparkling lace.
NONESSENTIAL CLAUSE	Edgar Allan Poe, **who wrote "The Tell-Tale Heart,"** is a master of the macabre.

Do not set off an ***essential*** (or ***restrictive***) phrase or clause. Since such a phrase or clause tells *which one* or *which ones*, it cannot be omitted without changing the meaning of the sentence.

ESSENTIAL PHRASE	The discovery **made by Zenta** saved Tokubei fifty gold pieces. [Which discovery?]
ESSENTIAL CLAUSE	The book **that you bought** is not here. [Which book?]

(2) Use commas to set off an appositive or an appositive phrase that is nonessential.

APPOSITIVE	Smiley's frog, **Dan'l Webster,** lost the contest.
APPOSITIVE PHRASE	Robert Frost, **my favorite poet,** won four Pulitzer Prizes.

(3) Use commas to set off words used in direct address.

Do you know, **Elena,** who wrote the book *Pride and Prejudice*?

Do not set off an appositive that tells *which one* (or *ones*) about the word it identifies. Such an appositive is essential to the meaning of the sentence.

My ancestor **Alberto Pazienza** immigrated to America on the ship ***Marianna***. [Which ancestor? Which ship?]

(4) Use commas to set off a parenthetical expression.

A ***parenthetical expression*** is a side remark that adds information or relates ideas.

Amy should have known, **of course,** that Nishith would be late.

Commonly Used Parenthetical Expressions		
after all	for example	for instance
at any rate	in my opinion	I believe
by the way	of course	in general
in fact	on the other hand	in the first place

Some parenthetical expressions are not always used as interrupters. Use commas only when the expressions are parenthetical.

PARENTHETICAL	What**, in your opinion,** would be the best solution?
NOT PARENTHETICAL	We all have faith **in your opinion**.

INTRODUCTORY WORDS, PHRASES, AND CLAUSES

13j. Use a comma after certain introductory elements.

(1) Use a comma after *yes, no,* or any mild exclamation such as *well* or *why* at the beginning of a sentence.

Yes, I read "A Smart Cookie."

Why, if it isn't Nathan.

(2) Use a comma after an introductory prepositional phrase if the phrase is long or if two or more phrases appear together.

Underneath the moss-covered rock, a shiny, fat earthworm wiggled.

By the end of the second day of the journey, they were exhausted.

(3) Use a comma after a participial phrase or an infinitive phrase that introduces a sentence.

PARTICIPIAL PHRASE **Forced onto the sidelines by a sprained ankle,** Carlos was restless and unhappy.

INFINITIVE PHRASE **To defend the honor of King Arthur's knights,** Sir Gawain accepted the Green Knight's challenge.

(4) Use a comma after an introductory adverb clause.

As soon as I can, I'll let him know.

CONVENTIONAL SITUATIONS

13k. **Use commas in certain conventional situations.**

(1) Use commas to separate items in dates and addresses.

The delegates signed the document on Monday, September 17, 1787.

Her address is 64 Fig Road, Rome, IL 61562.

(2) Use a comma after the salutation of a friendly letter and after the closing of any letter.

Dear Mrs. Flowers, Sincerely yours,

Semicolons

A ***semicolon*** separates complete thoughts as a period does and also separates items within a sentence as a comma does.

13l. **Use a semicolon instead of a comma between closely related independent clauses when they are not joined by *and, but, or, nor, for, so,* or *yet.***

Motor activity is impaired; there is a general reduction of glandular activity; there is an accelerated loss of coordination.

—Daniel Keyes, *Flowers for Algernon*

13m. **Use a semicolon between independent clauses joined by a *conjunctive adverb* or a *transitional expression.***

A ***conjunctive adverb*** or a ***transitional expression*** shows how the independent clauses that it joins are related.

Mr. Scratch was formidable**; however,** he was no match for Daniel Webster.

He decided not to pay the ransom**; in fact,** he demanded money from the kidnappers.

Commonly Used Conjunctive Adverbs		
besides	consequently	furthermore
however	instead	meanwhile
nevertheless	otherwise	therefore

Commonly Used Transitional Expressions		
as a result	for example	for instance
in addition	in conclusion	in fact
in spite of	on the contrary	that is

When a conjunctive adverb or a transitional expression *joins* clauses, it is preceded by a semicolon and followed by a comma. When it *interrupts* a clause, however, it is set off by commas.

You are entitled to your opinion**; however,** you can't ignore the facts.

You are entitled to your opinion; you can't**, however,** ignore the facts.

13n. **Use a semicolon rather than a comma before a coordinating conjunction to join independent clauses that contain commas.**

We will practice Act I on Monday, Act II on Wednesday, and Act III on Friday; and on Saturday only Bill, Maya, and José will rehearse their scenes.

Colons

13o. **Use a colon before a list of items, especially after expressions like *as follows* or *the following.***

Robert Frost wrote the following: "The Runaway," "The Road Not Taken," and "A Time to Talk."

13p. **Use a colon before a statement that explains or clarifies a preceding statement.**

When a list of words, phrases, or subordinate clauses follows a colon, the first word of the list is lowercase. When an independent clause follows a colon, the first word of the clause begins with a capital letter.

There are two kinds of people: **c**at lovers and dog lovers.

She asked us only one question: **C**ould we finish the work in time?

13q. **Use a colon in certain conventional situations.**

(1) Use a colon between the hour and the minute.
11:30 P.M.

(2) Use a colon after the salutation of a business letter.
Dear Sir or Madam**:**

(3) Use a colon between chapter and verse in referring to passages from the Bible and between a title and a subtitle.
John 3**:**16
"A Tragedy Revealed**:** A Heroine's Last Days"

Never use a colon directly after a verb or a preposition that comes before a list of items.

INCORRECT	Please bring: garbage bags, shovels, loppers, and rakes.
CORRECT	Please bring garbage bags, shovels, loppers, and rakes.
INCORRECT	This sauce is made of: tomatoes, onions, oregano, and garlic.
CORRECT	This sauce is made of tomatoes, onions, oregano, and garlic.

Your Turn Using Punctuation Correctly

Read each of the following sentences, and revise any sentence that is too heavily punctuated.

1. Mary was just eighteen years old, but she had nerve and stood her ground; in the days to come, the family would have reason to be grateful to her.
2. She had run away, she bore scars, and she wouldn't say much about herself; because the family had no money, little food, and too much work for one man, Pa did not want to take her along with them, and, once he did, he did not even speak to her.
3. Life on the prairie broke the spirits of many people, such as those that the family met along the way; the people were glum and frightened, and many of them were past despair, yet they would give their help.
4. As you can well imagine, it must have been hard for the homesteaders to share their venison; food was difficult to come by, and they had little for themselves.
5. Mary prepared the mushroom, frying it in a pan; then, she ate some and sat up all night, waiting to see if death would come.

14. Punctuation

Underlining (Italics)

Italics are printed letters that lean to the right, such as *the letters in these words*. In your handwritten or typewritten work, indicate italics by underlining.

Monica Sone wrote <u>Nisei Daughter</u>.

In print this sentence would look like this:

Monica Sone wrote *Nisei Daughter*.

If you use a computer, you can set words in italics yourself.

14a. **Use underlining (italics) for titles of books, plays, periodicals, works of art, films, television programs, recordings, long musical compositions, trains, ships, aircraft, and spacecraft.**

Type Of Title	Examples
Books	*The Incredible Journey, Black Beauty*
Plays	*Let Me Hear You Whisper*
Periodicals	*Newsweek, The Wall Street Journal*
Works of Art	*The Last Supper, Bird in Space*
Films	*The Wizard of Oz, Batman*
Television Programs	*The Simpsons, Law & Order*

Type of Title	Examples
Recordings	*Music Box, No Fences*
Long Musical Compositions	*A Sea Symphony, Peer Gynt Suite*
Ships and Trains	*Queen Elizabeth 2, Orient Express*
Aircraft and Spacecraft	*Spruce Goose,* USS *Enterprise*

The article *the* before the title of a magazine or a newspaper is usually neither italicized nor capitalized when it is written within a sentence. Some periodicals do include *the* in their titles.

We subscribe to **the** *Chicago Tribune*.
He wrote for ***The*** *New York Times*.

14b. **Use underlining (italics) for words, letters, and figures referred to as such.**

The word is *emigrate* not *immigrate*.
Drop the final *e* before add *–ing* to *dine*.
Is this number a *3* or an *8*?

Quotation Marks

14c. **Use quotation marks to enclose a *direct* quotation—a person's exact words.**

"Have you read the book?**"** she asked.

Do not use quotation marks for an ***indirect quotation***—a rewording of a direct quotation.

She asked me whether I had read the book.

14d. **A direct quotation begins with a capital letter.**

Abe Lincoln shouted, "**T**he ballot is stronger than the bullet."

When the expression identifying the speaker interrupts a quoted sentence, the second part of the quotation begins with a lowercase letter.

"What are some of the things," asked Mrs. Perkins, "**t**hat the astronauts discovered?"

When only part of a sentence is being quoted, the quotation generally begins with a lowercase letter.

Abe Lincoln described the ballot as "**s**tronger than the bullet."

When the second part of a divided quotation is a separate sentence, it begins with a capital letter.

"Sandra and Alfonso went bike riding," remarked Mrs. Perkins. "**T**hey left an hour ago." [Notice that a period, not a comma, follows the interrupting expression.]

14e. **A direct quotation is set off from the rest of the sentence by a comma, a question mark, or an exclamation point, but not by a period.**

Set off means "separated." If a quotation appears at the beginning of a sentence, a comma follows it. If a quotation falls at the end of a sentence, a comma comes before it. If a quoted sentence is interrupted, a comma follows the first part and comes before the second part.

"I've just finished the book**,**" Alison said.
Jaime said**,** "He's my favorite writer."
"Did you know**,**" asked Helen**,** "that O. Henry is not his real name?"

14f. **A period or a comma is always placed inside the closing quotation marks.**

She said, "The story is set in California**.**"

14g. **A question mark or an exclamation point is placed inside the closing quotation marks when the quotation itself is a question or exclamation. Otherwise the question mark or exclamation point is placed outside.**

"Did Rawlings write *The Yearling***?"** asked Ken. [The quotation is a question.]
She exclaimed, "I can't find my homework**!"** [The quotation is an exclamation.]
What did the captain mean when he said "Hard aport"**?** [The sentence, not the quotation, is a question.]

When both the sentence and the quotation at the end of the sentence are questions (or exclamations), only one end mark is used. It is placed inside the closing quotation marks.

Who wrote the poem that begins "How do I love thee**?"**

When a quotation ends with a question mark or with an exclamation point, no comma is needed.

"What did they wish**?**" asked Cynthia.
"What a surprise**!**" exclaimed Meryl.

14h. **When you write dialogue (conversation), begin a new paragraph each time you change speakers.**

"I'm listening," said the latter, grimly surveying the board as he stretched out his hand. "Check."

"I should hardly think that he'd come tonight," said his father, with his hand poised over the board.

"Mate," replied the son.

—W. W. Jacobs, "The Monkey's Paw"

14i. **When a quotation consists of several sentences, place quotation marks at the beginning and at the end of the whole quotation.**

"Oh, please come in. I'm so happy to see you. Let me take your hat," said Ms. Davis.

14j. **Use single quotation marks to enclose a quotation within a quotation.**

"What Longfellow poem begins 'Listen, my children, and you shall hear'?" Carol asked.

14k. **Use quotation marks to enclose titles of short works such as short stories, poems, articles, songs, episodes of television programs, and chapters and other parts of books.**

Type of Title	Examples
Short Stories, Poems	"Raymond's Run," "The Runaway"
Articles	"New Computers," "The Best Word"
Songs	"Greensleeves," "Yesterday"
Episodes of Television Programs	"Theo's Future," "Mr. Likable"
Chapters and Other Parts of Books	"Workers' Rights," "Word Games"

Your Turn Using Quotation Marks

You have conducted an interview with a famous writer named F. A. Moss. During the interview, Mr. Moss made the statements listed below. Write a paragraph or two based on Mr. Moss's quotations. Be sure to use at least three direct quotations.

1. "A poem can come at any time, so I always carry a small notebook."
2. "Some of my best ideas occur to me in the middle of the night."
3. "Poetry is the heart of literature."
4. "I once wrote a haiku while waiting for a traffic light to change."
5. "Anyone can write poetry if only he or she speaks the truth."

15. Punctuation

Apostrophes

POSSESSIVE CASE

15a. **The *possessive case* of a noun or a pronoun shows ownership or relationship.**

(1) To form the possessive case of a singular noun, add an apostrophe and an *s*.
the boy**'s** bike, Charles**'s** father

A proper noun ending in *s* may take only an apostrophe to form the possessive case if the addition of *'s* would make the name awkward to pronounce.
Buenos Aires**'** climate, Hercules**'** strength

(2) To form the possessive case of a plural noun ending in *s*, add only the apostrophe.
students' records, citizens' committee

(3) To form the possessive case of a plural noun that does not end in *s*, add an apostrophe and an *s*.
mice**'s** tracks, children**'s** voices

(4) To form the possessive case of most indefinite pronouns, add an apostrophe and an *s*.
everyone**'s** opinion, somebody**'s** umbrella

CONTRACTIONS

15b. **To form a contraction, use an apostrophe to show where letters have been left out.**

A ***contraction*** is a shortened form of a word, a figure, or a group of words.

Common Contractions	
he is → he**'s**	you will → you**'ll**
let us → let**'s**	they had → they**'d**
we are → we**'re**	where is → where**'s**

The word *not* can be shortened to *–n't* and added to a verb, usually without changing the verb's spelling.

are not → aren**'t** have not → haven**'t**
does not → doesn**'t** do not → don**'t**
should not → shouldn**'t** was not → wasn**'t**

EXCEPTIONS
will not → won**'t** cannot → can**'t**

Do not confuse contractions with possessive pronouns.

Contractions	Possessive Pronouns
It's raining. [It is]	**Its** wing is broken.
There's only one left. [There is]	This car is **theirs.**
You're a good student. [You are]	**Your** story is interesting.

PLURALS

15c. **Use an apostrophe and an *s* to form the plurals of letters, numerals, and signs, and of words referred to as words.**

The word has two *r***'s**, not one
My brother is learning to count by *5***'s**.
Don't use *&***'s** in place of *and***'s**.

Hyphens

15d. **Use a hyphen to divide a word at the end of a line, using the rules that follow.**

(1) Divide a word only between syllables.
INCORRECT Charlene has four questions about Shakespeare.
CORRECT Charlene has four questions about Shakespeare.

(2) Do not divide a word so that one letter stands alone.
INCORRECT Tokubei and Zenta stayed o-
vernight in an unusual inn.
CORRECT Tokubei and Zenta stayed overnight in an unusual inn.

(3) Divide an already hyphenated word at a hyphen.
INCORRECT We are going to see my sis-
ter-in-law tomorrow.
CORRECT We are going to see my sister-in-
law tomorrow.

(4) Do not divide a one-syllable word.
INCORRECT Hopefully, Mr. White wished for two hundred pounds.
CORRECT Hopefully, Mr. White wished for
two hundred pounds.

15e. **Use a hyphen with compound numbers from *twenty-one* to *ninety-nine* and with fractions used as adjectives.**

twenty-five dollars, **one-half** cup of flour [*but* one half of the class].

Parentheses

15f. Use parentheses to enclose material that is added to a sentence but is not considered of major importance

Saki (1870–1916) wrote "The Open Window."

A short sentence in parentheses may stand by itself or be contained within another sentence.

Fill in the form carefully. **(Do not use a pencil.)**
The fort **(used during the war)** has been rebuilt.

Dashes

15g. Use a dash to indicate an abrupt break in thought or speech.

Rob don't—I mean, doesn't—want to face Sandra.
The new library has windows—a real improvement.

Your Turn Correcting Punctuation

Correct the punctuation in the following sentences by inserting apostrophes, hyphens, dashes, or parentheses as needed.

1. The Civil War 1861–1865 was one of the bloodiest wars in the nations history.
2. The war ended with the defeat of the Confederates at the Battle of Appomattox pronounced ap uh MAT uhks Courthouse.
3. For extra credit our teacher asked us to read Stephen Cranes *The Red Badge of Courage.*
4. Im planning to read the first fifty one pages.
5. The book is about a young soldiers struggles with fear something we can all understand.

16. Spelling

Using Word Parts

Many English words are made up of two or more word parts. Some word parts have more than one form.

ROOTS

The ***root*** of a word is the part that carries the word's core meaning.

Commonly Used Roots		
ROOT	MEANING	EXAMPLES
–port	carry	portable, transport
–scrib–, –script–	write	describe, manuscript
–spec–	look	spectator, spectacles

PREFIXES

A ***prefix*** is one or more letters or syllables added to the beginning of a word or word part to create a new word.

Commonly Used Prefixes		
PREFIX	MEANING	EXAMPLES
dis–	not, opposing	disable, disagree
mis–	badly, wrong	misbehave, misdeed
re–	back, again	rebuild, reclaim

SUFFIXES

A ***suffix*** is one or more letters or syllables added to the end of a word or a word part to create a new word.

Commonly Used Suffixes		
SUFFIX	MEANING	EXAMPLES
–er, –or	doer, native of	actor, westerner
–ful	full of, characteristic of	joyful, truthful
–tion	action, condition	rotation, selection

Spelling Rules

ie AND *ei*

16a. Except after *c*, write *ie* when the sound is long *e*.

ach**ie**ve shi**e**ld c**ei**ling dec**ei**ve

EXCEPTIONS

either n**ei**ther prot**ei**n

16b. Write *ei* when the sound is not long *e*, especially when the sound is long *a*.

for**ei**gn fr**ei**ght h**ei**ght h**ei**r

EXCEPTIONS

anc**ie**nt consc**ie**nce p**ie**

This time-tested verse may help you remember the *ie* rule.

I before *e*
Except after *c*
Or when sounded like *a*,
As in *neighbor* and *weigh*.

The rhyme above and rules 16a and 16b apply only when the *i* and the *e* are in the same syllable.

–cede, –ceed, AND *–sede*

16c. The only English word ending in *–sede* is *supersede*. The only words ending in *–ceed* are *exceed, proceed,* and *succeed.* Most other words with this sound end in *–cede*.

con**cede**, inter**cede**, pre**cede**, re**cede**

ADDING PREFIXES

16d. When adding a prefix to a word, do not change the spelling of the word itself.

over + see = **over**see il + legal = **il**legal

ADDING SUFFIXES

16e. When adding the suffix *–ly* or *–ness* to a word, do not change the spelling of the word itself.

usual + ly = usual**ly**
eager + ness = eager**ness**

EXCEPTIONS For words that end in *y* and have more than one syllable, change the *y* to *i* before adding *–ly* or *–ness*:
happy + ly = happ**ily**
lazy + ness = laz**iness**

16f. Drop the final silent *e* before a suffix beginning with a vowel.

live + ing = liv**ing** give + er = giv**er**

EXCEPTIONS Keep the final silent *e* in a word ending in *ce* or *ge* before a suffix beginning with *a* or *o*:
notice + able = notic**eable,**
courage + ous = courag**eous.**

When adding *–ing* to words that end in *ie*, drop the e and change the *i* to *y*.

lie + ing = l**ying** die + ing = d**ying**

16g. Keep the final silent *e* before a suffix beginning with a consonant.

hope + ful = hope**ful** care + less = care**less**

EXCEPTIONS true + ly = tru**ly**,
judge + ment = judg**ment**

16h. For words ending in *y* preceded by a consonant, change the *y* to *i* before any suffix that does not begin with *i*.

easy + ly = eas**ily** cry + ing = cr**ying**

16i. For words ending in *y* preceded by a vowel, keep the *y* when adding a suffix.

obey + ed = obey**ed**

EXCEPTIONS day—da**ily**
lay—la**id**
say—sa**id**

16j. Double the final consonant before a suffix beginning with a vowel if the word (1) has only one syllable or has the accent on the last syllable *and* (2) ends in a single consonant preceded by a single vowel.

dim + ing = di**mm**ing occur + ed = occu**rr**ed

However, do not double the final consonant in words ending in *w* or *x*.

mow + ing = mowing wax + ed = waxed

FORMING THE PLURALS OF NOUNS

16k. For most nouns, add *–s.*

SINGULAR	desk	idea	shoe
PLURAL	desk**s**	idea**s**	shoe**s**

16l. For most nouns ending in *s, x, z, ch,* or *sh,* add *–es.*

SINGULAR	bus	fox	waltz
PLURAL	bus**es**	fox**es**	waltz**es**

16m. For nouns ending in *y* preceded by a vowel, add *–s.*

SINGULAR	decoy	highway	alley
PLURAL	decoy**s**	highway**s**	alley**s**

16n. For nouns ending in *y* preceded by a consonant, change the *y* to *i* and add *–es.*

SINGULAR	army	country	city
PLURAL	arm**ies**	countr**ies**	cit**ies**
EXCEPTIONS	For proper nouns ending in *y*, just add *–s*: Brady—Brady**s.**		

16o. For some nouns ending in *f* or *fe*, add *–s.* For others, change the *f* or *fe* to *v* and add *–es.*

SINGULAR	belief	giraffe	thief
PLURAL	belief**s**	giraffe**s**	thie**ves**

16p. For nouns ending in *o* preceded by a vowel, add *–s.*

SINGULAR	radio	patio	stereo
PLURAL	radio**s**	patio**s**	stereo**s**

16q. For nouns ending in *o* preceded by a consonant, add *–es.*

SINGULAR	tomato	potato	echo
PLURAL	tomato**es**	potato**es**	echo**es**
EXCEPTIONS	For musical terms and proper nouns, add *–s*: solo—solo**s**, Aquino—Aquino**s**		

16r. The plural of a few nouns is formed in irregular ways.

SINGULAR	ox	foot	mouse
PLURAL	ox**en**	f**ee**t	m**ice**

16s. For most compound nouns, form the plural of the last word in the compound.

SINGULAR	bookshelf	push-up
PLURALS	bookshel**ves**	push-up**s**

16t. For compound nouns in which one of the words is modified by the other word or words, form the plural of the word modified.

SINGULAR	brother-in-law	maid of honor
PLURAL	brother**s**-in-law	maid**s** of honor

16u. For some nouns, the singular and the plural forms are the same.

trout, sheep, pliers, series, aircraft, Chinese

16v. For numbers, letters, symbols, and words used as words, add an apostrophe and *–s.*

four *2*'**s**, two *m*'**s,** missing *$*'**s**, many *and*'**s**

SPELLING NUMBERS

16w. Spell out a number that begins a sentence.

Five hundred people went to see the game.

16x. Within a sentence, spell out numbers that can be written in one or two words. Use numerals for other numbers.

In all, **fifty-two** people attended the reunion.
More than **160** people were invited.

16y. Spell out numbers used to indicate order.

She came in **second** [*not* 2nd] in the race.

If you use several numbers, some of which could be spelled out, write them all as numerals.

He wrote **37** plays and **154** poems.

Your Turn Using Apostrophes Correctly

Insert apostrophes where appropriate in each of the following sentences.

1. Do not use *its* to refer to people.
2. These *hers* should be written with *ss*.
3. In computing, */s* are very important.
4. In the Middle Ages, 62 great romances were written.
5. How many *is* are in the word *billion*?

17. Glossary of Usage

This Glossary of Usage is an alphabetical list of words and expressions that are commonly misused in English. Throughout this section some examples are labeled *standard* or *nonstandard*. ***Standard English*** is the most widely accepted form of English. It is used in *formal* situations, such as in speeches and writing for school, and in *informal* situations, such as in conversation and everyday writing. ***Nonstandard English*** is language that does not follow the rules and guidelines of standard English.

a, an Use *a* before words beginning with consonant sounds. Use *an* before words beginning with vowel sounds.

He did not consider himself **a** hero.
An oryx is a large antelope.

accept, except *Accept* is a verb that means "receive." *Except* may be either a verb or a preposition. As a verb, *except* means "leave out" or "exclude"; as a preposition, *except* means "other than" or "excluding."

Squeaky **accepts** the responsibility. [verb]
Some students will be **excepted**. [verb]
No one **except** Diego finished. [preposition]

affect, effect *Affect* is a verb meaning "influence." The noun *effect* means "the result of some action."

His test score will **affect** his final grade.
The **effect** of the medicine was immediate.

ain't Avoid this word in speaking and writing; it is nonstandard English.

a lot *A lot* should always be written as two words, but should not be overused. As you revise your own writing, try to replace *a lot* with a more exact word or phrase.

I spent **a lot** of time making this poster.
I spent **three hours** making this poster.

all ready, already *All ready* means "completely prepared." *Already* means "before a certain point in time."

We were **all ready** for the quiz.
I had **already** read "Flowers for Algernon."

all together, altogether The expression *all together* means "everyone or everything in the same place." The adverb *altogether* means "entirely."

He called us **all together** for the rehearsal.
He is **altogether** pleased with his victory.

at Do not use at after *where*.

Where does she live? [*not* Where does she live at?]

bad, badly *Bad* is an adjective. *Badly* is an adverb.

The tea tastes **bad**. [*Bad* modifies the noun *tea*.]
The boy's wrist was sprained *badly*. [*Badly* modifies the verb phrase *was sprained*.]

between, among Use *between* when referring to two things, even though they may be part of a group of more than two.

Alfonso avoided Sandra **between** classes.

Use *among* to refer to a group rather than to separate individuals.

It was divided **among** the four of them.

bust, busted Avoid using these words as verbs. Use a form of either *burst* or *break*.

The balloon may **burst** [*not* bust].
Alfonso's bicycle chain **broke** [*not* busted].

choose, chose *Choose* is the present tense form of the verb *choose*. It rhymes with *whose* and means "select." *Chose* is the past tense form of *choose*. It rhymes with *grows* and means "selected."

What did you **choose** as your topic?
Trish **chose** to do her report on Shel Silverstein.

could of Do not write *of* with the helping verb *could*. Write *could have*. Also avoid *had of, ought to of, should of, would of, might of,* and *must of*. *Of* is also unnecessary with *had*.

Jim **could have** [*not* could of] done it.
If he **had** [*not* had of], we would know.

fewer, less *Fewer* is used with plural words. *Less* is used with singular words. *Fewer* tells "how many"; *less* tells "how much."

I have **fewer** errors to correct than I thought.
The kidnappers asked for **less** money.

good, well *Good* is an adjective. Never use *good* as an adverb. Instead, use *well*. *Well* may also be used as an adjective to mean "healthy."

She works **well** [*not* good] with the others.
Mary and the children didn't look **well**.

had ought, hadn't ought *Had* should not be used with *ought*.

He **ought** [*not* had ought] to read more.

he, she, they Avoid using a pronoun along with its antecedent as the subject of a verb. This error is called the ***double subject.***

NONSTANDARD Bambara she is a writer.
STANDARD Bambara is a writer.

hisself *Hisself* is nonstandard English. Use *himself.*

He finds **himself** [*not* hisself] in a dilemma.

how come In informal situations, *how come* is often used instead of *why*. In formal situations, *why* should always be used.

INFORMAL I know how come he did that.
FORMAL I know **why** he did that.

kind of, sort of In informal situations, *kind of* and *sort of* are often used to mean "somewhat" or "rather." In formal English, *somewhat* or *rather* is preferred.

INFORMAL Alfonso was kind of shy.
FORMAL Alfonso was **rather** shy.

learn, teach *Learn* means "gain knowledge." *Teach* means "instruct."

What did he **learn** from the professor?
What did the professor **teach** him?

like, as In informal situations, the preposition *like* is often used instead of the conjunction *as* to introduce a clause. In formal situations, *as* is preferred.

Do you think Marga memorized a poem, **as** [*not* like] Mrs. Cobb had suggested?

like, as if, as though In informal situations, the preposition *like* is often used for the compound conjunctions *as if* or *as though*. In formal situations, *as if* or *as though* is preferred.

He acted **as if** [*not* like] he hadn't done it.

of Do not use *off* with other prepositions such as *inside, off,* and *outside.*

The bun is **inside** [*not* inside of] the box.

real In informal situations, *real* is often used as an adverb meaning "very" or "extremely." In formal situations, *very* or *extremely* is preferred.

INFORMAL Max became real quiet.
FORMAL Max became **extremely** quiet.

reason . . . because In informal situations, *reason . . . because* is often used instead of *reason . . . that*. In formal situations, use *reason . . . that*, or revise your sentence.

INFORMAL The reason I like the story is because I identify with the protagonist.
FORMAL The **reason** I like the story is **that** I identify with the protagonist.

some, somewhat Do not use *some* for *somewhat* as an adverb.

Her writing improved **somewhat** [*not* some].

than, then *Than* is a conjunction used in making comparisons. *Then* is an adverb that means "at that time."

Squeaky is a faster runner **than** Gretchen.
First we shopped; **then** we studied.

theirself, theirselves *Theirself* and *theirselves* are nonstandard English. Use *themselves*.

They bought **themselves** [*not* theirself *or* theirselves] a telescope.

them *Them* should not be used as an adjective. Use *those.*

Karen gave you **those** [*not* them] magazines.

try and In informal situations, *try and* is often used instead of *try to*. In formal situations, *try to* should be used.

INFORMAL I will try and do it.
FORMAL I will **try to** do it.

when, where Do not use *when* or *where* incorrectly in stating a definition.

INCORRECT A flashback is when a writer interrupts the action in a story to tell about something that happened earlier.
CORRECT A flashback is an interruption of the action in a story to tell about something that happened earlier.

where Do not use *where* for *that.*

I read **that** [*not* where] he went to prison.

Your Turn Using Standard English

Revise the following paragraph according to the rules of Standard English.

[**1**] When the twins tried to fix the toilet, the pipe busted. [**2**] Dad hadn't ought to have asked the twins to do the job. [**3**] Jedd and Jamie they are always breaking things. [**4**] Dad should have done the work hisself rather than ask the twins. [**5**] In fact, I wonder how come he didn't call a plumber.

Glossary

The glossary that follows is an alphabetical list of words found in the selections in this book. Use this glossary just as you would use a dictionary—to find out the meaning of unfamiliar words. (Some technical, foreign, and more obscure words in this book are not listed here but instead are defined for you in the footnotes that accompany many of the selections.)

Many words in the English language have more than one meaning. This glossary gives the meanings that apply to the words as they are used in the selections in this book. Words closely related in form and meaning are usually listed together in one entry (for instance, *cower* and *cowered*), and the definition is given for the first form.

The following abbreviations are used:

adj.	adjective
adv.	adverb
n.	noun
v.	verb

Each word's pronunciation is given in parentheses. For more information about the words in this glossary or for information about words not listed here, consult a dictionary

A

abide (uh BYD) (with *by*) *v.* accept and follow.
abnormal (ab NAWR muhl) *adj.* not normal; unusual.
acquisition (ak wuh ZIHSH uhn) *n.* something purchased or gained.
aghast (uh GAST) *adj.* shocked; horrified.
amend (uh MEHND) *v.* make better.
amiably (AY mee uh blee) *adv.* good-naturedly.
ample (AM puhl) *adj.* as much as is needed; enough.
anguish (ANG gwihsh) *n.* emotional pain.
annihilation (uh ny uh LAY shuhn) *n.* complete destruction.
antiquated (AN tuh kway tihd) *adj.* old-fashioned.
appeal (uh PEEL) *n.* request for help or sympathy.
archaic (ahr KAY ihk) *adj.* out of date; old-fashioned.
arrogant (AR uh guhnt) *adj.* overly proud.
audacity (aw DAS uh tee) *n.* boldness.
authentic (aw THEHN tihk) *adj.* genuine.
authorization (aw thuhr uh ZAY shuhn) *n.* official permission.

B

barracks (BAR ehks) *n.* large buildings or groups of buildings in which many people live.
benign (bih NYN) *adj.* kindly; harmless.
boundaries (BOWN duh reez) *n.* where one thing ends and another begins.
breach (breech) *n.* opening caused by a break, such as in a wall or in a line of defense.

C

chaotic (kay AHT ihk) *adj.* confused.
cherished (CHEHR ihsht) *v.* used as *adj.* valued; well-loved.
circuit (SUR kiht) *n.* regular route of a job.
clemency (KLEHM uhn see) *n.* mercy; tolerance.
commemorate (kuh MEHM uh rayt) *v.* honor the memory of.
commotion (kuh MOH shuhn) *n.* noisy confusion; disturbance.
competition (kahm puh TIHSH uhn) *n.* contest.
compressed (KUHM prehsd) *adj.* pressed together.
comrade (KAHM rad) *n.* companion; friend; associate.
conceded (kuhn SEED ihd) *v.* admitted; acknowledged.
confines (KAHN fynz) *n.* borders; boundaries.
conspicuous (kuhn SPIHK yoo uhs) *adj.* noticeable.
contradictory (kahn truh DIHK tuhr ee) *adj.* in disagreement; opposing.
corps (kawr) *n.* group of people with special training; a military unit.
correlate (KAWR uh layt) *v.* show the connection between things.
corresponding (kawr uh SPAHN dihng) *adj.* matching; equivalent.

credulity (kruh DOO luh tee) *n.* quality of believing too readily.
creed (kreed) *n.* statement of belief or principles.

D

defiance (dih FY uhns) *n.* willingness to fight; rebellious feelings.
denounce (dih NOWNS) *v.* speak against.
derision (dih RIHZH uhn) *n.* contempt; ridicule.
descendants (dih SEHN duhnts) *n.* all the generations who come from one person.
desolate (DEHS uh liht) *adj.* lonely; miserable.
detect (dih TEHKT) *v.* discover; notice.
deterioration (dih tihr ee uh RAY shuhn) *n.* used as an *adj.* worsening; declining.
detract (dih TRAKT) *v.* take away from; make less important.
diplomat (DIHP luh mat) *n.* person who handles issues with other countries.
disconnected (dihs kuh NEHK tihd) *v.* used as *adj.* not connected; cut off; separated.
discontinued (dihs kuhn TIHN yood) *v.* used as *adj.* not continued; stopped; ended.
dispel (dihs PEHL) *v.* get rid of by driving away.
displeasure (dihs PLEHZH uhr) *n.* annoyance; dissatisfaction.
dissuade (dih SWAYD) *v.* change someone's mind against; convince not to do.
domination (dahm ih NAY shuhn) *n.* act of controlling; power.
drifting (DRIHF tihng) *v.* being carried along as if by a current of air or water.
drone (drohn) *n.* continuous buzzing sound.

E

eloquence (EHL uh kwehns) *n.* ability to write or speak gracefully and convincingly.
elusive (ih LOO sihv) *adj.* hard to catch.
emaciated (ih MAY shee ay tihd) *v.* used as *adj.* extremely thin, as from starvation.
empowered (ehm POW uhrd) *adj.* given the power to do something.
excessive (ehk SEHS ihv) *adj.* too much; too great.

F

fate (fayt) *n.* what becomes of someone or something.
fatigue (fuh TEEG) *n.* exhaustion; tiredness.
ferocious (fuh ROH shuhs) *adj.* brutal; cruel.
fixated (FIHK sayt uhd) *adj.* focused with full attention.
forlorn (fawr LAWRN) *adj.* abandoned and lonely.
formulated (FAWR myuh lay tihd) *v.* stated clearly and logically.
foster (FAWS tuhr) *adj.* given shelter and care by people other than one's parents.
foundered (FOWN duhrd) *v.* broke down; failed.
frail (frayl) *adj.* weak; fragile.
frayed (frayd) *adj.* worn away; unraveled.
fugitives (FYOO juh tihvz) *n.* people fleeing from danger or oppression.
functions (FUHNGK shuhnz) *n.* uses; purposes.

G

gesticulations (jehs TIHK yuh LAY shuhnz) *n.* energetic movements or gestures.
gnarled (nahrld) *adj.* covered with knots; twisted.
grueling (GROO uhl ihng) *adj.* very tiring; demanding.

H

hazards (HAZ uhrdz) *n.* dangers; things that can cause danger.
hospitality (hahs puh TAL uh tee) *n.* friendly or generous treatment of guests.
host (hohst) *n.* army; large number.
hypocrisy (hih PAHK ruh see) *n.* false show of virtue or goodness.
hypothesis (hy PAHTH uh sihs) *n.* possible explanation or answer.
hysterically (hihs TEHR uh klee) *adv.* in an uncontrolled or wild manner.

I

immortality (ihm awr TAL uh tee) *n.* endless life.
impeccably (ihm PEHK uh blee) *adv.* flawlessly.
impetuous (ihm PEHCH yoo uhs) *adj.* impulsive; eager.
impromptu (ihm PRAHMP too) *adj.* unplanned.
incentive (ihn SEHN tihv) *n.* reason to do something; motivation.
incomprehensible (ihn kahm prih HEHN suh buhl) *adj.* impossible to understand.

indignantly (ihn DIHG nuhnt lee) *adv.* with anger caused by something felt to be unjust.
inert (ihn URT) *adj.* not moving; still.
inexplicable (ihn ihk SPLIHK uh buhl) *adj.* unable to be explained.
innumerable (ih NOO muhr uh buhl) *adj.* very many.
inquiring (ihn KWYR ihng) *v.* looking for answers; asking.
instinctively (ihn STIHNGK tihv lee) *adv.* automatically.
insulated (IHN suh layt ihd) *v.* shielded; protected.
intensified (ihn TEHN suh fyd) *v.* increased; strengthened.
intently (ihn TEHNT lee) *adv.* with close attention.
intolerant (ihn TAHL uhr uhnt) *adj.* unwilling to accept something.
introspective (ihn truh SPEHK tihv) *adj.* looking inward.
invasion (ihn VAY zhuhn) *n.* act of entering by force.

L

legitimate (luh JIHT uh miht) *adj.* allowed by law.
liable (LY uh buhl) *adj.* legally responsible.
liberation (lihb uh RAY shuhn) *n.* release from imprisonment or enemy occupation.
loathed (lohthd) *v.* hated.

M

majority (muh JAWR uh tee) *n.* larger part of something.
mass (mas) *n.* large group, in this case, of people.
mastered (MAS tuhrd) *v.* made oneself the master of; became skillful at.
merit (MEHR iht) *n.* worth.
mesmerized (MEHS muh ryzd) *v.* used as *adv.* hypnotized.
mimicking (MIHM ihk ihng) *v.* imitating; copying.
mind (mynd) *v.* take care of.
minority (muh NAWR uh tee) *n.* smaller part of something.
misled (mihs LEHD) *v.* fooled; led to believe something wrong.
monopoly (muh NAHP uh lee) *n.* total control over a particular business.
mournful (MAWRN fuhl) *adj.* full of deep sadness.

N

necessarily (nehs uh SAIR uh lee) *adv.* unavoidably; in every case.
negotiated (nih GOH shee ayt ihd) *v.* came to an agreement through discussion; talked.
negotiation (nih goh shee AY shuhn) *n.* process of reaching an agreement.
nobly (NOH blee) *adv.* in a manner that is excellent or heroic.

O

oasis (oh AY sihs) *n.* place or thing offering relief.
obscure (uhb SKYUR) *v.* hide.
observation (ahb zuhr VAY shuhn) *n.* act of noticing.
ominous (AHM uh nuhs) *adj.* threatening.
ostentatiously (ahs tehn TAY shuhs lee) *adv.* in a showy way.

P

patriots (PAY tree uhts) *n.* people who love and support their country.
perpetuate (puhr PEHCH yoo ayt) *v.* cause to continue.
petrified (PEHT ruh fyd) *adj.* paralyzed with fear.
poignant (POYN yuhnt) *adj.* causing sadness or pain; touching.
populated (PAHP yuh layt ihd) *v.* used as *adj.* lived in.
potentially (poh TEHN shuh lee) *adv.* possibly.
premonition (prehm uh NIHSH uhn) *n.* feeling that something bad will happen.
presumptuous (prih ZUHMP choo uhs) *adj.* overly bold or confident; expecting too much.
probing (PROHB ihng) *v.* used as *adj.* searching or investigating.
procession (proh SEHSH uhn) *n.* parade.
prodigy (PROD uh jee) *n.* child with exceptional talent.
proposal (pruh POHZ uhl) *n.* suggestion.
prototype (PROH tuh typ) *n.* first or original model of something.
proximity (prahk SIHM uh tee) *n.* state of being close by; nearness.
purge (purj) *v.* get rid of something harmful.

R

raucous (RAW kuhs) *adj.* loud and rough.
recite (rih SYT) *v.* present a memorized text orally, often in a formal manner.
refugees (rehf yuh JEEZ) *n.* people who seek refuge, or safety, especially in another country.
regression (rih GREHSH uhn) *n.* return to an earlier or less advanced condition.
rehabilitate (ree huh BIHL uh tayt) *v.* restore to good standing.
reigns (raynz) *v.* dominates; exists.
re-invented (ree in VEHNT ihd) *v.* created again, or made new.
reputation (rehp yuh TAY shuhn) *n.* the way others see a person.
resembles (rih ZEHM buhlz) *v.* looks like.
riveted (RIHV iht ihd) *v.* used as *adj.* intensely focused on.
rueful (ROO fuhl) *adj.* regretful.
ruefully (ROO fuhl lee) *adv.* with regret and embarrassment.
ruin (ROO uhn) *n.* great damage; devastation.

S

scholarship (SKAHL uhr shihp) *n.* money given to help a student continue to study.
scorn (skawrn) *n.* obvious disrespect or dislike for someone or something.
secure (sih KYUR) *v.* fix firmly in place.
serene (suh REEN) *adj.* calm; undisturbed.
shunning (SHUHN ihng) *v.* avoiding; having little to do with.
solace (SAHL ihs) *n.* comfort.
somber (SAHM buhr) *adj.* dark, melancholy.
spent (spehnt) *adj.* worn-out.
spirit (SPIHR iht) *n.* courage; liveliness.
stirred (sturd) *v.* moved; roused.
stoically (STOH uh kuhl lee) *adv.* here, stubbornly.
subject (SUHB jehkt) *adj.* likely to have; having a tendency.
summoned (SUHM uhnd) *v.* called; requested to come.
superiors (suh PIHR ee uhrz) *n.* people of higher rank.

T

taut (tawt) *adj.* pulled tight.
tax (taks) *v.* here, burden; strain.
tedious (TEE dee uhs) *adj.* long and boring.
teeming (TEEM ihng) *adj.* full (in this case, of people); crowded.
tentatively (TEHN tuh tihv lee) *adv.* in an uncertain or hesitant way.
tersely (TURS lee) *adv.* briefly and clearly; without unnecessary words.
tranquility (trang KWIHL uh tee) *n.* calm; peace.
traumatic (traw MAT ihk) *adj.* emotionally painful; causing shock.
tremor (TREHM uhr) *n.* shaking movement; vibration.
tyranny (TIHR uh nee) *n.* cruel and unjust use of power.

V

vaguely (VAYG lee) *adv.* unclearly.
vehemently (VEE uh muhnt lee) *adv.* forcefully; passionately.
verify (VEHR uh fy) *v.* show to be true; confirm.
versatility (vur suh TIHL uh tee) *n.* ability to do many things well.
vexed (vehkst) *v.* disturbed; annoyed.
vigil (VIHJ uhl) *n.* keeping guard; act of staying awake to keep watch.
vile (vyl) *adj.* very unpleasant.
vital (VY tuhl) *adj.* of great importance or need.

W

weathered (WEHTH uhrd) *v.* survived; came through safely.
wholesome (HOHL suhm) *adj.* good for the mind and spirit.
writhed (rythd) *v.* twisted and turned.

Y

yearning (YURN ihng) *v.* used as *adj.* longing for; wanting badly.

Spanish Glossary

A

aborrecer *v.* odiar.
abundante *adj.* suficiente; tanto como se necesite.
acogido *adj.* que otras personas distintas de sus padres lo llevaron a su hogar y lo cuidaron.
acongojado *adj.* que tiene una tristeza profunda.
admitir *v.* reconocer; aceptar.
adquisición *sust.* algo que se compra o se obtiene.
afablemente *adv.* con amabilidad.
aislar *v.* apartar, proteger.
alivio *sust.* consuelo.
angustia *sust.* sensación de dolor o sufrimiento emocional.
anhelo *sust.* ansia; deseo grande.
aniquilación *sust.* destrucción completa.
anormal *adj.* que no es normal; inusual.
anticuado *adj.* pasado de moda.
apesadumbradamente *adv.* con arrepentimiento y vergüenza.
apreciado *adj.* valorado, querido.
arcaico *adj.* muy viejo o anticuado.
arrogante *adj.* excesivamente orgulloso.
asegurar *v.* fijar con firmeza en el lugar.
asemejarse *v.* ser parecido a.
atender *v.* ocuparse de.
atenerse *v.* aceptar algo y actuar acorde a ello.
atentamente *adv.* prestando mucha atención.
aterrorizado *adj.* alarmado; horrorizado.
audacia *sust.* atrevimiento; osadía.
autorización *sust.* permiso oficial.
autorizado *adj.* que tiene el poder de hacer algo.

B

barraca *sust.* edificio grande o grupo de edificios en los que viven muchas personas.
beca *sust.* dinero que se da a un estudiante para que continúe sus estudios.
benigno *adj.* amable; inofensivo.
brecha *sust.* abertura, en general se refiere a una ruptura en una pared o en una línea de defensa.

C

camarada *sust.* compañero; amigo; socio.
caótico *adj.* confuso.
chillón *adj.* ruidoso y brusco.
circuito *sust.* recorrido habitual.
clemencia *sust.* compasión; tolerancia.
competición *sust.* competencia; partido.
comprimido *adj.* apretado.
confines *sust.* fronteras; límites.
conmemorar *v.* honrar la memoria de alguien.
conmoción *sust.* gran confusión; perturbación.
conmovedor *adj.* que causa tristeza o dolor; tierno.
conmover *v.* emocionar profundamente.
contorsionarse *v.* retorcerse.
contradictorio *adj.* que está en desacuerdo; que se opone.
convocar *v.* llamar; pedir que alguien asista a un lugar.
correlacionar *v.* establecer una relación entre dos o más cosas.
correspondiente *adj.* que coincide con algo; equivalente.
credo *sust.* proclamación de las creencias o principios.
credulidad *sust.* tendencia a creer algo con mucha facilidad.
cuerpo *sust.* grupo de personas con entrenamiento especial; unidad militar.

D

demacrar *v.* provocar extrema delgadez, por ejemplo, a causa del hambre.
denunciar *v.* expresarse en contra de algo.
deriva (ir a la) loc. *adv.* moverse empujado por una corriente de aire o agua.
desamparado *adj.* solo y abandonado.
descendientes *sust.* todas las generaciones que vienen de una persona.
desconectado *adj.* que no está conectado; aislado; separado.
desdén *sust.* falta de respeto o antipatía evidente por alguien o algo.

desmerecer *v.* quitar importancia; restar mérito.
desolado *adj.* desierto; triste.
destino *sust.* lo que le sucederá a alguien en el futuro.
detectar *v.* descubrir; darse cuenta de algo.
deteriorado *adj.* estropeado; dañado.
diplomático *sust.* persona que se encarga de las relaciones con otros países.
disgusto *sust.* desagrado; insatisfacción.
disipar *v.* hacer que algo desaparezca.
disuadir *v.* aconsejar a alguien que no haga algo; convencerlo para que no lo haga.
dominación *sust.* acción de controlar; poder.
dominar *v.* sobresalir en algo; adquirir la habilidad de hacer algo.
dudosamente *adv.* de manera incierta o dubitativa.

E

elocuencia *sust.* habilidad para hablar o escribir con gracia y de manera convincente.
embaucar *v.* engañar; hacer creer a alguien algo que no es cierto.
emular *v.* imitar; copiar.
endeble *adj.* débil; frágil.
enmendar *v.* corregir, mejorar.
escarnio *sust.* desdén; burla.
escurridizo *adj.* difícil de atrapar.
espíritu *sust.* vigor; vivacidad.
estoicamente *adv.* aquí, testarudamente.
examinar *v.* investigar, explorar.
excesivo *adj.* que es demasiado; exagerado; desmesurado.
extenuante *adj.* que cansa; agotador.

F

fascinar *v.* hipnotizar.
fatiga *sust.* agotamiento; cansancio.
feroz *adj.* brutal; cruel.
formular *v.* explicar de manera clara y lógica.
fugitivo *sust.* persona que escapa del peligro o la opresión.
función *sust.* uso; objetivo.

G

genuino *adj.* auténtico.
gesticulación *sust.* movimientos enérgicos.
gravar *v.* aquí, cargar, pesar sobre alguien o algo.

H

hipocresía *sust.* acto de fingir virtudes o bondad.
hipótesis *sust.* explicación o repuesta posible.
histéricamente *adv.* de manera salvaje e incontrolada.
hospitalidad *sust.* trato generoso y amigable hacia los invitados.
hueste *sust.* ejército.

I

impecablemente *adv.* sin errores.
impetuoso *adj.* impulsivo; precipitado.
improvisado *adj.* que no estaba planeado.
incentivo *sust.* razón para hacer algo; motivación.
incomprensible *adj.* imposible de entender.
indagar *v.* buscar respuestas, preguntar.
indignadamente *adv.* con enojo causado por algo que se siente como una injusticia.
inerte *adj.* que no se mueve; quieto.
inexplicable *adj.* que no se puede explicar.
inmortalidad *sust.* vida sin fin.
innumerable *adj.* numeroso; incalculable.
inquietante *adj.* amenazante.
instintivamente *adv.* automáticamente.
intensificar *v.* aumentar, reforzar.
interrumpir *v.* hacer que algo se detenga, que no continúe.
intolerante *adj.* que no está dispuesto a aceptar algo.
introspectivo *adj.* que mira hacia el interior de sí mismo.
invasión *adj.* acto de entrar por la fuerza.
irritar *sust.* molestar; enojar.

Spanish Glossary

A

aborrecer *v.* odiar.
abundante *adj.* suficiente; tanto como se necesite.
acogido *adj.* que otras personas distintas de sus padres lo llevaron a su hogar y lo cuidaron.
acongojado *adj.* que tiene una tristeza profunda.
admitir *v.* reconocer; aceptar.
adquisición *sust.* algo que se compra o se obtiene.
afablemente *adv.* con amabilidad.
aislar *v.* apartar, proteger.
alivio *sust.* consuelo.
angustia *sust.* sensación de dolor o sufrimiento emocional.
anhelo *sust.* ansia; deseo grande.
aniquilación *sust.* destrucción completa.
anormal *adj.* que no es normal; inusual.
anticuado *adj.* pasado de moda.
apesadumbradamente *adv.* con arrepentimiento y vergüenza.
apreciado *adj.* valorado, querido.
arcaico *adj.* muy viejo o anticuado.
arrogante *adj.* excesivamente orgulloso.
asegurar *v.* fijar con firmeza en el lugar.
asemejarse *v.* ser parecido a.
atender *v.* ocuparse de.
atenerse *v.* aceptar algo y actuar acorde a ello.
atentamente *adv.* prestando mucha atención.
aterrorizado *adj.* alarmado; horrorizado.
audacia *sust.* atrevimiento; osadía.
autorización *sust.* permiso oficial.
autorizado *adj.* que tiene el poder de hacer algo.

B

barraca *sust.* edificio grande o grupo de edificios en los que viven muchas personas.
beca *sust.* dinero que se da a un estudiante para que continúe sus estudios.
benigno *adj.* amable; inofensivo.
brecha *sust.* abertura, en general se refiere a una ruptura en una pared o en una línea de defensa.

C

camarada *sust.* compañero; amigo; socio.
caótico *adj.* confuso.
chillón *adj.* ruidoso y brusco.
circuito *sust.* recorrido habitual.
clemencia *sust.* compasión; tolerancia.
competición *sust.* competencia; partido.
comprimido *adj.* apretado.
confines *sust.* fronteras; límites.
conmemorar *v.* honrar la memoria de alguien.
conmoción *sust.* gran confusión; perturbación.
conmovedor *adj.* que causa tristeza o dolor; tierno.
conmover *v.* emocionar profundamente.
contorsionarse *v.* retorcerse.
contradictorio *adj.* que está en desacuerdo; que se opone.
convocar *v.* llamar; pedir que alguien asista a un lugar.
correlacionar *v.* establecer una relación entre dos o más cosas.
correspondiente *adj.* que coincide con algo; equivalente.
credo *sust.* proclamación de las creencias o principios.
credulidad *sust.* tendencia a creer algo con mucha facilidad.
cuerpo *sust.* grupo de personas con entrenamiento especial; unidad militar.

D

demacrar *v.* provocar extrema delgadez, por ejemplo, a causa del hambre.
denunciar *v.* expresarse en contra de algo.
deriva (ir a la) loc. *adv.* moverse empujado por una corriente de aire o agua.
desamparado *adj.* solo y abandonado.
descendientes *sust.* todas las generaciones que vienen de una persona.
desconectado *adj.* que no está conectado; aislado; separado.
desdén *sust.* falta de respeto o antipatía evidente por alguien o algo.

S

saludable *adj.* bueno para el cuerpo y el alma.
sereno *adj.* en calma; tranquilo.
sombrío *adj.* oscuro; melancólico.
sortear *v.* sobrellevar; sobrevivir a algo y quedar a salvo.
sujeto *adj.* propenso; que tiene tendencia a.
sumirse *v.* concentrarse mucho en algo.
superior *sust.* persona que tiene un cargo o rango más alto.
súplica *sust.* petición de ayuda o compasión.

T

tedioso *adj.* aburrido.
tedioso *adj.* extenso y aburrido.
temblor *sust.* sacudida; vibración.
tenso *adj.* tirante.
tiranía *sust.* ejercicio del poder de una manera cruel e injusta.
tranquilidad *sust.* calma; paz.
traumático *adj.* doloroso emocionalmente; que causa una impresión fuerte.

U

usado *adj.* gastado.

V

vagamente *adv.* sin claridad.
vehementemente *adv.* con fuerza; apasionadamente.
verificar *v.* probar que algo es cierto; confirmar.
versatilidad *sust.* habilidad para hacer bien muchas cosas.
vigilia *sust.* vigilancia; acción de estar despierto para hacer guardia.
vil *adj.* muy desagradable.
vital *adj.* de gran importancia o necesidad.

Z

zumbido *sust.* ruido continuo y bronco.

Academic Vocabulary Glossary

English/Spanish

The Academic Vocabulary Glossary in this section is an alphabetical list of the academic vocabulary words found in this textbook. Use this glossary just as you would use a dictionary—to find out the meanings of words used in your literature class to talk about and write about literary and informational texts and to talk about and write about concepts and topics in your other academic classes.

For each word, the glossary includes the pronunciation, part of speech, and meaning. A Spanish version of the glossary immediately follows the English version. For more information about the words in the Academic Vocabulary Glossary, please consult a dictionary.

English

A

associations (uh soh see AY shuhnz) *n.* connections in the mind between different things.

C

consequence (KAHN suh kwehns) *n.* result of something that happened earlier.
contribute to (kuhn TRIHB yoot too) *v.* play a part in; bring about.
convey (kuhn VAY) *v.* communicate; express.
critical (KRIHT ih kuhl) *adj.* vital, very important.

D

define (dih FYN) *v.* make clear the meaning of; explain.
distinctive (dihs TIHNGK tihv) *adj.* special; different from others.

E

effective (uh FEHK tihv) *adj.* bringing about a desired result.
emphasize (EHM fuh syz) *v.* give importance to; pay special attention to.
establish (ehs TAB lihsh) *v.* bring about; set up.
evident (EHV uh duhnt) *adj.* plain; clear; obvious.
evoke (ih VOHK) *v.* draw out; elicit.
express (ehk SPREHS) *v.* show; put into words.

F

factor (FAK tuhr) *n.* something that has an influence on something else.
fundamental (fuhn duh MEHN tuhl) *adj.* basic; essential.

I

impact (IHM pakt) *n.* strong or forceful effect.
impression (ihm PREHSH uhn) *n.* idea or notion.
incident (IHN suh duhnt) *n.* event or occurrence.
indicate (IHN duh kayt) *v.* point out; suggest.
insight (IHN syt) *n.* act of understanding how things work or how people think or act.
intent (ihn TEHNT) *n.* purpose; plan; aim.
interact (ihn tuhr AKT) *v.* behave toward one another.
interpretation (ihn tur pruh TAY shuhn) *n.* explanation of the meaning.

O

observation (ahb zuhr VAY shuhn) *n.* act of taking notice of something for some special purpose; study.
outcome (OWT kuhm) *n.* result; ending.

R

reactions (ree AK shuhnz) *n.* responses.
response (rih SPAHNS) *n.* reply or reaction.
reveal (rih VEEL) *v.* make known.

S

sequence (SEE kwuhns) *n.* order.
significant (sihg NIHF uh kuhnt) *adj.* meaningful; important.
specify (SPEHS uh fy) *v.* mention or describe in detail; give as a condition.
structure (STRUHK chuhr) *n.* arrangement of parts.

Spanish

A

asociación *sust.* relación que se hace mentalmente entre cosas distintas.

C

consecuencia *v.* resultado de algo que pasó con anterioridad.
contribuir *v.* participar; colaborar.
crìtico *adj.* vital; muy importante.

D

definir *v.* aclarar el significado de algo; explicar.
distintivo *adj.* característico; que lo hace diferente de otros.

E

efectivo *adj.* que produce el resultado deseado.
enfatizar *v.* dar importancia; prestar especial atención a algo.
especificar *v.* explicar o describir en detalle; fijar una condición.
establecer *v.* instaurar; crear.
estructura *sust.* disposición de las partes.
evidente *adj.* patente; claro; obvio.
expresar *v.* demostrar; poner en palabras.

F

factor *sust.* algo que influye en otra cosa.
fundamental *adj.* básico; esencial.

I

impacto *sust.* efecto brusco o fuerte.
impresión *sust.* idea o noción.
incidente *sust.* suceso o hecho.
indicar *v.* señalar; sugerir.
intención *sust.* objetivo; plan; propósito.
interactuar *v.* actuar conjuntamente.
interpretación *sust.* explicación del significado.

O

observación *sust.* acción de examinar algo con un propósito determinado; estudio.

P

perspicacia *sust.* capacidad para entender cómo funcionan las cosas o cómo piensan las personas.

R

reacción *sust.* respuesta.
réplica *sust.* respuesta o reacción.
representar *v.* comunicar, expresar.
resultado *sust.* efecto; conclusión.
revelar *v.* dar a conocer.

S

secuencia *sust.* orden.
significativo *adj.* importante.
suscitar *v.* provocar.

ACKNOWLEDGMENTS

For permission to reproduce copyrighted material, grateful acknowledgment is made to the following sources:

"Hawaiian Teen Named Top Young Scientist." Copyright © 2006 by **The Associated Press** and MetroSource. Reproduced by permission of the publisher.

"My Mother Pieced Quilts" by **Teresa Palomo Acosta** from *Festival de Flor y Canto: An Anthology of Chicano Literature*, edited by Alurista et al. Copyright © 1976 by El Centro Chicano, University of Southern California. Reproduced by permission of the author.

From "Oda a las gracias" from *Navegaciones y Regresos* by Pablo Neruda. Copyright © 1959, 2007 by Fundación Pablo Neruda. Reproduced by permission of **Agencia Literaria Carmen Balcells on behalf of Fundación Pablo Neruda.**

"The Treasure of Lemon Brown" by Walter Dean Myers from *Boys' Life Magazine*, March 1983. Copyright © 1983 by Walter Dean Myers. Reproduced by permission of **Miriam Altshuler Literary Agency, on behalf of Walter Dean Myers.**

Quote by James Baldwin from *Nobody Knows My Name: More Notes of a Native Son*. Copyright © 1954, 1956, 1958, 1959, 1960, 1961 by James Baldwin. Published by Vintage Books. Reproduced by permission of the **James Baldwin Estate.**

"The Wise Old Woman" from *The Sea of Gold and Other Tales from Japan* adapted by Yoshiko Uchida. Copyright © 1965 by Yoshiko Uchida. Reproduced by permission of **Bancroft Library, University of California, Berkeley.**

From "A Smart Cookie" from *The House on Mango Street* by Sandra Cisneros. Copyright © 1984 by Sandra Cisneros. Published by Vintage Books, a division of Random House, Inc., and in hardcover by Alfred A. Knopf in 1994. All rights reserved. Reproduced by permission of **Susan Bergholz Literary Services, New York, NY, and Lamy, NM.**

"Gil's Furniture Bought and Sold" from *The House on Mango Street* by Sandra Cisneros. Copyright © 1984 by Sandra Cisneros. Published by Vintage Books, a division of Random House, Inc., and in hardcover by Alfred A. Knopf in 1994. All rights reserved. Reproduced by permission of **Susan Bergholz Literary Services, New York, NY, and Lamy, NM.**

"Redwing Sonnets" from *Homecoming: New and Collected Poems* by Julia Alvarez. Copyright © 1984, 1996 by Julia Alvarez. Published by Plume, an imprint of The Penguin Group (USA); originally published by Grove Press. All rights reserved. Reproduced by permission of **Susan Bergholz Literary Services, New York, NY, and Lamy, NM.**

"Valentine for Ernest Mann" from *Red Suitcase: Poems* by Naomi Shihab Nye. Copyright © 1994 by Naomi Shihab Nye. Reproduced by permission of **BOA Editions, Ltd.**

From *The Glass Menagerie* by Tennessee Williams. Copyright © 1945 by Tennessee Williams and Edwina D. Williams; copyright renewed © 1973 by Tennessee Williams. Reproduced by permission of **Georges Borchardt, Inc.**

"Saying Yes" by Diana Chang. Copyright © 2000 by **Diana Chang.** Reproduced by permission of the author.

"Drumbeats and Bullets" from *The Boys' War* by Jim Murphy. Copyright © 1990 by Jim Murphy. All rights reserved. Reproduced by permission of **Clarion Books, an imprint of Houghton Mifflin Company, www.hmco.com.**

"The Word" by Manuel Ulacia, translated by Jennifer Clement. Translation copyright © 1995 by **Jennifer Clement.** Reproduced by permission of the translator.

"The Inn of Lost Time" by Lensey Namioka from *Short Stories by Outstanding Writers for Young Adults*, edited by Donald R. Gallo. Copyright © 1989 by Lensey Namioka. All rights reserved. Reproduced by permission of **Ruth Cohen, for Lensey Namioka.**

"The Drummer Boy of Shiloh" by Ray Bradbury from *The Saturday Evening Post*, April 30, 1960. Copyright © 1960 by The Curtis Publishing Company; copyright renewed © 1988 by Ray Bradbury. Reproduced by permission of **Don Congdon Associates, Inc.**

"The Flying Machine" from *Golden Apples of the Sun* by Ray Bradbury. Copyright © 1953 and renewed © 1986 by Ray Bradbury. Reproduced by permission of **Don Congdon Associates, Inc.**

"The Fog Horn" by Ray Bradbury from *The Saturday Evening Post*, June 23, 1951. Copyright © 1951 by the Curtis Publishing Company; copyright renewed © 1979 by Ray Bradbury. Reproduced by permission of **Don Congdon Associates, Inc.**

The Dragon (Graphic Version) by Ray Bradbury with art by Vicente Segrelles. Copyright © 1955 and renewed © 1983 by Ray Bradbury. Reproduced by permission of **Don Congdon Associates, Inc.**

Introduction to *The Dragon* (Graphic Version) by Ray Bradbury with art by Vicente Segrelles. Copyright © 1955 and renewed © 1983 by Ray Bradbury. Reproduced by permission of **Don Congdon Associates, Inc.**

Author's comments on "The Drummer Boy of Shiloh." Copyright © 2003 by Ray Bradbury. Reproduced by permission of **Don Congdon Associates, Inc.**

From "A Shot at It" from *When I Was Puerto Rican* by Esmeralda Santiago. Copyright © 1993 by Esmeralda Santiago. Reproduced by permission of **Da Capo Press, a member of Perseus Books, L.L.C.**

"How I Learned English" from *Falling Deeply into America* by Gregory Djanikian. Copyright © 1989 by **Gregory Djanikian.** First published in *Poetry*, 1986. Reproduced by permission of the author.

From *The Cay* by Theodore Taylor. Copyright © 1969 by Theodore Taylor. Reproduced by permission of **Doubleday, a division of Random House, Inc.** and electronic format by permission of **Watkins/Loomis Agency, Inc.**

From *The Diary of a Young Girl: The Definitive Edition* by Anne Frank, edited by Otto H. Frank and Mirjam Pressler, translated by Susan Massoty. Copyright © 1995 by Doubleday, a division of Random House, Inc. Reproduced by permission of **Doubleday, a division of Random House, Inc., www.randomhouse.com.**

"A Nincompoop" from *Anton Chekhov: Selected Stories*, translated by Ann Dunnigan. Translation copyright © 1960 by Ann Dunnigan. Reproduced by permission of **Dutton Signet, a division of Penguin Group (USA) Inc.** and electronic format by permission of **GRM Associates, Inc., Agents for the Ann Elmo Agency.**

"The Puppy" from *Stories and Prose Poems* by Aleksandr Solzhenitsyn, translated by Michael Glenny. Translation copyright © 1971 by Michael Glenny. Reproduced by permission of **Farrar, Straus and Giroux, LLC.**

"Dancer" from *Simple Songs* by Vickie Sears. Copyright © 1990 by Vickie Sears. Reproduced by permission of **Firebrand Books.**

"Suéter" from *Despertar* by Alberto Forcada. Copyright © 1992 by Alberto Forcada. Published by Centro de Información y Desarrollo de la Literatura Infantiles (CIDCLI). Reproduced by permission of **Alberto Forcada.**

Act II, Scene I of *Alice in Wonderland* by Lewis Carroll, adapted for the stage by **Eva Le Gallienne and Florida Friebus.** Copyright © 1948, 1949, 1960, 1976, 1977 by Eva Le Gallienne and Florida Friebus. Reproduced by permission of the estates of the authors.

"Those Three Wishes" from *A Taste for Quiet and Other Disquieting Tales* by Judith Gorog. Copyright © 1982 by **Judith Gorog.** Reproduced by permission of the author.

Quote from *To Kill A Mockingbird* by Harper Lee. Copyright © 1960 and renewed 1988 by Harper Lee. All rights reserved. Reproduced by permission of **HarperCollins Publishers Inc.**

"Americans All" from *Paper Trail* by Michael Dorris. Copyright © 1994 by Michael Dorris. Reproduced by permission of **HarperCollins Publishers, Inc.**

"A word is dead" from *The Poems of Emily Dickinson*, edited by Thomas H. Johnson. Copyright © 1951, 1955, 1979, 1983 by the President and Fellows of Harvard College. Published by The Belknap Press of Harvard University Press, Cambridge, Mass. Reproduced by permission of **Harvard University Press and the Trustees of Amherst College.**

"Sweater" by Alberto Forcada, translated by Judith Infante. Copyright © 1995 by Judith Infante. Reproduced by permission of **Judith Infante.**

"Flowers for Algernon" (short story version) by **Daniel Keyes** from *The Magazine of Fantasy & Science Fiction*. Copyright © 1959, 1987 by Daniel Keyes. Book length paperback version published by Harcourt. Companion book, *Algernon, Charlie and I: A Writer's Journey*. Reproduced by permission of the author.

Essay by Ursula Le Guin. Copyright © 2007 by Ursula Le Guin. Reproduced by permission of **Virginia Kidd Agency, Inc.**

From *My Childhood Under Fire: A Sarajevo Diary* by Najda Halilbegovich. Copyright © 2006 by Najda Halilbegovich. Reproduced by permission of **Kids Can Press Ltd., Toronto.**

"I Have a Dream" by Martin Luther King, Jr. Copyright © 1963 by Martin Luther King, Jr.; copyright renewed © 1991 by Coretta Scott King. Reproduced by permission of **The Heirs to the Estate of Martin Luther King, Jr., c/o Writers House, Inc. as agent for the proprietor, New York, NY.**

"I, Too" from *The Collected Poems of Langston Hughes*. Copyright © 1994 by The Estate of Langston Hughes. Reproduced by permission of **Alfred A. Knopf, a division of Random House, Inc.** and electronic format by permission of **Harold Ober Associates Inc.**

"Refugee in America" from *The Collected Poems of Langston Hughes*. Copyright © 1994 by The Estate of Langston Hughes. Reproduced by permission of **Alfred A. Knopf, a division of Random House, Inc.** and electronic format by permission of **Harold Ober Associates Incorporated.**

"Birdfoot's Grampa" by Joseph Bruchac. Copyright © 1978 by Joseph Bruchac. Reproduced by permission of **Barbara S. Kouts on behalf of Joseph Bruchac.**

Essay by Joseph Bruchac. Copyright © 2007 by Joseph Bruchac. Reproduced by permission of **Barbara S. Kouts on behalf of Joseph Bruchac.**

From *Passage to Freedom: The Sugihara Story* by Ken Mochizuki. Text copyright ©1997 by Ken Mochizuki. Reproduced by permission of **Lee & Low Books, Inc., 95 Madison Ave., New York, NY 10016.**

"The Cub" by Lois Dykeman Kleihauer. Reproduced by permission of **Brent D. Kleihauer.**

"The Old Grandfather and His Little Grandson" from *Twenty-two Russian Tales for Young Children* by Leo Tolstoy, translated by Miriam Morton. English translation copyright © 1969 by Miriam Morton. Reproduced by permission of **Little Simon, an imprint of Simon & Schuster Children's Publishing Division.**

"Ode to Thanks" from *Odes to Opposites* by Pablo Neruda. Copyright © 1995 by Pablo Neruda and Fundación Pablo Neruda; English translation copyright © 1995 by Ken Krabbenhoft. Reproduced by permission of **Little, Brown and Company, Inc.**

Excerpt (retitled "Camp Harmony") from *Nisei Daughter* by Monica Sone. Copyright © 1953 and renewed © 1981 by Monica Sone. Reproduced by permission of **Little, Brown and Company, Inc.** and electronic format by permission of **Philip G. Sone for Monica K. Sone.**

"Apologies for Past Actions are Still Appropriate Today" from *The Macon Telegraph*. Copyright © 2007 by Macon Telegraph Georgia. Reproduced by permission of **The Macon Telegraph, GA; Knight-Ridder/Tribune Business News.**

Essay by **Cassandra Medley.** Copyright © 2007 by Cassandra Medley. Reproduced by permission of the author.

"Walking with Living Feet" by Dara Horn from *Merlyn's Pen*, October/November 1993. Copyright © 1993 by Merlyn's Pen, Inc. First appeared in *Merlyn's Pen: Fiction, Essays, and Poems by America's Teens.* All rights reserved. Reproduced by permission of **The Merlyn's Pen Foundation.**

"The Border: A Glare of Truth" from *Nepantla: essays from the land in the middle* by **Pat Mora.** Copyright © 1993 by Pat Mora. Reproduced by permission of the author.

Essay by **Aimee Nezhukumatathil.** Copyright © 2007 by Aimee Nezhukumatathil. Reproduced by permission of the author.

"Hamadi" by Naomi Shihab Nye from *America Street: A Multicultural Anthology of Stories*. Copyright © 1999 by **Naomi Shihab Nye.** Reproduced by permission of the author.

Quote by **Naomi Shihab Nye** from *HarperChildren's* Web site, accessed October 5, 2000 at http://www.harperchildrens.com/hch/authorpage/index.asp?authorID=15255. Copyright © 2000 by Naomi Shihab Nye. Reproduced by permission of the author.

"Stop the Sun" by **Gary Paulsen** from *Boy's Life*, January 1986. Copyright © 1986 by Gary Paulsen. Reproduced by permission of the author.

Quote by Fernando Pessoa from Preface of *The Book of Disquiet* by Fernando Pessoa, translated by Richard Zenith. Copyright © 1998 by Assírio & Alvim and the heirs of Fernando Pessoa; translation copyright © 2001 by Richard Zenith. Reproduced by permission of **Penguin Books Ltd., www.penguin.co.uk.**

From "I'm laughing so hard I'm crying" from *If Life is a Bowl of Cherries—What Am I Doing in the Pits?* Copyright © 1978 by Erma Bombeck. Reproduced by permission of **The Aaron M. Priest Literary Agency.**

From "A Sort of Preface" from *Gorilla, My Love* by Toni Cade Bambara. Copyright © 1960, 1963, 1964, 1965, 1968, 1970, 1971, 1972 by Toni Cade Bambara. Reproduced by permission of **Random House, Inc., www.randomhouse.com.**

"Raymond's Run" from *Gorilla, My Love* by Toni Cade Bambara. Copyright © 1960, 1963, 1964, 1965, 1968, 1970, 1971, 1972 by Toni Cade Bambara. Reproduced by permission of **Random House, Inc., www.randomhouse.com.**

The Diary of Anne Frank by Albert Hackett, Frances Goodrich Hackett. Copyright © 1956 by Albert Hackett, Frances Goodrich Hackett, and Otto Frank. Reproduced by permission of **Random House, Inc.** and electronic format by permission of **Abrams Artists Agency.**

Excerpts (retitled "Mrs. Flowers") from *I Know Why the Caged Bird Sings* by Maya Angelou. Copyright © 1969 and renewed © 1997 by Maya Angelou. Reproduced by permission of **Random House, Inc., www.randomhouse.com.**

From *Beowulf*, translated by Burton Raffel. Translation copyright © 1962 and renewed © 1990 by Burton Raffel. Reproduced by permission of **Dutton Signet, a division of Penguin Group (USA) Inc.** and electronic format by permission of **Russell & Volkening as agents for the author.**

"Go On or Die" and "The Railroad Runs to Canada" from *Harriet Tubman: Conductor on the Underground Railroad* by Ann Petry. Copyright © 1955 and renewed © 1983 by Ann Petry. Reproduced by permission of **Russell & Volkening as agents for Ann Petry.**

"Ed McMahon Is Iranian" by Mariam Salari from *A World Between: Poems, Short Stories & Essays*. Copyright © 1999 by **Mariam Salari.** Reproduced by permission of the author.

From "Ray Bradbury is on fire!" by James Hibberd from *Salon.com* Web site, accessed December 23, 2002 at http://archive.salon.com/people/feature/2001/08/29/bradbury/index.html. Copyright © 2002 Salon Media Group, Inc. Reproduced by permission of **Salon.com.**

From *Ploughman of the Moon* by Robert Service. Copyright © 1945 by Dodd, Mead & Company, Inc. Reproduced by permission of the **Estate of Robert Service.**

"The Medicine Bag" by Virginia Driving Hawk Sneve. Copyright © by **Virginia Driving Hawk Sneve.** Reproduced by permission of the author.

"Riding Lesson" from *An Afternoon of Pocket Billards* by Henry Taylor. Copyright © 1975, 1992 by **Henry Taylor.** Reproduced by permission of the author.

From *Contemporary Authors: Autobiography Series*, vol. 6, by Ann Petry, ed. Adele Sarkissian. Copyright © 1988 by Gale Research Company Inc. Reproduced by permission of **Thomson Learning, www.thomsonrights.com.**

"Pyramus and Thisbe" from *A Midsummer Night's Dream* by William Shakespeare, edited with a modern English translation and illustrated by Simon Greaves. Copyright © 2005 by Simon Greaves. Reproduced by permission of **Timber Frame Publications Ltd, www.shakespearecomics.com.**

"La Palabra" from *El rio y la piedra valencia* by Manuel Ulacia, published by Pretextos, Mexico. Copyright © 1989 by **Manuel Ulacia.** Reproduced by permission of the author.

"Introduction to Poetry" from *The Apple that Astonished Paris* by Billy Collins. Copyright © 1998 by Billy Collins. Reproduced by permission of **University of Arkansas Press.**

"The Circuit" by Francisco Jiménez from *Cuentos Chicanos: A Short Story Anthology*, edited by Rodolfo A. Anaya and Antonio Marquez. Copyright © 1984 by the University of New Mexico Press. Published for *New America* by the University of New Mexico Press. Reproduced by permission of **University of New Mexico Press.**

From "John Lewis: Hand in Hand Together" (retitled "The Power of Nonviolence") from *From Camelot to Kent State* by Joan Morrison and Robert K. Morrison. Copyright © 1987 by Joan Morrison and Robert K. Morrison. Reproduced by permission of **John A. Ware Literary Agency.**

"The Scientific Method" from *Current Science*, vol. 87, Issue 5, pg 7-7, October 26, 2001. Copyright © 2001 by **Weekly Reader Corporation.** All rights reserved. Reproduced by permission of the publisher.

From "Don't Know Much About Liberty" from *Weekly Reader Senior Edition*, April 21, 2006. Copyright © 2006 by **Weekly Reader Corporation;** illustrations copyright © 2006 by **Chris Murphy.** All rights reserved. Reproduced by permission of the publisher and the illustrator.

Quote by Judy Collins. Copyright © by Judy Collins. Reproduced by permission of **Wildflower Records.**

"A Tragedy Revealed: A Heroine's Last Days" by Ernst Schnabel translated by Richard and Clara Winston from *Life*, vol. 45, no. 7, August 18, 1958. Copyright © 1958 by Time, Inc.; copyright renewed © 1986 by Justina Winston Gregory and Krishna Winston. Reproduced by permission of **Krishna Winston on behalf of The Estate of Richard and Clara Winston.**

"The Struggle to Be an All-American Girl" by **Elizabeth Wong.** Copyright © 1995 by Elizabeth Wong. Reproduced by permission of the author.

"Pronunciation Key" from *World Book Online Reference Center* at www.worldbook.com. Reproduced by permission of **World Book, Inc.**

"Separation" from *The Moving Target*. Copyright © 1963 by W.S. Merwin. Reproduced by permission of **The Wylie Agency.**

Sources Cited

"Shiloh, Battle of" from *Microsoft® Encarta® Online Encyclopedia 2004*, http://encarta.msn.com.

From "Waiting for the Hmmm" by Jim Murphy from *Children's Book Council* web site, accessed November 25, 2002 at www.cbcbooks.org/html/jim_murphy.html.

Quotes by Sandra Cisneros from *Interviews with Writers of the Post-Colonial World*, conducted and edited by Feroza Jussawalla and Reed Way Dasenbrock. Published by University Press of Mississippi, Jackson, MI, 1992.

Quote by Francisco Jimenez from *Santa Clara Magazine*, vol. 38, no. 2, Spring 1999. Published by Santa Clara University, Santa Clara, CA.

PICTURE CREDITS

The illustrations and photographs on the Contents pages are picked up from pages in the textbook. Credits for those can be found either on the textbook page on which they appear or in the listing below.

Photo credits: iii, (all) Sam Dudgeon/HRW Photo; **iv,** (l, c, r) Sam Dudgeon/HRW Photo; (cl) Courtesy of Héctor Rivera; (cr) Courtesy of Eric Cooper; **v,** (l) Courtesy of Mabel Rivera; (cl, r) Sam Dudgeon/HRW Photo; (cr) Courtesy of Margaret McKeown; **vi,** (all) Sam Dudgeon/HRW Photo; **vii,** (tl) ©Dan Tuffs; (tr) ©Michael Greenlar/The Image Works; (bl) Photo courtesy of Aimee Nezhukumatathil; (br) Photo courtesy of Cassandra Medley; **A04,** (detail) © 2007 Artists Rights Society (ARS), New York / ADAGP, Paris. Private Collection, Paris, France, Giraudon/Art Resource, NY; **A05,** (l) ©David Hosking/Photo Researchers, Inc.; (r) Smithsonian American Art Museum, Washington, DC, U.S.A./Art Resource, NY; **A06,** (detail) Gift of the Harmon Foundation. Smithsonian American Art Museum, Washington, DC, U.S.A./Art Resource, NY; **A07,** (t) ©Paul Doyle/Alamy; (b) Victoria & Albert Museum, London, UK/The Bridgeman Art Library; **A08,** ©Randy Faris/CORBIS; **A09,** (t) Jerry Jacka Photography, (b) ©Stu Smucker/Lonely Planet Images; **A10,** (t) (detail) Collection Manu Sassoonian, New York, NY, U.S.A., Manu Sassoonian/Art Resource, NY; (b) ©Daniel Arsenault/Stone/Getty Images; **A11,** ©JUPITERIMAGES/Creatas/Alamy; **A12,** ©AP Images/Jon Super; **A13,** (l) Smithsonian American Art Museum, Washington, DC, U.S.A./Art Resource, NY; (bkgd) ©David Muench/CORBIS; **A14,** Stefano Paltera/North American Solar Challenge; **A15,** (t) ©David Young-Wolff/PhotoEdit, Inc.; (b) Darrell Lecorre/Masterfile; **A16,** ©amana productions inc/Getty Images; **A17,**(detail) ©Gilbert Mayers/SuperStock; **A18,** (t) ©Pixtal/PunchStock; (b) © Joan Marcus; **A19,** Netherlands Institute for War Documentation; **A30–A31,** (bkgd: wood surface) © Burke/Triolo Productions/Brand X/CORBIS; **A30,** White wall: © Digital Vision/Getty Images; Gray Wolf: © Alan and Sandy Carey/ Photodisc/Getty Images; Gavel: © Glenn Mitsui/Photodisc/Getty Images; Round base for gavel: © PhotoSpin, Inc/Alamy; Steamed broccoli: © Foodcollection/Getty Images; Blue print of house: © Rupert King/Digital Vision/Getty Images; **A31,** File folder: ©Brand X Pictures; Teenagers in library: © Nancy Honey/Photonica/Getty Images; Press badge: © Photodisc/Alamy; Photo of Kylene Beers: Sam Dudgeon/HRW Photo; Yellow notepad: © Photodisc; 0, (l) ©Dan Tuffs; (cl) Cover image from Very Far Away from Anywhere Else by Ursula K. Le Guin. Copyright © 1976 by **Harcourt, Inc.** Reproduced by permission of the publisher.; (r) Cover image from A Wizard of Earthsea by Ursula K. Le Guin. Copyright © 1968 by **Bantam Books, a division of Random House, Inc.** Reproduced by permission of the publisher.; (bkgd) Image courtesy of the Virginia Kidd Agency, Inc.; **2-3,** Private Collection, Paris, France, Giraudon/Art Resource, NY; **3,** (r) ©John William Banagan/Photodisc Red/Getty Images; **7,** ©Private Collection/The Stapleton Collection/The Bridgeman Art Library; **12,** (b) Photo courtesy of Judith Gorog;(bkgd) ©Bob Krist/CORBIS; **14,** ©Private Collection/The Bridgeman Art Library; **16,** (l) Photo ©Miriam Berkley; (r) ©Jochen Tack/Alamy; **19,** Smithsonian American Art Museum, Washington, DC, U.S.A./Art Resource, NY; **22,** ©StockAB/Alamy; **26,** ©Takuya Inokuma/amana images/Getty Images; **32,** (l) Richard McNamee; (r) ©Kaz Chiba/The Image Bank/Getty Images; **33, 34,** ©Chad Ehlers/Stone/Getty Images; **37, 39,** Fitzwilliam Museum, University of Cambridge, UK/The Bridgeman Art Library; **41,** ©Chad Ehlers/Stone/Getty Images; **42, 43,** Freer Gallery of Art, Smithsonian Institution, Washington, D.C., Gift of Charles Lang Freer, F1897.31a-b; **45,** ©Chad Ehlers/Stone/Getty Images; **46,** Bibliotheque des Arts Decoratifs Paris/Dagli Orti/The Art Archive; **48,** ©Chad Ehlers/Stone/Getty Images; **51,** Toho Company/Photofest; **52,** (t) ©Frank Krahmer/zefa/CORBIS; (b) ©Tetra Images/CORBIS; **54,** (l) Photo ©Miriam Berkley;(r) Courtesy Everett Collection; **55,** ©Frank Krahmer/zefa/CORBIS; **56,** Courtesy Everett Collection; **59,** ©Spencer Grant/PhotoEdit, Inc.; **61,** Courtesy Everett Collection; **62,** ©David Hosking/Photo Researchers, Inc.; **64, 67,** Courtesy Everett Collection; **68,** ©David Hosking/Photo Researchers, Inc.; **71,** Kirchoff and Wohlberg/HRW; **73,** (l) ©Josh Westrich/zefa/CORBIS; (c) ©Frank Krahmer/zefa/CORBIS; (r) ©David Hosking/Photo Researchers, Inc.; **75,** ABC Pictures Corp./Photofest; **76,** ©David Hosking/Photo Researchers, Inc.; **78,** Courtesy Everett Collection; **81,** ©David Hosking/Photo Researchers, Inc.; **83,** ABC Picture Corp./Photofest; **88,** National Gallery of Art, Washington, DC, U.S.A., Banque d'Images, ADAGP/Art Resource, NY.; **90,** (t) ©reserved; collection The National Portrait Gallery, London.; (b) Photo ©Miriam Berkley; **108,** National Oceanic and Atmospheric Administration/Department of Commerce; **118,** Bill Fitz-Patrick Photography; **119,** ©Galen Rowell/CORBIS; **122,** ©Jonathan Daniel/Getty Images; **124,** ©Steve Satushek/The Image Bank/Getty Images; 130, Victoria Smith/HRW; **139,** ©Kevin Schafer/Alamy; **146,** (tl) Cover image from *Kit's Wilderness* by David Almond. Copyright © 1999 by **Dell Publishing, a division of Penguin Group (USA) Inc.** Reproduced by permission of the publisher.; (tr) Cover image from *Ella Enchanted* by Gail Levine. Copyright © 1997 by **HarperCollins Children's Books, a division of HarperCollins Publishers, Inc.** Reproduced by permission of the publisher.; (bl) Cover image from Hatchet by Gary Paulsen. Copyright © 1987 by **Holt, Rinehart and Winston.** Reproduced by permission of the publisher. (br) Cover image from Ice Drift by Theodore Taylor. Copyright ©2006 by Theodore Taylor. Reproduced by permission of **Harcourt, Inc.; 147,** (tl) Cover image from Samurai by Caroline Leavitt, cover image by Erik Von Weber. Copyright ©2007 by **Capstone Press.** Reproduced by permission of the copyright holder.; (tr) Cover image from *Guinea Pig Scientists* by Leslie Dendy and Mel Boring. Copyright © 2005 by **Henry Holt and Company, Inc.** Reproduced by permission of the publisher.; (bl) Cover image from *Black Pioneers of Science and Invention* by Louis Haber. Copyright © 1970 by **Harcourt, Inc.** Reproduced by permission of the publisher.; (br) Cover image from Forensics by Richard Pratt. Copyright © 2005 Kingfisher Publications Plc. All rights reserved. Reproduced by permission of **Kingfisher Publications Plc., an imprint of Houghton Mifflin Company.; 148–149,** Gift of the Harmon Foundation. Smithsonian American Art Museum, Washington, DC, U.S.A./Art Resource, NY; **149,** (r) ©Philip Scalia/Alamy; **152, 153,** Musee d'Orsay, Paris, France, Erich Lessing/Art Resource, NY; **155,** (tl, bl) Matthias Kulka/Masterfile; (tr, br) sgame/iStockphoto; **157,** ©Ned Frisk/CORBIS; **160,** (bkgd) ©Michael Juno/Alamy; **164,** (l) ©Nancy Kaszerman/ZUMA; (r) ©Roger Cracknell/Alamy; **167,** ©Paul Doyle/Alamy; **168,** ©Michael Newman/PhotoEdit, Inc.; **172,** Pankaj Shah & Insy Shah/Gulf Images; **173,** Food Image Source/Dennis Gottlieb/StockFood; **174,** ©Sandy Felsenthal/CORBIS; **178,** ©Ingram Publishing/Getty Images; **180,** (l) ©Bettmann/CORBIS; (r) ©Michael Pasdzior/Riser/Getty Images; **182,** Image courtesy of The Advertising Archives; **185,** Advertising Ephemera Collection- Database #A0132, Emergence of Advertising On-Line Project, John W. Hartman Center for Sales, Advertising & Marketing History, Duke University Rare Book, Manuscript, and Special Collections Library; **187,** National

Gallery Budapest/Dagli Orti/The Art Archive; **192,** (t) (detail) United States Holocaust Memorial Museum, courtesy of Markus & Mary Nowogrodzki; (b) ©AP Images/Kevin Frayer; **194,** (l) Photo courtesy of Ken Mochizuki and Lee & Low Books; (r) ©Wolfgang KaehlerAlamy; **195,** (both) (details) United States Holocaust Memorial Museum, courtesy of Markus & Mary Nowogrodzki; **198–99,** (bkgd) (detail) United States Holocaust Memorial Museum, courtesy of Markus & Mary Nowogrodzki; **198,** (l) United States Holocaust Memorial Museum, courtesy of Hiroki Sugihara; (r) Photo by Setsuko Kikuchi, United States Holocaust Memorial Museum, courtesy of Hiroki Sugihara; **199,** (r) Courtesy Visas for Life Foundation, reproduced by permission; **206,** (b) ©Dave Allocca/DMI/Time & Life Pictures/Getty Images; **211,** Victoria & Albert Museum, London, UK/The Bridgeman Art Library; **214,** Gift of the Harmon Foundation. Smithsonian American Art Museum, Washington, DC, U.S.A./Art Resource, NY; **215,** Smithsonian American Art Museum, Washington, DC, U.S.A./Art Resource, NY; **220,** ©AP Images/Mary Ataffer; **222,** Smithsonian American Art Museum, Washington, DC, U.S.A./Art Resource, NY; **225,** ©Bob Krist/CORBIS; **234,** Kinzie-Riehm Inc/HRW; **250,**(tl) Cover image from *The Call of the Wild* by Jack London. Copyright © 1998 by **Holt, Rinehart and Winston.** Reproduced by permission of the publisher.; (tr) Cover image from *The Clay Marble* by Minfong Ho. Copyright © 1991 by Holt, Rinehart and Winston. Reproduced by permission of the publisher.; (bl) Cover image from *Number the Stars* by Lois Lowry. Copyright © 1989 by **Bantam Books, a division of Random House, Inc.** Reproduced by permission of the publisher.; (br) Cover image from *Call Me Maria* by Judith Ortiz Cofer. Copyright ©2004 by Judith Ortiz Cofer. Reproduced by permission of **Orchard Books, an imprint of Scholastic, Inc.; 251,** (tl) Cover image from *Freedom's Children* by Ellen Levine. Copyright © 1993 by **Puffin Books, a division of Penguin Group (USA) Inc.** Reproduced by permission of the publisher.; (tr) Cover image from *Lives of the Musicians* by Kathleen Krull. Copyright © 1993 by **Harcourt, Inc.** Reproduced by permission of the publisher.; (bl) Cover image from *The Story of My Life* by Helen Keller. Copyright © 1990 by **Bantam Books, a division of Random House, Inc.** Reproduced by permission of the publisher.; (br) Cover image from *Rescue: The Story of How Gentiles Saved Jews in the Holocaust* by Milton Metzer. Copyright © 1988 by **HarperCollins Children's Books, a division of HarperCollins Publishers, Inc.** Reproduced by permission of the publisher.; **252–253,** ©Randy Faris/CORBIS; **253,** (r) ©Herbert Spichtinger/zefa/CORBIS; **257,** Private Collection/The Bridgeman Art Library; **264,** ©Anne Rippy/Iconica/Getty Images; **266** ©Stu Smucker/Lonely Planet Images; **268,** (both) ©AP Images/Al Grillo; **271,** Department of Defense, Washington/The Art Archive; **272,** ©John Borthwick/Lonely Planet Images; **274,** (both) ©Stu Smucker/Lonely Planet Images; **276,** US Army Center of Military History; **280,** NativeStock Pictures; **282,** (l) Photo courtesy of Virginia Sneve; (bkgd) ©Annie Griffiths Belt/CORBIS; **283, 285, 286,** ©Werner Forman/CORBIS; **287,** Jerry Jacka Photography; **288,** (l) Jerry Jacka Photography; (r) NativeStock Pictures; **291,** NativeStock Pictures; **298,** ©Jan Butchofsky-Houser/CORBIS; **301,** ©Michael Cogliantry/Taxi/Getty Images; **306,** Jon Feingersh/Masterfile; **308,** (tl) ©Frank Cantor; (tr) Photo courtesy of Greg Djanikian and The University of Pennslyvania; (bl) Ruth T. Wong; (br) Photo courtesy of Mariam Salari; **309,** (bkgd) Uladzimir Bakunovich/iStockphoto; **311,** Courtesy Babcock Galleries; **312,** (bkgd) Uladzimir Bakunovich/iStockphoto; **314,** ©Michael Newman/PhotoEdit, Inc.; (bkgd) Uladzimir Bakunovich/iStockphoto; **317,** ©Peter Hvizdak/The Image Works;(bkgd) Uladzimir Bakunovich/iStockphoto; **319, 320,** Courtesy of Bill Goff, Inc.; **323,** ©JUPITERIMAGES/BananaStock/Alamy; **326,** ©AP Images/Douglas C. Pizac; **330,** ©AP Images/Mark Duncan; **332,** (l) Independence National Historical Park; (r) ©Topham/The Image Works; **333,** National Oceanic and Atmospheric Administration/Department of Commerce; **335,** (t) ©Smithsonian Institution/CORBIS; (b) North Wind Picture Archives; **338,** (t) Map Division. Astor, Lenox and Tilden Foundations, The New York Public Library/Art Resource, NY; (b) ©AP Images/James Woodcock/Billings Gazette; **340–341,** (t) ©AP Images/Charles Rex Arbogast; **341,**(c) ©AP Photo/Charles Rex Arbogast; (b) ©AP Images/Robin Loznak/Great Falls Tribune; **342,** (t) ©James L. Amos/CORBIS; (c) North Wind Picture Archives; (b) Jeff Olson/NPS; **348,** Sam Dudgeon/HRW; **362,** (tl) Cover image from *Bud, Not Buddy* by Christopher Paul Curtis. Copyright ©1999 by Christopher Paul Curtis. Reproduced by permission of **Random House Children's Books, a division of Random House, Inc.;** (tr) Cover image from *Goodbye, VietNam* by Gloria Whelan. Copyright 1992 by **Holt, Rinehart and Winston.** Reproduced by permission of the publisher.; (postcard on book cover) Cameramann International; (bkgd on book cover) Cliff Hollenbeck/Image State; (bl) Cover image from *The Maze* by Will Hobbs. Copyright © 1998 by **Morrow Jr. Books, a division of HarperCollins Publishers, Inc.** Reproduced by permission of the publisher.; (br) Cover image from *The Friends* by Rosa Guy. Copyright ©1973 by **Bantam Books Inc., a division of Random House, Inc.** Reproduced by permission of the publisher.; **363,** (tl) Cover image from *The Captain's Dog: My Journey with the Lewis and Clark Tribe* by Roland Smith. Copyright ©1999 by Bryn Barnard. Reproduced by permission of **Harcourt, Inc.;** (tr) Cover image from *The Flight of Red Bird: The Life of Zitkala-Sa* by Doreen Rappaport. Copyright © 1997 by **Puffin Books, a division of Penguin Group (USA) Inc.** Reproduced by permission of the publisher.; (bl) Cover image from *Sacajawea* by Joseph Bruchac. Copyright © 2000 by **Harcourt, Inc.** Reproduced by permission of the publisher.; (br) Cover image from *Immigrant Kids* by Russell Freedman. Copyright © 1980 by **Puffin Books, a division of Random House, Inc.** Reproduced by permission of the publisher.; **364–365,** Collection Manu Sassoonian, New York, NY, U.S.A., Manu Sassoonian/Art Resource, NY; **365,** (r) ©Simon Marcus/CORBIS; **368,** Private Collection, Art Resource, NY; **372,** ©Image Source Pink/Getty Images; **373,** ©Image Source Pink/Alamy; **374,** (both) ©Bryce Harper; **378,** (l) ©Bettmann/CORBIS; (r) ©Uwe Walz/CORBIS; **381, 383, 384, 387,** Culver Pictures, Inc.; 388, Debra LaCappola and Charles Meier/HRW; **390,** (l) ©Susan J. Ross; (r) ©Rudy Sulgan/CORBIS; **393,** Debra LaCappola and Charles Meier/HRW; **394,** (bkgd) © Thomas Rodriguez/CORBIS, (teenage girls) ©Thinkstock/CORBIS; **397,** ©MM Productions/CORBIS; **398,** Debra LaCappola and Charles Meier/HRW; **399,** ©Tom & Dee Ann McCarthy/CORBIS; **400,** Debra LaCappola and Charles Meier/HRW; **403,** ©Ty Milford/Aurora/Getty Images; **404,**©J. Emilio Flores/CORBIS; **406,** (l) Photo courtesy of Francisco Jimenez; (r) ©Gail Shumway/Photographer's Choice/Getty Images; **407,** (t) OlgaLIS/iStockphoto;(top bkgd) Duncan Walker/iStockphoto;(top bkgd) earl arena/iStockphoto; (b) Pattie Steib/iStockphoto; (bottom bkgd) Duncan Walker/iStockphoto; (bottom bkgd) earl arena/iStockphoto; **409,** ©Jim Sugar/CORBIS; **410,** ©Phillip Gould/CORBIS; (bkgd) Duncan Walker/iStockphoto; (bkgd) earl arena/iStockphoto; **412,** ©Oleksiy Maksymenko/Alamy; (bkgd) Duncan Walker/iStockphoto; (bkgd) earl arena/iStockphoto; **416,** NativeStock Pictures; **418,** (l) ©Gay Bumgarner/Alamy, (bkgd) NativeStock Pictures; **420,** ©Dennis MacDonald/Alamy; **421,** ©Luc

Novovitch/Alamy; **422,** NativeStock Pictures; **426,** ©Steven Georges/Press-Telegram/CORBIS; 428, ©Jean-Claude Amiel/ Kipa/CORBIS; **429,** (t, b) ©CSA Plastock/Getty Images; (c) ©Douglas Kirkland/CORBIS; **430,** (t) ©Daniel Arsenault/Stone/ Getty Images; **431,** (tr) ©Dorling Kindersley/Getty Images; (cr) ©CSA Plastock/Getty Images; **433,** Private Collection, Photo ©Christie's Images/The Bridgeman Art Library; **435,** ©Christie's Image/CORBIS; **438,** ©imagebroker/Alamy; **444,** ©Bruce Wheadon/Alamy; **446–447,** ©Steve Bloom/Taxi/Getty Images; **448,** ©Fortean/Topham/The Image Works; **450,** ©Jan Pittman/ Getty Images; **454,** ©JUPITERIMAGES/Creatas/Alamy; **456,** ©Jim Richardson/CORBIS; **457,** ©MPI/Hulton Archive/Getty Images; **459,** (t) Used with permission of Documenting the American South, The University of North Carolina at Chapel Hill Libraries.; (b) ©Buddy Mays/CORBIS; **466,** ©Myrleen Ferguson Cate/ PhotoEdit, Inc.; **480,** (tl) Cover image from *River Rats* by Caroline Stevermer. Copyright ©1992 by Caroline Stevermer. Reproduced by permission of **Harcourt, Inc.;** (tr) Cover image from *Roll of Thunder, Hear My Cry* by Mildred D. Taylor. Copyright ©1976 by **Puffin Books, a division of Penguin Group (USA) Inc.** Reproduced by permission of the publisher.; (bl) Cover image from *Out of the Dust* by Karen Hesse. Copyright © 1997 by **Scholastic, Inc.** Reproduced by permission of the publisher.; (br) Cover image from *A Christmas Carol* by Charles Dickens. Copyright © 1998 by **Holt, Rinehart and Winston.** Reproduced by permission of the publisher.; **481,** (tl) Cover image from *There Comes a Time: The Struggle for Civil Rights* by Milton Meltzer. Copyright © 2001 by **Random House Children's Books, a division of Random House, Inc.** Reproduced by permission of the publisher.; (tr) Cover image from *Savion: My Life in Tap* by Savion Glover and Bruce Weber. Copyright ©2000 by Savion Glover and Bruce Weber. Reproduced by permission of **Morrow Jr. Books, a division of HarperCollins Publishers, Inc.;** (bl) Cover image from *Travels With Charley In Search of America* by John Steinbeck. Copyright © 1962 by **Penguin Group (USA) Inc.** Reproduced by permission of the publisher.; (br) Cover image from *Black Hands, White Sails* by Patricia C. McKissack. Copyright © 1999 by **Scholastic Inc.** Reproduced by permission of the publisher.; **482,** (l) ©Michael Greenlar/The Image Works; (cl) Cover image from *Jim Thorpe: Original All-American* by Joseph Bruchac. Cover design by Christian Fuenfhausen. Copyright © 2006 by **Dial Books, a division of Penguin Books for Young Readers, a member of Penguin Group (USA) Inc.** All rights reserved. Reproduced by permission of the publisher.; (cr) Cover image from *Sacajawea* by Joseph Bruchac. Copyright © 2000 by **Harcourt, Inc.** Reproduced by permission of the publisher.; (r) Cover image of *Pocahontas* by Joseph Bruchac. Copyright © 2003 by **Harcourt, Inc.** Reproduced by permission of the publisher.; (bkgd) Masterfile; **484–485,** ©AP Images/Jon Super; **485,** (r) ©Andy Stewart/Digital Vision/Getty Images; **493,** ©JUPITERIMAGES/ Creatas / Alamy; **494,** (l) ©AP Images; (c, r) ©Tom Bean/CORBIS; **496,** Smithsonian American Art Museum, Washington, DC, U.S.A./Art Resource, NY; **498,** (l) ©Richard Meek/Time & Life Pictures/Getty Images; (r) ©Scott Lituchy/Star Ledger/CORBIS; **500–501,** (border) amygdala imagery/ShutterStock; **500,** (b) ©CORBIS; **501,** (r) ©CORBIS; **502-503,** (border) amygdala imagery/ShutterStock; **503,** (b) ©Bettmann/CORBIS; **504–505,**(border) amygdala imagery/ ShutterStock; **505,** (r) ©Mary Evans Picture Library/Alamy; **506–507,** (detail) Collection of The New-York Historical Society, Album file, PR-002-347.20; Digital id #aa02038; negative #37629; **507, 508,** (borders) amygdala imagery/ShutterStock; **512,** National Archives (210-GC-839); 514, Photo courtesy of Monica Sone; **516, 518,** Fair Street Pictures; **520,** Department of Special Collections, Charles E. Young Research Library, UCLA. Collection 2010 Japanese American Research Project: Estelle Ishigo Papers, Box 719, Painting titled "Home". ; **524,** (detail) Bob Adelman/Magnum Photos; **526,** (t) Fair Street Pictures; (b) ©Flip Schulke/CORBIS; **527,** ©North Wind Picture Archives/Alamy; **528,** ©Thad Samuels Abell II/National Geographic/Getty Images; **529,** ©Robert W. Kelley/Time & Life Pictures/Getty Images; **530,** John Rottet/The News and Observer; **534,** Private Collection/ The Bridgeman Art Library; **536,** (l) Photography by Cheron Bayna, Courtesy of Pat Mora; (r) ©George H. H. Huey/CORBIS; **538,** ©Hector Mata/AFP/Getty Images; **538–539,** (border) ©Brooklyn Museum/CORBIS; **540,** (b) ©Hector Mata/AFP/Getty Images; (border) ©Brooklyn Museum/ CORBIS; **544,** ©Collection of the New-York Historical Society, USA/The Bridgeman Art Library; **546,** (t) Arthur Cohen Photography; (b) ©Sophie Bassouls/CORBIS Sygma; **547,** (t) ©Philip Gould/CORBIS; **548,** ©Medford Historical Society Collection/CORBIS; **549,** ©Tria Giovan/CORBIS; **550–551,** ©Bettmann/CORBIS; **552,** ©CORBIS; **554,** (l) ©Richard T. Nowitz/CORBIS, (border) ©Ed Young/CORBIS; **557,** Brooklyn Museum of Art, New York, USA/The Bridgeman Art Library; **558,** ©Kevin Fleming/CORBIS; **560,** ©David Muench/CORBIS; **561,** (photograph) Culver Pictures, Inc.; (picture frame) ©Bettmann/CORBIS; **564,** Dreamworks SKG/Photofest; **566,** (t) christine balderas/iStockphoto; (b) ©The Corcoran Gallery of Art/CORBIS; **567,** National Portrait Gallery, Smithsonian Institution, Washington DC, U.S.A./Art Resource, NY,; **571,** ©imagebroker/Alamy; **578,** HRW Photo; **587,** ©Bettmann/ CORBIS; **594,** (tl) Cover image from *The Glory Field* by Walter Dean Myers. Copyright © 1994 by **Holt, Rinehart and Winston.** Reproduced by permission of the publisher.; (tr) Cover image from *Little Women* by Louisa May Alcott. Copyright © 1994 by **Tom Doherty Associates, LLC.** Reproduced by permission of the publisher.; (bl) Cover image from *North by Night* by Katherine Ayres. Copyright © 1998 by **Dell Publishing, a division of Random House, Inc.** Reproduced by permission of the publisher.; (br) Cover image from *Journey Home* by Yoshiko Uchida. Copyright © 1978 by **Simon & Schuster Books for Young Readers, an imprint of Simon & Schuster Children's Publishing Division.** Reproduced by permission of the publisher.; **595,** (tl) Cover image from *The Boys' War* by Jim Murphy. Copyright © 1990 by **Houghton Mifflin Company.** Reproduced by permission of the publisher.; (tr) Cover image from *Behind Barbed Wire* by Daniel S. Davis. Copyright ©1982 by **Dutton Children's books, a division of Penguin Group (USA) Inc.** Reproduced by permission of the publisher.;(bl) Cover image from *Behind Rebel Lines* by Seymour Riet. Copyright © 1988 by **Harcourt, Inc.** Reproduced by permission of the publisher.; (br) Cover image from *To Be a Slave* by Julius Lester. Copyright © 1968 by **Penguin Putnam Books for Young Readers, a division of Penguin Group (USA) Inc.** Reproduced by permission of the publisher.; **596-597,** Stefano Paltera/North American Solar Challenge; **601,** Ailvin Ailey/Andrew Eccles/ JBGPhoto; **604,** Courtesy of Media Relation Division, Space and Missile Systems Center, Los Angeles Air Force Base; **610,** ©Ursula Klawitter/zefa/CORBIS; **613,** ©David Young-Wolff/PhotoEdit, Inc.; **614,** Pacifica Skatepark, Department of Parks, Beaches and Recreation, City Hall, Pacifica, California; **615,** ©Ryan McVay/ Photodisc/Getty Images; **618,** ©Jeff Greenberg/PhotoEdit, Inc.; **619,** Mark Raycroft/Minden Pictures; **621,** (t) Mike Randolph/ Masterfile, (b) ©Geraint Lewis/Alamy; **622,** (t) Darrell Lecorre/ Masterfile; (b) ©Ron Chapple Stock/CORBIS; **624,** ©Mike Kemp/ Rubberball Productions/Gettty Images; **626,** (l) ©Stockbyte/ Getty Images, (r) Alex Gumerov/iStockphoto; (bkgd and push pins) ©Peter Dazeley/Photodisc/Getty Images; **630,** (Satisfaction Guaranteed stamp) Grafissimo/iStockphoto; **632,** ©Jack Hollingsworth/Photodisc/Getty Images; **633, 634,** (bkgds) doodlemachine/iStockphoto; **635, 636,** (bkgds) ©Chad Baker/Photodisc/Getty Images; **638,** ©Ken Kaminesky/Take 2 Productions/CORBIS; 652, Kinzie-Riehm, Inc./HRW; **664,** (tl) Cover image from *Cobblestone Magazine*, February 1981, vol. 2, no. 2. Copyright © 1981 by Cobblestone Publishing Company, 30 Grove Street, Suite C, Peterborough, NH 03458. All rights reserved. Reproduced by permission of **Carus Publishing Company.;** (tr) Cover image from *National Geographic Kids*, March 2007. Copyright © 2007 by National Geographic Kids. Reproduced by permission of **National Geographic Society.;** (bl) Cover image from *Cricket Magazine*, June 1998, vol. 25, no. 10. Copyright © 1998 by Cobblestone Publishing Company, 30 Grove Street, Suite C, Peterborough, NH 03458. All rights reserved. Reproduced by permission of Carus Publishing Company.; (br) Cover image from *Muse Magazine*, May/June 2003. Copyright © 2003 by Cobblestone Publishing Company, 30 Grove Street, Suite C, Peterborough, NH 03458. All rights reserved. Reproduced by permission of **Carus Publishing Company.; 665** (tl, br) ©Suza Scalora/Photodisc/Getty Images; (tr, bl) ©Image Source/CORBIS; **666,** (l) Photo courtesy of Aimee Nezhukumatathil; (c) Cover image from *Miracle Fruit* by Aimee Nezhukumatathil. Copyright © 2003 by **Tupelo Press.** Reproduced by permission of the publisher.; (r) Cover image from *At The Drive-In Volcano* by Aimee Nezhukumatathil. Copyright © 2003 by **Tupelo Press.** Reproduced by permission of the publisher.; (bkgd) ©Jagdish Agarwal/CORBIS; **668-669,** ©amana productions inc/Getty Images; **669,** (r) ©Comstock Select/CORBIS; **670,** ©2007; Reprinted courtesy of Bunny Hoest and Parade Magazine; **672,** (l) Erik Enervold/iStockphoto; **675,** Private Collection, Malcah Zeldis/Art Resource, NY; **678,** ©Steve McDonough/CORBIS; **679,** ©Michael Blann/Digital Vision/Getty Images; **680,** (t) ©AP Images/Debbie Brown; (b) ©AP Images/Beth A. Keiser; **682,** www.tafatafa.com; **684,** (t) ©Michael Greenlar/The Image Works; (b) ©Nancy Kaszerman/ZUMA; **685,** (c) ©AP Images/Robin Loznak/Great Falls Tribune; (bkgd) ©imagebroker/Alamy; **687,** Boden/Ledingham/Masterfile; **690,** (tl) Courtesy Teresa Palomo Acosta; (tr) Private Collection/The Bridgeman Art Library; **691,** ©Buddy Mays/CORBIS; **692,** (l) ©Ariel Skelley/CORBIS; (r) ©Pixland/CORBIS; **693,** (l, r) ©David P. Hall/CORBIS; (c) Smithsonian Institution, Washington DC, USA/The Bridgeman Art Library; **694,** ©Buddy Mays/CORBIS; **695,** ©Tony Arruza/CORBIS; **699,** ©Philadelphia Museum of Art/CORBIS; **702,** Regional Gallery of Art, Astrakhan, Russia, Scala /Art Resource, NY; **704,** (t) ©Stock Montage/Hulton Archive/Getty Images; **705,** (b) ©Randy Wells/Photographer's Choice/Getty Images; (bkgd) ©Charles O'Rear/CORBIS; **706–707,** (border) ©Charles O'Rear/CORBIS; **707,** (l) ©Kevin Fleming/CORBIS; **708–709,** (border) ©Charles O'Rear/CORBIS; **709,** (t) © Bettmann/CORBIS; **710,** (b) Simple Stock Shots/IPN Stock Independent Photo Network; (bkgd) ©Charles O'Rear/CORBIS; **711, 712–713,** (bkgds) ©Greg Pease/Photographer's Choice/Getty Images; **716,** ©AP Images; **717,** (t) © 2007 Daryl Pederson/AlaskaStock Images; (b) © 2007 Jeff Schultz/AlaskaStock Images; **718–719,** (b) © 2007 Jeff Schultz/AlaskaStock Images; **719,** (t) ©Carol Kohen/The Image Bank/Getty Images; **720–721,** (b) © 2007 Jeff Schultz/AlaskaStock Images; **721,** (r) ©Ashley Cooper/CORBIS; **722,** (r) ©Smithsonian Institution/CORBIS; **722–723,** (bkgd) ©Jon Arnold Images/Alamy; **726,** (tr) British Library/The Art Archive; (bl) Courtesy of the Harvard University Archives; (br) ©Steve Dunwell /Index Stock Imagery, Inc.; **727,** (b) National Museum, Copenhagen, Denmark, Erich Lessing/Art Resource, NY; (bkgd) ©Ted Spiegel/CORBIS; **728–729,** (bkgd) ©Ted Spiegel/CORBIS; **730–733,** Mary Evans Picture Library; **736,** Private Collection, U.S.A., Erich Lessing/Art Resource, NY; **738,** (l) *John Keats* (detail) (circa 1822) by William Hilton, after Joseph Severn. Oil on canvas, 30 in. x 25 in. (762 mm x 635 mm), National Portrait Gallery, London; (r) ©Massimo Listri/CORBIS; **739,** (t) Private Collection/The Bridgeman Art Library; **742,** (l) ©AP Images/Michel Lipchitz; (r) Jo Ann Snover/iStockphoto; **743,** ©altrendo nature/Altrendo/Getty Images; **744,** (flower) ©Dirk v. Mallinckrodt/Alamy; (bkgd) ©altrendo nature/Altrendo/Getty Images; **747,** (l) Fair Street Pictures; (r) ©Corey Hochachka/Design Pics/CORBIS; **748,** (l) Prints & Photographs Division, Library of Congress, LC-USZ62-112729; **748-749,** (bkgd) Peter Christopher/Masterfile; **752,** ©CORBIS; **753,** ©Todd Davidson/Stock Illustration Source/Getty Images; **754,** ©Gilbert Mayers/SuperStock; **758,** ©Andre Jenny/Alamy; **760,** (t) ©Richard T. Nowitz/CORBIS; (b) Prints & Photographs Division, Library of Congress, LC-USZ62-116102; **761,** (leaves) ©Sean Justice/CORBIS; **762, 763,** ©Johannes Kroemer/The Image Bank/Getty Images; **766,** Kevin Dietsch/UPI/Landov; **768,** (t) ©Picture History; (c) ©CORBIS; (b) Photo courtesy of Diana Chang; **769,** ©David Buffington/Photodisc/Getty Images; **770,** (b) Culver Pictures, Inc.; **771,** (t) American Jewish Joint Distribution Committee; (c) Image courtesy of National Park Service, Statue of Liberty, National Monument; (b) Brown Brothers; **773,** ©Jeff Greenberg/The Image Works; **774,** (r) Chad Johnston/Masterfile; **776,** (border) ©M. Timothy O'Keefe/Alamy; **777,** (t) ©Peter Turnley/CORBIS; (bkgd) ©M. Timothy O'Keefe/Alamy; **779,** (t) ©CORBIS; (b) ©Horace Bristol/CORBIS; (bkgd) ©M. Timothy O'Keefe/Alamy; **786,** © image100/CORBIS; **794,** (tl) Cover image from *In The Eyes of the Cat* by Demi. Copyright © 1992 by **Henry Holt and Company, LLC.** Reproduced by permission of the publisher.; (tr) Cover image from *You Come Too: Favorite Poems for Young Readers* by Robert Frost. Copyright © 1959 by **Henry Holt and Company, LLC.** Reproduced by permission of the publisher.; (bl) Cover image from *Canto Familiar* by Gary Soto. Copyright © 1995 by **Harcourt, Inc.** Reproduced by permission of the publisher.; (br) Cover image from *This Same Sky*, selected by Naomi Shihab Nye. Copyright © 1992 by **Simon & Schuster Books for Young Readers, an imprint of Simon & Schuster Children's Publishing Division.** Reproduced by permission of the publisher.; **795,** (tl) Cover image for *Island of Hope* by Martin W. Sandler. Copyright ©2004 by Martin W. Sandler. Reproduced by permission of **Scholastic, Inc.;** (tr) Cover image from *Lincoln: A Photobiography* by Russell Freedman. Copyright © 1987 by **Houghton Mifflin Company.** Reproduced by permission of the publisher; (bl) Cover image from *A Great and Glorious Game* by A. Bartlett Giamatti. Copyright © 1998 by **Algonquin Books of Chapel Hill, a division of Workman Publishing.** Reproduced by permission of the publisher.; (br) Cover image from *The Harlem Renaissance* by Veronica Chambers. Copyright © 1997 by **Chelsea House Publishers, a subsidiary of a subsidiary of Haights Cross Communications.** Reproduced by permission of the publisher.; 796, (l) Photo courtesy of Cassandra Medley; (c) Cover image from *3 by E.S.T.* by Cassandra Medley, Greg Germann, and Laura Cahill. Copyright © 1997 by **Dramatists Play Service Inc.** Reproduced by permission of the publisher.; (r) Cover image from *Relativity* by Cassandra Medley. Copyright © 2006 by **Broadway Play Publishing, Inc.** Reproduced by permission of the publisher.; (bkgd) altrendo images/Altrendo/Getty Images; **798–799,** ©Pixtal/PunchStock; **799,** (r) David Muir/Masterfile; **807,** Private Collection, ©Chris Beetles, London, U.K./The Bridgeman Art Library; **809,** Private Collection,

Archives Charmet/The Bridgeman Art Library; **810,** (l) ©Bettmann/CORBIS; (r) ©Michael S. Yamashita/CORBIS; **814,** (t) AK Purkiss/Lebrecht Music & Art; (b) ©Bettmann/CORBIS; **815,** ©Adam Woolfitt/CORBIS; **828,** (b) © Collection of the Earl of Leicester, Holkham Hall, Norfolk/The Bridgeman Art Library; **832,** (both) ©Anne Frank House/Hulton Archive/Getty Images; **834,** ©Bettmann/CORBIS, **835,** ©Anne Frank House/Hulton Archive/Getty Images; (bkgd) ©Pedro Ugarte/AFP/Getty Images; **836,** (l) ©Hulton-Deutsch Collection/CORBIS; **837,** (tl, cl)©Anne Frank House/Hulton Archive/Getty Images; (tr) Library of Congress; (bkgd) Maxim Pushkarev/iStockphoto; **838,** (r) ©Bettmann/CORBIS; (bkgd) Maxim Pushkarev/iStockphoto; **839,** (top bkgd) ©Pedro Ugarte/AFP/Getty Images;(bkgd) Maxim Pushkarev/iStockphoto; **842,** ©Anne Frank House/ Hulton Archive/Getty Images; **845,** ©Bob Krist/CORBIS; **847,** (b) ©Anne Frank House/Hulton Archive/Getty Images; (bkgd) ©Pedro Ugarte/AFP/Getty Images; **849,** (bkgd) Maxim Pushkarev/iStockphoto; **850,**(b) ©Anne Frank House/Hulton Archive/Getty Images; (bkgd) ©Pedro Ugarte/AFP/Getty Images; **857,** (bkgd) Maxim Pushkarev/iStockphoto; **858,** (both) Netherlands Institute for War Documentation; **861,** (b) ©Anne Frank House/Hulton Archive/Getty Images; (bkgd) ©Pedro Ugarte/AFP/Getty Images; **862,** (bkgd) Maxim Pushkarev/ iStockphoto; **865,** Dutch Resistance Museum, Amsterdam; **867,** (r) ©Anne Frank House/Hulton Archive/Getty Images; (bkgd) ©Pedro Ugarte/AFP/Getty Images; **871,** (r) ©Anne Frank House/Hulton Archive/Getty Images; (bkgd) ©Pedro Ugarte/ AFP/Getty Images; **879,** ©Purestock/Getty Images; **885,** (top bkgd) ©Pedro Ugarte/AFP/Getty Images; (bkgd) Maxim Pushkarev/iStockphoto; **887,** (b) ©Anne Frank House/Hulton Archive/Getty Images; (bkgd) ©Pedro Ugarte/AFP/Getty Images; **889,** (bkgd) Maxim Pushkarev/iStockphoto; **891,** ©James P. Blair/CORBIS; **892,** ©Anne Frank House/Hulton Archive/Getty Images; 897, (bkgd) Maxim Pushkarev/iStockphoto; **899,** (b) ©Anne Frank House/Hulton Archive/Getty Images; (bkgd) ©Pedro Ugarte/AFP/Getty Images; **905,** (bkgd) Maxim Pushkarev/iStockphoto; **907,** (l, r) ©Anne Frank House/Hulton Archive/Getty Images;(bkgd) ©Pedro Ugarte/AFP/Getty Images; **908,** (t) ©Anne Frank House/Hulton Archive/Getty Images; (b) Maria Austria/Maria Austria Institute (MAI); (bkgd) ©Pedro Ugarte/AFP/Getty Images; **916,** ©AP Images/Karsten Thielker; **918,** (t) ©Anne Frank House/Hulton Archive/Getty Images; (b) Photo courtesy of Nadja Halilbegovich and Kids Can Press; **919, 920, 921,** (all) ©Anne Frank House/Hulton Archive/Getty Images; **923,** ©Jon Jones/Sygma/CORBIS; **925,** Photo courtesy of Nadja Halilbegovich and Kids Can Press; **928,** ©David Sutherland/CORBIS; **930,** ©Michael St. Maur Sheil/CORBIS; **933,** (r) ©Michael Jenner/Robert Harding World Imagery/Getty Images; (bkgd) ©Bettmann/CORBIS; **935,** ©Anne Frank House/ Hulton Archive/Getty Images; **938,** (t) ©epa/CORBIS; (b) ©Hulton Archive/Getty Images; **941,** United States Holocaust Memorial Museum; **943,** ©Sean Gallup/Getty Images; **944, 946,** ©Anne Frank House/Hulton Archive/Getty Images; **949,** Photodisc/Getty Images; **951,** akg-images/Michael Teller; **958,** Sam Dudgeon/HRW; **974,** (tl) Cover image from *Favorite Stories for Performance.* Copyright © 2000 by **Holt, Rinehart and Winston.** Reproduced by permission of the publisher.; (tr) Cover image from *Tunes for Bears to Dance To* by Robert Cormier. Copyright ©1992 by **Doubleday, a division of Random House, Inc.** Reproduced by permission of the publisher.; (bl) Cover image from *A Gathering of Days* by Joan Blos. Copyright © 1979 by **Simon & Schuster Books for Young Readers, an imprint of Simon & Schuster's Children's Publishing Division.** Reproduced by permission of the publisher.; (br) Cover illustration copyright ©2001 by Rafal Olbinski.; **975,** (tl) Cover image from *I Am David* by Anne Holm. Copyright ©1993 by **Harcourt, Inc.** Reproduced by permission of the publisher.; (tr) Cover image from *Hitler Youth* by Susan Campbell. Cover photos by ©Bettmann/CORBIS (Hitler Youth giving "Heil" salute)and ©CORBIS (Hitler and Nazi youth). Copyright © 2005 by **Scholastic, Inc.** Reproduced by permission of the publisher.; (bl) Cover image from *Zlata's Diary* by Zlata Filipovic. Copyright © 1993 by **Puffin Books, a division of Penguin Group (USA) Inc.** Reproduced by permission of the publisher.; (br) Cover image from *The Upstairs Room* by Johanna Reiss. Copyright © 1972 by **HarperCollins Publishers, Inc.** Reproduced by permission of the publisher.; **977,** © ColorBlind Images/Iconica/Getty Images; **1018,** (t) Tom Bachtell ©2001/represented by Chris Glenn; (b) Tim O'Brien ©2005/represented by Peter Lott; **1019** (both) Peter Van Steen/HRW

INDEX OF SKILLS

The boldface page numbers indicate an extensive treatment of the topic.

The Index of Skills is divided into the following categories:

LITERARY SKILLS

Informational Text Skills

Reading Skills

Vocabulary Skills

Writing Skills

Standardized Test Practice

Language Skills (Grammar, Usage, and Mechanics)

Listening and Speaking Skills

Read On

INDEX OF AUTHORS AND TITLES

RESOURCE CENTER

Index of Authors and Titles